THE NEW INTERPRETER'S® BIBLE

OLD

TESTAMENT

SURVEY

THE NEW INTERPRETER'S® BIBLE

OLD

TESTAMENT

SURVEY

ABINGDON PRESS

Nashville

THE NEW INTERPRETER'S® BIBLE
OLD TESTAMENT SURVEY

Library of Congress Cataloging-in-Publication Data

The New Interpreter's Bible. Old Testament Survey.
        p. cm.
Includes bibliographical references and index.
ISBN 0-687-05344-7 (9780687053445 : alk. paper)
1. Bible. O.T.--Introductions. I. Title: Old Testament Survey.

BS1140.3.N49 2006
221.6'1--dc22

The HebraicaII® and GraecaII® fonts used to print this work are available from Linguist's Software, Inc., PO Box 580, Edmonds, WA 98020-0580.
Tel (425) 775-1130. Web www.linguistsoftware.com

PUBLICATION STAFF
President and Publisher: Neil M. Alexander
Editorial Director: Harriett Jane Olson
Reference Unit Director: Paul Franklyn
Reference Project Manager: Marianne Blickenstaff
Development Editor: Heather R. McMurray
Editorial Consultant: John S. Cook
Production and Design Manager: Ed Wynne
Composition Specialist: Brenda Gayl Hinton
Print Procurement Coordinator: Paul Shoulders

Publisher's Foreword

"While it is appropriate to distinguish historical and literary explanation of the text as a work of the past from reflection on its import in various situations today, it is also necessary to ground the later in the former. The fact that most writers of the *NIB* are professional Bible scholars reflects the conviction that what effective and imaginative interpretation needs most is solid grounding in an explanation of the text that engages the religious and moral content of scripture."

—Leander E. Keck,
General Editor of *The New Interpreter's® Bible*

The success of *The New Interpreter's® Bible* (12 volumes) as a standard of contemporary biblical scholarship prompts the creation of two surveys based on the introductory materials included in this commentary set. The *Old Testament Survey* and *New Testament Survey* are easily accessible to students who are seeking an expert overview of every book of the Old or New Testament. These volumes can be used as primary texts alongside the Bible, or as supplements to other textbooks.

The New Interpreter's® Bible Old Testament Survey provides the introductory content for each book of the Old Testament and Apocrypha. As an added bonus, the Survey also provides introductions to genres of literature contained in the Bible. The articles in the Survey cover essential historical, socio-cultural, literary, and theological issues, which are illustrated with maps and charts. For students interested in key points related to the original languages of the Bible, we have provided the Hebrew, Aramaic, and Greek languages along with transliterations and translations. Each chapter includes an updated list of suggested readings.

The New Interpreter's® Bible line is committed to providing balanced coverage of critical issues for seminary and church audiences. Perhaps the best reason to consider the *Old Testament Survey* as a textbook is that it represents a collection of noteworthy biblical scholars, each writing in their own field of expertise. Moreover, these collections represent a diversity of scholarship that includes perspectives of women and men, racial and ethnic minorities, Protestantism and Catholicism.

Contributors

Elizabeth Achtemeier[†]
Adjunct Professor of Bible and Homiletics
Union Theological Seminary in Virginia
Richmond, Virginia
(Presbyterian Church [U.S.A.])
Joel

Leslie C. Allen
Professor of Old Testament
Fuller Theological Seminary
Pasadena, California
(Baptist)
1 & 2 Chronicles

Robert A. Bennett
Professor of Old Testament
Episcopal Divinity School
Cambridge, Massachusetts
(The Episcopal Church)
Zephaniah

Adele Berlin
Robert H. Smith Professor of Biblical Studies
Department of English and Jewish Studies Program
University of Maryland
College Park, Maryland
Introduction to Hebrew Poetry

Bruce C. Birch
Dean
Woodrow W. and Mildred B. Miller Professor of Biblical Theology
Wesley Theological Seminary
Washington, DC
(The United Methodist Church)
1 & 2 Samuel

Joseph Blenkinsopp
John A. O'Brien Professor of Biblical Studies, Emeritus
Department of Theology
University of Notre Dame
Notre Dame, Indiana
(The Roman Catholic Church)
Introduction to the Pentateuch

Walter Brueggemann
William Marcellus McPheeters Professor of Old Testament, Emeritus
Columbia Theological Seminary
Decatur, Georgia
(United Church of Christ)
Exodus

Ronald E. Clements
Samuel Davidson Professor of Old Testament, Emeritus
King's College
University of London
London, England
(Baptist Union of Great Britain and Ireland)
Deuteronomy

Richard J. Clifford, S.J.
Professor of Old Testament
Weston Jesuit School of Theology
Cambridge, Massachusetts
(The Roman Catholic Church)
Introduction to Wisdom Literature

Robert B. Coote
Professor of Old Testament
San Francisco Theological Seminary
San Anselmo, California
(Presbyterian Church [U.S.A.])
Joshua

Sidnie White Crawford
Professor and Chair of Classics and Religious Studies
Department of Classics and Religious Studies
University of Nebraska-Lincoln
Lincoln, Nebraska
(The Episcopal Church)
Esther; Additions to Esther

James L. Crenshaw
Robert L. Flowers Professor of Old Testament
The Divinity School
Duke University
Durham, North Carolina
(Baptist)
Sirach

[†]*deceased*

KATHERYN PFISTERER DARR
Professor of Hebrew Bible
The School of Theology
Boston University
Boston, Massachusetts
(The United Methodist Church)
Ezekiel

ROBERT DORAN
Samuel Williston Professor of Greek and Hebrew
(Religion)
Religion Department
Amherst College
Amherst, Massachusetts
1 & 2 Maccabees

THOMAS B. DOZEMAN
Professor of Old Testament
United Theological Seminary
Dayton, Ohio
(Presbyterian Church [U.S.A.])
Numbers

KATHLEEN A. ROBERTSON FARMER
Professor of Old Testament, Emerita
United Theological Seminary
Dayton, Ohio
(The United Methodist Church)
Ruth

TERENCE E. FRETHEIM
Elva B. Lovell Professor of Old Testament
Luther Seminary
Saint Paul, Minnesota
(Evangelical Lutheran Church in America)
Genesis

FRANCISCO O. GARCÍA-TRETO
Jennie Farris Railey King Professor of Religion
Department of Religion
Trinity University
San Antonio, Texas
(Presbyterian Church [U.S.A.])
Nahum

DONALD E. GOWAN
Robert Cleveland Holland Professor of Old
Testament, Emeritus
Pittsburgh Theological Seminary
Pittsburgh, Pennsylvania
(Presbyterian Church [U.S.A.])
Amos

THEODORE HIEBERT
Francis A. McGaw Professor of Old Testament
McCormick Theological Seminary
Chicago, Illinois
(Mennonite Church)
Habakkuk

WALTER C. KAISER, JR.
President
Colman M. Mockler Distinguished Professor of
Old Testament
Gordon-Conwell Theological Seminary
South Hamilton, Massachusetts
(The Evangelical Free Church of America)
Leviticus

RALPH W. KLEIN
Christ Seminary-Seminex Professor of Old Testament
Lutheran School of Theology at Chicago
Chicago, Illinois
(Evangelical Lutheran Church in America)
Ezra; Nehemiah

MICHAEL KOLARCIK, S.J.
Associate Professor of Old Testament
Regis College
Toronto, Ontario
Canada
(The Roman Catholic Church)
Book of Wisdom

J. CLINTON MCCANN, JR.
Evangelical Professor of Biblical Interpretation
Eden Theological Seminary
St. Louis, Missouri
(Presbyterian Church [U.S.A.])
Psalms

W. EUGENE MARCH
Arnold Black Rhodes Professor of Old Testament,
Emeritus
Louisville Presbyterian Theological Seminary
Louisville, Kentucky
(Presbyterian Church [U.S.A.])
Haggai

PATRICK D. MILLER
Charles T. Haley Professor of Old Testament
Theology, Emeritus
Princeton Theological Seminary
Princeton, New Jersey
(Presbyterian Church [U.S.A.])
Jeremiah

PETER D. MISCALL
Denver, Colorado
(The Episcopal Church)
Introduction to Narrative Literature

FREDERICK J. MURPHY
Professor
Department of Religious Studies
College of the Holy Cross
Worcester, Massachusetts
(The Roman Catholic Church)
Introduction to Apocalyptic Literature

CAROL A. NEWSOM
Charles Howard Candler Professor of Old Testament
Candler School of Theology
Emory University
Atlanta, Georgia
(The Episcopal Church)
Job

IRENE NOWELL, O.S.B.
Associate Professor of Religious Studies
Benedictine College
Atchison, Kansas
(The Roman Catholic Church)
Tobit

KATHLEEN M. O'CONNOR
William Marcellus McPheeters Professor of Old
Testament
Columbia Theological Seminary
Decatur, Georgia
(The Roman Catholic Church)
Lamentations

BEN C. OLLENBURGER
Professor of Biblical Theology
Associated Mennonite Biblical Seminaries
Elkhart, Indiana
(Mennonite Church)
Zechariah

DENNIS T. OLSON
Professor of Old Testament
Princeton Theological Seminary
Princeton, New Jersey
(Evangelical Lutheran Church in America)
Judges

Samuel Pagán
Professor
Evangelical Seminary of Puerto Rico
San Juan, Puerto Rico
(Christian Church [Disciples of Christ])
Obadiah

[†] *deceased*

DAVID L. PETERSEN
Professor of Old Testament
Candler School of Theology
Emory University
Atlanta, GA 30322
(Presbyterian Church [U.S.A.])
Introduction to Prophetic Literature

ANTHONY J. SALDARINI[†]
Professor of Biblical Studies
Boston College
Chestnut Hill, Massachusetts
(The Roman Catholic Church)
Baruch; Letter of Jeremiah

EILEEN M. SCHULLER
Professor
Department of Religious Studies
McMaster University
Hamilton, Ontario
Canada
(The Roman Catholic Church)
Malachi

CHRISTOPHER R. SEITZ
Professor of Old Testament and Theological Studies
Saint Mary's College
The Divinity School at the University of Saint
Andrews
Saint Andrews, Scotland
(The Episcopal Church)
Isaiah 40-66

CHOON-LEONG SEOW
Henry Snyder Gehman Professor of Old Testament
Language and Literature
Princeton Theological Seminary
Princeton, New Jersey
(Presbyterian Church [U.S.A.])
1 & 2 Kings

DANIEL J. SIMUNDSON
Professor of Old Testament, Emeritus
Luther Seminary
Saint Paul, Minnesota
(Evangelical Lutheran Church in America)
Micah

DANIEL L. SMITH-CHRISTOPHER
Professor of Theological Studies
Department of Theology
Loyola Marymount University
Los Angeles, California
(The Society of Friends [Quaker])
Daniel; The Additions to Daniel

CONTRIBUTORS

W. SIBLEY TOWNER
  The Reverend Archibald McFadyen Professor of
  Biblical Interpretation, Emeritus
  Union Theological Seminary in Virginia
  Richmond, Virginia
  (Presbyterian Church [U.S.A.])
    Ecclesiastes

PHYLLIS TRIBLE
  University Professor of Biblical Studies
  Wake Forest University Divinity School
  Winston-Salem, North Carolina
    Jonah

GENE M. TUCKER
  Professor of Old Testament, Emeritus
  Candler School of Theology
  Emory University
  Atlanta, Georgia
  (The United Methodist Church)
    Isaiah 1-39

RAYMOND C. VAN LEEUWEN
  Professor of Biblical Studies
  Christian Studies Department
  Eastern College
  Saint Davids, Pennsylvania
  (Christian Reformed Church in North America)
    Proverbs

RENITA J. WEEMS
  Ordained Elder, African Methodist Episcopal Church
  Public Lecturer
  (African Methodist Episcopal Church)
    Song of Songs

LAWRENCE M. WILLS
  Ethelbert Talbot Professor of Biblical Studies
  The Episcopal Divinity School
  Cambridge, Massachusetts
  (The Episcopal Church)
    Judith

GALE A. YEE
  Professor of Hebrew Bible
  Episcopal Divinity School
  Cambridge, Massachusetts
  (The Roman Catholic Church)
    Hosea

CONTENTS

CONTENTS

CONTENTS

ABBREVIATIONS AND INDEX OF CHARTS, ILLUSTRATIONS, AND MAPS

PART ONE:
THE WRITINGS
OF THE OLD TESTAMENT

INTRODUCTION TO THE PENTATEUCH

JOSEPH BLENKINSOPP

THE PENTATEUCH
IN THE BIBLICAL CANON

The designation Pentateuch, deriving from the Greek ἡ πεντάτευχος βίβλος (hē penta-teuchos biblos, "the fivefold book"), is not attested before the second century CE, though the fivefold division was in place much earlier. Josephus gives pride of place to the five books of Moses among authoritative Jewish records, which he compares favorably with those of the Greeks, but does not name the individual books.[1] The titles were, however, known to his older contemporary Philo, who refers to Deuteronomy as "The Protreptics," a not inappropriate title.[2] Occasional allusions in the New Testament (NT) to "the law and the prophets" (e.g., Matt 5:17; Luke 16:16; Rom 3:21) reflect contemporary Jewish usage, but the NT nowhere refers to the fivefold division or names any of the individual books. This division was, nevertheless, in place no later than the time of Ben Sira, who wrote his treatise in the early decades of the second century BCE; the fact that this author is familiar with the division of Latter Prophets into three and twelve (Sir 48:20–49:10) creates a strong presumption that he also knew the fivefold division of Torah. Frequent allusions to "the law," "the law of Moses," and "the book of the law" in earlier Second Temple compositions (e.g., 2 Chr 30:16; Ezra 10:3; Neh 8:3) refer to the legal content of the corpus, most frequently the Deuteronomic law, rather than to the entire Pentateuch. Designations current in Judaism—התורה חמישה חומשי (hămîšâ hûmšê hattôrâ , "the five fifths of the Law") or, more briefly, חומש (hûmāš, "the fivefold book") and, of course, תורה (tôrâ, "instruction, law")—imply the preeminence of the legal material that takes up more than one fifth of the Pentateuch. And since all the laws were believed to have been delivered to Israel through Moses, it was practically inevitable that the entire corpus came to be attributed to him as sole author.

In due course, the Pentateuch, or Torah, became the first and most important segment of the tripartite canon for Jews, and it alone enjoyed canonical status in the Samaritan community. We should add, however, that the term *canon*, meaning an authoritative corpus of sacred writings, originated in a Christian milieu no earlier than the fourth century (in Athanasius's *Decrees of the Council of Nicaea*, c. 350), though lists of biblical books were in circulation from the early second century. In Judaism there is nothing comparable prior to the well-known passage in *b. B. Bat.* 14b-15a listing the biblical books and their reputed authors. The process by which the canon in its different forms (Jewish, Protestant, Catholic, Eastern Orthodox) reached its final formulation is now acknowledged to have been much more complex and less clearly defined than was once thought, and the role of "the men of the Great Assembly" at the time of Ezra and "the Council of Jamnia [Yavneh]" after the fall of Jerusalem to the Romans in 70 CE is now known to be anachronistic and unhistorical. In any case, the Pentateuch had in all essentials reached its final form much earlier in the Second Temple period.

THE PENTATEUCHAL NARRATIVE

In spite of the designation Torah current in Judaism, the Pentateuch is basically a narrative. The sequence of events begins with creation and the early history of humanity in which the structurally decisive event is the deluge, after which the descendants of Noah are dispersed around the earth. In the tenth generation after the deluge, Abram (later Abraham) is called by God to leave Mesopotamia for a new land, with the promise of divine blessing and numerous progeny contingent

1

on his answering this call. The history of Israel's ancestors is traced through four generations, particular attention being devoted to the twenty-year exile of Jacob (later called Israel) in Mesopotamia, his eventual return to the promised land, and the emigration of his family, now seventy in number, to Egypt. The story of the ancestors, therefore, begins and ends outside the land, hence the promise made initially to Abraham and often repeated awaits fulfillment in the future. In Egypt the original settlers grow into a numerous and powerful people until a new pharaoh ascends the throne and, for reasons that are not entirely clear, launches a genocidal campaign against them.

One of Jacob's descendants called Moses, son of Levitical parents, survived the massacre of Hebrew male infants decreed by Pharaoh and, after killing an Egyptian overseer, was forced to take refuge in Midian. There he had the extraordinary experience of a deity's self-revelation to him as Yahweh, God of the ancestors, who sent him on a mission to persuade Pharaoh to let the oppressed Hebrews leave Egypt. A first attempt proved unsuccessful, but with the assistance from his brother, Aaron, and after a series of ecological disasters visited on the Egyptians culminated in the death of their first-born, a second mission succeeded. The Israelites headed out into the wilderness and the pursuing Egyptians were destroyed as they attempted to cross a body of water. After further vicissitudes, the Israelites, now 600,000 strong, not counting women and children, reached the wilderness of Sinai. There Moses received laws from Yahweh: First, ten commandments promulgated to the people at once; then a collection of laws communicated to Moses alone. There followed a covenant ritual and the revelation of the plan for the construction of the sanctuary and detailed instructions for the cult to be carried on in it. During Moses' absence on the mountain, an act of apostasy by the people, aided and abetted by Aaron, led to the breaking and remaking of the Law tablets and the giving of further statutes, mostly of a ritual sort. The cult was then set up as prescribed, the priesthood under Aaron was inaugurated, and after a lapse of about a year the Israelites continued on their way.

After an abortive attempt to invade Canaan, the Israelite throng under Moses arrived in Moab east of the Jordan. The attempt of the Moabite king to block their passage by hiring a seer to curse them was thwarted, and those Israelites who succumbed to the temptation to engage in sexual rites were executed. Preparations were made for occupying land both east and west of the Jordan, and on the last day of his life Moses addressed the people, reminding them of past favors bestowed on them by their God and the obligations they had thereby incurred. This last address included a new set of laws and was followed by a new covenant. Moses commissioned Joshua as his successor before his death and burial in an unmarked grave at the age of 120.

NARRATIVE ANOMALIES

The uneven narrative tempo of the Pentateuch story will be obvious even on a cursory reading. According to the chronology provided by the narrative itself, the events unfold over a period of 2,706 years, yet the sojourn at Sinai, the account of which occupies about one fifth of the total length, lasts less than one year (Exod 19:1; Num 10:11), while another fifth is dedicated to the last day in the life of Moses (Deut 1:3; 32:48). The most obvious explanation of this anomalous feature is that all laws, whenever promulgated, came in the course of time to be backdated to the lifetime of Moses. But the narrative also contains numerous repetitions and digressions and is punctuated at frequent intervals by genealogies and lists. These features suggest that the Pentateuchal story has been formed as the result of an incremental process over a considerable period of time.

Another structural problem is that the ending, with Moses and his people camped in Moab, east of the Jordan, appears to leave the promise of land, prominent in the history of the ancestors, up in the air. According to the Deuteronomic author-editor of Joshua, the conquest of Canaan was viewed as the fulfillment of that promise (see esp. Josh 21:43-45), so that it might seem more appropriate to speak of a Hexateuch (Pentateuch plus Joshua) as the basic literary unit and explain the omission of the conquest from the Pentateuch as a later move dictated by the needs of the post-exilic community. But in the context of the dominant documentary hypothesis (see below), we then have the problem that the principal continuous early sources—namely, J and E—are not clearly attested in Joshua, which reflects, rather, the language and ideology of Deuteronomy. This has led several scholars, conspicuously Martin Noth, to read Deuteronomy as the preface to the Deuteronomic History (Joshua–2 Kings) and the first four books as a more or less self-contained Tetrateuch. But a glance at the conclusion of Numbers will suffice to show that the Tetrateuch is no more a well-rounded and self-contained narrative than the Pentateuch; indeed, less so, since it not only leaves Israel outside the land but also omits the death of Moses. Noth's Tetrateuchal hypothesis would be further weakened if, as several scholars have since argued, the Deuteronomic hand is much more in evidence in Genesis–Numbers than he and others at that time were prepared to allow.

It is at least clear that the present divisions in the narrative continuum from creation to the Babylonian exile resulted from successive editorial adjustments. The most important of these was the inclusion of the Deuteronomic law and its homiletic framework in the narrative of Israelite origins, a move that necessitated the displacement of the commissioning of Joshua and the death of Moses from their original position in the Priestly narrative (Num 27:12-23) to the end of Deuteronomy (32:48-52 and 34:1, 7-9, also of P origin). Once this was done, Moses' death marked the closing of the normative epoch in which everything necessary for the sustenance of the Israelite commonwealth had been revealed and promulgated. In its final form, therefore, the Pentateuch is centered on the law and the unique mediatorial role of Moses.

STRUCTURE, DIVISIONS, THEME

The chapter divisions of the Pentateuch begin to appear in Hebrew MSS in the later Middle Ages, but had already been introduced into the Vulgate by Stephen Langton, Archbishop of Canterbury (1150–1228). By the Talmudic period, individual sentences or brief pericopes were being identified by words or phrases (סימנים *sîmānîm*, "signs"), but verse numbering is first attested in Christian Bibles at the time of the Reformation. The division of the Hebrew Bible (HB) into longer pericopes for liturgical reading is also attested from an early date. These sections (סדרים *sĕdārîm*) were subdivided into short paragraphs (פסקות *pisqôt*) separated by

a space of at least three letters, a practice already attested in the Qumran biblical texts. According to an early tradition, this had the purpose of giving Moses time to reflect on the meaning of the text between each subsection.[3]

While the division of the Pentateuch into five books clearly owed something to the need for convenient scroll handling, it is equally clear that the material could have been divided in a different way. Genesis and Deuteronomy have their own distinctive character as self-contained narratives, though the former could as well have concluded with the recapitulating genealogy of the Israelite family in Egypt in Gen 46:8-27. This is not the case with Exodus and Numbers, which are almost exactly equal in length. The break between Exodus and Leviticus is quite artificial, for the latter falls within the Sinai pericope that ends only in Numbers 10. Moreover, the ordination ceremony in Leviticus 8 is the sequel to the prescriptions for carrying out that ceremony in Exodus 29. It is possible that the fivefold arrangement had the purpose of highlighting Leviticus, by far the shortest of the five books, as the central panel defining Israel as a holy community distinct from other nations. The structure itself could then be read as encoding an important aspect of the self-understanding of the emergent Jewish commonwealth after the return from exile.

Another significant structural feature is the division of Genesis into sections entitled אלה תולדות (*'ēlleh tôlĕdôt*, "these are the generations . . . "). They are arranged in two pentads (groups of five) covering, respectively, the early history of humanity (Gen 2:4a; 5:1; 6:9; 10:1; 11:10) and the ancestral history (Gen 11:27; 25:12, 19; 36:1; 37:2). As with the fivefold division of the Pentateuch itself, this arrangement draws attention to the central panel of each pentad—namely, the deluge in the first and the vicissitudes of Jacob/Israel in the second. While the title *tôlĕdôt* is particularly apt for genealogical material, most of these sections contain far more narrative than genealogy.

A structuring and periodizing feature of a different kind is the series of precise chronological markers punctuating the narrative, especially in Genesis (e.g., Gen 7:6, 11; Exod 12:40-41; Num 10:11). Attempts to decode this chronological schema are complicated by the different numbers in the MT, LXX, and Samaritan Pentateuch, and no one solution has won universal acceptance. What can be said is that the schema is undoubtedly fictive and that it extends beyond the Pentateuch, taking in the building of Solomon's Temple (1 Kgs 6:1) and the 430 years between the construction and the destruction of the Temple, identical with the length of the sojourn in Egypt, according to Exod 12:40. It has also been observed that the interval of 2,666 years between creation and the exodus is two-thirds of a total of 4,000 years, which may have been thought of as a world epoch or "Great Year." Whatever the solution, this chronological grid expresses the conviction that the course of events has a direction and a goal predetermined and willed by God.

Since the Pentateuch contains materials from successive periods in the history of Israel and early Judaism that have been combined and reshaped in response to different situations, it is difficult to identify a single theme or organizing principle. The fact that it concludes with the death of Moses prior to the occupation of and residence in the land suggests that what is centrally important is the complex of institutions and laws that serve as a kind of blueprint for the commonwealth and polity to be established. But the story of the ancestors begins with the command to Abraham to go to a land in which his descendants would become a great nation replete with blessing and a source of blessing for other peoples (Gen 12:1-3). For those who postulate a Hexateuch from which the Pentateuch was formed by detaching Joshua, the fulfillment of these promises would be seen in the conquest and settlement of Canaan (see Josh 21:43-45 which reads like a finale to the story); and for those who postulate a Yahwist (J) source from the early monarchy, the terminus would be the "Greater Israel" of David and Solomon. If, however, the Pentateuch *in its final form* is read in the context of the emergent Judaism that produced it, the ancestral promises would reflect the aspirations of those who elected to return to the homeland under Persian rule. The addition of the early history of humanity in Genesis 1-11, in keeping with well-established historiographical tradition in the Near East and the Levant (the countries bordering the eastern edge of the Mediterranean Sea), placed the history of the nation in the context of world history and allowed for a realistic and profound diagnosis of the human condition.

THE FORMATION
OF THE PENTATEUCH

From Ibn Ezra to Wellhausen. The view long traditional in both Judaism and Christianity, and still maintained in the more conservative denominations of both religions, is that Moses authored the entire Pentateuch with the possible exception of the last verses recounting his death and burial. The beginnings of this belief can be traced to the close association between Moses and the law. From a fairly early time, it became standard procedure to attribute all laws to Moses in the same way that sapiential compositions came to be attributed to Solomon and Psalms to David. And since the laws are embedded in narrative, it was a short step to assigning the entire corpus to Moses in spite of the fact that this is nowhere affirmed in the Pentateuch itself.

One of the earliest to raise questions about the attribution was the twelfth-century Jewish scholar Abraham Ibn Ezra, who alluded cryptically, in his commentary on Deuteronomy, to certain passages that presuppose situations and events long after the time of Moses; e.g., the remark that at that time the Canaanites were in the land Gen 12:6 and the allusion to the iron bed of King Og of Bashan, which was a tourist attraction at the time of his writing (Deut 3:11). Further difficulties were raised by other commentators in the following centuries, with the result that by the seventeenth century writers as diverse as Spinoza and Hobbes simply rejected Mosaic authorship altogether. Even scholars within the ecclesiastical mainstream, while not denying the traditional view outright, were beginning to acknowledge the composite nature of the Pentateuch. One of the earliest of these was the French Oratorian priest Richard Simon. In his *Histoire Critique du Vieux Testament* (1678) he acknowledged the role of Moses in the production of the Pentateuch but went on to suggest that it owed its final form to scribes at the time of Ezra. The outcome was that his work was placed on the Roman Catholic Index of Prohibited Books and most of the copies printed were destroyed. One of the surviving copies was, however, translated into German by Johann Salomo Semler about a century later and, in that form, contributed significantly to research on the Pentateuch, then well underway in German universities.

By the early eighteenth century, evidence for the use of sources was becoming more and more apparent. Repetitions, parallel versions of the same event, and notable differences in language and point of view seemed to render this conclusion inevitable. The first to exploit the occurrence of divine names—Elohim and Yahweh—as a means of distinguishing between sources was Henning Bernhard Witter, Lutheran pastor of Hildesheim, who wrote a monograph on the subject in 1711 that remained practically unnoticed until rediscovered by the French biblical scholar Adolphe Lods in 1925. Somewhat along the same lines, the French physician and amateur Old Testament (OT) scholar Jean Astruc published a book forty-two years later in which he distinguished three sources in the Pentateuch, the first two of which were characterized by use of the names Elohim and Yahweh respectively. By assuming that these sources were used by Moses in compiling the Pentateuch, Astruc sought to preserve the traditional dogma. By the end of that century, nevertheless, the existence of parallel sources was widely acknowledged, at least for Genesis and the first part of Exodus up to the point where the divine name YHWH (Yahweh) was revealed to Moses (Exod 3:13-15).

A minority opinion, first proposed by the Scottish Roman Catholic priest Alexander Geddes in the late eighteenth century and developed by J. S. Vater, professor at Halle in the early years of the following century, rejected the hypothesis of two continuous parallel sources in favor of a much greater number of quite disparate blocks of material that were combined long after the time of Moses to form the Pentateuch (the Fragmentary Hypothesis). Another alternative assumed that a single base narrative, or *Grundschrift*, was subsequently filled out with additional material (the Supplementary Hypothesis). But in whatever form it was proposed, the view that the Pentateuch is the result of a long process of literary formation was firmly established by the early nineteenth century, in academic if not in ecclesiastical circles.

During that period of political and cultural upheaval, the most important contribution to understanding the formation of the Pentateuch was that of Wilhelm Martin Leberecht de Wette (1780–1849), colleague of Schleiermacher at the newly founded University of Berlin. De Wette's study of Chronicles persuaded him that the legal and cultic system that the author of Chronicles presumes to have been in place since Mosaic times or, with respect to the Jerusalem cult, from the time of David, is unattested in the early records and must, therefore, be a projection into the past of the situation obtaining at the time of writing in the post-exilic period. The greater part of the legal and cultic material in the Pentateuch, therefore, belongs to the early history of Judaism rather than to that of Israel. In keeping with this conclusion, de Wette divided his *Biblical Dogmatics* (1813) into two sections entitled "Hebraism" and "Judaism." True to the dominant Romanticism of the time, de Wette contrasted the spontaneity and vigor of early Israelite religion with the formalism and empty ritualism that he believed characterized early Judaism and Judaism as a whole, a contrast that would be set out in much starker terms by Wellhausen toward the end of the same century. In another important monograph, de Wette identified the lawbook that the priest Hilkiah claimed to have found in the Temple during the reign of Josiah (640–609 BCE) with an early draft of Deuteronomy (see 2 Kgs 22:8-10). According to de Wette, this composition claimed for itself Mosaic authorship but was actually a recent pseudepigraphal work "planted" by the priests to serve as a basis for the religious reforms that followed its "discovery." By thus placing the Deuteronomic Law (Deuteronomy 12–26) in the seventh century BCE, de Wette believed it possible to distinguish between earlier legislation unfamiliar with this compilation and later laws that presupposed it.

Throughout the nineteenth century OT scholars concentrated on the identification and dating of sources, rather less so on the editorial processes by which they were assembled into a coherent whole. Briefly, the most important advances following de Wette were, first, the discovery that the Elohist source (E), by most considered the earliest, contained an earlier and a later strand. First suggested by Karl David Ilgen in 1798, the distinction was worked out in detail about a half century later by Hermann Hupfeld, resulting in the emergence of a priestly and theocratic source (later to be known under the siglum P). The second and decisive proposal, already implicit in the results obtained by de Wette at the beginning of the century, was that this newly discovered Priestly source was to be located at the end, not the beginning, of the process of for-

Documentary Hypothesis

	Source	Approximate Date	Characteristics
J	the Yahwistic source	10th century BCE	Use of name YHWH for God; Promises and Blessings; Southern Version
E	the Elohistic source	9th century BCE	Use of name Elohim for God; Nonpriestly; Northern Version
D	the Deuteronomistic source	7th century BCE	Law Codes; Centralization of Worship; Theme of the Promised Land; Election and Covenant
P	the Priestly source	6th century BCE	Use of name Elohim for God; Specialized Vocabulary (ex. Israel as a Congregation); Ordered, Unconditional, Eternal Covenant

mation. First advanced by Edouard Reuss in lectures delivered at the University of Strasbourg, the hypothesis of the late P source appeared in print in a book published by Karl Heinrich Graf, student of Reuss, in 1866. The way was thus cleared for the definitive formulation of what came to be known as "the newer documentary hypothesis," with the sources in the chronological order JEDP, in the *Prolegomena to the History of Israel* of Julius Wellhausen (1883).

With benefit of hindsight, it is not too difficult to detect the philosophical and cultural determinants of this lengthy and persistent attempt to identify and date sources. It is important to bear in mind that the goal of this massive effort to identify and date sources was not so much a theological or aesthetic appreciation of the texts in themselves but rather the reconstruction of the history, and especially the religious history, of Israel. Throughout the nineteenth century, scholars emphasized development, specifically of ideas. Although sometimes exaggerated, the impact of Hegel's dialectical philosophy of history was felt in both OT and NT studies. It can be detected, for example, in the tendency for a tripartite periodization of the history— typically, Mosaism, propheticism, early Judaism. As noted above, influences were also felt from the Romantic movement, especially in the positive evaluation of the early and naive stage of religious development, the high estimation of the prophet as the religious individualist *par excellence*, and the marked lack of enthusiasm for post-exilic Judaism, generally characterized as a decline into religious formalism and ritualism. While, perhaps, few OT scholars professed to be anti-Jewish, academic study of the Pentateuch, and the OT in general, was carried on in an atmosphere decidedly unfavorable to Judaism. It is, therefore, not surprising that Jewish scholars, with few exceptions, turned their attention elsewhere.

From Wellhausen to the Mid-Twentieth Century. The four-source or newer documentary hypothesis as set out by Wellhausen soon became the critical orthodoxy, though opposed by scholars of more conservative ecclesiastical affiliation. It was not clearly perceived at the time, but the Graf-Wellhausenian construct was threatened less from conservative reaction than it was from the ongoing analysis of the sources themselves. The requirement of a fairly high level of consistency in terminology, style, and theme had already led to the division of an originally unitary E source into P and E, and it was not long before the E source itself suffered the same fate,[4] resulting in E^1 and E^2. However, J proved to be especially friable, resulting either in J^1 and J^2 as constituent sources[5] or in the postulation of a more primitive strand within J, variously described as of lay origin,[6] or of Kenite,[7] Edomite,[8] or nomadic provenance.[9] Wellhausen himself had argued for two strands in Deuteronomy, and the existence of a Josian and exilic redaction, from the seventh and sixth centuries BCE respectively, is now widely accepted. At the beginning of the century, Bruno Baentsch identified as many as seven strands in P, each with its own redactional history, and while few were prepared to press source division to that extreme, many agreed that additions were made at different times to the P narrative and laws,[10] though there is still no agreement as to whether P is a distinct source or an editorial reworking of earlier material.

The problem inherent in this kind of detailed analysis of sources is not difficult to detect. To the degree that the requirement of inner consistency is pressed, the sources tend to disintegrate into a bewildering variety of smaller units or strands, and the entire hypothesis is undermined. A challenge of a different nature emerged from the work of Hermann Gunkel (1852–1932), the first edition of whose commentary on Genesis appeared in 1901. Gunkel accepted the Graf-Wellhausen construct, but the innovative study of literary forms, in his work and that of his students Gressmann and Baumgartner, was to create serious problems for the documentary hypothesis. The influence of the History of Religions school on Gunkel can be seen in his first significant publication, entitled *Creation and Chaos* (*Schöpfung und Chaos*, 1895); following the lead of this school, Gunkel brought a comparative study of genres to bear on the narrative material in Genesis, concentrating on the smallest literary units, their oral prehistory, and the social situations that generated them. His description of these narratives as saga has occasioned difficulties, since in English the term applies to medieval Icelandic prose narratives, not necessarily composed and transmitted orally. In German, however, the corresponding term *Sage* can have a more general meaning, including legend and folktale, and it is in this sense that Gunkel used it, depending on the work of the Danish folklorist Axel Olrik. Gunkel's application of this kind of literary analysis, which he called *Literaturgeschichte* (literary history) or *Gattungsforschung* (the investigation of genres), but which has since been known as *Formgeschichte* (the history of forms, form criticism), shifted the emphasis away from extensive written documents to individual pericopes and the oral tradition underlying them. Although it was not clearly perceived at the time, Gunkel's investigations were to lead in a quite different direction from that of Graf and Wellhausen.

The concept of oral tradition also played an important role in the work of von Rad, whose study entitled "The Form-Critical Problem of the Hexateuch," published in 1938, proved very influential, and whose ideas were further developed in his commentaries on Genesis and Deuteronomy as well as in the first volume of his *Old Testament Theology*.[11] According to von Rad, the Hexateuchal narrative was elaborated on the basis of the kind of liturgical and confessional statement found in Deut 26:5-9, the form of words pronounced by the Israelite farmer at the offering of the firstfruits. He observed that this "Hexateuch in a nutshell," as he called it, memorialized the descent into Egypt, the exodus, and settlement in the land but omitted any mention of the giving of the Law. To explain this omission, he postulated two separate streams of tradition that came together only in the work of the Yahwist author (J): the exodus-occupation tradition rooted in the Festival of Weeks at Gilgal; and the Sinai tradition, originating in the Festival of Tabernacles at the ancient tribal sanctuary of Shechem. The Yahwist prefaced the literary elaboration of these conflated traditions with the early history of humanity in Genesis 1–11 and the ancestral history in Genesis 12–50, thus laying the groundwork for the Hexateuch as we have it. Cultic recital rooted in the tribal federation of the prestate period was thus transformed into religious literature, the catalyst for the transformation being what von Rad called "the Solomonic enlightenment."

Von Rad's high evaluation of the Yahwist as a literary and religious genius was very influential, especially during the heyday of the "biblical theology movement" in the two decades following World War II and residually down to the present. Books and articles began to appear on the kerygma, or the theology, of the Yahwist.[12] There were even attempts to penetrate the veil of anonymity by identifying him as a member of Solomon's entourage, the favored candidates being Nathan, Abiathar, and Ahimaaz. In recent years serious questions have been raised about the date, extent, and even existence of J as a continuous and integral narrative source.

Other proponents of a cultic origin for the narrative and legal traditions of ancient Israel were the Norwegian scholar Sigmund Mowinckel, who located the Decalogue in a pre-monarchic New Year festival; Johannes Pedersen, who read Exodus 1–15 as the deposit of cultic recital for Passover; and Albrecht Alt, whose influential essay "The Origins of Israelite Law"[13] grounded the apodictic laws in the cult of the Israelite amphictyony. Following the same form-critical and traditio-historical procedures, Martin Noth[14] identified five major themes (guidance out of Egypt, progress through the wilderness, entry into the arable land, promise to the ancestors, and the revelation at Sinai) whose origin and early development were in the tribal amphictyony and its cult. These traditions were combined and molded into a consecutive narrative to form the Tetrateuch. Noth's acceptance of the documentary hypothesis was fairly laconic, since he maintained that the essential lines of the narrative tradition had been present from the beginning, whether in oral or written form is unclear (his reference to a base narrative or *Grundschrift* remained undeveloped).

Noth's studies provided the basis for his account of the origins and early development of Israel in his *A History of Israel*.[15] His main point was that the combination of the five themes, originating in different segments of what later became Israel, went hand in hand with the consolidation of these diverse groups into the Israelite tribal federation, or amphictyony, of the pre-monarchic period. Here, too, more recent studies have called into question Noth's amphictyonic thesis, first advanced in 1930, and his understanding of Israelite origins in general. His hypothesis of a Deuteronomistic historical work (Dtr) covering Joshua through 2 Kings, first advanced in 1943, has on the other hand stood the test of time and is still almost universally accepted.

We can see now how von Rad and Noth, neither of whom questioned the regnant documentary hypothesis, followed Gunkel in shifting the emphasis back into the preliterary origin of the Pentateuchal traditions. While this displacement has had important consequences, many of the specific conclusions of both scholars have since been called into question. The creedal statements von Rad took as the starting point of the literary development eventuating in the Hexateuch, especially Deut 26:1-15, are now seen to be Deuteronomic and, therefore, no earlier than the seventh century BCE. The separate origin of the exodus-occupation and Sinai traditions has been generally abandoned, and the high antiquity of the covenant formulation can no longer be taken for granted. More recent comparative studies of oral tradition have given us a better understanding of the relation between oral and written transmission and have made it more difficult to determine the oral origin of written narrative.[16] Moreover, one might ask how the cult, which can certainly serve to transmit a narrative tradition, can also originate it.

During the same period, more radical theories of oral tradition were popular with Scandinavian scholars, especially with respect to the Pentateuch and the prophetic books. Drawing on the work of the Uppsala scholars H. S. Nyberg and Harris Birkeland, Ivan Engnell argued strongly for a traditio-historical approach rather than the Wellhausenian emphasis on literary sources. Engnell maintained that the narrative material in the Tetrateuch was transmitted orally throughout the pre-exilic period and was committed to writing only after the Babylonian exile in what he called "the P circle." This final redaction was quite distinct from the roughly contemporary "D work" comprising Deuteronomy and Dtr. At some point Deuteronomy was detached from the history and built into the Priestly Tetrateuch, resulting in the Pentateuch more or less as we have it. Some aspects of Engnell's critique of the documentary hypothesis are reproduced in recent revisionist writings, but his extreme advocacy of oral tradition has since been abandoned.

Recent Developments. While there have always been those who rejected the documentary hypothesis outright[17] and others who were critical of some aspect of it,[18] it is only in the last two decades or so that the Graf-Wellhausen construct can be said to be in serious and possibly terminal crisis. The main line of attack has focused on the existence of *continuous* sources from the early period of the monarchy. It has become apparent that Otto Eissfeldt's description of J as expressing "enthusiastic acceptance of agricultural life and national-political power and cultus"[19] may apply to some parts of the narrative but not at all to the substantial J component of Genesis 1–11, which speaks of the curse on the soil and emphasizes the vanity of human pretensions in general and in the political sphere in particular. Considerations such as this have led several scholars—Norman Wagner, Rolf Rendtorff, Erhard Blum, among others[20]—to argue that the several narrative blocks in the Pentateuch had their own distinctive processes of formation until they were redacted together at a late date. Doubts about the early dating of J (in the tenth or ninth century BCE) have coalesced to the point where such an early date can no longer be taken for granted. The Canadian scholar F. V. Winnett[21] argued for a post-exilic J in Genesis, while John Van Seters, one of his students, postulated an exilic J whose work reflects the exigencies and aspirations of the Jewish community at that time. In later studies, Van Seters went on to argue that the Yahwist, an individual author and not a school or circle, produced a historiographical work that can be profitably compared with, and was influenced by, early Greek mythography and historiography, including Herodotus and the Hesiodic *Catalogue of Women.*[22] It is still too early to evaluate adequately this new direction, but at least one scholar of note has taken a similar line.[23]

Another development threatening to undermine the existing paradigm involves the contribution of Deuteronomic authors to the narrative in the first four books of the Bible. We have seen that Martin Noth made a sharp distinction between the Tetrateuch and Dtr prefaced by Deuteronomy; until recently, this position was widely accepted. In recent years, however, several scholars have argued for a substantial D contribution to the narrative continuum in Genesis–Numbers, especially in key passages such as "the covenant of the pieces" in Genesis 15 and the Sinai/Horeb pericope in Exodus 19–34.[24] Others have noted prophetic and Deuteronomic features in passages routinely attributed to J—e.g., the call of Moses in Exodus 3–4, reminiscent of prophetic commissionings—and have concluded that the first consecutive account of the founding events was put together by members of the Deuteronomic school who linked existing units of tradition by means of the promise of land, nationhood, and divine blessing.[25] These conclusions—the displacement of J to a much later period, a significant D component in Genesis–Numbers, the absorption of J into the D school—are still open to debate, but if they are sustained it is difficult to see how the documentary hypothesis can survive in anything like its classical form. And it goes without saying that they would lead to a very different way of reconstructing the history and religion of Israel.

A more radical attack on the documentary hypothesis, and the historical-critical methods employed by its advocates, has come in recent years from a quite different direction, that of literary-critical theory. The emergence of the New Criticism in the twenties and thirties of this century marked a decisive turning away from the historical, philological, and referential approach to literature with an emphasis on the circumstances of the production and first reception of texts, the psychology and intention of the author, and the like. The proponents of this theory, including such major figures as I. A. Richards and William Empson, favored a text-immanent approach that concentrated on the internal organization and aesthetics of the literary composition without regard to its social and psychological coordinates. A similar concentration on "the text in itself," the text as a closed system, characterizes more recent trends in formalist, structuralist, and post-structuralist interpretation, and it was inevitable that sooner or later such approaches would be applied to biblical texts.

Methodologies for the Study of the Pentateuch with Prominent Proponents	
Fragmentary Hypothesis	A. Beddes
	J. Vater
Newer Documentary Hypothesis	J. Wellhausen (P later than D)
	Y. Kaufman (P earlier than D)
Form Criticism	H. Gunkel
	A. Alt
Traditon-History	G. von Rad
	M. Noth
	I. Egnell
Redaction Critiscism	R. Rendtorff
	E. Blum
New Supplementary Hypothesis	J. Van Seters
New Criticism	R. Alter
Canonical Criticism	B. S. Childs

This is not the place to evaluate the many essays in interpretation of Pentateuchal narratives of these kinds that have appeared over the last two decades or so. Several (e.g., Roland Barthes's analysis of the Jabbok ford narrative in Genesis 32) have been stimulating, but the results have been uneven, and the best readings have come from professional literary critics familiar with and sensitive to the original language.[26] Synchronic analysis, which takes the text as it is can open up valuable new perspectives, but without disposing of the need for diachronic—i.e., historical-critical—reconstructions, the principal aim of which has never been aesthetic appreciation of the text.

Similar in some respects is the approach that, since the 1970s, has come to be known as "canonical criticism."[27] Both the new critical and the canonical approaches concentrate on the final form of the text, but with the difference that the latter has an explicitly theological agenda. The contribution of Brevard S. Childs in particular seems to aim at reaffirming the nature of the Bible as a confessional document originating in a faith community. Attention is, therefore, focused on the final form, rather than on the hypothetical origins or sources, of the biblical texts as the proper object of theological inquiry. With respect to the Pentateuch, therefore, Childs seeks to show how the five books are related thematically and how the final editorial stage was based on a reading of the Pentateuch as a whole.[28]

The Final Stage of Formation. It is generally agreed that the Pentateuch achieved its final form during the two centuries (538–334 BCE) when Jews in the province of Judah, and most Jews elsewhere, were subject to Iranian rule. Some, including Wellhausen himself, have been prepared to go further and identify the Pentateuch, or at least its legal content, with the law, which Ezra was commissioned to teach and enforce in the Transeuphrates satrapy of the Achaemenid Empire (Ezra 7:1-26). This hypothesis has ancient precedent in the Ezra Apocalypse (late first century CE), which depicts Ezra's reproducing under divine inspiration the sacred books after they had perished in the fall of Jerusalem (2 Esdras 14). The law administered by Ezra was certainly no innovation, since it was presumed to be familiar to Jews in the area under Ezra's jurisdiction Ezra 7:25. It would be reasonable to assume that, at least in the mind of the author of the Ezra narrative, it was identical with the law referred to on numerous occasions elsewhere in Chronicles–Ezra–Nehemiah, and therefore included legal material from both Deuteronomy and the Priestly writers. But there is no evidence that Ezra "canonized" the law in such a way that no further additions or modifications could be introduced into it. Thus the Temple tax, which is a third of a shekel in Neh 10:33-34, has increased to half a shekel in Exod 30:11-16 (see also 38:25), and the solemn day of fasting and repentance occurs on the twenty-fourth of Tishri, according to Neh 9:1, and on the tenth of the same month in the Priestly law (Lev 16:29; 23:27-32; Num 29:7-11). Admittedly, these divergences could be explained otherwise, but they are consistent with the conclusion that the Pentateuchal law had not attained its final form by the mid-fifth century BCE but was well on its way to doing so.

Our knowledge of Achaemenid imperial administration also suggests that the Pentateuchal law came to serve as the civic constitution of the Jewish ethnos at that time. It was the Persian custom to insist on the codification of local and traditional laws and entrust their implementation to the provincial authorities, including priesthoods, with the backing of the central government. A document example comes from Egypt, since we know from the Demotic chronicle[29] that Darius I appointed a commission composed of representatives of the different orders charged with the task of codifying the traditional laws. After a labor of several years, these laws were redacted in Aramaic and demotic Egyptian. While there is no direct evidence of such activity in Judah, the proximity of Judah to Egypt and its location in the same satrapy, as well as the consistency of Persian policy in this respect, suggest that something similar may have happened in Judah.

The circumstances under which the narrative achieved its final form are even more obscure. The great importance of the laws as the civic constitution of the nascent Jewish commonwealth would help to explain why the story ends with the death of the lawgiver, and the exclusion of the conquest narrative would be understandable in view of the delicate situation of a small subject province in the vast Achaemenid Empire. The need for a comprehensive corpus of laws resulted in the incorporation of the Deuteronomic law with its historical and homiletic framework into the structure of the Priestly work, which also features law and narrative. This was accomplished by the simple expedient of adding a date of the P type at the beginning of Deuteronomy (1:3), which aligned the book with the overall P chronology. It appears that in the original form of the P narrative Moses' death, preceded by the commissioning of Joshua as his successor, occurred at an earlier point in the wilderness itinerary (Num 27:12-23) following on the deaths of Miriam and Aaron (Num 20:1, 22-29). God commands Moses to ascend Mount Abarim, view the land, and die; the natural implication is that this is to happen at once, delayed only by the need to appoint a successor. But Moses' death is not recorded at this point, because he must first promulgate the second law and covenant in Moab. Only toward the end of

Deuteronomy, therefore, do we find a revised version of the appointment of Joshua as successor (32:48-52) and an account of Moses' death (34:1, 7-9), both passages from the hand of a later P writer. The work is then rounded off with a statement denying parity between the Mosaic revelation and prophetic revelations subsequent to Moses' death; a statement that, in effect, establishes the Mosaic age as normative and confers authoritative status on the record of Moses' life and work (Deut 34:10). By this means the post-exilic commonwealth laid a firm foundation in the past for its own self-understanding as a community based on covenant and law.

If, then, we view the process of formation beginning with this final stage and working backward we must assign a decisive role to the Priestly and Deuteronomic writers. The former, whose contribution is relatively easy to detect, were responsible for the basic structuring of the work. The narrative framework within which the massive corpus of Priestly law is presented begins with creation and ends with the establishment of the sanctuary in the promised land (Joshua 18–19). The Deuteronomic contribution is not confined to the book of Deuteronomy but is in evidence elsewhere in the Pentateuch (e.g., Genesis 15; Exodus 32–34), though to what extent still remains to be clarified. If, for the sake of continuity, we continue to speak of J and E, we must now acknowledge that there is no longer any certainty about the origin, date, and extent of these sources. Some of the material assigned to them is either Deuteronomic or of unknown provenance. The J material in Genesis 1–11 may even be later than P, serving as a reflective supplement and commentary in the manner of the later stages. Both D and P have certainly incorporated early traditions and written sources in prose and verse, but the entire issue of pre-exilic source material in the Pentateuch—its extent, its origins written and oral, and its editorial history—remains to be clarified.

READING THE PENTATEUCH THEOLOGICALLY

A theological reading of the Pentateuch must take account not only of the final form but also of the successive restructurings, re-editings and expansions that, according to a historical-critical reading, eventuated in the final form. This process implies that any theologically significant theme will have undergone a process of development. In addition, different traditions, notably those of the Priestly and Deuteronomic writers, have been allowed to coexist even where they differ in significant respects. Reducing these perspectives to a common theological denominator would risk missing the richness and variety of religious thinking in the Pentateuch.

Theological understanding is also conditioned by the point of view, the perspective, of the reader and the convictions of the community within which the text is read. Neither Judaism nor Christianity has assigned absolute and exclusive authority to the Pentateuch. In Judaism functional canonicity includes Mishnah, Gemarah, and Toseftah, understood as the deposit of the oral law. Early Christianity continued to regard the Law and the Prophets as authoritative but read them in the light of the new reality in Christ. Persons and events in the Pentateuch were interpreted as prefiguring this new reality and the prophets as predicting it. The laws in the Pentateuch were evaluated in widely different ways from the apostolic period on. From an early date, the Decalogue served as a compendium of moral teaching (e.g., in the *Didache*), a circumstance that, when taken with the neglect of the ritual laws, explains why it played a very minor role in Jewish teaching. (It is mentioned only twice in the Mishnah.) This issue came to the fore with particular clarity at the Reformation. The Lutheran distinction between law and gospel, reinforced by Luther's own often-expressed aversion to Judaism, resulted in a distinct undervaluation of the legal content of the Pentateuch. Calvinism, on the other hand, tended rather to overestimate the place of law in Christian theology and church polity. The result is that only in recent years have Christian biblical scholars begun to give serious and unprejudiced attention to the legal material, including the ritual law.

While this is clearly not the place to attempt a comprehensive survey or synthesis of religious ideas in the Pentateuch, which would be tantamount to writing a history of Israelite religion, some account should be given of the leading theological symbols and ideas in the major literary strands.

The Priestly Writers (P). While several Jewish scholars have followed Yehezkel Kaufmann[30] in dating P to the pre-exilic period, the majority opinion has placed this school in the sixth or fifth century BCE while allowing that much of the legal and cultic material may have originated earlier. There is no consensus on the issue of P's relation to earlier narrative material, some viewing it as basically commentary and editorial expansion and others as an independent narrative source. In favor of the latter alternative, at least with regard to the narrative core of the P material, are the thematic and linguistic correspondences between the creation account in Gen 1:1–2:3, the construction of the wilderness sanctuary in Exodus 35–40 (see especially 39:32; 40:33), and its establishment at Shiloh in the land of Canaan (Josh 18:1; 19:51).[31] One implication of this structural feature is that the created order exists for the worship and praise of God. The seven days of creation represent the liturgical week. Sabbath is rooted in the created order, and the fact that its celebration concludes the construction of the wilderness sanctuary signals a close association between world building and sanctuary building (Exod 31:12-17). The heavenly bodies are created on the fourth day as a means of establishing the religious calendar. If we confine ourselves to the P strand, the Sinai event consists exclusively in the reception by Moses in a vision of the specifications for the sanctuary and its cult (Exod 19:1; 24:15-18; 25-31), which can be inaugurated only after the ordination of priests, a ceremony that also lasts seven days (Leviticus 8–9).

Even if it is argued that the P version was intended to be read together with other, and presumably earlier, accounts of the Sinai/Horeb event, it is still remarkable that this source omits any reference to a covenant. The P source in fact represents a rather radical rethinking of the covenant idea, no doubt in response to the situation of exile. The first covenant is made with the new humanity after the flood, long before Israel appears on the historical scene (Gen 9:8-17). All of humanity had received a religious qualification at creation (Gen 1:26-28), and now is offered a new dispensation, including the so-called Noachide laws, and an unconditional commitment on the part of God to preserve the new creation. The only covenant with Israel recorded in P is with Abraham, to whom is promised nationhood, land, and the divine presence (Gen 17:1-21). Both of these covenants, with humanity and with Israel, are unilateral and unconditional, since circumcision is the sign of Israel's

covenant and not a stipulation on the observance of which God's promise is contingent. Both are also "everlasting covenants" (Gen 9:16; 17:7-8, 13) that, therefore, do not require periodic renewal as do most covenants. All that is called for is that God *remember* the covenant commitment, which God does when the people are languishing in exile (Exod 2:24; 6:5; Lev 26:42, 45).

According to P the covenant promise of divine presence is fulfilled through the erection of the sanctuary and the inauguration of the cult, a conclusion implicit in the structure of the core narrative. Throughout the wilderness journey, presence is signified by the mysterious glory or effulgence (כבוד *kābôd*) that comes to rest in the sanctuary (Exod 40:34-35), appears when important decisions have to be taken (e.g., Num 14:10; 16:19), and guides Israel in its progress to the land. In P, all aspects of the liturgical life of the people are revealed in orderly fashion. Only rituals not requiring presence in the sanctuary and the participation of the priesthood are revealed before the cult is inaugurated; namely, sabbath (Exod 31:12-17; cf. 16:22-30), circumcision (Gen 17:9-14), and Passover (Exod 12:1-28). The P version of the flood story, therefore, omits mention of the distinction between clean and unclean animals and Noah's sacrifice on leaving the ark. The basic rationale for the sacrificial cult, as of the laws governing clean and unclean and sexual relations, is to preserve and, where necessary, restore the cosmic order established at creation. That order is disturbed by sin, even involuntary sin (e.g., bodily discharges), and can be restored only by the mandatory purgation and reparation sacrifices (Lev 4:1–6:7). The tenfold occurrence in the creation recital of the phrase "according to its/their kind" suggests that the distinction between clean and unclean fauna (Leviticus 11–15) was intended to preserve the norms established in creation and to inculcate a reverent regard for the created order. Although often dismissed as archaic and irrational, these and similar regulations reflect an ecological concern in the broadest sense, a discriminating ethical attitude to the taking of life for human nourishment, and a concern for the body as that part of the world for which each one is more directly responsible.

The Deuteronomists (D). A significantly different perspective is apparent in the Deuteronomic corpus, consisting in Deuteronomy, the

Deuteronomistic History (Joshua–2 Kings), additions to the narrative in the Tetrateuch, and editorial accretions in several prophetic books, especially Jeremiah. Deuteronomy presents not so much a law as a program or polity for the future Israelite commonwealth. Endowed with the authority of Moses as lawgiver and founder of the nation, it grounds the social existence of the people on the new covenant made on the eve of entry into the land. Unlike the P covenant, that of the Deuteronomists is genuinely bilateral and conditional in that its maintenance is contingent on a faithful and trustful commitment on the part of Israel to the observance of the Law. In this respect, it is comparable to, and was probably influenced in its formulation by, more or less contemporary Assyrian vassal treaties. The emphasis, therefore, is on Israel as a moral community. The connection between the fulfillment of the promises and faith that finds expression in fidelity to the law is already clearly articulated in the Deuteronomic profile of Abraham (Gen 18:17-19; 22:16-18; 26:4-5), the starting point for the presentation of Abraham in both Judaism and Christianity as the model and paradigm of faith (e.g., Heb 11:8-12). On numerous occasions, the Mosaic homilies in Deuteronomy emphasize that the gift of land is contingent on fidelity to the Law, and it is made abundantly clear that without faith Israel cannot fulfill its destiny (see Deut 1:32; 9:23).

The covenant is also the basis for Israel's election and its consequent special status vis-à-vis the nations of the world. While the dangerous ambiguities inherent in this idea of election are abundantly clear, the Deuteronomists emphasize repeatedly both its origin in a divine initiative (see Deut 4:32-40; 7:7-11) and the obligations it entails (7:7-11). The uniqueness of Israel, thus defined and circumscribed, is emphasized at every turn. Thus the law is seen as the counterpart of the intellectual tradition or wisdom of other peoples (Deut 4:5-8), and prophecy is contrasted with divination and similar forms of mediation practiced elsewhere (13:1-5; 18:9-22). Most important, Deuteronomy insists on an exclusive relationship with one God: Yahweh, God of Israel. This conviction, of immense significance for the future, is enshrined in the שמע šěma (Deut 6:4-9), a confessional formula that has sustained the faith of the Jewish people down to the present.

The incorporation of Deuteronomy into the framework of the P narrative resulted in the juxtaposition within the same corpus of different theological perspectives, those of the two major schools and those of their sources. Thus the covenant of obligation of D is balanced against the promissory and indefectible covenant of the P writers, and the more limited and nationalistic perspective of Deuteronomy is offset by the more universalistic range of the P work. The extension of the narrative back to creation and the early history of humanity also permitted the grounding of institutions—sabbath and covenant—in antecedents of unimpeachable antiquity. This combination also provides an illustration of the tension between tradition and situation. Like Israel, both synagogue and church draw their self-understanding, their ability to survive and flourish, from the myth of their origins, constantly repeated and reactualized in recital and ritual. Appeal to a shared memory, so prominent in Deuteronomy, is a central feature of the Pentateuch. It appears with particular clarity in the festivals that memorialize the founding events of the community. It is also a prominent feature of the legal tradition. It is noteworthy, for example, how care for the rights of the resident alien is enjoined on the grounds of collective memory: "You shall not oppress a resident alien; you know the heart of an alien, for you were aliens in the land of Egypt" (Exod 23:9 NRSV). But allegiance to the past must also allow for openness to the demands imposed by life in a changing world, requiring an ongoing testing and reinterpreting of what has been received. A careful and critical reading of the Pentateuch shows that this process of incorporating and reinterpreting the past continued throughout the history of Israel.

Other Sources. While the existence of continuous early, pre-exilic sources can no longer be taken for granted, the Pentateuch in its final, postexilic form has clearly incorporated much pre-exilic narrative and legal source material. With the possible exception of Abraham, of whom we first begin to hear in exilic texts (Ezek 33:24), traditions about the ancestors were in circulation from an early time (e.g., Hos 12:4-5, 13), as also about the exodus (e.g., Amos 3:1; 9:7; Hos 2:15; 11:1) and wilderness period (e.g., Hos 2:14-15; 9:10). In whatever form these traditions circulated, they served to sustain a sense of corporate identity strong enough to survive the destruction of the state and the experience of exile, and they have continued down to the present to exercise this function for the different "interpretive communities" that have accepted them.

The J version of the early history of humanity in Genesis 1–11 has generally been assigned a date in the early monarchy period, perhaps as early as Solomon's reign, though we have seen reason to suspect that a much later date would be more appropriate. Using ancient Mesopotamian mythic traditions as a model, the author projects on to human origins a psychologically profound and disturbing diagnosis of human existence. In a manner reminiscent of some of the later prophets (e.g., Jer 17:9-10) and sages (e.g., Job 14:1-6), the author emphasizes both the ineradicable human tendency to evil (see especially Gen 6:5 and 8:21) and the reality of divine mercy and forgiveness. In their own quite different way, the stories about the ancestors (however they originated and in whatever form they were known to the post-exilic redactors) also succeed in rendering the richness and complexity of human existence in the presence of God. These stories are unified by the promise of land, progeny, and divine blessing, announced at the outset (Gen 12:1-3) and repeated at regular intervals throughout (e.g., 13:14-17; 15:7-21; 26:2-4; 46:2-3). Yet at the crucial points of the narrative—at the beginning, in the middle, and at the end—the protagonists are outside the land, and the story ends with exile in Egypt. In this situation of deferred fulfillment, Abraham is presented as the model of trust and fidelity, especially in the climactic scene of the near-sacrifice of Isaac (Genesis 22). The Jacob narrative, less schematic and psychologically more realistic than that of Abraham, is organized around the twenty-year exile of the protagonist and the transformation he must undergo in order to bear the name Israel (Gen 32:22-32; cf. 35:9-15 P).

The "Song at the Sea" (Exod 15:1-18), one of the oldest poems in the HB, celebrates deliverance from slavery in Egypt by miraculous, divine intervention. The accompanying prose account narrating the sequence of events leading up to this point is also based on ancient tradition, though we are no longer able to identify its earliest formulation or trace its development in detail. These events were decisive for Israel's self-identity and its relationship with its God ("I am Yahweh your God from the land of Egypt" [Hos 12:9; 13:4]). Commemorated in the Passover ceremony, they achieved paradigmatic status for both community and individual: "In every generation one must look upon oneself as if one had in one's own person come out of Egypt." Something similar can be said of the wilderness narratives (Exod 15:22–18:27; Num 10:29–36:13), also based on ancient tradition, as exemplifying divine guidance and providence and legitimating the institutional life of the community. This context, then, confers on the law given at Sinai/Horeb its character as gift and grace.

FOR FURTHER READING

Commentaries:

Alter, Robert. *The Art of Biblical Narrative*. New York: Basic Books, 1981.

Blenkinsopp, Joseph. *The Pentateuch: An Introduction to the First Five Books of the Bible*. Anchor Bible Reference Library. New York: Doubleday, 1992.

_____. *Prophecy and Canon*. Notre Dame: University of Notre Dame Press, 1977.

Friedman, Richard Elliot. *The Bible with Sources Revealed: A New View of the Five Books of Moses*. San Francisco: Harper Collins, 2003.

Knight, Douglas A. "The Pentateuch." In Douglas A. Knight and Gene M. Tucker, eds. *The Hebrew Bible and Its Modern Interpreters*. Chico, Calif.: Scholars Press, 1985.

Noth, Martin. *A History of Pentateuchal Traditions*. Englewood Cliffs, N.J.: Prentice-Hall, 1972.

Rendtorff, Rolf. "Pentateuchal Studies on the Move," *JSOT* 3 (1977) 2-10, 43-45.

_____. *The Problem of the Process of Transmission in the Pentateuch*. Translated by John. J. Scullion. JSOTSup 89. Sheffield: JSOT Press, 1990.

Rofé, Alexander. *Introduction to the Composition of the Pentateuch*. Translated by Harvey N. Boch. Biblical Seminar 58. Sheffield: Sheffield Academic Press, 1999.

Sparks, Kenton L. *The Pentateuch: An Annotated Bibliography*. IBR Bibliographies 1. Grand Rapids, Mich.: Baker, 2002.

Van Seters, John. *In Search of History: Historiography in the Ancient World and the Origins of Biblical History*. New Haven: Yale University Press, 1983.

_____. *The Pentateuch: A Social Science Commentary.* Trajectories 1. Sheffield Academic Press, 1999.

_____. "Recent Studies on the Pentateuch: A Crisis in Method," *JAOS* 99 (1979) 663-67.

von Rad, Gerhard. "The Form-Critical Problem of the Hexateuch." Pages1-78 in *The Problem of the Hexateuch and Other Essays.* New York: McGraw-Hill, 1966.

_____. *Old Testament Theology.* Vol. 1: *The Theology of Israel's Historical Traditions.* Translated by D. M. G. Stalker. New York: Harper & Row, 1962.

Whybray, R. Norman. *The Making of the Pentateuch: A Methodological Study.* Sheffield: JSOT, 1987.

Winnett, F. V. "Re-examining the Foundations," *JBL* 84 (1965) 1-19.

ENDNOTES

1. *Against Apion* 1:37-41.

2. *De Fuga et Inventione* 170.

3. *Sipra* 1:1.

4. See Abraham Kuenen, *Historisch-Kritische Einleitung in die Bücher des Alten Testaments ihrer Entstehung und Sammlung* (Leipzig: J. C. Hinrichs, 1887); Otto Procksch, *Das nordhebräische Sagenbuch. Die Elohimquelle* (Leipzig: J. C. Hinrichs, 1906).

5. See Karl Budde, *Die Biblische Urgeschichte (Gen. 1–12, 5)* (Giessen: A. Töpelmann, 1883); Rudolph Smend, *Die Erzählung des Hexateuch. Aufe ihre Quellen untersucht* (Berlin: Walter de Gruyter, 1912); Cuthbert Simpson, *The Early Traditions of Israel: A Critical Analysis of the Pre-Deuteronomistic Narrative of the Hexateuch* (Oxford: Blackwell, 1948).

6. *Laienquelle* is a source of the Pentateuch, according to Otto Eissfeldt. See his *The Old Testament: An Introduction* (Oxford: Blackwell, 1965).

7. Julius Morgenstern, "The Oldest Document of the Hexateuch," *Hebrew Union College Annual* 4 (1927) 1-138.

8. Robert Pfeiffer, "A Non-Israelite Source of the Book of Genesis," *Zeitschrift für die alttestamentliche Wissenschaft* 48 (1930) 66-73.

9. Georg Fohrer, *Introduction to the Old Testament* (Nashville: Abingdon, 1968).

10. See Gerhard von Rad, *Die Priesterschrift im Hexateuch literarisch untersucht und theologisch gewertet* (Stuttgart: W. Kohlhammer, 1934).

11. Published in English in *The Problem of the Hexateuch and Other Essays* (New York: McGraw-Hill, 1966) 1-78. See *Genesis: A Commentary*, rev. ed. (Philadelphia: Westminster, 1973), first published in 1953; *Deuteronomy: A Commentary* (Philadelphia: Westminster, 1966), first published in 1964; *Old Testament Theology*, vol. 1: *The Theology of Israel's Historical Traditions*, trans. D. M. G. Stalker (New York: Harper and Row, 1962), first published in 1957.

12. See Hans-Walter Wolff, "Das Kerygma des Yahwisten," *Evanglische Theologie* 24 (1964) 73-98; Peter Ellis, *The Yahwist: The Bible's First Theologian* (Collegeville: Liturgical Press, 1968).

13. Albrecht Alt, "Die Ursprünge des israelitischen Rechts," *Bericht über die Verhandlungen der Sächischen Akademie der Wissenschaften zu Leipzig. Philologisch-historische Klasse*, vol. 86, 1 (Leipzig: S. Hirzel, 1934).

14. Martin Noth, *A History of Pentateuchal Traditions* (Englewood Cliffs, N.J.: Prentice-Hall, 1972). First published in 1948.

15. Martin Noth, *A History of Israel*, 2nd ed. (New York: Harper and Row, 1960), first published in 1950.

16. Robert Culley, *Studies in the Structure of Hebrew Narrative* (Philadelphia: Fortress, 1976).

17. E.g., the Jewish scholar Umberto Cassuto, *Torat hatte 'udot vesiddurim shel sifre hattorah* (Jerusalem: Magnes, 1941).

18. E.g., Wilhem Rudolph and Paul Volz, *der Elohist also Erzähler. Ein Irrweg der Penteteuchkritik? An der Genesis erlautert* (Berlin: Walter de Gruyter, 1933).

19. Otto Eissfeldt, *The Old Testament: An Introduction* (Oxford: Blackwell, 1965) 200.

20. Norman E. Wagner, "Pentateuchal Criticism: No Clear Future," *Canadian Journal of Theology* 13 (1967) 225-32; Rolf Rendtorff, "Pentateuchal Studies on the Move," *JSOT* 3 (1977) 2-10, 43-45; Erhard Blum, *Die Komposition der Vätergeschichte* (Neukirchen-Vluyn: Neukirchener Verlag, 1984), and *Studien zur Komposition des Pentateuch* (Berlin: Walter de Gruyter, 1990).

21. F. V. Winnett, "Re-examining the Foundations," *JBL* 84 (1965) 1-19.

22. John Van Seters, "Recent Studies on the Pentateuch: A Crisis in Method," *JAOS* 99 (1979) 663-67; and *In Search of History: Historiography*

in the Ancient World and the Origins of Biblical History (New Haven: Yale University Press, 1983).

23. R. N. Whybray, *The Making of the Pentateuch: A Methodological Study* (Sheffield: JSOT Press, 1987).

24. See Lothar Perlitt, *Bundestheologie im Alten Testament (Neukirchen-Vluyn: Neukirchener Verlag, 1969)*; and Ernst Kutsch, *Verheissung und Gesetz* (Berlin: Walter de Gruyter, 1973).

25. See esp. Hans Heinrich Schmid, *Der sogenannte Jahwist: Beobachtungen und Fragen zur Pentateuchforschung* (Zurich: Theologischer Verlag, 1976).

26. E.g., Robert Alter, *The Art of Biblical Narrative* (New York: Basic Books, 1981).

27. Brevard S. Childs, *Introduction to the Old Testament as Scripture* (Philadelphia: Fortress, 1979); and *Old Testament Theology in a Canonical Context* (London: S.C.M., 1985).

28. Brevard S. Childs, *Introduction to the Old Testament as Scripture,* 112-35.

29. Papyrus 215 of the Bibliothèque Nationale in Paris.

30. Y. Kaufmann, *The Religion of Israel from Its Beginnings to the Babylonian Exile* (New York: Schocken, 1972).

31. J. Blenkinsopp, "The Structure of P," *CBQ* 38 (1976) 275-92.

The Book of
Genesis

TERENCE E. FRETHEIM

The book of Genesis stands at the head of the canon. Its range is breathtaking, moving from cosmos to family, from ordered world to reconciled brothers, from the seven days of the creation of the universe to the seventy descendants of Jacob entering the land of their sojourn. Hence, it stands as a monumental challenge to the interpreter.

The canonical placement of Genesis is important for various reasons. Genesis is a book about beginnings, from the beginnings of the universe and various orderings of humankind to the beginnings of the people of Israel. It also witnesses to the beginnings of God's activity in the life of the world. But creation is more than chronology. Genesis stands at the beginning because creation is such a fundamental theological category for the rest of the canon. God's continuing blessing and ordering work at every level is creational. Moreover, only in relationship to the creation can God's subsequent actions in and through Israel be properly understood. The placement of creation demonstrates that God's purposes with Israel are universal in scope. God's work in redemption serves creation, the *entire* creation, since it reclaims a creation that labors under the deep and pervasive effects of sin. Even more, the canonical placement makes clear that God's redemptive work does not occur in a vacuum; it occurs in a context that has been shaped in decisive ways by the life-giving, creative work of God. Redemption can never be understood as *ex nihilo* without denigrating God's gifts given in creation.

THE CRITICAL STUDY OF GENESIS

For more than two hundred years, *source criticism* has provided the predominant literary approach to the study of Genesis and the Pentateuch. In fact, Genesis has often been studied only as part of this larger literary whole. Hence, Genesis is usually seen as a composite work, consisting primarily of three interwoven sources (Yahwist [J], Elohist [E], Priestly [P]), with some texts attributed to other traditions (e.g., chaps. 14 and 49). Genesis thus grew over time, with these sources gradually brought together by redactors over five hundred years or more, from the United Monarchy to the post-exilic era.

This long-prevailing scholarly consensus has come under sharp challenge from a number of perspectives in the last generation. From within the source-critical perspective, the nature, scope, and dating of the sources have been regular subjects of debate. Few doubt that Genesis consists of traditions from various historical periods, but there is little consensus regarding the way in which they have been brought together into their present form.[1]

I view Genesis as a patchwork quilt of traditions from various periods in Israel's life. The earliest stories date from before the monarchy; over time certain traditions began to coalesce around key figures, such as Abraham and Jacob, and more extensive blocks were gradually built up. The fact that the major sections of Genesis (generally, chaps. 1–11; 12–25; 26–36; 37–50) remain identifiable clusters within a relatively thin, overarching framework sustains this theory. A redactor (probably J) wove these clusters of tradition together into a coherent whole, provided a basic framework (perhaps focused on the ancestral promises), and integrated them with the larger story of the Pentateuch. While J probably worked early in the monarchical period, arguments for a later date for the Yahwist are attractive (not least because of the sophisticated form of its anthropomorphisms). Over the centuries reworkings of this collection took place, drawing on other, as yet unintegrated, traditions (the Elohist may be one such supplementary reworking). One major redaction is to be identified with P (probably during the exile); this redactor drew on materials from a wide variety of sources, older and more recent, and placed a decisive stamp on the entire corpus. It is possible that deuteronomistic redactors worked over this material at a later time, integrating it into a still larger collection with only minor touch-ups.

The purpose of these retellings of the material is not entirely clear and may vary, involving sociopolitical and religious issues. Each reworking made it ever more difficult to discern where the inherited traditions and the retellings begin and end. It is likely, however, that theological and kerygmatic interests come more and more into play, so that finally one must speak of the essential testimonial character of the material, a witness to the complex interrelationships of divine action and human response.[2]

Newer literary approaches have also called into question many of the assumptions and conclusions of the source-critical consensus. These strategies focus on issues of literary criticism rather than literary history, on the texts as they are rather than any history prior to their present shape. Such readers attempt to hear the texts as we now have them and to discern their various rhetorical features as they work together to form a coherent whole. At times, this analysis has been undertaken with an eye to literary parallels in other ancient Near Eastern literature (e.g., the *Gilgamesh Epic*).[3]

The book of Genesis has been one of the most popular workshops for these approaches. Over the last two decades hundreds of articles and sections of books have mined the literary riches of these chapters and unearthed many insights into the ways in which they can be read with greater profit. Yet, it is not so clear how these gains are to be integrated with the more historical approaches. While historical issues continue to be important, this commentary will emphasize literary approaches in order to perceive what makes these texts work.

Literary studies and analyses of the theological movement within these texts have not kept pace with one another. For example, many literary (and other) studies simply work with the assumptions and conclusions of classical theism in the analysis of the theological material the texts present. On the other hand, some studies take pains to treat the theological elements at the same level as any other (e.g., God becomes a character like every other). I will attend to the theological dynamic of the text and recognize its special stature in view of the community of faith that produced it and the canonical place eventually given to it.[4]

Another lively concern in Genesis studies has to do with ancient Near Eastern parallels (and beyond, possibly even Greece). Since the unearthing of the Mesopotamian accounts of creation and the flood over a century ago, augmented since by numerous discoveries, scholars have devoted considerable attention to discerning possible links with Genesis. While this is true of Genesis as a whole, parallels to chaps. 1–11 have constituted a special focus. Although direct points of dependence do not seem common, it is clear that Israel participated in a comprehensive ancient Near Eastern culture that had considerable impact on its ways of thinking and writing, both in details and with larger themes. Apart from more formal links, such as language, some have tended to view these parallels largely in negative terms. At the same time, Israel's deep dependence upon its cultural context extends even to theological matters (e.g., the understanding of moral order or creation by word) and to the very creation-disruption-flood structure of chaps. 1–11. Interpreters must maintain a fine balance between recognizing such dependence (finally, a witness to the work of the Creator) and Israel's genuinely new and imaginative ideas and formulations.

Feminist scholarship has produced important studies that have influenced this commentary at numerous points. This work has attended particularly to the place of the woman in chaps. 1–3 and the prominent role of women in the ancestral narratives. Phyllis Trible's work, in particular, has had an immense and salutary influence. In addition, anthropological and sociological studies have expanded our knowledge of the issues of kinship and culture.[5] Generally, a proliferation of approaches is elucidating ever new dimensions of these important biblical materials.

LITERARY FORM

There are basically two types of literature in Genesis, narrative and numerative, to use Westermann's language.[6] Poetic pieces are integrated into the narratives as well (e.g., 2:23; 3:14-19; 16:11-12; 25:23; 27:27-29, 39-40; 49:1-27).

1. Narratives. Little consensus has emerged regarding the proper label for these narratives, though *saga* has been used often. The issues in chaps. 1–11 are particularly complex. "Family narrative (story)" emphasizes the family unit as central to these texts, and in a way that has no real parallel elsewhere in the OT. While not historiographical in character and with much imagination used in the telling, the narratives do possess certain features associated with history writing, e.g., a chronological framework and some cumulative and developmental character.[7]

The language of story may be most helpful in determining how these materials functioned for Israel.[8] They are told in such a way that they could become the story of each ensuing generation. The readers could participate in a great, yet often quite hidden, drama of divine action and human response. At this juncture of past story and present reality Israel came to know what it meant to be the people of God. The faith was not fundamentally an idea, but an embodiment, a way of life. The language and experience of faith thus remained concrete and personal. Thus it has the capacity to keep the reader anchored in this world. It does not dissolve into myth, into some mystical world of the gods that suppresses the human or the natural, or some religious world far removed from the secular sphere. By and large, the world reflected in these stories is ordinary, everyday, and familiar, filled with the surprises and joys, the sufferings and the troubles, the complexities and ambiguities known to every community.

At the same time, the story form allows (in a way that history proper does not) an admixture of Israel's story and God's story. But even the latter is seen to be this-worldly, as God works toward the divine purposes in and through less than perfect individuals and world. And God's story has the ultimate purpose, not of bringing people into some heavenly sphere, but of enabling a transformation of this life.

The capacity of the story to draw one into it in such a way as to encompass the full life of the reader has the effect of overcoming the distance between past story and present reader; the horizons merge. At the same time, readers will encounter that which is often different from their own stories; there are surprises and discontinuities as past and present life stories come into contact with one another. Some hearers may reject the story, but for those who respond positively the story may provide a means of shaping identity (a constitutive function), a mirror for self-identity (a descriptive function), or a model for the life of faith (a paradigmatic function). One may thereby not only become a member of the people of God, but also come to know who one is, and what shape the life of faith ought to take in the world.

The narratives offer an exercise in self-understanding. They become a vehicle through which a new generation can learn its identity once again as the people of Abraham, a people who have trod in his footsteps, who have taken his journey. It is one more retelling of the past, not to find patterns for moral behavior, but to understand who we are as the people of God who have inherited these commands and promises, who have ventured down similar paths. We can thereby see where we have been, who we now are, and the shape of our paths into the future.

2. Genealogies. "Genesis is a book whose plot is genealogy."[9] Israel formulated family trees, often with social and political overtones. As with us, they were concerned about kinship interrelationships and tracking family origins and "pedigrees," especially for important figures. Also similar is the way in which genealogies are woven into family stories. Major portions of seven chapters in Genesis consist of genealogies, an interest evident in other OT texts (e.g., Chronicles) as well as in the NT (see Matthew 1; Luke 1).

The ten תולדות (tôlĕdôt translated either "genealogy"/"generations" or "account"/"story") —2:4 (heaven and earth); 5:1 (Adam); 6:9 (Noah); 10:1 (Noah's sons); 11:10 (Shem); 11:27 (Terah); 25:12 (Ishmael); 25:19 (Isaac); 36:1, 9 (Esau); 37:2 (Jacob)—constitute a prominent structuring device in Genesis. These Priestly genealogies are supplemented by a few others (e.g., that of Cain, 4:17-26). Genealogies have an enumerative style, but at times they are "broken" by narrative pieces (e.g., 10:8-12). They usually introduce a section, but at times they look both backward and forward (2:4; 37:2). One type of genealogy is linear (one person in each generation, 5:1-32); the other is segmented (multiple lines of descent), characteristic of branches of the family outside the chosen line (table of nations; Ishmael; Esau). Because genealogies cut across the break between chaps. 11 and 12, they witness to the fundamental creational unity of Genesis.

The historical value of the genealogies is much debated, but their function of providing continuity over these chapters probably means that they were understood as some kind of historical anchor for the larger story. Their original setting was the family or tribe, those most interested in such matters, and within which they were often transmitted orally over many generations. They show that every character is kin to every other, a key to Israelite self-identity, especially in times of conflict or dispersion. Hence, Genesis is fundamentally about one big extended family. The genealogies also demonstrate that Israel is truly kin to all the surrounding peoples, a fact that helps to develop the meaning of the people's special role. The genealogies thus are integrally related to the essential concerns of the narratives.

Because genealogies order people into families, and witness to the continued existence of families in spite of much difficulty and dysfunctionality, they fit most fundamentally within a theology of creation (so explicitly in 5:1-2). They present "the steady, ongoing rhythm of events which stamp the course of human existence—birth, length of life, begetting, death" in which both God and human beings participate.[10] Moreover, because the first of the *tôlĕdôt* includes the nonhuman, genealogies link human and nonhuman into a larger *creational family*, in which every creature is, in effect, kin to every other. Even more, because genealogies also encompass larger human groupings (10:1-32; 25:12-18), they witness to the range of the divine creative activity in the ordering of the world.

The narratives, on the other hand, "are inherently messy . . . take account of much that is problematic and contingent, all the vagaries of human life . . . pursuing a far less predictable course of surprise and unanticipated events."[11] Naomi Steinberg speaks of genealogies reintroducing equilibrium into such messy family lives, restabilizing them for the next journey into a volatile future. Yet, she shows that this perspective is too simple. Some genealogies also contain elements of disequilibrium, contingency, and open-endedness (see 11:30; 25:19-26; 37:2); hence, the genealogies do not witness so univocally to order and stability as one might initially think.[12] Indeed, most genealogies contain such an unusual element (e.g., 5:24 on Enoch; 5:29; 6:9 on Noah; 10:8-12 on Nimrod). Such features integrate narrative messiness into the very heart of the genealogical order. They show thereby that the genealogies do not witness to a *determined* order of reality. Cain's genealogy (4:17-26) testifies further to this integration; it *intensifies* the contingencies of the prior narratives. Genealogies are finally *insufficient* for ordering purposes; another type of divine activity will be needed in order to reclaim the creation—namely, redemption.

FAITH AND HISTORY IN GENESIS

The book of Genesis does not present the reader with historical narrative, at least in any modern sense. Its primary concerns are theological and kerygmatic. Those responsible for the material as we now have it (and no doubt at other stages in its transmission) were persons of faith concerned to speak or reflect on a word of God to other persons of faith. The voice of a living community of faith resounds through these texts. Rooted in history in this way, Genesis is not socially or historically disinterested; it was written—at each stage of transmission—with the problems and possibilities of a particular audience in view.

Although scholars have a difficult time discerning those audiences, the text is linked to specific times and places. While the latest redactors may well have made the witness of the text more generally available to ongoing communities of faith, the material has not been flattened out into generalities. The most basic shaping of Genesis probably occurred in exile. Traditions in Genesis are consistent with other examples of creation language during this era, as evidenced by Isaiah 40–55, which relates Israel's future to the universal purposes of God. Affirmations of divine faithfulness to ancient promises—a veritable litany in these texts—speak volumes in a time when the future appears to stand in jeopardy. In attending to Israel's ancestral heritage, both in narrative and in genealogy, the authors address sharp issues of communal identity. The various stories of the ancestors often seem to mirror the history of Israel, assisting the exiles in coming to terms with their own past (this will often be noted in the commentary; e.g., the parallels between 12:10-20 and the exodus). These texts spoke a clear word of God to exiled people.

The literary vehicle in and through which this word of God is addressed narrates a story of the past. Although the ancient writers were not concerned with reconstructing a history of this early era, modern scholars have had a great interest in determining the extent to which these texts reflect "what actually happened". This task has been made difficult by the nature of the texts themselves as well as by the difficulties of assessing extra-biblical parallels.

Scholarly efforts at historical reconstruction of the ancestral period have had mixed results.[13] A period of some confidence in the basic historicity of these texts within the second millennium BCE has faded in recent years in view of the character of the texts and challenges to the interpretation of putative archaeological evidence. Since the biblical texts underwent a long period of transmission, they reflect aspects of Israel's history all along the way. For example, relationships between these texts and other tribal and genealogical OT materials suggest that various historical realities from both before and after the United Monarchy are reflected in them. Various ancient Near Eastern parallels to patriarchal names, customs, and modes of life have at times been overdrawn; yet they are not finally without historical value, even for a second-millennium dating at some points. While it is not possible to determine whether the women and men of Genesis were actual historical persons, it seems reasonable to claim that the narratives carry some authentic memories of Israel's pre-exodus heritage. At the same time, Israel's valuing of these materials for its own faith and life appears not to have centered on issues of historicity; however, it is likely that Israel thought these traditions derived from pre-exodus times.

The religion of the ancestors reflected in the texts also figures in this discussion about historical background. The religious (and other) practices of these chapters are often distinctive when compared to later Israelite convention.[14] Hence, later Israelites did not simply read their own religious lives back into these texts (though nothing seems to be incompatible with later Yahwism). They preserved some memories of earlier practices, including worship of God under various forms of the name El (see 16:13; 21:33; 33:20; El is the high god in the Canaanite pantheon), referred to as the God of my/our/your father(s), the God of Abraham, the God of Isaac, and the God of Jacob. The ancestral God was understood to be a personal deity who accompanied this family on its journeys, providing care and protection. Some traditions understand that Yahweh was a name revealed only at the time of Moses (Exod 3:14-16; Exod 6:2-3) and that El was an earlier name for God (although the OT generally understands El to be an alternate name for Yahweh). The frequent use of Yahweh in Genesis is anachronistic in some ways, but it conveys an important theological conviction—namely, that the God whom the ancestors worshiped under the name El had characteristics common to Yahweh and, in fact, is to be identified with Yahweh.

UNITY, STRUCTURE, AND THEME

It has long been the practice in Genesis study to drive a sharp wedge between chaps. 1–11, the so-called Primeval History (Story), and chaps. 12–50, the Patriarchal (Ancestral) History. More recently, under the impact of literary-critical readings, there has been renewed interest in the integrity of Genesis as a whole.[15]

In some ways this division is appropriate, with chap. 12 marking a new stage in God's relationship with the world. Even those who sharpen this division often note that 12:1-3 is a fulcrum text, linking Abraham with "all the families of the earth." Hence, it has been common to claim that God's choice of Abraham had a universal purpose: to extend God's salvific goals through this family to the entire world. Even more, this theme has been tracked through chaps. 12–50, with particular attention not only to its verbal repetition (e.g., 18:18; 22:18; 26:4; 28:14), but also to the numerous contacts made between Israel's ancestors and the "nonchosen" peoples. Remarkably little polemic is directed against outsiders in the Genesis text. The promises of God to Abraham are intended for the world. The way in which Israel's ancestors did or did not respond to this intention served as a negative or positive model for every generation.

The focus of such discussion has been so sharply placed on "salvation history" that creation themes have been neglected. Even more, it is striking the extent to which the more emphatic themes of chaps. 12–50 are grounded in chaps. 1–11, wherein God promises and blesses, elects and saves. God first establishes a covenant and makes promises, not to Abraham, but to Noah (6:18 and 9:8-17); God's promissory activity in Israel participates in God's promissory relation to the larger world (see the manifold promises to Ishmael and Esau). God's work of blessing in the world does not begin with Abraham; it is integral to chaps. 1–11 (see 9:1, 26) and so God's blessing work through Abraham must involve intensification and pervasiveness, not a new reality. Since God saves Noah, his family, and the animals (Ps 36:6), God does not become a savior with Abraham or Israel. Issues of creation and redemption are integrated throughout Genesis. God's promises and salvific acts must finally be seen as serving all of creation. God acts to free people, indeed the entire world, to be what they were created to be.[16]

Scholars have noted various forms of evidence for structured unity in Genesis, especially in the genealogies (extending from 2:4 to 37:2 and the divine promises (from 8:21 to 50:24). More refined efforts to discern structures throughout the book have been less successful, with the focus of attention on the four major, distinct sections.[17] Links within Genesis have been discerned in chaps. 1–11 and 37–50, from family discord/harmony, to fertility (1:28 and 47:27), to the extension of life to a flood/famine-filled world (41:57), to the "good" that God is about in the creation and through this family (50:20); in some sense Joseph functions as a new Adam (41:38).

At the same time, the Joseph story does not occasion a return to Eden. Sin and its ill effects remain very much in place. Human life, more generally, becomes ever more complex as one moves from Adam to Joseph. These developments are matched by shifts in the imaging of God, whose words and deeds become less direct and obtrusive. God's actions are never all-controlling in Genesis, but a more prominent role is given to the human in the Joseph story, from the transmission of promises to the exercise of leadership. These developments correlate with narratives that become less and less episodic.[18]

The following themes in Genesis as a whole may be gathered; creation themes remain prominent throughout. (1) The presence and activity of God in every sphere of life, among nonchosen and chosen, for purposes of judgment and salvation. These two themes tie chaps. 1–11 closely to chaps. 12–50: God responds to ongoing human sinfulness through sentence and judgment (often involving creational realities, from flood to plague to fire and brimstone); God also responds in a gracious way to humankind, even though their lives have been deeply affected by sin and its consequences. (2) Blessing is a creational category in which both God and humankind, nonchosen and chosen, are engaged. This theme includes the continuity of the family through the struggles of barrenness and birth, and the fertility of fields and animals, often juxtaposed with famine. Blessing also relates to land, raising ecological considerations that are not far from the surface (from the flood to Sodom and Gomorrah). (3) The pervasive concern for kinship and family, an order of creation. One contemporary way of looking at chaps. 12–50 is through the lens of family systems theory and the manifestations of a dysfunctional family one sees throughout. The various dimensions of family life belong within the sphere of God's concern. God is at work in and through family problems and possibilities for purposes of reconciliation (50:20). (4) Concern for the life of the nation also entails one of the most basic orders of creation. In the Joseph story especially, the writers devote attention to issues of economics, agriculture, and the dynamics of political and governmental life more generally, in and through which God is at work for blessing (41:53-57; 47:13-26). (5) The role of the human in the divine economy. It is not uncommon to denigrate the importance of human activity in these chapters. For example, von Rad states: "The story of Hagar shows us a fainthearted faith that cannot leave things to God and believes it necessary to help things along. . . . [A child] conceived . . . in little faith cannot be the heir of promise."[19] But divine promise, appropriated by faith, does not entail human passivity in working toward God's goals for the creation. The high place given to the human role, from creation to Joseph, testifies to the depth of God's engagement with human beings as the instruments of God's purpose.

FOR FURTHER READING

1. The following are standard commentaries that deal with the full range of issues faced by the interpreter. Those by Westermann contain the most extensive discussions of issues the text presents, from textual matters to the history of interpretation to end of Bibliography.

Hamilton, Victor. *The Book of Genesis, Chapters 1–17.* NICOT. Grand Rapids: Eerdmans, 1990.

Sarna, Nahum. *Genesis.* JPS Torah Commentary. Philadelphia: Jewish Publication Society, 1989.

Von Rad, Gerhard. *Genesis.* OTL. Philadelphia: Westminster, 1972.

Wenham, Gordon. *Genesis 1–15; Genesis 15–50.* Word Biblical Commentary. 1–2 Waco: Word, 1987–1993.

Westermann, Claus. *Genesis 1–11: A Commentary; Genesis 12–36: A Commentary;* and *Genesis 37–50: A Commentary.* Minneapolis: Augsburg, 1984–86.

2. The following are commentaries or studies on Genesis geared for use in preaching, teaching, and personal study. The commentary of Brueggemann should be cited for its thoughtful discussions of the text in view of the issues presented by contemporary American culture.

Brueggemann, Walter. *Genesis*. Interpretation. Atlanta: John Knox, 1982.

Fretheim, Terence. *Creation, Fall and Flood: Studies in Genesis 1–11*. Minneapolis: Augsburg, 1969.

Gowan, Donald E. *From Eden to Babel: A Commentary on the Book of Genesis 1–11*. Grand Rapids: Eerdmans, 1988.

Jeansonne, Sharon. *The Women of Genesis*. Minneapolis: Fortress, 1990.

Mann, Thomas. *The Book of the Torah: The Narrative Integrity of the Pentateuch*. Atlanta: John Knox, 1988.

Rogerson, John. *Genesis 1–11*. Old Testament Guides. Sheffield, England: *JSOT*, 1991.

Roop, Eugene F. *Genesis*. Scottdale, Pa.: Herald, 1987.

3. The following are studies of special issues in Genesis from a particular angle of vision. Various articles of interest are cited in appropriate sections of the commentary.

Alter, Robert. *The Art of Biblical Narrative*. New York: Basic Books, 1981.

Anderson, B. W., ed. *Creation in the Old Testament*. IRT 6. Philadelphia: Fortress, 1984.

Blenkinsopp, Joseph. *The Pentateuch: An Introduction to the First Five Books of the Bible*. ABRL. New York: Doubleday, 1992.

Bonhoeffer, Dietrich. *Creation and Fall: Temptation*. New York: Macmillan, 1966.

Brenner, Athalya, ed. *A Feminist Companion to Genesis*. The Feminist Companion to the Bible, 2. Sheffield: Sheffield Academic Press, 1993.

———. *Genesis: The Feminist Companion to the Bible*. Second Series. Sheffield: Sheffield Academic Press, 1998.

Brueggemann, Walter, and H. W. Wolff. *The Vitality of Old Testament Traditions*. Atlanta: John Knox, 1982.

Clines, David. *The Theme of the Pentateuch*. JSOTSup 10. Sheffield JSOT, 1978.

Coats, George W. *From Canaan to Egypt: Structural and Theological Context for the Joseph Story*. CBQMS 4. Washington: Catholic Biblical Association of America, 1976.

———. *Genesis: With an Introduction to Narrative Literature*. The Forms of the Old Testament Literature 1. Grand Rapids: Eerdmans, 1983.

Damrosch, David. *The Narrative Covenant*. San Francisco: Harper & Row, 1987.

Fishbane, Michael. *Text and Texture: Close Readings of Selected Biblical Texts*. New York: Schocken, 1979.

Fokkelman, J. P. *Narrative Art in Genesis*. Assen: Van Gorcum, 1975.

Fretheim, Terence. *Deuteronomic History*. Nashville: Abingdon, 1983.

Gunkel, Hermann. *The Legends of Genesis: The Biblical Saga and History*. New York: Schocken, 1964.

Hendel, Ronald. *The Epic of the Patriarch: The Jacob Cycle and the Narrative Traditions of Canaan and Israel*. HSM 42. Atlanta: Scholars Press, 1987.

Humphreys, W. L. *Joseph and His Family: A Literary Study*. Studies in Personalities of the Old Testament. Columbia: University of South Carolina Press, 1988.

Levenson, Jon. *Creation and the Persistence of Evil*. San Francisco: Harper & Row, 1988.

Meyers, Carol. *Discovering Eve: Ancient Israelite Women in Context*. New York: Oxford University Press, 1988.

Miller, Patrick D., Jr. *Genesis 1–11: Studies in Structure and Theme*. JSOTSup 8. Sheffield JSOT, 1978.

Moberly, R. W. L. *The Old Testament of the Old Testament: Patriarchal Narratives and Mosaic Yahwism*. Minneapolis: Fortress, 1992.

Niditch, Susan. *Chaos to Cosmos: Studies in Biblical Patterns of Creation*. Chico: Scholars Press, 1985.

———. *Underdogs and Tricksters: A Prelude to Biblical Folklore*. San Francisco: Harper & Row, 1987.

Rendsburg, Gary. *The Redaction of Genesis*. Winona Lake, Ind.: Eisenbrauns, 1986.

Rendtorff, Rolf. *The Problem of the Process of Transmission in the Pentateuch*. JSOTSup 89. Sheffield JSOT, 1990.

Steinmetz, Devorah. *From Father to Son: Kinship, Conflict and Continuity in Genesis*. Louisville: Westminster/John Knox, 1991.

Sternberg, Meir. *The Poetics of Biblical Narrative.* Bloomington: Indiana University Press, 1985.

Thompson, Thomas. *The Historicity of the Patriarchal Narratives.* BZAW 133. Berlin: de Gruyter, 1974.

Trible, Phyllis. *God and the Rhetoric of Sexuality.* Overtures to Biblical Theology. Philadelphia: Fortress, 1978.

Turner, Lawrence. *Announcements of Plot in Genesis.* JSOTSup 96. Sheffield JSOT, 1990.

Van Seters, John. *Abraham in History and Tradition.* New Haven: Yale University Press, 1975.

_____. *Prologue to History: The Yahwist as Historian in Genesis.* Louisville: Westminster/John Knox, 1992.

Wallace, Howard. *The Eden Narrative.* HSM 32. Atlanta: Scholars Press, 1985.

White, Hugh C. *Narration and Discourse in the Book of Genesis.* Cambridge: Cambridge University Press, 1991.

Whybray, R. N. *The Making of the Pentateuch.* JSOTSup 53. Sheffield JSOT, 1987.

Wilson, R. R. *Genealogy and History in the Biblical World.* New Haven: Yale University Press, 1977.

ENDNOTES

1. For a recent survey, see R. N. Whybray, *The Making of the Pentateuch* (Sheffield JSOT, 1987); and J. Blenkinsopp, *The Pentateuch: An Introduction to the First Five Books of the Bible* (New York: Doubleday, 1992) 1-30.

2. See W. Brueggemann and H. W. Wolff, *The Vitality of Old Testament Traditions* (Atlanta: John Knox, 1982).

3. On new literary approaches, see R. Alter, *The Art of Biblical Narrative* (New York: Basic Books, 1981). On extra-biblical parallels, see D. Damrosch, *The Narrative Covenant* (San Francisco: Harper & Row, 1987).

4. On theology and narrative, see Terence E. Fretheim, *Exodus,* Interpretation (Louisville: Westminster/John Knox, 1990) 10-12.

5. Phyllis Trible, *God and the Rhetoric of Sexuality* (Philadelphia: Fortress, 1978) 72-143; see also the work of R. Hendel and C. Meyers, listed in the bibliography.

6. C. Westermann, *Genesis 1–11: A Commentary* (Minneapolis: Augsburg, 1984) 6.

7. On the Pentateuch as a historiographical work in comparison with early Greek histories, see the assessment of John van Seters in J. Blenkinsopp, *The Pentateuch: An Introduction to the First Five Books of the Bible,* 37-42.

8. See T. Fretheim, *Deuteronomic History* (Nashville: Abingdon, 1983) 39-40; R. W. L. Moberly, *The Old Testament of the Old Testament: Patriarchal Narratives and Mosaic Yahwism* (Minneapolis: Fortress, 1992) 130-46; D. Steinmetz, *From Father to Son: Kinship, Conflict and Continuity in Genesis* (Louisville: Westminster/John Knox, 1991) 134-55.

9. N. Steinberg, "The Genealogical Framework of the Family Stories in Genesis," *Semeia* 46 (1989) 41. Generally, see R. Wilson, *Genealogy and History in the Biblical World* (New Haven: Yale University Press, 1977).

10. C. Westermann, *Genesis 1–11: A Commentary,* 7.

11. R. Robinson, "Literary Functions of the Genealogies of Genesis," *CBQ* 48 (1986) 597.

12. N. Steinberg, "The Genealogical Framework of the Family Stories in Genesis," 43.

13. See a survey in G. Ramsey, *The Quest for the Historical Israel* (Atlanta: John Knox, 1981) 28-43. See also K. McCarter, "The Historical Abraham," *Int* 42 (1988) 341-52.

14. For a review, see R. W. L. Moberly, *The Old of the Old Testament: Patriarchal Narratives and Mosaic Yahwism.*

15. See D. Clines, *The Theme of the Pentateuch* (Sheffield JSOT, 1978); B. Childs, *Introduction to the Old Testament as Scripture* (Philadelphia: Fortress, 1979) 136-60; B. Dahlberg, "On Recognizing the Unity of Genesis," *TD* 24 (1977) 360-67; T. Mann, "All the Families of the Earth: The Theological Unity of Genesis," *Int* 45 (1991) 341-53.

16. See T. Fretheim, "The Reclamation of Creation," *Int* 45 (1991) 354-65.

17. G. Rendsburg, *The Redaction of Genesis* (Winona Lake: Eisenbrauns, 1986).

18. See R. Cohn, "Narrative Structure and Canonical Perspective in Genesis," *JSOT* 25 (1983) 3-16.

19. G. Von Rad, *Genesis* (Philadelphia: Westminster, 1972) 196.

THE BOOK OF
EXODUS

WALTER BRUEGGEMANN

The book of Exodus is, according to tradition, the "Second Book of Moses"—i.e., the second book of the Pentateuch. This traditional formula refers not to Mosaic authorship but to the foundational character of the literature in relation to the unrivaled authority of Moses. The book of Exodus stands at the center of Israel's normative faith tradition.

RELATIONSHIPS WITHIN THE PENTATEUCH

We may identify three relationships within the Pentateuch that are pertinent to the book of Exodus.

1. The relation between the books of Genesis and Exodus is important but uneasy.[1] On critical grounds, it is clear that the community of the Exodus has no direct (historical) connection to the "ancestors" of Genesis. Nonetheless, the text itself gives considerable attention to that connection, which is theologically crucial. On the one hand, the God known in Genesis is only in Exodus made fully known by name (see 3:14; 6:2). On the other hand, the text is insistent that the old promises of Genesis are still operative in Exodus—promises made at creation (Gen 1:28; Exod 1:7), and promises of land to the ancestors (Gen 12:1). Indeed, those promises are the driving force that causes God to be engaged on behalf of the slaves (see Exod 2:24; 3:16-17; 6:8). Thus the connection between the two pieces of literature is promissory (i.e., theological rather than historical) but for that no less decisive.

2. The relation of the book of Exodus to the books of Leviticus and Numbers is very different. Insofar as these later books are the extended proclamation of the Torah, they simply continue the work of Moses at Sinai. They belong completely within the orbit of Moses' authorizing work and in fact constitute no new theme.

3. The relation of Exodus to Deuteronomy is again very different. Deuteronomy consists of a restatement of the Ten Commandments (5:6-21), which then receive a full and belated exposition that is placed in the mouth of Moses. There is enormous interpretive freedom in Deuteronomy, so that what we are given is what Moses could have said in a later, very different circumstance.

Thus the book of Exodus reaches in three quite different directions to gather together the main threads and themes of Israel's faith. As the focal point of all this literature, it is the force of the book of Exodus that makes the Torah (Pentateuch) a profoundly Mosaic book, relying primarily upon his authority.

THE DOCUMENTARY HYPOTHESIS

It is not necessary to review here the complex account of recent critical scholarship, which for the past two centuries has been preoccupied with the complex history of the literature that now bears the authority of Moses. Specifically, this complexity is articulated by scholars in "the Documentary Hypothesis," which identifies four major recastings (sources) of the material around four demanding theological crises. This hypothesis is a way of speaking in critical fashion (largely in nineteenth-century modes) about dynamic vitality in the ongoing development of the tradition. Current scholarship finds the hypothesis in its classical form less and less useful.

Specifically, it has been necessary to recognize that the "Priestly texts" are of a peculiar kind, easy to recognize, with very specific ideological interests. I have not found any way to avoid the odd juxtaposition of the liberation narrative and the "sacerdotal" accent.[2] Acknowledging the juxtaposition, what has interested me is the way in which the final form of the text has been able to bring these very different accents into serious, sustained interaction.

MAJOR THEOLOGICAL THEMES

We may identify four major theological themes that order the book of Exodus and that provide focal points for interpretation.

1. Liberation. The "narrative of liberation" (chaps. 1–15) is primarily concerned with the transformation of a social situation from oppression to freedom. This liberation is indeed a sociopolitical-economic operation that delegitimates and overthrows the throne of Egypt. The odd claim of this literature is that social transformation of revolutionary proportion is wrought through the holy intentionality of a "new God" (see Judg 5:8), whose name is known only in and through this wondrous happening.

2. Law. The meeting at Sinai (which continues through Num 10:10) is the announcement of God's will for all aspects of Israel's personal and public life. The God who liberates refuses to be limited with reference only to "religion." Three aspects of this proclamation of law may be noted. First, the giving of the Law is situated in a frightening theophany, whereby the holy God intimidates and threatens Israel (19:16-25). The purpose of the theophany, so far as the canonical form of the literature is concerned, is to ground law in holy authority beyond any human agent or construct. This Law is God's law! Second, the Ten Commandments, and only they, come directly from God's own mouth. This is an extraordinary phenomenon, an act of sovereignty that orders the world, and an act of graciousness whereby Israel need not guess about God's intention for it or for the world. Third, the rest of the laws in Exodus (20:22-26; 21:1–23:19; 34:11-26) are given by Moses, who is the designated and accepted mediator (20:18-21). That is, Israel has devised a stable human arrangement whereby God's will and purpose continue to be available.

3. Covenant. The proclamation of Law has as its purpose the making of a covenant, a binding relation whereby Yahweh and Israel are intimately, profoundly, and non-negotiably committed to each other. In this act, a social novelty is introduced into the world, a community founded on nothing other than an act of faith and loyalty.

Moreover, the present form of Exodus 32–34 is now positioned as a new or renewed covenant, after the nullification of the covenant of 19–24. The relation between 19–24 and 32–34 suggests that covenant is a once-for-all commitment. It is endlessly impinged upon by the contingencies of history, so that the covenant rooted in fidelity must struggle with the reality of infidelity. This dynamic, on the one hand, permits the savage warning of the pre-exilic prophets that the relation will end because Israel persists in disobedience. On the other hand, this same dynamic of fidelity in the face of infidelity permits the daring assertion in the Exile that the God who "plucks up and tears down" will also "plant and build" a new covenant people (Jer 1:10; 31:27-28). Thus the theme of covenant permits the terrible tension of judgment and hope already anticipated in 34:6-7 and asserted in pre-exilic prophets (e.g., Hosea), but worked out in the great prophets of the Exile— Jeremiah, Isaiah 40–55, and Ezekiel.[3]

4. Presence. The book of Exodus is concerned not only with an *event* of liberation, but with a *structure* that will ensure in some concrete institutional form the continued presence of God in the midst of Israel. This God, however, is not casually or easily available to Israel, and the emerging problem is to find a viable way in which to host the Holy. The second half of the book of Exodus is preoccupied with this problem and this possibility (25:1–40:38). Israel devises, through daring theological imagination, structure (tabernacle) that makes possible "glory" both as abiding presence and as traveling assurance (40:34-38).

These four themes converge to make the poignant claim that Israel is a profound *novum* in human history. It is a community like none that had yet been—the recipient of God's liberating power, practitioner of God's sovereign Law, partner in God's ongoing covenant, and host of God's awesome presence. This astonishingly odd community is, of course, made possible only by this incomparable God who dares to impinge upon the human process in extravagant and unprecedented ways (see 33:16).

LOCUS

The current view of scholarship is that the book of Exodus reached its present, final form during the sixth-century exile or soon thereafter, with the final shaping of the Priestly tradition. This judgment provides a chronological reference point for the literature. More important, however, this critical judgment also suggests a context in which to understand the pastoral intention and interpretive issues at work in the literature as it comes to us.

The exilic (or post-exilic) community had to practice its faith in a context where the primary guarantees of the Jerusalem establishment (both political and religious) had been terminated, and where foreign powers (Babylon, Persia) governed. The book of Exodus thus is to be understood as a literary, pastoral, liturgical, and theological response to an acute crisis. Texts that ostensibly concern thirteenth-century matters in fact are heard in a sixth- to fourth-century crisis.

This judgment that Exodus is an exilic document does two things. On the one hand, it requires a rereading of the main themes of the book. Thus *liberation* now concerns the freedom given in faith in an imperial context of a Babylonian or Persian "pharaoh." *Law* concerns a counter-ethic in an empire that wants to preempt and commandeer all of life. *Covenant* is a membership alternative to accommodation to the empire. And *presence* is a sense of energy, courage, and divine accompaniment in an empire that wants to "empty" life of such resources. In that imperial context, the book of Exodus becomes a counterdocument that voices and legitimates the odd identity of this community in the face of an empire that wants to crush such oddity.

On the other hand, the identity of the book of Exodus as an exilic document suggests the interpretive vitality that belongs inherently to this text. Our own interpretive work, then, is not to reflect on an ancient history lesson about Egypt or about cult, but to see how this text, in new, demanding, and dangerous circumstances, continues to offer subversive possibilities for our future.

METHOD

The older critical commentaries (of which Noth's is a primary example) largely reflect and build upon nineteenth-century questions and methods.[4] They are especially concerned with the history behind the present text, both concerning what happened as "event," and how the text itself was developed and formed. It is increasingly clear that the older "critical perspective" is a product and example of the prevailing epistemological situation in the service of modernism. Any probe of these commentaries suggests how greatly our epis-

temological situation is changed by the receding of modernity. We are, however, only beginning to articulate new methods, none of which yet claims any consensus of scholarly support.

1. Literary Criticism. The newer "literary criticism" is no longer preoccupied with the history of hypothetical sources and documents, but seeks to focus on the internal, rhetorical workings of the text, assuming that the text itself "enacts a world" in which the reader may participate. Focus is not on external references, but on what is happening in the transactions of the text itself. This approach devotes great attention to the details, dramatic tensions, and rhetorical claims of the text itself. Such an approach requires great discipline to stay inside the world of text, and great patience in noticing the subtle nuances of the text. From a theological perspective, it operates with a "high view" of the text, suggesting that the world inside the text may be more real, more compelling, and more authoritative than other worlds construed behind or beyond the text.

While this method is everywhere important, Exodus 32–34 provides a marvelous example of its fruitfulness. In these chapters the demanding, insistent role of Moses over against God is noteworthy. Such a role requires that God should also be considered a character who can be impinged upon by action in the text, and who is placed at risk by the rhetoric and transactions of the text. Thus the decision of 34:10 that God will grant a new covenant to Israel results from Moses' insistent petition in v. 9, which in turn results from God's statement of available options in vv. 6-7. Moreover, in 32:10, Yahweh seems almost to be seeking Moses' consent or permission to "burn hot" and consume Israel. Such a dramatic treatment of God in the text does not serve well the interests of either conventional historicism or conventional orthodoxy. It does, however, let the text become a field of imagination in which the listening community catches a glimpse of an alternative world that lives in and through the text.

2. Social Criticism. "Social criticism" sees the text itself as a practice of discourse that is loaded with ideological power and interest. Texts are never innocent or disinterested, but are always acts of advocacy. Most especially, textual material about God is never "mere religion," but is discourse in which God is a party to social conflict and social interest.

In Exodus are many such voices of interest and advocacy; we will comment on two. First, in the narrative of liberation (chaps. 1-15), the dominant voice of the text is that of revolutionary criticism, which mounts a vigorous assault on every (Pharaonic) establishment of abusive power. The work of such revolutionary discourse is to expose the power of Pharaoh as null and void, and to assert that other social possibilities are available, if enacted with freedom, courage, and faith.

Conversely, in chaps. 25–37, 35–40, and more specifically in 28–29 and 39, the centrality of the Aaronide priesthood is established.[5] There can be no doubt that these texts are ideologically interested and that they work hard to establish the preeminence and monopoly of the Aaronide priesthood.[6] Thus even a text about presence is a form of political discourse about power. Theological terms and social forces are always and everywhere intimately connected and cannot be rent asunder. Indeed, to imagine that they can be separated is a maneuver that keeps real power masked in benign God-talk.

In the book of Exodus, the ideological force of the liberation narrative (1–15) and the monopolizing program of the Aaronides (25–40) are in profound tension with each other, one being revolutionary and the other consolidating if not reactionary.[7] It may be that Exodus leaves us with that tension. However, it is also possible that in its final form, the book intends to show the victory of the "liberation narrative" over the "pattern of presence." This may be subtly suggested in the fact that in 25–31 and 35–40, Aaron does nothing, but passively depends on Moses, who takes all the initiatives. Thus the priest of presence is derivative from the authority of the great liberator. More directly, Exodus 32–34 constitutes a massive critique of the Aaronides and establishes Moses' Levites as the faithful priests.

3. Canonical Criticism. "Canonical criticism" is based on the insistence that one gains very little by probing the complexity of the pre-history of the text. One must seek to read the text in its final, canonical form, taking the joints and seams in the text as clues to the intention of the text.

The final form of the book of Exodus follows a definite sequence from liberation to covenantal law to abiding presence. That is, the purpose of liberation is to live in covenantal obedience, in communion with God's glory. As Yahweh "gets glory" over Pharaoh (14:4, 17), the book of Exodus intends to wean Israel away from the glory of Pharaoh to an alternative glory encountered on the mountain of covenantal law. For Christians, that "alternative glory," a "greater glory," is found in Jesus (see 2 Cor 3:10-11). For the book of Exodus, the culmination of glory in 40:34-38 is already in view in Exodus 1. In bondage, as the story begins, Israel has no glory and has no access to glory. By this sequence from liberation through covenantal encounter to assured presence, it is clear that the distinct political and religious themes of liberation, covenant, and presence cannot be kept separated.

In reading from liberation to glory, one may attend to the deep ideological tension present in Exodus. Thus the Mosaic accent on emancipation wrought through the destabilization and overthrow of Pharaoh is uneasy with the stable "presence" linked to Aaron. I suggest that 29:43-46 shows that traditionists are aware of the tension and deliberately establish the juxtaposition of the two. A canonical reading must take seriously a sociocritical reading.[8] The canonical reading does not nullify the sociocritical dimension of the text, but makes a second-level, intentional use of them. Only in this way is the final form genuinely "post-critical."

INTERPRETIVE ISSUES

The fact that the old memory can serve a later (exilic) community in a pastoral, liturgical way suggests that questions of the recurring contemporaneity of the text are not inappropriate, even concerning our own context as "contemporary." From the very beginning, Israel's authorizing text must always be reread and reinterpreted.

1. This text is understood as dynamic and under way, open to a fresh hearing. The mode of such a text is liturgical—i.e., it is used regularly in public worship, where texts are always and inevitably heard with enormously liberated imagination. In worship one does not ask historical-critical questions of when and where, nor does one ask scientific questions of rational possibility. For the moment, one agrees to a willing suspension of disbelief, giving oneself over to the voice of the text.

The Exodus text itself shows Israel practicing exactly that kind of imaginative freedom. Thus the "report" of the Exodus eventuates in the festival of remembrance, whereby new generations enter into the memory and possibility of liberations (12–13). In parallel fashion, I imagine many generations of girls and boys, upon hearing the "pattern of the tabernacle," imagine it, construct it, and at least for a moment "see" the glory that is there.

2. There is no doubt that the core claim of the book of Exodus is covenantal liberation. The text, and a long Jewish history of Passover celebration, has been a voice of alternative possibilities in the world. The structures, policies, and agents of oppression that have seemed ordained to perpetuity are here delegitimated and overthrown. The text permits the entertainment of a world that is different, which in turn permits different kinds of behavior. What happens in the text thus serves to make abused, oppressed persons subjects of their own history, able and authorized to take responsibility for their future. In liturgical celebration, one is not given strategies, policies, or procedures for freedom. Rather, what is given are imaginative possibilities in which the God who hears the cries of the abused Hebrews hears the cries of other abused persons as well and enacts promises that authorize and embolden.

There are, to be sure, current objections to the notion that the Exodus text is related to "liberation theology"; Fretheim offers three objections to such a construal of the material.[9] However, his objections are largely based on a caricature, infused by a kind of dualism that splits religious affirmation and social reality. Thus when Fretheim insists that the exodus is God's doing, and not "violent revolutionary activity," he fails to see that Moses is indeed engaged in such activity in the center of the narrative, and that it is precisely Moses' words and actions that delegitimate the Egyptian power structure. No one imagines that it is Moses alone who liberates. But if the text is taken seriously, it also is not "Yahweh alone" who liberates; for Moses, not Yahweh, must "go to Pharaoh." Fretheim's separation of religious idea from social practice ends with a kind of "idealism," an approach that Gottwald has decisively critiqued.[10]

Gottwald has rightly argued that Yahweh is a "function" of the revolution, even as the revolution is a "function" of Yahweh. The text precludes and denies a separation between the powerful intentionality of Yahweh and the determined action of disobedience that brings freedom to the slaves. The same ill-advised split is evident in Fretheim's second objection that separates "anti-God" activity from "political" activity. Such a split fails to see that God-talk is intrinsically and inevitably political talk. I propose, thus, that one can resist the agenda of liberation in the text only by a seriously distorted reading of the text.

3. Conversely, Fretheim is enormously helpful in suggesting that Exodus champions the theme of creation. The book of Exodus is indeed concerned with God's will for creation and with the destructive capacity of Pharaoh to undo creation.[11] In a context where one might think about "sustainable creation," this text is urgent. Just as Pharaoh defeats creation, so also the laws of Yahweh are intended as ways to honor and enhance creation.

4. Because this text refuses to remain "history," but insists on contemporary liturgical engagement, the contemporary interpreter is permitted considerable imaginative maneuverability, disciplined, of course, by the detailed specificity of the text. As hearers of this text, we are like youths entering into the Passover liturgy and hearing with our own ears the wonder of God's power over Pharaoh. Or we are like children in a ritual of covenant renewal, watching again the frightful theophany, frightened to death, hearing the law proclaimed afresh, claimed in innocent obedience. Or we are like children dazzled by the "pattern of presence," free to imagine how the glory comes and where it dwells, in our midst. Then, upon hearing the wonder of liberation and the poignancy of the law proclaimed, and being dazzled by the presence, we break out in an innocent *Te Deum*, when it is all "finished" (39:32; 40:33)!

Scholarly niceties are not unimportant, but must, in the end, be mobilized for our own work of contemporary interpretation. The book of Exodus is now, for us in our reading, set down in a context of profane, self-indulgent consumer culture, in which technological capacity is matched and mobilized by self-serving ideology. In such a culture (either in market-driven licentiousness or in state-practiced brutality), human beings, human community, and human possibility are increasingly neglected and muted, if not nullified. In such a culture, the voice of Exodus sounds where it has courageous interpreters, who simply and uncompromisingly voice the alternative intention the

Holy One has for creation.

The dramatic rendition of *liberation* takes place in a society where the question of liberation is little honored. Ours is increasingly a shut-down culture in which "freedom" is reduced to a range of "product choices," but in which the soaring of the human spirit, the dignity of the human body, and the health of the body politic are little cared for, honored, or financed. The question posed by the Exodus tradition is whether liberation is possible in such a shut-down world. The answer given by this Jewish voice of God is that God's own will to end the bondage status of the marginated is relentless and cannot finally be resisted.

The revolutionary possibility of *covenant* is resisted when power is closed, settled, and monopolized. Covenant, the text claims, is a revolutionary possibility. Against both authoritarianism and individual autonomy, the Sinai text enacts a covenant rooted in a holy authority that deabsolutizes every other authority. Moreover, in law and command the God of Sinai grounds human dignity and mobilizes the strong for the sake of the weak. Since those awesome days at Sinai, Jews and Christians have believed that a community of mutuality, rooted in the command of God, is indeed a social possibility and a social mandate.

The pattern for *presence* imagines God's awesome magisterial, life-giving glory being present concretely in the world. That "pattern" given us in the text makes its statement now in an utterly profane cultural context in which sacrament is reduced to technique and magisterial "signs" are driven out by mindless slogans and manipulative ideology. The text continues to ask whether sacramental power and presence are possible in an "emptied" culture.[12] This text asserts that God is willing and yearning to be present, but that presence requires a community of generous faith, which gives its best skills, disciplines, and goods for the housing of the holy.

When we depart the text of Exodus, our world is not miraculously transformed by our reading and interpretation. What is effected by our reading and interpretation is only the slow, unnoticed work of transformed imagination. The book of Exodus invites the reader to Passover imagination (i.e., counterimagination), rooted in the sufferings of our ancestors who cried out. It is powered by our ancestors of the Exile who treasured the alternative. Now our reading, amid the suffering of the world, in the presence of exiles and of exile-producing institutions and policies, invites us to leave off the paralyzing fantasy of Pharaoh for the One who will be gracious.

THREE NEW TESTAMENT EXTRAPOLATIONS

Richard Hays has shown with reference to Paul that the Christian use of the Old Testament (OT) is done in rich and varied modes, but always with respect for and a careful reading of the OT.[13] This is clearly true of the New Testament (NT) use of the book of Exodus. The interrelations between the book of Exodus and the NT take many forms, and one cannot reduce that usage to any single interpretive principle of method. Each such usage attends carefully to the claim of Exodus, and each usage focuses on the decisiveness and finality of Jesus. Here I will mention characteristic interactions that refer to each of the three great themes of the book of Exodus.

1. Exodus Deliverance and Liberation. The entire Moses recital of deliverance becomes the center piece and primary material of Stephen's great sermon (Acts 7:17-44). One is especially impressed with the detailed way in which the Moses narrative is followed all the way from the birth of Moses in the midst of a death-dealing Egyptian regime (v. 19) to the "tent of testimony" (v. 44). The story of Moses is for Stephen the primary model for the work of the Holy Spirit and for the persecution of the prophets. (See a different casting of the same recital in Heb 11:23-29.)

2. The Covenant at Sinai. The Covenant at Sinai is clearly definitional for Christians. Paul, however, in relating "Moses and Sinai" to his own generation of Jews and the continuing community of Judaism, which did not accept Jesus as Messiah, speaks of a "new covenant" (1 Cor 11:25; 2 Cor 3:6; and the subtle argument of Romans 9–11). Yet for all his brave language of "new covenant," Paul can never cleanly and unambiguously declare that the old covenant is null and void.[14]

3. The Presence. The argument of Hebrews 7–10 depends completely on the Levitical-Aaronide theory of priesthood and presence in Exod 25–40. Again, a complete contrast is made between the once-for-all priestly work of Jesus and the priesthood of Aaron, which is said to be unreliable and insufficient.

In these several uses the New Testament writers are passionately focused on the distinctiveness and finality of Jesus. In our ecumenical and reconciling context, this supersessionism is awkward, but nonetheless evident in the text. It is equally clear, however, that for all such bold claims, the New Testament can never freely and fully escape the claims and categories of the Old Testament and the faith of Moses. Even when the claim of Christian displacement is most powerful, the truth of the Mosaic witness persists in the New Testament. Thus, for example, the thematic use of Exodus in the Gospel of Mark argues for a sense of continuity between the narrative of the God of Exodus and the story of Jesus.

FOR FURTHER READING

Commentaries:

Calvin, John. *Commentaries on the Last Four Books of Moses (Arranged in the Form of a Harmony)*. Vols. II, III. Grand Rapids: Baker, 1979.

Childs, Brevard. *The Book of Exodus*. OTL. Philadelphia: Westminster, 1974.

Fretheim, Terence. *Exodus*. Interpretation. Louisville: Westminster/John Knox, 1991.

Greenberg, Moshe. *Understanding Exodus*. New York: Behrman House, 1969.

Noth, Martin. *Exodus*. OTL. Philadelphia: Westminster, 1962.

Pixley, George V. *On Exodus, a Liberation Perspective*. Maryknoll, N.Y.: Orbis, 1987.

Sarna, Nahum. *The JPS Torah Commentary: Exodus*. Philadelphia: JPS, 1991.

Other Studies:

Bloom, Harold, ed. *Exodus: Modern Critical Interpretations*. New York: Chelsea House, 1987.

Brenner, Athalya, ed. *A Feminist Companion to Exodus to Deuteronomy*. The Feminist Companion to the Bible 6. Sheffield: Sheffield Academic Press, 1994.

———. *Exodus to Deuteronomy: A Feminist Companion to the Bible*. Feminist Companion to the Bible, Second Series 5. Sheffield: Sheffield Academic Press, 2000.

van Iersel, Bas, and Anton Weiler, eds. *Exodus: A Lasting Paradigm*. Concilium. Edinburgh: T & T Clark, 1987.

Van Seters, John. *The Life of Moses: The Yahwist as Historian in Exodus-Numbers*. Westminster/John Knox, 1994.

Walzer, Michael. *Exodus and Revolution*. New York: Basic Books, 1985.

ENDNOTES

1. R. W. L. Moberly, *The Old Testament of the Old Testament: Patriarchal Narratives and Mosaic Yahwism*, OBT (Minneapolis: Fortress, 1992).

2. George V. Pixley, *On Exodus: A Liberation Perspective* (Maryknoll, N.Y.: Orbis, 1987) 35 and *passim*, has used the term *sacerdotal* rather than the more conventional *Priestly*, escaping a bit the pejorative usage attached to *Priestly* and suggesting that this layer of tradition is a continuing angle of interpretation, rather than a late, "degenerate" form of faith.

3. See W. Brueggemann, *Hopeful Imagination: Prophetic Voices in Exile* (Philadelphia: Fortress, 1986); Gerhard von Rad, *Old Testament Theology II* (London: Oliver and Boyd, 1965) 188-278.

4. Martin Noth, *Exodus: A Commentary*, OTL (Philadelphia: Westminster, 1962).

5. Ellis Rivkin, "The Revolution of the Aaronides," in *The Shapers of Jewish History* (New York: Charles Scribner's Sons, 1971) 21-41.

6. See Frank M. Cross, *Canaanite Myth and Hebrew Epic: Essays in the History of the Religion of Israel* (Cambridge, Mass.: Harvard University Press, 1973) 195-215; Paul D. Hanson, *The Dawn of Apocalyptic* (Philadelphia: Fortress, 1975); O. Plöger, *Theocracy and Eschatology* (Richmond: John Knox, 1968); and Morton Smith, *Palestinian Parties and Politics That Shaped the Old Testament* (New York: Columbia University Press, 1971).

7. See the statement on this ongoing tension between "the constitutive" and the "prophetic" by James A. Sanders, "Hermeneutics," *IDBSup*, ed. Keith Crim (Nashville: Abingdon, 1976) 402-7.

8. Norman K. Gottwald, "Social Matrix and Canonical Shape," *TToday* 42 (1985) 307-21.

9. See Terence E. Fretheim, *Exodus*, Interpretation (Louisville: Westminster/John Knox, 1990) 18-20. See also Lyle Eslinger, "Freedom or Knowledge? Perspective and Purpose in the Exodus Narrative (Exodus 1–15)," *JSOT* 52 (1991) 43-60; Jon D. Levenson, "Exodus and Liberation," *HBT* 13 (1991) 134-74; and in response, Walter Bruegge-

mann, "Pharaoh as Vassal: A Study of a Political Metaphor," *CBQ* 57(1995) 27-51.

10. Norman K. Gottwald, *The Tribes of Yahweh: A Sociology of the Religion of Liberated Israel 1250–1050 BCE* (Maryknoll, N.Y.: Orbis, 1979) 592-607.

11. Terence E. Fretheim, "The Plagues as Ecological Signs of Historical Disaster," *JBL* 110 (1991) 385-96. Fretheim has elaborated this suggestive theme in his commentary, *Exodus*.

12. See George Steiner, *Real Presences* (Chicago: University of Chicago Press, 1989). Concerning an "emptied, shut-down" culture, see Herbert Marcuse, *One-Dimensional Man* (Boston: Beacon, 1964).

13. Richard B. Hays, *Echoes of Scripture in the Letters of Paul* (New Haven: Yale University Press, 1989).

14. See the carefully nuanced discussion by Paul M. van Buren, *A Theology of the Jewish-Christian Reality. Part 3; Christ in Context* (San Francisco: Harper & Row, 1988); and Norbert Lohfink, *The Covenant Never Revoked: Biblical Reflections on Christian-Jewish Dialogue* (New York: Paulist, 1991).

THE BOOK OF
LEVITICUS

WALTER C. KAISER, JR.

Few books of the Bible challenge modern readers like Leviticus. In fact, even the most venturesome individuals, who aspire to read through the whole Bible, usually run out of enthusiasm as they begin to read this third book of the Bible. However, such initial discouragement may be mitigated when we realize that Leviticus discloses the character of God in important ways. One central concern involves the oft-repeated injunction: "Be holy, for I am holy" (11:44-45; 19:2; 20:26). (The Hebrew root for "holy" [קדש *qdš*] occurs as a verb, noun, or adjective 150 times in Leviticus.) Moreover, this book calls upon both priests and people constantly to "distinguish between the holy and the profane [common], between the unclean and the clean" (10:10).

THE NAME LEVITICUS

The Greek translators called this third book of the Bible *Leuitikon*, "the Levitical book." Our English title derives from the Greek one, but through the Latin translation. Oddly, the Levites, as such, are mentioned only in 25:32-34, even though all Israelite priests were members of the tribe of Levi.

Leviticus belongs to the section of the Bible that Jewish tradition designated as the *Torah*, "law" or "instruction." This sense of תורה (*tôrâ*)—an extension of that noun in passages such as Deut 1:5; 4:8; 17:18-20; 33:4—applies to everything from Genesis to Deuteronomy. Eventually this same corpus of material came to be known (since 160 CE) by the Greek term *Pentateuch*, the "five-sectioned" work.

As with most works in antiquity, this third book of the Torah is identified by its opening word ויקרא (*wayyiqrā*), "And he [the LORD] called"). The rabbinic name for this book is *tôrat kōhănîm*, a title that can be translated "instruction *for* the priests" (hence, rules and regulations by which

priests will conduct their services) or "instruction *of* [or *by*] the priests" (hence, teaching and guidance offered to the people by the priests). This double dimension of the rabbinic title allows us to understand the dual focus of Leviticus: The priesthood is instructed in proper rules for officiating, observing purification, and administering at the sanctuary; but the priests also teach the people what God requires of all Israelites.

THE CONTENT OF LEVITICUS

Except for the brief historical narratives in 10:1-7 and 24:10-16, the book of Leviticus focuses initially on instructions, many of which involve worship of the most holy God as well as the purity of the people. Oversight of such worship is given over to Aaron and his sons, that part of the tribe of Levi designated for the task of officiating at the altar.

The first seven chapters present the laws of sacrifice. Chapters 1–3 articulate the spontaneously motivated sacrifices (burnt, grain, and peace), chaps. 4–5 deal with sacrifices required for expiation of sin (sin and guilt), and chaps. 6–7 rehearse these same five sacrifices, with special emphasis on directions for the priests.

The second main section (chaps. 8–10) concentrates on the priesthood. After their installation (chap. 8), the priests begin to officiate (chap. 9). However, improper officiating could lead to death, as in the case of Aaron's two sons, Nadab and Abihu (chap. 10).

The focus changes to matters of purity in chaps. 11–15. Chapter 11 lists the marks and the names of clean and unclean animals. But impurity of various sorts may also arise from childbirth (chap. 12), from skin diseases and various infections in houses and clothing (chaps. 13–14), and from aspects relating to the sexual life (chap. 15).

Chapter 16 appears central to the life of the worshiping community. One of the best known of all the sections in Leviticus, it is read in the synagogue on Yom Kippur. On this day, according to the ancient prescriptions, the high priest entered the innermost sanctum of the sanctuary with the blood of a goat that had been sacrificed as a sin offering. Afterward, a second goat was released, never to be seen again in the camp.

With chaps. 1–16 as the first major block, chaps. 17–27 constitute the second division, most of which is often termed the Holiness Code. It opens with a prologue (chap. 17) and ends with an epilogue (26:3-46). Chapters 18–20 deal with holiness in the family, especially its sexual activity. Chapters 21–25 return to the ritual life of the community with regulations for the priests, Israelite marriages, mourning rites, and the holy days and feasts. Probably no biblical chapter is quoted or alluded to more in prophetic literature than Leviticus 26. It portrays the alternative prospects for either reward or punishment, depending on Israel's obedience or disobedience.

Most scholars consider chap. 27 to be an appendix. It speaks to the matters of redemption of persons, animals, or lands dedicated to the Lord by vow. Its closing formula (v. 34) is almost a repetition of 26:46.

The content of Leviticus exhibits a plan and a reasonably clear structure. Basically, chaps. 1–16 are addressed to the priests, while chaps. 17–27 focus on priestly instructions for the people. The first division provides directions concerning acts of officiating and purifying directed to the priests, while the second division emphasizes holiness among all Israelites. Despite this basic distinction, chap. 11 fits better in the holiness section (chaps. 17–27), since it provides the first reference to the theme of holiness (11:44-45). Indeed, 11:46-47 ("These are the regulations [tōrâ] concerning animals. . . . You must distinguish between the unclean and the clean") may have originally been part of the holiness law, but it may have been moved forward since it stipulates a basic duty of the priests—namely, to "distinguish between the holy and the profane, between the unclean and the clean" (10:10).[1]

LITERARY FORM OF LEVITICUS

The formula "the LORD said to Moses" (or a similar one) occurs fifty-six times. (In three of these fifty-six formulations, Aaron is named along with Moses [11:1; 14:33; 15:1], and once Aaron is addressed alone [10:8].) Seventeen of the twenty-seven chapters begin with the formula "And the LORD said. . . ." Leviticus, more than any other OT book, claims to be a divine word for humanity.

Even though the Greek and Latin origins for the name of this book would tend to limit it as a manual for priests from the tribe of Levi, who indeed are mentioned nearly two hundred times, approximately half of the divine address formulas specifically involve all the people. For example, 1:2 states, "Speak to the Israelites and say to them."

Only in the epilogue to the Holiness Code (26:3-46) does a prose composition appear. Two other narratives make brief appearances: the tragic death of Aaron's sons Nadab and Abihu (10:1-7), and the incarceration and stoning of the blasphemer (24:10-16).

Aside from these brief narratives, Leviticus is a book of rituals and laws. The style we encounter here is very similar to what we would expect in legal documents. Leviticus is filled with specialized terminology, technical vocabulary, and repeated formulaic statements. Even words used frequently in other parts of Scripture are often highly nuanced in their usages in this book.[2]

To summarize: Leviticus is a book that offers rituals and prescriptions for officiating priests and a purified people.

THE PURPOSE OF LEVITICUS

The book is given to Israel so that the people might live holy lives in fellowship with a holy God. But that intent does not tell the whole story, for a greater purpose is also served in furnishing Israel with laws that secure their well-being: They are to be a blessing to the nations. As expressed in the covenant with Abraham (see Gen 12:2-3), these beneficiaries of God's covenant are to be mediators of blessing to the nations at large. Seen in this light, the Levitical laws are intended to train, teach, and prepare the people to be God's instruments of grace to others. Consequently, one of the key purposes for the law of Leviticus is to prepare Israel for its world mission. What Israel communicates most immediately to the nations is the character of God, especially the deity's unapproachable holiness. Israel's disclosure of God's holiness to the nations is visible primarily through the sacrificial system. All can see that any sin, no matter what the status or rank of the individual, is an offense against a holy God.

The importance of God's holiness is also evident in the severity of the penalties attached to some of the laws in Leviticus. Although we mortals are often tempted to play down the seriousness of sin, God's holiness demands intolerance of sin and impurity.

However, God's holiness also involves a positive side: "The LORD, the LORD, the compassionate and gracious God, slow to anger, abounding in love and faithfulness, maintaining love to thousands, and forgiving wickedness, rebellion and sin" (Exod 34:6-7 NIV). What the austere law demands, and what mortals find themselves unable to do, a loving and forgiving Lord provides in the same law that upholds so high a standard. Mercy and remission of sins are available for all who turn to God with a repentant heart.

One of the most frequently repeated terms in Leviticus is *atonement*; it occurs almost fifty times. In connection with the sacrifices, the members of the Israelite community heard the reassuring words repeatedly offered: "The priest will make atonement for [that person's] sin, and [that one] will be forgiven" (e.g., 4:20, 26, 31, 35).

Leviticus 17:11, 14 provides a key statement regarding atonement: "Because the life of a creature [literally life of the flesh] is in the blood." Blood outside the flesh is equivalent to death; however, blood in all creatures makes possible life. Somehow, according to the prevailing belief among ancient Israelites, animal blood could affect mortal sin. Some have suggested that a sacrifice was effective because of an accompanying divine word.

Some Christian readers think the Levitical law was intended to be typical and prophetic of Messiah and his work of redemption. Perhaps some such thought pattern prepared John the Baptist for his sudden declaration when he met Jesus of Nazareth for the first time: "Look, the Lamb of God, who takes away the sin of the world!" (John 1:29b NIV).

One more purpose for Leviticus must be noted: to teach Israel and all subsequent readers how to worship God. True worship can best be expressed by joining the visible forms of the religious life with holiness of the worshiper's life. The external forms are important, but they do not suffice to denote the proper worth and value that a person is attempting to express to God. Although persons must not divorce the sacred from the secular, since God is Lord over all, they must be able to distinguish between what is holy and what is common or profane, between the clean and the unclean. But the holiness of God dictates that any approach to God must acknowledge the yawning gulf between the character of God and the character of all humans. Thus the distinctions between the holy and the ordinary help mortals to realize that God is unapproachably different from humans.

THE MEANING OF SACRIFICE

Whereas the word *sacrifice* in today's common usage means something of value that a person gives up for the sake of some greater value, it did not have that connotation in the ancient world of Israel and its neighbors. For the ancients, *sacrifice* meant a religious rite, something someone offered to some deity or power.

Our English word *sacrifice* comes from a Latin word meaning "to make something sacred, [or] holy." As the object is offered, it passes from the common or mundane world to the sacred realm; it is consecrated. The heart of the sacrificial act, then, is the transference of property from the profane to the sacred realm. The most common Hebrew equivalent for "sacrifice" is קרבן (*qorbān*), meaning "something [that is] brought near [to the altar]." Thus the connection of sacrifice with the altar and meeting place with God is evident in the OT. But what is brought must be a מתנה (*mattānâ*, a "gift"). That probably explains why game and fish were unacceptable as sacrifices, since, as David declared, "I will not sacrifice to the LORD my God burnt offerings that cost me nothing" (2 Sam 24:24 NIV).

In the last century, a huge literature has developed on both the *origin* and the *significance* of sacrifice in the OT and the ancient Near East.[3] Of the two, the question of origin has been the most exasperating, since neither the OT nor the cultures of the ancient Near East provide clear evidence about the subject. Scholars have propounded a number of theories, but no theory has ever commanded anything approaching a consensus. Some have suggested that sacrifices originally belonged either to totemic practices or to ancestor worship.[4] But such speculative theories have now been abandoned.

Generally, researchers in comparative religions have identified four purposes for sacrifice: (1) to provide food for the deity; (2) to assimilate the life force of the sacrificial animal; (3) to effect a union with the deity; and (4) to persuade the deity to give the offerer help as a result of the gift.[5] Some think the first three purposes are not found in

Israel and the fourth is in evidence only to a lesser degree than elsewhere in the Near East.

"The feature which distinguishes Israelite and Canaanite rituals from those of other Semitic peoples is that, when an animal is sacrificed, the victim, or at least a part of it, is burnt upon the altar. This rite did not exist in Mesopotamia or in Arabia, but it did exist among the Moabites and the Ammonites, according to allusions in the Bible [1 Kgs 11:8; 1 Kings 18; 2 Kgs 5:17; John 10:18-27; Jer 7:9; 11:12, 13, 17; 32:29]."[6] Clearly, there are strong affinities in the terms and practices for sacrifice between the west Semitic peoples.

MAJOR INDIVIDUAL SACRIFICES PRESCRIBED BY LEVITICUS Requirements (in order of presentation):				
Reason for Offering	Atoning sacrifices		Burnt Offering	Grain Offering
	Guilt Offering	Sin Offering		
For violations of the Lord's holy things (5:14-19)	A ram without defect Value of profaned item plus 20%			
For violations of human property rights (6:1-7)	A ram without defect Full restitution plus 20%			
For lepers (14:4f.) when cleansed	A male lamb and a log of oil (as a wave offering) and	A male lamb and	A ewe lamb a year old and	3/10 ephah, mixed with oil
or if poor	A male lamb and	A turtledove or a pigeon and	A turtledove or a pigeon and	1/10 ephah, a log of oil
Inadvertent Sins (4:3—5:10): for Priests		A young bull		
for Congregation		A young bull		
for Ruler		A male goat		
for Individuals		A female goat or lamb		
if poor		A turtledove or a pigeon and	A turtledove or a pigeon or	1/10 ephah, no oil or incense
For purification after childbirth (12:6)		A pigeon or a turtledove and	A year-old lamb	
or if poor		A turtledove or a pigeon and	A turtledove or a pigeon	
for discharges (15:1-33)		A turtledove or a pigeon and	A dove or a pigeon	
voluntary (1:3-17)			A male animal from the herd or flock or a turtledove or pigeon or	Fine flour, oil incense, and salt If cooked, no yeast or honey
Peace Offerings (3:1-17)			A male or female from the herd or flock and	Bread, no yeast, made with oil
Thank Offerings (7:12-15)				Wafers, no yeast spread with oil
Votive Offerings (7:16-18) Freewill Offerings				Cakes, mixed with oil

Our knowledge of west Semitic peoples comes from three sources: (1) allusions to or condemnations of the ritual practices in Moab, Ammon, and Edom found in the Bible; (2) inscriptions from Phoenicia or its colonies to its cultic practice; and

(3) the terms for sacrifice used in the texts from Ras Shamra, i.e., ancient Ugarit. De Vaux provides evidence for the first source in the quotation above. Evidence for the second can be found in the Phoenician and Punic inscriptions. The most

important of these are the Carthage price list and the price list of Marseilles, a stone taken from North Africa. These lists fix the amount of money to be paid for each type of sacrifice, including the portion of the sacrifice that is given to the priest and the part that is given to the person making the sacrifice. The four sacrifices mentioned are the *minḥâ*, the *kālîl*, the *sewaʿat*, and the *šelem kalil*. In the *kālîl*, almost everything is burned on the altar except for a small portion given to the priest. In the *sewaʿat*, the breast and the leg are given to the priest and the rest to the person making the sacrifice. At Ras Shamra, archaeologists have discovered texts dating from the fourteenth century BCE with a number of similar terms to those used in Israel's sacrificial vocabulary. They include *dbh*, "sacrifice" (cf. Hebrew זבח *zebaḥ*); *šlmm*, "peace offering" (cf. Hebrew שׁלמים *šělāmîm*); *šrp*, "burnt offering"; and perhaps *ʾtm*, "guilt offering(?)" (cf. Hebrew אשׁם *ʾāšām*).

Accordingly, whether through close contact with each other or through other means as yet unnoticed, there were some very strong connections with at least the sacrificial terms, and in some cases with some of the practices, in the west Semitic world of the first and second millennia BCE.

But if the origin of sacrifice in Israel and the ancient Near East remains elusive, what may we say about the religious significance of sacrifice? Some anthropologists and historians of religion offer explanations based on cross-cultural comparisons and emphasize the social function of such rituals.[7] These judgments may be based on slim analogies. Also, some Christian readers have moved beyond the evidence by using NT sacrificial concepts to explain the meaning of the OT sacrificial system. Both parties can err by reading into the situation outside materials before the text itself is given a chance to speak.

Some scholars have argued that sacrifice symbolically expresses the interior feelings of the person making the offering. But, as such, it can be an act with many aspects: It is a gift to God, but it is more; it is a means of achieving union with God, but it is more; it is a means of expiating sin, but it is more. Often all three aspects are present, including a response of a conscience motivated by a desire to obey God.

As a *gift*, the act of sacrifice acknowledges that everything a person has comes from God (see 1

Chron 29:14). And just as a contract between men is often sealed by sharing a meal together (cf. Gen 26:28-30; 31:44-54), so also *communion* and *union with God* are often achieved by sharing a sacrificial meal together. Moreover, since the life of the sacrificial animal is symbolized by its blood (Lev 17:11), sacrifice also carries *expiatory* value.

Some scholars have focused on the polemics of the prophets against sacrifices as an indication that they condemned outright the practice of sacrifice (e.g., Isa 1:11-17; Jer 7:21-22; Hos 6:6; Amos 5:21-27; Mic 6:6-8). But such a conclusion misunderstands the prophets. Never did they intend their words to be taken as an unconditional condemnation of the cult and its sacrifices. Instead, theirs was a qualified negation in which they said in effect, "What is the use of *this* [offering sacrifices] without *that* [a proper heart relationship as the basis for offering sacrifices to God]?" Or to put the proverb in another form: "Not this, but that," which is another way of saying, "Not so much this as that." The prophets were opposed to formalism and the mere external practice of religion without corresponding interior affections or repentance of the heart (e.g., 1 Sam 15:22; Isa 29:13).

No less concerned were the wisdom writers who verbalize the same message: "The LORD detests the sacrifice of the wicked,/but the prayer of the upright pleases him" (Prov 15:8 NIV); or "The sacrifice of the wicked is detestable—/how much more so when brought with evil intent" (Prov 21:27 NIV); and "To do what is right and just/is more acceptable to the LORD than sacrifice" (Prov 21:3 NIV).

As a result of such evidence, the older thesis that the pre-exilic prophets repudiated rituals, especially sacrifice, has now been abandoned.[8] It was the abuse, not the practice, of the cult itself that the prophets so thoroughly condemned. For them, ritual activity had no efficacy or value if it was not preceded and motivated by genuine repentance and a proper intention.

However, two texts have continued to haunt biblical scholars since they seem to claim that Israel did not offer sacrifices in the wilderness and was not commanded to do so. The two texts are found in Jeremiah and Amos:

> This is what the LORD Almighty, the God of Israel, says: Go ahead, add your burnt offerings to your other sacrifices and eat the meat yourselves! For

when I brought your forefathers out of Egypt and spoke to them, I did not just give them commands about burnt offerings and sacrifices, but I gave them this command: Obey me, and I will be your God and you will be my people.

(Jer 7:21-23a NIV)

Even though you bring me burnt offerings and
grain offerings,
I will not accept them . . . .
Did you bring me sacrifices and offerings
forty years in the desert, O house of Israel?

(Amos 5:22, 25 NIV)

The NIV has added "just" to Jer 7:22, but this is of little help in rendering the עַל־דְּבַר ('al-debar, NRSV "concerning"; NIV "about"). The dilemma posed by Jeremiah's text, which appears to disclaim any command or knowledge of a practice of sacrifice in the wilderness, is solved by translating 'al-debar as "for the sake of." This meaning for 'al-debar is clearly attested in passages such as Gen 20:11, 18; and Ps 79:9. Jeremiah announced that God had not spoken "for the sake of" sacrifices and offerings, i.e., for sacrifices in and of themselves. Jeremiah (chaps. 7–10) provided a strong denunciation of the people's penchant for carrying out external religion without any corresponding interior intentions and desires. Indeed, the very sacrifices named by Jeremiah, the עלה ('ōlâ) and the זבח (zebaḥ), could apply only to those voluntarily brought by individuals and not to those of the community as a whole.

The solution for the Amos text is different. His question drips with sarcasm and hyperbole. Did Israel indeed bring sacrifices and offerings to the Lord during those forty years in the wilderness? Amos inquired with more than a slight touch of sarcasm. The implication of Amos's pointed barb seems to be that Israel had lifted their sacrifices up to the idols they had made for themselves. Once again the priority of the heart and the intentions is asserted over the mere external performance of the cult.

But this whole discussion raises a further point: What counts for righteous behavior in the OT? Is it the act itself, or does it also involve the disposition and the intent of the sacrificer? Even though many have tried to make the case for the former, attributing most, if not all, of OT cultic and moral practice to the mere carrying out of perfunctory acts, forms, and rituals, the case for intentionality

as a major factor in OT cult cannot be avoided. Proverbs 21:27 denounces bringing sacrifices with evil intent (בזמה bezimmâ). Sanctification begins with a declaration that someone intends to sacrifice and then continues with an announcement that the individual intends to follow through with it. One story in Scripture reports how a mother attempted to dedicate stolen money to the Lord by making an oral declaration (see Judg 17:3).

At times, scholars have offered rationalistic explanations for the sacrificial system in the OT. Moses Maimonides (1135–1204 CE) develops such an approach to the sacrificial legislation when he describes it as a concession to human frailty. As this line of thinking goes, the Israelites could not imagine a religion without sacrifice, such as they had witnessed while in Egypt. Thus sacrifices to Yahweh were permitted to wean the Israelites away from making sacrifices to other deities. In this view, sacrifices were a temporary expedient due to the pressure of idolatry. However, Maimonides draws no such conclusion but goes on to affirm that when Messiah returns, the sacrificial rites must again be ready and the Temple must be rebuilt for Messiah's use.[9]

The sacrificial cult came to an end when the Romans burned the Temple in 70 CE and ordered that it not be rebuilt. Another institution, the synagogue, had arisen during the years of the Babylonian captivity. It was a place of prayer and study, but it made no provision for sacrifices.

THE HOLINESS CODE

Leviticus 18–23 and 25–26 were first identified as an independent corpus in 1866 by K. Graf.[10] Graf also proposed Ezekiel as the author of this corpus, for Graf found many linguistic ties with the book of Ezekiel. In 1874, A. Kayser accepted Graf's thesis and noted other linguistic characteristics that he had observed, while adding, most significantly, Leviticus 17.[11] Then in 1877, A. Klostermann gave the corpus, Leviticus 17–26, its name—the Holiness Code—and explored its ties with Ezekiel.[12] However, Julius Wellhausen ensured that this hypothesis would have a permanent berth in the scholarly literature.[13] Wellhausen maintained that Leviticus 17–26 occupied a singularly distinct position within the Priestly (P) document, which he dated to the last years of the exile.

In the late nineteenth and early twentieth centuries the debate about Leviticus 17–26 continued. In 1894 and 1899, L. Paton published several articles in which he sought to identify three primary strata in this code: the original holiness material, a pre-Priestly corpus that was built on the deuteronomistic program for centralization, and a work by a Priestly redactor.[14] In 1912, B. D. Eerdmans attacked the concept of an independent Holiness Code, for in his view no basic structure held the whole corpus together. He complained that other texts in the Pentateuch issued calls for holiness (e.g., Exod 19:6; 22:30 [31]; Lev 11:44-45; Deut 7:6; 14:2, 21; 26:19; 28:9), so holiness could not be limited to this section.[15] Moreover, the alleged distinctive vocabulary of the Holiness Code occurred in other OT texts. S. Küchler supported Eerdmans's position,[16] but scholars, in the main, were not persuaded by Eerdmans's and Küchler's objections.

G. von Rad's *Studies in Deuteronomy* (1947 [German]; 1953 [English ed.]) marked a dramatic change in the direction of research on the Holiness Code.[17] Von Rad emphasized that this material ought to be attributed to the Yahwist, since the deity's role as speaker was emphasized by the repeated formula "I am Yahweh." With this argument, von Rad started a trend that focused on the growth and development of the sections within the Holiness Code.

Cultic Calendars in Leviticus 23 and Numbers 28-29*

Leviticus 23
1. Daily Sacrifice (Not Included)

2. Sabbath (Lev 23:3)
   Emphasis: No Work by Israelites
3. Monthly Sacrifice (Not Included)

4. Yearly Festivals (Lev 23:5-43)
   A. Month 1
      (1) Day 14
         Passover (23:5)
         Emphasis: Time (Twilight)
      (2) Days 15-21
         Unleavened Bread (23:6-8)
         Emphasis: Days 15 and 21
         Convocation by Israel
   B. First Fruits (23:9-22)
      Emphasis: Role of Lay Israelites
      (1) First Frits to Priest
      (2) Sacrifice by Israelites
      (3) Determining Date
   C. Month 7
      (1) Day 1
         Blowing the Horn (23:23-25)
         Emphasis: Convocation by Israel
         No Work
      (2) Day 10
         Day of Atonement (23:26-32)
         Emphasis: Convocation by Israel
         No Work
      (3) Days 15-21
         Feast of Booths (23:33-43)
         Emphasis: Role of Lay Israelites
            (a) Construction of Booths
            (b) Interpretation

Numbers 28-29
1. Daily Sacrifice (Num 28:2-6)
   Emphasis: sacrifices by Priests
2. Sabbath (28:9-10)
   Emphasis: Sacrifices by Priests
3. Monthly Sacrifice (Num 28:11-15)
   Emphasis: Sacrifices by Priests

4. Yearly Festivals (Num 28:16—29:39)
   A. Month 1
      (1) Day 14
         Passover (28:16)

      (2) Days 15-21
         Unleavened Bread (28:17-24)
         Emphasis: Daily Offerings
            by Priests
   B. First Fruits (28:26-31)
      Emphasis: Sacrifices by Priests

   C. Month 7
      (1) Day 1
         Blowing the Horn (29:1-6)
         Emphasis: Sacrifices by Priests

      (2) Day 10
         Not Named (29:7-11)
         Emphasis: Sacrifices by Priests

      (3) Days 15-21
         Not named (29:12-28)
         Emphasis: Sacrifice by Priests

*NIB 2:231

In 1961, H. G. Reventlow completed a comprehensive study on the code in which he argued that this corpus evolved at the ancient yearly covenant festival, including traditions from Israel's arrival at Mount Sinai.[18] Older materials came from the wilderness period but were supplemented by later elements. The preacher who delivered the sermons found in this code was probably Moses' successor.

R. Kilian returned to the source-critical approach in 1963 as a means for identifying two major redactions in the basic code.[19] And again, in 1964, C. Feucht promoted the independent existence of the Holiness Code, declaring that it was made up of two collections.[20] But in 1966, K. Elliger published his commentary on Leviticus with a denial that the Holiness Code ever had an independent existence.[21] He theorized that the material was grafted onto the Priestly materials in two stages, each with a supplement, thereby leaving us with four identifiable layers in Leviticus 17–26. In 1976, A. Cholewiński concluded that the Holiness Code had not gone through a major Priestly redaction; instead, Leviticus 17–26 was composed by members of a priesthood who belonged to the deuteronomistic circle.[22]

Most recently, H. T. C. Sun has analyzed both the history of the discussion and the compositional history of the Holiness Code.[23] In his view, the Holiness Code had no existence prior to its present location in the text. His conclusion was based on three arguments: (a) The texts in the Holiness Code appear to be of widely varying ages; (b) there is no conclusive evidence that a compositional layer extends throughout the entire corpus; and (c) some texts appear to have been composed as supplements for other materials in the corpus. Therefore, even though blocks of material appear to stand together (e.g., 18–20, 21–22, 23 and 25), no overall structure unites all of Leviticus 17–26.

Consistent with Sun's work, some scholars express doubts about the Holiness Code as a self-contained, independent document. As a result, some conclude that the holiness corpus was composed in its present position in Leviticus as a continuation of the concerns for ritual purity found in chaps. 11–15.[24]

These chapters, more than any others in the book, emphasize the holiness of God and the fact that Israel is also called to be holy. One command

is repeated: "Be holy because I, the LORD your God, am holy" (19:2; 20:7, 26; 21:6, 8), along with a similar declaration: "I am the LORD, who makes them holy" (21:15, 23; 22:9, 16, 32).

The book consistently reminds the reader, "I am the LORD." This refrain, or the expanded one listed below, appears more than thirty times in this latter section (e.g., 18:5; 19:14; 21:12; 22:2; 26:2). Or again: "I am the LORD your God" (e.g., 18:4; 19:3; 20:7; 24:22; 26:1). Finally, this holiness section in Leviticus repeatedly admonishes the reader, "You must obey my laws and be careful to follow my decrees" (e.g., 18:4; 19:3; 20:8; 22:31; 25:18; and throughout chap. 26).

Although these chapters have a distinctive style and content, the absence of any introductory formula in 17:1 would seem to work against the hypothesis that they constitute a volume of laws inserted into Leviticus. Moreover, scholars have been unable to discern an overarching organization, which, if present, would indicate that the chapters had a life of their own outside the book.

Readers may find it difficult to locate chap. 17 in the Holiness Code. It could just as easily be grouped with the preceding chapters with their emphasis on directions for the priests. Yet, though it does not specifically mention the concept of holiness, chap. 17 contains some of the other terminology typical of the holiness section. Chapter 17 may be best regarded as a transitional chapter between the two major sections of the book.

To summarize: Leviticus 17–26 does not appear to be a single, systematic, and consistently ordered document; instead, it is a collection of materials grounded in the affirmation of God's holiness. Chapter 17 functions as a hinge chapter between the first major division, addressed mainly to the priests, and this second major division, which concerns itself with the conduct of the general public.

UNITY, AUTHORSHIP, AND DATE OF LEVITICUS

The colophon at the conclusion of the book places the site for its composition at Sinai at the time when Israel stopped during the first year of the exodus from Egypt: "These are the commands the LORD gave Moses on Mount Sinai for the Israelites" (27:34). This sentiment, of course, stands in contrast with Num 36:13, which has a similar colophon but locates the place for the composition of the materials "on the plains of Moab by the Jordan across from Jericho" (NIV).

Much in Leviticus is consistent with the claim that Israel was still in the wilderness wanderings at the time that most of these laws were promulgated, e.g., the people were dwelling "in the camp" (4:12; 9:11; 10:4-5; 14:3; 17:3; 24:10). Their sanctuary is routinely referred to as the "tent of meeting." Outside the camp lies "the desert" (16:21-22). And entrance into the land of Canaan lies in the future (14:34; 18:3; 19:23; 20:22; 25:2).

The aforementioned references, along with the prominent formula "The LORD said to Moses," help explain why both the synagogue and the church held to the essential unity of this book and to a Mosaic authorship until well into medieval times. The internal claims of the book, in their present shape, argue for the beginning of the forty years of wandering as the canonical setting for Leviticus, with Moses, Aaron, and the Israelites of that generation as the ones who are addressed.

This traditional view stood as the scholarly consensus, with very few exceptions, until the rise of the critical method in the sixteenth and seventeenth centuries. Today, most biblical scholars think that Leviticus (and parts of Genesis, Exodus, and Numbers) originated during post-exilic times in conjunction with the Priestly source, often designated as "P." Julius Wellhausen provided one important formulation of that position.[25]

In Wellhausen's view, the earliest days of Israel's worship were simple, spontaneous, and fairly unstructured. Accordingly, whereas it seemed possible to sacrifice wherever one chose in the days of Samuel (see 1 Sam 16:2), King Josiah, during the 621 BCE revival, made a strong case for limiting sacrifice to the Temple in Jerusalem (see 2 Kings 23). As a result, many scholars have argued that Leviticus reflects this notion of worship at a central shrine. Moreover, with the collapse of the institutions of the kingdom and the Davidic monarchy, the priestly guild in Israel had its first real opportunity to assert its point of view—especially after the Babylonian exile.

Another argument often used on behalf of a late dating for P, and therefore of Leviticus, depends on differences between the books of Kings and Chronicles. Since most scholars agree that Chronicles is post-exilic, and since Chronicles has much to say about worship, whereas Kings has very little to offer on the subject, the similarities between P and Chronicles, especially emphasis on ritual matters, suggest that most of the materials in Leviticus derive from the same period as Chronicles—namely, the post-exilic era.

More recently, Yehezkel Kaufmann, among others, has put forth a third and mediating position. Taking aim at the central thesis of Wellhausen, Kaufmann observes that "fixity in times and rites and absence of 'natural spontaneity' characterize the festivals of ancient Babylonia, Egypt, and all known civilizations. Annual purifications are likewise ubiquitous. . . . That these elements are found in P rather than in JE or D is, in itself, no indication of lateness."[26]

Kaufmann argues that P is pre-exilic but not Mosaic. His reasons are: (a) the laws, institutions, and the terminology of P do not fit in with the post-exilic books of Chronicles, Ezra, and Nehemiah; (b) Deuteronomy and Joshua quote Leviticus along with other P passages, suggesting that P comes before, not after, D;[27] and (c) the rules for war and certain other rituals more closely approximate those mentioned in Judges and Samuel than any other period of time. Scholars who follow this mediating position tend to date P to the early seventh century BCE.

For those who have watched the accumulation of the epigraphic materials gathered from the archaeological discoveries of this century, it comes as little surprise that substantial material in Leviticus appears similar to ancient Near Eastern materials from the second millennium BCE.[28]

Still, it is too early to call for a conclusion to this debate between the traditional, critical, and mediating positions on the date and authorship of Leviticus. If we were to emphasize comparisons with ancient Near Eastern texts, some might discern a tendency for dating Leviticus to the pre-exilic period. Scholars who focus primarily on the internal data will tend to side with the critical resolution, i.e., a post-exilic date, to this question. Pentateuchal studies remain in flux, as the recent studies of Blenkinsopp, Cross, Moberly, and Rendtorff, among others, demonstrate.[29] It is now abundantly clear that there is no sole, higher-critical position; rather, there are a number of quite diverse ways by means of which to understand the origins of the Pentateuch and, hence, Leviticus.

THE THEOLOGY OF LEVITICUS

The keynote to the book of Leviticus is holiness to the Lord, a phrase occurring some 152 times. Leviticus 20:26 exemplifies this concept: "You are to be holy to me because I, the LORD, am holy, and I have set you apart from the nations to be my own."[30]

Leading the way and serving as a model for all other aspects of holiness is the holiness of the deity. In its basic ideology, holiness involves a double separation: distinct *from* and separate *unto/to* someone or something. Thus, God as creator is separate from all creatures. This is the so-called *ontological* gulf that separates beings. God is immortal, omnipotent, omniscient, and totally different from all creatures. But there is another gulf: a *moral* gap between humanity and God because of human sinfulness.

This latter emphasis appears in the second major division of Leviticus (chaps. 17–26). Here individuals are called to act, think, and live holy lives patterned after the norm established by the character of God. The accent is, normally, on the moral rather than the ceremonial and ritual aspects of life.

The first major division of Leviticus treats primarily the sacrificial order and the distinctions between the unclean and the clean. Although the theme of holiness is mentioned directly only once (11:44-45), behind both the sacrificial instructions and the concerns over defilements is the overriding concern for the holiness of God. A holy God graciously provides these rituals to make it possible for mere mortals, who are also sinners, to walk in fellowship with one who is pure. Israel is taught, both in word and in deed, what the holiness of God entails.

The laws of holiness are addressed not to selected individuals but to the entire community of Israel. Instead of attempting to produce a selected group of pure individuals, the laws aim at producing a holy people, a holy nation, who collectively will be a royal priesthood, a rich treasure belonging to God (see Exod 19:5-6). The demonstration of this consecration to God is to be displayed by the whole nation in every walk and area of life: family life, community affairs, farming, commerce, and worship of God. Among the ethical duties entailed in this life of holiness by the total community, the book singles out sexual holiness for spe-cial emphasis. Even in this most intimate area, holiness of life demands control and regard for the sanctity of life (and not ascetic abstinence).

Holiness has more dimensions than just the vertical aspect of our relations with the divine and the interior dimension of basic self-integrity. There is also the horizontal relationship with others, which comes to full expression in 19:18*b* (often termed the Golden Rule): "Love your neighbor as yourself." Hillel used this verse to summarize the entire Torah: "What is hateful to you, do not do to your fellow."[31] Likewise, Jesus declared that this commandment is second in importance only to the command to "love the LORD your God with all your heart and with all your soul and with all your mind and with all your strength" (Mark 12:28-31 NIV; quoting Deut 6:4-5).

Many have suggested that the "neighbor" in 19:18*b* is a fellow Israelite, but lest some think that this observation limits the scope of this injunction, 19:34 requires this same love to be shown to the resident alien in their midst. And the love extended to such non-Israelites is to be the same sort of love with which Israelites love each other (v. 34*b*).

For those who fail to measure up to the standard of God's holiness, this same Lord has provided a number of reconciling sacrifices. Leviticus describes five major sacrifices. These Israelite sacrifices are unique (even though the institution of sacrifices is common throughout the ancient Near East, many with some of the same names for the sacrifice and often specifying some of the same parts of the animal in the ritual) in their treatment of blood, especially in the expiatory sacrifices.[32]

The word for and notion of "atonement" become important at this point; it occurs forty-five times in this book. The verb כפר (*kipper*, "to atone") used to be understood as cognate with the Arabic root that means "to cover."[33] Thus it was said that the sins in the OT were covered over by the blood of the animals (and in Christian terms, until the final and all-sufficient sacrifice of Christ). However, the meaning "cover" does not adequately convey the meaning of this term in Leviticus. The Hebrew verb is used in causative stem (the *piel*) and as such probably is a denominative verb taken from the noun *kōper*, which means "a ransom." Consequently, the verb carries the meaning "to pay a ransom" or "to ransom, deliver by a substitute."

The related noun *kappōret* is used as the name for the lid on the ark, variously translated as the "mercy seat" or "atonement cover." The same lid is labeled in Greek the ἱλαστήριον (*hilastērion*), a word directly applied to Christ's atoning work in Rom 3:25: "God presented him [Jesus] as a sacrifice of atonement" (NIV).

This concept of delivering and ransoming from sin by means of a substitute is most forcefully expressed in Leviticus 16 and the great Day of Atonement, Yom Kippur. In part it is a ritual of purification for the sanctuary itself and its furniture. It does involve that, to be sure; but three times the text refers explicitly to the atonement made "on behalf of" (literal translation of בעד *ba ʾad*; "make atonement *on behalf of*" the high priest and his family [16:11]; "make atonement *on behalf of*" all the congregation of Israel [16:17, 24]), whereas this combination of prepositions is not used with reference to the tabernacle. The uncleanness of the sanctuary and its furniture is due to ("because of," מן *min*, literally "from" [16:16, 19]) the uncleanness and sinfulness of the Israelites.

The one sin offering on the great Day of Atonement is divided into two parts, as the presence of the two goats attests. The first goat is slain and its blood is taken into the holy of holies, behind the veil, where the high priest dares to enter only on this one day every year. The blood of the first goat is placed on the lid of the ark of the covenant, called here the "atonement cover" (16:14-15). After Aaron emerges from the tent of meeting, he is to lay his hands on the head of the second goat, confess all the sins of all Israel, and send the goat away into the desert. In graphic and concrete terms, the rite symbolizes two aspects in the remission of sins: Sins are *forgiven* on the basis of a substitute that gives its life so the people can go free, and sins are *forgotten* and removed, as the psalmist says, "As far as the east is from the west,/so far has he removed our transgressions from us" (Ps 103:12 NIV).

This does not, of course, exhaust all possible meanings of the various sacrifices. In addition to the expiatory sacrifices, mainly in the sin and guilt offerings, the sacrifices bring the believer closer to God through communion, dedication, service, worship, and thanksgiving. However, foundational to all of the offerings is the atonement for sin by blood, i.e., through the life of a victim, which serves as a substitute for the offerer.

Leviticus has as one of its main purposes to teach Israel how to distinguish "between the holy and the common, and between the unclean and the clean" (10:10). No less significant is the theology of cleanness in this book, for the word *unclean* occurs 132 times and the word *clean* appears 74 times!

Just as the sacrificial laws and the theology of atonement are provided to promote ethical holiness as separation from sin, so also the laws on the clean and the unclean are given to promote ritual holiness as a separation from defilements that come as barriers in the worship of God. Thus holiness has both an ethical and a ritual side. Being unclean does not mean the same thing as being dirty, just as being pure means more than being physically clean. "Cleanliness is next to godliness" is not the operating adage for chaps. 11–15. Instead, what is profane (literally what is distant or outside the Temple) and unclean temporarily disqualifies a person from coming into the presence of God. On the other hand, to be holy or clean indicates one who is fit or qualified to enter into the presence of God. It is not always possible to identify what makes something common/profane or unclean. Therefore, from the standpoint of many worshipers, some of the items in the lists of clean/unclean appear to have an arbitrary quality, just as the line drawn around Mount Sinai when Moses ascended it to receive the Ten Commandments was an arbitrary line that neither people nor beasts were to cross on penalty of death. When an individual comes into the presence of a holy God, a line of demarcation must be drawn; otherwise, the worshiper's entrance may trivialize what is absolutely set apart from all of life. And when the profane is blended into the sacred, there is always a loss of the absolute otherness and transcendence of God. Thus some of the boundaries drawn here may seem arbitrary, but drawing the line remains necessary.

When the Almighty confronts Moses at the burning bush (see Exod 3:1-6), the Almighty tells Moses to take off his sandals because the ground he is standing on is holy. It is conceivable to imagine that Moses might well have protested, "But why?" But Moses is informed it is imperative that he do so because the ground on which he is standing is holy ground. Again, Moses might have responded, "But, Lord, what do you mean this is holy ground? Didn't sheep and goats pass over this same spot as recently as this very day? How could such ordinary, common ground be holy?" And the answer is simply this: The presence of God at the burning bush demands that Moses worship God—visibly, concretely, bodily, as well as with his inner spirit. That episode helps us understand both a certain arbitrariness in distinguishing the sacred from the secular and the radical difference between God and everything else in creation.

Mary Douglas has argued that cleanness is a matter of wholeness or normality. Using anthropological categories, she presses the case that animals are clean when they conform wholly to the class to which they belong. Animals that split the hoof and chew the cud are "normal," but those who lack one of these characteristics are "unclean" according to this scheme: They do not wholly conform to their class.[34] However, it remains difficult to define what is normal or clean. All creatures, as they came from the hand of the Creator, were pronounced "good"; therefore, it is difficult to see why only the clean animals, for example, should be regarded as normal. There are many imponderables here that almost all interpreters frankly confess are baffling. But on the central point there can be little room for doubt: A holy God demands that we draw the line between the sacred and the secular, the clean and the unclean, the holy and the common.

THE PRESENT-DAY USE OF LEVITICUS

The question most contemporary readers of this book raise is this: Of what use can the book of Leviticus be for us today? The answer, of course, must not be contrived or involve a manipulation of the text, as some have done by allegorizing and reducing the book to a series of symbols with modern values and meanings. Philo, some of the early church fathers, and Cabalistic interpreters have already traversed this route—with minimal results!

First and foremost, in all attempts of modern persons to worship God, the fact of God's absolute otherness and transcendence must influence all initial thoughts about approaching or entering into the divine presence. However, that sense of divine transcendence must also signal the divine separateness from sin and help create the call for followers of God to be holy. God's mercy is available to those who are penitent, as exemplified in this book.

But if the age and strange features of these rituals cause a stumbling block, let us realize that, although the Aaronic priesthood and blood sacrifices have disappeared, the spiritual truth they signal remains constant. Some would say that what Leviticus depicts in a specific ritual points to a later type that would fulfill in the abstract what had earlier been put in a more figurative form.

In addition to ritual prescriptions, Leviticus includes civil laws. Nowhere are modern readers encouraged to attempt to reintroduce the theocracy of Israelite days to our generation. But just as contemporary legal experts read old legal cases to discern the abiding principles, so also readers of Leviticus can use the civil laws contained here in the same way. In so doing, we will find that impartiality in the administration of justice, fairness in the treatment of the poor, provision for unemployed persons, and scrupulous honesty in all business dealings are demanded as the minimal standard for people who are called to be holy as their Lord is holy.

Finally, for those who have difficulty understanding the abstract and theological language of the NT concerning the forgiveness of sins and atonement, the book of Leviticus could serve as an introduction, a primer with big pictures and big print. In it everything is put in the concrete rather than in abstract, philosophical, or theological terms. In the NT, the book of Hebrews capitalizes on this advantage and brilliantly argues its case about salvation and atonement.

In short, Leviticus helps present an overarching view of God, humans, and the physical world. We need only note that the eschatological picture of how history concludes involves a reference to God's holiness. For, on that day, even the bells on the horses and the inscriptions on the pots and pans will have emblazoned on them: "HOLY TO THE LORD" (Zech 14:20 NIV). Leviticus is the book par excellence about this holiness. God remains the quintessence of holiness; and the deity's creatures can hardly offer to be less in their aspirations and in their everyday conduct.

FOR FURTHER READING

Bamberger, Bernard J. *The Torah: A Modern Commentary: Leviticus.* New York: Union of American Hebrew Congregations, 1981.

Brenner, Athalya, ed. *A Feminist Companion to Exodus to Deuteronomy.* The Feminist Companion to the Bible 6. Sheffield: Sheffield Academic Press, 1994.

———. *Exodus to Deuteronomy: A Feminist Companion to the Bible.* Feminist Companion to the Bible, Second Series 5. Sheffield: Sheffield Academic Press, 2000.

Bush, George. *Notes, Critical and Practical on the Book of Leviticus.* New York: Newman and Ivison, 1852 (reprinted, Minneapolis: James & Klock, 1976).

Calvin, John. *Commentary on the Four Last Books of Moses.* Grand Rapids: Erdmans, reprint of 1852 translation.

Gammie, John G. *Holiness in Israel* OBT. Philadelphia: Fortress, 1989.

Harris, R. Laird. *The Expositor's Bible Commentary.* 12 vols. Grand Rapids: Zondervan, 1990. 2:500-654.

Harrison, Roland K. *Leviticus: An Introduction and Commentary.* Downers Grove, Ill.: InterVarsity, 1980.

Hartley, John E. *Leviticus.* WBC 4. Dallas: Word, 1992.

Keil, C. F., and Franz Delitzsch. *Biblical Commentary on the Old Testament.* Vol. 2, *The Pentateuch.* Translated by J. Martin. Grand Rapids: Eerdmans, 1956.

Kellogg, S. H. *The Book of Leviticus.* The Expositor's Bible. 3rd ed. Minneapolis: Klock & Klock, 1978 (reprint of 1899 edition published by A. C. Armstrong).

Levine, Baruch A. *The JPS Torah Commentary: Leviticus.* Philadelphia: JPS, 1989.

Micklem, Nathaniel. *The Interpreter's Bible.* 12 vols. Nashville: Abingdon-Cokesbury, 1953. 2:1-134.

Milgrom, Jacob. *Leviticus.* 3 vols. Anchor Bible 3—3B. New York: Doubleday, 1991—2001.

Noordtzij, A. *Bible Student's Commentary: Leviticus.* Translated by Raymond Togtman. Grand Rapids: Zondervan, 1982 (originally published in Dutch by J. H Kok, B. V. Kampen, 1950).

Noth, Martin. *Leviticus: A Commentary.* Old Testament Library. Philadelphia: Westminster, 1965.

Wenham, Gordon J. *The New International Commentary on the Old Testament: The Book of Leviticus.* Grand Rapids: Eerdmans, 1979.

ENDNOTES

1. Baruch A. Levine, *The JPS Torah Commentary: Leviticus* (Philadelphia: Jewish Publication Society, 1989) xvi-xvii.

2. As Levine (*JPS Torah Commentary,* xviii-xix) has shown by citing three such formulas.

3. For analysis of the earlier discussion, see D. Davies, "An Interpretation of Sacrifice in Leviticus," *ZAW* 89 (1977) 387-99.

4. One of the standard books is Roland de Vaux's *Ancient Israel: Its Life and Institutions,* trans. John McHugh (New York: McGraw-Hill, 1961); see chap. 12, "The Origin of Israelite Ritual," 433-46. De Vaux's work continues a line of study set forth in J. Pedersen, *Israel, Its Life and Culture* (Copenhagen: V. Pio-P. Branner, 1926) vols. 1 and 2 (Copenhagen: Branner og Korch, 1940) vols. 3 and 4.

5. As set forth by Jacob Milgrom, *Leviticus 1-16,* AB (New York: Doubleday, 1991) 440.

6. Roland de Vaux, *Ancient Israel: Its Life and Institutions,* 440, see also 438.

7. For an excellent recent example, see G. Anderson, "Sacrifice and Sacrificial Offerings (OT)," *The Anchor Bible Dictionary* 5:871-86.

8. For a convenient listing of these scholars dating from 1885 with Julius Wellhausen to P. Volz in 1937, see Jacob Milgrom, *Leviticus 1–16,* 482. The thesis of this group of scholars "has been unanimously and convincingly rejected by its successor," argues Milgrom, by scholars such as H. H. Rowley, Y. Kaufmann, R. Rendtorff, and R. de Vaux.

9. Nachmanides did not agree with the explanation that sacrifices were merely to protect Israel from falling into idolatry. He argued that Abel and Noah brought sacrifices at a time when idolatry had not yet appeared.

10. K. Graf, *Die geschichtlichen Bücher des Alten Testaments: Zwei historische-kritische Untersuchungen* (Leipzig: T. O. Weigel, 1866).

11. A. Kayser, *Das vorexilischen Büch der Urgeschichte Israels und seine Erweiterungen: Ein Beitrag zur Pentateuch-kritik* (Strassburg: C. F. Schmidt's Universitäts-Buchhandlung, 1874).

12. August Klostermann used the term *Holiness Code* for the first time in "Beiträge zur Entstehungsgeschichte des Pentateuchs," *Zeitschrift für Lutherische Theologie für die gesamte Lutherische Theologie und Kirche* 38 (1877) 416. Later he incorporated the term in *Der Pentateuch: Beiträge*

zu seinem Verständis und seiner Entstehungs-geschichte (Leipzig: U. Deichert'sche Verlags-buchandlung, 1893) 368-69. See also Kloster-mann's "Ezechiel und das Heiligkeitsgesetz" in the same volume, 419-47.

13. Julius Wellhausen, *Die Composition des Hexateuchs und der historischen Bücher des Alten Testaments* (Berlin: Georg Reimer, 1889) 152-54.

14. For a comprehensive analysis of the positions and bibliography in this discussion of the Holiness Code, see H. T. C. Sun, "An Investigation into the Compositional Integrity of the So-Called Holiness Code (Leviticus 17-26)" (Ph.D. diss., Claremont, 1990).

15. B. D. Eerdmans, *Alttestamentliche Studien 4: Das Buch Leviticus* (Giessen: Töpelmann, 1912).

16. S. Küchler, *Das Heiligkeitsgesetz Lev 17-26: Eine literarkritische Untersuchung* (Königs-berg: Kümmel, 1929).

17. G. von Rad, *Studies in Deuteronomy*, trans. D. Stalker (London: SCM, 1953).

18. H. G. Reventlow, *Das Heiligkeitsgesetz: Formgeschichtlich untersucht* (Neukirchen: Neukirchener Verlag, 1961).

19. R. Kilian, *Literarkritische und for-mgeschichtliche Untersuchung des Heiligkeitsge-setzes* (Bonn: Peter Hanstein, 1963).

20. C. Feucht, *Untersuchungen zum Heiligkeitsgesetz*, Theologische Arbeiten 20 (Berlin: Evangelische Verlagsantalt, 1964).

21. K. Elliger, *Leviticus*, HAT (Tübingen: Mohr, 1966).

22. A. Cholewiński, *Heiligkeitsgesetz und Deuteronomium: Eine vergleichende Studie*, AnBib 66 (Rome: Biblical Institute Press, 1976).

23. See note 14 above.

24. This is the conclusion of John E. Hartley, *Leviticus*, WBC (Dallas: Word, 1992) 259-60.

25. Julius Wellhausen, *Prolegomena to the His-tory of Israel*, trans. W. Robertson Smith (New York: Meridian, 1957). Originally published in 1878.

26. Yehezkel Kaufmann, *The Religion of Israel*, trans. and abr. M. Greenberg (Chicago: University of Chicago Press, 1960) 178.

27. See, for instance, Jacob Milgrom, *Leviticus 1–16*, 9-10. Milgrom follows this discussion with fifteen other arguments for P's antiquity.

28. For example, see E. A. Speiser, "Leviticus and the Critics," in *Yehezkel Kaufmann Jubilee Volume*, ed. M. Haran (Jerusalem: Magnes, 1960) 29-45. Also see William W. Hallo, "Leviticus and Ancient Near Eastern History," in *The Torah: A Modern Commentary*, ed. W. Gunther Plant (New York: Union of American Hebrew Congregations, 1981) 740-48.

29. See J. Blenkinsopp, *The Pentateuch: An Introduction to the First Five Books of the Bible*, ABRL (New York: Doubleday, 1992); Frank M. Cross, *Canaanite Myth and Hebrew Epic: Essays in the History of the Religion of Israel* (Cambridge, Mass.: Harvard University Press, 1973); R. Moberly, *The Old Testament of the Old Testa-ment: Patriarchal Narratives and Mosaic Yahwism* (Minneapolis: Fortress, 1992); and R. Rendtorff, *The Problem of the Process of the Transmission of the Pentateuch*, trans. J. Schullion, JSOTSup 89 (Sheffield: JSOT, 1990).

30. See John G. Gammie, *Holiness in Israel*, OBT (Philadelphia: Fortress, 1989).

31. Rabbi Hillel, *Sabb.* 31a.

32. See R. J. Daly, *The Origins of the Christian Doctrine of Sacrifice* (Philadelphia: Fortress, 1979) 30: "Comparative religion has been unable to find a highly illuminating parallel for the OT blood rites." Also, D. J. McCarthy, "The Symbol-ism of Blood Sacrifice," *JBL* 95 (1969) 167-76; and Leon Morris, *The Apostolic Preaching of the Cross* (Grand Rapids: Eerdmans, 1956) 110-11, 122-24.

33. See J. Hermann, "*kipper* and *koper*," in *Theological Dictionary of the New Testament*, trans. G. Bromiley (Grand Rapids: Eerdmans, 1965) 3:303-10. Hermann concluded by saying, "It would be useless to deny that the idea of sub-stitution is present to some degree" (310).

34. Mary Douglas, *Purity and Danger*, rev. ed. (London: Routledge & Kegan Paul, 1978) 53.

The Book of
Numbers

Thomas B. Dozeman

TITLE, STRUCTURE, AND CONTENT

Two titles are associated with the fourth book of Moses. The title "Numbers" comes from the Vulgate (Vg, *Numeri*) and the Septuagint (LXX, *Arithmoi*). The talmudic name חומש הפקודים (*ḥômeš happēqûddîm*, "the fifth of the census totals")[1] would also correlate most closely with the title "Numbers." A second title, "In the Wilderness," comes from the Masoretic Text (MT), where pentateuchal books are named either by their opening word or by a significant word in the first sentence. The two titles provide different points of view concerning the central themes and structure of Numbers.

Numbers. The title "Numbers" focuses on the characters in the book. It underscores the census of Israel, which takes place twice over a forty-year period. The first (or exodus) generation is counted in chap. 1 on Year 2, Month 2, Day 1 after the exodus (Num 1:1). A second generation is numbered in chap. 26, most likely in the fortieth year after the exodus. No date is given for this census, but it takes place after the death of Aaron in Num 20:22-29, which is dated as Year 40, Month 5, Day 1 in Num 33:38. Dennis T. Olson has argued that the numbering of Israel is the clue to the structure and thematic development of the book.[2] The two-part division results in the following structure: chapters 1–25, The Old Generation of Rebellion; chapters 26–36, The New Generation of Hope.

Comparison between the two halves of the book reveals thematic development. Numbers 1–25 contains stories of rebellion. The establishment of the wilderness camp in Numbers 1–10 provides background for conflict. The people complain about the lack of meat in Numbers 11:1. They refuse to risk their lives to conquer Canaan in Numbers 13–14. And they continue to rebel

against God and Moses in Numbers 16–17; 20–21; and 25. Rebellion leads to the death of the first generation. Numbers 26–36 focuses on the second generation. It is a story of hope. Rebellion gives way to negotiated solutions (Num 27:1-11; 31:14-15; 32:1-42), and the promise of land once again takes center stage (Numbers 27; 34–36).

In the Wilderness. The title "In the Wilderness" accentuates the setting of the book. The goal of Numbers is for Israel to leave the wilderness and enter the promised land of Canaan. The interrelationship of characters continues to be important to the book when the focus is on the setting. But it is their journey through the wilderness that provides the key to the plot structure. Numbers separates into three parts when the wilderness setting is emphasized: 1:1–10:10, Forming Community Around a Holy God; 10:11–21:35, The Wilderness Journey; 22:1–36:13, Preparing for Canaan on the Plains of Moab.

Numbers 1:1–10:10 contains revelation concerning the camp and the tabernacle. It takes place in the wilderness of Sinai. The purpose of instruction is to ready the people for Yahweh to dwell in the tabernacle at the center of the Israelite camp. The central theme is the holiness of God and its effects on Israel. Israel is counted in Numbers 1:1. The twelve tribes, priests, and Levites are arranged within the camp in Numbers 2:1. The Levites become the center of focus in Numbers 3–4. They guard the tabernacle at the center of the camp. Numbers 5–6 contain camp laws, which illustrate ways in which the holiness of God could be defiled. Numbers 7:1–10:10 narrows the subject matter from the social organization of the camp to the dedication of the tabernacle. This section includes sacrifices by each tribe, the observance of Passover, and preparation for the wilderness march.

Numbers 10:11–21:35 tells of the tragic wilderness journey of the first generation. The literature is organized around conflicts in which Israel rebels against God and the leadership of Moses. The people complain about food in Numbers 11–12 and question the ability of Moses to lead them through the wilderness. Israel doubts that God can bring them safely into the promised land in Numbers 13–15. The refusal of the first generation to enter Canaan leads to their death in the wilderness. Numbers 16–17 contains a series of conflict stories in which the priestly leadership of Moses and Aaron is challenged. Numbers 18–19 provide guidelines for approaching God. And Numbers 20–21 chronicles the deaths of Miriam and Aaron to provide the transition from the first to the second generation.

Numbers 22:1–36:13 describes the second generation of Israelites on the plains of Moab. The topics in this section anticipate an imminent possession of Canaan. Numbers 26:1 is a new census of the second generation. Numbers 28–29 provides instruction for worship in the land. Numbers 35:1 lists cities of asylum in Canaan. And Numbers 27:1; 32; 34; and 36 contain laws of inheritance. There is also a change of focus. Numbers 10:11–21:35 has an internal focus, exploring how rebellion by Israel threatens the holiness of God. Numbers 22:1–36:13 examines external threats to Israel in the story of Balak and Balaam in chapters 22–24 and the sin at Baal Peor in Numbers 25:1.

LITERARY FORM AND CONTEXT

Critical Study. Modern interpretation has focused on the literary formation of Numbers and its relation to the other books of the Pentateuch (Genesis, Exodus, Leviticus, and Deuteronomy). George Buchanan Gray outlined the literary formation of Numbers at the turn of the century using the documentary hypothesis.[3] According to this theory, the Pentateuch is composed of four literary sources (JEDP) written independently of each other. The Yahwist (J) was a tenth- or ninth-century BCE history. It was composed either during the united monarchy of David and Solomon (1000–922 BCE) or in the southern kingdom of Judah shortly after the split of the kingdoms (922 BCE). The Elohist (E) was an eighth-century BCE history, written for the northern kingdom of Israel (922–722 BCE). The book of Deuteronomy (D) is a seventh-century BCE document associated with the reform of Josiah in 621 BCE. And the Priestly (P) history was written in the sixth century BCE in the wake of the Babylonian exile (587–539 BCE).[4]

Gray concluded that Numbers was composed of J, E, and P. Examples of J include Israel's departure from Sinai (Num 10:29-32), request for meat (Num 11:4-15, 18-24*a*, 31-35), and a portion of the Balaam narrative (Num 22:22-35). The story of the seventy elders (Num 11:16, 17*a*, 24*b*-30), the vindication of Moses (Num 12:1-15), the embassies to Edom and to the Amorites (Num 20:14-21; 21:21-24*a*), and most of the Balaam narrative (Numbers 22–24) derive from E. J and E were separate histories that spanned the books of Genesis, Exodus, Numbers, and possibly also Joshua. They were combined in the seventh century BCE. The sign JE represents their combination.[5]

Gray also identified the work of a priestly school (P) in Numbers and concluded that most of the literature in Numbers belongs to this school. The symbol P represents a body of literature that includes both law and narrative. The distinctive literature within P is designated by the symbols Pg, Ps, and Px. Pg is a priestly history of sacred institutions, written after the Babylonian exile. It is composed independently of JE. Examples include the organization of the camp and dedication of the tabernacle in Num 1:1–10:10 and most of the laws dealing with life in the land of Canaan in Numbers 26–36. Gray also concluded that the priestly history (Pg) was expanded with additional stories (Ps) and legal material (Px). Thus the literature of the priestly school was not unified. He judged the war against Midian in Numbers 31:1 to be a narrative addition (Ps) and the directions concerning unintentional sin in Numbers 15:22-31 to be a legal addition (Px). The present form of Numbers results from the combination of the distinct literary sources (JE plus P).[6]

There are a number of lasting results from Gray's work. We know that Numbers was not written by one author, but contains literature spanning the history of Israel. This literature is preserved in two general histories, with different theological perspectives. There is a pre-priestly stratum of literature (JE), which makes up a small portion of the book. It consists of stories about Israel's wilderness wandering, beginning with their leaving Sinai in Numbers 10:29-36, and it continues through the account of Balaam in Numbers 22–24. Gray used the symbol JE to underscore that this literature was not unified. There is also a priestly stratum of literature (P). Most of Numbers derives from the priestly tradition. Priestly literature opens (Num 1:1–10:10) and closes (Numbers 26–36) the book. Priestly narrative and law are also woven throughout the middle portion of the book (e. g., Num 15:17-21, 22-31; 16:8-11; 17:1-5; 19). Two guidelines for interpretation emerge from the work of Gray. First, priestly theology dominates in the book of Numbers. Second, Numbers also contains a history of composition. Thus many stories will yield more than one meaning, since they include priestly and pre-priestly versions.

Two developments in pentateuchal studies are departures from the documentary hypothesis evident in Gray's commentary. The first is the character and date of pre-priestly literature in Numbers. Gray dated J in the ninth century and E in the eighth century BCE. A consequence of his early dating was the distinction of the J and E histories from Deuteronomy (D), written in the seventh century BCE. Thus, for Gray, there was no D literature in Numbers. Martin Noth sharpened this distinction by arguing that J and E in the Tetrateuch (Genesis, Exodus, Leviticus, and Numbers) were clearly separated from Deuteronomy (D).[7]

More recent research indicates a closer relationship between JE and D. The theme of covenant, for example, with Abraham (Genesis 15:1) and Israel (Exodus 19:1-34) carries through to Deuteronomy 1–11.[8] The same is true with other themes, such as the promise of land (e.g., Genesis 12:1; 24; Exodus 13:1; 30–33; Numbers 14:1; Deuteronomy 1–11; and Joshua 1:1).[9] The points of continuity between the Tetrateuch and Deuteronomy have prompted a reevaluation of the pre-priestly history.[10] John Van Seters maintains the name "Yahwist" to describe this history, but he redates the material from the early monarchical period to the exile. He also detects influence between J and Deuteronomy. But, according to Van Seters, J was written after Deuteronomy and the Deuteronomistic History (Joshua, Judges, Samuel, and Kings). Thus it represents a later perspective and not an earlier one.[11] Other names for the pre-priestly history include Erhard Blum's designation of it as "D-Composition." This term designates literature in the Tetrateuch, Deuteronomy

and the Deuteronomistic History.[12] Thus, for Blum also, there is a literary relationship between the Tetrateuch and Deuteronomy. In previous studies I have employed the term "deuteronomistic" to indicate the same close relationship between the pre-priestly Tetrateuch and Deuteronomy.[13]

The brief overview indicates how terminology is open to debate at the present time. I will simply use the term "pre-priestly" to indicate a history that is earlier than priestly tradition. It is composed in the late monarchical or the exilic period. It contains material from earlier periods in Israel's history as well, and it extends from Genesis through Kings.[14] Thus there is literary interdependence between the pre-priestly history in Numbers and Deuteronomy.

The second departure from the documentary hypothesis is the literary character of priestly tradition. Gray interpreted P as a history that was written independently of JE. The relationship between priestly and pre-priestly literature took place only when the distinct histories were combined to form the canonical Pentateuch. Thus the interweaving of the two histories was not important for interpretation. Martin Noth expressed doubts about this conclusion. He noticed more interaction between the two histories in the composition of P, concluding that P played a formative role in determining the literary shape of Numbers. This was true not only for the introduction (Numbers 1–10) and conclusion (Numbers 26–36), but also for the middle section, where Gray identified the JE narrative. Priestly writers provided the basic literary design of this section, according to Noth, by the way in which they had gathered the literature together in Numbers 11–12; 13–15; and 16–19.[15]

More recent scholars have continued to question whether the documentary hypothesis provides the best model for interpreting priestly tradition in Numbers. Wenham noted in passing that the composition of Numbers may be more the result of editors who interrelated older material with commentary.[16] Budd also questioned whether priestly tradition might better be interpreted as "midrashic commentary" on older literature, rather than an independent literary source. He took a middle position in his commentary. Priestly tradition is more than commentary, but not an independent document. P incorporates older material, according to Budd, along with interpretative comments, while also providing its own distinctive structure.[17] I, too, will interpret priestly tradition as a redaction of pre-priestly literature, rather than an independent history. This change in perspective assumes a dialogue between traditions in the formation of Numbers. As a result, interpretation must pay attention to the themes that arise in priestly literature and to the ways in which additions by priestly writers reinterpret and restructure the pre-priestly history.

Literary Form. According to Jacob Milgrom, Numbers contains the greatest variety of literature of any book in the Bible. He lists fourteen distinct genres: narrative (Num 4:1-3), poetry (Num 21:17-18), prophecy (Num 24:3-9), victory song (Num 21:27-30), prayer (Num 12:13), blessing (Num 6:24-26), lampoon (Num 22:22-35), diplomatic letter (Num 21:14-19), civil law (Num 27:1-11), cultic law (Num 15:17-21), oracular decision (Num 15:32-36), census list (Num 26:1-51), temple archive (Num 7:10-88), and itinerary (Num 33:1-49).[18] The literature, moreover, spans the history of Israel. The distinct literature within Numbers can be summarized in four stages of composition: (1) individual poetry, stories, records, and law; (2) the pre-priestly history; (3) the priestly history; and (4) the canonical book of Numbers.

Individual Poetry, Stories, Records, and Law. *Poetry.* Ancient poetry is concentrated in the story of Balaam in Numbers 22:1–24, but it is also woven throughout Numbers. The poems are very diverse in content. They include songs of war, water, blessing, prophecy, and even a foreign song:

6:24-26, priestly blessing;
10:35-36, Song of the Ark;
21:14-15, an excerpt from the Book of the Wars of Yahweh;
21:17-18, Song of the Well;
21:27-30, ballad over Heshbon;
23:7-10, 18-24; 24:3-9, 15-24, oracles of Balaam.

Stories, Inheritance Records, and Itineraries. Individual stories and other records were also in circulation prior to their incorporation into the pre-priestly and priestly histories. Topics include land inheritance, temple practice, and life experiences from the desert. Numbers also contains travels lists, known as itineraries. These lists are most likely from royal archives, perhaps associated with military campaigns:[19]

20–21,*[20] conquest in the Transjordan;
21:4-9, cult of Nehushtan;
21:10-20, itinerary list;
25:1-5, sin at Baal Peor;
32,* inheritance;
33,* itinerary list.

Law. There is debate surrounding the origin of priestly law. The majority view in the modern era was that priestly law is exilic or post-exilic in origin.[21] This conclusion has been countered by more recent arguments in favor of locating early forms of priestly law in the monarchical period.[22] The debate is difficult to resolve because all priestly law has been edited well into the post-exilic period. Possible examples of pre-exilic priestly law include the following:

5:5-10, restitution
5:11-28, the wife suspected of adultery
6:1-22, Nazirite vow
15:1-31,* law of sacrifice
19, red heifer
28–29,* aspects of the cultic calendar
30,* law of vows
34,* inheritance
35,* levitical cities.

The Pre-priestly History. Pre-priestly literature is concentrated in the middle portion of Numbers. It begins with Israel's departure from Mt. Yahweh in Num 10:29-36 and ends with a summary of the wilderness travel in Numbers 33:1. The pre-priestly history separates into two parts. It begins by outlining the complaints of Israel over food, water, and leadership (Numbers 11–12; 16) and the loss of the land by the first generation (Numbers 13–14). Numbers 20–21 provides transition from wilderness wandering to conquest of the Transjordan by the second generation. Numbers 22–24 and 25:1-5 explore threats to Israel by other nations. The story concludes with an account of Israel's inheritance of the Transjordan (Numbers 32:1) and a summary of the wilderness journey (Numbers 33:1). Pre-priestly literature includes the following:

10:29-36,* departure from Mt. Yahweh;
11:1-3, murmuring;
11:4-35, complaint about food and the selection of the seventy elders;

12,* conflict between Moses, Miriam, and
　　perhaps Aaron;
13–14,* loss of the land;
16,* conflict between Moses and Dathan
　　and Abiram;
20:14-21, conflict with Edom;
21:1-3, defeat of the king of Arad;
21:4-9, fiery serpents;
21:10-20, leaving the wilderness;
21:21-35, defeat of the Amorite kings Sihon
　　and Og;
22–24,* the threat of Balak and the blessing
　　of Balaam;
25:1-5, sin at Baal Peor;
32, inheritance of the Transjordan;
33,* summary of itinerary stops.

Pre-priestly literature in Numbers is part of a history that includes the promise of land and nationhood to the ancestors in Genesis, as well as liberation from Egypt and the establishment of covenant at the mountain of God in Exodus. The departure of Israel from Mt. Yahweh in Numbers 10:29-36 indicates that the pre-priestly history once followed immediately after the establishment of covenant in Exodus 19–34. The role of the tent of meeting in Exodus 33:1 and Numbers 11–12 provides further support for this conclusion. In both Exodus 33:1 and Numbers 11–12, the tent of meeting is located outside the Israelite camp. This is unusual in the Pentateuch, because priestly writers place the tabernacle at the center of the camp in Exodus 35–40, Leviticus, and Numbers 1–10. As a result, Exodus 33:1 and Numbers 11–12 stand out in their present narrative context. But, in the pre-priestly history, Exodus 33:1 and Numbers 11–12 would have followed in rapid succession. The return of the tent of meeting in Deut 31:14-23 as the setting for the commissioning of Joshua to replace Moses suggests that the pre-priestly history also incorporated the book of Deuteronomy. The commissioning of Joshua leads into the conquest stories of the book of Joshua. Central themes of the pre-priestly history include the unfulfilled promise of land to the ancestors and the necessity of conquest to acquire it, salvation from Egypt as an event of liberation that provides an initial stage toward conquest, faith as fear of God that is able to withstand tests in the wilderness, the revelation of law, the establishment of covenant, and the idealization of Moses as a prophetic leader and teacher of law.

The Priestly History. Most literature in Numbers belongs to the priestly history. The priestly

writers frame the pre-priestly history with law. Camp legislation is introduced in Numbers 1–10, while inheritance law and cultic legislation now conclude the book in Numbers 26–36. The priestly writers also add their interpretation to the conflict stories in Numbers 11–25 and interweave law with the narratives in Numbers 15:1; 18–19. The story of the loss of land in Numbers 13–14 includes a priestly interpretation, and it concludes with laws concerning life in the land in Numbers 15:1. A priestly leader, Korah, is added to the conflict with Dathan and Abiram in Numbers 16–17. This conflict, too, is followed by legislation in Numbers 18–19. Numbers 20–21 is less of a transition to the second generation for the priestly writers. They emphasize instead the death of Miriam and Aaron, as well as the sin of Moses. Israel's arrival on the plains of Moab in Numbers 22:1 signals transition from wilderness wandering to preparation for Canaan in the priestly history, although the death of the first generation is not complete until the second census in chap. 26. Priestly literature includes the following:

1:1–10:10, legislation concerning the camp
　　and the tabernacle;
10:11-28, departure from Sinai;
12,* conflict between Moses, Miriam, and
　　Aaron;
13–14,* loss of the land;
15,* law concerning life in the land;
16–17,* conflict between Moses and Korah;
18–19, law concerning the priesthood and
　　death;
20:1, death of Miriam;
20:2-13, sin of
　　Moses and Aaron;
20:22-29, death of Aaron;
25:6-18, sin at Baal Peor;
26, second census;
27:1-11, inheritance of the daughters of
　　Zelophehad;
27:12-23, death of Moses;
28–29,* offerings and cultic calendar;
30,* law of vows;
31, law of booty;
33,* summary of Israel's itinerary stops;
34,* inheritance;
35,* levitical cities;
36, inheritance of the daughters of
　　Zelophehad.

Priestly literature in Numbers is part of a history that begins with the story of creation in Genesis 1:1. It also includes the promise of land and nationhood to the ancestors in Genesis, the liberation from Egypt, and the establishment of the nation at the mountain of God in Exodus. The central event at Mt. Sinai is the revelation of the tabernacle cult. Its plans are revealed to Moses in Exodus 25–31, when the יהוה כבוד (kĕbôd YHWH, "the glory of Yahweh") descends on Mt. Sinai in Exod 24:15-18. Exodus 35–40 describes the construction of the tabernacle. It concludes with a theophany in Exod 40:16-38, when the kĕbôd YHWH leaves Mt. Sinai to enter the tabernacle. The book of Leviticus recounts the revelation of the sacrificial cult and the sanctification of the priesthood. These events also conclude with a theophany in Lev 9:23-24, when the kĕbôd YHWH appears at the altar in front of the tabernacle. The formation of the camp in Numbers 1–10 completes the revelation at Mt. Sinai in the priestly history. This episode, too, is marked by a theophany in Nums 7:89, when Moses enters the tabernacle to speak with God before the mercy seat.

The conclusion to the priestly history is not clear. There is evidence of editing by priestly writers in Deuteronomy. In particular, they enclose the book of Deuteronomy with the death of Moses. It is announced in Num 27:12-23 and 31:1-2, but not fulfilled until Deut 32:48-32 and 34:1-8. The framing may indicate that their history ends with the death of Moses.

The priestly history addresses the tragedy of the exile (587 BCE), when Israel lost their land to the Babylonians. One of its aims is to explore how Israel can once again be the people of God in the land of Canaan in the post-exilic period (539 BCE). Central themes of the priestly history include creation as the primary context for interpreting salvation, the relationship of creation and covenant, the unfulfilled promise of land, the holiness of God and the demand that it places on Israel to be holy like God, the importance of the sanctuary, the revelation of law, the atoning power of cultic ritual, the need for a sanctified priesthood, the danger of impurity, and the idealization of Moses as a priestly mediator.

The Canonical Book of Numbers. Numbers undergoes a final literary transformation. It is indicated by the way in which the book is presently framed. Numbers 1:1 opens with the statement, "The LORD spoke to Moses in the wilderness of Sinai, in the tent of meeting." The book closes in Num 36:13 with the similar theme: "These are the commandments and the ordinances that the LORD commanded through Moses to the Israelites." The effect of these verses is to separate the literature in Numbers to some degree from the other books in the Pentateuch. The opening and closing verses emphasize the authoritative nature of the literature. The framing also suggests a transformation of genre from history to law. The literature is not so much an episode in a larger history, when it is confined to Numbers. Instead, it resembles more a book of divine law revealed by God to Moses.

METHOD OF STUDY AND PRIESTLY RELIGION

Method of Study. The prominence of priestly ritual law in Numbers has made interpretation difficult. The rituals are not explained; their meaning is assumed. The layout of the camp (Numbers 2:1); distinctions between priests, Levites, and laity (Numbers 3–4); the dedication of the tabernacle with sacrifices (Numbers 7–9); and laws of inheritance (Numbers 27:1; 34–36) are outlined in detail without explanation. Gordon Wenham notes that the "sheer bulk of ritual law in the Pentateuch indicates its importance to biblical writers." Yet few of these texts have worked their way into the lectionary cycles of the church. Readings from Numbers in the *Revised Common Lectionary* are limited to three: the priestly blessing in Num 6:22-27, the selection of the seventy elders in Numbers 11:1, and the healing power of the copper snake in Num 21:4-9. The reason for the absence of Numbers in Christian teaching and preaching, according to Wenham, is that priestly ritual has been judged "dull to read, hard to understand, and apparently quite irrelevant to the church in the twentieth century."[23]

Social anthropologists have opened a window of interpretation into ritual law within the Bible. Anthropologists are trained to interpret living societies. Their research ranges from the most important events in a society to the everyday exchange between members. In most instances, the rules of interaction are known by all and thus usually unexplained. These rules reflect the deepest values of a people, and adhering to them gives rise to ritual behavior. They include important events like birth, marriage, worship practices, and burial of the dead. Yet other rules are mundane, like how and what people eat or acceptable forms of greeting each other on the street.[24] It is usually the outsider or foreigner who becomes aware of such rituals by unintentionally breaking them. All travelers know how easy it is to break the rules of another society.

Priestly laws are the unexplained rituals of ancient Israel. They take up most of the Pentateuch because they reveal their deepest values. Anthropologist Mary Douglas brought insight into the interpretation of priestly law with her study of Leviticus 11.[25] This text outlines the laws for clean and unclean food, known as "kashrut" (כשרות *kašrût*), kosher food law. The chapter consists of a long list of animals, fish, birds, and insects that are edible (clean) and inedible (unclean). Yet the underlying reason why only some split-hoofed animals were edible or why certain fish and birds were clean while others were not elude modern interpreters. Priestly writers gave no explanation, and the study of individual laws provides no insight.

Douglas assumed that the meaning of the text was in the interrelationship of all the laws and not in any one law. She concluded that what made something unclean was that it did not move as other land, air, or water creatures. Unclean animals, therefore, did not clearly conform to their species. The same was true for fish, birds, and insects. They broke the order (or natural law) of creation and thus were not fit for human consumption (at least by godly people). Priestly writers never state this principle. It only emerges when all the laws in Leviticus 11 are read together. The study of food laws in Leviticus 11 provides three important guidelines for interpreting priestly law in Numbers.

(1) Priestly law is concerned with the order of creation. Order, purity, and even holiness are interrelated in priestly law. The source of life is the holiness of God, which fashions order in the world. Life flourishes in a well-ordered creation. Disorder creates a condition that is threatening to holiness and all life in creation. It allows for impurity, which is not simply disorder, but, in its most extreme form, death.[26] Impurity is like a virus to the holiness of God. It can spread through contact, creating chaos and death in its wake. Priestly law is meant to safeguard the holiness of God from contagious impurity by reinforcing the order of creation. Eating habits are part of the system of safeguards for the holiness of God. So are the camp regulations in Numbers.

(2) The meaning of priestly ritual is not in any one law, but in the interrelationship of all the laws. Only by examining all the laws in Leviticus 11 was Douglas able to show that the principle of locomotion was the decisive factor for biblical writers in judging animals clean or unclean. The same is true for priestly law in Numbers. Theological insight requires that all the laws be interrelated. As a result, individual stories or laws in Numbers must be interpreted within the larger complex of literature.

(3) Priestly ritual has symbolic meaning. It creates a comprehensive worldview in which God, humans, and the created order are interrelated. Douglas concluded that in Leviticus 11 laws about animals were carried over into the human world. Thus just as animals separated into unclean (inedible), clean (edible), and sacrificial, so also humans separated into Gentile (unclean), Israelite (clean), and priest (sacrificial). Clean people eat clean food, and only priests sacrifice. The laws concerning the layout of the Israelite camp in Numbers will also have symbolic significance about God, about humans, and about creation.

Priestly Religion. Interpretation of Numbers requires an understanding of priestly religion. This is not an easy task for a modern Christian. We envision God as an intimate friend who dwells within us. We sing about "what a friend we have in Jesus." The focus of our piety is not on the vast gulf between God and ourselves, but on our own close, personal, and individual relationship with God. We may fear God, but it is the respect due a powerful companion. Our friendship with God leads to spontaneous prayer. These conversations take place at any time and in any location. They are not restricted to organized worship. They do not require special rituals. There is no need for a priest to mediate our prayer. And prayer certainly is not confined to church buildings. In fact, we envision our own bodies as the temple of God. The temple, sacrificial rituals, and God's relationship to humans are different in priestly religion.

Temple. The center of priestly religion is God dwelling in the Temple. When Solomon completed the Jerusalem Temple, he stated to Yahweh, "I have built you an exalted house, a place for you to dwell in forever." The same is true for the tabernacle in priestly religion. It is where God dwells on earth. Yahweh states to Moses, "Have [Israel] make me a sanctuary, so that I may dwell among them." The plans for the tabernacle in Exodus 25–31 are a pattern of God's heavenly home. Construction of the tabernacle allows God to descend to earth. Thus it connects heaven and earth. It is the *axis mundi*—the central point of creation where heaven and earth link.[27] All communication with God is channeled through cultic rituals in the tabernacle.

Temples are located on symbolic mountains. Solomon's Temple is on Mt. Zion (Psalm 48:1). Pre-priestly writers associate the tent of meeting in Exodus 33:1 with Mt. Horeb, which is also the mountain of theophany in Deuteronomy 4–5. Numbers 10:33-34 identifies the desert sanctuary of God as Mt. Yahweh. Priestly writers locate the tabernacle on Mt. Sinai (Exod 24:15-18). Yahweh has many mountain homes. Mountains symbolize the presence of God in the Temple and the role of the Temple in connecting heaven and earth. Different mountains indicate distinct forms of worship. Contemporary church architecture provides a partial analogy. Denominations favor distinct styles for church buildings because of different forms of worship. Churches are built with and without altars, with center aisles or in the round. But nearly all churches have steeples. Steeples convey the same message as mountains: They reach up to heaven and indicate communication between heaven and earth. The difference is that for ancient Israel temples are the only place where God can be approached.[28]

Sacrificial Ritual. Sacrifice and liturgical rituals result from the indwelling of God in the Temple. Worship rituals in the tabernacle, therefore, do not conjure up the presence of God. They are a response to Yahweh, who is already there. The word for worship is "work" or "service" (עבדה *'abōdâ*). It states that sacrifice and worship rituals are acts of service to God, who has chosen to dwell with Israel.[29] Two-way communication results from the work of worship. Humans serve God through sacrifice. They also express their hopes and fears and seek blessing from God. In the process, God reveals law and makes promises.[30]

Thus the act of worship manifests the presence of God in the sanctuary in a more concrete way through ritual drama.

Sacrificial ritual in priestly religion continues in Christian sacraments. Baptism and eucharist result from prior actions of Jesus. Thus their observance by Christians is a response to God, who has chosen to dwell with us. Observance in worship is an act of service to God, in which Christ is made manifest through two-way communication. In baptism, for example, God forgives sins and defeats death. The congregation makes confession of faith to live a sin-free life and celebrates new life in Christ. Sacraments also provide partial analogy to the central role of the tabernacle in priestly religion. In most cases, they require ordained clergy for their administration. And they are usually performed publically at a sanctuary with established rituals.

God and Humans. Priestly religion does not envision God as an intimate friend of individuals. The starting point for priestly writers in Numbers is the gulf between God and humans. They achieve this by emphasizing the holiness of God. The word "holy" (קדש *qōdeš*) means "to be separate." God is separate from humans in two different ways.

First, holiness distinguishes God from all things common. This is the separation between the sacred and the profane. God is sacred (holy), and humans are profane (common). This contrast makes God dangerous to humans.[31] Priestly writers convey this message by symbolizing the holiness of God as fire. Fire destroys life, but when applied carefully it can also purify. Priestly writers introduce the *kēbôd* YHWH in Exod 24:17 as a devouring fire. Wholeness is another metaphor to contrast the sacred and the profane. Holiness is complete, and the profane world is not. The contrast between the sacred and the profane is prominent in the arrangement of the camp in Numbers 1–4.

Second, holiness also creates a contrast between health (purity) and disease (impurity). The contrast between purity and impurity intensifies the danger of God to humans. God embodies health, purity, and life. Death is the source of disease and all impurity. Thus corpses become a source of impurity for the priestly writers. Evil actions are also disease that pollutes and eventually kills a society. God is repelled by all forms of impurity. The contrast between purity and impurity is a central topic in the laws of defilement in Numbers 5–6.

The goal of priestly religion is to bring a holy God and a profane people together through the tabernacle cult. The arrangement of the camp and selection of Levites provides an ordered way for the sacred and the profane to dwell together. The *kĕbôd YHWH* also seeks to purify the tabernacle and the priesthood (Exodus 29:1; 40; Leviticus 9:1), allowing God to dwell with Israel. Ritual observance at the tabernacle monitors the health of Israel and transforms them into a holy people. But this transformation is not a story of intimate friendship. It is more an epic drama. Communication with God is not spontaneous and individual. It is ritualized and communal, requiring priestly intercessors. The reason for the heroic or grand scale to the drama is the holiness of God: Israel needs the *kĕbôd YHWH* for life, but the source of their life can be a consuming fire.

THEOLOGICAL THEMES

The book of Numbers is a rich resource of theological reflection on community. Israel's formation at Sinai and the journey with God through the wilderness are intended to be a continuing model of how the people of God live out their faith in this world. The central theological themes in Numbers are embedded in the interplay of the wilderness setting, the journey toward the promised land, and the interaction of characters along the way.

Wilderness Setting. The wilderness is the primary setting for the book of Numbers. Israel is encamped in the wilderness of Sinai (Num 1:1) at the outset of the book, and the wilderness continues to be the setting for their journey toward the promised land of Canaan through Numbers 21:1. It is replaced by "the plains of Moab" in the Transjordan in Num 22:1. The following map provides the geographical boundaries of the wilderness.

The wilderness provides more than geographical background in Numbers. Biblical writers also use it to reflect theologically on salvation history. Gerhard von Rad characterized salvation history as a "canonical history."[32] It is a mixture of historical experience and cultic legend, recounting divine acts of salvation that formed the nation of Israel. The central topics of salvation history include the promise of land to the ancestors, the exodus, the wilderness wandering, the revelation at Sinai, and future life in the land of Canaan. The wilderness setting takes on a wide range of theological meanings in Numbers.

Place of Birth. The wilderness can represent Israel's birth as a nation. It is the setting for stories of Israel's youth and innocence, when they were courted by God (see Hos 2:16-17; 9:10). The formation of the camp in Numbers 1–10 is part of these positive stories. The wilderness is the place where Israel is organized, when structures of leadership are defined, when their relationship to God is revealed, and when systems of worship and government are developed.

Place of Testing. The wilderness also symbolizes a time of transition between slavery in Egypt and life in the land. A time of transition is not the same as a time of origin. This is a more complex meaning, in which an age of innocence is replaced by a time of testing. The test is whether Israel is able to live the life of faith outside the promised land. Testing gives rise to the possibility of failure, in which case the wilderness may be a negative time of rebellion, rather than a positive time of innocence and courtship (see Ezek 20:10-17). The failed journey of the first generation in Num 10:11–21:35 contains many negative stories of testing and rebellion.

Homeless Place. The destruction of a city or an entire land is often symbolized by the wilderness. The prophet Isaiah, for example, writes, "The fortified city is solitary, a habitation deserted and forsaken, like the wilderness" (Isa 27:10). Desolation imagery underscores that biblical writers do not view the wilderness as a natural home or an inviting setting.[33] It lies outside the security of civilized structures and is a dangerous place. Stories of complaint about food (Numbers 11) and water (Num 20:2-13) accentuate the danger of traveling through the wilderness. Divine judgment on the "rabble" in Numbers 11 and Moses' loss of the promised land in Num 20:2-13 underscore the need for faithful action in the desert.

A Place Outside of Civilization. The wilderness can take on a more subversive theological meaning as a symbol that criticizes civilization and encourages one to seek God outside its structures.[34] Yahweh is a God of the desert in Israel's oldest poetry, and not a God of the city (Deut 33:2; Judg

5:5; Ps 68:9, 18; Hab 3:3-4).[35] Often biblical heroes like Hagar (Genesis 16–18) and Moses (Exodus 3) must flee oppressive structures of civilization to find some form of salvation or relief in the wilderness. In these stories, Yahweh is presented as a God who is encountered outside of the confines of civilization and the nation-state. Encountering God in the desert puts one in tension with culture at large. Numbers participates in this subversive imagery. That Yahweh chooses to live in a desert tabernacle, rather than the temple of a king, is a criticism of civilization, with its many forms of security that seek to subvert faith in God. Failure to see the threats of society leads to death in the wilderness, while critical insight provides a path toward new life in the land.

New Creation. The wilderness is also the location for God's continuing work in creation. Sabbath re-emerges in the wilderness for the first time after Genesis 1. Signs of providence in water and food bring to the foreground the implications of salvation for all of creation. God is certainly active in creation within the wilderness, but the wilderness is not sacred or holy.[36] The land of Canaan represents a different quality of divine presence in creation, where God will actually dwell in the land. It represents the fulfillment of salvation for Israel and for this world. Second Isaiah underscores the distinction between the wilderness and the promised land, which he symbolizes as a garden in Zion. The wilderness is a road (Isa 40:3) and a place of miracles (Isa 41:18-19) that signals and may even lead to the return of Zion (Isa 53:3). But the wilderness is not Zion. The same is true for the wilderness in Numbers. It is a place of journey and miracles.[37] But the goal of the story is envisioned at the end of the book. One day God will dwell in the land with Israel (Num 35:34).

Promise of Land. The promise of land is central to the plot of Numbers for both pre-priestly and priestly writers. But theological reflection on how Israel achieves their promised home is different in the two histories. The distinct theologies are indicated by divergent travel routes through the wilderness. The two routes can be illustrated as follows:

Pre-priestly Kadesh Sequence of Travel	Priestly Paran Sequence of Travel [a] Sinai to Paran (10:12)
[1] from Mt. Yahweh (10:33) (Three days journey) [2] Kibrothhattaqvah to Hazeroth (11:35)	
	[b] Hazeroth to Paran (12:16)
KADESH/ZIN —Spy Story (13:21, 26) —Korah (Num 16:1–19) —Edom (20:14-21)	PARAN —Dathan and Abiram (chap. 16) —Spy Story (Num 13:3, 26)
[3] Kadesh to Mount Hor (20:22)	[c] to Kadesh/Zin (20:1)

The sequence of travel in the pre-priestly history begins with Israel's departure from Mt. Yahweh on a three-day journey (10:33) to Hazeroth (11:35). The wilderness of Zin, or Kadesh, is an important setting in the pre-priestly history, even though it lacks a clear itinerary notice in the present form of Numbers. Israel arrives at Kadesh in the second year of their exodus from Egypt. It is the setting for the loss of the land in Numbers 13–14 (13:21, 26). The challenge to the leadership of Moses by Dathan and Abiram (chap. 16) and an unsuccessful negotiation with the Edomite king to cross his land (20:14-21) also take place at Kadesh. Israel leaves Kadesh when they journey to Mt. Hor (20:22).

Priestly writers change the sequence of travel. Israel departs from Sinai rather than Mt. Yahweh. Their next significant stopping point is the wilderness of Paran. This is stated both at the outset of their journey from Sinai (Num 10:12) and immediately preceding the spy story (Num 12:16). As a result, Paran is firmly established as the location of the spy story, which creates confusion in the present form of Numbers 13–14. The insertion of Paran results in Israel's arriving at Kadesh at the end of their wilderness trek in the fortieth year after they left Egypt (Num 20:1).

The two versions of travel represent different theologies of the promised land. Pre-priestly writers view the promised land from the wilderness location of Kadesh. Priestly writers achieve a different vantage point from Paran.[38] The two perspectives are expressed most clearly in the story of Israel's loss of the promised land in Numbers 13–14.

Kadesh and Holy War. Pre-priestly writers emphasize that Israel must acquire the courage to undertake holy war to leave the wilderness and to enter the promised land. Possession of the promised land requires a conquest of indigenous peoples no matter how dangerous such a war may appear. Holy war is an act of faith in the promises of God. The failure of the first generation to leave the wilderness in Numbers 13–14 is because they lack the courage of conquest. Joshua sends out spies from Kadesh to reconnoiter the southern border regions of the land. Upon their return, they report the goodness of the land and how fearsome the people appear to be, like the giant Anakim (Num 13:22-24, 26-30), which prompts rebellion (Num 14:2-4). Rebellion in this account is fear of the giants to the point where the people lose faith in God to lead them to conquest. Divine judgment and the subsequent failure of the first generation to leave the wilderness is because the people lack the courage of conquest.

Paran and the Goodness of Creation. Priestly writers change the setting of Numbers 13–14 to Paran, and they introduce a new theology of the promised land. These writers eliminate the central role of conquest as the means for leaving the wilderness. Instead, they emphasize Israel's need to see the goodness of God in creation. In this account, Moses no longer sends out spies, but "explorers" from each tribe to evaluate the entire land of Canaan. Their goal is not espionage on the fortifications at the southern border of Canaan, but assessment of the quality of the whole land that Yahweh has promised. Thus the spies travel to the northernmost border of the land of Canaan (Num 13:21 *b*). Rebellion is not the fear of conquest, but the failure of the people to judge the land "good" (Num 13:31-33). The first generation still dies, but the plot no longer pushes ahead to an account of holy war. Priestly writers interpret the wilderness more in relationship to creation than to an exodus and conquest. Entering the promised land, in their version of the story, requires proper perception of its goodness, rather than a conquest of indigenous peoples.

Characters. The development of characters in Numbers evolves around the problem of how to build a theocratic society in the wilderness. The central character is Yahweh, and all other characters are defined in relation to God. The goal is to devise a way in which a holy God can be brought into relationship with humans who do not share this quality, and, hence, are at risk in the presence of God. Characters separate into three general groups: God, who embodies holiness; Israel, who lives in the sphere of holiness; and the nations, who live outside of the sphere of holiness.

God. There is unresolved tension in God that is central to the book of Numbers. It is the tension between holiness and covenant. Divine holiness results in separation from humans and creation. Holiness means that God is unlike creation and even repulsed by the pollution of sin. Covenant describes God's commitment to humans and creation in spite of sin.[39] God enters into a covenant with all of creation at the end of the flood in Gen 9:1-17. God makes a covenant with Abraham in Genesis 17, and God forms a covenant treaty with Israel in Exodus 19–34. Covenant is not easily harmonized with holiness, because it describes the relationship between God and humans, rather than separation. The result is a tension between divine holiness and Yahweh's commitment to creation and relationship with humans. The formation of a theocratic society around the wilderness tabernacle is the attempt to fulfill the divine obligations of covenant while safeguarding holiness.

The tension between holiness and covenant is never really resolved in the book of Numbers. Divine obligation to creation and to Israel fuels the plot of the story. Covenant prompts the exodus (Exod 6:2-8). It is also the driving force in the establishment of the wilderness sanctuary, when God descends from Mt. Sinai into the tabernacle (Exod 40:35-36). Covenantal concern is manifested in divine communication with Moses (Num 1:1), in leading and guiding through the wilderness (Num 9:15-23), in the providential care of food and water (Numbers 11; 20), in healing (Num 21:1-9), in the quality of loving kindness (Num 14:18, 20), and in blessing (Num 6:21-27). The holiness of God emphasizes that divine leading is never casual and that divine grace is anything but cheap. Yahweh's repulsion to sin is underscored by the holy war imagery of the ark of the covenant (Num 10:33-36), by the precise details of the camp and priesthood (Num 1:1–10:10), and by the destructive power of divine wrath conceived in the wilderness (Num 11:1-3; 25).

The tension between holiness and covenant makes God dynamic and open to change. Obedience reinforces divine obligation (Caleb and Joshua in Numbers 13–14). Resistance to divine leading (Num 11:1-3), lack of faith in divine providence (Numbers 11:1), rejection of God's new creation (Numbers 13–14), and the worship of other gods (Numbers 25:1) prompt judgment and separation between God and Israel. Yet, even at these times, zealous action on behalf of God (Numbers 25:1), healing icons (Num 20:4-9), cultic rituals (Numbers 15:1), and intercession (Numbers 14:1) can persuade God to relent from acts of judgment.

Israel. Israel is the direct object of God's saving activity. They are formed out of divine covenantal obligation. Israelites are singled out for divine favor with the promise of land (Numbers 15:1). They experience special providence (Numbers 11:1) and divine guidance (Num 9:15-23). They are the ones who gather around the sanctuary and live in close proximity to God (Num 1:1–10:10). And, because of their special status, they are required to embody the qualities of divine holiness through cultic observances (Num 1:1–10:10; chaps. 28-29), in their march through the wilderness (Numbers 11–21; 25), and in their future life in the land of Canaan (Numbers 15:1; 35). Failure to do so results in death (Numbers 13–14; 25).

Numbers also explores forms of leadership for Israel. Leaders provide different ways for Israel to approach God, who dwells at the center of the camp. Divine holiness in the tabernacle is protected through the hierarchy of priests and Levites camped around it. Priestly leaders also provide a safe means for Israel to approach God through worship (Numbers 3-4; 8; 16-18). The seventy elders provide prophetic leadership in governing the people (Numbers 11). Numbers also outlines the role of lay tribal leaders (Numbers 1) and Nazirites (Numbers 6). The role of Moses throughout Numbers also provides theological reflection on both prophetic and priestly leadership. He models prophetic, charismatic leadership (Numbers 11–12); priestly, non-charismatic leadership (Numbers 16–18); and other intercessory roles (Numbers 13–14; 25).

The Nations. The nations are defined more in relationship to divine holiness than to covenant. They are separate from God and live outside of the wilderness camp. Some are associated with Canaan. They may be mythologized as giants, such as Anak, or the descendants of the Nephilim (Num 13:25-33). Others are simply described as ethnic groups, like the Amalekites, the Hittites, the Jebusites, and the Amorites (Num 13:27-29). In general, the nations are opponents of God who must be defeated by Israel in holy war, like Sihon, the Amorite king (Num 21:21-32), and Og of Bashan (Num 21:33-35). Divine concern for the nations is also evident in Numbers. The intercession of Moses in Num 14:13-19 is successful in part because of God's concern for the nations.

Other people and groups blur the line between "Israel" and "the nations." Resident aliens are one example of non-Israelites included in the camp (Num 9:1-14) and in Israel's future life in the land (Numbers 15; 35). "The rabble" in Num 11:4, on the other hand, represent members of the camp who belong outside the sphere of holiness. Balaam is a non-Israelite seer who knows Yahweh (Numbers 22–24), and the Midianites represent an entire ethnic group whose relationship with Israel is ambiguous. Jethro, or Hobab, the father-in-law of Moses, is a Midianite, whose guidance Moses requests (Num 10:29-32). Yet a Midianite woman threatens the purity of the Israelite camp in Numbers 25.

FOR FURTHER READING

Ashley, Timothy R. *Numbers.* NICOT. Grand Rapids: Eerdmans, 1993.

Budd, Phillip J. *Numbers.* WBC 5. Waco, Tex.: Word, 1984.

Gray, George Buchanan. *Numbers.* ICC. Edinburgh: T & T Clark, 1903.

Davies, Eryl W. *Numbers.* NCB. Grand Rapids: Eerdmans, 1995.

Levine, Baruch A. *Numbers 1:1–20.* AB 4A. New York: Doubleday, 1993.

Milgrom, Jacob. *Numbers.* JPS Torah Commentary. Philadelphia: JPS, 1990.

Noth, Martin. *Numbers.* OTL. Philadelphia: Westminster, 1968.

Olson, Dennis T. *Numbers.* Interpretation. Louisville: Westminster John Knox, 1996.

Sakenfeld, Katharine Doob. *Journeying with God: A Commentary on the Book of Numbers.* ITC. Grand Rapids: Eerdmans, 1995.

Wenham, Gordon J. *Numbers: An Introduction and Commentary.* Tyndale Old Testament Commentaries. Leicester: Inter-Varsity, 1981.

ENDNOTES

1. See *m. Yoma* 7:1; *m. Menaḥot* 4:3.

2. Dennis T. Olson, *The Death of the Old and the Birth of the New: The Framework of the Book of Numbers and the Pentateuch,* BJS 71 (Chico, Calif.: Scholars Press, 1985) 83-124.

3. George Buchanan Gray, *Numbers,* ICC (Edinburgh, T & T Clark, 1903) xxxi-xxxii.

4. Joseph Blenkinsopp, "Introduction to the Pentateuch," in *The New Interpreter's Bible,* vol. 1 (Nashville: Abingdon, 1994) 310-12.

5. Gray, *Numbers,* xxxi-xxxii.

6. Gray, *Numbers,* xxxiii-xxxix.

7. Martin Noth, *Numbers,* trans. James D. Martin, OTL (Philadelphia: Westminster, 1968) 4-11. Noth extended the argument to include later deuteronomistic (Dtr) additions, which tied Deuteronomy to the Deuteronomistic History (Joshua, Judges, Samuel, and Kings).

8. See Lothar Perlitt, *Bundestheologie im Alten Testament,* WMANT 36 (Neukirchen-Vluyn: Neukirchener Verlag, 1969); and Thomas B. Dozeman, *God on the Mountain,* SBLMS 37 (Atlanta: Scholars Press, 1988) 37-86.

9. Susan Boorer, *The Promise of Land as Oath: A Key to the Formation of the Pentateuch,* BZAW 205 (Berlin: de Gruyter, 1992); and Thomas B. Dozeman, *God at War: Power in the Exodus Tradition* (Oxford: Oxford University Press, 1996) 42-100.

10. Blenkinsopp, "Introduction to the Pentateuch," 312-13.

11. John Van Seters, *In Search of History: Historiography in the Ancient World and the Origins of Biblical History* (New Haven: Yale University Press, 1983); and *The Life of Moses: The Yahwist as Historian in Exodus-Numbers* (Louisville: Westminster/John Knox, 1994).

12. Erhard Blum, *Studien zur Komposition des Pentateuch,* BZAW 189 (Berlin: de Gruyter, 1990).

13. Dozeman, *God on the Mountain* and *God at War.*

14. See Dozeman, *God at War,* 42-100, 171-83, for discussion of the pre-priestly history as including Genesis through Kings. For further discussion of terminology, see D. Carr, *Reading the Fractures of Genesis: Historical and Literary Approaches* (Louisville: Westminster John Knox, 1996) 143-293, who uses "Non-P" to designate pre-priestly tradition.

15. Noth, *Numbers,* 4-12.

16. Gordon J. Wenham, *Numbers: An Introduction and Commentary,* Tyndale Old Testament Commentaries (Leicester: Inter-Varsity, 1981) 20-21.

17. Philip J. Budd, *Numbers,* WBC 5 (Waco, Tex.: Word, 1984) xxii.

18. Jacob Milgrom, *Numbers,* JPS Torah Commentary (Philadelphia: JPS, 1990) xiii.

19. See G. I. Davies, "The Wilderness Itineraries and the Composition of the Pentateuch," *VT* 33 (1983) 1-13.

20. The asterisk (*) indicates that a section of literature contains writing from more than one author.

21. See Julius Wellhausen, *Prolegomena to the History of Ancient Israel,* trans. J. S. Menzies and A. Black (Gloucester: Peter Smith, 1983; first published in 1883).

22. See Y. Kaufmann, *The Religion of Israel,* trans M. Greenberg (Chicago: University of Chicago Press, 1961).

23. Gordon J. Wenham, *Numbers: An Introduction and Commentary,* 25-29.

24. See, e.g., Thomas W. Overholt, *Cultural Anthropology and the Old Testament,* Guides to Biblical Scholarship, Old Testament (Minneapolis: Augsburg Fortress, 1996); and Robert R. Wilson, *Sociological Approaches to the Old Testament* (Philadelphia: Fortress, 1984).

25. Mary Douglas, *Purity and Danger: An Analysis of the Concepts of Pollution and Taboo* (London: Routledge and Kegan Paul, 1966), 41-57.

26. See Jacob Milgrom, *Numbers,* 344-46; and Kathrine Doob Sakenfeld, *Numbers: Journeying with God,* ITC (Grand Rapids: Eerdmans, 1995) 17-20.

27. Gary A. Anderson, "Introduction to Israelite Religion," *NIB* 1:277-79.

28. Thomas B. Dozeman, *God on the Mountain.*

29. Anderson, "Introduction to Israelite Religion," 279-80.

30. Wenham, *Numbers*, 29-30.

31. David P. Wright, "Holiness: Old Testament," in *Anchor Bible Dictionary*, 6 vols. (New York: Doubleday, 1992) 3:237-49.

32. Gerhard von Rad, *Old Testament Theology I*, trans. D. M. G. Stalker (New York: Harper and Bros., 1962) 126, 129. See also Thomas L. Thompson, "Historiography [Israelite]," *ABD* 3:209-10.

33. Shemaryahu Talmon, "The 'Desert Motif' in the Bible and in Qumran Literature," in *Biblical Motifs in Origins and Transformations*, ed. A. Altmann, Philip W. Lown Institute of Advanced Judaic Studies, Brandeis University Studies and Texts 3 (Cambridge, Mass.: Harvard University Press, 1966) 39-44.

34. Herbert N. Schneidau, *Sacred Discontent: The Bible and Western Tradition* (Baton Rouge: Louisiana State University Press, 1976) esp. 104-57.

35. The poems are characterized as the "March in the South" theophany tradition. A common feature of this poetry is that Yahweh dwells in the desert, not in the city. See Dozeman, *God on the Mountain*, 121-26; and Richard J. Clifford, *The Cosmic Mountain in Canaan and the Old Testament*, HSM 4 (Cambridge, Mass.: Harvard University Press, 1972).

36. Max Oelschlaeger, *The Idea of the Wilderness: From Prehistory to the Age of Ecology* (New Haven: Yale University Press, 1991) 41-53, esp. 50-51.

37. Robert L. Cohn, "Liminality in the Wilderness," in *The Shape of Sacred Space: Four Biblical Studies*, AAR Studies in Religion 23 (Missoula, Mont.: Scholars Press, 1981) 7-20.

38. See the detailed study of the different travel routes by Baruch A. Levine, *Numbers 1:1–20*, AB 4A (New York: Doubleday, 1993) 48-72.

39. See Dozeman, *God on the Mountain*, 57-65.

THE BOOK OF DEUTERONOMY

RONALD E. CLEMENTS

THE BOOK AND
ITS LITERARY SETTING

The Contents of the Book. Deuteronomy is the fifth book of the Hebrew Bible and is ascribed to Moses, making it the concluding book, or scroll, of the Pentateuch. Its title, which derives from the Greek (Septuagint, or LXX) text of Deut 17:18, indicates that it is a "second law." The title is wholly appropriate, since it describes the law given by Moses in the plains of Moab immediately prior to the crossing of the river Jordan and Israel's entry into the land promised to its ancestors, Abraham, Isaac, and Jacob. It is, therefore, a "second law," or more precisely a second giving of the law that had first been given as the terms of the covenant concluded through the mediation of Moses on Mt. Sinai between the Lord as God and the people of Israel, immediately after their deliverance from slavery in Egypt.

Although it contains two main collections of legal, or quasi-legal, material, the book of Deuteronomy is much more than a book of law. The first of these collections is set out in Deut 5:6-21, where the Ten Commandments are repeated from their first disclosure in Exod 20:2-17. The second collection is to be found in chapters 12–26 and contains an extensive collection of laws and legislative prescriptions (concerning, for example, how law is to be administered). The relationship between the Ten Commandments and the laws of chapter 26 has remained a very important issue for the understanding of the book and its background.

In addition to these collections of commandments and laws there is a narrative beginning in chapters 1–3 that summarizes the story of Israel's life in the wilderness from the first revelation on Mt. Sinai (which Deuteronomy consistently refers to as Mt. Horeb) to the time when the people were ready to launch their assault upon the promised land under Joshua. The narrative conclusion (chap. 34) tells of the death of Moses in the plains of Moab, before the crossing of the Jordan. In addition to this narrative framework there is a significant series of exhortations and warnings in chapters 6–11 and similar admonitory speeches, presented as blessings and curses, in chapters 27–28. Further hortatory addresses and poems in chapters 29–33 complete the framework of the law code. Scholars, therefore, have found it useful to distinguish between the "law code" of chapters 12–26 and the "framework" of chapters 1–11 and 27–34.

Sermon-like speeches and laws may at first appear as unlikely companions in a single literary work, but throughout there is a high level of consistency and homogeneity of style in Deuteronomy that makes it in general the most easily recognized of the entire OT. This closeness of stylistic presentation does not point to one single author, but to a particular group of writers, preachers, and reformers who shared a consistency of purpose that has created a work of coherence, clarity, and intense passion. The writers very evidently set out to compose a comprehensive guidebook for Israel to live as the people of the LORD God.

The Form and Forms of the Book. When we inquire as to the overall form and character of the book, the overall title of "law" proves to be inadequate. Deuteronomy describes its own chief contents as being composed of "law" (תורה *tôrâ,* "instruction," "directive," "guidance") and further defines this as being made up of "decrees, statutes, and ordinances" (Deut 4:44). Certainly there are laws, such as would appear in a statute book for the handling of criminal cases, which are present in the book, but there is much else besides. Moreover, many of the so-called laws are in the nature of religious regulations; some are ethical directives concerning good behavior in the home and in society in general, and some are institutional directives for setting up governmental organizations. Besides all these there are regulations controlling family law and custom. If we seek a comprehensive term to describe what is to be found in the book, then "polity" is almost certainly the most helpful term.

From a formal perspective, there is a surprising shift between the high prominence given to Moses in the framework, particularly in chapters 1–11, and in the lack of reference to Moses in the law code of chapters 12–26, apart from being referred to by inference in the regulation concerning prophecy in Deut 18:18. This accords with the very marked rhetorical style of the exhortations of the framework and the more crisp style of the law code. Obviously the authors of the finished book have drawn material from different sources over an extended period of time. Although they have imposed a general level of stylistic and theological consistency on the work, this variety in the different types of material and its varied origins still shows through.

If the subject matter of the book can best be described as declaring a national "polity" for Israel,[1] extending from constitutional permission for a monarchy (Deut 17:14-20) to rules of personal hygiene in a military encampment (Deut 23:12-14), then its form can best be described as "preached law."[2] It is law only in a modified sense, however, since it is addressed to an entire nation, even demanding that its most important requirements be taught to children (Deut 6:7) and making use of a high degree of exhortation and rhetorical persuasion. Even specific laws that call for precise and careful definition are sometimes supplemented by exhortations to observe them for religious reasons (e.g., in showing generosity to former slaves, Deut 15:12-18).

The formal legal parts of the book can be usefully compared with earlier formulations of laws covering similar cases, most particularly in the law code of Exod 20:22–23:19, which has come to be described as "the book of the covenant" (cf. Exod 24:7). This older law code can clearly be seen to have been available to the authors of the laws of Deuteronomy, who can be shown to have based many of their own rulings on it.[3]

The form of the Ten Commandments has a distinctiveness all its own and requires to be considered separately for its importance in regard to the origins both of these commandments and of the book of Deuteronomy.

The law code proper of chapters 12–26 necessarily invites comparison with the form and structure of comparable law codes of the ancient Near East. The similarities and the contrasts are both worthy of close attention and can be considered in connection with the introduction to that code.

The speeches of warning and exhortation ascribed to Moses are distinctive in their style and represent the most marked and characteristically "deuteronomic" feature of the book. Whoever the authors were, it is evident that they were accomplished speakers and preachers. A further aspect of the form of the book as a whole relates to the possibility that ancient Near Eastern treaty forms, themselves originally secular in character, may have been employed by its authors to shape the work.[4] While not in itself implausible, at most the extent of this influence would appear to be limited to the introduction of the blessing and curse formulas of chapters 27–29 and will be considered in that connection. Beyond this, support for the assumption of the influence of ancient Near Eastern treaty forms is chiefly in the awareness that the book of Deuteronomy displays many affinities in its forms and vocabulary with the bureaucratic language and conventions of a state administrative circle.

Deuteronomy in the Old Testament. Deuteronomy now appears as the fifth and final book of the five books of Moses that make up the Pentateuch (Genesis–Deuteronomy). In Jewish tradition, all of them are ascribed to the authorship of Moses, and they form the first, and most foundational, part of the canon of the Hebrew Bible. Taken as a whole, they provide the basis for the heirs of Abraham, who are also viewed as persons bound in covenant to the LORD God through the revelation given through Moses on Mt. Sinai (Horeb), to govern their lives as the people of God.

However, so extensive a work as the Pentateuch was certainly not written at one period of history and by one writer alone. It has been brought together from a variety of source documents and traditions in order to present the fullest and most basic constitution of Israel. Within this great anthology, which shows many features of being a "collection of collections," Deuteronomy is neither the earliest nor the latest to have been composed, even though it now forms the last of the five books. Rather, it stands very much as a midpoint, and even a balance point, for the Pentateuch as a whole.

Because Deuteronomy has such a distinctive style and lays down such precise and specific requirements over a number of major issues relating to worship, it has proved helpful in enabling scholars to identify (within certain limits) what is "pre-deuteronomic" from what is "post-deuteronomic." It is not surprising, therefore, that in the course of critical biblical scholarship, which has sought to trace, as far as possible, the main lines of the literary growth of the Pentateuch, the attention to Deuteronomy has been very pronounced. It represents a kind of center, both for the literary composition of the Pentateuch and for the development of Israel's religious life.

Seen in such a light, the book of Deuteronomy, or at least some major part of it, can be said to have once formed an independent work that was later joined to other writings, before finally being given its present position. Whereas we might have expected that these other writings would have been the other books of the Pentateuch, the majority opinion among present-day scholars is that this was certainly not the case. It was instead first joined with the six historical books of Joshua–2 Kings, which in the Hebrew canon make up the Former Prophets (Joshua, Judges, 1–2 Samuel, 1–2 Kings). As a consequence, it has become a widespread scholarly practice to refer to these six books as "the deuteronomic (or deuteronomistic) history" because they explicitly presuppose a tradition of divinely given law by which events and persons are judged. This law, which is sometimes explicitly referred to as a law book, is clearly a body of the laws contained in Deuteronomy. There is also a consensus to accept that the first three chapters of Deuteronomy were composed in order to provide an introduction to this large work, comprising both law book and historical narrative. At most, some parts of Deuteronomy 1–3 may have provided a much more brief introduction to the original deuteronomic law book before it was combined with the history.

During the post-exilic period, the deuteronomic writings were supplemented by a large body of additional material, consisting partly of narrative and partly of additional rulings of a priestly and ritual character. This additional material has usually been described as belonging to a priestly (or P) documentary source, although much of it may actually have been incorporated piecemeal into a combined work. Essentially the Pentateuch can be seen to have been composed of the combined deuteronomic and priestly material, together with such earlier (pre-deuteronomic) traditions as had been preserved in conjunction with Deuteronomy.

At this stage, the book of Deuteronomy was separated from the history of the Former Prophets, of which it had at one time been a part, to constitute a separate work that is our present Pentateuch. This contains all the essential traditions and rulings governing the existence and life of Israel as the people of the LORD God, given before Israel entered the promised land. Within this immensely formative document, Deuteronomy can readily be seen to have a most important place. In terms of religious ideas and practice, it marks the first great comprehensive stage in the collecting, harmonizing, and unifying of regulations governing Israelite belief and practice. It represents, therefore, a primary stage in the formation of the Hebrew canon, or "rule," of faith, even though the term as such is not used. Nevertheless, all the main features of defining, controlling, and focusing faith and practice, which later the provision of a scriptural canon sought to supply, are evident in Deuteronomy. It can justifiably be regarded, therefore, as providing a center for the Pentateuch and for the Hebrew Bible as a whole.

In addition to the links between Deuteronomy and the historical books of the Former Prophets, it is also important to note that there are significant contacts between Deuteronomy and the prophecies of Jeremiah. At one time these were explained in terms of an influence, either from the prophet Jeremiah upon the authors of the law book, or vice versa. If the deuteronomic law book, with its distinctive preaching style, were part of a contemporary tradition that the prophet Jeremiah was familiar with, then it could be argued that Jeremiah sometimes made use of this high-flown rhetorical style.

However, all such explanations must now be set aside in favor of a more literary, but potentially more complex, explanation for such noteworthy contacts between a prophet and the authors of a law book. Certainly the evidence that these contacts provide is important for determining the date of Deuteronomy, but their origin can be explained in a rather different fashion from supposing that a direct influence of a prophet upon lawmakers took place. The use of the so-called deuteronomic style in the book of Jeremiah, which is in reality more a matter of a distinctive vocabulary and a distinctive set of theological ideas than a matter of style in the technical sense, is not uniformly present throughout the book. It appears particularly in the narrative sections and in a series of homilies on specific themes and topics. The reason for the presence of these homilies and for the use of this narrative style is to be found in the fact that the extant book of Jeremiah has come down to us in a deuteronomic dress. It has, in fact, been edited in circles that stood close to the authors of Deuteronomy.

Taken overall, therefore, we can identify a situation in which, besides the book of Deuteronomy, the scribes who produced the final form of the history of Joshua–2 Kings and the extant written version of the prophecies of Jeremiah were all deeply influenced by the belief in a Mosaic law given by Moses in the plains of Moab. The law book of Deuteronomy can then be seen to provide an excellent viewpoint for understanding one of the most formative periods in the development of Israel's faith and of the formation of a central part of the biblical literature.

THE CHARACTER OF DEUTERONOMY

Having drawn attention to what has been described as the style of the deuteronomic authors, it is now possible to consider what precisely this style consisted of.[5] In a broad sense, the features that mark a particular author, or group of authors, have to do with the way in which ideas are presented so that the literary purpose is achieved. We can infer the purpose of the authors of Deuteronomy with considerable confidence. It was first and foremost to define a pattern of conduct, especially religious conduct, which was regarded as conforming to the terms of the covenant the LORD God had made with Israel. Such conduct required especially single-minded and exclusive allegiance to worship the LORD God alone. No other God was to be set alongside this one deity, nor was any form of image or physical representation of any god, even of the LORD, to be tolerated. In accordance with this purpose, sacrificial worship was to be restricted to one location only, which the LORD God would signify. Sanctuaries, cult objects, and religious practices pertaining to other gods and goddesses were all banned and condemned to be actively destroyed. A particular program of festivals was further defined as appropriate to the worship of the LORD God.

Alongside this very stringent code of religious practice was placed a related, and interwoven, code of moral and social behavior, which was partly defined in terms of dealing with criminal behavior through an established, although rather mixed, legal administration. Much further than this, however, were many rules governing family life, military commitments, and commercial dealings that were all intended to bear the stamp of the covenant made between the LORD and Israel.

If defining what God's covenant implied was the primary purpose of the book of Deuteronomy, in parallel with it went the goal of persuading the readers of the book of the rightness and necessity of this. To this end a highly developed rhetorical style of speech is employed, marked by long parentheses, many repetitions, and a strong probing into questions of motive and attitude that search the hearts of the reader. The psychology of faith is richly explored, more so than anywhere else in the entire Bible, with constant appeals to remember, not to forget, to avoid self-satisfied complacency, and to bear constantly in mind the deceitfulness of the human heart. The overall evaluation that the deuteronomic authors place upon the goodwill and good intentions of their readers is not high! They are assumed to be prone to disloyalty, as the deuteronomic authors insist their ancestors had been.

In line with this rich and often intensely passionate appeal to religious loyalty and steadfastness is a deep feeling that Israel is one single people throughout all its generations. The chosen setting in which the laws and exhortations of the book are given is that of Israel, standing poised in the plains of Moab and waiting to cross the river Jordan to take possession of the land. Yet, the author is fully aware that this was a generation that lay in the very distant past, so that the fiction of such a time and place is only thinly maintained. The reality that Israel has long been in the land and that its experience there has often been painful and distressing is frequently evident in the book. Yet, the author uses extensively the phrase "all Israel" and views the passing of the generations as a fact that changes nothing concerning the way in which Israel stands face to face before God. The "here and now" of the authors is both the situation recognized for the readers and that which is selected for the setting of the speeches and laws given through Moses. Moreover, even this collapsing of the interval of time between the generation that first awaited entry into the land and that of the readers is stretched further to embrace the generation that stood at the foot of Mt. Horeb to whom Moses first brought the tablets of law. Israel is one people, and this oneness stretches laterally across all twelve of its member tribes and vertically through its generations.

It is in the rhetorical flourishes and insights into human psychology that the distinctiveness of the deuteronomic vocabulary shows itself most markedly. This is what we should expect, since the defining of behavior requisite to the careful formulation of laws was necessarily governed by the subject matter dealt with. However, alongside the distinctive vocabulary of this preaching style there is also a very evident theological vocabulary relating to the way in which Israel is regarded as being bound to the LORD God and, therefore, must repudiate the forms of illicit religion through which the people have been tempted. These religious traditions, which are ascribed to the former occupants of the land, are regarded as particularly alluring and contrary to the attitude of mind that is appropriate to true worship. So we find that the concept of covenant, the dangers of idolatry, the persistence of the worship of the Baals and Asherah, and the importance of gratitude as an essential component of serving God all stand prominently in view within the deuteronomic horizon.

Whether we consider the topic from a theological, a historical, a political, or a sociological perspective, the subject of the land that had been promised to the ancestors of Israel—Abraham, Isaac, and Jacob—is of paramount significance.[6] The primary gift of God to Israel under the terms of the covenant is this land. Consequently, the most serious consequence of disobeying the terms of the covenant is threatened as the loss of this land and the possibility of being expelled from it.

However, besides these broad theological and literary features that characterize Deuteronomy, there are other features that are of great interest to the careful reader. Not least among these is the contribution that Deuteronomy makes to the knowledge and evaluation of the development of a system of law in ancient Israel. The fact that it is possible to compare closely the text of the deuteronomic laws with those made earlier in the Book of the Covenant makes it possible to see how new questions had arisen in legal administration and how this had been progressively improved and elaborated. Conversely, several features of the deuteronomic law code reveal that this administration had displayed shortcomings and serious limitations. Furthermore, the fact that, in some cases, later versions of rulings dealing with essentially the same problem are also preserved in the latest parts of the Pentateuch enable us to construct a valuable chronology of legal and ethical development.

THE DATE OF DEUTERONOMY

A question that has loomed prominently in the modern study of the book of Deuteronomy concerns the question of the date at which it was written. In 2 Kings 22–23, the biblical historian recounts how a "book of the law," which was subsequently identified as "the law of the covenant between God and Israel" (2 Kgs 22:11–23:3), was found in the Temple during renovations in the reign of King Josiah (639–609 BCE). This led to an extensive cultic reform in which a complete destruction of the ancient sanctuary of Bethel took place and many of the old Canaanite rural shrines were destroyed in order to centralize sacrificial worship exclusively in Jerusalem. Since the work of the great nineteenth-century biblical scholar W. M. L. de Wette, this law book has been identified with some part, if not the whole, of the book of Deuteronomy. For a time, there was something of a scholarly consensus that the law book thus rediscovered was probably only the law code of Deuteronomy 12–26. Such conclusions must now certainly be substantially modified.

In the present reconsideration of the issues, the value of this piece of historical criticism has been heavily undermined by the recognition that the account of how the law book was discovered is clearly an attempt by the biblical historian to introduce to the reader the law book of Deuteronomy. The story is itself, therefore, a part of the deuteronomic character of the presentation of history in 1–2 Kings and by itself neither confirms nor denies that the book of Deuteronomy was composed somewhere close to that time.[7]

The report of the discovery of the law book in Josiah's time, then, is relevant to an understanding of the date of origin of the book of Deuteronomy, but does not settle the issue. In reality it never could have done, since it leaves unclear how much older the law book was at the time when it was rediscovered. Nor does it explain what part or form of the book of Deuteronomy was given a new life at this time.

Some parts of Deuteronomy cannot have been written as early as King Josiah's reign, since they make allusion to the disasters that befell Jerusalem in the sixth century BCE (e.g., Deut 29:21-28). Other parts could be, and have frequently been held to be, considerably older. Much depends, then, on which part of Deuteronomy is being discussed when the question of time of composition is under consideration. Too much has been built on the assumption that the law code of chapters 12–26 was significantly older in its complete form than the framework of chapters 1–11 and 27–34. The position adopted in the present author is that the original law code on which the present code was based almost certainly did originate in Josiah's reign, but that this has been extensively revised and added to in the wake of the disasters that overtook Judah in the sixth century BCE.

Overall the question of the date at which the book was composed must be regarded as dependent in part on a careful analysis of the various component sections and layers that are evident within the book. Neither the law code of chapters 12–26, nor the book as a whole was composed at a stroke and at one time.

Of great significance is the question of how much of the book was composed after the disastrous events that overtook the kingdom of Judah at the hands of the Babylonian forces at the beginning of the sixth century. Some reflections of these events are evident in the book, although they have frequently been held to be present only in the concluding parts of the framework. The view adopted here is that these events are far more strongly reflected than this and have deeply influenced several major features of Deuteronomy. Most prominent are the demand for cult centralization, the greatly weakened role ascribed to the king, the desacralizing of several aspects of the cultus, and most probably the overall awareness that, in the future, the true Israelite who is loyal to the covenant will be dependent on a written law for guidance. If this is the case, then a great deal of the spiritual character and strategy that have contributed to making the book of Deuteronomy what it is are a consequence of what happened to Judah at the beginning of the sixth century BCE.

However, this does not properly settle the issue of the date of Deuteronomy as a written document. Those scholars are undoubtedly correct who have recognized that some form of connection exists between the book and the steps taken by King Josiah in the late seventh century to reform worship around Jerusalem. The relationship is more oblique, however, than has often been assumed, and in signficant measure the book of Deuteronomy in its final form must be regarded as a long-term product of the reforms initiated by Josiah, rather than simply the prompting cause of those reforms.

After the breakup of the united Israelite kingdom at Solomon's death, the divided kingdoms of Israel and Judah pursued separate paths and eventually the northern kingdom fell prey to Assyrian intervention by the end of the eighth century. Judah survived, though at the cost of painful and humiliating submission to Assyrian demands that only slackened when, by the middle of the seventh century, the Mesopotamian influence weakened. Josiah's measures were essentially an attempt to rebuild a united kingdom of Israel, with its capital in Jerusalem and under a Davidic king, along the lines that tradition credited to David and Solomon.

Josiah was only partially successful in achieving his goal, and his death in battle in 609 BCE set a limit to further restoration of the ideal kingdom of "all Israel." In these reforms, clearly the role of the Davidic monarchy had of necessity been significantly curtailed, since it was the excessive impositions of the monarchy under Solomon that had brought about the earlier breakup (1 Kgs 12:4). However, the relief from Assyrian control in Judah proved to be only short-lived, and Babylonian power swiftly replaced it, thereby putting an end to the belief that God had spared and preserved Jerusalem during the preceding centuries for the sake of Jerusalem and the Davidic kingship.

The disastrous events that brought a fearful siege and eventual surrender of Jerusalem to the Babylonians in 598 and again in 587 BCE ended with the destruction of the Temple in Jerusalem and the removal of the last of the Davidic kings from his Jerusalem throne. All of these events form part of the background to the composition of the book of Deuteronomy and are, in varied ways, reflected in its pronouncements and exhortations. What was left of the old kingdom of Israel, which Josiah had sought to restore and revive, now found itself in ruins. The people were once again in a situation closely akin to that chosen by the author of Deuteronomy for the setting of the book. They stood at the borders of the land, sorely stricken by military defeats that seemed to defy explanation and in danger of losing altogether their sense of nationhood, of commitment to the LORD as God, and of any direction as to how to prepare for a difficult future. More than at any other period in its history the threat of a return to the "old gods" of the land presented Israel with a temptation and appeal that were almost irresistible.

The book of Deuteronomy, together with its supporting historical and prophetic writings, is a magnificent response to this situation of political and religious crisis. It is a serious review of Israel's past and a challenge to renew commitment and loyalty to God and to look for the time when a new Israel would take shape and the land would once again belong to those who had kept faith with the God who gave it.

THE AUTHORS OF THE BOOK

The Authors and Their Interests. To some extent the answers that we have sought to provide to the date of the book go some way toward also answering the question concerning who the authors were. If they were persons who were active over a period of more than a century, then clearly they represented not simply a small interest group that emerged at one moment of crisis, but a movement that retained momentum for a significant length of time. We can best seek to track down more fully who they were from the particular interests they reveal in the book they have left.

Among such interests we can certainly place the high premium they set on the commitment to an exclusive worship of the LORD God alone. No image was to be tolerated of any kind, and no other God was to be set alongside this one deity. That this falls short of an absolute monotheism in which the very existence of any other God is altogether denied may be admitted, but nevertheless the portrayal that is made of such deities is so negative and derisive in its tone as to present them as powerless nonentities that deserve little more than contempt. Certainly the deuteronomic doctrine of God contributed greatly to the emergence of a more fully explicit monotheism in subsequent biblical writings.[8]

It is unlikely that this movement, which aimed at worshiping "the LORD alone," originated among these deuteronomic authors. It certainly found support among several of the eighth-century prophets, and it seems likely that this prophetic influence was an important factor. But so, too, were the political crises that had beset Israel during the eighth century, when the incursions from Mesopotamia effectively broke up the temporary stability that had left the Lev-

ant to sort out its own affairs, looking chiefly to Egypt as the major external power to be reckoned with.

The very concept of a law book, the markedly literate social world the book presumes, and the polished rhetorical style, which shares many features in common with the Israelite tradition of wisdom,[9] point us also to recognize that the authors of Deuteronomy had close links with the royal administration, where education flourished. Certainly this must have been the Jerusalem court, even though the general tenor of the deuteronomic attitude to kingship is certainly not that of an ardent pro-Davidic court circle. Many of its most marked features represent a strong expression of antipathy to the high-flown and exaggerated court style of the royal psalms, with their mythological coloring for the place of the king in the world of lesser mortals.

Strongly supportive of the conclusion that the deuteronomic authors themselves stood close to the circles of power that hovered around the king is the fact that the authors of this law book display every confidence in their ability to control the administration of the nation. King Josiah had assumed the throne in Jerusalem as a mere boy, placed there by those described as "the people of the land" (2 Kgs 21:23-24). In particular the control of legal affairs, the expectation of enforcing new legal rulings, combined with the assumption of a right to speak for "all Israel," points to a circle of patrician and skilled administrators.

A further feature of the deuteronomic legislation is to be found in its interest in the cultus and in the levitical priesthood. This has led several scholars to look to a circle of levitical priests, or ex-priests, as the authors of Deuteronomy, perhaps drawn from among those who had been forced from their duties and service in sanctuaries during the eighth-century incursions of Assyria. Yet, overall the intellectual outlook and concern of the book are not priestly. It is, on the contrary, very distinctively non-mystical and unsympathetic to the ideas of priestly cultic power, redolent of a holiness that could kill, which echoes in several of the priestly (P) sections of the Pentateuch.[10] It seems certain that the authors of Deuteronomy were not traditional priests, even though they recognized the value and authority of the services that Israel's priests performed.

Taken together, all of these considerations point to the recognition that the authors of Deuteronomy are unlikely to have belonged to any one professional class. If this were the case, then they have contrived to show a considerable knowledge, not only of governmental administration, but also of ideas that were current among both the prophetic and the priestly circles current in Judah during the seventh and sixth centuries BCE. This is by no means impossible. Nevertheless, if we think in terms of a deuteronomic movement, encouraged and inspired by the strong nationalistic and Yahwistic faith that arose in the wake of the humiliations and sufferings inflicted by Assyria, then we shall certainly be close to the truth. Since, in any case, we know and understand the aims and thinking of the deuteronomic authors from the literature that they have given to us, it is perhaps of only limited value to endeavor to define more precisely who they were. For the most part they remain anonymous, although it is tempting to speculate from the names of men linked with King Josiah, and later the prophet Jeremiah, who may have been among their number.

Deuteronomy and the Northern Kingdom. One of the features of the book of Deuteronomy that has repeatedly attracted the attention of biblical scholars is the extent to which it shows familiarity with, and even a strong empathy with, traditions that appear to have originated within the old northern, or Ephraimite, kingdom of Israel. This region had broken from any allegiance to the Davidic monarchy when Rehoboam became king, and it was effectively dismembered as a political entity at the end of the eighth century BCE by Assyrian intrusion and territorial realignments, including mass deportations of sections of the population.

Scholars as distinct as A. C. Welch,[11] Albrecht Alt,[12] and G. von Rad[13] have drawn attention to different features of the book that show a stong link to territorial, political, and religious aspects of the dismembered northern kingdom. But they have not agreed as to what these northern interests are. More recently, the commentary by E. Nielsen[14] has added further support for such a conclusion. Josiah clearly had political ambitions to regain as much of this lost territory as it was possible to achieve and to restore it to a reborn kingdom of a united Israel. That he was only partially successful in doing so does not weaken the insight that this had been a prime goal he sought to achieve.

The insights gained from this can all too readily be overpressed. In particular, we must conclude that many aspects of the book are to be traced to the devastating effect that Babylonian interventions in Judah at the beginning of the sixth century had upon the veneration for the Davidic dynasty of kings and the Jerusalem Temple. Josiah's reform had encouraged hope that a new era of prosperity for Israel was about to dawn. Now the discrediting of an overconfident and complacent faith in both the Temple and the kingship demanded a major reappraisal of them. It is this reappraisal, and not the resurgence of old northern Israelite traditions, that is most prominent in the deuteronomic legislation.

Nevertheless, set in a guarded perspective, it seems evident that the deuteronomic ambition to present a legislative program that was designed for, and acceptable to, "all Israel" was genuine enough. It could not hope to achieve this by simply retaining the excessive Judahite claims that had first broken the kingdoms apart in the tenth century. It would appear, then, that the deuteronomic movement did not ultimately prevail to establish the final form of the Mosaic Torah. More cult-oriented traditions, almost certainly originating in a central circle of the Jerusalem priestly aristocracy, acquired new impetus and dominance in the post-exilic period. Fundamental, therefore, as the deuteronomic movement was in establishing the central lines of the post-exilic Jewish faith, the final definition of this called for a noticeably different tradition from that of Deuteronomy to be added to it, and in substantial measure to overlay it.

Moses in the Book of Deuteronomy. It is a feature of the book that cannot easily be overlooked that it is prominently presented as the product and teaching of Moses. In chapters 1–11 and again in 31–34, this great leader of Israel's formative beginnings dominates the scene. Not only is much of the book presented under the form of a speech of Moses, but also his figure is set in the forefront of faith. To a remarkable extent he is presented as a man who stands over against the great majority of his people. He is a leader, and they need to be led. His faith contrasts with their mean-spiritedness. He is a person of prayer, but they are faithless and full of complaints. He is for going on, when they are for going back. It is not simply that Moses stands between the people and God, as a chosen mediator would inevitably do, but that he is of a different temper and insight from all of them. In heeding the words of Moses, the people of Israel are assured that they will be drawing inspiration from the most worthy of sources.

Certainly the earlier traditions of Israel's origins had given a significant role to Moses as the one who had led the people out of slavery in Egypt, but none of this material had placed so high a valuation upon his person. He is a figure of faith in a way that shows a remarkable new sensitivity concerning what is needed in such a person. He appears as the most worthy of national leaders.

There is no easy, simple explanation of why the deuteronomic authors display so great an interest in Moses. In part it can be seen as a consequence of the feeling of leaderless malaise that the deuteronomic authors diagnosed as part of their nation's ills. They needed a new Moses! Yet this is not sufficient to explain such a prominent new interest in this historic figure. Certainly it cannot be traced to the belief that the authors of the book held any specific professional attachment to Moses, either as a prophet or a priest, for they do not place any significant emphasis on either task, even though Moses is more prophet than priest. Rather, it must lie chiefly in the feeling of disillusionment with the institution of kingship, and in particular with the kings who were of the dynasty of David. They had promised much and had, in the person of Josiah, given cause for hope that the LORD God would once again hold all nations in derision before the power vested in the chosen scion of the house of David (see Ps 2:4-11). This had proved to be a tragically misguided faith, as even those who had placed great confidence in the ambitions of Josiah and his less honorable successors found out so tragically (see 2 Kgs 23:29-30).

We must also recognize that there is present in all the deuteronomic literature a refreshing, if sometimes startling, consciousness that all human institutions are no more than human. Claims to divinity or to possess unlimited access to divine power, when vested in any human being become a serious threat to fundamental features of human society. So the deuteronomic authors put more trust in law than in lawmakers, and more in God than in human beings.

They also shared a remarkably insightful and commendable awareness of the way in which human beings are easily led. The markedly dismissive portrait they present of the contemporaries of Moses, with very few exceptions, reveals much of this social awareness that all human leaders seem readily capable of commanding a following, even when leading their people astray. Accordingly, by presenting the true ideal of human leadership in a figure of the past, who is forthrightly declared to have been more cognizant of the divine ways than any other (Deut 34:10-12), the deuteronomists establish a firm role model through whom all other expressions of human leadership are to be judged. In painting such a picture of the great leader of the nation, they reinforce their claims that the Mosaic law deserves the most urgent and undeviating attention.

DEUTERONOMY IN JEWISH AND CHRISTIAN TRADITION

Deuteronomy in the Hebrew Bible and in Jewish Tradition. To a quite remarkable degree the book of Deuteronomy establishes a standard for the interpretation of the entire Hebrew Bible. This is not surprising, since it is in Deuteronomy that we first hear defined the content of the Mosaic teaching as *torah*. Subsequently, such a title has been employed to characterize the entire contents of the Pentateuch and to establish its essential purpose. Its English translation as "law," by means of its ancient Greek and Latin counterparts, has meant that from a Jewish perspective the entire biblical tradition is understood to consist of law. That it could equally well have been translated as "instruction" or "guidance" is undoubtedly true, although had this been the case the note of authority that has so characterized its reception in Judaism (and Christianity) would certainly have been much reduced.

Moreover, as has already been noted, the fact that the deuteronomic law expresses a development of an earlier code of laws and was itself subsequently used as the basis for yet further elaboration and clarification has meant that it provides a pattern for all subsequent Jewish biblical interpretation. The eventual formulation and publication of a code of Mishnah stands very much in a straight line with the idea that Deuteronomy itself represents a "second giving" of the law of God's covenant. If we are at all to understand the Jewish perspective on the interpretation of the biblical tradition, then we shall undoubtedly need to pay full attention to the fact that Deuteronomy presents its contents as *torah*, and what it implies by doing so.

Deuteronomy in New Testament Perspective. From a New Testament viewpoint, the book of Deuteronomy was clearly a work of immense importance as a central formative work that had shaped contemporary Jewish practice. Allusions to and citations from the book in the New Testament writings are to be found more frequently than is the case with any other Old Testament book. Moreover, it cannot be overlooked that the teaching of Jesus concerning the first, and most important, of all the commandments takes the form of a quotation from Deut 6:4-5 (see Luke 10:25-28). In a similar fashion, the story of the temptation of Jesus in the wilderness uses citations from Deuteronomy as the primary means for countering the suggestions made by Satan (Matt 4:1-11).

However, it is not simply in these specific key moments that the teaching of Deuteronomy has exercised a major influence on the New Testament tradition. More pervasively, it can be recognized that the inward psychologizing and spiritualizing of religious commitment, which is so marked a feature of the deuteronomic teaching, pervades the early Christian tradition. It is the inwardness of faith, the emphasis on attitude beside action, and the focus on love, obedience, and gratitude that have made the deuteronomic teaching so fundamental to New Testament faith.

Moreover, one of the significant aspects of the deuteronomic interpretation of a divine *torah* lies in the way it brings together religious, ethical, and social concerns under a single umbrella. It may be held to have desacralized religion, removing much of the mystical and quasi-magical notions of cultic power. As such it promotes a rather "secularized" interpretation of religious commitment. In another direction, however, it can be held to have spiritualized a wide range of everyday activities, spiritualizing their significance. It can be seen to have moralized and personalized ideas of religious loyalty to a remarkable degree. Not only is the individual called upon to respond to God in obedience, but also such obedience is made the subject of deep heart searching and self-examination. Without the teaching of Deuteronomy, it is hard to see how the religious and ethical arguments that characterize the conflicts between Jesus and his Jewish contemporaries could have arisen. From the perspective of grasping the nature of the New Testament and its reflection of Christian controversies with the contemporary Jewish tradition, a close study of the teaching of Deuteronomy becomes essential.

Deuteronomy in Historical and Ethical Perspective. What has been noted in regard to the place of Deuteronomy in Old and New Testament tradition has viewed it in a predominantly positive and constructive light. On any reckoning its influ-
ence in shaping the main lines of biblical tradition has been very strong. Yet, once it is viewed in a wider historical and ethical perspective, a number of serious questions arise that can only be answered negatively.[15] Most prominent in this regard is the uncompromising vehemence with which Deuteronomy demands the wholesale extermination of all ethnic and religious communities that had occupied the land prior to the Israelite conquest. Moreover the very assumption that Israel could be the beneficiary of a divinely given entitlement to conquer, repress, and exterminate an entire population in order to gain possession of their land undermines the many richer ethical and spiritual insights the book contains.[16] It reflects deeply upon not only the concept of Israel as a people of God, but also on the understanding of God that it exemplifies.

From a historical perspective, therefore, the influence of Deuteronomy has been far from uniform and not at all consistently helpful. That there are inherent dangers and defects in its teaching must be frankly reckoned with. Certainly we can moderate this ethical criticism of the book with the help of two important provisos, neither of which adequately resolves the problems raised.

The first of these provisos concerns the fact that the book is an uneven composition; it has many strands. The stratum of legislative demand that calls for the extermination of all the previous occupants of the land and the death penalty for any Israelite who tolerates or encourages the perpetuation of their religion stands alongside much more tolerant and humane considerations for the weak and the oppressed. Even informing on one's neighbor is encouraged if religious loyalty is at stake (Deut 13:6-11). To this extent, the punishment demanded for those who presume to practice the religions of Baal and Asherah and the other traditions of the land's previous occupants stands in contrast with a more considered awareness of the need to show consideration and compassion to the oppressed and to distinguish between distinct categories of foreign aliens (Deut 23:3-8). How and why the frenetic and cruel demand for a rigid exclusivism in promoting the worship of the LORD alone was to be applied in the light of the parallel concern for love and compassion is never adequately made clear from the book's contents. Presumably it was an attitude the authors felt to be necessary when the very survival of their religious tradition was under threat.

The second proviso concerns the fact that, in calling for the extermination of the previous inhabitants of the land, the book was undoubtedly propagating a historical anachronism. These peoples had long since ceased to retain any clear and separate ethnic identity, having undoubtedly largely been absorbed into the Israelite kingdom that flourished under David and Solomon. Yet this does not properly resolve the difficulty, since almost certainly the deuteronomic authors did have in mind a real contemporary community and its leaders, whom they regarded as enemies and who were believed to pose a danger to the program that they themselves were seeking to propagate. Thus we are left with the difficulty that, in seeking to promote a richly ethical and responsible interpretation of Israel's religious faith, the authors of Deuteronomy were prepared to recommend the most uncompromising and repressive measures. Sadly, the long history of humankind's subsequent religious conflicts has shown how many have been willing to follow that lead and have failed to set it under a necessary critical scrutiny.

A further critical perspective on the teaching of Deuteronomy is also a necessary part of the introduction to the book. From within the biblical tradition, one of its most innovative features has been its emphasis on the ideas of Israel's divine election, of its privileged covenant status in relationship to God, and of the many claims to advantage and power that this covenant relationship confers. In itself such teaching can be seen as an important step in seeking to theologize and rationalize the inherited ideas that flourished in the ancient world of competing national powers with national deities, each seeking advantage over others. In many respects the history of international conflict that characterized the ancient Near East during the half millennium from the days of David to the end of the Davidic monarchy witnessed the absurdity of such notions. The impetus toward monotheism and to a concept of one world rendered the belief in many competing gods totally obsolete.

So Deuteronomy stands apart from the confused and confusing picture of a world in which many gods fought for the allegiance of human beings. It moves strongly in the direction of a true monotheism. Yet in order to accommodate its national, as well as its more universal, concepts appropriate to belief in a deity who wielded supreme authority over the universe, it makes use of ideas that have themselves become fraught with danger. In spite of the high place given to the notion of a covenant between the supreme deity and human beings in Deuteronomy and the biblical tradition that drew from it, it remains a limiting and imperfect concept for the expression of religious ideas. All too readily conferred privileges, rather than the call to a spiritual obedience, have assumed the most prominent place, sometimes with disastrous consequences.

FOR FURTHER READING

Commentaries:

Brueggeman, Walter. *Deuteronomy*. Abingdon Old Testament Commentaries. Nashville: Abingdon, 2001.

Craigie, P. C. *The Book of Deuteronomy*. NICOT. Grand Rapids: Eerdmans, 1976.

Driver, S. R. *Deuteronomy*. 3rd ed. ICC. Edinburgh: T & T Clark, 1902.

Mayes, A. D. H. *Deuteronomy*. NCB. London: Marshall, Morgan & Scott, 1979.

Miller, P. D. *Deuteronomy*. Interpretation. Louisville: Westminster John Knox, 1990.

Nelson, Richard D. *Deuteronomy: A Commentary*. OTL. Louisville: Westminster/John Knox, 2002.

von Rad, G. *Deuteronomy*. OTL. Philadelphia: Westminster, 1966.

Thompson, J. A. *Deuteronomy*. Tyndale Old Testament Commentaries. London: IVF, 1974.

Tigay, Jeffrey H. *Deuteronomy*. JPS Torah Commentary. Philadelphia: Jewish Publication Society, 1996.

Weinfeld, M. *Deuteronomy 1:1–11*. AB 5. New York: Doubleday, 1991.

Other Studies:

Braulik, G. *The Theology of Deuteronomy. Collected Essays of Georg Braulik OSB*. Bibal Collected Essays 2. Translated by Ulrika Lindblad. N. Richland Hills, Tex.: Bibal, 1994.

Brenner, Athalya, ed. *A Feminist Companion to Exodus to Deuteronomy*: The Feminist Companion to the Bible 6. Sheffield: Sheffield Academic Press, 1994.

———. *Exodus to Deuteronomy*: A Feminist Companion to the Bible. Feminist Companion to the Bible, Second Series 5. Sheffield: Sheffield Academic Press, 2000.

Christensen, D. L., ed. *A Song of Power and the Power of Song: Essays on the Book of Deuteronomy*. Sources for Biblical and Theological Study 3. Winona Lake: Eisenbrauns, 1993.

Haran, M. *Temples and Temple Service in Ancient Israel*. Oxford: Oxford University Press, 1978.

Harrelson, W. *The Ten Commandments and Human Rights*. OBT. Philadelphia: Fortress, 1980.

N. Lohfink, ed. *Das Deuteronomium: Entstehung, Gestalt und Botschaft*. BETL 68. Leuven: J. P. Peeters, 1985.

————. *Studien zum Deuteronomium und zur deuteronomistischen Literatur I*. SBA 8. Stuttgart: Katholisches Bibelwerk, 1990.

————. *Studien zum Deuteronomium und zur deuteronomistischen Literatur II*. SBA 12. Stuttgart: Katholisches Bibelwerk, 1991.

————. *Studien zum Deuteronomium und zur deuteronomistischen Literatur III*. SBA 20. Stuttgart: Katholisches Bibelwerk, 1995.

————. *Theology of the Pentateuch: Themes of the Priestly Narrative and Deuteronomy*. Translated by L. M. Maloney. Minneapolis: Augsburg Fortress, 1994

Olson, D. T. *Deuteronomy and the Death of Moses*. OBT. Minneapolis: Augsburg Fortress, 1994.

von Rad, G. *Studies in Deuteronomy*. Translated by D. Stalker. SBT 9. London: SCM, 1953.

Weinfeld, M. *Deuteronomy and the Deuteronomic School*. Oxford: Oxford University Press, 1972.

ENDNOTES

1. S. Dean McBride, "Polity of the Covenant People: The Book of Deuteronomy," *Int* 41 (1987) 229-44.

2. G. von Rad, *Studies in Deuteronomy*, trans. D. Stalker, SBT 9 (London: SCM, 1953) 11-24

3. Cf. E. Otto, *Theologische Ethik des Alten Testaments* (Stuttgart: W. Kohlhammer, 1994) 18-31.

4. See J. G. McConville, *Law and Theology in Deuteronomy*, JSOTSup 33 (Sheffield: JSOT, 1984). A more cautious and critical position is presented by Dennis J. McCarthy, *Treaty and Covenant*, AnBib 21A (Rome: Pontifical Biblical Institute, 1978) 157-205.

5. See the comprehensive survey in M. Weinfeld, *Deuteronomy and the Deuteronomic School* (Oxford: Oxford University Press, 1972) 320-65.

6. L. Perlitt, "Motive und Schichten der Landtheologie im Deuteronomium," *Deuteronomium-Studien* (Tübingen: J. C. B. Mohr, 1994) 97-108.

7. See E. Würthwein, "Die Josianische Reform und das Deuteronomium" *ZTK* 73 (1976) 395-423.

8. Cf. N. Lohfink, "Gott im Buch Deuteronomium," *Studien zum Deuteronomium und zur deuteronomistischen Literatur* II, SBA 12 (Stuttgart: Katholisches Bibelwerk, 1991) 25-53.

9. M. Weinfeld, *Deuteronomy and the Deuteronomic School* (Oxford: Oxford University Press, 1972) 244-81.

10. M. Weinfeld, *Deuteronomy and the Deuteronomic School* (Oxford: Oxford University Press, 1972), 282-97.

11. A. C. Welch, *The Code of Deuteronomy: A New Theory of Its Origin* (London: Nisbet, 1924).

12. A. Alt, "Die Heimat des Deuteronomiums," *Kleine Schriften zur Geschichte des Volkes Israel II* (Munich: C. H. Beck, 1953) 250-75.

13. G. von Rad, *Deuteronomy*, OTL (Philadelphia: Westminster, 1966).

14. E. Nielsen, *Deuteronomium*, HAT I/6 (Tübingen: J. C. B. Mohr, 1995).

15. See F. E. Deist, "The Dangers of Deuteronomy: A Page from the Reception History of the Book," in *Studies in Deuteronomy in Honour of C. J. Labuschagne*, ed. F. Garcia Martinez et al. (Leiden: E. J. Brill, 1994) 13-30.

16. Cf. Susan Niditch, *Warfare in the Hebrew Bible* (New York: Oxford University Press, 1994).

INTRODUCTION TO
NARRATIVE LITERATURE

PETER D. MISCALL

In the late 1960s increasing numbers of scholars suggested that the methods of historical criticism, particularly source and form analysis, had reached an impasse and new approaches were needed. In subsequent years, literary criticism, in its many contemporary forms, has become the area most consistently explored for new ways of studying biblical literature, particularly narrative. Muilenburg's influential essay "Form Criticism and Beyond" built the foundation for rhetorical criticism, one of the first of the new ways to read biblical narratives as they appear in the canonical text.[1] Rhetorical criticism is defined as "the isolation of a discrete literary unity, the analysis of its structure and balance, and the attention to key words and motifs."[2] Its early results are enshrined in the 1974 Muilenberg festschrift, *Rhetorical Criticism*. This approach can contribute much to the close reading of a text, but because of its limited focus, it has not developed into a major approach to biblical narrative.

Rhetorical criticism competed with the influx of French structuralism and of other traditional brands of literary criticism that were influenced by the American New Criticism of the 1930s through the 1960s. A 1971 collection of French essays appeared in translation in 1974 as *Structural Analysis and Biblical Exegesis*.[3] *Semeia*, a journal devoted to new trends in biblical studies, issued its first volume in 1974, "A Structuralist Approach to the Parables." "Classical Hebrew Narrative," its third volume, appeared the following year. The issue included both structuralist and traditional literary approaches. *Semeia: An Experimental Journal for Biblical Criticism* continues to be a major sounding board for new approaches to biblical studies. In its issues, one can track most of the developments in biblical studies over the past two and a half decades, whether these developments flowered and lasted or withered on the vine.

Structuralism is noted for its attention to structure, both manifest and deep. Rhetorical criticism shares its concern for the obvious textual marks of structure, such as repeated terms and phrases, plot elements, and characters. Deep structure, however, is a theoretical category referring to the arrangement of a story—e.g., in terms of plot elements or of the relationships of the characters—that is abstracted from the actual text through the application of modes of structural analysis. Structuralism is characterized by this abstract concern, by its fascination with specialist terminology—"synchronic," "diachronic," "actant" (instead of character)—and by its use of diagrams and quasi-mathematical formulas, such as the semiotic square and cube. Structuralism and rhetorical criticism remain valuable to biblical studies for the detailed textual focus they demand and for the original insights they produce.

Structuralism in particular, with its technical terminology and quasi-scientific claims, contrasts with "standard" literary approaches—those that employ the more familiar terminology of plot, setting, character, and theme and focus on these issues. They are no less probing or fruitful in their analyses. A collection of essays entitled *Literary Interpretations of Biblical Narratives* was published in 1974.[4] Intended for literature teachers in secondary schools and colleges, the collection had an impact on biblical studies and was one of the earliest of a long series of works devoted to the study of biblical narrative. The entire methodological shift that was occurring in the 1970s affected all areas of biblical studies—Old and New Testaments—including narrative, prophetic, wisdom, and epistolary literature. Our concern, however, lies with the Hebrew narrative in the OT; comments on other areas will be indirect.

The Sheffield periodical, *Journal for the Study of the Old Testament*, began appearing in 1976. It continues to be a major forum for diverse studies of biblical narrative. As with Semeia, one can track in its pages many of the changes and developments over the past twenty years of biblical studies.

Robert Alter's "A Literary Approach to the Bible" appeared in December 1975; it was devoted to Hebrew narrative and was followed in ensuing years by a series of articles on biblical narrative.[5] These articles, rewritten to various degrees, were gathered into Alter's influential *The Art of Biblical Narrative*, published in 1981.[6] Without arguing for a strict dividing line, I use this book and date to mark the beginning of a new stage in work on Hebrew narrative.

To simplify the work of a decade, we can say that in the 1970s those biblical scholars who were disenchanted, for a variety of reasons, with the methods and results of historical criticism were in search of new approaches to biblical study. This was a time of experimentation and often of heated debate between historical critics and the practitioners of various types of literary study of narrative. In particular, those debates addressed the central issue of whether one should focus on the biblical text in its canonical form or attempt to reconstruct earlier forms of the text. "The text-as-it-stands" and "the final form of the text" were two catchphrases of the period. The debate continues to the present day, although it is less heated and less prevalent.

The 1980s and 1990s witnessed the multiplication of methods and of in-depth interpretations of biblical narrative. Alongside the traditional historical-critical approaches were others: narratology, literary criticism, feminism, post-structuralism, and ideology critique. Scholars who employed the newer approaches could be as, if not more, acrimonious in their disputes among themselves as in those with historical critics. The recent *The Postmodern Bible* is an excellent overview of this diversity as it has developed over the last few decades and as it stands today.[7] I turn now from these controversies to a presentation of the literary study of biblical narrative as it has developed in the last generation. The presentation is general, but with pointers to some of the twists that individual critics give to both method and interpretation.

NARRATIVE AND NARRATOLOGY

A *narrative* is the telling, by a *narrator* to an audience, of a connected series or sequence of events. The series of events involve characters and their interrelationships, and the events occur in a place or places, the *setting*. The *plot* is the events selected and the particular order in which they are presented. A *theme* is an idea, an abstract concept, that emerges from the narrative's presentation and treatment of its material.

"Narrative" can refer to a short piece, to an episode (e.g., Rebekah and Jacob's deception of Isaac in Genesis 27:1), or to a larger work, such as Genesis itself or even the whole of Genesis through 2 Kings. Although others may make a distinction, I use "story" as a synonym for narrative—e.g., the story of Sarah and Hagar in Genesis 16:1 and Israel's primary story in Genesis–2 Kings.

Twentieth-century study of narrative, ancient and modern, from the epic to the novel, has developed into the specialized area of *narratology*, which endeavors to define narrative and its categories (e.g., narrator and character) on a theoretical and abstract level. Narratology is a subdivision of the larger field of *poetics* (not to be equated with the study of poetry only), which strives for a science of literature, a study of the basic elements and rules of any type of literature. Poetics is to literature what the study of grammar and syntax is to language. In such theoretical studies, actual narratives provide examples and illustrations. Narratology and poetics describe specific categories, with various subdivisions, that can be applied in the analysis of any narrative (or other type of literature); they offer tools to the literary critic, but do not engage in the in-depth reading and interpretation of texts for their own sake. These are the fields that have both refined and expanded our understanding of the mechanics and intricacies of, for example, characterization and point of view.

The works of Berlin,[8] Bar-Efrat,[9] and Gunn-Fewell[10] are fine examples of the genre that focuses on Hebrew narrative. They all employ extended examples of analysis, and Gunn-Fewell intersperse their theoretical presentations with extended readings of given narratives, including the fiery furnace episode in Daniel 3:1. Both Alter's The *Art of Biblical Narrative*[11] and Sternberg's *The Poetics of Biblical Narrative*[12] are inextricable mixes of theoretical comments and involved readings of chosen stories, mainly from Genesis–2 Kings.

One of the more important changes in this methodological shift is the explicit concern to describe and to appreciate biblical narrative in its own right as a literary category. Scholars engaged in this work describe the narratives as they appear in the Bible, rather than judging them according to norms and expectations developed from other Western literature, especially those of the modern realistic novel.

In the works just listed, the authors take pains to explicate the narratological terms and concepts they employ and, at the same time, to show in detail how they apply to actual biblical narratives. Narrative study is a contemporary response to the original, critical insight and demand of Spinoza and others that the Bible be read like other literature. At relevant points, I will note the impact of this shift in focus for the specific categories I am presenting.

Narrative and History. Before proceeding to biblical narrative itself, I address one final methodological issue: the relation of narrative study to the study of the history of Israel, on the one hand, and the history of biblical writing, on the other hand. Although it can have significant impact on both, expecially the latter, narrative study can proceed on its own by bracketing historical questions that are presently characterized by wide-ranging diversity of opinion and heated controversy. That is, we can discuss the narrative of Samuel, Saul, and David in 1 Samuel and beyond without having to answer, or even ask, the question of what "really happened" in those ancient times. This does not deny the relevance of issues of historicity. It neither affirms nor denies the historicity of specific characters and events, whether Joshua and the conquest, Samson and his exploits, David's relationship with Bathsheba, or the courtship of Ruth and Boaz. It asserts that these stories can be fruitfully read for what they tell us about people and how they relate to others, including God, and for what they tell us about the workings of biblical narrative, general and specific.

Moreover, it allows us to bracket questions of the historical development of narrative style—not to deny the relevance of the issues, but to be able to proceed with narrative analysis without becoming embroiled in all the debates about the history of the writing and editing of the biblical text. Narrative and literary analyses have enough debates and diversity of opinion of their own!

The Narrative and the Author. This topic takes us immediately to a central distinction developed in twentieth-century criticism that is relevant to all narrative, ancient and modern. The author is the actual historical person (or persons) who wrote the work in question. (In reference to the Bible, I am not taking a stand on the issue of oral or written composition.) For example, Herman Melville wrote *Moby Dick* in the mid-nineteenth century. The narrator, on the other hand, is a literary and abstract personage. Within the text, he tells us the story that we are reading and must be distinguished from the actual author. *Moby Dick* is narrated by Ishmael ("Call me Ishmael"), not by Melville.

This distinction allows biblical readers to discuss the narratives in depth, and in the detail of their presentation, without having to identify an actual author by name or impersonal title, by place, and by date. There is, in addition, the category of the "implied author," the hypothetical person inferred as the author from the text's style and content. This person might or might not be similar to the actual author. However, this category is too abstract and debated to be explored in this article.

STYLE

Style refers to form, to how a narrative is told. Style can be used across the spectrum to describe a single story (e.g., Genesis 27), a traditional section (e.g., the Pentateuch), or an entire corpus (e.g., Genesis–2 Kings). At this point I shall describe three primary, and often noted, characteristics of biblical narrative—indeed, of the whole OT. Then I shall discuss how these and other stylistic features affect the respective narrative categories. These three traits are the *episodic nature* of the material; the great *diversity* in terms of both form and content; and the prevalence of *repetition* of many different aspects of narrative.

The *episodic nature* is my phrase for the quality that allows us to read stories individually and separate from their context without feeling that we have lost the heart of the tale. This quality creates the impression that large segments of narrative are composed of stories strung together in a loose chronological frame, without further significant connection or relation. Examples are the Abraham cycle in Genesis 12–25, the wilderness wanderings episodes in Numbers 11–36, the judges stories in Judges 3–16, and the accounts of the last years of Israel and Judah in 2 Kings. These share a *paratactic style*—that is, scenes or stories are juxtaposed without connecting or transitional phrases.

The paratactic style is present at the level of individual sentences in the narrator's preference for "and" over subordinating conjunctions such as "so," "then," or "because." This characteristic is often obscured in modern translations, including the NIV and the NRSV, that use subordinating conjunctions in order to avoid too many repetitions of "and." The story of the war of the kings and of Abram's rescue of

Lot in Genesis 14 closes with Abram's declaration that he will accept nothing from the king of Sodom. The following episode of promise and covenant is introduced by the indefinite phrase "after these things" (NRSV) or "after this" (NIV). The narrator gives us no hint of how much time, if any, has elapsed or whether we should think of a change of place. And he relates the story in chapter 15 with sentences connected by "and"; both the NIV and the NRSV use "but," "then," and "also" in place of some of the simple connectives. The story closes with the Lord's far-reaching promise to Abram and his descendants. Genesis 16, like chapter 15, opens abruptly with no indication of any time lapse or change in locale: "And Sarai, the wife of Abram, bore him no children." Both the NIV and the NRSV attempt to lessen the abruptness by using "now" as an introduction. Others, such as the NJB and the REB, mirror the terseness with a plain "Abram's wife Sarai. . . . " (Note, however, the shift in the order of the characters such that Abram is named first; the NIV and the NRSV keep Sarai first.)

Another well-known and diversely interpreted juxtaposition of two stories occurs in the two creation stories in Gen 1:1–2:4*a* and 2:4*b*-25. To cite this example does not mean that we must accept the hypothesis that two different sources or authors are in evidence here, nor does it mean that we must attempt to harmonize the two stories and explain away all contrasts. Rather, we should accept the juxtaposition, even if it produces sharp contrasts or even contradictions, as part of the narrative style and then work at describing its effects upon readers and intepreters. Episodic and paratactic are descriptive, and not judgmental or evaluative, terms.

The narrator frequently proceeds by presenting contrasting or opposing views, stories, character portrayals, and such, whether placed side-by-side or at some remove. One example of the latter is the Moses who displays weaknesses in Exodus 17–18 and the Moses of Exod 33:7-11 and 34:29-35, who speaks with God face to face. Another is the near-silent Bathsheba of 2 Samuel 11–12 and the politically effective speaker of 1 Kings 1–2. This episodic style leaves room for readers to infer and to conjecture possible transitions and connections, but it never provides enough textual evidence to cinch any one interpretation. The myriad ways that have been proposed for relating or not relating the two creation stories is ample evidence for the process of unending inference triggered by this stylistic trait.

Diversity is a second catchword frequently used to describe biblical narrative. Not only do the two creation stories differ in their depictions of God, of creation, and of humanity, but also they differ in how the narrator presents the material. The first story is so highly and tightly structured that some question whether narrative or story adequately describes the text; perhaps a theological treatise or an ancient "scientific" document is a better descriptor. The second tale is a looser narrative with characters in potential conflict, and with the segment on the rivers in 2:10-14 in the center but without explicit relevance to the rest of the story. It is a fine example of the paratactic style.

This diversity in both content and form, along with the episodic aspect, confronts the reader constantly from the opening pages of Genesis through the close of 2 Kings and beyond. Genesis comprises narratives ranging from the terseness of the depiction of Lamech in 4:18-24 and of the tale of divine beings and human women in 6:1-4 to the lengthy and tightly woven story of Joseph and his brothers. The sagas of Abraham and his family, and of Jacob and his family or families, lie between these two poles, with the Abraham story the more episodic. Indeed, the latter has been referred to as the "Abraham Cycle," but never as a tightly woven tale. The strictly narrative portions of Genesis are broken at points by genealogies (e.g., chaps 5 and 36) and a poem, Jacob's blessing (49:1-27).

Once readers move beyond Genesis to the rest of the Pentateuch, however, they are confronted with an even greater range of diversity. The strictly narrative portions are mixed with genealogies; a wide variety of ritual, legal, and technical descriptions and prescriptions; and the lengthy rehearsal of all of this in the sermons in Deuteronomy. "Strictly narrative portions" refers to separate stories such as the call of Moses in Exodus 3–4, the manna in Exodus 16, spying out the land in Numbers 13:1–14, and Moses' final moments in Deuteronomy 34, as opposed to other materials. But all of this material, including stories, "laws," the description of the tabernacle, poems, and sermons, is still part of the overall narrative of Genesis–2 Kings. The flow of the narrative, the forward movement in time and events, may slow or even stop for the presentation of these other materials, but the latter are still part of the narrative. Much of Exodus through Deuteronomy consists of lengthy speeches by characters, mainly God and Moses. We must keep all of this together in order to describe accurately the narrative corpus of Genesis–2 Kings. Awareness of diversity in form and content is also necessary for reading other narrative portions of the OT, such as Chronicles, Ezra-Nehemiah, and Ruth. Diversity may appear in different aspects and ways in these works than in Genesis–2 Kings, but it is present nonetheless.

Joshua–2 Kings continues the mixing. In these books, the narrator relates the history of Israel in the land from conquest to exile. He does so with the same variation in style—from the comparatively tightly woven story of Samuel, Saul, and then David in 1–2 Samuel to the much looser episodes of Judges and 2 Kings. (I use the traditional term "books" without regarding them—e.g., Genesis and Joshua—as separate works by separate authors; for Genesis–2 Kings, I take the "books" to be more like chapters in a contemporary work.) At points the material is punctuated with poems, such as those in Judges 5, 1 Samuel 2, and 2 Samuel 22, and by the speeches of characters, e.g., of Jotham in Judges 9, of Samuel in 1 Samuel 12, and of Ahijah in 1 Kings 11. The speeches, including overviews by the narrator, such as in 2 Kings 17, place the particular narratives in the larger setting of the story of Israel from its creation to the disaster of the exile.

Repetition is the third and final trait I shall discuss. It, like the other traits, appears in the opening pages of the OT. Genesis 1 is divided into six days by the formula "And there was evening and there was morning, the X day." Genesis 2 "repeats" the first chapter. There are two genealogies for Lamech (Gen 4:17-24; 5:1-31), and three stories of a patriarch (Abraham, Isaac) claiming that his wife (Sarah, Rebekah) is his sister (Gen 12:10-20; and 26:6-11). Ten plagues ravage Egypt, and God produces two copies of the stone tablets. In Exodus 25–31 the Lord, in great detail, commands Moses and the Israelites to build a tabernacle; in Exodus 35–40, with much the same detail, the narrator describes the actual construction of the tabernacle. This is the longest and most detailed repetition in the OT.

One of the most, if not the most, repeated stories is that of Israel from Genesis through 2 Kings and beyond, which is recited by the narrator, by God, or by another character at many different stages in the larger narrative. The story is anticipated in the Lord's declarations to Abraham in Gen 15:13-16 and to Moses in Exod 23:20-33 and Deut 31:16-21. Moses refers to it often in his speeches in Deuteronomy (e.g., Deut 26:1-11; 31:26-29; Joshua summarizes it in Josh 24:1-15, as does the narrator in 2 Kgs 17:7-20).

The story is repeated in a wide variety of ways from the brief declaration of the first commandment, "I am the Lord your God, who brought you out of the land of Egypt, out of the house of slavery" (Exod 20:2), to the lengthy versions in Deuteronomy 31 and Joshua 24. The repetition of Israel's story exemplifies both diversity and *diversity amid regularity*, since the same story is repeated. Diversity in biblical narrative is not endless or unlimited, but variation within set boundaries and a set number of narrative elements. A notable example is the Decalogue. It appears first as the Lord's direct speech in Exodus 20:1 and then is cited by Moses, in slightly different form, in Deuteronomy 5:1.

The versions of the story of God and Israel vary not only in terms of their length, but also in terms of their content. The sentence cited from Exod 20:2 refers only to the exodus from Egypt, while Joshua traces the story from the days of Abraham to the entrance into the land in his own day. In Deut 31:16-21, the Lord begins the tale with Moses and then looks off into Israel's future of sin and misery. Moses himself speaks of this distant future in Deut 4:25-31 with a more optimistic view of the outcome. An unnamed prophet tells of the exodus and entrance into the land with no mention of patriarchs or the wandering in the wilderness (Judg 6:8-10). Ezra's recital in Neh 9:6-37 is a full, detailed version that includes all the stages down to Ezra's own day, a time of suffering for past sins.

THE NARRATOR

In accepted literary terms, the biblical narrator is *omniscient* in the sense of possessing potential knowledge of all the characters and events presented, even the thoughts of God (see Gen 6:5-7; 18:17-21). The narrator is *reliable* to the extent that we can trust what we are told. Gunn and Fewell define this characteristic:

> A reliable narrator always gives us accurate information; or put another way, does not make mistakes, give false or unintentionally misleading information, or deliberately deceive us.[13]

They recognize, however, that the many factual contrasts and contradictions in Genesis–2 Kings, the focus of many source and traditio-historical studies, and the presence of ironic statements require us to modify our understanding of what is reliable. Their general rule is the one followed in this article: "In practice, some such scale of reliability is a helpful rule of thumb in reading biblical narrative."[14] Finally, this is a *third-person* narrator who is not identified by name or title and who does not use "I."

In most ancient literature, narrators are voices, disembodied presences who narrate what we are reading and who seldom explicitly identify themselves or mark their presence. Genesis opens, "In the beginning God created the heavens and the earth," with no textual comment as to who is telling us this. The same narratorial style is employed throughout Genesis–2 Kings. For contrast, we can turn to Nehemiah ("In the month of Chislev, in the twentieth year, while I was in Susa" [1:1]) or to Ecclesiastes/Qoheleth ("I, the Teacher [Qoheleth], when king over Israel in Jerusalem, applied my mind" [1:12]). These are the exceptions and not the rule in biblical narrative.

The narrator's *point of view* is generally from outside or above the characters and the actions of the narrative, but material can be presented through the eyes of a character. For example, part of the formula that closes each day of creation is the repeated "and God saw that it was good"—a report of God's reaction and evaluation, not of the narrator's. Genesis 18:1 opens with the narrator's report, followed by what Abraham himself saw: "The LORD appeared to Abraham. . . . He looked up and saw three men standing near him" (NRSV). A similar contrast is drawn between the report and a character's perception in Exod 3:2. "There the angel of the LORD appeared to him in a flame of fire out of a bush: he looked, and the bush was blazing, yet it was not consumed" (NRSV).

In narratology, both within and beyond biblical studies, critics have proposed a wide range of distinctions and subdivisions to deal with all the complexities and nuances of the narrator and the point of view in narrative, ancient and modern. These can be valuable in the close reading and analysis of a narrative, but they are beyond the scope of this article. I refer the reader to the works of Berlin,[15] Bar-Efrat,[16] and Bal[17] for both the complexities and the varieties. There is little critical consensus in this matter of further distinctions.

These characteristics are only the general framework within which the very capable and resourceful narrator works. This storyteller may be able to know all about the characters and events but is very selective and deliberate in exactly what is told us about them and how and when we are told. Such sparseness of narrative detail, whether in terms of characters, events, or setting, has long been noted in biblical narrative. What has changed in the contemporary scene is the judgment and evaluation of this stylistic trait; this change applies to many of the other stylistic traits discussed above, particularly the episodic and repetitive nature of the narrative. These traits have been variously observed in the past, but have almost always been judged as marks of the primitive and simplistic nature of biblical narrative. Critics took them as signs of a lack of literary ability and sophistication and not as essential keys to reading and analyzing the narrative. Contemporary literary critics speak, on the other hand, of the art of biblical narrative and of the artistic sophistication of the narrator, who can accomplish so much with apparently so little.

I turn now to discuss each of the other aspects of narrative: theme, setting, plot, and character. I deal with the initial three first because they can be presented more briefly. This is not to turn our backs completely on the narrator, since all that we know about these other four comes through the narration. We will have opportunity to comment further on the narrator's style—diversity, repetition, selectivity, etc.—and to relate it to the particulars of the narrative.

THEME, SETTING, AND PLOT

Theme is a rich, overarching category containing all of the ideas, concepts, and issues that a narrative treats, explicitly or implicitly, in what it says and how it says it. Thematic content can derive from both narrative form and content, and it is developed from the study of all other aspects of a narrative. Themes are generally spoken of in abstract terms: e.g., covenant, divine and human responsibilities, justice and injustice, mercy, prophetic (charismatic) and monarchic (dynastic) leadership, war, wisdom, law, love, the strengths and the failings of families, friendship, loyalty, and betrayal. This short list illustrates the wide range of issues that biblical narrative addresses. In addition, themes can be grouped into comprehensive classifications, such as political, theological, sociological, and historical, and then studied in relation to other topics within those classifications. The relation of one classification to another can be developed—e.g., what does the depiction of the monarchy in Samuel–Kings tell us about the narrator's (or author's) theology of state and of history?

Plot comprises the events that occur in the course of a narrative and can be looked at from two different perspectives. First, plot reflects a *pattern*, since the events, the actions, occur in a certain order and arrangement; they form a series. Second, one central binding element in the series is a *temporal framework*. The events form a sequence, a continuum that is bound in large part by chronology, by the flow of time. Genesis–2 Kings presents the story of humanity, especially Israel, from the creation of the world to the fall of Judah and Jerusalem c. 600–580 BCE. But there is great variety in the presentation of the plot—e.g., the amount of space and detail accorded a given event or period of time and the clarity, or lack thereof, in noting the passage of time.

Focus on plot raises the issues of causality and resolution. They, especially the former, are complicated by the episodic nature and brevity of biblical narrative, whether on the level of individual scenes and even sentences of one story, or on the level of the grouping of narratives into larger works, such as Exodus or all of Genesis–2 Kings. Specific events, stories, and even whole books frequently follow one upon another in time with little or no indication of any other connection between them. I included one example of this in the discussion of Genesis 15–16. The final statement in the clash between Michal and David (2 Samuel 6) is another good example of paratactic style characterized by the use of "and." The mutual anger and resentment between Michal and her husband are revealed in their heated exchange. The story closes: "And Michal the daughter of Saul had no child to the day of her death" (2 Sam 6:23 NRSV). The narrator thereby reports "the objective fact of Michal's barrenness . . . but carefully avoids any subordinate conjunction or syntactical signal that would indicate a clear causal connection between the fact stated and the dialogue that precedes it."[18] Is the childlessness divine punishment, one spouse refusing conjugal relations with the other, or "a bitter coincidence, the last painful twist of a wronged woman's fate"?[19]

The transition from Joshua to Judges provides another example of a reading difficulty caused by the juxtaposition of stories without an explicit statement of chronology and the flow of events. The book of Joshua closes with Israel in firm possession of much of the land and unified in its worship of the Lord; Josh 24:31 speaks of Israel in the singular: "Israel served the Lord." In the final verses, the narrator reports the passing of Joshua and his generation. The book of Judges opens with "after the death of Joshua" without, however, specifying the amount of elapsed time. Further, we immediately encounter "the children of Israel," who see themselves as a group of tribes without a leader, not as the united people, the singular "Israel" of Josh 24:31 led by Joshua and his comrades.

The division and isolation of the tribes narrated in Judges 1:1 is mirrored in the narrator's jagged style, which recounts each event, however brief, separately. Narrative form reflects content. A brief speech from a divine messenger (Judg 2:1-5) in part accounts for this sorry state of affairs. In Judg 2:6–3:6, the narrator provides a lengthy explanation both for what has happened and for what will continue to happen. The narrator's exposition breaks the chronology by backing up and telling us, after the reports in chap. 1, what happened after the death of Joshua and his generation, and then by looking ahead to the pattern of the future, the careers of the judges (Judges 3–16). The narrative of Judges 17–21 is not explicitly anticipated in this overview.

Both the stories of the judges and those about the characters and tribes in Judges 17–21 are presented in an episodic manner. They are apparently bound by chronology, with one judge and crisis following upon the other in time; they are also connected by themes of violence and war, both foreign and civil, and by themes of ignorance, confusion, and anonymity. As with chap. 1, the confusions and divisions narrated continue to be mirrored in the broken, paratactic form of the narration. The narrator forces readers to experience some of the bewilderment and bafflement of the characters of the narrative.

The chronological ties are only apparent. The narrator punctuates the text with explicit statements of elapsed time—e.g., "the Israelites served Cushan-rishathaim eight years" (Judg 3:8 NRSV); "the land had rest forty years" (Judg 3:11; 5:31 NRSV); and "he [Samson] had judged Israel twenty years" (Judg 16:31 NRSV). Depending on how one adds up or overlaps the figures, a two- to three-century period is covered in the stories of the judges. However, the narrator, in an aside, jolts us with the information that Israel has moved only one generation from the close of Joshua. The last verse of the book of Joshua reports the passing of Eleazar, son of Aaron; and Judg 20:27-28 notes that "Phinehas son of Eleazar, son of Aaron, ministered before [the ark] in those days." This genealogical notice forces us to rethink the previous material in Judges as simultaneous events or as events narrated after or before they have occurred, and not as events narrated in a straightforward plot line.

In historical-critical analyses, Judges has served as a prime target for different types of source and traditio-historical methods that divide the book into separate stories, groups of stories, or redactional levels. Critics employing these methods regard the narrative traits as pointing to the lack of a consistent narrative and conclude that the book cannot be read as a whole.[20] A contemporary literary critic, such as Josipovici, recognizes the literary problems and then, reflecting the shift in how such literary characteristics are evaluated, accepts them as part of the book: "The book of Judges is indeed oddly fragmented and jagged, even by the standards of the Bible, but that is part of what it is about, not something to be condemned."[21]

Plot, finally, leads us to question whether a narrative leaves its reader with a sense of resolution, a feeling that all the loose ends have been tied up. This applies to a single episode such as the Tamar and Shechem story in Genesis 34, the entire Abraham cycle in Gen 11:10–25:18, the book of Genesis, or the whole of Genesis–2 Kings. The endings of both the Abraham story and the entire book of Genesis leave the reader with a sense of completion. Abraham "died in a good old age, an old man and full of years, and was gathered to his people" (Gen 25:8); he was blessed by the Lord in all things (Gen 24:1). He had seen to the proper marriage of his son Isaac; and the matter of his other wives and sons, including Ishmael, is summarized in the genealogies in Gen 25:1-6 and chaps. 12–18. Genesis ends with the proper burial of Jacob in the family plot at Machpelah, and with all his remaining family in Egypt having finally reached a high degree of trust and reconciliation. The story continues in Exodus but centuries later, and with an almost entirely new cast of characters, except for God and Jacob's "sons," who have now become the people Israel.

On the other hand, Genesis 34 ends with the city of Shechem plundered and Jacob terrified that the violent acts of his sons will result in his and his house's destruction by the Canaanites. The story ends with a question: "Should our sister be treated like a whore?" Thus the story is left open-ended, in regard both to Jacob's fears and to the query itself. All of Genesis–2 Kings ends, perhaps "stops" is a better

term, with the description of King Jehoiachin residing in Babylon and being maintained in fine style by the king of Babylon. The ambiguity of the scene is evident, in the divided opinion of many commentators. Is it a positive sign that the Judean king yet lives on with ample support, or is it a negative sign of pathetic subjection and a fast-fading, last glimmer of hope? Is eating at another king's table a mark of honor or of humiliation? Note the similar ambiguity surrounding Mephibosheth's presence at David's table (2 Samuel 9:1). Is this only the fulfillment of a pledge to Jonathan, or is it an effective way of keeping an eye on a survivor of the house of Saul?[22]

Setting is the locale, the place where events happen, where characters reside. It refers to the cosmic, the heavens and earth of Genesis 1; to the large scale of countries and areas such as Canaan, Egypt, and the wilderness; to the smaller scale of cities, towns, and designated sites such as Shechem, Zoar, and the field of Machpelah, and to particular places within these sites. When the Lord appears to Abraham, it is "by the oaks of Mamre, as he sat at the entrance of his tent in the heat of the day" (Gen 18:1). Such details, including the notice of the time of day, add specificity to the narrative and, in this case, can lead us to wonder if Abraham first thinks he is seeing a heat mirage. The absence of any explicit indication of setting can serve to keep our attention on other aspects of the narrative. Genesis 15 and 17, both covenant stories, are appropriate examples.

In Genesis–2 Kings one broad concern is whether the setting is in Canaan/Israel, in a foreign country such as Egypt or Babylon, or in the intermediate zone of the wilderness. The setting may be actual or potential—i.e., promised or threatened—and is closely related to the actions of the people Israel, of God, and of the other nations and people involved in the ongoing narrative. This relation of setting with plot and character is a major part of the entire thematics and pattern of covenant and promise, possession or loss of the land, and both exodus and exile.

On a smaller scale, setting, especially as it fits or does not fit with the characters and actions placed there, can be significant in a story. Abram, in Egypt, expects the Egyptians to be amoral and to resort to murder to avoid adultery (Gen 12:10-20). Pharaoh and the Egyptians do nothing of the sort, and Pharaoh is shocked at Abram's behavior when he learns the truth. In the future, an Israelite king in the holy city of Jerusalem will act in just this way as he arranges for Uriah's death to cover his adultery with Bathsheba (2 Samuel 11). Awareness of similarities and contrasts in plot and setting heightens our appreciation of the characterization of the main players, particularly Abram and David.

A contrasting example of the significance of Jerusalem occurs in Judges 19. Late in the day a servant suggests to his Levite master that they spend the night in "Jebus" (i.e., Jerusalem), but the Levite wants to press on to Gibeah of Benjamin, since Jebus is "a city of foreigners, who do not belong to the people of Israel" (Judg 19:10-12). It soon turns out that the men of Gibeah are more like the men of Sodom than like those whom the Levite and most readers would expect to encounter in an Israelite city.

Sisera, the commander of Jabin's army and a man of cities and broad battlefields, dies at the hand of a woman, Jael, in the confines of her tent (Judges 4). The male space of cities and the great outdoors contrasts with the female space of indoors and tents to the detriment of males. Sisera dies in a tent, and Barak discovers his enemy's corpse there and not on a battlefield. The same contrast is found between Michal's looking "out of the window" at David dancing in the street (2 Sam 6:16) and Jezebel's looking "out of the window" at Jehu (2 Kgs 9:30). The contrast of male and female space at the beginning of the David and Bathsheba episode in 2 Samuel 11 anticipates the dark portrayal of David—one already foreshadowed by the story of Pharaoh in Gen 12:10-20. David is in Jerusalem in the king's house, while Joab and the army are away at war with the Ammonites; from the roof of his house, he sees Bathsheba, and this sets the sordid tale in motion.

Genesis ends and Exodus begins in Egypt. The same setting allows us to focus on the passage of time and on the change in characters and situation. The narrator passes over the intervening centuries in silence, but the arrival of a new king "who did not know Joseph" (Exod 1:8) expresses, in as brief a manner as possible, the potentially threatening new conditions. The gap in time does not pose a problem for the plot, since the narrator's concern is with how Israel first came to Egypt and then with why and how they left. Judges ends, in accord with its episodic style, with the grotesque story of the rape of the young women of Shiloh at the annual festival. In terms of plot resolution the book ends or stops with the noncommittal statement about Israel's having no king and the people's doing whatever they want.

In the Hebrew Bible, but not in the Septuagint arrangement that underlies most English Bibles, 1 Samuel follows immediately with the story of Hannah, Elkanah, and Samuel. It is set in Shiloh and revolves about events at the annual festival in that city. But this common setting with the close of Judges is not accompanied by common elements of plot or character. We have no idea of elapsed time, if there is any; perhaps we are to read 1 Samuel 1:1 as saying that Hannah and her family were at Shiloh during the mass rape. Only after reading further into 1 Samuel do we realize that the narrative is finally moving on beyond the repetitive cycles of Judges. The narrator does not signal this shift at the start.

CHARACTER AND CHARACTERIZATION

I discuss this topic last because many, if not most, contemporary narrative studies focus on it and, directly or indirectly, relate the treatment of other narrative aspects to the development of characters. This includes works such as Moyers's Genesis television series and Miles's *God: A Biography,*[23] both of which are outside the mainstream of biblical studies. Many of my previous examples point to the significance of plot, setting, and style for our appreciation of characters. *Character* refers to the personages depicted in the narrative—e.g., Abraham and Rebekah—while *characterization* refers to all of the means that the narrator employs to portray them.

Characterization was not dealt with in any depth by either rhetorical criticism or structuralism because of their central concern with the text's structure, apparent or deep, and because of the latter's strong tendency to regard characters as actants. An actant is described in terms of relationships to others and by the use of adjectives attached to the actant. This technical terminology reflects structuralism's desire to align itself with science.

Before the advent of contemporary literary approaches, biblical studies regarded characterization in biblical narrative as minimal because of its lack of many of the devices for character development (e.g., detailed physical descriptions and in-depth psychological portraits) employed in other literature, especially the modern novel. The inability to describe the portrayal of characters in biblical narrative left mainline biblical studies unable to explain or engage the testimony of so many artists, teachers, and other expositors—Jewish and Christian—to the existence of such powerful individual characters as Abraham, Sarah, Moses, Ruth, and David.

The change in the evaluation of the biblical style of characterization is signaled in the title of one of Alter's chapters, "Characterization and the Art of Reticence."[24] He, and many others, now celebrate the Bible's sparseness and laconic style, seeking to describe how the biblical narrator can depict such powerful and memorable individuals without employing all of the familiar narrative modes.

Alter describes an ascending scale of reliability in the ways that the narrator presents a character. Although his is not the final word on the subject, it is a solid and accessible starting point. The lowest level of the scale includes a character's actions or appearance; these facts reveal little or nothing about motivations for actions or about the significance of the physical trait. Next is direct speech, by a character or by other characters concerning him or her. This moves us into the realm of claims and assertions about motives, feelings, intentions, etc., but here too we have to evaluate the assertions, weighing them against what others, including the narrator, tell us about the situation. The Amalekite's claim to have killed Saul (2 Samuel 1) is a lie that contradicts the narrator's reliable report that Saul killed himself in battle (1 Samuel 31).

Next comes inward speech, a character's interior monologue, which gives us some certainty regarding what she or he feels and thinks. In Gen 18:17-19, we learn precisely why the Lord's plans for Sodom and Gomorrah will be revealed to Abraham; in contrast, we know *what* Abraham argues for regarding the city, but we do not know *why*. Because the men with the Lord are going toward Sodom (Gen 18:16, 22), we assume that Abraham means Sodom when he says "the city." Perhaps Lot and his family are at the front of his mind, and not just the righteous in general. Such assumptions and conjectures are typical of the process a reader goes through in evaluating and developing a portrait of a character.

Finally there is the reliable narrator's report of what the characters feel, think, and plan. Even here, however, the narrator may only state the feeling or intention without offering any explanation or motive for it. At the center of the story of Absalom's revolt, the narrator informs us that "the

LORD had ordained to defeat the good counsel of Ahithophel, so that the LORD might bring ruin on Absalom" (2 Sam 17:14 NRSV). This announces the intention but not the motives of the Lord, especially whether this ruin of Absalom is meant for the benefit of David. In Genesis 37, Joseph's reports of his dreams result in his brother's hatred and jealousy, "but his father kept the matter in mind" (37:11 NRSV).

Since brevity and selectivity play major roles in the depiction of character, reliability needs qualification in the sense that we cannot rely on the narrator to tell us all the facts, motives, intentions, etc., that we need. The modes that grant certainty are employed sparingly and usually report minimal amounts of information. This reticence can clothe characters in varying ways and degrees in ambiguity, mystery, and depth. Abner's death at Joab's hands is the convenient removal of a potential rival of David, and readers have wondered whether David had some role in this murder, as he will in the subsequent death of Uriah (2 Samuel 11). The narrator could resolve this question for us, but instead only asserts the king's popularity with the people and their conviction of his innocence: "All the people and all Israel understood that day that the king had no part in the killing of Abner son of Ner" (2 Sam 3:37). We learn that Isaac and Rebekah favor Esau and Jacob respectively; a motive is provided for Isaac's love but not for Rebekah's: "Isaac loved Esau, because he was fond of game; but Rebekah loved Jacob" (Gen 25:28 NRSV).

The narrator employs repetition to great effect in the depiction of characters. Repetition extends from specific details to whole stories and is one of the most, if not the most, employed devices in the narrator's literary tool kit. A character's own statement can be repeated at a different time or in a different place. We gain insight into God's frustration with and eventual toleration of human sin in that God first sends the flood and then promises never to send another because the human heart is always inclined to evil (Gen 6:5; 8:21). The narrator can tell us one thing and the character another. The character may be lying outright or simply tailoring the facts to fit an agenda. Both David and Solomon speak of the Lord's presence and establishment of Solomon's reign (1 Kgs 2:45 NRSV). Solomon proclaims to Shimei that "King Solomon shall be blessed, and the throne of David shall be established before the LORD forever" (1 Kgs 2:44-45). But the narrator makes no mention of the Lord in the closing report: "The kingdom was established in the hand of Solomon" (1 Kgs 2:46 NRSV; see 2:12).

Similar are the many instances when a character repeats what another character has said but alters it. Determining what the alterations are and how they reflect on the characters and the situation is a central process in our development and appreciation of biblical characterization. In Isaac's proposal to bless Esau, he emphasizes the hunt and food and does not mention the Lord. When Rebekah repeats this to Jacob, she shortens the description of the hunt and adds that the blessing is to be "before the LORD" (Gen 27:1-7). She tailors the repetition to impress Jacob more strongly. When Elisha first hears of Naaman's request for healing, he asks that Naaman be sent to Elisha "that he may learn that there is a prophet in Israel" (2 Kgs 5:8 NRSV). Once Naaman, an Aramean, is healed, he asserts, "Now I know that there is no God in all the earth except in Israel" (5:15). The contrast redounds to the honor of the foreigner and to the disgrace of the self-centered prophet.

Issues of change and complexity are central to appreciating biblical characterization. Characters can change for the better or for the worse. Judah develops from the self-centered brother and father-in-law of Genesis 37–38 into the responsible and knowledgeable son and brother of Genesis 43–44. In 1 Samuel, Saul gradually degenerates from the capable, although wary, king and soldier of his early career into the crazed and jealous ruler who spends his time and resources in the pursuit of David. David, at the same time, learns a lesson about the political and personal value of restraint in his chance encounter with Saul in the cave and through Abigail's argument that killing Nabal would haunt him in the future (1 Samuel 24–25). David then applies this lesson in deliberate fashion by hunting down Saul and demonstrating that he will not kill him, even though he has the ability to do so whenever he wants (1 Samuel 26).

On the other hand, lack of change or the persistence of personality, particularly in new situations, adds to characterization. Esau's impetuous nature leads him to sell his birthright in Gen 25:29-34, but results in his emotional welcome of Jacob in Genesis 33. In both instances Esau is a man of the moment

who does not consider matters of the future or of the past. Samuel, even in death, remains the harsh prophet and Saul's implacable foe (1 Samuel 13–15; 28). Jacob, unlike David, does not learn from his own experience that parental favoritism can tear a family apart; he plays favorites with Joseph, who, like Jacob, ends up spending twenty years in a foreign land before seeing his brothers again.

Complexity points to the multifaceted aspect of many character portrayals, including both the change and the persistence of personality traits. Seldom do characters fit into simple moral categories, and seldom can they be described using only one or two adjectives. They are portrayed with personal and moral strengths and weaknesses, and they demonstrate these in a variety of settings. Complexity combines with the capability of change to produce the rich and full individuals we meet in the pages of the OT. Even characters who appear once are seldom mere stereotypes, present only to advance the plot or to serve as a foil to other people, as evidenced by Abraham's servant (Genesis 24), by Rahab (Joshua 2), by Samson's parents (Judges 13:1), and by Abigail (1 Samuel 25).

Characters. Discussion of the portraits of a few individuals furthers the presentation and underlines differences in how specific biblical people have been perceived. The 1970s produced a growing number of studies of major personalities such as Joseph, Moses, and David that developed some of the aspects of complexity and change. In the 1980s, the rate of growth accelerated, and the tenor of many of these studies shifted. Again, Alter's work is a helpful benchmark.

Besides complexity and change, Alter discussed the role of ambiguity in the depiction of a character such as David. I use David as a major illustration because a large number of works treat him directly or indirectly and because of the distinct shift in the evaluation of his character. Ambiguity of character arises when we are given some information that leads us to speculate about a particular trait, motive, or such, but we are not given enough information finally to resolve the question. In the example from Genesis 25, we know that Rebekah loves Jacob. Because we are given a motive for Isaac's love of Esau, we can wonder what Rebekah's reasons might be.

At various points in his discussion, Alter draws attention to this mainly in the portrayal of David.

We are at times told how others view and react to David, whether in fear or in love. Saul, Jonathan, Michal, and all the people love David (1 Sam 16:21, 18:1-3, 16, 20), and Saul comes to fear him (1 Sam 18:12, 29). But we are never told what David feels toward any of these people. David is "very much afraid of King Achish" (1 Sam 21:12 NRSV), so it is not that the narrator never tells us what David feels or thinks. When Saul proposes that David marry one of his daughters, Merab and then Michal, the narrator uses inner monologue to reveal Saul's ulterior motive (that David would die in battle with the Philistines, 1 Sam 18:17, 21, 25). Of David, he tells us that he "was well pleased to be the king's son-in-law" (1 Sam 18:26 NRSV) but not why he was pleased or whether he has any inkling of Saul's intentions. David kills two hundred Philistines to collect double the required number of foreskins, but the narrator provides no light on David's reasons.

In evaluating David's—indeed, any character's—assertions and claims about self, about others, and about the general situation, we must take account of the setting for the statements. It is striking how many of David's pronouncements are made publicly so that, in evaluating them for their sincerity and truth, we have to ask whether David speaks honestly, only for public effect, or for a mix of the two. When David confronts Goliath in view of both the Israelite and Philistine armies, he proclaims the Lord's power (1 Sam 18:45-47). Once Goliath is dead, however, no one—including David and the narrator—makes any mention of the Lord or of the assembled people coming to acknowledge his feat. At a crucial point in his flight from Saul, David speaks "in his heart" or "to himself" of the necessity of fleeing to the Philistines to escape Saul; in this very private moment David says nothing of the Lord.

Ambiguity means that we are presented a choice of ways of understanding David, or any character depicted in this mode. Is David only the pious shepherd and chosen king of Jewish and Christian tradition? Is he a violent, grasping man who will stop at almost nothing to achieve his goals? Or is he a complex mix of both of these, a true "political animal" to use a contemporary phrase? He ends his life displaying the same mixture of piety and power. He speaks to Solomon of fidelity to the Lord and then gives him a "hit list" of potential enemies (2 Kgs 2:1-9). The various studies and commentaries of the last twenty or so years have developed, in their own ways, each of these views with a variety of nuances and perspectives.

Character studies of David are prime examples of changes in the study of biblical narrative in both method and content. The brevity, selectivity, and repetitive nature of the narrator are now celebrated as integral parts of the depiction of characters. In addition, the characters themselves are regarded as complex, multifaceted, and capable of change, and not as cardboard stereotypes of righteousness or sin, faith or disobedience, success or failure. This includes a willingness to recognize that the biblical narrators are deliberately portraying both positive and negative sides of people and institutions. Biblical narrative is not a one-sided story of saints versus sinners, evil kings versus good prophets, and so forth.

Instead of dividing 1 Samuel into pro-monarchical and anti-monarchical sources, for example, we can read the book as a sophisticated and multifaceted evaluation of monarchy. The presentation includes kingship and the related systems of priests, judges, and prophets. This mode of reading works with both the abstract (prophecy) and the concrete (Samuel) without trying fully to separate them. That is, we cannot talk of the narrator's view(s) of monarchy separate from the personalities of Samuel, Saul, David, and the others associated with them. The many, and often contradictory, critical and historical stands that scholars have taken concerning 1 Samuel reflect, in part, the very complexity of the multiple viewpoints and beliefs expressed in the text.

Samuel is another example of rich characterization. He is a leader with aspects of priest, judge, and prophet; and he is a leader who is asked by the people and commanded by God to appoint his own successor. In 1 Samuel 8, Samuel threatens the people with the reality of kingship, but both the people and the Lord repeat their request and command. Samuel responds ambiguously, and not with immediate obedience: "Samuel then said to the people of Israel, 'Each of you return home' " (1 Sam 8:22 NRSV). Chapters 10–11, then, depict a prophet dragging his feet in carrying out his commission. Since Samuel is unwilling to appoint a king immediately, God sends him a candidate, Saul. Samuel has a love/hate relationship with Saul that carries both personal and political implications. Saul, for his part, is a capable military leader in his campaign against the Ammonites, but he can never envision himself totally separate from Samuel. Because of this latter trait, Samuel, perhaps, thinks of Saul as a leader whom he can influence or even control. Hence Samuel's angry reaction to the Lord's regret at ever making Saul king is a complex mix of emotions (1 Sam 15:10-11).

The Role of Women. Concern with characters has heightened our awareness of the roles women play in biblical narrative. This awareness has been accompanied by a focus on the issue of gender in both biblical narrative and commentary. Phyllis Trible, in her rhetorical and feminist readings, was one of the first to focus on questions of gender in the creation stories and other biblical narratives.[25] She challenges traditional views that assert God's strict maleness in Genesis 1 and that see a straightforward story of disobedience in Genesis 3. Starting with her work, critics have produced more readings of the opening chapters of Genesis that explore in detail the ways the narrator develops the plot, setting, and characters of the story.[26] In these readings, the garden story becomes a fuller and richer narrative, not the simple story of sin committed by the one-dimensional figures Adam and Eve.

This leads into the large and growing number of feminist studies of biblical narrative. Many focus on the women in the narratives, whether they are major or minor characters, and portray them in depth and with independence. Sarah, Rebekah, Miriam, Deborah, Michal, Bathsheba—all take on a life of their own and no longer exist solely as the mothers, daughters, or wives of men. This holds even if the women are not given proper names of their own—e.g., the wife of Manoach, Samson's mother, and the daughter of Jephthah.

In addition, and just as significant, feminist studies draw our attention to the patriarchal and male society that forms a narrative's setting. These studies do not have to deal only or mainly with women in the text. Setting here refers to the entire range of social, religious, and political beliefs, perspectives, and assumptions that form the often unspoken background for the stories. Setting in this sense is usually evident only after close study of the text. The fact that most studies refer to the biblical narrator as "he" reflects the dominant male perspective of the narrative. Feminist studies, however, show us that it is a dominant, but not a totally commanding, per-

spective. Finally, reflecting the contemporary willingness to look at the darker parts and aspects of the Bible, feminist studies can confront us with troubling issues such as the role and treatment of women in the world of biblical narrative.[27]

The Character of God. The LORD (*YHWH*), God (*Elohim*), has seldom been treated as a character, mainly because of the powerful influence of Christianity and Judaism. However, as with the shift to full character portrayal with humans, God as a character with strengths and weaknesses is often a major part of the study of biblical narrative. God is not viewed as above or outside of the story, but as an integral part of it: "We can read the character of God in Hebrew narrative more elusively, positing of God the enigmatic ambiguities found in complex human characters."[28] A character portrayal of God takes into account all divine actions and statements, as well as whatever is said of or to God by another, including the narrator. This data is then evaluated as with any human character.

The divine presence varies from the implicit to the explicit. As an explicit presence, the Lord speaks and acts as in Genesis 1–11 and 12–25 (the primeval and the Abraham stories, respectively) while as an implicit presence, the Lord is referred to by others, as in the Joseph story, but seldom appears directly. (The book of Esther is an extreme example of the latter.) The Lord appears only once in the Joseph story, when in a vision of God, Jacob is assured of divine presence and support during his upcoming stay in Egypt. True to the narrator's selective style, the Lord says, "Joseph's own hand will close your eyes," and neither confirms nor negates Joseph's claims that his rise to power in Egypt was part of a divine plan to preserve the family (Gen 45:4-9; 50:19-20). This relates to the variation between clarity and ambiguity of the portrait in terms of whether the Lord is actually determining and involved in events and of any possible motives for such activity. Previously I noted the limited extent of the narrator's ascription of Absalom's fall to the divine intention (2 Sam 17:14).

Narrative critics are willing to look at the dark side of human characters like Abraham and David, and of human society in general. The latter is evidenced in the mistreatment of women and in the prevalence of violence as the chief way to deal with problems. The focus on the human side is matched by a concern with understanding and evaluating

God, who is not only involved with this human scene but is often also the initiator, the one who sets violent events in motion. The flood, the conquest, the seemingly unending wars of Samuel–Kings, and the destruction of Judah and Jerusalem are prime examples. Humans, whether individuals or the whole people, are flawed or far worse; and God is the One who chooses them to play a role in the divine plan. Critics have begun raising the question of how all of this reflects on God.

Biblical studies are presently enmeshed in assessing and debating the impact and relevance of all these changes, particularly the emphasis on the dark side, both human and divine, of the story. The task is to read the Bible as it is and to hold together its glory and its dread, and not to deny one to maintain only the other.

FOR FURTHER READING

Alter, Robert. *The Art of Biblical Narrative.* New York: Basic, 1981.

Bal, Mieke. *Narratology: An Introduction to the Theory of Narrative.* Toronto: University of Toronto Press, 1985.

Bar-Efrat, Shimon. *Narrative Art in the Bible.* Sheffield: Almond, 1989 (Hebrew ed., 1979).

Berlin, Adele. *Poetics and Interpretation of Biblical Narrative.* Sheffield: Almond, 1983.

The Bible and Culture Collective. *The Postmodern Bible.* New York: Yale University Press, 1995.

Gunn, David M., and Danna N. Fewell. *Narrative in the Hebrew Bible.* New York: Oxford, 1993.

Josipovici, Gabriel. *The Book of God: A Response to the Bible.* New Haven: Yale University Press, 1988.

Miles, Jack. *God: A Biography.* New York: Random House, 1995.

Moyers, Bill, *Genesis: A Living Conversation.* New York: Doubleday, 1996.

Sternberg, Meir. *The Poetics of Biblical Narrative: Ideological Literature and the Drama of Reading.* Bloomington: Indiana University Press, 1985.

ENDNOTES

1. James Muilenberg, "Form Criticism and Beyond," JBL 88 (1969) 1-18.

2. Bernhard W. Anderson, "Introduction," *Rhetorical Criticism: Essays in Honor of James Muilenberg,* ed. Jared J. Jackson and Martin Kessler (Pittsburgh: Pickwick, 1974) xi.

3. R. Barthes, F. Bovon, et al., eds., *Structural Analysis and Biblical Exegesis* (Pittsburgh: Pickwick, 1974).

4. K. R. R. Gros Louis, J. S. Ackerman, and T. S. Warshaw, eds., *Literary Interpretations of Biblical Narratives* (Nashville: Abingdon, 1974).

5. Robert Alter, "A Literary Approach to the Bible," *Commentary* 60 (1975), 70-77.

6. Robert Alter, *The Art of Biblical Narrative* (New York: Basic, 1981).

7. The Bible and Culture Collective, *The Postmodern Bible* (New York: Yale University Press, 1995).

8. Adele Berlin, *Poetics and Interpretation of Biblical Narrative* (Sheffield: Almond, 1983).

9. Shimon Bar-Efrat, *Narrative Art in the Bible* (Sheffield: Almond, 1989; Hebrew ed., 1979).

10. David M. Gunn and Danna N. Fewell, *Narrative in the Hebrew Bible* (New York: Oxford, 1993).

11. Alter, *The Art of Biblical Narrative.*

12. Meir Sternberg, *The Poetics of Biblical Narrative: Ideological Literature and the Drama of Reading* (Bloomington: Indiana University Press, 1985).

13. Gunn and Fewell, *Narrative in the Hebrew Bible,* 53.

14. Gunn and Fewell, *Narrative in the Hebrew Bible,* 54.

15. Berlin, *Poetics and Interpretation of Biblical Narrative.*

16. Bar-Efrat, *Narrative Art in the Bible.*

17. Mieke Bal, *Narratology: An Introduction to the Theory of Narrative* (Toronto: University of Toronto Press, 1985).

18. Alter, *Art of Biblical Narrative,* 125.

19. Alter, *Art of Biblical Narrative,* 125.

20. See Robert G. Boling, *Judges,* AB 6A (Garden City, N.Y.: Doubleday, 1975).

21. Gabriel Josipovici, *The Book of God: A Response to the Bible* (New Haven: Yale University Press, 1988) 110.

22. Leo G. Perdue, " 'Is There Anyone Left of the House of Saul . . .?' Ambiguity and the Characterization of David in the Succession Narrative," *JSOT* 30 (1984) 67-84.

23. See Bill Moyers, *Genesis: A Living Conversation* (New York: Doubleday, 1996); Jack Miles,

God: A Biography (New York: Random House, 1995).

24. Alter, *The Art of Biblical Narrative*, 114-30.

25. Phyllis Trible, *God and the Rhetoric of Sexuality* (Philadelphia: Fortress, 1978), and *Texts of Terror: Literary-Feminist Readings of Biblical Narratives* (Philadelphia: Fortress, 1984).

26. Gunn and Fewell, *Narrative in the Hebrew Bible*, 194-205.

27. For example, see Danna N. Fewell and David M. Gunn, *Gender, Power, and Promise: The Subject of the Bible's First Story* (Nashville: Abingdon, 1993); J. Cheryl Exum, *Fragmented Women: Feminist (Sub)Versions of Biblical Narratives* (Valley Forge, Pa.: Trinity, 1993).

28. Gunn and Fewell, *Narrative in the Hebrew Bible*, 85.

THE BOOK OF
JOSHUA

ROBERT B. COOTE

The book of Joshua tells of Israel's conquest of Canaan, which appears to climax the long opening story of the Bible. In Genesis, God promises to give the land of Canaan to the descendants of Abraham, Isaac, and Israel. After delivering the descendants of Israel from Egypt and forcing them to remain in the desert long enough for an entire generation to die out and a new generation to take their place, God fulfills this promise. Near the end of the book of Numbers, with Moses still in command, the Israelites conquer the promised land east of the Jordan River and finally arrive at the Jordan. Deuteronomy consists of a long speech by Moses to Israel, including the last major installment of the law Moses passes on to Israel. At the end of Deuteronomy, Moses dies.

The book of Joshua continues the story from this point. First God commissions Joshua. Then, in an orgy of terror, violence, and mayhem, God takes the land of Canaan west of the Jordan away from its inhabitants and gives it to Israel under Joshua's command. Joshua, with the help of the priest Eleazar, distributes the conquered land to the tribes of Israel. Having aged, like Moses he bids his people farewell, dies, and is buried. Thus the book of Joshua explains how under Joshua's command Canaan was conquered, the Canaanites were slaughtered, and their lands were expropriated and redistributed to the tribes of Israel. It forms a triumphant finale to the Bible's foundational epic of liberation, the savage goal toward which God's creation of Israel and delivery of Israel from slavery in Egypt appears to point from the start.

COMPOSITION DURING
THE MONARCHICAL PERIOD

It is possible, but unlikely, that this story was recorded as it happened in history. The story is composed of diverse ingredients. These include set speeches, folk narratives (some with auxiliary additions), echoes of rituals, excerpts from supposed ancient sources, lists, territorial descriptions of differing kinds, material repeated elsewhere in the Bible but in different form, and a double ending. The story purports to be about tribal warfare, but several features point to a monarchical as much as a tribal viewpoint. These include the precise delineation of territory covering a sweeping area, the notion of a unified conquest involving mass murder, and the portrayal of strict military loyalty and absolute obedience to a single commander. While Joshua plays a singular role in the story, however, he appears only sporadically, mostly in frameworks, large and small, as though he might not have belonged originally to all the parts—or to any of them. It is surprising that a hero from the tribe of Ephraim, whose territory lay at the heart of early Israel, should be the protagonist of a conquest narrative that focuses almost entirely on the territory of Benjamin, with scarcely anything at all to say about Ephraim. Similarly, Joshua rarely, if ever, acts on his own initiative, but moves only on Yahweh's orders. This contrasts, for example, with the account of David, who acts for himself, albeit in response to God's election; but it comports, as will become clear, with the scheme behind the later composition of the book of Joshua. This scheme held that for centuries Joshua, together with Israel under his command, was unique in his obedience to Yahweh. The first five books of the Bible are composed of at least five distinctive layers and strands, and the book of Joshua appears to be in line with at least two of these, long known as D and P, the first in a major way and the second in a minor way. Many towns are destroyed in Joshua, and these often do not agree with the archaeological evidence of the period before the Israelite monarchy, when the story is supposed to have taken place. In sum, these features of the book of

Joshua indicate that it was not composed all at once as an accurate account of an episode in the history of pre-monarchic Israel. Instead, they point to a gradual composition, which took place mainly during the period of the monarchy, from two hundred to six hundred years after the supposed events occurred. Other features make clear that the monarchic perspective of Joshua derives specifically from the house of David.

The book of Joshua is not a simple account of historical events. It is a complex narrative shaped by writers belonging to several different contexts. Most of these contexts can be identified with at least some probability. The clearest is what most scholars regard as the basic context of the D strand, or Deuteronomistic History—namely, the reform of Josiah (c. 640–609 BCE) in the late seventh century. A significant part of Josiah's reform was the reconquest of what had been Israel, and Joshua's conquest of Canaan was taken as a precursor of Josiah's reconquest of Israel. Another earlier context was the reign of Hezekiah (c. 714–687 BCE). Hezekiah was the first Davidic king to begin his reign after the fall of Samaria in 722 BCE, when the non-Davidic kingdom of Israel came to an end. Analysis has shown that much of the books of Kings was composed under Hezekiah, and it is possible that much in the books of Joshua and Judges comes from his reign as well. He, too, wanted to reconquer Israel. The likelihood is that it was Hezekiah who adopted Joshua as a Davidic hero. Before Hezekiah, Joshua was an Israelite hero, probably introduced into wider popularity by Jeroboam I, the usurper of what had been Davidic Israel, whose home was not far from the tomb of Joshua. While it is not always possible to assign particular parts of Joshua to an exact source, these are the main events that helped to shape the book prior to the Babylonian exile of the house of David. During the exile, a few minor changes may have been made in line with the exilic revision of the entire Deuteronomistic History. After the exile, the parts of Joshua that seem related to the priestly strand in the Pentateuch were written, during the Persian period. The source and context of a few parts of Joshua remain a mystery.

That the book of Joshua was written mainly during the period of the Davidic monarchy no longer occasions surprise. In the last twenty years, much research has been devoted to the study of early Israel, particularly with regard to the tide of village settlements that arose in the hill country of Palestine during the Early Iron Age.[1] The Early Iron Age lasted during the twelfth and eleventh centuries BCE, after the supposed time of Joshua and before the time of David. While an exact identification between these new settlements and early Israel cannot be proved, historians and archaeologists believe that the inhabitants of most of these villages were related in some way to Israel as described in the Bible.

Settlement shifts are not uncommon in the history of Palestine. They have been going on for at least five thousand years, and many are comparable to the Early Iron Age shift. While the interpretation of these shifts will remain under investigation for the foreseeable future, so far one thing is clear: Century-long settlement shifts in Palestine are not typically caused by blitzkriegs; therefore, it is improbable that the Early Iron Age settlement shift was prompted by an onslaught of tribal outsiders of the sort described by the book of Joshua. Most scholars now think that the people of Israel were indigenous to Palestine, and were not outsiders. There is nothing in the archaeological record to suggest that the Early Iron Age population of highland Palestine had a mainly pastoral-nomadic background, as suggested by the Bible, or that any sizable segment of the population of Palestine at that time originated outside of Palestine, again as suggested by the Bible, except the Aegean "Sea Peoples," represented by the Philistines. (Hittites are named in Joshua, where they are seen as indigenous; it is conceivable that they settled in Palestine during the Late Bronze Age, but more likely the term has its Neo-Assyrian meaning of the inhabitants of greater Syria.)

Several passages in Joshua itself, as well as in Judges, contradict the picture of a single triumphant assault. Moreover, the picture in Joshua leaves an important question unanswered: What was the nature of early Israel? One of the biggest mistakes readers of the Bible can make is to project modern notions of nationalism onto the ancient world or to assume, with the eighteenth-century thinker Johann Gottfried Herder and his Romantic and modern followers, that a given people whose existence as such is mistakenly taken for granted naturally expresses its singularity through a homogeneous folk spirit. In this introduction, "nation" refers to what historians call the "political nation," rulers over a changing body of subjects. Early Israel represented not a nation, but a shifting confederation of tribes.

A tribe was a political network of families united by external threat and claiming a common putative ancestor. Tribal loyalty competed with other political and social loyalties and tended to be stronger among the stronger members of the alliance. Thus "tribe," like "nation," referred mainly to the political identity and function of an elite. Anthropological study of tribal societies, combined with historical evidence, shows that notions of defined patriarchal descent and kinship like those described in the Bible tend to be putative and fictional, reflecting not historical kinship but political relations, both among tribes and tribal alliances and between tribes and a central government. The biblical descriptions of the tribes of Israel, like those in J and P, reflect the interests of a state or governing elite with the ability or desire to centralize. The description of the "tribes" in Joshua is no different: It reflects, not the disorderly tribal relations that must have characterized early Israel, as illustrated in the early "Song of Deborah" in Judges 5, but the politics of radical reform and centralization. Thus in Joshua the tribes of Israel are presented in a rationalized manner, united in harmonious kinship.

The sources used by the writers of the book of Joshua may contain sparse material going back in some way to early Israel, but the book of Joshua in its present form was written long after the time of early Israel. The emergence of Israel and its settlement of the central highlands of Palestine are now understood mainly through archaeology and comparative history rather than the Bible.[2] To inquire about the historical contexts of the book of Joshua means to look at the house of David, and not early Israel. In this regard, Joshua resembles the Pentateuch, which precedes it. Virtually all of the Pentateuch, while purporting to describe early Israel, was written during the period of the Israelite and Davidic monarchies or later and reflects chiefly their circumstances and concerns.

CONTEXT OF DEUTERONOMISTIC HISTORY

To understand the book of Joshua, it is important to recognize that it is part, and how it is part, of a much larger work: the Deuteronomistic History. This is a conglomerate of monarchic historical sources, some of them probably tracing back to the court of David himself, that have been edited according to a single overarching conception. That conception is the house of David's claim to the sovereignty of Israel. The Deuteronomistic History was composed out of these sources mainly during the reigns of Hezekiah and later Josiah to support their programs of centralization. Joshua cannot be understood apart from the Deuteronomistic History. But what about the story of the Tetrateuch, the first four books of the Bible, which precedes the Deuteronomistic History? Should Joshua also be read in the light of the Tetrateuch, especially the parts that pre-date the great priestly revision of it in the late sixth century BCE? Joshua presumes aspects of the Tetrateuch's story, but there is little of importance in Joshua that must be understood mainly in terms of the pre-priestly Tetrateuch. For example, Joshua assumes the Tetrateuch's representation of Davidic sovereignty, even though the Tetrateuch contains hardly a hint of a forthcoming conquest. Joshua also contains priestly passages.

If we ask what gave God the right to dispossess the Canaanites of their land, the scriptural answer is to be found near the beginning of the Tetrateuch, in Noah's curse of Canaan in Gen 9:25-26: "Cursed be Canaan;/lowest of slaves shall he be to his brothers. . . . Blessed by [Yahweh] my God be Shem [an ancestor of Israel];/and let Canaan be his slave" (NRSV; cf. Josh 16:10; 17:13; Judg 1:28; 1 Kgs 9:20-21). The reason why Noah cursed Canaan was that Canaan's father, Ham, had seen Noah naked when Noah lay drunk in his tent (Gen 9:21-22). This curse laid the basis for God's promise to Abram made "between Bethel and Ai" (Gen 13:3): "All the land that you see I will give to you and to your offspring forever" (Gen 13:15 NRSV; Bethel and Ai lie about a mile and a half apart; cf. Josh 12:19).

The source of this myth was the court of the house of David, which early on produced the "history" of the world and of Israel that forms the basis of the Tetrateuch. The myth of God's promise of land to Israel, essential to the story of Joshua, together with the related myths of a unified nation descended from a single family arriving from outside, originated in its present form to help the house of David explain its sovereignty over greater Israel. However, the house of David exercised such sovereignty for only a short period in its five-hundred-year history, during the reigns of its founder David and his son Solomon in the tenth century BCE. Thereafter the house of David ruled little more than the highland territory of Judah, while the rest of Israel had its own kings and foreign rulers. For centuries the house of David looked back on the reigns of David and Solomon as the Golden Age and never gave up the hope of reconquering Israel and restoring Davidic rule to its original glory.

Such claims are not uncommon in dynastic histories. For instance, in the Mayflower Compact of 1621, the Pilgrims acknowledged the sovereignty of their king, James I (of the King James Bible), whom they called "king of Great Britain, *France*, and Ireland." The kings of England had not ruled in France for a long time, but they maintained the title in theory up through the eighteenth century. James I inherited this proprietary title from his great-grandmother on both sides, Margaret Tudor, daughter of Henry VII, and she from distant forebears. In the same way, the house of David maintained its title to Israel, inherited from David, in theory for hundreds of years. The ambition to reconquer Israel and make that title real again became pronounced in the late Assyrian period, after the fall of Samaria, Israel's capital, in 722 BCE, when there were no more opposing kings of Israel. Two Davidic kings in particular are known to have pursued policies leading to a projected reconquest of Israel: Hezekiah in the late eighth century BCE and Josiah in the late seventh century.

To the extent that the promise of the land plays an important role in the Tetrateuch, the book of Joshua appears to bring the Tetrateuch's story to its expected conclusion. However, originally the book of Joshua was *not* the ending of this story. When this story was first composed, the book of Joshua had not even been thought of. As already indicated, the Romantic idea that a single popular folk narrative lies behind the various strands of the biblical story from Genesis to Joshua has no basis. Even within the Pentateuch, Deuteronomy does not belong to the original story, but begins a new story, the Deuteronomistic History, which apparently was meant to be a sequel to the original pre-priestly Tetrateuch story.[3]

Two strands of narrative made up the bulk of the pre-priestly Tetrateuch story. These were the early house of David's history of Israel, called J, and a slightly later northern Israelite supplement, called E. The J and E strands give little indication of how God's promise of land is to be fulfilled. They seem to take it for granted that David (in the case of J) and the kings of Israel (in the case of E) possess sovereignty over the land of Israel, as sanctioned by God, and devote most of their attention to other concerns. These strands cannot be traced into Deuteronomy and Joshua. They end, not with a conquest, as in Joshua, but with the culmination of their own distinctive themes, in Exodus (for E) and in Numbers (for J).[4]

Not only do the earliest strands of the Pentateuch conclude before Deuteronomy and Joshua, fail to appear in Deuteronomy and Joshua, and fail to refer to a conquest, but they also give no indication that the promise of the land is to be fulfilled in a blitzkrieg and attempted ethnic cleansing. Nor is there a hint of God's command to exterminate the Canaanites, to say nothing of the particular contours and emphases of the book of Joshua. The curse of slavery on Canaan is not the same as extermination, as recognized in the book of Joshua (Josh 16:10; 17:13). The figure of Joshua himself appears in the Tetrateuch, but he has little if anything to do with the main themes of J and E, and was probably introduced there by scribes in the court of Hezekiah or Josiah. In Exod 17:8-16, a text that belongs to neither J nor E, Joshua appears out of nowhere to help defeat the Amalekites. He appears again in Numbers 13–14, also in connection with the Amalekites. This is a J story about the Judahite town of Hebron, later David's first capital, and its eventual Judahite conqueror, Caleb. Here Joshua, an Ephraimite, is introduced rather artificially as a new character (Num 13:8, 16) to play a supplementary and presumably secondary role to Caleb, who is of primary interest in the J strand. It is even implied in Josh 14:12 that Joshua was not one of the spies.

The Amalekites play a major role in the Deuteronomistic History (Deut 25:17, 19; Judg 3:13; 5:14; 6:3, 33; 7:12; 10:12; 12:15; 1 Sam 14:48; 15:2-3, 5-7, 18, 20, 32; 28:18; 30:1, 13, 18; 2 Sam 1:1, 8, 13; 8:12; most of these passages have a connection with the founding of the house of David), but only a minor part in the Tetrateuch, except for these two passages involving Joshua (Gen 14:7; 36:12, 16; Num 24:20).[5] As for the notion of mass extermination, it figures in the Tetrateuch in only two stories, Joshua's attack on the Amalekites in Exodus 17 and Israel's attack on Hormah in Numbers 21, a duplicate of the attack on the Amalekites in Num 14:39-45.[6] It may be no coincidence that the Amalekites were later said to have been finally exterminated under Hezekiah (1 Chr 4:41-43).[7] It was probably in the court of Hezekiah, where the overall plot of the Deuteronomistic History was first conceived and Joshua was first given a significant role in the Davidic history of Israel, that the association of Joshua with the Amalekites was apparently introduced into the Tetrateuch.

NARRATIVE STRUCTURE

The story of Joshua has two parts. Israel's land east of the Jordan has already been conquered under Moses. The story of Joshua concerns mainly the west side of the Jordan.[8] First, Joshua leads the tribes of Israel in the conquest of the west side of the Jordan. What begins in Josh 1:1-6 concludes in 12:7-24. Second, Joshua oversees the distribution to the twelve tribes of all the land conquered (Joshua 13–31). The distribution includes the designation of refuges for manslayers and the assignment of towns and pasture to the Levites. After giving permission to the tribes from east of the Jordan to build an altar beside the Jordan to witness to their desire not to be separated from the west-bank tribes, and after giving a double farewell—a speech followed by a covenanting ceremony, ending with the erection of a stone as a witness that all Israel has committed to Joshua's Yahweh—Joshua dies and is buried (Joshua 22–24).

The plot of conquest and distribution represents only the bare bones of the narrative. By the time most of the account of the conquest is completed (Joshua 1–9), only two towns have been captured and destroyed, Jericho and Ai, and the inhabitants of another town, Gibeon, accommodated. The three towns that dominate the narrative of conquest lie in the small territory of Benjamin, nearly within sight of one another. They represent a tiny part of the land to be conquered. Why is this the case? The story uses conquest not only to foreshadow the house of David's reconquest, but also to confirm its sovereignty and elaborate on its policy of centralization.

Most of the narrative of conquest is taken up with three localities of great significance for the house of David's claim to sovereignty: Gilgal, Bethel, and Gibeon. (This assumes that the story of Ai bears on its neighbor Bethel.) At Gilgal, Samuel determined to depose Saul in favor of David, thereby establishing the house of David. Bethel plays a critical role in the entire Deuteronomistic History. Its altar symbolized the "sin of Jeroboam." By usurping the sovereignty of the house of David in Israel, Jeroboam violated the first law of Moses, which stipulates that the service of Yahweh has to be performed at one shrine only. The sin of Jeroboam was then committed by all the subsequent kings of Israel, who thus stood in the way of the house of David's reconquest of Israel. Gibeon played a decisive role in the conflict between the house of Saul and the house of David, which led to David's usurping the throne and becoming king of Israel. It was at Gibeon that David's men defeated Abner's men and launched David's war of usurpation (2 Sam 2:12–3:1). David later consolidated his sovereignty by complying with the Gibeonites' demand for the execution of seven remaining sons and grandsons of Saul on the grounds that Saul had "put the Gibeonites to death." Although the incident referred to is not mentioned elsewhere, it makes direct reference to Josh 9:3-27 (2 Sam 21:1-14).

The story signals radical Davidic centralization by highlighting Joshua's fulfillment of Yahweh's command. Following the quasi-royal commissioning of Joshua, in which he begins his career as not only a second Moses but also the prototype of the ideal king in the Deuteronomistic History, the main narrative focuses on three examples (involving the three localities Gilgal, Ai, and Gibeon) of how the law of חרם (ḥērem; Deut 7:1; 20:16-18), which requires that all opponents be killed and no booty be taken, applies in order to sharpen the definition of how people are to relate to Yahweh's command, as enforced by Joshua, and to God's service, or cult, in its extraordinary deuteronomistic form. The first example involves Rahab and her family. They are Canaanites, but because Rahab shows loyalty to Yahweh by saving the Israelite spies and making possible the conquest of Jericho, at Joshua's direction she and her family are not slaughtered with the rest of the people of Jericho. In contrast, in the second example the Judahite Achan violates the law of ḥērem by withholding booty from Jericho. Achan and his family are Israelites, but this does not protect them from the consequences of their disloyalty.

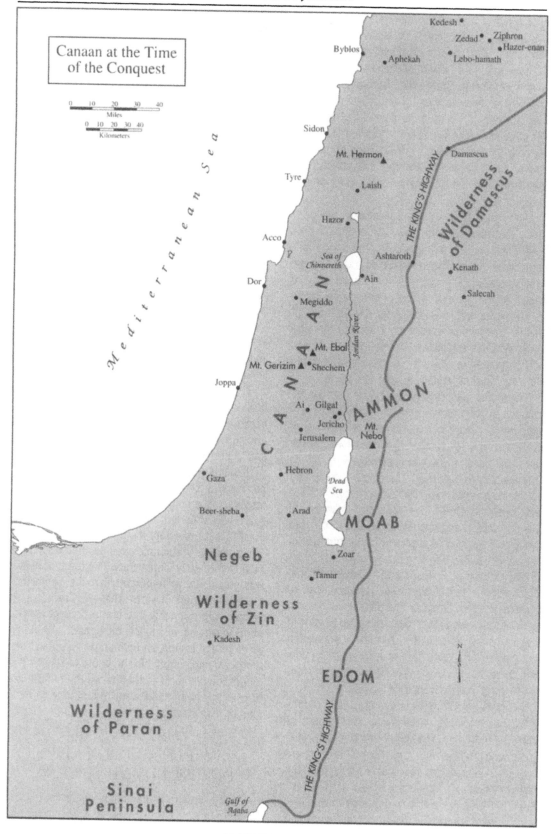

Canaan at the Time
of the Conquest

As a result of Achan's violation, at Joshua's direction, Achan and his family are stoned to death by "all Israel." The stoning of Achan makes possible the conquest of Ai.[9] The third example involves the Hivites of Gibeon. They trick Joshua into thinking they live far away, and in line with Deut 20:10-15 Joshua exempts them from *ḥērem* annihilation. When he finds that he has been deceived, he keeps his oath to them and does not destroy them, but makes them slaves of Yahweh's cult, laying the foundation for David's later annihilation of the house of Saul.

The concluding section concerning the conquest in Joshua relates two short campaigns of extermination. The first was prompted by Joshua's compact with the Gibeonites and instigated by the Amorite king of Jerusalem, the future city of David. In the second, Joshua overthrows a horde of Canaanite and alien kings led by the king of Hazor. The section ends with a list of thirty-one kings defeated and killed, largely in the order in which they were killed in the narrative, starting with the kings of Jericho, Ai, and Jerusalem.

The second half of Joshua's story concerns the distribution of the conquered land. Following an age-old pattern, victory in war ensues in the division of the spoils. The spoils other than land have mostly been "dedicated" to Yahweh through *ḥērem*, leaving only the land to distribute. The distribution of land places the greatest weight on Judah (Joshua 14–15) and Benjamin (Josh 18:11-28). As followers of David, Judahites ended up in Jerusalem (15:63), but the town itself was located within the territory of Benjamin (18:28). The distribution of land is by lot at Gilgal for Judah, Ephraim, and Manasseh, then at Shiloh for the remaining tribes. The land goes to tribes defined in terms of specified territories, an artificial conception that reflects the point of view of a central state concerned to regulate a population that threatens to regard itself as opposed to the state and, therefore, ready to make its own use of tribal designations and tribal rhetoric.

Centralizing monarchs strove to curtail not only tribal independence, but also acts of revenge that subverted the rule of the king through royally sanctioned law. Hence, once the tribal allotments are defined, Joshua assigns the cities of refuge from the avenger of blood, required in Deut 19:1-13 (cf. Num 35:9-34). According to deuteronomistic law, Levites are to control the document of the law laid down by Moses and thus oversee the house of David's jurisdiction. Members of the tribe of Levi do not receive a tribal territory, but are assigned towns and pasturage throughout the other territories (Joshua 21). Then a lengthy account in Joshua 22 details how Joshua helps to settle a dispute over an altar that threatens to duplicate the altar destined to be located at the Davidic Temple in Jerusalem. This ostensible exception to the deuteronomistic law of centralization must be meticulously justified.

Finally, Joshua pronounces two farewells. In the first he stresses absolute obedience to the command of Yahweh, the same emphasis with which the entire narrative began. In the second farewell, he performs a covenanting ceremony at Shechem, deep in the heartland of Israel, where little else has happened to this point. Here the gathered people in formation are encouraged to vow their loyalty to Joshua's, or the deuteronomist's, Yahweh. This ceremony has points of contact with Deuteronomy 27 and Josh 8:30-35, though it does not appear to belong to the monarchic Deuteronomistic History.

The narrative concludes with the death and burial of Joshua. Joshua's burial is important, because Joshua was likely to have been revered as a local hero, or saint, after his death, in a saint's cult centered at his tomb. Especially after death, such saints (Elijah and Elisha are probably examples) could become the focal point of political movements among villagers in the countryside, and it was important for central authorities to suppress them or to co-opt them. This is probably why few instances of such movements are found in the Bible before early Christianity. The tomb of Moses was potentially so important that the deuteronomistic historian asserts that its location is unknown, presumably in a bid to prevent anyone from starting a resistance movement around it. The figure of Joshua, an Ephraimite hero, has been thoroughly pre-empted in the house of David's history of the conquest so that he will be of little use to Israelites who might want to continue to resist the house of David.

MAIN FEATURES OF THE DEUTERONOMISTIC HISTORY

Since Joshua must be understood as part of the Deuteronomistic History, it is essential to recall the main features of that work. It is a lengthy and mul-tifarious work, a corpus of manifold overlapping sources in successive editions that probably span almost four hundred years. However, its basic story is straightforward. Like most basic stories in the Bible, it treats of sovereignty expressed in terms of jurisdiction exercised through a religious shrine and cult. In the world of the Bible, government, politics, and religion are inseparable. Translations using "religious" language, like "worship" in place of "fear," which occurs several times in Joshua, often do not adequately express the political signif-icance of shrines and cults in the Bible. The reason is that such translations do not have a juridical and jurisdictional connotation in modern English, as terms referring to the services in and of cults invariably have in the Bible.[10] The deuterono-mistic story is the story of a set of laws that must be obeyed and eventually established through a particular shrine and its cult if the promised land is to be kept. If this story is thought to be mainly "religious," despite the essential role of this law, then it may be seriously misunderstood.

The deuteronomistic story begins when this law is delivered to the "nation" by Moses. Keeping the law, Joshua conquers Canaan. After Joshua dies, the nation fails to keep the law. Enemies afflict the nation, as one "judge" after another suc-ceeds only in temporarily saving some of them. The first law of Moses delivered at the Jordan calls for centering the cult of Yahweh at one shrine only (Deut 12:1-14). David captures Jerusalem, and there his son Solomon builds the Temple, and this turns out to be the one shrine. Solomon, however, tolerates other shrines. Therefore, Yahweh takes the sovereignty of Israel away from the house of David and gives it to Jeroboam, who is no better. He immediately reactivates the cult of Bethel, vio-lating Moses' cardinal law. As a result, the sover-eignty of Israel must ultimately revert to the house of David. The story leaves no doubt how: At the precise moment Jeroboam is to inaugurate the secessionist cult of Bethel at its forbidden altar, a "man of God" from Judah, still held by the house of David, suddenly appears. He proclaims that a future scion of the house of David, whose name, here revealed three hundred years in advance, will be Josiah, is destined to destroy that very altar (1 Kgs 13:1-6). Two hundred years later, the story reaches a preliminary climax. The kingdom of Israel, whose kings have persisted in the "sin of Jeroboam," is obliterated, and the sovereignty of what had been Israel is taken over by the king of Assyria. The cult at Bethel, however, remains intact. Within three more generations, the long-awaited Josiah is born. During refurbishment of the Temple, ordered by Josiah, the law of Moses, which seems to have dropped out of sight, is redis-covered. Like Joshua, Josiah obeys it. He embarks on a triumphant rampage, destroying every shrine in sight other than the Temple—and most notably Bethel—throughout Judah and what had been Israel, which now may be reconstituted and brought once again under the sovereignty and direct jurisdiction of the house of David.

In sum, the Deuteronomistic History tells of how Israel under Joshua acquired its land in the first place, then how the house of David took it over, lost it, and under Josiah looked to recover it. It is a story of revanchism: The land once lost is to be reconquered. At the end of the story, the recon-quest is not told in detail. In fact, it seems scarcely to be mentioned (cf. 2 Kgs 23:19-20). It is not clear whether the writer of this stage of the Deuterono-mistic History meant to end his work by referring to the reconquest in this highly abbreviated form or simply to present the basis for a policy of recon-quest. Whether Josiah's reconquest ever actually took place, the structure of the overall deuterono-mistic story shows clearly how that reconquest was conceived. The story begins with the proclamation and recording of the law of Moses and the conquest of the land. It ends with the rediscovery of the law of Moses and the reconquest of the land. Thus the earlier conquest pre-figures the later reconquest. Joshua, as will become evident, pre-figures Josiah and may be said to be modeled on Josiah. In essence, the book of Joshua is a representation, incorporating sources of various kinds, of either the plan for or the course of the house of David's recon-quest of Israel under Josiah.

The main deuteronomistic account ended with Josiah. The debacle of the Babylonian exile of the house of David necessitated updating the history. Minor additions appear in several places, and a coda brings the story to about 560 BCE. This updat-ing had little effect on Joshua. Joshua 23:15-16 is the best candidate for an exilic addition.

Josiah's reform is the goal of the Deuterono-mistic History and the event that more than any other provides the context for the book of Joshua. Josiah's reform is an example of a practice known throughout ancient history, including numerous times in the Bible, in which a ruler refurbished the state shrine or temple and, in the name of the state god(s), promulgated a roster of reform laws that headlined the easement of debts. Such appeals to commoners were a standard feature of the reigns of the protodemocratic rulers called "tyrants" (an impartial term) in Greece during the seventh century BCE. The famous reforms of Draco (624 BCE) and Solon (594 BCE) in Athens were nearly contemporary with Josiah's reform. The centerpiece of such reform laws was usually debt remission. Other forms of debt easement included the manumission of debt slaves (indentured servants trapped in interminable indebtedness), the prohibition or limiting of interest, and regulations governing the holding of securities for loans. All these are found in Josiah's deuteronomistic reform law (Deut 15:1-18; 23:19-20; 24:6, 10-13, 17-18).

The purposes of such ruler reforms are well known. They are summarized by Chaney, who studied the many ancient parallels to the abundant biblical texts related to such reforms.[11] In the ancient world, the lower classes were usually heavily in debt. Periodically their accumulated indebtedness threatened economic, social, and political order. One purpose of debt reform was to "ameliorate economic abuses severe enough to threaten the viability of the state." By the time of Josiah's reform in 622 BCE, economy and society under the house of David had been extensively commercialized in the context of the Assyrian "peace." Such commercialization typically had the effect of concentrating agricultural land in the hands of the wealthy through a combination of high rents and taxation and manipulation of the debt mechanism. It is not difficult to imagine that Josiah's reform answered to a clamor for debt relief.

A second purpose was to restore the reputation of the ruler, to allow him to "project a public image as a just statesman who took good care of his subjects, especially the weak and disadvantaged." Josiah's reform came after eighty years of Assyrian domination of the house of David. The dynasty's tradition of strength, longevity, and autonomy only served to point up its current weakness, since it had been suffered to govern for the last three generations only by the indulgence of and at the behest of its imperial master. It is almost certain that the house of David encouraged the commercialization that swelled indebtedness in its realm, and at the same time was poorly positioned to prevent disregard for and abuse of debt easement provisions sanctioned by age-old custom or spelled out in existing law rosters. Thus the house of David was in need of a policy that would counteract charges of callousness and injustice from the impoverished.

The third purpose of such reforms was to undermine opponents by implementing debt remission laws in a selective, partial manner, in order to "weaken elite factions that threatened the ruler's hold on power." The dominant political relations and political conflicts concerned the ruling class, who were also the creditor class. This class typically divided into contending factions. The reform of Josiah appears to have been partly the work of a faction only recently come to power. Josiah himself, who became king at the age of eight, would have reached his majority only a few years before the reform. Upon coming of age, he had either to break out of the clutches of his regents altogether or to gain control of them and join forces with them to enhance their combined power. It is likely that Josiah followed the second course. It seems that with the backing of the court newcomers who had held the regency, he promulgated a policy of debt remission designed to weaken eminent households long in power in the court and its Temple in Jerusalem, some perhaps going as far back as the early years of the house of David.

The modern reader may react very differently to two of the most important aspects of Josiah's reform: debt easement, on the one hand, and, on the other hand, a revanchist reconquest patterned after the destructive devotion of Canaan's indigenous populace—men, women, and children—which amounts to ethnic cleansing if not genocide. Group-based debt easement may be regarded by most people today as a laudable policy, even an acceptable foundation for an entire ethical program, though in practice usually only so long as, unlike the ideal in Deuteronomy, creditors can control the process. The same people today, however, would probably regard ethnic cleansing as wholly outside the bounds of ethics, categorically indefensible under any circumstances. Yet God, through Moses, commands both, and both as part of the *same* policy and program, within the space of five chapters in Deuteronomy. Clearly the world of Joshua is not the same as our world, and this ambiguity, like many other features of the book of Joshua, requires careful attention to the ancient context.

The deuteronomistic account of Josiah's reform is based largely on typical elements of ancient royal reforms (2 Kgs 22:3–23:24). These include the repair of the dynastic Temple, the announcement of a reform law featuring debt remission, radical centralization of cult and jurisdiction, and territorial expansion. These elements are integral to one another and together enhance the reforming monarch's sovereignty and jurisdiction. Such acts were performed by Josiah with one end in view: the greater power of the house of David embodied in Josiah.

In the deuteronomist's account, the reform begins when Josiah orders his high priest Hilkiah to supervise the refurbishing of the Davidic Temple. In the ancient Near East, repairing a temple was tantamount to rebuilding it, or even building it in the first place. It represented the reassertion of strong rule through the reconfirmation of the dynasty. According to the deuteronomist, only one previous Davidic king had ordered the Temple repaired, and that was Jehoash (2 Kgs 11:1–12:16). Jehoash and Josiah had much in common. Jehoash's father, Ahaziah, had been assassinated, just as Josiah's father, Amon, was. Like Josiah, Jehoash needed to overcome the detriment of a lengthy minority, begun when he was seven years old, much like Josiah at eight. Jehoash's minority, like Josiah's, began with the aggressive restoration of the house of David by a forceful priest. The restoration of the dynasty was carried out in spite of alien overlords controlling Jerusalem, in Jehoash's case the Omrids, in Josiah's the Assyrians. In both cases the overlords promoted exceptional commercial development, producing the need for a temple-centered debt reform.

In the course of the repair ordered by Josiah, Hilkiah discovers the law of Moses, ostensibly long lost or long in desuetude. This is the law laid out in Deuteronomy 12–26, which was immediately written down and then heeded, or nearly so, under Joshua (Josh 1:7-8). As noted, although it is possible that this document, the "document of the law" within the Deuteronomistic History, contains archaic elements predating the monarchy, it is not

likely, and the whole clearly reflects a radical monarchic reform. The writing of supposedly ancient, hidden books of vision, law, and wisdom for discovery is a commonplace of history.[12] The writer of Deuteronomy may well have consulted ancient sources, but by and large those parts of the law in Deuteronomy not already composed for Hezekiah's reform were probably composed under Josiah, in preparation for Josiah's centralizing reform, the aim of the history as a whole. Moses had introduced his law by insisting over and over that it was essential if the Israelites were to keep the land they were about to conquer. No law of Moses, no land of Israel. Having transgressed this law, the political nation of Israel lost its land with the fall of Samaria. The only hope for recovering the land of Israel, to say nothing of keeping the land of Judah, is to recover the law. And here it is, in the hands of Josiah's priest Hilkiah, ready to launch the house of David on its long-anticipated reconquest of Israel.

The two primary accents of this law have been mentioned: centralization, both cultic and judicial, and the periodic remission of debt. These policies are effected by radical rulings indeed, in all likelihood previously unheard of among Israelites in the form in which they occur in Deuteronomy. The Temple of the house of David, the shrine that Yahweh is to choose to place his name there, makes all other shrines, including other shrines dedicated to Yahweh, illegitimate (Deut 12:2-12; 12:29–13:18). Throughout the Deuteronomistic History, the presence of Yahweh is signified by the presence of Yahweh's name. In the deuteronomistic conception, the name of Yahweh encapsulates the political character of the central cult, which, like all cults, combines the religious and judicial aspects of the cult. The name of Yahweh is invoked not only in worship and supplication, but also, equally important and sometimes simultaneously, in judicial oaths that sanction true witness and just judgment in the adjudication of cases and disputes. To judge from the account in Deuteronomy of Moses' appointment of the judiciary (which may borrow from the E-strand account in the Tetrateuch, Exod 18:13-27). Josiah proposed to extend and rationalize central Davidic jurisdiction and to this end planned, for judicial purposes, to organize the entire subject people into surveillance cells of ten households each (Deut 1:9-18; cf. Deut 16:18-20).

Shrines and their jurisdictions outlawed by Moses' first law include those devoted to other Palestinian deities like Baal, Astarte, and Asherah, as well as the sun, the moon, and the host of heaven (stars, constellations). The status of the cults of the foreign peoples deported to Palestine by the Assyrians (identified in 2 Kgs 17:29-31) is ambiguous, since Josiah is not said to destroy them. The outlawed shrines include those devoted to departed heroes similar to Joshua and Moses. Josiah preempts the shrine of Joshua rather than outlawing it. Preempting the shrine or shrines of Moses, which must have existed, was apparently thought to be beyond even the militant, insurgent power of Josiah. Accordingly, it was officially declared not only that Moses died on the far side of the Jordan (probably an accepted tradition, although neither J nor E had addressed the matter), but also that "no one knows the burial place of Moses to this day" (Deut 34:6). It is not likely that this was a popular or widely accepted view. In the face of popular piety and practice to the contrary, it probably is one of the pronouncements and rulings put forward in their account of Moses that Josiah and his faction were unable to maintain.

The main rite of the central shrine, like nearly all ancient shrines, is sacrifice, which often entails the eating of meat; so the deuteronomistic historian goes into where and how meat may be eaten (Deut 12:13-27; 14:3-29). This subject resumes in Deut 15:19-23 and continues by implication through the rulings regarding keeping the three main feasts at the central shrine (Deut 16:1-17). In addition, this opening section of laws regarding centralization deals with the disposition of the Judahite levitical priests, who seemed to preside at now outlawed non-Jerusalemite shrines. They are made wards of the central shrine, but are expected to reside throughout the kingdom (Joshua 21).

In Deuteronomy 15, the historian reaches the second primary accent of the law: debt remission. This was a radical law: "At the end of seven years you shall remit all debts" held by fellow Israelites, that is, subjects of the house of David who have covenanted to keep the laws of Moses. Foreigners may be dunned indefinitely; as Frick points out, the Deuteronomistic History, like the Tetrateuch, presents "national" identity, not class, as the primary social category and takes little interest in the amelioration of poverty in the rest of the history

outside Deuteronomy.[13] Like all land-reform and debt-reform laws, this one was short-lived, even though similar laws occur, like ruler's reforms, throughout biblical history (cf. Exod 22:25-27; Lev 25:8-55; Neh 5:1-13; and numerous prophetic oracles that assume such laws, like Isa 3:13-15 and Amos 2:6-8; Jer 34:8-22 is reminiscent of Deut 15:1-18 but seems not to represent a full-scale royal reform). The lender is not permitted to deny the needy person's request for a loan, no matter how close the seventh year, the year of remission, may be. The condition described in Deut 15:11 is frequently misunderstood because of the use of this verse in the New Testament (Matt 26:11; Mark 14:7; John 12:8); the Hebrew text in Deuteronomy does not say that the poor will never cease, an outcome that would be quite unlikely given this law as formulated and given the abundant produce of the land (Deut 15:4). Instead, it says that when you enter the land, "since the poor shall not yet have ceased," open your hand to them. An exceptional feature of this legislation is the optimism and goodwill it expresses: The Israelite is not only to forgive debts owed, but to do so readily and joyously. This attitude is expressed particularly in regard to the release of the debt slave, another form of debt remission, which in the deuteronomistic conception recapitulates the deliverance from Egypt.

Josiah's reform continues when he orders all the elders of Judah—those town and village heads who are referred to throughout the law—to gather in Jerusalem, together with all the nobles, priests, cult emissaries, courtiers, and plebs already there. "In the ears" of this great assembled gathering, the entire nation under the house of David, Josiah himself reads the complete law of Moses, discovered in the Temple. Josiah then makes a covenant to keep the law in all its parts, and the assembled nation joins him with one accord (2 Kgs 23:1-3).

This pristine accord, reminiscent of Joshua's fighting nation, ignites Josiah's campaign of cult purification, beginning with Judah. In obedience to the first law, Josiah purges and purifies the cult of the Temple and suppresses or purges all other cults as rivals to the one shrine and one cult serving the one Yahweh (2 Kgs 23:4-14). He dislodges and demolishes or incinerates the apparatus and artifacts of the cults of Baal, Asherah, and the sun, the moon, and the stars, presumably with Astarte and

Ashtar at their head. These are the Canaanite deities that helped to advance the house of David's long-standing trade relations and are associated particularly with Solomon and, for the Assyrian period, with Ahaz and Manasseh. Like most populist reforms, Josiah's reform touts its aversion to commerce, a root cause of the creation of debt slaves out of villagers forced to mortgage their labor and of the amassing of landholdings mortgaged by debt slaves into cash-crop estates. Altars and high places in and about Jerusalem he destroys, as well as all altars in Judah, "from Geba to Beer-sheba." These include the "high places" at the gate of the governor of the city, whose name happens to be Joshua; these high places at the gate probably sanction the jurisdiction assumed by this strong man, until Josiah puts an end to his insubordination (2 Kgs 23:8). The priests of all these abolished cults are left in their localities, but now they are dependent on the central cult, to which are owed all the contributions previously made to the demolished shrines (2 Kgs 23:9). This has been taken as a signal expression of the economic exploitation entailed in cult centralization, as the priests called Levites in Deuteronomy are forced to become wards of the Davidic Temple.[14] Many scholars theorize that these priests were installed by the house of David early in its history as partisans for Davidic rule in the hinterland. Apparently Josiah feels this settlement calls for reorganization (cf. Josh 21:1-42). Josiah puts a stop to child sacrifice in Jerusalem, thus confirming his right to supplant household patriarchs in determining the fate of their sons and daughters. The culmination of Josiah's purge of Judah comes with the wrecking of the shrines installed by Solomon (23:13-14). These were the shrines that, in the reformers' view, brought about the house of David's loss of Israel in the first place. With their destruction, the way is cleared for the reconquest of Israel.

Having thus purged Judah, Josiah turns to Israel. The revanchism of the house of David, dormant for more than three hundred years but festering for the preceding one hundred years, has come to a head. The ancient prophecy of the man from Judah at the altar of Jeroboam in Bethel—the altar by which generations of kings of Israel presumed to sanction the hated non-Davidic jurisdictions of Israel, jurisdictions condemned from the very start by Moses as recorded in the document found in the Davidic Temple—is to be fulfilled. Josiah begins with the altar at Bethel (23:15-18). He destroys the altar and its shrine. He removes the bones from saints' tombs nearby and incinerates them on the remains of the altar, as the man from Judah foretold. The remains of that same man lie in his own tomb; his bones Josiah leaves in peace, a relic of three centuries of impudence and its epochal requital.

Josiah continues on from Bethel, ravaging the remaining shrines of Israel founded under the kings of Israel, treating them all as he had the shrine at Bethel. Apparently, Josiah spares the priests of the outlawed shrines in Judah, but slaughters the priests in Israel. Finally he returns to Jerusalem (23:19-20). The brevity of this account has been noted. The historian may leave the details of the reconquest of Israel to be worked out, having previewed its salient highlights in the conquest of Canaan by Joshua. The key detail of Josiah's rampage through Israel is what is not said; as noted, Josiah does not attack the cults of the Assyrian populace planted by imperial force within the territory of what had been Israel (2 Kgs 17:34), but only "the shrines of the high places . . . which kings of Israel had made" (2 Kgs 23:19 NRSV).

Josiah's historian thus makes a clear distinction between indigenous cults and alien cults. The significance of this distinction goes beyond the possibility that the writer wished to avoid arousing Assyrian ire or resistance over the extent of Josiah's reconquest. Josiah accepts Assyrian settlement policy in this territory, just as he defines the territory in terms of Assyrian bounds, and he respects the separate jurisdictions sanctioned by these recently established cults. These were presumably limited jurisdictions for each imperial local group represented, like the Babylonians, Cuthites, and Hamathites. In the absence of any indication to the contrary, Josiah apparently lets these groups be, along with the judicial and property relations, including landholdings, under their aegis.

Josiah's concern lies not only with the pre-Assyrian populace and their leaders and cults, represented both by the so-called Canaanite people and by the contemporary inhabitants who correspond to the other distinct groups peopling the land Joshua fought to possess. These were the Canaanite "nations," called in varying order and combinations Canaanites, Hittites, Hivites, Perizzites, Girgashites, Amorites, and Jebusites (Josh

3:10; 9:1; 11:3; 12:8; 24:11; later they were idealistically regarded as seven in number). These Canaanite entities are also thought of in general as either Canaanites or Amorites. The latter distinction appears to represent the notion that the Amorites are native to the uplands of Palestine and the Canaanites to the lowlands (Num 13:29; Josh 11:3; 13:2-5). The cultures of the uplands and lowlands were distinct from each other during both the Late Bronze and Iron ages in Palestine.[15]

Most of the leaders of this native populace, especially of those who were subject to the kings of Israel, had been dispersed and deported a hundred years earlier than Josiah. The populace came under the new leaders planted by the Assyrians. These, the deuteronomistic historian explains, had been forced by Yahweh to acknowledge the cult of Bethel and hence its laws and jurisdiction, as part of their duty for taking over landholding rights and privileges in territory disposed of by Yahweh (2 Kgs 17:24-28).[16] The primary landholding relations of the newcomers, in other words, were those regulated from Bethel, and these were abolished when Josiah ransacked Bethel. Their private cults, which they had set up after the arrangement with Bethel and continued to practice following Josiah's reconquest, had little or no bearing on the loyalty of landholders, including themselves, to Jerusalem. As the historian explains at length in 2 Kgs 17:24-41, the descendants of these people do not now adhere to the law of Yahweh (Bethel having been destroyed) and, falling for the most part outside the scope of rural landholding in Israel, do not come under the jurisdiction of the house of David. From the Josianic deuteronomist's perspective, their overlord remains the king of Assyria.

Some may find it surprising that the presence of Assyria, rather than its absence, figures in the background of Josiah's reform. It used to be thought that the main event that made Josiah's reform possible was the collapse of Assyria at the end of the seventh century BCE, leaving a temporary power vacuum into which Josiah could step. The great Assurbanipal died in 627, Nineveh fell in 612, and by 609 virtually nothing was left of the once great empire. Assyria was fast being replaced by Babylon. Here was a window of opportunity, it seemed, that induced Josiah to reform.

However, in recent years views have changed. It is true that Josiah's reform advanced a nationalist and populist revival in which all things foreign were open to ridicule. This meant that any natives of Palestine who as the result of a hundred years of Assyrian cultural domination continued to imitate Assyrian style or custom or tout Assyrian ties were fair game for disparagement. But such disparagement leaves no trace in the deuteronomistic account of Josiah's reform, or anywhere in the Deuteronomistic History. It is now clear that the Assyrians did not require conquered peoples to worship Assyrian gods and that Josiah's purging of the Temple and the cults of Judah was not an anti-Assyrian act.[17] Apparently the deuteronomist makes a distinction between regional and indigenous people, on the one hand, and the newcomers planted by the Assyrians, the people of Babylon, Cuth, Hamath, and Sepharvaim, and the Assyrians themselves, who were still in place in 622 BCE, on the other hand. Josiah attacks the cults of the indigenous, but not of the Assyrian newcomers.[18]

Astonishingly, Josiah's historian says nothing about Assyria or Assyrians at either the beginning or the end of his history. Moses says nothing about them, nor, most remarkably, do they appear at all after Hezekiah's reign. The Assyrians are treated with an understandably negative slant in the account of Hezekiah's reign, since Hezekiah was known to have rebelled against Assyria. That account may incorporate a source from Hezekiah's time, as indicated by the ample role played by the prophet Isaiah. The deuteronomistic writers themselves do not give the named prophets so much attention, except when distinct sources are incorporated in their history, as with Samuel, Elijah, and Elisha. Thus it is not surprising that the Assyrians appear in a somewhat unsympathetic light in relation to Hezekiah. The deuteronomistic view is better seen in the treatment of the fall of Samaria, which immediately precedes the account of Hezekiah's reign. Here the king of Assyria is presented as simply carrying out God's judgment (2 Kgs 17:1-34).

In his attack against rivals in Israel, Josiah seems to defer to long-standing Assyrian administrative boundaries. Josiah probably remained a nominal Assyrian vassal to the end of his reign and never had a reason to be anti-Assyrian. If the main impulse of Josiah's reform was anti-Assyrian, there is no sign of it in the Deuteronomistic History.

Thus for understanding Joshua as much as Josiah, the account of Josiah's campaign against the cults of the north is significant as much for what it does not say as for what it does say. By not having to attack the Assyrian newcomers, Josiah's historian makes it all the easier to develop the era of Joshua as the prototype for Josiah's reconquest, in which the long-resident peoples, "Amorite" and "Canaanite" agriculturists and commercialists, are the primary target.

When Josiah arrives back in Jerusalem, two final acts bring his reform to a close. The first is the keeping of the feast of Passover "as prescribed in this document of the covenant" (2 Kgs 23:21-23). The deuteronomistic law of Moses requires that the feast be kept at the central shrine. Like most of the reform legislation, this is a radical innovation. As described in the Tetrateuch, the Passover is an intrinsically local, household rite, centered on the extended family as the patriarch's household. By now it comes as no surprise that Josiah wishes to suppress such extended family rites, as is implied clearly in Deut 16:1-17. In the deuteronomistic conception, as seen above, the Passover celebrates the archetypal release from debt. The history of the nation as the Davidic "nation" in the land of Canaan, therefore, begins and ends with a Passover. The first Passover is represented by the national crossing of the Jordan, followed by the celebration of Passover (Josh 3:1–5:10). On apparently the second day of that first Passover in the land, the manna ceases and the nation eats for the first time of the produce of the land (Josh 5:11-12). The second Passover comes under Josiah, at the conclusion of his reform, and is the first in history to be in full compliance with the final law of Moses. For this alone, Josiah would have ranked supreme among the kings of Israel in deuteronomistic terms.

The second of Josiah's final acts is to remove from Judah "the mediums, wizards, teraphim, idols, and all the abominations . . . in Judah and Jerusalem" (2 Kgs 23:24 NRSV). To the extent that these are not redundant, they refer to local saints and their devices and representations, of the kind prohibited in Deut 18:9-14. The burden of this act is clear from the juxtaposition of the prohibition in Deuteronomy 18 with the text in which Moses says that "Yahweh will raise up a prophet like myself, whom you shall heed" (18:15). To obey Moses is to refuse to consult an oracle or saint who does not represent Moses. Elijah, and to a lesser extent

Elisha, came close to looking something like Moses, but no one in the Deuteronomistic History actually both looks and sounds like Moses. The only way Moses does reappear is in the document containing his words, found in the Temple at Josiah's instigation. The authenticity of this document is confirmed by the prophet Huldah, so no further search for judgment, wisdom, or truth is required.

THE POLITICAL CONTEXT OF JOSIAH'S REFORM

The political context of Josiah's reform forms the primary backdrop for the story of Joshua. Josiah's support came not from the political middle, but instead from the two political extremes. One was the empires in control of Palestine: Egypt and its ally Assyria.[19] The other was a particular rural family and its allies and clients, a non-Jerusalemite family with deep Israelite roots, whose most famous member was Jeremiah, from Anathoth in Benjamin, just north of Jerusalem. This family traced its putative lineage back to Shiloh and was eager to promote a populist correction. From Shiloh's once venerable shrine came the prophet Samuel, who anointed David and sanctioned his usurpation of Saul, and the prophet Ahijah, who sanctioned Jeroboam's usurpation of the house of David (1 Kgs 11:29-39; 12:15) and then turned to a third dynasty (14:1-18). Jeroboam bypassed Shiloh when he restored the cult of Israel at his borders, a common strategy, in Bethel and Dan. The importance of traditions from Benjamin in the book of Joshua and its failure to mention Egypt or Assyria are among the direct reflexes of this twofold source of support for Josiah.

Not everyone, conceivably even the partisans' original backers, was enthusiastic about Josiah's pretensions. The Deuteronomistic History deals extensively with opponents of and foils to centralization. Indeed, its treatment of opponents, whether actual or metaphorical, comprises the great bulk of the history, and an understanding of these opponents as the deuteronomist presents them is of great importance for interpreting the book of Joshua. First there are the "Canaanites" of various kinds, who play an essential role in the preview of Josiah's reconquest and reassignment of land titles played out under Joshua. Then there are the local heroes of the type represented by the "saviors" and "judges" of the book of Judges, climaxing with Saul, in all of whose days the Israelites, in the absence of a rightful king, do "each what is right in his own eyes," contrary to the deuteronomistic law of centralization. Then come the opponents of David from among the house of Saul and its supporters and from David's own sons, possibly not unlike bypassed sons of Manasseh. Then follow the several dynasties of the kings of Israel (especially Jeroboam I and Ahab) who reject the pretensions of the house of David and its cult in Jerusalem, even when allied with it. All of these represent in Josiah's own day the kinds of opponents he must vanquish if his plan of conquest and political dominance is to succeed: men who, like Hiel of Bethel, fortify strategic sites like Jericho to their own advantage (Josh 6:26; 1 Kgs 16:34); indigenous landholders and traders in the Assyrian provinces who may identify themselves as Israelites following the norms of Bethel but not of Jerusalem; popular regional warlords, strongmen, and outlaws; prophets other than those who directly support the house of David; opposing claimants to the sovereignty of Israel from rival elite households or from the house of David itself. None can rival Josiah, the Deuteronomistic History proclaims, for the cogency and legitimacy of his claim of sovereignty.[20]

Josiah and his supporters promote a policy of "ethnic" cleansing based on the idea that "Canaanites"—that is, opponents in both Judah and the north headed by landowners and urban elite with commercial affiliations and their families, a large group under the Assyrian and Egyptian empires in Palestine—deserved to be murdered and all their property destroyed by the monarchy. As a "nationality," the category "Canaanite," like that of "Israelite," was a social construction, not an unchangeable historical reality. In the world of the Bible, there were no such nations as we understand the term.[21] Like virtually all distinctions of race, ethnic identity, and nationality, as well as the very definitions of such concepts, categories like "Canaan" and "Israel" were not natural but cultural.

The several kinds of opponents to Josiah treated throughout the Deuteronomistic History appear in the book of Joshua in the character of the seven "great and strong nations" named in Josh 3:10 (cf. Deut 7:1; Josh 11:3; Acts 13:19). In the deuteronomistic conception, these are the original inhabitants of the land of Canaan, of whom the "Canaan-

ites" in particular are only one group. "Canaan" was a general term of uncertain origin for the southeastern Mediterranean coast and its hinterland, for which the terms "Palestine" and "the land of Israel" are often used in modern academic literature. Use of the term "Canaan" goes back to the Egyptian New Kingdom period, when Egypt held imperial sovereignty in Palestine, and even earlier. The term occurs in the phrases "the inhabitants [i.e., landholding elite] of Canaan" (Exod 15:15) and "the kings of Canaan" (Judg 5:19) already in early Israelite women's battle songs. It refers to the territory destined to come under David's sovereignty in the J strand, which adapts early Israelite tribal traditions so as implicitly to pit David against the king of Egypt in the post–New Kingdom struggle for Canaan. In J, the land of Canaan is mythically pictured as a "land oozing milk and honey"— that is, a largely uncultivated land (cf. Isa 7:18-25), peopled almost exclusively by city dwellers, the "Canaanite" elite descended from Ham (Gen 10:15-18). In a few texts in the Bible, "Canaanite" appears to mean "merchant," functionaries of the "kings of Canaan." The most interesting of these texts is Zeph 1:11, in which the "people of Canaan" are condemned. In this text, probably written in the time of Josiah, and perhaps in his court, "the people of Canaan" parallel "all who weigh out silver"—i.e., traders from "Canaan" resident in Jerusalem—precisely the people Josiah was most determined to suppress. The deuteronomistic historian, therefore, appears to have taken over the term "Canaan" from the house of David's history of early Israel and added to it the nuance of "trader," if that nuance was not already present.

Then, still using traditional sources and with no independent knowledge of his own (note, for example, that six of the "nations" are listed in Exod 3:8, probably an original J text), the deuteronomistic historian peoples the land of Canaan with a multifarious ancient elite of seven or so "nations" (Canaanites, Amorites, Hittites, Hivites, Girgashites, Perizzites, Jebusites; in the MT, the group numbers seven only in Deut 7:1; Josh 3:10; 24:11). Some of their names occur in the historical record outside the Bible. This is particularly the case with "Hittite" and "Amorite," a Semitic term (meaning "Westerner") used by the Egyptians like "Canaan" as a general geographic designation, this time for the Mediterranean coast and its hinterland north of

Canaan. All may have existed at some time in ancient Canaan. It is important to realize that although modern historians can show that among these "nations" at least so-called Amorites, Hittites, and possibly Hivites lived long before the time of Josiah, mainly outside of Canaan, Josiah's historian, like scribes of the house of David probably going back to its beginning, believed that all these "nations" were, unlike "Israel," indigenous to Canaan. Thus they were all "Canaanites" in the sense of the original elites of the land of "Canaan," and all, in terms of J's genealogy of the "nations," sons of Ham as distinct from the sons of Shem, from whom Israel was descended.

In sum, for his understanding of "Canaan" and "Canaanite," which in his history figure almost exclusively prior to Saul and David, the deuteronomist had to look no further than the scrolls available to him in Josiah's scriptorium. He simply followed the written tradition of the house of David, to which he belonged. In line with this tradition, the ancient "land of Canaan" was the territory destined to be held by the united tribes of Israel ruled by the house of David. The original "inhabitants" or "kings" of Canaan would have to be dispossessed. The list of thirty-one kings (petty city lords) of Canaan in Josh 12:9-24, however fictional, fits exactly the Davidic concept of pre-Davidic Canaan as the land of the "kings of Canaan." Such a concept of Canaan apparently existed among tribal Israelites who formed their ostensible political identity partly over against the petty states of Canaan long before David. But this pre-existence makes little difference for understanding the book of Joshua, since it has little to do with early Israel. In the context of Davidic sovereignty in "Canaan," "Canaanite" meant "not Israelite," and as a fictive representation of contemporary political identity it meant "not submitting to the sovereignty of the house of David."

As an expression of Josiah's reform, the story of Joshua's conquest, patterned on Josiah's reconquest, "functions as an instrument of coercion" and intimidation, encouraging the submission of all subjects.[22] The historian wants to terrorize the populace, particularly its recalcitrant political leaders, into submission to Josiah by showing what happens to a class of people ("Canaanites") whose interests are opposed to the interests of Josiah's monarchy and of the peasantry under him. The

writer also shows that obedience to Josiah can take precedence over supposed ethnic affiliation: Canaanites can submit and be saved (Rahab, the Gibeonites), and if a Judahite belonging to the Israelite in-group disobeys the commander-in-chief, he can be repudiated and killed (Achan). "The primary purpose of the conquest narrative is to send a message to internal rivals, potential Achans, that they can make themselves into outsiders very easily."[23] Josiah's historian "uses the rhetoric of warfare and nationalism as an encouragement and a threat to its own population to submit voluntarily to the central authority of a government struggling to organize itself and to [re]create its own ideological framework of inclusion. In order to justify violent action [to that end], the dynamics of the literature of warfare usually consist of a division [often outrageously overstated] between self and other," us and them.[24]

VALUES IN THE BOOK OF JOSHUA

Much about the book of Joshua is repulsive, starting with ethnic cleansing, the savage dispossession and genocide of native peoples, and the massacre of women and children—all not simply condoned but ordered by God. These features are worse than abhorrent; they are far beyond the pale. Excoriable deeds and many others of at least questionable justifiability have been committed with the sanction of the book of Joshua, such as the decimation of the Native American peoples. People who regard themselves as peaceable Christians tend to shun the book of Joshua as not simply unedifying but irreconcilable with their faith, or to justify a tacit Marcionism by equating the worst parts of the book of Joshua with the entire OT. The book of Joshua scarcely appears in the ecumenical lectionary for preaching used in many denominations; not only are its most repugnant passages ignored, but most of the rest of the book is too. The current lectionary prescribes only three passages from Joshua, all innocuous: the crossing of the Jordan (3:7-17), the keeping of Passover at Gilgal (5:9-12), and the covenant at Shechem (24:1-3, 14-25). That the last pericope, with its lofty if paternalistic avowal "as for me and my household, we will serve the LORD," is assigned twice while most of the book is assigned not at all only corroborates the aversion and bowdlerizing selectivity with which people attuned to "family values" tend to hold Joshua at arm's length.

It is possible to abstract the narrative of Joshua so as to extract from it pure qualities or values that are positive and affirmable. The stories can be taken to illustrate reliance on the power of God, whose provision, both short-term and long-run, does not fail. They illustrate the importance of grace, allegiance, obedience to authority, community solidarity, the family, and deterring hasty revenge. This is one way to rescue the text of Joshua from peremptory dismissal. However, with such a sidestepping approach study is not necessary, and commentaries need play no role.

The purpose of a careful study of the book of Joshua is not in the first place to redeem it but to understand it better, and through it to understand ourselves better. In order to understand the book of Joshua better, along with other helps we need to use the imperfect knowledge of it that is available—with all its mere likelihoods and probabilities, its uncertainties, puzzles, gaps, and voids. When looked at in terms of its historical context, the values represented in the book of Joshua, whether ostensibly bad or good, are not pure, like offhand abstractions, but multifaceted, mixed, and ambiguous. Even within the limited and relatively well understood context of Josiah's reform, significant interpretive issues arise that are difficult to address. Josiah marshaled the harsh forces of centralization for the sake of his poor subjects, promulgating a program of debt remission, which, if carried out, would have eliminated poverty among his subjects within his lifetime—an unheard-of boon. Or did he marshal the sympathies of the poor for the sake of his program of centralization? Where does the balance lie? Such ambiguities cannot finally be resolved but must be grappled with if the Word of God is to be discovered in the book of Joshua.

What does the book of Joshua show us about ourselves? If we attend to it carefully, it may suggest to us our own affinities with the atrocities, violence, coercion, and prejudicial categorizing as means to social betterment that are its main events. The point of such insight through God's Word is not to exaggerate our sins or grovel in them, but to encounter a greater reality in which we may not be as innocent as we suppose when averting our gaze from this book or disavowing it out of hand. The book of Joshua can help us to overcome consciousnesses mystified through the ignorance, fear, and conflict that to one degree or another affect all human beings.

PRIESTLY ADDITIONS TO JOSHUA

The main priestly strand (P) as a unified composition is confined to the Tetrateuch. But at least one passage of priestly character is found in Deut 32:48-52. Some historians have argued that the priestly strand predates and hence provides a source for at least the beginning parts of the Deuteronomistic History. Most, however, continue to believe that, while preserving earlier tradition from the time of their service as the priesthood of the house of David in Jerusalem, P was composed in its present form during or just after the Babylonian exile of the house of David. This sequence suggests what is probably the simplest explanation for the quasi-priestly additions to the Deuteronomistic History as well, which are most evident in the book of Joshua.

The Deuteronomistic History reflects a levitical control of tradition against the established priesthood. In contrast, in the post-exilic period the reestablished priesthood, who identified with the figure of Aaron, again found themselves in power and thus in a position to modify the Deuteronomistic History to make it conform more with the priestly Tetrateuch and express their special interests, and this they seem to have done in a modest way. For example, while the list of levitical cities in Joshua 21 may date originally from the late eighth or seventh century BCE, in its present form it is a priestly composition that was probably composed in the post-exilic period. Thus its assignment of Anathoth to the Aaronid priests (Josh 21:18) may represent, not long-standing tradition, but a form of Aaronid revenge against the deuteronomistic cabal of more than a century earlier. The similar bias can be seen in the account of Josiah's reform in 2 Chronicles 34–35, which, like the rest of Chronicles, reflects the influence of both the Aaronid rulers of the post-exilic period and the Levite underlings. Ignoring a foundational theme of the Deuteronomistic History, the account in Chronicles makes no mention at all of Josiah's attack against Bethel, the erstwhile Aaronid shrine.

A less likely explanation of the priestly additions to Joshua is to suppose that an exilic deuteronomist used priestly sources. Either way, the priestly tradition met in Joshua should be understood primarily in relation to the priestly strand in the Tetrateuch rather than in relation to the Deuteronomistic History, even though it is doubtful that a continuation of the P strand or any other unified priestly substratum underlies the present book of Joshua.

A notable instance of a priestly addition is the insertion of Eleazar in Josh 14:1; 17:4; and 21:1. Eleazar was the third son of Aaron and his designated heir. In later genealogies, he is the link between Aaron and the Zadokite Aaronids displaced by Josiah but restored to power following the Babylonian exile, at least putatively (1 Chr 6:3-15, 50-53; Ezra 7:1-5). In the deuteronomistic view, Joshua is the direct successor of Moses and is obedient to Moses' charge and commands, both without intermediary. In Josh 14:1; 17:4; 19:51; and 21:1, however, Eleazar appears to come between Moses and Joshua, as in Num 32:28 and 34:17. This contrasts with the deuteronomistic emphasis. (Eleazar is mentioned in Deut 10:6, but this is likely to be a priestly addition.) In the priestly strand, Eleazar joins Moses to hear Yahweh's order to enumerate the clans of the tribes of Israel in preparation for the apportionment of the conquered land (Numbers 26). This order is given before Joshua is commissioned (Num 27:12-23). Then, at Joshua's commissioning, Yahweh makes it explicit to Moses that Joshua is subordinate to Eleazar (Num 27:20-21).

In Joshua 13:1–21, the word מטה (*maṭṭeh*) rather than שבט (*šēbeṭ*) is sometimes used for "tribe," and scholars have sometimes taken this, together with other supposed differences, to indicate a comprehensive priestly source for the account of the allotment of territories to the tribes. This remains doubtful. Clearly Joshua 13–21 as currently phrased fulfills priestly directions given in the book of Numbers, tying together the themes of promise and fulfillment in the Tetrateuch and Joshua. This is true even when there are differences between the two books on the same subject. Thus priestly writers had a hand in composing the agreements between Numbers and Joshua, and it is not necessary to look further to explain the priestly characteristics found in these chapters.

Others have noted similarities between the book of Joshua and Chronicles. Such may be particularly significant in the account of the crossing of the Jordan (Joshua 3–4). The liturgical character of this account, which apparently originated in a ritual reenactment, is enhanced by the ceremonial role of the priests, much in the style of Chronicles. Because circumcision appears nowhere else in the Deuteronomistic History but plays a cardinal role in the priestly strand, the account of circumcision in Josh 5:2-8, which appears to interrupt the narrative, represents a priestly addition.

FOR FURTHER READING

Boling, Robert G., and G. Ernest Wright. *Joshua.* AB 6 Garden City, N.Y.: Doubleday, 1982.

Chaney, Marvin L. "Debt Easement in Israelite History and Tradition." In *The Bible and the Politics of Exegesis.* Edited by David Jobling, Peggy L. Day, and Gerald T. Sheppard. Cleveland: Pilgrim, 1991. 127-39.

———. "Joshua." In *The Books of the Bible.* Edited by Bernhard W. Anderson. New York: Charles Scribner's Sons, 1989.

Coogan, Michael D. "Joshua." In *The New Jerome Biblical Commentary.* Edited by Raymond E. Brown, Joseph A. Fitzmyer, and Roland E. Murphy. Englewood Cliffs, N.J.: Prentice Hall, 1990. 110-31.

Creach, Jerome F. D. *Joshua.* IBC. Louisville, Ky.: Westminster/John Knox, 2003.

Curtis, Andrian H. *Joshua.* Sheffield: Sheffield Academic, 1994.

Doorly, William J. *Obsession with Justice: The Story of the Deuteronomists.* New York: Paulist, 1994.

Hamlin, E. John. *Inheriting the Land: A Commentary on the Book of Joshua.* Grand Rapids: Eerdmans, 1983.

Harris, J. Gordon, Cheryl A. Brown, and Michael S. Moore. *Joshua, Judges, Ruth.* NIBCOT 5. Peabody, Mass.: Hendrickson, 2000.

Hawk, Daniel J. *Joshua.* Berit Olam. Collegeville, Minn.: Liturgical Press, 2000.

Hess, Richard S. *Joshua: An Introduction and Commentary.* Downer's Grove, Ill.: Inter-Varsity, 1996.

Na'aman, Nadav. "The 'Conquest of Canaan' in the Book of Joshua and in History." In *From Nomadism to Monarchy: Archaeological and Historical Aspects of Early Israel.* Edited by Israel Finkelstein and Nadav Na'aman. Jerusalem: Israel Exploration Society (1994) 218-81.

Nelson, Richard D. *Joshua.* OTL. Louisville: Westminster/John Knox, 1997.

Niditch, Susan N. *War in the Hebrew Bible: A Study in the Ethics of Violence.* New York: Oxford University Press, 1993.

Pressler, Carolyn. *Joshua, Judges, and Ruth.* Westminster Bible Companion. Louisville, Ky.: Westminster/John Knox, 2002.

Pury, Albert de, Thomas Römer, and Jean Daniel Macchi. *Israel Constructs its History: Deuteronomistic Historiography in Recent Research.* JSOTSupp 306. Sheffield: Sheffield Academic Press, 2000.

Soggin, J. Alberto. *Joshua: A Commentary.* Philadelphia: Westminster, 1972.

Woudstra, Marten H. *The Book of Joshua.* Grand Rapids: Eerdmans, 1981.

ENDNOTES

1. The standard work is Israel Finkelstein, *The Archaeology of the Israelite Settlement* (Jerusalem: Israel Exploration Society, 1988).

2. For early Israel, see Robert B. Coote, *Early Israel: A New Horizon* (Minneapolis: Fortress, 1990); Coote, "Early Israel," *Scandinavian Journal of the Old Testament* 5 (1991) 35-46; Coote, "Conquest: Biblical Narrative," in *Eerdmans Dictionary of the Bible*, ed. David Noel Freedman, Astrid B. Beck, and Allen C. Myers (Grand Rapids: Eerdmans, 2000) 274-276; Michael G. Hasel, "Israel in the Merneptah Stela," *BASOR* 296 (1994) 45-61; Israel Finkelstein and Nadav Na'aman, eds., *From Nomadism to Monarchy: Archaeological and Historical Aspects of Early Israel* (Jerusalem: Israel Exploration Society, 1994); Israel Finkelstein, "The Great Transformation: The 'Conquest' of the Highlands Frontiers and the Rise of the Territorial States," in *The Archaeology of Society in the Holy Land*, ed. Thomas E. Levy (New York: Facts on File, 1995) 349-65.

3. Deuteronomy became a part of a five-book Pentateuch, or Torah, late in the OT period, when the notion of an "Age of Moses" became a primary basis for partitioning Scripture. At that time the rest of the Deuteronomistic History, beginning with Joshua, became a part of the section of the Scriptures later called the Prophets.

4. Hans Walter Wolff, "The Kerygma of the Yahwist," in *The Vitality of Old Testament Traditions*, eds. Walter Brueggemann and Hans Walter Wolff, 2nd ed. (Atlanta: John Knox, 1982) 41-66; Robert B. Coote and David Robert Ord, *The Bible's First History* (Philadelphia: Fortress, 1989); Robert B. Coote, *In Defense of Revolution: The Elohist History* (Minneapolis: Fortress, 1991).

5. The first and last of these passages probably belong to the J strand. The middle two belong to a separate text regarding the Edomites that may have been incorporated into the J strand.

6. The verb הֶחֱרִם (*heḥerîm*, "dedicate" in the sense of "exterminate") occurs in the Tetrateuch only in Num 21:2-3, as a folk explanation of the name "Hormah," "Extermination" (cf. Josh 12:14). The name probably derives from the notion of a sacred or prohibited precinct.

7. Outside of Exodus 17 and Numbers 13–14, Joshua appears parenthetically in Exod 24:13; 32:17 (texts that belong to neither J nor E); 33:11 (Joshua is introduced as an aside, with no close tie to the story); Num 11:28 (Joshua is a superfluous double to the "young man" in v. 27); and Num 27:18, 22; 32:12, 28; 34:17, all texts, basically priestly, that come after the end of J and E. See George W. Ramsey, "Joshua," *ABD*, 3:999.

8. In the long history of Palestine, the Jordan has rarely formed a prominent natural boundary as it does in the Deuteronomistic History. The tribe of Manasseh traditionally occupied both sides of the Jordan precisely because it was not a boundary. In the biblical period, the Jordan as boundary appears to be attested for the first time in the eighth and seventh centuries BCE, as an administrative expedient instituted by the Assyrians, who, not surprisingly, were outsiders.

9. This episode also sets up a contrast with the Judahite Caleb, whose clan figures in the rise of David (Joshua 14). Because once Caleb, unlike Achan, alone obeyed Yahweh's command in battle, he later became the first member of the first tribe to receive a land grant on the west side of the Jordan.

10. The NRSV translates forms of חרם (*ḥārm*, "devote," "consecrate," "sanctify") with "destroy" or "annihilate," thereby misleadingly excluding the "religious" sense of the term, presumably because the practice was perceived by the translators as highly negative and hence not religious, and limiting its meaning to a "secular" sense; this is the reverse of the translators' approach to "fear," where they chose to exclude its secular sense,

which takes in the entire sphere of jurisdiction, and limit its meaning to the religious sense of "worship," a term that, perhaps, was felt to make "fear," which here was unmistakably religious, sound more positive. The traditional translation of *hērem* is "ban," emphasizing the prohibition.

11. Marvin L. Chaney, "Debt Easement in Israelite History and Tradition," in *The Bible and the Politics of Exegesis*, ed. David Jobling, Peggy L. Day, and Gerald T. Sheppard (Cleveland: Pilgrim, 1991) 131. The quotations on this subject that follow are from this article.

12. See Jonathan Z. Smith, "The Temple and the Magician," in *Map Is Not Territory: Studies in the History of Religions* (Leiden: Brill, 1978) 176, esp. note 19.

13. Frank S. Frick, *"Cui Bono?*—History in the Service of Political Nationalism: The Deuteronomistic History as Political Propaganda," *Semeia* 66 (1994) 79-92.

14. W. Eugene Claburn, "The Fiscal Basis of Josiah's Reforms," *JBL* 92 (1973) 11-22.

15. Rivka Gonen, *Burial Patterns and Cultural Diversity in Late Bronze Age Canaan* (Winona Lake, Ind.: Eisenbrauns, 1992), esp. 38-39; Elizabeth M. Bloch-Smith, "The Cult of the Dead in Judah: Interpreting the Material Remains," *JBL* 111 (1992) 213-24, esp. 214-19.

16. The lions sent by God to ravage the Assyrian plantations for not acknowledging the judicial authority of Bethel (2 Kgs 17:26) are ironically akin to the lion sent by God to kill the man of God from Judah for dining with the anonymous old prophet in Bethel (1 Kgs 13:11-32).

17. Mordechai Cogan, "Judah Under Assyrian Hegemony: A Reexamination of *Imperialism and Religion*," *JBL* 112 (1993) 403-14.

18. This distinction may have been disregarded or found unacceptable by the later writer who added 2 Kgs 17:34*b*-40 to the history written under Josiah. See *The New Oxford Annotated Bible*, ed. Bruce M. Metzger and Roland E. Murphy (New York: Oxford University Press, 1991) 489.

19. In this regard, Josiah followed in the footsteps of his grandfather Manasseh. See Anson F. Rainey, "Manasseh, King of Judah, in the Whirlpool of the Seventh Century BCE," in *Kinattūtu ša dārâti: Raphael Kutscher Memorial Volume*, ed. Anson F. Rainey (Tel Aviv: Institute of Archaeology, 1993) 147-64; J. P. J. Olivier,

"Money Matters: Some Remarks on the Economic Situation in the Kingdom of Judah During the Seventh Century B.C.," *Biblische Notizen* 73 (1994) 90-100; Israel Finkelstein, "The Archaeology of the Days of Manasseh," in *Scripture and Other Artifacts: Essays on the Bible and Archaeology in Honor of Philip J. King*, ed. Michael D. Coogan, J. Cheryl Exum, and Lawrence E. Stager (Louisville: Westminster John Knox, 1994) 169-87; Richard Nelson, *"Realpolitik* in Judah (687–609 BCE)," in *Scripture in Context II: More Essays on the Comparative Method*, ed. William W. Hallo, James C. Moyer, and Leo G. Perdue (Winona Lake, Ind.: Eisenbrauns, 1983) 177-89; J. Maxwell Miller and John H. Hayes, *A History of Ancient Israel and Judah* (Philadelphia: Westminster, 1986) 365-401; Duane L. Christensen, "Zephaniah 2:4-15: A Theological Basis for Josiah's Program of Political Expansion," *CBQ* 46 (1984) 669-82, esp. 678-81; Robert Althann, "Josiah," *ABD* 3:1015-18.

20. Richard D. Nelson, *The Double Redaction of the Deuteronomistic History* (Sheffield: JSOT, 1981) 122.

21. Benedict Anderson, *Imagined Communities: Reflections on the Origin and Spread of Nationalism* (New York: Verso, 1983); Ernest Gellner, *Nations and Nationalism* (Ithaca: Cornell University Press, 1983); Eric J. Hobsbawm, *Nations and Nationalism Since 1780* (New York: Cambridge University Press, 1990); Mario Liverani, "Nationality and Political Identity," *ABD* 4:1031-37; John Hutchinson and Anthony D. Smith, eds., *Nationalism* (New York: Oxford University Press, 1994).

22. Lori L. Rowlett, "Inclusion, Exclusion and Marginality in the Book of Joshua," *JSOT* 55 (1992) 15-23; Rowlett, *Joshua and the Rhetoric of Violence: A "New Historicist" Analysis* (Sheffield: Sheffield Academic, 1996).

23. Rowlett, "Inclusion, Exclusion and Marginality in the Book of Joshua," 23.

24. Rowlett, "Inclusion, Exclusion and Marginality in the Book of Joshua," 23. See also Danna Nolan Fewell, "Joshua," in *The Women's Bible Commentary*, ed. Carol A. Newsom and Sharon H. Ringe (Louisville: Westminster/John Knox, 1992) 63-66; Peter Machinist, "Outsiders or Insiders: The Biblical View of Emergent Israel and Its Contexts," in *The Other in Jewish Thought and History: Constructions of Jewish Culture and Identity*, ed. L. J. Silver-

stein and R. I. Cohn (New York: New York University Press, 1994) 35-60; E. Theodore Mullen, *Narrative History and Ethnic Boundaries: The Deuteronomistic History and the Creation of Israelite National Identity* (Atlanta: Scholars Press, 1992), which holds that the Deuteronomistic History is mainly an exilic composition. For more on Josiah's reform and the Deuteronomistic History, see Steven L. McKenzie, "Deuteronomistic History," *ABD* 2:160-68; Jeffries M. Hamilton, *Social Justice and Deuteronomy: The Case of Deuteronomy* 15:1 (Atlanta: Scholars Press, 1992); Shigeyuki Nakanose, *Josiah's Passover: Sociology and the Liberating Bible* (Maryknoll, N.Y.: Orbis, 1993); Gary N. Knoppers, *Two Nations Under God: The Deuteronomistic History of Solomon and the Dual Monarchies*, vol. 1: *The Reign of Solomon and the Rise of Jeroboam* (Atlanta: Scholars Press, 1993), vol. 2: *The Reign of Jeroboam, the Fall of Israel, and the Reign of Josiah* (Atlanta: Scholars Press, 1994); William G. Dever, "The Silence of the Text: An Archaeological Commentary on 2 Kings 23:1," in *Scripture and Other Artifacts: Essays on the Bible and Archaeology in Honor of Philip J. Kings*, ed. Michael D. Coogan, J. Cheryl Exum, and Lawrence E. Stager (Louisville: Westminster John Knox, 1994) 143-68; Erik Eynikel, *The Reform of King Josiah and the Composition of the Deuteronomistic History* (Leiden: E. J. Brill, 1995); Hieronymus Cruz, "Centralization of Cult by Josiah: A Biblical Perspective in Relation to Globalization," *Jeevadhara* 25 (1995) 65-71; William Schniedewind, "The Problem with Kings: Recent Study of the Deuteronomistic History," *Religious Studies Review* 22 (1996) 22-27.

THE BOOK OF
JUDGES

DENNIS T. OLSON

The book of Judges is one of the most exciting, colorful, and disturbing books of the Bible. It combines stories of political intrigue and assassination, lies and deception, rape and murder, courage and fear, great faith and idolatry, power and greed, sex and suicide, love and death, military victories and civil war. The book portrays a major transition in the biblical story of Israel. Before the book of Judges, Israel was under the leadership of Moses in the wilderness (Exodus–Deuteronomy) and then Joshua in the initial conquest of the land of Canaan (Joshua). After the book of Judges, Israel was ruled by kings, beginning with Saul, David, and Solomon and concluding with Judah's defeat and exile to Babylon (1–2 Samuel; 1–2 Kings; see 2 Kings 24–25). The turbulent transition between Moses and Joshua, on one hand, and the kings of Israel, on the other hand, is portrayed in the book of Judges. The book presents the varied tales of twelve warrior rulers, called judges, who led ancient Israel for brief periods in times of military emergency.

The book's title, "Judges," may bring to mind images of wise people who arbitrate legal cases in courts. Indeed, one of the so-called judges, Deborah, appears to function in this way as a mediator of disputes (4:4-5). However, the term "judge" (שֹׁפֵט *šōpēṭ*) in Hebrew can also mean "rule" or "ruler," and it is this meaning of the term that applies to the major characters in the book.[1] They are primarily warrior rulers who led Israel in fighting oppressive enemies. The judges were also involved in maintaining Israel's religious life and institutions with varying degrees of success (2:17; 5:1-31; 6:25-27; 8:22-28).

JUDGES AND HISTORY

Scholars have debated the value of the book of Judges in reconstructing the early history of ancient Israel after its settlement in the land of Canaan in the twelfth and eleventh centuries BCE. Some commentators assume that many of the events and people recounted in Judges do reflect actual historical situations in this early period, although the stories have been significantly reshaped and edited.[2] For example, scholars argue that the ongoing struggle of the Israelites with other nations in Canaan over a long period of time in Judges may provide a more accurate picture of the conquest of Canaan than does the quick and total conquest as depicted in some parts of Joshua (Josh 11:23). Scholars also point to the Song of Deborah and Barak in Judges 5 as one of the most ancient parts of the Bible, with its origin in the period of the judges or the early monarchy.

Yet, scholars are also cautious about using Judges to reconstruct early Israelite history.[3] For example, if one adds all of the years of enemy oppression and the length of the judges' rule throughout the book (e.g., 3:8, 11), the total comes to 480 years. But, that is far too long a period to fit the roughly 300 years between the exodus, dated sometime in the thirteenth century, and the rise of kingship in the tenth century BCE. Moreover, some of the judges' stories may have originally been tales of local heroes and chieftains of small clan or tribal groups. The tales were then later rewritten so that they became stories of leaders of larger Israelite coalitions as they were incorporated into the book of Judges. Still other scholars believe that we simply do not have adequate evidence from archaeological or other textual sources to evaluate the overall historicity of the events in Judges.

METHODS IN THE
INTERPRETATION OF JUDGES

The lively characters, the moral difficulties, the turbulent social context, and the theological questions that animate the book of Judges have occasioned a wide spectrum of response in the history of biblical interpretation. The rabbinic debate over whether Jephthah's daughter was actually offered as a burnt sacrifice and the ancient Christian interpretation of the death of Samson as a typological prefigurement of the death of Jesus are only two of many intriguing examples of the ancient approportion of Judges. Modern historical-critical interpretation of Judges has paid the most attention to the history of the composition of the book in the light of proposals for the growth of the larger Deuteronomistic History (Deuteronomy and Joshua–2 Kings). Most scholars agree that Judges emerged through several stages of collecting, writing, and editing.[4] Originally separate stories of local clan or tribal heroes were assembled into a larger connected narrative. Editorial sections were added at key junctures in and around the stories. A definitive two-part introduction (1:1–2:5; 2:6–3:6) and a two-part conclusion (17:1–18:31; 19:1–21:25) were also added in two or more editorial stages. This process occurred over many generations, culminating in two or three definitive periods of editorial shaping, including the time of King Hezekiah (eighth century BCE), King Josiah (seventh century BCE), and sometime after the exile of Judah to Babylon (sixth–fifth century BCE). The audience for the final form of Judges probably included the people of Judah, who had experienced the exile to Babylon and the disintegration of their social, political, and religious life (2 Kings 24–25). Judges continued to be read and interpreted in new contexts and thus lived on as a biblical paradigm for future generations.

The book of Judges has been an exceptionally fertile ground for a wide variety of newer approaches to biblical interpretation.[5] Narrative analyses of plot, character, point of view, repetition, and theme have proved to be profitable avenues of study. Judges contains one of the Bible's largest concentrations of female characters, nineteen in all. The variety of women in Judges has offered a rich resource for feminist scholarship on the relationship of women, power, and violence. Social-scientific criticism has found grist for its mill in the questions of the formation of Israelite society in the judges period, the function of kinship association in a tribal society, and the role of the judges as chieftains in the rise of Israelite kingship. Structuralist, deconstructive, and ideological criticisms have also found Judges to be amenable to

their various strategies and methods of reading. The study of Judges is also informed by the Russian literary theorist Mikhail Bakhtin and his notion of competing dialogical voices and themes that are held together but not absorbed into one another.[6]

THE SHIFT FROM REPETITIVE CYCLES TO GRADUAL DECLINE

The book of Judges is often associated with a repetitive pattern or cycle outlined in 2:11-19 and repeated throughout the narratives of individual judges: Israel does evil, God sends an enemy; Israel cries in distress, God sends a judge or deliverer; Israel again does evil, and the cycle repeats. The cyclical pattern probably defined an earlier editorial layer of Judges. However, editors of the final form made important changes and additions that redefined the basic movement of the book's plot. These changes redefined the judges era from its characterization as a series of flat cycles in endless repetition to a downward slide and increasingly severe disintegration of Israel's social and religious life. These changes included altering the two-part introduction to Judges so that it described the gradual deterioration of the twelve tribes' conquest of Canaan (1:1–2:5) and the gradual decline of Israel's faithfulness to the covenant with God (2:6–3:6).

The stories of the individual judges (3:7–16:31) also have been edited to exhibit a similar gradual decline from initial success and faithfulness among the early judges (Othniel, Ehud, Deborah, and Barak) to eventual ineffectiveness and unfaithfulness among the later judges (Jephthah, Samson). In the final chapters of Judges, Israel is portrayed as having no king or ruler, and "all the people did what was right in their own eyes" (17:6; 21:25). Israel disintegrates into religious and social chaos in this final phase of the judges era (17:1–21:25). God allowed Israel to hit bottom as punishment for its increasing sinfulness and idolatry. Yet in the midst of Israel's unraveling and near-death experiences, glimpses of hope emerge. Samson's shaved hair began to grow back (16:22). A faithful house of God remained functioning in northern Israel at Shiloh in spite of the idolatrous cult at Dan (18:30). The tribe of Benjamin was pulled back from the brink of extinction and death (20:46–21:24). God remained present and active even in the midst of sinful and tragic circumstances (20:18, 21, 28, 35).

IMPORTANT THEMES
IN DIALOGICAL TENSION

The book of Judges contains a wide array of dialogical perspectives on key themes. The book holds together seemingly opposed or disjunctive viewpoints on the same subject. Only a few examples are cited here. This dialectical character of Judges was the basis for Martin Buber's proposal that Judges contains two "books," an anti-monarchical book that opposes dynastic kingship (chaps. 1–12) and a pro-monarchical book that supports dynastic kingship (chaps. 13–21).[7] The first anti-kingship section offers a critique of foreign kings, like Adoni-bezek (1:5-7), fat King Eglon (3:15-25), and King Jabin of Canaan (4:23-24). In this same section, Gideon rejects the offer to become a king over Israel (8:22-23), and Jotham ridicules Abimelech's disastrous attempt to become an Israelite king (9:7-15). In contrast, Buber argued that the second half of Judges, chapters 13–21, is pro-kingship in that it laments the chaos and disintegration of Israel in a time when "there was no king in Israel" and "all the people did what was right in their own eyes" (17:6; 18:1; 19:1; 21:25).

However, in my judgment the book's view of kingship is more consistent throughout the book than Buber suggests, but no less dialectical.[8] The book of Judges affirms the need for human kingship in Israel *at this particular time in Israel's history* at the end of the judges era. However, the editors and readers of the final form of Judges and the Deuteronomistic History also know that kingship, like the institution of judgeship, will be flawed, temporary, and eventually collapse. Kingship in Israel, like the judges, will in time be replaced by another form of human leadership, which will be necessary but also provisional and imperfect. The era of the judges thus becomes a paradigm of any human institution, mode of governance, or ideology—necessary but provisional, helpful for a time, but eventually replaced by another.

Examples of other themes held in dialogical tension throughout Judges include the interplay of religion and politics, the well-being of women and the health of society, the benefits and threats of relationships with people of other nations, human character as both noble and deeply flawed, the subtle interplay of divine and human agency and actions, and small signs of hope in the midst of horrendous chaos and social disintegration. One final and overriding tension throughout Judges is the interplay of God's justice or punishment and God's mercy or compassion. God repeatedly punishes Israel for its continual evil, and yet God cannot let Israel go. This increasingly intense dance between divine justice and mercy raises questions as the reader moves through the chapters of Judges: How far can God's patience and mercy be stretched until it reaches a breaking point? How far can Israel stray from the covenant before God gives up on Israel altogether? The angel's words in 2:1-5 pose the tension. On one hand, God affirms to Israel, "I will never break my covenant with you" (2:1). But on the other hand, God promises to punish Israel because "you have not obeyed my command" (2:2). In the end, God's mercy will sustain God's relationship with Israel, but Israel will go through a time of national chaos and death in order for a new generation to be born and a new way forward to emerge as Israel's experiment in kingship opens up into the narratives about the rise of kingship in 1–2 Samuel.

FOR FURTHER READING

Commentaries:

Boling, Robert G. *Judges*, AB 6A. Garden City, N.Y.: Doubleday, 1975.

Gray, John. *Joshua, Judges, Ruth*. NCBC. Grand Rapids: Eerdmans, 1986.

Hamlin, E. John. *Judges: At Risk in the Promised Land*. ITC. Grand Rapids: Eerdmans, 1990.

Harris, J. Gordon, Cheryl A. Brown, and Michael S. Moore. *Joshua, Judges, Ruth*. NIBCOT 5. Peabody, Mass.: Hendrickson, 2000.

Matthews, Victor H. *Judges and Ruth*. New Cambridge Bible Commentary. New York: Cambridge University Press, 2004.

McCann, J. Clinton, Jr. *Judges*. IBC. Louisville, Ky.: Westminster/John Knox, 2002

Pressler, Carolyn. *Joshua, Judges, and Ruth*. Westminster Bible Companion. Louisville, Ky.: Westminster/John Knox, 2002.

Schneider, Tammi J. *Judges*. Berit Olam. Collegeville, Minn.: Liturgical Press, 2000.

Soggin, J. Alberto. *Judges*. OTL. Philadelphia: Westminster, 1981.

Other studies:

Bal, Mieke. *Death and Dissymmetry: The Politics of Coherence in the Book of Judges*. Chicago: University of Chicago Press, 1988.

Brenner, Athalya, ed. *A Feminist Companion to Judges*. Sheffield: JSOT, 1993.

———. ed. *Judges: A Feminist Companion to the Bible*. Feminist Companion to the Bible. Second Series 8. Sheffield: Sheffield Academic Press, 1999.

Jeter, Joseph R. *Preaching Judges*. Preaching Classic Texts. Saint Louis: Chalice Press, 2003

Klein, Lillian R. *The Triumph of Irony in the Book of Judges*. Sheffield: Almond, 1989.

Marcus, David. *Jephthah and His Vow*. Lubbock, Tex.: Texas Tech Press, 1986.

Polzin, Robert. *Moses and the Deuteronomist: A Literary Study of the Deuteronomic History*. New York: Seabury, 1980.

Trible, Phyllis. *Texts of Terror: Literary-Feminist Readings of Biblical Narratives*. Philadelphia: Fortress, 1984.

Stone, Lawson. "From Tribal Confederation to Monarchic State: The Editorial Perspective of the Book of Judges." Ph.D. dissertation, Yale University. Ann Arbor: University Microfilms, 1987.

Webb, Barry. *The Book of the Judges: An Integrated Reading*. Sheffield: JSOT, 1987.

Yee, Gale A., ed. *Judges and Method: New Approaches in Biblical Studies*. Minneapolis: Fortress, 1995.

ENDNOTES

1. Temba L. J. Mafico, "Judge, Judging," in *The Anchor Bible Dictionary*, 6 vols. (New York: Doubleday, 1992) 3:1104.

2. Robert G. Boling, *Judges*, AB 6A (Garden City, N.Y.: Doubleday, 1975) 9-29.

3. J. Alberto Soggin, *Judges*, OTL (Philadelphia: Westminster, 1981) 6-12.

4. An insightful survey and proposal for the editorial shaping of Judges is offered by Lawson Stone, "From Tribal Confederation to Monarchic State: The Editorial Perspective of the Book of Judges" (Ph.D. diss., Yale University; Ann Arbor: University Microfilms, 1987). Much of my view of the overall structure and movement of Judges is indebted to Stone's work.

5. A survey of new methods as applied to Judges is Gale Yee, ed., *Judges and Method: New Approaches in Biblical Studies* (Minneapolis: Fortress, 1995).

6. Among other works, see Mikhail Bakhtin, *Problems of Dostoevsky's Poetics*, ed. and trans. Caryl Emerson (Minneapolis: University of Minnesota Press, 1984), and *The Dialogic Imagination: Four Essays by M. M. Bakhtin*, ed. Michael Holquist (Austin: University of Texas Press, 1981). An example of a biblical scholar's application of Bakhtin's insights to some aspects of Judges is Robert Polzin, *Moses and the Deuteronomist: A Literary Study of the Deuteronomic History* (New York: Seabury, 1980).

7. Martin Buber, "The Books of Judges and the Book of Judges," in *The Kingship of God* (New York: Harper & Row, 1967) 66-84.

8. Stone, "From Tribal Confederation to Monarchic State," 77-84, 373-89. Stone reaches similar but not identical conclusions on Buber and Judges' view of kingship.

THE BOOK OF
RUTH

KATHLEEN A. ROBERTSON FARMER

The book of Ruth contains an artistically constructed, kaleidoscopic narrative that is more like an extended parable than a historical report. The story is told with extreme narrative economy (a style that includes deliberate gaps or silences that leave many details unexplained) and with a characteristic disregard for historical or political details. The narrator uses symbolic names (such as the names of Naomi's sons, signifying in advance that they are not long for this world), word play (such as puns and double entendres), and the purposeful repetition of words and phrases to highlight themes and underline ambiguities. The "sophisticated literary artistry of the author" is marked by "the conscious intentional employment of multiple levels of meaning in the narrative."[1]

THE INTERPRETIVE CHALLENGE

In form and function, the book of Ruth closely resembles both the book of Jonah and the story Nathan tells to David in 2 Sam 12:1-7, without Nathan's accusatory line ("You are the man!") at the end. Like Nathan's story, and like Jonah, Ruth has the power of revealing us to ourselves *as we are* rather than as we think we ought to be. But unlike Nathan's story, Ruth and Jonah are *not* presented to us by a prophet who is willing and able to tell us who we are within the dynamics of the story.

Thus the interpretive challenge in both stories lies in the area of identification. We can rather easily argue that Jonah was a personification of the Jewish audience to whom the book itself was addressed. "Israel itself is symbolized in Jonah's person, a stubborn and self-isolating Israel that is always occupied with itself, evading the actual will of God, and unaware that God loves other peoples just as much as Israel itself."[2] But which of the characters in the book of Ruth can be said to mirror the people of God?

Generations of interpreters have held up the character of Ruth as a model of morality. Like the "good Samaritan" in Luke 10:30-37, Ruth is an admirable character from an ethnic group that was despised and rejected by those who considered themselves to be the "people of God." Ruth's admirability tempts interpreters to tell themselves and their audiences, "We *ought* to be or act like this." But an interpreter's advice to "go and do likewise" (as wise as it may be) never comes to an audience with the force of revelation. Nathan's exclamation in 2 Sam 12:7 has revelatory power because it uses the mirror of the story to reveal David to himself. But seeing themselves mirrored in the character for whom the book of Ruth is named will not lead an audience either to repentance or to hope for their own redemption.

REDEMPTION AND IDENTIFICATION

The purposeful repetition of key terms in the book of Ruth encourages us to consider Naomi as the character who most closely mirrors the attitudes and experiences of the people of God, including both Israel and the church. Repetition indicates that "redemption" is a key concern in the story of Ruth. The book is only eighty-five verses long, but the word "redeem" (גאל *gāʾal*) and its derivatives ("redeemer," "redemption") are used some twenty-three times. Asking who or what is redeemed leads to the discovery that Naomi is the ultimate recipient of redemption in the story.

On a superficial level, we might say that the story of Ruth is about redemption defined in a secular manner, as the restoration of property to its original owners or as the healing of a break in a branch of a family tree. The final scene in the story (4:13-17), however, hints at a deeper level of meaning. In 4:14 the audience discovers that Naomi is to be "redeemed" through the child

113

whose conception was said to have been given by the LORD (4:13). The women of Bethlehem, who know how bitter Naomi has been about the emptiness of her life, tell us that this "redeemer" will "restore" or "reverse" Naomi's "life" (using the word וֶפֶשׁ [nepeš], which is often translated "soul").

Reversal is the essence of redemption. Within the story world Naomi is the primary object of redemption. It is Naomi whose life is turned around, whose feelings of bitterness, emptiness, and hopelessness are reversed. Ruth's faithfulness is only the *instrument* God uses to accomplish Naomi's redemption.

If the story told in the book of Ruth is to be redemptive for the people of God, then the people of God must identify themselves with the one who *is* redeemed. The story of Ruth becomes a story of redemption for Israel only if Israel can be persuaded to believe that the redemptive efforts made by God on Naomi's behalf will be made by God on Israel's behalf as well.

Ruth, the outsider, the representative of a group that Deut 23:3 refuses to admit to "the assembly of the LORD," is the agent or tool God uses to bring about the redemption of Israel/Naomi. The parable-like form of the narrative encourages us to see not just that we *ought* to be like Ruth but that we *are* like Naomi. And when we see ourselves reflected in the story as we really are (rather than as we think we ought to be), the good news comes to us as revelation rather than application.

Thus a redemptive reading of Ruth will assume that the story is primarily concerned with the faithfulness of God rather than with the faithfulness of the people of God. In Ruth, redemption is based on grace, not merit. Redemption is not a reward given to Naomi because of her exemplary behavior. God chooses to redeem those who seem to have done little to deserve redemption. And God chooses to use those who seem unqualified according to human standards of judgment to accomplish God's purposes in the world. The admirability of the "other" in the story (be they Samaritan or Moabite) should serve primarily to convict us of our own repeated failures to recognize the despised "other" as an agent of God's redemptive activity in the world.

CANONICAL LOCATIONS AND THEIR IMPLICATIONS

Different Bibles place the book of Ruth in different locations. In Christian Bibles (following the Septuagint), Ruth is found in the "Former Prophets," the traditional name for the narrative sequence from Joshua to 2 Kings. But the Hebrew Bible puts Ruth among the Writings, the division of the canon that includes wisdom literature and Psalms. In the Hebrew text, Ruth is one of the *Megilloth* ("The Five Scrolls") set apart for liturgical use in the major religious festivals of Judaism. Ruth is read aloud in the synagogue as a part of the two-day celebration of *Shavuot*, the Feast of Weeks (which is also called Pentecost because it falls fifty days—seven weeks plus one day—after the beginning of Passover). The Feast of Weeks celebrates both the end of the grain harvest season and the giving of the Torah, marking the covenant between Yahweh and the people of Israel.[3] The connection between the festival and the book is both seasonal (the action in Ruth takes place during the grain harvest) and symbolic (God's love for Israel culminates in a marriage/covenant oriented toward redemption).

The canonizers responsible for the order of the books in Christian Bibles may not have intended to convey any particular theological meaning by their placement of Ruth between Judges and 1 Samuel. They may have intended merely to put as many books as possible in chronological order. However, once it was done (for whatever reason) it must be acknowledged that "the narrative that includes [Ruth] differs from the narrative that excludes it."[4] When Ruth is read in between Judges and Samuel, it functions both as a spacer and as a bridge between the end of the period when "there was no king in Israel" (Judg 21:25) and the beginning of the united monarchy. On the one hand, the opening of Ruth ("In the days when the Judges ruled") implies that the period of the judges is an era now gone by, making the book of Judges seem quite distant and separate from the action in 1 Samuel. On the other hand, the way Ruth begins with a reference to the judges and ends with a reference to David informs the reader in advance that the episodes in Samuel dealing with Saul are little more than a detour on the road to the dynasty that really matters, the Davidic line of kings.[5]

Taken together, Judges 19–21 and Ruth seem to condemn the origins of Saul and commend the origins of David for ethical rather than ethnic reasons.[6] God's rejection of Saul can be anticipated by the reader who notes that Saul comes from Gibeah (the source of the appalling behavior described in Judges 19–21). Saul has an ethnically "pure" family tree, but he seems to have inherited his ancestors' tendency to disregard God's sovereignty. In contrast, David's family tree is rooted in the remarkably loyal behavior of a foreigner who has voluntarily chosen to join herself and her future to the Lord. Thus if Ruth is read in between Judges and 1 Samuel, it seems to function as a "witness to the moral legitimacy of the Davidic monarchy."[7] When Judges, Ruth, and Samuel are read together as a single story, it seems that David, with his "outsider" blood, is more of an insider with God than is Saul, whose bloodlines are not tainted by intermarriage but whose ancestors *acted* in a tainted way.

In the Hebrew Bible, Ruth is surrounded by post-exilic, poetic and wisdom-oriented texts. The reader who encounters Ruth among the Writings is more inclined to see the story as a parable than as an apology, or as an example story rather than royal propaganda. Many of the psalms are assigned to David, and a large section of 1 Chronicles (chaps. 10–29) is devoted to the kingship of David. In this literary context, the book of Ruth seems to assume the greatness rather than defend the legitimacy of the Davidic line of kings. Thus readers of Ruth in the Hebrew Bible are more likely to conclude that it teaches a lesson that could function equally well in any historical setting. An early rabbinic interpreter says Ruth was written "to teach how great is the reward of those who do deeds of kindness,"[8] and a modern literary critic says that the moral of the story is, "Common people achieve uncommon ends when they act unselfishly toward each other."[9]

Since many of the Writings are obviously post-exilic in origin, Ruth's placement in the Hebrew Bible tends to support those who think the story of Ruth was developed in the fifth century BCE as a way of casting doubt on the wisdom of Ezra and Nehemiah's attempt to cast all foreign wives out of the restoration community of Israel.[10]

THE AMBIGUITY OF DATING

We cannot date the composition of the book of Ruth with any degree of certainty. The linguistic evidence is so ambiguous that equally valid arguments can be formulated to support either an early or a late date.[11]

Some readers jump from the observation of Ruth's function in its literary context in Christian Bibles to the conclusion that Ruth was *written* in David's time as an attempt to establish David's right to the throne. However, an apology for the righteous origins of the Davidic dynasty might have served the purposes of later writers as well. The exilic editors of the Deuteronomic History (the narrative sequence from Joshua to Kings) were interested in reflecting on faithful and unfaithful forms of leadership in Israel and Judah, and the post-exilic work of the chronicler was dedicated to exalting the successful kingship of David over against the failures of Saul.

In his own lifetime, David would have been known as a successful and powerful king who had overcome the military opponents of Israel and expanded the borders of the kingdom, while creating a sense of national identity among various tribal and ethnic groups. But David's greatest fame in Israel came in retrospect, as people in later times looked back on the beginnings of the Davidic dynasty, which had become remarkable for its stability and longevity. Long after David's own time, as the gap between the theological ideals projected onto human kingship and the historical realities perpetrated by human kings continued to widen, the faithful in Israel began to look for a future king descended from David (a "messiah" [מָשִׁיחַ *māšîaḥ*], meaning "an anointed one") whose reign would bring about true security, justice, and well-being. Thus David's significance did not diminish with time but grew even greater in the years just before and just after the Babylonian Exile (587–539 BCE).

READING RUTH IN VARIOUS LIFE SETTINGS

Reading history through the lens of Ruth is more like looking through a kaleidoscope than a microscope. While the dominant themes of redemption and insider/outsider dynamics remain constant within the story, every rotation of the proposed background against which the story is read causes these themes to fall into a different pattern. Every attempt to fill in the silences in the story produces a new shade of meaning.

If we imagine an audience of people in David's own time concerned with the purity of David's bloodline, we can see how reading Ruth might have persuaded them that the Moabite "taint" in David's ancestry was "redeemed" when the Moabite in question was shown to be an admirable convert to Judaism.[12] If we imagine an audience at a later date concerned with what it was that qualified one line of kings to rule "forever," we can see how reading Ruth may have convinced them that lovingkindness (not ethnic purity) gave birth to the messianic line of kings. If Ruth is read by people who are gravely concerned over the fragmentation of Israel, it may seem that "in the reunion of Ruth and Naomi, whom even death will not separate, the old sad break between the families of Lot and Abraham is repaired, and from that reforging of patriarchal bonds, there will be a new birth of salvation."[13] And if the book is read and studied by people who are being forced to choose between those who want to cast all foreign influences out of their community of faith (Neh 13:1-3) and those who insist that the "house of the LORD" should be a "house of prayer for all peoples" (Isa 56:1-8), such an audience must have heard the story of Ruth as supporting the fruitfulness of the inclusive position.

In fact, the parabolic nature of the narrative makes tenuous every attempt to pin its origins down to one particular setting in the life of Israel. The enduring appeal of Ruth depends precisely upon this non-specificity, which allows the story to function effectively as revelation in our own as well as in Israel's eyes. When the kaleidoscope of history spins into our own time, we must consider how people in a country that is in the process of tightening its immigration laws in order to protect its cultural identity will see or hear themselves reflected in the dynamics of the text. Every new reader is challenged afresh to recognize his or her own present reality mirrored in a narrative that both convicts us of our lack of merit and assures us of God's redemptive inclinations.

FOR FURTHER READING

Commentaries:

Bush, Frederic. *Ruth/Esther*. WBC 9. Dallas: Word, 1996.

Campbell, Edward F., Jr. *Ruth*. AB 7. Garden City, N.Y.: Doubleday, 1975.

Hubbard, Robert L., Jr. *The Book of Ruth*. NICOT. Grand Rapids: Eerdmans, 1988.

Linafelt, Tod, and Timothy K. Beal. *Ruth and Esther*. Berit Olam. Collegeville, Minn.: Liturgical Press, 1999.

Sakenfeld, Katharine Doob. *Ruth*. IBC. Louisville, Ky.: Westminster/John Knox, 1999.

Other studies:

Bos, Johanna W. H. *Ruth, Esther, Jonah*. Knox Preaching Guides. Edited by John H. Hayes. Atlanta: John Knox, 1986.

Brenner, Athalya, ed. *A Feminist Companion to Ruth*. Feminist Companion to the Bible. First Series 3. Sheffield: Sheffield Academic Press, 1993.

———. *Ruth and Esther: A Feminist Companion to the Bible*. Feminist Companion to the Bible. Second Series 3. Sheffield: Sheffield Academic Press, 1999.

Fewell, Danna Nolan, and David Miller Gunn. *Compromising Redemption: Relating Characters in the Book of Ruth*. Literary Currents in Biblical Interpretation. Louisville: Westminster/John Knox, 1990.

Kates, Judith A., and Gail Twersky Reimer, eds. *Reading Ruth: Contemporary Women Reclaim a Sacred Story*. New York: Ballantine, 1994.

Korpel, Marjo C. A. *The Structure of the Book of Ruth*. Pericope 2. Assen: Van Gorcum, 2001.

LaCocque, André. "Ruth." In *The Feminine Unconventional: Four Subversive Figures in Israel's Tradition*. OBT. Minneapolis: Fortress, 1990.

Sasson, Jack M. *Ruth: A New Translation with a Philological Commentary and a Formalist-Folklorist Interpretation*. Baltimore: John Hopkins University Press, 1979.

Trible, Phyllis. "A Human Comedy." In *God and the Rhetoric of Sexuality*. OBT. Philadelphia: Fortress, 1978.

ENDNOTES

1. Moshe J. Bernstein, "Two Multivalent Readings in the Ruth Narrative," *JSOT* 50 (1991) 15-16.

2. Gerhard Lohfink, *The Bible: Now I Get It! A Form-Criticism Handbook*, trans. Daniel Coogan (Garden City, N.Y.: Doubleday, 1979) 83.

3. See Abraham P. Bloch, *The Biblical and Historical Background of the Jewish Holy Days* (New York: KTAV, 1978) 179-89.

4. David Jobling, "Ruth Finds a Home: Canon, Politics, Method," in *The New Literary Criticism and the Hebrew Bible*, ed. J. Cheryl Exum and David J. A. Clines (Valley Forge: Trinity Press International, 1993) 126.

5. David Jobling, "Ruth Finds a Home: Canon, Politics, Method," 130-31.

6. See Warren Austin Gage, "Ruth Upon the Threshing Floor and the Sin of Gibeah: A Biblical-Theological Study," *Westminster Theological Journal* 51 (1989) 369-75.

7. See Warren Austin Gage, "Ruth Upon the Threshing Floor and the Sin of Gibeah: A Biblical-Theological Study," *Westminster Theological Journal* 51 (1989), 370.

8. *Ruth Rabbah* II.14, L. Rabinowitz, trans. (London: Socino Press, 1939).

9. Jack M. Sasson, "Ruth," in *The Literary Guide to the Bible*, ed. Robert Alter and Frank Kermode (Cambridge, Mass.: Harvard University Press, 1987) 321.

10. Although this idea has circulated since the early 1800s, it has been given its best modern presentation by André LaCocque, "Ruth," in *The Feminine Unconventional: Four Subversive Figures in Israel's Tradition* (Minneapolis: Fortress, 1990) 84-116.

11. Edward L. Greenstein, *Essays on Biblical Method and Translation*, BJS 92 (Atlanta, 1989) 14-15.

12. Murray D. Gow, *The Book of Ruth: Its Structure, Theme, and Purpose* (Leicester: Apollos, 1992) 182.

13. Harold Fisch, "Ruth and the Structure of Covenant History," *VT* 32 (1982) 435.

THE FIRST AND SECOND BOOKS OF SAMUEL

BRUCE C. BIRCH

The books of 1 and 2 Samuel witness to one of the most crucial periods of transition and change in the story of ancient Israel. At the opening of 1 Samuel, Israel is a loose federation of tribes, experiencing both external threat from the militarily superior Philistines and internal crisis because of the corruption of the priestly house of Eli at Shiloh, where the ark was maintained and covenant traditions were preserved. At the conclusion of 2 Samuel, an emerging monarchy is firmly in place under David. He has weathered various threats to the integrity of the kingdom, and is preparing to establish a hereditary dynasty in Israel. The momentous changes necessitated by this transition to kingship provide some of the most dramatic stories in the Old Testament. These stories not only narrate dramatic events but also introduce us to some of the most striking characters in the biblical story. Samuel, Saul, and David, whose stories overlap, dominate the pages of the books of Samuel. Moreover, even the supporting cast is remarkable for the variety of sharply drawn characters that flesh out the pages of these stories—Hannah, Eli, Jonathan, Michal, Joab, Abigail, Abishai, Abner, Bathsheba, Nathan, Amnon, Tamar, Absalom, Mephibosheth, to name only a few. Yet, beyond these personalities and events, the books of Samuel make clear that the Lord is at work in these turbulent times. On the surface, these stories may seem preoccupied with political power, but we will discover that these narratives testify to the true power of the Lord, acting in and through personalities and events to bring Israel to a new future in keeping with God's purposes.

TITLE AND DIVISION OF THE BOOKS OF SAMUEL

The books of 1 and 2 Samuel were originally one book. The oldest Hebrew manuscript from Qumran (4QSam[a]) includes both 1 and 2 Samuel on a single scroll. Moreover, the Talmud references allude to a single book of Samuel. The division into two books was probably introduced by the Greek translators (the Septuagint), perhaps to create scrolls of a more manageable size. In Septuagint manuscripts, the books of Samuel and Kings are divided into four books called 1–4 Kingdoms. This division and its designations were adopted by Jerome in his Latin translation (the Vulgate) and became the common designation in Roman Catholic Bibles until the mid-twentieth century. The manuscripts of the Masoretic text (Hebrew) assume a one-book arrangement. The division into 1 and 2 Samuel did not appear until the fifteenth century and became common with the first printed editions of the Hebrew Bible in the sixteenth century.[1]

The decision about the place at which to divide the books was undoubtedly influenced by the custom of concluding books with the death of a major figure (e.g., Joseph/Genesis; Moses/Deuteronomy; Joshua/Joshua). Thus the division of the books of Samuel was placed after the death of Saul. It is curious, however, that the two versions of Saul's death are separated by this division (1 Samuel 31; 2 Samuel 1). The retention of the name "Samuel" for the divided arrangement also creates the anomaly of a 2 Samuel named for the prophet Samuel, who does not appear at all in the book.

TEXT OF THE BOOKS OF SAMUEL

The Hebrew text of 1 and 2 Samuel (the Masoretic text) on which English translations have been routinely based is in extremely poor condition.[2] Its text for these books is much shorter than the text of the ancient Greek translation of the Hebrew Bible, the Septuagint (LXX), and other ancient versions of the text of 1 and 2 Samuel. Until recently, many scholars assumed that the Greek translators had simply added traditions known to them and thus expanded the text. However, other scholars offered a different explanation—namely, that the Hebrew text had suffered numerous omissions and copying errors. This latter assumption was confirmed by the discovery, beginning in 1952, of three fragmentary Samuel manuscripts in the library of the ancient community of Qumran, beside the shores of the Dead Sea.[3] The most important of these, 4QSam[a], was written in the first century BCE and contains large portions of 1 and 2 Samuel in a well-preserved condition. The second, 4QSam[b], dates from the mid-third century but contains only poorly preserved fragments of a small portion of 1 Samuel. And the third, 4QSam[c], also from the first century, contains only fragments of 1 Samuel 25:1 and 2 Samuel 14:1–15.

The failure to publish many of the Qumran texts promptly has delayed the impact of this material on English translations of the books of Samuel. However, the work of Ulrich and McCarter (both cited above) has given wide circulation to the longer LXX/Qumran readings for 1 and 2 Samuel. Frank Cross used the Qumran material in translating the books of Samuel for the NAB (1970). More recent translations (including the NRSV and the NIV) have been able to use this textual material, and as a consequence have often adopted many of the longer readings reflected in the LXX and Qumran texts.

LITERARY COMPOSITION
OF THE BOOKS OF SAMUEL

It is generally agreed that analysis of the process by which the books of Samuel were composed comprises one of the most complex subjects in twentieth-century biblical study. Current views on the literary composition of 1 and 2 Samuel offer no clear-cut consensus. I can only summarize briefly some of the major positions and approaches concerning the formation of the books of Samuel.

Earlier Approaches. Repetitions, doublets, contradictions, and contrasting viewpoints in the stories and traditions of 1 and 2 Samuel led scholars in the late nineteenth and early twentieth centuries to look for multiple literary strands or sources that could be traced throughout the books of Samuel.[4] Some identified literary sources in the books of Samuel that they thought were continuations of those present in the Pentateuch, but this view was largely abandoned in the early twentieth century. A more prominent theory involved the view that the books of Samuel were made up of an early and a late source. Although details differed, many scholars until the mid-twentieth century defended some variation on this hypothesis. The early source was thought to offer a more positive assessment of the development of monarchy in Israel and also to be more historically reliable. The late source was responsible for additions to the text that created inconsistencies and redundancies. This late source was negative toward kingship and considered to provide a less reliable historical source for the period. This theory of an early and a late source has been largely abandoned. Both supportive and antagonistic attitudes toward kingship in Israel are likely to have arisen from Saul's time onward and not simply to be the product of late experience with kings. Furthermore, the negative views associated with the kingship of Saul disappear in positive approval of David when he enters the story. In sum, theories of composition for the books of Samuel have become more complex. Moreover, few scholars think that the traditions now included in the books of Samuel offer a neutral historical reconstruction of that period.

In 1926, Leonhard Rost published his influential study of 2 Samuel 9:1–20 and 1 Kings 1:1–2,[5] which he identified as an independent narrative written by a single author who lived close to the time of the events themselves. Rost believed that the focus for this narrative was in answering the question, Who will succeed David on the throne? Building on Rost's hypothesis, Gerhard von Rad argued that the succession narrative was an early example of history writing, albeit a history that assumes divine providence acted through persons and events in the narrative.[6] Rost's work has been the starting point for an unusual degree of interest in these chapters of 2 Samuel, and many of Rost's conclusions have been modified, including the contention that succession is the central interest of these chapters.

Nevertheless, his view of a coherent pre-existing narrative used as a source by the author of 1 and 2 Samuel is still widely accepted.

This claim for the existence of a succession narrative as a source document for the compiler of 1 and 2 Samuel has influenced a flurry of claims for other independent pre-existing sources that were incorporated into the books of Samuel—not as intertwined sources but as stories in a sequence. Other proposed sources included an ark narrative (1 Samuel 4:1–6; 2 Samuel 6), a history of David's rise (1 Samuel 16:1–2 Samuel 5:10), and a birth story of Samuel (1 Samuel 1:1–3).

In 1943, Martin Noth proposed that the whole of the Former Prophets (Joshua–2 Kings, excluding Ruth in the English Bible) constituted a single great history work influenced by deuteronomic theological perspectives and written during the time of the Babylonian exile.[7] His basic argument for a deuteronomistic historian (Dtr) is still widely accepted, although some now argue persuasively that this Deuteronomistic History was written before the destruction of Jerusalem and was then supplemented to take account of those events. Noth did identify the deuteronomic historian with most of the material and viewpoint attributed to the so-called Late Source of earlier scholarship—that is, negative to kingship and historically unreliable. This broad identification is no longer accepted. Most now regard the final shape of 1 and 2 Samuel to be the work of the deuteronomistic historian, but the extent of that role is debated, with some claiming that the deuteronomist did little more than mechanical redaction with occasional theological comment and others claiming single, unified authorship of the whole of 1 and 2 Samuel by the deuteronomist.[8]

Recent Emphases. Scholarship on the books of Samuel since 1960 has been prolific and varied, but one may highlight several prominent areas in the discussion. Many scholars continued to work with the traditional tools and approaches of historical-critical scholarship but with much greater attention to the complexity of the Samuel material. In addition, they have tended to examine longer segments of the Samuel narratives and with greater attention to the final form of the text in these segments as well as in the books of Samuel as a whole. Significant studies, based on

historical-critical methods, have focused on the ark narrative, the rise of kingship in Israel, the history of David's rise, David's consolidation of his kingdom, the court history of David (the succession narrative), and the so-called appendixes to the books of Samuel.

Some scholars still discern evidence of pre-deuteronomistic editions of Samuel traditions incorporating, and in some cases helping to form, the larger narrative segments just mentioned above. Perhaps the most thoroughgoing example of such a viewpoint appears in McCarter's Anchor Bible commentary. Building on the work of Weiser and Birch, McCarter argues that

> the First Book of Samuel derives its basic shape from a prophetic history of the origin of the monarchy that was intended to present the advent of kingship in Israel as a concession to a wanton demand of the people . . . the history was written to set forth according to a prophetic perspective the essential elements of the new system by which Israel would be governed. The prophet, whom the example of Samuel showed to be capable of ruling alone, would continue to be the people's intercessor with Yahweh. The king . . . would be subject not only to the instruction and admonition of the prophet acting in his capacity as Yahweh's spokesman but even to prophetic election and rejection.[9]

This prophetic history, dating to the late eighth century, is especially evident in segments of narrative on the birth of Samuel (1 Samuel 1:1–3), the role of Samuel as judge and deliverer (1 Samuel 7), the rise of kingship and the role of the prophet in those events (1 Samuel 8:1–12), the rejection of Saul (1 Samuel 13 and 15), the anointing of David (1 Samuel 16), Saul's consultation with the ghost of Samuel (1 Samuel 28), elements of the dynastic oracle (2 Samuel 7), the sin of David and his confrontation by Nathan (2 Samuel 11:1–12), and David's census and God's judgment (2 Samuel 24).

Recent decades have seen the impact of social-scientific methods and comparative social-world models on study of the books of Samuel and the transition period these traditions represent in the history of Israel. The publication of Gottwald's groundbreaking study on tribal Israel in the period of Joshua and Judges[10] had a catalytic effect on Samuel studies. Interest focused on describing the centralization process that moved

Israel from its tribal existence to a monarchic nation-state. Most social-world critics think a complex pattern of social and economic pressures led toward centralization, but also produced resistance to that centralization. Many believe the political reality of the Philistines' pressure and the economic reality of limited resources led not to a full-fledged kingship under Saul and David, but to something more like a paramount tribal chieftaincy, which was not free politically or economically to embrace fully the model of a royal state.[11] That remains for Solomon to accomplish. The narratives of Samuel represent not history per se but a telling of Israel's story that seeks to unify diverse perspectives in the service of a social unity centered in Jerusalem and based on Yahwistic religion.

> Differences and contradictions in the stories have ecological, political, social, economic, and religious bases. By their existence, the texts signal continuing hope for social unity grounded in belief. The unifying force of Yahwist religion is central to the stories. Tensions among factions and perspectives that can be felt, for the most part, follow from contemporary differences rather than successive revisions of the texts. Hence, 1–2 Samuel, although formed from separate traditions, cycles, and stories, is a unified account that captures the urgency of the compilers' time.[12]

Recent scholarship has also seen the application of literary-critical methodologies to 1 and 2 Samuel. These studies have focused on the final form of the text with little interest in traditional questions of sources or processes of composition. Literary critics assume that the narrative as it stands possesses artistic integrity and must be analyzed as such. These approaches have been largely uninterested in historical questions and are largely skeptical that genuine correlations are possible between these stories and the actual course of Israel's history. The study by David Gunn, devoted to the succession narrative, represented a break with many of the assumptions of traditional historical criticism and treated the succession narrative as a part of a larger integrated whole in the books of Samuel.[13] More recently, works by Polzin and Fokkelman involve a close literary reading of the texts of 1 and 2 Samuel that has moved in an entirely different direction from traditional historical-critical scholarship on the books of Samuel.[14]

Their treatments postulate and seek to demonstrate a literary integrity in the books of Samuel that neither admits to previous sources or editions in these narratives nor shows any interest or confidence in these texts as sources for Israel's history in the time of Saul and David. The narrative is understood to be largely the product of the literary efforts and theological concerns of a later single author (for Polzin, it is the deuteronomist).

Finally, there has been a resurgence of interest in the theological interpretation of the books of Samuel. In the search for sources and in the effort to identify various historical elements in the text, the theological importance of the books of Samuel as a whole had been neglected. However, this situation has changed dramatically since 1970. There is increasing recognition that the books of Samuel represent Israel's theological struggle to adapt its faith to radically changed social realities and that many of the issues concerning the relationship of God's providence to human power are of continuing concern to the Jewish and Christian communities. The work of Walter Brueggemann has been of critical importance in the renewal of theological interest in the books of Samuel. In countless articles, monographs, and books he has pioneered the reshaping of traditional assumptions that these books are only of "historical" interest. His commentary on the books of Samuel represents the culminating statement of his work on this literature.[15]

Recent Samuel scholarship has been rich and eclectic. There is no clear consensus on many of the critical issues in interpreting the book, but a general agreement seems to be emerging that scholarship on the books of Samuel in the future is likely to draw on a variety of approaches and methodologies (historical-critical, social-world, literary, theological). Perhaps such multifaceted approaches are the best hope of doing justice to the complexity and richness of these books.

CRITICAL ASSUMPTIONS

1. This overview emphasizes the *final form* of 1 and 2 Samuel as a literary witness whose integrity and meaning do not depend on analysis and recovery of the earlier sources and editions that have brought the narrative to its present final form. This final form is probably the product of the deuteronomistic historian, who allowed earlier sources and editions to remain visible. These earlier elements may contribute distinctive emphases to the narrative. The concern, however, will not be to separate and recover these earlier sources and editions from the final form of the text, but to examine how they contribute to the books of Samuel in their present form. The long process by which these traditions have been shaped is not recoverable.

Earlier sources and editions include:

Independent literary units that existed prior to the work of the narrator and are responsible for the final shape of the books of Samuel. These include an ark narrative (1 Samuel 4:1–6); a history of the rise of David (1 Sam 16:1–2 Sam 5:10); and a court history (so-called succession narrative; 2 Samuel 9:1–20). Other narrative segments of 1 and 2 Samuel seem intentionally shaped as literary units, but it is less clear that they predate the work of the artistic hand responsible for the whole of these books.

A prophetic edition of these narratives may have joined and interpreted early traditions and sources prior to the work of the deuteronomist. The conclusions of McCarter, mentioned earlier, seem to have merit, though I am not as confident as McCarter that the work of this prophetic editor can be as precisely identified as he believes. It is not possible to isolate a prophetic edition in the present form of the books of Samuel. Rather, one may identify a prophetic theology of kingship and an emphasis on the peculiar role of the prophets in relation to kings within certain narratives. These prophetic interests and emphases will be noted as they appear in the final form of the text. This emphasis is apparent especially in 1 Samuel 1:1–3; 7–15; 16; 28; and 2 Samuel 7:1; 11–12; 24 .

Even if the deuteronomistic historian is responsible for the whole of 1 and 2 Samuel, there are certain *narrative segments that reflect deuteronomistic language and theological interests.* Compared to other portions of the Deuteronomistic History, there are fewer of these distinctively deuteronomistic passages, which suggests that a large part of the narrative of 1 and 2 Samuel already existed in a form that the deuteronomistic historian found congenial. Many of the distinctly deuteronomistic passages incorporate the Samuel narratives into the form and structure adopted

elsewhere for the Deuteronomistic History—e.g., elements of the farewell speech of Samuel (1 Samuel 12) or the archival notices on Saul's kingship (1 Sam 13:1-2; 14:47-51). In general, I do not try to identify every verse that might be argued as distinctively deuteronomistic;[16] instead, I simply note those places where a deuteronomistic perspective or use of language influences the analysis of the larger narrative. I do not regard the deuteronomist as simply an annotator. By what has been included, excluded, and added to earlier sources, the deuteronomist has worked as the literary artist and theological commentator responsible for the books of Samuel as we now have them.

2. There is an identifiable and significant *socio-historical context* to which the narratives of 1 and 2 Samuel give witness, even if that witness is now interpretively shaped by the perspectives and contexts of later Israelite generations. These stories are rooted in a time of considerable social and political transformation in the life of Israel, and these realities challenged the theological categories by which Israel understood its life in relation to God. This transformative period was so crucial to Israel's understanding of itself that its events and personalities were still being assessed politically and theologically at the time of the exile, when the work of the deuteronomistic historian fixed these narratives in their present form.

The books of Samuel open with a loose federation of tribal groups gripped by a crisis, both external and internal, that threatens the very existence of Israel, and they end on the eve of an emergent hereditary monarchy that will preside over an established nation-state. This transformation represents a considerable achievement. The narratives in 1 and 2 Samuel are not historical in the sense of our modern positivistic understandings of history. Rather, they blend historical realism with artistic and theological imagination. Attention to the imaginative elements of these narratives has led some to miss the historically realistic style by which these narratives depict the nature of this historical crisis and social transformation. Likewise, the historically realistic style has led others mistakenly to treat the books of Samuel as history writing and to overlook the artistic and imaginative freedom with which many elements of the story have been shaped.

The socio-historical context at the beginning of 1 Samuel includes the external threat of incorporation into a Philistine empire that sought to expand into Israelite territory c. 1000 BCE (1 Samuel 4). The internal crisis in this same period is reflected in the loose tribal association that proves incapable of meeting such a crisis (1 Samuel 4) and the corruption of the institutions of Yahwism, which gave tribal Israel whatever unity it possessed (1 Samuel 2:1-3). The end of the book of Judges describes a state of political chaos and moral decadence that results in idolatry and barbarous behavior (Judges 17:1-21), a time when "there was no king in Israel; every man did what was right in his own eyes" (Judg 17:6; 18:1; 19:1; 21:25). There is little reason to think that Israel could survive these internal and external crises.

Yet, by the end of 2 Samuel, Israel has been transformed socially and politically. Although details may be debated, it is clear that this transformation included political centralization and the emergence of governmental structures (first to chieftaincy then to monarchy) capable of uniting tribal Israel and coping with the crises it faced. This transformation included movement economically from marginal tribal, agrarian existence to a period of prosperity that included extended trade and the emergence of wealth. This development also required new structures of social management and practice. Many of the narratives of 1 and 2 Samuel are concerned to make legitimate, politically and theologically, these newly emerging political and economic structures. Saul, David, Jerusalem, the Temple—all in turn are the subject of narrative apologists in the books of Samuel (e.g., Saul, 1 Sam 9:1-10:16; David, 1 Sam 16:1-2 Sam 5:10; Jerusalem, 2 Sam 5:6-10; 6:1-19; Temple, 2 Sam 24:18-25). But the narratives also reflect the resistance to new centralized political and economic structures: Kingship is opposed (1 Samuel 8); David cannot build the Temple (2 Samuel 7); David's census brings judgment (2 Sam 24:1-17). These narratives reflect the challenge, tensions, and promise of a transformative moment in Israel's life. Elements of historical realism in the narratives allow us a view of the socio-historical context for this moment in Israel's story, but the narratives exercise artistic imagination in presenting the personalities, the events, and the divine will that mediated Israel's transformation.

3. The role of personality in Israel's story of this period is central. Samuel, Saul, and David loom over the story in overlapping domination of the narrative landscape (Samuel, 1 Samuel 1:1-28; Saul, 1 Samuel 9:1-2 Samuel 1:1; David, 1 Samuel 16:1-2 Samuel 24:1). First, Samuel, then Saul, and finally David are presented as crucial to Israel's future, but where any two are present in the story, tension and conflict arise, as if there is room for only one of these dominant personalities in the spotlight. In the end, it is David, "the man after God's own heart," who fascinates Israel's storytellers.

Yet, for all the intense interest in David, these narratives do not neglect the role of others in the story. No segment of the Old Testament is filled with a richer cast of characters, and their portraits are vividly drawn. Even characters that occupy a single episode (e.g., Abigail, 1 Samuel 25) are often drawn as full and intriguing figures who play crucial roles in the drama that will find its climax in David. More than in earlier narratives in the canon (the Pentateuch, Joshua, Judges) the personalities of 1 and 2 Samuel are described in terms of inner motives and struggles as well as actions.

The telling of these stories depicts the personalities in artistic as well as historical terms. A historically realistic style is blended with artistic imagination. The narrator is not concerned with just the "truth" of fact but with the "truth" of meaning for Israel, especially where David is concerned. It does not matter who really killed Goliath (David, 1 Samuel 17, or Elhanan, 2 Sam 21:19). The combination of piety and courage in the dramatic, but fanciful, story of a youthful David's triumph captures the imagination of Israel and allows one to be confident that Israel's new future is assured. The story of Israel's transformation from tribe to kingdom is grounded in a historical experience, but the story of this time is peopled by characters that are, at times, portrayed in painstakingly realistic terms and, at other times, seem to stride off the page larger than life. Both the imaginative and the realistic elements are important in conveying Israel's memory of this crucial time.

4. To paint David and other crucial characters solely in human historical terms might suggest that Israel's transformation in that period was simply the product of human activity. But the authors of 1 and 2 Samuel understand that Israel's new future results from the working of *the providence of God*. It is the Lord (Yahweh) who shapes the events and personalities of this time. Sociopolitical realities and leadership are bent to the divine purpose.

In a world of human politics preoccupied with the issues of power, the issue for the narratives of Samuel is, Where does true power lie? These narrators understand that, in the juxtaposition of human power and divine will, God possesses the final authority. The poetry of Hannah's song (1 Sam 2:1-10) and of David's song (2 Sam 22:2-51) frames the entirety of 1 and 2 Samuel by announcing a divine purpose at work in the world that overturns and reverses the usual patterns of power. Consistent with this literary frame, a barren woman can give birth to the prophet of God's future for Israel (1 Samuel 1), a devastating Philistine victory can be turned into Philistine defeat without human help (1 Samuel 4:1-6), the king demanded by the people can nevertheless become God's anointed one (1 Samuel 8:1-10), even anointed kings can be rejected for unfaithfulness (1 Samuel 13; 15), an eighth son of an obscure family can become the future of Israel and the man after God's own heart (1 Samuel 16), a fugitive with a renegade band of followers sought by the king can receive the divine promise of eternal dynasty (2 Samuel 7), and even Israel's greatest and most beloved king can be judged by God (2 Samuel 12) and bring tragedy upon his own family (2 Samuel 13:1-18). In human terms, many of these events seem unlikely, but the narratives of Samuel understand all of these (and more) as a part of God's providence at work to bring Israel's future into being.

In 1 and 2 Samuel, the divine shaping of events is assumed, and even stated by the main characters in the narrative. This working of divine power does not usually occur by direct intervention in events, although the ark narratives (1 Samuel 4:1-6) suggest that God's purposes might not require human agency. Nevertheless, God's will is usually brought to pass through human events and personalities. The narratives make clear that divine power lies behind the human drama. For example, the lengthy narration of David's rise (1 Samuel 16:1-2 Sam 5:10) has as its central theological motif the conviction that "God was with him" (1 Sam 16:18;

18:14, 28), and it concludes after David is fully enthroned over Israel and Judah, "David became greater and greater, for the LORD, the God of hosts, was with him" (2 Sam 5:10 NRSV).

NARRATIVE UNITS AND EMPHASES IN THE BOOKS OF SAMUEL

Completely apart from judgments about earlier independent sources still visible in 1 and 2 Samuel, there is a developing scholarly consensus about the major segments into which the narrative falls. A brief description of these units gives a sense of the flow of the narrative and its major emphases.

1 Sam 1:1–4:1a. As the books of Samuel open, Israel is faced with a grave crisis, both internal and external, but we are not introduced to that crisis directly. Instead, we hear the story of Hannah, a barren woman who prays to the Lord and makes a vow (1:11). She asks the Lord to remember her, which the story tells us the Lord does (1:19). The story of Hannah's barrenness opens to the story of Israel's barren future. She bears a son, Samuel, the prophet who leads Israel through its time of crisis and through whom God will establish a kingship in Israel. Hannah's song (2:1-10) speaks of a God who brings the future in dramatic reversals and foreshadows the remarkable emergence of David as the climax of this story, an eighth son who becomes king. Childs has identified this song as "an interpretive key for this history which is, above all, to be understood from a theocentric perspective."[17] He has also shown that it has a counterpart at the end of 2 Samuel (chap. 22), a song that celebrates the Lord as the power behind David's successes. Thus a story that will be rich in human characters and events is framed as the work of the Lord.

This opening segment of 1 Samuel goes on to depict the tragic corruption of the priestly house of Eli at Shiloh (2:11-36). But against this background of covenant disobedience at the heart of Israel, chaps. 1–3 provide a story of the birth, growth, legitimization, and establishment of Samuel as the prophetic leader who will bring Israel through crisis to a new day. By the end of chap. 3, Samuel is established as God's prophetic voice, and judgment has been pronounced on the house of Eli.

1 Sam 4:1b–7:1. This section of narrative identifies the external crisis of Israel. It tells a dramatic story of Philistine threat, defeat of Israel, and capture of the ark (chap. 4). Nevertheless, the Philistines do not turn out to have the upper hand. The ark of the covenant itself mediates the powerful presence of the Lord, defeating the Philistine god Dagon and bringing plagues upon the Philistine people. In humiliation, the Philistines finally send the ark on a cart back into Israelite territory (chaps. 5–6). I agree with those who have argued that this so-called ark history did not originally continue in 2 Samuel 6. That story does, of course, include the ark, but it focuses on David in a way quite unlike the style in 1 Samuel 4:1–6, where human characters play a small role.

These stories about the ark are remarkable, because Samuel, who was so carefully introduced in the preceding chapters, is absent. The only connection to chaps. 1–3 is the report of the death of Eli's sons when the ark is captured and of Eli's death when he hears the tragic news (4:12-22). Human leadership plays no role in these events; the divine power mediated by the ark is equal to the challenge of the Philistine crisis. As a result, the ensuing human demand for a king seems unnecessary. The Lord is sovereign and governs Israel's history, even in the face of threat from Philistine armies and gods. Whatever is to unfold in Israel's story in 1 and 2 Samuel will be because God allows or wills it.

1 Sam 7:2-17. Suddenly Samuel reappears in the story. In this unusual narrative, Samuel faces a Philistine threat and leads Israel to victory, but not through his own military leadership. Through prayer and mediation of divine power against the enemy, Samuel meets the threat (7:2-14). This victory is followed by the notice of a circuit that Samuel travels, "administering justice" in Israel (7:15-17). The portrait in this chapter is of Samuel single-handedly carrying on the covenant tradition and giving the leadership necessary for Israel's welfare. Once again, the narrative's effect is to render the coming request for a king unnecessary. Israel has the power of God and the leadership of Samuel. What more is needed? If kingship is nevertheless to come, then it is because God wills it, not because the situation of Israel demanded it.

1 Sam 8:1–15:35. These chapters focus on the establishment of kingship in Israel and the installation of Saul as the first holder of this office. There can be little doubt that these narratives have gone through a complex literary process that cannot be entirely recovered. There is also an emerging consensus that the socio-historical realities behind these narratives were more complex than response to the Philistine crisis. Economic developments leading to accumulation of wealth and to the centralized forms of government needed to safeguard that wealth undoubtedly played a role in the development of Israelite monarchy, but these processes lie in the background of the narrative.

As the narratives now stand, the internal and external crises of Israel have driven some to demand a king. These chapters preserve a divided opinion on this matter. Some narratives clearly view kingship as sinful, allowed by an indulgent God (chaps. 8 and 12), while other narratives see the choice of Saul and his kingship as an act of God's providential grace (9:1–10:16; 11:1-15). This divided opinion is now widely understood as being rooted in genuine division within Israel at an early time. These traditions undoubtedly reflect Israel's struggle over the appropriate relationship of human power to divine power as expressed in the institutions of governance in Israel. Economic and political pressures were demanding new patterns of institutional leadership, but how was covenant obedience and divine authority preserved when human power grew more centralized and prominent in Israel?

The prophet plays a crucial role in representing the initiative of God (anointing, 10), in voicing the covenant demands of God on king and people (Samuel's farewell address, chap. 12), and in holding kings accountable to God (Saul's rejection, 13:8-15; 15:1-35). This prophetic role also occurs in David's story. The roles of the prophet in these narratives have led some scholars to suggest a prophetic editing of significant portions of the narratives in 1 and 2 Samuel, including the diverse material on the establishment of kingship.

The political and theological interests reflected in 1 Samuel 8:1–15 are played out around the person of Saul. Many interpreters have noted the tragic character of his story. The narratives reflect an awareness that David is the true climax of the story and of God's purposes in the story. Saul, in spite of his gifts, beyond what seems deserved by his faults, appears destined for failure and tragedy. Saul's story is not his own; it is a preparation for David. Saul's shortcomings are exposed in these stories (esp. chaps. 13–15). He does not appear to have the gifts required to usher in Israel's new future. Yet, the narrator is aware that Saul pays the personal price for Israel's future as one destined to fail so that another might succeed. It is fitting that much later in the narrative, after David has become the focus of attention, there is a pause for compassion and tribute to Saul and his son Jonathan on the occasion of their tragic deaths (2 Samuel 1).

1 Sam 16:1–2 Sam 5:10. The focus shifts to David. Story after story celebrates the courage, leadership, resourcefulness, piety, and political skill of David. Saul appears as a foil to David—driven, impulsive, cruel, fickle, and ineffective. Many scholars believe these narratives existed as an earlier collection, often called the "History of David's Rise".

With the appearance of David, the divisions and struggles evident in 1 Samuel 8:1–15 begin to recede into the background. The theme of Hannah's song reappears forcefully in these stories; God is at work in great historical reversals—to bring low and to exalt. In 1 Samuel 16, we are introduced to an eighth son of an obscure family who tends sheep. By 2 Sam 5:3, he has become the king of Judah and Israel. The activity of God through these events is made explicit at the conclusion of the whole narrative segment, "David became greater and greater, for the LORD, the God of hosts, was with him" (2 Sam 5:10 NRSV). God's presence with David is a central theme of this narrative section (see 1 Sam 16:18; 17:37; 18:12, 14, 28; 20:13). David is portrayed as a man of piety and prayer alongside his prowess as warrior and leader (e.g., 1 Sam 17:45-47; 23:1-5).

The narrator is concerned to legitimize the kingship of David and to overcome objections that might be raised against his claim on the throne. Thus various episodes in this section seek to counter charges that might be made against David. McCarter has listed the following charges that these narratives seek to refute and explain:[18]

1. David sought to advance himself at Saul's expense.
2. David was a deserter.
3. David was an outlaw.
4. David was a Philistine mercenary.
5. David was implicated in Saul's death.
6. David was implicated in Abner's death.
7. David was implicated in Ishbaal's death.

Alongside these apologetic efforts is a growing procession of witnesses who acknowledge David's right and destiny to Israel's throne: Jonathan, Michal, the servants of Achish, Ahimelech, Abigail, and finally Saul himself (1 Sam 24:20). After Saul's death (1 Samuel 31:1; 2 Samuel 1:1), David first becomes king over Judah (2 Sam 2:1-4), and after a series of complicated events, which includes the deaths of Abner and Ishbaal, David becomes king over Israel as well (2 Sam 5:3). In the final event of this drama of David's rise, David takes Jerusalem as his capital city (2 Sam 5:6-9). In David and Jerusalem, God has established a new future for Israel.

2 Sam 5:11–8:18. David remains the focus of the narrative, but in this segment the tone is not as celebrative as it was for David's rise. Enthusiasm gives way to official records and affairs of state. David sits on the throne; bureaucracy and ideology seem to close around him. Flanagan has observed a symmetry of arrangement that suggests a shift from tribal, covenant realities to state, royal ideology.[19] Family genealogy (2 Sam 5:13-16) gives way to officers of the court (2 Sam 8:15-18). War to bring deliverance from the Philistine threat (2 Sam 5:17-25) gives way to wars of national expansion and empire building (2 Sam 8:1-14). The central symbol of tribal covenant relationship to God, the ark, is brought to Jerusalem (2 Sam 6:1-20) and made secondary by God's announcement through the prophet Nathan of an eternal covenant with David (2 Sam 7:1-29). The center of Israel's life has shifted. God's covenant promises for Israel's future are now identified with the future of the Davidic dynasty. Conflict in Israel over kingship has now disappeared or been overridden by the claim that David is the destiny for Israel toward which God has been moving.

2 Sam 9:1–20:26. This is the segment of 2 Samuel usually designated as the succession narrative or the court history of David. Most scholars agree that this narrative segment existed independently prior to the time it was incorporated into the larger narrative of the books of Samuel. However, recent arguments have been advanced against considering 1 Kings 1:1–2 to be the continuation or conclusion of this narrative.

There is a general consensus that, with these chapters, the narrative makes a sudden and dramatic shift in its portrayal of David. The key to this shift is 2 Samuel 11:1–12, which recount David's adultery with Bathsheba, his murder of Uriah, his marriage to Bathsheba, and his confrontation by the prophet Nathan. David's repentance spares his own life, but Nathan announces God's judgment of violence unleashed in David's own family. The remaining narratives provide detailed accounts of the tragic consequences of David's own sin: Amnon's rape of Tamar (13:1-22), Absalom's killing of Amnon and his banishment (13:23-39), Absalom's rebellion and David's humiliating retreat from Jerusalem (chaps. 14–17), the defeat and death of Absalom; David's overwhelming grief (chaps. 18–19), and continued rebellion in the kingdom (chap. 20).

As many have noted, literary style and emphasis change markedly in this segment of David's story. Gone is the assurance of state ideology that marked the previous narrative on David as king and the exuberance of the narrative on David's rise. These are stories in which the humanity, pathos, and vulnerability of David come to the fore. We are allowed to see David in decline and suffering. The literary style is unusually subtle and sensitive. It focuses on human agency in these stories of tragedy in David's family; yet, it makes clear, in understated ways, that God's providence nevertheless encompasses even these painful human moments (cf. 2 Sam 11:27b; 17:14b). The result of this intensely human portrait of David is that readers approach the end of the books of Samuel in a chastened mood. The achievement of human political power is not without its dangers. The temptation to think of human power as autonomous is considerable. To wield that power in the service of self-interest and in disregard of God's ultimate authority and rule is to incur judgment. Even David takes such a course of action at considerable cost.

2 Sam 21:1–24:25. These chapters, commonly called appendixes to the books of Samuel, have been most often treated as a miscellaneous collection of David traditions inserted by a rough hand prior to David's deathbed scene in 1 Kings 1:1-2. However, there is a symmetrical arrangement to these materials that suggests a significant intention. There are two narratives, one focused on expiation of Saul's guilt (2 Sam 21:1-14) and the other on expiation of David's guilt (2 Sam 24:1-25). There are two lists of heroes and their deeds (2 Sam 21:15-22; 23:8-39). Finally, at the heart of this section are two songs: a thanksgiving by David for the Lord's deliverance (2 Sam 22:1-51, parallel to Psalm 18:1) and a song that celebrates God's promise to David (2 Sam 23:1-7). This pattern reminds us of the pattern in 2 Sam 5:11–8:18 and has led some to suggest that the earlier movement from tribal to royal realities is being reversed in these appendixes—to reassert tribal, covenantal perspectives at the end of David's story.

In many ways the ideology of royal absolutism has been deconstructed by the judgment on David's sin with Bathsheba and Uriah, and the tragic events in David's family that ensued. Yet, at the end of chap. 20, David's power is reestablished, and he asserts that power to quell a rebellion. Without the so-called appendixes, the story would continue in 1 Kings 1:1–2 with deathbed vendettas by David and bloodbaths by Solomon. This material (chaps. 21–24) stays or moderates the reconstruction of royal absolutist power. The narratives in these chapters provide a reminder that, even when David feels most powerful, he is accountable to forces and authority beyond his own (the execution of Saul's son, chap. 21; the census, chap. 24). The lists of heroes make clear that it was never David alone through whom God was working to bring Israel's future. David was the leader of a heroic community. The two great songs at the heart of this section place into the mouth of David acknowledgment and celebration of the power of God working through him. In spite of earlier sin and judgment, these final appendixes return to the David anticipated by the song of Hannah at the start of the books of Samuel. It is the Lord who "brings low and exalts" and who "exalts the power of his anointed" (1 Sam 2:7b, 10b). Just as the Lord had heeded the prayer of Hannah (1 Sam 1:19) to open the story of kingship in Israel, so also that story concludes with the Lord heeding the prayer of David (2 Sam 24:25).

FOR FURTHER READING

Commentaries:

Anderson, A. A. *2 Samuel.* WBC 11. Waco: Word, 1989.

Brueggemann, Walter. *First and Second Samuel.* Interpretation. Louisville: John Knox, 1990.

Campbell, Anthony F. *1 Samuel.* FOLT 7. Grand Rapids, Mich.: Eerdmans, 2003.

Cartledge, Tony W. *1 & 2 Samuel*. Smyth & Helwys Bible Commentary. Macon, Ga.: Smyth & Helwys, 2001.

Gordon, R. P. *1 and 2 Samuel*. Old Testament Guides. Sheffield: JSOT, 1984.

Hertzberg, Hans Wilhelm. *I and II Samuel*. OTL. Philadelphia: Westminster, 1964.

Klein, Ralph W. *1 Samuel*. WBC 10. Waco: Word, 1983.

McCarter, P. Kyle. *I Samuel*. AB 8. Garden City, N.Y.: Doubleday, 1980.

————. *II Samuel*. AB 9. Garden City, N.Y.: Doubleday, 1984.

Other Studies:

Alter, Robert. *The Art of Biblical Narrative*. New York: Basic Books, 1981.

Birch, Bruce C. *The Rise of the Israelite Monarchy: The Growth and Development of I Samuel 7–15*. SBLDS 27. Missoula, Mont.: Scholars Press, 1976.

Brenner, Athalya, ed. *A Feminist Companion to Samuel and Kings*. Feminist Companion to the Bible. First Series 5. Sheffield Acadmic Press, 1994.

————. *Samuel and Kings: A Feminist Companion to the Bible*. Feminist Companion to the Bible. Second Series 7. Sheffield: Sheffield Academic Press, 2000.

Brueggemann, Walter. *David's Truth in Israel's Imagination and Memory*. Philadelphia: Fortress, 1985.

————. *Power, Providence, and Personality: Biblical Insight into Life and Ministry*. Louisville: Westminster/John Knox, 1990.

Carlson, R. A. *David, the Chosen King: A Traditio-Historical Approach to the Second Book of Samuel*. Stockholm: Almqvist och Wiksell, 1964.

Childs, Brevard S. *Introduction to the Old Testament as Scripture*. Philadelphia: Fortress, 1979.

Fokkelmann, J. P. *Narrative Art and Poetry in the Books of Samuel*. 4 vols. Assen: Van Gorcum, 1981—1983.

Gunn, David M. *The Fate of King Saul*. JSOTSup 14. Sheffield: JSOT, 1980.

————. *The Story of King David*. JSOTSup 6. Sheffield: JSOT, 1978.

Miller, Patrick D., Jr., and J. J. M. Roberts. *The Hand of the Lord: A Reassessment of the "Ark Narrative" of 1 Samuel*. Johns Hopkins Near Eastern Studies. Baltimore: Johns Hopkins University Press, 1977.

Polzin, Robert. *David and the Deuteronomist: A Literary Study of the Deuteronomic History. Part Three: 2 Samuel*. Bloomington: Indiana University Press, 1993.

————. *Samuel and the Deuteronomist: A Literary Study of the Deuteronomic History. Part Two: 1 Samuel*. San Francisco: Harper & Row, 1989.

Rad, Gerhard von. "Der Anfang der Geschichtsschreibung im alten Israel." *Archiv für Kulturgeschichte* 32 (1944) 1-42. English translation: "The Beginning of History Writing in Ancient Israel." In *The Problem of the Hexateuch and Other Essays*. Translated by E. W. Trueman Dicken. New York: McGraw-Hill, 1966.

Rost, Leonhard. *Die Überlieferung von der Thronnachfolge Davids*. BWANT 3/6. Stuttgart: Kohlhammer, 1926. English translation: *The Succession to the Throne of David*. Translated by Michael D. Rutter and David M. Gunn. Sheffield: Almond, 1982.

Van Seters, John. *In Search of History: Historiography in the Ancient World and the Origins of Biblical History*. Winona Lake, Ind.: Eisenbrauns, 1997.

ENDNOTES

1. See P. Kyle McCarter, *I Samuel*, AB 8 (Garden City, N.Y.: Doubleday, 1984) 3-4.

2. McCarter has the fullest description of the textual witnesses for the books of Samuel, and the textual sections of his chapter-by-chapter commentary represent the most detailed treatment of textual problems in these books. McCarter, *I Samuel*, 5-11.

3. See E. C. Ulrich, Jr., *The Qumran Text of Samuel and Josephus*, HSM 19 (Missoula, Mont.: Scholars Press, 1978).

4. For a detailed discussion of representative scholars and viewpoints in early and recent research on the books of Samuel, see James W. Flanagan, "Samuel, Book of 1-2: Text, Composition and Content," in *The Anchor Bible Dictionary*, 6 vols., ed. David Noel Freedman (New York: Doubleday, 1992) 5:958-61.

5. Leonhard Rost, *Die Überlieferung von der Thronnachfolge Davids*, BWANT 3/6 (Stuttgart:

Kohlhammer, 1926); English trans.: *The Succession to the Throne of David*, trans. Michael D. Rutter and David M. Gunn (Sheffield: Almond, 1982).

6. Gerhard von Rad, "Der Anfang der Geschichtsschreibung im alten Israel," *Archiv für Kulturgeschichte* 32 (1944) 1-42; English translation: "The Beginning of History Writing in Ancient Israel," in *The Problem of the Hexateuch and Other Essays*, trans. E. W. Trueman Dicken (New York: McGraw-Hill, 1966) 166-204.

7. Martin Noth, *Überlieferungsgeschichtliche Studien. Die sammeln and bearbeitenden Geschichtswerke im Alten Testament* (Tubingen: Niemeyer, 1943); English translation: *The Deuteronomistic History*, trans. J. Doull, JSOTSup 15 (Sheffield: JSOT, 1981).

8. The most careful and nuanced treatment of the deuteronomistic influences and traditions in the books of Samuel is that of T. Veijola, *Das Konigtum in der Beurteilung der deuteronomistischen Historiographie. Eine redaktionsgeschichtliche Untersuchung*, Annales Academiae Scientiarum Fennicae B, 193 (Helsinki: Suomalainen Tiedeakatemia, 1977). Robert Polzin has recently argued in a series of volumes that the text from Joshua through 2 Kings is the work of a single deuteronomistic author. His volumes on the books of Samuel are *Samuel and the Deuteronomist: A Literary Study of the Deuteronomic History, Part Two: 1 Samuel* (San Francisco: Harper & Row, 1989) and *David and the Deuteronomist: A Literary Study of the Deuteronomic History, Part Three: 2 Samuel* (Bloomington: Indiana University Press, 1993).

9. McCarter, *I Samuel*, 21. McCarter builds on work by Artur Weiser, *The Old Testament: Its Formation and Development*, trans. B. M. Barton (New York: Association Press, 1961; German original 1948); and Bruce C. Birch, *The Rise of the Israelite Monarchy: The Growth and Development of* 1 Samuel 7:1–15, SBLDS 27 (Missoula, Mont.: Scholars Press, 1976).

10. Norman K. Gottwald, *The Tribes of Yahweh: A Sociology of the Religion of Liberated Israel, 1250–1050 B.C.* (Maryknoll, N.Y.: Orbis, 1979).

11. See James W. Flanagan, "Chiefs in Israel," *JSOT* 20 (1981) 47-73; Frank S. Frick, *The Formation of the State in Ancient Israel: A Survey of Methods and Theories*, SWBA 4 (Sheffield: JSOT, 1985).

12. Flanagan, "Samuel, Books of 1-2," *ABD* 5:961.

13. David M. Gunn, *The Story of King David: Genre and Interpretation*, JSOTSup 6 (Sheffield: JSOT, 1978).

14. See Polzin, *Samuel and the Deuteronomist* and *David and the Deuteronomist*; J. P. Fokkelman, *Narrative Art and Poetry in the Books of Samuel*, 2 vols. (Assen: Van Gorcum, 1981; 1986).

15. Walter Brueggemann, *First and Second Samuel*, Interpretation (Louisville: John Knox, 1990). His many other articles and books related to the books of Samuel are too numerous to mention here.

16. A helpful and thoughtful delineation of the deuteronomistic portions of 1 and 2 Samuel may be found in McCarter, *I Samuel*, 14-17, and *II Samuel*, 4-8, although McCarter is generally more confident than I in arguing the presence of a deuteronomistic hand in very small additions to some chapters.

17. Brevard S. Childs, *Introduction to the Old Testament as Scripture* (Philadelphia: Fortress, 1979) 273.

18. P. Kyle McCarter, "The Apology of David," *JBL* 99 (1980) 499-502.

19. James W. Flanagan, "Social Transformation and Ritual in 2 Samuel 6:1," in *The Word of the Lord Shall Go Forth*, ed. Carol L. Meyers and M. O'Connor (Winona Lake, Ind.: Eisenbrauns, 1983) 361-72.

THE FIRST AND SECOND BOOKS OF KINGS

CHOON-LEONG SEOW

The books of 1 and 2 Kings cover more than four hundred years of Israelite history, from the death of David and the accession of Solomon in the tenth century, to the release of Judah's exiled king Jehoiachin in the sixth century BCE. The story begins with the court intrigues that propelled Solomon to power, dwells on his many worldly accomplishments and his widespread reputation, and focuses on the terrible precedent for syncretism that he set for other kings after him. From the start, one discerns the inevitable interplay of divine will and human will in history. That interplay of wills continues to be evident in the rest of the story of the monarchy, from the division of the kingdom into Judah and Samaria, through the reigns of various kings of Israel and Judah, to the fall of Samaria and, eventually, to the fall of Jerusalem. In the chaotic arena of history and amid the court intrigues, internecine warfare, and international conflicts, the story relentlessly conveys the confidence that God's will is being worked out. The story as a whole testifies to divine purposefulness in the messiness of history. Despite the impression that the affairs of the world are determined by political maneuverings and military strivings of rogues and scoundrels, it is God who will have the final say when all is said and done. History moves inexorably according to the will of the sovereign God.

THE UNITY OF 1 AND 2 KINGS

The two biblical books now known as 1 and 2 Kings originally constituted a single work. The artificial division into two books was first made in the Greek version, where the materials now known as 1–2 Samuel and 1–2 Kings are broken up into four manageable portions called the "books of Reigns/Kingdoms" (chapter and verse divisions were not introduced into biblical man-

uscripts until the medieval period). Thus the point of division between the books appears to be purely arbitrary; the end of 1 Kings (1 Kgs 22:51-53) and the beginning of 2 Kings (2 Kgs 1:1-18) together constitute a single literary unit, a report on the reign of King Ahaziah of Israel. The Hebrew tradition, in fact, assumed a single literary work, and it was only in the late Middle Ages when, under the influence of the Greek and Latin versions, the division began appearing in Hebrew manuscripts as well. Hence, from a literary viewpoint at least, it is more accurate to speak of a "book of Kings" rather than the "books of Kings."

In the Jewish tradition, the book of Kings belongs—together with the books of Joshua, Judges, and Samuel—to the Former Prophets, a collection of works that provide a prophetic interpretation of Israel's history from the conquest of Canaan to the end of the monarchy. Modern scholars call this biblical corpus "the deuteronomistic history" because the narratives therein share a common vocabulary, literary style, and theological perspective that is heavily influenced by the book of Deuteronomy, which many scholars now regard as the introduction to the corpus. Although it appears likely that there were earlier editions of the deuteronomistic history—in the reigns of Hezekiah (c. 715–686 BCE) and Josiah (c. 640–609 BCE)—it seems clear that the work was given its final form sometime during the exilic period (c. 586–539 BCE). Although it may be more accurate to speak of several deuteronomists, I will presume that the final form of the text is broadly coherent and will refer to the final editor as "the (deuteronomistic) narrator."

The book may be divided into three parts. The first part (1 Kings 1:1–11) is focused on the kingdom under Solomon. The narrator explains how

Solomon succeeded David, even though Solomon was not the heir apparent to the throne (1 Kings 1:1–2). This succession, to the narrator, was according to the will of God, for God's promise to David was being fulfilled in Solomon's accession to the throne. From the start, therefore, the reader gets the message that God's purpose was being worked out behind all the scandals and human schemes. God's will was fulfilled despite, and even through, human devices and plots. Then the reader is introduced to Solomon the king, and the picture of him is mixed (1 Kgs 3:1-15). Solomon loved God, but he had other loves as well, and his priorities were not always right (1 Kgs 3:1-3). Still, God responded to Solomon's imperfect love and graciously granted him a gift—a gift on which Solomon's reputation

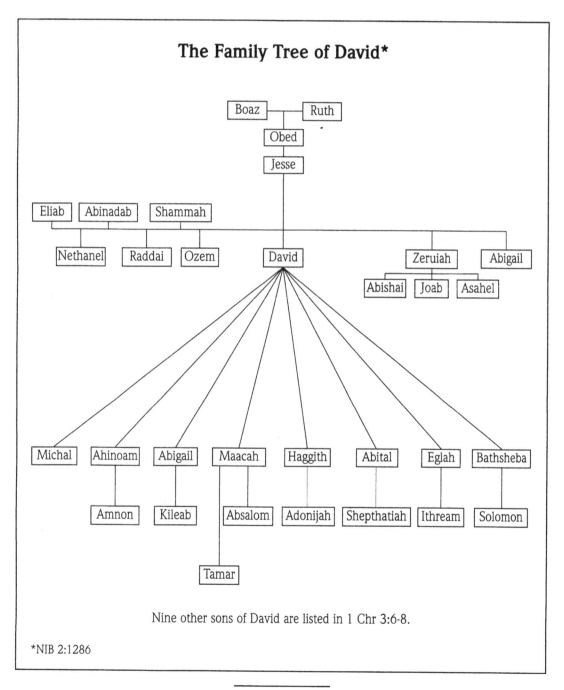

The Family Tree of David*

Nine other sons of David are listed in 1 Chr 3:6-8.

*NIB 2:1286

would be built. The rest of the account of Solomon's reign depicts him as a king who was successful in all the worldly ways: He was famous, rich, and powerful. Among his many accomplishments was his building of the Temple in Jerusalem. Clearly the dedication of the Temple (1 Kings 8:1) was a highpoint within the structure of the story, for the Temple was the very symbol of God's presence in the midst of the people, and God's presence was assured, as long as God's people were faithful. Yet, to the narrator, Solomon was no ideal king. Indeed, in many ways, Solomon violated the expectations of faithful kingship laid out in Deuteronomy (Deut 17:14-20). Above all, Solomon's many loves opened the doors to all kinds of compromises to faith in the Lord. Hence, God promised to divide the kingdom into two.

Narratives about the divided kingdom constitute the bulk of the second part of the book of Kings (1 Kings 12:1–2 Kings 17). It begins with the secession of the ten northern tribes under Jeroboam, who established two heterodox sanctuaries at Bethel and Dan to rival the Temple of the Lord in Jerusalem (1 Kgs 12:25-33). To the narrator, this was blatant apostasy, and Jeroboam had provided a horrible precedent for all his successors to follow. Henceforth, all the kings of Israel (the northern kingdom) would be judged according to their failure to depart from "the way of Jeroboam," and all of them would fail miserably (1 Kgs 15:30, 34; 16:2, 7, 19, 26, 31; 21:22; 22:52; 2 Kgs 3:3; 9:9; 10:29, 31; 13:2, 6, 11; 14:24; 15:9, 18, 24, 28; 17:21-22). Jeroboam had set an indelible pattern of apostasy in the north; it remained possible for each of his successors to turn back to the Lord, but none would do so. Hence, the destruction of the north was inevitable. Throughout the account of the kings of the north, the imperative of obedience to God's demands is emphasized, and the narrator makes the point that destruction is the consequence of Israel's will to disobey.

Meanwhile in Judah, God's promise of an enduring dynasty for David was being preserved by the sheer grace of God. Unlike Israel, there was continuity on the throne of David in Judah, as God had promised. Yet, there was the expectation of faithfulness to the Lord. Just as the kings of the north were judged according to failure to depart from the apostate ways of Jer-

oboam, so also the kings of the south were judged according to the standard of piety set by David (1 Kgs 14:8; 15:3-5, 11; 2 Kgs 14:3; 16:2). Unlike the northern kingdom, however, there were a few good kings in the south, reformists like Asa (1 Kgs 15:9-15), Jehoshaphat (1 Kgs 22:41-50), and Joash (2 Kgs 12:1-21). Yet, even these reformist kings failed to do all that was necessary to ensure the centralization of worship in Jerusalem. Hence, even though Judah would last a little longer than Israel, it was also set on a path of destruction.

The third major portion of the book focuses on the kingdom of Judah (2 Kings 18:1–25), the northern kingdom's having been destroyed because of its persistent will to disobey God (2 Kings 17:1). There is hope when one reads about the reign of reformist King Hezekiah. Indeed, when the Assyrians besieged Jerusalem, they were unable to take the city and had to turn back (2 Kings 18:1–19). The destiny of Judah appeared to be embodied in the person of Hezekiah, who was on the brink of death, but because of his piety was miraculously granted a reprieve and recovered to live for a while longer (2 Kgs 20:1-11). Yet, all was not well, because Hezekiah, who has been portrayed as one who trusted the Lord, instead trusted the Babylonians and finally cared most about preserving his own well-being (2 Kgs 20:12-21). Even worse for Judah, Hezekiah was succeeded by Manasseh, who thoroughly undid what good Hezekiah had done (2 Kings 21:1-18). Indeed, Manasseh's heretical counterreformation was so horrifying to the narrator that he portrayed this king as Judah's equivalent of Jeroboam of Israel: Just as Jeroboam had caused Israel to sin, so also Manasseh caused Judah to sin. On account of his offenses, the fate of Judah was sealed. The pious reforms of Hezekiah were rendered as nothing. Even the all-encompassing reformation of Josiah could not save Judah (2 Kgs 22:1–23:30). So Judah was finally destroyed; Jerusalem was devastated; the Temple, the symbol of God's presence, was razed to the ground; and the people of Judah were exiled.

Judah's monarchy survived the long years of Assyrian domination but fell then into Babylonian hands, which it did not survive.

KINGS OF ISRAEL AND JUDAH*

Kings of Judah	Kings of Israel	
Rehoboam (924–907)	Jeroboam I (924–903)	**Four decades of hostilities** (c. 924–855) From Solomon's death to Omri's rise to power, the two kingdoms were weak and often at war with each other.
Abijah (907-906)		
Asa (905-874)		
	Nadab (903–902)	
	Baasha (902–886)	
	Elah, Zimri (886–885)	
	Omri (885–873)	**Era of the Omride dynasty** (c. 885–843) Israel emerged in strength and played a significant role in international affairs. Judah, allied with Israel, also shared in the resulting prosperity.
Jehoshaphat (874–850)		
	Ahab (873–851)	
	Ahaziah (851–849)	
Jehoram (850-843)		
	Jehoram (849–843)	
Ahaziah (843)		
Athaliah (843–837)	Jehu (843-816)	**Era of the Jehu dynasty** (c. 843–745) Israel and Judah were overshadowed by Damascus, then recovered and, under Jeroboam II and Uzziah, experienced a brief period of prosperity and expansion.
Joash (837–?)		
Amaziah (?–?)	Jehoahaz (816–800)	
Uzziah (?–?)	Joash (800–785)	
	Jeroboam II (785–745)	
	Zechariah, Shallum (745)	
Jehoahaz I (742–727)	Menahem (745–736)	**Assyrian domination** (c. 745–605) Israel's monarchy ended with the fall of Samaria, and the former Israelite territory was annexed into the Assyrian province system.
	Pekahiah (736–735)	
	Pekah (735–732)	
	Hoshea (732–723)	
Hezekiah (727–698)	**Fall of Samaria (722)**	
Manasseh (697–642)		
Amon (642–640)		
Josiah (639–609)		
Jehoahaz II (609)		
Jehoiakim (608–598)		**Babylonian domination** (c. 605–539) Judah's monarchy survivied the long years of Assyrian domination but fell then into Babylonian hands, which it did not survive.
Jehoiachin (598–597)		
Zedekiah (597–586)		
Destruction of Jerusalem (586)		

*NIB 1:263

THE BOOK OF KINGS AS THEOLOGICAL NARRATIVE

Arguably the most challenging task for the interpreter of Kings is to make sense of it in one's own day and age. To be sure, there are the memorable stories that warm our hearts, like the story of Solomon's receipt of the gift of wisdom from God (1 Kgs 3:4-15) or his swift and simple administration of justice in a complex case (1 Kgs 3:16-28). There are also stories that obviously testify to the power of God and God's prophets, like Elijah's victory on Mt. Carmel (1 Kgs 18:1-46) or Elisha's healing of the leprous Aramean general through a cleansing at the Jordan River (2 Kgs 5:1-19). These are the passages that one finds repeatedly in lectionaries. Yet, there is much in the narratives that is difficult to appropriate as Scripture. The book is filled with all kinds of peculiar details, not only the unfamiliar names of many kings and the dates of their reigns, but also administrative lists (e.g., 1 Kgs 4:1-34) and pedantic descriptions of the Temple and its appurtenances (e.g., 1 Kgs 6:1–7:51). Many of the stories seem tedious and repetitive (cf. 1 Kgs 15:1–16:28), horribly violent (e.g., 2 Kgs 9:1–10:36), ethically challenging (e.g., 1 Kgs 1:1–2:46; 13:1-33), or just plain odd (e.g., 2 Kgs 6:1-7; 13:14-21). Our challenge in reading these texts—indeed, all of Kings—is to make theological sense of them. At one level, the book of Kings reads like a historical document. By presenting the events in a chronological sequence, by its frequent chronological notices and synchronisms (coordination of the reigns of the kings of Israel with the reigns of the kings of Judah), and by its use of and references to historical sources ("the Book of the Acts of Solomon"; "the Book of the Annals of the Kings of Israel"; "the Book of the Annals of the Kings of Judah"), the book of Kings seems to present itself as a work of history. Much of what we know of the history of Israel in this period is, indeed, derived from this source; some of its information has been corroborated by extra-biblical inscriptions and other archaeological sources.

Yet, the purpose of the book is not to present a comprehensive history of the period, as if it were written for general information about the period in question. Rather, by its frequent references to fuller accounts elsewhere (e.g., 1 Kgs 14:19, 29), the text implicitly admits to the selectivity of its data. Rather, the history is a decisively theological one. It has to do with the working out of God's will. Other historical data are of secondary interest to the narrator or, indeed, of no interest at all. So, for instance, Omri, who is known from extra-biblical sources to have been a powerful monarch, warrants only passing notice, for to the narrator he was merely an unfaithful king who was a failure in the eyes of God. Likewise, Ahab is known to have accomplished much politically and militarily, but the narrator presents him as a bungling and rather weak king. By the same token, there are many tantalizing historical allusions that cannot be verified from other records, historical details that cannot be easily reconciled with what we know from other sources, synchronisms that contradict one another, and places that cannot be identified and the significance of which cannot be discerned. Although the pursuit of such historical questions may yield satisfying results, the reader must keep in mind that the purpose of the book of Kings is to impart a theological message.

FOR FURTHER READING

Brenner, Athalya, ed. *A Feminist Companion to Samuel and Kings*. Feminist Companion to the Bible. First Series 5. Sheffield Acadmic Press, 1994.

————. *Samuel and Kings: A Feminist Companion to the Bible*. Feminist Companion to the Bible. Second Series 7. Sheffield: Sheffield Academic Press, 2000.

Brodie, Thomas L. *The Crucial Bridge: The Elijah-Elisha Narrative as an Interpretive Synthesis of Genesis-Kings and a Literary Model for the Gospels*. Collegeville, Minn.: Liturgical Press, 2000.

Brueggemann, Walter. *1 Kings*. KPG. Atlanta: John Knox, 1983.

————. *2 Kings*. KPG. Atlanta: John Knox, 1982.

————. *1 & 2 Kings*. Smythe & Helwys Bible Commentary Series. Macon, Ga.: Smyth & Helwys, 2001.

Cogan, Mordechai. *1 Kings*. New York: Doubleday, 2001.

Cogan, Mordechai, and Hayim Tadmor. *2 Kings*. AB 11. Garden City, N.Y.: Doubleday, 1988.

Cohn, Robert L. *2 Kings*. Berit Olam. Collegeville, Minn.: Liturgical Press, 2000.

De Vries, Simon J. *1 Kings*. WBC 12. Waco, Tex.: Word, 1985.

Fretheim, Terence E. *First and Second Kings*. Westminster Bible Companion. Louisville, Ky.: Westminster/John Knox Press, 1999.

Fritz, Volkmar. *1 and 2 Kings: A Continental Commentary*. Translated by Anselm C. Hagedorn. CC. Minneapolis: Augsburg Fortress, 2003.

Gray, John. *1 & 2 Kings, A Commentary*. OTL. Philadelphia: Westminster, 1970.

Hobbs, T. R. *2 Kings*. WBC 13. Waco, Tex.: Word, 1985.

Jones, Gwilym. H. *1 and 2 Kings*. NCB. 2 vols. Grand Rapids: Eerdmans, 1984.

Long, Burke O. *1 Kings, with an Introduction to Historical Literature*. FOTL 9. Grand Rapids: Eerdmans, 1984.

————. *2 Kings*. FOTL 10. Grand Rapids: Eerdmans, 1991.

Montgomery, James A., and Henry Snyder Gehman. *A Critical and Exegetical Commentary on the Book of Kings*. ICC. Edinburgh: T & T Clark, 1986.

Nelson, Richard D. *First and Second Kings*. Interpretation. Atlanta: John Knox, 1987.

Rice, G. *1 Kings: Nations Under God*. ITC. Grand Rapids: Eerdmans, 1990.

Walsh, Jerome T. *1 Kings*. Berit Olam. Collegeville, Minn.: Liturgical Press, 1996.

THE FIRST AND SECOND BOOK OF CHRONICLES

LESLIE C. ALLEN

The books of Chronicles are the Bible's best-kept secret. Pastors who base their preaching on *The Revised Common Lectionary*[1] will find Chronicles absent from its readings. In Christian tradition these books have suffered by being placed behind 1 and 2 Samuel and 1 and 2 Kings, as if they were some pale shadow instead of an epic work in their own right. In the Hebrew Bible they stand impressively at the end, at the close of the Writings, or else before Psalms and after Malachi. That canonical distance from Samuel–Kings is necessary to symbolize a later time frame and different perspective. Still, the first nine chapters of genealogies are like lions guarding the gates, driving away the fainthearted from the treasures inside. S. De Vries has testified: "I regard Chronicles as one of the richest mines of spirituality in all Scripture."[2] The assessment of an earlier commentator may be added: "Chronicles is one of the most stimulating books in the Bible, courageous and practical—a splendid achievement."[3]

THE DATING OF CHRONICLES

There is a growing tendency to regard Chronicles as distinct from Ezra–Nehemiah, over against the traditional view of the two texts as a composite document. Although more work needs to be done to establish their precise relationship, enough evidence of their basic independence has emerged.[4] This discovery has released the books of Chronicles from the burden of interpretation dictated by Ezra–Nehemiah, which as a post-exilic document dealing with post-exilic events has a plainer agenda than Chronicles.

Chronicles appears to have been written after the bulk of Ezra–Nehemiah. It cites the latter, just as it does other written texts. Ezra 1:1-3 is quoted in 2 Chr 36:22-23, and Neh 11:3-19 in 1 Chr 9:2-17, while Ezra 9:1–10 is reflected in 2 Chr 24:26.

Chronicles also depends on Zechariah 1:1–8, as it does on pre-exilic prophetic texts. Zechariah 1:2-4 is presupposed in 2 Chr 30:6-7, Zech 4:10 in 2 Chr 16:9, and Zech 8:10 in 2 Chr 15:5-6. Since Zechariah 1:1–8 was written in the early post-exilic period, Chronicles must have been written sometime later. Moreover, it is significant that Chronicles used the Pentateuch in its final form.[5]

Archaeologists have found that the Persian period of Judean history falls into two parts. The second part, from about 450 to 332 BCE, is marked by an increase in prosperity.[6] David's appeal for contributions to the Temple and prayer of praise for a generous response in 1 Chronicles 29 and the narrative of the people's provision of ample support for the temple personnel in 2 Chronicles 31 are significant in this respect. Both chapters are transparently addressed to the constituency for whom the book was intended. The difficulty to be surmounted was evidently not an inability to give but an unwillingness to do so. The motif of willingness pervades the account in 1 Chronicles 29, and it is accompanied by references to the wealthy patriarchs as models. Such references fit the relative affluence of the second part of the Persian period.

A late Persian period dating is also supported by the levitical claims made in the course of Chronicles. There seems to have been considerable development in the standing of subordinate personnel of the post-exilic Temple. At an early stage the singing musicians were not regarded as Levites (Ezra 2:41 = Neh 7:44). By Nehemiah's time they were considered as such and were composed of two groups, the descendants of Asaph and the descendants of Jeduthun (Neh 11:3-19). At a later period the choir of Heman was added; eventually it became more prominent than that of Asaph, while the choir of Jeduthun was displaced by that of Ethan.[7] The evidence of Chronicles spans both stages of the third period, the former in 1 Chr

16:37-42; 2 Chr 5:12; 29:13-14; 35:15, and the latter in 1 Chr 6:31-48; 15:16-21, while the citation of Neh 11:3-19 in 1 Chronicles 9 naturally echoes the second period. Similarly, the gatekeepers were not yet Levites at the time of Ezra 2:42 (= Neh 7:45), nor had they yet graduated to this position by Neh 11:19, cited at 1 Chr 9:17. However, a later source employed in 1 Chr 9:18 firmly identifies them as such.

The same impression of a dating late in the Persian period is given by the post-exilic continuation of the Davidic genealogy in 1 Chronicles 3. The exact number of generations involved cannot be ascertained, but the genealogy extends into the fourth century BCE and was presumably meant to reflect the time of Chronicles. In the light of this and the earlier evidence, the first half of the fourth century BCE seems to be the period when it was written. No Hellenistic features are present to warrant a later date.

THE SETTING AND PURPOSE OF CHRONICLES

A dominant feature of Chronicles is an emphasis on exile and restoration, both as a historical fact and as a metaphor that providentially relates the overall success or failure of the community to its spiritual relationship to the Lord. The chronicler—the homogeneity of most of the work suggests that an individual rather than a group was responsible, and one may presume that the author was male—envisioned in 2 Chronicles 28:1–36 not one exile but a series of exiles toward the end of the pre-exilic period. He conceived of not only one literal and national restoration but also a royal one in the case of Manasseh and a metaphorical one under Hezekiah, which repeated the restoration represented by David's reign after the "exilic" fate of Saul and Israel.[8]

The novelty of the chronicler lies in his application of the theme and not in his creation of it. A later author (Daniel 9) would claim that the exile was to last 490 years, not seventy, and was a negative condition still experienced by the so-called post-exilic community.[9] This notion of exile as a metaphor for a continuing experience is also found in earlier post-exilic literature. Psalm 126 celebrates the Lord's restoration of Zion's fortunes in the return from exile. Yet all was not well. The worshiping community prayed afresh, "Restore our fortunes." They were still suffering a virtual exile, though they lived in the land again. The same point is made in the first half of Psalm 85, where the Lord's past restoration of Jacob's fortunes is the basis for hope of a renewed restoration (Ps 85:1, 4). The cessation of divine anger indicated by the return from literal exile needed to be repeated, since the community was still suffering from that anger (Ps 85:3, 4-5). This superimposing of an exilic condition as a way to understand the post-exilic situation also occurs in Zech 1:2-6, which as has been observed is reflected in 2 Chr 30:6-7. The Lord's anger with the pre-exilic people, which resulted in their exile, is used as a symbol of warning for the post-exilic community.

The prayers in Ezra 9 and Nehemiah 9 demonstrate the ways in which exile as a metaphor can be traced to the present. In the former case it is lamented that "from the days of our ancestors to this day we have been deep in guilt, and for our iniquities we, our kings, and our priests have been handed over to the kings of the lands, to the sword, to captivity, to plundering, and to utter shame, as is now the case" (Ezra 9:7 NRSV). Divine alleviation of this condition is described in grudging terms (Ezra 9:8-9). Similarly, Nehemiah 9 speaks of the hardships endured by the community "since the time of the kings of Assyria until today" and of the "great distress" caused by foreign domination (Neh 9:32, 37). Despite domicile in the land, the people understood themselves to be "in exile."

In this connection the reader should consider the partial spiritualization of terms relating to the land in the psalms. Although the process began in the pre-exilic period, its continuing use in the post-exilic age is significant. The psalms use the levitical phrase "the LORD is my portion"—the Levites had received no portion of tribal land—to express the faith of the laity (Pss 16:5; 73:26; 142:6; cf. Lam 3:24). They also freely employ terms of inheriting the land as metaphors of blessing in store for the faithful (Pss 16:6; 25:13; 37 [5 times]; 44:4; 69:36-37).[10] The concept of a spiritual restoration to the land is reinforced by this use of language.

Chronicles acknowledges the problematic condition of metaphorical exile. The chronicler utilized this well-established imagery of exile and restoration, and he deliberately echoed it thoughout his work. He used three religious texts that deal with the literal exile and pointed forward to restoration, reapplying them to people in other conditions. These texts became guidelines for his constituency to follow, commending to them the cures advocated in the texts.

The first text is Lev 26:34-45, which reviews Israel's sin, exile, and return to the land. Leviticus 26:34 is given a structurally significant place in 2 Chr 36:21 to define the duration of the literal exile as limited to a set period of sabbath rest. According to Jeremiah 29, this exile was to last seventy years. There never was a fatalistic decree that exile should continue for centuries. The metaphorical exile was the people's fault, not the Lord's. To describe the spiritual conditions for such exile the chronicler drew upon the expression מעל מעל (māʿal maʿal), "practice unfaithfulness" (Lev 26:40; "committed treachery," NRSV). He used either the phrase or its separate elements of verb and noun as a key term. In the light of Lev 26:15, 43, this vocabulary is used in the general sense of breaking the covenant, though in a few contexts it gains a cultic nuance. He employed the term to define the cause of literal exile in 1 Chr 5:25 ("were unfaithful," NIV); 9:1; and 2 Chr 36:14. This same vocabulary appears elsewhere in his regular diagnosis for metaphorical exile, notably in the evaluation of the reigns of Saul and Ahaz (1 Chr 10:13; 2 Chr 29:6). The Leviticus passage also supplies one of the characteristic terms used by the chronicler when he refers to restoration, "to be humbled" (נכנע niknaʿ, in the niphal; Lev 26:41), e.g., in 2 Chr 7:14, a text that puts in a nutshell the chronicler's remedy for spiritual exile.

The second text imbued with religious authority to which the chronicler made frequent reference is Jer 29:10-19. It, too, discusses literal exile and restoration, and so might be used as a basis for comparison for their metaphorical counterparts. The description of the desolation of the land in Jer 29:18 is applied to the outworking of divine wrath inherited by Hezekiah in 2 Chr 29:8. The prophecy of seventy years of exile is used positively as a limit of the Lord's judgment of exile in 2 Chr 36:21-22. However, the passage was primarily used to define how God's people might be spiritually restored: "when you call upon me and come and pray to me, I will hear you . . . If you seek me with all your heart, I will let you find me, says the LORD, and I will restore your fortunes" (Jer 29:12-14 NRSV). The divine promise became the substance of the chronicler's own message. It is the basis of the epigrammatic 2 Chr 7:14 and of the spiritual principle, "If you seek [the Lord], he will be found by you" in 1 Chr 28:9 and 2 Chr 15:2. Most notably the Jeremian text supplies the chronicler's devotional key word דרש (dāraš, "seek"), which is extensively used to characterize repentant return to the Lord and normative worship and way of life. The chronicler uses the parallel verb בקש (biqqēš, "seek"), which occurs in Jer 29:13, less often.

The third text about exile and return from which the chronicler drew heavily is Ezekiel 18, which grounds an appeal to the exiles for repentance in a sequence of good and bad generations, and also generations who changed in midcourse from bad to good and from good to bad.[11] The text provides structural models for the royal narratives of both the divided kingdom in 2 Chronicles 10:1–28 and the reunited kingdom in chaps. 29–36. Moreover, it uses the idiom māʿal maʿal, "practice unfaithfulness" [Lev 26:40; Ezek 18:24]), in the general sense of breaking the Torah. The chronicler's teaching of immediate retribution is generally worked out at the level of individual kings, but who symbolize separate generations. We have learned to exegete Ezekiel 18 in terms of generations, and we must also do so in the case of Chronicles. The chronicler regarded members of each generation as controlling their own destiny, free to start again with or against the Lord.

A clue to the importance of each generation in Chronicles is the recurring phrase "the God of their/your/our fathers" (NIV). The NRSV, true to its inclusive concern, renders "the God of . . . ancestors," but this is rarely the meaning. The singular counterpart "the God of your/his father" in 1 Chr 28:9; 2 Chr 17:4 is significant. Each generation had the responsibility of appropriating the faith handed down by its immediate predecessors. The chronicler was calling on his own generation to pursue the path that led to spiritual restoration. It was this policy that, by God's grace, made possible a break with the oppressive past that otherwise haunted each post-exilic generation.

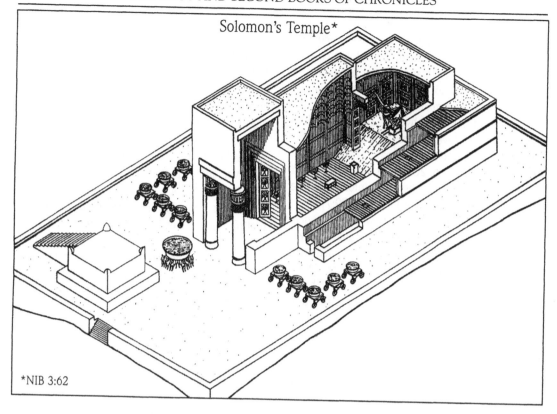

Solomon's Temple*

*NIB 3:62

THE DAVIDIC ERA

The literary backbone of Chronicles is the account of the joint reigns of David and Solomon, to which nearly half the work is devoted. Correspondingly their reigns constitute the theological mainstay of the book. The chronicler used the verb "choose" (בחר *bāḥar*) to indicate special agents or agencies in the Lord's long-term purposes. Of the seven entities so described, five are closely associated with these two reigns: David (2 Chr 6:6), Solomon (1 Chr 28:10), the Temple (2 Chr 7:12, 16; 33:7), Jerusalem (2 Chr 6:6, 34, 38; 12:13), and the tribe of Judah in its royal role (1 Chr 28:4). The two other entities, Israel (1 Chr 16:13) and the Levites (1 Chr 15:2; 2 Chr 29:11), are swept into this new work.

Another term for theological destiny used by the chronicler is "forever" (עד עולם *'ad 'ôlām*) or variations involving this word. Apart from two references to God, it is employed twenty-seven times in Chronicles, of which sixteen occurrences relate either to the Davidic dynasty (7 times) or to the Temple (9 times). Again the joint reigns supply the arena for the majority of cases. As for the other instances, three entities were radically affected by the two reigns, the land (3 times), Israel (twice),

and the covenant love (חסד *ḥesed*, "[steadfast] love") extended by the Lord to Israel (6 times).

The way these weighty terms are used discloses the chronicler's perception of a Davidic era launched under David and Solomon and continuing until the chronicler's own time. It superseded the Mosaic dispensation and covenant, to which Israel failed to adhere. Hence Chronicles plays down, though without denying, the exodus traditions. They are given a swan song in 1 Chr 17:21-22, to be replaced, in effect, by new traditions. The concept of a new dispensation was probably suggested to the chronicler by Psalm 78:1, especially vv. 67-72; the chronicler alludes to Ps 78:68, 70 in 1 Chr 28:4. There was continuity with the old dispensation; the religious and general duties of the Mosaic Torah were still obligatory for Israel. Yet the Jerusalem Temple now replaced the tabernacle of the Torah, and the Levites received a new role. The chronicler indulged in a host of typological parallels to demonstrate the divine authority of the new sanctuary, over against the representations of the writen Torah. And for those who broke the Torah and repented, there was a way back to the Lord.

There is also a concern to establish the permanent nature of the Davidic dynasty. It was guaranteed, the chronicler claimed, by Solomon's construction of the Temple and general obedience to the Torah (1 Chr 28:6-7). Thereby Israel's relationship to the Lord was made permanent, as especially 2 Chr 9:8 affirms. The hymnic snatch "for [the Lord's] [steadfast] love endures forever" ties Israel's covenant to the Davidic covenant (1 Chr 16:34, 41; 2 Chr 5:13; 7:3, 6; 20:21). The permanent gift of the land to the patriarchs was reinforced by the Davidic covenant (1 Chr 16:17; 2 Chr 20:7).

There is a delicate balance between the once-for-all theological privilege established under David and Solomon and the onus of covenant obedience laid on kings and commoners thereafter. These twin phenomena find common ground in 1 Chronicles 28. In v. 8 the latter responsibility is added to a declaration of the God-given privilege. Israel's future oscillates in Chronicles between objective certainty in principle (2 Chr 9:8) and subjective uncertainty in particular (2 Chr 7:19-20).

In the interests of a moral and spiritual challenge the royal narratives after David's and Solomon's reigns focus on tracing the obedience or disobedience of each king to the guidelines laid down in those reigns. Yet there are also reminders of the permanent nature of Davidic kingship (2 Chr 13:5; 21:7), reaffirming the earlier narratives. Similarly, in 1 Chronicles 2:1–9 the extension of the Davidic genealogy into the post-exilic period at 1 Chronicles 3:1 strikes a unique note of permanence. The Davidic covenant's divinely pledged permanence—and hence certainty of restoration—was also the sign of Israel's permanence. Pastoral needs loom large in the emphasis on Israel's responsibility after 2 Chronicles 9. The lack of any royal reaffirmation near or at the end of the book also reflects the historical fact of the Davidic dynasty's eclipse, an eclipse that stretched far into the post-exilic period. One suspects that the dynasty's restoration was a distant item on the chronicler's eschatological calendar, doubtless as a negative response to political and perhaps proto-apocalyptic pressures.[12] It would be restored in God's good time. Moreover, that restoration was separate from the blessings each post-exilic generation had the potential to inherit, even within the context of Persian hegemony (see 2 Chr 12:7-8).

The Temple provided a pivot between theological stability and spiritual alternatives in the chronicler's thought. Its choirs brought a constant reminder that the Lord's "[steadfast] love endures forever." The Temple was the divinely instituted setting for the normative obligations of worship and maintenance of its fabric and personnel. In the course of the royal narratives, the chronicler covered each of the Torah-based festivals in turn, the Feast of Tabernacles in 2 Chronicles 7, the Feast of Weeks in 2 Chronicles 15, and the double feast of Passover and Unleavened Bread in 2 Chronicles 30 and 35.[13] Both in these chapters and in 1 Chronicles 15:1–16, he affirmed the joy of celebrating regular worship. Yet the Temple was also the center of an emergency system that offered restoration to the repentant. Redemptive grace could prevail over the breaking of the Torah (see esp. 2 Chr 7:3-16; 30:18-20; 32:25-26).

AN INCLUSIVE ISRAEL

A constant issue in the teaching of Chronicles is the inclusiveness of the people of God. In this respect the work stands at a remarkable distance from Ezra and Nehemiah, who at an earlier period advocated a separatist community made up of Judeans who had returned from exile. Doubtless the chronicler judged that the time was ripe for a less rigorous policy, now that the community was more established. His insistence on the spiritual potential of a wider religious community made up of "all Israel" is integrated with his presentation of the united kingdom of David and Solomon, and that insistence is reaffirmed under the reunited kingdom of Hezekiah. In the genealogical prologue, it is undergirded by appeals to the traditions of the twelve tribes in the wilderness period, attested by the Torah, and affirmed in the settlement of the promised land.

In this respect the chronicler steered a middle course between separatist and assimilationist parties in Jerusalem.[14] He rigorously maintained the unique role of the Jerusalem Temple in Israel's worship. The well-established traditions of a united Israel laid on Judah the obligation to attempt to win back Israelites still in the north to allegiance to the God of the Temple. Hezekiah is presented as a model for this obligation (2 Chronicles 30).

THE LEVITES

The chronicler's attitude toward the Levites breaks the pattern of his overall teaching. Certainly it is stitched neatly into the Davidic organization of the Temple, and their work is thus invested with the highest religious authority. Yet his teaching would have been coherent, theologically and spiritually, without his pervasive attention to the Levites. The chronicler acted as advocate for the Levites, regarding them as a disadvantaged group. His enthusiasm, which extends to a call for affirmative action, opens for us an otherwise closed window to the music and song provided by the singing Levites and the security system operated by the gatekeeping Levites. The chronicler urges that they be given a greater role in sacrificial worship and attaches names and pedigrees to the faceless members of these lower ranks of the temple staff.

The chronicler's advocacy of the Levites led to the redactional introduction of material emphasizing the role of the priesthood. A pro-priestly reviser was active mainly in 1 Chronicles 23:1–27, but also in a few passages elsewhere; he may have lived a generation later than the chronicler.[15] The redactor's aim was not to silence his predecessor's advocacy but to supplement it and so redress the balance somewhat, making Chronicles more comprehensive in its outlook.

THE FORM OF CHRONICLES

Cronicles falls into four literary blocks. The longest and most important block deals with the reigns of David and Solomon, which established under God the institutions of the dynasty and the Temple. It is followed by accounts of the divided kingdom of Judah and of the reunited kingdom. These latter two blocks reaffirm the spiritual guidelines laid down in the main one, sometimes positively but more often negatively. The introduction to Chronicles provides a block of genealogies, which presents the themes of Israel's election, its inclusive nature as traditionally made up of twelve tribes, and its territorial heritage. These themes are set against a gradually emerging background of the people's unfaithfulness, exile, and restoration, which the royal narratives will repeat.

The chronicler had only a few tunes in his literary repertoire. He played them over and over again in the interests of spiritual challenge and encouragement, mainly with the present and immediate future in mind, but also on a long-term scale. It has been observed that Chronicles could "have been utilised section by section as a series of connected homilies."[16] I have traced in an article, the quasi-homiletic stylization of the subdivisions in the four literary blocks of Chronicles.[17] The chronicler used standard rhetorical devices to present his material in assimilable portions in order to stimulate spiritual commitment to theological principles.

The question of the relation of Chronicles to "real" history is often raised. A thorough answer would be complex. Sometimes the chronicler evidently reproduced ancient, authentic documents, for instance in 1 Chr 27:25-31; sometimes he wrote up a grand tale out of a little incident, for example in 2 Chr 20:1-30; and once he stood an earlier narrative on its head to adapt it to his own perspective, in 2 Chr 20:35-37. In general modern readers need to be warned against false expectations. The chronicler was writing to help his own generation. Hence readers must focus on his situation and message—and not only on earlier history—if they are to do him justice. His royal narratives in 2 Chronicles 10:1–36 are a series of spiritual parables, and the speeches put into the mouths of his characters are vehicles by means of which he interprets these stories. The earlier narratives of Samuel–Kings, which were his sources, are put through a hermeneutical filter to convey the truths his constituency needed to learn. The particular genre of historiography exhibited in Chronicles must be considered in the light of its homiletic function.

THE TEXT OF CHRONICLES

Discussion of the Masoretic Text (MT) has been limited to explaining cases of divergence from it by the NRSV and the NIV, which are both alert to textual problems, and between these versions and also to other instances judged to be of exegetical importance. For further discussion, readers will often be directed to my earlier work, *The Greek Chronicles: The Relation of the Septuagint of 1 and 2 Chronicles to the Massoretic Text.*[18]

An important issue is what type of text of Samuel–Kings was available to the chronicler. For Kings, he had the type preserved in the MT.[19] In the case of Samuel, his text was close to that of the first-century BCE Qumran manuscript

4QSam[a].[20] It is crucial to trace this textual relationship because a number of idiosyncratic features previously credited to the chronicler are now seen to be already part of the textual tradition of Samuel that he used.

EXEGETING AND APPLYING CHRONICLES

Chronicles is inspirational literature, and so an exegetical and hermeneutical interpretation has the duty to convey with warmth the inspirational message. The chronicler had a pastor's heart and a teacher's mind, and his concern for his constituency surfaces throughout. Application depends on the particular circumstances of the modern pastor. The chronicler does invite us to take an interest in his literary sources (see, e.g., 2 Chr 13:22). But the main endeavor will be to examine Chronicles as a work in its own right and to listen to the spiritual message it wants to bring. As we readers first overhear it and then make an effort to hear it in the context of our particular situations, we shall find that message to be both biblical and contemporary, both inspired and inspiring.[21]

FOR FURTHER READING

Ackroyd, P. R. *1 & 2 Chronicles, Ezra, Nehemiah*. Torch Bible. London: SCM, 1973.

Braun, R. L. *1 Chronicles*. WBC 14. Waco, Tex.: Word, 1986.

De Vries, S. J. *1 and 2 Chronicles*. FOTL 11. Grand Rapids: Eerdmans, 1989.

Dillard, R. B. *2 Chronicles*. WBC 15. Waco, Tex.: Word, 1987.

Graham, M. Patrick, Kenneth G. Hoglund, and Steven L. McKenzie, eds. *The Chronicler As Historian*. JSOTSup 238. Sheffield: Sheffield Academic Press, 1997.

Graham, M. Patrick, and Steven L. McKenzie, eds. *The Chronicler As Author: Studies in Text and Texture*. JSOTSup 263. Sheffield: Sheffield Academic Press, 1999.

Graham, M. Patrick, Steven L. McKenzie, and Gary N. Knoppers, eds. *The Chronicler As Theologian: Essays in Honor of Ralph W. Klein*. JSOTSup 371. New York: T&T Clark, 2003.

Japhet, S. *1 & 2 Chronicles*. OTL. Louisville: Westminster/John Knox, 1993.

———. *The Ideology of the Book of Chronicles and Its Place in Biblical Thought*. Translated by A. Barber. BEATAJ 9. Frankfurt am Main: Peter Lang, 1989.

Hognesius, Kjell. *The Text of 2 Chronicles 1–16: A Critical Edition With Textual Commentary*. ConBOT 51. Stockholm: Almqvist & Wiksell, 2003.

Hooker, Paul K. *First and Second Chronicles*. Westminster Bible Commentary. Louisville, Ky.: Westminster/John Knox, 2002.

Kalimi, Isaac. *The Book of Chronicles: Historical Writing and Literary Devices*. Jerusalem: Bialik Institute, 2000.

McConville, J. G. *1 & 2 Chronicles*. Daily Study Bible. Philadelphia: Westminster, 1984.

Selman, M. J. *1 Chronicles; 2 Chronicles*. TOTC. Downers Grove: Inter-Varsity, 1994.

Williamson, H. G. M. *1 and 2 Chronicles*. NCB. Grand Rapids: Eerdmans, 1982.

———. *Israel in the Books of Chronicles*. Cambridge: Cambridge University Press, 1977.

ENDNOTES

1. *The Revised Common Lectionary* (Nashville: Abingdon, 1992).

2. S. J. De Vries, *1 and 2 Chronicles*, FOTL 11 (Grand Rapids: Eerdmans, 1989) xiv.

3. W. A. Elmslie, *The First and Second Books of Chronicles*, IB, 12 vols. (New York: Abingdon, 1954) 3:341.

4. See T. C. Eskenazi, *In an Age of Prose: A Literary Approach to Ezra–Nehemiah*, SBLMS 36 (Atlanta: Scholars Press, 1988) 14-36; S. Japhet, *1 & 2 Chronicles*, OTL (Louisville: Westminster/John Knox, 1993) 3-5.

5. See W. M. Schniedewind, *The Word of God in Transition: From Prophet to Exegete in the Second Temple Period*, JSOTSup 197 (Sheffield: Sheffield Academic, 1995) 133n. 11, 194n. 16.

6. See C. L. Myers and E. M. Myers, *Zechariah 9:1–14*, AB 25C (Garden City, N.Y.: Doubleday, 1993) 22-26.

7. See H. Gese, "Zur Geschichte der Kultsänger am zweiten Tempel," *Abraham unser Vater: Juden und Christen im Gespräch über die Bibel*, ed. O. Betz et al. (Leiden: Brill, 1963) 222-34 (= *Vom Sinai zum Zion. Alttestamentliche Beiträge zur biblischen Theologie*, BEvT 64 [Munich: Chr.

Kaiser, 1974] 147-58); H. G. M. Williamson, "The Origins of the Twenty-four Priestly Courses: A Study of 1 Chronicles xxiii-xxvii," in Studies in the Historical Books of the Old Testament, ed. J. A. Emerton, VTSup 30 (Leiden: Brill, 1979) 251-68, esp. 263.

8. See R. Mosis, *Untersuchungen zur Theologie des chronisten Geschichtswerks*, Freiburger theologische Studien 92 (Freiburg: Herder, 1973) 31-43; P. R. Ackroyd, "The Chronicler as Exegete," *JSOT* 2 (1977) 2-32, esp. 3-9 (= *The Chronicler in His Age*, JSOTSup 101 [Sheffield: JSOT, 1991] 314-18).

9. See M. A. Knibb, "The Exile in the Literature of the Intertestamental Period," *HeyJ* 17 (1976) 253-72.

10. See H. D. Preuss, *Old Testament Theology I*, trans. L. G. Perdue (Louisville: Westminster/John Knox, 1995) 123.

11. See R. B. Dillard, "Reward and Punishment in Chronicles: The Theology of Immediate Retribution," *WTJ* 46 (1984) 164-72, esp. 171.

12. See H. H. Rowley's refusal to see eschatological significance in World War II in *The Relevance of Apocalyptic* (London: Lutterworth, 1944) 7-8. Very little is known of Judah's history in this period. For the unsettled political history of the later Persian period in the West, see E. Stern, *The Cambridge History of Judaism*, ed. W. D. Davies and L. Finkelstein (Cambridge: Cambridge University Press, 1984) 1:73-77.

13. See H. Cancik, "Des jüdische Fest," *TQ* 105 (1970) 335-48, esp. 338-39.

14. H. G. M. Williamson, *Israel in the Books of Chronicles* (Cambridge: Cambridge University Press, 1977) 139.

15. See H. G. M. Williamson, "The Origins of the Twenty-four Priestly Courses: A Study of 1 Chronicles xxiii-xxvii," in *Studies in the Historical Books of the Old Testament*, ed. J. A. Emerton, VTSup 30 (Leiden: Brill, 1979) 251-68, esp. 266; cf. in principle A. C. Welch, *The Work of the Chronicler: Its Purpose and Date* (London: British Academy, 1939) 71-73, 85-96.

16. P. R. Ackroyd, *The Age of the Chronicler* (Aukland: Colloquium, 1970) 45 (= *The Chronicler in His Age, JSOTSup 101* [Sheffield: JSOT, 1991] 64).

17. L. C. Allen, "Kerygmatic Units in 1 and 2 Chronicles," *JSOT* 41 (1988) 21-36.

18. L. C. Allen, *The Greek Chronicles: The Relation of the Septuagint of 1 and 2 Chronicles to the Massoretic Text*, Part 1: *The Translator's Craft;* Part 2: *Textual Criticism*, VTSup 25, 27 (Leiden: Brill, 1974).

19. See S. L. McKenzie, *The Chronicler's Use of the Deuteronomistic History*, HSM 33 (Atlanta: Scholars Press, 1985) 83-84, 33-81.

20. See S. L. McKenzie, *The Chronicler's Use of the Deuteronomistic History*, 83-84, 119-58.

21. Leslie C. Allen, *1, 2 Chronicles*, Communicator's Commentary 10 (Waco, Tex.: Word, 1987). Thanks are due to my colleague Francis I. Andersen for giving me a copy of the unpublished "A Key-Word-in-Context Concordance to Chronicles," edited by himself and A. D. Forbes, which proved of inestimable help; to the staff of the word processing office of Fuller Seminary for their labors on my behalf; and to my research assistant Curtis McNeil for his careful editing of the manuscript.

THE BOOK OF
EZRA & NEHEMIAH

RALPH W. KLEIN

The books of Ezra and Nehemiah were originally considered a single literary work called Ezra. Although this work was already separated into two books by Origen and Jerome, the division does not appear in the Hebrew Bible until the fifteenth century, and the statistics traditionally given at the end of a biblical book ("final massorah") come only at the end of the twenty-three chapters of Ezra–Nehemiah.

Ezra and Nehemiah consistently turn up in all canonical lists of Judaism and of Western Christianity, though they and 1–2 Chronicles are lacking in canonical lists of the Syrian church. In modern Hebrew Bibles the third section of the canon, the Writings, ends with Ezra–Nehemiah and then the books of Chronicles.

EXTENT AND DATE
OF THE ORIGINAL WORK

A principal issue in studies of Ezra and Nehemiah is whether they were once part of a longer chronicler's history or whether they formed from the beginning an independent work. Since the time of Leopold Zunz (1832) until the 1960s, the vast majority of scholars believed that the chronicler's history consisted of (all or most of) Chronicles and (all or parts of) Ezra–Nehemiah. Objections to this hypothesis were first raised by Sara Japhet on linguistic grounds, although subsequent discussion has questioned whether linguistic arguments alone can decide the question one way or the other.[1]

Other scholars have focused more on theological differences between Chronicles and Ezra–Nehemiah: (1) the concept of retribution and the terms related to it in Chronicles are almost entirely lacking in Ezra–Nehemiah; (2) the two works differ in their attitude toward the northern tribes, in particular the Samaritans; (3) Chronicles places a greater emphasis on the Davidic monarchy; (4) Ezra–Nehemiah mentions the election of Abraham and the exodus, whereas Chronicles concentrates on the patriarch Jacob (who is always called Israel) and de-emphasizes the exodus; (5) the frequent references to prophets in Chronicles make it a prophetic history; in Ezra–Nehemiah, by contrast, the prophetic influence has virtually ceased; (6) the נתינים (nĕtînîm, "temple servants") and the sons of Solomon's servants appear throughout Ezra–Nehemiah, but are absent from Chronicles, with the exception of 1 Chr 9:2; (7) in Chronicles, Israel comprises all twelve tribes, whereas in Ezra–Nehemiah Israel is limited to Judah and Benjamin.[2] This overview assumes that Chronicles and Ezra–Nehemiah are separate works.

While Tamara Eskenazi, through a literary reading, has made a strong case for the unity of Ezra–Nehemiah, including even the originality of the repetition of Ezra 2 in Nehemiah 7, David Kraemer and James VanderKam have proposed that Ezra and Nehemiah should be read as separate books.[3] Kraemer argues that Ezra is the work of the priesthood and limits the realm of the sacred to the Temple and the priests. Nehemiah, by way of contrast, is a lay composition that sees Torah as the focus of the sacred. VanderKam notes numerous minor differences in language between the two books, their different use of sources, and, most important, the alternate themes of the two books: Ezra focuses entirely on the restoration of the Temple and the people; Nehemiah centers on the rebuilding of the wall and the repopulating of Jerusalem. It is unclear whether these differences are due to the editor or to the sources (such as the Ezra and Nehemiah Memoirs) that were incorporated into the work. Perhaps the most suggestive aspect of this proposal is to understand Ezra's reading of the law in Nehemiah 8 within the literary context of Nehemiah, rather than in a reconstructed, "more original" position after Ezra 8 or Ezra 10. Here, Ezra's reading of the law will be interpreted in the context of Nehemiah 8, but I believe that Sara Japhet's proposed structure for Ezra–Nehemiah undercuts the proposals to read the books separately.

Scholars unanimously locate the author of this work in Palestine, but are somewhat more uncertain about the book's date. If we follow the traditional dates for Ezra (458 BCE) and Nehemiah (445–432?), then the composition must have taken place sometime later, but presumably well within the Persian period, since a favorable attitude is toward the Persians nearly everywhere in the book (except for Neh 9:37). A date in the first quarter of the fourth century, before the weakening of the Persian Empire, seems reasonable.

STRUCTURE OF EZRA–NEHEMIAH

Sara Japhet detects a historical periodization in Ezra–Nehemiah and divides the book into two units.[4] The first, Ezra 1:1–6, lasting one generation from the decree of Cyrus to the dedication of the Temple, includes two leaders, Zerubbabel and Jeshua, heads of the secular and religious establishments respectively. The building of the Temple is the main event in this unit, with events happening only in the first two and last two years of the unit. The intervening years, when work on the Temple was stopped, are described in one verse (Ezra 4:24). The status of the leaders is left undefined throughout the unit. Neither is present at the beginning of the unit, and neither was there at the Temple's dedication.

The second unit, Ezra 7–Nehemiah 13, again lasts one generation, from the arrival of Ezra in 458 BCE to the second term of Nehemiah in 432. This period is defined by its leaders, not by its projects. Ezra at first works by himself, then Nehemiah by himself, then the two together, and then Nehemiah again by himself. The two figures are active in 458 BCE (Ezra 7:1–10), 445 (Nehemiah 1:1–12), and 432 (Nehemiah 13:1), with nothing reported about the spaces between these activities. Nehemiah alone directs work on the walls, the social reform, and the repopulating of Jerusalem, but in the reading of the Torah and the dedication of the wall both Ezra and Nehemiah are present (Neh 8:1-2, 9; 12:26, 36).

For the first unit the author did not have a continuous literary source, but combined existing documents with his own narrative. For the second unit he was able to incorporate the memoirs of Ezra and Nehemiah, and he assigned both of them to the era of Artaxerxes I. By alternating between the two sources (Ezra 7:1–10; Nehemiah 1:1–7; Nehemiah 8 [Ezra material]; Neh 13:4-31), he created a synchronicity between the two leaders. Nehemiah 9:1–10 was added as material pertaining to the reading of Torah, and the lists in 11:1–12:26 provide information about the inhabitants of Jerusalem and Judah. Nehemiah 10; 11:1-2; and 12:27-43 are also excerpts from the Nehemiah Memoir. The author in the second unit did not include much of his own writing, but assigned the borrowed material to a chronological and historical framework he had created.

Throughout the work the author affirms that change and renewal in the life of Judah were the result of initiative on the part of the Persian kings—Cyrus, Darius, and Artaxerxes—and the Jews who had returned from exile in Babylon. God extended grace to those who returned from exile by means of the kings of Persia. Because of the author's method of composition, it is impossible to fully reconstruct his sources or the events they report.

HISTORICAL BACKGROUND

General Historical Outline. After Cyrus and the Persians conquered Babylon in 539 BCE, the king issued a decree that commanded the Jews, who had been exiled in 597 and 586, to return home and rebuild the Temple. Sheshbazzar led the first group home, and he was replaced at an unknown time by the governor (?) Zerubbabel and the high priest Jeshua. Their initial efforts to rebuild the Temple were interrupted by opposition from the peoples of the land, until Darius I reaffirmed the decree of Cyrus and ordered the rebuilding of the Temple to continue. The Temple was dedicated in 516 BCE.

About fifty-eight years later, Artaxerxes I (465–424) sent Ezra, the priest and scribe of the law of the God of heaven, to Jerusalem. The king's Aramaic decree (Ezra 7:12-26) commanded Ezra to lead Jews to Jerusalem, deliver gifts offered by the Persian authorities and by the people to the Temple, make inquiry about conformity to the law in

Judah and Jerusalem, and appoint magistrates and judges to teach the law. Within his first year Ezra led the people in a public confession of sin because of their intermarriage with foreigners and saw the creation of a commission that carried out the removal of the foreign wives and their children.

In 445 BCE Artaxerxes I sent Nehemiah to rebuild the walls of Jerusalem, a task completed within fifty-two days. Nehemiah also corrected abuses in the making of loans and the charging of interest and generously provided for others at his table without drawing on the taxes enjoyed by former governors (Neh 5:14-19). Before Nehemiah could carry out the repopulation of Jerusalem, Ezra reappeared and read the law to the people, who resolved to study it and then celebrated the Feast of Tabernacles. In a public ceremony, the people separated themselves from foreigners and confessed their sins and those of their parents. Next they entered a firm agreement to amend a number of activities with regard to mixed marriages, the sabbath, the wood offering, first fruits, levitical tithes, and proper care of the Temple.

The community also decided to relocate 10 percent of the population to Jerusalem, followed by a joyful celebration at the dedication of the city walls. The final chapter of the book lists specific corrections of abuses during Nehemiah's second stay in Jerusalem.

Perhaps the most contested historical question has been the date of Ezra's arrival. The order of the canonical texts suggests that Ezra came before Nehemiah, and since Nehemiah is firmly dated to the reign of Artaxerxes I, Ezra is traditionally assigned to this king as well. But Ezra and Nehemiah actually have little to do with each other in the book, and a number of Nehemiah's reforms do not seem to presuppose Ezra's establishment of the law in the land. Hence a number of scholars redate Ezra to the time of Artaxerxes II (404–358), although the traditional date has gained in favor. If Japhet is correct in her analysis of the compositional techniques of the editor who intentionally periodized the history, scholarship may never be able to decide definitively about the date of Ezra. Lester Grabbe even questions his existence![5]

Other debated historical issues include the following:

(1) The relationship of Sheshbazzar and Zerubbabel—Sheshbazzar's descent is unknown, and the transition between him and Zerubbabel, his successor, cannot be dated. According to data outside the corpus of Ezra–Nehemiah, Zerubbabel was both a son of David and a governor of the Persian province of Yehud, but neither of these facts is affirmed in Ezra–Nehemiah. Japhet believes this silence is ideological.

(2) The establishment of Judah as an independent province—Albrecht Alt contended that Judah was part of the province of Samaria under a Samarian governor until the coming of Nehemiah, but Nehemiah refers to his predecessors in Jerusalem as governors. The discovery of a group of bullae and seals from Yehud that identify several individuals as "governors," has permitted a reconstruction of a list of Judean governors in the fifth–fourth centuries, prior to Nehemiah.[6]

(3) Ezra's book of the law—the canonical text of Ezra–Nehemiah suggests that Ezra's law book was the Pentateuch, but scholars differ in their assessment of what that law may have been historically. Some identify it as the source P, others as an undefined group of laws now contained in the Pentateuch, others as Deuteronomy, and still others believe that the law of Ezra has been lost. Where the book seems to differ from the Pentateuch, we do not know whether the book cites the Pentateuch inexactly or whether it has reinterpreted ancient laws to meet the demands of the day.

(4) The Citizen-Temple community (Bürger Tempel Gemeinde)—Joel Weinberg describes the post-exilic community as a citizen-temple community, consisting of an assembly made up of free, property-owning citizens and temple personnel.[7] Weinberg distinguishes this type of community from that of the Persian province of Judah, even believing Nehemiah to be governor of the citizen-temple community and not of the province. Land belonged to the "fathers' houses" (בית אבות *bêt ʾābôt*), the household units that came to prominence in the post-exilic period. This community was loyal to the Persian government and was controlled by the people who had returned from exile in Babylon, much to the disadvantage of those who had remained in the land after 586. Weinberg has been criticized for his use of Ezra 2 and Nehemiah 7 to create artificially high population numbers, and his model departs somewhat from the extra-biblical parallels in which land was owned by the Temple. What we do not know—

and what surely must have been one of the most bitter sources of division within the community—was the way land ownership was transferred from those who had never left the land to those who had returned from exile. In any case, the books of Ezra and Nehemiah thoroughly back those who had returned from exile (the Golah) and virtually ignore those who had remained in the land.

MESSAGE

The main theological message of Ezra–Nehemiah may be summarized as (1) the return from exile and the rebuilding of the Temple; (2) the initial activities of Ezra; (3) Nehemiah and the rebuilding of the walls; (4) the climax of the work of Ezra and Nehemiah; and (5) the final acts of Nehemiah.

The Return from Exile and the Rebuilding of the Temple (Ezra 1:1–6). At the beginning (1:1-3) and end (6:22) of this section, the text asserts that Yahweh had brought about both the return of the exiles to Judah and Jerusalem and the rebuilding of the Temple through the favorable actions of the Persian kings toward Israel. Cyrus's decree permitted the rebuilding of the Temple and the restoration of its vessels (6:5), and Darius reinforced these privileges and added to them a curse against anyone who would attempt to countermand them (6:6-12).

The book fails to mention the Davidic ancestry of Sheshbazzar and Zerubbabel or the governors of Judah except in materials drawn from the author's sources, themes that might lead to a more eschatological or revolutionary orientation. Instead, the work of Cyrus fulfills the prophecy of Jeremiah (1:1), and contemporary prophets like Haggai and Zechariah merely encourage the building of the Temple (Ezra 5:2; 6:14) without setting forth any additional eschatological promises.

According to the books of Ezra and Nehemiah, the community in Jerusalem is made up only of those who returned from the exile (Ezra 2:1-70), who constitute the true Israel. In order to maintain continuity with the great pre-exilic traditions, all the temple vessels captured by Nebuchadnezzar are returned to Jerusalem through the agency of Sheshbazzar (Ezra 1:7-11; 5:14-15; 6:5), and both the altar (Ezra 3:3) and the Temple (Ezra 6:7) are re-erected on their former sites. The return from the exile (Ezra 1:5) and the rebuilding of the Temple (Ezra 3:7-13) show similarities to accounts of the first exodus and the construction of the First Temple respectively. The celebration of the Feast of Tabernacles after the completion of the altar (Ezra 3:4-5) anticipates the joyful dedication of the Temple (Ezra 6:16-18) and the equally joyful observation of the Passover a few months thereafter (Ezra 6:19-22).

The delay in the completion of the Temple is blamed not on the people's concern for their own comforts (as in Hag 1:4), but on the actions of the people of the land, who persistently opposed the work in Jerusalem and disheartened the returned exiles (Ezra 3:3; 4:1-24) and who later enlisted Artaxerxes I in their efforts to stop the building of the walls (Ezra 4:21-22). The laying of the foundation for the Temple was also a time for weeping for the older members of the community, who compared the foundation to that of the First Temple. The great noise produced by these emotions (Ezra 3:13) was heard by the adversaries, and it spurred them on to a deceptive offer to help with the temple building.

The Initial Activities of Ezra (Ezra 7:1–10). The second scene in Ezra–Nehemiah is formed by the initial activities of Ezra some fifty-eight years later (Ezra 7:1–10). Like Sheshbazzar and Zerubbabel, Ezra, too, led a group of exiles home (8:1-14; 8:15-34). His lineage is traced back to Aaron, the high priest (7:1-5), and his own attitude toward the law parallels that of Moses (7:10). The authority of the law is underscored by the decree of Artaxerxes (7:12-26).

After the leaders raise the problem of mixed marriages (9:1-5), the prayer of Ezra in 9:6-15 makes clear that the community is not yet the complete embodiment of Yahweh's will since it is still under bondage to Persian power. Yet, Yahweh's love for the community in these circumstances is considered a sign of God's favor and evidence for hope of a little reviving (Ezra 9:8-9). Ezra articulates the people's confession of sin, accompanied by public weeping (10:1) and fasting (10:6).

The people gathered together in a mass assembly during inclement weather to express their contrition publicly (10:6-12), and requested the creation of a special commission to carry out the removal of the foreign wives and their children (10:13-17). Within a year of Ezra's departure from

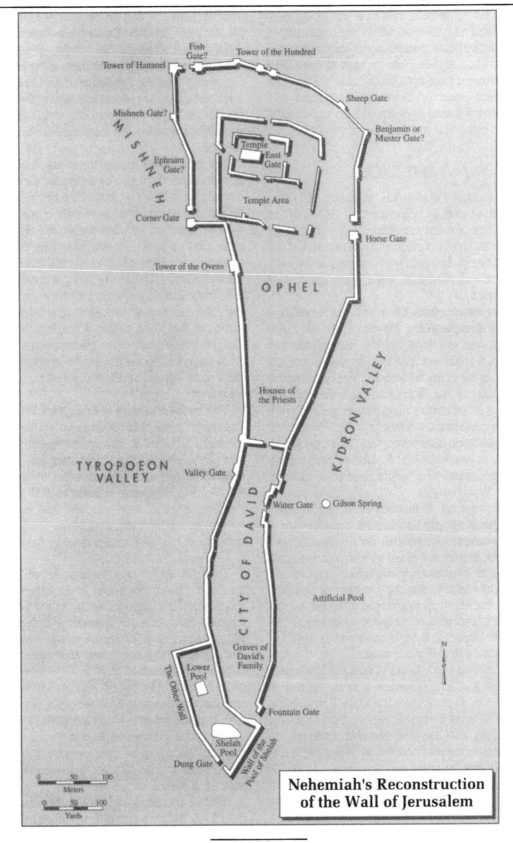

Nehemiah's Reconstruction of the Wall of Jerusalem

Babylon (cf. 7:9 with 10:17), a purified community was created in Jerusalem.

Nehemiah and the Rebuilding of the Walls (Neh 1:1–7:73a [HB 7:72a]). Nehemiah, too, led exiles home (cf. Sheshbazzar, Zerubbabel, and Ezra). Opposition from Sanballat and his allies was met by Nehemiah's defensive maneuvers (Neh 4:21-23 [HB 4:15-17]). Because he saw through the opponents' plots and their false charges about his desire for the office of king (6:1-14), he prayed for deliverance from them and placed an imprecation upon them (Neh 4:4-5 [HB 3:36-37]). The nations lost self-esteem when they perceived that the completion of the wall was the work of God (Neh 6:16). Nehemiah's work, then, authorized by Persian authorities (2:6-8), was ultimately successful: The purified community (Ezra 7:1–10) completed the building of walls (Neh 6:15) around the holy city (Ezra 1:1–6). Nehemiah corrected abuses in the making of loans and charging of interest (Neh 5:1-13) and generously provided for others at his table without drawing on the taxes enjoyed by former governors (5:14-19).

After the threefold restoration of the community and the city reported in Ezra 1:1–6; 7–10; and Nehemiah 1:1–6, Nehemiah decided to remedy the low population in the city by selecting people for relocation there whose genealogy could be correlated with the list of those who had returned with Zerubbabel (Neh 7:73a ; HB 7:5, 6-72a).

The Climax of the Work of Ezra and Nehemiah (Neh 7:73 [HB 7:72b]–10:39 [HB 40]). Before the actual repopulation of Jerusalem began, the people unanimously requested that Ezra read the law to them (Neh 8:1). Ezra reassured them that the joy of the Lord would offer protection against the judgments of the law against transgressors (Neh 8:10).

The people resolved to study the law (Neh 8:13) just as Ezra had done (Ezra 7:10). On the basis of this study, they held a unique celebration of the Feast of Tabernacles, unparalleled since the days of Joshua (Neh 8:17). This celebration in Nehemiah 8:1 recalls the Tabernacles celebration at the erection of the altar (Ezra 3:4) and the dedication celebration (Ezra 6:16-18) and Passover (Ezra 6:19-22) observed at the completion of the Temple.

Next the people separated themselves from foreigners and confessed their sins and those of their parents (Neh 9:2-3). A speech by an unnamed speaker (Neh 9:6; attributed by LXX to Ezra), which rehearses the sinfulness of Israel in the days of the wilderness wandering (9:16-18) and the people's stay in the land (9:26-30) includes the sinfulness of the present generation (9:33). Nevertheless, they had received Yahweh's repeated benefactions in creation (9:6); in the time of Abraham (9:7-8); in the exodus from Egypt and the giving of the law on Mt. Sinai (9:9-14); in the provision of food, water, and guidance in the wilderness (9:15, 19-21); in the gift of the land (9:22-25); and in the patient warning through the prophets in the land (9:27-30). Even the defeats at the time of the exile did not bring Yahweh's mercies to an end (9:31).

The confession concludes with an acknowledgment that the present Persian rulership, accepted elsewhere with equanimity in Ezra–Nehemiah, leaves the community in a less than perfect situation: "We are slaves this day . . . and we are in great distress" (9:36-37; cf. Ezra 9:8-9).

The community entered into a covenant to walk in God's law and to do all the commandments (10:28 [HB 10:29]; cf. Ezra 7:10). The community obligated itself to correct certain practices that later in the book require Nehemiah's direct actions.

Nehemiah 8–10, therefore, sets forth an ideal picture of the community. Made joyful by the reading of the law, after an initial reaction of grief, the people celebrated Tabernacles and confessed their previous sins and God's constant deliverance—and their less than perfect current status. The appropriate sequel to reading the law and offering a confession was a community-wide commitment to keep the proscriptions of the law.

Final Acts of Nehemiah (Neh 11:1–13:31). The perfected community decided to relocate one of every ten persons from the local towns to Jerusalem, thus carrying out what Nehemiah had begun in Neh 7:1-5. Subsequent lists identify those who lived in Jerusalem (11:3-24) and in the villages (11:25-36) and provide the names of priests, Levites, and high priests at various times of the restoration period (12:1-26). The dedication of the city's wall features a double procession in which both Ezra and Nehemiah play a role. The joy at the dedication (12:43) recalls the joy experienced at the reading of the law (Neh 8:12, 17), at the beginning of the rebuilding of the Temple (Ezra 3:12-13), and at its dedication (Ezra 6:16). The sounds of exaltation at the dedication of the wall were heard at a great distance (Neh 12:43; cf. Ezra 3:13).

After the appointment of supervisors of contributions, following the command and example of David (Neh 12:44-47), and a decision to separate from all foreigners (13:1-3), the rest of the book consists of specific corrections of abuses during Nehemiah's second stay in Jerusalem. He removed the Ammonite Tobiah from a chamber in the Temple (Neh 13:4-9), restored the portions due to the Levites (Neh 13:10-14), reinstituted proper observance of the Sabbath (Neh 13:15-22), remonstrated with those who had married foreign women and whose children could not speak Hebrew (Neh 13:23-27), chased away the son of the high priest who had married a daughter of Nehemiah's arch-rival Sanballat (Neh 13:28-29), cleansed the community from foreign contamination and established the duties of the priests and Levites (Neh 13:30), and provided for the wood offering and first fruits (13:31). These reforms were precisely in those areas in which the community had undertaken covenantal obligations according to Nehemiah 10.

The plea "Remember me, O my God, for good" (Neh 13:31) and similar expressions in Neh 13:14, 22, and 29, call attention in the canonical context to the virtue of Nehemiah, the wall builder and reformer of the community. At the same time, Nehemiah 13 reminds the reader that even the best intentions of the perfect community, under ideal leadership (see the ceremonies in Nehemiah 8:1–10), can fail and the people can lapse into sin. While the people confessed in chapter 9 that God's saving goal for them had not yet been achieved, the final chapter of Nehemiah concedes that the behavior of the restored community, too, was never fully perfected and often was in need of reform. The real circumstances in which people live—still under Persian rulership and in imperfection—set limits to the salvation that God gives in fulfillment of promises. The author leaves unresolved the relationship between the present and the future in the divine plan of salvation.

FOR FURTHER READING

Commentaries:

Allen, Leslie C., and Timothy S. Laniak. *Ezra, Nehemiah, Esther.* NIBCOT 9. Peabody, Mass.: Hendrickson, 2003.

Blenkinsopp, Joseph. *Ezra–Nehemiah.* OTL. Philadelphia: Westminster, 1988.

Clines, David J. A. *Ezra, Nehemiah, Esther.* NCB. Grand Rapids: Eerdmans, 1984.

Davies, Gordon F. *Ezra and Nehemiah.* Berit Olam. *Collegeville, Minn.: Liturgical Press, 1999.*

Gunneweg, A. H. J. *Esra.* KAT 19, 1. Gütersloh: Gütersloher Verlagshaus Gerd Mohn, 1985.

———. *Nehemia.* KAT 19, 2. Gütersloh: Gütersloher Verlagshaus Gerd Mohn, 1987.

Myers, Jacob. *Ezra–Nehemiah.* AB 14. Garden City, N.Y.: Doubleday, 1965.

Rudolph, Wilhelm. *Esra und Nehemia, samt 3. Esra.* HAT 20. Tübingen: J. C. B. Mohr [Paul Siebeck], 1949.

Throntveit, Mark A. *Ezra–Nehemiah.* Interpretation. Louisville: John Knox, 1992.

Williamson, H. G. M. *Ezra, Nehemiah.* WBC 16. Waco, Tex.: Word, 1985.

Other Studies:

Duggan, Michael W. *The Covenant Renewal in Ezra-Nehemiah (Neh 7:72B-10:40): An Exegetical Literary and Theological Study.* SBLDS 164. Atlanta: Society of Biblical Literature, 2001.

Eskenazi, Tamara C. *In an Age of Prose: A Literary Approach to Ezra–Nehemiah.* SBLMS 36. Atlanta: Scholars Press, 1988.

Hoglund, Kenneth G. *Achaemenid Imperial Administration in Syria-Palestine and the Missions of Ezra and Nehemiah.* SBLDS 125. Atlanta: Scholars Press, 1992.

Janzen, David. *Witch-hunts, Purity and Social Boundaries: The Expulsion of the Foreign Women in Ezra 9-10.* JSOTSup 350. New York: Continuum, 2002.

Klein, Ralph W. "Ezra–Nehemiah, Books of." In *Anchor Bible Dictionary.* Garden City, N.Y.: Doubleday, 1992, 2:731-42.

Stern, Ephraim. *Material Culture and the Land of the Bible in the Persian Period 538–322* BC. Jerusalem: Israel Exploration Society, 1982.

Weinberg, Joel P. *The Citizen-Temple Community.* JSOTSup 151. Sheffield: JSOT, 1992.

ENDNOTES

1. Sara Japhet, "The Supposed Common Authorship of Chronicles and Ezra-Nehemiah, Investigated Anew," *VT* 18 (1968) 330-71. See also the response and review of subsequent research in Mark Throntveit, "Linguistic Analysis

and the Question of Authorship in Chronicles, Ezra and Nehemiah," *VT 32 (1982) 201-16.*

2. See Kent Harold Richards, "Reshaping Chronicles and Ezra-Nehemiah Interpretation," in *Old Testament Interpretation: Past, Present, and Future*, ed. James Luther Mays, David L. Petersen, and Kent Harold Richards (Nashville: Abingdon, 1995) 211-24.

3. Tamara C. Eskenazi, *In an Age of Prose: A Literary Approach to Ezra–Nehemiah*, SBLMS 36 (Atlanta: Scholars Press, 1988); David Kraemer, "On the Relationship of the Books of Ezra and Nehemiah," *JSOT 59* (1993) 73-92; James C. VanderKam, "Ezra–Nehemiah or Ezra and Nehemiah?" *Priests, Prophets and Scribes: Essays on the Formation and Heritage of Second Temple Judaism in Honour of Joseph Blenkinsopp*, ed. Eugene Ulrich, John W. Wright, and Robert P. Carroll, JSOTSup 149 (Sheffield: Sheffield Academic, 1992) 55-75.

4. Sara Japhet, "Composition and Chronology in the Book of Ezra–Nehemiah," in *Temple Community in the Persian Period*, ed. Tamara C. Eskenazi and Kent Harold Richards, JSOTSup 175 (Sheffield: Sheffield Academic, 1994) 189-216.

5. Lester Grabbe, *Judaism from Cyrus to Hadrian, vol. 1: The Persian and Greek Periods* (Minneapolis: Fortress, 1992) 93.

6. Albrecht Alt, "Die Rolle Samarias bei der Entstehung des Judentums," *Kleine Schriften* 2 (Munich: Beck, 1953) 316-37; Nahman Avigad, *Bullae and Seals from a Post-Exilic Judean Archive, Qedem 4* (Jerusalem: The Hebrew University Press, 1966).

7. Joel Weinberg, *The Citizen-Temple Community*, JSOTSup 151 (Sheffield: Sheffield Academic, 1992).

THE BOOK OF ESTHER

SIDNIE WHITE CRAWFORD

The Hebrew book of Esther is an exciting, fast-paced story that has captured the imagination of Jews over the centuries, although it has been less well-received by the Christian church. It contains all the elements of a popular romance novel: a young and beautiful heroine; a wicked, scheming villain; a wise older father figure; and an inept and laughable ruler. In the story good triumphs, evil is destroyed, and all ends happily. It is no surprise, then, that the book of Esther was so popular that, despite certain objections, including its failure to mention God even once (see below), it made its way into the Jewish canon by popular acclaim. Beneath its lighthearted surface, however, the book of Esther explores darker themes: racial hatred, the threat of genocide, and the evil of overweening pride and vanity. These layers of meaning make this book a worthwhile object of study.

DATE AND PROVENANCE

The book of Esther is set in the Jewish diaspora of the Persian Empire, during the reign of Aha-suerus, who is to be identified with Emperor Xerxes (486–465 BCE). Therefore, the book was written no earlier than the fifth century BCE. A later date is more probable, however, given the book's distance from the actual events of Xerxes' reign (see below). It is unlikely that Esther was written later than the third century BCE, since it lacks all Hellenistic coloring (including any evidence of Greek vocabulary) and displays a much more positive attitude toward Gentiles and Gentile rulers than do later works, such as Judith or 1 Maccabees. In addition, the author's familiarity with the Persian court setting and customs suggests a date within or close to the period of the Persian Empire. Therefore, a date in the late fourth or early third century BCE seems most likely.[1]

It is probable that the book, set in the Persian diaspora, was written there as well. The characters evince no interest in the Judean homeland—not even, most strikingly, in the Jewish Temple in Jerusalem. Rather, the plot centers around the court in Susa, where Esther and Mordecai have made their lives. The author displays knowledge of the court of Susa and its immediate surroundings, as well as Persian court customs; but his knowledge about outlying provinces is quite hazy. Hence, Esther was most likely composed in the eastern diaspora of the Persian Empire for the Jews who resided there.

GENRE, STRUCTURE, AND STYLE

Any discussion of the genre of the book of Esther must begin with the acknowledgment that it is *written* literature, with no stylistic traits of oral literature. This work is meant to be read; in fact, the one rabbinic requirement concerning the Festival of Purim is the obligation to read the scroll publicly.[2] Further, although the author may have used sources in composing his work, the book is now a unified literary piece with a distinct and meaningful structure.

The genre of Esther is most easily described as an early Jewish novella (Wills) or short story (Fox).[3] Either term is acceptable if what is meant is a piece of literature with a single plot that has a clear beginning, middle, and end and whose action occurs within a specified length of time.[4] The Esther novella is related in type to the royal courtier tale, but it has a more complex plot and structure than a typical tale of that type (e.g., the stories in Daniel 2:1–6). As the book stands now, it is also a *Festlegende*, an explanation (or etiology) of the Festival of Purim, although the story's connection with that festival may be late and secondary. As either novella or *Festlegende*, the book is meant to be read as if it were history, even though it is clearly fictional. As Fox puts it, it is "a fictive text meant to be read by nonfictional conventions."[5]

Within the novella are several structuring elements that give the work a sense of symmetry and equilibrium. The most obvious structuring device is the use of banquets to form an elaborate envelope construction. Banquets occur in the book of Esther in pairs, with each one either opposing or complementing the other. A single banquet can belong to more than one pair, as shown in the following chart:

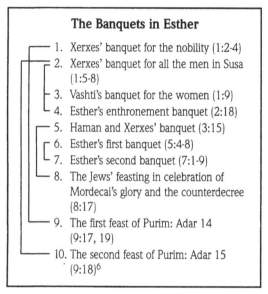

The Banquets in Esther

1. Xerxes' banquet for the nobility (1:2-4)
2. Xerxes' banquet for all the men in Susa (1:5-8)
3. Vashti's banquet for the women (1:9)
4. Esther's enthronement banquet (2:18)
5. Haman and Xerxes' banquet (3:15)
6. Esther's first banquet (5:4-8)
7. Esther's second banquet (7:1-9)
8. The Jews' feasting in celebration of Mordecai's glory and the counterdecree (8:17)
9. The first feast of Purim: Adar 14 (9:17, 19)
10. The second feast of Purim: Adar 15 (9:18)[6]

The first two and the last two banquets form a set: Numbers 1 and 9 are empire-wide, while numbers 2 and 10 are limited to the inhabitants of Susa. Banquet 2 for the men forms a pair with banquet 3, given for the women. Banquets 3 and 4 also form an oppositional pair, with banquet 3 given by Vashti and banquet 4 given for Esther. Banquets 5 and 8 oppose each other, while 6 and 7 complement each other. The resulting structure is a pleasing envelope construction.

Banquets are not the only things in the book that occur in pairs. The main characters appear in three pairs of men and women: (1) Ahasuerus and Vashti, (2) Esther and Mordecai, and (3) Haman and Zeresh. Further, the protagonists, in groups of two, revolve around King Ahasuerus in a clear progression. The first pair is Esther-Mordecai; the second, Mordecai-Haman; the third, Haman-Esther; and the fourth, Esther-Mordecai. Note the progression through pairs and the symmetry of the envelope construction. The pairs motif recurs throughout the book: two groups of seven servants/noblemen (1:10, 14; the names of the two groups are suspiciously similar); two helpful eunuchs (2:8-9; 7:9), two meetings of Haman and Zeresh (5:10-14; 6:13); two decrees (3:12-14; 8:9-14), and a two-day celebration of Purim (9:21).

Finally, the motif of pairs lends itself to a major theme of the book: ironic reversal (peripety). Throughout the book of Esther, the expected outcome is reversed; people's status and character undergo sudden changes. Vashti is queen; then she is banished. Esther changes from humble orphan to powerful queen. Haman is forced to honor his enemy Mordecai. Haman is hanged on the gallows prepared for Mordecai. Mordecai becomes grand vizier in place of Haman. Most important, the Jews move from mourning to rejoicing. These reversals signal pivotal moments in the plot: Esther's character change in 4:15-17 enables her to save the Jews; Haman's honoring of Mordecai signals the beginning of his downfall, as recognized by Zeresh (6:13); and Mordecai's elevation (8:15-16) completes the salvation of the Jews. As Levenson nicely puts it, this theme is summarized by a single phrase in 9:1: "the reverse occurred" (נהפוך הוא *nahăpôk hû*).[7] The theme gives the book its movement: The plot is never in stasis; something is always changing. This is also a hopeful message to Jews living in diaspora; the status quo is never such, and things can always change.

The book of Esther has received rather low marks for its prose style. Carey A. Moore comments that "the author of Esther was no master of the Hebrew language, writing timeless prose."[8] Indeed, the prose of Esther sometimes seems to sink under its own weight. There are long lists of names (1:10, 14; 9:7-9) and endless descriptions of palace procedures, such as the banquet arrangements (1:5-9) and the Persian postal system (8:9-14). The language appears repetitious; there is an extraordinary number of verbal dyads in the text, such as "Ahasuerus, the same Ahasuerus" (1:1) and "to the governors over all the provinces and to the officials of all the peoples" (3:12).[9] The text also contains verbal and nominal chains, some of which occur several times, such as "to destroy, to slay, and to annihilate" (3:13; 7:4; 8:11). All of these features tend to weigh down the prose.

However, as Levenson astutely points out, this is not a matter of bad writing, but the author's attempt to convey Persian "officialese," the style of writing common to bureaucracies both ancient and modern.[10] The story, after all, takes place in the Persian court, and if the events had actually happened, this is how they would have been reported.

The sometimes pompous language of the book is also part of a larger characteristic of this author: the use of humor to convey his message. The book, which was written for Jews living in exile, consistently lampoons their Gentile overlords. Ahasuerus is less an awe-inspiring ruler than an easily manipulated buffoon. Haman is an egomaniac whose vanity leads to his humiliation and downfall. The author also uses hyperbole to point to the surreality of the Persian Empire: Ahasuerus gives a banquet that lasts 180 days (six months! 1:4); the maidens are beautified for an entire year (2:12); and even at the denouement of the plot, when the Jews defend themselves against their enemies, the number of those slain (75,000) strains credibility (9:6, 15-16). Finally, the characters' reactions to events lead the reader to laugh. For example, Vashti's refusal to obey one order is thought to threaten the stability of the empire and leads to a decree declaring, of all things, that husbands should rule in their own houses and speak their own languages (1:21-22). The irony and humor found throughout the book mask, in a pleasant way, the author's very serious intent: to teach diaspora Jews that it is possible to lead a successful life in the sometimes inexplicable Gentile world in which they find themselves.[11]

HISTORICITY

Although much ink has been spilled in attempting to show that Esther, or some parts of it, is historical, it is clear that the book is a work of fiction that happens to contain some historical elements. The historical elements may be summarized as follows: Xerxes, identified as Ahasuerus, was a "great king" whose empire extended from the borders of India to the borders of Ethiopia. One of the four Persian capitals was located at Susa (the other three being Babylon, Ecbatana, and Persepolis). Non-Persians could attain to high office in the Persian court (witness Nehemiah), and the Persian

Empire consisted of a wide variety of peoples and ethnic groups. The author also displays a vague familiarity with the geography of Susa, knowing, for example, that the court was separate from the city itself.[12] Here, however, the author's historical veracity ends. Among the factual errors found in the book we may list these: Xerxes' queen was Amestris, to whom he was married throughout his reign; there is no record of a Haman or a Mordecai (or, indeed, of any non-Persian) as second to Xerxes at any time; there is no record of a great massacre in which thousands of people were killed at any point in Xerxes' reign. The book of Esther is not a historical record, even though its author may have wished to present it as history, since by doing so he could claim royal sanction for the purpose of his book: establishing Purim as an official Jewish festival.

The book of Esther, as stated above, is a *Festlegende*, an etiology for Purim, a festival probably originally celebrated in the eastern diaspora and slowly accepted in Judea (e.g., it is evidently not among the festivals celebrated among the Jews at Qumran). It is possible that Purim is a Jewish adaptation of a Persian festival, its connection with the story of Esther only secondary. However, the present book's intimate connection with the festival was probably the reason why it was ultimately allowed into the canon, unlike the very similar book of Judith. As Paton states, "It is connected in the closest way with the feast of Purim; and if the events here narrated did not create the feast, then the feast probably created the story."[13] Therefore, an investigation into the origins of Purim is warranted.[14]

Only two possibilities exist for the origins of Purim: the first that its origins lie in post-exilic Judaism, the second that it is an originally pagan festival adapted by the Jews. Those commentators who suspect a Jewish origin for Purim have searched through the known persecutions of Jews in the Hellenistic period to find a suitable antecedent. The most convincing argument, first put forth by Michaelis (1772),[15] holds that Purim was founded to commemorate the victory of Judas Maccabeus over Nicanor on 13 Adar 161 BCE. This argument, however, fails on several points. The book of Esther calls for the observance of Purim on the fourteenth and fifteenth of Adar, not on the thirteenth. Second Maccabees 15:36, which calls the fourteenth of Adar the "Day of Mordecai," carefully distinguishes it from the thirteenth, the "Day of Nicanor." The later rabbis (Jewish sages who, beginning in the second century, produced commentaries on the books of the HB) make the same distinction. Further, this identification, like all identifications with Jewish historical events, founders on the same rock: Purim is a feast whose character is essentially secular. Finally, the word "Purim" has no satisfactory Hebrew etymology; it appears to be a Hebrew corruption of either an original Aramaic form, פּוּרַיָּא (*pûrayyā*),[16] or the Babylonian *pūrū*, meaning "fate" or "lot." It seems best, therefore, to seek the origins of Purim in a Persian or Babylonian celebration. If Purim does have a foreign origin, then the Esther/Mordecai tale is easily explained as a justification for it. It is possible that the festival was originally a Persian feast, possibly the spring new year festival, adopted by the Jews of Susa that later spread to the rest of the Jewish community. Purim may also be connected to the Babylonian new year festival (which, however, was celebrated in Nisan, not Adar). All speculations on this subject run aground on the fact that we know very little about the eastern diaspora in the Persian period. Moore rightly declares, "Scholars have suggested much but proven very little about the probable origins of the festival of Purim."[17] In the end, a Persian origin for the festival seems most likely, with the tale of Esther and Mordecai added to bring it into the Jewish orbit.

TEXTS AND VERSIONS

The book of Esther differs from other books of the Hebrew Bible in that it exists not just in its Masoretic form and more or less similar translations, but instead in three different versions, each with integrity as a separate literary piece. These versions are the Hebrew Masoretic Text (MT), the Septuagint (LXX), and the Alpha Text (AT).

The Masoretic Text, written in Hebrew in the late fourth–early third centuries BCE, used as its source a Hebrew story concerning Esther and Mordecai. The MT author added the etiology of Purim to the original story, and this version gained canonical status in Jewish Scriptures and later in Protestant Bibles.

The Alpha Text is a Greek translation of a Hebrew text similar to, but not identical with, the original Hebrew source of the MT (the AT is approximately 20 percent shorter than the MT). It contains several conspicuous differences from the MT, indicating a different author/redactor: The conspiracy of the two eunuchs (2:21-23) is missing; Persian law is not characterized as irrevocable, an important plot device in the MT; there is no mention of Purim; and, very important, the AT explicitly mentions God. The AT came into being at about the same time as the MT,[18] but never enjoyed canonical status, although it may have been popular in Egypt in the second century BCE.

The Septuagint is a Greek translation of the Hebrew MT, made in the late second century BCE. It contains six long passages not found in the MT that were added to the LXX at the time of translation or later. These additions change the nature of the LXX, so that it is a distinctly different literary piece from the MT. The LXX has canonical status in the Eastern (Orthodox) churches and deuterocanonical status in the Roman Catholic Church (in the Vg, the Additions appear after the end of the Hebrew text). In modern translations, these Additions often appear in the apocrypha. In this volume they appear in the apocrypha section. The Additions were added to the Alpha Text of Esther sometime after the LXX came into being, evidently to bring the two Greek texts into conformity. The diagram on the following page illustrates the relations of the various versions, in which proto-Esther stands for the hypothetical source(s) behind the MT and the AT.

In addition, several other translations of both the MT and the LXX exist, including an Old Latin (OL) translation. The book of Esther also has two Targums (translations into Aramaic), which are more like midrashic free renderings than strict translations. Finally, the paraphrase of the first-century CE Jewish historian Josephus seems to show his familiarity with several of the versions, which he rendered freely.

THE ORIGINS OF ESTHER

It has long been suspected in the field of Esther studies that behind the three extant versions of the book of Esther (MT, LXX, and AT) lie sources that are no longer recoverable. Cazelles proposed a two-source theory for Esther. One source was liturgical, centered around Esther and the Jews in

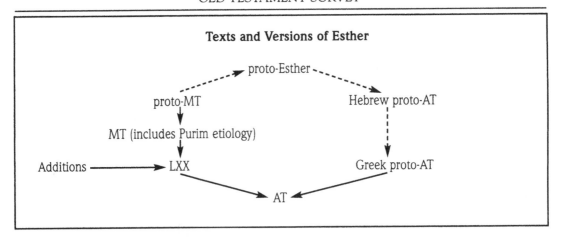

Texts and Versions of Esther

proto-Esther

proto-MT   Hebrew proto-AT

MT (includes Purim etiology)

Additions ⟶ LXX   Greek proto-AT

AT

the provinces, and was concerned with the celebration of a festival. The second source was historical and centered around Mordecai and court intrigues leading to a persecution of the Jews in Susa. The two sources would have had much in common, including the two main characters and the basic plot structure, making them relatively easy to combine.[19] In a later analysis, Bardtke suggested that the author of Esther drew on a Jewish "midrashic" source, from which he reworked three tales: an apocryphal harem story about Vashti; the story of Mordecai, concerning court intrigue and the persecution of Jews in Susa; and the Esther story, about a young Jewish girl who becomes the king's favorite and saves her people from persecution.[20] Other scholars have preferred to talk about traditions lying behind the Esther story. The argument is complicated by the presence of the expanded version of the LXX, for which Semitic sources have been posited for Additions A, C, D, and F. Torrey suggested that the Greek versions of Esther are translations of Aramaic originals and that the Hebrew version is late and secondary, but his conclusions have not been widely accepted.[21] Rather, it seems most probable that the Hebrew MT, from which the LXX was translated, and the Hebrew proto-AT, from which the Greek AT was translated (this Greek text was later expanded using the LXX Additions), were constructed from a common story about Esther and Mordecai, two Jews living in the court of a foreign king who by their wits defeated the plot of Haman to destroy all the Jews of Persia. However, this story no longer exists; it may be hypothetically reconstructed from the three extant versions. A further question remains: Are there

"sources" or "traditions" behind this tale and/or behind the Additions to the LXX?

Previous attempts to isolate sources, especially Cazelles's, have foundered on the attempt to assign blocks of material from the present form of MT Esther to specific sources. As shown above, the layers between MT Esther and its possible sources are too many, and the literary skill of the author too great, to allow for a convincing analysis. The search for plausible sources seemed to be stymied.

Some new light has been shed on the question. In 1992, Milik published fragments of an Aramaic manuscript(s) from Qumran Cave 4 that he entitled "4Qproto-Estheraramaic."[22] These fragments, Milik argued, contain the Aramaic source for the Greek source of the OL translation of Esther. Milik maintains that this Greek text was the original book of Esther. The LXX is, according to him, a revision of the OL's Greek source, while the Hebrew MT is a late (post–70 CE) and secondary translation. While Milik's arguments about the textual history of Esther are not at all convincing,[23] the fragments he presents may be an example of the type of source material the author of proto-Esther may have used when composing his story.

4Qproto-Estheraramaic, or as it is better named, *4QTales of the Persian Court*, consists of six manuscript fragments (4Q550), dating paleographically from the second half of the first century BCE.[24] The fragments appear to contain three distinct blocks of material, the first two of which contain clear parallels to the book of Esther. The first story, found in 4Q550a-c, is set in the court of King Xerxes and appears to be addressed to a man whose father was named Patireza.[25] The text of frags. a-c is as follows:

Frag. a:

1. . . . o]beyed Patireza your father [. . .
2. . . . and [am]ong your servants of the royal wardrobe [. . .] to serve
3. the service of the king like all which [you have] receiv[ed . . .] at the same hour
4. the temper of the king was stretched [. . . the bo]oks of his father should be read to him and among
5. the books was found a scroll [. . .] sealed with seven seals of Darius his father entitled:
6. . . . . Dar]ius the king to the servants of the empire which is the whol[e e]arth, Peace! On being opened and read, it was found written therein: Darius the king
7. . . .]reign after me and to the servants of the empire, Pe[ac]e! Let it be known to him who violates or falsifies . . .

Frag. b:

1. nobody but the king kn[ows] if there is [. . .
2. and his good name does not perish [and his] faithful[ness . . .
3. the king come to Patireza son of ?[. . .
4. fear of the house of the scribe fell on him [. . .
5. the messenger of the king, Comm[and] and let it be given [. . .
6. my house and possessions to all who [. . .
7. being measured. And you will receive the office of your father. [. . .

Frag. c:

1. . . .]the messenger of the king, Command the princess (?) [. . .]banish[ed . . .
2. . . . Patrieza [your] father, from Hama' who arose concerning the service of [. . .] before the king [. . .
3. . . .] and he was a faithful and tr[usty] servant before her [. . .
4. . . . and the messenger said, [. . .
5. . . . purp[le] . . .

Interesting parallels to the book of Esther may be noted: The story is set in the Persian court, it takes place during the reign of Xerxes (note "Darius his father" in frag. a, line 5); and it resembles the royal courtier tale in genre. Some parallels are even more specific: In frag. a, the king has the royal

annals read to him, as in Esth 6:1. Also, Patireza's son is rewarded by the king (frag. b), as is Mordecai in Esther 6:1. Finally, the name *Hama'* (חמא) in frag. c bears some resemblance to the name "Haman."

The differences between the two tales are also clear. First, the story in frags. a-c has no Jewish connection at all. Second, it is Patireza's son who is the object of the king's favor. If Patireza is to be equated with Mordecai, as Milik suggests (both being the son of Jair),[26] then 4Q550 mentions three generations: the father, Patireza, and his son, with the son being the protagonist of the story. Esther, of course, focuses on Mordecai. Third, a court conflict, which is at the heart of Esther, is not reflected in these fragments. And fourth, there are no direct linguistic connections between these fragments and any of the Esther versions.

The situation with frag. d, consisting of three columns, is similar:

Column 1:

1. Behold, you know [. . .] and because of the errors of my fathers
2. who sinned before you and [. . .] I went out, a man of
3. Judah, one of the leaders of Benjam[in . . .] an exile is standing to be received [. . .] goo[d
4. a good man who serves [. . .] What may I do for you? You know [that it is not] possib[le
5. that a man like me is responsible [. . . your ki]ngdom, standing in front of you [. . .
6. . . .] that which you desire, entrust me with, and when [you d]ie, I will bury you in [
7. being the master of all. It is possible that my elevation in service bef[ore . . .

Column 2:

1. . . .] the decree [. . .] they left [. . .
2. . . .] plagues [. . .]he left [. . .] in the wardrobe [. . .
3. . . .] coronet of go[ld . . .] her [h]ead and five years passed [. . .
4. . . .] alone [. . . and the s]ixth passed [. . .
5. . . . si]lver and gold [. . . possess]ions which belong to Bagoshe, in double amount [. . .

6. and the sev[enth passed . . .] then in peace Bagasraw went up to the court of the king [. . .

7. Bagosh[e . . .] pronoun[ced . . . he was k]illed. Then Bagasraw went up to the co[ur]t of the king.

8. And he took his han[d . . .] on [his] head [. . .] kissed him, answered and said [. . .] Bagasraw, who [. . .

Column 3:

1. . . .] the Most High whom you revere and [wo]rship, it is He who rules over [all the ea]rth. Everything that he wishes is within his p[ow]er [. . .

2. . . .] any man who says anything bad against Bagasraw [. . . will] be killed, because there is nothing [. . .

3. . . .] ? for [e]ver [. . . th]at he saw [in the] two [. . .] And the king commanded that it be writt[en . . .

4. . . . em]pi[re . . .] in the court of the king's house [. . .

5. . . . a]rise after Bagasraw, those who read in this book [. . .

6. . . .] his wickedness will return on his own [head . . .

7. . . .] his des[cendants].[27]

Notice that the characters are different from those in frags. a-c: Bagasraw, Bagoshe, the king (unidentified), and an unidentified woman. It, too, has parallels to Esther: Frag. d opens with a prayer, which has certain similarities to the prayer of Esther in LXX Addition C. The description of "a man of Judah, one of the leaders of Benjamin, an exile" (col. 1, ll. 2-3) corresponds to the description of Mordecai in Esth 2:5-6. There is a dialogue between the king and a female protagonist, in which an adversary is criticized. The period of five years mentioned in column 2 is the same as the time lapse between Esther's ascension to the throne and her actions to save the Jews from Haman's plot. There is evidently a power struggle between Bagoshe, a non-Jew, and Bagasraw, a Jew, like the struggle between Haman and Mordecai. Bagasraw is received by the king in a manner similar to Esther's reception in LXX Addition D (taking into account the obvious difference that Bagasraw is a man and not the spouse of the king). The king makes a proclamation praising God, as in LXX Addition E.

However, the following caveats to the comparison should be noted: The parallels are not exact. The prayer in frag. d laments "the errors of my fathers," rather than present wrongdoing, as in LXX Addition C. Many of the parallels may plausibly be regarded simply as motifs of the royal courtier tale genre; for example, the royal proclamation is equally reminiscent of those in Dan 2:46-47 and 6:25-27. Further, if Bagasraw is a seer, as suggested by col. 3, line 3, he more closely resembles Daniel than any character in the book of Esther.

Finally, frags. e-f of 4Q550:

Frag. e, frag. 1:

1. . . .] before the king of Assy[ria? . . .

2. . . .] went at the summons [. . .

3. . . .] on yo[ur] faces [. . .

4. . . . Ba]gasraw [. . .

Frag. e, frag. 2:

1. . . .] servant [. . .

2. . . .] remembrance [. . .

Frag. f:

1. . . .] behold from the north comes evil [. . .

2. . . .] the building of Zion and in her shelter all the poor of [the] people [

3. . . .] space

4. . . .] come up upon it. They swell up between Medea and Persia and Assyria and the [Great] Sea

5. . . .] space

The only possible parallels to be noted between these fragments and the book of Esther are the phrase "on your faces" in frag. e, frag. 1, line 3, which may refer to prostrating oneself before royalty, and the mention of Medea and Persia in frag. f, line 4. On the other hand, in frag. f, lines 1-2 contain a paraphrase of Isa 14:31-32, while the book of Esther contains no allusions to any other biblical book.

In sum, *4QTales of the Persian Court* contains several intriguing parallels to the book of Esther in both its Hebrew and its Greek versions. These parallels permit us to posit some type of generic relationship between the two texts, but not enough to argue for any type of direct dependence. *4QTales of the Persian Court* may have been an example of a popular type of story—a royal courtier tale in which a Jew, against all odds, rises to success in the court of the Persian king. The author of Esther may have drawn from this type of tale when constructing his story.

THE IMPLIED THEOLOGICAL STANCE OF THE BOOK OF ESTHER

Although enjoying unwavering popularity among Jews throughout most of its existence, the book of Esther has come into its share of theological criticism. The reasons for this are the absence of religious elements in the book, and, among Christians, its perceived hostility toward Gentiles. The lack of religiosity in Esther is indeed striking. The book does not mention God even once. In addition, there is no prayer, no mention of the Temple, and no clear indication of religious activity on the part of Esther or Mordecai. The possible exception is the fast ordered by Esther in 4:16; however, that fast is not explicitly directed to God and seems to have no purpose beyond communal solidarity.[28] Furthermore, there is no indication that either Esther or Mordecai is obedient to the Torah; in fact, quite the opposite is true. Esther is married to a Gentile, eats non-kosher food, and appears to be so thoroughly assimilated that her husband and his court are unaware that she is a Jew. Jewishness, in fact, is a matter of ethnic identification rather than religious practice.

This lack of religion was noticed early on. The proto-AT, which stems from either the same or a very similar Semitic source as the MT, mentions God several times in natural places in the text (AT 5:9, 11; 7:17; 8:2, 34).[29] The LXX, which is a translation of the MT, deliberately adds long passages, as well as short references, that insert a distinct tone of religiosity and change the character of the book. Esther and Mordecai both pray (Add. C), and Esther declares that she has kept the commandments and lived as a good Jew (Add. D). Josephus and the Targums also add religious elements to the book of Esther, as do the rabbis. The rabbis speculate, for example, that Mordecai refuses to bow down to Haman because Haman wears an idol pinned to his chest.[30] These additions show that the mention of God or of religious practice

would be natural in several places in the book; moreover, it is unlikely that an ancient Jewish reader, with even the vaguest familiarity with Israel's sacred history (e.g., the exodus) could have read a story of Jewish deliverance without understanding in it God's action.[31] Therefore, the lack of any theological statements in the book must be deliberate. What was the author's intention? The answer is not immediately apparent.

There are, however, two key passages in the book that contain theological implications. In the first, 4:13-14, Mordecai says to Esther:

> "Do not think that in the king's palace you will escape any more than all the other Jews. For if you keep silence at such a time as this, relief and deliverance will rise for the Jews from another quarter, but you and your father's family will perish. Who knows? Perhaps you have come to royal dignity for just such a time as this." (NRSV)

"Quarter" (מקום *māqôm*) is not a circumlocution for God, as is sometimes claimed, meaning that Mordecai is implying that if Esther does not act, God will (as God does in the book of Daniel). Rather, the passage indicates that Mordecai believes in a wider historical purpose, which includes the survival of the Jews; therefore, in this crisis, the deliverance of the Jews will occur somehow. Does this imply the hand of God in these events? It would seem so, for the only way the survival of the Jews as a historical issue makes any theological sense is for the Jews to be God's special chosen people. Therefore, for the author of Esther, there must be a God, and God must want the Jews to survive. How God will ensure their survival is unclear, however, especially to Mordecai. It is possible that Esther became queen just to fulfill God's purpose, but humans cannot know that. They must act, with profound hope that they are thereby participating in the divine scheme.

The second key passage would seem to support this interpretation. In 6:13*b*, Zeresh says to Haman: "If Mordecai, before whom your downfall has begun, is of the Jewish people, you will not prevail against him, but will surely fall before him." Why does Mordecai's Jewish identity guarantee his triumph and, consequently, Haman's downfall? It does so only if the Jews are somehow special; and in ancient Judaism their specialness is that of being God's people. Once again, belief in

God and God's action in history is implied, but not directly stated. However, this implication, coupled with the Jewish context in which the book was read, probably smoothed Esther's entry into the canon.

Another feature of the book that commentators have argued may point to the author's theology is the series of remarkable coincidences moving the plot forward. These include Vashti's dethronement, Esther's enthronement, the king's insomnia (this coincidence is seemingly so obvious that both the LXX and Josephus attribute the king's sleeplessness to God), the reading of the passage concerning Mordecai in the royal annals, and Haman's early arrival in the court, just in time to honor Mordecai. According to Berg, these coincidences help to show that "the narrator believed in a hidden causality behind the surface of human history, both concealing and governing the order and significance of events."[32] However, what is equally important to note is that not one of these coincidences would mean anything without corresponding human action. Esther's enthronement means nothing if she does not choose to act for her people. The reading of the passage concerning Mordecai is meaningless unless Ahasuerus decides to reward him. Coincidences may reveal the hand of God, but, once again, humans cannot know that for sure. All they can do is act, in the hope that their action corresponds to the plan and purpose of God.

The theological implications teased out above may have more direct relevance in our secular culture than stories in which God intervenes directly and miraculously, such as that of Daniel. Along with the implicit belief that within the realm of human history God's plan includes the salvation of the Jews, the book of Esther also holds out the possibility that in the immediate circumstances things might not work out. Esther might not sway the king; Haman may succeed in his murderous scheme. However, for the author, the failure of Esther and Mordecai would not prove the absence of God (as it would by necessity in Daniel), since Esther and Mordecai can never be completely sure that they are acting in concord with God. This is certainly theologically ambiguous, but it corresponds with the modern believer's daily struggle to discern the will of God. The best anyone can do, the author of Esther implies, is to act within those

circumstances in which one finds oneself and to take advantage of those opportunities with an attitude of hope, what Fox calls "an openness to the possibility of providence, even when history seems to weigh against its likelihood."[33] It is this openness that speaks to the skeptical end of the twentieth century and becomes a posture of profound faith.

The second charge, hostility toward Gentiles, is more easily disposed of. The book of Esther has never enjoyed great popularity in the Christian church, even to the present day. It had difficulty obtaining canonical status, particularly among the Eastern churches.[34] Esther is not quoted anywhere in the New Testament and is rarely mentioned by the church fathers. During the Reformation, Martin Luther was vehement in his dislike of the book. The attitude of many Christian commentators toward the book of Esther before the latter part of the twentieth century is nicely summarized by the remarks of L. B. Paton in 1908:

> There is not one noble character in this book. Xerxes is a sensual despot. Esther, for the chance of winning wealth and power, takes her place in the herd of maidens who become concubines of the King. She wins her victories not by skill or by character, but by her beauty. She conceals her origin, is relentless toward a fallen enemy, secures not merely that the Jews escape from danger, but that they fall upon their enemies, slay their wives and children, and plunder their property. Not satisfied with this slaughter, she asks that Haman's ten sons may be hanged, and that the Jews may be allowed another day for killing their enemies in Susa. The only redeeming traits in her character are her loyalty to her people and her bravery in trying to save them. Mordecai sacrifices his cousin to advance his interests, advises her to conceal her religion, displays wanton insolence in his refusal to bow to Haman, and helps Esther in carrying out her schemes of vengeance. All this the author narrates with interest and approval. He gloats over the wealth and the triumph of his heroes and is oblivious to their moral shortcomings. Morally Esther falls far below the general level of the Old Testament and even of the Apocrypha. The verdict of Luther is not too severe: "I am so hostile to this book that I wish it did not exist, for it Judaizes too much, and has too much heathen naughtiness."[35]

With the benefit of hindsight, it is clear that Paton fell victim to his own preconceptions of what a biblical book "should" be like, rather than reading the book for what it is: an entertaining story written for an oppressed minority that ties what was probably originally a pagan holiday into a Jewish context. The tone of the book is ironic and gives the audience a chance to chuckle at those who, in the reality of day-to-day life, rule over them. Ahasuerus is less a sensuous despot than a buffoon ruled by his emotions. Esther, who receives the bulk of Paton's criticisms, actually has no choice about entering the king's harem; once there, she makes the best of the situation and acts with courage and resourcefulness to save her people, who had been endangered by the bloated revenge fantasies of the Gentile Haman. Mordecai does not "sacrifice" his cousin but acts toward her with care and concern; when his personal quarrel with Haman threatens the whole Jewish people, he acts to save them in concert with Esther. The laconic reports in chapter 9 concerning the number of enemies killed may be disconcerting, particularly to Gentile readers, but it must be remembered that they are not real, that this is a work of fiction. What is more, it is reiterated that the Jewish people fight only in self-defense against their declared enemies. In this way, Esther is much less "anti-Gentile" than, for example, the book of Joshua, in which the Israelites fight aggressive wars leading to the wholesale slaughter of the Gentile inhabitants of Canaan. In fact, the book of Esther portrays a situation in which, under normal circumstances, Jews and Gentiles live harmoniously under Persian rule. Only the threat of annihilation causes the Jews to respond aggressively. Therefore, the objections of Paton (and others) to the book of Esther can be dismissed as, at best, misunderstanding, and, at worst, anti-Semitism.

S. Talmon has suggested a solution to the objections raised against Esther, especially its lack of religious elements, in his proposal to understand the book as a "historicized Wisdom tale."[36] Talmon sees the characters of the book as "types" of wisdom characters: Mordecai is the wise courtier; Haman is the foolish courtier; Esther is the adopted heir of the wise courtier; and Ahasuerus is the king manipulated by the court intrigues. While Esther should not be classified as wisdom literature,[37] it certainly falls within the parameters of the "royal courtier tale," in which a courtier rises to prominence, is endangered by the machinations of enemies, and is eventually vindicated. However, as Wills notes, Esther is more complex in its literary structure than a simple court legend (cf., e.g.,

Daniel 6).[38] There are two protagonists, Esther and Mordecai; there is a long subplot concerning Vashti; and the Jews act to secure their own rescue. Further, the book contains common folklore motifs—such as the stupid king, the clever court official, and the beautiful wise queen—so that the characters are not unique to wisdom literature.[39] Finally, as the book now stands, the establishment of the Festival of Purim is its *raison d'être*. Nevertheless, the book's emphasis on the ability to function well in a secular environment may point to an influence from wisdom literature (cf. Proverbs).

COMPARISON WITH JOSEPH, DANIEL, AND JUDITH

The book of Esther also lends itself to comparison with other stories of Jews in foreign courts, particularly those of Joseph (Genesis 37:1–50), Daniel, and Judith. The story of Joseph may have served as a model for the author of Esther.[40] Both are stories of Jews in a foreign court who overcome obstacles and achieve fabulous success. In both stories, the proximity of the protagonist to royal power results in the saving of his or her ethnic group, in Joseph's case his father's family, in Esther's the Jewish people. Both stories involve cases of concealed identity: Joseph is unrecognized by his brothers; Esther conceals her Jewishness. Most intriguing, several times the stories demonstrate almost exact linguistic correspondence, for example at Esth 6:11 and Gen 41:42-43:

Esther	Joseph
And he clothed Mordecai	And he clothed him . . .
and he caused him to ride	and he caused him to ride
in the square of the city	in his second chariot
and he cried out before him . . .	and they cried out before him . . .

However, the differences are also important, not the least of which is the fact that Joseph attributes the outcome of the story directly to God (Gen 45:5-8; 50:19), a declaration never found in Esther. Therefore, it seems best to presume that the author of Esther knew the Joseph story and used it when composing his story, but not in a relation of strict dependence.

Esther has also been compared to the book of Daniel, specifically to the cycle of royal courtier tales found in Daniel 2:1–6.[41] The correspondences are clear; both concern Jewish protagonists in foreign courts who, despite the machinations of enemies, rise to be trusted advisers to the king. Both stories display a tolerant attitude toward the Gentile ruler, and both assume that it is possible for Jews to lead comfortable, happy lives in the diaspora. These similarities, however, probably do not indicate dependence one way or the other, but rather adherence to the royal courtier tale genre, adapted for a Jewish audience.[42] The differences between the stories of Esther and Daniel and the conclusions their audiences are expected to reach are very striking. The character of Daniel is a pious Jew, keeping the dietary laws (Dan 1:8-16), praying several times a day facing Jerusalem (Dan 6:10), and, with his companions, bearing his identity as an observant religious Jew proudly and openly. Further, in every misadventure Daniel and his companions survive, God actively intervenes, causing them to interpret dreams (Dan 2:19-23; 4:19-27), providing mysterious signs (Dan 5:5, 24-28), and, in extreme cases, rescuing them from the fiery furnace and the lions' den (Dan 3:24-29; 6:20-23). The message of the Daniel cycle is clear: It is possible for Jews to achieve success under Gentile rule, but only if they are careful to live a pious and observant life, causing God to intervene directly on their behalf. This is radically different from Esther, in which Jewish observance is not an issue; God, if active at all, is only so in a veiled and indirect way, and human action is the primary tool of deliverance.

The third story with which Esther may be directly compared is that of Judith, found in the apocrypha. In fact, it may be argued that the author of the book of Judith, familiar with the story of Esther, set about to create a Jewish heroine more in keeping with the pious standards of his own time.[43] Both stories are supposedly historical tales (although Judith contains even wilder historic "bloopers" than does Esther; for example, Judith makes Nebuchadnezzar, the king of Babylon in the sixth century BCE, the king of Assyria with his capital at Nineveh!) about Jewish women who save their people from destruction at the hands of Gentiles. However, the character of Judith contrasts sharply with that of Esther. Judith is a pious widow who spends her time in constant prayer and fasting (Jdt 8:4-6). She is beautiful, as Esther is beautiful; but Judith's beauty is secondary to her piety. When the people of her town, Bethuliah, are endangered by the besieging army of Nebuchadnezzar's general Holofernes, she acts on their behalf, but only after beseeching God's aid in prayer (Jdt 9:1-14; this scene closely parallels Add. C in the LXX Esther, added to give Esther the appearance of piety). Judith then arrays herself beautifully and makes her way to the enemy camp (Jdt 10:1-13, parallel to Esth 5:1, also Add. D 1-6). However, once Judith is in the Gentile realm, she is careful to eat only kosher food (Jdt 12:1-2), and she prays and purifies herself daily (Jdt 12:5-9). This is in direct contrast to Esther, who does none of those things. Finally, when Judith is confronted by Holofernes' desire to sleep with her, she does not defile herself by having intercourse with a Gentile; rather, she waits until he is drunk, then cuts off his head and carries it back to Bethuliah in a sack (Jdt 13:1-10)! MT Esther marries the Gentile Ahasuerus without a qualm; the most the LXX author can do to repair the situation is to have Esther declare that she "abhors the bed of the uncircumcised" (Add. C 26). So, although Esther and Judith are often compared to each other,[44] it is their differences that are most striking. The pious Judith seems to be created as a foil for the perceived defects in the character of Esther.

How, then, can the book of Esther be understood by a contemporary audience? For the Jew, the function of the book of Esther as an etiology for the Festival of Purim takes priority. For the Christian, the question is harder to answer. I would suggest two related paths for entering the book of Esther. The first sees the character of Esther as a feminine model for the Jewish diaspora. The second sees the book of Esther as the story of an oppressed minority struggling for recognition, and for life itself, in a majority culture that is indifferent, or even hostile, to its existence.

ESTHER AS HEROINE

Although the book of Esther takes its name from its chief female protagonist, the character of Esther has suffered much in the history of interpretation, especially Christian interpretation. Mainstream scholars have insisted on seeing Mordecai as the primary hero of the book, in spite of the fact that at the moment of crisis, Mordecai (who has brought the situation into being by his refusal to bow before Haman) can only go to Esther and ask her to intercede with the king.[45] Esther then devises a plan, carries it out with admirable skill, and, in the end, arranges for Mordecai to inherit Haman's position. Without Esther there would be no story.

Feminist scholars as well find little to admire in Esther, often preferring the deposed Vashti. Alice Laffey sums up the position: "In contrast to Vashti, who refused to be men's sexual object and her husband's toy, Esther is the stereotypical woman in a man's world."[46] Esther, it seems, is neither "woman" enough nor "man" enough to satisfy any of her critics.

Neither of these positions does justice to the character of Esther as she appears within the cultural confines of the book named after her.[47] As will be shown in the Reflections, Esther serves as a model of the successful Jew living in diaspora, and she is able to function as a model precisely because she is a woman. Within the culture we call "Western" or "Judeo-Christian," a culture that is admittedly male-dominated and patriarchal, women have been the constantly marginalized and oppressed gender. Lacking public power, women have historically been able to gain individual or private strength only by successfully exploiting the male power structure around them, as Esther does so well. Her actions are presented as a model to the Jews who, living in exile, are marginalized and powerless minority members of Persian society. Esther also attains her success without the element of the miraculous, which is so often a part of these royal courtier tales (e.g., Daniel). Rather, the oblique references to the providential action of God are so subtle that they might be missed by the casual reader. God is on the side of the oppressed, but works through human instruments to achieve the divine purpose. Esther is a human heroine for a human situation and, as such, speaks powerfully to all oppressed people through the centuries.

ANTI-SEMITISM, OPPRESSION, AND GENOCIDE

Although the book of Esther is entertaining and thought-provoking in many respects, its most salient theme for a modern theological understanding of the book is the fact that it is the story of an attempt by a Gentile to exterminate the Jewish people. Its importance to both Christians and Jews resides in the survival of the Jews in the face of the threats posed by the Gentile characters' active anti-Semitism or, at best, indifference. The relevance of this theme to a modern audience lies in a fact of history that responsible readers are compelled to acknowledge: the sorry history of Western Christianity's anti-Semitism, culminating in the murder of six million Jews in the Holocaust.[48] In the light of that history, arguments concerning Esther's "anti-Gentile" bias seem self-serving, to say the least. The book of Esther is about Jewish survival in the face of Gentile threat, and an enlightened interpretation in the post-Holocaust period must acknowledge the reality of that threat.

The book of Esther, with its theological underpinning of belief in the providence of God manifest in human events, also offers a message of hope to other minorities living in majority cultures, such as African Americans in the white-dominated United States. To those who are oppressed the book gives a message of active faith and hope in the face of threat, and to those who rule that the rights of minorities are as important as the rulers' self-interest. For both groups, the greatest societal rewards come through tolerance and cooperation. Further, the book of Esther teaches that in every situation God is able to work through willing human agents (not by miraculous intervention) to ensure that justice is done. The message of the book of Esther is thus easily translatable to our contemporary situation.[49]

FOR FURTHER READING

Bechtel, Carol M. *Esther*. IBC. Louisville, Ky.: Westminster/John Knox, 2002.

Berg, Sandra Beth. *The Book of Esther: Motifs, Themes, and Structure*. SBLDS 44. Missoula, Mont.: Scholars Press, 1979.

Berlin, Adele. *Esther*. JPS Torah Commentary. Philadelphia: Jewish Publication Society, 2001.

Brenner, Athalya, ed. *A Feminist Companion to Esther, Judith, and Susanna*. Feminist Companion to the Bible. First Series 7. Sheffield: Sheffield Academic Press, 1995.

———. *Ruth and Esther: A Feminist Companion to the Bible.* Feminist Companion to the Bible. Second Series 3. Sheffield: Sheffield Academic Press, 1999.

Clines, David J. A. *The Esther Scroll: The Story of the Story.* JSOTSup 30. Sheffield: JSOT, 1984.

Crawford, Sidnie White, and Leonard J. Greenspoon, eds. *The Book of Esther in Modern Research.* JSOTSup 380. London: T&T Clark, 2003.

Fountain, Kay. *Literary and Empirical Readings of the Books of Esther.* Studies in Biblical Literature 43. New York: Peter Lang, 2002.

Fox, Michael V. *Character and Ideology in the Book of Esther.* Second Edition. Grand Rapids, Mich.: Eerdmans, 2001.

Harvey, Charles E. *Finding Morality in the Diaspora?: Moral Ambiguity and Transformed Morality in the Books of Esther.* BZAW 328. New York: de Gruyter, 2003.

Klein, Lillian R. *From Deborah to Esther: Sexual Politics in the Hebrew Bible.* Minneapolis, Minn.: Fortress, 2003.

Laniak, Timothy S. *Shame and Honor in the Book of Esther.* SBLDS 165. Atlanta: Scholars Press, 1998.

Levenson, Jon D. *Esther: A Commentary.* OTL. Louisville: Westminster/John Knox, 1997.

Moore, Carey A. *Daniel, Esther, and Jeremiah: The Additions.* AB 44. Garden City, N.Y.: Doubleday, 1977.

———. *Esther.* AB 7B. Garden City, N.Y.: Doubleday, 1971.

White, Sidnie A. "Esther." In *The Woman's Bible Commentary.* Edited by Carol A. Newsom and Sharon H. Ringe. Louisville: Westminster/John Knox, 1992, 124-29.

ENDNOTES

1. This is a revision of my previously stated position that Esther was written in the early fourth century BCE. While this date is still certainly possible, it is also possible to argue for the later date. See Sidnie A. White, "Esther," in *The Woman's Bible Commentary,* ed. Carol A. Newsom and Sharon H. Ringe (Louisville: Westminster/John Knox, 1992) 124.

2. *b. Meg.* 3.

3. Lawrence M. Wills, *The Jew in the Court of the Foreign King,* HDR 26 (Minneapolis: Fortress, 1990) 153-54; Michael V. Fox, *Character and Ideology in the Book of Esther,* 146.

4. Lawrence M. Wills, *The Jew in the Court of the Foreign King,* 153; Michael V. Fox, *Character and Ideology in the Book of Esther,* 45.

5. Michael V. Fox, *Character and Ideology in the Book of Esther,* 149 n. 22.

6. Michael V. Fox, *Character and Ideology in the Book of Esther,* 157.

7. Jon D. Levenson, *Esther,* OTL (Louisville: Westminster/John Knox, 1997) 8.

8. Carey A. Moore, *Esther,* AB 7B (Garden City, N.Y.: Doubleday, 1971) LIV.

9. Edward L. Greenstein, "A Jewish Reading of Esther," in *Judaic Perspectives on Ancient Israel,* ed. J. Neusner et al. (Philadelphia: Fortress, 1987) 238-39.

10. Jon D. Levenson, *Esther,* 11.

11. Bruce W. Jones, "Two Misconceptions About the Book of Esther," *CBQ* 39 (1977) 171-81.

12. Carey A. Moore, *Esther,* 5.

13. Lewis B. Paton, *Esther,* ICC (Edinburgh: T & T Clark, 1908) 77.

14. The following remarks are dependent upon Lewis B. Paton, *Esther* 77-94, and Carey A. Moore, *Esther,* XLVI-XLIX.

15. Cited in Lewis B. Paton, *Esther,* 78.

16. C. C. Torrey, "The Older Book of Esther," *HTR* XXXVII (1944) 6.

17. Carey A. Moore, *Esther,* XLIX.

18. See David J. A. Clines, *The Esther Scroll: The Story of the Story,* JSOTSup 30 (Sheffield: JSOT, 1984); Michael V. Fox, *The Redaction of the Books of Esther,* SBLMS 40 (Atlanta: Scholars Press, 1991); Karen H. Jobes, *The Alpha-Text of Esther: Its Character and Relationship to the Masoretic Text,* SBLDS 153 (Atlanta: Scholars Press, 1996); Carey A. Moore, *Daniel, Esther and Jeremiah: The Additions,* AB 44 (Garden City, N.Y.: Doubleday, 1977).

19. Henri Cazelles, "Note sur la composition du rouleau d'Esther," in *Lex tua veritas. Festschrift für Hubert Junker,* ed. H. Gross and F. Mussner (Trier: Paulinus Verlag, 1961) 17-29. David J. A. Clines, *The Esther Scroll,* 115-26, does a masterful job of presenting both the strengths and the weaknesses of Cazelles's theory. Clines concludes that in modified form Cazelles's two-source theory is possible, but it is still not preferable to posit separate Esther and Mordecai sources.

20. Hans Bardtke, *Das Buch Esther*, KAT XVII/5 (Gütersloh: G. Mohn, 1963) 248-52.

21. C. C. Torrey, "The Older Book of Esther," 1-40.

22. J. T. Milik, "Les Modèles Araméens du Livre d'Esther dans la Grotte 4 de Qumrân," *RQ* 15 (1992) 321-99.

23. Sidnie White Crawford, "Has Esther Been Found at Qumran? 4QProto-Esther and the Esther Corpus," *RQ* 17 (1996) 307-25.

24. J. T. Milik, "Les Modèles Araméens du Livre d'Esther dans la Grotte 4 de Qumrân," 384. A paleographic date indicates only when the MS was copied. It is much more difficult to determine a date of composition; the terminus ad quem is the reign of Xerxes (486–465 BCE), in which the stories are set. The lack of animosity toward Gentiles (indeed, most of the characters may be Gentiles) may indicate a date of composition before the upheavals in the reign of Antiochus IV Epiphanes in the second century BCE.

25. "Patireza" is a Persian name. See Shaul Shaked, "Qumran: Some Iranian Connections," in *Solving Riddles and Untying Knots: Biblical, Epigraphic and Semitic Studies in Honor of Jonas C. Greenfield*, ed. Z. Zevit, S. Gitin, M. Sokoloff (Winona Lake: Eisenbrauns, 1995) 278.

26. J. T. Milik, "Les Modèles Araméens du Livre d'Esther dans la Grotte 4 de Qumrân," 332, restores the name of Patireza's father as Jair, thus making the connection to Esther even closer.

27. My translation has been greatly improved by study of the translation of John J. Collins and Deborah A. Green, "The Tales from the Persian Court (4Q550a-c)," in *Antikes Judentum und Frühes Christentum* (Berlin, New York: Walter de Gruyter, 1999) 39-50.

28. However, see Jon D. Levenson, *Esther*, 19.

29. All verses of the AT are given according to the Cambridge Septuagint edition: *The Old Testament in Greek*, vol. 3, Part I: *Esther, Judith, Tobit*, ed. A. E. Brooke, N. McLean, H. S. J. Thackeray (London: Cambridge University Press, 1940).

30. For references, see Louis Ginzberg, *The Legends of the Jews* (Philadelphia: Jewish Publication Society, 1946) 6:463.

31. Richard Bauckham, *The Bible in Politics: How to Read the Bible Politically* (London: SPCK, 1989) 123.

32. Sandra Beth Berg, *The Book of Esther: Motifs, Themes, and Structure*, SBLDS 44 (Missoula, Mont.: Scholars Press, 1979) 178.

33. Michael V. Fox, *Character and Ideology in the Book of Esther*, 242.

34. For a thorough discussion of Esther's canonical status in early Christianity, see Carey A. Moore, *Esther*, xxi-xxx.

35. Lewis B. Paton, *Esther*, 96.

36. S. Talmon, " 'Wisdom' in the Book of Esther," *VT* 13 (1963) 419-55.

37. See the objections of James Crenshaw in "Method in Determining Wisdom Influence Upon 'Historical Literature,' " *JBL* 88 (1969) 129-42.

38. Lawrence M. Wills, *The Jew in the Court of the Foreign King*, 151.

39. Susan Niditch, "Legends of Wise Heroes and Heroines," in *The Hebrew Bible and Its Modern Interpreters*, ed. Douglas Knight and Gene Tucker (Philadelphia: Fortress, 1985) 450.

40. For the following remarks I am dependent on the work of sandra Beth Berg, *The Book of Esther*, 124-42.

41. It is probable that these tales, which once circulated separately from the apocalyptic material in Daniel 7:1–12, were composed in the late Persian period diaspora. See John Collins, *The Apocalyptic Imagination* (New York: Crossroad, 1984) 70-72.

42. Many similar correspondences could be cited for the *Tale of Ahiqar*, a royal courtier tale set in the Assyrian Empire, in which the protagonist is not Jewish. However, the tale was evidently popular with Jewish audiences, since a copy of Ahiqar was found in the Jewish colony of Elephantine. See W. Lee Humphreys, "A Life-Style for Diaspora: A Study of the Tales of Esther and Daniel," *JBL* 92 (1973) 211-23.

43. It is probable that Judith was written during the period of the Hasmoneans. See Carey A. Moore, *Judith*, AB 40 (Garden City, N.Y.: Doubleday, 1985) 67-70.

44. Moore notes that the Church Fathers especially made this connection. See C. A. Moore, "Why Wasn't the Book of Judith Included in the Hebrew Bible?" in *No One Spoke Ill of Her: Essays on Judith*, ed. James C. VanderKam (Atlanta: Scholars Press, 1992) 66.

45. See Carey A. Moore, *Esther*, lii, who states, "Between Mordecai and Esther the greater hero in the Hebrew is Mordecai, who supplied the brains while Esther simply followed his directions."

46. Alice Laffey, *An Introduction to the Old Testament: A Feminist Perspective* (Philadelphia: Fortress, 1988) 216.

47. Sidnie White, "Esther: A Feminine Model for Jewish Diaspora," in *Gender and Difference in Ancient Israel*, ed. Peggy L. Day (Philadelphia: Fortress) 161-77; Sidnie A. White, "Esther," in *The Women's Bible Commentary, ed. Carol A. Newsom and Sharon H. Ringe* (Louisville: Westminster/John Knox, 1992). See also Michael V. Fox, *Character and Ideology in the Book of Esther.*

48. Richard Bauckham, *The Bible in Politics: How to Read the Bible Politically* (London: SPCK, 1989) chap. 8.

49. I would like to thank the following institutions and people: Albright College, especially the staff of the Gingrich Library; The W. F. Albright Institute of Archaeological Research, my scholarly home in Jerusalem; Katheryn Pfisterer Darr, Thomas G. Long, John R. Spencer, and Benjamin G. Wright III for their helpful comments on earlier drafts; and my husband, Dan D. Crawford, for his constant support.

INTRODUCTION TO HEBREW POETRY

ADELE BERLIN

It has been recognized since ancient times that the Hebrew Bible contains poetry, but the definition of what constitutes biblical poetry, the description of poetic features, and the identification of poetic passages have varied greatly over the centuries. This article will present a summary of the poetic features considered most relevant by contemporary biblical scholars, and will show how an understanding of them may lead to better interpretations of biblical poetry.

INTERNAL EVIDENCE FOR THE DEFINITION OF POETRY

A good starting place would seem to be the Bible's own terminology. Certain terms occur in superscriptions or within passages that may indicate poetic genres. The broadest of these is *šîr* (שִׁיר) or *šîrâ* (שִׁירה), meaning "song" or "poem." *Šîr* may stand alone, as in Judg 5:12 and Ps 65:1, or it may be qualified, as in *šîr hamma'alôt* (שִׁיר המעלות, "pilgrimage song"; Psalms 120–134), *šîr ṣiyyôn* (שִׁיר ציון, "Zion song"; Ps 137:3), *šîr ḥādāš* (שִׁיר חדש, "new song"; Pss 96:1; 98:1; 149:1). For other types of *šîr*, see Pss 30:1; 45:1; 137:4. The "feminine" form, *šîrâ*, is found, e.g., in Exod 15:1; Deut 31:30; Num 21:17. Another frequent term is *mizmôr* (מזמור, "song," "psalm"), which appears in numerous psalms, sometimes in combination with *šîr* (e.g., Pss 67:1; 68:1). A third term, *qînâ* (קינה, "lament"), is known from 2 Sam 1:17; Amos 8:10. While these terms provide a useful entrée into ancient notions of literary, or perhaps musical, genres, they do not encompass every passage that a modern reader would consider poetry.

Likewise, the ancient scribal tradition, practiced from rabbinic times, of writing certain sections of the Hebrew Bible stichographically (i.e., with space left between lines of a poem; see, e.g., Exodus 15; Deuteronomy 32; Judges 5) is suggestive of what may have been perceived as poems. Yet it is not a sufficient criterion by today's standards because, like the term *šîr*, stichographic writing was not used for all poetic passages and is occasionally used for non-poetic lists (Josh 12:9-24; Esth 9:7-9).

The internal features of the biblical text neither adequately define nor identify poetry. Moreover, no ancient Israelite or ancient Near Eastern treatises on poetry or poetics have been found. Hence, scholars in each time and place, beginning with the Greco-Roman period, have applied to the biblical text definitions of poetry from their own literary tradition. Early Christian scholars discussed biblical poetry in terms of classical metrical systems, medieval Jewish scholars searched the Bible for the types of rhyme and metrical patterns found in medieval Hebrew poetry, and English Renaissance scholars sought the attributes of their style of poetry in the Bible. We do the same today, applying all we know of systems of versification, poetic syntax and vocabulary, symbolic and metaphoric representation—in short, all the ways in which language may be distinguished as poetic (as opposed to non-poetic)—to the study of biblical poetry. The result is an increasingly complex and sophisticated view of the Hebrew Bible's poetry and, by extension, all biblical language, as well as an ever-deepening aesthetic appreciation for it.

VERSE OR POETRY?

When we speak of verse we mean a type of discourse with formal properties, generally quantifiable, such as meter or rhyme, that distinguish it from other types of discourse. The search for such properties in biblical poetry has a long and largely unsuccessful history. For most of this history, attempts were made to uncover the Bible's metrical system. Biblical verse has been, at various times and places, described as quantitative, syllabic, or accentual. But despite much effort, no one has been able to demonstrate convincingly the existence of a consistently occurring metrical system. (See the section "Meter and Rhythm," below.)

M. O'Connor has suggested that instead of looking for formal arrangements built on the recurrence of phonological units (which is what most metrical systems are), we will find the formal properties of biblical verse in the arrangement of syntactic units. O'Connor proposed a system of syntactic constraints to define a line of verse.[1] The terms that he employs are *clause*, a verbal clause or a verbless clause; *constituent*, each verb and nominal phrase and the particles dependent on it; and *unit*, the independent verb or noun along with the particles dependent on it (generally equivalent to a word). According to this system, a line of biblical verse may contain no more than three clauses; it may contain between one and four constituents; and it may contain between two and five units. The dominant line form, according to O'Connor's description, contains one clause and either two or three constituents of two or three units. For example, Exod 15:7 may be analyzed as

7a.	וברב גאונך תהרס קמיך	*ûběrōb gě'ôněkā*
		tahărōs qāmêkā
7b.	תשלח חרנך	*těšallaḥ ḥărōněkā*
7c.	יאכלמו כקש	*yō'kělēmô kaqqaš*

In your great majesty, you smash your foes,
You send forth your anger,
It consumes them like stubble.[2]

Line 7a contains one clause of three constituents, 7b contains one clause of two constituents, and 7c contains one clause of two constituents. While O'Connor's work is frequently cited, and is generally recognized as an innovative description grounded on a sound linguistic basis, it has rarely been applied to analyses of biblical poetry. Perhaps his description has not replaced the older types of search for meter because it is technical and complex, or because it is difficult to imagine that a native poet would have thought in these syntactic categories.

Other scholars, including myself, feel that the quest for a formal system of versification should be abandoned because it does not exist. It is prefer-

able, therefore, to speak of "poetry" rather than "verse." By "poetry" I mean a type of discourse that employs a high degree of the tropes and figures that are described below. Poetry can be distinguished from non-poetic discourse (historical narrative, legal discourse) by the comparatively high density of these tropes and by the structuring of some of them into recurring patterns. Poetry also employs sound and joins it to meaning in interesting ways. In stating this, I espouse a Jakobsonian view, which sees poetry as focusing on the message for its own sake. A poem conveys thought, and, moreover, it conveys that thought in a self-conscious manner, through a special structuring of language that calls attention to the "how" of the message as well as to the "what." At the same time, the "how" and the "what" become indistinguishable. Robert Alter, taking his approach from New Criticism, puts it slightly differently: "Poetry . . . is not just a set of techniques for saying impressively what could be said otherwise. Rather, it is a particular way of imagining the world."[3]

GENRES OF BIBLICAL POETRY

There does not seem to have been a formal or structural distinction between different kinds of poems. Hebrew poetry has no fixed number of lines or type of patterning that is characteristic of a particular genre. If the ancient Israelites did make genre distinctions, those genres are largely lost to us. (They are presumably similar to the genres of other ancient Near Eastern literatures.)[4]

As one might have expected, form-critical studies have discovered genres or subtypes of poetry, especially as they can be related to a specific *Sitz im Leben*, such as victory songs or communal laments. Hermann Gunkel's work remains the classic source on form-critical types of psalms.[5] Following Gunkel, most scholars find the following genres in the book of Psalms: individual and communal laments, hymns of praise, thanksgiving songs, royal psalms, songs of Zion, and wisdom psalms.

Modern scholars tend to impose their own notions of genre, based for the most part on analogy with the tone and contents of genres in other literatures, when they divide up the poetic territory in the Bible. This division corresponds to a large degree with the biblical books in which the poems are found; thus Proverbs and Job are wisdom literature; Psalms contains praise (or lyric) or perhaps liturgy; Lamentations has laments; Song of Songs is love poetry (or perhaps wedding songs). In other books, one may find victory songs (Exodus 15; Judges 5; Num 21:28) or elegies (2 Sam 1:19-27; 3:33-34). Prophetic writing makes an interesting test case, as Robert Alter has observed, for some prophetic speeches are written as poetry and others as prose. Alter has suggested that the vocative (addressing the reader in the second person) and monitory (admonishing) nature of prophetic poetry distinguishes it from other poetic genres.

Actually, most studies of biblical poetry are not concerned with genre per se, but concentrate on the common features of all biblical poetry. These are presented in the following sections.

TERSENESS

Scholars of comparative literature who have searched for a universal definition of poetry have noticed that poetic lines tend to be shorter and terser than lines of prose. This feature seems to occur whether or not there are metrical constraints on the length of lines. Whatever the reason, poetry has a tendency to be more terse, more concise, than non-poetic discourse, both within a single line and, in the case of biblical poetry, over the discourse as a whole. Biblical poems are relatively short, usually thirty verses or less; there are no epic poems in the Bible. Lines are short, and the relationships or transitions between lines are often unexpressed. This gives the impression that in poetry each word or phrase is more loaded with meaning, since fewer words must bear the burden of the message. In biblical poetry, terseness within lines is achieved largely by the omission of the definite article (ה *ha*), the accusative marker (את *ēt*), and the relative pronoun (אשר *'ăšer*). The decreased usage of these particles has been documented in computerized counts.[6] The relationship between lines is frequently not made explicit, but is implied by the parallelism that compels the reader to construe some type of relationship.

We can see some of the terseness and the effect of parallelism in a comparison of Judg 4:19 and 5:25, a poetic and a prose version of the same incident:

Then he said to her, "Please give me a little water to drink; for I am thirsty." So she opened a skin of milk and gave him a drink and covered him.　　　　(Judg 4:19 NRSV)

He asked water and she gave him milk,
　　she brought him curds in a lordly bowl.
　　　　　　　　　　　　(Judg 5:25 NRSV)

The poetic version is both more concise and more redundant. The parallelism in 5:25 sets up an exact equivalence, a reciprocity, which brings into focus the contrast between what was requested and what was served. The addition of "she brought him curds in a lordly bowl" does not add to the sequence of actions but doubles back upon the milk, stressing once more its "dairiness" (as opposed to water) and the noble flourish with which it was offered. The prose version carries the reader step by step along the narrative sequence, giving more information but not highlighting any part of it as the poetic version does.

PARALLELISM

Since the work of Robert Lowth, parallelism has come to be viewed as one of the two identifying markers of poetry.[7] And since the other marker, meter, is notoriously resistant to analysis, parallelism, which is relatively easy to perceive (at least since Lowth called attention to it), has emerged as the predominant feature of biblical poetry. We should note at the outset, however, that parallelism is also present in non-poetic discourse, albeit to a more limited extent. So the mere existence of parallelism is not a sufficient indication of poetry, although a high frequency of parallelism in adjacent lines or verses has a high correlation with what we consider poetic discourse.

Parallelism may be defined as the repetition of similar or related semantic content or grammatical structure in adjacent lines or verses. The repetition is rarely identical, and it is the precise nature of the relationship between the two lines that has been the focus of most discussion. Indeed, the flexibility of this relationship, its capacity for variation, makes parallelism rhetorically interesting.

The Semantic Relationship. There have been two schools of thought on how to describe the semantic relationship between parallel lines. The first, introduced by Lowth and followed until recently, emphasizes the sameness of the relationship and the types and degree of correspondence between the lines. Lowth's classic definition is

> The correspondence of one Verse, or Line, with another I call Parallelism. When a proposition is delivered, and a second subjoined to it, or drawn under it, equivalent, or contrasted with it, in Sense; or similar to it in the form of Grammatical Construction; these I call Parallel Lines; and the words or phrases answering one to another in the corresponding Lines Parallel Terms.[8]

Lowth advanced his description by proposing discrete categories into which parallelisms could fit, depending on the nature of the correspondence of the lines. His categories are synonymous, antithetic, and synthetic. In synonymous parallelism, the same thought is expressed in different words, as in Ps 117:1:

> Praise the LORD, all you nations!
> Extol him, all you peoples! (NRSV)

In antithetic parallelism, the second line contradicts, or is opposed to, the first line, as in Prov 10:1:

> "A wise child makes a glad father,
> but a foolish child is a mother's grief" (NRSV).

Synthetic parallelism, a much looser designation, accounts for parallelisms that lack exact correspondence between their parts but show a more diffuse correspondence between the lines as a whole. An example is Cant 2:4:

> "He brought me to the banqueting house,
> and his intention toward me was love" (NRSV).

This tripartite system of categorization of types of parallelisms gained wide popularity, for it accounted for large numbers of parallel lines.

As scholars continued to study parallelism, they refined Lowth's original categories, furthering his typological approach by adding subcategories, such as staircase parallelism, in which the second line repeats part of the first but moves beyond it, as in Jer 31:21:

> "Return, O virgin Israel,
> return to these your cities" (NRSV)

and janus parallelism, hinging on the use of a single word with two different meanings, one relating to what precedes it and one to what follows, as in Cant 2:12:

> "The flowers appear on the earth;
> the time of singing [הזמיר *hazzāmîr* ; or "pruning"])
> has come
> and the voice of the turtledove/is heard in our land."

In such an approach, the weak link was synthetic parallelism, because at best it appeared to be nothing more than a catchall of undefined categories or, at worst, a grouping of lines containing no parallelism. But the weakness of synthetic parallelism began to spread, as it was observed that no set of parallel lines is exactly synonymous or antithetic.

A major turning point came in the 1980s with the work of Robert Alter and James Kugel. Whereas Lowth's approach emphasized the similarity between parallel lines, Alter and Kugel emphasized their differences. Kugel rejected the notion of the synonymity of parallel lines and substituted the notion of continuity, phrasing his definition of parallelism as "A, what's more, B." Alter, moving independently in the same direction, spoke of the "consequentiality" of parallel lines. He saw the relationship between the lines as one of progression or intensification.

Indeed, both approaches contain elements of truth, for parallelism contains relationships of both similarity and difference. Take, for example, Ps 18:9 (Eng. 18:8 = 2 Sam 22:9):

> Smoke went up from his nostrils,
> and devouring fire from his mouth;
> glowing coals flamed forth from him. (NRSV)

There is a grammatical and semantic similarity among the three lines: *smoke/fire/coals* coming forth from his *nostrils/mouth.* But at the same time, within the general sameness there is an intensification, an escalation of the sense of burning. A clearer example is Lam 5:11:

> They raped women in Zion,
> Virgins in the Judean towns.

At first glance, these lines are synonymous, but on further reflection one sees intensification as one moves from *women* to *virgins* and progresses from *Zion* to *the Judean towns.*

Parallel Word Pairs. Lowth's definition had called attention to "parallel terms"—that is, "words or phrases answering one to another in corresponding lines"—but it was only with the discovery of Ugaritic poetry and the widespread acceptance of the theory of oral composition that efforts to analyze parallelism focused on parallel word pairs, or, as they came to be called, "fixed word pairs." Scholars noticed that certain sets of terms regularly recurred in parallel lines, such as *day/night* (e.g., Ps 121:6: "The sun shall not strike you by day,/ nor the moon by night" [NRSV]) and *heaven/earth* (e.g., Isa 1:2: "Hear, O heavens, and listen, O earth" [NRSV]). Such pairs were taken to have been the functional equivalents of the formulas in Greek and Yugoslavian poetry that enabled the poet to compose orally. The pairs were thought to have been fixed—i.e., they were stock pairs of words learned by poets who would then use them as the building blocks around which a parallelism could be constructed. Much research concentrated on discovering and listing these pairs (which were often the same in Hebrew and Ugaritic) and charting their frequency, the order in which the members of a set occurred, their grammatical form, and the semantic relationship between them. This last element led to categories not unlike those elicited by Lowth: synonyms and antonyms. But new categories were also noted, such as a whole and a part, abstract and concrete, common term and archaic term, and the breakup of stereotyped phrases. Examples of recurring word pairs abound: *Jerusalem/Judah* (Isa 3:8; Jer 9:10); *father/mother* (Ezek 16:3; Prov 1:8); *right/left* (Gen 13:9; Ezek 16:46; Cant 2:6).

Research on word pairs advanced the scholarly understanding of the components of parallel lines and the lexical and poetic similarities between Hebrew and Ugaritic. But because the study was largely based on an unproven hypothesis about the oral composition of Greek poetry and a tenuous analogy between Greek formulas and Hebrew word pairs, it misconstrued the nature of word pairs. They are not "fixed," and they do not drive the composition of parallel lines. Rather, the process of composing parallel lines calls forth word pairs, which are nothing more than commonly associated terms that can be elicited by any speaker of the language (as word association games have shown). In fact, many of the same pairs occur together in non-parallel discourse (e.g., right/left, Num 20:17; 22:26).

Linguistic Models. In the 1970s and 1980s the focus of research on parallelism began to move away from word pairs and back to the lines as a whole. By then, however, there were new theories and models from the field of linguistics that offered new and better possibilities for understanding parallelism. Among the scholars employing linguistic models were A. Berlin, T. Collins, S. Geller, E. Greenstein, D. Pardee, and W. G. E. Watson. They drew on structural linguistics and transformational grammar for a grammatical analysis of parallelism. The major influence came from the work of Roman Jakobson, whose most famous dictum on parallelism was

> Pervasive parallelism inevitably activates all the levels of language—the distinctive features, inherent and prosodic, the morphological and syntactic categories and forms, the lexical units and their semantic classes in both their convergences and divergences acquire an autonomous poetic value.[9]

This statement suggests that not only lexical units (word pairs) or semantic relationships, but all linguistic features as well come into play in parallelism.

Parallelism can be viewed as a phenomenon involving linguistic equivalences or contrasts that may occur on the level of the word, the line, or across larger expanses of text. (However, the analysis of parallelism generally operates at the level of the line.) Linguistic equivalence not only means identity, but also refers to a term or construction that belongs to the same category or paradigm, or to the same sequence or syntagm. This kind of equivalence can easily be seen in word pairs. Pairs like day and night or father and mother belong to the same grammatical paradigm (nouns) and might be said to belong to the same semantic paradigm ("time" and "family members").

Similarly, entire lines can be grammatically equivalent—that is, contain the same grammatical deep structure (and perhaps surface structure). I call this the *grammatical aspect*. In fact, Lowth had called attention to lines with similar grammatical construction in his definition of parallelism, but this feature had never been carefully analyzed before. With the advent of transformational grammar, it began to receive major attention.

For example, Ps 103:10:

Not according to our sins did he deal with us,
And not according to our transgressions did he
   requite us.

These lines have the same surface structure as well
as the same deep structure. More often, though,
the surface structure varies in some way, while the
deep structure remains the same. For instance, in
Mic 6:2*b* a nominal clause is paired with a verbal
clause:

For the Lord has a quarrel with his people,
And with Israel will he dispute.

In Prov 6:20, a positive clause is paired with a negative clause:

Guard, my son, the commandments of your
   father,
And do not forsake the teaching of your mother.

The subject of one clause may become the object
in the parallel clause, as in Gen 27:29:

Be lord over your brothers,
   and may the sons of your mother bow down to
   you. (NIV)

Parallelism may pair lines of different grammatical
mood, as in Ps 6:6 (Eng. 6:5) where a negative
indicative clause parallels an interrogative one.

For in death there is no mention of you,
In Sheol, who can acclaim you?

All parallelism involves the pairing of terms, the
lexical aspect; as already suggested, the process
whereby specific terms are paired is similar to the
process that generates associations in psycholin-
guistic word association games. Linguists have discovered rules that account for the kinds of associations made, much as biblical scholars had tried to
discover the principles at work in "fixed word
pairs." They have noted that in word association
games a word may elicit itself; so, too, in parallelism a word may parallel itself or another word
from the same root—e.g., 2 Sam 22:7: *I called//I
called* ; Job 6:15: *stream//bed of streams*. Linguists have also noted that a word may have a
number of different associates and that some are

likely to be generated more often than are others,
thereby giving rise to the perception that some
associations are "fixed."

The rules for word association are categorized
by linguists as paradigmatic and syntagmatic (like
the rules for the grammatical, and other, aspects of
parallelism). Paradigmatic pairing involves the
selection of a word from the same class as a previous word. The most common type of paradigmatic
pairing is one with minimal contrast, which produces an "opposite," such as *good/bad* or *man/
woman*. Other linguistic rules explain other paradigmatic choices.

Syntagmatic responses involve the choice of an
associate from the same sequence rather than
from the same class. This is often realized in the
completion of idiomatic phrases or conventional
coordinates, like *horses/chariots* or *loyalty/truth*.
(This phenomenon is similar to what had been
called the breakup of stereotyped phrases.)
Another type of syntagmatic pairing involves the
splitting of the components of personal or geographic names; e.g., *Balak//king of Moab* (Num
23:7) and *Ephrathah//Bethlehem* (Ruth 4:11).

While this lexical aspect of parallelism generally
accompanies the grammatical aspect (the pairing of
lines with equivalent syntax), it may occur in the
absence of grammatical parallelism (strictly
speaing, lines with paradigmatic grammatical
equivalence). An example is Ps 111:6:

The power of his deeds he told to his *people*,
In giving to them the inheritance of *nations*.

The grammatical relationship of the lines is not
paradigmatically equivalent. Moreover, *people* and
nations do not refer to the same entity in this verse
(*people* refers to Israel, and *nations* refers to non-
Israelite nations). But the pair *people/nation* is a
known association that occurs frequently, usually
referring to the same entity. The manner in which
this pair is used is somewhat novel, but the use of
a common pair helps to draw the two lines
together, making them appear more parallel.

Even in the presence of grammatical equivalence, word pairs may run counter to this equivalence instead of reinforcing it, as is more usual. An
example is Job 5:14:

By day they encounter darkness,
And as at night they grope at noon.

Both lines express a similar thought (semantic content); during the daytime it will seem like nighttime. The semantic and syntactic equivalent terms here are *day/noon* and *darkness/night*. But the poet has employed a common word association, *day/night*, and has placed these terms in the same position in each line. In this case, the lexical pairing is at odds with the semantic and syntactic pairing, creating a tension between the two, which in turn sets up a competing relationship between the lines, thereby binding them even more closely together.

This illustration reminds us that the sense of the entire verse comes into play in the selection of word pairs, for words are chosen to express or emphasize a particular message. Just as the selection of parallel words is not totally random, so also it is not totally fixed. Through linguistics, we have come to understand better the process of word selection, and so to understand better the workings of parallelism and the effect of a particular word choice. Another illustration will demonstrate the subtle difference that the choice of a word pair can make. Compare, for example, Ps 102:13 [Eng. 102:12] with Lam 5:19:

> But you, O LORD, are enthroned forever;
> your *name* endures to all generations.
> (NRSV, italics added)

> But you, O LORD, reign forever;
> your *throne* endures to all generations.
> (NRSV, italics added)

The difference in the choice of one word underscores the difference in the messages of these two passages. Psalm 102 contrasts the weakness and fleetingness of a human being with the permanence of God. God's name—that is, God's existence—lasts forever. The author of Lamentations, on the other hand, laments the destruction of the Temple, the locus of God's throne. Despite its physical destruction, he maintains that God's throne—the metaphoric seat of God's rulership—will remain intact.

I have made reference to the *semantic aspect* of parallelism, which pertains to the relationship between the meaning of the parallel lines. Lowth characterized this relationship as synonymous, antithetic, or synthetic, and Kugel called it "A, what's more, B." From a linguistic perspective, the

semantic relationship between lines (like the lexical and grammatical relationships) can be described as either paradigmatic or syntagmatic. It is not always easy, however, to decide specific cases, for often one reader sees similarity where another sees sequential development (see above the discussion on Lowth vs. Alter and Kugel.) Part of the confusion arises because both paradigmatic and syntagmatic elements may be present.

> Ascend a high hill, Herald (to) Zion,
> Lift your voice aloud, herald (to) Jerusalem.
> (Isa 40:9)

The actions of the herald are sequential (syntagmatic), but the vocatives, "herald (to) Zion/Jerusalem," are paradigmatic. It seems to be the nature of parallelism to combine syntagmatic and paradigmatic relationships on different levels or in different aspects. The effect is to advance the thought, while at the same time creating a close relationship between the parallelism's constituent parts.

Another linguistic aspect that may come into play in parallelism is phonology. Equivalences in sound may be activated in parallelism just as equivalences in grammar are. This is the *phonological aspect*, which often takes the form of pairing words with similar consonants. These pairs may also be semantic or lexical pairs, such as שָׁלוֹם (šālôm) // שַׁלְוָה (šalvâ), "peace" // "tranquility" (Ps 122:7); or they may be unrelated, as in Ps 104:19:

> He made the moon for time-markers [מוֹעֲדִים mô'ǎdîm],
> The sun knows its setting [יָדַע מְבוֹאוֹ yāda' mĕbô'ô].

Sound pairs reinforce the bond between lines created by grammatical and lexical pairings, providing an additional type of linguistic equivalence in the parallelism. The more linguistic equivalences there are, the stronger is the sense of correspondence between one line and the next. Such similarity, in turn, promotes the sense of semantic unity.

There are infinite ways to activate linguistic equivalences, and hence there are infinite ways to construct a parallelism. No one type is "better" or "worse" than another. Each is designed for its own context and purpose.

METER AND RHYTHM

Although I earlier rejected meter as a demonstrably formal requirement of biblical verse, it is appropriate to summarize some of the modern analyses of meter because they are so pervasive in discussions of biblical poetry, and because they raise important questions about the nature of that poetry. Moreover, it is practically impossible for someone raised in a modern North American or European tradition to imagine poetry without meter.

Strictly speaking, meter requires the recurrence of an element or group of elements with mathematical regularity. The element to be measured may be the syllable (or a certain type or length of syllable), the accent or stress, or the word. (M. O'Connor's system of syntactic constraints is a substitute for meter, or a metrical system of a different order.) There have been various metrical theories of biblical poetry involving one or more of these elements. The theory of word meter assumes that there is a fixed number of word units in each line of verse. Related to word meter is the theory of thought meter, in which the thought unit (usually one or two words receiving one major stress) constitutes the basic unit of measurement. A third theory counts the number of syllables (without respect to whether they are open or closed, or stressed or unstressed). While technically not a metrical theory, syllable counting is related to discussions of syllabic meter. The most popular theory of biblical meter is accentual, which counts the number of accents or stresses per line. This approach is sometimes combined with the counting of the number of words or syllables.

All of these metrical theories suffer from several deficits. First, none has gained sufficient acceptance among scholars to place it clearly above its competitors. Second, all have had problems defining precisely the unit to be counted. For instance, what constitutes a "word"? Does it include affixed prepositions? Is a construct noun (a noun linked grammatically to an adjacent noun, as in "mountain top") a separate word? Finally, when the counting is done, the pattern of recurrence of the unit does not appear with sufficient regularity, even within a few lines, not to mention throughout an entire poem. While there are certain parameters for the number of words or syllables that may occur in a line, these parameters do not appear to result in a metrical system. They are, rather, a factor of the biblical Hebrew language, the terseness of poetic lines, and parallelis-

tic construction. It seems best, therefore, to abandon the quest for meter in the poetry of the Bible.

The absence of a real metrical system notwithstanding, sounds do seem to recur with some regularity in biblical poetry, and this recurrence can be differentiated from non-poetic discourse. I prefer to use the term *rhythm* rather than *meter* for this type of recurrence because *rhythm* conveys the notion of the recurrence of sound, or the patterning of sound, without the requirement of measured regularity.

The rhythm of biblical poetry results from terse parallel lines. The number of thoughts and, therefore, of words and of stresses in each line of a parallelism tends to be about the same—not necessarily precisely the same, but about the same. Benjamin Hrushovski has described this as "semantic-syntactic-accentual free parallelism,"[10] which, as far as the recurrence of sound is concerned, produces "free accentual meter." In this system, most lines have between two and four stresses. More important, the lines within a parallelism tend to have the same number of stresses. Thus parallel lines are rhythmically balanced. Lines throughout a poem may vary in number of stresses (within linguistic constraints), but sets of parallel lines tend to be of the same "length." An exception is the so-called *qinah* meter, the rhythm found in laments, which has an unbalanced 3-2 stress pattern. Many lines in the Songs of Ascent collection (Psalms 120–134) have similarly unbalanced lines, but the pattern is not consistent. On the whole, though, a rhythmic balance within a parallelism, and sometimes over larger textual expanses, seems to be present, no matter what elements are counted. This rhythm, a by-product of parallelism, may be viewed as the "metrical" aspect of biblical poetry.

REPETITION AND PATTERNING

All discourse entails repetition, but we have come to expect more of it in poetry because we expect poetry to be more formally organized around certain structures and patterns. Patterning depends on repetition. We have already seen that parallelism, the most dominant characteristic of biblical poetry, involves many types of linguistic repetition or equivalences—grammatical structures, semantic terms, words, and sounds. While much of the repetition described in this section occurs in parallelism, and some is a direct result of parallel structuring, other forms of repetition occur independently of parallelism. Whether or not they are found in discourse formally designated as poetic, they add to the poetic nature of the discourse because they encourage the reader to focus on the message for its own sake; in Jakobsonian terms, they contribute to the poetic function.

The repetition described below involves repeating the same word or triliteral Hebrew root, or the same or closely related basic sounds. The repetition may occur in various combinations or patterns. Sometimes it seems designed to emphasize the message or to focus attention on only a part of that message. At other times, the effect is less discernible, but nevertheless creates an agreeable impression.

Key Words. The same word or root may occur numerous times throughout a passage. For example, the root שׁמר (*šāmar*, "guard") occurs six times in the eight verses of Psalm 121. In Psalm 137 (nine verses) the root זכר (*zākar*, "remember") occurs three times, and the root שׁיר (*šîr*, "sing/song") occurs five times. In both cases, the key words point to the essence of the psalm's message. Psalm 121 assures us that God is the guardian who never sleeps, and Psalm 137 struggles with the conflict between remembering Zion and singing Zion-songs—that is, between the need to remember the Temple and the impossibility of performing the temple worship.

Anaphora. Several consecutive lines may begin with the same word or phrase. An excellent example is Psalm 150, in which every line begins with "praise him." Compare also Eccl 3:2-8: "a time to . . . and a time to. . . . " More often, the repetition occurs within just a few lines, as in Ps 13:2-3: "How long" (four times).

Cataphora (Epiphora). Consecutive lines end with the same word or phrase. This is rare in the Hebrew Bible and may be considered incidental. An example is Isa 40:13-14; both of these verses end with "instructed him."

Anadiplosis. In this type of repetition, the last word or phrase of a line is repeated at the beginning of the next line. Examples are Ps 96:13:

> before the LORD; for he is coming,
> for he is coming to judge the earth.
> He will judge the world with righteousness.
> (NRSV)

and Ps 98:4b-5:

> break forth into joyous song and sing praises.
> Sing praises to the LORD with the lyre,
> with the lyre and the sound of melody. (NRSV)

Side-by-side Repetition. This is the immediate repetition of the same word (a device used also in prose); for example, "Comfort, O comfort my people" (Isa 40:1 NRSV); "Awake, awake,/put on your strength" (Isa 52:1 NRSV). Isaiah 28:10 (NRSV) makes extensive use of this form:

> "For it is precept upon precept,
>   precept upon precept,
> line upon line, line upon line,
>   here a little, there a little."

Refrain. A refrain is a phrase that is repeated after every verse or at major subdivisions of the poem. The refrain may have been chanted by a chorus in liturgical poems, such as Psalm 136, in which every verse contains the refrain "for his steadfast love endures forever" (cf. Ps 107:1, 8, 15, 21, 31). An example of a refrain in a non-liturgical poem occurs in David's lament over the death of Saul and Jonathan: "How the mighty have fallen!" (2 Sam 1:19, 25, 27 NRSV).

Inclusio (Envelope Figure, Frame). In this figure, the passage or poem begins and ends with the same word or phrase. The inclusio in Psalm 8 is "O LORD, our Sovereign,/ how majestic is your name in all the earth!" (NRSV). In Psalm 103 it is "Bless the LORD, O my soul" (NRSV). The framing of a poem gives a sense of closure and completeness.

Chiasm (ABBA Word Patterning). There are many types of chiasm, or reverse patterning, ranging from within one verse to entire books. The figure has been widely documented. I cite here only two examples of the ABBA patterning of words in one verse or two.

> Ah, you who call evil good and good evil,
>   who put darkness for light
>   and light for darkness,
>   who put bitter for sweet
>   and sweet for bitter! (Isa 5:20 NRSV)

> Even youths will faint and be weary,
>   and the young will fall exhausted;
> but those who wait for the LORD
>   shall renew their strength,

they shall mount up with wings like eagles,
they shall run and not be weary,
  they shall walk and not faint.
(Isa 40:30-31 NRSV, italics added; this is part of a
larger patterning of these words)

ABAB Word Patterning. Isaiah 54:7-8:

For a brief *moment* I abandoned you,
But with great *compassion* I will gather you.
In overflowing wrath for a *moment* I hid my face
from
  you,
But with everlasting love I will have *compassion*
on
  you.

Notice that the patterned words in Isa 54:7-8 are
not semantically related, as they are in Isa 51:6:

Lift up your eyes to the *heavens,*
And look at the *earth* beneath.
For the *heavens* will vanish like smoke,
And the *earth* will wear out like a garment.

Sound Patterning. Various types of sound
patterning are possible in poetry. I have already
mentioned the use of sound pairs, terms in parallel
lines that share the same or similar phonemes (see
the section "Parallelism," above). The most common type of sound patterning that one might
expect is rhyme, but such rhyme as can be found
in the Bible is incidental. There are many examples
of alliteration, the repetition of the same sound or
sounds (or more precisely, consonance, the repetition of consonant sounds). For example, Isa 1:2
contains what may be viewed as consonance in an
AABB pattern: שמעו שמים והאזיני ארץ (*šimʿû
šāmayim wĕhaʾăzînî ʾereṣ*; cf. also Ps 46:10; Job
5:8).

Closely related to consonance and to parallel
sound pairs is paronomasia, or word play—the use
of words with different meanings but similar
sounds. This is a favorite technique in the Hebrew
Bible, and it occurs in prose as well as in poetry. A
classic example is in Isa 5:7:

ויקו למשפט והנה משפח   *wayĕqav lĕmišpāṭ
                         wĕhinnēh miśpāḥ*
לצדקה והנה צעקה   *liṣdāqâ wĕhinnēh ṣĕʿāqâ*

This play on words is rendered in the Tanakh
translation as:

And He hoped for justice,
But behold, injustice;
For equity,
But behold, iniquity! (See also Isa 61:3; Zeph 2:4.)

The discussion thus far has focused on repetition
and patterning within small passages of text, usually
a line or two. Many more possibilities may occur in
an entire poem. Of course, the most obvious structuring device is the alphabetic acrostic (Psalms
9–10; 25; 34; 37; 111; 112; 119; 145; Prov 31:10-
31; Lamentations 1–4). Daniel Grossberg has analyzed centripetal and centrifugal structures. An adequate appreciation of the ways in which poems may
be structured requires a separate study. I cite here
only an example of the manner in which the various
types of repetition presented above may intertwine
and interact in one poem, Psalm 122.[11]

The key words of the psalm are *Jerusalem* (3
times) and *peace* (3 times), and they are good
pointers to the message. The phonemes of
Jerusalem echo in the word *peace* (שלום *šālôm*)
and in several other words throughout the poem,
so the entire poem reverberates with the sound of
the city's name. *House of the Lord* (Temple) forms
an inclusio, and at the midpoint, in verse 5, is
House of David. Anadiplosis occurs in vv. 2-3 in the
repetition of *Jerusalem,* and in two lines in v. 4: "To
it the tribes go up,/the tribes of the LORD"
(NRSV). There is anaphora in the repetition of *there*
in vv. 4-5 and *for the sake of* in vv. 8-9. The words
שלום (*šālôm,* "peace") and שלוה שלה (*šālâ/šalvâ,*
"have peace"/ "ease") alternate in an ABAB pattern
in vv. 6-7; v. 6 has a high degree of consonance.
Moving away from the repetition of words and
sounds, we might note that the poem employs five
verbs of speaking (*say, praise, ask, speak, request*)
and four verbs of motion (*walk/go, stand, ascend,
sit*). All of these forms of repetition help to bind the
poem into a tight unity of sound and meaning.

IMAGERY

Metaphor and simile are hallmarks of poetry in
all languages, to the extent that some theorists
would define poetry in terms of the presence or
dominance of metaphor rather than in terms of formal linguistic structures, like meter or parallelism.
While biblical scholars generally do not view
metaphor as the *sine qua non* of poetry, there is
widespread   acknowledgment   that   metaphor

abounds in the Bible's poetic discourse. At the same time, there is widespread ignorance of how metaphor operates in biblical poetry, both from a theoretical point of view and on the practical level of how it affects the message of the poem.[12] An introductory article such as this one does not permit a full treatment of the theory of metaphor, or of the wealth of biblical examples, but a few observations on the use and effect of metaphor may be offered.

Imagery involves more than a simple comparison of one object to another. By placing the two objects in juxtaposition, a relationship between them is established such that their qualities become interchanged. This can be seen in Ps 42:2-3 [Eng. 42:1-2]:

> As a deer longs for flowing streams, [אפיק 'apîq]
>   so my soul longs for you, O God.
> My soul thirsts for God. (NRSV)

Water, the life-sustaining element, is equated with God; and the psalmist's thirst for God is like the deer's thirst for water. It is a natural, intuitive thirst for a basic substance. Thus the qualities of the deer image are transposed to the psalmist. But "longing" is not an emotion usually associated with a deer. It is a human emotion, transposed from the psalmist's longing for God onto the deer. The verb that one would expect in v. 1 in connection with the deer, "to thirst," is used for the psalmist in v. 2. There is a crossover effect: The deer longs (like a human) for water, and the human thirsts (like a deer) for God. (The psalm continues in v. 4 with "My tears have been my food day and night" [NIV]—continuing the parallelism between "water" and "food/bread" and doing so through another metaphor, equating "tears" [water, non-food, a symbol of despair] with "food.")

Even stock images like water can be used creatively. Let us see how the same term found in Ps 42:2, "stream" (āpîq), is used in two other passages.

> My brothers are treacherous like a wadi,
> Like a wadi-stream [āpîq] that runs dry. (Job 6:15)

> Restore our fortunes, O LORD,
> like streams [āpîq] in the Negev. (Ps 126:4 NIV)

The image in both verses is taken from nature: the wadis that flow with water in the winter and dry up in the summer. The primary transfer of qualities

in Job 6:15 is from the water to the friends. They are treacherously inconsistent like the wadis; they are unreliable, changing with the seasons. The choice of water imagery may also suggest that, like water, the friends should be life-giving and that, therefore, their betrayal is all the more disappointing. But there is also a transfer in the other direction. One does not normally think of wadis as traitors; yet that is what is suggested here in a hint of personification of the wadis. (The root "to betray, be treacherous" [בגד bāgad] is never used of inanimate objects.)

The same natural reference serves a more optimistic purpose in Ps 126:4, where the return of the streams in the rainy season forms the basis of the image. Is the restoration of fortunes, like the streams in their cyclical return, a certainty? Or is it unpredictable (as in the Job verse), and therefore an act of grace?

Sometimes multiple metaphors are linked to one subject, generally to clarify or to reinforce the thought. The metaphors derive from different images and are linked only in that they convey a shared idea.

[two different images for speed]:
> They go by like skiffs of reed,
>   like an eagle swooping on the prey. (Job 9:26 NRSV)

> And it [the sun] is like a bridegroom coming out
>   from his wedding canopy,
> It rejoices like a strong man in running his/its
>   course. (Ps 19:6 [Eng. 19:5])

In the example from Psalm 19, which I have translated literally, it is not clear whether both images have the same sense—eagerness—or whether the first represents happiness/brightness and the second eagerness/strength. Again there is a crossover, this time between the two images, for "rejoices" (שׂושׂ śûś) is a verb more aptly used for a bridegroom than for a runner. The NRSV has neatly bound the two images together:

> which comes out like a bridegroom from his
>   wedding canopy,
> and like a strong man runs its course with joy.[13]

There may also be a series of metaphors deriving from a central image—a conceit—as in Eccl 12:1-7; or a series of different metaphors for different parts of the subject, like the waṣfs in Song of Songs 4–7.

When the Bible talks about God, it must speak, by necessity, metaphorically. God is *sui generis* and abstract, having no form, shape, color, or size. The deity is not like anything else, hence the only way to picture God is to compare God to other things. The most commonly used metaphor is that of a human, which results in anthropomorphisms, but aspects of God may also be compared to natural phenomena (Deut 32:11; Ps 36:5-7) or to the works God created (Ps 48:13-15).

On occasion, the same image may recur in close proximity with a new twist that gives a jarring effect, thereby reinforcing the power of the image, as in Isa 1:9-10:

If the LORD of hosts
 had not left us a few *survivors*,
we would have been *like Sodom*,
 and become *like Gomorrah*.
Hear the word of the LORD,
 you rulers of *Sodom*!
Listen to the teaching of our God,
 you people of *Gomorrah*. (NRSV, italics added)

Because the Sodom-and-Gomorrah image has two different connotations, Isaiah is able to use it for two different effects. He first invokes the association of Sodom and Gomorrah with total destruction, suggesting that the destruction that he describes might have been, but for the grace of God, just as catastrophic. But then, in an arresting reversal, he calls upon the association of Sodom and Gomorrah with total corruption, equating his present audience with the wickedness of Sodom and Gomorrah, which must inevitably lead them to a similarly catastrophic end:

Raise your eyes to the heavens,
And look upon the earth beneath.
Though the heavens should evaporate like
 smoke,
And the earth wear out *like a garment*,
And its inhabitants in like manner die out,
My salvation shall stand forever.
My deliverance shall not cease.
Listen to me, you who know the right,
You people with my teaching in its heart.
Fear not human insults,
And be not dismayed at their jeers.
For the moth shall eat them up *like a garment*,
The caterpillar shall eat them like wool.
But my deliverance shall endure forever,
My salvation through the ages. (Isa 51:6-8)

The image of the earth's wearing out like a garment makes the earth, which does not wear out nearly so quickly, seem ephemeral compared to the permanence of God's victory. Then, in v. 8, the jeering enemy will be eaten as a garment eaten by a moth, making the enemy not only ephemeral but also powerless before the attack of a small insect that will come to punish it. While the single use of "Sodom and Gomorrah" and "being eaten like a garment" would be effective, the reuse of these images strengthens the rhetoric by forcing the audience to give deeper thought to the image and its range of associations.

Finally, when reading the Bible, especially Hebrew poetry, it is not always easy to know when to read the text figuratively and when literally. What are we to make of Ps 114:3-4?

The sea looked and fled;
 Jordan turned back.
The mountains skipped like rams,
 the hills like lambs. (NRSV)

It seems clear that the personification of the sea and the Jordan refers to a "literal" event, the crossing of the Reed Sea and the crossing of the Jordan, which form a frame around the wandering in the wilderness at the time of the exodus. But what of the animation of the mountains and hills? Was this earth imagery made up to match the water imagery, to provide a kind of figurative background? Or does it, perhaps, also refer to a "literal" event, the theophany at Sinai?

Psalm 133:1 presents a different case:

How very good and pleasant it is
 when kindred live together in unity! (NRSV)

Most modern scholars interpret this verse literally as a reference to family harmony. They perceive the entire psalm as a practical teaching on correct conduct. But, as I have shown elsewhere, this verse is both more concrete and more metaphoric than is generally understood. The phrase "live together in unity" is a technical legal term for joint tenancy (cf. Gen 13:6; 36:7; Deut 25:5), but the psalm uses the phrase metaphorically. The joint tenancy refers to the united monarchy. The psalm is expressing an idealistic hope for the reunification of Judah and Israel, with Zion as the capital and focal point.

FIGURES OF SPEECH

The notion of "figures of speech" is a Greek invention, as is much of the terminology used to describe poetic diction, but many of the phenomena that the Greeks identified in their own poetry and rhetoric may be found in other literatures as well. There is no clear consensus among modern scholars as to the figures of speech used in biblical poetry.[14] Among the figures of speech usually cited are allusion, apostrophe, hendiadys, hyperbole and litotes, irony, merismus, oxymoron, personification, and rhetorical questions. It should be noted that these figures also appear in the non-poetic sections of the Hebrew Bible, with the same rhetorical force. They are rhetorical figures, not poetic figures per se. These figures are not critical to the structuring of the poetry, nor do they dominate the poetic landscape like repetition or parallelism. They are merely decorative, enhancing the rhetorical effect of the message.

For example, in Ps 107:26 sailors tossed about in a storm are described through hyperbole (extravagant exaggeration) and merismus (the expression of a totality through mention of its representative components) as: " . . . mounted up to the heavens and went down to the depths" (NIV). Often hyperbole is conveyed through metaphor or simile, as in Obadiah 4: "If she [Edom] soars aloft like an eagle; if she places her nest among the stars."

Personification of death can be seen in Isa 28:15 and Ps 49:15; and wisdom is personified as a woman in Prov 1:20-33 and Proverbs 8.

Rhetorical questions may occur in series (Job 38; Amos 3) or singly. The effect can be as varied as the message in which the question is contained: anguish in Lam 5:21; sarcasm in Job 8:12 and Zeph 2:15; instruction in Prov 31:10; amazement in Ps 8:5. A rhetorical question is a good way to draw the listener into the argument, and it is effectively employed by the prophets, as in Isa 5:4 and Jer 5:7, 9.

MOTIFS AND THEMES

A number of motifs or themes recur throughout or are specific to certain types of biblical poetry. These devices, no less than parallelism and repetition, are part of the forms of poetic expression. The recognition of motifs and themes allows the reader to understand them as overarching cultural references or metaphors and to compare their use in different contexts. They may be taken from the natural world, from human relationships, or from historical or mythical references.

Some themes are well-known, but even these have rarely been studied systematically. Among these are the prophetic use of familial relationships—i.e., husband-wife, father-child—to represent the relationship between God and Israel. Familial imagery is found throughout prophetic writing and reaches its height in the book of Hosea. Brief examples are:

> I accounted to your favor
> The devotion of your youth,
> Your love as a bride. (Jer 2:2)

> For I am ever a father to Israel,
> Ephraim is my firstborn. (Jer 31:9)

Another pervasive theme is creation, which may be used to demonstrate God's infinite power over the enemy (Isaiah 40); God's benevolence to the natural world (Psalm 104); the awe and mystery of God's deeds (Job 38); the appreciation of the place of humans in the cosmos (Psalm 8); or the venerability of wisdom (Proverbs 8). Each iteration of the creation theme is different—in the wording used, in the items enumerated, in the aspects omitted or emphasized—so that the effect in each instance is tailored to the specific tone and message of the poem in which it is located.[15]

Other common motifs include God as a shepherd (Ps 23:1; Isa 40:11) and water as a metaphor for the life-sustaining nature of God (Ps 1:3; Jer 2:13). Less commonly recognized as a motif, but used frequently in the psalms, is the enemy or foe. This may be taken literally, but it is just as likely that it is intended to be an image for a more generalized type of danger or distress, physical or psychological.

> O LORD, how many are my foes!
> Many are rising against me.   (Ps 3:1 NRSV)

> O LORD my God, I take refuge in you;
> save and deliver me from all who pursue me.
> (Ps 7:1 NIV)

> Lest my enemy say, "I have overcome him,"
> My foes exult when I totter.   (Ps 13:5)

An individual poet or prophet may have his own motifs or refrains, as Jeremiah does with "to uproot and tear down, to destroy and overthrow, to build and to plant" (Jer 1:10 NIV; 18:7-9 and passim) and Ezekiel does with "O, human being" (12:2, 9 and passim).

READING A POEM

Most scholarly analysis of biblical poetry has concentrated on its measurable features, such as formal structuring devices, repetition, parallelism, meter, and the like. Commentaries generally offer line-by-line interpretations focusing on difficult words and constructions or unusual references. Occasionally provided by the exegete, but often left to the reader, has been the actual reading of the poem—the making of sense and beauty from its sounds, words, and structures, the perception that it is a unified entity with a distinctive message. This, after all, is the raison d'etre for all the analysis, but because it requires more art than science, there has been some reluctance to engage in it. But there are ways to approach the reading of poetry and some guidelines to direct the reading process. One might look for the movement within the poem, the repeated words or phrases, unexpected expressions or images, and the general tone and the effect that it produces. It is also useful to compare similar passages, with an eye to their differences. (Meir Weiss does this with great skill and insight.) An introductory article does not permit a full-blown discussion of these points, but a few examples may be offered.

Movement in Psalm 13. The psalm begins at the depths of despair: "How long, O LORD? Will you forget me forever?" (v. 1 NRSV). It slowly moves toward the possibility of hope: "Look at me, answer me, O Lord, my God" (v. 3). Then it reaches its climax in hope and exultation: "But I trust in your faithfulness . . . I will sing to the Lord for he has been good to me." The reader of this psalm, if identifying with the speaker, traverses the same emotional path from despair to hope.

Repetition in Job 38. Job 38 contains numerous rhetorical questions that involve first- and second-person pronouns: "Where were you when I laid the earth's foundation?" (v. 4 NIV); "Do you know who fixed its dimensions?" (v. 5); "Who closed the sea behind doors . . . when I clothed it in clouds?" (vv. 8-9); "Have you ever commanded the day to break?" (v. 12); "Have you penetrated the vaults of snow . . . which I have put aside for a time of adversity?" (v. 22). The effect of these pronouns is to create an opposition between the "you" and the "I"—Job and God—and the answers to the rhetorical questions prove that Job lacks even a fraction of God's knowledge and power. The combined effect is to show that Job is no match for God.

FOR FURTHER READING

The bibliography on biblical poetry is extensive, and much of it is extremely technical. It includes monographs and articles on specific features of poetry as well as explanations of poetic verses and sections in the Hebrew Bible. I have listed here only the most broad-based studies. References to more narrowly focused studies were made in the body of the discussion when appropriate. For additional bibliography, see Berlin, *The Dynamics of Biblical Parallelism*; O'Connor, *Hebrew Verse Structure*; and Watson, *Classical Hebrew Poetry* (all cited below).

Alonso Schökel, L. *A Manual of Hebrew Poetics.* Rome: Pontificio Istituto Biblico, 1988.

Alter, R. *The Art of Biblical Poetry.* New York: Basic Books, 1985.

Berlin, A. *Biblical Poetry Through Medieval Jewish Eyes.* Bloomington: Indiana University Press, 1991.

———. *The Dynamics of Biblical Parallelism.* Bloomington: Indiana University Press, 1985.

———. "Parallelism." *Anchor Bible Dictionary.* New York: Doubleday, 1992. 5:155-62.

Fisch, H. *Poetry with a Purpose.* Bloomington: Indiana University Press, 1988.

Freedman, D. N. "Pottery." In *Poetry and Prophecy: Collected Essays on Hebrew Poetry.* Winona Lake, Ind.: Eisenbrauns, 1980.

Fokkelman, J. P. *Reading Biblical Poetry: An Introductory Guide.* Translated by Ieke Smit. Tools for Biblical Study 1. Louisville: Westminster/John Knox Press, 2001.

Garr, W. "The Qinah: A Study of Poetic Meter, Syntax and Style," *ZAW* 95 (1983) 54-75.

Grossberg, D. *Centripetal and Centrifugal Structures in Biblical Poetry.* Atlanta: Scholars Press, 1989.

Hrushovski, B. "Prosody, Hebrew." In *EncJud.* 13:1195-1203.

Kugel, J. *The Idea of Biblical Poetry: Parallelism and Its History.* New Haven: Yale University Press, 1981.

Kuntz, J. K. "Recent Perspectives on Biblical Poetry," *RelSRev* 19, 4 (1993) 321-27.

O'Connor, M. *Hebrew Verse Structure.* Winona Lake, Ind.: Eisenbrauns, 1980.

Petersen, D., and K. Richards. *Interpreting Hebrew Poetry.* Minneapolis: Fortress, 1992.

Watson, W. G. E. *Classical Hebrew Poetry.* Sheffield: JSOT, 1986.

Weiss, M. *The Bible from Within.* Jerusalem: Magnes, 1984.

ENDNOTES

1. M. O'Connor, *Hebrew Verse Structure* (Winona Lake, Ind.: Eisenbrauns, 1980).

2. Unless otherwise specified, translations of the biblical text are the author's.

3. Robert Alter, *The Art of Biblical Poetry* (New York: Basic Books, 1985) 151.

4. For biblical terms that may possibly indicate different genres see above, "Internal Evidence for the Definition of Poetry."

5. Hermann Gunkel, *Einleitung in die Psalmen. Die Gattingen der religiösen Lyrik Israels* (Göttingen, 1933).

6. See F. I. Andersen and A. D. Forbes, " 'Prose Particle' Counts of the Hebrew Bible," in *The Word of the Lord Shall Go Forth*, ed. C. Meyers and M. O'Connor (Winona Lake: Eisenbrauns, 1983) 165-83.

7. Robert Lowth, *De sacra poesi Hebraeorum* (*Lectures on the Sacred Poetry of the Hebrews*), 1753; *Isaiah: A New Translation with a Preliminary Dissertation and Notes Critical, Philological, and Explanatory*, 1778.

8. Lowth, *Isaiah*, 10-11.

9. Roman Jakobson, "Grammatical Parallelism and Its Russian Facet," *Language* 42 (1966) 423.

10. "Note on the Systems of Hebrew Versification," in *The Penguin Book of Hebrew Verse*, ed. T. Carmi (New York: Penguin, 1981) 58.

11. See also Grossberg's analysis of this poem in Daniel Grossberg, *Centripetal and Centrifugal Structures in Biblical Poetry* (Atlanta: Scholars Press, 1989).

12. One of the few volumes devoted to this topic, G. B. Caird, *The Language and Imagery of the Bible* (London: 1980), is not helpful except as a catalogue of common images. The interpretations of Harold Fisch and Meir Weiss on specific passages are much more successful in explaining the workings of metaphor. See Harold Fisch, *Poetry with a Purpose* (Bloomington: Indiana University Press, 1988); Meir Weiss, *The Bible from Within* (Jerusalem: Magnes, 1984).

13. But the NRSV may have gone astray here. The word occurs in Job 39:21 in connection with strength or eagerness. It may well be that the image in Psalm 19 is not one of joy, but of virility. See my article "On Reading Biblical Poetry: The Role of Metaphor" in J. A. Emerton, ed. *Congress Volume: Cambridge 1995*, VT Sup 66 (Leiden: Brill, 1997) 25-36

14. The standard reference is W. Bühlmann and K. Scherer, *Stilfiguren der Bibel* (Fribourg: 1973), but compare, for example, the list of "Figures of Speech" in L. Alonso Schökel, *A Manual of Hebrew Poetics* (Rome: Pontificio Istituto Biblico, 1988), and the list of "Poetic Devices" in W. G. E. Watson, *Classical Hebrew Poetry* (Sheffield: JSOT, 1986).

15. See A. Berlin, "Motif and Creativity in Biblical Poetry," *Prooftexts* 3 (1983) 231-41.

THE BOOK OF JOB

CAROL A. NEWSOM

"There was once a man in the land of Uz whose name was Job." With these words, the Bible introduces one of its most memorable characters. In the popular imagination Job is an icon, emblematic of the sufferer who endures the unendurable without complaint. Yet what many generations have tended to remember about Job is only one aspect of his story. The "patience of Job" has become a cliché that obscures the much more complex figure who appears in the biblical book. Although the book of Job begins with just such a depiction of Job the pious, patiently enduring calamity, that initial image serves as a foil for the contrasting representation of Job that follows: Job the rebel, who debunks the piety of his friends and boldly accuses God of injustice. In contrast to the majority of Jewish and Christian interpreters over the centuries, who have often seemed somewhat embarrassed by Job's unrestrained blasphemies, many twentieth-century readers, reeling from a century of unparalleled horror, have been drawn to Job's anger as a voice of moral outrage against a God who could permit such atrocities. The attempt to claim Job as the patron saint of religious rebellion, however, also encounters embarrassment, for at the end of the book, after God's speech from the whirlwind, Job withdraws his words against God. Neither the character nor the book of Job yields to an easy appropriation. To the reader who is willing to forgo simplistic answers, however, the book offers a challenging exploration of religious issues of fundamental importance: the motivation for piety, the meaning of suffering, the nature of God, the place of justice in the world, and the relationship of order and chaos in God's design of creation.

READING THE BOOK OF JOB: ISSUES OF STRUCTURE AND UNITY

Job is a challenging book to read, not only because of the theological issues it treats but also because of the form in which it is written. It begins with a simple prose story (1:1–2:13) describing Job's piety, the conversation between God and the *satan*, which leads to a decision to test Job, and the disasters that befall Job as the test of his piety. Abruptly, the style of the book changes in chap. 3, as Job and the friends who have gathered to comfort him begin to debate the meaning of what has befallen him and the proper posture Job should assume toward God. In contrast to the simple prose of the first two chapters, this dialogue is composed in elegant, sophisticated poetry, full of rare words and striking images. The climax of this section is the long speech of God from the whirlwind and Job's brief reply (38:1–42:6). At that point, just as abruptly, the style again shifts back to simple prose for the conclusion, as Job's well-being is restored and the remainder of his long life is briefly described (42:7-17). The changes between the beginning, middle, and end of the book are not merely stylistic, but also correspond to changes in the representation of characters and in the nature of the religious issues under consideration.

Although the relationship between the prose and the poetic sections poses the most intriguing questions about how one is to read the book of Job, the form of the central poetic dialogue also presents issues that affect one's understanding of the book. The dialogue takes shape initially as an exchange between Job and the three friends who have come to comfort him. Following Job's initial speech (chap. 3), this exchange exhibits a regular and symmetrical pattern throughout two cycles, but appears to break down in the third (see "Dialogue Between Job and the Three Friends," below). In this third cycle, Bildad's speech is only six verses long (25:1-6), and Zophar has no speech at all. Even more perplexing, what Job says in parts of chaps. 24, 26, and 27 seems to contradict his own previous words and to assert views like those of the friends.

Dialogue Between Job and the Three Friends							
		Eliphaz	Job	Bildad	Job	Zophar	Job
First cycle:	chaps.	4-5	6-7	8	9-10	11	12-14
Second cycle:	chaps.	15	16-17	18	19	20	21
Third cycle:	chaps.	22	23-24	25	26	—	27

Between the end of the third cycle and Job's long speech in chaps. 29–31 comes a poem on the elusiveness of wisdom (chap. 28). No heading introduces the chapter, yet its style and content are so different from the surrounding speeches that it is difficult to imagine its being spoken by any of the characters. Job's long closing speech in chaps. 29–31 is no longer addressed to the friends as part of the dialogue but contains a challenge to God (31:35-37). Yet instead of God's reply, the following chapters introduce a new character, Elihu, whose speech is uninterrupted for six chapters (chaps. 32–37). Only then does the divine speech occur, bringing an end to the poetic section of the book.

In scholarly discussions of the past century, these various elements have usually been interpreted as evidence that the book of Job grew by stages, the various parts attributable to different authors working at different times. Although there are many different versions of this hypothesis,[1] it usually includes at least the following claims.

Stage 1. The oldest form of the book would have been the prose tale, an ancient story, originally told orally, about Job the pious. This stage is represented by chaps. 1–2 and 42:7-17. The middle part of this form of the story is no longer extant, but would have included some sort of brief dialogue between Job and his friends in which they spoke disparagingly of God, while Job steadfastly refused to curse God.

Stage 2. An Israelite author who considered the old story inadequate and in need of critique decided to use it as the framework for a much more ambitious, sophisticated retelling of the story in which the figure of Job does not remain the patiently enduring character of the traditional tale, but challenges God's treatment of him. According to this hypothesis, the author substituted a new poetic dialogue between Job and his friends (3:1–31:37) in place of the discussion in which they engaged in the older story and added a long

speech by God as the climax (38:1–42:6). The author used the conclusion of the old story (42:7-17) as the conclusion of his thoroughly transformed new version of the book. The poem on wisdom in chap. 28 may be a composition by this author, who used it as a transition between Job's dialogue with his friends and Job's dialogue with God, or it may be an addition by a later hand.

Stage 3. Another author, writing sometime later, considered the new version of the book of Job unsatisfactory, because he perceived that Job had gotten the better of his three friends in their argument, and because he did not find the divine speeches to be an entirely adequate answer to Job. Consequently, he created a new character, Elihu, and inserted his long speech into the book in order to provide what seemed to him a decisive refutation of Job's arguments.

Stage 4. Sometime during the transmission of the book, copyists who were shocked by Job's blasphemous words attempted to soften their impact by rearranging the third cycle of speeches, putting some of Bildad's and Zophar's speeches into Job's mouth.

Perhaps the least persuasive part of the hypothesis is the supposed rearrangement of the third cycle of speeches. Although some disruption may have occurred, the final result suggests incoherence more than a depiction of Job in the process of rethinking his views. Much more persuasive is the claim that the Elihu speeches are a secondary intrusion. The removal of his speeches would create no disruption in the rest of the book, for Elihu is not mentioned outside of chaps. 32–37, either in the frame story or in the dialogues. The absence of Elihu from the conclusion of the story is difficult to explain if he were an original part of the composition of either the prose frame story or the poetic dialogue. Also pointing to the secondary nature of the Elihu material is the fact that Elihu's speeches stand apart as a long monologue, unlike the speeches of Job's three friends, which are interspersed more or less regularly with Job's replies in the body of the dialogue. Elihu's discourse is also written differently, as he is the only character who explicitly cites other characters' words, a feature that suggests that the author of this section had the book of Job before him as he composed Elihu's speech. Since Elihu is the only character who bears a Hebrew name, it is possible, although quite speculative, that Elihu is actually the name of the writer who added these chapters—i.e., that he is a disgruntled reader who quite literally wrote himself into the book.

The hypothesis of growth by stages also provides a plausible account of the relationship between the prose tale and the poetic dialogue, and it offers an explanation for the incongruity that exists between the end of the poetic section and the final prose conclusion. In 42:7-9, God rebukes the friends for not having spoken correctly about God, as Job has done. This comment is difficult to reconcile with the book as we know it, but it seems to point back to a different form of the story, the "missing middle" that was displaced to make room for the poetic dialogues. No direct evidence for the independent existence of the old prose tale exists, but there is indirect testimony. Bishop Theodore of Mopsuestia (c. 350–428 CE) was familiar with an oral version of the story of the pious Job that did not contain the angry speeches of the canonical book and that was popular among both Jews and others. Indeed, Bishop Theodore considered the oral story to be the true story of Job, considering the biblical version as a literary production composed to show off the learning and poetic skill of its author.[2]

Critics who argue that the book of Job developed in this way rarely address the question of how one is supposed to read the book as it now exists. Indeed, one of the unfortunate consequences of this hypothesis about the composition of Job is that it has often led to interpretations of the book that fail to take its final or canonical form seriously. In recent years there has been a reaction against this tendency to treat the book as an assortment of parts rather than a single whole. Increasingly, even commentators who consider that the book may well have undergone some form of growth and redaction have nevertheless argued that one should read the book "as if" it were the product of a single author.[3] Occasionally, the claim

is made that the book possesses a literary, thematic, and even stylistic unity best accounted for as the work of a single author.[4] Supporting the argument in favor of a single author is the contention that the prose tale in chapters 1–2 and 42 cannot be understood as more or less a transcription of an oral folktale but is a highly sophisticated piece of narrative art written in a deliberately "pseudo-naive" style.[5] To make that claim is not to reject the evidence for the existence of oral tales and traditions about Job, but only to recognize that the form of the story as we have it in Job 1–2; 42 is the product of a skilled author who has written an artistic imitation of such a popular story as the framework for his retelling of the story of Job.

Apart from the Elihu speeches, which seem quite clearly to be a later addition to the book, I confess to being an agnostic on the question of whether the book of Job grew by stages or was written by a single author, although I incline to the latter view. Interpretively, the important issue is not how the book attained its present form but how the shape of the book contributes to its meaning. In this regard, the presence of Elihu, the incoherence of the third cycle, and the role of the poem on wisdom raise interesting but relatively minor interpretive issues. The vital question is how one understands the significance of the abrupt juxtaposition of the two very different ways of telling the story of Job one finds in the prose and poetic parts of the book. The position taken in this commentary is that the incongruities produced by the transition to the prose conclusion in 42:7-9 are intentionally designed to call attention to these differences and to frustrate attempts to read the book as a single coherent narrative.[6] Whether this structure was produced by an editor who chose to let the discrepancies stand when the prose tale was adopted as a framing device, or whether it was produced by a single author who composed both prose and poetry, cleverly planning the incongruities, the effect is of a book "at odds with itself."[7]

Far from being an embarrassment, recognition that the book is at odds with itself is key to understanding its meaning and purpose. Dialogue is at the heart of the book of Job. The clash of divergent perspectives is represented in the three cycles of disputation between Job and his friends (chaps. 3–27). Job's final speech of self-justification (chaps. 29–31) stands over against God's answer from the whirlwind (chaps. 38–41) in dialogical relationship. By means of the cleverness of editor or author, the book as a whole is also structured as a dialogue of two very different prose and poetic voices, two very different ways of telling the same story that cannot be harmonized into a single perspective.

Representing two different ways of telling the same story within a single composition presents an artistic challenge. One could, of course, tell one version of the story in its entirety and then tell the other. The dialogic relationship is enhanced, however, by having one way of telling the story interrupt the other, as happens in the book of Job. This structure of two intersecting ways of telling the story may be visualized as follows:

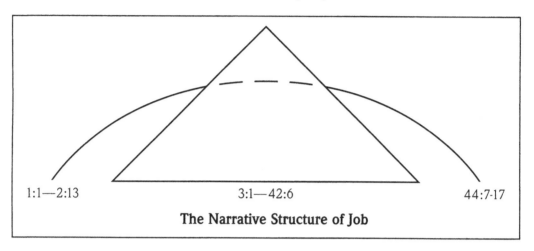

1:1—2:13   3:1—42:6   44:7-17

The Narrative Structure of Job

This design works artistically because the frame story, whether considered as a naive popular tale or a "pseudo-naive" tale, invokes certain narrative conventions belonging to traditional storytelling that give such stories a high degree of predictability. As surely as a story that begins "Once upon a time . . . " must end with " . . . and they all lived happily ever after," readers know almost immediately what kind of story is being told in Job 1–2, how it will develop, and how it must end. One can plot the trajectory of the story line on the basis of these conventions. After God and the narrator have vouched for Job's character against the detractions of the *satan*, there can be no doubt about how Job will conduct himself. Since significant features often cluster in sequences of three in traditional storytelling, one expects three trials of Job's piety, before the obligatory happy ending. Thus, when the author of Job interrupts the frame story with the very different material in 3:1–42:6, a dialogical relationship is set up between what one knows is "supposed" to happen in this sort of a tale and what is actually happening in the story.

The tension set up by this structure is not only an aesthetic one. Social, moral, and religious values and assumptions are always embedded in particular modes of telling a story. By disrupting the prose tale, the poetic section of Job also challenges its assumptions about the nature of piety, the grounds of the relationship between humans and God, the proper stance toward suffering, etc.

If the book of Job had ended with a smooth transition from the poetic section to the concluding prose, then perhaps a synthesis of perspectives might have been fashioned. In the book as we have it, however, the transition to the prose tale is both abrupt and incongruous. The prose conclusion takes no account of the poetic dialogue but gestures back to the missing middle of the traditional tale, to what was "supposed" to happen according to its conventions. Moreover, the presence of the prose conclusion following the dialogue and divine speeches actually creates both dissonance and irony, which threaten to unravel the sense of closure created by God's speech and Job's reply at the end of the poetic section. The book of Job thus presents the reader with unresolved perspectives. The theological implications of this structure are considered below.

DATE AND PROVENANCE

When, by whom, and for whom a book is written are important in understanding its meaning and significance. As the preceding discussion already suggests, those are difficult questions to answer with respect to Job, since different parts of the book may have been composed at different times for different audiences. Estimates for the date of the book as a whole (excepting the Elihu speeches), have ranged from the tenth century to the second century BCE, with most scholars opting for dates between the seventh and fifth centuries BCE.[8] Part of the difficulty in establishing a date for the book is that it contains no references to historical events or persons. Attempts to date the book according to its themes or place within the history of the religion of Israel are precarious, since it is difficult to demonstrate that the issues and religious values of the book of Job would be at home in only one era. More persuasive is the argument that certain motifs, such as the representation of the *satan* in chaps. 1–2, have their closest parallels in literature from the early post-exilic period (cf. 1 Chr 21:1; Zech 3:1-2).

Linguistic evidence has also been used to date the book; yet even here one encounters ambiguity. The poetic dialogues contain linguistic forms that one would expect to find in archaic Hebrew, from approximately the tenth century BCE.[9] Since these speeches appear to be written in a deliberately archaizing style and lack other poetic features one associates with very ancient Hebrew poetry, the argument for such an early date has not been generally accepted. The prose tale also contains narrative and stylistic details that suggest great antiquity.[10] Yet here, too, one must distinguish between what is genuinely archaic from an artistic imitation of archaic style. The most careful linguistic study has argued that the prose tale in its present form is no older than the sixth century BCE.[11] If that is the case, the book of Job as a whole is best taken as a composition of the early post-exilic period (sixth–fifth centuries BCE), whether one considers the book to have been composed by a single author, writing in two different styles, or by an author who appropriated an existing prose tale as the framework for a new composition.[12]

The Elihu speeches are difficult to date for many of the same reasons. The latest date for their composition is determined by their presence in the Aramaic translation of Job found in the Dead Sea Scrolls. Although that manuscript dates from the first century CE, the translation may have taken place as early as the second century BCE.[13] The only other basis upon which to date the Elihu speeches is the similarity of their ideas and expressions to other literature. While such evidence is not decisive, recent scholarship on the Elihu speeches has tended to place them in the third century BCE.[14]

Arguably more important than date is the question of by whom and for whom the book was written. Since no independent evidence exists, this question has to be posed in terms of the assumptions and values embodied in the book. Although much remains elusive, there are certain clues to its intellectual context and social class perspectives.

The book of Job is an immensely learned and cosmopolitan work. One recognizes this quality in the texture of the language itself, which is full of rare vocabulary and archaic verbal forms. The complex and beautiful poetry contains numerous mythological allusions, some of which appear to be based on Egyptian and Mesopotamian traditions. Furthermore, the poetic dialogue presents Job in terms of a sophisticated reworking of the Mesopotamian tradition of "the righteous sufferer" (see "The Book of Job and Ancient Near Eastern Tradition"). This same command of cultural and literary forms is evident in the author's treatment of genres and stylistic features drawn from Israelite tradition. The speeches of Job and his friends are largely shaped as disputations and make use of a rich variety of rhetorical devices one finds in wisdom, prophetic, and legal argumentation (e.g., rhetorical questions, wisdom sayings, appeals to ancient tradition). The author also displays a similar command of the genres of Israelite piety, in particular the hymn, the psalm of praise, and the complaint psalm. Not only are these forms cited in their traditional modes, but in the speeches of Job they are also rendered as exquisite parodies. Legal vocabulary, categories, and practices are similarly drawn upon for the development of a forensic metaphor through which to explore Job's relationship with God. The overall impression is of an author who has a remarkable command of the religious literature and traditions of Israel and its neighbors.

Although the author of Job orchestrates motifs, genres, and themes from a variety of different discourses in a way that is not characteristic of the books of Proverbs and Ecclesiastes, one should identify the book of Job primarily with the wisdom tradition. The very subject matter of the book suggests as much. Wisdom literature is centrally concerned with the nature of the proper moral and religious conduct of an individual and with the relation of such conduct to personal and communal well-being. Moreover, wisdom tends to pursue such questions in ways that do not make use of distinctively national religious traditions so much as they employ the conventions, styles, and language of an international discourse of wisdom. This orientation characterizes the book of Job, in which traditions about the non-Israelite Job are used to develop a critical reflection on the assumption that good conduct and well-being are related. More specifically, the theme of "fearing God," which is programmatic for the book of Proverbs (Prov 1:7; 9:10), also occurs in significant places in the framing of the book of Job, not only in the prose tale but also in the poem that concludes the dialogue between Job and his friends (1:1, 8; 2:3; 28:28). The friends' speeches, too, contain the sort of advice and admonition that has been described as "sapiential counseling."[15] The theme of wisdom is most explicit in the poem in chap. 28, in the refrain, "'But where shall wisdom be found?'" (28:12, 20 NRSV). The prominence of creation motifs, both in chap. 28 and especially in the divine speeches, is also characteristic of wisdom, which often sets the question of the moral order of the world in terms of the structures of creation (e.g., Proverbs 3; 8; Ecclesiastes 1; Sirach 24). Finally, the wisdom tradition as a whole is typified both by conventional voices, which one largely hears in Proverbs, and skeptical, subversive voices, such as Ecclesiastes. In Job these two voices are joined in dialogue, not only in the dialogue between Job and his friends but also in the very form of the book, as discussed above. Thus the book of Job, although unique in many respects, is best understood as a part of the intellectual and cultural world of wisdom.

There is little consensus about the social identity of Israel's sages.[16] Although the sources of wisdom thought may lie in the social structures of families and tribes, wisdom *books* like Job are likely to emerge from a different institutional setting. Analogies with Egyptian wisdom literature suggest that such works were the product of a scribal class, the members of which served as administrators in the court or temple. Alternatively, it has been suggested that schools for the education of upper-class youths provided the social context for the composition of wisdom books. But the existence of such institutions is speculative. Although it is clear that Job is the product of an intellectual milieu, the exact nature of the social context in which it was produced and read cannot be known.

The issue of social class perspectives in the book of Job is complicated by the fictional setting of the book. Simply because the characters are depicted as wealthy aristocrats, one cannot necessarily assume that the author and audience are of that class. The more appropriate question to ask is what ethos is reflected in the book; when the issue is framed in those terms it is easy to agree that, whatever the actual social class of the author, the book addresses issues through the perspective of aristocratic sensibilities and values. In particular, Job's final speech (chaps. 29–31) provides an extended statement of the moral values of an aristocratic and patriarchal culture.[17] Attempts have been made to locate the social context of Job more specifically within the socioeconomic changes of the Persian period, when disruptions in traditional economic and social relations threatened to displace many old aristocratic families and brought increased suffering to the very poor, while the *nouveau riche*, who lacked traditional aristocratic religious and social values, exploited the new possibilities for their own benefit (cf. Nehemiah 5).[18] Although it is plausible to consider the author of the Joban dialogues as representing the perspectives of the old aristocratic culture in the context of the economic upheavals of the Persian period, it would be difficult to claim that the social conflicts presupposed by Job and his friends were unique to that period.

THE BOOK OF JOB AND ANCIENT NEAR EASTERN TRADITION

Scholars agree that neither the character Job nor the story about his misfortunes originated in Israel. The name "Job" is not a typically Israelite name, although forms of the name are attested in Syria-Palestine in the second millennium BCE.[19] Moreover, the story itself associates Job with the land of Uz, a place that is to be located either in Edomite or Aramean territory. Job's three friends—Eliphaz the Temanite, Bildad the Shuhite, and Zophar the Naamathite—also come from non-Israelite locales. The story as we have it in the Bible has been adapted for an Israelite religious context, however, so that Yahweh is assumed to be the God whom Job serves.

Although no trace of a pre-Israelite Job story exists in sources yet discovered from the ancient Near East, there is one biblical text that associates Job with two other non-Israelite characters whose stories had been incorporated into Israelite tradition. The prophet Ezekiel refers to Job in the context of an oracle from God concerning judgment against Jerusalem:

> "Mortal, when a land sins against me by acting faithlessly, and I stretch out my hand against it, and break its staff of bread and send famine upon it, and cut off from it human beings and animals, even if Noah, Daniel, and Job, these three, were in it, they would save only their own lives by their righteousness, says the Lord [Yahweh] . . . as I live, says the Lord [Yahweh], they would save neither son nor daughter; they would save only their own lives by their righteousness." (14:13, 20 NRSV)

Noah, the hero of the flood story, is a non-Israelite (or pre-Israelite) character whose story is told in Genesis 6–9. Although the name "Noah" is known only from biblical tradition, the character and his story originate in Mesopotamia, where he is variously known as Utnapishtim and Atrahasis.[20] Dan'el is not the Judean exile, hero of the book of Daniel, but a legendary Canaanite king. Although he is otherwise mentioned in the Bible only in Ezek 28:3, his story is told in the Ugaritic epic of Aqhat, the text of which was found in the second millennium BCE tablets excavated at Ras Shamra.[21]

Ezekiel's brief allusion takes for granted that his audience knows the stories of all these ancient paragons of righteousness. Yet it is difficult to say in detail exactly what stories about these figures Ezekiel and his audience know, whether they are the same ones preserved in the written accounts or from different oral traditions. The reference in Ezek 14:20 appears to suggest that all three some-how save their children from danger by means of their own righteousness. In Genesis 6–9, Noah's righteousness saves not only his own life but also those of his children when he takes them aboard the ark. Dan'el's story from the Ugaritic tablets is unfortunately broken off at a critical place, but it does involve the death of his son at the hand of the goddess Anat, the recovery of his body, and Dan'el's seven years of mourning for Aqhat. Whether the story told of Aqhat's restoration to life because of Dan'el's righteousness, as Ezekiel's allusion might suggest, is not known. With respect to Job, Ezekiel's allusion may refer to Job's attempting to protect his children by sacrificing on their behalf, in case "my children have sinned, and cursed God in their hearts" (Job 1:5 NRSV). In the canonical story of Job, the children are eventually killed as a part of the test of Job's righteousness. Ezekiel, however, may have known versions of the stories different from the ones preserved in written sources. Like Noah and Dan'el, Job appears to have been an ancient non-Israelite or pre-Israelite whose story, originally developed in other parts of the ancient Near East, had been incorporated into Israelite religious culture by the sixth century BCE.

In contrast to the prose tale, for which there are only tantalizing hints but no clear ancient Near Eastern parallels, the poetic dialogue in the book of Job has been compared to a variety of ancient Near Eastern texts from Egypt, Mesopotamia, and Ugarit.[22] For the most part, however, the similarities are much too general to be significant and do little to illumine the specific literary tradition to which the poetic dialogue of Job belongs. Only two categories of texts warrant discussion. The first is the tradition of Mesopotamian liturgical texts from the second millennium BCE in which a sufferer praises his god for deliverance from suffering. Among these are the Sumerian composition known as "Man and His God: A Sumerian Variation on the 'Job' Motif"[23] and the Babylonian text "I Will Praise the Lord of Wisdom," often called the "Babylonian Job."[24] Although these texts offer some parallels to the description of suffering one finds in Job, their importance for understanding the literary tradition to which Job belongs has been overrated. They are much closer in form and function to biblical psalms of thanksgiving than to the book of Job.[25] At most they provide background for the general ancient Near Eastern conventions for describing physical suffering and social ostracism.[26]

Much more significant is the striking similarity of form and content between Job and the text known as the Babylonian Theodicy. In contrast to the liturgical poems discussed above, the Babylonian Theodicy is a wisdom text.[27] Written c. 1000 BCE, the text was apparently quite popular even in the Hellenistic period, when a commentary on it was written by a Mesopotamian scribe from Sippar.[28] The Babylonian Theodicy consists of a dialogue between a sufferer and his friend and is composed as an acrostic poem of twenty-seven stanzas of eleven lines each, with a strict alternation of stanzas between the two characters. This formal design is quite similar to the dialogue in Job, although in Job the role of the friend is divided among three characters: Eliphaz, Bildad, and Zophar. Equally striking is the similarity in the way the individual speeches begin. In the Babylonian Theodicy, most of the stanzas begin with a compliment to the general intelligence of the other party. When the friend speaks, this general compliment is followed by a criticism that in this particular case the sufferer has said something irrational, erroneous, or blasphemous. For example:

> "Respected friend, what you say is gloomy.
> You let your mind dwell on evil, my dear fellow.
> You make your fine discretion like an imbecile's"
> (ll. 12-14)
> "My reliable fellow, holder of knowledge, your
> thoughts are perverse.
> You have forsaken right and blaspheme against
> your god's designs." (ll. 78-79)[29]

Similarly, when the sufferer speaks, his opening compliment is followed by a request that his friend truly listen to what he has to say:

> "My friend, your mind is a river whose spring
> never fails,
> The accumulated mass of the sea, which knows
> no decrease.
> I will ask you a question; listen to what I say.
> Pay attention for a moment; hear my words"
> (ll. 23-26).

In Job many of the speeches begin with a similar characterization of the previous speaker's words and wisdom, although the tone is generally sarcastic rather than the polite-but-frank tone that typifies the Babylonian Theodicy. As Job says:

> "Doubtless you are the people,
> and wisdom will die with you!
> But I have a mind as well as you;
> I am not inferior to you.
> Who does not know all these things?"
> (12:2-3 NIV)

Similarly, Eliphaz replies:

> "Would a wise man answer with empty notions
> or fill his belly with the hot east wind?
> . . . . .
> But you even undermine piety
> and hinder devotion to God." (15:2, 4 NIV)

Like the sufferer of the Babylonian Theodicy, Job asks that his words be heard, yet Job spoke without the confidence that his friends are capable of true understanding: "'Listen carefully to my words,/and let this be your consolation./Bear with me, and I will speak;/then after I have spoken, mock on'" (21:2-3 NRSV).

The content of the "Babylonian Theodicy" and of the Joban dialogues contains close parallels. In each of his speeches, the Babylonian sufferer complains about either personal misfortune or his perception that the world itself is morally disordered, with the unworthy and the criminal prospering while the deserving and the pious languish in misery.

> "My body is a wreck, emaciation darkens [me,]
> My success has vanished, my stability has gone.
> My strength is enfeebled, my prosperity has
> ended,
> Moaning and grief have blackened my features."

Compare Job:

> "My skin grows black and peels;
> my body burns with fever.
> My harp is tuned to mourning,
> and my flute to the sound of wailing."
> (30:30-31 NRSV)

The Babylonian sufferer complains that the impious flourish:

> "[...]the nouveau riche who has multiplied his
> wealth,
> Did he weigh out precious gold for the goddess
> Mami?" (ll. 52-53).
> "Those who neglect the god go the way of
> prosperity,
> While those who pray to the goddess are
> impoverished and dispossessed" (ll. 70-71).

Similarly, Job:

"Why do the wicked live on,
reach old age, and grow mighty in power?
. . . . .
They say to God, 'Leave us alone!
We do not desire to know your ways.'"
(21:7, 14 NRSV)

Like Job's friends, the friend in the Babylonian Theodicy argues that retribution will come eventually to the wicked, whereas the pious one who bears temporary distress patiently will have his prosperity returned to him:

"The godless cheat who has wealth,
A death-dealing weapon pursues him.
Unless you seek the will of the god, what luck
have you?
He that bears his god's yoke never lacks food,
though it be sparse.
Seek the kindly wind of the god,
What you have lost over a year you will make up
in a moment" (ll. 237-42).

Compare Eliphaz's words:

"Consider now: Who, being innocent, has ever
perished?
Where were the upright ever destroyed?
As I have observed, those who plow evil
and those who sow trouble reap it."
(4:7-8 NIV; cf. 5:17-26).

Similarly, just as the Babylonian friend argues that "the divine mind, like the centre of the heavens, is remote; Knowledge of it is difficult; the masses do not know it" (ll. 256-57), so also Zophar asks Job:

"Can you fathom the mysteries of God?
Can you probe the limits of the Almighty?
They are higher than the
heavens—what can you do?
They are deeper than the depths of
the grave—what can you know?
Their measure is longer than the earth
and wider than the sea." (11:7-8 NIV)

Despite the striking similarities between particular arguments, the dialogues end quite differently. In the Babylonian Theodicy, when the sufferer complains that people praise the wicked and abuse the honest person, his friend not only agrees with him but also attributes this sad state of affairs to the gods, who "gave perverse speech to the human race. With lies, and not truth, they endowed them for ever" (ll. 279-80). Apparently satisfied that he has been heard, the sufferer thanks his friend, repeats his claim that he has suffered even though he has behaved properly, and concludes with an appeal to the mercy of the gods:

"May the god who has thrown me off give help,
May the goddess who has [abandoned me] show
mercy,
For the shepherd Shamash guides the peoples like
a god" (295-97).

By contrast, there is no rapprochement between Job and his friends. Following Job's lengthy concluding defense of his conduct, he does not appeal for God's mercy but wishes for a legal confrontation with his divine adversary (31:35-37). The Babylonian Theodicy contains nothing like the speech from the whirlwind, which forms the climax of the book of Job.

Although it is possible that the author of Job knew and drew upon the Babylonian Theodicy itself, it is more likely that the relationship is indirect and that there was a larger tradition of wisdom dialogues about the problem of the righteous sufferer and the general issue of moral disorder in a world supposedly governed by divine justice.[30] If that is so, then the similarities between Job and the Babylonian Theodicy, coming from different times and different national and religious contexts, allow one at least to identify the contours of that genre: the formal structuring of the dialogue, the rhetorical acknowledgment by speakers of each other, the characteristic arguments for and against the just ordering of the world. The lack of a narrative framework, as in the Babylonian Theodicy, is probably also a characteristic of the genre. Even if one assumes that the dialogue in Job was written explicitly with the frame tale in mind, it is striking that, except for the names of the characters, the dialogue makes no reference whatsoever to the particulars of the frame story. The dialogue appears to have been left intentionally unintegrated. As compared to the Babylonian Theodicy, the Joban dialogue is a much more sophisticated literary work. Without other examples, however, one cannot say whether the more ambitious scope and daring tone of the Joban dialogues mark a radical departure from the tradition or build on examples more fully developed than the Babylonian Theodicy.

Having traced what can be known of the ancient Near Eastern background to the prose and poetic parts of the book of Job, it is possible to venture a suggestion about the composition of the biblical book. All suggestions are necessarily speculative. They amount to claims that the shape of the book and its component parts make the most sense if one assumes that it arose in such and such a fashion. They are in that sense suggestions about how one should read the book. With that caution in mind, I suggest that one read the book "as if" it came into existence in the following fashion. One might assume that an Israelite sage from the sixth or fifth century knew various oral traditions about the legendary Job and also knew the literary wisdom tradition of the dialogue of a righteous sufferer and his friend. Since Job was such an archetypal righteous sufferer, it is possible that the name "Job" had already been attached to versions of such dialogues. The religious perspectives of the two traditions, however, would have been sharply different, the tale of Job stressing a model of righteousness that takes the form of legendary endurance of extraordinary misfortune without protest, and the dialogue tradition casting Job in the role of skeptical protester against unwarranted personal misfortune and general moral disorder. How might one bring these traditions together so that they may both assert their claims and be challenged by the other's vision of reality? The solution devised by this clever Israelite sage was the artistic device of inter-cutting, beginning the book with a version of the traditional story, then sharply interrupting the telling of the tale with a version of the skeptical dialogue of the righteous sufferer, abruptly followed by the resumption of the traditional tale. Although it is possible that the speech from the whirlwind has antecedents in some other literary tradition, one might be inclined to think that the divine speech is the author's innovation, a reinterpretation of wisdom traditions about creation that serves to set the entire conversation about the experience of suffering in a quite different context than that envisioned either by the old tale or by the conventions of the dialogue of the righteous sufferer.

THEOLOGICAL ISSUES

However the book of Job achieved its present form, it presents a series of thought-provoking theological issues. The initial theological question of the book is framed in the prose tale by the *satan*, who asks about the motives of piety (1:9-11). Why does Job, and by extension any person, reverence God? Is it an implicit bargain for security and well-being, or is the relationship independent of circumstances? Traditional religion often talks about the blessings that come from piety and obedience to God, and the *satan*'s probing question asks whether such expectations subtly corrupt the relationship between human beings and God. The prose story, taken by itself, describes Job's piety as unshaken by extreme and inexplicable misfortune, and so affirms the possibility of wholly unconditional love of God. As important as such a question is, the way in which it is treated in the prose tale leaves a great deal unexplored. *Should* one serve God unconditionally and without question? What *is* the nature of the relationship between God and human beings? What is the character of God, and how does one have knowledge of that character? The dialogue and the divine speeches serve as a vehicle for considering these further questions, as well as other religious issues as they emerge from the experience of suffering.

Perhaps the most prominent issue in the dialogues is that of the proper conduct of a person in suffering. For the friends, suffering is an occasion for moral and religious self-examination and reflection. Although there is no single "meaning" for suffering, it is to be understood in some way as a communication from God. For the wicked, it is judgment (15:20-35); for the ethically unsteady, it is a warning (33:14-30); for the morally immature, it is a form of educational discipline (5:17-19); and for the righteous, it is simply something to be borne with the confidence that God will eventually restore well-being (4:4-7; 8:20-21). In every case the proper response is to turn to God in humility, trust, and prayer (5:8; 8:5; 11:13-19; 22:21-30). Implicit in the friends' view is the assumption that God is always right and that it is the human being who must make use of the experience to learn what God is trying to communicate. Although Job does not engage the friends' arguments explicitly, his own stance toward God implies a very different understanding of the divine-human relationship. Rather than turning inward in self-examination, Job demands an explanation from God (7:20; 10:2; 13:23; 23:5; 31:35). For Job, God has no right to cause suffering to come upon a person unless that person deserves punishment. The proper response where suffering appears to be undeserved is not humble prayer but confrontation of God. Thus Job rejects the notion of unconditional piety, at least insofar as it would mean submission to a God who acts without regard to what is just.

The differences between Job and the friends on the matter of proper conduct in suffering also bring into focus the issue of the character of God and God's governance of the world. In contrast to the conventional views of the friends, which take God's goodness and justice to be axiomatic (8:3; 34:12), Job often depicts God as a violator of justice (27:2) who acts out of obsessive and malicious curiosity (7:17-20; 10:8-14) or in a spirit of sadistic rage (16:9-14). The world over which God exercises supposed "moral" governance is characterized by anarchic destruction (12:14-25), the prosperity of the wicked (21:30-33), and the pervasive abuse of the poor (24:1-12). If Job is correct when he depicts God in these ways, then the very possibility of reverence for God is at an end, for God is a monster of cruelty. Job's speeches set up the theological issue in a more complex fashion, however, for Job's view of God's character is contradictory. He cannot give up the idea that, despite the evidence of his experience and his observations, God will ultimately be revealed as a God of justice (13:15-22; 23:3-7). The theological and emotional power of the book is due in large measure to the apparently insoluble nature of this contradictory experience. Job is not unique in raising the problem of a just God and the existence of injustice in the world (cf. Psalm 73). What is unusual about Job is the way in which he attempts to pursue and ultimately resolve this excruciating dilemma.

Some of the most intriguing theological issues in the book are never raised to the level of explicit debate between Job and his friends but can be teased out by attentive readers. One of these is the way claims to knowledge are authorized. Job and his friends not only hold different positions about the nature of God, the moral order of the world, and the meaning of what has befallen Job, but they also authorize their claims on very different grounds. The friends appeal to common sense, what "everybody" knows (4:7). Consequently, they assume that Job, too, will share their perceptions (5:27). Sometimes they argue deductively from what they consider to be universally agreed principles (34:10-12). At other times they cite anecdotal evidence (4:8; 5:3) or even the transcendent authority of private revelation (4:13-16). Most important of all, however, is their reliance on the authority of tradition. Not only do they appeal explicitly to ancestral tradition (8:8-10), but by filling their speeches with the forms of traditional religious language (e.g., sayings, didactic examples, doxologies), they also embody that authority. Job opposes this arsenal of common sense, rational argument, revelation, and tradition because he knows that what the friends claim is inconsistent with his own experience. Job often expresses the vivid immediacy of this experience and the claims to knowledge that it warrants in terms of the body's organs of perception (tongue, eyes, ears; 6:30; 13:1). Thus the book stages a conflict between different ways of grounding and authorizing knowledge.

Related to the conflict over the grounds for knowledge of truth is the book's exploration of the adequacy and limits of various kinds of religious language. Job's parodies of traditional psalmic and hymnic forms (7:17-19; 12:13-25) expose what appears to him to be their pervasive hypocrisy about the real nature of the divine-human relationship. Such forms of religious speech allow one to speak only of the goodness of God's transforming power, care for human beings, etc., but exclude from view the terrible experiences that give rise to the crisis of religious doubt about the nature of God. Traditional prayer also, which the friends keep urging upon him, is inadequate for the kind of conversation Job seeks to have with God, because it has no means of imposing accountability on God. Rejecting the conventional alternatives, Job's speeches gradually explore the possibilities of a new religious language based on a radically different underlying metaphor of the divine-human relationship. Job reimagines the relationship in legal categories, most concretely in terms of the possibility of a trial with God. This idea occurs first as parody (9:2-4) but eventually develops into a serious model for engaging God (23:3-7; 31:35-37). It serves Job's purposes well, for the model envisions a relationship of mutual accountability, undistorted by discrepancies of power, in which both parties acknowledge common standards of justice as binding. Such a way of talking about God and with God would have radical implications for the nature of religion. The book never fully develops these implications but leaves them as a provocative possibility.

Throughout the long dialogues between Job and his friends, theological issues and options are set up as alternatives between the traditional positions championed by the friends and the radical challenges posed by Job. The friends argue for the goodness of God, the moral order of the world, the purposiveness of suffering, and the importance of humble submission to God. Job questions the justice of God, describes the world as a moral chaos, depicts suffering in terms of victimization, and stakes his life on the possibility of legal confrontation with God. What goes largely unnoticed is the extent to which both positions depend on the same paradigm of understanding. They both take as unquestionable the assumption that justice, specifically retributive justice, should be the central principle of reality. They disagree only as to whether such justice is operative in the world or whether God should be called to account for failing to enforce such justice. The speeches of God from the whirlwind, however, challenge the paradigm that both Job and the friends have taken for granted. When God speaks of the "design" of the cosmos, which Job has obscured (38:2), the categories that underlie God's descriptions are not categories of justice/injustice but order/chaos.

The divine speeches do not explicitly engage the particular arguments Job had made but implicitly call into question their fundamental assumptions. As the juxtaposition of Job's final speech (chaps. 29–31) and the divine speeches (chaps. 38–41) shows, Job's theological categories had been derived from the social and moral assumptions that structured community life and social roles in his own experience. From these assumptions Job had extrapolated his expectations concerning God and the world. God's speeches, by beginning with the great structures of creation and speaking scarcely at all of the place of human beings in the cosmos, expose the limits of Job's anthropocentric categories. Similarly, Job's legal model for understanding divine-human relationships is also implicitly challenged. In Job's understanding, the fundamental categories are "right and wrong." No place exists in such a schema for

the chaotic. Yet in God's speeches, the play between fundamental order and the restricted but still powerful forces of the chaotic is crucial for understanding the nature of reality. Through images of the sea (38:8-11), the criminal (38:12-15), the anarchic wild animals (38:39–39:30), and finally the legendary beasts Behemoth and Leviathan (40:15–41:34[41:26]), God confronts Job with things that his legal categories cannot possibly comprehend. The evocative but elusive language of the divine speeches provides resources for the reconstruction of theological language of a very different sort than that employed by Job and his friends, but the divine speeches do not do that work themselves. Theological construction properly remains a human task.

The provocative challenge of the divine speeches, which incorporate an image of God and the world quite different from that embodied in either the prose tale or the dialogues, brings one back to the original theological issue of the book: Why does one reverence God? What had been a question about the nature of human piety in the prose tale was transformed in the dialogues into a question about the character of God. Job's reply suggests that the divine speeches have provided him with a transformed vision of God and thus a very different basis for reverence (42:5); but his brief and enigmatic words (42:1-6) do not make clear exactly how his understanding has changed. If the author had made Job's interpretation of the divine speeches more explicit, then the reader would have been left with little to do beyond approving or disapproving of Job's response. By making Job's response so elusive, however, the author forces the reader to grapple more directly with the meaning of the divine speeches and so enter into the work of theological reconstruction that they invite.

One final theological issue remains to be considered, an issue that arises from the overall structure of the book, as discussed above. This issue might be stated in language taken from the book of Job itself: "Where can wisdom be found?" (28:12 NIV)—i.e., to which of the many voices in the book should one listen for the word of truth? One might reasonably assume that the divine speeches contain the essential truth of the book of Job. Not only does the voice of God carry transcendent authority, but the structure of the book up to that point seems to encourage such a judgment as well. The book appears to have been directing the reader from less to more adequate perspectives. The naive prose tale presents a moral perspective that is made to appear inadequate by the more literarily and theologically sophisticated dialogues. Within the dialogues, the friends' moral perspectives are shown to be inadequate by the compelling power of Job's words. The inadequacy of Job's perspective, however, is disclosed by the extraordinary speeches of God from the whirlwind. Surely one is supposed to adopt and endorse the perspective articulated by none other than God. Yet the book gives the last word to the prose tale. Moreover, the transition to the prose conclusion creates ironies that undermine the conviction that the book as a whole endorses the perspective of the divine speeches as the one true point of view. By having God declare that *Job* has spoken rightly (42:7), and by having events turn out just as the *friends* had predicted, the book wryly affirms perspectives that had appeared to be superseded and rejected.

What gets challenged in this process is the very notion that discerning truth is a matter of choosing one perspective and rejecting all others, that the truth about a complex question can be contained in a single perspective. Each perspective in the book of Job, taken by itself, contains valid insights. Yet each one, by virtue of its distinctive angle of vision, is of necessity oblivious to other dimensions of the question. When one looks back at the various views articulated by the different voices in the text, one finds that they are not so much contradictory as incommensurable.

It may be that the truth about a complex question can only be spoken by a plurality of voices that can never be merged into one, because they speak from different experiences and different perspectives. This is not to suggest that every position has equal validity or that with enough conversation consensus will be reached. As the book of Job illustrates, serious theological conversation places different voices in relationship precisely so that their limitations as well as their insights may be clearly identified. The dialogic truth that emerges from such a conversation is not to be found either in the triumph of one voice over the others or in an emerging consensus. It is to be found in the intersection of the various voices in their mutual interrogation. Such a perspective does not mean that

one never gets beyond talk to decision. On the contrary, every person must choose how to live. In terms of the issues posed by the book of Job, choosing how to live involves deciding about the character of God, the structure of creation, the place of suffering in the world, and the significance of the moral and pious life. What the structure of the book challenges, however, is the assumption that such a decision, once made, accounts for everything and resolves every question. Instead, the significance of a choice can be appreciated only when it is questioned from other perspectives and by persons who have made different choices. The book of Job models a kind of theological inquiry in which multiple perspectives are not merely helpful but essential. By closing in a manner that frustrates closure, the book signals that the conversation it has begun about the nature of divine-human relations is not finished but requires to be continued by new communities of voices.

FOR FURTHER READING

1. Commentaries

Andersen, F. I. *Job: An Introduction and Commentary.* Tyndale Old Testament Commentaries. Downers Grove, Ill.: Inter-Varsity, 1976.

Clines, David J. A. *Job 1–20.* WBC 17. Dallas: Word, 1989.

Good, Edwin M. *In Turns of Tempest: A Reading of Job with a Translation.* Stanford, Calif.: Stanford University Press, 1990.

Habel, Norman C. C. *The Book of Job.* OTL. Philadelphia: Westminster, 1985.

Hartley, John E. *The Book of Job.* NICOT. Grand Rapids, Mich.: Eerdmans, 1988.

Janzen, J. Gerald. *Job.* Interpretation. Atlanta: John Knox, 1985.

Pope, Marvin H. *Job.* 3rd ed. AB 15. Garden City, N.Y.: Doubleday, 1979.

2. The following books and collections of essays by biblical scholars and theologians are particularly recommended.

Duquoc, Christian, and Casiano Floristan, eds. *Job and the Silence of God.* New York: Seabury, 1983.

Gordis, R. *The Book of God and Man: A Study of Job.* Chicago: The University of Chicago Press, 1965.

Gutiérrez, Gustavo. *On Job: God-Talk and the Suffering of the Innocent*. Translated by M. J. O'Connell. Maryknoll, N.Y.: Orbis, 1987.

Nam, Duck-Woo. *Talking About God: Job 42:7-9 and the Nature of God in the Book of Job*. Studies in Biblical Literture 49. New York: Peter Lang 2003.

Newsome, Carol A. *The Book of Job: A Contest of Moral Imaginations*. New York: Oxford University Press, 2003.

Perdue, Leo G. *Wisdom in Revolt: Metaphorical Theology in the Book of Job*. JSOTSup 112. Sheffield: JSOT Press, 1991.

Perdue, Leo G., and W. Clark Gilpin, eds. *The Voice from the Whirlwind: Interpreting the Book of Job*. Nashville: Abingdon, 1992.

Pyeon, Yohan. *You Have Not Spoken What is Right About Me: Intertextuality and the Book of Job*. Studies in Biblical Literature 45. New York: Peter Lang, 2003.

Wolde, E J van, ed. *Job's God*. London: SCM Press, 2004.

Zuckerman, Bruce. *Job the Silent: A Study in Historical Counterpoint*. New York: Oxford University Press, 1991.

3. Job's status as literary classic as well as sacred Scripture for both Judaism and Christianity has encouraged many who are neither biblical scholars nor theologians to write about the book. The following are particularly engaging recent examples of such work.

Bloom, Harold, ed. *The Book of Job*. New York: Chelsea House, 1988.

Girard, Rene. *Job: The Victim of His People*. Translated by Yvonne Freccero. Stanford, Calif.: Stanford University Press, 1987.

Mitchell, Stephen. *The Book of Job*. San Francisco: North Point, 1987.

Wiesel, Elie. *The Trial of God: A Play in Three Acts*. Translated by M. Wiesel. New York: Schocken, 1979.

Wilcox, J. T. *The Bitterness of Job: A Philosophical Reading*. Ann Arbor: University of Michigan Press, 1989.

ENDNOTES

1. See the discussions in H. H. Rowley, "The Book of Job and Its Meaning," in *From Moses to Qumran* (London: Lutterworth, 1963) 151-61; M. Pope, *Job*, 3rd ed., AB 15 (Garden City, N.Y.: Doubleday, 1979) xxiii-xxx; J. E. Hartley, *The Book of Job*, NICOT (Grand Rapids: Eerdmans, 1988) 20-33.

2. See the report of Isho'dad of Merv, the ninth-century CE author who summarizes Bishop Theodore's views, cited in D. Zaharopoulos, *Theodore of Mopsuestia on the Bible: A Study of His Old Testament Exegesis* (New York: Paulist, 1989) 45-48. B. Zuckerman has suggested that the epistle of James alludes to the familiar oral tale rather than to the canonical book of Job when it says, "You have *heard* of the patience of Job" (James 5:11) rather than "you have *read* [in the Bible] of the patience of Job" (Zuckerman, *Job the Silent: A Study in Historical Counterpoint* [New York: Oxford University Press, 1991] 13-14).

3. E.g., F. Andersen, *Job: An Introduction and Commentary*, Tyndale Old Testament Commentaries (Downers Grove, Ill.: Inter-Varsity, 1976) 55; J. G. Janzen, *Job*, Interpretation (Atlanta: John Knox, 1985).

4. N. Habel, *The Book of Job*, OTL (Philadelphia: Westminster, 1985) 35-40. Cf. Hartley, *The Book of Job*, 20.

5. D. Clines, "False Naivete in the Prologue to Job," HAR 9 (1985) 127-36. The extensive and symmetrical repetition, highly stylized characters, and studied aura of remote antiquity imitate but exaggerate features of folktale style. Alongside these features are subtle word plays and verbal ambiguities that suggest an ironic distance from the aesthetic of simple naivete.

6. See C. Newsom, "Cultural Politics in the Book of Job," *Biblical Interpretation* 1 (1993) 119-34. In contrast, cf. the interpretive position taken by N. Habel, *The Book of Job*, 25-35.

7. B. Zuckerman, *Job the Silent*, 14.

8. See J. Roberts, "Job and the Israelite Religious Tradition," *ZAW* 89 (1977) 107-14.

9. D. Robertson, *Linguistic Evidence in Dating Early Hebrew Poetry*, SBLDS 3 (Missoula, Mont.: SBL, 1972) 153-56.

10. N. Sarna, "Epic Substratum in the Prose of Job," *JBL* 76 (1957) 13-25.

11. A. Hurvitz, "The Date of the Prose Tale of Job Linguistically Reconsidered," *HTR* 67 (1974) 17-34.

12. B. Zuckerman, *Job the Silent*, 26, however, argues that the linguistic evidence as a whole indicates that the dialogues are chronologically older than the prose tale.

13. Here, too, the basis for that date is linguistic. See J. P. M. van der Ploeg and A. S. van der Woude, *Le Targum de Job de la Grotte XI de Qumran* (Leiden: Brill, 1972) 4.

14. H.-M. Wahl, *Der Gerechte Schoepfer*, BZAW 207 (Berlin and New York: Walter de Gruyter, 1993) 182-87. Cf. T. Mende, *Durch Leiden zur Vollendung*, Trierer Theologische Studien 49 (Trier: Paulinus-Verlag, 1990) 419-27.

15. N. Habel, *The Book of Job*, 118.

16. See, e.g., R. N. Whybray, "The Social World of the Wisdom Writers," in R. E. Clements, *The World of Ancient Israel* (Cambridge: Cambridge University Press, 1989) 227-50; M. B. Dick, "Job 31, the Oath of Innocence, and the Sage," ZAW 95 (1983) 31-53.

17. C. Newsom, "Job," in *The Women's Bible Commentary*, ed. C. Newsom and S. Ringe (Philadelphia: Westminster/John Knox Press; London: SPCK, 1992) 133-35; M. B. Dick, "Job 31, the Oath of Innocence, and the Sage," 31-53.

18. See F. Cruesemann, "Hiob und Kohelet: Ein Beitrag zum Verstaendnis des Hiobbuches," *Werden und Wirken des Alten Testaments* (Westermann Festschrift), ed. R. Albertz et al. (Goettingen and Neukirchen: Vandenhoeck & Ruprecht and Neukirchener Verlag, 1980) 373-93; R. Albertz, "Der sozialgeschichtliche Hintergrund des Hiobbuches und der 'Babylonischen Theodizee,' " *Die Botschaft und die Boten* (Wolff Festschrift), ed. J. Jeremias and L. Perlitt (Neukirchen: Neukirchen Verlag, 1981) 349-72.

19. M. Pope, *Job*, 5-6.

20. For the Mesopotamian versions of the flood story, see James B. Pritchard, ed., *Ancient Near Eastern Texts Relating to the Old Testament* (*ANET*), 3rd ed. with supplement (Princeton: Princeton University Press, 1969) 93-95, 104-6.

21. *ANET*, 149-55.

22. See, e.g., J. Gray, "The Book of Job in the Context of Near Eastern Literature," *ZAW* 82 (1970) 251-69; J. Leveque, *Job et son Dieu* (Paris: J. Gabalda, 1970) 13-90; Pope, *Job*, lvi-lxxi.

23. *ANET*, 589-91.

24. *ANET*, 596-600.

25. M. Weinfeld, "Job and Its Mesopotamian Parallels—A Typological Analysis," in W. Claassen, ed., *Text and Context: Old Testament and Semitic Studies for F. C. Fensham* (Sheffield: Sheffield Academic Press, 1988) 217-26; Gray, "The Book of Job in the Context of Near Eastern Literature," 256.

26. But see Zuckerman, *Job the Silent*, 93-103, who suggests a larger role for this genre in the development of the book of Job.

27. J. Gray, "The Book of Job in the Context of Near Eastern Literature," 267-68; S. Denning-Bolle, *Wisdom in Akkadian Literature* (Leiden: Ex Oriente Lux, 1992) 136-58.

28. W. G. Lambert, *Babylonian Wisdom Literature* (Oxford: Oxford University Press, 1960) 63.

29. Translation according to W. G. Lambert, *Babylonian Wisdom Literature*, 71-89.

30. W. G. Lambert, *Babylonian Wisdom Literature*, 90-91, suggests that another very fragmentary text may be a second example of such a dialogue.

THE BOOK OF PSALMS

J. CLINTON MCCANN, JR.

One of the most outstanding and highly respected international leaders of the twentieth century was Sweden's Dag Hammarskjöld. As Secretary-General of the United Nations, he devoted the final years of his life to pursuing the principles espoused in the United Nations Charter—international cooperation and reconciliation toward a peaceful world. As Dorothy V. Jones points out, Hammarskjöld viewed his work not simply as a political role but as a religious calling. Jones reports:

> On his travels around the world Hammarskjöld always took three items with him. These items were found in his briefcase that was recovered after the plane crash that took his life in September 1961: a copy of the New Testament, a copy of the Psalms and a copy of the United Nations Charter.[1]

Hammarskjöld apparently understood—quite correctly—that the book of Psalms presents nothing short of God's claim upon the whole world and that it articulates God's will for justice, righteousness, and peace among all peoples and all nations. I write as a Christian biblical scholar and theologian, and, like Hammarskjöld, I consciously and constantly hold side by side the psalms and the New Testament. A careful reading of each reveals that the psalms anticipate Jesus' bold presentation of God's claim upon the whole world ("the kingdom of God has come near" [Mark 1:15 NRSV]) and that Jesus embodied the psalter's articulation of God's will for justice, righteousness, and peace among all peoples and all nations. In other words, my approach to the psalms is explicitly *theological*, and it takes seriously the canonical shape of the book of Psalms itself as well as the psalter's place in the larger canon of Scripture.

To be sure, this approach differs from the predominant scholarly approach to the psalms in the twentieth century. For the most part, Psalms scholarship has been explicitly *historical*. Undoubtedly, the historical-critical method has produced exciting, enduring, and important results. For instance, when scholars asked historical questions that were informed by sociological analysis (see below on form criticism), they arrived at the understanding that the psalms are not just the products of pious individuals in ancient Israel and Judah but that they are the liturgical materials used in ancient Israelite and Judean worship. In short, the psalter represents the hymnbook or the prayer book of the Second (and perhaps the First) Temple. This conclusion is not incorrect, but it is only partially correct. When scholars began to ask historical questions that were informed by literary sensitivity (see below on rhetorical criticism), they arrived at a new appreciation of the psalmists as highly skilled and sophisticated poets and of each psalm as a unique poetic creation. This conclusion is not incorrect either, but it too is only partially correct.

As important as it is to view the psalms as the sacred poetry that was used in ancient Israelite and Judean worship, this conclusion fails to do justice to another crucial dimension of the psalms: It fails to deal with the fact that the psalms were appropriated, preserved, and transmitted not only as records of human response to God but also as God's word to humanity. As Brevard Childs puts it:

> I would argue that the need for taking seriously the canonical form of the Psalter would greatly aid in making use of the Psalms in the life of the Christian Church. Such a move would not disregard the historical dimensions of the Psalter, but would attempt to profit from the shaping which the final redactors gave the older material in order to transform traditional poetry into Sacred Scripture for the later generations of the faithful.[2]

In short, the book of Psalms has been preserved and transmitted as Scripture, a dimension that is more evident when the final shape of the book of

Psalms is taken seriously and when the psalms are heard in conversation with the whole canon of Scripture.

It is my intent to interpret the psalms both as humanity's words to God and as God's word to humanity. Underlying this intent is a very *incarnational* view of Scripture, but the origin and transmission of the psalms in this regard is really no different from other parts of the canon. *All* Scripture originated as the record of humanity's encounter with and response to God, a record that generations of God's people judged to be authentic and true; thus it was preserved and transmitted as the Word of God. To be sure, such an incarnational view of Scripture is scandalously particularistic, but no more so than the fundamental Jewish and Christian convictions that God chose Israel or that God is fully known finally in one Jesus of Nazareth, who was "fully human"—"the Word became flesh and lived among us" (John 1:14 NRSV).

To interpret the psalms both as human words to God and as God's word to humans means that a multiplicity of methods is necessary. To appreciate the psalms as humanity's response to God—as sacred poetry as well as songs and prayers used in worship—it is necessary to employ form criticism and rhetorical criticism. To be sure, these methods may yield insights that lead to fruitful theological reflection; however, as Childs suggests, to appreciate the psalms more fully as God's word to humanity—as Scripture—it is helpful to consider the canonical shape of the psalter itself. I consciously employ a multiplicity of methods in an attempt to interpret the psalms both historically and theologically. To illustrate what this means in practice, it is helpful to consider the history of the critical study of the psalms in the twentieth century.

CRITICAL STUDY OF THE BOOK OF PSALMS

For centuries, interpreters of the psalms assumed that they were written by the persons whose names appear in the superscriptions. Since David's name appears in the superscriptions of seventy-three psalms, interpreters often have assumed by generalization that David must have written most of the untitled psalms as well. With the emergence of critical scholarship in the nineteenth century, these assumptions began to be questioned. Even so, at the beginning of the twentieth century, the psalms were still understood primarily as the work of pious individuals (although not necessarily the persons whose names appear in the superscriptions) who composed prayers and songs either for their private devotional use or in response to particular historical events. Thus scholars were intent upon determining and attempting to describe the authors of the psalms, to discern the historical circumstances of their composition, and to date each psalm as specifically as possible. The tendency was to date most of the psalms very late (third to second century BCE) and to view them as evidence of an individualized spirituality that was superior to the corporate worship of earlier centuries of Israelite and Judean history.

This approach has been characterized by W. H. Bellinger, Jr., as "the personal/historical method."[3] It is still being practiced in some circles, not only by interpreters who tend to read the Bible literally, but also by critical scholars. Michael Goulder, for instance, has recently proposed that Psalms 51–72, a collection attributed to David, actually date from David's time, that they were probably written by one of David's sons, and that they are in chronological order, with Psalm 51 deriving from the events of the David/Bathsheba episode in 2 Samuel 11–12 and subsequent psalms reflecting the succeeding events narrated in the rest of 2 Samuel through 1 Kings 1. Thus 1 Kings 1, which narrates Solomon's accession to the throne, corresponds to Psalm 72, which is attributed to Solomon.[4] A major weakness in Goulder's proposal is that the historical superscriptions of Psalms 52; 54; 56; 57; 59; 60; and 63 do not fit the scheme, since they allude to events much earlier in David's life. Thus most scholars remain unconvinced by Goulder's proposal, which, although ingenious and skillfully argued, contains a high degree of speculation. Nevertheless, Goulder's work illustrates well the variety of possible approaches to the psalms; and the personal/historical method at least reminds us that the psalms grew out of concrete historical situations in which real people sought to live their lives under God. While this reminder is valuable, most scholars agree that dating the psalms with any degree of precision or certainty is virtually impossible. To be sure, there are a few exceptions (see Psalm 137), and it often makes sense to relate certain psalms or groups of psalms to broad historical eras (see below on the shaping of the psalter in response to the exile). By and large, however, scholars have abandoned the personal/historical method in favor of a method that has dominated the study of Psalms in the twentieth century: form criticism.

Form Criticism. Early in the twentieth century, German scholar Hermann Gunkel became convinced of the inadequacy of the personal/historical method. He noted the many references in the psalter to liturgical activities (singing, dancing, shouting, sacrifice, prayer, etc.) and places (the Temple, the house of the Lord, gates, courts, etc.); he concluded that the psalms were as much or more related to the corporate worship of ancient Israel and Judah than to the meditation of pious persons. Gunkel pioneered a method known as form criticism. He classified the psalms as various forms or types or genres, and then sought to determine where each type would have fit into the worship of ancient Israel or Judah—its "setting in life."[5] Although Gunkel's work has been modified, extended, and refined (see below), it remains the foundation of a method that dominated psalms scholarship for much of the century and that still remains a viable and vital approach. Gunkel's types are described in the following sections, which also include observations concerning how subsequent scholars have responded to Gunkel's work.

Lament of an Individual. The lament of an individual, which some scholars prefer to call the complaint or prayer for help, is the most frequent type in the psalter. Characteristic elements include:

- ❖ Opening address, often including a vocative, such as, "O LORD"
- ❖ Description of the trouble or distress (the lament or complaint proper)
- ❖ Plea or petition for God's response (the prayer for help), often accompanied by reasons for God to hear and act
- ❖ Profession of trust or confidence in God (Gunkel's "certainty of being heard")
- ❖ Promise or vow to praise God or to offer a sacrifice

Not all of the typical elements appear in every prayer. Furthermore, the order of the elements varies from psalm to psalm, and the elements vary considerably in length and intensity among the prayers. This means that each lament has some degree of uniqueness, an observation that is especially important to rhetorical critics (see below).

When it came to the question of the setting in life for the laments of an individual, Gunkel did not break completely with the older personal/historical approach. He still maintained that the prayers were late spiritual compositions by individuals, but he claimed that the authors based their creations upon prototypes that had originated in the worship of an earlier period. In Gunkel's view, the cultic prototypes arose out of a situation in which a sick person came to the Temple to pray for God's help. Recurring features of the prayers were explained in relation to this basic situation. For instance, the dramatic turn from complaint and petition to trust and praise is explained as the psalmist's response to a priestly salvation oracle, which is not preserved in the text. The wicked or enemies are those who slandered or sought to take advantage of the psalmist's distress. Some prayers include the psalmist's plea for revenge against the enemies (Gunkel's Imprecatory Psalms). In some prayers, as a way of asserting that the distress is undeserved, the psalmist explicitly defends his or her behavior (Gunkel's Protestations of Innocence). In other prayers, the psalmist admits her or his guilt and is content to leave the situation with God (Gunkel's Penitential Psalms).

Needless to say, subsequent scholarship has not been entirely content with Gunkel's conclusions. In particular, the question of the setting in life of the laments has been and still is much debated. While it is true that the language and imagery of several of the laments of an individual clearly suggest an original situation of sickness (see Psalms 6; 38; 41; 88), such is not the case with many others. Rather than sickness, the primary distress in some cases seems to be persecution by ruthless opponents. Consequently, several scholars have suggested that some of the prayers have arisen out of a situation in which the psalmist was falsely accused of some offense (see Psalms 5; 7; 11; 17; 26; 59; 109). According to this view, the psalmist has come to the Temple—perhaps has even taken up residence there—to seek asylum and to request redress from God (see 1 Kgs 1:50-53). This situation explains the protestations of innocence and the need to request revenge against the enemies, or in short, to ask that justice be done. The existence of praise following the complaint and petition is explained as a portion of the psalm that was added later, when the psalmist had been exonerated.

Still other laments of an individual seem to have arisen from circumstances involving neither sickness nor false accusation. The imagery is primarily military (see Psalms 3; 35; 56–57). This has led some scholars to identify the speaker in these psalms as the king, the military leader of the people. In the absence of any explicit indications in this regard, however, it is more likely that the military imagery is metaphorical. Indeed, the imagery of sickness and accusation may also be metaphorical. If this is the case, then the attempt to specify precisely the original circumstances of these prayers is finally futile and unnecessary. The work of Erhard Gerstenberger points to this conclusion. Maintaining that scholars "know little about the exact use of individual complaint psalms," Gerstenberger concludes that they "belonged to the realm of special offices for suffering people who, probably assisted by their kinfolk, participated in a service of supplication and curing under the guidance of a ritual expert."[6] While Gerstenberger's work is clearly historical and form critical, it is to be noted that his conclusions are fairly modest in comparison to earlier attempts and that his focus is on primary social groups, like the family, rather than on the Temple and its rituals.

Regardless of the circumstances out of which the prayers arose, the language and imagery were eventually heard and appropriated metaphorically (and perhaps were even *intended* to function metaphorically from the beginning). This means that the language and imagery are symbolic and stereotypical enough to be applicable to a variety of situations. While this may be a frustration to scholars who are attempting to pin down precisely the historical circumstances of a psalm's origin, it is a distinct advantage to faithful communities and people who actually pray the prayers and look to them for a word about God and their own lives under God. As Patrick D. Miller, Jr., suggests:

> The search for a readily identifiable situation as the context for understanding the laments may, however, be illusory or unnecessary. The language of these psalms with its stereotypical, generalizing, and figurative style is so open-ended that later readers, on the one hand are stopped from peering behind them to one or more clearly definable sets of circumstances or settings in life, and on the other hand, are intentionally set free to adapt them to varying circumstances and settings.[7]

In other words, the really pertinent questions in approaching the laments are *not*, What was wrong with the psalmist? Who were her or his enemies? Rather, the crucial interpretive questions are these: What is wrong *with us?* Who or what are *our* enemies? This approach opens the way for an explicitly *theological*, as well as historical, understanding of the laments of an individual. For instance, rather than approaching the transition from complaint/petition to trust/praise chronologically or liturgically, the interpreter can take the simultaneity of complaint and praise as an expression of the perennial reality of the life of faith. Such an approach has profound implications for understanding human suffering and the suffering of God (see below on "The Theology of the Psalms").

Thanksgiving Song of an Individual. The thanksgiving song of an individual can be thought of as the offering of the praise that is regularly promised in the concluding sections of the laments (see above). It may have originally accompanied a sacrifice offered in the Temple, including perhaps a sacrificial meal. Typical elements include:

- ❖ expressions of praise and gratitude to God
- ❖ description of the trouble or distress from which the psalmist has been delivered
- ❖ testimony to others concerning God's saving deeds
- ❖ exhortation to others to join in praising God and acknowledging God's ways

Because the thanksgiving songs seem to look back on the kinds of distressing situations described in the laments, the same basic interpretive issues come into play (see above). In fact, because of the difficulty of translating Hebrew verb tenses, scholars sometimes disagree on whether a psalm should be classified as a lament or a thanksgiving song (see Psalms 28; 56; 57). From a theological perspective, the difference is not crucial, since the larger context of the book of Psalms suggests that deliverance is finally experienced not beyond but in the midst of suffering. Historical matters should not be ignored, but the emphasis will fall on the consideration of what it means to make gratitude one's fundamental posture toward God.

Lament of the Community. The characteristic elements of the lament of the community are essentially the same as those of the lament of the individual (see above), but the prayer is offered in the first-person plural. In addition, the communal prayers frequently include a reminder to God of the history of God's relationship with the people and of God's mighty deeds on behalf of the people. The communal prayers are less likely to include the turn from complaint and petition to trust and praise. Like the laments of an individual, however, each communal prayer is unique.

The communal prayers obviously originated amid situations of communal distress, and scholars offer a range of proposals for each psalm. The most dramatic communal setback in the biblical period was the destruction of Jerusalem in 587 BCE and the subsequent exile. While it is not clear that all of the communal laments arose in response to this crisis, it is likely that several of them did; it is even more likely that all of them were eventually read and heard in view of this crisis. Attention will be given to the apparently intentional attempt to place strategically the communal laments in the final form of the psalter. The second psalms in Books II and III are communal laments (Psalms 44; 74), and several more communal prayers appear in Book III (Psalms 79; 80; 83; and perhaps 77; 85; and 89; see "The Shape and Shaping of the Psalter"). The placement of these prayers encourages a theological as well as a historical approach to them, and it gives them a significance greater than their relative paucity might indicate. In particular, the communal laments encourage reflection on what it means to continue to profess faith in God's sovereignty in situations of severe extremity (see "The Theology of the Book of Psalms").

Hymn or Song of Praise. Whereas there are elements of praise in the above-mentioned types, the hymn or song of praise is oriented exclusively in this direction. The basic form is very simple:

❖ Opening invitation to praise
❖ Reasons for praise, often introduced by the Hebrew particle translated "for" (כִּי *kî*)
❖ Recapitulation of invitation to praise

As with the other types, these elements may vary in length and arrangement, thus giving each song of praise a certain individuality. For instance, in some hymns, the invitation is greatly extended and occupies most or all of the psalm (see Psalms 100; 148; 150). Then, too, the reasons for praise cite a variety of events, themes, and characteristics of God, and they employ a variety of vocabulary and imagery.

The songs of praise ordinarily refer to God in the third person rather than addressing God directly, as in the prayers, but there are exceptions (see Psalm 8). While it is clear that the communal laments are the corporate correlate of the laments of individuals, it seems to be that the hymns or songs of praise serve as the corporate correlate of the thanksgiving songs of individuals. In several cases where God is addressed directly in praise, however, some scholars prefer to categorize the psalm as a thanksgiving song of the community (see Psalms 65–67). In the final analysis, though, precision of categorization is not crucial. Claus Westermann, for instance, has chosen not to use "song of thanksgiving" at all in categorizing the psalms. Rather, he prefers to distinguish between descriptive praise, which celebrates God's general character and activity, and declarative praise, which celebrates God's deliverance in a specific situation of distress.[8]

Usually treated as sub-categories of the songs of praise are two more groupings customarily known as the enthronement psalms and the songs of Zion. The enthronement psalms are those that explicitly proclaim the reign of God (see Psalms 29; 47; 93; 95–99), and the songs of Zion are poems that focus praise on the city of Jerusalem (see Psalms 46; 48; 76; 84; 87; 122). While Gunkel was inclined to treat these psalms as "Eschatological Hymns" directed toward a vision of the end of time, his form-critical successors sought a liturgical setting for these psalms. For instance, Sigmund Mowinckel began by criticizing Gunkel's view that cultic prototypes had been spiritualized. Mowinckel characterized his own approach as the cult-functional method, and he made the enthronement psalms the foundation for an overarching proposal for a liturgical setting in life of many psalms. In particular, Mowinckel suggested that the enthronement psalms can be taken as evidence that Israel, like certain other ancient Near Eastern peoples, celebrated annually the enthronement or re-enthronement of their deity, Yahweh, as king of the universe.[9] According to Mowinckel, this New

Year Festival formed the setting in life of not just the enthronement psalms but many others as well. In a similar move, but one that went in a different direction, Hans-Joachim Kraus focused on the songs of Zion and the royal psalms (see below) in his proposal that many of the psalms were used liturgically in an annual Royal Zion Festival, which celebrated God's choice of Jerusalem and the Davidic dynasty. The basic problem with these two proposals, as well as with Artur Weiser's attempt to relate many psalms to a Covenant Renewal Festival, is that there is simply no solid biblical evidence for such festivals.[10]

Because of the lack of biblical evidence, subsequent scholarship has generally abandoned the proposals of Mowinckel, Kraus, and Weiser. Even so, they were not totally misguided. They had the value of emphasizing the liturgical origins and use of the psalms, and they served to highlight crucial themes in the psalter, especially the reign of God and the centrality of Zion. While the proposals of Mowinckel and Kraus may have gone beyond the confines of the evidence, it can hardly be doubted that the kingship of God and God's choice of Zion were celebrated culticly in some manner in ancient Israel or Judah. Neither can it be doubted that the songs of praise played a major role in such celebrations and more generally in worship at the major pilgrimage festivals (see the festal calendars in Exod 23:14-17; Lev 23:3-44; Deut 16:1-17).

Possible liturgical origins and uses of the songs of praise should be noted; however, in keeping with the shape of the psalter itself (see below, "The Shape and Shaping of the Psalter"), interpreters should emphasize hearing the hymns as proclamations of the reign of God. Not only do the enthronement psalms proclaim God's reign (see Psalms 29; 47; 96), but so also do the other songs of praise (see Psalms 8; 33; 100; 103; 104; 113), including the songs of Zion (see Psalms 46; 48; 122).

Royal Psalms. The royal psalms are actually not a form-critical category but rather a grouping based on a particular *content*. In this category, Gunkel included all the psalms that deal primarily with the Israelite or Judean king or the monarchy. For instance, Psalm 2 seems to be a portion of a coronation ritual; Psalm 45 celebrates a royal wedding; Psalm 72 is a prayer for the king, perhaps originally upon his coronation day (see also Psalms 18; 20; 21; 89; 101; 110; 132; 144).

Form-critical appropriation of the royal psalms involves the attempt to determine a precise setting for each psalm. More emphasis will be given, however, to the function of the royal psalms in the final form of the psalter. Gerald Wilson has noted that royal psalms occur at the "seams" of Books I–III.[11] It may also be important, as Childs suggests, that the royal psalms are generally scattered throughout the psalter (see below "The Shape and Shaping of the Psalter").[12] The effect is to give these psalms themselves and the psalter as a whole a messianic orientation; that is to say, the royal psalms are not only poetic relics from the days of the Davidic dynasty but are also expressions of the ongoing hope that God will continue to manifest God's sovereignty in concrete ways in the life of God's people and in the life of the world. Such an appropriation of the royal psalms takes seriously the historical fact that they were preserved and were found meaningful long after the disappearance of the monarchy (see below on "The Theology of the Book of Psalms".

Wisdom/Torah Psalms. Gunkel suggested that certain psalms should be identified as wisdom poetry (see Psalms 1; 37; 73; 128). Like the royal psalms, wisdom poetry is not strictly a form-critical category. Rather, for Gunkel, wisdom psalms "consist entirely of pious reflections."[13] Mowinckel also distinguished certain psalms as wisdom poetry, and he suggested that these poems were the only non-cultic material in the psalter.[14] Subsequent scholars have debated these conclusions, sometimes trying to identify various characteristics or themes as constitutive of wisdom psalmody and sometimes seeking a cultic setting for the wisdom psalms.[15]

Some psalms share characteristics and themes with the wisdom literature. More important, however, is the fact that one of the wisdom psalms opens the psalter and serves as a kind of preface. Psalm 1, along with Psalms 19 and 119, is often identified as a torah psalm (NIV and NRSV "law" in Ps 1:2 translates the Hebrew word תורה [tôrâ]; see also Ps 19:7; 119). As James L. Mays points out, these three psalms, along with numerous other expressions throughout the psalter of a didactic intent (see Psalms 18; 25; 33; 78; 89; 93; 94; 99; 103; 105; 111; 112; 147; 148), serve to give the whole psalter an instructional orientation. The effect, according to Mays, is this: "Form-critical and cult-functional questions are subordinated and questions of *content and theology* become more important."[16] In short, the existence of the wisdom/torah psalms is finally a stimulus to interpret the psalms theologically as well as historically (see below on "The Shape and Shaping of the Psalter").

Entrance Liturgies. Although a relatively minor category, since it contains only Psalms 15 and 24, the psalms that Gunkel called entrance liturgies have commanded a good deal of scholarly attention. The similarity between the two psalms is evident:

❖ The question apparently asked by those approaching the Temple or sanctuary
❖ The answer, perhaps delivered by a priestly voice, involving standards of admission
❖ Concluding blessing or affirmation

While the liturgical origin and use of Psalms 15 and 24 are perhaps more evident than with any other genre, the entrance liturgies invite theological reflection on what it means to enter God's reign and to submit to God's sovereign claim upon the life of God's people and the world.

Prophetic Exhortation. Gunkel noticed prophetic sayings or oracles in several psalms, an insight developed by Mowinckel and subsequent scholars to the point that Psalms 50, 81, and 95 are often called prophetic exhortations. More recently, Gerstenberger has suggested that these psalms may represent what he calls a "liturgical sermon."[17] In any case, as with the wisdom/torah psalms, the instructional intent is evident. These psalms challenge the reader to make a decision regarding God's sovereign claim.

Psalms of Confidence/Trust. According to Gunkel, the psalms of confidence are to be explained as derivatives of the lament of an individual; that is, when the "certainty of being heard" (see above) became detached from the elements of complaint and petition, the result was psalms like Psalms 16, 23, and 91. It is not at all clear that this explanation is correct; however, it has been largely adopted by subsequent scholars, and it does make sense to categorize certain psalms under the rubric of confidence or trust. That these psalms offer eloquent professions of faith in God's protective presence and power amid threatening circumstances. In short, these psalms assert God's sovereignty, despite appearances to the contrary.

Mixed Types and the Move Beyond Form Criticism. Even though his methodological emphasis would seem to belie it, Gunkel was well aware of the individuality of each psalm. When psalms were especially unique, and thus resistant to easy categorization, Gunkel resorted to a category that he called "mixed types."[18] In retrospect, it is clear that the very existence of this category would eventually undermine the basic goals of the form-critical and cult-functional approaches. Gunkel, Mowinckel, and their successors sought first of all to discern what was *typical* about particular psalms. Thus practitioners of the form-critical and cult-functional methods tended to overlook the *individuality* of each psalm. This neglect opened the way for James Muilenburg and others to issue the call for scholars to supplement form criticism with rhetorical criticism in an attempt to appreciate the unique literary features of each psalm. It is to rhetorical criticism, the immediate successor of form criticism, that we now turn. But first, it should be noted that Gunkel's explanation of the existence of mixed types also anticipates a further scholarly move beyond form criticism. In Gunkel's words: "Mixtures or inner transformations occur with great frequency when the literature we are discussing becomes old, especially when the original setting of the literary types has been forgotten or is no longer clear."[19]

In short, Gunkel recognizes that discernment of the types and liturgical origins of the psalms is not sufficient for understanding them in their final form and literary setting. It is precisely this recognition that eventually invited the movement beyond a method that aims at appreciating the *typical* and the *original* to methods that aim at appreciating the *individual* and the *final*. In other words, the limited aims of form criticism invited the movement first toward rhetorical criticism and then toward a consideration of the importance of the shape and the shaping of the book of Psalms as a literary context for interpreting the individual psalms.

Rhetorical Criticism. In 1968, James Muilenburg issued his widely heeded call for biblical scholarship "to venture beyond the confines of form criticism into an inquiry into other literary features which are all too often ignored today."[20] Muilenburg did not advocate the abandonment of form criticism, but rather suggested that it be supplemented by what he called rhetorical criticism.

As applied to the book of Psalms, rhetorical criticism has meant an attention to literary features that leads to an appreciation of each psalm as a unique poetic creation.

Parallelism. Perhaps the most persistent poetic feature of the psalms is parallelism. While several of the psalms' poetic features cannot readily be captured in translation, parallelism can be, and even a casual reader is likely to notice that the second half of a typical poetic line is often related somehow to the first half of the line. Earlier generations of scholars categorized parallelism as either synonymous (the second part of the line echoes the first), antithetical (the second part of the line states opposition to the first), or synthetic (which is a catch-all category and often really meant that no parallelism could be detected). In these terms, the most frequent type of parallelism is synonymous; however, recent scholars have pointed out that the echoing involved is only rarely precisely synonymous. Rather, the second part of the poetic line usually has the effect of intensifying or specifying or concretizing the thought expressed in the first part of the line.[21]

Repetition. Another very common, and probably the most important, poetic feature of the psalms is repetition. While it is often considered bad writing style to use the same word repeatedly, such apparently was not the case in Hebrew. Consequently, repetition occurs frequently in a variety of patterns and for a variety of purposes. For instance, the same word will occur several times in a psalm in order to draw the reader's attention to a key word or concept, such as salvation/deliverance (Psalm 3), righteousness (Psalms 71; 85), justice/judgment (Psalm 82), or steadfast love (Psalms 103; 109; 136). Unfortunately, both the NIV and the NRSV sometimes obscure the Hebrew repetition by choosing different English words to translate the same Hebrew word.

When a word, phrase, or poetic line occurs in both the opening and the closing line of a psalm or section of a psalm, the repetition is called an *inclusio*, or envelope structure. This framing technique again often identifies a crucial theological theme or concept (see Psalms 8; 21; 67; 73; 103; 107; 118). The same effect is frequently achieved by the use of a refrain, a poetic line that occurs in exactly or essentially the same form two or more times in the psalm (see Psalms 8; 42–43; 46; 49; 56; 57; 59; 62; 80; 99; 107; 116; 136). Still another form of repetition is known as step-like or stair-like repetition, since it involves repeating a word either in both parts of the same line or in juxtaposed lines. Not coincidentally, it occurs most frequently in the Songs of Ascents or Songs of the Steps (Psalms 120–134). While it is not necessary to categorize every instance of repetition, and while some instances are clearly more noticeable and significant than others, repetition is a primary stylistic clue for discerning the theological message and significance of the psalms.

Chiasm. A special form of repetition is known as a chiasm. *Chiasm* is a word derived from the Greek letter *chi* (X), and it denotes the arrangement of elements in an ABBA or ABCBA pattern. The number of elements in a chiasm may vary, but the effect is to provide a sort of multiple envelope structure that focuses attention on the center of the chiasm. Chiasm occurs frequently, and on various scales, in the psalms. It may involve the arrangement of words in a single poetic line (see Pss 3:7; 6:10; 25:9; 83:1; 100:3; 142:2); it may involve the arrangement of corresponding words or phrases in several poetic lines (see Pss 1:5-6; 3:1-2; 36:6-7, 10-11; 56:3-4; 72:1-2; 87:3-7; 90:1-2, 5-6; 97:6-7; 101:3-7; 137:5-6); or it may involve the arrangement of the poetic lines or sections of a psalm with the effect of focusing attention on a central panel or pivotal verse (see Psalms 1; 5; 11; 12; 17; 26; 67; 86; 92). Chiasm is not only an important literary device but also is a clue to appropriate directions for theological reflection and appropriation.

Structure. Whereas form critics are interested in the structure of a psalm in order to discern characteristic elements and their typical arrangement, rhetorical critics are more interested in what is unique about the way a psalm is structured. The structure of a psalm is not only a literary issue but also is a clue to theological significance and appropriation. To be sure, some psalms are more amenable to such analysis than others (e.g., Psalms 8; 73; 122). In many cases, it seems fairly clear that a poem falls into distinct sections, sometimes even into formal stanzas or strophes (although I have avoided these terms because such formal regularity is rare). In several cases, however, the structure of a psalm can justifiably be perceived in several ways, depending upon which structural clues one chooses to focus. In this case, it is not necessary to declare one structural proposal correct to the exclusion of others. Rather, it is proper to conclude that the structure or movement of the psalm occurs at more than one level (see Psalms 62; 77; 87; 94; 101; 113; 122; 128; 129; 136; 140; 142; 145; 146).

Other Figurative Uses of Language. The literary features described above can be captured in English translation, at least to a certain extent. Nevertheless, other figurative uses of language in the psalms are virtually impossible to render recognizably into English. For instance, although there is disagreement over how to define it and even over whether it exists, most scholars are willing to speak of the meter of Hebrew poetry. There is no really satisfactory way to capture the rhythmical quality of psalms, except perhaps to render the psalms in poetic lines rather than as continuous prose; and both the NIV and the NRSV do this. Also difficult to capture in English are instances in which Hebrew syntax or word order is unique or striking (see Pss 3:1-2, 6-7; 5:1; 22:9-10; 31:15; 36:5-6; 38:15; 62:7; 90:4; 93:2; 114:7; 123:3). So will other figures of speech that cannot be readily rendered into English, such as alliteration (see Pss 54:3-4; 63:1, 11; 122:6-8), onomatopoeia (see Pss 29:3-7; 140:3), and plays on words (see Pss 28:5; 39:4-5; 48:4; 146:3-4).

Another literary feature of the psalms that cannot be captured in English is the apparently intentional ambiguity of some Hebrew words, phrases, and grammatical constructions (see Pss 1:3; 25:12; 40:9; 51:14; 71:7; 87:4-5; 96:13; 100:3; 122:3; 127:3; 135:3; 147:1).

Aside from specific instances of intentional ambiguity, however, there is a sense in which all poetry is inevitably ambiguous. That is, poetry aims not so much at describing things objectively as it does at evoking the reader's imagination. As Thomas G. Long puts it, "Psalms operate at the level of the imagination, often swiveling the universe on the hinges of a single image."[22] This means that the psalms put the reader in touch with a source of mystery that cannot be precisely defined, objectively described, or even fully comprehended. As S. E. Gillingham says of biblical poetry, including the book of Psalms:

Its diction is full of ambiguity of meaning. As with all poetry, but perhaps especially in this case, the concealing/revealing aspect of biblical verse

means that any interpretation involves as much the power of imaginative insight as any so-called "objective" analysis. . . .

. . . The language of theology needs the poetic medium for much of its expression, for poetry, with its power of allusion, reminds us of the more hidden and mysterious truths which theology seeks to express. Poetry is a form which illustrates our need for a sense of balance in our study of theology. On the one hand, good poetry still testifies to the need to be properly analytical in our pursuit of knowledge, but on the other, it illustrates the importance of being open to the possibility of mystery and ambiguity in our pursuit of meaning.[23]

In keeping with the direction Gillingham suggests, interpretation should attend analytically to the literary and stylistic devices that make the psalms good poetry, but always with an eye toward theology—that is, to the way the psalms encounter the reader with the majesty of God and with the mystery of God's involvement with the world.

The Shape and Shaping of the Psalter. As already suggested, Hermann Gunkel's own conclusions about the psalms left the way open for the emergence of rhetorical criticism and for the scholarly consideration of individual psalms in the context of their final *literary* setting within the book of Psalms. It is in the latter direction that Psalms scholarship has moved in the past fifteen years. Although they did not make much of them, scholars have long been aware of various features that pointed to a process involving the gradual collection of individual psalms and groups of psalms into what we now have as the book of Psalms.

Superscriptions. Of the 150 psalms, 117 have a superscription, ranging from a single phrase (see Psalms 25–28) to several lines (see Psalms 18; 60; 88). The superscriptions contain three kinds of information:

(1) *Personal Names.* The superscriptions of seventy-three psalms mention David; others mention Jeduthun (Psalms 39; 62; 77; see 1 Chr 16:41-42; 25:1-8), Heman (Psalm 88; see 1 Kgs 4:31; 1 Chr 2:6; 6:17; 16:41-42; 25:1-8), Ethan (Psalm 89; see 1 Kgs 4:31; 1 Chr 2:6), Solomon (Psalms 72; 127), Moses (Psalm 90), the Korahites (Psalms 42; 44–49; 84–85; 87–88), and the Asaphites (Psalms 50; 73–83). While it is possible in some cases that these names indicate authorship (see above on the personal/historical method), it is more likely that they originated in the process of collection. David,

for instance, was remembered as the initiator of psalmody in worship (see 1 Chr 16:7-43). To be sure, the chronicler wrote hundreds of years after the actual time of David, but the memory may be an ancient one. In any case, it is more likely that many psalms were attributed to David as a result of this memory rather than as a result of Davidic authorship. Similarly, the process of collection accounts for the association of thirteen psalms with specific moments in David's life (see Psalms 3; 7; 18; 34; 51; 52; 54; 56; 57; 59; 60; 63; 142). These references should not be construed as historically accurate, but neither should they be dismissed as irrelevant. Rather, they provide an illustrative narrative context for hearing and interpreting particular psalms as well as a clue to the appropriateness of imagining narrative contexts for other psalms that do not contain superscriptions.

Not surprisingly, several of the other names found in the superscriptions are also associated with David's establishment of worship—Jeduthun, Heman, Korah (see 1 Chr 6:22, 37; 9:19), and Asaph (1 Chr 6:39; 9:15; 16:5, 7; 37; 25:1-8). The significant Korahite and Asaphite collections probably point to a process of both authorship and collection of psalms within Levitical guilds. It is not clear how well these collections reflect the actual work of these guilds, and this issue remains the subject of scholarly debate.[24] Of more relevance for the consideration of the shape and shaping of the psalter is the appearance of those collections at the beginning of Books II and III. Interestingly, too, the name Solomon occurs at the end of Book II and the name Moses at the beginning of Book IV. This pattern seems more than coincidental, and I shall return to these observations later.

(2) *Liturgical Instructions.* Fifty-five superscriptions contain the phrase "to the leader" (למנצח *lamnasṣēaḥ;* see NRSV). As the NIV suggests with its translation, "for the director of music," this phrase is probably some sort of liturgical instruction (see NIV "directing" and NRSV "lead" in 1 Chr 15:21, where the Hebrew word occurs as a verb). Its precise significance is unknown, as is that of other words and phrases that probably indicate moods, modes, or even melodies accompanying the original singing of certain psalms (see *sheminith* [השמינית *haššĕmînît*] in Psalms 6; 12; and 1 Chr 15:21; *gittith* [הגתית *haggittît*] in Psalms 8; 81; 84; NRSV, *Muth-labben* [עלמות לבן *'almût*

labbēn]; NIV, "the tune of 'The Death of the Son'" in Psalm 9; NRSV, "The Deer of the Dawn"; NIV, "the tune of 'The Doe of the Morning' " in Psalm 22 [אילת השחר *'ayyelet haššaḥar*]; "Lilies" [שושנים *šōšannîm*] in Psalms 45 and 69; "Lily of the Covenant" [שושן עדות *šûšan 'ēdût*] in Psalm 60; NRSV, "Lilies, a Covenant"; NIV, "the tune of 'The Lilies of the Covenant' " in Psalm 80 [*šōšannîm 'ēdût*]; *alamoth* [עלמות *'ălāmôt*] in Psalm 46 and 1 Chr 15:20; *mahalath* [מחלת *māḥălat*] in Psalm 53; *mahalath leannoth* [מחלת לענות *māḥălat lĕ'annôt*] in Psalm 88; NRSV, "Dove on Far-off Terebinths"; NIV, "to the tune of 'A Dove on Distant Oaks' " in Psalm 56 [יונת אלם רחקים *yônat 'ēlem rĕḥōqîm*]; and "Do Not Destroy" in Psalms 57–59; 75 [אל-תשחת *'al-tašḥēt*]). According to some scholars, however, these mysterious terms may designate musical instruments or the original liturgical settings of certain psalms, as is more clearly the case with other words and phrases. For instance, musical instruments are mentioned in the superscriptions of Psalms 4; 5; 6; 54; 55; 61; 67; 76, and several superscriptions indicate a particular setting or use for their psalms. Psalms 30 and 92 are the most specific in this regard, but the superscriptions of Psalms 38; 45; 70; and 100 may also point to cultic occasions. The liturgical instructions in the superscriptions clearly suggest that many of the psalms were meant to be sung, but we know very little about actual performance. The same applies to the term *selah*, which occurs in the body of several psalms. While it almost certainly represents a liturgical instruction of some kind—perhaps a signal to the musical director or levitical choir—its precise meaning and significance are not known.

(3) *Genre Designations.* The term "Genre designation" may be misleading, since it is clear that the ancient authors and performers of the psalms were not form critics in the contemporary sense (see above). For instance, while the most important contemporary rubrics are "prayer" and "praise," these terms occur infrequently in the superscriptions—"praise" only in Psalm 145 and "prayer" only in Psalms 17; 86; 90; and 102 (and only in Psalm 102 does the superscription further identify the prayer as a "lament"; see the NIV). Even so, the ancient collectors did apparently distinguish among types of poems. The most frequent designation in the superscriptions is the Hebrew word מזמור (*mizmôr*; 57 times), which is traditionally rendered "psalm," an

English transliteration of the Greek translation (ψαλμός *psalmos*) of *mizmôr* and the term that has provided the Greek and English names for the entire collection (the Hebrew title of the book is תהלים [*těhillîm*, "Praises"]). The Hebrew root occurs frequently in the Psalms as a verb, and it describes both singing and the musical accompaniment to singing. Aside from "psalm," the most frequent designation in the superscriptions is "song" (שיר *šîr*), and it too points to the musical performance of the poems. What difference the ancient authors and collectors perceived between a "psalm" and a "song" is not clear, especially in view of the fact that thirteen psalms are identified as both and that both labels are applied to psalms that contemporary form critics categorize in a variety of ways. Psalm 88 is even triply identified as a "song," a "psalm," and a "maskil" (משכיל *maśkîl*). This term, which occurs in the superscriptions of thirteen psalms as well as in Ps 47:7 (see NIV and NRSV notes), appears to derive from a root that means "be attentive, prudent, wise." Thus it may mean something like "contemplative poem" or "didactic poem." Certainty of meaning is impossible, however, and the term is best left untranslated. The same conclusion applies to the terms מכתם (*miktām*, Psalms 16; 56–60) and שגיון (*šiggāyôn*, Psalm 7; see the similar term in Hab 3:1), which are even more obscure.

Collections. The existence of collections within the Psalter has long been obvious, but the exact process behind the compilation of these collections to form the book of Psalms remains unknown. While the superscriptions of many psalms may not be original, they do offer a clue as to which psalms were perceived as somehow belonging together. For instance, psalms with the same ancient genre designation often occur in sequence (see Psalms 42–45; 52–55; 56–60), but more important, the personal names mentioned in the superscriptions indicate the existence of a collection. With the exception of Psalms 1–2; 10; and 33, the superscription of every psalm in Book I mentions David. Another Davidic collection is formed by Psalms 51–72. While Psalms 66–67 and 71–72 do not mention David, the notice in 72:20 suggests the ancient editors' awareness of a collection. Interestingly, most of the psalms in the two Davidic collections are laments of an individual, although the ancient genre designations vary.

Between the two Davidic collections that form the bulk of Books I–II are a Korahite collection (Psalms 42–49) and a single Asaph psalm (Psalm 50) that anticipates the Asaphite collection (Psalms 73–83), which forms the bulk of Book III.

A mysterious feature of Books II–III is the existence of another kind of collection, the so-called Elohistic psalter (Psalms 42–83), a grouping in which the divine name *Elohim* occurs far more frequently than it does in Psalms 1–41 or 84–150 (*Elohim* occurs 244 times in Psalms 42–83 as opposed to only 49 times in Psalms 1–41 and 70 times in Psalms 84–150). For years, scholars have usually concluded that the Elohistic psalter is the result of the work of a redactor who changed many of the occurrences of *Yahweh* to *Elohim*; however, this conclusion is questionable. For instance, it does not satisfactorily explain why 44 occurrences of *Yahweh* remain in Psalms 42–83 or why the redactor would have stopped with Psalm 83 rather than continuing through Psalm 89, the end of Book III. Thus it appears likely that the occurrences of *Elohim* are original to the composition of Psalms 42–83 and that these psalms originated and existed independently. Only later, it seems, were they joined to Psalms 3–41 (or 1–41) and only later were Psalms 84–89 attached as a sort of appendix to form Books I–III.[25]

It appears that Books I–III were in place prior to Books IV–V. Indications to this effect include the facts that 28 of the 33 untitled psalms occur in Books IV–V and that the psalters found at Qumran show a great deal more variation from the MT in Books IV–V than they do in Books I–III.[26] In short, it is likely that a different and later process of collection was operative for Books IV–V. For instance, the name of David is not nearly so prominent (see only Psalms 101; 103; 108–110; 122; 124; 131; and the Davidic collection, Psalms 138–145). At the same time, the laments of an individual are far less prominent and songs of praise become predominant (see below). Collections are marked more by the theme of praise, as with Psalms 93–99 (the reign of God) and Psalms 113–118 (or 111–118). More formally, Psalms 146–150 all begin and end with the imperative "Praise the LORD!" Book V contains what is clearly a discrete collection, the Songs of Ascents (Psalms 120–134).

While scholars have long noticed the existence of various collections, only recently have they begun to try to discern the significance of the shape of the whole book of Psalms. While much about the process of collection remains and will undoubtedly always remain unknown, certain directions can be detected and will be discussed under the heading "The Editorial Purpose of the Psalter."

The Five-Book Arrangement. As both the NIV and the NRSV suggest, the doxologies in Pss 41:13; 72:19; 89:52; and 106:48 have the effect of dividing the psalter into five books:

Book I	Psalms 1–41
Book II	Psalms 42–72
Book III	Psalms 73–89
Book IV	Psalms 90–106
Book V	Psalms 107–150

This is not a new observation. Indeed, the *Midrash Tehillim* states, "As Moses gave five books of laws to Israel, so David gave five books of Psalms to Israel."[27] Despite this ancient tradition, some scholars conclude that the five-book arrangement is coincidental rather than intentional; that is, the doxologies are simply original parts of Psalms 41; 72; 89; and 106 and were never meant to serve any editorial function. This conclusion has recently been definitively refuted by Gerald H. Wilson, who points out that the movements from Psalms 41 to 42, 72 to 73, and 89 to 90 are marked not only by doxologies but also by shifts in the ancient genre designation and in the personal names mentioned in the superscriptions.[28] Thus, while a five-book arrangement may not have been the original goal of the earliest editors or collectors, it did become a goal of those who put the psalter in its final form. Wilson's work has been a major stimulus in moving Psalms scholarship in the direction of attempting to discern the editorial purpose of the psalter, and it is to this issue that we now turn.

The Editorial Purpose of the Psalter. The detection and description of an editorial purpose for the psalter does not involve the attempt to explain how each individual psalm reached its current literary placement. There are relationships among several psalms that seem to form a coherent sequence or pattern, and these literary relationships need to be taken seriously as a context for theological interpretation. At the same time,

however, an interpretation must attempt not to force relationships or to read too much into patterns that may simply be coincidental. By no means can every psalm tied to an overarching editorial purpose, but rather the psalter in its final form often reflects the earlier shape of the smaller collections of which it is composed. Following Wilson's lead, editorial activity most likely took place at the "seams" of the psalter—that is, at the beginning or conclusion of the whole or of the various books.[29] Proceeding on this assumption, the interpreter of the whole psalter notices several patterns that seem too striking to be coincidental.

Books I–III (Psalms 1–89). The most striking observation about Books I–III is that royal psalms occur near the beginning of Book I (Psalm 2) and at the conclusion of Books II (Psalm 72) and III (Psalm 89). To be sure, the pattern would be even more striking if Psalm 41 were a royal psalm; but even so, it is impressive enough as Psalm 2 forms with Psalm 72 an envelope structure for Books I–II and with Psalm 89 an envelope structure for Books I–III. As Wilson points out, the progression from Psalms 2 to 72 to 89 is revealing. Psalm 2 establishes the intimate relationship between God and the Davidic king; Psalm 72 reinforces this relationship; and while Psalm 89 begins as a comprehensive rehearsal of all the features of this relationship (vv. 1-37), it concludes with a wrenching description of God's rejection of the covenant with David (vv. 38-45) and with the pained, poignant prayer of the spurned anointed one (vv. 45-51). As Wilson concludes concerning the effect of this progression, "The Davidic covenant introduced in Psalm 2 has come to nothing and the combination of these books concludes with the anguished cry of the Davidic descendants."[30] In other words, Books I–III document the failure of the Davidic covenant—at least as traditionally understood—that was made evident by the destruction of Jerusalem in 587 BCE and the subsequent exile. Thus Books I–III call out for a response, and, according to Wilson, this response is offered by the proclamation of God's reign, which is prominent in Books IV–V.

Before considering Books IV–V in detail, however, it should be noted that the opening psalms of Books II–III already begin both to anticipate the crisis of exile that is fully articulated in Psalm 89 and to point toward a constructive response.

Again, a strikingly similar pattern exists between Books II and III. Not only does each of these books conclude with royal psalms, but also each begins with psalms in which an individual voice expresses deep alienation from God and God's place (Psalms 42–43; 73). In each case, these opening psalms are followed by communal laments that are strongly reminiscent of the destruction of Jerusalem and the exile (Psalms 44; 74). Furthermore, impressive verbal links exist between Psalms 42–43 and 44 and between Psalms 73 and 74. The effect is to provide a corporate orientation and context for hearing Psalms 42–43; 73 as well as other individual expressions of opposition and defeat in Books II–III. Such expressions predominate in Book II (see Psalms 51–71). They occur also in Book III (see Psalms 86; 88), although Book III is actually pervaded by communal laments (Psalms 74; 79; 80; 83; 89:38-51), which suggests that the whole book may have been decisively shaped by the experience of exile. In any case, the opening psalms of Books II–III effectively instruct the community to face exile (Psalms 44; 74) with "Hope in God" (Pss 42:5, 11; 43:5) and with the assurance that "God is the strength of my heart and my portion forever" (Ps 73:26 NRSV).[31]

Although not exactly the same as the opening of Books II and III, a similar pattern creates the same effect at the beginning of Book I. Psalm 1 states the problem of the wicked and the righteous in individual terms, and then Psalm 2 states the same problem in corporate terms. Like Psalms 42–44 and 73–74, Psalms 1 and 2 are connected by significant verbal links. Although, unlike Psalms 44 and 74, Psalm 2 is a royal psalm, it does feature a problem that was preeminent in the exilic and postexilic eras: the reality and continuing threat of the domination of Israel by the nations. By portraying God as judge of the wicked (Ps 1:4-6) and ruler of the nations (Psalm 2), Psalms 1–2 affirm the possibility of hope amid the hard realities of the exilic and postexilic eras. By standing at the head of Book I (and the whole psalter; see further below), Psalms 1 and 2 provide a literary context for hearing Psalms 3–41. As in the case of Book II, the shape of Book I suggests that the laments of an individual, which heavily dominate Book I, may be heard also as expressions of communal plight. In short, the final form serves to instruct the community to face crises in the same manner as the "I" of

the laments, who always accompanies the articulation of distress with expressions of trust and praise (see above on the laments of an individual).

Because the laments of an individual are so numerous in Book I, psalms of other types are quite noticeable (see Psalms 8; 15; 19; 24; 29; 33; 37). It may be that these other psalms have been placed intentionally between small collections of laments.[32] In any case, however, the juxtaposition of complaint and praise both within a single psalm and between psalms is theologically significant.

In view of the foregoing discussion of Books I–III and in anticipation of the consideration of Books IV–V, it is necessary to define further what is meant here by reference to the exile. To be sure, the exile was a historical event that began with the deportation of Judeans to Babylon in 597 BCE, continued with the destruction of Jerusalem in 587 by the Babylonians, and lasted until 539 when Cyrus permitted the Judean exiles in Babylon to return to Palestine. But in a broader sense, the exile was a theological problem, and it represented an ongoing theological crisis well beyond 539. The destruction of Jerusalem and the deportation to Babylon meant that the people of God lost their three most fundamental and cherished religious institutions: the Temple, the land, and the monarchy. To say that this loss precipitated a crisis is an understatement. Although some of the exiles returned to Palestine after 539, and although the Temple was rebuilt by 515, things were never really the same as before. National autonomy was never achieved again except briefly in the second century BCE. Furthermore, the Davidic monarchy was never reestablished. The Davidic king had been viewed as nothing less than God's own adopted son (see Ps 2:7), and the monarchy represented theologically the concrete embodiment of God's purposes on earth (see Psalm 72). The loss of the monarchy was thus an ongoing theological crisis that made it necessary for the people of God to come to a new understanding of God and of their existence under God. When this introduction refers to the exile, it means primarily not the historical event but the ongoing theological crisis.[33] Because this theological crisis persisted for centuries, the fact that we cannot precisely date the final formation of the psalter is not of crucial significance. The Hebrew psalter may have taken final form in the fourth to third centuries BCE, as many scholars suggest; however, the manuscript evidence from Qumran complicates this conclusion, since it suggests the fluidity of Books IV–V into the second century BCE or beyond.[34] But even if the psalter did not take final form until the first century CE, its shape can still be understood as a response to the exile in the sense of an ongoing theological crisis. This crisis called for new understandings of God and of human faithfulness to God. The shape of the psalter indicates that its editors intended the psalms to participate in the theological dialogue that resulted in new perspectives on both divine and human sovereignty and suffering (see further below on "The Theology of the Psalms").

Books IV–V (Psalms 90–150). The anguished questions of the Davidic descendants (Ps 89:46; 49) cry out for a response, and a fitting answer is provided by Psalm 90 and the subsequent psalms in Book IV—namely, Israel's true home is, always has been, and always will be God alone (Ps 90:1-2). There is, of course, no better voice to deliver this assurance than that of Moses, whose intimate experience of God and leadership of the people occurred before there ever was a temple or a monarchy and before entry into the land! Not coincidentally, the superscription of Psalm 90 is the only one to bear the name of Moses, and seven of the eight references to Moses in Psalms occur in Book IV.[35]

Furthermore, Book IV affirms that Israel's true monarch is not the Davidic king but Yahweh—again, the way it was in Moses' time (see Exod 15:18) and before the monarchy (see 1 Samuel 8). This affirmation is found explicitly in Book IV in the so-called enthronement psalms (Psalms 93; 95–99), a collection that dominates Book IV and that Wilson properly called "the theological 'heart'" of the psalter.[36] While it appears at first sight that Psalm 94 is an intrusion into this collection, it has significant thematic parallels with the enthronement psalms. This fact, plus the verbal links between Psalms 92 and 94, suggest that the placement of Psalm 94 may be intended to bind the enthronement collection more closely to Psalms 90–92, which also share significant verbal links .[37] It may also be more than coincidental that Psalms 95 and 100 are similar (cf. 95:7 and 100:3) and that they form a frame around Psalms 96–99. Furthermore, Psalm 100 recalls Psalm 2, since 2:11 and 100:2 are the only two occurrences in the psalter of the imperative, "Serve

the LORD" (NIV and NRSV "Worship" in 100:2). That the theological heart of the psalter recalls its beginning may be a coincidence, but if so, it is an auspicious one that reinforces the psalter's pervasive proclamation of God's sovereignty (see further on "The Theology of the Psalms").

The intent of Book IV to address the crisis of exile helps to explain the placement of Psalms 101–102, which have proven extremely enigmatic in the light of earlier approaches. If Psalm 89 has documented the failure of the Davidic monarchy, for instance, why is a royal psalm like Psalm 101 in Book IV at all? While absolute certainty is elusive, it is crucial to note that when 101:2 is not emended (cf. the NIV with the NRSV), Psalm 101 can be reasonably read as a royal lament. In view of the concluding verses of Psalm 89 (see above), the placement of this royal complaint makes perfect sense. As a lament out of the experience of exile, Psalm 101 also anticipates Psalm 102, vv. 12-17 of which have baffled commentators, since these verses represent a corporate profession out of exile following an apparently individual prayer in vv. 1-11. But together, Psalms 101–102 rehearse the three crucial elements of the crisis of exile: loss of monarchy, Zion/Temple, and land. Fittingly, and congruent with the move from Psalms 89 to 90, Psalm 103 returns the reader to a Mosaic perspective, even though it is labeled "Of David." Not surprisingly, Book IV ends with a historical review, which concludes with the exile (Ps 106:40-46) and the people's plea to be gathered "from among the nations" (Ps 106:47).

In view of the sevenfold occurrence of the Hebrew word for "steadfast love" (חֶסֶד ḥesed, NRSV) in Psalm 89, culminating in the question of v. 49 ("Lord, where is your steadfast love of old . . . ?" [NRSV]), it is significant that Ps 90:14 prays for God's steadfast love and that Psalm 106 features this word as well (see vv. 1, 7, 45). Furthermore, Psalm 103, which follows immediately the two psalms in Book IV that most clearly articulate the pain of exile (see above on Psalms 101–102), contains four occurrences of the word (vv. 4, 8, 11, 17; see also Pss 92:2; 94:18; 98:3; 100:5). What is more, the six occurrences of the word in Psalm 107, the opening psalm of Book V, suggest that Book V picks up where Book IV left off—that is, it continues the response to the crisis of exile (cf. also Pss 106:47 and 107:2-3). Indeed, Psalm

107 can properly be considered a sermon on God's steadfast love that sounds as if it could have been written in response to Ps 89:49. Psalms 108 (v. 3) and 109 (vv. 21, 26) continue the focus on God's steadfast love, and the opening verse of Psalm 107 reappears as the first and last verses of Psalm 118. While Psalms 113–118 are a traditional liturgical unit within Judaism, the literary connections between Psalms 107 and 118 (107:1; 118:1, 29) suggest that Psalms 107–118 may form a redactional unit within Book V. Psalms 107 and 118 both recall the exodus, but the language is also appropriate for describing the return from exile. Significant in this regard, however, Psalm 118 moves toward a petition for continuing help (see v. 25). In short, even after the historical return from exile (see Pss 107:2-3; 118:21-24), the crisis persisted, and the shape of Book V continues the psalter's response.

The imposing Psalm 119, for instance, whenever it may have originated, admirably articulates the experience of the post-exilic generations. While the psalmist is faithful to God and God's instruction, he or she nonetheless is scorned and persecuted and so must live in waiting as a suffering servant—just like the post-exilic generations. This perspective is "eschatological," since it involves the proclamation of God's reign amid circumstances that seem to deny and belie it—that is, it leaves the people simultaneously celebrating and awaiting God's reign (see below on "The Theology of the Psalms").

This same eschatological perspective characterizes the movement of the Songs of Ascents (Psalms 120–134) and is particularly evident in Psalm 126. Not surprisingly, the final three psalms (135–137), which form a sort of appendix to the Songs of Ascents, are the most explicit statement in the psalter of the pain of exile. Psalms 135–137 are the prelude to a final Davidic collection, the first and last psalms of which return to the theme of God's steadfast love, which is prominent at key points in Books IV–V (see Pss 138:2, 8; 145:8; see above on Psalms 89; 90; 106; 107; 118). The core of this collection consists of psalms of lament, culminating in Psalm 144, which is a royal lament. Thus, near the end of both Books IV and V, there are royal laments (see above on Psalm 101) that effectively call to mind the ongoing theological crisis of exile. Significantly, Psalm 145 responds to

Psalm 144 by affirming God's steadfast love, just as Psalm 103 had responded to Psalms 101–102 (see Pss 103:8; 145:8). Of further significance, Psalm 145 begins by addressing God as "King," thus also recalling Psalms 93; 95–99, the dominant collection of Book IV and the theological heart of the psalter.

Actually, Psalm 145 proves to be transitional. Not only does it conclude the Davidic collection, forming with Psalm 138 an envelope of praise around a core of laments, but it also anticipates Psalms 146–150. Each psalm in this concluding collection is bounded by "Praise the LORD [הַלְלוּ־יָהּ *hallelu-yah*]!" The psalter's final invitation to praise (150:6) has been anticipated by 145:21. Furthermore, the explicit proclamation of God's sovereignty, reintroduced in Ps 145:1, recurs in Pss 146:10 and 149:2, thus recalling the theological heart of the psalter and its beginning as well. More particularly, Ps 149:6-9 features the same cast of characters present in Psalm 2: the rebellious "nations" and "peoples" and "kings." In contrast to Psalm 2, however, Psalm 149 assigns to the "faithful" (see vv. 1, 5, 9)—*not* to the Davidic king as in Psalm 2—the task of concretely implementing God's reign in the world. Thus Psalm 149 completes a direction that was initiated earlier in Books IV–V and that is another piece of the psalter's response to the crisis of exile—namely, the transfer to the whole people of claims and promises formerly attached to the Davidic monarchy. The literary and conceptual links and contrasts between Psalms 2 and 149 are another reminder of the crucial significance of Psalms 1–2, and further consideration of their role is necessary.

Psalms 1–2 as an Introduction to the Psalter. As already suggested, Psalms 1–2 are a fitting introduction to Books I and to Books I–III as a unit. As the psalter progresses, however, it becomes increasingly clear that Psalms 1–2 have set the interpretive agenda and provided an orientation for reading the whole book of Psalms. Scholars have traditionally concluded that Psalm 1 represents an intentional preface or introduction to the psalter, but the introductory function clearly belongs to Psalms 1 and 2 together. Neither psalm has a superscription, and they are bound by several literary links, including the crucial word translated "happy" (אַשְׁרֵי *'ašrê*), which forms an envelope structure (Pss 1:1; 2:12).

Psalm 1 portrays happiness as constant openness to God's "instruction" (v. 2; NIV and NRSV "law"), the fundamental orientation of life to God. The repetition of "instruction" (תורה *tôrâ*) is emphatic and suggests that the book of Psalms itself will serve as a source of divine instruction. While Psalm 1 counsels the reader to be open to God's instruction, including the subsequent psalms, Psalm 2 introduces the basic content of that instruction—namely, that God rules the world. Although the role of the Davidic monarch as an agent of God's rule will change as the psalter proceeds (see above), nothing will alter the pervasive proclamation of God's reign, which is first articulated in Ps 2:11-12. Thus happiness essentially belongs to those who "take refuge in" *God* (Ps 2:12), *not* in the Davidic monarch! In short, happiness is essentially trusting God, living in dependence upon God, an affirmation to which the conclusion of the psalter will return (see Ps 146:5). As Psalms 1 and 2 already make clear, and as subsequent psalms will clarify even further, the rule of God is persistently opposed. Thus the perspective of the psalter from the beginning is eschatological—that is, God's reign is proclaimed as a present reality, but it is always experienced by the faithful amid opposition. In this sense, the faithful live both with fulfillment and in waiting (see below, "The Theology of the Psalms").

Beyond Psalms 1 and 2, the rest of the psalter will portray the shape of the faithful life—including what it looks like and feels like and leads people to say and do—and it will reveal how the faithful life constitutes happiness. The portrayal of the faithful life is congruent with the portrayal of the character of God in Psalms, and both portrayals constitute a profoundly important revelation about the nature of divine sovereignty. In other words, while the book of Psalms originated as liturgical responses to God, it has been preserved and transmitted as God's word to humanity. As such, it not only represents a theological resource for dealing with the crisis of exile, but is also a theological resource for the people of God in every generation.

Methodological Conclusion. To be sure, it is theologically significant that Israel sang songs of praise to God, addressed honest and heartfelt prayers to God, and composed sacred poetry either addressed to or devoted to God. As traditionally practiced, however, form criticism and rhetorical

criticism have not yielded theological conclusions. It is sustained attention to the shaping and final form of the psalter that pushes the interpreter toward theological interpretation. Klaus Seybold summarizes well the purpose of the psalter in its final form:

> With the new preface ([Psalm] 1) and the weight of the reflexive proverbial poem ([Psalm] 119), which in terms of its range is effectively a small collection in itself, the existing Psalter now takes on the character of a documentation of divine revelation, to be used in a way analogous to the Torah, the first part of the canon, and becomes an instruction manual for the theological study of the divine order of salvation, and for meditation.[38]

As a theological instruction manual that aims at nothing less than the "documentation of divine revelation," the psalter in its final form demands to be interpreted theologically. Thus, while form criticism and rhetorical criticism will regularly be employed to arrive at historical, sociological, and literary conclusions, the ultimate purpose in the commentary is "to compose a commentary based on the book itself as the interpretive context of the psalms."[39] In short, I shall attempt to discern how the psalter was for Israel and is for us "an instruction manual for the theological study of the divine order of salvation"—in other words, what the psalter reveals about the life of God and the life God intends for humankind and for the world.

THE THEOLOGY OF THE PSALMS

Given the importance of the final form of the psalter, it is necessary to begin a consideration of the theology of the psalms with Psalms 1–2; even more specifically, with the very first word of the psalter: "Happy" (NRSV). In a real sense, the rest of the psalter will portray the shape of human happiness, and it is clear from the beginning and throughout Psalms that the definition of human happiness is thoroughly God-centered. The "happy" are those who constantly delight in God's "instruction" (תורה *tôrâ*, Ps 1:2; NIV and NRSV, "law"). In short, happiness derives from the complete orientation of life to God, including perpetual openness to God's instruction. Not only does Ps 1:2 have the effect of orienting the reader to approach the rest of the psalter as Scripture, as "an instruction manual for the theological study of the divine order of salvation" (see Seybold quotation above), but it also introduces a key concept—happiness—and begins to give it a thoroughly theocentric definition. Not surprisingly, the word for "happy" (אַשְׁרֵי *'ašrê*) will occur throughout Book I and the rest of the psalter, including as soon as the conclusion of Psalm 2 (see also Pss 32:1-2; 33:12; 34:8; 40:4; 41:4; 65:4; 84:4-5, 12; 89:15; 94:12; 106:3; 112:1; 119:1-2; 127:5; 128:1; 137:8-9; 144:15; 146:5).

Psalm 2:12 begins to fill out the portrait of the happy person, and it does so by introducing another key word that will also occur throughout Book I and the rest of the psalter: "refuge" (חסה *ḥāsâ*; see Pss 5:12; 7:1; 11:1; 14:6; 16:1; 18:30; 25:20; 31:1, 19; 34:8, 22; 36:7; 37:40; 46:1; 57:1; 61:3-4; 62:7-8; 64:10; 71:1, 17; 73:28; 91:2, 4, 9; 94:22; 118:8-9; 141:8; 142:5; 144:2). The happy are those who "take refuge in" God. In short, happiness derives from living in complete dependence upon God rather than upon the self. The word *ḥāsâ* has several synonyms that also occur frequently throughout the psalms (variously translated as "refuge," "fortress," "stronghold"), the most important of which is "trust" (see Pss 4:5; 9:10; 13:5; 21:7; 22:4-6; 25:2; 26:1; 28:7; 31:6, 14; 32:10; 37:3, 5; 40:3; 52:8; 55:23; 56:3-4, 11; 62:8; 84:12; 86:2; 91:2; 115:9-11; 125:1; 143:8). To be happy is to entrust one's whole self, existence, and future to God. As one would expect, there are several instances in which the words for "refuge" and "trust" occur in the same context (see Pss 31:1, 4, 6, 14, 19; 52:7-8; 62:7-8; 71:1, 3, 5; 91:2, 4, 9; 143:8-9); in addition to 2:12, the word "happy" is associated with either "refuge" or "trust" in Pss 34:8; 84:12; and 146:3, 5. Not surprisingly too, several of the occurrences of *ḥāsâ* or related words occur at key places in the psalter (see Pss 2:12; 91:2, 4, 9; 146:3, 5). Indeed, Jerome F. D. Creach argues that the editors of the psalter intended by the placement of certain psalms to call particular attention to the word *ḥāsâ* and related words.[40] In any case, whether intentional or not, the sheer repetition of "refuge," "trust," and several other synonyms effectively portrays the happy, faithful life as one characterized by complete dependence upon God.

This fundamental dependence upon God for life and future defines another key word in Psalms, at least insofar as it applies to human beings: "right-eousness" (צדק *ṣĕdeq*) or "the righteous" (צדיק *ṣaddîq*). "Righteousness" is not primarily a moral category but a relational term. To be sure, behavior follows from one's commitments, but the righteous in the psalms should not be seen as morally superior persons whose good behavior lays an obligation on God to reward them. Rather, the righteous are persons who acknowledge their fundamental dependence upon God for life and future. Their happiness derives ultimately from God's forgiveness (see Ps 32:1-2) and the gift of God's faithful love (see Ps 32:10-11). In short, the happy, the righteous, are those who live by grace. As is evident from Psalm 1 onward, the righteous live constantly in the presence of the wicked, who are also called "scoffers," "sinners," "enemies," "foes," "adversaries," etc. As follows from the above definition of the righteous, the wicked are not outrageously or even obviously bad people, but are persons who live in fundamental dependence upon the self rather than upon God. In short, the wicked are persons who consider themselves to be autonomous, which means literally "a law unto oneself." Self-centered, self-directed, and self-ruled, the wicked see no need for dependence upon God or for consideration of others. The really frightening thing about this conclusion is that the essence of wickedness in the psalms—autonomy—is often what North American culture promotes as the highest virtue.

The definitions of "happiness" and "righteousness" in terms of refuge, the fundamental dependence upon God for life and future, makes sense only in the light of the affirmation that lies at what has been identified as the theological heart of the psalter: the Lord reigns (Psalms 93–99)! Indeed, this affirmation pervades the psalter. God is frequently addressed as "King" (see Pss 5:2; 10:16; 24:7-10; 29:10; 44:4; 47:2, 7; 48:2; 68:24; 74:12; 84:3; 95:3; 98:6; 145:1; 149:2), but even when the language of kingship and reigning is not explicitly present, God's rule is articulated by means of other words and concepts. For instance, God's role as universal judge is a function of God's cosmic sovereignty (see Pss 7:7-11; 9:7-8), as is God's role as the divine warrior who enacts the divine will for the world (see Pss 24:8; 68:1-3; 89:5-18).

Furthermore, the royal psalms, which are scattered throughout the psalter, located in strategic places (see above, "Royal Psalms"), serve to articulate God's sovereignty. To be sure, these psalms focus directly on the earthly kings of Israel and Judah, but the earthly kings are presented as agents of God's rule. Psalm 2, for instance, culminates not in an invitation to serve the earthly king but to "Serve the LORD" (v. 11 NRSV). God's reign involves the enactment of justice and righteousness among all people (see Pss 96:10-13; 97:1-2; 98:4-9), and it is precisely the mission of the earthly king as God's agent to embody justice and righteousness on a cosmic scale (see Psalm 72). In this way, too, the royal psalms articulate God's sovereign claim on the whole world.

Even the songs of Zion, although they focus on a very particular place, are finally affirmations of God's universal reign. Psalms 46 and 48, for instance, surround Psalm 47, which explicitly celebrates God's kingship. Not surprisingly, both Psalms 46 and 48 portray God in the role of a warrior who wages peace (see also Ps 76:4-9), and Psalm 48 addresses God as "King" and describes the effect of God's worldwide involvement as "righteousness" (v. 10 NIV) and justice (v. 11; cf. "judgments" in NIV and NRSV; see Ps 122:5). In short, a particular place, Jerusalem, has become a concrete symbol of the extension of God's rule in all places and times. God claims the whole world and all its peoples (see Psalm 87).

At the same time that they affirm God's cosmic reign, however, the royal psalms and songs of Zion also make it clear that God's rule is constantly and pervasively opposed. As the psalter begins, the nations and peoples are aligned against God and God's chosen king (Ps 2:1-3). Jerusalem is regularly the target of attack (see Pss 46:6; 48:5; 76:3-6). This apparent anomaly—constant and powerful opposition to the cosmic rule of God—calls attention to a crucial characteristic of the psalter that I refer to as its *eschatological* perspective. Because this word may be subject to misunderstanding, it needs to be carefully defined. By *eschatological*, I mean the proclamation of God's universal reign amid circumstances that seem to deny it and belie it. The word *eschatological* literally means "a word about last things," and it is popularly perceived as having to do primarily with the future. But the word focuses attention on the *present*. That is, the psalms regularly affirm God's reign as a *present* reality. To be sure, the reality of opposition implies the future consummation of God's reign, but the emphasis in the psalms is clearly on the

presence of God's reign as the only true source of refuge, happiness, and, indeed, life.

While the eschatological perspective of the psalter is clear enough from Psalm 2, the movement from Psalm 2 to Psalm 3 makes it clear that not only are God's chosen king and God's chosen place constantly opposed, but so also are God's people. In other words, happiness (Pss 1:1; 2:12), prosperity (Ps 1:3), and refuge (Ps 2:12) exist not beyond but rather in the midst of opposition and suffering. Consequently, in addition to "the righteous" and synonyms such as "the upright," the most frequent designations the psalmists use for themselves include "the poor," "the afflicted," "the meek," "the humble," "the needy," "the helpless," and "the oppressed" (see Psalms 9–10). Not surprisingly, therefore, the dominant voice in the psalter is that of prayer. Indeed, prayer is a way of life for those who entrust themselves fully to God's care. Prayer is the offering of the whole self to God, including pain, grief, fear, loneliness, and sinfulness as well as expressions of innocence and desire for vengeance (which in the final form of the psalter are to be understood as pleas for justice; see Psalms 58; 109; 137).

Although prayer and praise are usually treated as separate voices involving distinct categories of psalms (that is, laments/complaints and songs of praise; see above on form criticism), it is of crucial theological significance to notice that prayer and praise are finally inseparable. Almost without exception, each prayer for help moves toward expressions of trust and praise. Furthermore, Books I–III, the portions of the psalter dominated by laments, include songs of praise at regular intervals, that are often linked verbally to the preceding prayer as if to remind the reader of the inseparability of prayer and praise. Thus, while laments and songs of praise may have represented in ancient Israel separate liturgical movements or moments, their regular juxtaposition within the same psalm and in the final arrangement of the psalter suggests theological connections. The juxtaposition prevents the conclusion that the songs of praise represent merely the ideology of the rich and powerful that is used to celebrate the status quo.[41] To state it positively, the juxtaposition means that for the faithful, suffering and glory are inseparable. In explicitly Christian terms, the people of God are inevitably and always identified by *both* the cross and the resurrection.

When construed as ultimately inseparable voices, both prayer and praise are means of expressing complete dependence upon God. While prayer is the offering of the whole self to God by way of direct address to God involving bitter complaint, brutally honest confession of sin or innocence, and poignant petition and intercession, praise is the offering of the whole self to God by way of joyful affirmation of God's sovereignty, enthusiastic celebration of God's character and activity, and direct address to others to invite them to join in the song. Praise affirms a simple but profound good news—namely, that the whole cosmos and all its peoples, creatures, and things belong to God. This good news has extraordinary political, socioeconomic, and ecological implications.

Because our lives belong to God, we are not our own. Thus the autonomy that much of North American culture promotes is a dead end; it will lead only to a society of isolated selves rather than to the community of justice and righteousness that God wills among all people.

Because our lives belong to God, and because God wills life for all people, "justice for all" becomes far more than a phrase out of a pledge or a matter of democratic fairness. Rather, "justice for all" means that God wills political and economic systems that exclude *no one* from access to provision for life and future; God will be content with nothing less than peace on earth. Because God wills life for the whole creation as well as for all people, ecological awareness becomes not simply a matter of preserving limited natural resources in order to maintain for ourselves and our children the standard of living to which we have grown accustomed. Rather, ecology and theology are inseparable. To live under God's rule is to live in partnership with all other species of creature and in partnership with the earth itself.

The psalter's eschatological character has profound significance for understanding the fundamental identity of both humanity and God. As for humanity, the psalms teach us that human happiness—indeed, authentic human life—exists only when people acknowledge God's reign and respond by taking refuge in God. Because God's reign is constantly opposed by humans, however, happiness and life inevitably involve suffering. Therefore, the faithful, righteous life consists of suffering servanthood.

As for God, the reality of constant opposition to God's reign calls for an understanding of divine sovereignty that differs from the usual view of sovereignty. Sovereignty is ordinarily thought of as the power to enforce one's will. But God simply does not do this. Rather, God invites, encourages, and empowers people to do God's will. But from the very beginning of the biblical story, people have chosen *not* to do God's will (see Genesis 3). God's only choice is either to enforce the divine will, which will mean the destruction of humanity, or to suffer the consequences of human disobedience (see Genesis 6–9). God chooses the latter, and it is a monumentally important choice, for it means that God willingly becomes vulnerable for the sake of relating genuinely to humankind. Terence Fretheim calls God's choice "a divine *kenosis*, a self-emptying, an act of self-sacrifice," and he concludes, "The very act of creation thus might be called the beginning of the passion of God."[42] In other words, God suffers, too, and it is necessary to conclude that divine sovereignty consists not of sheer force but of sheer love. The eschatological perspective of the psalter—the proclamation of God's reign amid persistent opposition—reinforces the conclusion that God's power is essentially that of pure, unbounded love. God's life, too, consists of suffering servanthood!

This being the case, it is not an exaggeration to say that the most important theological concept in the book of Psalms is represented by the Hebrew word חסד (*ḥesed*), which the NIV often translates as "unfailing love" and the NRSV regularly translates as "steadfast love." It occurs as early as Ps 5:7 and frequently thereafter in all five books of the psalter, often in crucially placed psalms (see Psalms 42; 89; 90; 106; 107; 118; 138; 145). Its range is not restricted to a particular type. Rather, Israel appeals to God's *ḥesed* in prayer, and Israel celebrates God's *ḥesed* in songs of praise (see Psalms 33; 100; 103; 136; 145; 147). Indeed, the opening line of several psalms constitutes a brief hymn in itself as it celebrates God's *ḥesed* (see Pss 107:1; 118:1; 136:1; cf. 100:5; 113:2), and this formulation appears to have functioned as a sort of "favorite hymn," which also has the character of a basic profession of faith (see 2 Chr 5:13; 7:3; 20:21; Ezra 3:11).

Given that the final form of the psalter has the character of "instruction" (*tôrâ* ; see above), it is not surprising that the importance of *hesed* in the psalms matches its importance in the Pentateuch, the Torah. At a crucial turning point when the future of Israel hangs in the balance, God reveals Godself to be "merciful and gracious, slow to anger, and abounding in steadfast love and faithfulness" (Exod 34:6 NRSV). In fact, this or a very similar formulation occurs several more times in the Pentateuch and beyond; it seems to constitute a basic profession of Israel's faith (see Num 14:18; Neh 9:17; Joel 2:13; Jonah 4:2). Not unexpectedly, it also occurs in the psalms (see Pss 86:15; 103:8; 145:8). The other terms in the formulation of Exod 34:6 are also important in the psalms. The NRSV's "merciful" (רחום *rahûm*) is from the same root as a noun that means "womb" (רחם *rhm*); thus it conveys God's motherly compassion (see also Pss 25:6; 40:11; 51:1; 69:16; 79:8; 106:45; 111:4). The word "gracious" (חנון *hanûn*) is regularly paired with "merciful" (*rahûm*), and another form of the root indicates that God's grace is the basis for appeals to God for help (e.g., see "Be gracious" in Pss 4:1; 6:2). The words "faithfulness" (אמת *'emet*) and "steadfast love" (*hesed*) are paired frequently in the psalms as in Exod 34:6 (see Pss 25:10; 36:5; 40:10-11; 57:3; 61:7; 85:10; 89:14; 117:2). The word "faithfulness" occurs alone as well (see Pss 54:5; 71:22; 91:4; 143:1), but the word *hesed* appears more frequently and serves virtually as a one-word summary of Israel's understanding of the character of God.

That God is fundamentally compassionate, gracious, faithful, and loving does not mean that anything goes with God. From the beginning, the psalter recognizes the wrath of God (see Ps 2:5, 12). The psalmists appeal to God's wrath against their enemies (Pss 56:7; 59:13), and they are aware of experiencing God's wrath (Pss 6:1; 38:1; 78:59, 62; 88:7, 16; 89:38, 46; 90:7, 9, 11). Again, this picture is consistent with Exodus 34, where God's self-revelation as *hesed* (v. 6) is followed closely by the statement that God "does not leave the guilty unpunished" (v. 7 NIV). But how can God be both loving and wrathful, gracious and just, forgiving and punishing? The question is not easily answered for us—or for God! Indeed, this very dilemma is the inevitable result of God's choice to love a sinful humanity, and it bespeaks God's willingness to be vulnerable and to suffer for love's sake. What we can say is that retribution is clearly not operative as a mechanistic scheme. Rather, reward is the experience of authentic life in dependence upon God, and punishment is the inevitable outcome of the choice not to be related to God. The book of Psalms affirms that evil will not endure (see Psalm 1). But given Israel's awareness of its own sinfulness (see Psalms 32; 51; 78; 106; 130) and the sinfulness of all humanity (see Psalms 1–2; 14; 143), one must finally conclude that God's justice is ultimately manifest as love. For Christian readers, the psalter's presentation of the mystery of sovereignty made perfect in steadfast love comes into sharpest focus on the cross of Jesus Christ.

THE PSALMS AND THE NEW TESTAMENT

The early church's use of the psalms was in keeping with both major directions suggested by recent scholarly study of the book of Psalms—that is, the church used the psalms both as liturgical materials in early Christian worship and as a theological resource. Evidence for the first use is found in Paul's advice to the Colossians to "sing psalms, hymns, and spiritual songs to God" (3:16 NRSV; see also Eph 5:19). Although it is not clear precisely what each of these three terms designates, it is almost certain that "psalms" (and perhaps "hymns") refers to material from the book of Psalms. After all, the earliest followers of Jesus were Jews, so it only makes sense that they would continue to use in worship some of the same materials they had always used. To be sure, new materials were used in Christian worship as well, and it is likely that "spiritual songs" refers explicitly to Christian material that may have been created with inspiration from the psalms. For instance, Mary's Song (Luke 1:46-55) contains echoes of Psalms 98 and 113, and the Song of Simeon (Luke 2:28-32) echoes Ps 119:123.

While it is likely that the early Christians prayed and sang the psalms, it is absolutely clear that they used the psalms as a theological resource. The book of Psalms is quoted and alluded to in the NT more than any other OT book. This is not at all surprising in view of the fact that the theology of the psalms is congruent with the core of Jesus' preaching and teaching. What was identified earlier as the theological heart of the psalter—God reigns—is precisely the fundamental good news that Jesus announced from the beginning of his public ministry (see Mark

1:14-15). Jesus proclaimed the reign of God as a present reality, and he invited people to enter it and experience it immediately. Thus Jesus' preaching was eschatological in the sense in which this term was defined—that is, he proclaimed the reign of God amid constant opposition. This persistent opposition meant that Jesus' own life, as well as the lives of his followers and of those to whom his ministry was most often directed, may be characterized in the same terms that regularly describe the psalmists: *afflicted, oppressed, poor, needy, weak, meek,* and *persecuted.* But like the psalms, it is precisely the afflicted whom Jesus pronounces "Happy" or "Blessed" (see Matt 5:1-11; Luke 6:20-23).

In short, like the psalms, Jesus' ministry of suffering servanthood pushes toward a radical redefinition of the usual understanding of sovereignty. Sovereignty is not the demonstration of sheer power but the embodiment of sheer love, which ultimately is revealed to be the most powerful reality of all. The gracious, incarnational involvement of God with humanity, already evident in the psalms (and elsewhere in the OT), is, from the Christian perspective, completed in Jesus' ministry of suffering servanthood. Thus, in reflecting on Jesus' identity, the early Christians concluded that Jesus was nothing less than God incarnate, "the Word became flesh and lived among us" (John 1:14 NRSV). Because Jesus had fully revealed what God is like, thus fulfilling the role of the ancient kings of Judah and Israel to enact God's justice and righteousness, the early church saw in Jesus the culmination of the monarchical ideal. Thus they accorded Jesus the royal titles "anointed" (מָשִׁיחַ *māšîah*; Χριστός *Christos* ; see Ps 2:4; Mark 1:1) and Son of God (see Mark 1:1; Ps 2:7). The cross, far from being a sign of defeat, was the clearest demonstration of God's character and sovereignty. The resurrection did not remove the scandal of the cross but instead validated its revelation that the power of sheer love is the only authentic source of life. Thus Jesus' invitation to discipleship is essentially an invitation for people to share his ministry of suffering servanthood: "let them deny themselves and take up their cross and follow me" (Mark 8:34 NRSV). The lives of Jesus' followers, like Jesus' own life, will replicate the lives of the psalmists, who are pronounced "happy" not beyond but in the midst of their constant affliction.

Given the congruence between the portrayal of God and the faithful life in the psalms and by Jesus,

it is not surprising that the Gospel writers cannot tell the story of Jesus without frequently referring or alluding to a psalm. For instance, the words of the heavenly beings in Luke's account of Jesus' birth recall the content and movement of Psalm 29, thus suggesting that Jesus' birth signals the presence of God's reign (see Luke 2:13-14). The heavenly voice at Jesus' baptism quotes a portion of Ps 2:7, thus introducing Jesus as the one who would ultimately embody God's will and finally fulfill the purpose of the monarchy (see Matt 3:17; Mark 1:11; Luke 3:22). Psalm 2:7 is cited again at Jesus' transfiguration, immediately after the first prediction of his passion in the synoptic Gospels (see Matt 17:5; Mark 9:7; Luke 9:35). The effect is to reinforce the message that Jesus will embody God's character and will do so precisely by way of his suffering servanthood.

This message is, of course, regularly reinforced as well by Jesus' ministry of compassion and his teaching (see Psalms 41; 126). But it is seen most clearly in Jesus' passion, and in telling this part of Jesus' story, the Gospel writers rely most heavily on the psalms. Jesus' entry into Jerusalem is narrated with reference to Psalm 118, thus suggesting that Jesus' upcoming passion is to be viewed in sequence with the exodus and return from exile, God's saving deeds of old (see Matt 21:9; Mark 11:9-10; Luke 19:38; John 12:12). The account of the crucifixion in all four Gospels has been shaped by Psalm 22, and in Matt 27:46 and Mark 15:34, the words Jesus speaks from the cross are a quotation of Ps 22:1. These words are not present in Luke and John, but Jesus' final words in Luke are a quotation of Ps 31:5 (Luke 23:46), and Jesus' final words in John seem also to allude to Ps 31:5 and perhaps to Ps 22:31 (John 19:30). The passion accounts have also been influenced by Psalm 69 (cf. Matt 27:48; Mark 15:36; John 19:28-29 with Ps 69:21; and Ps 69:4 with John 15:25). In short, the Gospel writers drew upon the three longest and most impressive of the laments of an individual in order to relate the story of Jesus' suffering (see also Psalms 38; 41). In other words, Jesus is presented as the ultimate paradigm of the faithful sufferer. What is more, it is precisely Jesus' faithful suffering on behalf of others that reveals what God is like. Thus, as suggested already, the cross is for Christians the ultimate revelation of the mystery the Psalms present—that is, divine sovereignty manifested as perfect love.

The paradox of strength made perfect in weakness (see 2 Cor 12:9), although "a stumbling block to Jews and foolishness to Gentiles" (1 Cor 1:23 NRSV), should not be misunderstood. God's strength—the power of sheer love—is *real* strength. As William Placher, citing Jürgen Moltmann's *The Crucified God*, puts it: "It would be a weak, poor God . . . who could not love or suffer. Such a God would be caught in a prison of impassability."[43] It is precisely the God revealed in Psalms and in Jesus Christ that is strong enough to be vulnerable. This apparent weakness turns out to be the greatest strength of all, as the resurrection of Jesus demonstrated. For us to understand properly the paradox of divine sovereignty, the cross and the resurrection must be inseparable, and the NT always presents them this way.[44] Indeed, the inseparability of cross and resurrection is analogous to the way in which lament and praise are finally inseparable in the psalms (see above). Given this analogy, it is appropriate that the resurrection as well as the crucifixion is proclaimed in the NT by way of the psalms. The first recorded Christian sermon—Peter's sermon on the Day of Pentecost—is based primarily on Pss 16:8-11; 110:1; and 132:11 (see Acts 8:25-34); Psalm 110 is often quoted or alluded to in articulating the glory of the crucified one (see 1 Cor 15:25; Eph 1:20; Col 3:1; Heb 1:3; 8:1; 10:12-13; 12:2).

The radical implications of Jesus' embodiment of God's sovereignty in suffering love were not lost on the apostle Paul. As Elsa Tamez points out, Jesus' proclamation of the reign of God becomes, in Pauline terms, justification by grace—or better yet, "the revelation of the justice of God."[45] As Jesus revealed and as Paul clearly understood, God's justice is ultimately manifested as grace. The traditional exposition of justification by faith as the forgiveness of sins is not incorrect, but it is not broad enough. The revelation of God's justice involves fundamentally the good news that God's gracious love extends to *all* people. God's justice means the affirmation of life for all people, not based on any system of human merit but as a result of God's loving gift. The message is again congruent with that of the psalms, and Paul appeals to the psalms to support his case. No human being can deserve God's gift of life (see Rom 3:9-20, where Paul cites several psalms, including 14:1-3; 143:2). The gift of divine forgiveness (see Rom 4:7-8, which cites Ps

32:1-2) means the leveling of all distinctions and human systems that exclude. This theology of divine justice revealed as gracious love—which Paul found in the psalms and which Jesus had embodied—led Paul to the radical step of casting aside sacred but exclusivistic symbols, such as circumcision and dietary regulations, in order to open the church to all people. It is appropriate that Paul found warrant for this step in the psalms (see Rom 15:9-11, which quotes Pss 89:49; 117:1).

It is appropriate that a final word about the psalms and the NT come from the Revelation to John. While direct quotation of the psalms is rare (see only Rev 2:26-27, which cites Ps 2:8-9), the Revelation is full of singing and songs that could well have been inspired by the psalter. The Revelation shares the psalter's fundamental conviction that God rules the world (see Rev 11:15; 12:10; 15:3), and the mention of "a new song" (Rev 5:9; 14:3) explicitly recalls Psalms 96; 98; and 149, all of which assert God's reign. It is particularly interesting that the Revelation, like Psalm 149, envisions God's people reigning with God in a redeemed world that includes "the healing of the nations" (Rev 22:1-5 NRSV; see also 2:26-27; 5:10; and cf. Ps 149:5-9). While the Revelation is usually classified as apocalyptic literature, it should not be construed as a timetable for the chronological end of the world. Rather, it portrays the future that God wills, which is possible because God rules the world, and which, indeed, becomes a present reality for those who acknowledge God's claim and enter God's realm of life. Insofar as it depicts the "end" or destiny of the world, it portrays the faithful gathered to God and singing a song that recalls Pss 86:9-10 and 145:17 (see Rev 15:3-4). As a vision of the "end," it might be beneficial for contemporary folk to hold this scenario alongside secular apocalyptic scenarios like nuclear winter, nuclear holocaust, or an earth laid waste by the radiation that enters through an atmosphere depleted of ozone. To be sure, such warnings should not be dismissed, although it is unlikely that we shall be frightened into reform. What will go further than anything else to prevent such catastrophes will be living toward a different vision, the biblical vision of faithful folk from all times and places, gathered, as the psalmists of old, to acknowledge God's reign by singing a new song.

FOR FURTHER READING

Commentaries:

Allen, Leslie C. *Psalms 101–150*. WBC 21. Waco: Word, 1983.

Bratcher, Robert G., and William D. Reyburn. *A Translator's Handbook on the Book of Psalms*. New York: United Bible Societies, 1991.

Brueggemann, Walter. *The Message of the Psalms: A Theological Commentary*. Minneapolis: Augsburg, 1984.

Clifford, Richard J. *Psalms 1-72*. Abingdon Old Testament Commentaries. Nashville, Abingdon, 2002.

———. *Psalms 73-150*. Abingdon Old Testament Commentaries. Nashville, Abingdon, 2003.

Craigie, Peter. *Psalms 1–50*. WBC 19. Waco: Word, 1983.

Gerstenberger, Erhard S. *Psalms: Part 1, with an Introduction to Cultic Poetry*. Forms of the OT Literature 14. Grand Rapids: Eerdmans, 1988.

Kraus, Hans-Joachim. *Psalms 1–59* and *Psalms 60–150*. Translated by H. C. Oswald. Minneapolis: Augsburg, 1988 and 1989.

Mays, James L. *Psalms*. Interpretation. Louisville: John Knox, 1994.

Schaeffer, Konrad R. *Psalms*. Berit Olam. Collegeville, Minn.: Liturgical Press, 2001.

Stulmueller, Carroll. *Psalms 1* and *Psalms 2*. OT Message 21 and 22. Wilmington, Del.: Michael Glazier, 1983.

Tate, Marvin E. *Psalms 51–100*. WBC 20. Dallas: Word, 1990.

Terrien, Samuel L. *The Psalms: Strophic Structure and Theological Commentary*. Eerdmans Critical Commnentary. Grand Rapids, Mich.: Eerdmans, 2003.

Weiser, Artur. *The Psalms*. Translated by H. Hartwell. OTL. Philadelphia: Westminster, 1962.

Westermann, Claus. *The Living Psalms*. Translated by J. R. Porter. Grand Rapids: Eerdmans, 1989.

Other Studies:

Bellinger, W. H., Jr. *Psalms: Reading and Studying the Book of Praises*. Peabody, Mass.: Hendrickson, 1990.

Brenner, Athalya, and Carole R. Fontaine, eds. *Wisdom and Psalms*. Feminist Companion to the Bible. Second Series 2. Sheffield: Sheffield Academic Press, 1998.

Brown, William P. *Seeing the Psalms: A Theology of Metaphor*. Louisville, Ky.: Westminster/John Knox Press, 2002.

Brueggemann, Walter. *Praying the Psalms*. Winona, Minn.: St. Mary's, 1982.

Gillingham, S. E. *The Poems and Psalms of the Hebrew Bible*. Oxford Bible Series. Oxford: Oxford University Press, 1994.

Gunkel, Hermann. *The Psalms: A Form-Critical Introduction*. Translated by T. M. Horner. FBBS 19. Philadelphia: Fortress, 1967.

Guthrie, Harvey H. *Israel's Sacred Songs: A Study of Dominant Themes*. New York: Seabury, 1966.

Holladay, William L. *The Psalms Through Three Thousand Years: Prayerbook of a Cloud of Witnesses*. Minneapolis: Fortress, 1993.

Hopkins, Denise Dombkowski. *Journey Through the Psalms*. Revised and Expanded Edition. St. Louis: Chalice Press, 2002.

Kraus, Hans-Joachim. *Theology of the Psalms*. Translated by Keith Crim. Minneapolis: Augsburg, 1986.

Levine, Herbert J. *Sing Unto God a New Song: A Contemporary Reading of the Psalms*. Bloomington: Indiana University Press, 1995.

Limburg, James. *Psalms for Sojourners*. Minneapolis: Augsburg, 1986.

McCann, J. Clinton, Jr. *A Theological Introduction to the Book of Psalms: The Psalms as Torah*. Nashville: Abingdon, 1993.

Mays, James L. *The Lord Reigns: A Theological Handbook to the Psalms*. Louisville: Westminster John Knox, 1994.

Miller, Patrick D., Jr. *Interpreting the Psalms*. Philadelphia: Fortress, 1986.

Mowinckel, Sigmund. *The Psalms in Israel's Worship*. Translated by D. R. Ap-Thomas. Nashville: Abingdon, 1962.

Nowell, Irene. *Sing a New Song: The Psalms in the Sunday Lectionary*. Collegeville, Minn.: Liturgical Press, 1993.

Parrish, V. Stephen. *A Story of the Psalms: Conversation, Canon, and Congregation*. Colegeville, Minn.: Liturgical Press, 2003.

Peterson, Eugene H. *Answering God: The Psalms as Tools for Prayer*. San Francisco: Harper & Row, 1989.

Pleins, J. David. *The Psalms: Songs of Tragedy, Hope, and Justice*. Maryknoll, N.Y.: Orbis, 1993.

Prothero, Rowland E. *The Psalms in Human Life and Experience.* New York: E. P. Dutton, 1903.

Sarna, Nahum M. *Songs of the Heart: An Introduction to the Book of Psalms.* New York: Schocken, 1993.

Smith, Mark S. *Psalms: The Divine Journey.* New York: Paulist, 1987.

Wilson, Gerald H. *The Editing of the Hebrew Psalter.* SBLDS 76. Chico, Calif.: Scholars Press, 1985.

Zenger, Erich. *A God of Vengeance? Understanding the Psalms of Enmity.* Translated by Linda M. Maloney. Louisville: Westminster John Knox, 1995.

ENDNOTES

1. Dorothy V. Jones, "The Example of Dag Hammarskjöld: Style and Effectiveness at the UN," *The Christian Century* 111, 32 (Nov. 9, 1994) 1050.

2. Brevard Childs, "Reflections on the Modern Study of the Psalms" in *Magnalia Dei, the Mighty Acts of God: Essays in Memory of G. Ernest Wright*, eds. F. M. Cross, W. E. Lemke, P. D. Miller, Jr. (Garden City, N.Y.: Doubleday, 1976) 385.

3. W. H. Bellinger, Jr., *Psalms: Reading and Studying the Book of Praises* (Peabody, Mass.: Hendrickson, 1990) 15.

4. Michael Goulder, *The Prayers of David (Psalms 51–72)*: Studies in the Psalter II, JSOTSup 102 (Sheffield: JSOT, 1990) 24-30.

5. See Hermann Gunkel, *The Psalms: A Form-Critical Introduction*, trans. T. M. Horner, FBBS 19 (Philadelphia: Fortress, 1967).

6. Erhard S. Gerstenberger, *Psalms: Part 1, with an Introduction to Cultic Poetry*, OT 14 (Grand Rapids: Eerdmans, 1988) 13-14.

7. Patrick D. Miller, Jr., *Interpreting the Psalms* (Philadelphia: Fortress, 1986) 8; see also 48-52.

8. Claus Westermann, *Praise and Lament in the Psalms*, trans. K. R. Crim and R. N. Soulen (Atlanta: John Knox, 1981) 30-35.

9. Sigmund Mowinckel, *The Psalms in Israel's Worship*, 2 vols., trans. D. R. Ap-Thomas (Nashville: Abingdon, 1962) 1:106-92.

10. See H.-J. Kraus, *Psalms 1–59: A Commentary*, trans. H. C. Oswald (Minneapolis: Augsburg, 1988) 56-58; Artur Weiser, *The Psalms*, OTL, trans. H. Hartwell (Philadelphia: Westminster, 1962) 23-52.

11. Gerald H. Wilson, *The Editing of the Hebrew Psalter*, SBLDS 76 (Chico, Calif.: Scholars Press, 1985) 207-8.

12. Brevard Childs, *Introduction to the Old Testament as Scripture* (Philadelphia: Fortress, 1979) 515-16.

13. Hermann Gunkel, *The Psalms: A Form-Critical Introduction*, 38.

14. Sigmund Mowinckel, *The Psalms in Israel's Worship*, 2:104-25.

15. See Roland E. Murphy, "A Consideration of the Classification 'Wisdom Psalms'," VTSup 9 (1962) 156-67; J. K. Kuntz, "The Canonical Wisdom Psalms of Ancient Israel—Their Rhetorical, Thematic, and Formal Dimensions," in *Rhetorical Criticism: Essays in Honor of J. Muilenburg*, eds. J. J. Jackson and M. Kessler (Pittsburgh: Pickwick, 1994) 186-22; L. Perdue, *Wisdom and Cult: A Critical Analysis of the View of Cult in the Wisdom Literature of Israel and the Ancient Near East*, SBLDS 30 (Missoula, Mont.: Scholars Press, 1977).

16. James L. Mays, "The Place of the Torah-Psalms in the Psalter," *JBL* 106 (1987) 12; italics added.

17. Erhard S. Gerstenberger, *Psalms: Part 1, with an Introduction to Cultic Poetry*, 210.

18. Hermann Gunkel, *The Psalms: A Form-Critical Introduction*, 36-39.

19. Hermann Gunkel, *The Psalms: A Form-Critical Introduction*, 36.

20. James Muilenburg, "Form Criticism and Beyond," *JBL* 88 (1969) 4.

21. See James L. Kugel, *The Idea of Biblical Poetry* (New Haven: Yale University Press, 1981); Robert Alter, *The Art of Biblical Poetry* (New York: Basic Books, 1985). For a more technical discussion that proposes a broader understanding of parallelism, see Adele Berlin, *The Dynamics of Biblical Parallelism* (Bloomington: Indiana University Press, 1985).

22. Thomas G. Long, *Preaching and the Literary Forms of the Bible* (Philadelphia: Fortress, 1989) 47.

23. S. E. Gillingham, *The Poems and Psalms of the Hebrew Bible*, Oxford Bible Series (Oxford: Oxford University Press, 1994) 277-78.

24. See M. D. Goulder, *The Psalms of the Sons of Korah*, JSOTSup 20 (Sheffield: JSOT, 1982); H. D. Nasuti, *Tradition History and the Psalms of Asaph*, SBLDS 88 (Atlanta: Scholars Press, 1988).

25. Beth L. Tanner, " 'Where Is Your God?' The Shape of the Elohistic Psalter," unpublished paper

delivered at the Annual Meeting of the SBL, Nov. 20, 1994, Chicago, Illinois.

26. Gerald H. Wilson, "Shaping the Psalter: A Consideration of Editorial Linkage in the Book of Psalms" in *The Shape and Shaping of the Psalter*, ed. J. C. McCann, Jr., JSOTSup 159 (Sheffield: JSOT, 1993) 73-74.

27. William G. Braude, *The Midrash on Psalms* (New Haven: Yale University Press, 1954) 1:5.

28. Gerald H. Wilson, *The Editing of the Hebrew Psalter*, 139-97.

29. See Gerald H. Wilson, *The Editing of the Hebrew Psalter*, 207-8; see also G. H. Wilson, "The Use of Royal Psalms at the 'Seams' of the Hebrew Psalter," *JSOT* 35 (1986) 85-94. For a survey, see David M. Howard, Jr., "Editorial Activity in the Psalter: A State-of-the-Field Survey," in *The Shape and Shaping of the Psalter*, 52-70.

30. Gerald H. Wilson, *The Editing of the Hebrew Psalter*, 213.

31. See J. C. McCann, Jr., "Books I–III and the Editorial Purpose of the Hebrew Psalter" in *The Shape and Shaping of the Psalter*, 93-107.

32. See Lawrence Boadt and William J. Urbrock, "Book I of the Psalter: Unity, Direction, and Development," unpublished paper delivered at the Annual Meeting of the SBL, Nov. 20, 1994, Chicago, Illinois.

33. See Ralph W. Klein, *Israel in Exile: A Theological Interpretation* (Philadelphia: Fortress, 1979) 1-8.

34. G. H. Wilson, "A First Century CE Date for the Closing of the Hebrew Psalter?" in *Haim M. I. Geraryahu Memorial Volume* (Jerusalem: World Jewish Bible Center, 1990) 136-43.

35. See Marvin E. Tate, *Psalms 51–100*, WBC 20 (Dallas: Word, 1990) xxvi. Tate characterizes Book IV as a "Moses-book."

36. Gerald H. Wilson, "The Use of Royal Psalms at the 'Seams' of the Hebrew Psalter," 92. See also James L. Mays, *The Lord Reigns: A Theological Handbook to the Psalms* (Louisville: Westminster John Knox, 1994) 12-22.

37. Gerald H. Wilson, "Shaping the Psalter: A Consideration of Editorial Linkage in the Book of Psalms" 75-76. See also David M. Howard, "A Contextual Reading of Psalms 90–94," in *The Shape and Shaping of the Psalter*, 114-22.

38. Klaus Seybold, *Introducing the Psalms*, trans. R. G. Dunphy (Edinburgh: T & T Clark, 1990) 24. See also Harvey H. Guthrie, Jr., *Israel's Sacred Songs: A Study of Dominant Themes* (New York: Seabury, 1966) 188-93; J. Clinton McCann, Jr., "The Psalms as Instruction," *Int.* 46 (1992) 117-28.

39. James L. Mayo, *Psalms,* Interpretation (Louisville: John Knox, 1994) 19.

40. See Jerome F. D. Creach, *Yahweh as Refuge and the Editing of the Hebrew Psalter*, JSOTSup 217 (Sheffield: Sheffield Academic Press, 1996).

41. See Walter Brueggemann, *Israel's Praise: Doxology Against Idolatry and Ideology* (Philadelphia: Fortress, 1988).

42. Terence Fretheim, *The Suffering of God: An Old Testament Perspective* (Philadelphia: Fortress, 1984) 58.

43. William C. Placher, *Narratives of a Vulnerable God: Christ, Theology, and Scripture* (Louisville: Westminster John Knox, 1994) 19.

44. See Charles B. Cousar, *A Theology of the Cross: The Death of Jesus in the Pauline Letters* (Philadelphia: Fortress, 1990) 103-8.

45. Elsa Tamez, *The Amnesty of Grace: Justification by Faith from a Latin American Perspective*, trans. Sharon H. Ringe (Nashville: Abingdon, 1993) 157.

INTRODUCTION TO
WISDOM LITERATURE

RICHARD J. CLIFFORD, S. J.

DEFINITION OF
WISDOM LITERATURE

In biblical studies, "wisdom literature" designates the books of Proverbs, Job, Qohelet (Ecclesiastes), and, in the Apocrypha or deuterocanonical books, Sirach and the Wisdom of Solomon. Other biblical literature is sometimes put under the wisdom umbrella. Tobit in the Apocrypha has been called a sapiential short story because of its concern with the morality of everyday life. The Song of Songs is often included on the grounds that it, like the wisdom books, is "of Solomon" (Cant 1:1). Psalms such as 37, 49, 73, 112, and 127 are aphoristic, or meditate on the problem of the innocent righteous person; but to call them wisdom psalms broadens the category unduly in the opinion of many scholars; moreover, there is no consensus on which psalms belong to the group.

Scholars have occasionally regarded whole sections of the Bible as being influenced by wisdom themes, such as wisdom and life, worldly success resulting from shrewdness, or the inherent consequences of human actions. Genesis 1–11 is indeed concerned with cosmic order and with wisdom and life (esp. chaps. 2–3), but these themes come more from "international" epics like *The Epic of Gilgamesh* and the story of Atrahasis than from wisdom books. Genesis 37–50, detailing Joseph's rise at court through sagacity and skill at interpreting dreams, resembles court tales like Ahiqar and Daniel more than wisdom books. The sophisticated court history (2 Samuel 9–20; 1 Kings 1–2) portrays Yahweh as being hidden in the course of human events, as one finds in the wisdom portrayal, but such a shared perspective is no argument for literary dependence. Finally, some think that Deuteronomy and wisdom literature are related because both were written by the

Jerusalem scribal class. Such a view is possible, for these literatures share common vocabulary, and Deuteronomy reckons obedience to Yahweh as wisdom (Deut 4:5-8; 32:6, 21, 28-31). Rather than wisdom books influencing other biblical books, however, it is more likely that wisdom thinking was in the main stream of biblical literary production from whence its style and ideas radiated throughout biblical writings.

Jerome (died 420), in his *Prologue to the Books of Solomon*, attributed the unity of the traditional wisdom books to their connection with Solomon, although he was aware that the connection is loose in some instances. The Christian Bible groups the wisdom books together (with the psalms) after the historical books and before the prophetic books. The Jewish Bible places the wisdom literature in the third section of the Tanakh— the Writings (a miscellaneous collection) —after the Torah and the Prophets.

There are good reasons for grouping the wisdom books together. First, few of the books except the latest wisdom books, Sirach 44–50 and the book of Wisdom 10–19, say anything about the history of Israel, its major institutions of covenant and kingship, and its great personalities, such as Abraham and Sarah, Moses, and David. The name of Israel's God, Yahweh, does not even occur in Qohelet and the Job dialogues (Job 3–37; Yahweh in Job 12:9 is anomalous). Righteousness in the books is not linked to observance of the law and covenant or to performance of rituals as it is elsewhere in the Bible. Genres and themes of neighboring literatures are far more obvious in the wisdom books than in other sections of the Bible. Second, the books all share a strong didactic tone. The word "wisdom" pervades all the books: forty-two times in Proverbs, eighteen times in Job, twenty-eight times in Qohelet, sixty times in Sirach (σοφία *sophia*), and thirty times in the book of

Wisdom; the numbers are much higher if synonyms of "wisdom" are counted. There is persistent attention to wisdom in itself, which makes these biblical books different from their canonical counterparts. The books are, of course, concerned with practical wisdom—knowing how to live well, how to perform one's tasks, and how to understand the secrets of the universe. But the Bible goes beyond specific instances of wisdom to explore the nature of wisdom, its importance and limits, and its relationship to Yahweh.

Within this grouping of canonical wisdom literature, there are considerable differences deriving from the presence of distinct literary genres and from the different meanings of wisdom in antiquity. Proverbs includes the distinct genres of wisdom poem, instruction, and proverb; Job is a dialogue on divine justice set within a narrative; Qohelet is (among other things) a royal pseudo-autobiography; Sirach is a vast compendium of instructions and proverbs; and the book of Wisdom is a philosophical exhortation to a way of life (λόγος προτρεπτικός logos protreptikos). Each major genre develops different themes in a distinctive way. The concept of wisdom is not univocal; it may signify aphorisms, instructions for the younger generation, magical knowledge derived from the gods (as in oaths), royal and judicial discernment (as of Solomon), and critical, skeptical inquiry. All of these different concepts are included under the umbrella of ancient wisdom.

Modern interest in wisdom literature has gone through several phases since the foundations of contemporary biblical scholarship were laid in the sixteenth century. Renaissance creativity was based on freeing human activity from connection with ultimate and hierarchical patterns of order. Reformation theology was interested in the God of history rather than in the Author of a static system; human destiny was perceived as the realization of spiritual capacities in time. Given the presuppositions regnant at the dawn of modern historical-critical study of the Bible, it is no wonder that wisdom literature took second place to the study of the Pentateuch, historical and prophetic books, and Psalms. Sapiential writings were regarded by many as derivative, a quasi-philosophical distillation of the law and the prophets. Dependence on the prophets was, in fact, thought to account for two traits of wisdom: the doctrine of retribution

and the (alleged) suspicion of cult that surfaces in Prov 15:8: "The sacrifice of the wicked is an/abomination to the LORD,/ but the prayer of the upright is his delight" (NRSV; cf. Prov 21:27; Eccl 5:1; Heb 4:17). It is important to remind ourselves that this neglect of the wisdom literature is relatively modern and that it reflects neither the outlook of the Bible nor that of many centuries of Jewish and Christian interpretation, which have considered every aspect of the world to have been created for the divine purpose. To regard wisdom literature as a foreign body in the Bible, as some scholars still do, is a hermeneutical decision based on the assumption that the historical and prophetic books are normative for what is genuinely biblical.

Three twentieth-century developments have pushed wisdom books to the forefront of scholarly interest:

First, Hermann Gunkel (1862–1932), applying his new form criticism, proposed that much wisdom literature came from ancient oral models and originated in a particular group in Israel: the sages. Thus was introduced the impulse to search for the social location of the wisdom books, an impulse that has become stronger in recent times. Second, the recovery (beginning in the mid-nineteenth century) of texts comparable to biblical wisdom literature in Egypt and Mesopotamia, civilizations far older than Israel, challenged the old assumption that the biblical wisdom books were late systematizings of traditional teaching in accord with a view of religion as obedience to the law. Third, the theological bias against wisdom books was challenged by prominent scholars, such as Walther Zimmerli and Gerhard von Rad, who found a basis for the theological study of wisdom books in the concepts of creation and cosmic order, which attest that every aspect of God's world is good and worthy of study. Their discernment of wisdom literature's theological value prepared the way for the lively interest it holds today.

WISDOM LITERATURE
IN THE ANCIENT NEAR EAST

The title "wisdom literature" has been applied to certain literary genres from Egypt and Mesopotamia. Were it not for the example of the biblical wisdom books, however, the extra-biblical texts probably would not be regarded as constituting a special group. Comparison between these other texts and their biblical counterparts is fruitful, nonetheless, chiefly because the foreign examples illuminate two vitally important topics: literary genres (the set of conventions ruling the work) and the social location of the writers. On these points the Bible provides scant information.

Wisdom texts comprise some of the most ancient literature. Some wisdom genres, such as the instruction and the proverb collection, are attested from the first appearance of *belles lettres* (c. 2600 BCE for Mesopotamia, some two centuries later for Egypt) and continued in use long past the biblical period. The following section surveys Mesopotamian, Egyptian, and Canaanite parallels as they are relevant to the Bible, with particular attention to genres and the social location of the scribes.

Mesopotamia. Many wisdom texts entered the "stream of tradition" of cuneiform literature— i.e., texts controlled and maintained by generations of professional scribes, who copied them as part of their elaborate training. Preserved in temple archives and private collections, the works were widely known and accepted, in other words "canonical." They were widely distributed throughout the East including the Levant, and some of them influenced the Bible.

The oldest genre relevant to the Bible is *instruction.* The *Instructions of Šuruppak* was widely known and is extant in two archaic Sumerian versions dating to 2600–2400 BCE: a "classical" Sumerian version of c. 1800 BCE and two Akkadian translations of c. 1500–1100 BCE.[1] *Šuruppak* was king of the last antediluvian city (reminiscent of the biblical Noah) and was endowed with the divine wisdom of that privileged time. The text was used in schools, where students practiced cuneiform writing by copying it. In this collection, the father instructs his son, the customary recipient of ancient instructions. Some scholars believe that the father is a personification of the city of Šuruppak. The advice is not as specific and literal as Egyptian instructions, which are generally imparted through metaphor and indirection. Most of the counsels appear in a twofold structure: a command and a reason—e.g., "Do not go surety for another. They shall seize you." Incidentally, the fact that agricultural concerns are prominent in this and other instructions does not mean that

instructions originated with peasants rather than with the scribal class. The productivity of the land was such an abiding concern for all classes of an agrarian society that herds and crops occur often in the sayings of urban scribes. *Šuruppak* advises even the nobles to do their share at harvest time: "At the time of the harvest, days are precious. Collect like a slave girl, eat like a queen!"

Another well-attested genre was the *proverb collection.* No less than twenty-four collections are attested in Sumerian, though only a few survive in bilingual (Sumerian and Akkadian) translations.[2] A few independent Akkadian examples are extant.[3] Kassite scribes of the late second millennium BCE for some reason did not consider these texts worthy of copying. Biblical proverbs were not directly influenced by Sumerian collections, though there are general similarities in form and content.

Some literary works represent a skeptical and critical spirit for which the *edubba* ("tablet house," Sumerian for "the academy") was renowned. The sufferer in the "Sumerian Job" complains bitterly of his treatment by others and of his fate; the composition ends happily with the god's return.[4] The Babylonian Theodicy of c. 1000 BCE, an acrostic poem of twenty-seven stanzas, each of eleven lines, is a Job-like dialogue between a sufferer and a friend.[5] In one stanza, the protagonist complains of his sufferings, and in the next, his friend counters with the conventional pieties: Suffering is the fate of all, justice will ultimately be done, and the gods are remote and inscrutable. Eventually the friend concedes that the righteous poor are vulnerable and unhappy, and the sufferer utters a prayer for divine protection. Another poem, often compared with Job since its partial publication in 1885, is the "Babylonian Job," sometimes cited by its first line: "I will praise the lord of wisdom" (*ludlul bēl nēmeqi).*[6] The full publication of its first tablet in 1980 shows that it can no longer be used as a parallel to Job, for it is not a treatise on the problem of suffering but a bold proclamation of Marduk as the supplicant god. In the midst of terrible personal anguish, the sufferer rejects his personal god in favor of Marduk. (Marduk had become important in the late second millennium BCE.)

Another Mesopotamian genre only recently recognized as relevant to the Bible is the pseudo-autobiography of a king, in which the king makes a lesson of his life and records it for posterity. Especially relevant to the Bible is the standard version of the *Epic of Gilgamesh* in eleven tablets, apparently completed around the thirteenth century BCE.[7] A didactic purpose was imposed on the Old Babylonian version by a new introduction and conclusion as well as the inclusion of wisdom themes. Gilgamesh's opening and closing speeches in the standard version emphasize not his strength but his experience and knowledge gained through sufferings. The work addresses the reader as "thou" as it instructs. The flood story, which has been added in tablet XI, omits giving a reason for the flood (although the tradition attested in the Atra-hases epic did include a reason) to underline the wisdom theme of the inscrutability of the gods. The plant of life that slips away from the hero instances another wisdom theme: the fragility of life. Qohelet quotes the alewife's advice to Gilgamesh as he seeks immortality "You will not find the eternal life you seek. . . . Go eat your bread with enjoyment. . . . Enjoy life with the wife whom you love" (Old Babylonian version). The book of Proverbs may also draw from Gilgamesh; the goddess Ishtar's false offer of life to the hero seems to have influenced the depiction of Woman Folly's false offer of life to the young man in Prov 5:3-6; 7; and 9:13-18.

Mesopotamian literature reflects the world of the scribes. Despite their various specializations, scribes are described with one term: *ṭupšarru,* "scribe." They wrote the literature and saw to its transmission. Literature was by definition what they copied and kept in libraries. This practice accounts for multiple copies of the limited number of works in the stream of tradition. Scribes had three functions—bureaucrat, poet, and scholar. As bureaucrats, they recorded the intake and outflow of palace goods; as poets, they composed literary works, such as hymns, epics, annals, and inscriptions; as scholars, they recorded and arranged omens and practiced divination. For the writing of literature, the royal court was far more important than was the temple; the latter lost its economic and political importance to the palace at an early period. The king sponsored the cultural establishment as an ongoing part of his responsibility to uphold political and economic order and stability.

In contrast to other societies, Mesopotamian scribes were not *ex officio* connected with sanctuaries or other religious institutions, nor did they operate with a body of normative or "classical" texts. They functioned within the palace organization or, with the economic prosperity of the first millennium BCE, independently, selling their "scholarly" services (omens and divination) to wealthy individuals.

Egypt. Literature comparable to the biblical wisdom books was composed as early as the mid-third millennium in Egypt. Egyptologists include three major genres under the heading of wisdom: *instructions, laments* or *complaints,* and *political propaganda.* The first two, instructions and complaints, are relevant to the Bible. Since instruction is such an abundant source of information on the scribal profession, information on the social context will be provided within the discussion of instructions.

Instruction was a pervasive genre; seventeen examples are extant.[8] The oldest is the *Instruction of Prince Hardjedef* (composed c. 2450–2300 BCE),[9] and the youngest, the *Instruction of Papyrus Insinger* of the first century CE, written in Demotic, the vernacular language.[10] One instruction, that of Amenemope, dating to c. 1100 BCE,[11] has directly influenced Prov 22:17–24:22.

Instructions gave advice to enable the young person to lead a life free of undue difficulties and costly mistakes. Instructions make concrete and pragmatic suggestions rather than hold out abstract ideals to live up to—e.g., Don't lie to a judge, since telling the truth will render the judge benevolent the next time around, and in the long run lies don't work anyway. Such pragmatic counsels provide no indication that Egyptian instructions were secular. On the contrary, they were thoroughly religious. Like other ancient peoples, Egyptians believed that God implanted order (*ma'at*) in the world. *Ma'at* can be variously translated—"truth," "order," "justice"—and is found in nature (the seasons, fruitfulness) no less than in the human world (civic and social order, laws, right relationships within families and professions, among neighbors, and in relation to the king). In mythology, *Ma'at* is the daughter of Re, the god of the sun and of justice. She is portrayed as crouching with a feather on her knees or head. *Ma'at* was not revealed directly to humans, but "read off" the course of the world and communicated through the maxims and exhortations of instructions. To help readers fulfill the demands of *ma' at* in every walk of life was the aim of the instructions. Some scholars see *ma' at* as the model for personified Wisdom in Proverbs, though it must be noted that Wisdom in Proverbs, by her vigorous speeches and pursuit of her lovers, goes far beyond the abstract Egyptian goddess. Finally, the scope of the instruction is the guidance of the individual rather than the reform of society; one accepted the world and lived according to its rhythms.

Some themes of the instructions are explained by their context in Egyptian society. The career of the young person was played out, at least initially, within the *famulus* ("private secretary") system; one entered the household of high officials (mostly of royal blood) who trained their successors in their household. The young person served the great personage, establishing a solid relationship, like Joseph with Potiphar (Gen 39:2) and with Pharaoh (Gen 41:40). Eventually formal classes came to be conducted at the royal court. In that world, fidelity to one's master was important. The apprenticeship context explains exhortations to deliver messages accurately, to avoid (domestic) quarrels, and to guard against entanglements with women of the household.

In portraying human beings, the instructions use the "heart" as the seat of feeling and, especially, of intelligence. A "hard-hearted" person lacks good sense rather than compassion. Human beings are characterized by a fundamental polarity—the wise person and the fool, the hot and the silent person. Fools do not follow the advice of their "father," or elder, and thus do not act according to *ma 'at*. The cleverness of the wise is the result of education, nature, and their own shrewd assessment of people and situations. "Hearing" (in the sense of heeding) is an important verb in the exhortations. Egyptian society was open, allowing poor and ambitious young people to rise to positions of power. Such people needed guide books to success.

Instructions were composed in every period during the three millennia of Egyptian history, and they reflect changes in society. The genre arose with the Egyptian state in the third millennium BCE, when the need to administer vast territories required the king's servants to leave behind their village routine to travel and to respond to situations requiring more than just their personal experience. Instructions of the Old Kingdom (2650–2135 BCE) arose within the court and revolved around the king, but with the decline of the monarchy and the social disorder of the First Intermediate Period (2135–2040 BCE), the instructions turned from royal service to private concerns. With the restoration of monarchy in the Middle Kingdom (2040–1650 BCE), instructions once again stressed loyalty to the king. New Kingdom authors came from all levels of society, for daily business was now conducted by a broad range of people. With the *Instructions of Any* in the Eighteenth Dynasty (c. 1550–1305 BCE), concern for the individual and for the acquiring of inner peace reappears and dominates the genre down to Hellenistic and Roman times. Another reflection of societal change is the way success was interpreted. In the Old Kingdom, when courtiers were the intended readers, success meant getting ahead at court. When the readership became less tied to a particular social class, exhortations became more general and more personal—how to avoid suffering, conflicts, and disappointments in life.

In contrast to the Egyptian principle that artists be anonymous, instructions name their authors, presenting them as real people—kings or prominent scribes. The authority of instructions, after all, rested on the repute of their writers no less than on their antiquity. Reverence for authority and for antiquity did not, however, prevent critical editing and recasting of the ancient wisdom.

Composing, studying, teaching, and copying texts took place in a kind of academy known as the House of Life, which was usually located near a temple and had a cultic function. Instructions were copied out by school children as they learned the Egyptian script; their frequently faulty copies are often the chief manuscript source for instructions. Instructions were never meant solely to be school texts, however. The addressee in instructions was a "son," a broader term than its English equivalent, one that expressed any close relationship with a younger person—one's child, student, or successor. The texts reveal a high level of personal involvement, for the prestige of the "father" depended on the success of the "son." The instructions were class-specific up to the first millennium, at which time general formulations became more common.

At the end of the third millennium another type of writing appeared: pessimistic and cynical attacks on traditional ways of thinking. The *Admonitions of Ipu-wer*, after a grim recital of the troubles of the land (a common topos), blames the creator-god using the form of dialogue.[12] *The Protests of the Eloquent Peasant* is a confrontation in nine speeches between a peasant and a high official.[13] *A Song of the Harper* urges one to enjoy today for who knows about tomorrow.[14] The *Satire on the Trades* criticizes non-scribal activities to glorify the profession of the scribe.[15] The *Dispute of a Person with His Ba* (i.e., vital force) vividly describes the miseries of life.[16] These works show that scribes in Egypt, as in Mesopotamia, were free to criticize the tradition. One should not regard skeptical works *ipso facto* as the products of alienated or marginalized groups, therefore; they could arise within the scribal guild.

Canaan. The larger context for Israel was in the "Canaanite" culture common to the entire Levant (with local variations). Unfortunately, few wisdom writings survive from this culture. The Ugaritic texts, which provide a northern sampling of Canaanite culture, contain a few didactic texts. Most such texts are Babylonian: the *Counsels of Shube'awilum*,[17] collections of sayings, and a hymn of trust to Marduk (similar to the Babylonian "I will praise the Lord of wisdom"). These and other Babylonian texts appear in the Akkadian language, showing that the Ugaritic scribes read and appreciated Mesopotamian literature. One wisdom text, the book of Ahiqar, originally written in Aramaic around the eighth or seventh century BCE, is possibly of Canaanite origin. The book contains the tale of Ahiqar, an official of the Assyrian king, and a collection of his sayings. The tale is similar to stories of courtiers such as those of Joseph and Daniel, in which the courtier loses his high position at court through the envy of others and then regains it through his patience and sagacity. Ahiqar has some links to the book of Tobit. It is noteworthy that the courtier Ahiqar, who has experienced many things and suffered much, is celebrated as the author of sayings, exhortations, and wisdom poems. Practical wisdom is connected with age and experience.

SOCIAL CONTEXT

Form criticism, from its beginnings in the early twentieth century, has inquired about the origin of literary forms in specific arenas of human life. Recent scholarship, with its consciousness of class interest lurking in literary works, asks even more intensely about the social location of authors and their works.

Who were the authors of the wisdom books, and what social class interest(s) did they promote? Were they scribes on the staff of palace and temple, or teachers in schools? Were they elders of tribes or families inculcating tribal traditions and values onto the younger generation? Unfortunately, the Bible does not provide sufficient information about everyday life to answer these questions with certainty.

The complicated writing systems of Mesopotamia and Egypt virtually ensured that authors of literary works were professional scribes and poets. The scribe in Mesopotamia and Egypt belonged to a well-defined profession. Egypt had its House of Life, and Mesopotamia its tablet house.

Scholars have theorized about two different settings for Israel's wisdom literature: the school (under royal sponsorship) and the tribe. Some scholars, on the basis of foreign examples, suggest that the monarchy, beginning in the tenth century BCE, built up a skilled or "wise" bureaucracy for the keeping of records and accounts, for diplomatic correspondence with foreign powers (requiring a knowledge of Akkadian and Egyptian), and for composing didactic material. From this circle would have come the authors of the instructions and other wisdom literature. King Solomon was recognized by the historian both for establishing administrative structures and for possessing preeminent wisdom (cf. 1 Kings 3; 1 Kings 4:29; 1 Kings 11:41). His name is associated with wisdom books (Prov 1:1; 25:1; Eccl 1:12; Cant 1:1; Sir 47:13; Wisdom 7–9).

Proponents of the tribal theory point out that the wisdom books do not mention any class of sages. Noting the strong family and tribal traditions of Israel, they propose that the admonitions and warnings of the wisdom books have their roots in prohibitions laid down by tribal elders that regulated social relations within the tribe. A variant of the tribal theory finds the folk element not so much in the admonitions and warnings as in the sayings and comparisons. The latter arose from real-life experiences of ordinary people; the sayings were made concise and memorable by removing details of their originating situations.

In assessing the origin and context of wisdom writings, indeed of other biblical writings, one must concede some influence from tribal tradition on wisdom material, for the family was a dominant institution in ancient Israel. Nonetheless, it is likely that professional scribes or poets, under the general sponsorship of the king, composed the biblical wisdom books, since all of these books represent genres well known in the ancient literary world. Only people able to read and appreciate such writings could have adopted their conventions with the skill and sophistication so evident in the biblical books. References to rural life and farming cannot be used as evidence for tribal origins, for they reflect almost universal anxiety about crops and herds in the precarious economy of the ancient world. Many Israelites, it is true, were able to read the relatively simple alphabetic Hebrew, and they would have constituted a broad readership; but the authors of the biblical books came from the ranks of professional scribes and sages. Skeptical and critical books like Job and Qohelet could have come from these ranks also, for a critical and skeptical spirit was at home among ancient scribes, as is clear in the writings from Mesopotamia and Egypt. The author of Qohelet is called a sage, a collector, and a sifter of maxims (Eccl 12:9-11). Ben Sira, in the first quarter of the second century BCE, was a professional sage, though not necessarily in the employ of temple or court. He lauds the profession of scribe (Sir 38:24–39:11) and invites young people to his school (Sir 51:13-30). The role the Israelite sage played is difficult to detail, however. Like the Mesopotamian scribe, some Israelite scribes may have been in the employ of the royal court, whereas others may have been privately employed. African societies, where proverb experts provided the king with appropriate maxims, may offer a valuable analogy. Given the small population of Judah and Jerusalem and the limits on the monarchy (and later to the high priesthood) from tribal loyalty and ancient religious traditions, however, one cannot in simple fashion apply to Israel observations about the scribe in neighboring cultures.

FORMAL CHARACTERISTICS OF WISDOM LITERATURE

Biblical and other ancient literatures were ruled by conventions, far more so than is the case with modern literature. Attention to the major genre and smaller genres or forms of each work as well as to other formal features sheds considerable light on biblical wisdom literature. Genre refers to the kind of literature, the literary species of a complete work, such as comedy, tragedy, biography, law code, or instruction. Unfortunately, ancient Near Eastern authors did not commit their theories of literature to writing, forcing modern readers to infer each text's category.

Discussion of the precise literary forms in each work will be found in each commentary. Only the large-scale genres, those that incorporate smaller genres, will be noted here: instructions, proverb collections, dialogues on divine justice and human suffering, pseudo-autobiographies, and philosophical exhortations to a certain way of life.

Instruction. This widely attested wisdom genre is found in both Egypt and Mesopotamia from the mid-third millennium to the beginning of the common era. Most such writings are Egyptian. Formally, Mesopotamian and Egyptian instructions are of two types: those with a title and main text, and those with a title, prologue, and main text (with subtitles and other divisions). The author is always referred to in the third person, often with titles and epithets. There is always a direct address of the son in the prologue, sometimes also in the body of the work. The main text is made up of units consisting of one to seven lines, the two-line couplet by far the most common. The couplet (also called distich or bicolon) occurs in synonymous, antithetic, or synthetic parallelism, or in balanced phrases. Because early instructions are lengthy and sophisticated, attempts to show historical development from short sayings to long essays, or from simple to complex argumentation or forms, are not persuasive. Instructions always contain proverbs and exhortations.

Proverb Collections. Although proverbs or pithy sayings were part and parcel of all ancient literature, *collections* of proverbs were not always present. Besides sayings, the many Sumerian proverb collections contain anecdotes, extracts from works of literature, short fables, and other unidentifiable material. Some sayings occur in parallel lines, whereas others consist of just one line.

Dialogues on Divine Justice and Human Suffering. From a formal point of view, the Egyptian *Dispute Between a Man and His Ba* (second-millennium BCE) mingles prose, symmetrically structured speech, and lyric poetry. From the same period, *The Protests of the Eloquent Peasant* consists of nine carefully framed petitions in poetic form (with prose explanation) framed by a prose narrative describing the injustice done to the peasant. The whole is shaped and unified by irony and contrast. The Mesopotamian "Sumerian Job" has a brief introduction and ending, between which a sufferer addresses god in a long complaint, using pithy sayings. The Babylonian Theodicy has a remarkably regular structure—twenty-seven stanzas of eleven lines, one stanza for the sufferer's complaints, and one stanza for the friend's notions of divine justice. The argument proceeds with concrete examples of justice and injustice and short sayings rather than with abstract reasoning.

Pseudo-Autobiography. The Akkadian genre of autobiography narrates the great deeds of a hero, drawing morals from them. Related to this form of writing is the genre of royal pseudo-autobiography, narrated partly in the first person, in which legendary and historical elements blend. Both adventures and interactions between characters appear in it.

Philosophical Exhortation. Exhortations to follow a particular philosophy or life of wisdom, known as protreptic in classical Greek and Latin literature, employ a variety of arguments and styles to persuade their audience. Some forms of writing that fall within this genre are the diatribe, in which imaginary opponents are chided, and the (elaborate) comparison. The biblical book of Wisdom is such an exhortation.

Brief Forms. The most pervasive small forms in wisdom literature are the *saying* and the *command* or *prohibition*. The saying is a sentence, usually written in the indicative mode. It can be divided into three types: the proverb, the experiential saying, and the didactic saying. The definition of a proverb is controverted, but the following is widely accepted: a concise statement of an apparent truth that has currency. The word *apparent* is used because a proverb is not always and everywhere true but proven so by context—e.g., "many hands make light work" and "too many cooks spoil the broth" are true according to the situation. *Currency* means that people "use" proverbs; they are not just clever sayings. The experiential saying presents some aspect of reality, "telling it like it is," and lets the hearer or reader draw the practical conclusions from it. The saying, "Some pretend to be rich, yet have nothing;/others pretend to be

poor, yet have great wealth" (Prov 13:7 NRSV), is open to further verification or qualification. The didactic saying is more than a statement about reality; it characterizes an action or attitude so as to influence human conduct—e.g., "Those who oppress the poor insult their Maker" (Prov 14:31 NRSV).

The sages can impose their will directly through commands (imperative or jussive mood) and prohibitions. Occasionally a command is placed parallel to a saying, moving the saying from observation to command.

MAIN TEACHINGS
OF WISDOM LITERATURE

The theology found within the wisdom books does not add up to a system, for the writers did not have a speculative aim; rather, they sought to instruct the next generation, to solve specific problems, to collect, critique, and hand on ancestral traditions. The central assumption of all the books is that God made the world, an order within which the human race must learn to live. That order was given privileged expression on the day of creation. Through wisdom, human beings can cope with the world and live happy and successful lives. Of great concern to the sages was the consequences of human choices ("retribution") upon individuals and society. Wisdom authors saw human beings as active agents, often dramatizing the moral life as involving two ways: the way of the righteous and the way of the wicked. Experience of life forced the sages to confront that surd in the cosmic system, the problem of evil. The sages recognized wisdom to be more than human ability to master life; it was hidden with God and had to be given to human beings. Attempts to consider wisdom in itself led to the personification of wisdom as a woman. Such are the themes constituting a theology of wisdom.

God. The word for "God"—אֱלֹהִים (*'ĕlōhîm*), יהוה (*Yahweh*), or one of the several names for God in the Joban dialogues (e.g., "the Almighty" [שַׁדַּי *šadday*, Job 6:4])—occurs throughout the wisdom books, naming One who creates, sustains the universe, and brings all human acts to completion. Although the wisdom mode of understanding the divine presence differs from that of the historical and prophetic books, it is no less real. Scholarly hypotheses that early wisdom was profane and only later made religious by incorporation into Yahwism have rightly been rejected, for all ancient Near Eastern wisdom presupposed the gods even when gods and worship of gods are not mentioned. Skeptical Qohelet, who avoids the name "Yahweh," mentions "Elohim" four times in twelve chapters. In the monotheism of orthodox Yahwism, according to which the Bible has been edited, there is no order beyond Yahweh's will, unlike neighboring cultures.

Cosmic Order. Wisdom literature assumes that there is a divinely implanted order in the universe, embracing the "natural" and the human worlds. The modern, dichotomous distinction between human beings and nature (deriving largely from Greek thought) was unknown in the ancient Near East. The purposeful activity of a colony of ants is as much an example of order as is the purposeful activity of human beings (see Prov 6:6-11). Job's claim that he, as a righteous man, had not experienced any order in the universe (Job 38:2) is refuted by Yahweh's listing of the activity of the inanimate and animate spheres. Analogies are constantly being drawn between human and non-human beings and activities (Prov 5:15; 11:28-29; 26:21; 27:17, 21). These dispositions are all "righteous" examples of the way the world works.

Cosmic order was perceived in two basic ways in the ancient Near East: order as the result of divine planning and order as being above and beyond divine plans and powers. In the first perspective, the gods in their wisdom justly reward or punish an individual with success or failure in this life. Coexisting with this view, in an existential contradiction, is the second perspective—a deterministic view according to which the course of one's life is fixed from birth. An Akkadian word illustrates well this notion. *Šimtu* (Sumerian *nam-tar*), inexactly rendered "fate" or "destiny," was "a disposition originating from an agency empowered to act and to dispose, such as the deity, king, or any individual"; it refers to the share of fortune and misfortune that determines the direction and temper of life. Other Mesopotamian vocabulary is even more deterministic; e.g., Akkadian *uṣurtu* (Sumerian *gišḫur*), means "drawing" or "design." These two views of cosmic order reflect diverse, even contradictory, experiences of the world.

Israel's monotheism affected, at least implicitly, this ancient Near Eastern interpretive blend of fate and freedom. Instead of an interplay between unchangeable order and divine decree, the sole God, Yahweh, is consistently portrayed as all-powerful and all-wise, utterly responsive to human actions. Yahweh is not capricious, for there are always reasons for divine action. Cosmic order in the Bible, therefore, must be understood as less absolute than elsewhere in the East; it is associated closely with Yahweh's will (on occasion even personified as Yahweh's word or a female friend).

Creation. Unlike modern scientific concepts of creation, which envision only the physical world (typically in its astral and planetary aspects), ancient cosmogonies narrated the creation and organization of human society within the universe. In all cosmogonies, the gods created the world to benefit themselves; humans were slaves of the gods, their task being to ensure that everything operated for the divine service. Elements of the universe were given their purpose on the day of creation; the origin of a reality was its essence. Thus it is not surprising that cosmogonies were common in the ancient world, narrated to ground or to legitimate realities important to human life, such as the stars, the sun, and the moon, which determined time (especially sacred time), temple, king, and other institutions. Cosmogonies or cosmogonic language appear frequently in the Bible (see Genesis 1–11; Psalms 33; 77; 89; 93; 96–98; 104; Isaiah 40–66; and the wisdom literature).

Each wisdom book devotes considerable attention to creation. Proverbs has two cosmogonies: Prov 3:19-20 and 8:22-31. Job contains many allusions to creation, especially in chaps. 38–41. The opening of Qohelet (Eccl 1:3-11) presents a cosmology grounding the sage's ethical teaching about God and human actions. Sirach treats creation in 16:24–18:14; 39:12-35; and 42:15–43:38. In Sir 16:24–18:14, Yahweh creates the world, determining boundaries and arranging forever all their works that never disobey the divine word (Sir 16:26-28). The created world includes human beings whose obedience is not automatic but is given freely to their creator. Formed with a fixed number of days and with "fear of the Lord" and understanding, they are called to live obediently and worshipfully within the covenant (Sir 17:1-17). A lengthy address to the human race follows the cosmogony:

Turn back to your righteous and merciful God (Sir 17:17–18:14). For Ben Sira, the nature and purpose of human beings (including Israel) were fixed at creation. The book of Wisdom develops the parallel between creation and redemption that the books of Genesis and Exodus had already drawn through cross-referencing. According to Wisdom, the world was created as salvific by wisdom (Wis 1:14); the cosmos itself is intrinsically involved in the divine judgment that restores the original righteous order (Wis 19:18-21).

Proverbs 8 and Job 38–41 are worth singling out to show the relation between wisdom and creation. The cosmogony in Prov 8:22-31 legitimates the speech of Woman Wisdom in which she promises her friends life and prosperity. Proverbs 3:19-20 likewise grounds the promise of wisdom in Prov 3:13-18. The full cosmogony in Prov 8:22-31 is structured chiastically:

A   Yahweh creates Wisdom in honored first
　　place vv. 22-23;
　B   Creation "negatively" described vv. 24-28;
　B´ Creation "positively" described vv. 28-30a;
A´ Wisdom's intimacy with Yahweh vv. 30b-31.

The final two verses (vv. 30b-31), which come after the actual creating, are crucial for understanding Wisdom's appeal:

and I was daily [his] delight,
　[playing] before him at all times,
　[playing] in his inhabited world
　and delighting in the human race. (NRSV)

The chiastic placement of "delight" and "play" makes Wisdom's delighting in Yahweh parallel to Wisdom's delighting in the human race. Just as Wisdom is Yahweh's delight "daily" in v. 30b, so also her friends are to wait at her doors "daily" in v. 34. The intimate relationship between Woman Wisdom and human beings on earth is a reflection of the intimate relationship between Woman Wisdom and Yahweh in heaven. Woman Wisdom might be expected to ground her authority on the fact that she has seen Yahweh create and can communicate to her friends the secrets of how the world works. Yet she bases her authority solely on her intimacy with Yahweh; from the beginning she has been with God. She enables those who love her to know the all-wise God as well.

Proverbs 8 goes a step beyond Prov 3:19-20 by personifying wisdom, which the sages traditionally associated with the divine act of creation and the cosmic order. Now the vivid personification in Proverbs 8 grounds Wisdom's claim that only those who court her will enjoy blessing. The search for wisdom in Proverbs 8 becomes more than performing or avoiding certain actions. Rather, one is to seek Wisdom herself. To court her is to touch a quality of Yahweh the creator, and to enter into a relationship with her is to receive every divine blessing. This cosmogony explains how life may have a more profound meaning; it may be not only life in the sense of enjoyment of health, good name, and family happiness, but also "life with" association with Yahweh.

In Job, creation themes and language are vital to the argument. God's first speech (Job 38:1–40:2) refutes Job's denial of order, and the second (Job 40:6–41:34) refutes his charge of injustice (in the sense of God's being unable to restrain evil). The first speech is a list of created things, showing them to be a mix of the useful, the bizarre, and even the playful. God, it appears, creates not for human beings (Job) but for the divine pleasure, which is inscrutable. The second speech simply describes the two primordial beasts, Behemoth and Leviathan. Any cosmogony based on the combat myth, as it was then current in Canaan, would have told how God defeated the primordial monsters as the first act of creation (cf. Isa 51:9); but in Job they are not defeated, and their cosmic menace and hostility to the human race are actually celebrated by the deity! Rather than destroying them to create an orderly world, Yahweh chooses to let them be (although on a leash). God tells Job that these monsters, the very symbols of evil, are alive and well, and that Job must live in the universe where they roam. Creation language here and elsewhere in Job shows paradoxically that the universe is not orderly as some traditional sages had thought. Yahweh remains, however, the powerful if inscrutable friend of such stalwarts as Job.

Wisdom. The rules or laws structured into the world at creation can be discovered through wisdom. Moreover, these norms can be expressed in artful words and communicated to others. Although wisdom cannot be defined solely as a response to cosmic order, the literature accepts this order. The sages hoped to instruct others about how to live in accord with wisdom (see Proverbs), to investigate scandal in that order—namely, the failure of a righteous person to enjoy appropriate blessings (see Job)—to point out why tradition cannot explain the world or ensure happiness (see Ecclesiastes), to anthologize and arrange ancient wisdom and relate it to Israel's literary heritage (see Sirach), and to locate wisdom in a seemingly unjust world for an audience familiar with the philosophical tradition of middle Platonism (see book of Wisdom).

Wisdom cannot be satisfactorily captured in a single brief definition because it has at least four aspects. First, it is practical, involving knowledge about how the world works so that one can master and enjoy life fully. This aspect of wisdom is expressed well in the French term *savoir-faire*, "to know how to act or do," rather than "to know" in an absolute sense, divorced from action. Practical knowledge can involve judicial activity, as when kings exercise their role as judge. David discerns the true intent of the woman from Tekoa (2 Sam 14:1-24, esp. v. 20), and Solomon shrewdly decides which of the two prostitutes is telling the truth (1 Kgs 3:16-28). It can mean skillful composition of proverbs and songs (1 Kgs 4:32) or cataloging related objects (1 Kgs 4:33). Jewelers and artisans can be "wise," like the artisans who constructed the tabernacle (Exod 35:30–36:1). More generally, wisdom designates knowing how to live life; human life, as such, is a constant theme in wisdom literature. Most of the sayings in the wisdom books do not give advice but state a thesis about the world. "Hope deferred makes the heart sick,/but a desire fulfilled is a tree of life" (Prov 13:12 NRSV) is not advice to finish projects for the sake of psychological health; rather, it states the way people ordinarily respond to disappointment and fulfillment of desires. Life is sufficiently regular that the sage can discover its rhythms and formulate them into theses or statements.

Second, human wisdom has limits. Proverbs, which is sometimes regarded as naively optimistic, has as its heroine Woman Wisdom, who from her place with God gives wisdom to those who wait upon her. Proverbs 26:4-5 wittily expresses the limits of wisdom sayings to fit every occasion: "Do not answer fools according to their folly,/or you will be a fool yourself./Answer fools according to their folly, or they will be wise in their own eyes"

(NRSV). Wisdom in Proverbs involves the careful application of the tradition to individual situations. Job, that legendary wise man, refutes the traditional wisdom of his friends by using his own case; yet, he in turn is refuted by God's description of a vast, complex, and totally theocentric universe. Qohelet poses as the weary king who has seen all in order to put down any claim of wisdom to master life. The moments of life are hidden with God and parceled out to the foolish and the wise alike (Eccl 3:1-15). Ben Sira, though confident in the wisdom project, nonetheless writes long hymns to the divine wisdom (Sir 16:29–18:14; 39:12-35; 42:15–43:33) and pays court to her (Sir 51:13-30). The book of Wisdom focuses on divine wisdom; the model sage (Solomon) desires and prays intensely that it will be given to him (Wisdom 7–9).

The third point develops naturally from the foregoing one: Wisdom generally is both a human task and a divine gift, acquired through experience and obedience *and* given by God. Reconciling divine sovereignty with human freedom may be a major problem in the Western philosophical tradition, but the Bible does not perceive this dual affirmation to be a problem requiring a solution.

Fourth, wisdom in the Bible is itself an object of constant reflection. A major difference between the wisdom books of neighboring cultures and those of Israel is the constant occurrence of the word "wisdom" (חכמה *ḥokmâ*) in the biblical books. Job 28 declares that wisdom is hidden with God and that the only way to wisdom is fear of the Lord (Job 28:28). Proverbs 1–9 goes further and personifies wisdom as an attractive woman who offers to share with her friends the life she shares with God (Proverbs 8–9). She shares in the divine governance of the world, doing what Yahweh elsewhere is depicted as doing. Sirach 24 identifies wisdom with "the book of the covenant of the Most High God" (Sir 24:23 NRSV), part of Ben Sira's project of incorporating wisdom into the other literature of Israel. In the Wisdom of Solomon, wisdom is closely associated with God and is like an ether permeating the cosmos (Wis 7:22–8:1); wisdom is revealed to human beings after prayer and pursuit (Sir 7:1-22; 8:2–9:18).

Consequences of Human Choice. Because biblical wisdom is so linked to action, the sages were much concerned with the effects of human action on each individual and on the community. The term "retribution" is often used to describe the relation between deed and consequence, but its negative connotation in English (punishment from an external source) makes it an unsatisfactory term to use. The effects of actions, according to the sages, could come from the very actions themselves as well as externally—i.e., directly from God, who sees all. Klaus Koch has emphasized the deed/consequence side of human acts: The deed creates its own effect, that consequences are latent in all significant good and evil actions.[18] The theory is an instance of cosmic order applied to human activity. God acts as "midwife" (Koch's term) to the law. A good example is the parent's warning to their offspring not to join a band of robbers on the grounds that a life of brigandage is inherently self-destructive. The robbers

lie in wait—to kill themselves!
  and set an ambush—for their own lives!
Such is the end of all who are greedy for gain;
  it takes away the life of its possessors.
                    (Prov 1:18 -19 NRSV)

Another example of inherent outcomes is Prov 26:27 (NRSV): "Whoever digs a pit [to trap enemies] will fall into it,/and a stone will come back on the one who starts it rolling." Inherent outcomes, however, are only one side of human action, for God is depicted as intervening directly: Yahweh "does not let the righteous go hungry,/but he thwarts the craving of the wicked" (Prov 10:3 NRSV; cf. Prov 15:29; 16:4; 17:15). Job disproves his friends' belief that the deeds of the wicked always come back on them even as God is the ultimate source of Job's undeserved afflictions. The internal and the external perspectives that seem exclusive to modern readers remain valid for the biblical authors.

Doctrine of the Two Ways. The Bible, especially the book of Proverbs, imagines the moral life as presenting two ways, each with an intrinsic dynamism. Sometimes the two ways are explicitly contrasted, as in Woman Wisdom and Woman Folly in Proverbs 1–9 (esp. Prov 4:10-19) and in the persistent contrast in the sayings between the wise or the righteous and the fool or the wicked; Psalm 1 is also a good example of the inherent dynamism of two ways of life. The parental warning that opens Proverbs (1:8-19)

envisions the future of the child as a way of life (Prov 1:15) shared with others ("we will all have one purse" [Prov 1:14 NRSV]). The doctrine of the two ways has sometimes been interpreted statically, as if it described a class of people who meticulously observe the law and a class who do not; but this reading is incorrect. The concept is dynamic: There are two ways of living, one blessed and the other cursed, and people are invited to follow the way of the righteous and to avoid the way of the wicked. There is no room for pride or smugness, for one can leave the righteous way at any time. The way of the righteous is protected and guaranteed by God, but people must walk in it—that is, act accordingly. The doctrine is implicit in Job, where the point at issue is the result of righteous living, and also in Ecclesiastes, where, since one cannot fully understand human behavior, Qohelet denies the epistemological basis for the two ways. The book of Wisdom contrasts the wicked (Wis 2:1-24; 4:20–5:23) with the righteous child of God, interpreted individually (Wis 2:12-20; 5:15-16) or corporately as Israel (Wisdom 19). In the Qumran texts and in the New Testament, the notion of two ways is expressed in the concepts of the children of light and the children of darkness.

The Problem of Evil. A skeptical and critical thread runs throughout ancient wisdom literature. The problem of evil was often formulated as a case—the sufferer who is not aware of having sinned or, conversely, the prosperous scoundrel. Proverbs does not subject the problem of evil to explicit reflection, though it does not necessarily regard its sayings as the ultimate answer to life's mysteries. Job narrates a case of the innocent just person. Qohelet's skepticism and criticism of traditional wisdom attempts to explain inconsistencies in the world. Ben Sira is aware of inexplicable evil in life but simply affirms the divine origin of evil as well as good (Sir 39:12-35), and he insists that God has created all things in pairs, corresponding to the human ability to choose between right and wrong (Sir 15:11-20; 33:7-15). The suffering of the innocent just person is so important in the book of Wisdom that it led to the teaching on immortality as its solution.

Biblical exploration of inexplicable suffering differs from that of Israel's neighbors. In Mesopotamia there was, strictly speaking, no such thing as a righteous sufferer. If one is afflicted without apparent reason, it can only be that one has infringed upon the sovereign order of the gods. This perception continues throughout the history of ancient Mesopotamia:

In the Old Babylonian period this theology may find expression in a simple confession of bewilderment and ignorance of what one has done, or in the acceptance of one's sinfulness, along with its necessary consequences, as another manifestation of *fragilitas humana* common to all men. Later, one may infer from a clear conscience and a life re-examined and found, according to the known rules, faultless, that the gods hold men to the observance of other rules that he cannot know. To these thoughts one may join a contempt for man as the minion of many moods, a creature that may live gloriously only to die miserably. Or one may make the problem of the mind a problem of the heart, and solve it with reasons of the heart. Instead of wisdom, belief; instead of reflection and argument, a hymn to paradox and contraction. *Credo quia absurdum.* Attitudes and expression change; the theology does not.[19]

Against that background, Job is unique: "An explicit, unyielding declaration of innocence is not found before the book of Job."[20] The Bible's confession of one God, all-wise and all-powerful, makes its exploration of the problem of evil and of the righteous sufferer more pressing and more poignant than that of neighboring cultures. Who but God is ultimately responsible for whatever happens in the world?

Personification of Wisdom. Israelite wisdom literature attended to wisdom itself alongside pragmatic wisdom. This "theoretical" interest is first clearly visible in Proverbs 1–9 (also in Job 28), where traditional teacher-disciple instructions exhort one not only to proper conduct but also to the acquisition of wisdom, which is portrayed as the source of long life, wealth, honor, and closeness to Yahweh. Although Israel had long singled out divine attributes such as power, love, and fidelity, occasionally even personifying them ("love and faithfulness go before you" [Ps 89:14 NRSV]; "Awake, awake, put on strength,/O arm of the LORD!" [Isa 51:9 NRSV]), the consistent and vivid personification of wisdom as an attractive woman in Proverbs 1–9; Sirach 24; Bar 3:9–4:4; and Wisdom 7–9 stands on a different level. Wisdom acts and speaks, threatening or promising her audience,

exulting in her intimacy and privileged place with Yahweh. For explanation, scholars have adduced venerable parallels such as an alleged Canaanite goddess; Ma 'at, the Egyptian goddess of order; or the type scene found in the Mesopotamian Gilgamesh epic, the Canaanite Aqhat epic, and the Greek *Odyssey* (Calypso in Book V and Circe in Book X), in which a goddess offers life to a young hero only to destroy or transform him later on. Although personified Wisdom probably has non-Israelite roots, one must also reckon with influences from the social roles of real women in Israelite history and literary traditions about them—e.g., wife, harlot, wise woman—and with folk literature motifs such as the "sought-for person" (princess/bride).

In Prov 1:10-33 and chap. 8 (the frame for Proverbs 1–9), Wisdom invites the young disciple into a relationship with her, using language of love and courtship that is found also in Song of Songs (seeking and finding amid danger, waiting for the beloved). Her intimacy with Yahweh is the model of her relationship to the disciple; it enables her to give other gifts as well (Prov 8:30-36). Scholars grope for the right term for this presentation of Wisdom in Proverbs. Is it a hypostatization of a divine attribute or of the divinely implanted order in the world, or is it straightforward literary personification? Whatever explanation is adopted, Proverbs provides the primary interpretive context: Wisdom is a symbol of divine presence as well as of revelation; she is closely related to the instruction of the human teacher and to wisdom; a countervoice parodies Wisdom's message (Prov 2:16-19; Proverbs 5; 6:20-35; Proverbs 7; 9:13-18); and the quest for her is modeled on human love.

Personified wisdom appears in later books of the Bible as well. Sirach 24 (written c. 180 BCE) develops the link of wisdom and Yahweh and the old question of where wisdom dwells (Job 28) in a narrative in which Wisdom tells how she "came forth from the mouth of the Most High" (Sir 24:3 NRSV) and, at God's command, settled with Israel in Jerusalem (Sir 24:10-12). The author then identifies Wisdom with "the book of the covenant of the Most High God" (Sir 24:23 NRSV). Baruch 3:9–4:4 similarly identifies wisdom with the Torah. Wisdom of Solomon (c. first century BCE) combines the tradition of personified Wisdom living at God's side with Greek philosophical notions to assign a cosmic role to wisdom. The famous twenty-one qualities of Wisdom enumerated in Wis 7:22-23 highlight her pervasive agency in all things. For the influence of Wisdom on early Christian reflection about the cosmic role of Christ, see the section "New Testament" below.

THE CONTINUATION OF WISDOM LITERATURE

Judaism. The wisdom genres of instruction, saying, dialogue, and its themes of the blessed life and of cosmic order continued in the writings of early Judaism. Many literary works of the period used the technique of "relecture"—that is, rereading and recasting the classic texts. In the second century BCE, Sirach 24 rereads Proverbs 8, and Sirach 44–50 rereads the historical books, viewing the great personalities of Israel's history as individuals inspired by wisdom. Baruch 3:9–4:4 rereads Job 28 and Sirach 24, showing how the rulers of nations never found Wisdom, unlike Israel, who finds her in the book of the commandments of the law (Bar 4:1). Wisdom 10–19 interprets the books of Exodus and Numbers in seven great comparisons. *Pirqe 'Abot* (*The Sayings of the Fathers*) is a collection of sayings from the "men of the Great Assembly" (between the late fifth and the third centuries BCE) down to the descendants of Rabbi Judah the Prince in the third century CE. One of the treatises in the Talmud became the object of commentary in 'Abot de Rabbi Nathan. Its opening sentence places the men of the Great Assembly in a line from Moses, Joshua, the elders, and the prophets. The wisdom text of the Cairo Geniza, which some date in the first century CE but more likely dates to the early medieval period, continues the old wisdom tradition. Hebrew ethical wills, in which parents hand on to their children their wisdom, draw on traditional wisdom instruction.

The New Testament. Early Christians saw Jesus as a wisdom teacher and employed the tradition of personified wisdom to express his incarnation. Among the various influences on the New Testament was the wisdom teaching of "the Scriptures" (i.e., the Old Testament)—the themes of wisdom hidden with God and revealed to human beings, its identification with divine Spirit, Word, and Law, as well as the forms of instruction and admonition.

Unique among New Testament writings is the Letter of James, for it is an instruction. Although classed among the seven catholic epistles, it is a letter only in its opening address, "James, a slave of God and of the Lord Jesus Christ, to the twelve tribes in the dispersion, greetings" (Jas 1:1 NRSV). The rest of the work comprises a series of instructions using the familiar exhortatory verbs (imperatives, jussives), followed by reasons, which are often sayings or proverbs. Old wisdom themes appear: the dangers of an unbridled tongue (James 3; cf. Prov 10:18-21), of presumptuous planning (Jas 4:13-17; cf. Prov 16:1), or of ill-gotten wealth (Jas 5:1-6; cf. Prov 10:2-3). Although commonsensical in the style of the instruction, James nonetheless exalts "wisdom from above" (Jas 3:13-18 NRSV; cf. Jas 1:17), invoking the tradition of wisdom beyond human capacity but graciously given to human beings (see Job 28; Proverbs 8; Sirach 24). In Jas 3:17, wisdom from above is designated by seven qualities, recalling the famous twenty-one qualities of wisdom in Wis 7:22-23. The wisdom instruction does not remain unchanged, however, for it is altered by the addition of prophetic denunciations of the callous rich (Jas 1:27; 2:1-13; 4:1-10; 5:1-6).

Paul's argument against those who are scandalized by the cross (1 Cor 1:17–2:13) employs the traditional wisdom literature contrast between the wise and the foolish as well as that between human wisdom and divine wisdom (see Job 28; Proverbs 8): "For since in the wisdom of God the world did not come to know God through wisdom, it was the will of God through the foolishness of the proclamation to save those who have faith" (1 Cor 1:21 NAB). So harsh is Paul's judgment on the ability of the sage to know Christ that one may question whether this passage singlehandedly eliminated wisdom genres as vehicles for the early Christian message.

Wisdom traditions influenced the putative written source of the synoptic Gospels Matthew and Luke: Q, for *Quelle*, the German word for "source." Most scholars believe that Q emphasized Jesus' teachings rather than his death and resurrection. A few scholars even hypothesize a trajectory of the genre "words of the wise" from early collections of wisdom sayings, such as Proverbs, to gnostic collections of sayings, such as the *Gospel of Thomas* (late first century BCE), with Q falling somewhere in the middle of the trajectory. In its pure form the hypothesis runs into serious problems, for Q at some stage had eschatological statements incompatible with gnostic timelessness and lacking distinctively gnostic sayings. Wisdom themes nonetheless are strong in Q, as is illustrated by Matt 11:27//Luke 10:22: "All things have been handed over to me by my Father. No one knows the Son except the Father, and no one knows the Father except the Son and anyone to whom the Son wishes to reveal him" (NAB). The saying is part of the Jewish (and early Christian) debate about what and where wisdom is. Is it to be identified with the law (Sirach 24), with heavenly mysteries (*1 Enoch* 42:1-3), or with Christ (John 1:1-18; Col 1:15-20)? Is wisdom to be found in the Jerusalem Temple (Sir 24:8-12), everywhere in the cosmos (Wis 7:24-26), in heaven (*1 Enoch* 42:1-3), or in the church (Col 1:18)? Jesus in the text is divine wisdom incarnate, for to know him is to know God, who is wisdom itself. The immediately following verses, "Come to me, all you that are weary and are carrying heavy burdens, and I will give you rest. Take my yoke upon you, and learn from me" (Matt 11:28-29 NRSV), echo Sir 51:23-30, which is an invitation to attend Ben Sira's school and become his disciple. Matthew, therefore, answers the question of the early debate: Wisdom is found in Jesus and in his teaching.

Of all the Gospels, John is the most persistent in regarding Jesus as incarnate wisdom descended from on high to offer human beings light and truth. The Gospel expresses Jesus' heavenly origin by identifying him with personified Wisdom. Just as Woman Wisdom was with God from the beginning, even before the earth (Prov 8:22-23; Sir 24:9; Wis 6:22), so also Jesus is the Word in the beginning (John 1:1), with God before the world existed (John 17:5). Just as Wisdom teaches human beings heavenly secrets (Job 11:6-7; Wis 9:16-18) and shows them how to walk in the way that leads to life (Prov 2:20-22; 3:13-26; 8:32-35; Sir 4:12) and immortality (Wis 6:18-19), so also Jesus functions as the revealer in John. Jesus speaks in long discourses, as did Woman Wisdom (Prov 1:20-33; 8). Wisdom invites people to partake of her rich banquet, where food and drink symbolize life and closeness to God (Prov 9:2-5; Sir 24:19-21). Jesus does the same: "I am the bread of life. Whoever comes to me will never be hungry, and whoever believes in me will never be thirsty" (John 6:35 NRSV; cf. Prov 9:1-6, 11). Just as Wis-

dom seeks friends (Prov 1:20-21; 8:1-4; Wis 6:16), so also Jesus recruits followers (John 1:36-38, 43), though an individual might reject Wisdom (Prov 1:24-25; Bar 3:12; *1 Enoch* 42:2) or Jesus (John 8:46; 10:25).

Two early Christian hymns identify Jesus with God's creative Word and with heavenly wisdom: John 1:1-18 and Col 1:15-20. The Greek word λόγος (*logos*, "word") in John 1 has more in common with Old Testament wisdom than with merely a word. Sirach 24:3 ("From the mouth of the Most High I came forth," NAB) and Wis 9:1-2 had already made "wisdom" and "word" parallel. Proverbs 8:22-23 ("The LORD created me at the beginning. . . . Ages ago I was set up . . ." [NRSV]) and Sir 1:1 affirmed that Wisdom comes from God and remains with God forever. The Johannine prologue states that the Word was always with God. Wisdom as an aura of the might of God and pure effusion of the glory of the Almighty (Wis 7:25-26) seems to be echoed in John 1:14, where Jesus is the refulgence of eternal light (cf. Heb 1:1-2). Wisdom 7:22 says that Wisdom is unique (μονογενής *monogenēs*), and the prologue declares that the Word is God's unique (*monogenēs*) son. Wisdom sets up her tent in Sir 24:8, as does Jesus in John 1:14 (ἐσκήνωσεν *eskēnōsen*, "to tent"). In Sir 24:16, Wisdom has "glory" (δόξα *doxa*) and "grace" (χάρις *charis*), as does Jesus in John 1:14.

The hymn about creation in Col 1:15-20 (NAB) applies to Christ the creative role of wisdom:

> He is the image of the invisible God,
> the first born of all creation.
> For in him were created all things in heaven and
> on earth,
> · · · · · ·
> He is the head of the body, the church.
> He is the beginning, the firstborn from the
> dead.

He is the beginning, the firstborn from the dead. As in John 1, the hymn combines vocabulary of Genesis 1 with ideas from Proverbs 8 and Wisdom 7 to show that Christ, who created and governs the world, is now redeeming it. Creation and redemption stand in structural parallelism. Colossians 1:15-17 affirms that Christ was the model for the human race (created in the image of God, Gen 1:27-28) and is now the model for all members of the body, the church, and the means by which they are reconciled and exist together.

SUMMARY

The people of the ancient Near East, like people today, were interested in learning how to live optimally in a world they found only partially understandable. They took note of successful and unsuccessful ways of coping with life, stated them memorably, and handed them on to others. They also observed that life is often inexplicable and the lot of human beings to be miserable, and they explored such problems in complaints and dialogues. It was the human task to observe carefully the world the gods had made and to record their observations. Because of this common commitment to attend to the world and its rhythms and laws, there is remarkable continuity among the wisdom literatures of antiquity.

The people of Israel lived in that world and responded to it in literature similar to that of its neighbors. Belief in the sole God, Yahweh, made things different, however. The relation of wisdom to Yahweh had to be explained. The problem of evil was an especially vexing problem, because there were no demons to blame or a fate beyond God; there was only Yahweh, whom they celebrated as all-wise and all-just.

The wisdom books now appear in the Bible, a book of books. In the perennial dialectic of the Bible, the wisdom books "charge" other books and themselves receive a charge from them. They are incorporated into a story, which Christians and Jews regard as still ongoing. The wisdom books remind readers that one must take hold of life as both gift and task, that there are many possibilities but also profound limits, and that honest observation and fidelity to one's experience of life can put one in touch with a wondrous order whose source is God. The wisdom books' starting point of everyday experience and honest observations create common ground for Bible readers to engage with other people just as it once did for ancient Israel and its neighbors.

FOR FURTHER READING

Ancient Near Eastern Wisdom Literature:

Brunner, H. *Die Weisheitsbücher der Ägypter: Lehren für das Leben.* Munich: Artemis, 1991.

Pritchard, J. B. *Ancient Near Eastern Texts Relating to the Old Testament.* Princeton: Princeton University Press, 1955.

Lambert, W. G. *Babylonian Wisdom Literature.* Oxford: Clarendon, 1960.

Foster, B. B. *Before the Muses: An Anthology of Akkadian Literature.* 2 vols. Bethesda: CDL, 1993.

Lichtheim, Miriam. *Ancient Egyptian Literature.* 3 vols. Berkeley: University of California Press, 1973–1980.

Biblical Wisdom Literature:

Barré, M. L. " 'Fear of God' and the World View of Wisdom," *BTB* 11 (1981) 41-43.

Brenner, Athalya, ed. *A Feminist Companion to Wisdom Literature.* Sheffield: Sheffield Academic Press, 1995.

Brenner, Athalya, and Carole R. Fontaine, eds. *Wisdom and Psalms.* Feminist Companion to the Bible. Second Series 2. Sheffield: Sheffield Academic Press, 1998.

Hempel, Charlotte, Armin Lange, and Hermann Lichtenberger, eds. *The Wisdom Texts from Qumran and the Development of Sapential Thought: Studies in Wisdom at Qumran and its Relationship to Sapential Thought in the Ancient Near East, the Hebrew Bible, Ancient Judaism, and the New Testament.* BETL 159. Sterling, Va.: Peeters, 2001.

Murphy, R. *The Forms of Old Testament Literature.* FOTL 13. Grand Rapids: Eerdmans, 1981.

————. *The Tree of Life: An Exploration of Biblical Wisdom Literature.* 2nd ed. Grand Rapids: Eerdmans, 1996.

Gammie, J. G., and L. G. Perdue, eds. The Sage in Israel and the Ancient Near East. Winona Lake, Wis.: Eisenbrauns, 1990.

Smalley, B. *Medieval Exegesis of Wisdom Literature.* Edited by R. Murphy. Atlanta: Scholars Press, 1986.

Crenshaw, J. L., ed. Studies in Ancient Israelite Wisdom. New York: KTAV, 1976.

————. Theodicy in the Old Testament. Philadelphia: Fortress, 1983.

Vanel, A. "Sagesse," *Supplément au Dictionnaire de la Bible* (1986) 7:4-58.

von Rad, G. *Wisdom in Israel.* Nashville: Abingdon, 1972.

Whybray, R. N. *The Intellectual Tradition in the Old Testament.* BZAW 135. Berlin: de Gruyter, 1974.

ENDNOTES

1. See Bendt Alster, *The Instructions of Šurup-pak: A Sumerian Proverb Collection* (Copenhagan: Akademisk Forlag, 1974).

2. B. B. Foster, *Before the Muses: An Anthology of Akkadian Literature*, 2 vols. (Bethesda: CDL, 1993) 1:337-48.

3. See *Ancient Near Eastern Texts Relating to the Old Testament*, ed. James B. Pritchard, 3rd ed. (Princeton, N.J.: Princeton University Press, 1969) 595-96.

4. *ANET* 595-96.

5. *ANET* 601-4; B. B. Foster, *Before the Muses: An Anthology of Akkadian Literature*, 2:806-14.

6. B. B. Foster, *Before the Muses: An Anthology of Akkadian Literature*, 1:308-25.

7. *ANET*, 72-99.

8. Helmut Brunner, *Die Weisheitsbücher der Ägypter: Lehren für das Leben* (Munich: Artemis, 1991).

9. Miriam Lichtheim, *Ancient Egyptian Literature*, 3 vols. (Berkeley: University of California Press, 1973–1980) 1:58-59.

10. Miriam Lichtheim, *AEL* 3:184-217.

11. *ANET*, 421-25; Miriam Lichtheim, *AEL*, 2:146-63.

12. *ANET*, 441-44; Miriam Lichtheim, *AEL*, 1:159-63.

13. *ANET*, 407-10; Miriam Lichtheim, *AEL*, 1:169-82.

14. *ANET*, 467; Miriam Lichtheim, *AEL*, 1:194-97.

15. *ANET*, 432-34; Miriam Lichtheim, *AEL*, 1:184-92.

16. *ANET*, 407-07; Miriam Lichtheim, *AEL*, 1:163-69.

17. B. B. Foster, *Before the Muses: An Anthology of Akkadian Literature*, 332-25.

18. Klaus Koch, "Is There a Doctrine of Retribution in the Old Testament?" in *Theodicy in the Old Testament*, ed. James L. Crenshaw (Philadelphia: Fortress, 1983) 57-87.

19. W. L. Moran, "Rib Adda: Job at Byblos?" *Biblical and Related Studies Presented to Samuel Iwry* (Winona Lake: Eisenbrauns, 1985) 176-77.

20. W. L. Moran, "Rib Adda: Job at Byblos?" 177n. 16.

THE BOOK OF
PROVERBS

RAYMOND C. VAN LEEUWEN

Every human needs wisdom for living, and every healthy society hands its wisdom on to the next generation. Proverbs is a literary anthology of Israel's traditional wisdom, gathered from diverse spheres of life. The book's purpose is to help people become wise and godly (1:2-7). Yet its writers were aware of a hermeneutical circle of living and reading, in which one needs godly wisdom to get wisdom (2:1-6; 8:9). The book's entry into this circle of life and learning is generational. In traditional oral cultures, mothers and fathers, teachers and leaders pass on their own life experience and ancestral wisdom to their "children," both real and figurative (1:8; 4:3-4; 6:20; 31:1). Proverbs is a literary gathering of such diverse wisdom. Its readers are invited to walk the path of wisdom and "the fear of the LORD."

Although many readers find Proverbs full of "common sense" with which they can connect, there are still many difficulties in a book whose world, culture, and language are ancient and foreign. We often find ourselves listening in on a fragmentary conversation intended for someone else and filled with hidden assumptions and references. In addition to the challenges faced by all readers, feminism has made us aware that women face additional barriers in appropriating the wisdom of Proverbs, because it is addressed to men and presents women in terms of their relations with men. In the Hebrew of Proverbs, the word translated "my child" or "children" (NRSV) is invariably literally "my son" (בני *běnî*) or "sons" (בנים *bānîm*). Presumably, Israelite parents taught daughters as well as sons, but this book gives no sign thereof. Many readers today find this androcentric focus objectionable. Moreover, some women declare Proverbs to be oppressive because of its ancient patriarchal worldview, because it lacks a (nonpatriarchal) woman's

voice, and because of its portrayal of women.[1] It is, perhaps, important to remember that the male focus of Proverbs is a reflection not only of patriarchal culture but also of the book's genre (see below).

Proverbs is a challenge to all modern and post-modern readers whose world and worldviews can make it difficult to connect with aspects of this ancient book. Biblical scholars have shown the naivete of selectively domesticating the Bible to fit present cultural patterns (so that the Bible's own voice is silenced, as we assume it means what we mean), or of attempting to transform the present society into an ancient Israel (so that the particularity of the present culture and society is not taken seriously). Wisdom, however, requires that we see new situations fittingly. This means seeing not just the different or the particular in a new situation, but also recognizing in it those old fundamental patterns of life described by the sages of Proverbs. Wisdom requires a humble, earnest effort to hear what the other says and a willingness to see our world in the other's terms (18:13).

TITLE AND DATE

The English title "Proverbs" stems from *Proverbia*, the Latin title that Jerome gave the book in the Vulgate. In Hebrew, the book is known by its first word, [שלמה] משלי (*mišlê* [*šělōmōh*]), "The Proverbs [of Solomon]." *Mišlê* (sg., *māšāl*), however, has a wider range of reference than English "proverb." The word's meaning suggests "comparison," though some think it connotes "mastery" (over life or language). It is used to refer to a variety of oral and literary genres, including not only sayings and admonitions, but also parables, poems, and songs (see Num 21:27; 23:7; Ps 49:5; Isa 14:4; Ezek 17:2; 21:5).

The title "Proverbs of Solomon" is traditional and honorific, for it is clear that Solomon is not the author of the book in its present form (see 25:1; 30:1; 31:1), though some have argued for the origin of sections of the book in the Solomonic court. Solomon is Israel's paradigmatic wise king (1 Kings 3–4; 10). To him the ancients ascribed not only Proverbs, but also the Song of Songs, Ecclesiastes, the book of Wisdom (written in Greek!), and other works. In much the same way, all Psalms are conventionally ascribed to David and all of Israel's laws to Moses. The issue for the ancients was not authorship in the modern sense, but the authority of works written in the "spirit" of the archetypal lawgiver, psalmist, or sage.

Proverbs is a collection of collections, organized and edited with an Israelite character of its own. It was compiled over several centuries and bears the stamp of its diverse origins in the headings of its subcollections and sections (1:1; 10:1; 22:17; 24:23; 25:1; 30:1; 31:1) and in the variety of its materials.

Generally scholars consider the "Solomonic Collections" (10:1–22:16; 25:1–29:27) to be the earliest monarchical sections of the book. Though some have pointed out early ancient Near Eastern parallels to the personification of Wisdom in Proverbs 8,[2] the first nine chapters and the thirty-first chapter are usually dated in the early Persian period, after the return from the Babylonian exile (538 BCE).[3] However, the possibility of a Greek-Hebrew word play in 31:27 may mean that the final sections of the book were composed after Alexander the Great's conquest of Palestine (332 BCE). The Septuagint (LXX), with its different ordering of the last sections and its pluses and minuses, constitutes in effect another edition of the book. Thus different versions of the book existed during the Hellenistic period.[4]

The nature of this literature makes it extremely difficult to date. Proverbs (sayings and admonitions) refer to the common structures and patterns of human life. Sayings and admonitions are traditional and can preserve wisdom from earlier times in fossilized form (as in English, "Pride goeth before a fall"). The problem is made more difficult by the extremely brief scope of the various sayings and admonitions. In addition, there are virtually no historical "hooks" on which to hang a secure date or dates for the whole and its parts. Aside from the references to Solomon (1:1; 10:1) and to Hezekiah (25:1), there are no specific historical references in the book (Lemuel and Agur are otherwise unknown). Proverbs is entirely silent concerning Israel's history of redemption (patriarchal promises, covenants, exodus, law, gift of the land, exile and return—but see 2:21-22; 10:30; 22:28).

This silence does not imply that the various authors of the book had no interest in matters of redemptive history or in other biblical books. Like most books, Proverbs does not reveal the full range of its authors' concerns. Similarly, the New Testament wisdom book called James bypasses the events of the life of Jesus, a matter that displeased Martin Luther. Such silences in wisdom writings are a function of their genre and purpose, and too much should not be concluded concerning the isolation of the sages from Israel's historical traditions. To borrow a remark on Psalm 119, the sage "so focuses upon *ethos* that he barely notices *mythos*, in this case, the history of redemption."[5] The same holds true for the book's infrequent mention of worship.[6] The clues for dating that remain are the uncertain ones of language, culture, and social location.

SOCIAL LOCATIONS: ORAL AND LITERARY

Like the quest for firm dates, the attempt to establish the social location of the book, its sections, and sayings has proved difficult.[7] Arguments in these matters are especially prone to circular reasoning: One posits a date and social location for a section of the book and then proceeds to explain that section in terms of the proposed location. Neither have scholars always clearly distinguished among (1) the original *sources* of sections and proverbs (whether oral or written); (2) the *persons, processes*, and *places* of literary collection; (3) editorial *composition*; and (4) the Hebrew book in its final form, embodying all the earlier collections, but reflecting the shape, scope, and purpose of the final editors and ultimately of the Holy Spirit.[8] These writer-editors have put all their materials together for a new purpose, in which the whole is more than the sum of its parts.

The embodiment of oral traditions in literary works raises problems with which biblical scholars still struggle.[9] A number of scholars have compared sayings and admonitions in Proverbs to oral traditions from Africa to argue that the source of the biblical sayings and admonitions is the Israelite "folk," in family, clan, and village.[10] For R. N. Whybray, many of the sayings reflect the perspective of the Israelite peasant. For them life was hard and difficult, a matter of survival. Yet he notes that chaps. 1–9 and 22:16–24:22 have a more aristocratic social level, as does chap. 31.[11] Others believe that the book reflects the aristocratic world of the royal court. Although the sayings and admonitions of the Solomonic collections appear to arise from a variety of social locations and periods, the royal court remains the most plausible location for their literary compilation (10:1; 25:1; cf. 31:1). Even a scholar such as F. Golka (an advocate of the "folk" origin of proverbs), who claims to show that sayings about the king do not require a courtly origin, assumes that the sayings were collected and redacted in the royal court.[12]

The theory that the book (or its parts) arose from a school setting remains disputed, suffering from a lack of conclusive evidence that Israelite schools existed independently in the pre-exilic period.[13] The probable final editing of the book took place in the early Hellenistic period (after 322 BCE). The final editors of Proverbs were among the scribal sages who gave the Hebrew Bible its canonical shape. Parallels to these redactors may be found in literary sages like Ben Sira and the poet-writers of Qumran.[14]

The foregoing uncertainties about dating and social location are partly due to the variety and even contradictory character of sayings gathered in the book. It is likely that differing social groups produced and made use of originally independent sections and that the final author-editors collected, augmented, and edited the parts to provide a complex and diverse compendium of wisdom.[15] One group learns from another, borrowing and adapting its wisdom for its own ends. This is entirely in keeping with the amazing mobility of proverbial wisdom. Each group in a society produces its own sayings, some of which become universal. For example, everyone today knows the computer proverb, "Garbage in, garbage out." Proverbs not only cross social boundaries within a society, but they can even cross linguistic and cultural barriers as well.[16] Erasmus domesticated ancient and medieval Latin proverbs in his *Adages*. Western anthropologists and missionaries have collected sayings throughout the world.

When proverbs are contradictory, it is not necessarily a sign of different origins or conflicting worldviews. Proverbs even from a single group or person can be contradictory, because life is complex. In a proverb collection, or in the collective oral memory of a culture, we find a "universe" of wisdom, a world of discourse. The collection is undergirded by a common view of reality, but may be diverse and even contradictory in its particulars. Thus users of proverbs must choose from the diverse sayings and admonitions the one that best "hits the nail on the head." With proverbs, one may say, "If the shoe fits, wear it." Proverb use is always situational.

Another factor is at work in a written compendium of wisdom such as Proverbs. Whether individual units were originally oral or written, their juxtaposition cheek by jowl in a book creates a *literary* context for the reader. Their original oral settings have disappeared; we have only a literary context to clarify their meaning. Often proverbs are juxtaposed in such a way that one "comments" on its neighbor. Among these "proverb pairs," the Yahweh sayings are particularly sharp in qualifying their fellows.

In addition, within each section of Proverbs, certain themes, genres, or patterns are more prominent than in other sections. While the differences among the collections are not absolute, they are significant, for they create typical patterns of emphasis and concern. For example, the contrast between righteous and wicked in chapters 10–15 is typical of the first Solomonic subcollection (chaps. 10–15). It creates an orderly view of reality and justice in which good and bad actions are met with corresponding consequences. In contrast, the second Solomonic subcollection (16:1–22:16) presents a more complex view of acts and consequences. Here the focus on God's freedom and on the king (16:1-15) introduces the notion of limits to human wisdom and of mystery in the divine disposition of events. Here we see that sometimes the righteous suffer while the wicked prosper.

A further, crucial aid to interpreting Proverbs is the existence of long-distance literary context, created by repetitions of themes, of phrases, and even of lines and couplets.[17] This literary context is first of all within and among sections of Proverbs itself, but the alert reader will find many connections among Proverbs, the rest of the Bible, and other Jewish and Christian writings. Finally, comparative study of ancient Near Eastern and Egyptian cultures greatly enriches our understanding of Proverbs.

GENRE AND CONTENT

Proverbs has affinities in genre and content to a long list of Egyptian "instructions" and other ancient Near Eastern works.[18] Indeed, many scholars believe that the section titled "Sayings of the Wise" (22:17–24:22) adapts parts of the Egyptian *Instruction of Amenemope* for its own purposes.[19] The book begins with a brief title, an extended statement of purpose, and a motto: The fear of the Lord is the beginning of knowledge (1:1-7). The remainder of Proverbs 1–9 comprises a series of speeches by parents to a young son. These speeches especially are akin to the Egyptian "instructions" in which a royal father left a testament of wisdom to his heir. A similar medieval Jewish genre is the "Ethical Will." This sort of literature is based on oral "rites of passage." The parent—often portrayed as being on the point of death—gives advice to a son (occasionally a daughter) about to enter the responsibilities of adulthood (see 1 Kgs 2:1-9; Tob 4:1-21; Sir 3:1-16.[20]

Within the book, however, chapters 1–9 have a literary function. Together with chapters 30–31, they form an interpretive "frame" through which to view the small wisdom utterances they enclose. The worldview of these chapters—to change the image—gives the reader lenses through which to read the diverse sayings and admonitions in chapters 10–29. Even when contemplating the minutia of table manners, of farming, or of the law court, all of life expresses "the fear of the LORD"—or lack thereof (1:7; 9:10; 31:30). No aspect of reality is irrelevant to wisdom, because the Lord made all things through wisdom (3:19-20; 8:22-31).

The wisdom of Proverbs requires a knowledge of the common structures and patterns of the world and of human life as ordained by God. Globally, this is presented in the imagery of chaps. 1–9, in which "ways," "women," and "houses" in relation to the young male addressee form a metaphorical system for Wisdom and Folly that communicates the basic character of life in God's world. On a smaller scale, this is often true of the sayings and admonitions as well (chaps. 10–29). Sayings are often narratives in a nutshell; they distill the manifold patterns of life down to their basic elements. Thus Mario Puzo can expand the insight of Prov 10:21*b* into an entire novel.[21] The reader familiar with biblical stories will find in them many proverbs "writ large," as the commentary attempts to show.

Wisdom requires reverence for God and a general knowledge of how the world and humans work. Wise folk know the way things "ought to be," and they have a sense of right and wrong.[22] Wisdom also demands an understanding of concrete situations, of particular institutions and persons with their individuality and quirks (this job, this company, this boss, this employee, this woman or man, this teacher, this country, etc.). Wise people know what the present moment and its constituents require. Wise action and speech are *fitting*. Consequently, proverbs can be contradictory on verbal and social levels because different sayings apply to different persons, circumstances, and times. The wise person recognizes which is which and acts appropriately. The conceptual adequacy of Proverbs to illumine reality comes only when the rich diversity of proverbs is wisely exploited (see 26:7, 9).

The use of proverbs can be even more complex or subtle than suggested so far. The same proverb can be legitimately used for quite different purposes and to communicate quite different things, depending on who speaks, to whom, and in what way and circumstances. For a disadvantaged poor person to say, "Money talks," has a different meaning than when someone rich and powerful says it.[23] Social location and relations matter.

Even on something so basic as the "act-consequence connection" (the basic wisdom doctrine that people reap what they sow), the book of Proverbs can be contradictory. Its basic teaching (chaps. 1–15) is that right living produces wealth and well-being. Folly and wickedness produce poverty, disgrace, and even death. This is true because God made the world in wisdom, and God is faithful to its principles. But as the book proceeds (chaps. 16–29), we learn that there are exceptions to the general rules of life. Not even the wise can comprehend all the contradictions and mysteries of life, of God and cosmos. The wicked can prosper, especially in a time of chaos, and the righteous can suffer unjustly. (These themes are developed more extensively in Job and Ecclesiastes.) Still, Proverbs insists that it is better to be poor and godly than rich and wicked. Ultimately Proverbs is a book of faith (1:7), insisting on the reality of God's justice and righteousness, even when experience seems to contradict it (see Hebrews 11).[24] God's justice often remains hidden, since much of life—and God's own self—is beyond human grasping.[25]

The bulk of the book is devoted to short, mostly two-line indicative "sayings" or "sentences" of the sort commonly called "proverbs" (esp. 10:1– 22:16; 25:1–29:27). A middle section of the book (22:17–24:22) is largely devoted to "admonitions," brief second-person precepts that usually provide reasons or motive clauses for doing or not doing something. These motives can be practical (looking at positive or negative consequences) or explanatory (appealing to the nature of things). Ultimately, and sometimes explicitly, they are theological, rooted in the God who made and rules all things wisely. Both genres, sayings and admonitions, appear throughout the book, sometimes embedded in larger structures.

This diversity of sayings and admonitions constitutes one of the main problems in understanding the book. A master scholar of world proverbs has declared that "the proverb in a collection is dead," because readers have no direct access to the life situation in which they are used.[26] Proverbs (both sayings and admonitions) are generally short, pithy utterances that require a social and cultural context for us to understand them fully. Proverbs are addressed to particular people in particular situations, and yet, they embody common human truths, recurring patterns in ordinary life. Wisdom applies old truths to new situations, because in a certain sense, "There is nothing new under the sun" (see Matt 13:52). A mother tells a sluggish college student that "the early bird catches the worm." A Nigerian father tells a teenager who hangs out with the wrong crowd that those "who sleep with puppies catch fleas." One child needs to be told, "Look before you leap," another, "She who hesitates is lost."

Proverbs also embody a culture's commitments, contradictions, and myths. Many Americans believe that "money talks" and that "sex sells." Yet we emblazon "In God we trust" on our currency, perhaps to remind ourselves that "money isn't everything." And advertisers fervently exploit our belief that "the sky's the limit"—meaning that for us there are no limits, whether ecological, moral, or divine—to self-gratification.[27]

THEOLOGY

Some scholars believe that the God of Proverbs was a mere variant of the deities in other ancient Near Eastern wisdom writings. An extreme form of this view argues that the God of Proverbs is *not* the God of the rest of the OT.[28] This position, however, presupposes the widespread (and mistaken) belief that the uniqueness of Israel's God had to do with Yahweh's involvement in history; it also entailed a corresponding marginalization of creation.[29] A related position, using the method of tradition history, separates creation of the cosmos from creation of humans, so that the theology of Proverbs 1–9 (cosmos) has little to do with Proverbs 10–29 (humans).[30] This position, however, ignores the actual coexistence of both traditions in Proverbs and the editors' evident intent in chaps. 1–9 to create a cosmic context for understanding the sayings of chaps. 10–29. It is also anachronistic because, unlike the modern West with its separation of nature and culture, ancient Near Eastern anthropologies presuppose cosmologies, which may be largely implicit (as in chaps. 10–29) or explicit (as in chaps. 1–9). On another front, some scholars seek in Lady Wisdom evidence for an Israelite goddess whose existence was suppressed by the monotheistic editors of the book.[31] One's hermeneutical approach to these theological-exegetical questions greatly influences one's reading of the evidence and the conclusions drawn from it. On this point leading scholars are divided. James L. Crenshaw, writing in honor of Roland E. Murphy, put it succinctly: "For me, the crucial issue concerns whether or not ancient sages accepted the world view of Yahwism. Murphy thinks they did; I am not able to accept that position."[32]

Yet, the writer-editors of Proverbs clearly considered the God of wisdom to be Israel's God, Yahweh. This is evident in their almost exclusive reference to God by that name. That there are features common to both Israel's God and the gods of the nations is a theological problem not unique to Proverbs and the wisdom literature.[33] The evidence of Proverbs itself and its inter-textual relations within the larger canon leads one to see these commonalities in the light of the particular grace given to Israel.[34] At the same time, these commonalities, and the cosmic context of Israel's wisdom, lead one to recognize the God of Israel as the wise creator of all things and persons. Thus this commentary will begin with the book as a whole and assume it and the OT are the primary, though not only, literary context for theological interpretation.[35]

Because proverbs presuppose both specific life situations and a larger cultural context to make sense of them, their interpretation can be difficult. The sayings and admonitions are so short that they require some larger context for understanding. For ancient Israelites that larger context came naturally. Their sayings reflected their own culture and experience. Moreover, they used sayings (as do we) to comment on real-life situations. The truth of many sayings is only realized when they are "fittingly" applied.[36] Unfortunately, we do not have access to these life situations, though certain biblical stories and cross-cultural comparisons can give us some idea of how the Israelites actually used their proverbs.[37]

Consequently, finding the meaning of ancient biblical proverbs can be difficult. Sometimes knowledge of archaeology and ancient Near Eastern cultures and languages can help us. But our main resource is the language of the sayings themselves. Proverbs, in any language, never exist in isolation. One proverb comments on or contrasts with another. Thus proverbs can happily "contradict" each other: "Haste makes waste," but "whoever hesitates is lost." Again, when it comes to marriage and friendships, a recent authoritative study tells us that "birds of a feather flock together."[38] Yet, there are some marriages in which "opposites attract." Indeed, without the latter truth, the sexes would never get together.

The great German poet Goethe once said of languages that "whoever knows only one, knows none." This saying is all the more true of proverbs. One proverb may not fit a situation, but another will. One saying calls for another to qualify it, or for a biblical story to flesh it out. Often a proverb theme will appear more than once. Brief as proverbs are, no one saying contains the whole truth. Reality is too rich and complex for that.

EXCURSUS:
THE "HEART" IN THE
OLD TESTAMENT

The Hebrew term for "heart" (לב *lēb* or לבב *lēbāb*), often translated as "mind," is easily misunderstood in English translation. In both languages, the heart can simply be the organ in one's chest. But of greater interest biblically is its metaphorical use for the internal wellspring of the acting self. In the modern West, heart and head are often opposed as the loci of feeling and thinking respectively. But the ancient Hebrews used "heart" comprehensively to indicate the inner person, the "I" that is the locus of a person's will, thought (Prov 16:1, 9; 19:21), and feeling (Prov 14:10, 13; 17:22). Thus all of a person's actions (Prov 15:13; 2 Sam 7:3), especially speech (Prov 16:23), flow from the heart, expressing its content, whether good or bad (Gen 6:5; 8:21; Sir 37:17-18; Matt 12:33-35; 18:18-19). Scripture can use related terms, such as "belly" and "kidneys" (כליות *kělāyôt*; Jer 11:20; 17:10) in much the same way as "heart" (cf. John 7:38 NRSV).

Most important, one's basic disposition toward God is a matter of the "heart" (Prov 3:5; 19:3; Deut 6:5; 1 Sam 12:20). Like a deep well, the heart has a hidden depth (Prov 20:5). Its deepest depths, what modern psychologists might call the subconscious or the unconscious, only God can plumb (Prov 25:2-3), though hidden even from the heart's owner and friends: "The heart is devious above all else, and beyond cure—who can understand it? I the LORD test the mind and search the heart" (Jer 17:9-10 NRSV and NIV collated; cf. Prov 21:2; 15:11).

When seeking to replace Saul, the Lord finds in

David "a man after his own heart" (1 Sam 13:14 NRSV). But even the seer Samuel is not able to recognize the Lord's chosen, because mortals "look on the outward appearance, but the LORD looks on the heart" (1 Sam 16:7 NRSV). In Proverbs, since the heart is the locus of wisdom, it often stands in metonymy for wisdom: Those who are not wise "lack heart" (Prov 7:7; 10:13). Israel shared the general structure of its anthropology concerning heart and other bodily members with its neighbors. The famous "Memphis Theology" from Egypt illustrates the biblical conception well:

> The sight of the eyes, the hearing of the ears, and the smelling the air by the nose, they report to the heart. It is this which causes every completed (concept) to come forth, and it is the tongue which announces what the heart thinks.[39]

Against this background, we can understand the absolute urgency of the admonition in Prov 4:23: "Above all else, guard your heart" (NIV). This is a fundamental precept, like Socrates' "know thyself"; but it goes beyond Socrates in depth and scope. For Israel, all human hearts are inescapably related to the one Lord, whether in loving service, in uncertain vacillation (1 Kgs 18:21; Ps 86:11), or in grievous rebellion (Prov 19:3). Thus in a prayer that plumbs anthropological depths, the psalmist, wary of personal sin and self-deception, concludes, "Search me, O God, and know my heart" (Ps 139:23 NRSV). Augustine understood the biblical heart well: "Our hearts are restless until they find their rest in thee."[40] And when the prophets anticipate God's final renewal of a wounded and disobedient human race, they do it in terms of the heart, as it is the hidden seed of the new humanity: "A new heart I will give you, and a new spirit I will put within you. . . . I will put my spirit within you, and make you follow my statutes . . . and you shall be my people, and I will be your God" (Ezek 36:26-28 NRSV; cf. Ps 51:7-11; Jer 24:7; 31:33).

Even though the heart can stand in metonymy for the whole person in its "mental," inner aspect (what my heart thinks is what I think), there is in the admonition to guard one's heart an awareness of the mysterious reflexivity that humans possess: I can look at myself and make even my inmost self the object of care, reflection, improvement, and betterment. Some commentators have looked upon guarding the heart (Prov 4:23) as equivalent to keeping it from sin. The admonition is more comprehensive than that, but certainly does not exclude it, as is evident from Prov 4:24.

FOR FURTHER READING

Commentaries:

Alonso-Schökel, L., and J. Vilchez. *Proverbios.* Madrid: Ediciones Cristiandad, 1984.

Fox, Micahel V. *Proverbs 1-9: A New Translation with Introduction and Commentary.* AB 18A. New York: Doubleday, 2000.

McKane, William. *Proverbs: A New Approach.* OTL. Philadelphia: Westminster, 1970.

Perdue, Leo G. *Proverbs.* Interpretation Bible Commentary. Louisville, Ky.: Westminster/John Knox Press, 2000.

Toy, Crawford H. *The Book of Proverbs.* ICC. New York: Scribner's Sons, 1902.

Whybray, R. N. *Proverbs.* NCBC. Grand Rapids: Eerdmans, 1994.

Other Studies:

Camp, Claudia V. *Wisdom and the Feminine in the Book of Proverbs.* Sheffield: Almond, 1985.

Fontaine, Carole R. *Smooth Words: Women, Proverbs and Performance in Biblical Wisdom.* JSOTSup 356. New York: Continuum, 2002.

———. *Traditional Sayings in the Old Testament.* Sheffield: Almond, 1982.

Mieder, Wolfgang, and Alan Dundes, eds. *The Wisdom of Many: Essays on the Proverb.* New York: Garland, 1981.

Murphy, Roland E. *The Tree of Life: An Exploration of Biblical Wisdom Literature.* Third Edition. Grand Rapids, Mich.: Eerdmans, 2002.

Schroer, Silvia. *Widsom Has Built Her House: Studies on the Figure of Sophia in the Bible.* Translated by William C. McDonough and Linda M. Mahoney. Collegeville, Minn.: Liturgical Press, 2000.

Van Leeuwen, Raymond C. *Context and Meaning in Proverbs 25–27.* Atlanta: Scholars Press, 1988.

von Rad, Gerhard. *Wisdom in Israel.* Nashville:

Abingdon, 1972.

Washington, Harold C. *Wealth and Poverty in the Instruction of Amenemope and the Hebrew Proverbs*. Atlanta: Scholars Press, 1994.

Weeks, Stuart. *Early Israelite Wisdom*. Oxford: Clarendon, 1994.

Whybray, R. N. *The Book of Proverbs: A Survey of Modern Study*. Leiden: Brill, 1995.

———. *The Composition of the Book of Proverbs*. Sheffield: JSOT, 1994.

———. *Wealth and Poverty in the Book of Proverbs*. Sheffield: JSOT, 1990.

Williams, James G. *Those Who Ponder Proverbs*. Sheffield: JSOT, 1981.

Yoder, Christine Roy. *Wisdom As a Woman of Substance: A Socioeconomic Reading of Proverbs 1-9 and 31:10-31*. BZAW 304. Berlin: de Gruyter, 2001.

ENDNOTES

1. Sharon H. Ringe lists a variety of women's approaches to interpretation of the Bible in her essay "When Women Interpret the Bible," in Carol A. Newsom and Sharon H. Ringe, eds., *The Women's Bible Commentary* (Louisville: Westminster, 1992) 4-5.

2. Christa Kayatz, *Studien zu Proverbien 1-9*, WMANT 22 (Neukirchen-Vluyn: Neukirchener Verlag, 1966); G. von Rad, *Wisdom in Israel* (Nashville: Abingdon, 1972) 143-76.

3. Claudia V. Camp, *Wisdom and the Feminine in the Book of Proverbs* (Sheffield: JSOT, 1985) 179-208, 233-254.

4. E. Tov, *Textual Criticism of the Hebrew Bible* (Minneapolis: Fortress, 1992) 337.

5. Jon D. Levenson, "The Sources of Torah," in *Ancient Israelite Religion*, Patrick D. Miller, Jr., Paul D. Hanson, and S. Dean McBride, eds. (Philadelphia: Fortress, 1987) 568, 559-74. See J. J. Collins, "Proverbial Wisdom and the Yahwist Vision," *Semeia* 17 (1980) 1-17.

6. See Leo G. Perdue, *Wisdom and Cult* (Missoula: Scholars Press, 1977).

7. R.E. Murphy, "Form Criticism and Wisdom Literature," *CBQ* 31 (1969) 481; J.L. Crenshaw, "Wisdom," in John L. Hayes, ed., *Old Testament Form Criticism* (San Antonio: Trinity University Press, 1974) 236.

8. For an astute defense of God's speaking in the diverse texts of Scripture, see N. Wolterstorff, *Divine Discourse: Philosophical Reflections on the Claim That God Speaks* (Cambridge: Cambridge University Press, 1996).

9. Walter J. Ong, *Orality and Literacy: The Technologizing of the Word* (London: Methuen, 1982); Jack Goody, *The Logic of Writing and the Organization of Society* (Cambridge: Cambridge University Press, 1986). For the ancient Near East, see J. Bottero, *Mesopotamia: Writing, Reasoning, and the Gods* (Chicago: University of Chicago Press, 1992) 4, 67-137.

10. Most recently, C. Westermann, *The Roots of Wisdom: The Oldest Proverbs of Israel and Other Peoples* (Louisville: Westminster John Knox, 1995)

11. R.N. Whybray, *Wealth and Poverty in the Book of Proverbs* (Sheffield: JSOT, 1990); and *The Composition of the Book of Proverbs* (Sheffield: JSOT, 1994)

12. Friedemann W. Golka, "Die Königs und Hofsprüche und der Ursprung der Israelitischen Weisheit," *VT* 36 (1986) 13-36, here 13. See Michael V. Fox, "The Social Location of the Book of Proverbs," in Fox et al., eds., *Texts, Temples and Traditions: A Tribute to Menahem Haran* (Winona Lake: Eisenbrauns, 1996) 227-39.

13. See James L. Crenshaw, "Education in Ancient Israel," *JBL* 104 (1985) 601-5; S. Weeks, *Early Israelite Wisdom* (Oxford: Clarendon, 1994) 132-56. Cf. Andre Lemaire, "The Sage in School and Temple," in *The Sage in Israel and the Ancient Near East*, ed. John G. Gammie and Leo G. Perdue (Winona Lake: Eisenbrauns, 1990) 165-81.

14. See R. C. Van Leeuwen, "Scribal Wisdom and Theodicy in the Book of the Twelve," in Leo G. Perdue, et al., eds., *In Search of Wisdom: Essays in Memory of John G. Gammie* (Louisville: Westminster/John Knox, 1993) 31-49.

15. James L. Crenshaw, "The Sage in Proverbs," in Gammie and Perdue, *The Sage in Israel*, 205-16. See also the essays by Camp, Fontaine, Whybray, and Lemaire in the same volume.

16. The classic, essential work remains Archer Taylor, *The Proverb* (Cambridge, Mass.: Harvard University Press, 1931; reprint edited by W. Mieder [Bern: Peter Lang, 1985]). See also W. Mieder, *Proverbs Are Never Out of Season: Popular Wisdom in the Modern Age* (New York:

Oxford University Press, 1993).

17. Daniel C. Snell, *Twice Told Proverbs and the Composition of the Book of Proverbs* (Winona Lake: Eisenbrauns, 1993).

18. Stuart Weeks, *Early Israelite Wisdom* (Oxford: Clarendon, 1994) 162-89; Miriam Lichtheim, *Ancient Egyptian Literature,* 3 vols. (Berkeley: University of California Press, 1973-80) and *Late Egyptian Wisdom Literature in the International Context* (Freiburg and Göttingen: Vandenhoeck & Ruprecht, 1983).

19. Harold C. Washington, *Wealth and Poverty in the Instruction of Amenemope and the Hebrew Proverbs,* SBLDS 142 (Atlanta: Scholars Press, 1994).

20. See Michael V. Fox, "The Social Location of the Book of Proverbs," 232. For examples, see *Ancient Near Eastern Texts Relating to the Old Testament,* ed. James B. Pritchard, 3rd ed. (Princeton, N.J.: Princeton University Press, 1969). 412-25 or *AEL* 1:58-80, 134-39; 2:135-63; 3:159-217.

21. Mario Puzo, *Fools Die* (New York: Putnam, 1978).

22. Cornelius Plantinga, Jr., *Not the Way It's Supposed to Be: A Breviary of Sin* (Grand Rapids: Eerdmans, 1995) 113-28.

23. Barbara Kirshenblatt-Gimblett, "Toward a Theory of Proverb Meaning," in *The Wisdom of Many: Essays on the Proverb,* W. Mieder and A. Dundes, eds. (New York: Garland, 1981) 111-21; Peter Seitel, "Proverbs: A Social Use of Metaphor," 122-39 in the same volume; Carole R. Fontaine, *The Use of the Traditional Saying in the Old Testament* (Sheffield: JSOT, 1982).

24. R. C. Van Leeuwen, "On Wealth and Poverty: System and Contradiction in Proverbs," *Hebrew Studies* 33 (1992) 25-36.

25. G. von Rad's work remains basic, *Wisdom in Israel* (Nashville: Abingdon, 1972) 97-110.

26. Wolfgang Mieder, cited by Carole R. Fontaine, *The Use of the Traditional Saying in the Old Testament,* (Sheffield: JSOT, 1982) 54.

27. Alan Dundes, "Folk Ideas as Units of Worldview," *American Journal of Folklore* 84 (1971) 93-103.

28. H. D. Preuss, "Das Gottesbild der älteren Weisheit Israels," *VTS* 23 (1972) 117-45.

29. See H. G. Reventlow, *Problems of Old Testament Theology in the Twentieth Century* (Philadelphia: Fortress, 1985) 59-124; Rolf P.

Knierim, "Cosmos and History in Israel's Theology," in *The Task of Old Testament Theology: Substance, Method, and Cases* (Grand Rapids: Eerdmans, 1995) 171-224.

30. P. Doll, *Menschenschöpfung und Weltschöpfung in der alttestamentlichen Weisheit,* SBS 117 (Stuttgart: Verlag Katholisches Bibelwerk, 1985); C. Westermann, *The Roots of Wisdom: The Oldest Proverbs of Israel and Other Peoples.*

31. B. Lang, *Wisdom and the Book of Proverbs: An Israelite Goddess Redefined* (New York: Pilgrim, 1986); C. Camp, "Woman Wisdom as Root Metaphor: A Theological Consideration," in *The Listening Heart,* ed. K. G. Hoglund et al. (Sheffield: JSOT, 1987) 45-76.

32. James L. Crenshaw, "Murphy's Axiom: Every Gnomic Saying Needs a Balancing Corrective," in *Urgent Advice and Probing Questions: Collected Writings on Old Testament Wisdom* (Macon, Ga.: Mercer University Press, 1995) 352, 344-54. See Roland E. Murphy, "Wisdom and Yahwism," in *No Famine in the Land,* ed. J. Flanagan and A. Robinson (Missoula: Scholars Press, 1975) 117-26; "Wisdom and Creation," *JBL* 104 (1985) 3-11.

33. Bertil Albrektson, *History and the Gods* (Lund: Gleerup, 1967); J. J. M. Roberts, "The Ancient Near Eastern Environment," in *The Hebrew Bible and Its Modern Interpreters,* Douglas A. Knight and Gene M. Tucker, eds. (Chico, Calif.: Scholars Press, 1985) 75-121.

34. G. von Rad, *Wisdom in Israel* (Nashville: Abingdon, 1972), remains basic. See also L. Bostrom, *The God of the Sages: The Portrayal of God in the Book of Proverbs* (Stockholm: Almquist & Wiksell, 1990); R. E. Clements, *Wisdom in Theology* (Grand Rapids: Eerdmans, 1992).

35. See Raymond C. Van Leeuwen, "Heuristic Assumptions," in *Context and Meaning in Proverbs 25–27* (Atlanta: Scholars Press, 1988) 29-38; Jon Levenson, *Hebrew Bible, Old Testament, and Historical Criticism: Jews and Christians in Biblical Studies* (Louisville: Westminster/John Knox, 1993) 106-26, 177-79.

36. C. E. Carlston, "Proverbs, Maxims, and the Historical Jesus," *JBL* 99 (1980) 87-105.

37. See Carole Fontaine, *The Use of the Traditional Saying in the Old Testament* (Sheffield: JSOT, 1982); Susan Niditch, *Folklore and the Hebrew Bible*

(Minneapolis: Fortress, 1993) 67-91; Wolfgang Mieder and Alan Dundes, eds., *The Wisdom of Many: Essays on the Proverb* (New York: Garland, 1981).

38. Robert T. Michael, John H. Gagnon, Edward O. Laumann, Gina Collati, *Sex in America: A Definitive Study* (Boston: Little, Brown, 1994).

39. *ANET*, ed. James B. Britchard, 3rd ed. (Princeton, N.J.: Princeton University Press, 1969) 5; cf. Prov 6:12-19.

40. Augustine *Confessions* 1.1.

THE BOOK OF
ECCLESIASTES

W. SIBLEY TOWNER

Ecclesiastes has always had its fans among the original thinkers of the Jewish and Christian communities: skeptics, people with a dark vision of reality, recovering alcoholics. The rest of us know and love some of its individual epigrams and its more lyrical passages. On the whole, however, believers have found it at least baffling and at most wrongheaded. From the beginning serious efforts were made to exclude it from the list of sacred books, and even now in liturgical practice it enjoys only a very small place. The *Revised Common Lectionary* would have us read Eccl 3:1-13 every New Year's Day—not a day for much pious observance, except when it falls on Sunday—and offers Eccl 1:2, 12-14; 2:18-23 as the Old Testament alternative to Hos 11:1-11 on Proper 13 in cycle C. That's it! Theoretically, its place in Jewish liturgical practice is greater because it is one of the five "scrolls" (*megillot*) that are read during festivals. The book of Ecclesiastes is to be read in its entirety during the Feast of Sukkot (Tabernacles), but the number of worshipers who will sit still to hear all twelve chapters through or even, in modern synagogues, will have the opportunity to do so is surely small. Frequently this book excites talk about its partial grasp of the truth, its need for fulfillment, and its function as the dark background against which the light of the gospel shines forth.

All dismissive talk about the book of Ecclesiastes is banned from the following pages. Time and time again one is driven to admit the truth of what Ecclesiastes has to say, even though one might not want to hear it. Here is the most real of the realists of the sacred writers. Here is the Hebrew writer least comfortable with conventional wisdom, and the most willing to challenge unexamined assumptions. No faith can survive long that is founded on the slippery slope of conceptually muddled piety, and in Qohelet, God has given us a tonic for our biblical faith.

THE NAMES OF THE BOOK: QOHELET AND ECCLESIASTES

We know the writer of the book of Ecclesiastes not by name but by the title קהלה (*qōhelet*). In two of its seven occurrences in the book, that title even appears in Hebrew with the definite article (7:27 [as amended]; 12:8). Traditionally this title has come over into English as "the Preacher." The real identity of the author is masked by this title, however. True, the word *qōhelet* offers slight warrant for claiming that the author was a woman, because it has the form of a feminine singular participle of the Hebrew verbal root קהל (*qhl*, "assemble"). Arrayed against this suggestion, however, are two weightier considerations: (1) Other titles, presumably of male persons, can be found in the Hebrew Bible in exactly the same grammatical form (e.g., Hassophereth ["the leatherworker"]; Pochereth-hazzebaim ["the gazelle-tender"] in Ezra 2:55, 57). This leads to the conclusion that the "feminine" form of the participle is merely an alternative form of the masculine. (2) A clearly male appellation, "the son of David," is appended to the title in Eccl 1:1, and the verbs accompanying the title here and in two of its other appearances (Eccl 12:8-9) are masculine. For better or for worse, then, in this introduction, the speaker in the book of Ecclesiastes will be referred to as "him."

Now, one of the functions of the Hebrew participle is to serve as the noun that names the one who does the action of the verb. So a *qōhelet* is the agent of "assembly," the "assembler." If what he assembles is a קהל (*qāhāl*, "congregation"), one can translate *qōhelet* as "leader of the assembly" (see NIV note) or even, to use the title most frequently given by us to such a functionary, "preacher" (see NRSV note). Already in antiquity, the Greek translators of the Hebrew Bible accepted this sense of the term *qōhelet*. Their Septuagint translates it as Ἐκκλησιαστής (*Ekklēsiastēs*), "one who leads a congregation [ἐκκλησία *ekklēsia*]," and it is from them that the name reached the English language.

Working from the basic root meaning of "assemble" for the verb קהל (*qāhal*), some argue that a *qōhelet* is one who assembles sentences or proverbs or wisdom.[1] The translation "Teacher," favored by both the NIV and the NRSV, attempts to capture some of both of these senses of the term. A teacher not only assembles information to convey to students but also carries out this function in an assembly, perhaps even in a place of congregational worship. There are other perfectly good and far more common Hebrew words for "teacher," of course, and whether *qōhelet* would have been understood as a synonym for them is difficult to judge because this title occurs only in the book of Ecclesiastes. If this writer is essentially a teacher, then by the standards of the wisdom literature of the Hebrew Bible he is a highly original thinker, capable of uncommonly sustained argument.

A title always implies a social setting. No one is called "judge" except in a place in which decisions are handed down. People receive the title "pilot" by virtue of their vocation in the maritime or aeronautical industries. If we could be sure which way to construe it, we could provide Qohelet with at least a sketchy sociological setting from his title alone. If it is taken to mean "Preacher," the name Qohelet conjures up a social setting of a congregation of believers—e.g., an early synagogue. Taken to mean "Teacher," it suggests a place of instruction for one or more pupils—e.g., a tutor's chamber in a royal or high priestly household or another early school. Unfortunately, we know next to nothing about either places of worship (other than the Second Temple) or schools in third-century BCE Judea. So whichever way we go with the title, we gain only a hint about the work of the man.

It makes sense that the author of the book of Ecclesiastes should be referred to by his title, "the Teacher," only four times in the book: in the superscription (1:1) and in its reprise (12:8), once in the main body (7:27), and once in the epilogue (12:9). After all, he is presented as having written the book, and having done so mostly in the first person! In these four instances, some narrator or editor of the teacher's work butts in to say something about the man. Although the definite article

appears in the Hebrew only in 7:27 (as amended) and 12:8, the NRSV and the NIV make all four occurrences definite: He is always "the Teacher."

LANGUAGE AND GENRE

The Hebrew language in which Qohelet wrote is distinctive. Either it is a late dialect peculiar to his place and time or, because his task was to offer a philosophical discussion of issues, he had to shape a new language for the purpose. Ancient Hebrew was not a literature given to abstract philosophy; however, if there was a philosopher in ancient Hebrew, Qohelet was the one, and to him fell the task of making the language of his people work for the purpose of sustained reflection.

Like other post-exilic writings in the Hebrew Bible, Qohelet's Hebrew betrays significant influence of the Aramaic language. Because Aramaic, like Hebrew, is a member of the family of northwest Semitic languages, the two always drew on a common vocabulary base. Periodically, however, new words or grammatical constructions would flood into Hebrew from Aramaic, leaving behind enriched linguistic soil. This happened during the period of the divided monarchy, especially in the northern kingdom of Israel, which had much intercourse with the Aramean kingdoms of Damascus and Hamath. It happened again after the exile. From the seventh century BCE down into Hellenistic times as late as 200 BCE, Official or Imperial Aramaic was the lingua franca of the Near East. The royal epistles and decrees preserved in the book of Ezra are written in this language. The Hebrew spoken and written in Judea during these years in this Aramaic milieu is distinctive enough to have been given its own name, Late Biblical Hebrew. Probable Aramaisms that occur only in Ecclesiastes in the Hebrew text of the Bible (though they often become common in Mishnaic and even modern Hebrew) include ענין (*'inyan*, "business"; 1:13 and seven other times as a noun); כבר (*kĕbār*, "already"; 1:10 and eight other times); חשבון (*ḥešbôn*, "sum"; 7:25, 27; 9:10); פשר (*pēšer*, "interpretation"; 8:1); and גומץ (*gûmmāṣ*, "pit"; 10:8). Many other Aramaic loan words and grammatical forms occur as well, including the synonymous terms רעיון (*ra'yôn*) and רעות (*rĕ'ût*), "chasing [after wind]," alternatively translated "feeding [on wind]" in the NRSV note (1:14 and seven other times). In all, 3.1 percent of Qohelet's vocabulary consists of Aramaisms.[2]

Quite apart from linguistic evidences of origin in late post-exilic culture, Qohelet simply forged his own distinctive literary style out of a repertoire both of standard clichés and of unique words or inflections of words. Five of his favorite terms are discussed below (see the section "The Vocabulary of Qohelet's Thought"), and others are pointed out along the way.

The very genre of the book of Ecclesiastes is a matter of debate. The editors of the NIV consider 60 percent of the text to be poetry, while the NRSV thinks it is 75 percent prose. The translators of the Good News Bible and the Revised English Bible think the only poetic passage in the entire book is 3:2-8. The criteria for identifying poetry in biblical Hebrew are subtle, and with Ecclesiastes they function hardly at all. As to the literary form of the book as a whole, von Rad's proposal that it follows the Egyptian genre of "royal testament" is now generally rejected because the pretense of kingly authorship is dropped after chap. 2. The Hellenistic genre "diatribe," too, has failed to convince critics, largely because of the absence of any explicit dialogue. Numerous sub-genres can be recognized (e.g., autobiographical narrative, rhetorical questions, parable, curses and blessings, proverbs), but for the book as a whole the very general rubrics "instruction" and "reflection" seem to be most satisfactory.[3]

AUTHORSHIP, DATE, AND HISTORICAL SETTING

The language of Ecclesiastes demands that it be placed among the later books of the Hebrew canon. Its language is not as late as that of Daniel, however. Almost half of Daniel is written in the so-called Middle Aramaic dialect that slowly displaced Official Aramaic in written texts after Greek became the more widely used official language in the Hellenistic period (after 200 BCE). Embedded in that Aramaic and in the Hebrew half of Daniel as well are loan words from Greek; furthermore, that book is rich with veiled historical allusions to the Ptolemaic and Seleucid successors of Alexander in Egypt and Antioch respectively. Indeed, because of those allusions, we can date

Daniel in its canonical form quite confidently to 164 BCE. The language of Ecclesiastes shows no discernible influence from Hellenistic Greek, nor is it particularly reminiscent of the Hebrew of Daniel. It should, therefore, be dated earlier than 164 BCE. This terminus ante quem (the date before which it must have been written) is supported by the presence of fragmentary Ecclesiastes texts among the Dead Sea Scrolls of Cave 4, dated mid-second century BCE.

The book exhibits the "philosophical" spirit of the Hellenistic period to a degree more pronounced than any other book of the Hebrew canon, even though none of the Teacher's ideas can be directly linked to Greek originals. All things considered, it seems sensible to date the book to the period between 332 BCE, when Alexander the Great put an end to Persian political dominance in the Middle East and cemented the hold of Greek cultural influence in the area, and 200 BCE. Had Qohelet known of the wrenching political crises associated with the change from Ptolemaic to Seleucid suzerainty in Palestine around that time, he might have alluded to them. Without attempting a definitive statement on the matter, this exposition will assume that Ecclesiastes was written in the middle of the third century BCE, perhaps around 250.

Other books, such as Daniel, offer historical evidences that corroborate linguistic judgments about their dates. The narrator of the final form of the book of Ecclesiastes also offers a historical setting to the reader, though without reference to the Egyptian Ptolemies of his own day or to their rivals, the Seleucid monarchs of Antioch in Syria. Instead he reaches over centuries to the era of monarchy in Jerusalem. It is no surprise that the superscription (Eccl 1:1) attributes the book to a king. That a king would concern himself with wisdom might surprise people today, but it certainly would not have done so in antiquity. The importance of circles of scribes, seers, and teachers at the courts of Babylon, Persia, and Egypt can hardly be overestimated. In ancient Israel the court—whether royal, gubernatorial, or high priestly—was paired with the Temple as the center of learning, the patron of scribes and teachers, the arbiter of etiquette. Joseph and Daniel in their respective times act the parts of wise and learned courtiers. The wisdom writer, Jesus ben Sira, who may even have been a late contemporary of the author of Ecclesiastes, instructed the patrician youth of his age in the things that make for successful living, boldly claiming, "Hear but a little of my instruction,/and through me you will acquire silver and gold" (Sir 51:28 NRSV).

It comes as no surprise either that "the Teacher" is not only a king but is, in the literary presentation given to his work, no other than "the son of David," King Solomon. After all, it was Solomon who, having asked God for the gift of wisdom, received it so abundantly that it "surpassed the wisdom of all the people of the east, and all the wisdom of Egypt." It was he who "composed three thousand proverbs, and his songs numbered a thousand and five." It was to hear his wisdom that "people came from all the nations . . . [and] from all the kings of the earth who had heard of his wisdom" (1 Kgs 4:29-34 NRSV). Pre-eminent among these visitors was the Queen of Sheba, who exclaimed to him, "Your wisdom and prosperity far surpass the report that I had heard" (1 Kgs 10:7). His father, David, might have been both warrior and lyricist, but to Solomon were attributed, among the canonical books, whole sections of the book of Proverbs, Ecclesiastes, and the great lyric of erotic love, the Song of Solomon (NRSV), or Song of Songs (NIV). Apocryphal works attributed to the wise king include a long sapiental book, the book of Wisdom, the *Psalms of Solomon, Odes of Solomon*, and a pseudepigraphical *Testament of Solomon*, which touts his greatness as a magician.

However, when all is said and done, one person who almost certainly was not the author of the book of Ecclesiastes was Solomon. First of all, the author drops any pretense of being a king after the fictional narrative of the royal experiment (Eccl 2:1-11). In the middle of the book, he offers advice to courtiers who come into the presence of the king as if he were standing beside them and whispering words of etiquette into their ears (Eccl 8:2-6; 10:4). He expresses views of monarchy very unlikely to have emanated from any actual royal throne (Eccl 4:13-16; 5:8-9). Finally, he is identified in the epilogue as a wise man or sage, who worked among the people (Eccl 12:9). Apart from these bits of internal evidence that the writer of Ecclesiastes, or the Teacher himself (if they are not one and the same person), was not a king of any kind is the linguistic evidence already alluded to, which places the book well after the time of any monarchy in Israel.

Who, then, was the author of Qohelet? For the purposes of this introduction, let us assume that the author of the bulk of the book is also the one who speaks in the first person. Only the epilogists and the author of the first verse of the book stand apart from the man who teaches through the rest of the text, and their identities are too pallid to obscure the thought and personality of the Teacher in any significant way.

He is a "sage" (Eccl 12:9). It is generally agreed that sages played important roles in the royal courts of the ancient Near East. This does not necessarily mean, however, that Qohelet was either a member or a servant of the elite, or that he shared their "upper-crust" attitudes. Some commentators find the bent of a patrician in passages like 7:21 and 11:1-2, but others dismiss as routine the references to a personal servant and investment of capital. The assertion that he worked among the common people (Eccl 12:9) might suggest a link with the traditional wisdom circles of the rural folk of Palestine. Nevertheless, a man who could read and write and who could draw even indirectly upon resources of the ancient Near Eastern sapiental tradition seems unlikely to have been a common peasant. At the same time, too little is known about the sages as a class (if, indeed, they constituted anything as definable as a class in ancient Israel) to make generalizations about their place in the social order.[4]

As for the provenance of the book of Ecclesiastes, efforts to show settings as diverse as Egypt and Phoenicia have not gained much support. While nothing in the book requires that its author had worked in Judea or Jerusalem, neither is there any compelling reason not to make that assumption.

THE CANONICITY OF QOHELET

Although not much is known about the process by which Qohelet came to be regarded as sacred scripture, controversy evidently surrounded its candidacy for the first few centuries. Fragments of Ecclesiastes from about 150 BCE appear at Qumran, but a book did not have to be regarded as Scripture in order to be included in the library of the Dead Sea community. The Mishnah reports challenges in rabbinic circles to the sacredness of Qohelet down to the time of Rabbi Akiba (died c. 135 CE). After setting forth the general principle that "All the holy writings render the hands [ritually] unclean," *M. Yad* 3:5 states, "The Song of Songs and Ecclesiastes render the hands unclean." The rabbis argued about the matter, however. Rabbi Akiba gave a ringing endorsement of the canonicity of the Song of Songs with these words: "God forbid!—no man in Israel ever disputed about the Song of Songs [that he should say] that it does not render the hands unclean . . . for all the Writings are holy, but the Song of Songs is the Holy of Holies." Then, as if to suggest that the argument about Qohelet continued on, the passage concludes, "And if aught was in dispute the dispute was about Ecclesiastes alone."[5] Ecclesiastes is mentioned in the very earliest Christian lists of canonical writings as well, such as that of Melito of Sardis (died c. 190 CE).

QOHELET'S RELATIONSHIP WITH ANCIENT WISDOM

The book of Ecclesiastes belongs to that third part of the canon of the Hebrew Scriptures known as the Ketubim ("Writings"). Into this section of the Bible the scribes of ancient Israel gathered all sacred texts that were neither Torah nor prophets: Ezra, Nehemiah, and the books of Chronicles (late historical writings); the book of Psalms (hymns of the Second Temple, though certain ones, such as Psalms 1; 37; 49; 73; 112; and 128, are recognized as "wisdom" psalms); Lamentations (a collection of laments or dirges over the loss of Judah that are traditionally treated as an appendix to Jeremiah); Daniel (placed among the prophets in the order of the Christian canon); Ruth and Esther (short stories); and the Song of Songs (nuptial poetry). Only the remaining three "Writings"—Proverbs, Job, and Ecclesiastes—remain in the true "wisdom" canon of the Hebrew Bible.

That Ecclesiastes belongs in the company of Job and Proverbs cannot be doubted. The genres of writing, the strongly secular perspective, the sophisticated quarrel with conventional piety and theology—all belong to the effort of wisdom writers to make sense of life based on observation and practical experience. Like all of wisdom literature, both courtly and popular, the focus is on human nature, and the goal is to guide human beings into the path of successful living. Rules of proper behavior (i.e., etiquette), observations of natural phenomena, and even some sustained theological reflections (such as those on Dame Wisdom in Proverbs 1–9 and on theodicy in the book of Job) are the stuff of the classical sapiental writings of Israel.

The world of wisdom, however, stretched far beyond the narrow borders of Israel. Any reflection on the wisdom bed in which Ecclesiastes nestles, therefore, has to take account of this larger environment. The relationship was richer and more complex than a few sentences can indicate; the examples given here are merely illustrative. Mesopotamian wisdom traditions must have been known to writers and thinkers in Israel for nearly the first millennium of its existence as a people, since Assyria, Babylon, and finally Persia dominated the Levant during most of that time. The Babylonian exile may have given the displaced intellectuals of Jerusalem fresh purchase on the actual sapiental texts of their conquerors—the image of Daniel and his friends successfully gobbling up learning while picking delicately at their victuals in the Babylonian Academy of Wisdom (Dan 1:3-7, 18-21) might not be far off the mark. Among several witnesses to Babylonian theological pessimism about fair treatment for the righteous at the hands of the gods is *A Dialogue About Human Misery*, or "The Babylonian Ecclesiastes."[6] Ecclesiastes 3:11 resonates in a particularly striking way with v. 24 of this text, which says: "The mind of the god, like the center of the heavens, is remote; His knowledge is difficult, men cannot understand it."

Even a document as different in genre from Qohelet as the Mesopotamian epic of the primeval hero Gilgamesh provides evidence of the ubiquity of sage advice. The alewife, Siduri, tries to deflect the hero's quest for immortality with words of realism that have often been compared to the wisdom of the Teacher in Eccl 9:7-10:

Gilgamesh, whither rovest thou?
The life thou pursuest thou shalt not find.
When the gods created mankind,
Death for mankind they set aside,
Life in their own hand retaining.
Thou, Gilgamesh, let full be thy belly,
Make thou merry by day and by night.
Of each day make thou a feast of rejoicing,

Day and night dance thou and play!
Let thy garments be sparkling fresh,
Thy head be washed; bathe thou in water.
Pay heed to the little one that holds on to thy
    hand,
Let thy spouse delight in thy bosom!
For this is the task of [humankind]![7]

How the sapiental tradition of Egypt was mediated to the late post-exilic intellectual community in Judah is not entirely clear, although we know that a great deal of intellectual and cultural exchange between the two cultures took place right alongside commercial enterprise and the usual military incursions. That the sages of Egypt served in the ancient and universal role as counselors to nobility is demonstrated conclusively in wall paintings, tomb furnishings, and in such written works as *The Instruction of Amenemope.*[8] It is a role with which Qohelet was evidently familiar as well (e.g., Eccl 8:2-6). Other commonalities, if not direct influences, can be demonstrated in such works as *The Song of the Harper,*[9] which sounds the theme of *carpe diem* ("seize the day!") with words like these: "Fulfill thy needs upon earth, after the command of thy heart, until there come for thee that day of mourning" (cf. Eccl 7:14). *The Instruction of Ani*[10] offers admonitions about the proper approach to God, similar to those found in Eccl 5:1-7.

As far as relationship with Greek tradition, the consensus of scholars is that the parallels of ideas are frequent and broad enough to justify the contention that Qohelet was very much influenced by the Hellenistic culture that had spread throughout the domain of the Ptolemies, including Judea, in the third century BCE. Attempts to identify specific Greek influences in the terminology of the book or to discern overt borrowing by Qohelet from Greek philosophers or literature have all failed. It is clear, however, that he shared the quest of Greek philosophy in general, which was to help a human being live happily in a world that is not very friendly to human happiness.[11]

It remains to say something of the relation of Ecclesiastes to the two great deuterocanonical Jewish sapiental works of the last centuries before the turn of the era, Ecclesiasticus (the Wisdom of Ben Sira) and the book of Wisdom (also known as the Wisdom of Solomon). Many efforts have been made to link Qohelet's work with that of Ben Sira, whose book is dated about 180 BCE. Certainly, the two authors held one pedagogical objective in common: Both wished to imbue their students with ideas and etiquette sufficient to move successfully in the highest levels of society. Ben Sira differs markedly from Qohelet on the major wisdom theme of retribution by generally following the conventional expectation of his age that the system will requite fools and knaves for their deeds. Qohelet, of course, will have none of that. The two do agree that justice, if there is any, has to be achieved here and now because there is no life after death and in Sheol there is neither hope nor praise.

As far as the relationships with the first-century CE book of Wisdom, much effort has been made to show that it is in part an intentional refutation of Ecclesiastes. This polemic is centered particularly in Wisdom 2, which seems to target such passages in Ecclesiastes as 3:16-22 and 9:5-6 that speak of nonexistence after death. One major innovation by the Wisdom of Solomon over against Ecclesiastes (and the rest of the canonical Hebrew wisdom writings, as well as Sirach) is the doctrine of blessed immortality. That doctrine, of course, takes care of a number of the laments raised by Ecclesiastes, including the obscure but poignant agnostic statement about the wise and the righteous in the hands of God: "whether it is love or hate, one does not know" (Eccl 9:1). The writer of Wisdom knows. He believes that in the life beyond death a loving God makes good with those who trust that God.

Nevertheless, rather than argue that the writer of the book of Wisdom is specifically attacking Ecclesiastes on this point, it seems preferable to take the later work as simply a fresh meditation for another generation on the great themes of justice and death, which were perennially raised by the Israelite wisdom tradition and were addressed powerfully in his own time by Qohelet.

THE PLOT OF THE BOOK

Every piece of literature, down to and including one's laundry list, has a plot. That is to say, it moves according to some logic. It aims at some end and follows some structure in order to reach that end. Certain essays and books display their plots prominently, while others conceal them in elaborate ways. People tend to enjoy reading the former more than the latter. The same is true of biblical texts. They all have internal emphases, main points, punch lines, and the like. Some, such as Jonah or the Joseph narrative, are novellas with rising action, climactic moment, and falling action—just like *Tom Jones* or *A Farewell to Arms*. Others, such as the epistles of Paul, follow a more tortuous route toward their main emphases.

Either the book of Ecclesiastes has one of the most tortuous plots of any book of the Hebrew Bible, or else it has an extremely minimal one. The latter seems to be more likely. There is no story line. Unlike any one of the prophetic books, the seams between individual units in Ecclesiastes are often invisible. In fact, it is more difficult to identify most of the individual pericopes of Ecclesiastes than in any other book of the Hebrew Bible, except perhaps the book of Proverbs. This much, however, is agreed upon by all: There is a narrator of all the material between Eccl 1:2 and Eccl 12:8. All of this material presents itself as being the thought of Qohelet, whose book it is. Ecclesiastes 1:1 is always conceded to be a superscription or title for the book, probably by some other hand, and nearly all commentators agree that the last two units of the book (12:9-11, 12-14) are by one or two other persons who have added some words at the end of the work of Qohelet to integrate that work somehow into the stream of canonical literature. Beyond this, there is no universally agreed-upon analysis of the structure of the book.

Efforts to provide such an analysis range from claims that the book is a systematic philosophical treatise with a discernible architecture,[12] through proposals that it is a series of intentionally created antitheses or "polar structures" by which the Teacher set his thought off against conventional wisdom,[13] to proposals that the book is given unity by one concept or another (e.g., ephemerality, goodness, divine freedom), to denials that any overarching structure is demonstrable.[14] Crenshaw simply lists twenty-five units, comparing their sequence to the apparently random but sometimes illuminating configurations of a kaleidoscope.[15] Murphy, on the other hand, adopts and adapts the structural analysis of Addison G. Wright.[16] This approach, based initially on repetition of key phrases, was elaborated by Wright's discovery of a numerological pattern that places the conceptual midpoint of the book exactly where the Masoretes, who were only counting verses, placed

it—namely, after 6:9 (the 111th of the 222 verses in the book).

More recent commentators seem less eager than those of a generation ago to invoke a slew of editors and glossators (as Barton, e.g., did)[17] or extensive cryptic quotations from other sources (as Gordis did)[18] to account for the numerous and often-remarked upon contradictions within the book. Now its tensions strike people more as the natural inevitabilities of experience than as a dialectic between various voices. From one angle or another, everything that is said is true. Indeed, one might ask whether the failure of experience and observation to convince the writer of the truth either of traditional reward-and-punishment ideology or of an untraditional outlook of total moral randomness may have led him to despair of ever arriving at a working philosophy of life. Perhaps it led the writer to what is now called, in psychological jargon, "the doubting syndrome," in which he found reason to question everything simply because its opposite could also be found.

The outline of the book is merely descriptive of the contents and discerns no major organizing structure in the work. Certain structural features do stand out, however. (1) Specialized vocabulary, clichés, and refrains often signal the presence of major teachings. (2) Several important units can easily be demarcated: the thematic statement (Eccl 1:2; 12:8), the poem on times and seasons (Eccl 3:1-8), the sad but beautiful evocation of the ravages of old age (Eccl 12:1-7), and many individual epigrams and proverbs. (3) Elsewhere, it seems to be the case that the practice of gathering thematically related materials together in little collections is operative. (4) Beyond that, it is noteworthy that some sentences are stated in the first-person singular as if they were "reflections" by the author, and others, which can be called "instruction," are directed to the student in the second-person singular or even with the use of the imperative mood of the verb. These "reflections" and "instructions" interface throughout the book in a way that is almost as seamless as the tongue-and-groove joining of a good oak floor.

Perhaps Ecclesiastes is best viewed as a notebook of ideas by a philosopher/theologian about the downside and upside of life. In this notebook he reports much of his own inner life and then turns to his students or his public with instructions that flow from that inner life. All of this reflection and instruction is framed by the famous slogan of the book, "Vanity of vanities! All is vanity" (1:2; 12:8 NRSV). Perhaps that slogan itself, together with a few other key terms, provides the most solid principle of organization that we can grasp. As G. von Rad puts it, "There is . . . an inner unity which can find expression otherwise than through a linear development of thought or through a logical progression in the thought process, namely through the unity of style and topic and theme. . . . A specific, unifying function is fulfilled by a small number of leading concepts to which Koheleth returns again and again, concepts such as 'vanity,' 'striving after wind,' 'toil,' 'lot,' etc."[19]

THE VOCABULARY
OF QOHELET'S THOUGHT

"All" (כל *kōl*). In the opening thematic statement of the book (Eccl 1:2), Qohelet uses the word "all," and he never lets up after that. The word occurs in 41 percent of the 222 verses of the book. The text of Ecclesiastes constitutes about 1.2 percent of the volume of the Hebrew Bible, and yet 2.1 percent of the verses in which "all" is used are in this book, almost double the expected rate. This frequency of the use of "all" in Ecclesiastes far outdistances any competitor in the Hebrew Bible. Other wisdom texts do not stress it. In Proverbs it occurs in 8.3 percent of the verses, and in Job 6.2 percent. This statistical study suggests that the universal perspective conveyed by the word "all" belongs in a very special way to Qohelet, the philosopher and theologian. It is useful to him because of his determination to reflect on the meaning of all of life—not just Israelite life, not even just human life, but all of life. Alone within the canon of the Hebrew Bible, Qohelet makes this kind of meditation a central concern; more than any other book of the Old Testament, this one attempts to arrive at understandings that will work everywhere and in every time.

"Vanity" (הבל *hebel*). The noun *hebel* occurs some sixty-nine times in the entire Hebrew Bible, five of which can be subtracted because they are the name of Abel, Cain's unfortunate younger sibling. Of the sixty-four remaining occurrences, thirty-eight, or almost 60 percent, occur in the book of Ecclesiastes alone, beginning in the open-

ing thematic statement (Eccl 1:2). As if the great partiality of the Preacher for this term were not enough to drive home the centrality of the concept to his thought, the locations of most of its occurrences further underscore its importance. Usually it appears at the end of a discussion in the position of a punch line or a coda; furthermore, it is often used in longer formulas with one or both of two other stock expressions, "a chasing after the wind" and "under the sun."

In the light of this high visibility, one would suppose that the meaning of the Hebrew term *hebel* would be clear to all translators and interpreters. But such is not the case. This can quickly be illustrated by looking at the words used by various English versions simply to translate the first clause of Eccl 1:2: "Vanity of vanities" (KJV, RSV, NRSV, JB); "utterly vain, utterly vain" (Moffatt); "emptiness, emptiness" (NEB); "futility, utter futility" (REB); "it is useless, useless" (GNB); "utter futility!" (TNK); "nothing is worthwhile" (TLB); "utterly absurd" (Fox); "a vapor of vapors!" (Scott); "meaningless! meaningless!" (NIV).

These English renditions of the Hebrew word *hebel* do not all mean the same thing. They are not even all the same part of speech. Although most translators take the word to be a noun, the NIV treats it as an adjective. To say that something is a "vapor" captures a sense of ephemerality, but ephemerality and "utter futility" are not really the same thing. Something can be extremely substantial and not at all vaporous but still be utterly futile. Similarly, something can be meaningless without necessarily being worthless or vain. Perhaps the least satisfactory translation of the term *hebel*, because of the broadness of its meaning in English, is the traditional "vanity of vanities." What does that mean? That things are proud and stuck up? That things are a waste of time? That they are ineffectual?

Here, then, is the most important term in the book of Ecclesiastes, and its English equivalent is not agreed upon. No wonder. Even in Hebrew its sense is ambiguous. One way, of course, to make precise the meaning of the term in Ecclesiastes would be to go to the other 40 percent of its occurrences elsewhere in the Hebrew Bible to see what kind of sense can be made of it there. The standard biblical Hebrew dictionary gives the root meaning of the word as "vapor" or "breath"; that sense of the term in fact fits best with its use in Isa 57:13, where, in a polemic against idols, it is used in parallel with wind: "The wind will carry them off,/a breath [hebel] will take them away" (NRSV). This sense of the term can also be found in post-biblical Hebrew texts. Other occurrences translated by the NRSV as "breath" (Job 7:16; Pss 39:5-6, 11; 62:9; 78:33; 94:11; 144:4; Prov 21:6) do not demand this rendition alone. The parallel with "shadow" in Pss 39:5-6 and 144:4 and the comparison with weightlessness in Ps 62:9 suggest "ephemerality." Qohelet, too, uses the term in this sense at least once (Eccl 11:10). Other texts imply a meaning of emptiness or worthlessness, as in Jer 10:15: "They are worthless, a work of delusion" (NRSV; see also Job 35:16; Jer 51:18). Elsewhere hebel means "falsehood" (e.g., 2 Kgs 17:15; Job 21:34; Zech 10:2).

From these comparisons it is evident that the term hebel describes something that is without merit, an unreliable, probably useless thing. Perhaps, in the manner of creative thinkers everywhere, the Teacher has welded new meaning onto this already extant term so that it can better serve his special purposes. Michael Fox thinks so, arguing that the most appropriate English rendition of hebel as Qohelet uses it is "absurd," "absurdity." In order to define "absurd," he appeals to the contention of Albert Camus that absurdity arises when two ideas that ought to be joined by links of causality and harmony are in fact divorced from each other. Something that is absurd just makes no sense. "To call something 'absurd' is to claim a certain understanding of its nature: It is contrary to reason."[20] That, says Fox, is what hebel is in Ecclesiastes. (Murphy agrees with the sense of "absurd, absurdity" for Qohelet's hebel, but thinks that "irrational" goes one nuance too far for the meaning of "absurd." "Incomprehensible" is plenty for him.)[21]

Fox follows the many uses of the term hebel in Qohelet as it is applied to human behavior, living beings, and divine behavior and finds that this sense of "absurdity" for the notion of hebel best comprehends them all. Human labor produces goods and achievement, and yet all avails for nothing in the face of chance and death. It is possible to find pleasure, wisdom, and the like, and yet they do not guarantee happiness or long life. Even the behavior that, according to the normal piety of ancient Israel and of many people today, ought to be rewarded by God appears instead to be punished: The system of reward and punishment is out of order. In all of these things a disparity exists between what people expect and what actually happens to them. By his widespread application of hebel, "there is not, Qohelet avows, a single unspoiled value in this life."[22]

"Toil" (עמל 'āmāl). This Hebrew noun occurs some fifty-five times in the Bible. It has nothing to do with the honest, goal-oriented labor of what we know as the "work ethic," but almost always conveys such negative ideas as trouble (Job 3:10; 5:6), weariness (Ps 73:16), sorrow (Jer 20:18), mischief (Job 4:8; Ps 140:9), and even oppression (Deut 26:7). In Ecclesiastes alone the term appears twenty-two times as a noun (40 percent of its usage), which means that, as in the case of hebel, it supplies a major motif to the message of this book. The accents of suffering and pain remain even though the Teacher uses the term in a more focused way to refer to hard labor of the sort best conveyed in English by the word toil (see also Ps 107:12). For Qohelet, toil and life are practically identical.[23] Like the writer of the story of the fall in Genesis 3, he places human beings in a world from which both the presence and the friendship of God are withdrawn and people are left to fend for themselves on an accursed ground in lives of toil that end only in death.

"Wisdom" (חכמה ḥokmâ). This noun occurs some twenty-six times in Ecclesiastes, beginning with 1:13. The related noun/adjective חכם (ḥākām, "sage," "wise") also occurs nearly as frequently (22 times), and the verb occurs four times, twice in its usual stative sense, "to be wise" (2:15; 7:23), once in the unique preterit sense of "to act wisely" (2:19), and once in a reflexive form (7:16). These terms are part of the distinctive semantic repertoire of the Teacher, though their occurrence is not uniform throughout the book but clusters in those pericopes in which he reflects on the value of "wisdom" as such (1:12-18; 2; 7:10-13, 15-25; 9:10-18). Qohelet does not employ the entire semantic range that the word ḥokmâ enjoys elsewhere in the Hebrew Bible. For example, he does not use it to mean the inspired skill of a craftsman (cf. Exod 35:35; 36:2, 8; 1 Kgs 7:13-14); nor does he personify it as Dame Wisdom, God's first creation and co-worker in the making of the world (cf. Prov 8:22-31; Sir 24:1-12; Wis 7:22–8:18).

Unlike the other "wisdom" books of the Hebrew Bible, Ecclesiastes never explicitly identifies wisdom as "the fear of the LORD" (cf. Job

28:28; Ps 111:10; Prov 15:33; Sir 1:14), though he often recommends fearing God (e.g., Eccl 5:7; 7:18; 8:12); nor does he use it as a synonym for Torah, God's revealed will (cf. Sir 24:23; Bar 4:10). By *ḥokmâ* Qohelet never means the rich tradition of mantic wisdom—the interpretation of dreams, the solution of riddles, and other occult arts at which, for example, the Jewish sage Daniel excelled (Dan 5:11) and with which Solomon was credited by later generations (Wis 7:15-22).

For all that, however, the Teacher does mean a variety of things by the term "wisdom." It is an intellectual skill to be used in the discovery of truth (e.g., 2:3; 7:23), or at least the discovery that truth is undiscoverable (1:12-14). It is the mental endowment of "wise" people (e.g., 2:9), from whose instruction one gains great profit (7:5; 9:17). It can be construed as a moral value, the opposite of folly (e.g., 10:1). Perhaps most frequently, it is a rich body of lore (1:16) that, because it provides the only possible avenue to the understanding of all of life (8:16), is a most precious asset (2:9; 7:11), even though the training necessary to acquire it can only be called vexing (1:18). The first epilogist sums up the work of the "wise" Teacher under the headings of teaching knowledge, studying, and "arranging" (i.e., writing down) proverbs (12:9).

Not only the intense preoccupation with "wisdom" as demonstrated by the frequency of the term but also the literary style and subject matter of the book won Ecclesiastes its place alongside Job and Proverbs in ancient Israel's canon of sapiential literature. As Israel practiced it in these books, and in the deuterocanonical books of Sirach and Wisdom, wisdom aimed at "practical knowledge of the laws of life and of the world, based upon experience."[24] Many of the values that are prominent in the earlier sections of the Hebrew Bible—Torah and Former and Latter Prophets—are largely absent in this wisdom canon: covenant, election of Israel, sacrificial cultus, God's action in history. The outlook of these books is anthropocentric rather than theocentric and universal rather than particular. God is not mentioned very often, but stands in the background as the providential upholder of a world of such orders as the connection of deed to consequence and the certainty of death. These orders work themselves out dependably and inexorably, without any need for direct divine intervention.

As is quite evident, Qohelet shares these same understandings. However, he radicalizes them in that he rejects the commonly held conviction of his age that the linkage of cause and effect can be resolved in the moral sphere into a scheme of distributive justice by which good is rewarded and evil punished. For him, bad things happen to good people, too. The only transcendent truths are God's sovereignty over all things and the universality of death. All other supposed moral orders are absurd. No wonder orthodox theologians have found this book objectionable!

In short, the "wisdom" this book seeks and offers bears the distinctive accents of the Teacher. Although challenging to standard thinking, this wisdom was, nevertheless, recognized by Israel as a gift from God. It won and maintained its place in the sacred canon in spite of attempts to purge it.

"Fate" (מקרה *miqreh*). At the end of 2:14, the Teacher mentions for the first time the word *miqreh*, "fate," "chance," "destiny." Seven of the ten biblical occurrences of the word are in Ecclesiastes. The other three occurrences of the word are in more or less mundane contexts: (1) When David, suspecting a plot against his life, fails for two days to turn up at Saul's table, Saul says to himself, "Something has befallen him; he is not clean, surely he is not clean" (1 Sam 20:26 NRSV). (2) Ruth happened to glean in the part of the field that belonged to Boaz (Ruth 2:3). Of course, neither of these was really a random and mysterious event, for which our word "fate" would be the appropriate translation. The protagonist and the reader can easily see that these occurrences have been engineered very consciously. (3) Readers know that the great harm the Philistines suffered after they captured the ark of God was not mere "chance"; however, the Philistines themselves could be sure of that fact only by putting the ark on an ox cart and letting it go (1 Sam 6:9).

In Ecclesiastes, the outcome of life's struggles is described with the same word (2:14-15; three times in 3:19; 9:2-3). Here, too, the "fate" that awaits human beings is far from mere chance or a random event, though from our point of view it may seem purely contingent since it overtakes us without apparent connection either to our behavior or to our wishes. For the Teacher, "fate" is fact. It is decreed by God, even though one can learn nothing about this decree; it is death.

THE IDEOLOGY OF THE BOOK OF ECCLESIASTES

The thought of any book flows out of its vocabulary. The five components of the vocabulary of Qohelet discussed in the preceding section are pillars upon which its view of the world rests. "All" of human experience is "absurd"—i.e., incomprehensible, even senseless. Life is "toil." With the help of "wisdom" a person may find happiness amid the toil, but only if that person is utterly realistic about the inevitable "fate" of death.

Murphy sagely remarks that "the message of Ecclesiastes has suffered from excessive summarizing."[25] The epilogist, perhaps even the Teacher himself, started doing it right within the book itself ("All is absurd" [1:2]; "The end of the matter. . . . Fear God, and keep his commandments" [12:13]), and the practice has continued to this present day. Yet, what are we interpreters to do? We need handles on this book of Scripture. We need pedagogical and homiletical strategies that flow straight out of the book's own current of thought and ultimately make confluence with our own.

Ecclesiastes is not a book about God; it is a book about ideas. That is why one speaks of its ideology in preference to its theology. Its ideas are about human survival in a world in which work is pain, overwork is foolish, pleasure soon pales in the face of death, and wisdom is unable to comprehend even the simplest sequences that would make possible real understanding of the world. Such a world is absurd. Yet life in the face of the absurd did not create a Qohelet who, with desperate shouts of *carpe diem* ("seize the day!"), merely snatches at a few shreds of superficial happiness or lives a few fitful moments of bright joy against a relentlessly dark background. No, he comes forward as the Teacher, with sober and yet caring countenance, ready to help his pupils deal with such a world. He holds God in profound respect but will never claim to know too much about God. Above all he will not commit God to the program of distributive justice that Job's friends advocated. Is his God just, then? Is his God even good? Qohelet does not tell us, perhaps cannot tell us. His is not a book about God.

In his magisterial commentary on Qohelet, Robert Gordis identifies four themes that are basic to the thought of Qohelet: (1) Human achievement is weak and impermanent; (2) the fate of human beings is uncertain; (3) human beings find it impossible to attain to true knowledge and insight into the world; (4) the goal of human endeavors needs to be joy, which is the divine imperative.[26] Clearly, the fourth theme is the only one that boldly affirms life. The other three only point to the limitations and impossibilities within which human beings live. For Gordis, too, the book has no proper "theology" or doctrine of God other than that God exists in limitless sovereignty; its ideology is "anthropology." Deep within human nature is "an ineradicable desire for happiness," planted there by God.[27] To live a moral life by doing the will of God, then, is to pursue happiness.

Other commentators introduce at least a theological dimension into their summations of the meaning of the book of Ecclesiastes. Gerhard von Rad, for example, finds that the book continually circles around three basic ideas: "1. A thorough, rational examination of life is unable to find any satisfactory meaning; everything is 'vanity.' 2. God determines every event. 3. Man is unable to discern these decrees, the 'works of God' in the world."[28]

The notion that "God determines every event," based in large part on the famous passage in Eccl 3:1-8 , leads Murphy to write an entire section on who is the God of Qohelet.[29] He agrees that Qohelet teaches that whatever God is doing in the world is unintelligible to human beings and that little personal relationship with God can, therefore, exist apart from human attitudes of fear and awe. God is not revealed in any way in history. However, Murphy is convinced that Qohelet's God is not simply a god of origins who sets into motion inexorable natural laws and then walks away. Such a god is not the God of Israel, and Qohelet—though he never calls God "Yahweh," the name revealed to Moses at Sinai and uses only the generic name אלהים (*ĕlōhîm*)—is an Israelite writer who stands squarely within the give and take of Israel's tradition of theological reflection. Qohelet believes that "everything happens because of the Lord's action. . . . God is portrayed as intimately involved in all that occurs."[30] Murphy quotes with favor L. Gorssen's remark that "God is utterly present and at the same time utterly absent. God is 'present' in each event and yet no event is a 'place of encounter' with God. . . . Events do not speak any longer the language of a saving God. They are there, simply."[31]

Here is the ideological crux of the book. Von Rad and Murphy are by and large correct in saying that for Qohelet events are both impenetrable and preordained by God. There can be no question of mastery of events, because they are out of human hands. The position is deterministic, but not fatalistic, as Murphy understands it, because human beings are still perfectly free and responsible to act. At the same time, it seems unnecessary to insist that this assertion about the predetermination of times by God is the central idea of the book. True, God "has made everything suitable for its time . . . yet they cannot find out what God has done from the beginning to the end" (Eccl 3:11 NRSV). Nevertheless, charges that God is arbitrary and capricious or even just plain absent pale beside the positive assertion that, by taking charge of what they can in their lives, human beings can find joy and happiness (Eccl 2:24-26; 3:12-13; 5:18-20; 8:15; 9:7-10; 11:7-10). This advice culminates in the remarkable sentence, "Follow the inclination of your heart and the desire of your eyes, but know that for all these things God will bring you into judgment" (Eccl 11:9 NRSV), in which the latter clause should be taken to mean that God holds every person responsible for following the heart and the eyes to find happiness. Even in the middle of a maddeningly absurd world in which the fatal shadow of death hangs equally over the wise and the foolish (Eccl 2:10), human being and beast (Eccl 3:19), this passionate possibility exists for those who, with prudence and respect for the unknown and all-determining God, can seize it!

By the simple device of shifting the emphasis from the admitted determinism of an order in which God has already ordained everything to the human responsibility or freedom that Qohelet also admittedly affirms, the weight comes down not on a tragic fatalism—human beings in the hands of a distant, all-powerful, and arbitrary God who causes good and evil alike—but on the opportunity for human happiness in a world in which God is utterly sovereign and people are truly free.

Can we have it both ways—divine sovereignty over all things *and* human freedom? Let us hope so! Every book of the Bible mixes these ingredients of theological truth in different proportions. In the Hebrew Bible, the books of Samuel and Kings, Esther, and Ruth concern themselves largely with the free actions of human beings in the world,

while the book of Daniel hints at a plan for the ages set down before ever a king or a saint began to act. Ecclesiastes pours heavy doses of sovereignty and predestination into the theological mixture, but it too reckons with the responsive human heart and the obedient human will. Even though God remains cloaked in obscurity, God's predetermination sometimes seems more like prevenient grace; sometimes the ordained times and seasons seem more like the blessed and secure orders of nature. It is good that divine sovereignty and human freedom find a blend in this book, too, because faith assents to both ideas and finds each vital. If Qohelet spoke only for predetermined necessity, synagogue and church alike might have to put it aside, for most of us find such a doctrine both theologically obnoxious and intellectually impossible. But he does not; in the end, he seeks to lead his pupils to their own decision to walk humbly, sensitively, harmoniously with their God.

FOR FURTHER READING

Barton, George A. *A Critical and Exegetical Commentary on the Book of Ecclesiastes.* ICC. New York: Scribner's, 1908.

Brown, William P. *Ecclesiastes.* Interpretation. Louisville, Ky.: Westminster/John Knox Press, 2000.

Crenshaw, James L. *Ecclesiastes.* OTL. Philadelphia: Westminster, 1987.

Farmer, Kathleen A. *Who Knows What Is Good? A Commentary on the Books of Proverbs and Ecclesiastes.* ITC. Grand Rapids: Eerdmans, 1991.

Fox, Michael. V. *Qoheleth and His Contradictions.* BLS 18. Sheffield: Almond, 1989.

———. *Ecclesiastes.* JPS Torah Commentary. Philadelphia: Jewish Publication Society, 2004.

Gordis, Robert. *Koheleth: The Man and His World.* 1st ed. New York: Schocken, 1951; 3rd ed., 1968.

Miller, Douglas B. *Symbol and Rhetoric in Ecclesiastes: The Place of Hebel in Qohelet's Work.* SBL Academia Biblica 2. Atlanta, Ga.: Society of Biblical Literature, 2002.

Murphy, Roland E. *Ecclesiastes.* WBC 23A. Waco, Tex.: Word, 1992.

Rankin, O. S., and G. G. Atkins. "The Book of Ecclesiastes." In *The Interpreter's Bible.* Vol.

5. Edited by George A. Buttrick et al. Nashville: Abingdon, 1956.

Rudman, Dominic. *Determinism in the Book of Ecclesiastes.* JSOTSup 316. Sheffield: Sheffield Academic Press, 2001.

Salyer, Gary D. *Vain Rhetoric: Private Insight and Public Debate in Ecclesiastes.* JSOTSup 327. Sheffield: Sheffield Academic Press, 2001.

Scott, R. B. Y. *Proverbs, Ecclesiastes.* AB 18. Garden City, N.Y.: Doubleday, 1965.

Whitley, C. F. *Koheleth: His Language and Thought.* BZAW 148. Berlin: de Gruyter, 1979.

Whybray, R. N. *Ecclesiastes.* NCB. Grand Rapids: Eerdmans, 1989.

ENDNOTES

1. James L. Crenshaw, *Ecclesiastes*, OTL (Philadelphia: Westminster, 1987) 33-34.

2. James L. Crenshaw, *Ecclesiastes*, 31.

3. Roland E. Murphy, *Ecclesiastes*, WBC 23A (Wao, Tex.: Word, 1992) xxxi-xxxii.

4. Roland E. Murphy, *Ecclesiastes*, xxi.

5. Herbert Danby, trans. and ed., "The Mishnah" (Oxford: Oxford University Press, 1933) 782.

6. *Ancient Near Eastern Texts Relating to the Old Testament*, ed. James B. Pritchard, 3rd ed. (Princeton, N.J.: Princeton University Press, 1969) 438-40.

7. *ANET*, 90.

8. *ANET*, 421-25.

9. *ANET*, 467.

10. *ANET*, 420-21.

11. M. V. Fox, *Qoheleth and His Contradictions*, BLS 18 (Sheffield: Almond, 1989) 16.

12. Norbert Lohfink, *Kohelet, Die neue Echter Bibel* (Würzberg: Echter Verlag, 1980).

13. J. A. Loader, *Ecclesiastes*, Text and Interpretation (Grand Rapids: Eerdmans, 1986).

14. R. N. Whybray, *Ecclesiastes*, NCB (Grand Rapids: Eerdmans, 1989).

15. James L. Crenshaw, *Ecclesiastes*, 47-49.

16. Roland E. Murphy, *Ecclesiastes*, xxxviii-xli.

17. George A. Barton, *A Critical and Exegetical Commentary on the Book of Ecclesiastes*, ICC (New York: Scribner's, 1908).

18. Robert Gordis, *Koheleth: The Man and His World*, 1st ed. (New York: Schocken, 1951; 3rd ed., 1968).

19. Gerhard von Rad, *Wisdom in Israel* (Nashville: Abingdon, 1972) 227.

20. M. V. Fox, "The Meaning of Hebel," *JBL* 105 (1986) 413.

21. Roland E. Murphy, *Ecclesiastes*, lix.

22. Roland E. Murphy, *Ecclesiastes*, lix.

23. M. V. Fox, *Qoheleth and His Contradictions*, 54.

24. Gerhard von Rad, *Old Testament Theology* (New York: Harper & Row, 1962) 1:418.

25. Murphy, *Ecclesiastes*, lviii.

26. Robert Gordis, *Koheleth*, 252.

27. Robert Gordis, *Koheleth*, 113.

28. Gerhard Von Rad, *Wisdom in Israel*, 227-28.

29. Roland E. Murphy, *Ecclesiastes*, lxviii-lxix.

30. Roland E. Murphy, *Ecclesiastes,*, lxvi.

31. L. Gorssen, "La cohérence de la conception de Dieu dans l'Ecclésiaste," *ETL* 46 (1970) 314-15; quoted in Murphy, *Ecclesiastes*, lxviii-lxix.

SONG OF SONGS

RENITA J. WEEMS

The content of Song of Songs, sometimes referred to as the Song of Solomon, represents a remarkable departure from that of other books in the Bible. To open the pages of this brief volume of poetry is to leave the world of exceptional heroism, tribal conflict, political disputes, royal intrigue, religious reforms, and divine judgment and to enter the world of domestic relations, private sentiments, and interpersonal discourse. Filled with language of sensuality, longing, intimacy, playfulness, and human affection, Song of Songs introduces the reader to the non-public world of ancient Israel. The relationships are private (i.e., a man and a woman), the conversation is between intimates (e.g., "darling," "beloved," "friend"), and the language hints of kinship bonds (e.g., mother, sister, brother, daughter). At last, readers of Scripture have the opportunity to focus not so much on the external politics that organized and dominated the lives of Hebrew people (e.g., palace intrigue, temple politics, prophetic conflict, international doom, natural disasters) but on the internal systems and attitudes that also shaped the lives of the people of Israel.

Song of Songs stands out in sharp contrast to the rest of the biblical books in two other ways. First, nowhere in its eight chapters is God mentioned. The book of Esther is the only work that shares this distinction. Although the religious significance of the latter is frequently debated as well, its religious significance is a little more self-evident, referring as it does to the rituals of fasting and prayer (Esth 4:16) and to the celebration of the Feast of Purim (Esth 9:20-32). A decidedly secular tone permeates Song of Songs; not only is God's name not mentioned in the book, but also no allusions are made to any of Israel's sacred religious traditions, be they covenant traditions (the Davidic or Sinai covenants) or God's saving acts in Israel's history (e.g., deliverance at the sea). One possible allusion to a religious theme may indicate that the book had "religious"

origins: The lovers exchange their love poems against the backdrop of a pastoral, utopian garden setting where images of animals, hillsides, and exotic flowers predominate. Such allusions suggest intimations of the Garden of Eden story (Genesis 2), with its focus on the first human couple and their portentous dealings with each other. (More will be said about this topic below.)

Second, Song of Songs is the only biblical book in which a female voice predominates. In fact, the protagonist's voice in Song of Songs is the only unmediated female voice in all of Scripture. Elsewhere, women's perspectives are rehearsed through the voice of narrators, presumably male (e.g., Esther and Ruth), and their contributions are overshadowed by male heroism and assorted male-identified dramas. But in Song of Songs, where more than fifty-six verses are ascribed to a female speaker (compared to the man's thirty-six), the experiences, thoughts, imagination, emotions, and words of this anonymous black-skinned woman are central to the book's unfolding. Moreover, the protagonist is not merely verbal; unlike many of the women in the Bible, she is assertive, uninhibited, and unabashed about her sexual desires.

The book's pronounced and unrelenting female point of view is reinforced further by its strong female imagery. The several interjections of the Jerusalem daughters into the lovers' discourse (5:9; 6:1, 13a) and the repeated mention of the "mother's house" (בית אם bêt 'ēm, 3:4; 8:2) as opposed to the customary "father's house" (בית אב bêt 'āb), the patriarchal household, contribute to the book's impression of giving readers insights into the decidedly private, unexplored world of Hebrew women's special viewpoints and private sentiments. The presence of such important female imagery allows Song of Songs to be seen as a collection of meditations from a woman's heart. Casting the book as the private, journal-like reflections of a female may provide us just the insight needed to unlock the mystery behind the decision to include such patently erotic and secular musings within the canon. As meditations of a woman's heart, Song of Songs might have been viewed as the feminine counterpart to a book like, say, Ecclesiastes. In the latter, an unnamed speaker, who is most likely male, reflects on the chasm between traditional wisdom teachings and actual human experience. He does not hesitate to express profound disdain for traditional wisdom, arguing that even the best of life is plagued with transience, unpredictability, absurdity, vanity, and ultimately ends in death. And he is openly cynical about the contradictions he has observed in life, one being that good deeds do not always lead to good consequences. In the light of the patent limitation of human wisdom, and in the face of death and vanity, the Preacher repeatedly urges his audience to indulge themselves in life's few genuine pleasures—food, drink, love, work, and play—as gifts of God.

One might argue that the protagonist in Song of Songs accepts the author of Ecclesiastes' invitation and revels in the joys of nature, work, and play when one is in love. In its own way, Song of Songs meditates, among other things, on traditional thinking about (female) sexuality and a certain protagonist's life experiences as a woman in love. Speaking in the first person, as does the protagonist in Ecclesiastes, the woman allows herself a few outbursts of impatience and effrontery (1:6; 6:13b; 8:1, 10), making it very clear that she is well aware that her own words and actions violate traditional teachings pertaining to womanhood and modesty. In the end, she is as impatient with traditional wisdom as her male counterpart in Ecclesiastes is scornful. But instead of expressing openly her contempt for and cynicism toward traditional wisdom, the speaker in Song of Songs takes the subtle approach and extols the erotic happiness she has found—despite all of its complications and limitations. One can see from both the striking amount of female speech and the decidedly female angle of vision of the book how easy it is to imagine that a female sage is responsible for the stirring meditations contained in Song of Songs.

AUTHOR AND TITLE

On the surface, the allusion to King Solomon in the superscription to the book (1:1) rules out a female as the author of Song of Songs. But the attri-

bution to the last king of the united monarchy should not be taken as decisive. Because he was rumored to have married hundreds of wives (1 Kgs 11:3), many traditions inspired by Solomon's presumed vast knowledge about romance and matters of the heart no doubt emerged over the centuries. Song of Songs was likely one such composition. Attributing the love poems to Solomon probably represents an attempt by the scribes to associate the work with the wisest and most notorious king in Israel's history. Appending his name to the book would place it foremost within an intellectual stream of respected and authoritative theological reflection, the wisdom tradition. The king's reputation as a sage with more than several thousand wise sayings to his credit and a composer of more than one thousand lyrics (1 Kgs 4:32) lent to Song of Songs, especially in the light of the wisdom homily attached near the end of the book (Cant 8:6-7), the kind of sublimity and inspiration befitting royal compositions. This might explain one rendering of the book's title, "The Most Sublime of Songs."

There is no way to determine the gender of the person actually responsible for having written this collection of love poetry (although the preponderance of female speakers and experiences in the book has led me to refer to the lyricist throughout as female). But the book's class origins are conspicuous. Its author was acquainted with the accoutrements of the privileged class (e.g., the reference to the woman's vineyard in 1:6; the lavish royal wedding procession in 3:6-11; the scattered references to fine spices, fruits, and perfumes; the mention of Tirzah, once the capital city of the northern kingdom [6:4]). It is not farfetched to imagine that the lyrics were inspired by someone (a woman) from an elite class who, at least modestly educated, was familiar with the Hebrew lyrical heritage and aware of prevailing assumptions about the role of women and the prohibitions against marriages crossing class and ethnic lines.

The title of the book (שִׁיר הַשִּׁירִים *šîr haššîrîm*) cleverly hints at the work's contents. Although its flat translation is better known among English-speaking audiences as the Song of Songs (NIV) and the Song of Solomon (NRSV), the title actually bears rich connotations ranging from the Song Comprised of Songs to the Most Excellent of Songs. The book is a collection of love lyrics filled with candid longing and tender expressions of desire and desperation by both the lover and her beloved.

Although it is difficult to discern any straightforward rationale or logic to the book's structure, the poems' lyrical quality is unmistakable. These brief, evocative, unpredictable units of material, which were brought together on the basis of alliteration, intonation, and possibly rhythm surely made for memorable musical performances. In the second century CE, the lyrics to Song of Songs became a favorite in bawdy quarters, prompting Rabbi Aqiba (c. 135 CE) reportedly to protest that "he who trills his voice in chanting the Song of Songs in the banquet house and treats it as a sort of song has no part in the world to come."[1] We are not sure how successful the rabbi was in quelling secular enthusiasm for the lyrics. Nevertheless, for those who appreciate its subliminal nature, the content and character of Song of Songs continue to stir the religious imagination. Even today in some Jewish traditions, the text of Song of Songs is chanted at the end of the eight-day celebration of Passover. In other Jewish traditions, it is sung weekly in services prior to the sabbath. Even in many Protestant Christian traditions, some of the book's important themes continue to find their way into the church's most stirring compositions about human longing, divine compassion, and the beauty of creation.

LOVE LYRICS AND THEIR CONTENT

Lyrical poems cast as passionate dialogues, erotic soliloquies, and private dreams function in Song of Songs as the discourse of interior life and the rhetoric of heartfelt emotions. Hardly anything written in classical secular romance literature can match the exquisitely provocative exchanges between the anonymous female protagonist and her shepherd suitor in Song of Songs. To see Song of Songs merely as a collection of love poems that reclaims human sexuality and celebrates female sexuality, however, poems embodying gender balance and mutuality, is to fail to appreciate the deep and complicated emotions expressed in the book. Love lyrics are powerful forms of persuasion; they provide a modest way for communicating immodest sentiments, and they allow one to talk disingenuously about experiences and identities that defy official moral codes and fall outside the official cultural ideology. That being the case, the poetry of Song of Songs is the poetry of personal sentiment.[2] Its vocabulary and expressions are obscure because they are the private language of intimates. Identifying the speakers is complicated so as to protect the privacy of the partners. The descriptions of human longing, vulnerability, dependence, and yearning are intended to capture the imagination and sympathy of the audience, forcing them to identify with the universal plight of lovers who want to be loved by the man or woman of their own choosing. Love poetry permits the speakers to comment on subjects from perspectives the audience might otherwise never consider. The woman argues for her right to pursue love, and her lover argues that in his eyes his maiden is beautiful.

When we compare the lyrics in Song of Songs with some of the psalms, we see that all lyrics are not the same. They differ according to their content, emotional tone, and social context. In our culture, gospel music, Scottish hymns, anthems, rap music, country music, hard rock, rock and roll, reggae, and jazz, to name a few, are all examples of oral literature that, while formulaic, ultimately originated out of very particular social contexts and represent unique forms of social commentary. The closest American musical parallel to the kind of material we find in Song of Songs may be the American blues tradition because of its comparable poignant interest in personal, individual struggles, the joys and sorrows of love, and the confounding chasm that exists between domestic reality and domestic fantasy. In both musical traditions, the speaker speaks in the first-person singular voice and the subject matter is deeply personal and gripping in intensity.

Many of the specific themes covered in Song of Songs also appear in classical women's romantic literature (e.g., personal relationships, thwarted love, sexual passion, the female body). In the classics, male self-identity develops and grows through a series of adventures that inevitably takes him away from his country and home, especially away from his intimate connections with women (e.g., mother, wife, sister). However, the female self in classic literature develops invariably through the woman's experiences with the impediments and frustrations of romantic love. In other words, women's education traditionally is "in or on the periphery of marriage."[3] Similarly, the lyrics of Song of Songs record the personal predicament of a certain black-skinned maiden—her struggles to love and be loved by a man for whom she has been deemed, for reasons not exactly clear to modern readers, an unsuitable mate. Readers are asked to understand the innocence of their love, to recognize the purity of their longing, and to empathize with the absurdity of the obstacles and frustrations, both internal and external, they are forced to endure. We watch the protagonist's selfhood unfold before our eyes as we observe her (1) as the innocent romantic who is propelled by her passion and her dreams of being loved and caressed by the man of her dreams (e.g., 1:2-4); (2) as defiant and impatient (1:5-6; 6:13*b*); (3) as a mature, intelligent, knowledgeable woman who passes on what she has learned in her experience of frustrated love to her impressionable female audience (2:7; 3:5; 8:4); and (4) as self-assured but pragmatic about the way the world operates and resolved to find happiness, despite the limitations imposed on her (8:10, 13-14).

The book's charm is its ability to elaborate on the erotic while at the same time critiquing prevailing cultural norms. In fact, the poet cunningly uses the former subtly to denounce the latter. So forward, so uncompromising, so urgent is the maiden's desire for and attachment to her lover that her comments border on the contentious in some places. Her insistence on three occasions that her beloved suitor belongs to her (2:16; 6:3; 7:10) is not mere assertion. Rather, seen in the context of her defense of her complexion (1:4), her bodily integrity (1:5; 6:13*b*), her small breasts (8:10), her continual adjuration (2:7; 3:5; 8:4), and in view of the Jerusalem daughters' continual skepticism (5:9; 6:13*a*), the protagonist's words have a polemical tone. For one thing, her black skin color, she suspects, immediately places her at odds with those around her (1:5-6).

The woman's daring love talk and explicit sexual longing invariably raise questions about the place of this book within the Bible. This is especially the case when one considers that the lovestruck female is as straightforward and aggressive about satisfying her libidinous urges as is her male suitor, or any other male character in Scripture. How, then, do we explain the radically different portraits of female sexuality in the Bible when we compare the sexually vivacious protagonist in Song of Songs with the sexually constrained women in so many other portions of Scripture? The former speaks openly and immodestly about her erotic desires, while the latter are portrayed as the archetypal other whose sexuality must be regulated and guarded against. These are not questions easily answered by cursory readings of the book. In fact, it has been difficult for scholars to arrive at answers to such important questions. Per-

haps we are not supposed to come up with satisfying answers. Perhaps the fact that the book has been included in the canon is evidence enough of the rich, complex, and often ambivalent thinking about women, sex, and matters of the heart that existed in Israel throughout the centuries.

INTERTEXTUAL ALLUSIONS

Lyrical compositions, like all discursive forms, rely on a great store of intertextual comparisons for their affect and effect on their audiences. We have already seen how associating the book with King Solomon gave it an air of authority and legitimacy. When Song of Songs is viewed within its ancient Near Eastern setting, the influence of broader, extra-canonical texts lends the book a cosmopolitan note and situates it within the larger stream of internationally acclaimed compositions. For example, Song of Songs shares striking parallels with Egyptian love poetry. Both favor openness, tenderness, and frankness in their romantic speeches; the female lover in both traditions is referred to as "sister" (Cant 4:9, 10, 12) and is frequently addressed in superlative terms ("the most beautiful of women," Cant 5:9; 6:1).

Song of Songs also resonates with intertextual allusions to the story of the first human couple (Genesis 2–3).[4] Repeated mention of "garden" and garden-like settings in Song of Songs, whether used as a metaphor for the woman's sexuality (e.g., 4:12, 16; 5:1) or as a special location for the couple's lovemaking (6:11-12), may suggest that the book is a response to the "love story that goes awry"[5] back in the garden in Genesis 2–3. As a result of what happened in Eden, there is rupture in creation, disharmony between the first human couple, resulting in the subjugation of the woman and, by implication, the demise of mutual sexual fulfillment. In the garden of Song of Songs, by contrast, mutuality is reestablished and intimacy is renewed. Audiences encountering the content of Song of Songs for the first time would have had a repertoire of cultural information upon which to draw as they listened to the poems and placed them within the framework of what they understood love, relationships, and sex were or should entail.

A less commented upon, but equally suggestive parallel may be drawn between Song of Songs and Hosea 2.[6] Both use the trope of aggressive female sexuality to comment ambivalently on the relationship between love and power, on the one hand, and the erotic and the divine, on the other. In both texts, male figures threaten to imprison the women if they prove unchaste (cf. Cant 8:9 and Hos 2:6-7), and the women are beaten for pursuing the men they love (cf. Cant 5:2-8 and Hos 2:6-13). The woman in Song of Songs tells the woman's side of the drama; she is not depraved and incorrigible, as in Hosea. Instead, she is a woman in love and in trouble.

Whether Song of Songs was indeed written in response to these canonical examples of female/human sexuality is debatable. What is certain, however, is that like all poets, the author of Song of Songs appealed to what at that time was a store of cultural "texts" familiar to an ideal audience—some written and fixed, some oral and evolving, some ancient and tried, some contemporary and trendy, some expressly religious, and others, though secular, nevertheless inspired. Some of those texts are recoverable, such as the Garden of Eden story in Genesis and Egyptian love poems; but many of those intertextual allusions remain unrecoverable for the outsider. Regardless, they represent the kinds of material all readers bring to the reading process, consciously or unconsciously, that act as a sieve through which new information is assessed and organized, appropriated or resisted.

THE "BODY" IN SONG OF SONGS

With abandon, the lovers in Song of Songs delight in the physical pleasures of love. They revel in each other's body: taste (2:3; 4:11; 5:1), touch (7:6-9), smell (1:12-14; 4:16), and the sound (2:8, 14; 5:16) of each other's voice. The female body poses no ethical problems in Song of Songs, although in other parts of Scripture it is problematic. It bleeds (cf. Leviticus 12; 15:19-30); it breeds (Leviticus 12); it confounds male wisdom (Numbers 5); and it has enormous power over the male imagination (Lev 21:7; cf. 2 Samuel 11), or so it seems. So mysteriously powerful is a woman's body that it can compete with a man's religious obligations (Exod 19:15). Only in Song of Songs is the female body extolled and praised for its difference and its beauty. With daring abandon the shepherd describes the maiden's eyes, neck, hair, feet, thighs, and navel using extravagant metaphors and sexually suggestive imagery. In fact, both lovers, using the genre of the *wasf*, or poetic passages describing with a series of images the various parts of the body, celebrate the

integrity and uniqueness of the other's body. Four *wasfs* (Arabic for "description") can be found in Song of Songs (4:1-7; 5:10-16; 6:4-10; 7:1-9).[7] Three of the four *wasfs* praise the woman's form and flawless appearance, suggesting that the poet assumed that her audience might otherwise find some aspect of her physical makeup (perhaps her complexion?) objectionable (4:1-7; 5:10-16; 7:1-9). While only one *wasfs* praises the man's body (6:4-10), nevertheless it stands out in both Song of Songs and in Scripture because it is the only description of masculinity and male beauty from the female point of view. No doubt drawn from the conventional stock of imagery and language poets and lyricists used during that period to describe the human body, *wasfs* do not attempt to be precise and concrete in their descriptions. They are deliberately imprecise and playful, where the intention is upon evoking the imagination and stirring the senses.[8] The focus on the human body allows both the poet and the audience to reflect simultaneously on at least three complex and highly symbolic themes that body imagery invokes in a culture: race, sex, and power.

The protagonist is unapologetic about the way she looks and relaxes in her beloved's desire for her. On one occasion she insists that her beloved's desire is for her only, presumably despite what others think (7:10). This is the talk of a woman under pressure both to conform and to relinquish her rights to be loved by the man of her choice. A possible context for the poem's origin was the post-exilic period, when the inhabitants of the tiny province of Judah were struggling to reestablish their identity. There are indications that canons of legal prescriptions were codified during this period to legitimate women's subjugation and that aggressive measures were taken to restrict social intermingling and to monitor marriage affiliations (Ezra 9:1–10:44; Neh 13:23-29; cf. Leviticus 12; 15; Numbers 5).

INTERPRETATION

Various proposals have been made for interpreting the book's secular and erotic contents. The major interpretations have viewed Song of Songs as (1) a dramatization of an ancient fertility rite in which the deity and humans were ceremonially united in sacred marriage;[9] (2) a single love poem structured around repetitive words, phrases, and motifs;[10] (3) a cycle of marriage songs;[11] and (4) an allegory idealizing, from the Jewish point of view, God's love for Israel, and from the Christian perspective, Christ's love for the church or for the individual's soul.[12] As for the latter, it is surprising to note that while Protestants have for the most part rejected the allegorical and tropological modes of interpretation that were characteristic of medieval biblical interpretation, when it comes to Song of Songs they are willing to rely on medieval and mystical allegorical interpretations to guide their thinking about the book's contents.

Readers tend to see the book as an allegory in part because the vocabulary of love poetry is obscure, the images are condensed, and the referents are ambiguous. The view that the lovers' pulsating passion and titillating sexual fantasies do not represent or point to any higher theological reality, that the book's significance is revealed in its literal meaning, and that the poet and editors who shaped the final poetry were not interested in elaborating on the nature of God and mediating sound religious doctrine has proved too incredible for those who remain bent on reading Song of Songs allegorically.

Today more and more interpreters are willing to read the book as a collection or anthology of love lyrics that capture the joys and sufferings of intimate relationships and of sensual love. The book chronicles one woman's journey to find fulfilling love with a man who, for reasons unknown to us, comes across as both enamored of her and forever elusive to her. Although the matter is never put so boldly in the poems, everyone who listens to the couple's plaintive outbursts empathizes with their dilemma, "to love or not to love." And although the drama appears to center around the heterosexual, erotic exchange between a woman and a man, Song of Songs is not in the end *about* heterosexual sex. Instead, it teaches us about the power and politics of human love. The lovers' humanity, not their genders, intends to captivate the audience. Audiences are supposed to recognize their own flawed demonstration and practice of love in these two characters, not because they recognize themselves in the characters' genders, but because they recognize themselves in their humanity. Audiences are first lured into contemplating the universal need by all to be loved, and then forced to confront their ambivalences about sexuality.

The black-skinned protagonist remains in many ways a product of her culture in her ambitions and her fantasies. Her continuous struggle to fulfill her desire to be loved and to retain her dignity as a woman invites audiences to ignore for the moment their inbred ethnic prejudices (against a Shulammite?), their class assumptions (about women who labor in the sun?), and their religious judgments about female sexuality, modesty, and impurity. The hope is that readers, whether male or female, will recognize themselves in this woman's very human need and desire simply to be loved.

STRUCTURE AND COMPOSITION

While the archaic grammatical and linguistic forms found in the book suggest that some version of the book dates back to the early period in Israel's history, lyrical compositions are notoriously difficult to date with any accuracy. In fact, much of their appeal is the result of their seemingly timeless, universal application to the human situation. The themes of Song of Songs are those that belong to the commonplaces of human courtship and human sexual attraction: yearning for the lover's presence, the joys of physical intimacy, coded speech, and elusive behavior, intoxication with the charms and beauty of one's lover, overcoming social obstacles and impediments to be together. Such themes are typical of love lyrics both ancient and modern. In fact, scholars have long noted the similarities between the mood and lyrics in Song of Songs and those of ancient Egyptian love poetry dating from the period of the New Kingdom (c. 1567–1085 BCE).[13] Observing particular stylized features of Egyptian love songs associated with the Ramesside texts, Michael Fox posits that these ancient songs may have been composed for entertainment and were performed by professional singers at private banquets and public festivals.[14] This music, performed over centuries and for generations, was created to charm audiences through its use of erotic allusions, veiled speeches, and extravagant imagery. Indeed, in the Song of Songs, audiences are at least implicitly invited to assume the identities of the lovers, to identify with their plight, to sympathize with their dilemma, to share their resolve, to relish their tenacity, to enjoy their clever disguises, to mourn their losses and flaws, to celebrate their joys and strength, and to endure with them unto the end.[15] The mood and tone of the book change, sometimes within a few verses, as speakers move in and out of the drama, wooing, pleading, teasing, doubting, and interrupting each other. Audiences (and readers) are expected to be able to perceive within the poem's "progression" all the ambiguities, uncertainties, tensions, shortcomings, and suspense of love itself. In other words, drama and contents come together in the Song of Songs to create a poem intent upon gripping its audience.

Readers trained within the Western literary tradition invariably find a book like Song of Songs difficult to follow. Western readers expect literature to proceed in an orderly fashion and are frequently dismayed when a book like Song of Songs defies expectations of linearity, uniformity, transparency, and plot development. Whereas the presence of speakers, dialogue, and audiences gives the book an unmistakably dramatic quality, modern readers are struck by the way speakers, imagery, moods, and perspectives shift back and forth, seemingly without logic, sometimes within a span of one, two, or three verses. These otherwise oral speeches, which originally had their own performance quality, have been committed to a written form that has caused some tensions in its narrative development. Finding a uniform structure and consistent pattern to the book's content is not always possible. Those who perceive any literary unity to the poetry usually argue on the basis of their own aesthetic insights and not on the basis of any straightforward criteria. Commentators who divide the work into poems see it as a composition of fourteen, eighteen, twenty-eight, or thirty-one (to name just a few examples) units of poetry.

The position taken in this introduction to divide the poem into eleven lyrical units is not based on unassailable perceptions into its unfolding direction. Although the poem seems to be framed by an inclusio (the book opens [1:2-6] and closes [8:8-14] on similar themes; e.g., vineyard, the protagonist's brothers, her bodily integrity), the major indications of the book's "organization" are shifts in speakers and moods. Of course, in the numerous instances where it is difficult to determine exactly who speaks and who is the referent (e.g., 2:1; 6:11-12; 8:11-12), guesses are hazarded.

Although we see changing sides of the protagonist (romantic, defender, sage, and pragmatist), she switches back and forth between these different shades of herself, depending on the obscure attitudes challenging her right to love and to be loved by whomever she chooses. By the poem's end, the protagonist is leaning in her lover's arms in a satisfying embrace (8:5). But her fulfillment is short-lived. The curtain closes on the lovers' thwarted passion; the maiden hurries her lover's pleasure for fear of retaliation. As a woman in the Hebrew culture, she is aggressive and audacious, but as a sage and observer of human nature she is also profoundly realistic. The homily on wisdom in 8:6-7 may be correct that love is a powerful force, one that in the end conquers everything that opposes it. But love's victory does not come without a price.

Finally, Western readers expect compositions to exhibit some interest in progression or development of character(s) and plot. This cultural expectation is only casually satisfied in the Song of Songs. In the first five chapters the lovers yearn for each other, delight in each other's charms, and sing each other's praises. In the last three chapters of the book, having defended their relationship against forces from without and from within, they eventually embrace, consummate their love, and pledge that their love, though costly, is more powerful than the forces opposing it. Under no circumstances can one argue that the book closes on a note of resolution or conclusion. At the end the maiden is forced to shoo her lover away, leaving the audience to wonder whether the two are ever allowed to relax and revel in their relationship. What could be the meaning of such an unresolved ending? Is love worth it? Perhaps that is precisely the question the song wants the audience to ponder.

FOR FURTHER READING

Commentaries:

Bergant, Dianne. Song of Songs. Berit Olam. Collegeville, Minn.: Liturgical Press, 2001.

Falk, Marcia. The Song of Songs: A New Translation and Interpretation. San Francisco: HarperCollins, 1990.

Murphy, Roland. The Song of Songs. Hermeneia. Minneapolis: Fortress, 1990.

Pope, Marvin. Song of Songs. AB 7C. New York: Doubleday, 1977.

Other Studies:

Abu-Lughod, Lila. Veiled Sentiments: Honor and Poetry in a Bedouin Society. Berkeley: University of California Press, 1986.

Baruch, Elaine Hoffman. Women, Love, and Power: Literary and Psychoanalytic Perspectives. New York: New York University Press, 1991.

Biale, David. Eros and the Jews: From Biblical Israel to Contemporary America. New York: Basic, 1992.

Brenner, Athalya, ed. *A Feminist Companion to the Song of Songs.* Sheffield: JSOT, 1993.

Brenner, Athalya, and Carole R. Fontaine, eds. *The Song of Songs.* Feminist Companion to the Bible. Second Series 6. Sheffield: Sheffield Academic Press, 2000.

Horine, Steve. *Interpretive Images in the Song of Songs: From Wedding Chariots to Bridal Chambers.* Studies in the Humanities 55. New York: Peter Lang, 2001.

Merkin, Daphne. "The Woman on the Balcony: On Reading the Song of Songs," *Tikkun* 9, 3 (May–June 1994) 59-64.

Meyers, Carol. *Discovering Eve: Ancient Israelite Women in Context.* New York: Oxford University Press, 1988.

Miles, Margaret R. *Carnal Knowing: Female Nakedness and Religious Meaning in the Christian West.* Boston: Beacon, 1989.

Nelson, James, and Sandra P. Longfellow, eds. *Sexuality and the Sacred: Sources for Theological Reflection.* Louisville: Westminster John Knox, 1994.

Trible, Phyllis. *God and the Rhetoric of Sexuality.* Philadelphia: Fortress, 1978.

Walsh, Carey Ellen. *Exquisite Desire: Religion, the Erotic, and the Song of Songs.* Minneapolis: Fortess, 2000.

Winsor, Ann Roberts. *A King is Bound in Tresses: Allusions to the Song of Songs in the Fourth Gospel.* Studies in Biblical Literature 6. New York: Peter Lang, 1999.

ENDNOTES

1. Tosefta, *Sandedrin* XII 10.

2. For an illuminating discussion of the way poetry and songs are used to express personal, often unconventional sentiments in Arab bedouin communities, see Lila Abu-Lughod, *Veiled Sentiments: Honor and Poetry in a Bedouin Society* (Berkeley: University of California Press, 1986).

3. Elaine Hoffman Baruch, "The Feminine *Bildungsroman:* Education Through Marriage," in *Women, Love, and Power: Literary and Psychoanalytic Perspectives* (New York: New York University Press, 1991) 122-44.

4. Phyllis Trible argues that Song of Songs was written as a counterpoint or response to the Genesis story and points to a number of remarkable resonances between the two in her work *God and the Rhetoric of Sexuality* (Philadelphia: Fortress, 1978) chap. 5.

5. This is the title of Trible's chapter on Genesis 2–3 in *God and the Rhetoric of Sexuality*, 72-143.

6. A frequently overlooked study of the parallels between Song of Songs and Hosea 2 that deserves more attention is Fokkelien van Dijk-Hemmes, "The Imagination of Power and the Power of Imagination," *JSOT* 44 (1989) 75-88.

7. Richard N. Soulen, "The *Wasfs* in the Song of Songs and Hermeneutic," *JBL* 86 (1967) 183-90.

8. See Marcia Falk's keen insights on *wasfs* in *The Song of Songs: A New Translation and Interpretation* (San Francisco: HarperCollins, 1990) 125-36.

9. T. J. Meek, "Canticles and the Tammuz Cult," *AJSL* 39 (1922-23) 1-14.

10. J. Cheryl Exum, "A Literary and Structural Analysis of the Song of Songs," *ZAW* 85 (1973) 47-79.

11. Michael D. Goulder, *The Song of Fourteen Songs,* JSOTSup 36 (Sheffield: JSOT, 1986).

12. This line of interpretation began, of course, with the Targum, but one European Catholic scholar in modern times was very influential in arguing the claim. See Paul Joüon, *Le Cantique des Cantiques: commentaire philogique et exégétique* (Paris: Gabriel Beauchesne, 1909).

13. See Adolf Erman, *The Literature of the Ancient Egyptians,* trans. Aylward M. Blackman (London: Methuen, 1927); John Bradley White, *A Study of the Language of Love in the Song of Songs and Ancient Egyptian Poetry,* SBLDS 38 (Missoula, Mont.: Scholars Press, 1978).

14. Michael Fox, *The Song of Songs and the Ancient Egyptian Love Songs* (Madison: University of Wisconsin Press, 1985) 244-47

15. Roland Murphy, *The Song of Songs,* Hermeneia (Minneapolis: Fortress, 1990) 47.

Introduction to Prophetic Literature

DAVID L. PETERSEN

PROPHETIC LITERATURE: DEFINITIONS AND ORIGINS

What is prophetic literature? Prophetic literature involves far more than words that prophets spoke. That much is clear. But how much more? Study of biblical literature offers several possible answers: the canonical answer, the authorial answer, and the redactional answer.

One important definition of prophetic literature derives from the traditional divisions of the Hebrew Bible canon.[1] This is the "canonical" answer. Both early Jewish and Christian traditions attest a tripartite understanding of the Hebrew Bible: Torah (torah), Prophets (nebi'im), and Writings (ketubim). The second of these divisions, "the Prophets," is made up of Joshua, Judges, 1 and 2 Samuel, 1 and 2 Kings, as well as the major (Isaiah, Jeremiah, Ezekiel) and the minor (Hosea–Malachi) prophets. This list might appear odd. One would expect to find the books attributed to prophets here, but why is narrative, historical literature—the "former prophets"—also classified as prophetic literature?

Scholars have offered several different answers to this question, but their answers remain suggestive rather than definitive. First, the Deuteronomistic History (Deuteronomy–2 Kings) attests that God spoke to Israel through prophets during the course of its existence. The first book of that history, Deuteronomy, views Moses as a prophet (Deut 18:15-18), and the last book, 2 Kings, affirms that God had "warned Israel and Judah by every prophet and every seer" (2 Kgs 17:13).[2] These various historical books may attest to an understanding of history in which the prophets as those who admonished, indicted, and judged was of critical importance. Although kings are important, hence the title "Kings," prophets are even more so, especially since they were present—as personified by Moses, Deborah, Samuel, to name just three—even before kingship commenced in Israel.

A second reason for classifying these historical books—or "former prophets"—as prophetic literature derives from a different understanding of prophets. The books of Chronicles provide a key. There prophets are presented as historians. For example, 1 Chr 29:29 states, "Now the acts of King David, from first to last, are written in the records of the seer Samuel, and in the records of the prophet Nathan, and in the records of the seer Gad." To be sure, the books of Kings refer to sources that were used by the historian: for example, "Now the rest of the acts of Manasseh, all that he did, and the sin that he committed, are they not written in the Book of the Annals of the Kings of Judah?" (2 Kgs 21:17). However, no author for these sources is ever identified in Kings. In contrast, Chronicles attributes such sources to prophets, whom the chronicler apparently understood as historians. Hence, historical works, such as "Kings" (though not apparently Chronicles), may be understood as "the prophets," since prophets were viewed as Israel's early historians.

Both of these answers share an important underlying and often unstated assumption—namely, that Israel's prophets were of fundamental importance for understanding Israelite history. Their presence testifies to God's concern for the people Israel. Still, valuable as this understanding might be, it presents problems. Few readers today would want to count Joshua or 2 Samuel as prophetic literature.

One may identify a second kind of answer to the question about prophetic literature: the "authorial" response. Some would suggest that prophetic literature is that which prophets wrote or spoke. One could count the words of Micah, Amos, or Haggai as prophetic literature. Here prophets are not so much historians as authors, those who created literature—whether oral or written—that has been preserved in the Old Testament.

An important component of the authorial definition for prophetic literature is a high evaluation of that which prophets are understood to have said. That is, such speeches are often understood to be God's own speech. Many utterances in the books attributed to prophets commence with the phrase "Thus says the Lord" (e.g., Amos 1:3). To hear these words is, as it were, to hear God's words. Moreover, some interpreters view poetry as "inspired" language, and, in the case of the Old Testament, inspired not simply by one of the muses but by Israel's God. Finally, if wisdom literature is written or spoken by Israel's sages, then by analogy prophetic literature must have been written or spoken by Israel's prophets.

Regrettably, the matter is not so simple. There is considerable literature *about* prophets, but not all of it was written by them. The Bible presents two clear examples. The first involves the prophet Elisha and the literature associated with him. The book of 2 Kings includes a number of stories about this prophet. These stories are routinely included in assessments of Israel's prophets, even though someone other than Elijah must have been the author. As we shall see, these stories most probably originated in an oral, storytelling environment. In fact, the Bible attests to such a setting:

Now the king was talking with Gehazi the servant of the man of God, saying, "Tell me all the great things that Elisha has done." While he was telling the king how Elisha had restored a dead person to life. . . . (2 Kgs 8:4-5)

One can read the story about Elisha, the Shunamite woman, and her son (2 Kgs 4:8-37) and well imagine Gehazi, or another of Elisha's supporters, the so-called sons of the prophets, as its author. Someone like Gehazi, not Elisha, is the author of these stories.

The same could be said about Baruch, Jeremiah's scribe. The book of Jeremiah includes a number of stories told about the turbulent character whose name heads the book. These stories are clearly biographical, not autobiographical. Someone other than the prophet wrote about important episodes (e.g., Jeremiah 28) or major periods in his life (Jeremiah 37–44). A good candidate for the author is Baruch, the scribe who wrote down words that Jeremiah had spoken (see Jer 45). Unless we want to exclude such chapters from the corpus of prophetic literature, we will need to think about scribes like Baruch, and not just people like Jeremiah, as authors of prophetic literature.

In short, some of the literature attributed to a prophet was clearly written by someone other than the prophet. The previous cases involved literature in which the prophet was described. However, one may also refer to instances in which the prophet ostensibly speaks or writes, but the content of the text makes it difficult to think that the prophet in question actually wrote or spoke such words.

We enter here a range of biblical scholarship that some may find troubling—namely, the attempt to discern the difference between "authentic" and "secondary" prophetic literature. For example, for over a century scholars have pored over the book of Isaiah, in part attempting to determine what portions of that book might be attributed to Isaiah ben Amoz, who lived in the late eighth and early seventh centuriesBCE. There is now a consensus that much in that book (particularly in chaps. 40–66) dates to the sixth and fifth centuries. Put another way, Isaiah ben Amoz could not have written major portions of the book attributed to him. If one wants to construe most of the book of Isaiah as prophetic literature, then one must accept someone other than Isaiah as the author of that prophetic literature. This same situation also holds for sections of many other prophetic books (e.g., Zechariah 9–14). Unless one is willing to deny that such material in prophetic books is prophetic literature, the authorial answer will not suffice.

What, then, is prophetic literature? Prophetic literature is literature that attests to or grows out of (i.e., is generated by) the activity of Israel's prophets. This is the generative answer. One can count the words of a prophet as prophetic literature, but one can also deem a story about a prophet to be prophetic literature. Prophets can produce prophetic literature, but so can someone who is not known as a prophet. Moreover, as the examples suggest, prophetic literature can be composed not only as poetry, but also as prose.

These considerations lead us to ask about the origins of prophetic literature. Obviously, one essential element is the presence and activity of a prophet or an intermediary.[3] That individual could either write or speak prophetic literature—such was the case with Isaiah and Habakkuk, who are attested as both speakers and writers (Isaiah 7–8; Habakkuk 1–2). However, as we have already seen, other individuals contemporaneous with "prophets"—Gehazi and Baruch—could also speak or pen prophetic literature.

These two sorts of prophetic literature (prose accounts and poetic speeches), dating to roughly the period in which a prophet was active, possessed remarkable generative abilities. For example, the images of Zion present in the accounts and speeches of and about Isaiah ben Amoz offered later Israelites profound and productive ways for thinking about Zion—Jerusalem as God's chosen abode. In times long after that of the eighth-century prophet Isaiah, such as the Persian period (fifth cent.), authors composed literature that made its way into the book of Isaiah (material that can be found in chaps. 56–66). These anonymous individuals—whether or not we understand them to be prophets is an interesting question—produced a significant percentage of what appears in prophetic books. We need to look to these anonymous individuals and their times for the origins of prophetic literature as well as to the times of the originating prophets (e.g., an Amos or Isaiah).

In sum, prophetic literature can be understood from multiple perspectives. Moreover, a search for the origins of prophetic literature may end at various places—with the prophet, with a contemporary of the prophet, or with tradents, the anonymous authors and editors who preserved and added to the emerging corpus of prophetic literature. The words of a prophet or the prophet's contemporaries generated remarkable literary activity. The prophet's sayings and accounts, or those of the prophet's contemporaries, remained alive and elicited new words and accounts, a process that resulted in extensive books like Isaiah or Jeremiah. Israelite prophetic literature seems to have had an almost inherent capacity to elicit elucidation at a later time.

ISRAEL'S PROPHETS

Although prophetic literature is the primary focus of this volume, we also need to keep the prophet in the field of vision. The term "prophet" derives from the Greek noun προφήτης (prophētēs). The Greek root means, primarily, "to foresee." To understand prophets in the Old Testament as "prophets" in this sense is unfortunate and misleading for at least two reasons. First, the notion of seeing into the future, of predicting what will happen, is only one facet of what Israel's prophets were about. To be sure, Israel's prophets could and did speak about the future, but they also addressed the present and referred as well to the past. They were not essentially in the business of providing horoscopes for those in Judah and Israel.

Diverse Roles. Second, the use of one title, "prophet," belies the diversity among Israel's prophets. We possess various evidence of this diversity. Perhaps most indicative are the various titles or role labels used to describe those individuals whom we consider prophets. There are four such titles in the Hebrew Bible: חזה (ḥōzeh, "seer"), ראה (rō'eh, "diviner") איש האלהים ('îš hā'ělōhîm, "man of God"), and נביא (nābî', "prophet"). As the typical English equivalents suggest, two of the four nouns derive from words meaning "to see." The first noun, ḥōzeh, apparently means quite simply an individual who receives and reports visions, (e.g., Amos 7:12), but it also appears to function interchangeably with the noun nābî' (so Isa 29:10; 30:10). The noun rō'eh is associated primarily with the figure of Samuel. In the pivotal scene in which this noun appears (1 Samuel 9), Samuel functions rather like a diviner—that is, someone who is able to communicate with the world of the sacred in order to discover information that will be useful to those who consult him: "Perhaps he will tell us about the journey on which we have set out" (1 Sam 9:6). After Saul and his companion reach the town, they must go with Samuel to a shrine and then eat with him. Divinatory activity may have taken place in either context.

The third title, *'îš hā'ĕlōhîm*, "man of God," is especially prominent in the stories about Elijah and Elisha, particularly the latter. The literary character of these stories corroborates a judgment that the "man of God" can best be understood as a "holy man," a type of individual attested in numerous religious traditions. Such people possess the power of the holy and, hence, are dangerous, powerful, and due appropriate respect. Unlike visionaries, who occasionally engage in trance or possession behavior, the holy man personifies the deity in the midst of the profane world. A classic example is provided by 2 Kgs 6:1-7. Elisha, here characterized as "the man of God," makes an iron ax head float to the surface of the Jordan River, into which it had accidentally fallen. Such powers belong to the world of the sacred. Elisha does not need to pray; he can simply act, since he possesses those powers.

The most frequent term for "prophet" is *nābî'*. Scholars have not reached a consensus about its root meaning, but the term probably signifies someone called to a certain task. Hence it is no accident that call or commissioning narratives appear in several prophetic books (e.g., Isaiah 6; Jeremiah 1; Ezekiel 1–2). Over time, this term became the standard one by means of which prophets were known, as 1 Sam 9:9 reflects: "for the one who is now called a prophet [*nābî'*] was formerly called a seer."

One suspects that the use of these four role labels for a prophet reflected linguistic usage in different times and places. Moreover, they surely emphasized different things a prophet did; for example, report visions or utter oracles. However, as a roster of contemporary role labels, such as clergyperson, priest, pastor, or minister, suggests, there was probably considerable overlap in what various prophets were about. Israel's prophets were writers and/or speakers. They could receive communications from the deity in various ways (i.e., auditions and visions). Still, it is possible to

identify one element common to all prophets. They functioned as *intermediaries* between the human and the divine worlds. They could represent humans to God (e.g., Amos 7:2) or God to humans (Amos 5:4). They could act with the power of God within the mundane world (so Elisha). They could envision the cosmic world (Amos 7:4; Zech 1:7-17); they could participate in the divine council (1 Kings 22; Isaiah 6); and they could analyze the machinations of humans (Micah 3). Prophets were truly boundary figures.

If prophets are to be understood as boundary figures, as intermediaries, then some comment is necessary about the relationship between the two major classes of what might be called religious professionals: priests and prophets. An absolute distinction between prophets and priests did not exist in ancient Israel. Some prophets were also priests. Jeremiah was born into a priestly lineage that resided in Anathoth, a small town not far from Jerusalem. This priestly house probably traced its roots to Abiathar, who was exiled to Anathoth, the ancestral dwelling, for having supported Adonijah rather than Solomon (1 Kgs 2:26-27). Ezekiel, too, is accorded priestly status (Ezek 1:3), again as a function of his birth. Unlike Jeremiah, Ezekiel was probably a member of the priestly line of the Zadokites, who had primary responsibility for the Temple in Jerusalem. Zechariah was another prophet born into a priestly family. His genealogy, "Zechariah son of Berechiah son of Iddo" (Zech 1:1), is also attested in the book of Nehemiah (Neh 12:16), where the genealogy is part of the listing for priestly ancestral houses. At least three prophets—Jeremiah, Ezekiel, and Zechariah—belonged to priestly families.

The priest-prophet connection is even stronger than matters of lineage. The book of Joel offers a remarkable scenario in which the prophet appears to function as a priest. In a time of national crisis, Joel calls the Israelites to engage in ritual lamentation at the Temple (Joel 1:13-14). He then utters the words that the priest would have spoken to the deity (Joel 1:19). In response to their calls for help, the deity then speaks through the prophet, affirming that the concerns of the people have been heard (Joel 2:18-20). The prophet Joel undertakes just such work as one might expect from an intercessory priest. Another prophetic book, Zephaniah, depicts the prophet's (Zeph 3:14-15) calling

Israelites to the service of song. They are to praise the deity for having moved from a time of judgment to a time of restoration.

In sum, we do well to remember that prophets not only could exercise various roles but also could even be, even act as, priests. Such behavior should prevent us from thinking about prophets in a simple and/or monolithic fashion.

Historical and Social Settings. Prophets, as a class of religious specialists, are not present in all times or, for that matter, in all societies. Similarly, prophets were not present in all periods of Israel's existence. For reasons made clear in the article "Introduction to the History of Ancient Israel,"[4] it is difficult to speak about Israelite society in any strong historical sense much before the time of David (c. 1000 BCE). In literature that depicts Israel's understanding of itself prior to that time (the Pentateuch or the books of Joshua and Judges), references to prophets are rare or unusual. Moses is a significant exception, which will be examined below. Abraham (Gen 20:7), Miriam (Exod 15:20), and Deborah (Judg 4:4) are labeled as prophets; yet, they seem so strange when viewed as prophets that other labels for these individuals seem more appropriate; for example, Deborah is better understood as a judge and Abraham as a patriarch. Certain notions of the prophetic role (e.g., intercession) have affected the ways in which Israelite authors viewed these individuals. An ancient Israelite writer may view Abraham as a prophet when he prays on someone else's behalf, even though intercession may be characteristic neither of much prophetic activity nor of Abraham's own behavior.

Individuals who function as intermediaries and who are known as prophets begin to appear at the time when Israel adopted statehood as its form of government—in biblical terms, when Israel gained a king. Moreover, within seventy-five years from the time Judah was destroyed (as an independent state with a king), individually named prophets seem to have become a thing of the past. Thus there is a strong correlation between Israel's existence as a monarchic state and the presence of prophets in its midst.

This correlation may reflect several different features of prophetic behavior. As Overholt and others have demonstrated, prophecy requires certain conditions to exist.[5] Among them are an "audience" that will recognize someone as a prophet. Moreover, moving beyond Overholt, there may be a need for someone to protect a prophet from harm due to his proclaiming something unpopular; for example, the powerful individuals who helped Jeremiah (Ahikam son of Shaphan [Jer 26:24] or Ebed-melech the Cushite [Jer 38:7-13]). Finally, certain historical moments may produce greater needs for prophecy than do other times. Israel, from roughly 1000 to 500 BCE—though not uniformly during this half-millennium—met these conditions.

During these five hundred years, Israel lived through a number of major changes or crises: the inception of statehood, national schism, Neo-Assyrian threats and the destruction of the northern kingdom, the Neo-Babylonian threat and the destruction of Judah, life in exile, and attempts at restoration in the land. Prophets addressed each one of these pivotal moments.

For example, Nathan and Gad appeared during the lifetime of David, Israel's first true king. Both these prophets interacted directly with the king; they did not speak to a larger public.[6] Nathan confronted David after he had impregnated Bathsheba and had her husband killed (2 Samuel 11–12) and is able to trick David into indicting himself for this blatant misuse of royal power. Gad, too, critiqued the king after he had undertaken a census designed to assay the number of men available for battle (2 Samuel 24). In both cases, the prophet challenges the holder of a new political office, the king, by calling him to account based on Israel's ancient religious and ethical traditions. In the midst of this new political configuration, Israelites must have been asking the question, What does it mean for a king to function in an Israelite/Yahwistic setting? In some measure, then, these prophets are a voice from the past, attempting to relate Israel's defining norms to a new political situation.

David's grandson faced the next critical challenge. Could the diversity represented by the northern and southern tribes remain integrated in the united monarchy that David had forged? The Deuteronomistic History reports that even before Rehoboam had angered representatives from northern tribes, a prophet, Ahijah the Shilonite, had informed Jeroboam that he would be king of the new northern kingdom (1 Kings 11). These events (c. 922 BCE) spelled the end of the united monarchy and the creation of two nations, both of which claimed Yahweh as their state god. What is important to note for our purposes is that writers of Israelite history affirm that a prophet played a critical role in the creation of the divided monarchy.

The next major development on the political landscape was the threat posed by the reconsolidated Neo-Assyrian Empire in the eighth century. Although his predecessors should be credited with major initiatives, it was Tiglath-Pileser III (745–727 BCE) who began military campaigns in Syria-Palestine. These attacks in the decade between 740 and 730 BCE are attested both in biblical texts (2 Kings 15) and Assyrian annals. Moreover, they provide the context for two prophetic books: Amos and Hosea.

During this period, Amos, a Judahite who came to Israel, and Hosea, a native Israelite, addressed those in the northern kingdom, which was subject to greater pressure from the Neo-Assyrians than was its southern neighbor Judah. Both Amos and Hosea understood the dire straits facing Israel. One can comb the books and discover various images of military attack and destruction. Amos speaks of people being taken into exile (e.g., Amos 6:7), forcibly removed from their homes and resettled elsewhere, a practice used by the Neo-Assyrians when assuming control of a new area. Hosea, likewise, refers to the decimation of warfare:

Therefore the tumult of war shall rise against
   your people,
and all your fortresses shall be destroyed.
                     (Hos 10:14)

However, Hosea and Amos do more than simply see the signs of the times and state them in a poetic way. Instead, these individuals, as did those who came after them, interpreted these events from the perspective of Israelite religious and ethical traditions. These prophets understand Yahweh's hand to be at work behind whatever the Neo-Assyrians are doing. It is for this reason that Hosea continually describes the deity's work in the first person:

I will cast my net over them;
I will bring them down like birds of the air;
I will discipline them. (Hos 7:12)

Although Neo-Assyrian chariotry may set out against Israelite troops, Hosea understands that it is really Yahweh who is disciplining the Israelites.

In addition, Amos and Hosea tried to explain to those in Israel why they were to suffer such a dire fate. Interestingly, the reasons they offer are diverse. Amos inveighs against social and economic practices in the northern kingdom, whereas Hosea focuses on religious and political misdeeds. Still, although they offer different kinds of critiques, the prophets share two basic assumptions: (1) that the destruction is a punishment and (2) that Israel had violated that which they had earlier agreed to do. The prophets do not indict Israel for violating some new norm. If anything is new, it is the freedom with which the prophets talk about the deity. One might say that their theologies are more creative than their ethics.

The next pivotal moment involved the same empire, but now confronting Judah. New prophets are involved: Micah and Isaiah. Although it would be a mistake to read all prophetic texts as direct reflections of historical circumstances, some texts do attest to particular moments in a stark way. Micah 1:10-16 is such a text. These verses contain a number of city names. Those that have been identified with actual sites all sit to the south and west of Jerusalem. The Neo-Assyrian annals report that Sennacherib destroyed a number of Judahite cities. One of these, Lachish (Mic 1:13), has been excavated. There is one layer attesting to destruction brought by military means and that almost certainly reflects Sennacherib's campaign in 701 BCE. Micah sets such Neo-Assyrian action within the context of a Judah, and especially a Jerusalem, that is filled with rampant violence. Micah 3:1-4 indicts those who rule from Jerusalem. They are responsible for both the suffering they inflict in the capital and the suffering the Neo-Assyrians are inflicting throughout the land.

Isaiah, too, knows of this same set of events c. 701 BCE, events that were of such significance that they were narrated in both Isaiah and Kings (Isaiah 36–37; cf. 2 Kings 18–19). Moreover, what transpires provides a key for understanding much in the book of Isaiah. These chapters address a question that must have vexed those who heard Micah's words: Whom does the Lord support? One could hear Micah (and Amos and Hosea) and think that Yahweh supported the efforts of those who were attacking Judah. The Assyrians were the means by which God was punishing the people. According to Isa 36:10, the Assyrians themselves were making this very point. Isaiah, through a divine oracle, responds that God will protect Jerusalem, "for my own sake and for the sake of my servant David" (Isa 37:35). Isaiah, finally, knows more about what God will do—and why—than do the Assyrians. Through him, and other prophets, Israelites can understand such moments as an attack by an imperial enemy.

Almost a century passed before prophets appear prominently again, which they do as the Neo-Assyrian Empire is ousted from the ancient Near Eastern stage by the Neo-Babylonians. The book of Nahum might be read as a treatise on the necessity for such destruction. However, this is a minor chapter when compared with the role the Neo-Babylonians will play within Syria-Palestine. The Babylonians defeated Nineveh, the Neo-Assyrian capital, in 612 BCE. Then, in 597 and again in 587, they attacked Judah, destroying Jerusalem in the second campaign. It is, therefore, no accident that two of the three so-called major prophets date to this time. If Judahites had been asking questions in 701, they must have been shouting them in 587. How could Yahweh let Judah and the Temple in Jerusalem be destroyed? Before 587, Jeremiah and Ezekiel affirm the necessity of such punishment. And both before and after that date, they explain why such radical action had become necessary. Ezekiel focuses on the ways in which Judah had insulted God's holiness, whereas Jeremiah continues a line of attack begun by Hosea, but now directed against Judah: They have acted in a promiscuous fashion, worshiping other gods. Moreover, their political policies stand at odds with what Yahweh desires them to do. Here again, times of radical change elicit the need for radical explanations.

Both Jeremiah and Ezekiel stand astride the decisive date of 587 BCE. After the time of destruction, they and other prophets (e.g., Haggai and Zechariah) wrestle with questions about what comes next. Will God be with this people? Will there still be a covenant? Will the new chapter be written with those in exile or those who return to the land? Prophets, and not priests or sages, were the ones providing responses to such questions. Ezekiel addresses these questions by using visionary language about a field of bones: Could they live again (Ezekiel 37)? Deutero-Isaiah (the prophet responsible for Isaiah 40–55) thought about a Jerusalem that would have its streets paved with gold (Isa 54:11-12). Jeremiah spoke in terms of a new covenant (Jer 31:31). Haggai anticipated a restoration of the prior monarchic order (Hag 2:20-23). Zechariah envisioned a new order, with both priest and king in leading roles (Zechariah 4). Different though these perspectives are, they share one essential affirmation: God will continue to be with the people.

With the rebuilding of the Temple and its rededication in 515 BCE, such individually named intermediaries begin to pass from the scene. Prophetic literature continues to be written, but it now occurs in the form of notes, additions, and supplements to earlier words. As a province in the Persian Empire, Judah may no longer have required prophets or possessed the prerequisites for prophetic activity. Moreover, the very character of Yahwism had changed, from the religion of a nation-state roughly coextensive with the boundaries of Judah and Israel to a religion that could be practiced not only in the land, but also elsewhere, such as in Egypt and Mesopotamia. This new form of religion, oriented around divine instruction, did not so much need new "words," new oracles from the deity, as it needed interpreters of words that already existed, particularly those of the Torah or the Pentateuch. Judaism, this new religion, did not need prophets, as had its forebear religion, Yahwism.

Historical circumstance provides only one way in which to contextualize Israel's prophets. Social setting offers another fruitful angle of vision. A number of popular understandings of Israelite prophecy picture prophets as something akin to desert mystics, walking into Israelite cities and raving at the residential population.[7] Earlier comments about prophets as priests suggested problems with such a view. However, the question of the social setting for prophecy deserves even more attention.

Wilson and Petersen, among others, have attempted to classify the social location of Israel's prophets and then to compare that location with intermediaries in other cultures.[8] Such anthropological research has resulted in understandings of prophets quite different from earlier models. For example, most prophets appear to undertake their activities within an urban setting. In fact, most appear to have lived in cities or, at a minimum, to be associated with specific towns (e.g., Amos of Tekoa; Jeremiah of Anathoth).

The anthropologist Ioan Lewis theorized that intermediaries could appear either in a central or a peripheral setting.[9] By that, he meant that prophets could function in different places within society. An intermediary might be located in or near the circles of power. Alternatively, a prophet might be part of a disenfranchised group. Many popular understandings of Israel's prophets have placed them in the latter setting. Rarely, however, was that the case either in Israel or throughout the ancient Near East. One of the first prophets, Nathan, is embedded in the structure of the royal court. He has the direct ear of the king; he can judge the king and name the son who will succeed David. Likewise, over four hundred years later, one of the last prophets, Haggai, in the oracle with which the book named for him concludes, speaks to an heir of the Davidic house. Such proximity to the king or prince symbolizes the prophet's close connection to political power during many periods of ancient Israelite history.

To be sure, Israel's prophets spoke on behalf of those without power and on behalf of those oppressed by the powerful. Amos challenges those "who oppress the poor, who crush the needy" (Amos 4:1). However, Amos himself was apparently a well-off farmer who engaged in both animal husbandry and the production of crops. Micah indicts those who "covet fields, and seize them;/ houses, and take them away;/ they oppress householder and house,/ people and their inheritance" (Mic 2:2). Yet, Micah may well have belonged to the group of elders who were responsible for the governance of Moresheth, his village. In sum, there is considerable evidence for thinking that the prophets were not impoverished or members of a lower economic class. Instead, they articulate values that involve concern for those who might be oppressed by powerful groups or structures in Israelite and Judahite society.

A final comment needs to be made about prophecy as a form of intermediation in ancient Israel. Prophecy, as such, may have a fatal flaw. Prophecy can work well if there is one prophet speaking to somebody who will take that prophet seriously. The situation becomes problematic when two prophets appear and say things that are contradictory, especially if both prophets use the standard language of an Israelite prophet. This problem has often been termed the conflict between true and false prophecy.

Classic exemplars appear in 1 Kings 22 and Jeremiah 28. In the latter case, Jeremiah confronted another prophet, Hananiah, who presented a divine oracle (Jer 28:2-4) from Yahweh. However, Hananiah's words of hope stood in stark contrast to the words of judgment that Jeremiah had been proclaiming. Although Jeremiah responded with his own comments, Hananiah used a symbolic action, removing an ox yoke that Jeremiah had been wearing. Jeremiah, without any other prophetic alternative, left the scene. Later, after Jeremiah had received a divine oracle, he could challenge Hananiah in public.

One can imagine the difficulties encountered by those who had witnessed the initial confrontation. They had no easy way of knowing which prophet was telling the truth. In fact, the deuteronomic rules that govern such a case (Deut 18:15-22) stipulate that one should wait and see which individual's words would turn out to be true. But when prophets' words require action, such inactivity would not be possible. Moreover, prophets could disagree about assessments of the present and the past, not just about pronouncements concerning the future. This potential for conflict between prophets may have provoked such difficulty that other forms of seeking information from the deity developed, forms such as priestly admonition or scribal intermediation, neither of which allowed for a direct public challenge.

Prophets, then, appeared primarily in times of crisis during the period when Israel and Judah existed as monarchic states and shortly thereafter. And they addressed both the nation's leaders and the overall population based on their understanding of Israel's religious traditions. They were embedded in, rather than distinct from, the structures of Israelite society.

PROPHETIC LITERATURE IN THE ANCIENT NEAR EAST

Since intermediation is a well-attested form of religious behavior in many societies, it should come as no surprise that prophets appeared in ancient Near Eastern societies other than Israel. In fact, the OT reports both explicitly and implicitly—often polemically—that prophets of other religions existed. Deuteronomy 13:1-2 alerts us to the existence of such prophets:

If prophets or those who divine by dreams appear among you and promise you omens or portents, and the omens or the portents declared by them take place, and they say, "Let us follow other gods" (whom you have not known) "and let us serve them."

The authors of Deuteronomy not only knew about the existence of such prophets, but they also understood something about their power. A story like Elijah's confrontation with the prophets of Baal on Mt. Carmel (1 Kgs 18:20-40) makes sense only if Israelites had experience with these prophets and understood them to be effective intermediaries between Baal and those who venerated him.

For obvious reasons, most references to prophets for gods other than Yahweh are couched in a polemical tone, just as are references to the veneration of those gods. As a result, the case of Balaam son of Beor (Numbers 22–24) is particularly interesting. Balaam was a non-Israelite but also, according to Israelite tradition, was able to function as an intermediary between Israel's God and a Moabite and Midianite audience. He utters an "oracle of one who hears the words of God, who sees the vision of the Almighty" (Num 24:4). Although not an Israelite prophet, Balaam does the same sorts of things that one would expect from an Israelite prophet.

Our knowledge about this OT, but non-Israelite, prophet has been significantly enhanced by an important archaeological discovery in 1967. Archaeological work at Tell Deir 'Alla, which would have been part of ancient Ammon, revealed a fragmentary plaster inscription dating to the eighth century BCE. That inscription attests to the activities of an individual named Balaam, son of Beor, almost certainly the same individual whose work is described in Numbers 22–24. There could be no more graphic confirmation of Israelite prophecy as a phenomenon typical of the larger ancient Near Eastern environ.

The inscription begins with the following introduction:

The account of [Balaam, son of Beor], who was a seer of the gods. The gods came to him in the night, and he saw a vision like an oracle of El.[10]

Thereafter the text recounts the lamentation he undertakes after apprehending the vision, which he then recounts. The gods assembled in a council (cf. 1 Kings 22; Jer 23:18) in order to plan a devastating destruction. Darkness and the reversal of the social order will ensue (elements attested prominently in OT prophetic texts as well; see, e.g., Isa 3:4; Amos 8:9). Although much of the remainder of the text is so fractured that it is difficult to read, the text that is legible presents a picture of prophetic behavior essentially similar to that in other OT texts. Visions in the night (i.e., dreams; cf. the Greek notion of "sleeping vision") were a typical form of communication between the prophet and the world of the deity. The divine council, in which Yahweh is surrounded by minor deities (in the OT, "all the host of heaven" [1 Kgs 22:19]; "heavenly beings" [lit., "sons of God," Job 1:6]), is important in many prophetic texts. For example, Isaiah is commissioned to work as a herald on behalf of such a council (Isaiah 6). Balaam, like Israelite prophets, responded in a public way to the "private" communication at night. In so doing, that which he knew became public knowledge: "Sit Down! I will tell you what the Saddayin have done. Now, come, see the works of the gods!"[11] Finally, inside and outside Israel, such behavior was memorialized in written form to testify to the powerful revelation of what the gods were doing.

Perhaps the most important trove of ancient literature that illumines Israelite prophetic activity dates to a far earlier epoch than do Balaam or any Israelite prophets. On the upper Euphrates River, at the city of Mari, archaeologists have discovered an archive that dates to the eighteenth century BCE—just before Hammurabi, of law code fame, ruled in Babylon. This library contained not only economic and political records but also a series of clay tablets recording the work of various prophets. These Mari prophets were known by various titles, as were the Israelite prophets.

The Mari texts are all relatively brief, incised on clay tablets. One such text (ARM X 7) is here quoted in its entirety. Zimri-Lim is the king, Sibtu is his wife, and Selebum is a prophet situated at the temple of the deity Annunitum.

Speak to my lord: Thus Sibtu your maid-servant. The palace is safe and sound. In the temple of

Annunitu, on the third day of the month, Selebum went into a trance. Thus spoke Annunitum: "O Zimri-Lim, with a revolt they would put you to the test. Guard yourself. Put at your side servants, your controllers whom you love. Station them so they can guard you. Do not go about by yourself. And as for the men who would put you to the text, I shall deliver these men into your hand." I have now hereby dispatched to my lord the hair and fringe of the cult-player.[12]

This is a highly formulaic text; the phrase "Thus spoke Annunitum" is parallel to numerous OT texts, "Thus says Yahweh" (Amos 2:1). The prophetic messages are routinely addressed to the king. Some individual offers a message, which is then reported to the king by a confidant, whereas in ancient Israel the prophet often conveys his or her own message directly to the king (the case of Baruch's presenting Jeremiah's message is a notable exception). The text quoted above is typical of many Mari texts that focus on the safety and security of the king. Such focus on the monarch is present in Israel as well, though not always in preserving his safety (e.g., Isaiah 7; 38). Mari texts do on occasion challenge the king, especially if the prophet thinks that the monarch has not been providing properly for the maintenance of a temple.

This same Mari text (ARM X 7) includes two other elements that require mention. First, the text refers to the means by which the prophet received information: a trance. Anthropologists describe this as possession behavior, for which there is some evidence in the Hebrew Bible (e.g., 1 Sam 19:20). More to the point, prophetic literature often identifies the means by which a prophet receives information about the world of the divine—namely, through audition, vision, or possession. Second, the final sentence of the text refers to the hem of the garment and the hair from the head of Selebum. Such items were garnered in order to identify and verify the source of a particular prophetic message. Some scholars have suggested similar origins for superscriptions to or within prophetic collections (e.g., Isa 8:1, 16). The prophets' messages were powerful; they could influence military behavior and matters of state. Kings, especially, could not afford to put up with irresponsible prophetic speech. Hence, those who exercised the role of prophet were held accountable in this way.

The Mari texts, though stored in an archive, betray no attempt to create a collection associated with an individual. Also, there is no evidence of later additions or reflections, as one finds in Israelite prophetic literature.

A final set of texts must also be mentioned—namely, those that reflect prophetic activity in the Neo-Assyrian period (i.e., roughly eighth–seventh centuries BCE). Though less well known than the Mari texts, these tablets, which have been recently published by Simo Parpola, chronicle prophets contemporaneous with Isaiah and Micah. These texts apparently present the oracles of nine women and four men known as prophets, a striking divergence from the gender of Israelite prophets. One well preserved text reads:

Fear not, Esarhaddon!
I am Bel. (Even as) I speak to you,
    I watch over the beams of your heart.
When your mother gave birth to you,
    sixty great gods stood with me and protected you.
Sin was at your right side, Samas at your left;
    sixty great gods were standing around you
    and girded your loins.
Do not trust in man.
    Lift up your eyes, look to me!
I am Ishtar of Arbela; I reconciled Assur with you.
When you were small, I took you to me.
    Do not fear; praise me!
What enemy has attacked you while I remained silent?
The future shall be like the past.
I am u, lord of the stylus. Praise me!
By the mouth of the woman Baya, "son" of Arbela[13]

One feature of the Neo-Assyrian texts is particularly striking: More than one oracle is present on a tablet. One tablet from Nineveh includes five oracles, all apparently attributed to the same prophet. Moreover, the middle oracle seems to have been placed there because of its central importance for the overall sequence—namely, the basis for a covenant between the god Assur and the royal house of Assyria.[14] The third collection commences with a prologue or introduction prior to the citation of the oracles, and the oracles themselves have been arranged in a temporal sequence. One might view this text as a primal form of a prophetic book. The other collections include the utterances of different prophets. Still, Parpola writes: "It appears that the oracles collected in these tablets were arranged chronologically and, it seems, thematically, as well."[15]

In sum, we know that prophets were active both inside Israel and throughout the larger ancient Near Eastern cultural context. These prophets engaged in similar forms of activity, including reporting visions and uttering oracles. As a result, prophetic literature appears both in Israelite and other cultures. What is distinctive about things prophetic in ancient Israel is the monumental literary creations that derive from the work of these prophets. There is simply no prophetic text from ancient Mesopotamia, Syria-Palestine, or Egypt that can compare with the books of Isaiah and Hosea, whether viewed from the perspectives of length, breadth of vision, or literary complexity.

LITERARY PERSPECTIVES

Prophetic literature from the ancient Near East occurs in the form of single clay tablets or plaster inscriptions, each typically attesting to one prophetic performance. In contrast, the biblical prophetic books are, for the most part, collections of numerous speeches or incidents from a prophet's life. Most of these biblical books are more than a piling up of oracles, as if a series of clay tablets were simply lined up on a shelf and then copied. Some books represent a meaningful ordering and carefully structured presentation of speeches and reports. Ezekiel moves from indictment and judgment on Israel (chaps. 1–24) to judgment on foreign nations (chaps. 25–32) to hope for Israel (chaps. 33–48). Other books (e.g., Hosea) appear minimally ordered and without the aforementioned formulae. Some books include pre-existing collections (e.g., the oracles against the nations in Amos 1–2 or the series of oracles about kings in Jer 21:11–23:8). Others appear simply as one collection, without readily discernible subunits (e.g., Micah). Hence, the astute reader may recognize different levels of prophetic literature: the individual saying or report, intermediate collections of such units, and the prophetic book itself.

The categories of prose and poetry might seem to offer a convenient way of categorizing prophetic literature, if one meant that poetry equals speech and prose equals story, as some scholars have suggested. Unfortunately, the matter is not so simple for at least three reasons. First, the boundary between prose and poetry is not always easy to discern. For example, in comparing the RSV and the NRSV translations of Ezek 17:2-10, one discovers that the earlier group of translators deemed those verses to be prose, whereas the later group of translators deemed them to be poetry. The distinction between formal prose and loosely structured poetry is often difficult to discern. Second, some speeches, whether of the deity or of a prophet, are conveyed in prose (e.g., Ezekiel 25). Third, not all prose texts (apart from speeches) constitute stories—that is, prose that includes narrative structure. These difficulties notwithstanding, I propose two basic categories with which to understand prophetic literature: prose accounts and poetic speech.

Prose Accounts. Most exemplars of prophetic literature that report the activity of prophets are conveyed in prose. But they are not all stories, if by that we mean a prose narrative that includes what literary critics have described as an arc of tension or plot—namely, a beginning point, followed by a complication, which is then resolved. Put simply, a story may report, but not all chronicles or reports are stories in this strict sense.

Careful reading of accounts, most of which are composed in prose, should attend in the first instance to their literary features. For example, the accounts about Elisha present a peculiar figure, on occasion a troublesome miracle worker, on occasion a benevolent intercessor. One does well to ask questions such as, What sort of character has the writer depicted in an account? At what point does an account of his activity become a story?

It is helpful to identify at least seven basic types of prose accounts in Israelite prophetic literature:

1. Symbolic Action Report. The symbolic action report describes prophetic behavior that is designed to convey a message. Isaiah 20:1-6 provides a classic example of the straightforward form. God commands Isaiah to walk naked for three years "as a sign and a portent against Egypt and Ethiopia" (Isa 20:3). We are not told that Isaiah was to proclaim anything. Action, rather than words, provides the key element. As we work through this report, we discover that the message was directed not to these foreign nations but to "the inhabitants of this coastland," Judah's near neighbors. The text does not exhibit interest in any qualms Isaiah might have had about undertaking this task. Nor do we hear how those in Judah responded to this naked man in their midst. One can readily conceive an imaginative or entertaining story about Isaiah's having comported himself in this way. But the author was interested in using the form of the symbolic action report, not in exploring the narrative potential of such prophetic behavior. The book of Ezekiel includes a number of comparable examples of symbolic action reports (e.g., Ezek 4:1-3; 5:1-4). Reporting human behavior and its significance for an audience constitutes the key elements in such accounts.

2. Commissioning Report. These accounts, sometimes termed call narratives, do not occur in all prophetic books. But they are so interesting, and regular in general form, that they have elicited much attention.[16] Jeremiah 1:4-10; Isaiah 6; and Ezekiel 1–3 are the telling examples. (On formal grounds, Isa 40:1-11 may belong here as well.) All three texts identify a "conversation" between the deity and the prophet, which appears to depict the prophet's initiation into that role. However, these texts are not biography but, instead, highly theologized accounts, each one influenced by imagery and ideas important to the prophetic book of which it is a part (e.g., the prominence of word in the Jeremiah 1 versus the imagery of holiness in Ezekiel 1–3).

Commissioning reports are typically made up of six elements (divine confrontation, introductory word, commission, objection, reassurance, sign), all of which are present in another non-prophetic commissioning report: the commissioning of Abraham's servant, which may be found in Genesis 24. Norman Habel has argued that the regularity of the commissioning report in prophetic books is due to the use of such discourse in the commissioning of messengers throughout ancient Israel.

Like the symbolic action report, the report of commissioning does not comprise a story. One could easily imagine Isaiah 6 being told as a story— for example, an interest in whether Isaiah's "uncleanness" (v. 5) will prevent him from becoming a prophet—but the basic elements of narrative are absent. Instead, the ancient authors attest to the fact of commissioning, not why (or how) it happened. Moreover, these accounts focus on an essential element of an individual prophet's message or role (i.e., Jeremiah as a prophet to the nations who

announces both destroying/overthrowing and building/planting); they do not explore the prophet's personality or human capacities.

3. Vision Report. Two of the four role labels used to describe prophets may be translated "seer." Hence, it is not surprising that visionary behavior—"this is what the Lord God showed me" (Amos 7:1) or "I looked up and saw. . . ." (Zech 2:1)—figures prominently in prophetic books. Such behavior is also attested formulae that introduce prophetic books—e.g., "the book of the vision of Nahum" (Nah 1:1); "the vision of Obadiah" (Obad 1); or "the oracle that the prophet Habakkuk saw" (Hab 1:1).

Several prophetic books contain reports of that which a prophet "saw." Two of these visions occur in the commission reports (Isaiah 6; Ezekiel 1–3). However, elsewhere, prophets offer vision reports that attest not only to the inauguration of their roles as prophets but also to their ongoing work as prophets. Interestingly, these vision reports regularly occur in a series. Amos reports five visionary experiences (Amos 7:1-9; 8:1-3; 9:1-4). Ezekiel offers four vision reports; they begin in 1:1; 8:1; 37:1; and 40:1, respectively. And Zechariah 1–6 contains eight vision reports. (Jeremiah offers two very brief reports [Jer 1:11-13].) Each book presents its vision reports in a regular, one might even say stereotypical, manner. Whatever the prophet experienced has been conveyed in a regularized manner.

In this type of literature, one finds a prophet experiencing that which is happening or is about to happen. In the earliest vision reports, those of Amos, the seer understands immediately what he has experienced. For example, Amos perceives the deity "calling for a shower of fire, and it devoured the great [watery] deep and was eating up the land" (Amos 7:4). Immediately thereafter, the prophet intercedes on behalf of Israel, an act that implies that Amos understood all too well what he had seen. The same is true for the visions of Ezekiel, though this prophet is now accompanied on his visionary journey by the deity, who explains to Ezekiel the implications of what he sees (e.g., Ezek 8:17-18). By the time of Zechariah, the prophet is not so easily able to comprehend what he sees: "And I looked up and saw four horns. I asked the angel who talked with me, 'What are these?'" (Zech 1:18-19). By this time, there has been a major change in the vision reports. Earlier the prophet had a vision and understood what it meant; now the prophet sees and needs some other agent to explain the vision's significance. (This tradition of the vision as separate from the interpretation continues in the apocalyptic visions of the book of Daniel: "As for me, Daniel, my spirit was troubled within me, and the visions of my head terrified me. I approached one of the attendants to ask him the truth concerning all this" [Dan 7:15-16].)

4. Legend. The legend is another major exemplar of the prose account; it offers a report about something holy, whether an object (e.g., the ark of God; see 2 Sam 6:6-7) or a person. As we saw earlier, one of the role labels for a prophet was "man of God." From the perspective of the history of religions, such an individual can be understood as a holy person, someone who possesses supernatural powers. As with the previous two types of literature, a legend need not be a story (though there is a strong tendency in this direction). For example, 2 Kgs 2:23-24— just two verses—makes up one such account. Elisha encounters some boys who taunt him, whereupon he curses them, and they are killed. This is an account, not a story. There is no tension to be resolved, but simply a report that when someone bothers a holy man, that person is likely to end up dead. However, most biblical prophetic legends are written as narratives. A good example is found in 2 Kgs 4:1-7 (cf. 1 Kgs 17:8-16). Here the widow of one of Elisha's band of prophetic disciples lives in dire straits due to her poverty. Her children are about to be taken in debt slavery. Elisha saves the day by having olive oil appear in superabundant quantities behind the closed doors of her dwelling. The creditors are kept miraculously at bay. Moreover, there is a subtle subplot; the widow could have had even more oil than she did since the oil "stopped flowing" when she ran out of vessels that she had collected. Her notions of what might be possible limited the amount that she would receive. The legend has become a story, one with a didactic aside.

5. Prophetic Historiography.[17] Both the books of Isaiah and Jeremiah include chapters that overlap material found in Kings. Isaiah 36–39 is essentially the same as 2 Kgs 18:13–19:37, and Jeremiah 52 is coextensive with 2 Kgs 24:18–25:30. Isaiah the prophet appears in Isaiah 36–39, whereas Jeremiah is not mentioned in Jeremiah 52. However, what Jeremiah said and did help to set the context for this later overview of Jerusalem's defeat. What appears in the historical books can appear in a prophetic book as well. This fact has a bearing on how we think about prophetic literature— namely, as literature that can attest to the interplay between prophetic activity and the events that prophets address.

Isaiah 36–39 provides an account of Sennacherib's attack on Jerusalem during the reign of Hezekiah. The first chapter focuses on an Assyrian official's (the Rabshakeh) challenge to all those in Jerusalem. After Hezekiah laments this situation at the Temple, Isaiah offers an oracle (Isa 37:6-7) in which God promised to save Israel from this military threat: "I myself will put a spirit in him [Sennacherib], so that he shall hear a rumor, and return to his own land" (Isa 37:7). Then after another plea from Hezekiah, Isaiah again offers an oracle (Isa 37:21-35). After this speech, the Neo-Assyrian threat is lifted. For this historian, to narrate the events of Sennacherib's campaign is also to recount the prophetic oracles that this challenge elicited.

These chapters attest to the role of the prophet in major national affairs, especially those involving the monarch and military challenges to the nation. Moreover, such prophetic historiography presupposes that the prophet has a critically important role in times of national crisis. Hezekiah prays to God, and God offers a response through the prophet, so that the king, and others, know what will be happening. Not all Israelite history writing presumed such a role for the prophets, but even apart from such so-called prophetic historiography, there is evidence that ancient Israelites understood the prophetic word to have a major place in the historical process (e.g., "as he had foretold through all his servants the prophets," 2 Kgs 17:23; cf. 24:2).

6. Biography. Biography in the ancient world was not the same enterprise as the volumes we might purchase today. Along with an interest in an individual's life—a feature common to all biographies—ancient biographies included attention to a primary thesis or theme that could be elucidated

Historical Setting of the Prophetic Books*

Date**	Events	Prophet	Kings of Israel	Kings of Judah	Kings of Assyria/ Babylon/Persia	References
			Jehoahaz (816–800)		**Kings of Assyria** Adad-nirari III (810–783)	
805	Assyria defeats Damascus, opening the way for sixty years of Israelite and Judean expansion, a growing luxury class, and economic and religious excesses			Amaziah (?)		*ANET* 282
			Jeroboam II (785–745)			
		Jonah***		Uzziah (?)	Shalmaneser IV (782–773)	
					Ashur Dan (772–755)	
		Amos (760)			Ashur-nirari IV (754–745)	
				Jotham (?–742)		
		Hosea (750–724)				
745	Renewed Assyrian compaigns against Aram and Palestine		Zechariah Shallum (745)		Tiglath-pileser III (744–727)	2 Kgs 15:10
745–724	Political unrest in Israel: assassinations of Zechariah, Shallum, Menahem, Pekahiah, and Pekah		Menahem (745–736)			2 Kgs 15; *ANET* 282
				Jehoahaz I (742–727)		
735–733	Syro-Ephraimite War; Ahaz pays tribute to Assyria	Isaiah of Jerusalem (738–701)	Pekahiah (736–735) Pekah (735–732)			2 Kgs 16:5-8; Isa 7:1— 8:5-21
732	Damascus destroyed by Assyria, Aram becomes an Assyrian province; Israel made a vassal state	Micah (730–700)	Hoshea (732–723)	Hezekiah (727–698)	Shalmaneser V (726–722)	2 Kgs 16:2; *ANET* 282
722	Israel defeated by Assyria; Hoshea imprisoned				Sargon II (721–705)	2 Kgs 17:3-4
721	Samaria destroyed by Assyria, population deported					2 Kgs 17:5-6; 18:9-12; *ANET* 284-86
713–711	Assyria defeats coalition led by Ashdod					Isa 20:1-6; *ANET* 286-87
705	Hezekiah joins coalition against Assyria				Sennacherib (704–681)	*ANET* 287-88
701	Coalition defeated by Assyria; Jerusalem spare					2 Kgs 18:13— 19:37; 2 Chr 32:1-22; *ANET* 287
				Manasseh (697–642)		
689	Babylon destroyed by Assyria					
679–671	Assyrian campaigns against Egypt and Phoenicia Manasseh remains loyal to Assyria				Esarhaddon (680–669)	*ANET* 290-93
					Ashurbanipal (668–627)	
663	Thebes destroyed by Assyria					Nah 3:8-10; *ANET* 295

*NIB 7:844
**All dates are approximate.
***Based on 2 Kgs 14:25; the book of Jonah and the events that it reports are difficult, if not impossible, to date.

Historical Setting of the Prophetic Books, *continued**

Date**	Events	Prophet	Kings of Israel	Kings of Judah	Kings of Assyria/ Babylon/Persia	References
				Amon (642–640) Josiah (639–609)		
		Zephaniah (630–620)				
					Kings of Babylon	
626	Babylon gains freedom from Assyria; Josiah's "deuteronomic reform"	Jeremiah (627–583)			Nabopolassar (626–605)	*ANET* 304 2 Kgs 23:1-25; 2 Chr 34:1-33
614	City of Asshur destroyed by Medes					*ANET* 305
612	Nineveh destroyed by Medes and Babylonians	Nahum (612)				
609	Josiah killed; Judah under Egyptian control	Habakkuk (609–597)		Jehoahaz II (609)		2 Kgs 23:29-30, 33-35;
	Defeat of Assyrian and Egyptian forces of Haran			Jehoiakim (608–598)		2 Chr 35:20-24
605	Defeat of Egyptian forces at Carchemish and Hamath				Nebuchadnezzar (605–562)	Jer 46:1-12; *ANET* 307
604	Babylon gains control of Syria, Palestine, and Phonecia					
601/600	Egypt defeats Babylonian army; Jehoiakim withholds tribute					2 Kgs 24:1 *ANET* 564
598/597	Babylonians besiege Jerusalem; first deportation			Jehoiachin (598–597)		2 Kgs 24:8-17; 2 Chr 36:10; *ANET* 564
590/589	Zedekiah withholds tribute		Ezekiel (593–573)	Jedekiah (597–586)		2 Kgs 24:20*b*, 2 Chr 36:13
587	Jerusalem falls; Gadaliah appointed governor; second deportation	Obadiah (?)		Gedeliah (586–581?)		2 Kgs 25:1-24; 2 Chr 36:17-21 Jer 52:1-30; *ANET* 564
582/581	Gadaliah assasinated; third deportation					2 Kgs 25:25-26; Jer 40:7–42:18; 52:30
561	Jehoiachin released from prison; remains in Babylon				Evil-merodach (562–560)	2 Kgs 25:27-30; Jer 52:31-34
					Kings of Persia	
550	Cyrus the Persian begins campaigns against Lydia and media	Second Isaiah (550–538)			Cyrus (559–530)	*ANET* 305-6
538	The city of Babylon surrenders to Persia Edict of Cyrus; first return of exiles led by Sheshbazzar; Rebuilding of Temple begun, but soon halted					*ANET* 315-16 2 Chr 36:22-23; Ezra 1:1–2:70 Ezra 3:8–4:5
526/525	Persia defeats Egypt					
522	Accession of Darius; Temple rebuilding resumed	Haggai (520); Zechariah (520–518)			Darius (522–486)	Ezra 5:1–6:12
516/515	Temple completed and rededicated					Ezra 6:13-18
		Malachi (?) Second Zechariah (c. 450)				
458	Ezra travels to Jerusalem (?)					Ezra 7:1–8:36
445	Nehemiah travels to Jerusalem					Neh 2:1-11
		Joel (?)				

*NIB 7:844
**All dates are approximate.

by attention to that life. Not all accounts about a prophet are typical of ancient biographies. Some, however, are; Jeremiah 37–44 is one major example. These chapters cover both the last decade of Judah's existence and the early years of life after the defeat in 587. However, unlike prophetic historiography, to which they might seem similar, they refer to this history by focusing on the vagaries of Jeremiah's existence. The "primary" story of Israel in the early sixth century BCE involves life in the Babylonian exile. Thus 2 Kings 24 narrates two deportations, the first (597 BCE) during which King Jehoiachin, along with other leaders, was taken to Babylon, and the second (587 BCE) when King Zedekiah and another group were taken into exile. Only brief mention is made of an exile in another direction, one to Egypt (2 Kgs 25:26). In contrast, the way in which Judahites ended up in Egypt receives considerable attention in Jeremiah. Chapters 41–44 provide this account, one that runs counter to Jeremiah's own words; he prophesied on behalf of continued residence in the land. However, against his will, he was taken into Egypt, where he continued to work as a prophet, presumably until he died.

The author of these chapters seems as much interested in Jeremiah and his fate as he does the larger historical issues. Such focus on the person, and not on the message, is a hallmark of ancient biography. Moreover, there is, as one should expect, a thesis or principle being addressed by the author—namely, that Jeremiah's words received a positive response neither before nor after the devastating defeat of Jerusalem. One might have expected that the Judahites would pay attention to him after his earlier words had been borne out, but such was not the case. Even now, though God "persistently" continued to send prophets (Jer 44:4), the people did not respond. Such is the theme of this prophetic biography.

7. Divinatory Chronicle. The Hebrew Bible contains several texts that indicate the prophet could function like a diviner, an individual who could provide information or help from the world beyond that of normal human knowledge. Samuel functions this way in 1 Samuel 9. Ezekiel does as well. Ezekiel 20 presents a scene in which the prophet, living in exile, received representatives from "the elders of Israel." They had come to "inquire from Yahweh." Yahweh then speaks

through the prophet, thereby responding to the elders. Perhaps the most straightforward case of a prophet's receiving a request for a divine oracle and then providing the expected response occurs in Zechariah 7–8. The citizenry of Bethel empowered legates to ask: "Should I mourn and fast in the fifth month . . . ?" (Zech 7:3). The prophet then responds: "The fast of the fourth month, and the fast of the fifth, and the fast of the seventh, and the fast of the tenth, shall be to the house of Judah seasons of joy and gladness" (Zech 8:19 RSV).

In these and other cases (e.g., Jeremiah and Zedekiah, Jer 38:14), prophetic literature attests to interaction between the intermediary and those who want information from the deity. The deity's response, which is communicated by the prophet, is only one, though important, part of the literary form. The prophet as diviner is clearly attested in one type of prophetic literature, the divinatory chronicle.

In sum, accounts as a basic type of prophetic literature occur in a number of subgenres. Moreover, the impulses for the creation of these accounts are diverse. They do, however, tend to focus on action, people's behavior, rather than speech, which comprises the other basic type of prophetic literature.

Poetic Speech. Important though prose accounts are, structured speech is the predominant form of prophetic literature. Most, though not all, prophetic speech is set as poetry. Hence, readers need to attend to the rules of Hebrew poetry in general as well as to the special features of prophetic speech.[18] In addition to attending to matters of poetic technique, readers of prophetic structured speech should consider the formal characteristics of those speeches. Scholars have invested considerable energy in understanding the form (hence, the term "form criticism") of speeches in prophetic books. They have identified speeches that are traced to the deity—that is, when the deity speaks in the first person (e.g., "I, the Lord, am its keeper; every moment I water it" [Isa 27:3]). Although the prophet might mouth these words, he or she is clearly the rhetorical mouthpiece of the deity. Such speeches may be described as "divine oracles." And some form critics have distinguished these divine oracles from those speeches in which the prophet speaks about God in the third person, such as:

My joy is gone, grief is upon me,
  my heart is sick.
Hark, the cry of my poor people
  from far and wide in the land:
"Is the Lord not in Zion?
  Is her King not in her?" (Jer 8:18-19)

Here a different rhetoric is at work. The prophet speaks on behalf of the deity's perspective, but not with the voice of the deity. Hence these utterances are known as "prophetic speeches."

Those interested in the form of prophetic speeches or divine oracles have been particularly impressed and puzzled by texts like Amos 1–2 and Isa 10:5-19. Amos 1–2 is made up of a series of oracles that have a remarkably regular structure: "Thus says the Lord," followed by an indictment that is then linked to a judgment. Many of the oracles conclude with a brief formula, "says the Lord." Moreover, this basic form, known as the judgment oracle—an indictment followed by a sentence of judgment—appears in many other prophetic books (e.g., Jer 5:10-17; Mic 1:5-7). How should one explain such remarkable regularity? It seems very unlikely that Amos created such discourse, which was then copied by other prophets.

Form critics have observed the sorts of regularities we have just identified. They have then sought places in the ancient society in which such regular forms might have been created and preserved. In the aforementioned case, some form critics have argued that the language of indictment and sentence is most likely to have been at home in the law court. That social institution would have preserved such a form with great regularity, just as wills and contracts are preserved by our legal institutions today. Form critics suggest that prophets like Amos "borrowed" forms of speaking from various sectors of ancient Israelite society in order to make their points. Elsewhere in Amos, we find him using hymnic language, poetry created and preserved at the Temple or other ritual contexts (so Amos 4:13; 5:8-9; 9:5-6). So some poems that we find in the prophetic books have been forged using structures known both to prophets and to their audiences.

The readers of such poetry will need to be alert to the various forms they might encounter. The following incomplete list is designed to be suggestive rather than exhaustive: judgment oracle (Jer 6:16-21), woe oracle (Isa 10:1-4), lawsuit (Mic 1:2-7); lament (Jer 8:18-9:3), hymn (Hab 3:2-15), song (Isa 5:1-2), allegory (Ezek 17:2-10), and acrostic (Nah 1:2-8). As already mentioned, the judgment oracle is a speech made up of two basic parts: an indictment and a sentence. The woe oracle includes these same elements, though it commences with the Hebrew word הוי (hôy), which has been translated in various ways (e.g., "Ah," Isa 5:8; "Alas," Amos 5:18; "Ha," Isa 29:15; "Oh," Isa 30:1; "Woe," Isa 45:9). The woe formula (woe plus some name) was probably used originally to refer to someone who had just died. Both the judgment and the woe oracles pass a sentence on some individual or group, with the woe oracle offering the connotation that the party is as good as dead. In a similar legal vein, the lawsuit attests to the legal process that would have resulted in the passing of such a sentence. Parties are summoned, "Hear, you peoples" (Mic 1:2); interrogations are made, "What is the transgression of Jacob?" (Mic 1:5); and judgments are offered, "Therefore, I will make Samaria a heap in the open country" (Mic 1:6). As the notion of passing sentence or reference to a legal process suggests, these three forms of speech derive from Israel's law courts. The prophets used such legal forms of speech more than any other type. In contrast, the lament and the hymn derive from the world of ritual. The lament would have been used in funerary rites, whereas the hymn was sung at the Temple. Jeremiah used laments not only to express his concern for the people (Jer 8:18–9:3) but also to reflect about his own situation (Jer 15:10, 18). In addition, a number of prophets used the language of hymns (hymns typically begin with a plural imperative verb, like "Sing" or "Praise"), which is then followed by a statement expounding the character of the deity (e.g., Amos 9:5-6). This hymnic language attests to the character of the deity, who, despite judging the people, remains worthy of veneration and worship. Finally, the prophets used forms that one associates with the scribes or intellectuals: elaborate allegories (Ezek 17:2-10) and acrostics (Nah 2:1-8). Such formal variety attests to the broad cultural knowledge the prophets possessed along with their rhetorical abilities, which eled them to use such diverse forms of verbal expression.

Great value may be achieved by undertaking such a process of form-critical classification. It is terribly important to know what sort of literature one is reading. A lament, which derives from the language of ancient funerals, bears certain connotations. To utter a lament over someone who is still alive would have jarred ancient readers (so Amos 5:1-2).

THE GROWTH OF PROPHETIC LITERATURE

The dominant model for understanding the composition of prophetic books is one in which various discrete units of discourse—account or speech—were preserved, collected, and edited. Various speeches or accounts could be combined to create collections. We have already referred to one such collection outside the Bible—namely, in a Neo-Assyrian text. The legends collected about Elisha (e.g., 2 Kings 4–6) offer a good example of a prose collection, as does the assemblage of Zechariah's vision reports (Zechariah 1–6). The book of Jeremiah presents several compelling examples of collections that include both prose and poetry. Jeremiah 21:11–23:8 comprises an assemblage of sayings about Judahite kingship; the collection begins with the phrase "concerning the royal house of Judah." Jeremiah 23:9-40 offers a comparable collection of sayings, but now about prophets; this collection bears the title "concerning the prophets" (Jer 23:9). These labeled collections provide graphic evidence for the ways in which prophetic literature came to be formed. Either the prophet or an editor placed sayings addressing a similar topic together.

A quite different mode of collecting lies behind Hosea 12–14. Although the sayings are all composed in poetry, they are not similar in their content. Rather, their very dissimilarity—some very negative, others hopeful—permit the creation of a collection that moves the reader from sentiments of judgment to that of restoration. This and other sections of prophetic books represent the activity of an editor who confronted sayings of very different sorts. The result was an ordering that moved from punishment to promise. One can imagine oracles of admonition such as those in Hos 14:1-3 originally spoken prior to oracles of judgment. Now, however, within the prophetic book, they are meant to be read after Yahweh has spoken: "Compassion is hidden from my eyes" (Hos 13:14).

Other dynamics resulted in the growth of prophetic literature. Readers of earlier oracles often found them difficult to understand or otherwise problematic. As a result, scribes proceeded to interpret them and to include the interpretation as part of the biblical text. A comparison of the MT and LXX texts of Jeremiah presents a number of such examples. The reader of the LXX form of Jer 28:16 ("Therefore thus says the Lord: I am going to send you off the face of the earth. Within this year you shall be dead") might have asked, Why does Jeremiah offer such a harsh and abrupt sentence? The MT answers that question by adding the following clause to the end of the verse: "because you have spoken rebellion against the Lord." Such commentary or explication contributed to the growth of prophetic literature.

But much more than collection and exegetical interpretation were at work. The original prophetic sayings and accounts possessed a generative power that resulted in the creation of new literature, which is particularly evident in the books of Isaiah and Zechariah. This new literature, sometimes called "deutero-prophetic," represents an attempt by Israelites to understand their own times by reformulating earlier prophetic words and accounts. In some cases, the new literature arose in the form of rather short comments. Another prophet might update that which had been said earlier: "On that day the Lord will extend his hand yet *a second time* to recover the remnant that is left of his people" (Isa 11:11); "This was the word that the Lord spoke concerning Moab *in the past. But now* the Lord says . . ." (Isa 16:13-14). These texts represent brief notes from the hands of those who preserved and venerated the words of the earlier prophets as they contemporized those earlier texts. However, these later figures composed not only compact sayings but also major compositions in their own right. This ability of prophetic literature to elicit newer prophetic literature is one of its hallmarks. The book of Isaiah contains two major exemplars of this process. The chapters that have often been known as Second (chaps. 40–55) and Third (chaps. 56–66) Isaiah have been composed based on the sayings and accounts attributed to Isaiah ben Amoz and integrated into a composition that presents those earlier sayings and accounts as a response to Israelites living in the Persian period, long after Isaiah ben Amoz had died. In this process, major topics like the role of Jerusalem/ Zion and Babylon are explored over a long period of time.

The orientation of much prophetic rhetoric toward the future helps to explain this kind of literary creativity. Deuteronomy 18 informed Israelites that they could rely on a prophet's ora- cles if they proved true. To be sure, not all sayings were subject to clear verification. Nonetheless, one can imagine that when Jeremiah spoke of a seventy-year captivity (Jer 25:11), some would have started counting to see if he was correct. Both later prophetic (Zech 1:12) and non-prophetic (2 Chr 36:21) biblical writers reflected upon the nature and accuracy of that prediction.

There is a final type of literary development in prophetic literature, one exemplified by Hos 14:9 and Mal 4:4. The former text emphasizes the connection between Hosea's words and those who are wise, whereas the latter concludes the Minor Prophets, perhaps even the entire prophetic canon, by calling for obedience to torah. In both cases, these components of prophetic books link that literature to another portion of the canon: wisdom literature (e.g., Proverbs) and the pentateuchal torah respectively.

All of these elements—collection, comment, updating, and linkage—belong to the process by means of which the prophetic canon grew. Of these, the copious updating or contemporizing of prophetic words and traditions for a new generation seems to be a distinguishing feature of prophetic literature.

Ultimately, this process by means of which prophetic literature grew eventuated in the creation of prophetic collections and books. For much of the twentieth century, those who have studied prophetic literature have tried to discern the elemental building blocks of prophetic literature. For example, those who have written about Amos have taken pains to identify the constituent oracles in chapter 1. More recently, they have understood these oracles as part of a collection of oracles against nations, which makes up chapters 1–2. Now, most recently, they have studied the ways in which an entire prophetic book works. Such analysis has even moved to considering categories larger than an individual prophetic book. For example, some scholars have begun to read the so-called Minor Prophets, Hosea–Malachi, as one book, The Book of the Twelve.

To this end, some scholars have identified a "normative" form for a prophetic book: oracles against Judah, oracles against the nations, hope for Judah. Whereas this pattern appears in Isaiah,

LXX Jeremiah, and Ezekiel, it is absent from most other prophetic books. As a result, it is difficult, indeed, to talk about the typical format of a prophetic book. However, most prophetic books do possess one typical element, the superscription. This element often links the activity of a prophet to that of a period defined by the reign of a king (Isaiah, Jeremiah, Ezekiel, Hosea, Amos, Zephaniah, Haggai, Zechariah). In other cases, the superscription simply characterizes the book as "word" (Joel), "oracle" (Nahum, Habakkuk, Malachi), or "vision" (Obadiah). Although some superscriptions do refer to their books as "words" (e.g., Amos), the use of a singular noun predominates. This use of a singular noun to refer to books filled with diverse sayings and accounts may indicate that the editors who composed these superscriptions thought of them as literary entities, not simply as collections. These entities have, therefore, become the object of study, as scholars ask: How does Amos work as a book? How does Hosea work as a book? Are they similar to or different from each other?

The book of Habakkuk offers an interesting example for this kind of analysis. The reader sensitive to the diversity of rhetoric in prophetic literature will read Habakkuk and experience the sharp moves from dialogue (1:2–2:5) through woe oracles (2:6-20) to theophanic hymn (3:1-15) and prophetic response (3:16-19*a*). It would be possible to think about Habakkuk as simply a collection. However, the reader may move beyond the aforementioned variety to perceive an integrated booklet. The prophet's voice continues even after explicit dialogue with the deity has ceased. Instead of direct encounter, the prophet moves into the Temple (2:20), utters a prayer (3:2), sings a hymn (3:3-15), and then reflects or meditates upon what he has just sung (3:16-19*a*). The book of Habakkuk revolves around the prophetic voice, not a voice challenging the people but a voice speaking to or about the deity in various modes:

O Lord, how long shall I cry for help, and you will not listen? (1:2)

O Lord, I have heard of your renown, and I stand in awe, O Lord, of your work. (3:2)

God, the Lord, is my strength; he makes my feet like the feet of a deer. (3:19)

The book begins with complaint and concludes with the language of vow and thanksgiving. Hence, one may speak of the movement within and the coherence of this book. Such is also the case with other exemplars of prophetic literature.

RELIGIOUS AND ETHICAL ISSUES

Covenant and Imperium. If prophets are best understood as intermediaries, those who act and speak on behalf of Israel's deity, then they should, in principle, reflect the religious affirmations and theological norms of ancient Israel. And such is the case. But the emphasis here must be on diversity—norms, not norm. As a result, it is difficult, indeed, to talk about a single prophetic theology or a sole prophetic ethical perspective. One of the great strengths of von Rad's treatment of prophetic literature was his ability to discern the remarkable variety of theological traditions within the various prophetic books.[19] For example, traditions about Zion are constitutive of Isaiah, whereas they are absent from Hosea; the exodus is important in Hosea and unimportant in the literature attributed to Isaiah ben Amoz.

Despite such diversity, scholars have devoted considerable energy in attempting to discern a common core or element to prophetic literature. For example, Blenkinsopp has argued that prophecy in a military context was an essential early feature that continued to influence prophetic discourse.[20] Even more prominent have been assessments of the covenantal background of much prophetic literature.[21] For example, it is difficult to read Hos 4:2 and not hear echoes of the Ten Commandments, which are in some ways similar to the stipulations of a covenant or treaty. So, too, curses, as found in covenant texts (e.g., Deuteronomy 28), also appear in prophetic literature (e.g., Isa 34:11-17). In a similar vein, the lawsuits brought by God through the prophets reflect the covenant relationship between God and Israel (so Mic 6:1-8). Such observations have led many scholars to think about the prophets as spokespersons on behalf of Israel's covenant, calling Israel to obey that to which they had agreed at Sinai. Such a covenant background is difficult to deny, especially when some of the later prophets wrestle with a new way to understand Israel's relationship to its God and in so doing use the image of a new

covenant (Jer 31:31; cf. Ezek 36:26). The image of Moses, the quintessential covenant spokesman, as prophet (Deuteronomy 18, on which see below) adds further weight to this idea.

However, equally important is what I would term the imperial perspective of Israel's prophets. In prophetic literature, the image of God present in a theophany on Mt. Sinai is complemented by that of God enthroned in the divine council. This, after all, is the scene portrayed in the call narratives of both Isaiah and Ezekiel. The case of Isaiah is telling. The prophet envisions the deity in the Temple, which is the visible, earthly symbol for the heavenly divine council. In that context, Yahweh is surrounded by minor deities, to whom God speaks: "Whom shall I send, and who will go for us?" (Isa 6:8)—the "us" are the members of that council. Isaiah speaks up in that royal chamber, "Here am I; send me!" When he is given his "message"—"Go and say to this people. . . ." (Isa 6:9)—Isaiah then becomes nothing less than a herald from the divine council, empowered with its words and its power. Jeremiah 23:18 offers the same conciliar perspective.

Such a way of thinking about prophets helps to explain the remarkable sweep of their vision—a sweep considerably broader than that of the language of covenant between Israel and its God. Jeremiah provides a case in point. In his commissioning narrative, God designates Jeremiah as "a prophet to the nations" and says, "I appoint you over nations and over kingdoms" (Jer 1:5, 10). The prophet as one with an international role fits better with the notion of God as an imperial and cosmic sovereign than it does with the God who is covenant partner with Israel.

The international aspect of the prophet's work cannot be underestimated. Although Jeremiah is the only prophet officially designated as "a prophet to the nations," each of the "major" prophetic books includes a sizable collection of sayings and oracles devoted to nations other than Israel (Isa 13:1–23:18; Jer 46:1–51:58; Ezek 25:1–32:32). These chapters provide more than just jingoistic rhetoric. They exemplify a "plan" that God has for all people:

> This is the plan that is planned
>   concerning the whole earth;
> and this is the hand that is stretched out
>   over all the nations. (Isa 14:26)

Even among the Minor Prophets, this testimony to God's international imperium remains in place. The book of Amos begins with a short set of oracles concerning Israel's neighboring states. Joel is concerned with a northern army (2:20) and includes rhetoric proclaimed "among the nations" (3:9). Obadiah is concerned almost exclusively with Edom and its relation to Judah. Jonah's eyes are set toward Nineveh. Micah sees both woe and weal from an international perspective: "Peoples shall stream to it [Zion], and many nations shall come" (Mic 4:1-2). Nahum is titled "an oracle concerning [against] Nineveh" (Nah 1:1). Habakkuk's vision is palpably international: "Look at the nations, and see! . . . For I am rousing the Chaldeans" (Hab 1:5-6). Zephaniah, like Amos, includes a short section devoted to foreign nations (Zeph 2:4-15). Haggai, perhaps the most "domestic" prophetic book, understands Judah's weal and wealth to derive from God, acting on a cosmic scale: "I am about to shake the heavens and the earth, and to overthrow the throne of kingdoms" (Hag 2:21-22). Zechariah, too, is written from a grand scale. The very first vision reports that the divine patrol has moved throughout "the whole earth" (Zech 1:11). Finally, Malachi's theological perspective is international: "My name is great among the nations" (Mal 1:11).

The prophets lived in the world of politics, both international and domestic. They did not think that Israel, and more so Judah, could have an international policy (e.g., treaties, alliances) that did not take into account the divine king's imperial plans. In sum, Israel's prophets serve as heralds for a cosmic God. As such, they offer an international perspective for what happens to Israel even as they affirm the importance of God's covenant with Israel.

Ethical Norms. Ethical norms inform much of the critique offered by Israel's prophets. At the risk of oversimplification, one might suggest that there are two different levels of norms: those common to all humanity and those that Israel understands as specific to it. These two levels complement the aforementioned imperial and covenant perspectives. The former infuse those sayings and oracles devoted to foreign nations. One may read the judgment oracles that occur in Amos 1–2 and discover that those nations are indicted for behavior that all humans would ordinarily find heinous:

genocidal acts (1:6, 9), violence against noncombatants (1:13), acts of ritual degradation (2:1). Oracles against the nations also include indictments for prideful behavior that offended Israel's God. Isaiah 14 includes a dirge directed at an unnamed Neo-Assyrian emperor who, in the eyes of the poet, had attempted to "ascend to heaven." Finally, there is a strain of language according to which God had designated certain imperial powers—the Neo-Assyrians and the Neo-Babylonians—to act on God's behalf to punish Israel. However, in both cases, Israel experienced such devastation that some prophets maintained these two countries had overstepped the roles assigned to them by Yahweh (Assyria: Isa 10:12-15; Babylon: Jer 51:11-49). Hence, they are to be destroyed. But the norm is one common to all people: excessive violence in time of warfare.

When the prophets move to discourse about Israel, things change. There are more specific ethical categories at work. They are not unique to Israel, since they also appear on the stele that preserves Hammurabi's law code, but they pervade much of what the prophets say.[22] The categories are righteousness and justice. Quite simply, righteousness involves the principle of beneficence, doing the good thing (e.g., in Israelite language to aid the widow or orphan). Justice addresses the question of how. In concrete terms, should one offer ten pounds of wheat to one widow or one pound of wheat to ten widows? Considerations of justice are apt when one attempts to act out beneficence.

Some recent interpreters have noted that less overt and more troubling values underpin much rhetoric in the Hebrew Bible, particularly involving the place of violence. Although some have viewed language of slaughter as simply a concomitant of ancient warfare, on occasion there seems to be an interest in graphic descriptions of terror for its own sake (Isa 34:5-7; Jer 46:10). Also, violence against women—often bordering on the pornographic—cannot be gainsaid (e.g., Ezekiel 23).

As the reference to Hammurabi's law code suggests, the king was theoretically responsible for administering justice in the ancient Near East. Such was the case in Israel as well. To be sure, prophets did address kings, but they also challenged the entire population. One could say that they democratized the responsibility for justice and righteousness. To act in such a fashion was, ultimately, the responsibility of all, not simply the job of those elders, judges, who were most prominent in the legal system.

Israelite prophets during the Neo-Assyrian period seem concerned about a particular form of social and economic development in the eighth century BCE, a style of life that stood in tension with the realization of basic norms. It was increasingly difficult to provide for economic justice as larger estates were being created. People's land was being taken away, high interest rates made it difficult to retain financial independence, and debt slavery was rampant. When addressing these issues, the prophets were indicting societal structures as well as the behavior of individuals.

Along with these categories known both to moral philosophers and religious ethicists, there is another norm. Micah 6:8 speaks of walking humbly with one's God. Just as there can be prideful behavior on the international scene, so also too much arrogance can occur on the domestic front. As a result, some prophets argue on behalf of a proper relationship with Yahweh. What such a relationship involves is explored in various ways, but one important motif involves the absence of loyalty to any other deity. Hosea and Jeremiah, especially, attack the attraction of Baal, whereas Ezekiel 8 makes clear that the veneration of many other gods and goddesses was at stake. Only Obadiah, Jonah, and Haggai do not include overt polemics against the veneration of deities other than Yahweh. Of course, veneration of Yahweh alone is a characteristic feature of God's covenant with Israel (Exod 20:3), so the section "Covenant and Imperium."

Later prophets wrestled with the realities of human behavior. References to a new covenant (Jer 31:31) or a new heart (Ezek 36:26) could be read as utopian solutions to the intractable tendency of humans to do the errant thing. The ethical norms had not changed, but one recognizes a realization in Jeremiah, Ezekiel, and Zechariah that to enact them is terribly difficult, requiring a moral and religious capacity not hitherto realized.

Hope. Despite the propensity of prophetic literature to identify the many ways in which humans have fallen short of both universal and Israelite ethical norms—along with the ensuing results—that literature also often strikes a hopeful note. However, the vocabulary and images of hope in prophetic books have troubled many scholars.

How, they ask, could someone like Amos, who speaks about an end for Israel, also talk about a future of plenty (Amos 9:11-15)? The same question could be posed about Micah (Mic 2:12-13).

Scholars have offered a number of answers to explain this hopeful strain. Most prominent has been the judgment that the language of weal arises only after the disasters actually occurred. Hence, books like Micah, which speak of both disaster and hope for Judah, need to be read as composite compositions. According to these scholars, the negative material predates the assaults by the Neo-Assyrian and Neo-Babylonian empires, whereas the positive language (e.g., Mic 4:6-8) was added after 587 BCE.

Now, to be sure, as we have already seen, various additions did make their way into prophetic literature. However, the language of hope is truly pervasive in prophetic literature and, hence, requires an explanation beyond that of scribal addition. Westermann has maintained that such hopeful discourse in prophetic oracles is far more prominent than many readers have thought to be the case. Moreover, M. Sweeney has written, "In general, prophetic books tend to focus on the punishment and restoration of Israel/Judah, *with the emphasis on the latter.*"[23]

The sources for hope in prophetic literature are multiple. The vocabulary of hope may stem from rudimentary knowledge of what happens when there is military destruction; inevitably some people survive. The language of a remnant surely reflects this brute reality (e.g., Isa 11:11; cf. 7:3). Despite the thorough destruction of Jerusalem and deportation of many Judahites, the land was not left uninhabited. This reality would have been apparent even prior to the various defeats Israel and Judah experienced. An "end" did not mean the cessation of all human life.

Judah's theological traditions would also have contributed to the notion that God could continue to act on behalf of the people. The language of the so-called Davidic covenant included the expectation that this polity would continue "forever" (2 Sam 7:13). Hence, even well after the defeat of Judah, we hear about what "David" might mean for Israel, even when a prophet might mean something quite different from the restoration of the Davidic monarchy, as is almost certainly the case in Isa 55:3.

Finally, as masters of poetic expression, the prophets attest to the power of new words, of language itself. It is striking that Isaiah, Jeremiah, Ezekiel, and the Book of the Twelve all acknowledge that the future will see a renaming of Jerusalem. The city that for many prophets personified all that was wrong with Israel (e.g., Isa 1:21; Mic 3:12) will undergo the same sort of transformation as did Jacob, who became Israel. A new name will signify a new fate. Jeremiah thinks Jerusalem will be called "the throne of the Lord" (Jer 3:17). The book of Ezekiel concludes with a new name for Jerusalem: "The Lord Is There" (Ezek 48:35). Isaiah 62:4 refers to a new name that Yahweh will give, "Hephzibah," or "My Delight Is in Her." Finally, Zech 8:3, as part of the Book of the Twelve, offers the final exemplar: "City of Faithfulness" (TNK). In these diverse ways, prophetic literature attests to a future beyond the "end" that many of Israel's prophets foresaw.

Traditions About Prophets. Over time Israel was confronted with the task of thinking about prophets. To be sure, they knew that individuals known as prophets had been in their midst. But what was a prophet? Was there a typical or ideal prophet? Moreover, as canonical literature—the Torah, or Pentateuch, and the book of Psalms—began to emerge, Yahwists were confronted with the question of the relationship between prophetic literature and that of torah and that of the writings.[24] Moreover, as torah was increasingly understood to be canon—that is, a body of literature that was now essentially closed—how should one conceive of the relationship of prophetic literature to other parts of the canon? The phrase "the law and the prophets," which post-dates the formation of the Hebrew Bible, hints at a way of addressing the matter in a later time.

Those biblical writers who depicted Moses as a prophet offered one important way in which torah and prophets might be linked. If Moses were a paradigmatic prophet (Deut 18:15), and if Moses is responsible for torah, then prophecy becomes part of torah, though still subordinant to it. Prophetic literature may consequently be understood as an exposition or admonition based on torah, rather than an independent word of the deity. That is why Ezekiel appears to be such a dangerous text, since it purports to be a new torah, "the law of the temple" (Ezek 43:12), which might stand in competition with the pentateuchal torah.

However, Moses was only one of several possible paradigmatic prophets. Elijah is another; he had special credentials, since, according to biblical tradition, he had never died. As a result, writers both in the Persian and the Greco-Roman periods could look forward to the return of Elijah "before the great and terrible day of the Lord comes" (Mal 4:5; cf. Matt 17:10-13). Closed though the prophetic writings might finally become, there was still an expectation that a prophet or prophecy would appear in the future (see Joel 2:28-29; Acts 2).

Another important tradition about prophets as such involved the notion that they suffered a violent fate. Although this may have occasionally been the case in ancient Israel (see the brief chronicle about the death of Uriah son of Shemaiah in Jer 26:20-23), the Persian (2 Chr 24:20-22; Neh 9:26) and Greco-Roman periods saw the development of a notion that many prophets were treated in this way (e.g., Luke 13:34; Acts 7:52). Jeremiah's own rhetoric (e.g., Jer 11:19) may well have encouraged such an understanding. In contrast to this tradition, one may review the reports about prophets in ancient Israel and be surprised that they were not treated brutally more often.

Apart from traditions about prophets themselves, there were also canonical formulations that attempted to integrate prophetic literature with other portions of the canon. These texts are of several different types. On the one hand, considerable amounts of psalmic language are embedded within prophetic literature (e.g., the so-called Amos doxologies [4:13; 5:8-9; 9:5-6] and the catena of thanksgiving and hymn in Isaiah 12). On the other hand, there are texts at the end of prophetic books that call for the reader to reflect on that text from the perspective of another portion of the canon (Hos 14:9 points to wisdom texts, Mal 4:4 to torah). From this perspective, the law and the prophets were perceived by early readers as a far more coherent body than has been supposed.

SUMMARY

Prophetic literature derives from the activity of Israel's prophets. Just as there were different kinds of prophets, so also prophetic literature is itself diverse. Primary forms occur as account (symbolic action report, commissioning report, legend, prophetic historiography, biography) and structured speech (divine oracle and prophetic speech).

Although prophetic literature is known elsewhere in the ancient Near East—most notably Old Babylonian and Neo-Assyrian textual corpora—there are no extrabiblical exemplars comparable in size and sophistication to the biblical prophetic books, in considerable measure because of the generative power of Israelite prophetic literature. Prophetic literature is the product of creative speakers and writers who were influenced not only by contemporary events but also by a view of Yahweh as an international sovereign and by a profound understanding of God's relationship to Israel. These traditions contributed to a powerful theological and ethical amalgam. Phrases such as:

> Let justice roll down like waters,
>   and righteousness like an ever-flowing
>   stream. (Amos 5:24)

> They shall beat their swords into plowshares,
>   and their spears into pruning hooks;
> nation shall not lift up sword against nation,
>   neither shall they learn war any more.
>   (Mic 4:3)

> I am the first and I am the last;
>   besides me there is no god. (Isa 44:6)

embody some of the most enduring perspectives in prophetic literature—indeed, in all biblical literature.

FOR FURTHER READING

Blenkinsopp, J. *A History of Prophecy in Israel.* Louisville: Westminster/John Knox, 1996.

Clements, R. *Old Testament Prophecy: From Oracles to Canon.* Louisville: Westminster/John Knox, 1996.

Gitay, Y., ed. *Prophets and Prophecy.* Semeia Studies. Atlanta: Scholars Press, 1997.

Gordon, R., ed. *The Place Is Too Small for Us: The Israelite Prophets in Recent Scholarship.* SBTS 5. Winona Lake, Ind.: Eisenbrauns, 1995.

Lewis, I. *Ecstatic Religion: An Anthropological Study of Shamanism and Spirit Possession.* Baltimore: Penguin, 1975.

McLaughlin, John L. *The Marzēah in the Prophetic Literature: Reference and Allusions in Light of the Extra-Biblical Evidence.* VTSup 86. Leiden: Brill, 2001.

Nissinen, M. *References to Prophecy in Neo-Assyrian Sources.* SAAS 7. Helsinki: Helsinki University Press, 1998.

Nogalski, James and Marvin A. Sweeny. *Reading and Hearing the Book of the Twelve.* SBLSymS 15. Atlanta: Society of Biblical Literature, 2000.

Overholt, T. *Channels of Prophecy: The Social Dynamics of Prophetic Activity.* Minneapolis: Fortress, 1989.

Parpola, S. *Assyrian Prophecies.* SAA 9. Helsinki: Helsinki University Press, 1997.

Petersen, David L., ed. *Prophecy in Israel: Search for an Identity.* IRT. Philadelphia: Fortress, 1987.

———. *The Prophetic Literature: An Introduction.* Louisville, Ky: Westminster/John Knox, 2002.

Rad, G. von. *The Message of the Prophets.* New York: Harper and Bros., 1965.

Rofé, A. *The Prophetical Stories: The Narratives About the Prophets in the Hebrew Bible, Their Literary Types and History.* Jerusalem: Magnes, 1988.

———. *Introduction to Prophetic Literature.* Sheffield: Sheffield Academic, 1997.

Westermann, C. *Prophetic Oracles of Salvation.* Louisville: Westminster/John Knox, 1991.

Wilson, R. *Prophecy and Society in Ancient Israel.* Philadelphia: Fortress, 1980.

ENDNOTES

1. The term "Hebrew Bible" is a more ecumenical way of referring to that body of literature otherwise known as the Old Testament.

2. Unless otherwise noted, Scripture quotations are from the NRSV.

3. On the use of the term "intermediary," see R. Wilson, *Prophecy and Society in Ancient Israel* (Philadelphia: Fortress, 1980).

4. J. Maxwell Miller, "Introduction to the Religion of Ancient Israel," in *The New Interpreter's Bible,* 12 vols. (Nashville: Abingdon, 1994) 1:244-71.

5. See T. Overholt, *Channels of Prophecy: The Social Dynamics of Prophetic Activity* (Minneapolis: Fortress, 1989).

6. Other prophets would function in powerful ways with kings; e.g., one of Elisha's band anointed Jehu as king (2 Kgs 9:1-13); Ahijah the Shilonite proclaimed to Jeroboam that he would become king of Israel (1 Kgs 11:29-39).

7. Scholars differ in their judgments about the prominence of ecstatic behavior or trance possession among Israel's prophets. One might compare

S. Parker, "Possession Trance and Prophecy in Pre-exilic Israel," *VT* 28 (1978) 271-85, to R. Wilson, "Prophecy and Ecstasy: A Reexamination," *JBL* 98 (1979) 321-37.

8. See R. Wilson, *Prophecy and Society in Ancient Israel*, and D. Petersen, *The Roles of Israel's Prophets*, JSOTSup 17 (Sheffield: JSOT, 1981).

9. I. Lewis, *Ecstatic Religion: An Anthropological Study of Spirit Possession and Shamanism* (Baltimore: Penguin, 1975).

10. J. Hackett, *The Balaam Text from Deir 'Alla*, HSM 31 (Chico, Calif.: Scholars Press, 1980) 29.

11. J. Hackett, *The Balaam Text from Deir 'Alla*, 29.

12. W. Moran, "New Evidence from Mari on the History of Prophecy," *Biblica* 50 (1969) 29-30.

13. Text 1.4 in S. Parpola, *Assyrian Prophecies*, SAA 9 (Helsinki: Helsinki University Press, 1997) 6.

14. S. Parpola, Assyrian Prophecies, xix.

15. S. Parpola, Assyrian Prophecies, lxviii.

16. The classic study is N. Habel, "The Form and Significance of the Call Narrative," *ZAW* 77 (1965) 297-323.

17. See esp., A. Rofé, *The Prophetical Stories: The Narratives about the Prophets in the Hebrew Bible. Their Literary Types and History* (Jerusalem: Magnes, 1988) 75-105.

18. Adele Berlin's article "Introduction to Hebrew Poetry" provides an excellent guide for readers of ancient Hebrew poetry. See Adele Berlin, "Introduction to Hebrew Poetry," in *The New Interpreter's Bible*, 12 vols. (Nashville: Abingdon, 1996) 4:301-15 and in this volume.

19. G. von Rad, *The Message of the Prophets* (New York: Harper & Row, 1965).

20. J. Blenkinsopp, *A History of Prophecy in Israel* (Louisville: Westminster/John Knox, 1996).

21. D. McCarthy, *Old Testament Covenant: A Survey of Opinions* (Richmond: John Knox, 1972); R. Clements, *Prophecy and Covenant*, SBT 43 (Naperville: Allenson, 1965).

22. Shalom M. Paul, *Studies in the Book of the Covenant in the Light of Cuneiform and Biblical Law*, VTSup 18 (Leiden: Brill, 1970).

23. M. Sweeney, *Isaiah 1–39*, FOTL 16 (Grand Rapids: Eerdmans, 1996) 17.

24. Torah typically refers to the Pentateuch, whereas the Writings refers to the third part of the Hebrew canon (Torah, Prophets, Writings). Psalms is part of the Writings.

THE BOOK OF
ISAIAH 1–39

GENE M. TUCKER

The first rule of biblical interpretation should be this: Do not reverse the miracle at Cana. That is, do not turn wine into water. No interpretation, exegesis, commentary, or reflection can replace the text it addresses, particularly the rich and complex landscape that lies before all who read Isaiah 1–39. But herein lies a dilemma, for interpretation is both necessary and inevitable. Anyone who reads creates meaning. If a significant text—such as one in these chapters of Isaiah—is to have meaning and life, it will be only in the minds and hearts of its readers, each of whom will encounter something different based on various factors, including experience, culture, and their goals in reading. Moreover, the meaning of this text from antiquity seldom is self-evident; nor can it be taken for granted.

The aim of this overview is not to provide a substitute for reading the text, for there is none. The goal is to open up the text, to encourage an encounter with it, to make it more accessible. Disciplined interpretation wants to engage the text and not a preconceived notion about its meaning. Any exegesis that draws the reader into the text has served its main purpose.

Explanation and interpretation are not the same. Many features of ancient and foreign texts require explanation: Who was Hezekiah or Sennacherib? When was "the year that King Uzziah died"? Interpretation strives for more, for engagement with the text at the level of both its meaning and its potential implications. In short, interpretation strives for understanding.

ISAIAH 1–39 AS A BOOK WITHIN A BOOK

Until quite recently, no critical interpreter would have found it necessary to justify or even explain addressing Isaiah 1–39 apart from Isaiah 40–66. Biblical scholarship since the nineteenth century had demonstrated persuasively that the book was to be attributed to not one but at least three "Isaiahs," responsible in turn for chaps. 1–39, 40–55, and 56–66. Thus concern with the book as a whole in its canonical form had been overshadowed by the evidence for diverse authorship and date. In the last two decades of the twentieth century, however, the attention of scholarship has turned to the interpretation of the book as a whole and from a variety of perspectives. Virtually all such approaches continue to acknowledge the validity of the evidence for different dates and circumstances, but question the relative significance of the history of the development of the book.[1]

The move to consider the book as a whole is a long overdue change, and for at least two reasons. First, any text deserves to be interpreted in its context. That will include words in sentences, sentences in paragraphs or lines in stanzas, paragraphs in larger units, units within books, and books within the Scripture as a whole. In this respect, context within a book often has been neglected, but it is fundamental to understanding texts. Second, texts within books are the most accessible as well as the most important horizon for the interpreter. Both before and after one reaches conclusions concerning historical background or the history of the book's development (e.g., that a particular section is a secondary addition), the interpreter ought to face the text in its final form.

This shift in emphasis has generated a great deal of energy, bringing a variety of approaches to bear on the question of what the parts of the book of Isaiah have in common rather than what separates them. One commentator has focused on the entire sixty-six chapters as the work of an editor or author active c. 435 BCE.[2] Although most interpreters recognize that this date is too early for the latest material in the book, concern with the final editor's work is acknowledged as important. More widely accepted is the analysis of the book's unity in terms of a series of editorial productions, a redaction in the eighth century, another in the seventh century in the time of Josiah, an exilic, and a (final) post-exilic edition.[3] This position builds upon a great deal of redaction-critical analysis of particular parts of Isaiah.[4] One scholar has argued that an independent book of Deutero-Isaiah never existed; rather, the same poet who wrote chapters 40–55 edited what is now Isaiah 1–39 as the basis for his own work.[5]

Some have come to view the book as a whole from either a literary or a canonical perspective.[6] In many cases, they argue that concern with the history of the development of the literature or its historical context is beyond recovery, irrelevant, or distracts attention from the meaning of the text itself.[7]

Still others have recognized the coherence, if not necessarily the unity, of the book as a whole in terms of one or another theme.[8] One motif that doubtless contributes to the unity of Isaiah is that of kingship, including the importance of the Davidic dynasty, the expectation of an anointed ruler, and the servant of the Lord.[9] Others stress the theological centrality of Zion as a unifying theme.[10] The theme of the exodus, it has been argued, serves as one of the primary means of uniting the first and second halves of the book.[11] Another motif that persists throughout the book is "holy" (קדוש qādôš, 6:3), especially in "the Holy One of Israel" (1:4; 5:16, 19, 24; 10:20; 12:6; 17:7; 37:23; 41:14; 43:3, 14; 45:11; 48:17; 54:5; 60:9, 14) and in the identification of Zion as "the holy mountain" (11:9; 27:13; 56:7, 13; 65:11, 25; 66:20).

From the point of view of the history of the book's composition, these connections among the parts of the book disclose that the materials in Isaiah 40–66 were composed in the light of and in continuation of the tradition of Isaiah 1–39. From the point of view of reading and, therefore, interpreting the book, the links demonstrate the value of viewing any individual text from the perspective of the total book.

So is it legitimate any longer to present an introduction to Isaiah 1–39 as distinct from the canonical book? Is Isaiah 1–39 an artificial "book," especially since the division of Isaiah into three parts has been shaped by critical inquiry in the last century and more? Beyond the evidence for different authorship, there are sufficient reasons to address these chapters as a distinct part of the book. In the first place, it is

hardly possible to comprehend the whole of such a book all at once. One needs to pay attention to the particular parts, including individual units of discourse as well as large sections. In the interpretation of biblical literature, those parts need to be understood both on their own and in their context.

Second, in spite of major questions concerning the end of the book at various stages in the history of its composition (see below), there can be little doubt that the most distinct break falls between chaps. 39 and 40. Isaiah 1–39 is not an arbitrary unit. Although some parts of the first half are similar to chaps. 40–55 (chap. 35 in particular), the shift beginning with chap. 40 is dramatic in terms of style, historical horizon, and message. The superscription (Isa 1:1) appears to identify all that follows in the book with a particular prophet in a particular time, Isaiah the son of Amoz from (what we now know to be) the second half of the eighth century BCE. That verse has been the main basis, from the first century CE to the modern age, for attributing all sixty-six chapters to a single prophet. But closer scrutiny reveals problems and even contradictions within the literature. First, this is not the only superscription in the book, so we cannot take for granted that it was meant to cover the whole. One appears at Isa 2:1 and another at 14:1, the latter followed by a text concerning a much later period. Significantly, the last reference to the prophet Isaiah, son of Amoz, appears in chap. 39. Thus, for reasons that go beyond questions of authorship and date, Isaiah 1–39 presents itself as an appropriate unit of prophetic literature.

THE STRUCTURE AND COMPOSITION OF ISAIAH 1–39

Interpretation ought to begin with a description of the configuration or outline of the text in view, in this case Isaiah 1–39. Remarkably, there is widespread agreement among commentators on the major blocks of literature that comprise the book. That consensus points to the fact that these chapters have a great many clear markers that signal divisions, beginning with the superscriptions noted above. These markers include headings such as those ("Oracle concerning X") that both link the sections of chaps. 13–23 together in a series and separate them one from another, and the opening cries of "Woe" that function similarly in chaps.

28–32 (see also 5:8-24). Other indicators include genre, especially shifts from one to another. So Isaiah 36–39, consisting of a series of historical narratives, is readily recognized as a distinct section.

The meaning of those divisions, however, and particularly their relationship to one another, is far more disputed. One can hardly think of Isaiah 1–39 as a single composition, organized sequentially, either in terms of development of thought or chronologically. To be sure, there are elements of organization and development. First, some historical principles have guided the organization. Generally speaking, the prophetic speeches and narratives concerning the earlier events of the time of Isaiah come before the later ones. Thus the prophet's words and activities in relation to King Ahaz and the Syro-Ephramitic war (735–732 BCE) appear in chaps. 7–8, and those concerning King Hezekiah and the Assyrian crisis of 701 BCE come in chaps. 28–33 and in the historical narratives of chaps. 36–39. But this organization is far from rigid and is broken by material relating to events much later than the eighth century; and in any case, the historical references in many instances resist identification.

Second, some formal principles of organization reveal themselves. The initial chapter functions as a summary introduction to the whole and, some insist, to the entire book. In at least two instances (chap. 12 and chap. 33), liturgical materials conclude larger sections. A large section (chaps. 13–23) consists of a series of proclamations concerning foreign nations, each with the same heading, although there is no obvious principle for the organization of the individual proclamations within that section. The units of chaps. 24–27 have strong generic and thematic affinities, and those in chaps. 28–32 relate for the most part to the same historical events and theme.

Third, however, although certain themes recur throughout Isaiah 1–39, there is no obvious thematic development. There is not even a clear progression from words of judgment to those of salvation. In fact, the last word of the "book" is the announcement of the Babylonian exile (Isa 39:5-8). Organizational design and thematic development are more evident within some sections of the book, such as the interpretive summary in 1:2-31.

For the most part, the reader is faced with major blocks of material (such as 6:1–9:7; 13–23;

24–27; 28–33) that in turn consist of individual units of varying length. Since both the major building blocks and their individual components exhibit evidence of different historical horizons, it is more accurate to think of collections of traditions, subsequently more or less organized by scribes and editors over the years. Consequently, one must account for the shape of the book and its organization in terms of the history of its composition rather than, for instance, as the product of a self-conscious author or even a single editor.

How much one can know about the process of composition or why an editor placed material where it is rather than somewhere else is uncertain, and in that uncertainty lies the basis for disagreement about the meaning of the book's shape. Since all reconstructions of prior stages of development are hypothetical, some interpreters reject the effort out of hand. But the evidence, including the complexity of the book, reveals this much: Isaiah 1–39 developed over at least four centuries, and the actual process would have been more—not less—complicated than any theoretical model yet produced. This is by no means a call for ever more detailed division of the literature according to the stages of its development. It is to insist that the evidence does not allow recovery of all the steps through which the present text passed before reaching its final form. However, some steps along the way can be recognized.

The apportionment of Isaiah 1–66 among three distinct periods of activity remains fundamentally unshaken. But discernment of the relationship among those parts and the understanding of how Isaiah 1–39 itself developed have taken a turn. Until relatively recently, historians of the literature tended to view the major blocks of literature, such as chaps. 24–27 or 40–55, as arising independently before finally being incorporated into the book. These days the tendency is to attribute more thoughtfulness and craft to the tradents than did earlier generations of scholars. More and more scholars think of a process by which subsequent generations supplemented the tradition they had received. So even if it is acknowledged that Isaiah 24–27 had been composed independently of the present book, one asks why it was incorporated into the Isaiah tradition and why in its particular location. It has to be significant, and not arbitrary, that these eschatological prophecies concerning the whole world follow the proclamations against individual nations.[12] Moreover, Isaiah 1–39 could not have reached its final form before the addition of Isaiah 40–55, for some of its parts, including chaps. 24–27, originated later than Deutero-Isaiah. The development of the book was a complex process.

Nowhere is that complexity more obvious than with regard to the question of the end of the first book of Isaiah. So long as the source-critical divisions prevailed—into three sections according to authorship and date—the answer was clear: Chapters 1–39 were to be associated with Isaiah of Jerusalem. Now, however, and for various reasons, many commentators take the end of that book to be chap. 33.[13] This development means that chaps. 34–35 and chaps. 36–39 have become the keys to the organization of the book of Isaiah as a whole. The main impetus for taking chap. 33 to be the end has come from redaction criticism, the effort to write and understand the stages in the book's editorial development. Clearly both chaps. 34–35 and chaps. 36–39 are among the latest materials, and now widely regarded as transitional in some way between the First and Second Isaiahs. Isaiah 35 in particular is very similar to chaps. 40–55, but is sufficiently different to suggest that it was composed on the basis of those chapters. Moreover, there is persuasive evidence that an edition of the book in the seventh century in the time of Josiah closed the book with chap. 32 or 33.[14]

Against the position that chaps. 34–35 and 36–39 are to be associated more with what follows than with what precedes and, in favor of chap. 39 as the conclusion, is the subject matter of chaps. 36–39 in particular. Those narratives concern the prophet Isaiah, King Hezekiah, and the city of Jerusalem in the time of the Assyrian monarch Sennacherib. These chapters, as well as chaps. 34–35, almost certainly were added to the book even after chaps. 40–55, but they are about Isaiah.

ISAIAH THE PROPHET AND ISAIAH THE BOOK

None of this reflection on the questions concerning the shape of the book as a whole is to suggest that everything attributed to or concerning the prophet in the eighth century was written in his time. The issue of the meaning of the received form of the book or of its editorial stages can be distinguished from the question of the authorship, origin, or date of the individual parts. The material used by editors may be old or new.

It should not be surprising, therefore, that for more than a century many texts in Isaiah 1–39 have been recognized to be as late or even later than those in Isaiah 40–66. It is not some modern historical curiosity that provokes exploration of such matters, but the information in the texts themselves. What are we to believe: Isa 1:1, which attributes what follows to Isaiah in the eighth century BCE, or the allusions and explicit references to later events in the body of the material? For example, the superscription in Isa 13:1 claims directly that Isaiah son of Amoz was the author of what follows in chaps. 13–14, but there are clear and specific allusions in those chapters to events two centuries after the prophet. Moreover, some texts—such as the superscriptions and narratives about Isaiah—by their very perspective assume authors other than the prophet.

What, then, is the relationship between the book—specifically chaps. 1–39—and the prophet? Given the fact that some of the literature originated long after the eighth century BCE, is it possible to retrieve the words of Isaiah of Jerusalem? This was not a problem before the rise of critical inquiry, when tradition—including the citation of texts from all parts of the book in the NT—attributed everything to Isaiah. But once a Second and then a Third Isaiah had been recognized, it was inevitable that the same principles of investigation would be applied to Isaiah 1–39. These principles were the same that led to the documentary hypothesis of the Pentateuch. Is there evidence (allusions, perspective) of different historical periods? Are there significant or measurable differences in style (poetry, vocabulary, syntax, etc.)? Are there different theological perspectives? This last question led to some clear excesses, particularly with respect to the prophets. It was not uncommon through much of the twentieth century for scholars to conclude that the early prophets announced judgment and that any announcements of salvation must have been later additions to tone down or qualify the bad news. Although there are many instances where such conclusions are justified on other grounds (e.g., Amos 9:11-15), that approach is especially misleading with regard to Isaiah 1–39.

There were two particularly troubling aspects of this source-critical investigation of the prophets. First, although many readers of the prophetic books were disturbed by conclusions that such and such a passage did not originate with the prophet in question, even more misleading was the implication that one could, through such analysis, arrive at the authentic words of the prophet. Second, decisions concerning authorship or origin often entailed judgments about the relative value or validity of particular texts. Just as tradition valued the entire books as words of an inspired prophet, so also critics considered the "authentic" words of the prophet more valuable than those of the later editors. But it is only on the basis of a particular understanding of inspiration that the speeches of Isaiah of Jerusalem can be regarded as more theologically authoritative than later additions to the tradition. One is entitled to value judgments, but they should not be confused with judgments of fact concerning origin .

Early in the twentieth century, students of the Bible more and more acknowledged the importance of the oral tradition that had preceded the written texts. This concern was particularly significant with regard to the prophetic literature, which routinely reports the speeches of the prophets, often directly to individuals or to groups. Moreover, a great many of the genres present themselves as those of oral discourse.[15] The early prophets, such as Isaiah, were speakers whose words were written down and subsequently edited, expanded, and interpreted in new contexts. One effect of such form-critical analysis of prophetic literature was to extend earlier attempts to retrieve the original (oral) discourse of individual prophets. This view is appropriately chastened by the research and interpretation of recent decades, in which the recovery of the "original" speeches is recognized as difficult, if not impossible. Although one may remain convinced that the prophets were speakers, that does not at all mean that one can reconstruct individual speeches by the prophets whose names stand at the heading of the book, and even less the particular circumstances under which individual addresses were delivered.

Nevertheless, the questions posed by such analysis remain key interpretive steps in the study of prophetic texts. Introductory and concluding formulas enable the reader to recognize distinct units within the literature, structures common to particular genres show more clearly what is distinctive about a passage and how it relates to others, and the concern with social context (setting) helps one to understand how texts functioned in antiquity. Moreover, such questions have proved to be productive when applied to entire books as well as to small units of discourse.

The literary pursuit of authorship and the search for the original oral discourse of Isaiah are considered both more difficult and less significant than was the case only a few decades ago. If earlier generations of critical scholarship privileged the oldest, often at the expense of the actual written text, the current tendency is to privilege the latest, or canonical, form of the literature, sometimes at the expense of individual units and their precanonical history. This leads to what should be another rule for biblical interpretation: Throw nothing away. All texts in these chapters and all layers of their development are potentially significant. The serious reader who wants to understand and be confronted by the biblical text will not realize that potential by deciding in advance which is the more significant. There is life both in and behind the texts. Nor should one neglect the subsequent life of these texts as they came to echo in later biblical books, including the New Testament. So to read such rich and highly textured literature requires bifocals and more; its depths should not be sacrificed to a focus on one or another of its strata. Finally, if one level or one text is to be considered more valuable or more authoritative than another, that should not be determined on the basis of relative antiquity but on carefully considered theological grounds.

So is it possible to sort out the words of the prophet from the words of the book? The best one can do is to establish relative proximity to Isaiah's time and place, and that only when there is sufficient evidence. Such determination, when possible, is important, for it opens the door to deeper understanding. In any case, one needs to be occupied mainly with the text more than with its background, or even the text regardless of its background or origin. The book rather than the prophet Isaiah is what lies before us. Nevertheless, preoccupation with the unity of the entire book should not be allowed to obscure its individual parts or its pre-history.

HISTORICAL CONTEXT

As attention has shifted to the final form of the book, some have argued that the historical background is less important than the analysis of the literature as it stands. Although the main focus ought to be the text, consideration of its historical context is both all but unavoidable and essential to understanding. History is unavoidable because those who turn to this book from antiquity will take with them some image of that antiquity, and reading it will evoke further images. The issue for interpretation is whether that image of the past is a critical reconstruction—that is, whether or not the historical imagination is disciplined.

Attention to history is essential, for a great deal would be lost were it to be abandoned. Prophetic literature, and Isaiah 1–39 in particular, is filled with historical allusions, including references to events, kings, and circumstances. In many cases, the text would be mute if the reader did not comprehend the references. Who was Ahaz or Hezekiah or Sennacherib? At the most basic level of comprehending words and sentences, one cannot engage the details of the book without understanding what can be known about those individuals and circumstances. For the sake of making sense of the texts, the more one can know about its circumstances or those it refers to, the better. Unfortunately, many, if not most, of those allusions to circumstances are far more obscure than commonly assumed. Just as scholarship is less confident about reconstructing the history of the development of the book than only a few decades ago, so, too, there is greater caution about what can be known of the history of Israel. Nevertheless, the very contents of Isaiah 1–39 call attention to a historical horizon.

The history relevant to understanding Isaiah 1–39 could encompass most of the story of Israel and Judah, certainly at least from the time of David to well into the Persian period. The book—and the book of 2 Kings as well—locates Isaiah in the second half of the eighth century BCE. But these chapters include passages that originated as late as the fifth or possibly even the fourth century BCE, and they incorporate traditions stretching back to the time of David, around 1000 BCE. Moreover, the rise and fall of ancient Near Eastern empires come into play.

To begin with the center of attention, the prophet Isaiah son of Amoz was active in Jerusalem throughout most of the second half of the eighth century BCE. Little is known of his life, but some conclusions can be drawn from the book, mainly the narratives of his actions. That he had access to kings—although they did not always respect his messages—suggests he was inside rather than outside the central institutions of Judah. Although neither the prophet nor those who passed down the traditions show any interest in his biography, accounts of his symbolic actions indicate that he had children (Isa 7:3; 8:1-4). He probably had a group around him ("disciples," Isa 8:16) who would have been the first to collect and treasure his words.

The best evidence for the beginning of Isaiah's life as a prophet appears in the first-person account of his vocation in the Temple in Jerusalem (chap. 6). "The year that King Uzziah died" (6:1) probably was 742, but could have been as late as 736 BCE. Most important, that king's death signaled the end of an era of relative independence for Judah. Tiglath-pileser III came to power in Assyria in 745 BCE and soon began to expand his empire to include the small states of Syria and Palestine. His successors would continue his military and political policies. During most of Isaiah's lifetime, Judah lived under the threat of Assyrian domination. Most of the prophetic words and deeds that can be associated with historical events are related to the actions of a series of Assyrian monarchs or to events set into motion by their actions. More than once in Isaiah 1–39, Assyria appears as a tool of Yahweh's plan ("rod of my anger," 10:5).

One crisis not directly involving the Assyrians but caused by their advance toward Syria-Palestine was the so-called Syro-Ephraimitic war of c. 735–732 BCE. The initial response of the prophet and a summary of the events that prompted his intervention appear in Isa 7:1-9 (see also 2 Kgs 16:1-20; 2 Chr 28:5ff.). When Tiglath-pileser III of Assyria began to move against the small states of Syria and Palestine, the leaders of those states formed a coalition to oppose him. Apparently because Ahaz of Judah refused to join them, kings Rezin of Damascus and Pekah of Samaria, the capital of the northern kingdom, moved against Jerusalem (about 734 BCE) to topple Ahaz and replace him with someone more favorable to their policies. Their effort failed, but not because the Judean king heeded the prophet. In fact, both the books of Isaiah and 2 Kings present Ahaz as fearful and faithless. Much of Isaiah 7–8 concerns Ahaz and the time of the Syro-Ephraimitic war. Within a decade (722/21 BCE), the Assyrian army under Sargon II had destroyed the city of Samaria and settled the population of Israel around the empire, thus ending the history of the northern kingdom.

The next era of prophetic activity that can be identified with some confidence concerns another effort to mobilize opposition to the advance of Assyria. This time (c. 715 BCE), the rebellion was encouraged, if not instigated, by Egypt. Ashdod and other Philistine city-states revolted against Assyrian rule. According to Isa 20:1-6, when Sargon II attacked Ashdod, Isaiah walked naked in the streets of Jerusalem for three years as a sign. His action is interpreted as a warning against relying on Egypt in the face of Assyrian threats. Trust in Egyptian power proved to be vain, since Sargon managed to put down the rebellion. Isaiah 18 and 14:28-32 may also relate to the events of this time.

The final period of Isaiah's prophetic work was during the Assyrian crisis of 705–701 BCE. When Sargon II died c. 705 and Sennacherib came to the throne, there was widespread revolt across the empire, beginning when the Babylonian Merodach-baladan asserted his independence. In Jerusalem, Hezekiah declared Judah free from Assyrian control. The deuteronomistic historians (2 Kgs 18:1-8) credit him with a religious reformation. It did not take long, however, for Sennacherib to deal with Babylon and move toward Judah. Once again, the possibility of a Judean alliance with Egypt arises, and Isaiah is reported to have counseled against it (Isaiah 28–31). The Assyrian army decimated the cities and towns of Judah and laid siege to Jerusalem in 701 BCE (Isaiah 36–37). Complex sources, both biblical and Assyrian, render historical reconstruction difficult. However, whether because Hezekiah paid tribute or the Lord intervened directly as promised by Isaiah, the Assyrians withdrew without taking the city.

The last one hears of Isaiah (chap. 39) comes not from eighth-century traditions but from a later writer. Within a story about Babylonian exiles to Hezekiah, Isaiah is said to have prophesied the Babylonian exile. Thus the story goes on well beyond the end of the eighth century BCE, and a great deal of it is reflected in Isaiah 1–39. After Hezekiah would come other kings, including Josiah, who would centralize worship in Jerusalem yet die on a battlefield at the hands of Pharaoh Necho. After Sennacherib the Assyrian would come Nebuchadnezzar the Babylonian, who would first capture and then destroy Jerusalem with its Temple on Mt. Zion (597 and 587 BCE), carrying off the last Davidic king and much of the populace to Babylon. Then the exile would end (539 BCE) with the rise of the Persian Empire and Cyrus. The city of Jerusalem and the Temple would be rebuilt and worship renewed there. Also the institution and perspective of prophecy as reflected in the earlier traditions would gradually be transformed into apocalypticism. Some of the latest literature in Isaiah 1–39 (chaps. 24–27) reflects some of the steps in that direction.

TRADITIONS AND THEOLOGICAL THEMES

From what has been said thus far, it should be clear that one could hardly separate the message of Isaiah from the message of Isaiah 1–39. However, in many instances one can distinguish the earliest materials from the later ones. The heart of the eighth-century material—prophetic addresses and reports—lies in Isa 6:1–9:6 and 28–31, plus most of 1–5. Subsequent growth and development for the most part engaged that foundational tradition. Finally, the reader will need to come to terms with the book as it has finally been handed down. Throughout, there is some genuine continuity as well as significant differences. Some of that continuity continues throughout the entire book, although the differences become more pronounced after chap. 40.

Isaiah did not simply originate a theological message out of thin air. Rather, the prophet and the book are rooted in a number of foundational traditions.[16] The day is long past when one could think of a prophet like Isaiah as a solitary and creative individual who introduced a new way of thinking, radical ideas, or new legal or moral expectations.

First, there is the prophetic tradition itself. Although among the earliest of the prophets whose words have come down in a book with their name, both Isaiah the prophet and Isaiah 1–39 are part of a community that originated much earlier and stretches over centuries. This is confirmed not only by the accounts of earlier prophets, such as Nathan in the time of David, but also by the way Isaiah and most of his successors in these chapters speak and write. Patterns of speech and narrative are shaped by practices in communities over time. Consequently Isaiah's report of his call and the accounts of his symbolic actions closely parallel others in the Old Testament. The form and substance of the prophetic addresses reflect the essence of the prophetic self-understanding: They speak to others the word of the Lord, and that word concerns the future.

Second, neither Isaiah nor the other prophetic and poetic voices heard in these chapters introduced new laws. Rather, any indictment of people, groups, or kings is on the basis of ancient understandings of Israel's responsibilities to Yahweh. To be sure, specific concerns emerge in the indictments, and it is not always possible to identify particular laws behind accusations. Moreover, there seems to be little or no awareness of the covenant on Mt. Sinai when the laws were revealed. Still, Isa 5:24 can stand as a summary that links the legal with the prophetic tradition: "You have rejected the law [תורה *tôrâ*] of the Lord Almighty and spurned the word of the Holy One of Israel" (NIV; NRSV, "instruction"; see also Isa 2:3).

Two closely related theological traditions undergird the distinctive theology of Isaiah 1–39. These concern the chosen king and the chosen city. Again, these views did not originate with Isaiah in the eighth century BCE but were part of an ancient faith. To provide for the government of the people of God, the Lord had chosen the dynasty of David, promising that one of his sons would always sit on the throne (see 2 Samuel 7; Psalms 2; 89). Thus the dynasty was more than a symbol of the Lord's grace; it was the concrete means by which their security was established. When present kings prove faithless, as does Ahaz in Isaiah 7–8, this tradition turns to messianic expectations, as in Isa 9:1-7 and 11:1-9.

The Lord also chose Jerusalem as the sacred place and its center, Mt. Zion, as the place where the Lord would encounter the people in the Temple. And so Isaiah experienced the terrifying presence of the Lord there (Isaiah 6). Throughout these chapters there seems to be a struggle over the question of whether the Lord will allow an enemy to take the city or not, but the dominant expectation is that Yahweh will protect Jerusalem

(Isa 1:8; 3:17; 4:5; 10:24; 24:23; 29:8; 33:5). This tradition as well is firmly rooted in the Yahwistic faith. In the Song of Moses (Exodus 15), the holy place is the goal of the exodus (Exod 15:17), and Zion is praised and celebrated in worship (Pss 48:1-3; 52:2; 74:2; 132:13). So in the new age of peace among all peoples, Zion will be lifted up, and all nations will come to it (Isa 2:1-4).

It is not easy to summarize the message of Isaiah 1–39, or that of the earliest tradition. At the most basic level, was the message of Isaiah and of the book good news or bad? How can one reconcile the song of the vineyard (Isa 5:1-7), which proclaims judgment on the people of God, with that vision of Jerusalem as the center of world peace in Isa 2:1-4 or the promise of justice under a righteous king in Isa 9:1-7? Sorting out the layers of tradition or the specific historical circumstances of particular units helps to resolve some of the tensions and contradictions: The word of God could be different in diverse situations, and one generation's interpretation could supplement or revise that of its predecessors. But those efforts cannot resolve all the tensions into a consistent summary of the teachings of the prophet or of the book, and in any case the reader needs to come to terms with Isaiah 1–39 as it stands, with all its complexity.

Consequently, any statement of the book's themes must be cautious not to suggest more coherence than the work allows, not to replace a rich and textured landscape with a simple map. Although one might argue that one or another theme defines the others, that does not mean the others have been left behind. It would distort the book to ignore the harsh words against foreign nations or to rush past the announcements of judgment to those of salvation. After all, regardless of their own convictions, the final editors have handed down all this complexity. Nevertheless, it is important to identify some of the more pervasive and distinctive aspects of the book's message, even when they seem—or actually may be—in tension with one another.

One typically prophetic motif is the indictment of the Lord's people, as well as other nations, for their sins. The range of accusations is wide. Sin may be characterized broadly as rebellion against the Lord (Isa 1:2-3), as failure to know or acknowledge the Lord (Isa 1:4), or as rejection of the law of the Lord and the word of the Holy One of Israel (Isa 5:24). The people are accused of trusting in the trappings of worship when they should be seeking justice and caring for the oppressed (Isa 1:10-17). They are accused of specific unjust economic, judicial, and social activities (Isa 5:8-24; 10:1-4). Leaders and the powerful come in for particular attention (Isa 3:1-15), particularly for failing in their responsibilities (Isa 28:1-8) or scoffing at the word of the Lord (Isa 28:11-15). The accusations do not stop at Judah's boundary. Foreign powers are indicated as well, including the king of Assyria, the rod of the Lord's anger, who has become arrogant (Isa 10:5-19).

Second, Isaiah, as well as his successors in these chapters, announces that the Lord is coming in judgment. Often, but not always, that divine intervention is presented as punishment for offenses. The vineyard will be destroyed because it yielded bloodshed instead of justice, a cry instead of righteousness (Isa 5:1-7). People, nation, and city will be thrown into chaos (Isa 3:1-5). King and people will be carried into exile (Isa 39:6-8). Frequently, judgment is characterized as the coming of the day of the Lord (Isa 2:12, 20; 4:1; 7:20; 13:6). The wrath of the Lord is not limited to Israel and Judah but can include foreign nations (Isaiah 13-23; 34), the hosts of heaven (Isa 24:2), and even the world itself (Isa 24:1-23).

Third, in some of the most memorable passages of the Bible, the prophet and the book proclaim good news. The Lord will act to save, to redeem, and to transform. Here is where those two themes of the Davidic dynasty and the Lord's choice of Zion come into play most prominently. A new king will establish peace and justice (Isa 9:1-8), and the reign of the son of David will inaugurate a transformation in the relationship among all creatures (Isa 11:1-9). Jerusalem will be protected from the Assyrians (Isa 31:4-5; 37:6-7; 37:33-34). Exiles will return to Jerusalem (Isa 11:10-16; 35:1-10). Just as foreigners came in for punishment, so also they will participate in the new age of peace (Isa 2:1-4).

Finally, in the prophets generally, one encounters relatively few admonitions or instructions about what to believe or how to behave. For the most part, what they expect must be read as the reverse of what they criticize. One admonition in these chapters, however, is both distinctive and foundational. It is the summons to trust in the Lord, the Holy One of Israel. Kings in particular and the people as a whole are told to neither fear nor trust nations and armies, but the one who has authority over all things (Isa 31:1). Isaiah tells Ahaz, "If you do not stand firm in faith, you shall not stand at all" (Isa 7:9). With Jerusalem in trouble, the message from the Holy One of Israel is: "In returning and rest you shall be saved; in quietness and trust shall be your strength" (Isa 30:15). This summons has something to do with the content of belief, particularly that the Lord has chosen the dynasty of David and the city of Jerusalem. But fundamentally it is not faith as affirmation of doctrine or ideas that is encouraged. Rather, it is faith as trust in God, as commitment to the Holy One of Israel.

FOR FURTHER READING

Commentaries:

Barton, John. *Isaiah 1–39*. OTG. Sheffield: Sheffield Academic, 1995.

Blenkinsopp, Joseph. *Isaiah 1–39*. AB 19. Garden City, N.Y.: Doubleday, 2000.

Brueggemann, Walter. *Isaiah 1–39*. Westminster Bible Companion. Louisville: Westminster John Knox, 1998.

Childs, Brevard S. *Isaiah*. OTL. Louisville: Westminster John Knox, 2001.

Clements, R. E. *Isaiah 1–39*. NCNB. Grand Rapids: Eerdmans, 1980.

Goldingay, John. *Isaiah*. NIBCOT 13. Peabody, Mass.: Hendrickson, 2001.

Kaiser, O. *Isaiah 1–12: A Commentary*. Translated by R. A. Wilson. Philadelphia: Westminster, 1972.

———. *Isaiah 13–39: A Commentary*. Translated by R. A. Wilson. Philadelphia: Westminster, 1974.

Oswalt, John N. *The Book of Isaiah, Chapters 1–39*. NICOT. Grand Rapids: Eerdmans, 1986.

Seitz, Christopher R. *Isaiah 1–39*. Interpretation. Louisville: John Knox, 1993.

Sweeney, Marvin A. *Isaiah 1–39, With an Introduction to Prophetic Literature*. FOTL XVI. Grand Rapids: Eerdmans, 1996.

Watts, John D. W. *Isaiah 1–33*. WBC 24. Waco, Tex.: Word, 1985.

Wildberger, H. *Isaiah 1–12*. Translated by Thomas H. Trapp. Minneapolis: Fortress, 1991.

———. *Isaiah 13–27*. Minneapolis: Fortress, 1997.

Wildberger, Hans, and Thomas H. Trapp. *Isaiah 28-39*. CC. Minneapolis, Minn.: Fortress, 2002.

Other Studies:

Childs, Brevard S. *Isaiah and the Assyrian Crisis.* SBT. London: SCM, 1967.

Clements, R. E. *Isaiah and the Deliverance of Jerusalem: A Study in the Interpretation of Prophecy in the Old Testament.* JSOTSup 13. Sheffield: JSOT, 1980.

———. "The Unity of the Book of Isaiah." *Int.* 36 (1982).

Conrad, E. W. *Reading Isaiah.* OBT 27. Minneapolis: Fortress, 1979.

Fohrer, G. "The Origin, Composition and Tradition of Isaiah i–xxxix." *The Annual of the Lees University Oriental Society* 3 (1962–63).

Jensen, Joseph. *The Use of tora by Isaiah.* CBQMS 3. Washington: Catholic Biblical Association, 1973.

Melugin, Roy F., and Marvin A. Sweeney, eds. *New Visions of Isaiah.* JSOTSup 214. Sheffield: JSOT, 1996.

Seitz, Christopher R., ed. *Reading and Preaching the Book of Isaiah.* Philadelphia: Fortress, 1988.

———. *Zion's Final Destiny: The Development of the Book of Isaiah.* Minneapolis: Fortress, 1991.

Sweeney, Marvin A. *Isaiah 1–4 and the Post-Exilic Understanding of the Isaianic Tradition.* BZAW 171. Berlin: Walter de Gruyter, 1988.

Tate, Marvin E. "The Book of Isaiah in Recent Study." In *Forming Prophetic Literature: Essays on Isaiah and the Twelve in Honor of John D. W. Watts,* ed. James W. Watts and Paul R. House. JSOTSup 235. Sheffield: Sheffield Academic, 1996.

Tucker, Gene M. "The Role of the Prophets and the Role of the Church." *Quarterly Review* 5 (1981). Reprinted in *Prophecy in Israel,* ed. David L. Petersen. Philadelphia: Fortress, 1987.

Watts, James W., and Paul R. House. *Forming Prophetic Literature: Essays on Isaiah and the Twelve in Honor of John D. W. Watts.* JSOTSup 235. Sheffield: Sheffield Academic, 1996.

Whedbee, J. W. *Isaiah and Wisdom.* Nashville: Abingdon, 1971.

Williamson, H. G. M. *The Book Called Isaiah: Deutero-Isaiah's Role in Composition and Redaction.* Oxford: Oxford University Press, 1994.

———. *Variations on a Theme: King, Messiah, and the Servant in the Book of Isaiah.* Carlisle: Paternoster, 1998.

ENDNOTES

1. The exceptions are traditional approaches that focus on the book as a whole, considering all of it to be the work of the 8th-cent. BCE prophet. See John N. Oswalt, *The Book of Isaiah, Chapters 1–39,* NICOT (Grand Rapids: Eerdmans, 1986).

2. John D. W. Watts, *Isaiah 1–33,* WBC (Waco, Tex.: Word, 1985).

3. R. E. Clements, "The Unity of the Book of Isaiah," *Int.* 36 (1982) 117-29.

4. One of the most important of these is Hermann Barth, *Die Jesaja-Worte in der Josiazeit* (Neukirchen: Neukirchener Verlag, 1977). For such work on Isaiah 1–39, see esp. Marvin A. Sweeney, *Isaiah 1–39, With an Introduction to Prophetic Literature,* FOTL XVI (Grand Rapids: Eerdmans, 1996).

5. H. G. M. Williamson, *The Book Called Isaiah: Deutero-Isaiah's Role in Composition and Redaction* (Oxford: Oxford University Press, 1994).

6. See Brevard S. Childs, *Introduction to the Old Testament as Scripture* (Philadelphia: Fortress, 1979); Brevard S. Childs, *Isaiah: A Commentary* (Louisville: Westminster John Knox, 2001). Childs's central concern is to read and interpret biblical books finally as the scriptures of communities of faith. See also Christopher R. Seitz, "Isaiah 1–66: Making Sense of the Whole," in *Reading and Preaching the Book of Isaiah,* ed. Christopher R. Seitz (Philadelphia: Fortress, 1988) 105-26.

7. For an approach that emphasizes the role of the reader, see E. W. Conrad, *Reading Isaiah,* OBT 27 (Minneapolis: Fortress, 1979).

8. R. E. Clements, "A Light to the Nations: A Central Theme of the Book of Isaiah," in *Forming Prophetic Literature: Essays on Isaiah and the Twelve in Honor of John D. W. Watts,* ed. James W. Watts and Paul R. House, JSOTSup 235 (Sheffield: Sheffield Academic, 1996) 57-69. See also David M. Carr, "Reading for Unity in Isaiah," *JSOT* 57 (1993) 61-80.

9. H. G. M. Williamson, *Variations on a Theme: King, Messiah, and the Servant in the Book of Isaiah* (Carlisle: Paternoster, 1998).

10. Christopher R. Seitz, *Zion's Final Destiny: The Development of the Book of Isaiah* (Minneapolis: Fortress, 1991).

11. Marvin A. Sweeney, *Isaiah 1–4 and the Post-Exilic Understanding of the Isaianic Tradition,* BZAW 171 (Berlin: Walter de Gruyter, 1988) 17-21.

12. Ronald E. Clements, *Isaiah 1–39,* NCNB (Grand Rapids: Eerdmans, 1980) 198.

13. John D. W. Watts, *Isaiah 1–33.* For an excellent and detailed analysis of the structure and redactional history of Isaiah 1–39 in the context of the book as a whole, including an account of the critical scholarship on the question, see Marvin A. Sweeney, *Isaiah 1–39,* 39-62.

14. The work of Hermann Barth, *Die Jesaja-Worte in der Josiazeit,* has been widely accepted. See, also Ronald E. Clements, *Isaiah 1–39,* 5-6; Marvin H. Sweeney, *Isaiah 1–39,* 58-59.

15. For a summary see Gene M. Tucker, "Prophetic Speech," *Int.* 32 (1978) 31-45; reprinted in *Interpreting the Prophets,* ed. James Luther Mays and Paul J. Achtemeier (Philadelphia: Fortress, 1987) 27-40.

16. See esp. Gerhard von Rad, *Old Testament Theology,* vol. 2 (New York: Harper & Row, 1965).

THE BOOK OF
ISAIAH 40–66

CHRISTOPHER R. SEITZ

The reader who comes to the section of the book of Isaiah now popularly called "Second Isaiah" will expect some introductory material dealing with setting, author, religious context, major themes, and the like. A discussion of these matters can be found later in this overview. The first two sections to follow, however, discuss the suitability of providing an overview midway through a book of prophecy that, until the modern period, was treated as a single work. The discussion in these opening two sections takes its point of departure from more recent treatments of Isaiah 40–66, which view proper commentary on these twenty-seven chapters to demand at least a serious inquiry into the book's larger unity.

To be sure, some readers may find the discussion more comprehensible if the traditional sections (dealing with setting, historical period, author, and literary form and composition) are studied first. However, what is at issue is the justification of such introductory material following Isaiah 39, in spite of the fact that presentation of this material has been the standard operating procedure for roughly a century and a half.

THE LOGIC OF ISAIAH 40–66: FRONT MATTER, MIDDLE MATTER, OR NO MATTER?

Whatever one may make of divisions within biblical books, prophetic or otherwise, none calls for such a special and specialized examination as Isaiah 40–66. "Deutero" or "Trito" Zechariah, for example, or the prose narratives of Jeremiah or the Temple Vision of Ezekiel (chaps. 40–48) do not rise to the level of such individualized treatment as has been justified for for Isaiah 40–66. And yet in some sense, each of these acts of subdivision belonged to the same climate of assured or semiassured results of critical methodology, utilized for over a century.

In an almost breathtaking sense, the liberation of these twenty-seven chapters from the larger book of Isaiah also set free characters who have become household words within that narrow context better known as historical-critical education. Indeed, "Second" and "Third Isaiah" have now become so familiar in the vocabulary of the late modern West (whether one is ignorant of historical-critical labor or a devoted practioner of it) that one could imagine a major American newspaper referring to "Second Isaiah" without further ado. "Thus saith Second Isaiah" could easily ring out after a church reading from chapters 40–55.

In the *Interpreter's Bible* Isaiah volume, James Muilenberg produced a lengthy (disproportionately so) introductory front matter that summarized the findings of the day and also set forth his own characteristic approach to these twenty-seven chapters. Muilenberg took the opportunity to say things about his "rhetorical method" that had been said by him in lapidary or only more general terms before, thus making his front matter treatment a classic example of that approach. Indeed, his interest in rhetorical analysis, it could be said, was tailor-made to these chapters of prophecy from the book of Isaiah. It is worth noting, that Muilenberg's heavy investment in defending a rhetorical approach in Isaiah 40–66, integrated with and by no means at odds with previous critical (mostly form-critical) analyses, saw to it that the division of the book of Isaiah into two sections was maintained with the same high seriousness as had been true for over a century. It would be ironic if his rhetorical method succeeded both in capturing the distinctive character of these twenty-seven chapters and in assuring that they remained virtually unique in the history of critical interpretation, in terms of their special, independent treatment in the various commentary series. If a method claims to account for so much distinctiveness, it can literally displace the material, dissociating it from its own literary relations within the selfsame corpus of texts (the larger book of Isaiah).

So, in the last century and a half, the more one could say about the special character of these chapters of Isaiah, the more their rootedness in the larger book was rejected, ignored, or simply assumed as unworthy of, even passing, productive comment. Second Isaiah (and Third Isaiah) were here to stay. To produce commentary, with front matter the equivalent of, or more robust than, what was true for other prophetic books (including now a "First Isaiah") could pass without comment.

But for several reasons this is no longer true. On the one hand, these twenty-seven chapters have proved on the whole resistant to Muilenberg's rhetorical conclusions. This can be said here with deep appreciation for his learning and his sensitivity as an exegete; the problem is that continued division of the book of Isaiah into distinctive sections, as was for Muilenberg a truism, has succeeded in generating rival and contradictory accounts of the origins of, arrangement of, editing of, and independence and integrity of these same twenty-seven chapters. An older form-critical/rhetorical consensus, if such it was, has given way to literary analysis somewhat reminiscent of nineteenth-century approaches, with the focus on individual texts and editorial touches and highly complex reconstructions of redactional history. That these recent redactional approaches are now undertaken with an eye toward the larger book of Isaiah and its literary history is itself an ironic commentary on the history of critical reading of Second Isaiah. For these recent approaches, front matter, or "middle matter," would now not matter much. Yet it is difficult to see how such approaches are not the logical heirs of a method that divided the book firmly into two or more sections and gave such prominence to a "Second Isaiah," the great prophet of the exile.

On the other hand, renewed interest in the place of these twenty-seven chapters within the larger book of Isaiah has not found it necessary to reject the sort of integrative literary analysis deployed by Muilenberg, in favor of a complex redaction-historical conception. And yet precisely at this juncture, because of the interest in relating these chapters—as an integrated and rhetorically persuasive composition in something of the man-ner meant by Muilenberg—with the material found in chapters 1–39, it becomes far less clear how much of what belonged to the genre of "introduction" should properly be pursued. Matters of who, what, when, where, how—insofar as these are subsumed under attention to author, setting, historical period, literary analysis, and provenance, as in the standard introduction—are suitable within a historical-critical climate concerned with Second Isaiah, his life and times and message. But once one sees these questions as relevant only to the degree that they are correlated with an interpretation of the book of Isaiah as a whole, then the very genre of "introduction" in the middle of a major prophetic work like the book of Isaiah becomes problematic.

It is from such a vantage point, therefore, that we pause before commenting on Isaiah 40–66 to examine matters peculiar to the intepretation of these twenty-seven chapters. Is there a way forward that appreciates the literary advances manifest in Muilenberg's commentary, that integrates these with attention to the logic and coherence of Isaiah as a single (sixty-six chapters) work and that refuses so to honor the "life and times" of a "Second Isaiah" that the path back to reading these twenty-seven chapters as Isaiah's powerful conclusion is not blocked off or made unduly complex?

JUST WHAT IS AN "INTRODUCTION" TO ISAIAH 40–66?

In the middle of the twentieth century, form-critical readings of Isaiah 40–66 predominated. Yet, this predomination came with a caveat: The prophets Deutero and Trito-Isaiah utilized older forms and then, often radically, adapted them to new ends. This would require of the form-critic the skill to identify the scope and form of a unit of text and the creative adaptation of it, both in some measure the mark of the prophet's genius as inspired author. Interpreters spoke of the inspired freedom of Deutero-Isaiah, who "bent" older forms so as to fit them within a discourse suited for proclamation to Israelites languishing in Babylonian exile. Often it was said that this bending of forms was tied up with a new manner of proclamation. Rather than brief oral utterances, spontaneously delivered, the prophet had crafted longer rhetorical compositions (there was some disagreement about how long; this was a topic pursued with energy by Muilenburg in the *IB*), which were read or heard in a new "fuller-form" presentation. Perhaps this had to do with the social conditions under which the prophet labored; perhaps one should speak of an evolution in prophecy, undergoing modifications because of the awareness of prophecy as a written legacy, available and demanding correlation of some sort, in these special times of crisis and disruption. Perhaps one should simply say that the prophet is his own man, and what we see in these forms of speech has to do with Deutero-Isaiah and with his Trito-Isaiah disciple as inspired individuals. But whatever conclusion was reached, most recognized that in Isaiah 40–66 we stood on a borderline between older presuppositions about prophecy and later, new ones. Even the plain sense of the material in chapters 40–66 spoke this way when it used the language of "former things" and "latter" or "new things" to describe God's dealings with the people Israel.

It has taken several decades to recognize the full significance of the liminal state of these chapters as Israelite prophetic literature. The practice of simply treating the authors of Isaiah 40–66 as individuals, giving them names like Deuteroor Second Isaiah, and bestowing on them authorship of separate volumes of prophecy has held on, however, and is manifest in the majority of treatments available today (whether in commentary series or in general discussion).

Now this practical reality takes a further turn of significance in the case of Isaiah, because in recent decades the notion of independent prophets, following in some manner in the train of Isaiah and other pre-exilic voices, and therefore deserving of separate commentary treatment, is giving way to a different picture in the case of Isaiah 40–66. But this raises an important question, and it prepares the reader for meeting "Deutero-" and "Trito-Isaiah." The terms refer here not to literary sections of Isaiah, but to authors in fixed social settings that can be described, with this or that distinctive theological message, over against other Isaiahs and other prophets, working out of this or that historical setting, as was true of Jeremiah, Nahum, Hosea, or the Isaiah of the Syro-Ephraimite crisis of the eighth century BCE.

The older practice insisted upon, first, a reconstruction of the historical and social setting of the prophecy. This was to drive home the fact that the setting (i.e., social-historical setting) of chapters 40–66 was decidely not to be confused with the setting of Isaiah 1–39 (which presented its own problems). Second, the literature was classified as to form (units and larger organization) and situated within a developmental picture of Israelite prophecy attentive to the social and historical circumstances referred to at points in the literal sense. References to Babylon, Cyrus, fleeing from diaspora, and lack of mention of David, Temple, Assyria conspired to produce a reasonable picture of prophetic speech, in new forms of presentation, delivered to those in exile and, later, to those in the land, following some sort of return of exiles to Jerusalem. Then the limits for the contributions were set, with most assigning chapters 40–55 to a Second Isaiah author, while chapters 56–66 were the work of a Trito-Isaiah. A related task was, of course, determining additions to these major collections and rearrangements and dislocations. Recent work on chapters 40–66 indebted to this general manner of approach has focused in particular on matters of arrangement and on certain long-standing difficulties.[1] So some divide all of chapters 40–55 into various redactional levels and seek to coordinate these with similar features in chapters 56–66, or a major division is sought at chapter 49, or, more ambitiously, redactional levels are coordinated with portions of text in chapters 1–39. All of this has complicated any simple talk about who, what, when, where, or how as this pertains to Isaiah 40–66.

While there is at present interest in the larger unity and coherence of Isaiah as a whole book, it would not be fair to say that this interest is what presents the major challenge to any simple deployment of the genre of "introduction" for chapters 40–55 or 40–66. Recent redactional-critical studies, because they analyze the manifestly anonymous, often minute additions and rearrangements of this material, assigning to these theological significance within a study of the whole book's theological evolution, also cannot give easy answers to the old questions of author, social setting, audience, and historical location. Indeed, these recede in importance as the redactional decisions, made within the literature, carry the chief theological weight the material seeks to convey. To speak of a "Deutero-" or "Trito-Isaiah" has become more difficult than talking of a "Zion tradition" or a "pro-nations level" or an "anti-temple redaction." Setting stops being geographical location, historical moment, or individual "poetic" contribution ("The Great Prophet of the Exile") and becomes instead this or that literary evidence of this or that theological shift, within a much broader reconstruction of the later years of Israelite religion (exilic and post-exilic).

On all accounts, then, return to a simple "author, setting, audience" form-critical approach, with its usual introductory roll call of topics to be treated before reading chapter 40, must now face the challenge of a host of newer approaches. It is not just the existence of these chapters within a larger book that raises questions about the appropriateness of discussing author and setting; it is also the sheer complexification of form-critical methodology into redaction and *tendenz*-oriented literary criticism in recent years. The provenance of these chapters has become increasingly literary and scribal and anonymous, making use of the terms "Deutero-" and "Trito-Isaiah"—except as literary designations—nostalgic simplification.

SETTING

The term "setting" is used in its social-historical sense here, mindful that efforts to describe the setting of these chapters must rely quite heavily, if not exclusively, on the literary evidence of the chapters in question.

In an early reassessment, Childs raised the possibility that clearer signs of the book's historical and social location had been muted when the chapters were shaped to function in the larger book.[2] Another way to take Childs's suggestion is as a simple recognition that chapters 40–66 do not choose to highlight their historical and social setting in ways historical-critics might wish and in ways that do in fact exist in other parts of the canon (e.g., Jeremiah or Ezra-Nehemiah). To say such a thing is not a reflection of simple laziness or lack of resolve about historical questions (a century of work on these questions in Isaiah 40–66 shows otherwise). But it is significant to note, and often is not sufficiently noted, how content these chapters are to work with a low degree of historical referentiality. Whether the reason for that has to do with the existence of chapters 1–39 as its own "setting" for chapters 40–66 is a separate question, to be

taken up below. The "authorizing voice(s)" at work in our literature may have felt no need to stipulate a setting that, for the first audience, was everywhere pre-supposed and self-evident. This would be true whether such authorizing voices were aware of the voice of Isaiah or not (more on this below). What is noteworthy is that the material of chapters 40–66 was not supplied with editorial comment locating it in time and space, as is true of other prophetic books, and here the transmission of these oracles together with Isaiah 1–39 is surely relevant.

Reference to Cyrus in this discourse (Isa 45:1) does not appear to be an interpolation, but belongs intimately to the argument of the context. Cyrus was, of course, the Persian monarch who, history and parts of Scripture record (2 Chr 36:22-23; Ezra), brought about the end of Neo-Babylonian rule in the region and, indeed, saw to it that those in diaspora could return. It is not possible, given the form of the proclamation about him, more precisely to date the message of chapters 40–66. He is clearly modeled on typological grounds, in relationship to the depiction of Assyria earlier in Isaiah (10:5), and consistent with the new exodus language of much of these chapters, as a "second pharaoh" witnessing God's mighty acts. There is no reason to assume that the language about Cyrus is not roughly contemporaneous with his historical existence. But here again, it would probably be saying too much to argue that knowledge of Cyrus, in the terms expressed in these texts, requires the author and the audience to have been in Babylonian exile or to have been concerned about something so imminent as to fix this proclamation at one moment in time only.

At several points in chapters 40–55 reference is made to Israel in dispersion. The dispersion is global (e.g., Isa 43:5-7) and is not described with any constraint on our participating from only one point of view—say, with a "prophet of the exile." Indeed, from the standpoint of the literature's own presentation, as Duhm long ago noted,[3] the perspective is, if anything, Jerusalemite in orientation. This did not, however, prevent Duhm from locating the actual author in Phoenicia in an odd bit of exegesis, showing that Duhm knew the difference between the setting of the author (a matter for close literary and historical analysis) and the setting the literature itself appears to work with.

Hence, the words directed to those in dispersion in Babylon are to go forth *from there* (Isa 48:20), not, as it were, from here, and at other places, the Zion-orientation of the literature is unmistakeable (Isa 49:14–55:13). A handful of scholars has always registered objections to an exilic provenance.[4]

Once one respects Duhm's distinction between the literature's perspective and the author's actual historical location, a conclusion not unlike Childs's comes back into play. One need not conclude that these chapters once had a more concrete setting that was removed when the chapters began to form the conclusion of Isaiah 1–39. Rather, one need only respect the literature's Zion orientation and note the general concern for Israel in every compass point of dispersion (and the nations' similar location as anticipated recipients of God's name and glory). Then the constraining of the literature into some exilic context seems both unnecessary and less plausible, both on literary and on historical grounds.

Consequently, another major scholarly consensus will also need to be reviewed: the division of the book into two sections based upon the geographical reality of exile for one section (chaps. 40–55) and return for the other (chaps. 56–66), a distinction manifestly awkward when one notes the interest in Zion and its children running from chapter 49 to the final depiction of the book (66:10-16).

HISTORICAL PERIOD

As stated already, chapters 40–66 presuppose the collapse of the Neo-Babylonian Empire. Stated in the terms of Isaiah's own temporal bearings, the "former things" have passed away when we come to chapter 40. The period of judgment spoken of in Isaiah 6 has reached its conclusion, and only now are we in a position to hear about forgiveness and new things, on the other side of that judgment. Historically speaking, chapters 40–66 are self-consciously later speech than that of Isaiah of Jerusalem, from the period following Babylonian collapse.

This establishes a general *terminus ad quo* (earliest date) for the proclamation of Isaiah 40–66, but what of the *terminus ad quem* (latest possible date)? In some measure, this is both a historical and a literary question, for there is a time frame operating within the presentation of these twenty-seven chapters that allows us to note movement and change and development in the literature's argument, just as there is a narrower question about when such and such text was written, over against other texts, within and outside these twenty-seven chapters.

Beuken, more than any modern commentator, has taught us to pay attention to certain key words and themes in this discourse, and here he inadvertently raises a question of temporal location.[5] For all the centrality of the word "servant" in chapters 40–52, there is also some difficulty in knowing how to identify and interpret the servant's role and mission. Is the servant one and the same person, regardless of context? Is there a cycle of "servant songs" in which the servant is always the same person, or is to speak of a cycle already to prejudge the matter? What is beyond controversy, however, is that the plural form, "servants," appears only at chapter 54 and nowhere before that and that these "servants" (cf. also "seed/offspring") play a decidedly central role in the presentation of especially chapters 56–66. Beuken has established this beyond doubt in a series of important essays.

These servants are taken to be the followers of the servant, in the same manner as Isaiah raises up around himself disciples (8:16). That is, the servants function on analogy with the generation that were to carry out the will of God as manifested to the prophet Isaiah. In Isaiah's day, there had to be a period of waiting, for the prophet's speech was not to be heeded but ignored—indeed, it made hearers deaf and blind (6:10). So it was the task of the disciples to bind up the testimony that it might be preserved and opened for a later day (see also 29:11-12, 19). As at other places where prophets are described in the Old Testament, the prophet's followers can be understood as his children or offspring (e.g., in the Elijah/Elisha stories).

The time frame envisioned by this scenario of rejection and punishment is not overspecified in Isaiah; we know only that a period of judgment, devastating in scope, is to be visited upon God's people and that a remnant will survive (6:11-13). We know also that Hezekiah will be spared seeing this period of judgment (39:5-8). When we read into chapter 40 and following, it is clear that the day of judgment is past (40:2, "she has served her term—her penalty is paid"). The former things contained the record of this coming judgment and of God's commissioning of its agent of release (41:21-29). It is in the light of possession of this "former" record that Israel is a unique witness, able to produce what the nations cannot, and the possession of this knowledge is likewise testimony to the unique and sole lordship of Israel's God.

If the temporal relationship, in precise terms, between Isaiah and the testimony of the disciples released for a latter day is imprecise, we are able to infer that it involved movement from the period of Assyrian judgment and blasphemous threat (Isaiah 36–37), to a time centuries later (39:5-7), with Cyrus as the agent of release from judgment (cf. Isa 13:17 and 41:25).

The relationship, temporally, between the servant and the servants would appear more compressed. While the nomenclature "servants" is somewhat vague, there is no reason to assume that the "servants" of chapters 56–66 represent several successive generations; indeed, there is good evidence to believe that we are talking about the generation immediately after the servant, who is the author and subject of the core proclamation of Isaiah 40–66. At the close of chapter 59, we hear of a covenant made with several generations. God's spirit will be given to those ("offspring," "seed") who follow in the train of the servants, and the perspective is a future, not a past, one. At most, the book appears to describe a generation or two of servant disciples, and the steady attention of chapters 56–66, as Beuken has clearly shown, remains on them. They are the promised "seed" of the servant (53:10).

It remains to be established whether the temporal distinction represented by the movement in the literature from "servant" (singular) to "servants" (plural) also correlates with what was an alleged geographical distinction (exilic chapters, 40–55, and Jerusalemite-return chapters, 56–66). It is notable that the plural use of "servants" comes first in chapter 54, not in chapter 56. I have already registered my skepticism about whether the literature makes an important distinction between "Deutero" and "Trito" sections as traditionally held.In the final chapters of Isaiah, controversy over the Temple is clearly in evidence. Most of the language of restoration in Isaiah focuses on Zion's discovery of her many children, some birthed without any labor (66:7; cf. 54:1-2; 60:4). When reference is made to concrete restoration, it tends still to focus on Zion's resplendent dress (Isaiah 54;

60–61), and not on the sort of concrete scenario (foundation stone, altar, walls, city) envisioned in Ezra–Nehemiah. If it were necessary to set a *terminus ad quem* for the discourse of the servants in chapters 54–66, the most that could be safely said would be the period of the first generations concerned with the restoration of Zion. Chapter 66 is more about rival building proposals and false religion than about precise moments in the restoration of the cult as Ezra sets this forth.

In sum, the perspective of the literature is of several generations, during the time of return and restoration, depicted from the standpoint of Zion-Jerusalem, where the full return of all the dispersed is a lively hope and with that, the inclusion of the nations as worshipers of God and witnesses to the glory of YHWH (66:18-23).

AUTHOR

It is important that we understand what the term "author" means when we look at Isaiah 40–66. We can start by attending to "the author" on the literature's own terms:

(1) The author of the material in chapters 40:1–52:12 is not identified by name.

(2) The author of this material does not speak in the first person, as prophets do in reference to themselves (when not speaking for God); this changes at 48:16*d* ("and now the Lord God has sent me and his spirit").

(3) Thereafter, the author speaks of himself in the first person and as God's servant (49:1-7; 50:4-9), all the while maintaining his primary role as "divine voice" in the manner familiar in chapters 40–48, though now with special attention to discharging the responsibility to comfort Zion (in fulfillment of the charge of 40:1-11).

(4) This author does not use, nor do others ever use, the familiar term "prophet" (נביא *nābî*) to describe himself.

(5) The closest thing to what might be termed a "call narrative" (describing the setting apart of the individual for God's service) is to be found in 49:1-7, but it is more retrospective than prospective, and it entails a commissioning of the individual servant to be "Israel" (49:3), which gives rise to complaint about a past vocation.

Because the author is not called a prophet and because for much of the discourse he does not step forward (indeed, when he does so, it is due to divine compulsion and spirit possession; 48:16d), the term "author" must be understood along the lines of "authorizing" voice. This begs the question as to what sort of form-critical discourse the material of chapters 40–52:11 and 53:12–66:24 is (on this, see the section following).

In the opening chapters (chaps. 40–48) it is not necessary for the material to supply us with some account authorizing the speech. How is that possible? We are used to that in other prophetic material, even if it is only brief notices supplied clearly by an editor.

Several explanations lie close at hand. The first involves the relationship between the discourse of chapters 40–66 and what precedes in the book of Isaiah. The "former things" perspective assumed in chapters 40–48 operates with knowledge of a prior prophetic record, involving most crucially oracles from Isaiah of Jerusalem. The opening pericope (40:1-11) is not, as many have noted, a call narrative, however much we may feel entitled to one at the point of entry into this material and however much it may resemble such a narrative (e.g., Isaiah 6). The voices that speak are those from the heavenly council. We are meant to know that the voices who addressed Isaiah in former times with a word of judgment for God's people (see 6:3-5, 9-10) are here, as in chap. 6, deferential to the word the Lord has spoken: formerly for judgment (6:8-10), latterly for forgiveness (40:5), with the announcement of God's holy presence before all flesh (40:5, 10). What is missing in our account is a prophet on analogy with Isaiah. Instead we have voices speaking to one another, as before, but no named prophet. Consistent with this, in what follows we have divine speech without any presentation of the authorized voice. For that we must wait until 48:16d and 49:1-7, and even then what we find is indebted to former prophetic records (49:1-7 resembles Jer 1:4-10) and is not a full reproduction of them for a new prophet.

It is not clear that the speaker or his audience believes prophecy can exist at this period without further ado as a simple extension of what had pertained in the days of Isaiah, Jeremiah, or even Ezekiel (who is nearly contemporaneous). It is likely no accident that Isaiah 40–66 never circulated as a separate prophetic collection (in spite of Duhm's clever hypothesis to the contrary) in any reception-history capable of verification, and indeed that the only form we have of it is as it exists now: as the final chapters of a vision of Isaiah. As we shall see, the notion that there was to be a series of prophets, and a specific prophet "like Moses" (Deut 18:15), may have carried with it a further assumption—namely, that at some point prophecy would come to a close in eschatological fulfillment of God's plans for it. It is necessary here only to register that the peculiar depiction of the literature, focused on a servant and servants but not on a prophet, belongs to the specific presentation of the book of Isaiah as a whole and this particular moment in God's revelation of the word to Israel.

What stands out in Isaiah 40–66 is the notion of God's independent word accomplishing what God wills (55:11). This notion is rooted in the presentation of Isaiah 1–39, where we learn that Isaiah's word to one generation would go unheeded, but would remain God's word nonetheless for a later generation. The author lives under this perspective and does not seek to encroach upon it. Indeed, when in chapter 49 he speaks for himself, it is clear that he regards his vocation as heretofore fruitless, however, and in whatever form it took in chapters 40–48. His own hope is in God's accomplishing potential (49:4).

The servant is given in 49:3 the role announced as Israel's in 42:1-8, is persecuted and afflicted (50:4-9), and dies (52:13–53:12). He accomplishes what God had promised in comforting Zion, in removing sin, and in becoming thereby a light to the nations, if in an eschatological realm only (52:13-15). The moving tribute to the servant is provided by the servants, who glimpsed into the mystery of his death and saw there not an end but a fulfillment and an inauguration. The remainder of the book is their own written legacy.

Is it possible to assign this new mode of inspired speech to some social or religious setting? Yes, most certainly. What is less clear is whether this would add to or detract from our appreciation of the discourse as it lies before us in the book of Isaiah. I remain fairly certain that we are reading this material on something of the terms those who preserved it meant for us to—that is, as an extension of the vision of Isaiah. Reading these chapters, or hearing them read aloud, in other words, may not be far from how they first functioned. At points the intertextuality of the material (i.e., its reutilization of other parts of Scripture) is so strong that one must imagine a highly trained author and audience; trained, that is, in the knowledge of the specific literary content of Israel's legacy of divine speech. This, in turn, points to the strong possibility that the composition of these twenty-seven chapters never originated as public, spontaneous, brief utterances, in the manner understood by nineteenth and twentieth-century German scholars, only secondarily to be committed to writing, arranged and rearranged, until we have what sits before us now.

The sheer invisibility of the prophetic voice within the discourse itself may mean that the author was faced by oppression and challenge from within his circle. If this is true, it would provide an explanation for why such radically hopeful and forgiving speech exists together with descriptions of persecution and affliction, even unto death. In the final chapters, this conflict emerges into the full light of day, forms the center of the discourse, until the servants are separated from their wicked persecutors (65:13). Here as well, the descriptions of affliction and persecution sit right alongside language bursting with hope and promise.

We know that the office of prophet nearly tore Jeremiah in two. The servant-author and the servant followers move the discourse about Israel and the nations into truly unprecedented territory (cf. Jeremiah's appointment as prophet over nations and kingdoms in Jer 1:10) and therein may lie the source of the conflict. The servant and the servants insist that Israel be a light to the nations and that God may well use affliction and even death to accomplish this. It is hard to imagine a more difficult word to be given to deliver. The form of the presentation, with its hidden author who steps forward in the role of servant Israel, light to the nations, dies and gives birth to a new generation of servants, allows us to glimpse but partially the social world in which the message was first delivered. But that may not be an accident of history. The text from its beginning was felt to have an ongoing, eschatological import, beyond the circumstances of its first delivery, and that understanding goes back to Isaiah himself. To read the literature on its own terms is to respect this eschatological message and its capacity to transcend historical reconstructions.

In sum, I would argue for a single author, joined by a generation of servant followers, later termed those who tremble at God's word (66:2, 5). These latter form the core of a group who heard and transmitted the servant's oracles to a yet wider audience. In that transmission came friction and dissent. In the tribute to the servant and in the life of the servants we learn that this friction and dissent also belonged to God's plans for the people and inaugurated God's final purposes for all creation and all flesh.

LITERARY FORM AND COMPOSITION

Second Isaiah was a form-critical proving ground in the middle of the twentieth century. In the first phase, the focus was on exact delimitation of units and classification of them in terms of genre. These chapters seemed to lend themselves to this sort of task, because of the sharpness of transition and the general tidiness of expression. Still, sharp disagreements existed over both the number and the genre of the units discovered.

In the second phase, more attention was paid— in spite of these disagreements—to the life-setting of the speech units, now separated from their present literary arrangement ("situation-in-text"). Again, very little agreement was forthcoming about the social setting of the proclamation and the proper description of the office of the prophet Deutero-Isaiah. Some of this was the frustration of conjecturing about a setting for which we have very little collateral testimony (allegedly, life in Babylonian exile). Was the prophet operating in a cultic context, a preaching context, or some other context? Or was he, say, writing down his proclamation and sending it out piecemeal? Then an additional complicating factor extruded itself: What if the prophet was using genre familiar to him and his audience, but only in terms of literary imitation—that is, already at one stage removed from whatever situation-in-life they had first functioned in and had in turn affected their form? If this turned out to be the case, then form criticism could only point to its own built-in limitations, in the case of Isaiah 40–66.

In a third phase, then, attention returned to the text itself and to theories about the present structure and arrangement of the material. Here it seemed commentators felt themselves to be on firmer ground. Westermann and Melugin are classic examples of those who worked with the literary and formal aspects of the previous critical phase, but who sat easier to the search for setting-in-life, preferring instead an effort to account for the organization of the chapters in Isaiah 40–55.[6] Westermann extended his own analysis into chapters 56–66, and in large measure one could conclude that he was representative of a general trend, of seeing in "Third Isaiah" a much more heterogeneous and haphazardly arranged collection of formal units.

This interest in editorial shaping has continued, but it has taken two different directions. Mention has been made already about the newer redactional studies, and these represent one direction. A second direction can be seen in the work of Muilenberg and various other literary approaches.[7] These seek to see in the final form of Isaiah 40–55 a rhetorically effective, highly organized, only lightly redacted presentation. Redactional studies are more interested in identifying divergence and literary tension, and then delineating wide-scale levels of redaction and alteration, which run across tidy structural divisions—not only within chapters 40–55 or 56–66, but also across these sections (indeed, into the oracles of First Isaiah).

FOR FURTHER READING

Commentaries:

Baltzer, K. *Deutero-Isaiah: A Commentary on Isaiah 40–55.* Hermeneia. Minneapolis: Fortress, 2001.

Blenkinsopp, Joseph. *Isaiah 40-55: A New Translation with Introduction and Commentary.* AB 19A. New York: Doubleday, 2001.

Childs, B. S. *Isaiah.* OTL. Louisville: Westminster John Knox, 2001.

Hanson, P. D. *Isaiah 40–66.* Interpretation. Louisville: Westminster John Knox, 1995.

Koole, Joan Leunis. *Isaiah III, v 3: Isaiah 56-66.* Historical Commentary on the Old Testament. Leuven: Peeters, 2001.

Muilenburg, J. "The Book of Isaiah: Chapters 40–66." In *The Interpreter's Bible.* 12 vols. (Nashville: Abingdon, 1956). Vol. 5.

Westermann, C. *Isaiah 40–66.* Translated by David Stalker. OTL. Philadelphia: Westminster, 1969.

Other Studies:

Abma, R. *Bonds of Love: Methodic Studies of Prophetic Texts with Marriage Imagery, Isaiah 50:1-3 and 54:1-10, Hosea 1-3, Jeremiah 2-3.* SSN 40. Assen: Van Gorcum, 1999.

Bellinger, W. H., and W. R. Farmer, eds. *Jesus and the Suffering Servant: Isaiah 53 and Christian Origins.* Harrisburg, Pa.: Trinity Press International, 1998.

Beuken, W. A. M. "The Main Theme of Trito-Isaiah: 'The Servants of Yahweh.' " *JSOT 47* (1990).

Clements, R. "Beyond Tradition-History: Deutero-Isaianic Development of First Isaiah's Themes." *JSOT* 31 (1985).

Davies, Andrew. *Double Standards in Isaiah: Re-Evaulating Prophetic Ethics and Divine Justice.* Biblical Interpretation 46. Leiden: Brill, 2000.

Janowski, B., and P. Stuhlmacher, eds. *Der leidende Gottesknecht.* FAT 14. Tubingen: Mohr-Siebeck, 1996.

Leclerc, Thomas L. *Yahweh Is Exalted in Justice: Solidarity and Conflict in Isaiah.* Minneapolis, Minn.: Fortress, 2001.

Meade, D. G. "Authorship, Revelation and Canon in the Prophetic Tradition." In *Pseudonymity and Canon.* WUNT 39. Tubingen: Mohr-Siebeck, 1986.

Melugin, R. F. *The Formation of Isaiah 40–55.* BZAW 141. Berlin: Walter de Gruyter, 1976.

Melugin, R., and M. Sweeney, eds. *New Visions of Isaiah.* JSOTSup 214. Sheffield: JSOT, 1996.

Mouw, Richard J. *When the Kings Come Marching In: Isaiah and the New Jerusalem.* Revised and Expanded. Grand Rapids, Mich.: Eerdmans, 2003.

Seitz, C. R. "How Is the Prophet Isaiah Present in the Latter Half of the Book? The Logic of Chapters 40–66 Within the Book of Isaiah." *JBL* 115 (1996).

Smith, P. A. *Rhetoric and Redaction in Trito-Isaiah.* VTSup 62. Leiden: Brill, 1995.

Wilcox, P., and D. Paton-Williams. "The Servant Songs in Deutero-Isaiah." *JSOT* 42 (1988).

ENDNOTES

1. See esp. R. F. Melugin, *The Formation of Isaiah 40–55,* BZAW 141 (Berlin: Walter de Gruyter, 1976).

2. B. S. Childs, *Isaiah,* OTL (Louisville: Westminster John Knox, 2000). Trobisch discusses the concrete form such editorial efforts to "de-historicize" (Childs's term) literature might take in his treatment of the Pauline letters. See D. Trobisch, *Paul's Letter Collection: Tracing the Origin* (Minneapolis: Fortress, 1994).

3. Bernhard Duhm, *Das buch Jesaia,* HKAT (Göttingen: Vandenhoeck & Ruprecht, 1892).

4. J. D. Smart, *History and Theology in Second Isaiah* (Philadelphia: Westminster, 1965); C. C. Torrey, *The Second Isaiah* (New York: Scribner's, 1928); Recently questions have been raised afresh. See R. Clements, "Beyond Tradition-History: Deutero-Isaianic Development of First Isaiah's Themes," *JSOT* 31 (1985); J. van Oortschot, *Von Babel zum Zion,* BZAW 206 (Berlin: Walter de Gruyter, 1993).

5. W. A. M. Beuken, "The Main Theme of Trito-Isaiah: The Servants of Isaiah," *JSOT* 47 (1990).

6. C. Westermann, *Isaiah 40–66,* trans. David Stalker, OTL (Philadelphia: Westminster, 1969); R. F. Melugin, *The Formation of Isaiah 40–55.*

7. J. Muilenburg, "The Book of Isaiah: Chapters 40–66," in *The Interpreter's Bible* (Nashville: Abingdon, 1956) vol. 5.

THE BOOK OF
JEREMIAH

PATRICK D. MILLER

The book of Jeremiah is one of the longest books in the Bible, surpassed in number of pages of text only by the book of Psalms. While not all of the book is necessarily from the prophet Jeremiah himself, the vast extent of his prophetic career and its setting in one of the most critical times in the history of Israel—from the reform of Josiah through the downfall of Judah and into the time of exile—suggest why this book looms so large in Scripture. The great crisis of Israel's history in the Old Testament period involved the destruction of the Temple, the dwelling place of the Lord of Israel, and the exile of God's people. Much of the biblical literature either deals with those matters or comes from that time in Israel's history. No other biblical book so enables readers to comprehend theologically what was going on at that time—to hear both what happened and why it happened—as does the book of Jeremiah.

HISTORICAL CONTEXT

The two great events of Judah's history during the years of Jeremiah's prophecy were the religious reform of Josiah (622 BCE) and the destruction of Jerusalem and Judah (587 BCE) and the exile of many of its leaders and citizens (597 and 587 BCE). These events, however, took place in the context of major geopolitical upheavals in the ancient Near East, affairs of nations in conflict with one another that are constantly reflected in the book of Jeremiah and were often the focus of attention in his oracles. Jeremiah began to proclaim the divine word during the time of Assyrian decline and the ensuing conflict between Egypt and Babylon for domination of the Fertile Crescent. The demise of Assyria was under way during the first part of Josiah's reign (640–609 BCE). The last great king of Assyria, Asshurbanipal, died in the year given as the date of Jeremiah's call, 627 BCE (Jer 1:2). Thereafter, Assyria was unable to resist the rise of Babylon,

even with help from Egypt. Nabopolassar took Babylon from Assyrian control in 626 BCE and made himself its king. Having broken Egypt free from Assyrian control under Psammetichus, his successor, Necho, sought to help Assyria, probably to exercise some power in Syria-Palestine, but also to resist the greater threat of Babylonian dominance. Meanwhile, the Medes supported the Babylonians. Over the years there were various battles and engagements involving these nations against each other, which resulted in the loss of important Assyrian cities: Asshur, Nineveh, and Harran.

The loss of Assyrian control in Syria-Palestine permitted a more independent stance on the part of Judah, especially during the reign of Josiah. It was manifest especially in his religious reform, which included the removal of all Assyrian religious practices that had become a part of the religious life of Jerusalem and elsewhere and also in political reform, his taking control of the Assyrian provinces that had once constituted the northern kingdom, Israel.

The reform, which is dated to Josiah's eighteenth year (622 BCE) by 2 Kgs 22:3 and 23:3, may, in fact, have begun earlier (2 Chr 34:3-7). In any event, it seems to have been quite comprehensive, according to the account in 2 Kings 23, and even seems to have extended into the former northern kingdom (2 Kgs 23:15-20; 2 Chr 34:6). The reform was the most extensive and far-reaching in Israel's history, though its effects were not very lasting, if the prophecy of Jeremiah is any indication. It seems to have had its impetus in nationalistic stirrings during the decline of Assyrian domination. Josiah's ability to take control of northern territory inevitably meant conflict with the northern shrines, which were regarded as idolatrous by those in Jerusalem. The reform, however, was not only a political endeavor. The discovery of a law book while the Temple was being renovated, itself a part of Josiah's reforming activity, gave significant impetus to the

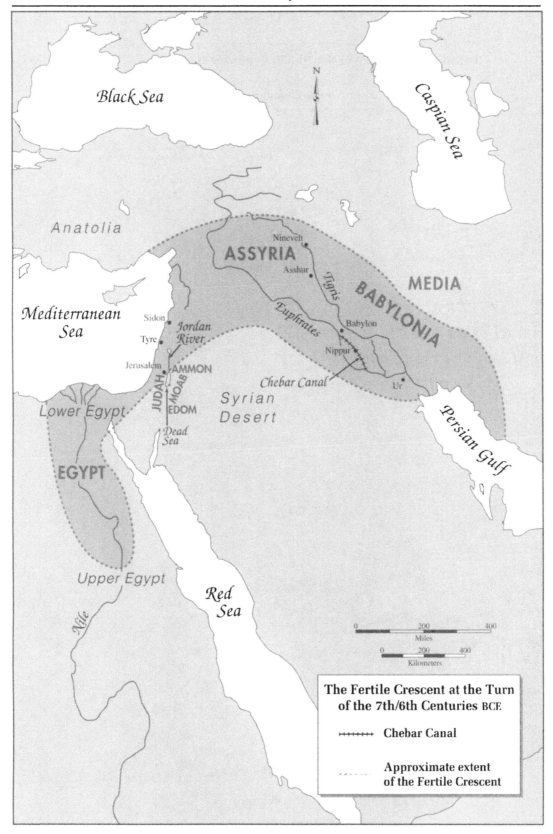

The Fertile Crescent at the Turn of the 7th/6th Centuries BCE

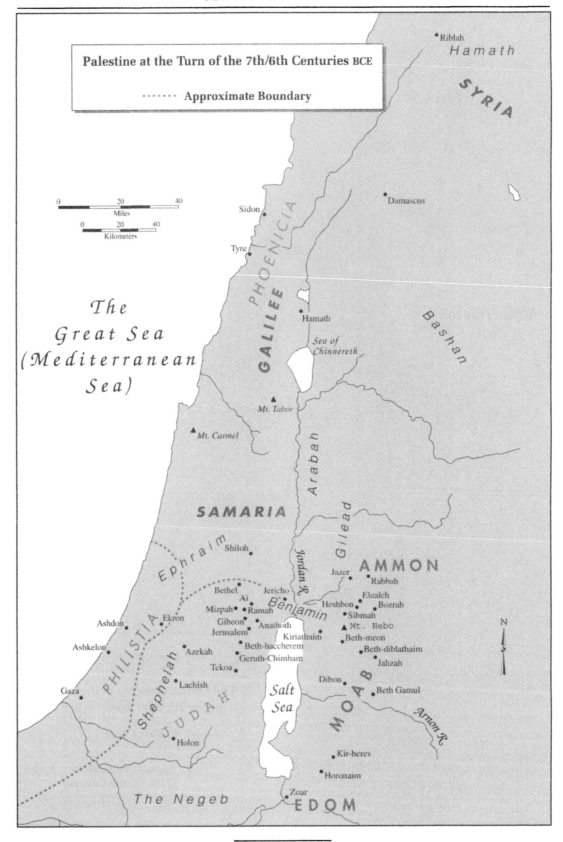

Palestine at the Turn of the 7th/6th Centuries BCE

- - - - - - Approximate Boundary

impulse for reform. There is no reason to doubt the judgment of Kings that Josiah was a committed Yahwist as well as an assertive nationalist.

During his reform, Josiah eliminated all non-Yahwistic cults and practices, both those manifest in the Temple and its paraphernalia and those in the high places or shrines. The reform was massive and involved the destruction of all the shrines outside Jerusalem, whether Yahwistic or not, and the complete centralization of worship in the capital city and its Temple. This reform meant the destruction especially of the shrines in the northern kingdom and their personnel, which would have been regarded as idolatrous almost by definition. The priests of the outlying shrines of Judah were invited to come to Jerusalem.

However successful Josiah's reform may have been, resistance to the reform is evident from the book of Jeremiah. Both the testimony of narrative texts in Jeremiah to the worship of other gods because of their apparent productivity (Jer 44:15-19) and his countereffort to insist that the other gods did not "profit" suggest that there was fairly widespread continuing devotion to other cults than the worship of Yahweh or that the single devotion to Yahweh in the one sanctuary was fairly short-lived.

Josiah was killed at Megiddo in 609 BCE when he met and sought to stop Necho, the king of Egypt, and his army from going to the assistance of Assyria when it tried to retake Harran. The Egyptian-Assyrian coalition failed to counter Babylon's strength, and by 605 BCE, with Nebuchadnezzar's defeat of the Egyptians at Carchemish (Jeremiah 46), Assyrian power was at an end. Meanwhile, Necho had sought, successfully, to regain Egyptian control of Palestine. The people of Judah had anointed Josiah's son Jehoahaz as king after Josiah's death, but Necho deposed him after only three months and deported him to Egypt, imposing tribute on Judah. He placed another son of Josiah on the throne and changed his name from "Eliakim" to "Jehoiakim." Jehoiakim paid the tribute by heavily taxing the citizenry.

Jehoiakim reigned until 598 BCE, when he died or possibly was assassinated. If Jeremiah's response to Jehoiakim (Jer 22:13-19) and the latter's disdain of Jeremiah's prophetic word (Jer 36:20-26) are any indication, Jehoiakim's rule served well the interests of those opposed to Josiah's reform, he showed no interest in the covenantal norms. Meanwhile, the defeat of the Egyptians at Carchemish in 605 BCE

allowed the Babylonians to move westward and begin to establish control of Syria-Palestine. In the period after the battle at Carchemish, Jehoiakim transferred his allegiance to Babylon (2 Kgs 24:1). That submission to Babylonian rule was, however, fairly short-lived. Within three years, Jehoiakim, probably in response to pro-Egyptian elements and nationalistic zeal, rebelled against the Babylonian king Nebuchadnezzar (2 Kgs 24:1). That was a big mistake. By 598 BCE, the Babylonian army was in Judah. Jehoiakim died that year, and his young son was made king. Within about three months, Jerusalem surrendered to the Babylonian army, and the young king, together with the queen mother and many officials and citizens, was deported to Babylon.

Jehoiachin's uncle Zedekiah was placed on the throne by the Babylonians, whereupon the nation went through a decade of unrest. Zedekiah was a relatively weak king. Jeremiah's encounters with him indicate that he had some good intentions but was unable to stand up to those who opposed him. The record of Zedekiah's reign, preserved primarily in the book of Jeremiah, shows a vacillating rule that ended in terrible defeat at the hands of those who had set him up as king. That some considered his predecessor, Jehoiachin, still to be the rightful king of Judah, even though in exile (see chap. 28), did not help him rule with the support of his subjects.

A rebellion in Babylon in 595 BCE seems to have stirred hopes of Judah's breaking free of Babylonian domination. In 594 (Jer 28:1), envoys from Edom, Moab, Ammon, Tyre, and Sidon met with Zedekiah in Jerusalem to plan a revolt against Babylon, a move that Jeremiah thought was a disaster, even contrary to God's will. The plans did not go anywhere, and Zedekiah sent to Babylon (Jer 29:3), or went to Babylon (Jer 51:59), to settle things with the Babylonians and assure them of his loyalty. Within five years, however, Judean leadership with pro-Egyptian and anti-Babylonian sympathies had pushed Zedekiah into open rebellion. The Babylonians reacted quickly. The account of their siege of Jerusalem and the end of Judah is preserved in the final chapters of the books of Kings and Jeremiah. Jerusalem and its Temple were destroyed after the Temple was looted. Many of the leaders were executed, and many people were taken into exile in Babylon. Zedekiah was forced to watch his sons being executed before the Babylonians put out his eyes and dragged him off to Babylon.

A number of Judeans were left behind, including Jeremiah. The Babylonians appointed Gedaliah, a member of an important Judean family whose father and grandfather had been officials in the court, as governor of Judah. He counseled the people to remain in the land and accept Babylonian control, the same message Jeremiah had offered. Unfortunately, Gedaliah was assassinated by Ishmael, a member of the royal family, who failed to gain any support for his action and fled to the Ammonites. Fearful of Babylonian retaliation because of the murder of Gedaliah, some of the remaining leaders ignored Jeremiah's counsel to stay put and insisted on fleeing to Egypt, taking Jeremiah and his scribe Baruch with them (Jeremiah 43). We last hear him preaching a sermon against the Judean refugees in Egypt, accusing them of idolatry and abandoning their allegiance to the Lord of Israel (Jeremiah 44).

THE PROPHET JEREMIAH

While the book of Jeremiah is not intended to tell the story of the prophet, the figure of Jeremiah is often the focus of attention in the book. In the commentary that follows, the treatment of particular texts seeks to show the ways in which the prophet's life—what happens to him, what he thinks, and how he acts—is a part of the message of the text. There are, however, two issues that need to be identified and discussed as a part of introducing the book.

One is the whole question of how much, if any, access to the "historical" Jeremiah is provided by the book of Jeremiah. Opinion on that question ranges from the conviction of William Holladay,[1] who proposes a detailed chronology of the prophet and believes that most of the oracles in the book of Jeremiah can be dated to some time in his prophetic career, to Robert Carroll's[2] equally vigorous argument that the book provides little access to the prophet and his words and thoughts because so much of the book is an editorial product from a later time. These two extremes, not surprisingly, do reflect features of the book. The prophet is so prominent in the book, proclaiming many oracles that were highly appropriate to specific circumstances, that one can hardly believe his prophetic activity is not attested in the book. Furthermore, the references to his dictating oracles and the iden-

tification of a scribe who wrote them down and who was himself involved in the story of the last days of Judah tend to move in the same direction. There is little doubt, however, that the process of formation of a prophetic book was long and complex with considerable creative editing activity as oracles were added and interpreted, sometimes moved from one place to another, expanded by words and phrases and the like. The existence of two different forms of the book in the Hebrew (or Masoretic) text and the Greek (or Septuagintal) text further confirms the complex growth of the book, which can hardly be confined to Jeremiah's prophetic activity. Nor can one refer even to the laments of Jeremiah as a presumably authentic view into the life and mind of the prophet. Their language is typical of the psalmic laments and are not peculiar to Jeremiah or to his experience.[3]

Out of the whole—remnants of Jeremiah's prophecy and editorial additions, expansions, and the like—there comes a picture of the prophet that cannot be labeled as either historical or unhistorical, fact or fiction. Some have spoken of this image as the *persona* of the prophet, a coherent depiction of the prophet as presented by the book. One may presume that much of what is recorded there accurately conveys the experiences and happenings of Jeremiah as well as his prophetic message. But that depiction is also the result of the growth of the book and so may involve embellishment from a later time. The reference to Baruch's recording of many of Jeremiah's oracles suggests that the book has a nucleus of Jeremiah's actual oracles. One may assume a high degree of consistency between the portrait of the prophet in the book and the actual events and experiences of Jeremiah's prophetic career. With regard to particular details and the ascription of particular oracles to the prophetic activity of Jeremiah, one may not always be able to say with certainty how close the connection is between the presentation of the prophet and the life of the prophet.

A second question addresses the beginning of Jeremiah's ministry. When did he receive his call and what oracles can be associated with his early career? The superscription at the beginning of the book places Jeremiah's call in the thirteenth year of Josiah's reign, which would be 627 BCE. That date is accepted by many scholars as accurate. Others observe that the book shows little indication of Jeremiah's connection with the reform of Josiah and no oracles can be assuredly dated to the time prior to Josiah's reform in 622 BCE. Only one passage, 3:6-11, is actually dated to "the days of Josiah," while the other references to him allude to his sons and assume Josiah's death (chap. 22). The oracle in 3:6-11 illustrates the problem. William Holladay, who tends to assign as many oracles as possible to Jeremiah, nevertheless says that these verses "are generally agreed to be late and unauthentic to Jrm."[4] John Bright associates them with prophetic preaching in Josiah's time, and Jack Lundbom sees that as a real possibility also. Bright, however, puts these verses prior to the reform of Josiah, while Lundbom says they would have to be late enough for the reform to have been judged a failure.[5] The association of Jeremiah's preaching with Josiah's time is further complicated by the problem of the identity of the "foe from the north," a topic prominent in the early chapters of the book. In Josiah's time, this could hardly have been Assyria, which was no longer attacking Syria-Palestine, or Babylon, which had not yet started to move west. The most likely candidate for the foe from the north is still Babylon, but, such an identification would involve dating those texts to a later time.

The absence of explicit date formulas in chaps. 2–20, where one would expect to find Jeremianic oracles from Josiah's time, creates an ambiguous situation. Some scholars have connected various oracles in chaps. 1–6 to that period.[6] Others have sought to explain in different ways the apparent silence about Josiah's time and his reform. Some have accepted the date in 1:2 but assumed long periods of inactivity on Jeremiah's part. Others see the superscription as conventional and stereotypical and thus unreliable for deriving biographical information.[7] The identification of Jeremiah as a boy when he was called and as having been called before he was even born (1:5-7) has led others to see in these references clues for distinguishing between his "call" and the time he actually began to act as a prophet. One solution is that of Holladay, who sees the dating of Jeremiah's call to the thirteenth year of Josiah as a reference to the prophet's birth—a plausible proposal in the light of the fact that Jeremiah was consecrated and appointed a prophet before he was born.[8] His actual public ministry as a prophet began sometime later. Lundbom distinguishes between Jeremiah's call (1:4-12) and the word of the Lord coming to Jeremiah "a second time" in 1:12-19. He would see in

this "second time" a commissioning of Jeremiah to begin his public ministry, an act that would have taken place at a later time than his call, which came when he was quite young.[9] Both Holladay and Lundbom put great weight on 15:16, where Jeremiah says: "Your words were found, and I ate them." They see here a reference to the "finding" of the book of the law in the Temple (2 Kgs 22:8, 13; 23:2) and Jeremiah's ingesting of these words as his acceptance of the call. For Lundbom, this means that the beginning of the prophetic ministry was in 622 BCE; for Holladay, it means simply that the public ministry began sometime after 622.

These difficulties cannot be resolved now. In the commentary that follows, there is no attempt to date precisely the individual oracles. The book does present most of Jeremiah's prophetic activity as stemming from the time of Jehoiakim and Zedekiah. If there are earlier oracles (and there probably are), they seem to be consistent with his proclamation from 609 BCE onward—in their condemnation of the religious and social practices of the Judeans. It is possible that some of that condemnation could have come before Josiah's reform. It is more likely, however, that such rhetoric followed the deterioration after the reform.

Jeremiah as a prophet is so prominent in the book that any interpretation is forced to pay attention to him and to see in his story and in his struggles something of the book's own proclamation. The anguish of the prophet over the heedlessness of the people overlaps with the anguish of God. Jeremiah's laments provide a glimpse into the inner struggle of those figures who were called by God to an often demanding and, indeed, terrible task. Jeremiah was not alone in resisting and fighting God over the burden laid upon him; witness Elijah and Jonah, for instance. But no other book so vividly portrays that inner anguish created by a burden imposed that cannot be laid down. The biographical material in the book tells the reader something of the cost of obedience to the prophetic calling, a testimony echoed in the lives of other prophets as well. As much as anything, therefore, the overall presentation of the prophet, which centers in his frequent conflicts with false prophets, with kings, with the religious and political leaders of the community, and finally with his God, provides important material for understanding and interpreting the prophetic role in the Old Testament.

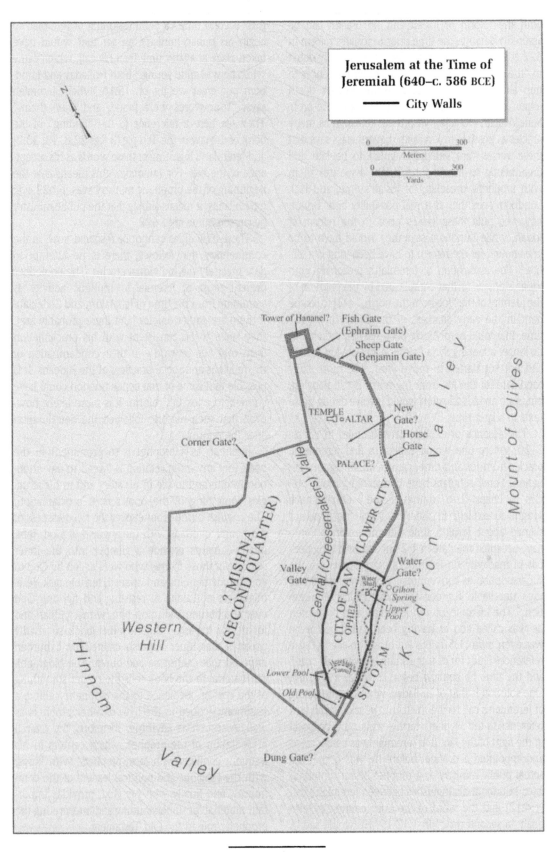

Jerusalem at the Time of
Jeremiah (640–c. 586 BCE)
——— City Walls

COMPOSITION

The beginning of the formation of the book of Jeremiah is evident within the book itself. The first indication is the reference to Jeremiah's dictation of a large collection of his oracles to Baruch, who wrote them down on a scroll (36:2; 45:1). This probably contained significant portions of what is now found in chaps. 1–25, though it could not have been too long if it was read three times in a single day (Jeremiah 36). The summary of Jeremiah's preaching in 25:1-13 is dated to the same year as Jeremiah's dictation to Baruch. Hence that year, 605 BCE, may be the starting point for the preservation and written transmission of Jeremiah's oracles.

That this initial writing down of Jeremiah's oracles did not constitute the final form of the book is indicated not only by the continuation of Jeremiah's prophetic activity for another twenty years but also by the information that after King Jehoiakim burned the scroll Baruch had written, Jeremiah redictated the oracles, Baruch wrote them down again, "and many similar words were added" (36:32). And these are not the only references to oracles being written down. The "Book of Consolation" (chaps. 30–31) receives its customary title from a statement at the beginning in which the Lord tells Jeremiah to "write in a *book*/scroll all that I have spoken to you" (30:2). It is another document that makes up part of the book of Jeremiah, though it, like the other collections, was probably edited and expanded in the process of transmission. Finally, at the end of the book, there is a reference to Jeremiah's writing down oracles against Babylon on a scroll (51:60), presumably what is now chaps. 50–51.

It is clear, therefore, that the process of recording a prophet's oracles does not happen all at once. Nor is it a matter of someone following him around and copying as he speaks, though that may have happened on occasion. That the text makes a point of indicating that the oracles of the first scroll covered a period of "twenty-three years" (25:3) suggests that there was a long process of oral communication. The oracles were first preserved in the memory of the prophet or of the prophet's disciples and then were written down. If the book of Isaiah is any indication, the purpose of writing them down was to provide a way of validating the truth of the prophet's message because, at a later time, one could read the record and see that the prophet had announced ahead of time what was going to happen (Isa 8:16-22). Like Baruch's scroll of Jeremiah's oracles, the process of writing down and adding continued.

It is not possible to say now what the two Baruch scrolls consisted of, though many hypotheses have been proposed. In the light of the Lord's desire to bring the people to repentance (36:2-3), expressed in the first scroll, one may assume that those oracles in the first part of the book that urge repentance in order that the Lord might forgive the people would have been prominent in the first scroll. Inasmuch as the Lord's instruction to write the words down a second time includes an announcement of punishment of the king and the people (36:28-31), the second scroll would probably have included the announcements of judgment that are so prominent in Jeremiah's prophecy. One may presume, further, that not only were the two scrolls brought together but additions were made to both over a considerable period of time.

There is considerable evidence of a long period of composition. The most obvious is the presence of two different textual witnesses to the Hebrew of Jeremiah: one in the Masoretic Text and the other in the Septuagint (see below). It is difficult to derive either one of these from the other. The Jeremianic tradition was dynamic and not fixed. A second indicator of a complex history of the formation of the book is the number of duplications and repetitions within it (e.g., 6:12-15 and 8:10-12 or 10:12-16 and 51:15-19). It is possible that some of the repetitions are the prophet's own reuse of stock material, but in some instances it appears as if they are the result of an editing process. Furthermore, there are also places where the words of the prophet are duplications of verses or passages from other prophetic books. Yet another signal to the reader that the book went through a process of growth that extended beyond Jeremiah's own words is the appendix at the end, Jeremiah 52, which is preceded by the sentence, "Thus far are the words of Jeremiah" (51:64). One might take that sentence as a testimony that everything in the first 51 chapters comes from Jeremiah, but when one notices how much of the book is *about* the prophet and not simply his words, it becomes clear that the book is built on Jeremiah's oracles but has grown both due to his long prophetic career and due to the editorial process that started with the narratives about Jeremiah.

Three kinds of material have been brought together in the composition of the book: (1) prophetic oracles in poetic style (esp. in chaps. 2–25); (2) biographical material (esp. chaps. 26–29 and 34–45); and (3) prose sayings by the prophet, often showing deuteronomic affinities. This last type occurs as long prose discourses (e.g., 7:1–8:3; 11:1-17; 25:1-11), as shorter prose oracles and sayings scattered throughout the poetry (e.g., 3:6-11), and as prose sayings transmitted in connection with the biographical material (e.g., 21:1-10). Considerable debate has arisen over the degree to which these different types of material, specifically the poetic oracles and the prose sayings, come from the prophet himself or represent later additions to the Jeremianic collection. It is generally assumed that the poetic oracles were proclaimed by the prophet. Certainly most of the pre-exilic prophetic writings are poetic in form. One must be careful, however, about assuming that the poetic form certifies authenticity. In other poetic books, such as Amos 9, there are clearly poetic additions to the original core of the book, and the same is probably the case with Jeremiah.

The prose prophetic sayings have provoked the most discussion. The clear presence of deuteronomic language in many has led some scholars to see them as essentially deuteronomic or deuteronomistic constructions from a later time. Others have argued that while the form may be prose, the language is as much Jeremianic as it is deuteronomic and not infrequently is anticipated in the poetic oracles. This would mean that either these prose sayings should be attributed to Jeremiah or that they at least originate with Jeremiah and preserve, as Bright puts it, the "gist" of Jeremiah's proclamation, now edited and cloaked in language that reflects verbal expansion or adaptation of the prophet's word by deuteronomic or other editors.[10] This process of preserving, transmitting, and reformulating Jeremiah's oracles sometimes may have produced prose versions that were close to the prophet's perspective and at other times may have led to more self-conscious theological reworking in the light of a new situation confronting those who preserved and transmitted Jeremiah's prophetic legacy.

Linguistic arguments have been used in various ways in this debate. The fact that language usage in these prose sermons can be interpreted in different ways suggests that the process of composition

whereby Jeremianic oracles were expanded and added to was multiform. That would include simple expansions and more thorough theological reworking with a particular *Tendenz*. But it also may have involved exegesis or comment on earlier texts in such a fashion that was quite particular and ad hoc, not part of a coherent theological or systematic reworking of the entire book.[11]

Brevard Childs has suggested that chap. 25 points to an oral communication of the oracles from Josiah's time to Jehoiakim's time (the poetic oracles) and then to a recording of them in "a written condensation of prophetic threat" (prose sermons), which interpreted the prophet's proclamation and ministry in relation to Scripture—namely Deuteronomy.

> From the perspective of the tradition a new understanding of Jeremiah emerged from the events of history, which, far from being a distortion, confirmed the prior word of scripture. The canonical shaping of the Jeremianic tradition accepted the Deuteronomic framework as an authentic interpretation of Jeremiah's ministry which it used to frame the earlier poetic material.[12]

Such an understanding may be too simple a handling of a complex problem and suggests more coherence than many see in the final outcome. To the extent, however, that one finds in the prose material a later editing that shows some significant affinities with deuteronomic language and theology, Childs's approach resists the tendency to dismiss this level of the text in favor of the authentic Jeremiah material, as many are wont to do. His interpretation refocuses the reader's attention on the final outcome, but without ignoring earlier levels of the text.

Variations of this effort to see a coherent and theological development arising out of the prose sayings and sermons can be found elsewhere. For example, Walter Brueggemann has proposed a two-stage development of the book, a move from judgment to hope that reflects the two literatures of the book, Jeremianic and deuteronomic.[13] This two-stage development has been argued in a more detailed way by Louis Stuhlman, who sees a move from dismantling the old world in chaps. 1–25 to new beginnings from that shattered world being worked out in chaps. 26–52. Stuhlman suggests that the prose discourses have been carefully placed to provide a framework for chaps. 1–25, one that helps to provide equilibrium, echoing and enunciating notes that are present in the poetry and ultimately creating "structural unity and cohesion." The result is a "narratorial construction" that makes three major claims: (1) Judah has rejected the prophetic word of Jeremiah, (2) the result of that rejection is an impending and just punishment, and (3) the end of the old system prepares the groundwork for a newly emergent community.[14] These salutary efforts to see some coherence in the various "sources" or tradition complexes and to affirm the significance of the later editorial stages of the book's composition should not cause the interpreter to ignore or smooth over inconcinnities in the text, signs of a less tidy growth that surely was a part of the creation of the book, as is clearly indicated in the different textual forms of Jeremiah.

TEXT

The significant variation between the two main ancient versions of the book of Jeremiah, the Hebrew (or Masoretic Text, MT) and the Greek (or Septuagint, LXX), presents the interpreter with major problems. The Greek text is about one-seventh to one-eighth shorter than the MT, which means that either a considerable amount of text has been lost by scribal error or intention in the Greek or text has been added to the Hebrew. Sometimes the differences are just a word or a phrase, but often they are several verses (e.g., 8:10-12; 33:14-26; 39:4-13 are not present in the Greek). Furthermore, the order of chapters in the LXX differs from that of the MT after 25:13a. The oracles against the foreign nations in chaps. 46–51 appear in the LXX after 25:13a and in a different order from that of the MT of chaps. 46–51. The discovery of some fragments of Jeremiah among the Hebrew texts from Qumran has put the discussion of this difference on a new footing, especially since the texts include Hebrew fragments reflecting the Hebrew behind both the Septuagint and the Masoretic Text.[15]

It is now the general consensus that we have, in effect, two texts of Jeremiah that reach back to earlier Hebrew forms of the book, one apparently coming from Egypt and preserved in the Septuagint and one apparently coming from Babylon or Palestine and preserved now in the Masoretic Text. It also seems that the Greek text is not generally an abbreviated text, while the MT tends to be expansionistic. This tendency of the MT is especially evident with regard to the addition of formulas, epithets, and the like. In this regard, the LXX testifies to a superior text, if one means by that an earlier form in which expansions evident in the Hebrew of the MT had not yet occurred.[16] But the divergences are significant enough that we must ask whether they do not reflect a development of the text in two different contexts such that the end result is not simply a superior text testifying to an earlier form of the Hebrew (that is, the LXX); rather, it may be a combination of two Hebrew texts that had a separate history over a long enough time to represent, in part at least, different developments of the book and not merely scribal mistakes and corrections in transmission. The MT and the LXX represent not simply two different stages but also two different streams in the literary history of the book—one given more to expansion, the other less so. Literary growth and textual transmission, therefore, have blurred considerably. The result, as one interpreter has put it, is "a fluid tradition, our written remains serving as 'snapshots' capturing the situation of a moment."[17] To what extent the differences in the growth of the text are systematic and wide-ranging or more ad hoc and particular remains debatable.

The position and order of the oracles against the nations (chaps. 46–51) are two elements within the larger differences. Janzen has argued plausibly that the oracles against the nations circulated separately as one of the component parts of the book of Jeremiah (like the Book of Consolation in chaps. 30–31, for instance).[18] They were inserted into the middle of the book (so the LXX), reflecting a tendency also evident in Isaiah and Ezekiel to put the oracles concerning other nations in the middle of a prophetic book. Chapter 25 already provided a connection with its oracular material having to do with foreign nations. Janzen further supposes that this new form of the Jeremianic corpus would have made other manuscripts obsolete in their existing form and that, rather than simply destroying them, scribes would have attached the corpus of oracles against the nations to the end of the book as an appendix. Because the order of the oracles in the Hebrew corresponds roughly to the order of the nations listed in 25:19-26, Janzen assumes that this is a secondary development designed to make these oracles conform to their context; there is no clear reason for a secondary development producing the Greek order of the oracles.[19]

If such an analysis is correct, and if there are other data to support it, then the reader is still confronted with two different traditions. One may grow out of the other, but the results are different traditions and texts. There is a sense in which once the egg is broken and scrambled this much, it is not possible to put it back together again. That is, the community of faith that carries forward the MT as its Scripture reads this material in a different way than is reflected in the LXX. The book comes to an end now in its Hebrew form with the oracles against the nations and especially with the oracle against Babylon. That ending gives a particular direction or shape to the book.

The interpreter, faced with this complex textual situation, may be able to use one version to help establish a "better" text or to make corrections of obvious mistakes in the transmission of the Jeremianic corpus. But in the end, it is still necessary to choose which of these two ancient textual traditions of the book of Jeremiah will function as the base text, the subject of interpretation for the interpreter and the community to which he or she belongs. Both texts have functioned as Scripture for parts of the Jewish and Christian communities. In this instance, the basis for comment and interpretation is the text that has been my own Scripture and that of most of the readers of this commentary series, the Hebrew Old Testament. This commentary, therefore, is based on the Masoretic Text and does not seek to reconstruct an earlier form of the text of Jeremiah, except in cases where obvious and unintentional errors have occurred.

FOR FURTHER READING

Commentaries:

Bright, John. *Jeremiah*. AB 21. Garden City: Doubleday, 1965.

Brueggemann, Walter. *A Commentary on Jeremiah: Exile and Homecoming*. Grand Rapids: Eerdmans, 1998.

Calvin, John. *Commentaries on the Book of the Prophet Jeremiah and the Lamentations*. 5 vols. Grand Rapids: Eerdmans, 1950.

Carroll, Robert P. *Jeremiah*. OTL. Philadelphia: Westminster, 1986.

Clements, Ronald. *Jeremiah*. Interpretation. Atlanta: John Knox, 1988.

Craigie, Peter, Page H. Kelley, and Joel F. Drinkard Jr. *Jeremiah 1–25*. WBC 26. Dallas: Word, 1991.

Fretheim, Terence E. *Jeremiah*. Smyth & Helwys Bible Commentary. Macon, Ga.: Smyth & Helwys, 2002.

Keown, Gerald L., Pamela J. Scalise, and Thomas J. Smothers. *Jeremiah 26–52*. WBC 27. Dallas: Word, 1995.

Holladay, William L. *Jeremiah 1: A Commentary on the Book of the Prophet Jeremiah Chapters 1–25*. Hermeneia. Philadelphia: Fortress, 1986.

———. *Jeremiah 2*. Hermeneia. Philadelphia: Fortress, 1989.

Lundbom, Jack R. *Jeremiah 1–20*. AB 21A. New York: Doubleday, 1999.

McKane, William. *A Critical and Exegetical Commentary on Jeremiah*. 2 vols. ICC. Edinburgh: T & T Clark, 1986, 1996.

O'Connor, Kathleen. "Jeremiah." In *The Women's Bible Commentary*. Edited by Carol A. Newsom and Sharon H. Ringe. Louisville: Westminster/John Knox, 1992.

Thompson, J. A. *The Book of Jeremiah*. NICOT. Grand Rapids: Eerdmans, 1980.

Other Studies:

Bauer, Angela. *Gender in the Book of Jeremiah: A Feminist-Literary Reading*. New York: Peter Lang, 1999.

Baumgartner, Walter. *Jeremiah's Poems of Lament*. Sheffield: Sheffield Academic Press, 1987.

Berridge, John MacLennan. *Prophet, People, and the Word of Yahweh: An Examination of Form and Content in the Proclamation of the Prophet Jeremiah*. Basel Studies of Theology 4. Zürich: EVZ-Verlag, 1970.

Friebel, Kelvin. *Jeremiah's and Ezekiel's Sign-Acts: Rhetorical Nonverbal Communication*. JSOTSupp 283. Sheffield: Sheffield Academic Press, 1999.

Holladay, William L. *The Architecture of Jeremiah 1–20*. Lewisburg: Bucknell University Press, 1976.

———. *Jeremiah: A Fresh Reading*. New York: Pilgrim, 1990.

Janzen, J. Gerald. *Studies in the Text of Jeremiah*. HSM 6. Cambridge, Mass.: Harvard University Press, 1973.

King, Philip J. *Jeremiah: An Archaeological Companion.* Louisville: Westminster/John Knox, 1993.

Laleman de-Winkel, Hetty. *Jeremiah in Prophetic Tradition: An Examination of the Book of Jeremiah in the Light of Israel's Prophetic Traditions.* Louvian: Peeters, 2000.

Lundbom, Jack R. *Jeremiah: A Study in Ancient Hebrew Rhetoric.* SBLDS 18. Missoula: Scholars Press, 1975; 2nd ed., Winona Lake: Eisenbrauns, 1997.

Nicholson, Ernest. *Preaching to the Exiles: A Study of the Prose Tradition in the Book of Jeremiah.* Oxford: Blackwell, 1970.

O'Connor, Kathleen M. *The Confessions of Jeremiah: Their Interpretation and Role in Chapters 1–25.* SBLDS 94. Atlanta: Scholars Press, 1988.

Overholt, Thomas W. *The Threat of Falsehood: A Study in the Theology of the Book of Jeremiah.* SBTSS 16. Naperville: Allenson, 1970.

Parke-Taylor, Geoffrey H. *The Formation of the Book of Jeremiah: Doublets and Recurring Phrases.* SBLMS 51. Atlanta, Ga.: Society of Biblical Literature, 2000.

Perdue, Leo G., and Brian W. Kovacs, eds. *A Prophet to the Nations: Essays in Jeremiah Studies.* Winona Lake: Eisenbrauns, 1984.

Sharp, Carolyn J. *Prophecy and Ideology in Jeremiah: Struggles for Authority in the Deutero-Jeremianic Prose.* New York: T&T Clark, 2003.

Stuhlman, Louis. *Order Amid Chaos: Jeremiah as Symbolic Tapestry.* The Biblical Seminar 57. Sheffield: Sheffield Academic, 1998.

ENDNOTES

1. W. L. Holladay, *Jeremiah 1: A Commentary on the Book of the Prophet Jeremiah, Chapters 1–25,* Hermeneia (Philadelphia: Fortress, 1986) 1-10.

2. R. P. Carroll, *Jeremiah,* OTL (Philadelphia: Westminster, 1986) 33-37.

3. On the relation of Jeremiah's laments to their narrative context and their use of typical lament language and expressions found in the book of Psalms, see Patrick D. Miller, *Interpreting the Psalms* (Philadelphia: Fortress, 1986).

4. W. L. Holladay, *Jeremiah 1,* 77.

5. John Bright, *Jeremiah,* AB 21 (Garden City, N.Y.: Doubleday, 1965) 26; Jack R. Lundbom, *Jeremiah 1–20,* AB 21A (Garden City, N.Y.: Doubleday, 1999) 308.

6. E.g., John Bright, *Jeremiah.*

7. E.g., R. P. Carroll, *Jeremiah.*

8. W. L. Holladay, *Jeremiah 1,* 1. See also W. L. Holladay, *Jeremiah: A Fresh Reading* (New York: Pilgrim, 1990) 13-15.

9. Jack R. Lundbom, *Jeremiah 1–20,* 107-9.

10. John Bright, *Jeremiah,* 59.

11. W. McKane, "Relations Between Poetry and Prose in the Book of Jeremiah with Special Reference to Jeremiah III 6–11 and XII 14–17," *Congress Volume Vienna 1980,* ed. J. A. Emerton, VTSup (Leiden: E. J. Brill, 1981) 220-37.

12. Brevard Childs, *Introduction to the Old Testament as Scripture* (Philadelphia: Fortress, 1979) 345-47.

13. Walter Brueggemann, "A Second Reading of Jeremiah After the Dismantling," *Ex Auditu* 1 (1985) 156-68.

14. Louis Stuhlman, *Order Amid Chaos: Jeremiah as Symbolic Tapestry,* The Biblical Seminar 57 (Sheffield: Sheffield Academic, 1998) chap. 1.

15. These fragments have been published in *Qumran Cave 4. X: The Prophets,* Discoveries in the Judean Desert 15, ed. Eugene Ulrich et al. (Oxford: Clarendon, 1997) 145-207. For a brief discussion of what is contained in the fragments, see Jack R. Lundbom, *Jeremiah 1–20,* 62-63. For the earliest and still primary discussion of the text-critical significance of the Qumran material, see J. Gerald Janzen, *Studies in the Text of Jeremiah,* HSM 6 (Cambridge, Mass.: Harvard University Press, 1973) 173-84.

16. Lundbom, *Jeremiah 1–20,* 57-62, has argued on behalf of the superiority of the Masoretic Text, claiming a much larger number of haplographies in the Hebrew lying behind the Greek than most text critics have been prepared to do.

17. David J. Reimer, *The Oracles Against Babylon in Jeremiah 50–51: A Horror Among the Nations* (San Francisco: Mellen, 1993) 155.

18. J. Gerald Janzen, *Studies in the Text of Jeremiah.*

19. J. Gerald Janzen, *Studies in the Text of Jeremiah.*

THE BOOK OF
LAMENTATIONS

KATHLEEN M. O'CONNOR

Lamentations is a searing book of taut, charged poetry on the subject of unspeakable suffering. The poems emerge from a deep wound, a whirlpool of pain, toward which the images, metaphors, and voices of the poetry can only point. It is, in part, the rawness of the hurt expressed in the book that has gained Lamentations a secure, if marginal, place in the liturgies of Judaism and Christianity. Its stinging cries for help, its voices begging God to see, its protests to God who hides behind a cloud—all create a space where communal and personal pain can be reexperienced, seen, and perhaps healed. Although the book of Lamentations is short, containing only five poems, it is a literary jewel and a rich resource for theological reflection and worship. Indeed, its recovery in our communal lives could lead to a greater flourishing of life amid our own wounds and the woundedness of the world.

HISTORICAL SETTING

A short collection of five poems, Lamentations is a poetic response to a national tragedy. Its poems reflect conditions following the invasion and collapse of the nation, particularly of its capital city, and of the destruction of economic and social life among the citizenry. A long-standing and firm tradition of interpretation places the book in the period following Babylonian military assaults on Judah in 597, 587, and 582BCE.

Iain Provan, however, has disputed the traditional dating and location of the book.[1] He claims that there is insufficient evidence to tie the book firmly to this or to any other precise historical period. Not only are the poems metaphoric and the language elusive, but also the author as a poet writes with great power in ways that do not represent particular events but simply evoke them. In Provan's view, other invasions and destructions of

Jerusalem could equally have produced the conditions that gave birth to this literature.

The helpful conclusion to be drawn from Provan's refreshing academic heresy is that the biblical text need not be tied to a particular historical setting to be moving and effective literature. By severing the book from precise historical connections, the interpreter quickly enables the book to serve as a metaphor that may illuminate many different situations of intense pain and suffering. Provan does not succeed, however, in dislodging Lamentations completely from the Babylonian era. Though he is correct about the paucity of evidence explicitly connecting the book to this time, he does not credit the traditional interpretations that locate the book in Palestine after the Babylonian invasion. If the invasion of Judah and Jerusalem is not the precise tragedy underlying Lamentations, then it is at least a central catastrophe in Israel's history that provides an illuminating backdrop for understanding the fury, grief, and disorientation that this book expresses.

In the aftermath of the Babylonian invasions of Jerusalem, survivors would have wondered whether they could continue to survive as a people. Leading families had been deported to Babylon; the king's palace, the Temple, and the city walls had been razed. A long siege of the city had left many dead, ill, and suffering from famine. Along with overwhelming physical and social devastation came the collapse of the community's entire theological and symbolic world. The words of the prophets and the promises to Abraham and to David had turned empty. Where was the God who promised to dwell with them in Zion, to be with the house of David forever? Where was the God who brought them to the land of promise? How had God contributed to the devastation of their world?

Whether the Babylonian invasion actually occasioned the writing and composition of this book or whether later tradition emerged from reflection on the book in the light of the nation's fall and assigned it to that time and place cannot be known for certain. But the traditional connections of Lamentations with the fall of Jerusalem and Judah to Babylon indicate the way the book served the community. The book came to be seen as an expression of grief and outrage at heart-stopping tragedy—and the tragedy that provoked its composition was massive.

AUTHORSHIP, VERSIONS, CANONICAL PLACEMENT

One of the reasons for the traditional dating of Lamentations to the Babylonian period is because tradition has also held that the prophet Jeremiah was its author. The Hebrew or Masoretic Text (MT) does not name any author, but the later Septuagint (LXX) translation adds an interpretive opening line. After the captivity of Israel and the desolation of Jerusalem, "Jeremiah sat weeping and lamented this lamentation over Jerusalem."

Other features of the book associate it with Jeremiah. The speaker in Lam 3:52-54 portrays his captivity in terms that vaguely resemble Jeremiah's captivities in the court of the guard in Jer 37:11-21 and 38:1-13. Jeremiah's own reputation is that of the weeping prophet, and hence, the spirit of Lamentations accords with some of his gloomy prophecy.

Jeremiah is the author of Lamentations in a symbolic sense but probably not in a literal sense. Authorship in the ancient world did not follow modern customs. In order to bring books under the aura of heroes and their moral authority, writings were often ascribed to them. Despite loose thematic and metaphorical connections between Lamentations and the book of Jeremiah, numerous features of Lamentations argue against his authorship, not the least of which is the fact that many positions in Lamentations appear to contradict Jeremiah's prophecies.[2]

Just as there is inadequate data to determine Jeremiah's possible role in the production of the book, so also no clear consensus has emerged regarding how many authors were involved in composing the poems. The work of one poet or several may be gathered here. This commentary does not attempt to decide these questions but assumes a unity of material in the book's present form.

The Masoretic Text separates Lamentations from Jeremiah and places Lamentations among the Writings, though that position has varied.[3] Hebrew practice places Lamentations among the *Megillot*, or five liturgical scrolls. By contrast, the LXX, which asserts Jeremianic authorship, also places Lamentations after the prophetic books, sometimes directly following Jeremiah and sometimes with the book of Baruch intervening between them. In addition to the MT and the LXX, there is a later Aramaic version, or targum, that translates the text in a midrashic manner to highlight and expand religious aspects of the Hebrew text.[4]

LITURGICAL USE

Lamentations holds a special place in liturgical services of Judaism and Christianity. The Jewish community reads the Lamentation scroll on the ninth of Ab. That date commemorates five calamities, including the destruction of the First and Second Temples and the destruction of Jerusalem by the Romans. The liturgical atmosphere for the reading is like a public funeral, and the text may be chanted.[5]

Christians use selections of Lamentations during Holy Week services in the recitation of Tenebrae and Good Friday liturgies. Christians lament the death of Jesus, their own sins, and, symbolically, their own eventual deaths. Beyond these special liturgical occasions, however, Lamentations is largely ignored in public worship, in preaching, and for meditative use. Many factors may contribute to this neglect of Lamentations, including its troubling content of relentless grief and anger and the predominance of denial in the dominant culture of North America.

STRUCTURE AND LITERARY FEATURES

Poetic beauty, dramatic power, and puzzling ambiguities converge in Lamentations. The book's artfulness gives it the capacity to draw readers into the overwhelming human struggles portrayed in the poems and to embroil readers in unanswerable questions. Alphabetical and formal structures, mixtures of voices, and the relationship of the five poems to each other contribute to the book's intense and terrible potency and raise key issues in its interpretation. These features overlap in interpretation, and decisions about form and voice contribute to the understanding of the relationships of the poems to each other.[6]

First, each of the five poems draws on the lament form and is built in some way upon the Hebrew alphabet, but within that framework are wide variations in form and structure. Second, a number of different voices or poetic speakers appear within and across the poems. Third, the relationships among the five poems are complex and strongly debated by modern interpreters, but readers must account for them in determining the book's purposes. What hangs in the balance in this decision are the purposes of the book and the status of hope in the book. Is the third, and only hopeful, poem the book's "monumental center,"[7] or is hope swallowed up by the doubt and despair of the surrounding poems?

By their very presence, these literary dilemmas prevent swift resolution and easy dismissal of the enormous sense of abandonment and injustice expressed in these poems. The book's literary puzzles, its mixtures of forms, voices, and unevenly shaped poems may give evidence of deliberate crafting, a chiseling and polishing of words, images, and poetic forms that draw readers into a maelstrom and force them to find their own way out.

Alphabetical Forms and Literary Genre. The Hebrew alphabet contributes to the structuring of the book's individual poems in two ways. First, the book's first four poems are acrostics. They are written in alphabetical order so that each verse or line begins with a sequential letter of the Hebrew alphabet. The poem in chapter 3 intensifies the acrostic form by including three lines in each verse that begin with the same alphabetical letter.[8]

The second way the alphabet structures the poems concerns their length. In accordance with the twenty-two lines of the Hebrew alphabet, all five poems contain twenty-two lines or multiples thereof. The first three poems are each sixty-six lines long. The fourth poem contains only forty-four lines, and the fifth, and only non-acrostic, poem contains only twenty-two lines. While the poems gain from alphabetical structuring, the diversity of their relationships to the alphabet indicates tensions among them. Each poem stands freely on its own, but how do they relate to each other?

Chapter One	Chapter Two
acrostic	acrostic
22 verses of three lines each	22 verses of three lines each
(66 lines)	(66 lines)

Chapter Three
acrostic
66 verses of one line each with three verses per letter

Chapter Four	Chapter Five
acrostic	not acrostic
22 verses of two lines each	22 verses of one line each
(44 lines)	(22 lines)

The acrostic form itself has been the subject of much scrutiny. What are the purposes of poetic alphabetizing? Acrostics may have been used for aesthetic purposes,[9] to show off the poet's skill, or as an aid to memory.[10] Mnemonic purposes alone, however, do not explain acrostic use, since there are many poems in the Hebrew Bible but few acrostics.[11] More evocative and symbolic purposes may better explain the use of the alphabet in Lamentations. Acrostics impose order and organization on shapeless chaos and unmanageable pain, and they imply that the suffering depicted in the poems is total. Nothing can be added to it, for suffering extends from "א to ת" (*aleph* to *taw*).

Whatever the motivation for their use, however, Daniel Grossberg observes that acrostics impose unity upon various voices, images, and perspectives within the individual poems.[12] Heater observes that the acrostics divide the content of the poems with the middle letters of the Hebrew alphabet.[13]

Besides their alphabetical structures, the poems in Lamentations also draw on lament forms and funeral dirges and, in particular, on the lament over the fallen city.[14] Laments abound in the Bible and in the literature of the ancient Near East. The book of Psalms contains communal laments that speak in the plural voice of the community, and individual laments in the voice of a single person.[15] Laments are prayers of protest, complaint, and grief over a disaster, and with great passion they appeal to God for deliverance. They arise from faith in the power and willingness of God to save. They insist that the world is an open system in which divine intervention is always possible.

The lament over the city was a common literary form in the ancient Near East. Mesopotamian city laments, for example, exhibit some common features with Lamentations, including their somber mood at the destruction, themes of divine abandonment and involvement in the destruction, descriptions of calamity, massive weeping, as well as the use of poetic devices of many voices or personas, personification of the city, and marked reversals in the city's fate.[16]

Lamentations, however, significantly adapts the Mesopotamian form. It transfers the Mesopotamian treatment of the city's patron goddess to the figure of personified Jerusalem. Goddesses were heavenly patrons of their city, but they were powerless to prevent destruction caused by other gods and often wept over the city's destruction.[17] In Lamentations, Jerusalem is personified as a female, but she is merely a city, not a goddess. The many similarities between the city laments and Lamentations indicate that the biblical book emerged from a world that possessed common artistic forms for the expression of grief, rage, and protest.

Interlaced with lament forms in the book are themes typical of the funeral dirge. These include a mournful cry for the one who has died, a proclamation of death, contrast with previous circumstances of the dead person, and the reaction of bystanders.[18] When the poet or poets of Lamentations sought to give expression to the unspeakable pain their community endured, they drew on the repertoire of form, imagery, and metaphor available in the ancient world. From this familiar and traditional raw material, they created a complex artistic expression in the interplay of acrostic, lament, and dirge.

Voices. One of Lamentations' most effective literary devices is its use of different speakers.[19] Multiple poetic voices interweave, overlap, and contradict each other. The speakers are literary creations who offer testimony in the thick of catastrophe. Voices of a narrator, Daughter Zion, an unidentified man, and the community lament, protest, and attempt to cope with the tragedy they have survived. The book is dramatized speech.

A narrator, an omniscient third-person reporter, appears in chapters 1, 2, and 4. In the first two chapters he introduces and comments upon the circumstances and words of Daughter Zion, who appears only in the first two chapters. She is the city of Jerusalem, personified as a woman, a princess, a lover, a widow, a daughter, and above all, a mother. The principal speaker in chapter 3 is a man, a shamed and humiliated captive, entrapped and reaching for hope. The voice of the community appears briefly in chapters 3 and 4 but takes over in speech directed to God in chapter 5.

The interplay of these voices allows the book to approach the massive suffering of the destroyed city from many viewpoints. The city itself becomes a person, weeping over its pain, screaming for aid, and protesting its deplorable conditions. The defeated man in chapter 3 grasps for hope, but in chapters 4 and 5 his words are quickly replaced by dour accounts of suffering from the narrator and the community. Westermann observes that the speakers are not individuals but "are at the same time both lamenters and the lamented."[20] They signify the destroyed city and its citizens. Each voice articulates the pain of the community.

The personification of Jerusalem as Daughter Zion, or "Daughter of Zion,"[21] has an ancient tradition that receives further development in Lamentations. The ancient world commonly understood cities as female and personified them as divine wives of the resident god. Biblical representations of Daughter Zion draw on these depictions but do not understand the city as a deity. In Lamentations, the personified city is the punished wife of Yahweh, who fulfills all the prophecies against her in the books of Jeremiah, Ezekiel, and Hosea.[22]

Female personification of Jerusalem and Judah in Lamentations comes with strong associations that lend themselves to poetry of woundedness and grief and shame. Daughter Zion is a woman with a past, a disastrous present, and no future. Mintz observes, "The serviceableness of Jerusalem as an abandoned fallen woman lies in the precise register of pain it articulates."[23] In contrast to the dead, whose sufferings are finished, the defiled woman who survives is a living witness to pain that knows no end.

Missing from the poetic voices in Lamentations is the voice of God. The missing voice looms over the book. The speakers refer to God, call for help, ask God to look, accuse God of hiding from them, of attacking and forgetting them—but God never responds. The speakers interpret, provide motives for, and attack the absent one, but God never steps into the sound studio. Thick, soundproof walls bar the suffering voices from the one who caused their suffering and the only one they believe can comfort them, save them, and stop the suffering. Unlike Job, who receives a divine response to his protestations, the suffering characters in this book never gain an audience. Why is God silent? No simple answer to this question emerges.

Relations Among the Poems. How the five poems with their diverse voices and viewpoints and their varied alphabetic structures fit together and interact is the major issue in the book's interpretation. Until recently, many interpreters, both Christian and Jewish, claimed that chapter 3 is the book's literary and theological center.[24] There are good reasons for such an interpretive decision. Located in the middle of the book, chapter 3 intensifies the acrostic form and expresses hope in an extended way to suggest that the triumph of hope over suffering is the book's main point.

Despite its midpoint location, however, chapter 3 is not bordered by symmetrically composed poems to clinch such an interpretive decision. The poems that precede chapter 3 do not match the poems that follow it in length or form. Instead, chapters 4 and 5 grow shorter, and the acrostic form disappears altogether in chapter 5. These formal variations create a lopsided structure of the whole, leading some interpreters to think that hope is drowned by the reality of suffering and by a silent God.

William Shea suggested that the book's asymmetrical shape imitates the rhythmic pattern found in funeral dirges in ancient Israel, called the "limping," or *qînâ* (קינה), meter.[25] This rhythmic pattern contains three long beats and two short ones. In Shea's analogy, the shortening of the poems and the disappearance of the acrostic form in the latter part of Lamentations construct an ending that drifts off, like the funeral dirge, in grief without resolution. The rhythmical pattern dies away "because it was written in remembrance of Jerusalem, the city that died away."[26]

Although the presence of this meter as a structuring device in the book is far from certain, since Shea transfers a meter found in single lines to five poems, his suggestion is provocative. His treatment of the book that decenters the importance of chapter 3 and its expressions of hope has found strong development in recent interpretation. Linafelt, Dobbs-Alsopp, and Provan deemphasize chapter 3 for a variety of reasons and point to the book's movement toward protest and doubt rather than faith and reconciliation.[27]

Linafelt identifies a number of interpretive biases that have led interpreters to find chapter 3 to be the book's hermeneutical key. These biases include preference for the male voice of the "strong man," Christian identification of the figure in chapter 3 with Christ, and preference for interpretation that favors human reconciliation with God through repentance.[28] But hope does not triumph in the book; it is merely one point of view, more tenuously arrived at even in chapter 3 than commentators have admitted. What the book offers instead of resolute hope, confidence, and reconciliation with God are "intersecting perspectival discourses,"[29] speeches that move across trauma, rage, hope, doubt, and tired dismay. No single speaker, no particular viewpoint silences the others. Instead, multiple speakers try to find expression for grief, "to articulate the inexpressible, and turn death into beauty."[30]

The poems try to house grief in familiar and ordered language commonly found in other biblical laments. But these poems in Lamentations use traditional lament language in ways that are gripping and concrete. Within the poems the same Hebrew roots and sounds appear, get repeated, disappear, and reappear.[31] Provan observes that the language is metaphorical, imagistic, and conventional, rather than representational.[32] The book is not trying to mimic reality but to evoke and re-create the suffering of the community. The poems are masterpieces of artistic intricacy in which the speakers hammer out their pain in rhythms and circles of sorrow. Ultimately the poems cannot build a shelter for grief and rage. Landy proposes that the poetry conveys its own inadequacy to the task by fading out in a whimper and in an effectual cry for revenge.[33]

LAMENTATIONS AND THE ARTS

A brief sampling of the artistic appropriations of Lamentations shows the potency of Lamentations in new contexts. Musicians have employed its lyrics for liturgical music and for more general compositions. In the sixteenth century, Thomas Tallis set "The Lamentations of Jeremiah" to music, and in the twentieth century Pablo Casals did likewise in "O Vos Omnes," known in English as "O Ye People." For Lent of 1956, Hungarian composer Lajos Bardos wrote a musical setting for eight verses of chapter 5 to lament national shame, entrapment, and guilt during the Soviet occupation of Hungary. Leonard Bernstein wrote a "Jeremiah" symphony that uses Lamentations, and Igor Stravinsky composed "Threni" in 1958.

Although Polish composer Henryk Gorecki's Symphony No. 3 has no direct connection with the book of Lamentations, the symphony is a haunting lament that employs lyrics of great sadness in the form of testimony from a prison wall and of a mother's lament for her disappeared child. In the exquisite sorrow of its music, this work expresses communal heartbreak at the unspeakable horrors of the twentieth century. The work's surprising popularity among classical music lovers in the United States may witness to the stored-up sorrow and unspoken anger in the general culture.

Among literary reincarnations of Lamentations two works demand attention. One is a short memoir by Naomi Seidman, "Burning the Book of Lamentations," in which Seidman yearns for the end of lamenting and for the day all Jews can burn laments forever. The other is a work of fiction by Cynthia Ozick entitled *The Shawl: A Story and Novella*, in which Daughter Zion's loss of her children is reenacted in a mother's exceedingly tragic loss of her small daughter in a concentration camp.[34]

A painting by Rembrandt, entitled *The Prophet Jeremiah Lamenting the Destruction of Jerusalem*, hangs in the Rijksmuseum in Amsterdam. For the Union Church of Pocantico Hills, New York, Marc Chagall created a small jewel of a stained-glass window of Jeremiah, whom he identified by referring to Lam 3:1-3. Fritz Eichenberg's etching of *The Lamentations of Jeremiah* pictures a man in chains, a woman clutching a baby, and a small child clinging to the captured man.[35]

THE BOOK'S TITLES

Because the Hebrew Bible names its books by their first word or words, the Hebrew title of Lamentations is ספר איכה (*seper ʾêkâ*), literally "the book of How."[36] איכה (*ʾêkâ*) is an exclamation of shock that means "how" or "alas," and should, perhaps, be pronounced with a catch in the voice or with a gasp: "How lonely lies the city upon the hill!" (Lam 1:1). Seidman suggests that behind the declarative *how* of the title lurks an interrogative "how" that questions the means and even the possibility of telling about this unspeakable catastrophe.[37] The opening exclamation of pity and astonishment hangs over the entire book and reappears as the first word of chapters 2 and 4. In the literal rendering of the title, "How," as opposed to "Lamentations," which derives from the Greek translation (θρῆνοι *Thrēnoi*), Jean-Marc Droin finds a close approximation to the book's meaning. In his view, Lamentations is a quest for understanding in disaster more than simply a sorrowful lament.[38] But a lamentation, by its very nature, is also a complaint, a protest, as well as a search for meaning.

Linafelt calls Lamentations a brutal book,[39] a book that assaults us, and it surely does, even in the violence-laden climate of media, entertainment, and the streets. But the book's unmitigated violence, its expression of loneliness, abandonment, and suffering, its descriptions of death, of helplessness, of the suffering of women, children, the elderly, all have a contemporaneity to them. The poems evoke an outer world and portray an inner landscape known to many contemporary people. The book's very brutality makes it a comfort, a recognition in its metaphorical construction of the way things are for many people. The book functions as a witness to pain, a testimony of survival, and an artistic transformation of dehumanizing suffering into exquisite literature. In the process, it raises profound questions about the justice of God.

FOR FURTHER READING

Commentaries:

Bergent, Dianne. *Lamentations*. Abingdon Old Testament Commentaries. Nashville: Abingdon, 2003.

Berlin, Adele. *Lamentations*. OTL. Louisville, Ky.: Westminster/John Knox Press, 2002.

Dobbs-Allsopp, F. W. *Lamentations*. Interpretation Biblical Commentary. Louisville, Ky.: Westminster/John Knox Press, 2002.

Hillers, Delbert. *Lamentations*. AB 7A. Garden City, N.Y.: Doubleday, 1972.

Provan, Iain. *Lamentations*. NCB. Grand Rapids: Eerdmans, 1991.

Westermann, Claus. *Lamentations: Issues and Interpretation*. Translated by Charles Muenchow. Minneapolis: Fortress, 1994.

Other Studies:

Dobbs-Allsopp, F. W. *Weep, O Daughter of Zion: A Study of the City Lament Genre in the Hebrew Bible*. BibOr 44. Rome: Editrice Pontifico Istituto Biblico, 1993.

Gottwald, Norman K. "The Book of Lamentations Reconsidered." In *The Hebrew Bible in Its Social World and Ours*. SBLSS. Atlanta: Scholars Press, 1993.

————. *Studies in the Book of Lamentations*. Chicago: Alec R. Allenson, 1954.

Grossberg, Daniel. *Centripetal and Centrifugal Structures in Biblical Poetry*. SBLMS 39. Atlanta: Scholars Press, 1989.

Linafelt, Tod, *Surviving Lamentations: Catastrophe, Lament, and Protest in the Afterlife of a Biblical Book*. Chicago: University of Chicago Press, 2000.

ENDNOTES

1. Iain Provan, *Lamentations*, NCB (Grand Rapids: Eerdmans, 1991) 7-19.

2. Delbert Hillers, *Lamentations*, AB 7A (Garden City, N.Y.: Doubleday, 1972) xxi-xxii.

3. Delbert Hillers, *Lamentations*, xvii.

4. Etan Levine, *The Aramaic Version of Lamentations* (New York: Hermon, 1976); Shaye J. D. Cohen, "The Destruction from Scripture to Midrash," *Prooftexts* 2 (1982) 1-17.

5. Ethan Levine, *The Aramaic Version of Lamentations*, 13.

6. Alan Mintz, "The Rhetoric of Lamentations and the Representation of Catastrophe," in *Hurban: Responses to Catastrophe in Hebrew Literature*, ed. G. A. Buttrick et al. (New York: Columbia University Press, 1984) 19-48; reprinted from *Prooftexts* 2 (1982) 1-17.

7. Alan Mintz, "The Rhetoric of Lamentations and the Representation of Catastrophe," 33.

8. In chaps. 2–4 the alphabet is disturbed, reversing the usual 'ayin-pê (ע-פ) order, but this may indicate that the alphabet itself was not yet stable. See Frank Moore Cross, "Studies in the Structure of Hebrew Verse: The Prosody of Lamentations 1:1-22," in *The Word of the Lord Shall Go Forth*, ed.

Carol L. Meyers and M. O'Connor (Winona Lake, Ind.: Eisenbrauns, 1984) 148.

9. Claus Westermann, *Lamentations: Issues and Interpretation* (Minneapolis: Fortress, 1994) 99.

10. N. Gottwald, *Studies in the Book of Lamentations*, SBT (Chicago: Alec R. Allenson, 1954) 26-28.

11. Other acrostics in the Hebrew Bible include Psalms 9–10; 25; 34; 37; 111–12; 119; 145; Prov 31:10-31; and Nah 1:2-8.

12. Daniel Grossberg, *Centripetal and Centrifugal Structures in Biblical Poetry*, SBLMS 39 (Atlanta: Scholars Press, 1989) 84-85.

13. Homer Heater, Jr., "Structure and Meaning in Lamentations," *BSac* 149 (1992) 304-15.

14. Claus Westermann, *Lamentations: Issues and Interpretation* (Minneapolis: Fortress, 1994) 1-23; F. W. Dobbs-Allsopp, *Weep, O Daughter of Zion: A Study of the City-Lament Genre in the Hebrew Bible*, BibOr 44 (Rome: Editrice Pontifico Istituto Biblico, 1993); Paul Wayne Ferris, *The Genre of Communal Lament in the Bible*, SBLDS 127 (Atlanta: Scholars Press, 1992); Norman K. Gottwald, "The Book of Lamentations Reconsidered," in *The Hebrew Bible and Its Social World and in Ours*, ed. Norman K. Gottwald, SBLSS (Atlanta: Scholars Press, 1993) 165-73.

15. See Patrick Miller, *They Cried to the Lord: The Form and Theology of Biblical Prayer* (Minneapolis: Fortress, 1994) 68-134.

16. F. W. Dobbs-Allsopp, *Weep, O Daughter of Zion*, 29-96.

17. J. J. M. Roberts, "The Motif of the Weeping God in Jeremiah and Its Background in the Lament Tradition of the Ancient Near East," *Old Testament Essays* 5 (1992) 361-74.

18. C. Westermann, *Lamentations*, 1-23.

19. William F. Lanahan, "The Speaking Voice in the Book of Lamentations," *JBL* 93 (1974) 41-49.

20. C. Westermann, *Lamentations*, 140.

21. F. W. Dobbs-Alsopp, "The Syntagma of *bat* Followed by a Geographical Name in the Hebrew Bible: A Reconsideration of Its Meaning and Grammar," *CBQ* (1995) 451-70.

22. Julie Galambush, *Jerusalem in the Book of Ezekiel: The City as Yahweh's Wife*, SBLDS 130 (Atlanta: Scholars Press, 1992) 25-59; F. W. Dobbs-Alsopp, *Weep, O Daughter of Zion*, 75-91; A. R. Pete Diamond and Kathleen M. O'Connor, "Unfaith-

ful Passions: Coding Women, Coding Men in Jeremiah 2–3 (4:2)," *Biblical Interpretation* (1996) 288-310; Elaine Follis, "The Holy City as Daughter," in *Directions in Biblical Hebrew Poetry*, ed. Elaine Follis, JSOTSup 40 (Sheffield: JSOT, 1987) 173-84; Renita J. Weems, *Battered Love: Marriage, Sex, and Violence in the Hebrew Prophets*, OBT (Minneapolis: Fortress, 1995).

23. Alan Mintz, "The Rhetoric of Lamentations and the Representation of Catastrophe," 24.

24. Norman K. Gottwald, "The Book of Lamentations Reconsidered," 165-73; Delbert Hillers, *Lamentations*, XVI; Alan Mintz, "The Rhetoric of Lamentations and the Representation of Catastrophe," 33.

25. William H. Shea, "The *qînāh* Structure of the Book of Lamentations," *Bib* 60 (1979) 103-7.

26. William H. Shea, "The *qînāh* Structure of the Book of Lamentations," 107.

27. Tod Linafelt, "Surviving Lamentations: A Literary-Theological Study of the Afterlife of a Biblical Text" (Ph.D. diss., Emory University, 1997); F. W. Dobbs-Allsopp, *Weep, O Daughter of Zion*, 22-24; Iain Provan, *Lamentations*.

28. Tod Linafelt, "Surviving Lamentations," 6-25.

29. Burke O'Connor Long, *Planting and Reaping Albright: Politics, Ideology and Interpreting the Bible* (University Park: Pennsylvania State University Press, 1997).

30. Francis Landy, "Lamentations," in *The Literary Guide to the Bible*, ed. Robert Alter and Frank Kermode (Cambridge, Mass.: Belknap, 1987) 329.

31. Frank Moore Cross, "Studies in the Structure of Hebrew Verse: The Prosody of Lamentations 1:1-22," 129-55.

32. Iain Provan, *Lamentations*, 13.

33. Francis Landy, "Lamentations," 329.

34. Cynthia Ozick, *The Shawl: A Story and a Novella* (New York: Knopf, 1981). Tod Linafelt, "Surviving Lamentations," studies the story as a "survival" of the biblical book.

35. *Fritz Eichenberg: Works of Mercy*, ed. Robert Ellsberg (Maryknoll: Orbis, 1992).

36. See Naomi Seidman, "Burning the Book of Lamentations," in *Out of the Garden: Women Writers on the Bible*, ed. Christian Buchmann and Celina Spiegel (New York: Fawcett Columbine, 1994) 282.

37. Naomi Seidman, "Burning the Book of Lamentations," 282.

38. Jean-Marc Droin, *Le Livre des Lamentations: "Comment?" Une Traduction et un commentaire*, La Bible, porte-Parole (Geneva: Labor et Fides, 1995).

39. Tod Linafelt, *Surviving Lamentations*, 2.

THE BOOK OF
EZEKIEL

KATHERYN PFISTERER DARR

"In the thirtieth year, in the fourth month, on the fifth day of the month, as I was among the exiles by the river Chebar, the heavens were opened, and I saw visions of God" (Ezek 1:1). With these words, readers enter the world and work of Ezekiel, son of Buzi, a Judean priest who, along with his upper-crust compatriots, was exiled to Babylonia in 597 BCE. Ezekiel was, it seems, part of a "brain drain" by which Babylonia's King Nebuchadrezzar II attempted to subdue the troublesome vassal state of Judah. Their deportation is described in 2 Kgs 24:14-16:

> [The king of Babylon] carried away all Jerusalem, all the officials, all the warriors, ten thousand captives, all the artisans and the smiths; no one remained, except the poorest people of the land. He carried away Jehoiachin to Babylon; the king's mother, the king's wives, his officials, and the elite of the land, he took into captivity from Jerusalem to Babylon. The king of Babylon brought captive to Babylon all the men of valor, seven thousand, the artisans and the smiths, one thousand, all of them strong and fit for war. (NRSV)

From the time that Ezekiel was commissioned as Yahweh's prophet to the house of Israel in 593 BCE, until the fall of Jerusalem in 586 BCE, he engaged in the harsh task of dismantling the orthodox Yahwistic theology of his day. That theology emphasized Yahweh's promises to the Israelites—e.g., the blessings attending the covenant forged at Sinai, God's absolute commitment to the Davidic dynasty, and the inviolability of Jerusalem, site of Yahweh's Temple. Such promises strengthened his fellow exiles' resistance to Ezekiel's relentless insistence that Yahweh had resolved utterly to destroy Judah on account of its long-lived and ongoing abominations. The end was approaching. Israel's failure to honor the obligations of its covenant with Yahweh was bringing upon its own head the full weight of the covenantal curses. Only after Nebuchadrezzar, Yahweh's weapon against Judah, destroyed Jerusalem

and devastated the land of Judah did the content and tone of Ezekiel's oracles change. Israel did have a future, but that future was under God's control and was designed to ensure that the sins of the past could never be repeated. After all, Yahweh's reputation among the nations was at stake!

HISTORICAL BACKGROUND

The Decline and Defeat of Judah. What historical circumstances caused Nebuchadrezzar II to treat Judah and its capital city, Jerusalem, so harshly? In order to answer this question, we must consider certain historical events in the ancient Near East. From the ninth century BCE onward, the small kingdoms of Syro-Palestine, including Israel and Judah, struggled to survive as the armies of Assyria, Egypt, and later Babylonia marched through the Fertile Crescent—the traversable arc of land linking Egypt to the west and Mesopotamia to the east.

Judah was one of only a few kingdoms to survive Assyrian aggression in the eighth century. During the reigns of Tiglath-pileser III (745–727 BCE), Shalmaneser V (726–722 BCE), and Sargon II (721–705 BCE), the Assyrian Empire subjected significant areas of Syro-Palestine to destruction, depopulation, and political reorganization into Assyrian provinces. Aram-Damascus fell in 732 BCE, and Samaria, capital of the northern kingdom of Israel, followed in 722/21 BCE. Jotham, Judah's king, survived because he had refused to join with the kings of Israel and Damascus when they formed a last-ditch coalition against the Assyrians. His son and successor, Ahaz, avoided an attempt to remove him from the throne and replace him with ben Tabeel by sending an appeal for help (and a generous gift) to Tiglath-pileser (2 Kgs 16:7-9). The Assyrian king intervened, but Judah paid the price of becoming an Assyrian vassal state.

Judah did not attempt to escape Assyrian domination until the reign of Hezekiah (715/14–687/ 86 BCE). According to 2 Kgs 18:4-8, Hezekiah undertook three primary tasks. First, he authorized cultic reforms, removing pagan artifacts from the Temple and reinstituting Passover observance. Second, he rebelled against the king of Assyria and refused to serve (pay tribute to) him. Third, he engaged in wars with the Philistines.

In 701 BCE, Sennacherib responded to Hezekiah's initiatives with a punitive campaign against the land of "Hatti" (Syro-Palestine). After quelling centers of rebellion in Phoenicia, Palestine, and a number of cities in Judah, he besieged the city of Jerusalem (2 Kgs 18:13–19:37; Isaiah 36–37). In his annals, Sennacherib boasts of imprisoning Hezekiah in his city "like a bird in a cage" and of exacting enormous tribute.[1] Jerusalem survived Sennacherib's campaign, but the land of Judah was severely crippled. Throughout the long reign of Hezekieh's son Manasseh (687/86–642 BCE), Judah remained an obsequious vassal of Assyria.

After Sennacherib was murdered, Esarhaddon became king of Assyria (680–669 BCE). He was followed by Ashurbanipal (668–627 BCE), whose early success in holding together the sprawling Assyrian Empire was compromised by the revolt of Pharaoh Psammetichus I, founder of the twenty-sixth Egyptian dynasty (554–610 BCE). Psammetichus both ended Assyrian domination of Egypt and planned campaigns into Syro-Palestine in order to reassert Egyptian control over the area. In Mesopotamia, Babylonia also was able to reassert its independence under Nabopolasar, the founder of the Neo-Babylonian Empire, with the help of the Medes (626 BCE).

During this period of waning Assyrian power, young Josiah (640–609 BCE) became king of Judah after his father, Amon (642–640 BCE), was assassinated in a palace intrigue. Like Hezekiah, Josiah sought to centralize worship in the Jerusalem Temple as well as to restore Judah to its earlier, broader borders. Assyria was too weak immediately to address Josiah's political ambitions and cultic reforms. Nevertheless, Josiah's attempts at reform were short-lived. Egypt and Babylonia engaged in a power struggle, and Pharaoh Necho launched a military expedition to Carchemish on the Euphrates River (609 BCE). He planned to join forces with Assuruballit, the king of Assyria, in order to prevent the Babylonians from defeating the Assyrians, lest the

Babylonians gain an upper hand over Egyptian ambitions. Recognizing the negative consequences of an Egyptian/Assyrian victory for Judah, Josiah attacked Necho's forces as they passed through the Megiddo valley and was killed in battle. Necho hurried on to Carchemish, leaving the Judeans to mourn their dead king and to place his son Jehoahaz (called Shallum in 1 Chr 3:15) upon the throne.

Jehoahaz ruled for only three months. Returning from Carchemish by way of Riblah, Necho appointed another of Josiah's sons, Eliakim (whom he renamed Jehoiakim, 2 Kgs 23:35), to reign in his stead. Jehoahaz was exiled to Egypt, where he died (2 Kgs 23:31-34; 2 Chr 36:34; Jer 22:1-12; Ezek 19:1-4). Egyptian control of Syro-Palestine lasted from 609 to 605 BCE, and Jehoiakim maintained a pro-Egyptian policy throughout that period.

In 605 BCE, the scales of power tipped in favor of Babylonia. Nebuchadrezzar II met the Egyptian army at Carchemish and won a decisive victory. He also launched military expeditions into the land of Hatti and demanded tribute from its local kings. When Ashkelon—a major Philistine city—refused to surrender, its king was captured, and the city was destroyed (see Jer 36:9). Following the Babylonian victory over Philistia, another Philistine city (c. 603/602 BCE), Jehoiakim abandoned his pro-Egyptian policies and became Nebuchadrezzar's vassal.

Jehoiakim continued to hope for an Egyptian revival, however. In 601 BCE, Nebuchadrezzar's forces met Necho's army near the frontier of Egypt. Both sides suffered enormous casualties, and neither could claim complete victory. Nebuchadrezzar went home to reorganize his troops, and he did not return to Syro-Palestine until 598/97 BCE. Jehoiakim decided that the time was ripe for revolt. Only three years after submitting to Nebuchadrezzar, he rebelled against his overlord, no doubt with the expectation of Egyptian assistance.

Nebuchadrezzar could not immediately crush Jehoiakim's rebellion, but he deployed Babylonian troops already in the region, along with bands of Syrians, Moabites, and Ammonites, to unsettle the area until he could attend to it personally (Jer 35:11). In 597 BCE, during the seventh year of his reign, Nebuchadrezzar mounted a campaign against Judah. The Babylonian Chronicles contain the following report: "Year 7, month Kislimu: The king of Akkad moved his army into Hatti land, laid siege to the city of Judah and the king took the city on the second day of the month Addaru. He appointed in it a (new) king of his liking, took heavy booty from it and brought it into Babylon."[2]

Nebuchadrezzar's stranglehold on Jerusalem ended when Jehoiakim's successor, Jehoiachin, surrendered in March 597 BCE. He and members of the royal household were forced into exile, along with nobles, craftsmen, and smiths, as well as "the men of valor" (see 2 Kgs 24:14-16 NRSV) and Ezekiel, the priest (Ezek 1:1-3). According to 2 Kgs 24:14, only "the poorest people of the land" escaped deportation, but this is likely an exaggeration. Many people living in outlying areas probably escaped, relatively unscathed by the event. The total number of persons exiled cannot be determined, because the biblical sources disagree.

Nebuchadrezzar chose Jehoiachin's uncle Mattaniah to occupy the exiled king's throne and changed his name to Zedekiah (2 Kgs 24:17). The choice was an unfortunate one for Judah. According to the biblical witness, Zedekiah was a weak, vacillating figure who lacked the strength to make decisions in the midst of conflicting advice from pro-Babylonian and pro-Egyptian advisers. During his initial years, the king apparently fulfilled his vassal obligations to Nebuchadrezzar. In 594/93 BCE, however, a conspiracy—either in Babylonia or in Syro-Palestine itself (encouraged, perhaps, by Pharaoh Psammetichus II [593–588 BCE])—rejuvenated hopes of national freedom and the exiles' speedy return home (see Jeremiah 27–28). The rebellion apparently dissipated quickly, however; and Judean envoys, perhaps even Zedekiah himself, traveled to Babylonia to demonstrate Judah's submission to its suzerain.

Zedekiah did not learn his lesson. Encouraged by pro-Egyptian advisers and by offers of assistance from Egypt's new pharaoh, Hophra (588–569 BCE), as well as by the soothing words of certain prophets (see Jer 5:12; 14:13), he rebelled openly against Babylonian overlordship in 589/88 BCE. The rebellion was ill-timed, ill-planned, and doomed to failure. Nebuchadrezzar reacted almost immediately by besieging the city of Jerusalem (2 Kgs 25:1-2). The land of Judah was devastated, and many of its cities were destroyed (Jer 34:7; 44:2; Lam 2:2-5). Jerusalem itself withstood the siege until August 586 BCE (see 2 Kgs 25; Jer 21:3-7; 39; 52:4-5; Ezek 24:1-2), but it was finally taken, despite limited military assistance from Pharaoh Hophra.

Zedekiah remained in Jerusalem throughout the siege, but when the city's walls were breached, he and his military advisers attempted to flee (2 Kgs 25:4). They were captured by Babylonian forces and taken to Riblah, where Nebuchadrezzar was headquartered. After witnessing the executions of his sons, Zedekiah was blinded, fettered, and taken to Babylon.

On the ninth of Ab, Nebuzaradan, commander of the Babylonian forces, supervised the systematic destruction of Jerusalem. Its significant structures, including the royal palace, were burned, its walls were torn down; and the Temple was first looted and then torched. A number of people, including Seraiah, the chief priest; Zephaniah, the second priest; and other cultic personnel, military leaders, and "sixty men of the people of the land who were found in the city" were taken to Riblah and executed (2 Kgs 25:18-21 NRSV).

No figures concerning the number of Judeans forced into exile in the wake of Jerusalem's defeat are provided in 2 Kings 25. Verse 11 states that "Nebuzaradan the captain of the guard carried into exile the rest of the people who were left in the city and the deserters who had defected to the king of Babylon—all the rest of the population" (2 Kgs 25:11 NRSV), save for the very poorest people in the land. Jeremiah 52:28-30 states that a total of 4,600 persons were deported in three waves (3,023 in 597 BCE, 832 in 586 BCE, and 745 in 581 BCE). We do not know how many people perished during the siege and devastation of Jerusalem.

Conditions in Judah During the Exilic Period. In accord with Babylonian imperial practice, Nebuchadrezzer neither repopulated the land of Judah with exiles from other countries nor set a foreign commander over the remaining people. Instead, he appointed a Judean nobleman, Gedaliah, son of Ahikam, to a position of leadership. Settling into the Benjaminite city of Mizpah, apparently the new provincial capital, Gedaliah began to gather and reorganize the survivors. At some point, he summoned "all the leaders of the forces in the open country" (Jer 40:7 NRSV; see 2 Kgs 25:23), some of whom were apparently hiding in caves or in the Judean desert (Ezek 33:27), to return to their homes and co-exist peacefully with the Babylonian overlords in their midst. Gedaliah's invitation that these captains "gather wine and summer fruits and oil, and store them in your vessels, and live in the towns that you have taken over" (Jer 40:10 NRSV) suggests that the devastation of Judah was neither so widespread nor so thorough as the biblical accounts state.

Precisely how many and what sorts of people lived under Gedaliah's supervision is difficult to determine. The biblical witness that only a few of the "poorest people of the land" remained after the deportations of both 597 BCE (2 Kgs 24:14) and 586 BCE (2 Kgs 25:12) has already been noted, but this is probably an exaggeration. Janssen has argued that the economic status of some who remained in the land actually improved after the deportations, since they were given property (including royal estates) previously belonging to the exiles.[3]

According to Jer 40:13–41:3, Gedaliah ignored a warning from Johanan that one of Johanan's fellow captains of the forces intended to kill him. Jeremiah 40:14 suggests that the assassin, Ishmael, son of Nethaniah, was encouraged by Baalis, king of Ammon. It is possible, however, that Ishmael instigated the plan himself, for he was a descendant of David; and he may well have regarded Gedaliah's cooperation with the Babylonians as traitorous. The assassination plot succeeded. Gedaliah was killed, as were "all the Judeans who were with Gedaliah at Mizpah, and the Chaldean soldiers who happened to be there" (Jer 41:3 NRSV). The next day, Ishmael also killed eighty mourners who had traveled to Jerusalem, save for ten men who bought their lives with promises of food for Ishmael and his men. Subsequently, Ishmael captured additional people at Mizpah and attempted to enter Ammon with them. Johanan aborted their flight, however, and released Ishmael's captives. The assassin and eight accomplices escaped (Jer 41:15).

Johanan and the people went to Geruth Chimham near Bethlehem and contemplated a trip to Egypt (Jer 41:16). Their fear of Babylonian reprisal was probably well-founded, since Babylonian soldiers, as well as Judeans, had been killed during the ordeal. Over Jeremiah's vehement protests, the people decided to flee (Jer 42:7–43:7), and "all the remnant of Judah" (Jer 43:5 NRSV) migrated to Tahpanhes, an Egyptian border fortress (Jer 43:7-8). Nothing is said of surviving communities within the land of Judah, but it is reasonable to suppose that people living in outlying areas did not leave with Johanan. Some of those who fled to escape Babylonian revenge may eventually have returned.

The book of Ezekiel has nothing positive to say about the Judeans who remained in Jerusalem following the deportations of 597 and 586 BCE. To the contrary, it excoriates those who were left behind in 597 BCE, heaping accusation after accusation against them and promising punishments such as had never occurred before. To Ezekiel's mind, Yahweh's destruction of Jerusalem was fully justified, and few would survive. To be sure, Ezekiel could be extremely critical of his fellow exiles as well. But he clearly believed that Israel's future depended upon Yahweh's dealings with the diaspora living in Babylonia. Hence, his assessment of the Judeans who remained in their homeland cannot be regarded as objective.

Conditions in Babylonia During the Exilic Period. Unfortunately, Hebrew Scripture provides little information about the conditions experienced by the Judean deportees of 597 and 586 BCE. After completing the long trek to Babylonia, the king and members of his family were imprisoned in its capital city (2 Kgs 25:27-30 states that Jehoiachin was released from prison in the thirty-seventh year of his exile, but says nothing about the fates of his subjects). However, many, if not most, of the exiles were settled at Tel Abib in the vicinity of Nippur near the Chebar Canal, part of an intricate system of canals carrying water from the Euphrates River throughout the city and its surroundings. The "tel" (mound) in Tel Abib suggests that the Babylonians placed the deportees in an area once inhabited, but subsequently destroyed. If this is the case, then many of the exiles would have spent their time rebuilding the ruins.

In his letter to the exiles of 597 BCE (Jer 29:1-23), Jeremiah rejected any hope of a quick return home. He urged them to "build houses and live in them; plant gardens and eat what they produce. Take wives and have sons and daughters; take wives for your sons, and give your daughters in marriage, that they may bear sons and daughters; multiply there, and do not decrease" (Jer 29:5-6 NRSV). If communication flowed between Syro-Palestine and Babylonia with relative efficiency, such that Jeremiah knew of the exiles' situation, then his letter can be taken as evidence that they could obey his advice if they resolved to do so. Nevertheless, we should not suppose that all of the exiles shared similar circumstances. Military leaders likely were conscripted into the Babylonian army. Expert craftsmen undoubtedly labored on some of Nebuchadrezzar's many building projects. Imprisonment, slavery, or forced conscription was surely the fate of some exiles. It seems likely, however, that most were able to practice their trades and support their families.

If the situation at Tel Abib was reasonably benign, however, we should not presume that its inhabitants endured no suffering or distress. Renz writes of their trauma:

> Having been part of Judah's upper class, they had left behind family, social status and material possessions. They had seen people dying during the siege and must have had further losses of life on the long and arduous journey to Babylonia, where they received a humiliating "welcome," as certainly as Nebuchadnezzar made sure that he received a hero's welcome. Even with these events receding somewhat in the background, the reality was that they had exchanged their hilly homeland and the pleasant climate of Jerusalem for the flat and hot Babylonian low lands, and at least some of them were certainly not used to the hard manual labour now required of them. To this must be added, at the time before the fall of Jerusalem, the mixture of hope and fear concerning their own and Jerusalem's situation.[4]

Psalm 137 expresses the exiles' grief, frustrated nationalism, and hunger for revenge in terms that could scarcely be more extreme. Perhaps this psalm was composed not long after the people reached Babylonia. Ezekiel 37:11 attests to the sense of resignation experienced by at least some of the exiles after years in Babylonia: "Our bones are dried up, and our hope is lost; we are cut off completely." We should not suppose that all of the deportees experienced the same reactions throughout the entire exilic period. While some clung with tenacity to their distinct ethnic identity, others probably assimilated into Babylonian culture rapidly. While some struggled mightily to maintain faith in Yahweh, others probably shifted their devotion to Babylonian deities.

EZEKIEL'S CRITIQUE OF THE ORTHODOX YAHWISM OF HIS DAY

Although we cannot assume that all of the exiles deported in 597 BCE subscribed to the same Yahwistic theology, it is helpful to understand prominent aspects of that theology, since doing so helps us to understand why Ezekiel's oracles were resisted by his audience prior to the fall of Jerusalem.

In his commentary, Block identifies four "pillars" of divine promise upon which the people of Judah rested their faith.[5] First, they believed that they were Yahweh's chosen people, enjoying the blessings of their covenant relationship with Yahweh forged at Sinai centuries earlier. From this belief, they derived a sense of confidence based on the power of their God to ensure their welfare and to protect them. To be sure, the Judeans knew that maintaining their covenant relationship with Yahweh brought obligations as well as benefits. Nevertheless, one can imagine that the latter were emphasized to the neglect of the former.

Second, they believed that Yahweh had granted land to Israel's ancestors and that they were inheritors of that land grant. Yahweh owned the land they inhabited, and their presence there was God's will. As their patron deity, Yahweh would fight to protect their land and to ensure that the people were not forced from it.

The third and fourth "pillars" of Israel's theology are particularly crucial for understanding the orthodox Yahwistic faith of Ezekiel's day. In both, the city of Jerusalem plays a crucial role. On the one hand, the people of Judah believed that Yahweh had entered into an eternal covenant with the descendants of David, promising that the Davidic dynasty would reign in Jerusalem in perpetuity. The people living in Jerusalem during the years leading up to the Babylonian onslaught knew well their traditions about David and about God's unconditional promise that one of his descendants would occupy Israel's throne forever. Presented as Yahweh's declaration to David through the prophet Nathan, 2 Sam 7:11*b*-16 is a classic statement that God established an ongoing Davidic dynasty in Israel:

> The Lord declares to you that the Lord will make you a house. When your days are fulfilled and you lie down with your ancestors, I will raise up your offspring after you, who shall come forth from your body, and I will establish his kingdom. He shall build a house for my name, and I will establish the throne of his kingdom forever. I will be a father to him, and he shall be a son to me. When he commits iniquity, I will punish him with a rod such as mortals use, with blows inflicted by human beings. But I will not take my steadfast love from him, as I took it from Saul, whom I put away from before you. Your house and your kingdom shall be made sure forever before me; your throne shall be established forever. (NRSV)

Other biblical literature declares, in exuberant poetry, the belief that Yahweh promised to ensure the continuity of the Davidic dynasty forever. Psalm 2, a royal psalm proclaiming the sovereignty of Judah's king over the nations, articulates the ongoing father/adopted son relationship between Yahweh and the Davidic king:

> I will tell of the decree of the Lord:
> He said to me, "You are my son;
>   today I have begotten you.
> Ask of me, and I will make the nations your
>   heritage,
>   and the ends of the earth your possession.
> You shall break them with a rod of iron,
>   and dash them in pieces like a potter's vessel."
>   (Ps 2:7-9 NRSV)

These two texts, and many others, affirm Yahweh's commitment to the Davidic kings who occupied Judah's throne throughout the pre-exilic period. The king was the adopted son of Yahweh, whom God would protect against attack by any and all nations. Israel did not go so far as to deify its kings, but it asserted that the relationship between Yahweh and the Davidic king was unique. This theological tenet had implications for all of the people, not just for the royal family, for through the king, Yahweh's blessings ostensibly were mediated to the nation as a whole. The Davidic king's rule was the earthly manifestation of Yahweh's heavenly rule. The political consequences of this theology served the Davidic dynasty well; the people were expected to give their total support and loyalty to the king, for he ruled with Yahweh's sanction and blessing.

On the other hand, Jerusalem was crucial to the theology of pre-exilic Judeans because the Solomonic Temple stood within its walls. The Temple built during Solomon's reign was likely very important from the time of its completion. But the Bible testifies to its increasing significance in succeeding centuries. A little more than three hundred years after it was constructed, Judah's King Josiah initiated a reform movement that sought to close down every other Yahwistic cultic site within Judah, and even in the territory of the former northern kingdom. Josiah believed that the Solomonic Temple in Jerusalem alone was suitable for appropriate worship of Yahweh.

It follows from these beliefs that the people thought that their patron deity would not permit the city in which God's Temple stood to be destroyed. Their unswerving faith is expressed in Psalm 48:

> Great is the Lord and greatly to be praised
>   in the city of our God.
> His holy mountain, beautiful in elevation,
>   is the joy of all the earth,
> Mount Zion, in the far north,
>   the city of the great King.
> Within its citadels God
>   has shown himself a sure defense.
>
> . . . .
> Your name, O God, like your praise,
>   reaches to the ends of the earth.
> Your right hand is filled with victory.
>   Let Mount Zion be glad,
> let the towns of Judah rejoice
>   because of your judgments.
>   (Ps 48:1-3, 9-11 NRSV)

Like the prophet Jeremiah, Ezekiel's contemporary who remained in Jerusalem, Ezekiel scrutinized these four tenets of the Yahwistic theology of his day and subjected them to a radical critique. True, Yahweh and Israel were covenant partners, but the people had for centuries failed to fulfill their covenant obligations. While the covenant forged at Sinai demanded Israel's undivided fidelity to God, the people of Ezekiel's day were idolatrous. Indeed, their idols had even found their way into Yahweh's own Temple (see, e.g., chap. 8). While the covenant demanded that the people observe moral and ethical laws, these laws were abrogated by each generation (see, e.g., chap. 20). While the covenant demanded that Judean society be just, its leaders were oppressors, perpetrators of violence and bloodshed (see, e.g., chap. 22). Because the rebellious house of Israel had failed to honor its covenant obligations, Yahweh would bring the covenant curses upon them, including deportation, destruction, and death.

God had, indeed, granted to Israel the land promised to its ancestors, but its failure to obey the covenant regulations meant that Israel could and would lose its right to inhabit that territory. God was either going to expel the people from their homeland (e.g., chap. 14) or cover it with their corpses (see, e.g., chap. 6).

Yahweh had determined long ago that David's descendants would rule over God's people. But Judah's kings, and especially its last monarchs, blatantly broke God's laws and ravaged their subjects like lions (chap. 19), oppressing the very people

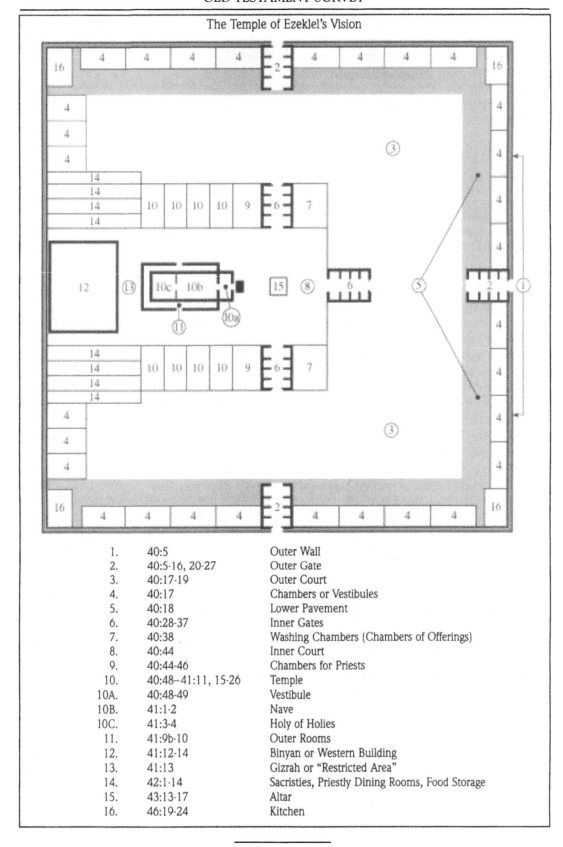

The Temple of Ezeklel's Vision

1.	40:5	Outer Wall
2.	40:5-16, 20-27	Outer Gate
3.	40:17-19	Outer Court
4.	40:17	Chambers or Vestibules
5.	40:18	Lower Pavement
6.	40:28-37	Inner Gates
7.	40:38	Washing Chambers (Chambers of Offerings)
8.	40:44	Inner Court
9.	40:44-46	Chambers for Priests
10.	40:48–41:11, 15-26	Temple
10A.	40:48-49	Vestibule
10B.	41:1-2	Nave
10C.	41:3-4	Holy of Holies
11.	41:9b-10	Outer Rooms
12.	41:12-14	Binyan or Western Building
13.	41:13	Gizrah or "Restricted Area"
14.	42:1-14	Sacristies, Priestly Dining Rooms, Food Storage
15.	43:13-17	Altar
16.	46:19-24	Kitchen

whose rights they were duty-bound to protect (chap. 22) and rebelling against the pro-Babylonian policy that Ezekiel insisted was Yahweh's will (chap. 17). Such kings would not go unpunished.

Ezekiel believed that God's glory had resided in the Temple in Jerusalem. But he insisted that Yahweh was abandoning that Temple, because the abominations committed within it had polluted the place completely. Without God's protective presence, the Temple was doomed to destruction, as was the city in which it stood—a city so corrupt that it had outsinned Sodom (see chaps. 16 and 23).

Ezekiel offered his fellow exiles no hope that their homeland might survive Babylonian aggression. To the contrary, he insisted that Yahweh was bringing about its downfall. The divine warrior was warring against "his" own people. Undergirding his pronouncements of judgment were certain presuppositions that Ezekiel steadfastly refused to abandon.[6]

First, Ezekiel asserts Yahweh's unparalleled sovereignty over history and the nations. His worldview is utterly theocentric. God is at work in the world, controlling nations and events according to God's own plan.

Second, that plan includes the destruction of Judah. Ezekiel insists that the approaching devastation is the doing, and not the undoing, of Israel's God. He spurns any notion that the Babylonian army will succeed because "The Lord does not see us; the Lord has abandoned the country" (Ezek 8:12 TNK), or that Jerusalem's demise will signal the victory of Marduk, patron deity of Babylon, over Israel's God. He ascribes historical events to Yahweh; he will not abandon Yahweh to history.

Third, Ezekiel insists that God's punishments are just. Yahweh's plan is not capricious, undertaken at the deity's whim, but the thoroughly merited response to Israel's long-lived sin. The punishment is proportionate to the crime. And because the anticipated punishment will be horrific, Israel's sins must be grievous, indeed.

In the years prior to Judah's collapse, Ezekiel ruthlessly opposes any notion that Yahweh is powerless, apathetic, or unjust. He insists that Yahweh is both in control of events and justified in the way those events are controlled. If the God who is both just and the Lord of history has determined to reduce Judean land and cities to uninhabited wasteland, and to exile or exterminate the population,

then this must be because the Judeans have sinned to such a degree that no other outcome is possible without violating divine justice. Both Judah's conviction and the deity who convicts it are just.

Ezekiel's oracles of judgment are filled with passion and utterly devoid of sentimentality. The God we witness through Ezekiel's words is consumed by wrath, bent on violence, and hungry for vengeance. Little wonder that Ezekiel's readers—ancient and modern—might recoil at his portrayal of Yahweh in chaps. 4–24. In the transitional chaps. 25–32, Ezekiel directs his ire at Israel's enemies (and at one potential ally, Egypt). His oracles against foreign nations and rulers likewise are replete with images of a wrathful, violent, and vengeful God, whose preferred method of dealing with these nations is extermination in order that all be forced to acknowledge that "I am Yahweh." The assertion that God would knock Israel's foes to their knees must have been good news, indeed, for Ezekiel's late exilic readers. For moderns, however, these oracles present formidable theological obstacles.

EZEKIEL'S ORACLES OF RESTORATION

Ezekiel's words of doom are not his only words, however. Chapters 33–48 contain the preponderance of the prophet's oracles of restoration. In them, he insists that Israel will not remain in exile forever, because the people's present plight dishonors Yahweh's reputation among the nations. For the sake of Yahweh's own name, God will regather the people from the nations, return them to their homeland, and ensure that the sins of the past are never repeated. Yahweh will enter into a new covenant with the people. Their God-given hearts and spirits will be incapable of abrogating Yahweh's statutes and ordinances; and their land will be transformed into a veritable Garden of Eden, prompting the astonishment of all who pass by (see Ezekiel 36). The people will be shepherded by a new David (see Ezekiel 34). All potential foes will be eliminated in God's final battle against Gog and his hordes (Ezekiel 38–39). And Yahweh's glory will return to a new and perfectly ordered Temple, situated at the center of a land inhabited by the reconstituted twelve tribes of Israel (Ezekiel 40–48).

THE PRIEST/PROPHET EZEKIEL

The book bearing Ezekiel's name provides readers with only a little biographical information about him. We know that his father's name was Buzi. His own name, which appears only in 1:3 and 24:24, means either "God strengthens" or "May God strengthen." He was a priest, or at least in training for the priesthood, at the time he was deported to Babylonia. We know that he had a residence in Tel Abib, for we are told that elders visited him in his house. He was married, although we do not know his wife's name. Nothing is said of their children, if any existed. We have no idea how he supported himself.

The Ezekiel we encounter in his book presents himself as an eccentric, even bizarre, figure. Little wonder that past scholars have sometimes subjected him to the psychiatrist's couch. Block acknowledges that Israel's prophets often acted and spoke in unusual ways, but he insists that Ezekiel was in a class of his own:

> The concentration of so many bizarre features in one individual is without precedent: his muteness; lying bound and naked [?]; digging holes in the walls of houses; emotional paralysis in the face of his wife's death; "spiritual" travels; images of strange creatures, of eyes, and of creeping things; hearing voices and the sounds of water; withdrawal symptoms; fascination with feces and blood; wild literary imagination, pornographic imagery; unreal if not surreal understanding of Israel's past; and the list goes on.[7]

Despite Ezekiel's apparent eccentricities, most contemporary scholars reject a psychoanalytical approach to understanding Ezekiel's personality. One exception, D. J. Halperin, believes that Ezekiel's writings betray a hatred of women and men rooted in child abuse.[8] But his speculations remain just that.

We know that Ezekiel was among the intellectual elite of his day. The book of Ezekiel reveals an author of extraordinary acumen, sophistication, and literary gifts. Ezekiel's intellect reveals itself in myriad ways: his mastery of technical vocabularies; his political expertise; his familiarity with Israel's religious traditions; and above all his creative revisions of those traditions to suit the challenges of his times. We should assume that his audience, Jerusalem's elite, was equipped to understand his words, for they shared with him a complex web of social, political, economic, military, and religious knowledge.

EZEKIEL AND HIS AUDIENCE

Like many, though not all, contemporary scholars, I think that Ezekiel's entire "ministry" took place in Babylonia and entailed the performance of certain sign acts, and especially the oral proclamation of oracles to his exilic audience. The notion that Ezekiel was a writer, not an orator, has deep roots within the discipline. In the nineteenth century, for example, Reuss denied Ezekiel any oral ministry:

> There is not a single page in the whole book which we must suppose to have been read or proclaimed publicly. Ezekiel was not an orator; he was a writer. What he gives us are literary reflections, the product of private study and the fruit of retirement and contemplation. We should have to shut our eyes to the evidence to arrive at the view that he had ever had occasion to interfere actively in affairs, and to go out from his retreat to appear on the scene where passions are aroused and events take place.[9]

But Reuss's statement, with its tinges of Romanticism, goes too far. I do not doubt that prior to his oral performances, Ezekiel frequently committed oracles to writing. Indeed, in the case of his longest and most detailed speeches (e.g., Ezekiel 16), that seems the most likely scenario. Nevertheless, in the book, Yahweh repeatedly instructs the priest-prophet to "speak" to his compatriots, and his late exilic readers (see below) will assume that he did so.

Like Renz, I think that the book of Ezekiel derives from an oral debate with his exilic audience.[10] Ezekiel's oracles are not disinterested theological essays. They are strategic speech by which the prophet seeks to persuade his audience to perceive events (e.g., the forthcoming destruction of Jerusalem), persons (e.g., Zedekiah and his pro-Egyptian advisers), and institutions (e.g., the monarchy) in his way, rather than in some other way. The exiles, clinging to the divine promises of their faith, resisted Ezekiel's message of doom and destruction. And one can imagine that the harshness of his pronouncements of judgment further hardened the hearts of many in his audience. Nevertheless, Ezekiel refused to soften his rhetoric or to concede that alternative interpretations of events were possible. His refusal to budge testifies to the depths of his convictions, and he everywhere insists that his words are actually *God's* words, which he must proclaim in order to save his own life.

EZEKIEL AND HIS READERS

Although some scholars think that the Ezekiel scroll reached essentially its final form years, perhaps even centuries, after the prophet's lifetime, I am not persuaded to that view. It is possible, perhaps likely, that during the post-exilic period, members of Ezekiel's "school" further supplemented his work. But the book as a whole does not address, or even seem knowledgeable about, conditions pertaining during the post-exilic period. Like Renz, I think that the book was virtually completed by the late exilic period; and I will place my reader (see below) in that time frame. Renz astutely observes that the book does not presuppose a great chronological gulf separating Ezekiel's original audience from the book's earliest readers:

> It is remarkable that the book of Ezekiel makes little effort to distinguish the audience of the book from the prophet's original audience; rather, the former is seen in continuity with the latter. This means that even if one assumes that the book was written for a post-exilic readership (an assumption . . . I do not share), one must not overlook the fact that the book invites its readers to identify with the exilic community. It does not address directly a world beyond the world of the prophet Ezekiel, but rather invites prospective readers to enter into the world of refugees in "Tel Aviv" and their prophet. The book of Ezekiel develops its argument with the reader by narrating the story of a prophet's unfolding argument with his exilic audience. In this way the book addresses its own audience by having the audience in the book addressed by the prophet. In other words, it is a communication by being a narrative about a communication.[11]

A significant factor distinguishes Ezekiel's original audience from his earliest readership, however. The latter constituency knows what the former did not until news of Jerusalem's destruction reached Babylonia: Ezekiel was right. His predictions that Nebuchadrezzar would breach Jerusalem's walls, torch the city, slaughter many of its inhabitants, and deport others were fulfilled. As a consequence of this knowledge, Ezekiel's earliest readers are, *from the outset*, predisposed to acknowledge his status as Yahweh's authentic prophet and to read his oracles as God's own words—precisely the posture that Ezekiel's original audience resists for reasons already identified. But more is involved than the simple verification of prophetic predictions. Renz is surely correct when he states that even the

reader who knows that Jerusalem was destroyed needs to understand *why* it was destroyed: "To this end the readers are put (in their imaginations) in the situation before the fall of Jerusalem. They are invited to 'judge' Jerusalem and thereby to pronounce Yahweh's judgment as just."[12] Once Jerusalem has been destroyed, and the news reaches Tel Abib, then the distance between Ezekiel's original audience and his late exilic readers diminishes. Now, both groups await the fulfillment of Ezekiel's outstanding oracles against the nations, and especially the restoration of Israel to its homeland and the restructuring of its society.

THE STRUCTURE OF THE BOOK OF EZEKIEL

Before turning to a discussion of the reading process, and of "my reader" of the book of Ezekiel, I offer the following observations about the structure of the book that are pertinent to that discussion. As noted earlier, the book of Ezekiel consists of three major sections. The first section, chaps. 1–24, consists primarily of sign acts and oracles of doom against Judah and Jerusalem. The second section, chaps. 25–32, contains most of Ezekiel's oracles against foreign nations and rulers, while the third section, chaps. 33–48, contains oracles concerning Israel's future restoration. Many of Ezekiel's oracles are dated (dates appear in 1:1-3; 3:16; 8:1; 20:1; 24:1; 26:1; 29:1, 17; 30:20; 31:1; 32:1, 17; 33:21; and 40:1), and with one understandable exception (29:17), these date notices appear in chronological order. This feature of the book contributes to the reader's sense of its coherence. This is no pastiche of oracles, but a carefully structured literary work anchored in historical events. The scroll has a beginning, a middle, and an end. Its contents can be read randomly, but it invites a sequential reading.

Moreover, four vision reports appear in the book. In 1:1–3:15, Ezekiel witnesses a vision in which "the glory of the Lord" comes to him over Babylonia in storm cloud and blazing light, and he is commissioned as Yahweh's prophet. In 8:1–11:24, Ezekiel is transported by the spirit to the Temple in Jerusalem, where he sees the abominations committed there and witnesses Yahweh's glory abandoning the city to its fate. In 37:1-14, Ezekiel is again transported by the spirit, this time to "the valley," which is filled with heaps of disconnected and thoroughly desiccated bones. Before his eyes, the bones are rejoined, bound by sinews, refleshed, covered with skin, and animated by the spirit. Finally, in chaps. 40–48, the hand of Yahweh brings Ezekiel to a "very high mountain," where he tours Yahweh's new Temple and witnesses God's glory enter it. These vision reports also tell a "story" of sorts, which unfolds chronologically. This is most obvious in the case of the second and fourth reports, which describe the departure of Yahweh's glory from the Temple and its return, respectively. The vision reports in the book also invite a sequential reading of the scroll. They can be read randomly. But a major structural component of the work is thereby obscured. One might imagine that after reading randomly in the book over a period of time, one could learn the relationship of any given pericope to another. What is lost in such a scenario, however, is the reader's experience of the *unfolding* prophetic message of Ezekiel as historical events develop. The late exilic reader whom I posit encounters Ezekiel's oracles sequentially, from beginning to end.

DISASSEMBLING AND RECONSTRUCTING THE BOOK OF EZEKIELXIII

The history of Ezekielian scholarship shows that in biblical studies, no less than in other disciplines, our presuppositions and methodologies influence the questions we ask of texts, and those questions inevitably influence the answers we discern. Early historical investigators of Israel's prophetic corpus, for example, sought primarily to recover the prophets' "authentic" words within their original historical contexts. They wished to distinguish later supplements from these "genuine" utterances in order that the prophets' own personalities, historical circumstances, and religious beliefs might be revealed. "To borrow from a description of sculpting attributed to the great Italian artist, Michelangelo, these scholars carved into the textual block until they reached a particular prophet's 'skin' and then stopped. When their work was completed, the statue before them looked precisely like their [mental] images of Amos, or Ezekiel, or 'Deutero-Isaiah.' But littered around its base lay chunks and shards of discarded text."[14]

Some contemporary scholars, frustrated by the "dismembering" tendencies of historical-critical methods, have turned to a variety of literary-critical approaches. Such approaches can contribute fresh and important insights into biblical books. But historical-critical approaches and literary criticism are not of necessity antithetical (as advocates of each sometimes suggest). Some literary-critical approaches, including my own, rely upon historical-critical discoveries. Such reliance is necessary when examining the book of Ezekiel, for, as noted above, it presents as a carefully structured literary work anchored in historical events. I often set aside certain traditional agendas, such as distinguishing between "authentic" and "inauthentic" materials, and carefully tracing the composition history of the book. But I do not concomitantly devalue the myriad contributions of historical criticism to our understanding of the Ezekiel scroll.

Ezekiel Among the Critics. In 1880, Smend could confidently pen the following assessment of the Ezekiel corpus: "The whole book is . . . the logical development of a series of ideas in accordance with a well thought out, and in part quite schematic, plan. We cannot remove any part without disturbing the whole structure."[15] Smend's assessment echoed that of Ewald, who declared in 1841 that the scroll, though not composed in a single stage, nevertheless owed its final form to Ezekiel himself.[16]

This judgment was attacked, however, in the late 1800s and early 1900s. G. Hölscher's *Die Profeten* constituted one such attack.[17] Having established to his satisfaction the ecstatic character of Ezekiel's genuine prophecies, Hölscher distinguished between the prophet's own utterances and the supplements of later redactors, whose efforts threaten to obfuscate the oracles of Ezekiel, the poet:

> By freeing the poetry of Ezekiel from the dry prosaic pattern in which the redaction has woven his poems, the poet Ezekiel appears once again in a clear light, with his brilliant, imaginative and passionate rhetoric. From a religio-historical point of view also the picture of Ezekiel changes completely: he is no longer the stiff priestly writer and pathfinder of a legalistic and ritualistic Judaism, for which he has been held, but a genuine prophet of Jewish antiquity, a spiritual companion of the authentic Jeremiah.[18]

Hölscher attributed only 144 of the book's 1,273 verses to Ezekiel![19]

Several years after Hölscher's commentary was published, V. Herntrich refuted the book's own claim that Ezekiel was among the exiles deported to Babylonia in 597 BCE, arguing instead that his prophetic ministry took place in Jerusalem.[20] Perhaps he was actually exiled in 587 BCE, after the city was destroyed. In any event, Ezekiel fell silent at that time. His earlier prophetic oracles were subsequently edited by a 597 BCE deportee who wished to buttress his assertion that true prophecy had traveled into exile with his own elite community. Herntrich attributed chaps. 40–48, as well as some material in prior chapters, to this editor.

Only a decade after Hölscher's commentary appeared, and beneath the cumulative weight of critical analysis, G. A. Cooke could point to an upheaval in Ezekiel studies: "In recent years the study of Ezekiel has undergone something of a revolution. . . . It is no longer possible to treat the Book as the product of a single mind and a single age."[21]

In a 1953 lecture, H. H. Rowley assessed the state of Ezekiel's studies to his own day. He rehearsed a variety of hypotheses about the book's unity, its date of composition, and Ezekiel's location(s) at the time of his prophetic career. But he also looked ahead to what he regarded as the future of Ezekiel studies. Today many, though not all, critics agree with Rowley's assessments:

> First, he noted that though the text undoubtedly contained some secondary elements, they probably were not present in large quantities. Second, he claimed that Ezekiel, a gifted poet, could not be ruled out as the author of prose passages as well, and that no compelling evidence discredited the scroll's own claims regarding the locus of his prophetic activities. Third, Rowley pointed out that the ostensible need to resort to psychological explanations of Ezekiel's behaviors and words was largely mitigated by appropriate consideration of the literary genre (for example, visions).[22]

DIACHRONIC AND SYNCHRONIC APPROACHES TO THE BOOK OF EZEKIEL

Rendtorff's observation about Isaian scholarship is true of Ezekiel studies as well: "The common starting point among scholars interested in the formation of the Book of Isaiah is the conviction, or at least the assumption, that the present shape of the book is not the result of more or less accidental or arbitrary developments but rather . . . of deliberate and intentional literary and theological work."[23] Like Rendtorff, I distinguish between two approaches current in contemporary Ezekiel scholarship. On the one hand, diachronic approaches attempt to reconstruct the history of a text, including its composition history. On the other hand, synchronic approaches pursue what the text, in all its complexity, means in its final form.

Diachronic Approaches and Redaction Criticism. An imposing group of scholars has applied diachronic methods to the book of Ezekiel. In the twentieth century, the most famous and influential of these was Walther Zimmerli, whose massive, two-volume commentary on the book of Ezekiel appeared first as part of the Biblischer Kommentar, Altes Testament series,[24] and later, in English translation, as part of the Hermeneia commentary series.[25] Zimmerli's approach lay between the extreme positions represented by Smend, on the one hand, and Hölscher and Herntrich, on the other. He located Ezekiel's entire ministry in Babylonia, attributed the scroll to the prophet and his "school," concluded that Ezekiel himself returned to and updated earlier oracles, and dated the book's composition largely to the exilic period.

A gifted text critic, Zimmerli both worked with the Hebrew Masoretic Text (MT) and resorted to the versions (e.g., the Greek Septuagint [LXX]) in order to produce an original text free of later accretions and scribal errors. (One can seriously question whether even an "original" text would be free of scribal errors. Text critics agree that the book of Ezekiel is difficult Hebrew. Moreover, the scroll contains many *hapax legomena,* terms found nowhere else in the Hebrew Bible. Zimmerli counted over 130 such terms in the work.)[26] He utilized methodological tools, especially form and traditio-historical criticism, with skill and verve; and he identified forms and speeches lying behind the final shape of the text. Indeed, he went so far as to rewrite certain passages, ostensibly restoring them to their "original" forms (see, e.g., his rewrite of Ezekiel 16).[27] But he also traced the diachronic processes whereby original versions of texts attained their final forms. Willing to attribute problematic textual features to inept redactors, he nevertheless dealt seriously, though separately, with their efforts, describing a process by which "kernel elements" underwent further development.[28]

Synchronic Approaches to the Book of Ezekiel.

As noted above, synchronic approaches to biblical books pursue the meaning of a text in its final form, irrespective of the process by which it attained that form. Rendtorff's defense of recent synchronic readings of Isaiah also is applicable to synchronic readings of Ezekiel:

A changing view on the Book of Isaiah should allow, and even require, studies on topics, themes, expressions, and even ideas characteristic for the book as a whole or significant parts of it, without at the same time discussing the questions of redaction or composition. A synchronic reading, if carried out with the necessary sophistication, should have its own right.[29]

The method employed by Moshe Greenberg in the first two volumes of his three-volume commentary on Ezekiel for the Anchor Bible series bears a close familial resemblance to synchronic approaches.[30] His "holistic" interpretations of Ezekiel's oracles reflect a dissatisfaction with what he deems the anachronistic criteria of certain methodologies. He asserts, for example, that criteria commonly employed to recover the original oracles of Ezekiel "are simply *a priori*, an array of unproved (and unprovable) modern assumptions and conventions that confirm themselves through the results obtained by forcing them on the text and altering, reducing, and reordering it accordingly."[31] Unlike Zimmerli, who seeks to recover original texts by removing later accretions, Greenberg attempts to make sense of the book both textually and structurally in its received (MT) form. "His interpretations demonstrate a deep appreciation for what texts reveal about themselves when patiently probed."[32] Yet Greenberg's method should be distinguished from synchronic readings proper, because he does not intend to bracket evidence of redaction and editorial shaping. Rather, his approach reflects his judgments concerning the book's authorship and arrangement, both of which he attributes to the prophet Ezekiel:

The present Book of Ezekiel is the product of art and intelligent design. . . . A consistent trend of thought expressed in a distinctive style has emerged, giving the impression of an individual mind of powerful and passionate proclivities. . . . The persuasion grows on one as piece after piece falls into the established patterns and ideas that a coherent world of vision is emerging, contemporary with the sixth-century prophet and decisively shaped by him, if not the very words of Ezekiel himself.[33]

In a review of both commentaries, J. D. Levenson contrasts the approaches of Zimmerli and Greenberg: "Whereas Zimmerli sees the book of Ezekiel as a puzzle which the exegete must put into an intelligible order, Moshe Greenberg sees it as a subtle work of art and the exegete's task as the demonstration of its intelligibility. Where Zimmerli is a plastic surgeon, Greenberg is a midwife, carefully uncovering ever more order and symmetry in a text before which he stands in obvious reverence."[34]

A READER-ORIENTED APPROACH TO THE BOOK OF EZEKIEL

Many biblical scholars no longer confine their interests to recovering a prophet's original words, cleansed of later accretions. To the contrary, recent scholarship displays considerable interest in redactors as gifted literary artists and theologians in their own right. Although I value the findings of diachronic analysis, I have chosen to focus upon a late exilic reader's construal (understanding) of the book. A reader-oriented approach differs from that of Zimmerli in many ways; notably, my reader does not bring to the text knowledge of the historical-critical methodologies developed especially in the nineteenth and twentieth centuries and of their goals. It also differs from that of Greenberg in that it focuses not only upon what is read, but also upon the reading process itself. In what follows, I am indebted to J. A. Darr, whose reader-oriented method approaches biblical books (in his case, Luke-Acts; in mine, Ezekiel) as potentially coherent literary works, rather than simply as quarries for historical data.[35]

Acknowledging the many literary methods available to critics, Darr emphasizes the importance of constructing a "text-specific" approach that is well-suited to a particular piece of literature. All too often, he observes, contemporary biblical scholars adopt literary methods developed with modern works in mind. Such anachronistic approaches inevitably prove inadequate. To paraphrase Darr, the complexities of interpreting an ancient religious text like the book of Ezekiel cannot be overlooked in our search for literary-critical methods.[36] Rather, we must construct an eclectic approach, whose features are fashioned in the light of the particular text at hand.

Three Critical Premises. Three critical premises ground Darr's method. First, he affirms that "literature functions rhetorically"—that is, "it achieves certain effects—esthetic, emotional, moral, ideological—in an audience by means of rhetorical strategies."[37] Second, he asserts that meaning arises from the "dynamic interaction of both the rhetorical strategies of the text and the interpretive strategies (a repertoire of conventions and expectations) of its reader."[38] In other words, *meaning depends not only upon what the text brings to the reader, but also upon what the reader brings to the text.* This second premise presupposes that scholars can gain access to both the text and at least some aspects of the reader's extra-textual repertoire, including: "(1) language; (2) social norms and cultural scripts; (3) classical or canonical literature; (4) literary conventions (e.g., genres, type scenes, standard plots, stock characters) and reading rules (e.g., how to categorize, rank, and process various textual data); and (5) commonly-known historical and geographical facts."[39]

Our knowledge of this repertoire remains incomplete; and like those engaged in purely historical-critical pursuits, we can never eliminate uncertainty or the necessity for conjecture. Nevertheless, Darr insists in his third premise that a variety of text-specific factors—historical, social, linguistic, literary—remain relevant for contemporary construals of ancient texts. Some of those factors function transculturally and are easily grasped. Others are elusive. But it behooves critics to reconstruct culture-specific factors pertaining when the book of Ezekiel could be read as a coherent literary work.

With these three premises in place, Darr locates his literary method among the categories identified by M. H. Abrams:

Abrams' analytic scheme consists of four elements: the work itself, the artist or author, the universe or nature, and the audience. While most critics blend all four of these elements in their interpretive endeavors, each "tends to derive from one of these terms his principle categories for defining, classifying and analyzing the work of art, as well as the major criteria by which he judges its value." All literary theories, by definition, pay some heed to the

text; however, some approaches concentrate on it in isolation (objective theories), whereas others explain the work by relating it to something or someone else—the author (expressive theories), the audience (pragmatic theories), or aspects of the universe (mimetic theories).[40]

Darr's premises place his method on the "pragmatic" axis of Abrams's categories. Pragmatic approaches are scarcely novel; they predominated from the time of Horace through the eighteenth century. In the following two centuries, however, they were supplanted—first by expressionism (Romanticism) and then by objectivism (Formalism and the New Criticism)—primarily as a reflex against Romanticism's propensities toward "psychologistic and biographical criticism."[41]

Objective theories, by contrast, approach the text as an object "solid and material as an urn or icon."[42] "Critics read, reread, and reify the text as a complete mental 'object' whose textual features, including plot, theme, motif, character, point of view, juxtaposition, ambiguity, etc., can be analyzed and described."[43] They may, for example, read about Yahweh's abandonment of the Temple in Jerusalem (Ezekiel 11) with God's return to a new temple (Ezekiel 43) in mind. Or they may read Ezekiel's accusations against personified Jerusalem in chap. 16 with those found in chap. 23 in mind. But first-time, sequential readers encounter texts without benefit of the "big picture." Only in retrospect can they reconsider the significance of an earlier text in the light of later ones.

Like Darr, I follow critics like W. Iser and W. Booth, who focus upon "the dynamic interaction between text and reader in the temporal, conventional process of reading."[44] Admittedly, Iser's approach includes an inevitable indeterminacy: "By bringing in the reader as co-creator of the work's meaning, Iser has left himself open to . . . charges of indeterminacy and relativism. . . . Will not each individual reading of a text be different? Are some readings better than others? If so, what criteria are used to make these sorts of judgments?"[45] Daunting though these questions are, they are better faced head-on than ignored, as if readers played no role in determining a text's meaning. Hence, Darr concludes that "responsibility for maintaining a delicate balance between text and reader in the dialectical production of literary meaning lies with the critic; at this point artistry enters the interpretive enterprise":

> We envision a dialectic in which the text guides, prefigures, and attempts to persuade a reader to choose a particular path or adopt a certain world-view. At the same time, the reader is only using these textual promptings as starting points for filling in the gaps left by the text . . . and anticipating what is to come as the reading progresses. Texts have a certain determinateness, but the meanings derived from these texts are qualified by the receptivity and creativity of the individual reader in an interpretive community.[46]

Focusing upon text, reader, and the reading process does not rule out appeals to other elements in the interpretive process. As noted, Darr's eclectic method admits those social, historical, and literary contexts pertaining when more or less completed biblical books were first read. It remains pragmatic, however, because of the ways in which these "extrinsic" elements are utilized: "In essence, author and historical context are brought into the process of interpretation through the portals of text and reader, respectively."[47]

"Optical Lenses" and the Critic's Task. Critics select, order, and balance elements that shape interpretation; and their choices are not, protestations notwithstanding, utterly disinterested. To the contrary, Darr writes, "what the critic writes is no less rhetorical than the text itself, for critics actively advance one reading over alternatives":[48]

> The critic is a creative re-reader whose selections specify and limit what is to be perceived and how "best" it is to be understood by others. . . . by reconstructing a particular social-historical setting, identifying specific literary influences, and accentuating selected textual phenomena (and ignoring others), the critic attempts to persuade others to accept his or her interpretation.[49]

One need only to compare the commentaries by Zimmerli and Greenberg to see that competent critics can construe texts in widely divergent ways.

Darr adopts Booth's "optical lens" imagery to describe how critics negotiate various interpretive options. "Our choices of a given inquiry work like our choices of optical instruments, each camera or microscope or telescope uncovering what other instruments conceal and obscuring what other instruments bring into focus."[50] Darr's "optical instrument" requires the manipulation of four lenses:

wide-angle, editorial, objective, and reading.[51] The wide-angle lens is located in the eye of the critic, and its field of vision is the broadest of the four because it includes all of the information (historical, cultural, social, literary, etc.) that critics bring to texts.

The editorial lens, Darr's second optical instrument, examines a smaller field, but at greater depth. It focuses upon a particular text; and through it, modern scholars can discern information unavailable to ancient readers—e.g., signs of multiple authorship and redactional layers.

Reading a literary work through the objective lens, critics can focus upon the entire text within the same field. As noted above, first-time sequential readers do not have access to this lens. But critics can read and reread a literary work until it becomes, in effect, a "complete mental object" whose recurring features assume their places within the larger design. "Through this lens," Darr writes, the critic "scans the entire work (in any sequence—end to beginning, beginning to end, or randomly) in an effort to compare the part to the whole."[52]

Finally, critics shape and position the reading lens. Although not always acknowledged as such, "the reader" is an interpretive construct:

> The reader is not a given (e.g., an innate property of the text), but rather, is implicitly or explicitly construed by the critic. Such a construal is inevitably based, at least in part, on the critic's own reading experience. Every audience-oriented approach is founded upon preconceived notions of (1) the nature of the reading process (in general, and with regard to the specific work in question), and (2) the identity (competence, learning, knowledge of literary and cultural codes) of the reader.[53]

Of course, critics inevitably create readers (at least to some degree) in their own image. Nevertheless, critic and reader are not simply the same. The modern critic has access to repositories of knowledge (e.g., critical methodologies) the ancient reader does not possess; and the ancient reader, native to the culture whence the book arose, has access to knowledge (historical, cultural, social, etc.) unavailable to modern scholars.

Identifying the Reader. The initial task is to construct a "text-specific" reader who possesses the knowledge necessary to interpret the book of Ezekiel competently. My reader is part of the second generation of Judeans living in Babylonia. Although he does not reside in Jerusalem, he has learned from

Israel's cognoscenti-in-exile about life there. Culturally literate and fully at home within his diaspora community, he knows—or at least thinks he knows—facts (historical, political, geographical, religious, ethnic) and conventions (social, cultural, literary, etc.) related to Israel and its world. Far better than those Judeans who remained in their homeland, he knows the sophisticated culture of a major Mesopotamian empire. Though this is his first reading of the Ezekiel scroll, he is familiar with other of Israel's existing religious texts. He also knows the literary "classics" of his larger culture. Finally, he enjoys the opportunity, access, expertise, and time to read and interpret the unfolding Ezekiel scroll.

As noted above, my reader reads the book of Ezekiel in order to understand why, from the perspective of this authentic prophet who proclaims God's own words, Jerusalem was destroyed, Judah collapsed, and part of the population was deported to Babylonia, where he now resides. He also reads to discover what the future of Yahweh's people, and their enemies, will be.

Aspects of the Reading Process. Iser describes the dynamic process of reading: "We look forward, we look back, we decide, we change our decisions, we form expectations, we are shocked by their nonfulfillment, we question, we muse, we accept, we reject."[54] From this quotation, Darr identifies four complementary, ongoing aspects of reading: anticipation and retrospection; consistency building; investment and identification; and defamiliarization.[55] I shall discuss each briefly.

As sequential readers progress through a text, they continually reassess earlier expectations and judgments as new insights and data emerge. "In the dialectic of reading," Darr states, "each word, sentence, or other textual unit both illuminates and is illumined by what precedes it." The further one reads, the more complex the process of anticipation and retrospection becomes.[56] This is especially true when one seeks to construe so long and complex a text as the book of Ezekiel.

Related to this first aspect is the reader's tendency toward consistency building: "By correlating discrete elements of the text . . . and adding extra-textual information when necessary, the audience [reader] is able to image patterns . . . which cover textual gaps, help to resolve tensions, and clarify ambiguities."[57] Again, consistency building is a more complex process when a

lengthy and eclectic piece of prophetic literature is at issue. Nevertheless, certain textual features (e.g., chronologically arranged oracles, the Ezekielian tendency to introduce topics briefly, only to return to them at greater length later in the scroll) encourage readers to construe texts on the basis of preceding chapters and verses.

The third aspect, "investment and identification," refers to the varying distance between the reader and the text. "Consciously or unconsciously," Darr observes, "the reader oscillates between a full-scale involvement in the [world of the text] and a more detached observation of it."[58]

How are Ezekiel's late exilic readers encouraged to accept his explanation of the tragic events of Israel's past and of Yahweh's role in those events, to assume responsibility for their own actions and those of their community, to remain faithful to God, and to live in anticipation of restoration to their homeland? Here, the focus shifts from the reader to the text itself: "The *text* provides a series of stimuli which elicit and guide audience responses. In other words, it is a rhetorical framework, designed strategically to foster a sequence of mental images and cognitive acts by the reader. The text also controls point of view, a vital element in the shaping of values"[59] Moreover, text and reader share an extratext—that is, common ground that facilitates communication: "The first-time reader must bring to a text a set of expectations which provide a context for processing it. Such a meeting point between reader and text is provided by the extra-text, the repertoire of shared conventions and canonical works that exists in any literate society."[60] The literature of the ancient Near East suggests that audiences prized established literary conventions. Yet innovation also had its place. What Iser calls "defamiliarization"—setting the well-known in unfamiliar terrain—could force readers to perceive traditional elements in new ways.[61] One need only think of Ezekiel's radically innovative account of Israel's exodus and wilderness experiences in chap. 20 to recognize the rhetorical power of defamiliarization.

CONCLUSION

The book of Ezekiel enriches our canon of Scripture with its architectural majesty, sophisticated and complex theology, and literary brilliance.

During a critical period in Israel's history, Ezekiel sought to teach his community about human responsibility and divine response, to convince his fellow exiles of the unparalleled power of their God, and to discern their future as the people of Yahweh. I can only respect his refusal to abandon faith in God in the midst of crippling tragedy.

In this overview, I have identified certain Ezekielian presuppositions and beliefs that, once recognized and understood, may ameliorate readers' discomfort somewhat. But beyond the acquisition of historical insight lies the responsibility to debate the issues the book of Ezekiel raises. If, in the course of such debates, readers challenge aspects of the Ezekielian tradition, they are not at odds with the priest-prophet of old. To the contrary, they are in a very real sense Ezekiel's true disciples.

FOR FURTHER READING

Commentaries:

Blenkinsopp, Joseph. *Ezekiel.* IBC. Louisville: John Knox, 1990.

Block, Daniel I. *The Book of Ezekiel: Chapters 1–24.* NICOT. Grand Rapids: Eerdmans, 1997.

———. *The Book of Ezekiel: Chapters 25–48,* NICOT. Grand Rapids: Eerdmans, 1998.

Eichrodt, Walther. *Ezekiel.* Translated by Cosslett Quin. OTL. Philadelphia: Westminster, 1970.

Greenberg, Moshe. *Ezekiel 1–20.* AB 22. Garden City, N.Y.: Doubleday, 1983; *Ezekiel 21–37.* AB 22A. Garden City, N.Y.: Doubleday, 1997.

Zimmerli, Walther. *Ezekiel 1: A Commentary on the Book of the Prophet Ezekiel, Chapters 1–24.* Translated by R. E. Clements. Hermeneia. Philadelphia: Fortress, 1979.

———. *Ezekiel 2: A Commentary on the Book of the Prophet Ezekiel, Chapters 25–48.* Translated by J. D. Martin. Hermeneia. Philadelphia: Fortress, 1983.

Other Studies:

Cook, Stephen L. and Corrine L. Patton, eds. *Ezekiel's Hierarchical World: Wrestling with a Tiered Reality.* SBLSymS 31. Atlanta, Ga.: Society of Biblical Literature, 2004.

Darr, John A. " 'Glorified in the Presence of Kings': A Literary-Critical Study of Herod the Tetrarch in Luke-Acts" (Ph.D. diss., Vanderbilt Univer-

sity, Nashville, 1987). Published as *Herod the Fox: Audience Criticism and Lukan Characterization.* JSNTSUP 163. Sheffield: Sheffield Academic, 1998.

———. *On Character Building: The Reader and the Rhetoric of Characterization in Luke-Acts.* Literary Currents in Biblical Interpretation. Edited by D. N. Fewell and D. M. Gunn. Louisville: Westminster/John Knox, 1992.

Darr, Katheryn Pfisterer. "Ezekiel." In *The Women's Bible Commentary.* Expanded Edition with Apocrypha. Edited by Carol A. Newsom and Sharon H. Ringe. Louisville: Westminster John Knox, 1998.

Davis, Ellen F. *Swallowing the Scroll: Textuality and the Dynamics of Discourse in Ezekiel's Prophecy.* Bible and Literature 21. Sheffield: Almond, 1989.

Galambush, Julie. *Jerusalem in the Book of Ezekiel: The City as Yahweh's Wife.* SBLDS 130. Atlanta: Scholars Press, 1992.

Hals, Ronald M. *Ezekiel.* FOTL 19. Grand Rapids: Eerdmans, 1989.

Joyce, Paul. *Divine Initiative and Human Response in Ezekiel.* JSPTSup 51. Sheffield: JSOT, 1989.

Kamionkowski, S. Tamar. *Gender Reversal and Cosmic Chaos: A Study on the Book of Ezekiel.* JSOTSup 368. New York: Sheffield Academic Press, 2003.

Kutsko, John F. *Between Heaven and Earth: Divine Presence and Absence in the Book of Ezekiel.* Biblical and Judaic Studies from the University of California, San Diego 7. Winona Lake, Ind.: Eisenbrauns, 2000.

Klein, Ralph W. *Ezekiel: The Prophet and His Message.* Studies on Personalities of the Old Testament. Columbia: University of South Carolina Press, 1988.

Lust, J., ed. *Ezekiel and His Book: Textual and Literary Criticism and Their Interrelation.* BETL 74. Leuven: Leuven University Press, 1986.

Mein, Andrew. *Ezekiel and the Ethics of Exile.* Oxford Theological Monographs. Oxford: Oxford University Press, 2001.

Odell, Margaret S., and John T. Strong, eds. *The Book of Ezekiel: Theological and Anthropological Perspectives.* SBLSymS 9. Atlanta: SBL, 2000.

Renz, Thomas. *The Rhetorical Function of the Book*

of Ezekiel. VTSup 76. Leiden: Brill, 1999.

Stevenson, Kalinda Rose. *The Vision of Transformation: The Territorial Rhetoric of Ezekiel 40–48.* SBLDS 154. Atlanta: Scholars Press, 1996.

ENDNOTES

1. J. B. Pritchard, *Ancient Near Eastern Texts Relating to the Old Testament,* 3rd ed. (Princeton: Princeton University Press, 1969) 88. This account conflicts with the biblical tradition that Sennacherib was forced to withdraw from the city when his army was decimated by "the messenger of the Lord" (see Isa 37:26-38; 2 Kgs 19:35).

2. J. B. Pritchard, *ANET,* 564. This passage names neither the Judean king who was defeated nor the man appointed by Nebuchadrezzar to take his place. The biblical historiographers differ in their accounts of the events. According to 2 Kgs 24:6-12, Jehoiakim died and was succeeded by his son, Jehoiachin, prior to the seige against Jerusalem. However, 2 Chr 36:6-10 states that Jehoiakim was bound in fetters and exiled to Babylon at the time of the siege, and Jehoiachin followed him into exile three months and ten days afterwards. The account in 2 Kings is likely more accurate (see also Jer 22:19; 36:30).

3. Enno Janssen, *Juda in der Exilszeit,* FRLANT 69 (Göttingen: Vandenhoeck & Ruprecht, 1956) 49-54.

4. Thomas Renz, *The Rhetorical Function of the Book of Ezekiel,* VTSup 76 (Leiden: Brill, 1999) 44-45.

5. D. I. Block, *The Book of Ezekiel: Chapters 1–24,* NICOT (Grand Rapids: Eerdmans, 1997) 7-8.

6. The following paragraphs are based on K. P. Darr, "Ezekiel's Justifications of God: Teaching Troubling Texts," *JSOT* 55 (1992) 98-117.

7. D. I. Block, *Ezekiel 1–24,* 10.

8. D. J. Halperin, *Seeking Ezekiel: Test and Psychology* (University Park: Penn State University Press, 1993).

9. E. Reuss, *Ancien Testament II, Les Prophètes Littérature* II (Paris: Sandoz & Fischbacher) 10; cited and translated in W. Zimmerli, *Ezekiel 1: A Commentary on the Book of the Prophet Ezekiel, Chapters 1–24,* trans. R. E. Clements, Hermeneia (Philadelphia: Fortress, 1979) 4.

10. Thomas Renz, *The Rhetorical Function of the Book of Ezekiel,* 16.

11. Thomas Renz, *The Rhetorical Function of the Book of Ezekiel,* 16.

12. Thomas Renz, *The Rhetorical Function of the Book of Ezekiel,* 41.

13. The following sections derive from my earlier research, specifically, K. P. Darr, "Ezekiel Among the Critics," *CurBS* 2 (1994) 9-24; and *Isaiah's Vision and the Family of God* (Louisville: Westminster John Knox, 1994) esp. 13-32.

14. K. P. Darr, *Isaiah's Vision and the Family of God,* 13.

15. R. Smend, *Der Prophet Ezechiel,* KHAT (Leipzig: Hirzel, 1880) xxi; cited by W. Zimmerli, *Ezekiel 1,* 3.

16. H. Ewald, *Die Propheten des Alten Bundes erklärt.* II. *Jeremja und Hezekiel* (Göttingen: Vandenhoeck & Ruprecht) 207.

17. G. Hölscher, *Die Profeten* (Leipzig: Hinrichs, 1914); that attack was further strengthened in his *Hesekiel, der Dichter und das Buch,* BZAW 39 (Giessen: Töpelmann, 1924).

18. Hölscher, *Hesekiel,* 5-6; cited in Zimmerli, *Ezekiel 1,* 5.

19. See W. Zimmerli, *Ezekiel 1,* 5. Even more extreme is J. Garscha, *Studien zum Ezechielbuch: Eine redaktionskritische Untersuchung von Ez 1–39,* Europaische Hochschulschriften 23.23 (Bern: Peter Lang, 1974). He argues that only about thirty verses of chaps. 1–39 are from the prophet himself (17:2-10; 23:2-25).

20. V. Herntrich, *Ezekielprobleme,* BZAW 61 (Giessen: Töpelmann, 1974).

21. G. A. Cooke, *A Critical and Exegetical Commentary on the Book of Ezekiel,* ICC (New York: Scribner's, 1936) 1:v.

22. K. P. Darr, "Ezekiel Among the Critics," 11-12. See also H. H. Rowley, "The Book of Ezekiel in Recent Study," *BJRL* 36 (1953–54) 149-90.

23. R. Rendtorff, "The Book of Isaiah: A Complex Unity. Synchronic and Diachronic Reading," *SBLSP* 30 (1991) 9.

24. W. Zimmerli, *Ezechiel,* I, *BKAT* 13.1 (Neukirchen-Vluyn: Neukirchener Verlag, 1969); *Ezechiel,* II, *BKAT* 13.2 (Neukirchen-Vluyn: Neukirchener Verlag, 1969).

25. W. Zimmerli, *Ezekiel 1: A Commentary on the Book of the Prophet Ezekiel, Chapters 1–24,* trans. R. E. Clements, Hermeneia (Philadelphia: Fortress, 1979) and *Ezekiel 2: A Commentary on the Book of*

the Prophet Ezekiel, Chapters 25–48, trans. J. D. Martin, Hermeneia (Philadelphia: Fortress, 1983).

26. W. Zimmerli, Ezekiel 1, 23.

27. W. Zimmerli, Ezekiel 1, 347-48.

28. Because Zimmerli dealt with "primary" verses before moving on to secondary accretions, it it difficult to grasp the dynamic of the text as a text.

29. R. Rendtorff, "The Book of Isaiah," 20.

30. Moshe Greenberg, Ezekiel 1–20, AB 22 (Garden City, N.Y.: Doubleday, 1983); Ezekiel 21–37, AB 22A (Garden City, N.Y.: Doubleday, 1997).

31. Moshe Greenberg, Ezekiel 1–20, 20.

32. K. P. Darr, "Ezekiel Among the Critics," 14.

33. Moshe Greenberg, Ezekiel 1-20, 26-27.

34. J. D. Levenson, "Ezekiel in the Perspective of Two Commentators," Int 38 (1984) 213.

35. See John A. Darr, "'Glorified in the Presence of Kings': A Literary-Critical Study of Herod the Tetrarch in Luke-Acts" (Ph.D. diss., Vanderbilt University, Nashville, 1987), published as Herod the Fox: Audience Criticism and Lukan Characterization, JSNTSup 163 (Sheffield: Sheffield Academic, 1998). He subsequently refined it in On Character Building: The Reader and the Rhetoric of Characterization in Luke-Acts, Literary Currents in Biblical Interpretation, ed. D. N. Fewell and D. M. Gunn (Louisville: Westminster/John Knox, 1992).

36. John A. Darr, "'Glorified in the Presence of Kings,'" 12-13.

37. John A. Darr, "'Glorified in the Presence of Kings,'" 15.

38. John A. Darr, "'Glorified in the Presence of Kings,'" 15.

39. John A. Darr, On Character Building, 22.

40. John A. Darr, "'Glorified in the Presence of Kings,'" 18, citing and discussing M. H. Abrams, The Mirror and the Lamp: Romantic Theory and the Critical Tradition (New York: Oxford University Press, 1953) 6.

41. John A. Darr, "'Glorified in the Presence of Kings,'" 23.

42. T. Eagleton, Literary Theory: An Introduc-

tion (Minneapolis: University of Minnesota Press, 1983) 47.

43. K. P. Darr, Isaiah's Vision and the Family of God (Louisville: Westminster John Knox, 1994) 25-26.

44. John A. Darr, "'Glorified in the Presence of Kings,'" 38. See also W. Iser, The Act of Reading: A Theory of Aesthetic Response (Baltimore: Johns Hopkins University Press, 1978); W. Iser, "The Reading Process: A Phenomenological Approach," New Literary History 3 (1972) 279-99; and W. C. Booth, The Rhetoric of Fiction, 2nd ed. (Chicago: University of Chicago Press, 1983).

45. John A. Darr, "'Glorified in the Presence of Kings,'" 30.

46. John A. Darr, "'Glorified in the Presence of Kings,'" 38-39.

47. John A. Darr, "'Glorified in the Presence of Kings,'" 19.

48. John A. Darr, "'Glorified in the Presence of Kings,'" 55.

49. John A. Darr, "'Glorified in the Presence of Kings,'" 56-57.

50. W. C. Booth, The Rhetoric of Fiction, 405.

51. John A. Darr, "'Glorified in the Presence of Kings,'" 57.

52. John A. Darr, "'Glorified in the Presence of Kings,'" 60.

53. John A. Darr, "'Glorified in the Presence of Kings,'" 61.

54. W. Iser, "The Reading Process," 293.

55. John A. Darr, On Character Building, 29.

56. John A. Darr, "'Glorified in the Presence of Kings,'" 64.

57. John A. Darr, "'Glorified in the Presence of Kings,'" 65.

58. John A. Darr, "'Glorified in the Presence of Kings,'" 65.

59. John A. Darr, On Character Building, 32.

60. John A. Darr, "'Glorified in the Presence of Kings,'" 67.

61. W. Iser, The Act of Reading, 69.

INTRODUCTION TO
APOCALYPTIC LITERATURE

FREDERICK J. MURPHY

The terms *apocalypticism, apocalypse,* and *apocalyptic* are widely used within biblical scholarship, and they also appear in more popular settings—literature, film, and the news media, for example. The words derive from the Greek ἀποκάλυψις (*apokalypsis*), which means "revelation." Modern use of these words to describe a certain kind of literature and a specific worldview is due to the book of Revelation, which begins, "The revelation [*apokalypsis*] of Jesus Christ." The book of Revelation is often called the Apocalypse, and the title "Revelation" is simply a translation of that term. Beginning in the nineteenth century, scholars perceived similarities of form and content between Revelation and other ancient Jewish and Christian works, so they began to call such works "apocalypses" by analogy. Other ancient works written after Revelation explicitly call themselves apocalypses, but none before. Nonetheless, many Jewish works written before Revelation share its literary genre.

Until the 1970s, the word *apocalyptic* was used as a noun, denoting a rather amorphous entity made up of certain texts, a specific kind of imagery, vision reports, a variety of worldviews, and particular social groups. A wide range of Jewish and Christian texts, many of them not apocalypses, were used in this construction of "apocalyptic." The resulting construct was then used to interpret specific texts, persons, and events. Ideas like "apocalyptic movement" emerged, implying that there was a single movement that could be called apocalyptic in which the various expressions of the phenomenon were included. The problem with this approach is that the theoretical "apocalyptic" that results does not always fit the apocalypses. There is tremendous variation in apocalypses with respect to form and content, beliefs, expectations, historical circumstances, political positions, and so on. Nothing like a single apoca-

lyptic movement ever existed. A basic worldview is common to all apocalypses, but it is common in the Hellenistic world even outside apocalypses, leaving room for a wide spectrum of particular apocalyptic theologies and ideologies.

Greater precision is attained through distinguishing between apocalypse as a literary genre, apocalypticism as a worldview, and "apocalyptic" as an adjective applied in the first instance to apocalypses and in a derivative way to texts and ideas that have much in common with apocalypses. What is apocalyptic is first of all what one finds in apocalypses. Anything else is apocalyptic by comparison. Further, it is no longer assumed that a given text necessarily represents a historical community or movement, rather than the point of view of an individual or of a small group fairly indistinguishable from society as a whole. The basics of the apocalyptic worldview were widespread enough in the Hellenistic world that apocalypses do not necessarily imply a sectarian group that produced and preserved them. The judgment about whether a sect stands behind a given apocalypse must be made anew for each text.

The book of Daniel in the Hebrew Bible and the book of Revelation in the New Testament are the only biblical examples of apocalypses. But apocalyptic influence in the Bible is far broader than that fact suggests. A number of prophetic texts written during and after the Babylonian exile share features of content and form with the apocalypses, so they are sometimes called "proto-apocalyptic." Apocalyptic influence is also evident throughout most of the New Testament. Of course, the Bible presents only aspects of ancient Judaism and Christianity, thus it is part of the task of biblical scholars to look beyond the canon to situate the biblical texts within their original contexts. In this connection, it is noteworthy that a substantial proportion of Jewish literature written between 300 BCE and

200 CE is either in the form of apocalypses or displays apocalyptic features. Likewise, apocalypses and apocalyptic thought played a prominent role in early Christianity. This article concentrates on the period between 300 BCE and 200 CE. References to and analyses of specific apocalypses are illustrative rather than exhaustive.

THE APOCALYPTIC GENRE

The first step in discussing apocalyptic literature is to decide which texts are apocalypses. In the late 1970s, a group of scholars examined all documents considered apocalypses and constructed a definition that fits all of them and distinguishes them from other sorts of ancient literature.[1] All apocalypses are narratives, stories describing the disclosure of otherwise inaccessible secrets to a human seer by a heavenly being. The disclosures are usually through visions. (The term *seer* literally means "see-er," one who sees visions.) Often the visions themselves are enigmatic and must be interpreted by a heavenly being, usually an angel. There are two main kinds of apocalyptic narratives. In the first, the seer travels to the heavenly realm or to parts of the cosmos usually inaccessible to human beings. The second type contains no otherworldly journey. This type often incorporates a review of history, culminating in an eschatological crisis and resolution, such as a conflict between the forces of good and evil, resulting in evil's defeat. That review is frequently in the form of fictive "prediction" of history (actually, the past of the real author) by the pseudonymous seer, a device known as *vaticinia ex eventu*, "prophecies after the event." At the end of such reviews is genuine prediction of things to happen in the author's future. A Jewish apocalypse from the end of the first century CE, the *Apocalypse of Abraham*, contains both an otherworldly journey and a review of history, but such a combination is unusual.

Apocalyptic revelation has temporal and spatial dimensions. The spatial aspect deals with the supernatural world, often conceived of as being above or below this world. It sometimes involves a heaven divided into levels, and it discloses the activities of supernatural beings, such as angels and demons. The natural and supernatural realms are closely interrelated. Decisions made in the supernatural realm or events that transpire there

affect and sometimes determine what happens on earth. Conversely, earthly events can have repercussions in the supernatural world. True understanding of historical events and concrete earthly circumstances requires knowledge of the heavenly world not generally available. The temporal aspect of apocalyptic revelation concerns eschatological judgment. That judgment can involve cosmic catastrophe and public judgment of all humanity, a scenario that conforms to what is popularly termed apocalyptic, but it might involve only individual judgment after death. The element common to all apocalypses is postmortem rewards and punishments, an idea that enters Judaism through the medium of apocalypticism, since it does not occur elsewhere in the Hebrew Bible. Israel's religion as presented in the Hebrew Bible is focused on this life. After death, good and bad alike descend into Sheol and live a shadowy existence that bears little resemblance to later concepts of heaven and hell. Daniel is the only biblical book in which transcendence of death through resurrection is clearly attested, and it is the last-written book to be included in the Hebrew Bible (c. 165 BCE). Even before Daniel, transcendence of death is expressed in the *Book of the Watchers*, a Jewish apocalypse from the third century BCE, now preserved as *1 Enoch* 1–36. Resurrection becomes a regular feature of apocalyptic scenarios of the eschaton. The future life is often conceived of as taking place in the supernatural realm. In Daniel 12 and *2 Baruch* 51, for example, the righteous join the stars. In other instances, there is a new heaven and a new earth in which the saved live. In Revelation 21–22, the new Jerusalem descends to earth, and God and Christ live on the new earth with the righteous.

All Jewish apocalypses and many Christian ones are pseudonymous. The seer is an ancient hero, such as Enoch, Abraham, Moses, Baruch, or Ezra. Such attributions enhance the authority of the works. The specific choice of seer is often appropriate. Three Jewish apocalypses were written as responses to the destruction of the Jerusalem Temple by the Romans in 70 CE. *Second Baruch* is attributed to a writer who lived through the earlier destruction of the Temple by the Babylonians in 587 BCE. Fourth Ezra is credited to the scribe who brought the Torah back to Israel after the Babylonian exile, and the work ends with Ezra reconstituting the Torah, which was burned in the destruction, by dictating it to scribes (4 Ezra 14). The *Apocalypse of Abraham* takes the vision experienced by Abraham in Genesis 15 as the occasion of a sweeping view of world history that puts the destruction of the Temple into perspective. A large number of apocalypses were assigned to Enoch. At least five such apocalypses are now preserved in a collection called *1 Enoch*, preserved in Ethiopic, in Aramaic fragments from Qumran, in several Greek fragments, and in one Latin fragment. Enoch appears in Gen 5:24 as one who walked with God—i.e., as righteous. It is stated enigmatically that "God took him," a phrase later interpreted as God's taking him to heaven. Enoch thus became an appropriate figure to whom heavenly revelations could be given. In *1 Enoch* 14, he makes a trip to the heavenly throne room, and in chapters 17–36 he tours parts of the cosmos not accessible to other humans.

Although apocalypses are often permeated by scriptural language, images, and patterns, they do not try to convince their readers through exegesis of Scripture. Nor is rational persuasion their technique. Rather, the authority of an apocalypse comes from the seer's direct reception of revelation. In effect, the author claims divine authority for the content of the apocalypse. Apocalypses are the more compelling in that they do not merely relay information, but allow their readers to accompany the seer through the process of revelation by describing that process in detail. So, for example, the readers experience Enoch's awe as he enters the heavenly sanctuary (*1 Enoch* 14), Daniel's terror as he sees mysterious beasts arising from the sea and a powerful angel descending from heaven (Daniel 7; 10), John's wonder as he sees the great harlot dressed in crimson and purple and riding on the seven-headed, ten-horned beast (Revelation 17). Through such means, apocalypses do more than convey information or demand specific behavior. They also contain a powerful emotional element that cannot be translated into other terms. They allow the reader to experience the supernatural world that affects this one and to see firsthand the coming eschatological judgment. Through that experience they can put their own circumstances into perspective. Through historical apocalypses, readers can contemplate history as a whole and understand their place in it. Apocalypses concerned with politics can allow readers to perceive

their struggles with evil rulers as part of a larger struggle between good and evil forces. They derive hope from the knowledge that as in the mythological combat between the most high God and forces inimical to divine order, good will be victorious.

Discussions of apocalyptic genre have been complicated by the fact that apocalypses are sometimes found embedded in other genres, that they frequently incorporate other genres, and that apocalyptic elements can be found in a variety of texts. Two other genres show particular affinities with apocalypses: testaments and oracle collections. Testaments are last words of major figures before their deaths. The form was popular in the period under consideration. A common element in testaments is prediction of the future. Such predictions often include eschatological scenarios and so are suited for apocalyptic predictions. There are many such passages in the *Testaments of the Twelve Patriarchs*, and one of the texts in that collection, the *Testament of Levi*, contains a short apocalypse in chapters 2–5. In the *Testament of Moses*, Moses predicts the course of Israel's history, culminating in the appearance of God's kingdom (chap. 10). Satan is destroyed, and God comes as the divine warrior to put an end to idols and to vindicate Israel.

The prophetic books in the Hebrew Bible are for the most part oracle collections. Their relevance for the apocalypses will be examined below. Another oracle collection that is very significant for the study of Jewish apocalyptic literature is the *Sibylline Oracles*. The notion of a woman prophet (sibyl) who utters prophecies of a political nature was taken over by the Jews from their environment in the Hellenistic period. Sibylline collections also figured largely in Greek and Roman settings. The *Sibylline Oracles* in standard editions are Jewish (books 3–5 and 11–14) and Christian (only books 6 and 7 were originally Christian; the others adapt Jewish works). Although the form of revelation is quite different from that found in apocalypses, they contain political prophecy that resembles what is found in many historical apocalypses. They employ mythological elements; criticize the present state of affairs, particularly Roman rulers; and predict future disaster.

WORLDVIEW

The form and content of apocalypses imply a basic worldview common to all of them. There is a supernatural world that is closely related to this one, and there is an eschatological judgment for humans and often for supernatural beings as well. This basic foundation allows for a wide variety of theologies, messages, and social ideologies.

Most past scholarship on apocalypticism has been dominated by Christian concerns. Since eschatology and messianism are so important to early Christian thought, those aspects of apocalypses, both Jewish and Christian, have often attracted attention disproportionate to their actual importance in apocalyptic literature. That imbalance is now being addressed by studies that do greater justice to the noneschatological and nonmessianic nature of many of the revelations in particular apocalypses. The heavenly journey apocalypses in particular show an interest in a wide range of topics—cosmology, meteorology, astronomy, astrology, calendar, angelology, etc.—in addition to eschatology. Many of the topics addressed by such apocalypses do not receive much attention in the Hebrew Bible. Such apocalypses may not conform to what is popularly thought of as apocalyptic, because they do not always contain cosmic upheavals or eschatological sufferings. But they share with the historical apocalypses interest in the supernatural world, a world that is crucial for understanding this one, and belief in rewards and punishments after death.

Apocalypses frequently display some degree of dualism. A distinction is drawn between this world and the supernatural realm and between life before and life after death. Some apocalypses go beyond these dualisms to see a cosmic dualism consisting of an opposition between supernatural forces of good and evil. This is not a thoroughgoing dualism, positing an evil entity equal to God. Rather, it opposes lesser forces, such as Michael against Satan (Revelation 12), Michael against Belial,[2] Gabriel and Michael against the heavenly patrons of Persia and Greece (Daniel 10; cf. Jesus against Satan in the Gospel of Mark). God is always supreme. The degree of cosmic dualism varies across the apocalypses, and so it cannot be taken as a universal characteristic of them.

Social dualism is also frequent in apocalypses and is correlated with cosmic dualism when present. Humanity is divided into good and evil, the elect and the rest, those who are being saved and those who are perishing (see 1 Cor 1:18). There is a final struggle between good and evil, which usually involves supernatural powers. The nature of human participation in that struggle varies. In Daniel, it is God who destroys Judaism's enemy, the Seleucid king Antiochus IV Epiphanes, and the heavenly patrons of various nations clash with Gabriel and Michael. In Revelation, Christians participate in the battle against Satan and Rome only through their witness to Christ and their refusal to accommodate themselves to Hellenistic culture and to the imperial cult. Christ has already defeated Satan in his death and resurrection. Satan has been ejected from heaven by Michael and the good angels (Revelation 12) and now wages war against Christians on earth. The final military victory is fought between Christ and his heavenly armies on the one side and Satan and his allies on the other.

All apocalypses involve eschatology, but some forms of apocalypticism have a strong eschatological focus. The conflict between good and evil will be resolved through victory for the forces of good. That victory is conceptualized in many ways. It may be renewal of the earth, where life will be lived as it should be, in union with God and without evil of any sort, or it may be a future heavenly existence for humans.

THE ORIGINS OF APOCALYPTICISM

The origins of apocalypses and apocalypticism have been a major preoccupation of scholars. The main debate has been between those who consider apocalypses to be a natural development of elements already existent within Judaism and those who see apocalypticism as a foreign entity, imported from the Gentile world. The most widely accepted position today is that apocalypses resulted from a complex interplay of foreign and domestic elements. The debate over whether apocalypticism is authentically Jewish can be misleading. Israel was always to some degree open to outside influences. Israelite and Jewish religion was full of elements adapted from its environment. The Hellenistic age saw a particularly fertile interaction of different cultures and national and ethnic heritages, and Judaism shared in that interaction. Writers of Jewish apocalypses responded to the new conditions and circumstances of the Hellenistic and Roman periods, and they used both domestic and foreign elements to do so.

The Hebrew Bible furnishes much raw material for apocalypticism. The idea that God communicates in mysterious dreams or visions that require inspired interpretation is found in the story of Joseph in Egypt (Genesis 40–41) as well as in the books of Zechariah and Ezekiel. That God controls human events from the heavenly court is clear in the story of the prophet Micaiah ben Imlah, who is granted a view of God deciding to send a lying spirit into Ahab's prophets so as to mislead him (1 Kings 22). The apocalyptic picture of a warrior God who intervenes in history to defeat evil has its roots in the notion of the divine warrior, a common biblical idea.

Efforts to find the origins of Jewish apocalypticism in Israel's proverbial and speculative wisdom tradition have not won many supporters, but the exilic and post-exilic prophets are a particularly fruitful source of comparison. Zechariah attests to the vision-reaction-interpretation pattern common in apocalypses. Ezekiel contains extended metaphors, such as the prostitute of chapter 16, which Revelation uses in chapter 17 (see also the oracles against Babylon in Jeremiah 50–51). Ezekiel's vision in chapters 40–48 of the restored Jerusalem inspired later apocalyptic visions. The visions of the heavenly throne room found in texts such as *1 Enoch* 14, Daniel 7, and Revelation 4–5 find counterparts in the earlier visions of Isaiah 6 and Ezekiel 1. Beyond formal similarities there are also similarities of content. Although prophetic texts never contain the idea of postmortem rewards and punishments, they do provide elements that were used in apocalyptic eschatological scenarios. A good example is Isaiah 24–27, often called the Isaiah Apocalypse, although it is not written in the form of an apocalypse. Isaiah 24:21-23 speaks of punishment of the heavenly host and earthly kings who are shut up in prison until a final punishment. This is like the scheme found in the *Book of the Watchers* (see also Revelation 20). Isaiah 26:19 calls for the rising of those who dwell in the dust, an apparent reference to resurrection. This may be simply a metaphor, as is the revivification of dry bones in Ezekiel 37, but it at least hints at the later apocalyptic idea of resurrection. Zechariah 14 and Ezekiel 38–39 speak of a great eschatological battle, and those texts inspired later versions of the final battle between forces for and against God.

Apocalypses differ from prophetic texts in their combination of heavy use of techniques like vision-reaction-interpretation and heavenly journeys, intense interest in the supernatural world, and eschatology that includes transcendence of death. Each of these elements was common in the Hellenistic world, as were pseudepigraphy, periodization of history, and *ex eventu* prophecy.

Scholars have noted phenomena in Persian, Egyptian, and Mesopotamian texts that correspond to features of Jewish apocalypses. Persian sources contain evidence of resurrection, postmortem judgment, division of history into periods, eschatological tumult, dualistic conflict between the forces of good and evil, and the ascent of the soul. Although the Persian sources are difficult to date, it is likely that many of these ideas go back at least to the Hellenistic period, if not before. Egyptian sources provide examples of political prophecy, as do Mesopotamian texts. Mesopotamia also furnishes examples of *ex eventu* prophecy combined with authentic prediction, as is found in Daniel 11. Daniel 8 betrays the influence of Mesopotamian astrology.

It is difficult to know precisely how these influences fed into Israel's traditions so as to emerge in apocalypses. It is possible that Jews in the eastern diaspora were the first to incorporate such features into their works and worldview. The seer of the two earliest extant Jewish apocalypses, the *Book of the Watchers* and the *Astronomical Book* (*1 Enoch* 72–82), is Enoch. The figure of Enoch originates in Gen 5:18-24, but it has been developed according to the model of the Enmeduranki, who was the seventh of the kings on the Sumerian king list. Enmeduranki founded an association of Babylonian diviners. The book of Daniel shows various Eastern influences, and the stories in the first six chapters of the book are set in the royal courts of Babylonia, Media, and Persia. Those stories may have originally existed independently of the book of Daniel and have come from the eastern diaspora. But given the fluid interchange of ideas, symbolism, and traditions that marked the Hellenistic age in general and the amount of Hellenistic influence that occurred even among Palestinian Jews, it is unwise to draw too sharp a distinction between the Jews in the diaspora and those who remained in the homeland. Both groups were influenced by their Hellenistic environment, thus both can be called Hellenistic Jews, although perhaps to different degrees and in different ways.

Apocalypses make creative use of mythology. Indeed, they are more heavily mythological than is the Hebrew Bible itself. Although the Hebrew Bible contains mythological elements, they are often historicized. They are not related as full myths, but are used to comment on or to embellish Israel's history. Nonetheless, some parts of the Hebrew Bible, the book of Psalms and Second Isaiah, for example, do attest to a certain vitality of mythology in Israel. Apocalypses tap into the deep wellsprings of ancient Near Eastern mythology. In doing so, they render fuller versions of some myths that are used more sparingly in the Hebrew Bible. For example, Gen 6:1-4 briefly recounts the descent of angels to have intercourse with human women, resulting in offspring who were giants. The story is mentioned, but not developed. A much fuller version of this story appears in the *Book of the Watchers*, where the watchers' development of their plan, their descent, and its consequences are related in much more detail. The angels' descent becomes the explanation for the existence of evil in the world. Another example of a more developed mythology concerns the punishment of humans and supernatural figures mentioned in passing in Isa 24:21-23. They "will be gathered together like prisoners in a pit" and "shut up in a prison" (Isa 24:22 NRSV) until the time of their punishment. This pattern is found in much greater detail in the *Book of the Watchers*, and it may have influenced the story of the binding, releasing, and defeat of Satan in Revelation 20. A last example involves the combat myth, the notion that there once was a great battle between supernatural figures that determined the subsequent course of the universe. One finds that myth in various forms throughout the ancient Near East. It serves as a model for Revelation 12 and Dan 8:10.

The proximate sources for the mythological traditions found in Jewish and Christian apocalypses are something of an open question. The cult may well have preserved mythological elements that are not entirely clear through our extant texts. Israel may also have passed down such elements in its general culture or adopted them from its environment at different stages of its history. Since Jews lived in the Hellenistic world, which was characterized by a fertile interaction of cultures, their literature may have received many elements from that interaction. In any case, scholarship will not grasp the meaning of apocalypses merely by tracing the origin of their individual traditions.

Apocalypses must be read as whole units and as creative responses to the new conditions of the Hellenistic world.

Another open question is to what extent apocalypses attest to actual visions experienced by their authors. There is not enough evidence to decide the answer to this question definitively. The descriptions of preparations to receive revelations found in some apocalypses suggest genuine techniques to induce visions. Some scholars have pointed to the scribal nature of apocalypses and their heavy use of tradition to argue against this position, but apocalypses may be the results of learned elaboration of an original experience rather than a simple description of what actually happened to the seer. Some scholars have attempted to develop criteria by which it might be decided which apocalyptic passages represent real visions and which are stylized accounts, but no set of criteria has won general approval. What is clear is that the authors of apocalypses expected their claims to visionary experience to be taken seriously and to affect their audiences profoundly.

Apocalypses have often been considered crisis literature, composed during times of oppression or even persecution. Two crises in the Second Temple period led to the production of apocalypses. When Antiochus IV Epiphanes, the Seleucid king, tried to outlaw Judaism in 167 BCE, one result was the Maccabean revolt, and another was the writing of apocalypses. Daniel dates to this time, as does a small apocalypse embedded in the collection called *1 Enoch:* the *Animal Apocalypse* (*1 Enoch* 85–90). The *Apocalypse of Weeks* (*1 Enoch* 93:1-10; 91:12-17) probably dates from about the same time. The *Animal Apocalypse* clearly supports the militant resistance of the Maccabees and sees it as the culmination of history, leading to the messianic era. But Daniel takes a more quietistic stand. Humans are not expected to take up arms, a fact that makes it seem unlikely that the author had much enthusiasm for the revolt. Daniel 11:34 may refer to the Maccabees as "a little help" (NRSV), judging them to be ultimately irrelevant to the solution of the problem. The real solution will be provided by God's direct intervention. The differing stands taken by these contemporary apocalypses show that the apocalyptic worldview does not imply any special political ideology. Another crisis that led to the writing of apocalypses was the

Roman destruction of Jerusalem and its Temple in 70 CE. Shortly afterward, four apocalypses appeared: 4 Ezra, *2 Baruch*, the *Apocalypse of Abraham*, and probably *3 Baruch.*

Although many apocalypses clearly arise from circumstances of crisis, that is not so clear for others. No public crisis is obvious in the *Similitudes of Enoch* (*1 Enoch* 37–71), the *Testament of Abraham, 2 Enoch*, or the *Apocalypse of Zephaniah*, for example. Of course, what constitutes a crisis may be in the eye of the beholder. What might look like a period of prosperity and peace from the viewpoint of the well-to-do can appear as a time of oppression and suffering to those at the bottom of the social hierarchy. Even those who are not poor or obviously oppressed might see a crisis in the fact that a foreign power rules their land. Recent research on Revelation and its social and political setting agrees that there was no large-scale persecution of Christianity in the late first century under Emperor Domitian, when Revelation was written. Opposition to Christianity, where it existed at all, was probably local and resulted not in Christians' being thrown to the beasts, but in informal social and economic sanctions on a small scale. The function of Revelation may have been less to comfort Christians at the onset of a major persecution than to warn them of the demonic nature of the Roman Empire so as to discourage the accommodation to Hellenistic and Roman culture that the author observed going on around him.

Although a crisis setting is not provable or even probable for many apocalypses, they all express, at least implicitly, a dissatisfaction with the temporal world. The impulse to explore the supernatural world and to look beyond death is due at least in part to a perception that all is not as it should be on earth. The wrong king may be on the throne, a foreign power may occupy the land, there may be laxity in ordering society according to God's will.

APOCALYPTIC DISCOURSE

The way that apocalypses make meaning is foreign to most modern people. Scholars have often dealt with the strangeness of apocalypticism by reducing it to more understandable terms. At times, apocalypses have been treated as encoded forms of exhortation, timeless truths, or descriptions of historical situations. At other times, they have been treated as sources from which to extract bits of information about topics of interest, such as messianism and eschatology. These approaches to understanding apocalypses are not without some justification. Apocalypses do make references to historical events and circumstances, and they sometimes express truths that speak to ages other than their own, and they can be used to supply information about messianic and eschatological beliefs. But to appreciate apocalypses for what they are, one must read them on their own terms.

Apocalyptic discourse has been called poetic and even mythopoetic. Apocalypses project experience onto a cosmic screen, using all the resources at their disposal, including elements from their own religious traditions as well as from their broader environment. The result is imaginative literature, which uses symbolic language to evoke aspects of reality that are beyond our powers of literal description. They allow their readers to see their own situations from the perspectives of the supernatural world and from the vantage point of life after death. This change of perspective allows a different consciousness to emerge, thereby changing experience itself. Human experience is found to be connected to larger, even cosmic realities. One's own historical period or personal life is viewed within a broad vista and can thereby be ordered correctly. This does not just make experience more tolerable; it actually changes experience, since experience is inseparable from perception. To change perception is to change the world.

A consideration of the use of mythology displayed in apocalypses can produce insight into the ways in which they make meaning. Ancient Near Eastern myths were stories about supernatural figures. Those stories shed light on human life, its institutions, hopes, fears, and struggles. Myths incorporate patterns that correspond to deeply held convictions, profound emotions, and basic attitudes toward life. To tap into this sort of discourse is to access the power of such stories and the images and symbols they contain. For many people, the beasts from the sea and the Son of Man coming on the clouds in Daniel 7 are still potent symbols of the victory of good over evil. The same is true of the battle between Christ and Satan depicted in Revelation and in the Gospels. If the strength of such symbols can still be felt today, the effect they had in ancient Mediterranean and Near Eastern cultures where they originated can be imagined as well.

Because apocalypses project human experience onto a broad screen, temporally and spatially, they have something to say not just to the particular circumstances in which they were written, but also to other times and situations. The history of interpretation of the two canonical apocalypses, Daniel and Revelation, bears eloquent testimony to the adaptability of apocalypses. Daniel itself was crucial to the writing of parts of the Enochic literature, and it was also important to Revelation and 4 Ezra, for example. Revelation supported the hopes of the early Christians who expected a thousand-year period of blessedness, was interpreted as a description of Christian life between Christ's resurrection and the parousia (by Augustine and many others), served as a map of church history, and has been seen by some contemporary Christians as the key to current events and a disclosure of the future. A solid understanding of the genre, the worldview, and the original historical circumstances of apocalypses can enable today's believers to benefit from their spiritual insights and strange beauty without being misled by simplistic and sometimes dangerous interpretations.

THE CANONICAL APOCALYPSES: DANIEL AND REVELATION

The two biblical apocalypses, Daniel and Revelation, are similar in many respects. Each responds to a specific crisis—Daniel to the persecution of the Jews by Antiochus IV Epiphanes in the second century BCE, Revelation to what the author perceives as an impending persecution of true Christians by the Roman Empire in the first century CE. Each document provides typically apocalyptic solutions to its crisis. In each case a revelation is granted to a human seer in which the seer has visions of the supernatural world—visions at least partially explained by an angelic interpreter. The visions reveal that the supernatural world determines the natural world and human history. It is disclosed that the earthly adversary of God's people will be defeated through divine intervention, and the righteous will live in union with God forever after. Each text anticipates resurrection. Each attempts to persuade readers of its viewpoint. Because Daniel and Revelation supply insights into the heavenly world and into God's own decisions, the points of view that each book advocates receive divine sanction and attain the status of divine revelation.

Daniel. This book falls into two parts. Chapters 1–6 are a prologue to the apocalypse proper, which occupies chapters 7–12. Chapters 1–6 are set in the royal courts of the Babylonian, Median, and Persian empires, where Daniel distinguishes himself both as a champion of Jewish piety and as a divinely inspired interpreter of dreams and signs. This portrait of Daniel makes him an ideal mediator of heavenly secrets. This is true particularly because Daniel credits God with his dream interpretations and does not attribute them to his own talents or efforts (2:28, 30). In chapters 7–12, Daniel has his own visions in the night, interpreted for him by an angel. His vision in chapter 7 contains the essential elements of the other dreams. He sees a succession of four beasts rising out of the sea. In the ancient Near East and in Israel, the sea represented the powers of chaos, a cosmic force opposed to God and to God's order. The beasts' origin in the sea reveals their nature as opponents of God. They are both like and unlike earthly animals. Because the beasts are in some ways similar to earthly creatures, the readers can get some idea of the strength and fearful qualities of these beasts. Since as a whole they correspond to no earthly creature but are a bizarre combination of known beasts, they assume an otherworldly and awful aspect. They are suitable, therefore, to represent powers that are both this-worldly and cosmic.

Later in the vision, Daniel learns that the beasts represent four kings (7:17), but in 7:23-24 it is clear that the fourth beast is also a kingdom and that its horns are individual kings. The fluidity of the imagery here should be a warning not to insist on a rigid, one-to-one correspondence between elements of the visions and the natural or supernatural realities to which they refer (see also Revelation 17). Such correspondences do occur, but the visions are mythopoetic, so their full import always exceeds such simple references. The fourth beast differs from those that precede it in its destructiveness. Then a horn arises on the fourth beast that supplants three other horns and begins to speak arrogantly. Commentators agree that the arrogant horn is Antiochus IV Epiphanes, whose rise to power was at the expense of other royal pretenders and whose persecution of Judaism was arrogant in the extreme, since by it he opposed God.

After the vision of the four beasts, the focus suddenly shifts to God's heavenly court, where God, the Ancient of Days, sits on a throne. As the court sits in judgment, books are opened. Abruptly, the focus leaves the heavenly court and is back on the fourth beast, who is slain. After some words about the fate of the other beasts, the scene again jumps to heaven, where one like a "son of man" comes on the clouds and is presented before God and receives kingship. The rest of the chapter indicates that just as the one like a son of man and the holy ones receive the kingdom in heaven, so also their people, Israel, receive sovereignty on earth. The holy ones are angels, and the one like a son of man is a prominent angel, probably Michael, Israel's heavenly patron (see Dan 10:21).

Daniel 8–11 covers much the same material as Daniel 7, but there is more detail concerning the Seleucids, especially Antiochus IV Epiphanes. In chapter 10, the mode of revelation shifts from vision and interpretation to direct instruction of Daniel by an angel, probably Gabriel. The angel tells Daniel that an angelic war is being waged in which he is fighting against a series of "princes" representing earthly empires (10:13, 20-21; 11:1). Gabriel has only Michael, Israel's heavenly patron (10:21), as an ally. The angel's words assume that each nation has its own patron angel and that conflicts between earthly nations reflect struggles between their supernatural patrons. This notion builds on ancient Near Eastern mythology as glimpsed in Psalms 82; 89:5-7; Deut 32:8-9, and serves apocalyptic purposes by emphasizing the close connection between entities and events in the natural and supernatural realms. In Daniel 12, Israel's protector, Michael, appears, and there is turmoil such as has never been seen in the world's history. There is a resurrection that does not seem to include all of humanity, but only certain select good and evil persons, and some of the elect "shine . . . like the stars" (Dan 12:3 NRSV) forever. Daniel is then told to seal up his book until the end.

This brief review of Daniel 7–12 highlights several elements typical of apocalypses. Daniel, a human seer, is granted visions mediated by an angel. He is allowed to see the supernatural world, even heaven itself, and to know of the divine decree for the eschatological defeat of Israel's enemy, Antiochus. Daniel thus learns the truth behind the historical events in the time of the actual author. True interpretation of events depends on divine revelation. Daniel does not come to this understanding through his own talents or insight. His understanding comes through the unveiling of heavenly mysteries.

In addition to features that Daniel shares with all apocalypses, there are a number of ways in which it fits the subgenre of historical apocalypses. There is a review of events that are actually in the real author's past, such as the rise of the Babylonian, Median, Persian, and Greek empires in the form of *ex eventu* prophecy, made possible by the attribution of the work to the ancient seer. When the review reaches Antiochus's persecution, in the real author's present, it shifts to genuine prediction. In fact, the prediction of Antiochus's death in chapter 11 is historically inaccurate in a number of ways. The review builds confidence in the real prediction contained in the text by showing how Daniel accurately foretells the rest of history. It also implies God's control of history. Since there are four beasts, history is periodized, another way of saying that it is controlled by God. History is seen as a whole, under the rubric of divine sovereignty and purpose. History leads to the ultimate goal of the defeat of God's (and so God's people's) enemies and the establishment of God's authority over a harmonious cosmos and a faithful people.

There is a complex and intimate connection between the natural and the supernatural worlds, illustrated especially well by Daniel 7. The scene undergoes several sudden and unexplained shifts between the earthly and the supernatural realms. The implication is that there is a close connection between decisions made in heaven and events in human history. The text does not say that explicitly; it demonstrates it graphically. Because Antiochus is judged in the heavenly court, he dies on earth. The earthly realm can also affect the heavenly, as when Antiochus's persecution is portrayed as an attack on heaven and the angels (Dan 8:10-12, 23-25). The lack of literary transition between the heavenly and the earthly parts of the vision reinforces the impression that the two realms are mutually dependent.

Revelation. The book of Revelation is a Christian work written in western Asia Minor at the end of the first century CE, when Roman Emperor Domitian was on the throne. In Revelation's environment, religious devotion to the goddess Roma and to past and present emperors as gods was an expression of loyalty to Rome. The author viewed the imperial cult as symbolic of Christian accommodation to Hellenistic culture. Such accommodation violated the Christian obligation to render worship to God alone. The letters in Revelation 2–3 bear witness to the extent to which some Christians were at home in Hellenistic and Roman culture, but Revelation's author was convinced that the empire that seduced some Christians and threatened others drew its power from Satan and would soon be defeated by God. Indeed, Satan had already been defeated in heaven by Michael and his angels. Satan's dominion on earth was visible in the oppression of the Christian churches, but his ultimate defeat was inevitable.

In Revelation 4, the seer John ascends to the heavenly throne room, where he sees God and the heavenly court. In God's hand is a sealed scroll containing the eschatological events. There is lamentation in heaven that no one is worthy to open the scroll because until the scroll is opened, the eschatological events cannot take place. In chapter 5, a slain lamb appears, representing the crucified and risen Christ. He takes the scroll from God, and the heavenly host sings a hymn that reveals that he is able to take the scroll and open it because of his death. Here we have the traditional Christian notion that the death and resurrection of Christ set in motion the events of the end time. As in Paul's letters, something eschatological has already happened—Satan's defeat through the death of Christ—and something is still to happen—Satan's ultimate defeat at the hands of Christ at the end of time. The conviction that the end time has already been inaugurated in the death and resurrection of Christ is the major point of difference between Jewish and Christian apocalypticism.

As the seals of the scroll are broken, the events of the end time unfold. The point is that God has a plan for the eschatological events—a plan set in motion by the Christ event. The rest of Revelation reinforces the idea that all of the final events on earth are initiated in heaven and implemented by angels. Eschatological judgment is evident throughout the book. In chapter 19, Christ emerges as the heavenly warrior at the head of his army. He defeats the first beast (the Roman Empire and its emperors) and the second beast (leaders of

the imperial cult), and he throws them into the lake of fire. Final judgment comes in chapter 20, where the dragon (Satan) is thrown into the fiery lake. Then the righteous live forever in God's and Christ's presence in the new Jerusalem, now descended onto earth.

Revelation never explicitly quotes Scripture, but it is permeated by biblical allusions and patterns. The use of Isaiah, Ezekiel, Jeremiah, Joel, and Daniel is particularly evident. But events in Revelation are never said to fulfill biblical prophecy. As with other apocalypses, Revelation draws its authority not from biblical proof but from the seer's visions. What he sees divulges what is happening in heaven itself, and this special knowledge grounds the entire book. The use of biblical allusions gives Revelation deep roots in Israel's sacred traditions and taps into their power. Revelation contextualizes its own revelations in the vast sweep of God's previous actions and revelations, but its authority remains steadily grounded in the seer's experience.

Although Daniel is a historical apocalypse and Revelation belongs to the otherworldly journey variety, these books are quite similar in form and content. Indeed, the definition of *apocalypticism* employed by many is dependent on the worldview shared by Daniel and Revelation. Eschatology plays a dominant role in both works, as it does in many definitions of *apocalypticism*. Both works expect public upheaval and eschatological woes. Both look forward to resurrection. Both see heavenly events, including conflict between supernatural beings, reflected on earth. Both symbolize evil powers in bizarre beasts coming from the sea (four in Daniel 7, one in Revelation 13). Both see society in somewhat dualistic terms, although both leave room for movement from the category of those who will perish to those who will be saved. Both refer to the Son of Man, a heavenly figure who plays a role in the eschatological events. Given the fact that Daniel and Revelation are the canonical examples of apocalypses, it is not surprising that the elements they share in common have assumed importance in the definition of *apocalypticism* that is in some cases out of proportion to the presence of these elements in apocalypses in general. Nonetheless, the basic elements of the apocalyptic genre and of its implied worldview are, indeed, shared with all other apocalypses from this period.

THE EARLIEST APOCALYPSES

The earliest extant apocalypses are embedded in *1 Enoch*. They are the *Book of the Watchers* (*1 Enoch* 1–36) and the *Astronomical Book* (*1 Enoch* 72–82). They both date from the third century BCE, and both involve otherworldly journeys. The *Book of the Watchers* is in three parts. The first part (chaps. 1–5) serves to introduce the *Book of the Watchers* in particular and the whole of *1 Enoch* in general. It describes the coming of the divine warrior in eschatological judgment. God comes to judge because humans have not followed the example of the cosmos in its obedience to divine commands. The second part (chaps. 6–16) concerns the introduction of evil into the world through the activity of angels, called "watchers," a name that may come from their original function as heavenly guards (see also Dan 4:13, 17, 23). Two strands of tradition are discernible here. One concerns intercourse between angels and human women, a tradition similar to but more fully developed than the fragmentary narrative in Gen 6:1-4. The other tradition concentrates on illicit revelation of heavenly secrets to humans by angels. Both strands see catastrophic consequences, including violence, following from these violations. The earth cries to heaven for relief, and the good angels bring the case before God, who decrees punishment. The sinful watchers enlist Enoch to intercede for them, but he is told of God's irrevocable sentence and is brought to the heavenly sanctuary (chap. 14). In chapters 17–36, Enoch tours the universe. Most of what he sees concerns eschatological judgment. For example, he sees the place of torment prepared for the sinful watchers and the chambers in which human souls await final judgment. Finally, he sees the preparations that have been made for the restoration of Jerusalem, in which the righteous will live.

The precise historical circumstances that led to the writing of the *Book of the Watchers* are unclear. Two suggestions are the suffering caused by the wars between successors of Alexander the Great and dissatisfaction caused by the laxity toward Torah of the Jerusalem priesthood. What is clear is that the author of the book is unhappy with present circumstances and sees their cause as the people's deviance from God's original plans for the cosmos. The solution is typically apocalyptic—sentence is passed in the supernatural world, evidence for which Enoch receives both directly from God and indirectly through his tour of the universe. Eschatological judgment is inevitable.

The *Astronomical Book* is an excellent example of how closely human history is interrelated with the cosmos. Most of the book is a somewhat dry review of astronomical laws. It takes the form of a tour of the cosmos by Enoch, guided by the angel Uriel. Enoch learns that because of human sinfulness, the universe is disrupted (chap. 80). Crops will not grow properly, rain is withheld, and the orbits of the heavenly bodies are disturbed. The book is presently integrated into *1 Enoch*, so it is not in its original form, but Enoch's tour of heaven assumes some sort of ascent as described in *1 Enoch* 14. In chapter 81, Enoch reads heavenly tablets that reveal the course of human history, and he is sent back to earth to write down what he has seen and to warn of eschatological judgment.

LATE APOCALYPSES

Four Jewish apocalypses were written in reaction to the destruction of Jerusalem in 70 CE: 4 Ezra, *2 Baruch*, the *Apocalypse of Abraham*, and *3 Baruch*. The book of 4 Ezra is now preserved as 2 Esdras 3–14; 2 Esdras 1–2 and 15–16 are Christian additions to the Jewish work, and 2:42-48 is itself a little apocalypse. Set in the time of the destruction of Solomon's Temple by the Babylonians in 587 BCE, 4 Ezra was really written after the destruction six and a half centuries later. It consists of seven sections. In the first three, Ezra argues with the angel Uriel and challenges the justice of a God who allows Israel to be punished at the hands of unrighteous Gentiles. Uriel offers Ezra an apocalyptic solution. The angel first stresses the inaccessibility of the heavenly information that is necessary to understand earthly events. Humans can no more achieve such understanding on their own than they can weigh fire, measure wind, or recall days that are past (4 Ezra 4:5). Nonetheless, God can choose to reveal such information, and that is precisely what happens as Uriel speaks to Ezra. Uriel says that God made two worlds, and it is only in the world to come that the righteous will receive their just reward and the wicked their punishment. Ezra protests that there are so few righteous people that the angel's words provide little comfort.

In the fourth section of the book, Ezra receives a vision of a woman weeping, whom he tries to distract by telling her of Zion's destruction. She is then transformed into a marvelous city, and the angel tells Ezra that she is Zion restored. From this point on, Ezra's attitude changes. He accepts God's judgments as expressed by the angel. Then follow two visions predicting the victory of the forces of good over the powers of evil. In the first vision, an eagle represents Rome. It is reproached and defeated by a lion, representing the Messiah. In the second vision, "something like the figure of a man" arises from the sea (a probable allusion to Daniel 7), does battle with the nations at Zion, and emerges victorious. In the last section of the book, Ezra preserves the Torah, which had been burned in the destruction. Under inspiration, he dictates it to scribes. The twenty-four books of the Torah are meant for the public. Ezra also dictates seventy other books that are to be revealed only to the elect, and those books appear to be held in even higher esteem than the Torah itself, "for in them is the spring of understanding, the fountain of wisdom, and the river of knowledge" (14:47). It would appear that these other books are apocalyptic revelations, necessary for true understanding.

An interesting aspect of 4 Ezra is that it polemicizes against the notion, common in other apocalypses, that anyone could possibly ascend to heaven (see John 3:13). It does so to emphasize human beings' inability to understand heavenly realities on their own, an understanding that is necessary to comprehend earthly happenings. Nonetheless, Uriel does reveal those heavenly secrets to Ezra.

A perennial problem of interpreting 4 Ezra is the question of why Ezra changes his attitude during the course of the book. In the first three visions and during part of the fourth, Ezra complains about God's ways, questions the angel sharply, and seems dissatisfied with the angel's answers. Even if, as some interpreters claim, Ezra does show some movement in his position in the first half of the book, there is still a remarkable change in his attitude after the fourth vision. Once he sees the woman transformed into the restored Zion, he accepts God's ways and the angel's answers. A plausible solution to this quandary is that Ezra's religious experience—his encounter with the grieving woman and her transformation into restored Zion—is necessary for him to transcend his sorrowful circumstances and accept the apocalyptic solution offered to him. The angel and the seer may represent two aspects of the real author, a person so anguished by the destruction of Jerusalem that he was torn between acceptance of God's ways and rebellion against them. It was only the author's own religious experience, perhaps the very visions described in this book, that led him to accept and to espouse the solution the book provides. Writing the book allowed the author to impart his experiences to others and lead them through the same process he had undergone. This explanation suggests that a real religious experience, perhaps an authentic vision or set of visions, underlies this apocalypse and perhaps others as well.

Another response to the destruction of the Second Temple in 70 CE is *2 Baruch*, which is also set in the time of the destruction of the previous Temple by the Babylonians in the sixth century BCE. This work stresses the foundational importance of the Torah for the continued existence of Israel, emphasizes the temporary nature of this world, and anticipates an eschatological judgment in which Israel's enemies will be punished and the righteous will be elevated to the positions of the stars. It thereby relativizes the loss of the Temple and helps to provide for Israel's survival without a sacrificial cult.

The *Apocalypse of Abraham* develops Abraham's vision in Genesis 15 into a full-blown apocalypse. The idea that Abraham received more extensive revelation than is narrated in Genesis 15 is also found in *2 Baruch* 4. The apocalypse is in two parts. Chapters 1–8 tell of Abraham's discovery of the falseness of idolatry and his rejection of it. In chapters 9–32, Abraham makes a heavenly journey assisted by the angel Yaoel. This twofold structure recalls that of Daniel, where the stories about Daniel in chapters 1–6 prepare for the apocalypse proper in chapters 7–12. During the cosmic journey, Abraham views the whole of human history. This section of the apocalypse has been adapted by Christians, but most of the material is Jewish. The review of history leads to eschatological judgment. As with the other apocalypses, the key to understanding human history lies in the supernatural world and is able to be known only through direct revelation.

The book of *3 Baruch* is a Jewish apocalypse dating from the early second century CE. It describes

Baruch's ascent through five levels of heaven. Baruch never enters the presence of God. There is a door in the fifth heaven through which the archangel Michael goes to bring the prayers of the faithful to God, but Baruch never passes through that door. Thus the apocalypse may envisage the more common scheme of seven heavens, even though Baruch sees only five. This apocalypse contains no cosmic upheavals, political turmoil, or public eschatology. Baruch observes the places of reward and punishment in heaven reserved for those who have died. Therefore, this apocalypse offers an example of personalized eschatology.

THE SIMILITUDES OF ENOCH

The *Similitudes of Enoch* has survived as part of the Ethiopic form of the collection called *1 Enoch* (chaps. 37–71). It is the only one of the five books in that collection not preserved at Qumran. (The Qumran fragments do contain part of another Enochic book called the *Book of the Giants*, not present in the Ethiopic manuscript.) The *Similitudes* is a fascinating document both as a witness to Jewish belief and thought and as a parallel to Christian notions. Because it is not attested in the Aramaic fragments at Qumran and because of its similarity to Christian ideas, some scholars have sought to date it quite late, perhaps in the third century CE. Scholarly opinion now tends strongly to a first century CE date.

The *Similitudes of Enoch* is an otherworldly journey apocalypse. Enoch is caught up to the heavenly throne room and is given revelations that make him understand the way the world is and the inevitability of eschatological judgment. The most common designation for God in this book is "Lord of the Spirits," which appears to be an adaptation of the biblical "Lord of Hosts." The change to "Spirits" indicates the view, common in apocalypticism, that an unseen world of spiritual beings determines what happens in this world. When Enoch first views God in heaven, he also sees another figure, called the "Elect One of righteousness" (*1 Enoch* 39). In chapter 46, the dependence of the *Similitudes* on Daniel 7 for its vision of heaven becomes clear. God is called one with a "head of days" who has a head "white like wool," recalling Dan 7:9, where God is called the Ancient of Days who wears white and has hair like pure wool. With God in *1 Enoch* 46 is one whose "face was like the appearance of a son of man." Else-

where in the *Similitudes* this mysterious figure is called the Righteous One, the Elect One, and the Messiah. The adjectives *righteous* and *elect* are also applied to faithful humans on earth, who recognize the authority of the Lord of Spirits. Just as the one like a son of man is hidden in heaven, known only to Enoch and to those to whom he reveals him, so also the righteous are hidden on earth, to be recognized only at the eschatological judgment (*1 Enoch* 38:1). The ultimate fate of the righteous will be to live with the one like a son of man forever (*1 Enoch* 62:14). In the *Similitudes*, the relation of the one like a son of man to the elect on earth is analogous to the relation between the one like a son of man and Israel in Daniel 7. In each case, the figure like a son of man is the heavenly patron of the faithful.

Contrasted with the righteous are the sinners. They are portrayed as the powerful and wealthy of the earth, those persons who trust in their own power and riches. They do not acknowledge the Lord of Spirits, nor do they admit that their status is due to the Lord. Therefore, the one like a son of man will judge them. He will sit on a throne to judge them (*1 Enoch* 62:1-12), and he will lift them from their own thrones (*1 Enoch* 46:4-8). Their acknowledgment of the Lord's authority and their pleas for mercy at the final judgment will go unheeded. They will be punished, together with the angels who disobeyed God (*1 Enoch* 67). Eschatological judgment is sure, and it will result in a reversal of fortune between those who are now wealthy, powerful, and arrogant and those who are now righteous and persecuted. This reversal is fairly common in Jewish and Christian eschatological thought of this period (e.g., the *Epistle of Enoch* [*1 Enoch* 91–104]; Matt 19:30; 20:16; Luke 1:46-55; 1 Cor 1:20-25; Revelation), and it is especially powerful in apocalyptic settings. For apocalypses, the certainty of reversal rests on divine revelation and involves rewards and punishments even after death. The *Similitudes* contain the idea that a certain number of righteous people must shed their blood before the eschatological judgment can take place (*1 Enoch* 47:3-4). According to 4 Ezra 4:36 and *2 Bar* 23:4-5; 48:46, the number of humans to be created is fixed, and must be completed before the end can come. Revelation 6:11 adapts that idea to its own purposes by making it a certain number of martyrs that must be fulfilled. The *Similitudes* is close to Revelation here.

All such schemes imply that history is determined by God in advance.

Enoch emphasizes the uniqueness of his revelation. He says, "Till the present day such wisdom has never been given by the Lord of Spirits as I have received" (*1 Enoch* 37:4). Chapter 42 claims that when personified Wisdom was sent out by God to find a dwelling place among humans, she had to return to heaven because she could find no such place. This contrasts with Sirach 24, where Wisdom finds a home in Zion and is equated with the Torah. The *Similitudes* claim that true wisdom can be found only in heaven, in the presence of the Lord of Spirits and the one like a son of man. Enoch must go there to find it. While there, he sees the founts of wisdom and reads the heavenly books (see Dan 7:10; Rev 3:5; 20:12). At the end of the apocalypse, Enoch is permanently exalted to heaven after having conveyed his revelations to humans (*1 Enoch* 70). In what is probably a later ending, he is identified with the son of man (*1 Enoch* 71:14).

The *Similitudes of Enoch* is certainly an apocalyptic text, with its otherworldly journey, its disclosure of secrets that explain this world and the next, and its anticipation of postmortem rewards and punishments. Its final judgment is public and involves a strong critique of the powerful and wealthy people of the earth. It is especially interesting for students of early Christianity because of the enigmatic figure of the one like a son of man, the Righteous One and the Elect One, who is to judge the world at the end and with whom the righteous will live forever. The similarities between this figure and the Christ of some early Christian documents have led to theories of Christian dependence on the *Similitudes* and, conversely, to suggestions that the *Similitudes* depend on Christian ideas. Dependence in either direction has never been convincingly argued. It is of great interest, however, that such a mediating figure is attested to in a Jewish document of the first century CE, because it helps to provide a context for early Christian concepts of Christ.

QUMRAN AND CHRISTIANITY AS APOCALYPTIC MOVEMENTS

If discussions of apocalypses and apocalypticism are rife with debates and disagreements, the diffi-culties increase when the topic is actual apocalyptic groups. Some scholars insist that a group can be considered apocalyptic only if it produces apocalypses. Others opt for a wider definition, considering those groups apocalyptic whose worldview is like that found in the apocalypses. In most cases, this means the particular worldview especially characteristic of historical apocalypses, including public eschatology. A good deal of discussion of this issue centers on two collections of documents: the Dead Sea Scrolls and the New Testament.

Qumran. The Dead Sea Scrolls are a collection of manuscripts, some fairly well preserved and others in fragmentary form, that were found in caves in the Judean desert in a series of discoveries beginning in 1947. They are commonly thought to have been the library of a community that inhabited a settlement nearby, whose ruins are called Qumran. The scrolls fall into three basic categories: biblical manuscripts, texts written by members of the community, and other texts that are neither biblical nor written by the sect. This is a somewhat simplified typology, since the community may have had a complex history involving several groups over time with varying relationships to one another and to the authorities at Jerusalem. To date there is no clear evidence that the sect living at Qumran produced any apocalypses. However, they seem to have had a high regard for Daniel and *1 Enoch*, both of which are found in multiple copies among the scrolls. They also possessed the book of *Jubilees*, a work of mixed genres with apocalyptic features, written in the second century BCE

Although the matter is disputed among scholars, most still consider the community at Qumran to have been an apocalyptic community. Its members were intensely interested in the supernatural world, explaining events in Israel's history and in the history of the sect itself in terms of that other world. They saw their own time as part of what they called the "Age of Wrath," an age dominated by Belial and the human and supernatural beings under his sway. They expected a great eschatological battle to be conducted in a preordained way, which would result in the victory of the forces of good over the powers of evil. The Qumran community thought itself to be allied with the good angels, chief of whom was Michael, who would fight alongside members of the community—the sons of light—against Satan and his supernatural allies and human allies—the sons of darkness. It considered that it had such knowledge through divine mysteries revealed to the Teacher of Righteousness, a key figure in the origins of the community. Because of the revelations made to the Teacher, the community knew the correct interpretation of Torah and therefore was able to please God and able to interpret the prophetic literature accurately. The people at Qumran saw history as culminating in themselves and interpreted the prophets and several psalms as predicting the community's own history.

Parallels between the Qumran community and early Christianity are plentiful and have been explored in depth. Each interpreted Scripture eschatologically and saw it as pointing to itself. Just as the Teacher of Righteousness unlocked the mysteries of Scripture for his followers, so also did Jesus for his own. Each had an authoritative interpretation of Torah that contradicted that of the ruling authorities. Each expected an eschatological resolution to the problems of this sinful world.

The Synoptic Gospels. Revelation is the only apocalypse in the New Testament, but apocalyptic influence is strong throughout the rest of the New Testament as well. The Synoptic Gospels have strong apocalyptic attributes. In each of them, Jesus delivers what is usually referred to as an apocalyptic discourse (Mark 13; Matthew 24–25; Luke 21), in which he predicts eschatological sufferings to be endured by his followers, followed by the return of the Son of Man to rescue the elect. Matthew repeatedly refers to the close of the age, and as part of his apocalyptic discourse he has Jesus tell of the last judgment for all humans, followed by eternal rewards and punishments (Matt 25:31-46; see also Matt 13:24-30, 36-43). Matthew associates Jesus' death and resurrection with other eschatological events (Matt 27:51-55). Whether Jesus himself thought in apocalyptic terms is highly debated. No one claims that Jesus wrote apocalypses. Many think that since he began his career as a follower of John the Baptist, an eschatological prophet, and since the New Testament documents present him in an apocalyptic light, Jesus himself probably thought in such terms. Others see the apocalyptic characteristic in the New Testament portrait of Jesus as a later development by the church, and they see Jesus as being similar to a wisdom teacher, a sort of countercultural figure who could be compared to other such teachers and philosophers in the ancient world.

Paul. The apostle Paul is often characterized as having an apocalyptic worldview. He traces his call to a "revelation" (*apokalypsis*; Gal 1:12). He claims to have made a heavenly journey and to have received other visions and revelations (2 Cor 12:1-7). He divides humanity into those being saved and those perishing (1 Cor 1:18). He thinks that his work is being hindered by Satan (1 Thess 2:18). He expects this world to pass away soon (1 Cor 7:26, 31; Rom 13:11). He even presents brief eschatological scenarios. In 1 Thess 4:13-18, he expects Christ to return with a trumpet blast, at which time the faithful dead will rise and be caught up together with the living believers into the clouds, to be with Christ forever. Paul insists, however, that the exact time of the end is unknowable (1 Thess 5:1-11). In 1 Cor 15:20-28, he says that Christ is the firstfruits of the dead. At the end of time, all of the righteous will rise, and then Christ will hand over the kingdom to God, having conquered "every ruler and every authority and power" (1 Cor 15:24 NRSV) and all his enemies. That these enemies are supernatural is supported by the fact that the last enemy to be overcome is death (1 Cor 15:26). In 1 Cor 15:50-57, Paul divulges an eschatological "mystery" about the transformation of the faithful at the end, and in Rom 11:25-32 he shares another "mystery" concerning the inclusion of the Jews among the saved at the end time. In Rom 8:18-25, Paul claims that the entire creation waits for the eschaton and the revelation of the righteous.

CONCLUSION

Apocalypticism played a far greater role in early Judaism and early Christianity than is attested by the presence of only two apocalypses in the Bible. The Jewish and Christian apocalypses written between 300 BCE and 200 CE constitute a substantial body of literature. Consideration of other genres that display features, imagery, patterns, and views typical of apocalypses leads to examination of a still larger body of texts. Discussions of apocalypses and apocalypticism are central to conversations about Second Temple Judaism, earliest Christianity, and the historical Jesus. They have helped to situate various forms of Judaism within both the sweep of

Israel's history and culture and the larger Hellenistic world. They have also shed light on Christianity's Jewish roots and on its relation to its Hellenistic environment. Studies of apocalypticism and of individual apocalypses will continue to contribute to biblical studies and to modern assessments of the two ancient religions for some time to come.

FOR FURTHER READING

Charlesworth, James H., ed. *The Old Testament Pseudepigrapha.* 2 vols. Garden City, N.Y.: Doubleday, 1983–1985.

Collins, John J., ed. *Apocalypse: The Morphology of a Genre.* Semeia 14. Missoula, Mont.: Scholars Press, 1979.

———. *The Apocalyptic Imagination: An Introduction to the Jewish Matrix of Christianity.* New York: Crossroad, 1984.

Collins, John J., and James H. Charlesworth, eds. *Mysteries and Revelations: Apocalyptic Studies Since the Uppsala Colloquium.* Sheffield: JSOT, 1991.

Cook, Stephen L. *The Apocalyptic Literature.* Interpreting Biblical Texts. Nashville, Tn.: Abingdon, 2003.

Grabbe, Lester L. and Robert D. Haak, eds. *Knowing the End from the Beginning: The Prophetic, the Apocalyptic and Their Relationships.* JSOP-Sup 46. London: T & T Clark, 2003.

Hanson, Paul D. *The Dawn of Apocalyptic: The Historical and Sociological Roots of Jewish Apocalyptic Eschatology.* Rev. ed. Philadelphia: Fortress, 1979; orig. ed. 1975.

Hellholm, David. *Apocalypticism in the Mediterranean World and the Near East: Proceedings of the International Colloquium on Apocalypticism, Uppsala, August 12-17, 1979.* Tübingen: Mohr, 1983.

Rowland, Christopher. *The Open Heaven: A Study of Apocalyptic in Judaism and Christianity.* New York: Crossroad, 1982.

Rowland, Christopher and John M. T. Barton, eds. *Apocalyptic in History and Tradition.* JSOP-Sup 43. London: Sheffield Academic Press, 2002.

Stone, Michael. "Apocalyptic Literature." In *Jewish Writings of the Second Temple Period.* Edited by Michael Stone. Philadelphia: Fortress, 1984.

ENDNOTES

1. See John J. Collins, ed., *Apocalypse: The Morphology of a Genre*, Semeia 14 (Missoula, Mont.: Scholars Press, 1979).

2. See 1QM 17.

THE BOOK OF
DANIEL

DANIEL L. SMITH-CHRISTOPHER

The book of Daniel is arguably the most unusual book of the Hebrew Bible. Certainly part of its notoriety can be attributed to the textual and literary problems that have perplexed scholars for generations. Some moderns would suggest that Daniel is also a notoriously dangerous book that has fueled religious speculation as well as contributing to social unrest and even revolution. In order to appreciate reading a biblical book of such multifaceted interest, one needs to place Daniel in some literary, historical, and—perhaps just as important—sociological and political context.

LITERARY CONTEXT:
THE COURT STORIES (DANIEL 1–6)
AND THE APOCALYPTIC VISIONS
(DANIEL 7–12)

The book of Daniel comes to us in two different, although related, Semitic languages. Chapters 1:1–2:4a and 8–12 are written in Hebrew, while chaps. 2:4b–7 are written in Aramaic, the *lingua franca* of the ancient Near East, especially in Mesopotamia, in the late Babylonian, Persian, and early Hellenistic periods (before Aramaic was replaced by Greek). There have been some attempts to relate these language changes in the book to stages in the composition of the book (suggesting, e.g., chaps. 2–7 as an original and early version of the text, before chaps. 1; 8–12 were added), but such theories have never achieved a general consensus in textual studies of the book. One of the main reasons for the difficulty is that the language differences do *not* coincide with the literary changes between chaps. 1–6 and 7–12.

Daniel 1–6. It is obvious to any reader of the book of Daniel that the first six chapters differ dramatically from the last six chapters. The first half of the book consists of six stories that have been called, variously, "diaspora novellas/stories,"[1]

"court stories,"[2] and even divided more specifically into "contest" stories (chaps. 2; 4–5) and "conflict" stories (chaps. 3; 6).[3] These first stories in the book are usually assumed to have derived from the life of the Jewish eastern diaspora after the time of the exile in 587/586, but usually are assigned to the Persian (539–333 BCE) or Hellenistic (333–63 BCE) periods rather than to the Babylonian period (597–539 BCE).[4] Although some of the court details seem, at first sight, to be impressive, most scholars argue that the Daniel stories as well as the stories of his friends Hananiah, Mishael, and Azariah are fictional accounts that represent the folklore of the diaspora communities. Furthermore, these details are something that a healthy imagination could create, drawing from the gossip and speculation of the surrounding peoples under Persian occupation. There was similar speculation about the pomp and circumstance of the Persian court among the Greeks as well.[5]

Recent attention to the stories in chaps. 1–6 has also emphasized their literary character as stories that recommend a "lifestyle for the Diaspora."[6] Most literary analysis of these stories, however, has tended to overlook their potent sociopolitical power as stories of resistance to cultural and spiritual assimilation of a minority by a dominant foreign power.[7] From this perspective, these stories take on a more ominous shade than from the perspective of purely folkloristic analysis.

Related to these questions is that of who actually wrote these stories. It is often suggested that these stories derived from an upper class of the Eastern diaspora community simply because only a member of the upper classes could aspire to service in the emperor's court. It is further assumed that these stories reflect a somewhat benign view of the foreign emperor and, therefore, are certainly much older than the assumed setting for the second half of the book of Daniel, which is much darker and more pessimistic about worldly powers, because of the persecution of the Palestinian Jewish communities under Antiochus IV Epiphanes, the reigning Seleucid Hellenistic ruler between 167 and 164 BCE.

It will be the perspective of this overview, however, that the authors of Daniel 1–6 did *not* aspire actually to work for the foreign emperor. Rather, the emperor's court served as an ideal setting for a political and religious folklore that speaks of surviving and flourishing in a foreign land, in a hostile environment. It effectively communicates as well the powerful images of lowly Jewish exiles standing with faith and courage before the very throne of the occupying (and militarily superior) emperor, overcoming his military and political power through the power of God. The perspective of the book of Daniel toward foreign conquerors, even in the first six chapters, is not nearly so benign as is often thought; in fact, it is openly hostile to their authority. This hostile challenge to authority provides one of the major unifying factors of Daniel as a whole, and is not merely an aspect of the latter half of the book.[8] This hostility requires a creative theology of confrontation as an essential aspect of the modern use of the book.

Court story narratives are not, of course, unique to Daniel. Besides the obvious similarities with Esther and the Joseph tales of Genesis (the striking similarities among these three texts were systematically noted as early as 1895) and even Ezra and Nehemiah (Nehemiah is a courtier), we should note the story of Zerubbabel in 1 Esdras. The discovery of the Dead Sea Scrolls and their publication since 1948 has provided other court stories of Jewish courtiers that resemble Daniel in some interesting details. The most dramatic example of such a story is the *Prayer of Nabonidus*, which many scholars believe is a more ancient form of a Daniel legend, even though Daniel is not explicitly mentioned in the fragments that have been found. The fragment reads as follows (with gaps and difficulties indicated by brackets):

1 Words of the prayer which Nabonidus, king of the la[nd of Baby]lon, [the great] king, pra[yed when we were afflicted]

2 by an evil inflammation, by the decree of God the All-Highest, in Teiman. [I Nabonidus] was afflicted [with an evil inflammation]

3 for seven years and was banished far from [men until I prayed to God the All Highest]

4 and an exorcist pardoned my sin. He was a Jewish [man] of the [exiles, and he said to me:]

5 Proclaim and write to the glory, exa[ltation and honor] of the name of Go[d the All-Highest. And I wrote as follows; When]

6 I was afflicted with an evil inflammation and I stayed in Teiman [by the decree of the all Highest God, I]

7 prayed for seven years [to all] Gods of silver and gold, [bronze, of iron]

8 of wood, of stone, of clay, for [I thought] they were Gods.[9]

This fragment contains a number of interesting details that relate to the study of Daniel. First, and most important, it specifically names and, therefore, connects Nabonidus, last king of Babylon, to the Daniel traditions. It is often assumed that the images of Nebuchadnezzar in many of the Daniel stories seem better suited to the historical Nabonidus (who was the historical father of Belshazzar of Daniel chap. 5), and this fragment would seem to confirm that suspicion. That Nebuchadnezzar was eventually substituted is not hard to understand, given that he was, after all, the conqueror of Jerusalem and responsible for the destruction of the Temple—and thus a more powerful symbol of Babylonian rule than was Nabonidus. Second, however, this fragment suggests that many Daniel stories may have circulated among the Jewish people in a kind of Daniel "folklore cycle" and that our present book of Daniel contains only a selection from that folklore tradition. Finally, there are some interesting specifics in this fragment, such as the list of materials in lines 7-8 that resembles lists in the book of Daniel and the story line that the Babylonian king had to learn that God is the true god, and not one of the gods of gold and silver. Although the historicity of many of the biblical and nonbiblical accounts must be doubted, given what we know from other sources, the theology of these stories (and the visions) is not significant for their time alone, but remains significant for modern Christians who seek to construct a biblically informed theology for contemporary living.

Daniel 7–12. The last six chapters of Daniel are the most important example of apocalyptic literature in the Hebrew Bible. A considerable amount of scholarly research has gone into the definition and description of apocalyptic literature, of which we have many examples outside the canon of the Old and the New Testaments.[10] Clearly, apocalyptic was an important style of theological writing for at least 500 years, during the Hellenistic and Roman periods (roughly 333 BCE–200 CE, although it may extend back into the Persian period, if some Persian influences are accepted).[11] We have both Jewish and Christian examples of this type of literature. Apocalyptic is most generally defined as literature that deals with the revelation and understanding of mysteries, but there have been attempts to be even more specific and comprehensive. For example, Collins has proposed the following definition:

"Apocalypse" is a genre of revelatory literature with a narrative framework, in which a revelation is mediated by an otherworldly being to a human recipient, disclosing a transcendent reality which is both temporal, insofar as it envisages eschatological salvation, and spatial insofar as it involves another, supernatural world.

An apocalypse is intended to interpret present earthly circumstances in the light of the supernatural world and of the future, and to influence both the understanding and the behavior of the audience by means of divine authority.[12]

The advantage of such a definition is not that it is finally complete, but that it gives students and scholars at least some kind of common language in their analysis of actual texts. The point is not to exclude certain texts from consideration (as if to create some kind of informal canon of "real" apocalyptic texts) but to facilitate our understanding of any particular text in all its unique originality as well as formal resemblances to other texts. Daniel, for example, has clear resemblances to books like *1 Enoch*, but they were not issued from some sort of theological or literary mold, and assumptions about their similarity can be hazardous.

Equally hazardous is the attempt to generalize about a sociological context for apocalyptic literature as a whole. Reid, for example, used a sophisticated sociological outline in order to compare *1 Enoch* and Daniel, and he concluded that they have quite different source communities.[13] Other scholars, however, are content to generalize that apocalyptic literature seems to come from "disenfranchised" communities, without being more specific.[14] It is not necessary, however, to suggest that

an entire genre has the same sociological setting in every specific case (attractive as such a conclusion may be!). The sociological setting of Daniel must also be determined on the basis of internal evidence as well as the genre of the stories and visions. That the authors of Daniel are hostile to foreign conquerors and to ancient Near Eastern empire building is clear from *what* the book says, and not only from *how* it is said. Furthermore, the social context of the exile itself and the realities of occupation from then on should alert the reader to certain attitudes that are revealed in Daniel. For this reason it is important to review the basic historical background before discussing the meaning of that background for a reading of the book of Daniel.

HISTORICAL BACKGROUND OF DANIEL: THE CONTEXT OF EMPIRE

The independent Jewish kingdom was short lived in the ancient Near East. Allowing for a 200-year period of decentralized tribal existence (roughly 1200–1000 BCE), the united kingdom existed under the Davidic monarchy from 1020 to 922 BCE, with the northern breakaway kingdom lasting until the Assyrian conquest of 722 BCE. The southern state of Judah continued until the Babylonian conquests began in 597 BCE and was completely overrun when Jerusalem was devastated in 587/586 BCE, the beginning of the Babylonian exile. Both the northern and the southern kingdoms ended tragically (but not atypically for the ancient Near East) in military conquest and deportation of a sizable segment of the populace—taken, it appears, from the institutional leadership of royal, military, and religious sectors. We know more about the Babylonian exiles than we do about the Assyrian captives because this community survived the ordeal. With the brief exception of the Hasmonean client state (which, given the realities of Hellenistic and Roman power, is not much of an exception), there was never again a military-royalist state of the ancient Hebrews in Palestine.

Around 539 BCE, Cyrus the Persian conquered Babylon and soon thereafter began allowing parties of Jews to return to Palestine (Ezra 1–6). This action is often interpreted as a freedom policy on the part of the Persians. But it must be kept in mind that these missions back to Palestine had particular Persian goals in mind—particularly the shoring up of the western flank of the Persian Empire when the Greeks became a troublesome presence in the Mediterranean rim.

The Persian period ended with the conquests of Alexander the Great in 333 BCE. After Alexander's death in 323 BCE in Babylon, his massive empire was divided among his generals. After a period of internal warfare, lines were drawn in the Near East between the eastern portion of the empire, based in Syria and Mesopotamia, and Egypt to the west. The Ptolemies ruled Egypt, which included Palestine until 198 BCE, when the Seleucids (Antiochus III), who ruled the eastern section of the empire, annexed Palestine to their region. Alexander's conquests brought an intensification of Hellenistic influence on life, but as Morton Smith has recently pointed out, western influence on Palestine is documented from the Philistine involvement in the early monarchy, and only intensifies in the Babylonian, Persian, and post-Alexandrian historical eras.[15] Following Alexander's death, and until Seleucid rule in 198 BCE, the Ptolemaic rule of Egypt was economically rigid, although most scholars doubt that there was any severe persecution when compared to the Seleucid period that followed. Newsome noted that, according to the Zenon Papyri from the Ptolemaic period, the Jews were "considered little more than serfs in that economic pyramid which placed the Greeks and Macedonians at the top."[16]

The era of Hellenistic rule that is of greatest interest for the study of the book of Daniel is the reign of Antiochus IV Epiphanes (175–164 BCE). Antiochus's father, Antiochus III, had already managed to expel the Ptolemies from Palestine by 200 BCE, and at first the Jewish residents welcomed him as a liberator (especially from Ptolemaic taxation!). Already during the years of Seleucus IV Philopater (187–175 BCE), the immediate successor of Antiochus III, the Jewish community was fractured into rival parties. A certain Simon denounced Onias III, at that time the high priest, and suggested that the high priest should not have such control of the great wealth of the temple treasury. Simon and his allies were pro-Seleucid, while Onias and Hyrcanus (the head of one of the aristocratic families named Tobias) were pro-Ptolemaic. When Onias traveled to Antioch-on-Orantes to appeal to the king, the new successor to the throne, Antiochus IV, imprisoned him. Jason, brother of Onias, paid a large sum

of money to Antiochus IV, who promptly made Jason the high priest. Jason was at the head of the move to modernize and Hellenize Jewish life, and he became a significant ally to Antiochus IV's efforts to rule the unruly Jews.

Matters took an even more complex turn when Simon's brother Menelaus, the old rival of Onias, outbid Jason for the office of high priest. So the situation involved two rival Hellenizing factions among the Jewish aristocracy and a third anti-Hellenistic party of Jews, led by the religious resistance known as the Hasidim (the "pious ones," although some have suggested the translation "the committed ones"); there were many other factions among the anti-Hellenistic parties as well. These events took a serious turn for the worse at the end of Antiochus IV's campaigns in Egypt. Antiochus IV managed to destroy the Egyptian army of Ptolemy VI Philometer (180–145 BCE) in 168 BCE. But instead of allowing Antiochus IV to consolidate power even over Egypt, Rome intervened to halt Antiochus IV's advance. Roman intervention is symbolized in the person of Popilius, who forced a humiliated Antiochus to withdraw his forces when they met at Eleusis. Back in Jerusalem, Jason had imprisoned Menelaus after hearing that Antiochus IV had been killed in battle. But the word that Jason had acted on was false, and when Antiochus assessed the situation in Jerusalem, it appeared to be open revolt against his authority, initiated perhaps by those who thought Antiochus was in a weakened position, even if not actually dead. Antiochus IV's response to the disarray in Jerusalem was violent. Not only were many Jews killed or sold into slavery, but also the Temple was violated; eventually certain aspects of Jewish traditional practice were banned as contributing factors to what Antiochus IV perceived as disloyalty. For some scholars, persecution of religiously motivated resisters to Antiochus's Hellenization policies under Jewish leaders like Jason makes sense—even in the context of otherwise tolerant policies that normally allowed diverse religious expressions: "If the revolt was led by Hasidim, for whom the commandments of the Torah were of the utmost sanctity, and if devotion to the Mosaic Law was the watchword of the uprising, then that Law had to be extirpated if the rebellion was to be put down."[17]

These political policies toward the rebellious Jews resulted in an intensification of intracommunal hostility as well as hostility toward the rulers. Antiochus IV's indulgences of rival priests who sought the office of high priest created internal struggles in the Jewish community that are now recognized as important to the strife of 167–164 BCE as were Antiochus IV's own policies. The emperor's endorsement of the move to make the Temple a home for an altar (rather than, most scholars think, an actual image) for Baal Shamem/Zeus Olympios as well as the strengthening of the Greek garrison (the Akra) and the building of such Hellenistic institutions as a gymnasium as a part of the process of Hellenizing the Jews all resulted in violent factionalism in the Jewish community. Part of Antiochus's policies clearly involved the strengthening of the military presence in Jerusalem—the garrison with whom the later Maccabees would have to contend for control of the city. One result of this action was the open Maccabean revolt (along with Josephus, 1 Maccabees is the most reliable source for this period). But the book of Daniel represents other forms of political and religious resistance during this same time. To summarize, scholars have discussed the outbreak of the resistance and the resultant repression of the Jews in different ways. Was it mainly the result of rival factions among the aristocratic Jewish families? Tcherikover, for one, has pointed out that we must not minimize the temptations that Hellenistic wealth and control offered to those members of local aristocracies who could successfully become part of the ruling elite.[18] Was it mainly the result of tensions between Ptolemaic and Seleucid sympathizers? Or was it a symptom of the larger conflict between the Seleucid and the Ptolemaic rulers of the Near East? How much of a role can we attribute to the desire for religious freedom among the Jews themselves, as portrayed in such pious documents as the books of the Maccabees? History, we know, is seldom so simple as a choice among opposing factors—all were clearly elements contributing to this period of severe disturbance, violence, and, for some, horrendous persecution. The precise causes are less significant to us than is the context of uncertainty and instability facing the average person, who then reflected on the words of the apocalyptic dreamers and speakers.

While Daniel 7–12 are usually dated to the time of greatest conflict under Antiochus IV Epiphanes (i.e., between 167, when the Temple was desecrated with the pagan altar, and 164 BCE, when the rule of Antiochus IV ended), it is important to keep in mind that one of the main reasons why so much attention is focused on this episode is because of the existence of 1 Maccabees. This can easily give the impression that Jewish life under the Ptolemies and the Seleucids was otherwise peaceful or without major incident, and therefore any language of resistance or unrest that we find in Daniel must also be from the time of Antiochus IV. This would be a false impression.

Morton Smith recently calculated that in the period between Alexander's conquest in 333 BCE, and the Roman takeover of Palestinian affairs around 63 BCE under Pompey, some 200 military campaigns were fought in or around Palestine and that "this military history alone shows that no part of the country can have escaped Greek influence."[19] Thus military conquest, the taking of slaves and the temptations of mercenary service (it appears that some Jews welcomed military opportunities), and Greek settlement would have taken their toll on Jewish traditional life throughout the period from the exile to the Roman occupation of Palestine. The background of Daniel must include the social and political realities of exile and occupation throughout this period, and not only during any specific crisis. Late Hebrew thought, the Bible itself as a document, and both Rabbinic Judaism and Christianity were all formed under one or another system of political domination or occupation. This social and political reality will help to inform our reading of the book of Daniel.

It is common for many biblical scholars of the twentieth century to deal with the exile in a most peculiar manner: as an event that may have begun tragically, but resulted in an exilic existence that "must not have been that bad" under the Babylonians. This situation then improved even more, it is thought, under the benevolent rule of the Persians from the time of Cyrus's conquest of Babylon in 539 BCE until the coming of Alexander the Great in 333 BCE. While the Hellenistic rule that followed Alexander was not exactly political independence, the Hellenistic rulers over Palestine—the Ptolemies first and then after 198 BCE the Seleucids—must not have been so bad with the one exception of Antiochus IV Epiphanes' severe persecution of the

Jews. Greek influence allowed for a blossoming of Jewish "philosophy" and the translation of the Septuagint (the Greek version of the Hebrew Bible).

There are a number of severe historical and sociological problems with the (admittedly somewhat exaggerated) summary of this dominant paradigm for understanding the exile and the post-exilic developments within Jewish society. The main problem with this perspective is the lack of sensitivity to, and awareness of, the realities of living in exile and under military occupation. Although we have understood for some time that the exile must have had a dramatic impact on the ancient Jewish communities, we are only recently confronting the wider sociological and political, not to mention psychological, impact of these experiences, largely because we are only recently hearing from modern "exiles," minorities who insist that their stories of disenfranchisement be heard. Even more recently, some of these voices are taking up the scholarly study of the Bible, maintaining their unique perspectives as racial or cultural minorities in a variety of political circumstances.[20] By listening to modern exiles, minorities whose stories reflect the powerlessness of captivity of various kinds, we become far more alive to the meaning of the stories of the Bible—especially stories that reflect the realities of captivity and subordination. Furthermore, these voices are being heard against a new awareness of the historical realities of Persian and Hellenistic imperial politics.

The influence of Hellenism is already under severe reassessment, led by important older works such as S. K. Eddy's *The King Is Dead*[21] and Peter Green, who states that the "civilizing and missionary aspects [of Hellenistic conquests] have been greatly exaggerated, not least by modern historians anxious to find some moral justification for aggressive imperialism."[22] Such a reassessment, however, must also extend to the widespread notion of Persian "benevolence" as well. In a recent popular commentary on Ezra and Nehemiah, Holmgren reflects this general perspective in a most interesting manner. In his comment on Neh 9:36-37, a text that contains one of the most significant and explicit complaints against the Persians, Holmgren recognizes that this passage indicates a measure of resentment and unrest, but then continues at some length to maintain the general assumption about Jewish attitudes to Persian rule:

To be "almost free" is never enough; if you are a slave, "almost free" means that you are still a slave. Under Persian rule the Jews were "almost free." Jews did not despise this "almost free" existence, however, because under benevolent monarchs the Jews were free to return to the land and there to rebuild the temple and the city of Jerusalem. The writings of both Ezra and Nehemiah portray the Persian rulers as cooperative and fair . . . toward the Jewish community.[23]

Thus the idea of Persian benevolence has become an almost unquestionable doctrine of research on the exilic and post-exilic periods of the Bible, and is obviously relevant to the study of the book of Daniel. Such a positive view is typically considered a reliable collective memory of the Jews in the diaspora. So Collins writes that "the benevolence of the king is assumed" in the court tales,[24] and Wills, in an otherwise very interesting study, further presumes the positive view of foreign rulers.[25] Blenkinsopp, commenting on Ezra and Nehemiah, also notes "the theme of the benevolence of the Persian kings."[26] Indeed, such a positive view is often used as an argument for dating the Daniel materials in an era other than that of the hated Antiochus Epiphanes IV, because it is hard to accept stories of a benign foreign ruler in that time. It is the argument of this introduction that such an assumption about the benign rulers of either Babylon or Persia overlooks many of the significant symbols of domination that are indicated in the stories themselves—threats of death from the king, fear of the king's rage, name changing as a sign of subordination, symbolic warfare in the visions, etc. Thus that assumption fails to appreciate fully the themes of resistance and opposition that are major aspects of these stories. In short, one need not find calls to open and violent revolution in order to recognize calls to resistance, even if it is nonviolent resistance. It is true that some passages from the Bible would seem to support such assumptions, perhaps most powerfully in the enthusiastic bestowal of the title "Messiah" on Cyrus in Isa 45:1 or the clearly more sympathetic portrayal of Darius in Daniel 6.

Finally, because Jewish names turn up among the Murashu Documents (an archive of business affairs from the Persian period, discovered in the ancient city of Nippur), many scholars have concluded that life must have been profitable for some of the community members. Zadok's studies, however, note that very few Jewish names turn up as officials or members of the upper echelons of society. Nehemiah, he argued, was a clear exception to the rule.[27] While there is nothing in the Elephantine correspondence[28] of Jewish soldiers under Persian mercenary employment in Egypt to suggest resentment, it must not be overlooked that it was a military colony in the service of the Persians, opposed to a hostile local Egyptian populace. What might a new view of Persian imperial policy do for a reading of the book of Daniel?

The "positive attitude" notion is based on very few biblical sources that have nevertheless been allowed to dominate the interpretation of all Persian period biblical literature and the Jewish experience of Achaemenid rule. This has led scholars to overlook important sociological and sociopsychological factors in biblical and nonbiblical literature that are crucial for a modern assessment of the historical and ideological understanding of the Persian period.

In a recent analysis, Root contrasts the Persians' own self-image and propaganda as portrayed in official artwork with actual practice: "The world was at peace on the walls of Persepolis as it never was in actuality. While news of the Persian sack of Miletus was striking terror in the Athenian soul, artisans from near and far were carving dreams in stone for Darius."[29] In her important reassessment of the implications of the famous Cyrus Cylinder, Amelie Kuhrt also warns against allowing "a blatant piece of Persian propaganda" to convince modern historians of the benevolence of Cyrus.[30] Finally, in a recent forum in which the historical image of Cyrus was examined again, Van der Spek also takes issue with the older view on the basis of the historical sources, concluding that "Cyrus and the other Persian kings ruled their empire in a way which was quite common in antiquity. . . . Cyrus introduced no new policy toward subdued nations, but acted in conformity with firmly established traditions, sometimes favorable, sometimes cruel. Under his responsibility temples were destroyed, Ecbatana was plundered, after the battle of Opis Cyrus 'carried off the plunder (and) slaughtered the people.'"[31]

This historical reconsideration is beginning to have an impact on biblical analysis. For example, Jenner considers the Cyrus decree recorded in Ezra 1 to be a falsification by Darius, who needed to legitimate a strong western flank, and the Jewish Temple would certainly serve his purposes. Fur-

thermore, that Cyrus is called "Messiah" should not be overread, since, Jenner suggests, the meaning attached to such a title could have been much cooler than many modern interpreters assume, since "Cyrus, being in a position of dependency and obedience to JHWH, was no more than a useful tool in the service of Jerusalem."[32] This conclusion will have an important impact on a reading of Daniel.

The most important recent voice along these lines is that of Kenneth Hoglund.[33] Hoglund argues convincingly for a reassessment of the role of such Jewish representatives of the Persians as Ezra and Nehemiah, but especially the military leader Nehemiah. Nehemiah, declares Hoglund, was a Persian official (courtier?) whose task was more military than spiritual and who was concerned with the further imposition of Persian control over Palestine, not with any supposed free expression of local religion by the Jewish residents there. The Persians built a series of garrisons that represented strong military control of their western flank; thus any Jewish "returns to the land" under the Persians must be seen now as part of this strategic plan and not as the result of enlightened Persian rulership. In short, as Hoglund summarizes, "the appearance of these garrisons in the mid-fifth century is the indelible fingerprint of the hand of the Achaemenid empire tightening its grip on local affairs in the Levant."[34]

How do such historical realities about both Persian and Hellenistic policies influence interpretation of Daniel? Perhaps they simply alert the reader to look for the realities of political occupation and to learn how to see those realities, by reading Daniel in new ways. Given the sociopolitical context of empire in the latter half of the first millennium, the era of world empire, a full understanding of such post-exilic books as Daniel (not to mention Ezra–Nehemiah, Malachi, Esther, and many others) requires an understanding of the meaning and the impact of the exile and the kind of captivity it represented. It also requires that portions of the Bible be read "in the shadows," in order to fully comprehend their meaning and significance to a subordinated minority population. For minorities throughout the world, certain conversations must take place in the shadows, away from the "king's ear"—informers or guards. These conversations include stories, jokes, or tales told in whispers. Where a minority feels subordinated by either tradition or law, these stories can become a creative world of resistance in which heroes are drawn from among their own people, standing against the dominant majority culture.[35]

RETHINKING THE CONDITIONS OF CONQUEST AND EXILE

The exile was an experience of military defeat, deportation, and oppression in a new and strange land, which ended the days of independence for ancient Israel. At the hands of Nebuchadnezzar, Jerusalem, its Temple, and much of the environs were devastated (2 Kings 25). As was their policy, the Babylonians exiled large sections of the conquered population. Josephus, in his review of the history of the prisoners of war taken to Babylon, spoke of their being bound and chained. Whether this report can be taken as historically reliable and how far it is reconstruction on the basis of Josephus's time period is unclear, but note the language about fetters in Jer 40:1 (cf. Nah 3:10). As recounted in 2 Kings 25 and Jeremiah 52, only the poorest of the land were left to be "vinedressers and plowmen."

We know that under imperial rule subject populations and conquered territories were treated as sources of resources and labor; scholars sum this up graphically as a huge military and administrative apparatus designed to secure a constant flow of goods from the periphery to the center. Biblical traditions of proclamation against Babylon lead the reader to believe that Babylonian policies were severe; the oracles in Jeremiah, for example, threaten punishment of Babylon for its severity (Jer 50:15-16, 29; 51:20-22) and idolatry (50:2, 36; 51:44). But clearly the most crushing reality of Babylonian policy was the deportation itself, the disruption of life and the constant reminder of being a conquered people.

As for the actual number of people exiled, the evidence is unclear. Second Kings 24:14 states that there were 10,000 captives, but 2 Kgs 24:26 lists 7,000 "men of valor" and 1,000 craftsmen. Jeremiah claims that in all 4,600 persons were taken to Babylonia, listing them by year as follows in Nebuchadnezzar's seventh year, 3,023 Jews; in his eighteenth year, 832; and in the twenty-third year, 745 (Jer 52:28-30).

The usual means of calculating the number of exiles is to multiply a "typical family" unit (four to five members of an immediate family) by the number 4,600—who are assumed to have been only men—which results in approximately 20,000-25,000. However, if only "important" men were counted (heads of households, etc.), then the total figure could easily be much higher.

It is often strongly asserted in studies of the Babylonian exile that the exiles were *not* slaves, although at least one important building inscription has Nebuchadnezzar bragging that he "imposed the brick basket" on exiles taken from the western reaches of his empire, most certainly including Palestine.[36] We have noted, even under the rule of the supposedly tolerant Persians, that Ezra mentions in his prayer to God that "we are slaves" (Ezra 9:9 NRSV; cf. Neh 9:36).[37] But do we really know what we are talking about when we say that the exiles were (or were not) slaves? For North Americans, the image of slavery is indelibly marked by African American slavery in the early United States. But that is not the only form slavery has taken throughout history. In his book *Slavery and Social Death*,[38] Orlando Patterson analyzes the structure of slave societies using data from over forty different slave systems from all over the world and in different times. Common to all is the significance of symbolic institutions, what Patterson calls "the symbolic whips of slavery . . . woven from many areas of culture." These symbols include forceable name changes, hair or clothing changes, body markers, and anything that symbolized the death of one's identity at birth by means of a "rebirth" to a new identity given by the dominant authorities. Patterson notes that in different slave systems, a slave may be forced to change his or her name or "eat" the old identity through a food ceremony. Hence, according to Patterson's analysis, slavery is, in essence, the removal of one's identity and a social death. Therefore, the reconstruction and resistance of an ethnic group can be seen as a potential response to just such a threat of social death. One of the ways we see Jewish resistance to the symbols of powerlessness in the exile and afterward is in the telling of stories of Jewish courage in the face of tremendous foreign power. The tales of the book of Daniel are stories and writings of this kind.

Once we consider the significance of the symbols of domination, we are better prepared to note their significance in the Bible. For example, name changing is a common symbol used by foreign rulers in the Bible. Even though the stories of Daniel and his friends come from a late era in their final form, the symbol of name changing is an important factor in their association with the Babylonians and may not be an incidental detail. Furthermore, Nebuchadnezzar also changed the name of Zedekiah, when he placed him on the throne of Judah in Jehoiachin's absence (2 Kgs 24:17). That biblical writers mention these policies seems to reflect an awareness of the symbols of power that the exiles had to live with and struggle against.

Clearly, one element of recognizing these symbols is to note the constant reminders of foreign imperial power over the Jews. Indeed, so often is this context of empire noted in Ezra–Nehemiah, Daniel, and Esther that we may overlook its significance. For example, simply to pay attention to the frequency of the word *decree* in these works is revealing. The vast majority of occurrences of this term in the Bible are commands of foreign emperors dealing with the Jewish minority. The terms translated into English as "decree" in these books have been borrowed from political and administrative vocabulary of Imperial Aramaic or Persian, the official languages of the time. This is hardly surprising, since minorities would learn quickly such words as "police," "papers," "command," "authorized," and "order."

Such terms signal that the Jewish community was trapped by the competing claims to authority made by the local non-Jewish officials and the Persian court ("Who gave you a decree to build this house?" [Ezra 5:3]). They depended on Persian benevolence and support and had to appeal to the Persian court for permission at every turn. The biblical books from this period exhibit a heightened consciousness of a people not in control of their own lives: "I, Darius, make a decree," "You are permitted to go to Jerusalem," "I decree that any of the people . . . may go with you," "the unchangeable law of the Persians." Once again, the exile's legacy casts its shadow— the shadow of the guard tower—whether real or symbolic. Read in the shadows, Daniel becomes a revolutionary book of resistance, albeit nonviolent resistance.

Finally, one of the reasons why the revolutionary nature of the call to resistance in Daniel is not noted more frequently is the tendency among many modern historians to regard only violent forms of resistance as evidence of any kind of resistance activity. If violence is not present, then the literature is deemed unrealistic or fantasy. Yet, 1 Maccabees is seldom criticized as being either, even though it proposes to celebrate the preposterous notion of a military confrontation between a divided Jewish community and a vastly superior force. It would appear that if we do not have texts that explicitly state that the people did not like the conditions under which they lived and that thus they would fight for independence, then some scholars conclude that conditions must not have been so bad. It is hard to avoid the conclusion that more than historical evidence is implicated in such viewpoints. Yet this perspective overlooks the subtleties of spiritual, social, and political resistance, which are not always obvious to those who simply equate violence with resistance. In short, the Maccabean uprising was not the only form of Jewish social resistance to world empire in the Persian and Hellenistic era. A reading of Daniel "in the shadows of empire" greatly facilitates this historical conclusion.

POSTSCRIPT

It is somewhat dangerous to ask a Quaker to write on Daniel. Quaker associations with this book are long and interesting—and not a little controversial. Indeed, there is no other Hebrew biblical book that is more a Quaker's book than Daniel. Quakerism arose, after all, in the throes of the English civil war. The founder of Quakerism, George Fox, was himself offered an officership in Cromwell's anti-Royalist forces. It was not an unusual offer, as there were certainly other (and similarly minded) Christian radicals who believed that dethroning and then beheading the king and fighting for a much wider participation in national affairs, including in some cases the extreme notion of the vote for all persons, was a fulfillment of the book of Daniel. Some of these radicals called themselves "The Fifth Monarchy Men," a term inspired directly from the sequence of four empires named in Daniel 2 and 7. Many of Cromwell's more theologically extreme soldiers, including many Fifth Monarchists, swelled the ranks of Quakerism in its first generation.

Daniel has engendered more bizarre speculations than those of the seventeenth-century Puritan revolutionaries, of course, and part of its continued appeal is precisely the sense of crisis out of which the book arose, which then seems to speak to the frequent recurrence of crises in human society over the centuries. In short, people who sense that the world is not right are drawn to a book that shares their conviction. One of the ways in which we will read Daniel "in the shadows" is to read two authors along the way: Franz Fanon and Albert Memmi. Fanon was an Algerian psychologist who wrote about the Algerian resistance to French colonialism. His work written in 1961, *The Wretched of the Earth*, remains a classic statement of the colonized perspective.[39] Already in 1957, however, the Tunisian Jewish author Albert Memmi had written *The Colonizer and the Colonized* with a similar interest in analyzing the impact of colonization on native peoples.[40] Both works will help us to understand important aspects of reading Daniel as a book that reflects the domination of the Jewish people by Babylonians, Persians, and Greeks. The situations, so different and so far apart historically, are not exactly the same, of course, but Fanon and Memmi provide provocative suggestions for helping us to rethink the implications of social context in a reading of Daniel. We may also draw on the experiences of minority peoples, drawing especially on Native American comments.[41]

The danger inherent in the book of Daniel is clear from the fact that Josephus found himself attempting to tone down the rhetoric, lest it offend his Roman readers. In short, Daniel directs its severe judgment toward human rulers, and a serious assumption of the work is that the people of faith will inevitably find themselves in opposition to the state and its accompanying forms of political loyalties and idolatrous patriotism. Albert Memmi summarized the position of anyone who would begin to be sympathetic to those who suffer under present political circumstances, which in his context meant the colonized of North Africa. He wrote that a European in North Africa who begins to have sympathy and then to identify with the colonized is to choose "treason" against the values of the powerful.[42] Such a position will generate a reaction: "Wonder has been expressed at the vehemence of colonizers against any among them who put colonization in jeopardy. It is clear that such a colonizer is nothing

but a traitor. He challenges their very existence."[43] The book of Daniel calls people of faith to just such a treason against the rule of the powerful, a treason based on loyalty to the rule of God.

Such thoughts should immediately bring pause to any modern pastor who would attempt to preach or teach on Daniel—you are venturing into subversive territory. There is no message of facile patriotism, of "good citizenship," or of merely personal, pietistic faith in Daniel. Thus there can be no such thing as a non-political reading of Daniel, if it is to be true to the living spirit of Scripture and to the suffering of those who wrote it under the inspiration of a God who first delivered slaves from Pharaoh.

Reading Daniel in some contexts raises disturbing questions. How can a book meant to encourage the faith of a politically subordinated people be made meaningful for those of us in a dominant culture, such as European Americans, European Canadians, or European Australians? In short, do we read Daniel as modern "Babylonians," "Persians" and "Greeks," or as their captive peoples?

Reference to the experiences of historically subordinated peoples is not intended to be an exercise in collective guilt but rather highlights the possible similarities in experience between the writers of Daniel and modern conquered or colonized peoples, and further suggests that if the Christian faith is to be one that challenges the modern world, then it must accept a certain alienation from the dominant culture and its religious traditions of dominance.

To read the book of Daniel in one hand while holding Fanon or modern Native American works in the other is to suggest that biblical faith will of necessity find significant social and spiritual parallels with the life of alienated peoples. This is because Christians know that they live in Babylon and not in the kingdom of God. To come to that realization means embracing a theology of Christ against culture, particularly where that culture is based on the products of military conquest and economic abuse of conquered peoples.

FOR FURTHER READING

Commentaries:

Bentzen, Aage. *Daniel.* HAT 19. Tübingen: Mohr, 1952.

Collins, John J. *Daniel*. Hermeneia. Minneapolis: Fortress, 1993.

Goldingay, John. *Daniel*. WBC 30. Dallas: Word, 1988.

Gowan, Donald E. *Daniel*. Abingdon Old Testament Commentaries. Nashville: Abingdon, 2001.

Hartman, Louis F., and Alexander A. DeLella. *The Book of Daniel*. AB 23. Garden City, N.Y.: Doubleday, 1978.

Koch, Klaus. *Das Buch Daniel*. Darmstadt: Wissenschaftliche Buchgesellschaft, 1980.

Lacocque, André. *The Book of Daniel*. Translated by D. Pellauer. Atlanta: John Knox, 1979.

Montgomery, James A. *A Critical and Exegetical Commentary on the Book of Daniel*. ICC. Edinburgh: T & T Clark, 1927.

Porteous, Norman W. *Daniel: A Commentary*. OTL. Philadelphia: Westminster, 1965.

Seow, Choon Leong. *Daniel*. Westminster Bible Companion. Louisville, Ky.: Westminster/John Knox Press, 2003.

Towner, W. Sibley. *Daniel*. Interpretation. Atlanta: John Knox, 1984.

Other Studies:

Brenner, Athalya, ed. *Prophets and Daniel*. Feminist Companion to the Bible. Second Series 8. London: Sheffield Academic Press, 2001.

Collins, John J. *The Apocalyptic Vision of the Book of Daniel*. Missoula, Mont.: Scholars Press, 1977.

Fewell, Danna Nolan. *Circle of Sovereignty: Plotting Politics in the Book of Daniel*. Nashville: Abingdon, 1991.

Ginsberg, Harold. "The Oldest Interpretation of the Suffering Servant." *VT* 3 (1953).

Hellholm, David, ed. *Apocalypticism in the Mediterranean World and the Near East: Proceedings of the International Colloquium on Apocalypticism*. Tübingen: Mohr-Siebeck, 1983.

Kippenberg, Hans G. *Religions und Klassenbildung im antiken Judaä: Eine Religions-soziologie Studie zum Verhätnes von Tradition und gesellschaftlicher Entwicklung*. Vandenhoeck und Ruprecht: Göttingen, 1982.

Kvanvig, Helge S. *The Roots of Apocalyptic: The Mesopotamian Background of the Enoch Figure and of the Son of Man*. Neukirchen-Vluyn: Neukirchener Verlag, 1988.

Otzen, Benedikt. *Judaism in Antiquity: Political Development and Religious Currents from Alexander to Hadrian*. Sheffield: JSOT, 1990.

Rowland, Christopher. *The Open Heaven: A Study of Apocalyptic in Judaism and Early Christianity*. London: SPCK, 1982.

Smith, Daniel. *The Religion of the Landless: The Sociology of the Babylonian Exile*. New York: Meyer-Stone, 1989.

Tcherikover, Victor. *Hellenistic Civilization and the Jews*. Atheneum: New York, 1970.

VanderKam, James C. *Enoch and the Growth of an Apocalyptic Tradition*. CBQMS 16. Washington, D.C.: Catholic Biblical Association, 1984.

Weinberg, Joel. *The Citizen Temple Community*. Sheffield: JSOT, 1992.

ENDNOTES

1. A. Meinhold, "Die Diasporanovelle: Eine Alttestamentliche Gattung" (Ph.D. diss., University of Greifswald, 1969).

2. L. Wills, *The Jew in the Court of the Foreign King* (Minneapolis: Fortress, 1990); S. Niditch and R. Doran, "The Success Story of the Wise Courtier: A Formal Approach," *JBL* 96 (1977) 179-93.

3. W. L. Humphreys, "A Life-Style for Diaspora: A Study of the Tales of Esther and Daniel," *JBL* 93 (1973) 211-23; John J. Collins, *The Apocalyptic Visions of the Book of Daniel* (Missoula, Mont.: Scholars Press, 1977) and John J. Collins, *Daniel*, Hermoneia (Minneapolis: Fortress, 1993).

4. Collins dates the "traditions," rather than the texts as we have them, to the late Persian period. The Aramaic of the book of Daniel is older than the Aramaic of the Dead Sea Scrolls. This suggests that the tales should be dated early in the Hellenistic era, which began in 333 BCE with the conquests of Alexander the Great.

5. J. M. Cook, *The Persian Empire* (New York: Schocken, 1983) 132-33.

6. The classic study is W. L. Humphreys, "A Life-Style for Diaspora," 211-23.

7. A notable exception is D. N. Fewell, *Circle of Sovereignty: A Story of Stories in Daniel 1–6* (Sheffield: Almond, 1988).

8. Note the perspective of D. Berrigan in his series on Daniel, "Till the End of Empire," in *The Other Side* (July-August 1990) 8-14; (September-October 1990) 8-17; (November-December 1990) 36-42.

9. 4QPrNab. Translation from F. García-Martínez, *Qumran and Apocalyptic: Studies on the Aramaic Texts from Qumran* (Leiden: Brill, 1992) 119-20.

10. See the article in this volume by Frederick J. Murphy, "Introduction to Apocalyptic Literature."

11. On Persian influences, see esp. A. Hultgård, "The Bahman Yasht: A Persian Perspective," in *Mysteries and Revelations: Apocalyptic Studies Since the Uppsala Colloquium*, ed. John J. Collins and J. H. Charlesworth (Sheffield: JSOT, 1991).

12. John J. Collins, "Genre, Ideology, and Social Movements in Jewish Apocalypticism," in *Mysteries and Revelations, Apocalyptic Studies Since the Uppsala Colloquium*, ed. J. J. Collins and J. H. Charleworth (Sheffield: JSOT, 1991) 19.

13. S. B. Reid, *Enoch and Daniel*, Bibal Monograph Series (Berkeley: Bibal, 1989).

14. G. W. F. Nickelsburg, "Social Aspects of Palestinian Jewish Apocalypticism," in D. Hellholm, ed., *Apocalypticism in the Mediterranean World and the Near East* (Tübingen: Mohr, 1983) 641-54; see also, in the same volume, E. P. Sanders, "The Genre of Palestinian Jewish Apocalypses," 447-59. Note recent disagreements in Stephen L. Cook, *Prophecy and Apocalypticism: The Postexilic Social Setting* (Minneapolis: Fortress, 1995).

15. M. Smith, "Hellenization," in M. Stone and D. Satran, eds., *Emerging Judaism* (Minneapolis: Fortress, 1989) 111-12.

16. J. D. Newsome, *Greeks, Romans, Jews* (Philadelphia: Trinity Press International, 1992) 37.

17. V. Tcherikover, *Hellenistic Civilization and the Jews* (New York: Atheneum, 1970) 198.

18. V. Tcherikover, *Hellenistic Civilization and the Jews*, 1970), 202-3.

19. M. Smith, "Hellenization," 111-12.

20. See the volume of essays, *Voices from the Margin: Interpreting the Bible in the Third World*, ed. R. S. Sugirtharajah (New York: Orbis, 1991) and Daniel Smith-Christopher, ed., *Text and Experience: Papers on Cultural Exegesis from the 1992 Casassa Conference* (Sheffield: Sheffield University Press, 1996).

21. S. K. Eddy, *The King Is Dead: Studies in the Near Eastern Resistance to Hellenism 334–31 BC* (Lincoln: University of Nebraska Press, 1961).

22. P. Green, "Greek Gifts?" *History Today* (June 1990) 27-34.

23. F. C. Holmgren, *Israel Alive Again* (Grand Rapids: Eerdmans, 1987) 134-35.

24. John J. Collins, *Daniel*, FOTL (Grand Rapids: Eerdmans, 1984) 72.

25. L. Wills, *The Jew in the Court of the Foreign King*. This view is maintained in recent commentaries, such as that of André Lacocque, *The Book of Daniel*, trans. D. Pellauer (Atlanta: John Knox, 1979) 113; N. Porteous, *Daniel: A Commentary*, OTL (Philadelphia: Westminster, 1965) 90; and O. Plöger, *Daniel*, KAT (Leipzig: Gütersloh, 1965) 98.

26. J. Blenkinsopp, *Ezra–Nehemiah* (London: SCM, 1988) 160.

27. R. Zadok, *The Jews in Babylonia During the Chaldean and Achaemenid Periods* (Haifa: University of Haifa, 1979) 86-90.

28. Part of a group of papyrus documents and fragments written in Aramaic in the fifth century BCE, originating at Elephantine, an island in the Nile opposite Aswan (ancient Syrene); they were discovered during the nineteenth and twentieth centuries CE.

29. M. C. Root, *The King and Kingship in Achaemenid Art: Essays on the Creation of an Iconography of Empire*, vol. 9 of Acta Iranica, Textes et Memoires (Leiden: Brill, 1979) 311.

30. A. Kuhrt, "The Cyrus Cylinder and Achaemenid Imperial Policy," *JSOT* 25 (1983) 94-95.

31. R. J. van der Spek, "Did Cyrus the Great Introduce a New Policy Towards Subdued Nations? Cyrus in Assyrian Perspective," *Persica* 10 (1982) 278-79, 281-82.

32. K. D. Jenner, "The Old Testament and Its Appreciation of Cyrus," *Persica* 10 (1982) 284.

33. K. G. Hoglund, *Achaemenid Imperial Administration in Syria-Palestine and the Missions of Ezra and Nehemiah*, SBLDS 125 (Atlanta: Scholars Press, 1992). See also A. Kuhrt, "The Cyrus Cylinder and Achaemenid Imperial Policy," 83-97; R. J. van der Spek, "Did Cyrus the Great Introduce a New Policy Towards Subdued Nations?" 278-83.

34. K. G. Hoglund, "Achaemeid Imperial Administration in Syria-Palestine and the Missions of Ezra and Nehemiah," 433.

35. See D. Smith, *The Religion of the Landless* (New York: Meyer-Stone, 1989).

36. F. H. Weissbach, *Das Haupttheiligtum des Marduk in Babylon* (Leipzig, 1938) 47. See also S.

Langdon, *Building Inscriptions of the Neo-Baby-lonian Empire* (Paris, 1905) 59, 149.

37. It has been suggested that this refers to the fact that all Persian citizens routinely referred to themselves as slaves of the emperor. But is this what Ezra and Nehemiah were referring to? In the context, it can hardly be read as merely an equivalent term to "citizen." J. M. Cook, *The Persian Empire*, 132.

38. Orlando Patterson, *Slavery and Social Death* (Cambridge, Mass.: Harvard University Press, 1982).

39. F. Fanon, *The Wretched of the Earth* (New York: Grove, 1963).

40. A. Memmi, *The Colonizer and the Colo-nized* (Boston: Beacon, 1965).

41. During the time I spent in research for the NIB commentary, I was able to sit with Lakota Christians and Traditionalists on the Rosebud Reservation in South Dakota and read chapters from the book of Daniel with them. Some of the comments in the commentary reflect that research. These interviews form part of an upcoming study on cultural influences on the reading of the Bible.

42. A. Memmi, *The Colonizer and the Colo-nized*, 22.

43. A. Memmi, *The Colonizer and the Colo-nized*, 22.

THE BOOK OF
HOSEA

GALE A. YEE

THE BOOK

The play *The Marriage of Hosea*, published in 1929 under the pseudonym Izachak, carries the subtitle "A Passion Play." In describing the work as a *passion* play, the anonymous twentieth-century author understood the ancient prophetic book of Hosea very well. The multivalent word *passion* captures the incendiary relations existing among the characters of the book. It typifies the feverish lust of a wife chasing after her various lovers. As profound suffering, passion describes the torment her husband experiences because of her infidelity. It also embodies the violent anger with which the husband lashes out against his wife to punish her and bring her to her senses. Finally, it embraces the ardor between the couple as they reconcile and commit themselves to each other again.

Structure and Theological Themes. The prophetic book of Hosea is indeed a passionate work. Its vivid metaphor of marriage for the covenant between God and Israel usually comes to mind when one thinks of this book. Hosea is the first biblical work to employ such an image to describe the God/Israel relationship. Although a major one, however, marriage is not the only covenantal metaphor for Hosea. The book's structure evinces another important image of the special God/Israel relationship and another kind of "passion" as well.

The book is divided into three sections, each highlighting a particular metaphor for the covenant between God and Israel. Hosea 1–3 concentrates on the husband/wife metaphor. The tragic marriage of Hosea to his promiscuous wife, Gomer, and the births of their three children (chap. 1) parallel Yahweh's tumultuous union with the faithless wife, Israel (chap. 2). Hosea represents Israel's worship of illicit gods figuratively as adultery, punishable by death if God so chooses. God's eventual reconciliation with "his wife," Israel, provides a model for Hosea's own reunion with Gomer (chap. 3).

Chapters 4–11, the second and largest section, contain the bulk of Hosea's oracles against Israelite politics and cult. Chapter 11, which summarizes and concludes this section, takes up the parent/child metaphor for the God/Israel relationship. God becomes the loving, caring parent, while Israel in its transgression of the covenant is the rebellious son. The passion of the mother/father God exhibits itself in the parent's compassionate refusal to kill the intractable child, even though the laws of the land would sanction death.

In the third and final section, chaps. 12–14, the prophet interweaves both the husband/wife metaphor and the rebellious son metaphor. The unwise son is threatened with destruction, unless he repents of his accumulated guilt (Hosea 13). The repentant wife returns to her husband and to the land from whence she was banished (Hosea 12). Symbolizing the wife and her reunion with the husband, the land that had formerly been devastated by the husband blossoms forth into a fruitful, luxurious plantation (Hosea 14).

The first and final verses of the work are structurally significant. Hosea 1:1 contextualizes the tradition of Hosea during a particular time in the history of the Israelite people. Hosea 14:9 concludes the book with a word of wisdom, enjoining the reader to heed God's Word inscribed therein.

Hosea 3, 11, and 14 also have structural importance. These chapters conclude the three major sections of the work. Each presents a story about the God/Israel relationship through the metaphor either of the husband/wife (Hosea 3; 14) or of the parent/child (Hosea 11). Each highlights the themes of human repentance/return (the Hebrew word שוב [šûb] encompasses both meanings) and divine forgiveness and mercy. Each chapter also unfolds a journey motif that occurs at two levels: the wife's/son's spiritual journey back to the husband/parent and the physical journey back to the homeland from exile.

In addition to the themes of repentance/return and journey home, each major section of the work is characterized by a movement from barrenness to fertility. In Hosea 2 the land that was ravaged and laid waste (2:3, 12) participates cosmically in the bounty that flows from the rebetrothal of husband and wife. The wife/Israel is figuratively sown in the land (2:18-23). In the 4–11 complex, the symbolic barrenness of the people is reflected in the destitution of the cosmos . Nevertheless, three hope passages (5:15–6:3; 10:12; 11:10-11) articulate a movement from barrenness to fertility. Hosea 1–3 concludes with the wife/Israel sown in the land. Hosea 14:5-8 manifests the wonderful results of the sowing by depicting the wife/Israel breaking forth as a lush and flourishing land.

Authorship. Over a hundred years of scholarship on the prophetic books reveal that not every saying or oracle in the work comes directly from the prophet himself.[1] A prophetic book is the literary result of a long traditioning process, encompassing not only the lifetime of the prophet but also centuries following his death. Successive generations who inherit the prophet's sayings reinterpret them for their own particular time, putting a distinctive stamp upon the different literary phases of the book.

Earlier biblical scholarship tended to value what it saw as the *ipsissima verba*, or the "authentic words," of the prophet.[2] Evidence of later editorial activity was regarded as secondary, not only chronologically, but also in theological importance. Recent critical studies, however, recognize the significance of later stages of the work: those of the collectors and redactors.[3] In their collection, arrangement, and commentary on the prophetic tradition they inherit, these later editors are responsible for the biblical work as we have it today.

Hence, the authorship of the book of Hosea is a complex matter that is still disputed. Many scholars insist that most of the book originated with the prophet Hosea.[4] Others think that redactional activity was more extensive than previously thought.[5] Relevant for the oracles of this eighth-century BCE prophet are three major interpretive stages that can be detected in the book of Hosea: an eighth–seventh-century BCE collection of the prophet's oracles; a seventh-century BCE deuteronomistic redaction during the time of the Judean king Josiah; and a sixth-century BCE deuteronomistic redaction during the Babylonian exile

(587–539 BCE). Whether one thinks that Hosea's original oracles were particularly influential for these later interpretive periods or whether one maintains that redactors expanded Hosea's original oracles during these later times with their own theologies, it is clear that these stages were critical in the book's formation.

Since the focus of *The New Interpreter's Bible* is the final canonical text itself, we must reckon very seriously with the later interpretive stages as well as the prophet's earlier oracles. Although not all of the sayings can be credited to the prophet Hosea, from a scriptural vantage point they *now* belong fully to him and his book. Acceptance of every stage in the formation of a prophetic book recognizes that God's word, spoken by the prophet in a specific historical context, was not limited to that context. Later eras appropriated Hosea's words as *tradition* that spoke in some way to their own circumstances, often expanding upon or even modifying them. The content of the original message was not dissipated when its initial context was past.

THE HISTORICAL CONTEXTS OF THE BOOK

The Period of the Eighth-Century BCE Prophet. Social Turmoil. Very little is known about the northern prophet Hosea. The superscription to his book, which was added later by a redactor, identifies Hosea as the son of Beeri, about whom nothing more can be said. The superscription situates Hosea between 750 and 724 BCE—i.e., between the last years of Jeroboam II (786–746 BCE) and three years before the fall of Israel to the Assyrians in 721 BCE. If the superscription is correct, Hosea prophesied during a politically turbulent period after the peaceful rule of Jeroboam II (cf. 2 Kgs 14:23–17:41). The monarchy was plagued by a number of assassinations. Of the six kings to ascend the throne, all but one died violently. Corruption at court and partisan intrigue were rampant (Hos 6:8-10; 7:1-7). The northern kingdom not only contended with the western encroachment of the Assyrian king Tiglath-pileser III, but also clashed with its southern rival, Judah, during the Syro-Ephraimite war (735–733 BCE). Israel's foreign policy was often unpredictable. The nation curried favor with international powers, such as Egypt and Assyria, who competed with each other in the political arena (Hos 7:8-15; 12:1).

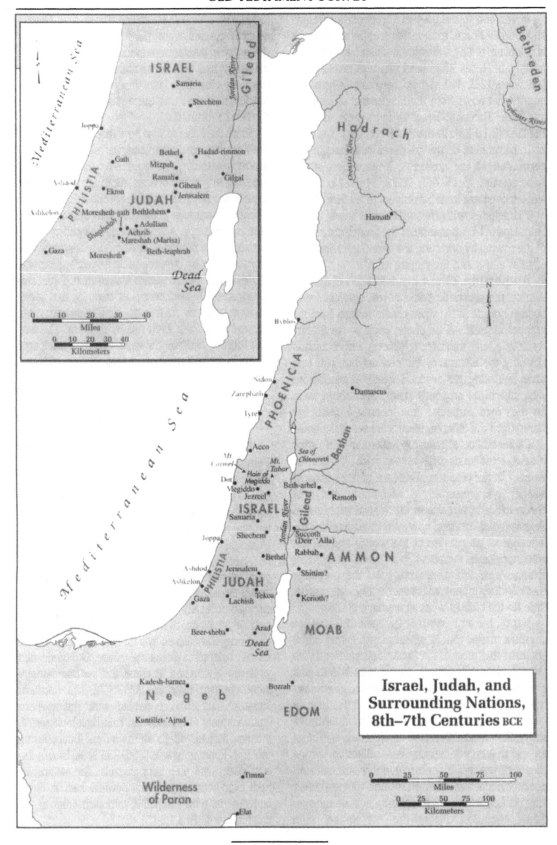

Israel, Judah, and Surrounding Nations, 8th–7th Centuries BCE

The nation was rife with economic abuses. The social inequities between rich and poor that were very much apparent during the time of Jeroboam II became exacerbated after his death. The war with Judah and heavy tribute to Assyria (Hos 8:10; 10:6) depleted economic resources. The richer classes intensified their exploitation of the peasants in order to pay these debts. Many resorted to fraud and cheating (Hos 12:7-8).

Cultic Turmoil. The book of Hosea is perhaps best known for its condemnation of Israel's cult. One gets the impression from reading this book (as well as many other books in the Hebrew Bible) that worship of Yahweh had become infected with the Canaanite religion of the land the Israelites had conquered. The wife/Israel is accused of chasing after her lovers, the *baals* (2:7-8, 13). In Canaanite mythology, Baal was the storm god responsible for life-giving rains. In an arid climate like Israel's, such rains were a matter of life and death. The fertility rituals grounded in this mythology supposedly involved orgiastic sex with temple prostitutes.

Recent scholarship calls into question this notion of Canaanite infiltration of a pure Yahwism.[6] Monotheism, belief in a single God to the exclusion of any other, was not always practiced in Israel. The monotheistic theology represented in the book of Hosea eventually became normative for Israel. In their formative stages, however, Israel's diverse religious beliefs and practices were influenced by those of other cultures.

Particularly important for understanding Hosea is recognizing that the religion of the ancient Israelites had a strong heritage in Canaanite religion. Although Yahweh was its primary God, early Israelite religion included the worship of several other deities. Veneration of the Canaanite deities El, Baal, and perhaps even the goddess Asherah,[7] was accepted or at least tolerated in the earlier stages of Israel's religious development. What stand condemned as Baal worship in Hosea—e.g., cultic rites on the high places (4:13; 10:8), pillars (3:4; 10:1-2), divining rods (4:12), images (4:17; 8:4; 14:8), and calf figurines (8:5-6; 10:5; 13:2)— were for centuries accepted components of the worship of Yahweh. Although these had been taken over from foreign cults, their appropriation had occurred much earlier and was no longer regarded as syncretistic by the people.[8] A number of complex factors, such as centralization of the cult, the rise of the monarchy, the increased use of writing that disseminated normative views, and a growing religious self-definition vis-à-vis other cultures, eventually led to an evolving monotheism and a rejection of much, though not all, of Israel's Canaanite heritage. Hence, the worship of Baal, once a legitimate part of Israelite religion, now stands condemned by the book of Hosea.

Although worship of Canaanite deities was most likely a long-established practice in ancient Israel, Canaanite religious rituals are very difficult to reconstruct on the basis of the biblical witness alone. Because of its increasing polemic against that religion, the biblical text presents biased and even distorted pictures of Canaanite rites. One alleged Canaanite practice that is specifically relevant to the book of Hosea is so-called cultic prostitution. We have learned much about Canaanite mythology from the Ras Shamra tablets, discovered some fifty years ago on the coast of Syria. According to these tablets, the storm god Baal was killed by Mot, god of barrenness and death. In its prescientific milieu, this myth explained the hot, dry period between May and September, when no rains fell on the land. Baal's sister-lover, the goddess Anat, came to the rescue by slaying Mot and bringing Baal back to life. Their passionate sexual intercourse, the Canaanites believed, initiated the rainy season that began in October.

Many scholars think that this mythic drama of death and renewed life was rehearsed every year in a religious new year festival that took place in the fall,[9] even though the festival itself is not described in the Ras Shamra tablets. Supposedly, part of this festival was a "sacred marriage" imitating Baal and Anat, during which Canaanite men, from the king on down, had ritual sex with cultic prostitutes in order to ensure fertility in the land. The religious intent behind these fertility cults was very serious, indeed—nothing less than the survival of the people in a hostile climate. Human nature being of a piece, however, some worshipers may have frequented these cultic prostitutes for less than religious reasons. In the minds of many interpreters, such rituals often degenerated into full-scale orgies at the sanctuaries and high places. Allegedly, it was these services that so offended Hosea (4:11-19; 9:1-3). Some critics even suggest that Hosea's wife, Gomer, like other Israelite women (see 4:14), was a cultic prostitute.[10]

Nevertheless, a number of scholars have questioned the phenomenon of cultic prostitution, not only in Canaan, but also in the rest of the ancient Near East.[11] No substantive textual or archaeological evidence verifies that such a class of prostitutes ever existed or that such sexual rites were ever performed. Although used by some to support the existence of cultic prostitution, the testimonies of certain ancient authors like the Greek writers Herodotus and Strabo are actually quite unreliable, because they were written at a far later date and are markedly tendentious. Although in the prophet's mind certain rituals involved sexual intercourse, it would be a mistake to accept this assertion at face value. The biblical text is simply too polemical, revealing more about the prophetic mind that leveled the accusation than about actual observances in the cult.

Thus far I have assumed that condemnations of Israel's cult originated with the eighth-century BCE prophet Hosea. If worship of Baal, along with rituals on the high places, pillars, calves, etc., had long been part and parcel of Israelite religion, then Hosea should not be considered a religious reformer, hearkening the Israelites back to "old time religion," the uncontaminated worship of Yahweh alone. Instead, Hosea would actually be a religious innovator, a spokesperson for a developing monotheistic theology.[12] His new theological ideas would influence the later deuteronomistic writers, for whom belief in the one God Yahweh was normative. Another possibility exists, however. It could be that censure of the "baalization" of the Israelite cult in the book of Hosea originated in the later deuteronomistic redaction of the book (see below).[13]

The Period of the Collector. In 721 BCE the prophet Hosea's predictions came true. The northern kingdom of Israel was destroyed by the Assyrians under Sargon II. Upper-class Israelites were exiled to other parts of the Assyrian Empire, while the poorer classes endured Assyrian occupation of the land. The lucky ones escaped to Judah in the south. Scholars think that Hosea's oracles survived the destruction because refugees brought them to Judah, where they were collected and preserved.[14]

The collector of Hosea's oracles played a crucial role in the literary formation of the book. He might have been a disciple of Hosea, or perhaps a scribe to whom the prophet dictated his words. We do not know his identity. Assuming that Hosea uttered more oracles than those actually preserved in the book, the collector's first task was the *selection* of sayings to be recorded for posterity. The book of Hosea is not simply a collection of Hosea's oracles. Rather, the oracles appear in the collector's work as selected traditions, vital enough to be retained. Moreover, the collector was important for the *arrangement* of the various oracles in a particular literary order. Unfortunate for the modern scholar, this order was not chronological. One critical task involves identifying the principles that guided the collector's organization of the material, as well as theorizing dates for it.

The collector thus created the first written tradition regarding Hosea, which later editing expanded, modified, and reinterpreted. Moreover, the collector seems to have been responsible for Hosea 1, the story of Yahweh's command that Hosea marry a promiscuous woman and have children by her. This divine commissioning (whether an actual event or not) marks the beginning of Hosea's prophetic service. Hosea 1 describes Hosea's "call" to be God's spokesperson. The collector had two reasons for prefacing the work with this call narrative. First, he grounded his oracular collection in the life of a particular person: the prophet Hosea. Without this contextualization it would be difficult to attribute the collected oracles to this eighth-century prophet. The collector thus established a stronger connection between the oracles contained in his work and the personality of the prophet.

Second, it was usually thought that a call narrative was written by the prophet to vindicate himself and to legitimate his office before his opponents. According to more recent scholarship, however, call narratives originated with the prophet's tradents, rather than with the prophet himself.[15] By including Hosea 1, the collector authenticated the prophet's ministry and his own work as well. He legitimized Hosea by anchoring his oracles in a selected moment of his ministry: the marriage and parenting the deity commanded. By prefacing his collection with a story of divine commissioning, the collector legitimated himself and the corpus he created. Lacking the call from God that authorizes a prophetic ministry, he carried on the prophet's work (now vindicated by events) by compiling and editing the sayings into a literary tradition for later generations.

The Period of the Josianic Redactor. Commentators often note strong affinities between the prophet Hosea and the tradents responsible for the book of Deuteronomy and the deuteronomistic history (Joshua, Judges, 1 and 2 Samuel, and 1 and 2 Kings). The two share a similar theology. Both insist upon worship of the one God Yahweh (Deut 4:39; 6:4; 1 Kgs 8:60; Hos 2:16-23; 12:9; 13:4). Both describe God's election of Israel (Deut 4:37; 7:6-8; Hos 9:10; 11:1). Both proclaim God's covenantal love of Israel and the people's own loving response (Deut 6:4-5; 7:8; 11:1; Josh 23:11; Hos 2:18-19; 3:1; 10:12; 14:4) and obedience to Yahweh's *torah* (Deut 30:8-10; Josh 1:7-8; 8:30-35; Hos 8:1, 12).Both vehemently condemn the people's idolatry (Deut 7:2-6; 12:2-4, 29-32; 31:16-22; Josh 24:14-20; Judg 2:11-15; 2 Kgs 17:7-18; Hos 2:8; 4:11-15; 8:5-6, 11; 10:1-2; 11:1-2; 14:8) and summon the people to repentance and return to God (Deut 4:29-31; 30:1-10; Josh 24:23; 1 Kgs 8:22-53; Hos 3:5; 6:1-3; 14:1-2).

Perhaps these similarities can be explained by regarding the prophet Hosea as an innovative theological forerunner of the deuteronomistic groups, an opinion held by those regarding most of the oracles in the book as authentic.[16] Alternatively, one could account for such correspondences by presuming a redaction of the book of Hosea by these circles, who updated and expanded Hosea's oracles for their own generation.[17] In either case, Hosea's oracles bore a fundamental theological relevance for the editors responsible for Deuteronomy and the deuteronomistic history.

The theological relationship between Deuteronomy and the deuteronomistic history was recognized by Martin Noth, who argued that a sixth-century BCE exilic author composed this distinct literary complex.[18] A number of scholars modify Noth's work by positing two major editions of the deuteronomistic history.[19] The first edition (Dtr 1) was produced in the seventh century BCE by a Judean author supportive of the religious reform policies of King Josiah (640–609 BCE). One of the principal themes of Dtr 1 is the crimes of Jeroboam I, the first king of Israel (922–901 BCE), and his northern successors against the cult of Yahweh. Jeroboam I appointed Bethel and Dan as the official sanctuaries of the northern kingdom, rivaling the Temple at Jerusalem. Setting up two golden calves at these holy places, he announced to the people: "You have gone up to Jerusalem long enough. Behold your gods, O Israel, who brought you up out of the land of Egypt" (1 Kgs 12:28). Dtr 1 blames the fall of Israel upon its supposedly "unlawful" cult and climaxes its history in the reforms of Josiah (c. 622 BCE), who tried to rid Judah of its idolatrous cult objects and personnel (2 Kings 22–23; cf. 1 Kgs 13:1-4).

Parts of Hosea can be contextualized in the seventh-century BCE in relation to Dtr 1, particularly in their similar condemnation of Israel's polluted worship. Like Dtr 1, Hosea protests against pilgrimages to northern sanctuaries like Bethel and Gilgal (Hos 4:15; 5:6; 9:15; 10:15), rejecting the calves set up there (Hos 8:5-6; 10:5-6). He denounces idolatrous cult practices, priests who should guarantee liturgical correctness, and the laity (Hos 2:13; 4:17-19; 5:6-7; 6:6; 9:4). He condemns the feasts, new moons, and cultic assemblies that Jeroboam I had established in the north (Hos 2:11; 9:5-6; cf. 1 Kgs 12:32-33). He prophesies that God will put an end to worship of the baals, with their altars and pillars (Hos 2:11-13, 17; 10:1-2, 8; 13:1-3), a prophecy fulfilled in the later purge under Josiah (2 Kings 23).

The Period of the Exilic Redactor. The second edition of the deuteronomistic history (Dtr 2) was composed during the Babylonian exile (587–539 BCE). This edition brings the nation's history up to date by including the fall of the southern kingdom of Judah. Addressed to the Judeans in exile, it explains the traumatic time of uprooting theologically: The Babylonian exile was the result of a long history of idolatry and faithlessness that began in Israel and continued in Judah.

Sections of the book of Hosea can be situated during this period, either as earlier oracles relevant during the exile or as redactional commentary updating earlier sayings so that they speak to the needs of the exiled people. Hosea 3:4; 9:3, 6-7, 16-17; 11:5-7; and 13:7-16 may refer to the destruction and exile of the north, yet be pertinent for the fall of the south as well.

Noteworthy in Hosea is the theme of repentance/return. On one hand, the nation is called to seek Yahweh and return to God (3:5; 5:15–6:1; 12:6; cf. 2:7; 7:10; 10:12; 14:2). On the other hand, the spiritual repentance of the people and their return to God has its counterpart in the physical return from exile. The spiritual journey back to Yahweh is bound up with the geographical journey back to the land. Hosea 1:11 speaks of a regathering of

Israel and Judah under one head. Hosea 3:5 explicitly names this leader as King David, an obviously exilic editorial comment. Hosea 11:11 announces the restoration of the people to their homes. In rich detail, 14:4-7 describes the healing and flourishing of the people back in the land (cf. 6:11*b*).

The later historical contexts of the collector, the Josianic redactor, and the exilic redactor represent important interpretive stages in the formation of the book of Hosea. The book is the result of an ongoing traditioning process, wherein each stage articulates a voice that recognizes in some way, whether by appropriation or by editing, the value of the Hosean tradition for its own time. Each stage makes its own distinctive imprint on the tradition, transmitting it to a brand-new audience.

ANCIENT ISRAELITE MARRIAGE, METAPHOR, AND THE THEOLOGICAL PROBLEM

In the biblical tradition, different metaphors are used to capture the unique covenantal relationship between God and Israel. Some biblical metaphors draw from the bonds between king and servant, lord and vassal, father and son, and even mother and child, to communicate different facets of the covenantal union. The book of Hosea was the first to employ the metaphor of husband for the deity, casting Israel in negative female imagery as God's adulterous wife.[20] This imaging reflects the historical situation of ancient Israel, where gender relationships were asymmetrical: The man occupied the more privileged position in this society, and the woman was subject to him. Appropriating this socially conditioned relationship as metaphor has deeply affected the theology of the book of Hosea, for this theology interprets the divine as male and the sinful as female. Using this imagery, the prophet describes God's legitimate punishment as physical abuse of the wife by her husband. Interpretive problems arise when the metaphorical character of the biblical image is forgotten.

The marriage metaphor for the God/Israel covenant becomes problematic for women who continue to be victims of sexual violence. Hosea's marriage metaphor arises from a particular ancient social context. Thus understanding Israel's institution of marriage and its laws regarding adultery is critical to its interpretation.

Two primary features of ancient Israelite society—its patrilineal, patrimonial, patrilocal kinship structure and its honor/shame value system—are especially pertinent to this discussion. Israel practiced a patrilineal kinship ideology, tracing descent through the male line. This ideology was supported by a number of social practices. Power and authority over a particular family household resided with the oldest living male. Ownership of goods and resources lay with this *paterfamilias*, who passed on his assets as patrimony to his eldest son, according to customs of primogeniture.

Marriage arrangements were patrilocal—i.e., the young woman had to leave the household of her birth and enter into the unfamiliar and often hostile abode of her husband's father, adapting herself to it as best she could. Love and romance were not major factors in joining a couple in wedlock. Fathers often used the marriages of daughters to forge or strengthen alliances with other households and larger clan groups.

A new wife occupied an ambiguous position when she entered her husband's household. She retained ties to her own family, who must support her if ever she left her husband's house (cf. Judg 19:2-3). She became a full member of her husband's household only when she bore a son. Furthermore, if the husband was polygamous, his new wife had to contend with other wives, who vied for the husband's attention and the ensuing status it could bring, particularly with the birth of sons. By its patrilineal descent, patrimonial inheritance, and patrilocal residence customs, then, ancient Israel privileged the male and disenfranchised the female in a hierarchy of gender.

In a labor-intensive agricultural society such as Israel's, the birth of children was crucial for survival. Sons were especially valued because they continued the patriline, were beneficiaries of the father, and did not leave the household. In fact, they brought additional human resources into the household in the persons of wives and the potential children they would bear. The wife's primary contribution to the household was to bear legitimate sons to carry on the family name in order to keep limited commodities such as land and other resources within the family.

The sexuality of wives, daughters, and sisters was carefully guarded and controlled, because it comprised the material basis for an ideology of honor and shame that legitimized the androcentric hierarchy of this society. Honor was one's reputation, the value of a person in his or her own eyes *and* in the eyes of his or her social group. Male honor was manifested in wealth, courage, aggression, the ability to provide for one's family and defend its honor, and the frank display of sexual virility. According to the male ideology of honor and shame, women could acquire or be ascribed honor, but their honor differed from that of men. If honor was exemplified through one's personal independence—based on wealth, status, kinship, care of the weak, etc.—then women occupied the lowest rank within this honor system. They were peripheral to the patriline and usually did not inherit any material resources.[21] As a result, they were socially and economically dependent upon men. Their honor was derived from the men with whom they were explicitly connected. Theirs was the honor of the weak, which exhibited itself in deference, modesty, and meekness toward men and in sexual propriety and concern for reputation.[22]

In the Hebrew Bible, shame or disgrace was the very opposite of honor, evoking negative feelings of inadequacy, inferiority, and worthlessness. Like the ideology of honor, notions of shame were divided along gender lines. A man was shamed by his lack of wealth, courage, aggression; by the inability to support his family and protect its honor; and by sexual passivity or impotence. A woman was shamed if she were strong willed, independent, assertive, disrespectful of men, or sexually immodest.

In a patrilineal kinship structure, a large measure of a man's honor depended on a woman's sexual behavior, whether his wife's, daughter's, sister's, or mother's. Men had various strategies for keeping their women (and, by extension, themselves) honorable, such as insisting that women remain veiled in public, segregating them, and restricting their social behavior. A woman's sexual shamelessness constituted a public statement that her husband, father, brother, or son had failed to preserve the family honor by his inability to control her. The male would consequently forfeit his honor in the community.

Adultery was a capital offense in a society that operated under patrilineal and honor/shame-based social systems. In the first place, it violated a man's absolute right to the sexuality of his wife and placed his paternity of her children very much in doubt. In a society governed by a patrilineal kinship structure, a man needed to know for sure that a particular son was his. Second, adultery resulted in a considerable loss of honor for the husband and his household. A "shameless" wife (one who defied his authority) revealed his failure to supervise her sexuality and preserve family honor.

Two types of punishment seem to have been applied to adulterous acts. The first was the stoning to death of both parties (Lev 20:10; Deut 22:22). In practice, however, this punishment was often incurred only by the woman (see Gen 38:24; John 7:53–8:11). According to the law, the couple had to be caught in the act by witnesses in order for the death penalty to be applied (Deut 19:15). This, of course, was not always feasible. Moreover, the woman was more vulnerable than the man to the accusation, because she could later become pregnant from the union. The second type of punishment is recorded in Hosea, that of publicly stripping the adulteress naked and exposing her shamelessness (Hos 2:2-3; cf. Ezek 16:37-39).

An implicit double standard existed in the biblical evaluation of a man who broke wedlock. Extramarital activity, which would have been inexcusable for the wife, was tolerated for the husband in many cases. From an honor/shame perspective, a lack of chastity in women placed in jeopardy their own family honor, accumulated in the patriline, whereas a lack of chastity in men threatened the honor of *other* families. A man was not punished for having sex unless an engaged or married woman was involved *and* he was caught in the act (Deut 22:22-29). Engaging the services of prostitutes was acceptable (see Gen 38:12-23; Josh 2:1-7; 1 Kgs 3:16-27). This double standard underscored the issues of honor and legal paternity that so characterized the ideological structure of Israelite society, making the woman the primary offender in adulterous acts.

As we will see, the husband/wife metaphor of the God/Israel covenant in the book of Hosea is embedded with specific, culturally conditioned notions of what it means to be male or female and how each should behave in a particular society. Present-day Euro-American societies are quite different in their understanding of marriage and gender relations. Biblical interpreters and readers must reckon with the adequacy of the husband/wife metaphor in describing the divine/human relationship today.

THE DYNAMICS OF RHETORIC AND METAPHOR

In order to assess the appropriateness of the marriage metaphor (and others) for God's covenant with Israel, one must pay close attention to the rhetoric in which this metaphor is couched. Rhetoric is the art of discourse, either spoken or written, to inform, to persuade, or to move an audience. Prophetic rhetoric is intended to call the nation to judgment, to denounce its social or religious abuses, to criticize its political dealings, to bring the people to repentance and return to God, and to inspire the renewal of their covenantal relationship with the divine. A significant aspect of Hosean rhetoric is his use of metaphor, through which he seizes the imagination of his (male) audience.

A metaphor is a comparison composed of two elements, the lesser-known element, the *tenor*, and the better known element, the *vehicle*.[23] In Hosea 1–3, the prophet attempts to convey something profound about the lesser known, God's covenant with Israel, through the vehicle of a better known institution in ancient Israel, the human marriage between husband and wife. (Hosea also uses the metaphor of the parent/child in Hosea 11–13.) The elements of the marriage metaphor break down as follows:

TENOR: lesser known	VEHICLE: better known
God's covenantal love	a husband's marital love
Israel's sin of idolatry	a wife's sexual infidelity
God's punishment of Israel	a husband's beating of wife
Israel's repentance/ return to God	a wife's repentance/ return to her husband
God's renewal of covenantal love	a husband's renewal of marital love

The metaphor of human marriage provides unique access into the depths of God's covenantal relationship with Israel. Understood from a twentieth-century Euro-American perspective (the perspective of many modern biblical scholars), marriage embodies both symbolically and physically the intimacy between two individuals who consciously choose each other out of many possible life partners. It involves a "revelation" on both sides of one's deepest self: one's fears, hopes, desires. This "knowledge," which is often shielded from other people, is bestowed upon the beloved in a daring act of trust. The revelation of this self-knowledge makes one vulnerable to the other. And yet, one will risk this vulnerability and its potential for hurt for the sake of the lover and for the deeper knowledge of self and of the other that love brings. Commitment, intimacy, enduring love, "being there" for the other, physical desire, sexual union—all are bound up in the human institution of marriage. In many ways, this contemporary understanding of marriage is imposed upon the words of Hosea.[24]

However, this modern notion is not what Hosea intends in adopting the marriage metaphor for God's covenant with Israel. Marriage in ancient Israel was certainly not a partnership of equals. Precisely the inequity in such unions determines why Hosea appropriates marriage as a vehicle for the divine/human covenantal relationship. The rhetoric in Hosea is one-sided and directed to a very specific audience: ancient Israelite men. The book of Hosea takes up the marriage analogy to teach these men about the depths of God's covenantal love by appealing to their personal experiences as husbands, as the superior partner in a marriage. In a patriarchal society in which notions of descent, inheritance, marital residence, and honor are intricately bound up with legitimate sons, a faithless wife and her illegitimate children are exceedingly threatening and disruptive. Hosea highlights rhetorically the tremendous effort an ancient Israelite man must make to forgive and take back an unfaithful wife and to accept her children as his own, even if they may have been fathered by another man.[25] To stand by his wife and her children, enduring the social stigma it entails, would be one of the most difficult experiences an Israelite man could undergo. And yet, God has precisely this kind of magnanimous love for faithless Israel. God's steadfast love for a people who certainly do not deserve it eventually compels their repentance and return.

The book of Hosea transforms the marriage of a husband to a promiscuous wife into a heuristic vehicle for the covenantal relationship between God and Israel. For modern readers, however, several interpretive problems become evident. In the first place, the metaphor conflates the deity and the human husband. God is cast as an all-forgiving male. The divine becomes a male, and inevitably the male becomes divine. Second, the sinful is embodied in the image of the licentious wife. As is typical in ancient Israelite culture, the female is considered the primary offender in adulterous affairs. In this covenantal metaphor, woman becomes the ultimate transgressor and the epitome of evil as an adulteress and a whore. Third, the metaphor comes perilously close to sanctioning a husband's domestic violence against his wife. The explicit punishment of the wife/Israel by God "for her own good" arises out of God's steadfast love in order "to make her see reason." As scholars point out, Hosea 1 and 3 do not provide any particulars of friction between Hosea and Gomer.[26] Instead, flanking the narrative of God's marriage in Hosea 2, the stories of their marriage are stereoscoped with the stormy relations between God and Israel. Hosea 3 implies what Hosea 2 describes in vivid detail: the physical abuse of Gomer in Hosea's attempts to "love" his adulterous wife into reason. Modeling the behavior of God toward Israel, Hosea isolates Gomer from her lovers (2:8-9; 3:3). He offers Gomer gifts, just as God offers gifts to Israel (2:19; 3:2). He ultimately makes a heroic effort to abstain from sex with Gomer during this period (3:3). What is not explicitly stated is that Hosea, like God, beats his wife into submission. If God's behavior is the model for Hosea, this battering is implied, but not articulated.

ENGLISH AND HEBREW VERSE NUMBERING

At different points in English translations of the book of Hosea, chapter and verse numbering diverges from the original Hebrew text. When checking the Hebrew text, one should note the following variations:

English trans.		Heb.	
1:10-11	=		2:1-2
2:1-23	=		2:3-25
11:12	=		12:1
12:1-14	=		12:2-15
13:16	=		14:1
14:1-9	=		14:2-10

FOR FURTHER READING

Andersen, Francis I., and David Noel Freedman. *Hosea.* AB 24. Garden City, N.Y.: Doubleday, 1980.

Brenner, Athalya, ed. *A Feminist Companion to the Latter Prophets.* Sheffield: Sheffield Academic, 1995.

Davies, Graham I. *Hosea.* Old Testament Guides. Sheffield: JSOT, 1993.

———. *Hosea.* NCB. Grand Rapids: Eerdmans, 1992.

Emmerson, Grace I. *Hosea: An Israelite Prophet in Judean Perspective.* JSOTSup 28. Sheffield: JSOT, 1984.

Keefe, Alice A. *Women's Body and the Social Body in Hosea.* JSOTSup 338. Sheffield: Sheffield Academic Press, 2001.

King, Philip J. *Amos, Hosea, Micah: An Archaeological Commentary.* Philadelphia: Westminster, 1988.

McComiskey, Thomas Edward. "Hosea." In *The Minor Prophets: An Exegetical and Expository Commentary.* Vol. 1. Edited by Thomas Edward McComiskey. Grand Rapids: Baker, 1992.

Mays, James L. *Hosea.* OTL. Philadelphia: Westminster, 1969.

Sherwood, Yvonne. *The Prostitute and the Prophet: Hosea's Marriage in Literary-Theological Perspective.* JSOTSup 212. Sheffield: Sheffield Academic Press, 1996.

Stuart, Douglas. *Hosea–Jonah.* WBC 31. Waco, Tex.: Word, 1987.

Trotter, James M. *Reading Hosea in Achaemenid Yehud.* JSOTSup 328. Sheffield: Sheffield Academic Press, 2001.

Ward, James M. *Hosea: A Theological Commentary.* New York: Harper & Row, 1966.

Wolff, Hans W. *Hosea.* Hermeneia. Philadelphia: Fortress, 1974.

Yee, Gale A. *Composition and Tradition in the Book of Hosea: A Redaction Critical Investigation.* SBLDS 102. Atlanta: Scholars Press, 1987.

ENDNOTES

1. I am assuming with good reason that the prophet and the collectors and redactors of his tradition are male.

2. The classic example was that of T. H. Robinson, *Prophecy and the Prophets in Ancient Israel* (London: Gerald Duckworth, 1923) 52-58. On Hosea in particular, see his commentary, *Die zwölf kleinen Propheten,* HAT 14 (Tübingen: J. C. B. Mohr, 1938) 1-2. For a review of the literature, see Graham I. Davies, *Hosea* (Sheffield: JSOT, 1993) 94-96.

3. See Grace I. Emmerson, *Hosea: An Israelite Prophet in Judean Perspective* (Sheffield: JSOT,

1984); Gale A. Yee, *Composition and Tradition in the Book of Hosea: A Redaction Critical Investigation*, SBLDS 102 (Atlanta: Scholars Press, 1987) 27-46; and Martti Nissinen, *Prophetie, Redaktion und Fortschreibung im Hoseabuch* (Kevelaer: Neukirchen-Vluyn, 1991).

4. For example, Francis I. Andersen and David Noel Freedman, *Hosea*, AB 24 (Garden City, N.Y.: Doubleday, 1980) 59.

5. See Gale A. Yee, *Composition and Tradition in the Book of Hosea: A Redaction Critical Investigation*, 1-25, for a review of the literature.

6. Mark S. Smith, *The Early History of God: Yahweh and the Other Deities in Ancient Israel* (San Francisco: Harper & Row, 1990) 145-60.

7. Cf. Saul M. Olyan, *Asherah and the Cult of Yahweh in Israel*, SBLMS 34 (Atlanta: Scholars Press, 1988).

8. Rainer Albertz, *A History of Israelite Religion in the Old Testament Period*, vol. 1: *From the Beginnings to the End of the Monarchy*, trans. John Bowden (Louisville: Westminster/John Knox, 1994) 172-75. Analogously, one would hardly think today that Christmas trees or Easter eggs represent a tainting of a pure Christian celebration of these events, even though trees and eggs were originally part of non-Christian religious rites.

9. For example, James L. Mays, *Hosea*, OTL (Philadelphia: Westminster, 1969) 25-26.

10. James L. Mays, *Hosea*, 3, and those cited in H. H. Rowley, "The Marriage of Hosea," in *Men of God* (London: Nelson, 1963) 76-77. Providing a feminist twist to the sacred prostitution argument, H. Balz-Cochois, "Gomer oder die Macht der Astarte: Versuch einer feministischen Interpretation von Hos 1-4," *EvT* 42 (1982) 37-65, thinks that such cultic sexual service was part of a larger cult of the goddess practiced by Israelite women.

11. Cf. Robert A. Oden, Jr., "Religious Identity and the Sacred Prostitution Accusation," in *The Bible Without Theology: The Theological Tradition and Alternatives to It*, New Voices in Biblical Studies (San Francisco: Harper & Row, 1987) 131-53, 187-93.

12. See the outline of the problem by Niels Peter Lemche, "The God of Hosea," in *Priests, Prophets and Scribes: Essays on the Formation and Heritage of Second Temple Judaism in Honor of Joseph Blenkinsopp*, Eugene Ulrich et al., eds., JSOTSup 149 (Sheffield: JSOT, 1992) 241-57. See

also Morton Smith, *Palestinian Parties That Shaped the Old Testament*, 2nd ed. (London: SCM, 1987) chap. 2; B. Lang, *Monotheism and the Prophetic Minority* (Sheffield: Almond, 1983) chap. 1 ; and Mark S. Smith, *The Early History of God*, chap. 6.

13. See Gale A. Yee, *Composition and Tradition in the Book of Hosea: A Redaction Critical Investigation*, 308-9. Niels Peter Lemche, "The God of Hosea," 255-57, also entertains this possibility.

14. For example, see Ina Willi-Plein, *Vorformen der Schriftexegese innerhalb des Alten Testaments: Üntersuchungen zum literarischen Werden der auf Amos, Hosea und Micha zurückgehenden Bücher im hebräischen Zwölfprophetenbuch*, BZAW 123 (Berlin: DeGruyter, 1971) 244.

15. B. O. Long, "Prophetic Authority as Social Reality," in *Canon and Authority*, G. W. Coats and B. O. Long, eds. (Philadelphia: Fortress, 1977) 13.

16. M. Weinfeld, "Appendix B: Hosea and Deuteronomy," in *Deuteronomy and the Deuteronomic School* (Oxford: Clarendon, 1972) 366-70.

17. For example, Hans Walter Wolff, *Hosea: Commentary on the Book of the Prophet Hosea*, Hermeneia (Philadelphia: Fortress, 1974) xxxi-xxxii; and Gale A. Yee, *Composition and Tradition in the Book of Hosea: A Redaction Critical Investigation*, 1987) 305-13.

18. Martin Noth, *The Deuteronomistic History*, JSOTSup 15 (Sheffield: JSOT, 1981). Originally published in German in 1943.

19. F. M. Cross, "The Themes of the Books of Kings and the Structure of the Deuteronomistic History," in *Canaanite Myth and Hebrew Epic* (Cambridge, Mass.: Harvard University Press, 1973) 274-89; Richard Elliott Friedman, *The Exile and Biblical Narrative: The Formation of the Deuteronomistic and Priestly Works* (Chico, Calif.: Scholars Press, 1981); Richard D. Nelson, *The Double Redaction of the Deuteronomistic History* (Sheffield: JSOT, 1981).

20. Parts of this section are similar to my comments in the article, "Hosea," in *The Women's Bible Commentary*, Carol A. Newsom and Sharon H. Ringe, eds. (Louisville: Westminster/John Knox, 1992) 195-202.

21. An exception would be Num 27:1-11, where the daughters of Zelophehad petition Moses to inherit their father's land.

22. See Lila Abu-Lughod, *Veiled Sentiments: Honor and Poetry in a Bedouin Society* (Berkeley: University of California Press, 1986) chaps. 2–4.

23. Cf. "Metaphor," in *A Handbook to Literature*, 5th ed., C. Hugh Holman and William Harmon, eds. (New York: Macmillan, 1986) 298-99.

24. For one example, among many others, of reading the marriage metaphor in Hosea from this twentieth-century perspective, see Karl A. Plank, "The Scarred Countenance: Inconstancy in the Book of Hosea," *Judaism* 32 (1983) 343-54, esp. 345-46.

25. According to Francis I. Andersen and David Noel Freedman, *Hosea*, AB 24 (Garden City, N.Y.: Doubleday, 1980) 187, the text allows for the possibility that Lo-ruhamah might be illegitimate. A faithless wife arouses her husband's suspicions, whether valid or not, about the paternity of his children.

26. In particular, see Renita J. Weems, "Gomer: Victim of Violence or Victim of Metaphor?" *Semeia* 47 (1989) 90-91.

THE BOOK OF
JOEL

ELIZABETH ACHTEMEIER

In first reading, the book of Joel may give the impression of being a narrow, nationalistic work that glorifies Israel at the expense of every other nation. Yet, on the basis of Joel 2:28-32, Peter interprets God's action on the day of Pentecost (Acts 2), and Paul makes Joel 2:32 the heart of his gospel (Rom 10:13). Similarly, the church has always turned to Joel 2:12-19 for its lection on Ash Wednesday. Few books are more pertinent to our time; indeed, Joel presents a message that is integral to the Christian gospel at any time.

We cannot pinpoint the date of the book. A few scholars have termed it as early as the ninth century BCE,[1] and some still argue that it is pre-exilic.[2] Most now are inclined to place it between 500 and 350 BCE. The Babylonian exile and dispersion are in the past, according to 3:1-3. Several passages assume the existence of the Second Temple, the priesthood, and daily sacrifices. There is no mention of a king or royal court, and priests and elders are the community's leaders. The walls of Jerusalem have been restored (2:7, 9) as happened under Nehemiah's direction. Tyre and Sidon have a commercial association with Philistia, known to have been the case before 343 BCE (3:4). The book relies heavily on earlier prophecy, including that of Obadiah, which was not written earlier than the fifth century BCE. No external unrest threatens the community. Thus the evidence seems to point to the conditions of Judah during the Persian period, when it was a tiny subprovince of the Persian Empire. Having said all that, we must acknowledge that establishing a precise date for Joel is not of ultimate importance for its interpretation. The book brings with it a message that was a matter of life or death for Judah, but Joel also deliberately directs that message to every age (cf. 1:3), and thus this prophetic literature is never out of date.

As it now stands in the canon, the book may be regarded as a unity. Earlier scholars[3] divided chapters 1–2:27 from 2:28–3:21, maintaining that the eschatological sections (including all references in chapters 1–2 to the day of the Lord) were later additions to the prophet's work, which originally concerned only a locust plague. However, many interpreters[4] have convincingly shown that the eschatological passages are integral to the book's message and that the book as a whole exhibits a remarkable literary symmetry between its two parts: 2:21-27 promises a reversal of the devastation described in 1:4-20; 3:1-17 describes events of the day of the Lord, foretold in 2:1-11; 2:28-32 portrays the "return" called for in 2:12-17; and 3:17 parallels 2:27. This does not, they believe, preclude later editorial additions (perhaps 3:4-8), and the final shape of the book may be the product of artistic literary arrangement. Nevertheless, the book now presents a unified message for our teaching and preaching.

Joel draws on centuries of Israelite tradition in the framing of his message. Principally, he uses the tradition, familiar from earlier prophecy, of the day of the Lord (Isaiah 13; Ezekiel 30; Obadiah; Zephaniah 1–2; Malachi 4), as well as those of the enemy from the north (Jeremiah 4–6) and of the judgment on foreign nations (Jeremiah and Ezekiel). Sometimes he borrows whole sentences from earlier prophets (e.g., 1:15 from Isa 13:6; 3:16 from Isa 1:2). Sometimes he appropriates smaller word groups (e.g., 3:18 from Amos 9:13; 2:32 from Obadiah 17). But Joel's prophecy is not a stereotyped word from the past. Rather, it is a forceful, sometimes eloquent testimony to the continued working of the prophetic word in history. Not only through immediate revelation to him, but also through the words of earlier prophets, Joel hears God speaking to Judah's present situation. He believes that much foretold in past prophecy has not yet been fulfilled and that the fulfillment is not only being worked out in his time but also stretches on into the future. Indeed, the future that he envisions reaches also into our time and gives to Joel's prophecies their pertinence for our lives.

Joel presents his message in a series of poetic oracles that are sometimes only one strophe or stanza in length (1:2-4; 1:19-20), but that may encompass two strophes (2:18-19, 20; 3:1-3, 4-8; 3:9-10, 11-12; 3:13-14, 15-17), sometimes three (1:5-7, 8-10, 11-12; 1:13, 14, 15-16; 2:12-14, 15-16, 17), or even four (2:1-2, 3-5, 6-9, 10-11). The division of strophes in Hebrew rhetoric can be made on the basis of initial imperative verbs, changes in subject matter, opening exclamations, inclusios, and other such rhetorical devices. Only two passages in the book are in prose (2:30-32; 3:4-8), indicating perhaps Joel's use of traditional prose material.

The prophet couches his message in a number of different forms or genres appropriate to their content. A didactic admonition opens the work (1:2-4), and there are also calls to lamentation (1:5-12; 1:13-16; 2:15-17), a prophetic cry of alarm from the watchmen (2:1-11), a call to repentance (2:12-14), oracles of salvation (2:18-27), oracles against the foreign nations (3:4-8), and apocalyptic fragments presenting signs of the approaching end of history (2:30-31). Such forms are employed with great flexibility, however, often being detached from their original life setting or being combined with other forms.

The Hebrew text of the book is in fairly good shape, so that few emendations are necessary, but anyone who works with the Hebrew text should note that the chapter divisions in the Hebrew differ from those in English versions. Joel 2:28-32 in English versions is 3:1-5 in Hebrew. Similarly, Joel 3:1-21 in English versions is 4:1-21 in Hebrew.

FOR FURTHER READING

Allen, Leslie C. *The Books of Joel, Obadiah, Jonah and Micah*. NICOT. Grand Rapids: Eerdmans, 1976.

Barton, John. *Joel and Obadiah: A Commentary*. OTL. Louisville, Ky.: Westminster/John Knox Press, 2001.

Bewer, Julius A. "Commentary on Joel." In *A Critical and Exegetical Commentary on Micah, Zephaniah, Nahum, Habakkuk, Obadiah, and Joel*. ICC. New York: Scribners, 1911.

Calvin, John. *Commentaries on the Twelve Minor Prophets*. Vol. 2. Edinburgh: Calvin Translation Society, 1896.

———. *Joel, Amos, Obadiah*. Edinburgh: Calvin Translation Society, 1896.

Driver, S. R. *The Books of Joel and Amos, with Introduction and Notes*. The Cambridge Bible for Schools and Colleges. Cambridge: Cambridge University Press, 1901.

Watts, John D. W. *The Books of Joel, Obadiah, Jonah, Nahum, Habakkuk, and Zephaniah*. The Cambridge Bible Commentary on the New English Bible. Cambridge: Cambridge University Press, 1975.

Whedee, J. William. "Joel." In *Harper's Bible Commentary*. San Francisco: Harper & Row, 1988.

Wolff, Hans Walter. *Joel and Amos*. Hermeneia. Philadelphia: Fortress, 1977.

ENDNOTES

1. G. Amon, "Die Abfassungszeit des Buches Joel" (Ph.D. diss., Würzburg, 1942); Milos Bic, *Das Buch Joel* (Berlin: Evangelische Verlagsanstalt, 1960).

2. A. S. Kapelrud, *Joel Studies*, UUÅ (Uppsala: Lundequist, 1948); W. Rudolph, "Wann Wirkte Joel?" in *Das Ferne und Nahe Wort: Festschrift Leonhard Rost*, ed. F. Maas, BZAW (Berlin: Töpelmann, 1967) 193-98.

3. B. Duhm, "Anmerkungen zu den Zwoelf Propheteten," *ZAW* 31 (1911) 1-43, 81-110, 161-204; E. Sellin, *Das Zwölfpropheten Buch*, KAT (Leipzig: Deichertsche, 1922); H. Robinson and F. Horst, *Die Zwölf Kleinen Propheten*, HAT (Tübingen: Mohr, 1938).

4. Principally H. W. Wolff, *Joel and Amos*, Hermeneia (Philadelphia: Fortress, 1977).

THE BOOK OF
AMOS

DONALD E. GOWAN

THE INFLUENCE
OF THE BOOK OF AMOS

There is almost unanimous agreement that the book of Amos is the earliest of the prophetic books. As such, it marks the beginning of a unique tradition in the history of religion: prophecies of the approaching end of the existence of God's people based upon God's judgment of them for failing to live according to the divine standards. The tradition continues from Amos through the books of Hosea, Micah, Isaiah, Zephaniah, and the early parts of Jeremiah and Ezekiel; then it comes to an end. Each of these later works takes up and reasserts the unacceptable message first announced in the book of Amos, but the message of Amos has no predecessors that we can identify. For this reason alone the book has rightly been marked by modern scholarship as one of the most important turning points in the history of the religion of Israel. More obvious to the contemporary reader, however, are two striking characteristics of the book: the power of its language and the passion of its concern for the oppressed. In the nineteenth and twentieth centuries, Amos has been appealed to regularly as the Old Testament's classic statement concerning social justice.

The existence of a prophetic tradition of judgment, from Amos through Ezekiel, shows that in the eighth and seventh centuries BCE Amos's message, with its announcement that God was about to do a new thing in history, had a profound effect on the theology of Israel. In the nineteenth and twentieth centuries CE its social message was taken up with enthusiasm, but during the many intervening centuries, Amos was one of the less influential parts of the canon. It was seldom quoted or even alluded to in Jewish or Christian writings.

The New Testament quotes it twice (5:25-27 in Acts 7:42-43 and 9:11-12 in Acts 15:16-17); it is cited once in the Apocrypha (Tob 2:6 quotes Amos 8:10); and the Mishnah quotes it twice (4:7 in *m. Ta'an.* 3:3 and 9:6 in *m. 'Abot* 3:6).

Once we note the typical ways the Old Testament has been used, prior to the nineteenth century, the reasons for the relative neglect of Amos become clear. Both Jewish and Christian interpreters typically sought messages of comfort and hope in the Old Testament, and there is little of that to be found in Amos. As a source of ethical teaching, the fact that the book contains only one exhortation, with a faint promise (5:14-15; cf. 5:4-6), made it less appealing than other books, which are filled with promises. The central message of the book, "The end has come upon my people Israel" (8:2 NRSV), has not been something many theologians have known how to use. This overview will attempt to show that Amos is more than a treatise on social ethics and more than an important document for understanding the development of the religion of Israel. It will take Amos's announcement of the impending exile of Israel, interpreted by him as the death of God's people, to be one of history's most profound insights into the true nature of the human dilemma and God's surprising—even shocking—ways of dealing with it. Amos speaks of death; he does not yet know of resurrection, about which the last of the line of judgment prophets spoke (Ezek 37:1-14), but he was the first to announce that Israel must die—the beginning of a new act in the Old Testament's story of redemption.

THE PROPHET AND THE BOOK

We know nothing about some of the prophets except their names (Obadiah, Habakkuk) or their name and place of residence (Nahum). Only the book of Jeremiah contains a lengthy series of stories about the life of a prophet. As for Amos, his book

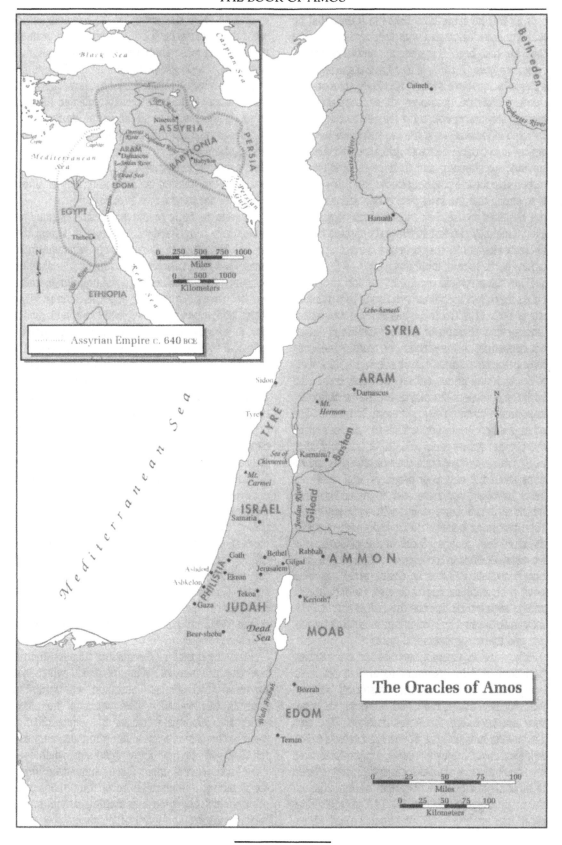

The Oracles of Amos

tells us that he came from Tekoa in Judah, that he was somehow associated with shepherds (1:1), and that he had been a herdsman and trimmer of sycamore trees (7:14). We also have the account of a single incident in his life (7:10-17). In spite of such slender evidence, however, other commentaries contain sections in which the life of Amos is reconstructed in various ways. It is clear that we have an almost unavoidable desire to gain access to the personality, experiences, and faith of the individuals responsible for the prophetic books, and that desire is so strong that the most responsible scholars have not hesitated to use their imaginations, along with every clue they can find in the texts of these books, to create biographies they believe to be fair representations of the lives of those prophets.

The "biographical approach" to the prophetic books may affect their interpretation in two different ways, both of them involving circular reasoning. One method attempts to recreate the life of Amos, but depending on the scholar one reads, Amos may have been: (a) a simple Judean shepherd; (b) a well-to-do and prominent citizen, perhaps connected with the Jerusalem Temple; or even (c) a politically important citizen of the northern kingdom. The other method (redaction criticism)[1] decides what the prophet Amos could and could not have said, using criteria derived from the text and presuppositions about the nature of prophecy, and attributes what he could not have said to redactors, after which the remaining passages will represent a consistent message believed to be appropriate for that eighth-century prophet. Some of the redaction critics make no effort to reconstruct a life of Amos (and may deny that this can be done), but I call their work a biographical approach also, for it proceeds on the assumptions that the thought of one individual can be isolated from additions made to it by others, and that it is important to do so.

My work on the prophets has led me to question both of those assumptions and to set aside every effort to recover the "historical Amos," focusing instead on the book of Amos, or what may also be called the Amos tradition. The first assumption fails because of the scarcity of explicit evidence about the life of Amos, which should call for an appropriate scholarly caution. I see no need to be as skeptical of the historicity of stories about the prophets (such as Amos 7:10-17 or Isaiah 7) as some scholars are, but I am skeptical of all efforts

to deduce from the words of the prophets either what their personal experiences may have been or clear standards as to what they could or could not have said. The book of Amos may all have come from him, may be mostly his with a few later additions, or may have been heavily redacted. Each of these opinions may be found in the work of very able scholars, but we cannot demonstrate that any one of them is true or false, and since that is the case, some might be driven to the skeptical conclusion that we cannot be sure that any of these words are the very words of Amos.

I prefer to think of this conclusion as cautious rather than truly skeptical, however. It is probably far less important to know exactly what the man Amos said than many have assumed. Certainly, in our time it is hard to avoid that assumption, because we do have a strong biographical interest. The words and stories preserved in the prophetic books lead us to want to know more about these individuals, and seldom has that desire been resisted. But the lives and religious experiences of the prophets seem to have been a subject of little or no interest to the Israelites who collected and produced the final editions of this material. The incidents from the lives of prophets that are contained in these books quite clearly have been preserved because they contain a message from God to Israel, and not because the prophets lived such interesting lives. The great bulk of material concerning Jeremiah's experiences during the last years of Judah might lead us to think otherwise, but there are clues enough in all the books containing stories about the prophets to show us that for Israel it was not the person of the prophet that was important, but the God the prophet represented. The book of Amos is almost anonymous; the pronouns "I" and "me" occur only in 7:1-9, 14-15; 8:1; and 9:1, and that prophetic anonymity ought to be taken seriously.

Thus the question of Amos's occupation (herdsman and trimmer of sycamore trees), which has drawn so much scholarly attention, will not find a place in this overview. The words of the book ascribed to him make it clear that Amos did not speak for herdsmen or sycamore trimmers; he spoke for God. We do not know how—or whether—those occupations might have influenced what Amos said, so the efforts to reconstruct that aspect of his life actually contribute nothing certain to our understanding of the words of his book.

Certainly, most of the prophetic books appear to be anthologies, and they may include the words of more than one prophet; but hypothetical reconstructions appear to be so subjective that scholarly caution should lead us to focus on what we have. We have the book of Amos, and we will call that the Amos tradition, rather than trying to identify all or certain parts of it with that person Amos about whom we know so little. Most, if not all, of that tradition makes good sense against a mid–eighth-century BCE background, so the commentary will we can interpret most of it with reference to the events of that period, without necessarily claiming that the eighth century date proves Amos was its author. The utter newness of the message that God had decreed the end of God's people Israel and the distinctive characteristics of style in the book strongly suggest that one writer was responsible for both its basic message and the ways in which it was expressed, but it should be emphasized again that for ancient Israel authorship seems not to have been a major concern. What was important was the authenticity of the words, which had been confirmed by history. Therefore, in our interpretation, we will be guided by Israel's primary interest in preserving the book and accepting it as canonical.

Having found redaction criticism too subjective an approach, we will focus on the more secure results to be obtained from the use of form criticism, elaborated by insights gained from rhetorical analysis, and the study of the history of the traditions that are reused by the prophet.

HISTORY OF THE PERIOD

The superscription of the book (1:1) dates it during the reigns of Uzziah, king of Judah (783–742 BCE), and Jeroboam II, king of Israel (785–745 BCE). The only part of the book that seems to refer to a different period is 9:11-15, although some scholars have dated that section in the eighth-century BCE also. The second quarter of the eighth century was a time of relative peace for both nations; both kings are said to have engaged in offensive campaigns to enlarge their territories rather than in defensive action (2 Kgs 14:22, 25-28). A major turn of events came shortly after the death of Jeroboam, with the accession of Tiglath-pileser III to the Assyrian throne in 745. He began to campaign actively in Syria by 740, received tribute from Israel in 738, occupied Galilee and Transjordan in 734 (2 Kgs 15:29), and took Damascus in 732. The government of the northern kingdom had fallen into chaos after Jeroboam's death, with six kings occupying the throne during the 24 years prior to the fall of Samaria. In 722 BCE, Samaria, the capital city of the northern kingdom, fell to the Assyrians under Sargon II.

The book of Amos is thus usually dated between 760 and 750 BCE, after Jeroboam's military successes in Gilead (2 Kgs 14:25; cf. Amos 6:13) and before the rise of Tiglath-pileser III made the Assyrian threat obvious. There is no evidence in Amos of any concern about Assyria; nor is there any reference to the rapid succession of kings in Israel following Jeroboam's death, as there is in Hosea. In Amos 7:11, the prophet is said to have foretold that Jeroboam would die by the sword, which did not happen, so this passage was almost certainly written before Jeroboam's death. Any effort to date the book more exactly than this calls for more explicit evidence than we have. Much has been made of the probability that Amos's ministry took place during a time of prosperity, but the evidence for that comes almost entirely from his own book, so it is inappropriate to describe that as if it were background for the book. What we can deduce concerning the social and economic circumstances to which these words are addressed thus belongs within the commentaryis open to discussion. In fact, the most important aspect of the historical setting of Amos is an event that occurred after most (if not all) of the book had been formulated, and that is the end of the northern kingdom in 722 BCE, for the impending death of Israel is the essential message of the book.

THE LITERARY FORM
OF THE BOOK OF AMOS

The book of Amos is considered to be one of the masterpieces of Hebrew literature. Only a few major examples of what form criticism and rhetorical analysis have revealed about the style and literary skill of this work can be offered here. The basic unit of speech is usually very short, from one to four sentences, but often these short units are combined into more elaborate structures. Whether the final compiler of the book had a clear plan for the organization of those larger structures is not yet clear, however, so commentaries will present outlines of the book that vary considerably from one another.

Individual Units. The form of speech used most prominently is the announcement of divine judgment combined with a reason, which is usually a description of Israel's sins (e.g., 2:4-5; 3:10-11; 5:11).[2] Either the reason or the announcement may be elaborated, as in 2:6-16. This genre, which occurs frequently throughout the prophetic books, is typically introduced by the messenger formula, "Thus says the LORD." The fact that the prophets use this form of speech more often than any other already tells us something essential about their mission. They seldom rebuke or argue; they seldom entreat or exhort; they have come with an announcement of what God is about to do, claiming that the message has come from God and offering the justification of God's intended act in the reason that goes with the announcement. There are only four exhortations in Amos, and they are severely qualified (4:12; 5:4-6, 14-15; 5:21-24). Other typical prophetic speech forms include the description of a vision (7:1-9; 8:1-3; 9:1-4) and the oracle of promise (9:11-15).

Other forms have been borrowed from daily life. Fragments of hymns are cited in 4:13; 5:8-9; and 9:5-6. Amos 4:5; 5:4-6, 14-15 are best understood as parodies of calls to worship. Chapters 1–2 make a new use of the old holy war oracle. A fragment of a funeral song appears in 5:1-2. The most significant feature of these reuses of familiar forms (except perhaps the hymns) is that the prophet has given them a shockingly new meaning, usually reversing what they originally were intended to say.

Larger Structures. The book contains a significant number of carefully organized series of sayings. The longest is the group of eight oracles against the nations in 1:3–2:16. Other series appear in 3:3-8; 4:6-12; 7:1-9. Within a unit, briefer sequences also occur, such as the seven disasters to befall the Israelite army in 2:14-16 and the five efforts to escape from God in 9:2-4. Other patterns of fives and sevens can be found throughout the book.

That the book may be subdivided into major units is suggested by the repetition of key words, such as "Hear!" in 3:1, 13; 4:1; 5:1; 8:4. Rhetorical analysis has found concentric (or chiastic)[3] patterns in 5:1-17 and elsewhere. The discussion offered below does not attempt to decipher the subtle and apparently inconsistent clues to major structures within the book, but will divide it for interpretive purposes according to certain important themes.

TRADITIONS

The prophets were innovators, with a radically new message concerning the approaching end of the way God and Israel had been related, but they made creative use of the traditions by which Israel had lived for a long time. Those of greatest importance for Amos will be noted here.

What has been called "holy war" or "Yahweh war" lies behind the oracles against nations in chapters 1–2 and the "Day of Yahweh" passage in 5:18-20. The battles in Judges and 1 Samuel have been described as following a consistent pattern. They are defensive wars: Israel has been attacked by a superior force, and defeat seems imminent until a charismatic leader announces that God intends to fight for Israel and give the enemy into their hands. Later messages of this type were pronounced under similar circumstances by prophets (1 Kgs 20:28; Isa 7:5-7), and there is additional evidence to show that prophets regularly played a role in assuring the king and his army that God would give them victory (1 Kings 22). The phrase "day of Yahweh" seems originally to have referred to such a day of God's triumph over Israel's enemies. Amos puts such traditions to a new use, announcing that Yahweh is now about to engage in holy war against Israel. Reference to specific aspects of the practice of war appear prominently throughout the book, and since death is a primary result, the practices of mourning for the dead are another tradition upon which Amos draws.

The hymns that appear in 4:13; 5:8-9; and 9:5-6 introduce elements of the creation tradition to the book. Since they emphasize God's power over nature, they function as part of the book's message that Yahweh is sovereign over all things, and they may be related to Amos's words concerning God's use of nature as a means of judgment (e.g., 4:6-9; 7:1-6).

Although the book does not contain word-for-word citations of any of the laws in the Pentateuch, clear references to specific parts of the legal tradition are recorded there, especially in 5:10-12 and 8:4-6, showing that the prophet was creating no new ethical standards, but that he appealed to what Israel should already have known to be God's will.

THE DISTINCTIVE THEMES OF THE BOOK

Amos represents the earliest collection of the words of a prophet into a book. Discovering what may have led to the creation and preservation of such a collection is thus one way of approaching the question of the distinctive themes of the book. It is logical to begin with the fact that its contents are mostly oracles of judgment. Unlike the earlier prophets, Amos declared that the whole people of Yahweh stood under divine judgment (Amos 3:1-2).

The book of Amos does not speak of reform, but of the end of normal life on the land, not of a better life for the poor but of a time when all will be reduced to despair. Its words of judgment thus should not be carelessly taken up and reapplied to new situations, for seldom is the future as dark for a given people as it was for eighth-century BCE Israel. That does not mean we should not be impressed by Amos's powerful words that claim that oppression of the weak and poor by the rich and powerful stands under the judgment of God. That is part of the message of Scripture for every age, but seldom has it been expressed with the impact of the book of Amos.

There is a great deal of continuity between the emphases of this book and the older traditions of Israel, but all of it has now been skewed by this terrible new message. We may consider what is distinctive in Amos's message concerning God and God's people, the nations, nature, and the future, by observing how what is utterly new ("The end has come upon my people Israel" [8:2 NRSV]) has changed things.

God. The destructive activity of God is emphasized. War dominates the thought of the book, and God is directly involved as the main participant in many passages, with twenty-eight different verbs being used to describe the divine role as warrior and destroyer. Except for 9:11-15, God's positive activity on Israel's behalf is confined to references to the past (2:10-11; 3:1), to temporary reprieves (7:3, 6), and to a highly conditional, partial promise of graciousness (5:15). Elsewhere, God kills (2:3; 4:10; 9:1), destroys (2:9; 9:8), and sends fire (1:4, 7, 10, 12; 2:2, 5), pestilence (4:10), and famine (8:11). This is not a completely new picture of God, for the accounts of the flood in Genesis 6–8, the plagues in Exodus

7–12, and the poems depicting God as a warrior (e.g., Deuteronomy 32; Isaiah 34; Habakkuk 3) also emphasize God's destructive power.

Amos is the only book, however, in which this aspect of God is so dominant, without the emphasis on faithfulness and mercy that almost always accompanies references to judgment elsewhere (e.g., Exod 34:6-7). The book of Amos is thus not to be taken as the last word about the nature of God. It is, rather, an overstatement of the judgmental aspect of God, which can be understood as the natural accompaniment of Amos's discovery that it was all over for Israel. That message was so new, and its implications so terrible, that it had to be stated in the most extreme form possible, and that included extreme statements about God.

God is by no means depicted as an arbitrary or vengeful enemy, however. The divine role as judge is justified again and again by the prophet's use of reason-announcement oracles. God is not described in this book; words like "just," "righteous," and "holy" are not used, in preference for verbs depicting divine destructive activity. That God is the upholder of justice is to be deduced instead from the particular reasons for God's action; for example, "because he [Edom] pursued his brother with the sword" (1:11 NRSV); "because they sell the righteous for silver" (2:6 NRSV); "because you trample on the poor" (5:11 NRSV). God's primary role in this book is to be the judge and the executioner of those persons who have refused to obey divine standards of justice—to which it is assumed God also adheres.

Israel. The wholly new part of Amos's message concerning Israel is the threat of exile (5:5, 27; 6:7; 7:11, 17).[4] Israel had been threatened before with defeat in war as a result of offending God, but there is no clear evidence that anyone prior to Amos spoke explicitly of the possibility that the Israelites might lose the promised land. (It is very doubtful that Leviticus 26 and Deuteronomy 28–29 can be dated earlier than Amos.) The idea is so new that no "theology of exile" appears as yet; deportation is simply announced. Later, Hosea attempted to connect it to Israel's sacred traditions, making exile a temporary return to the wilderness (2:14-15) or a reversal of the exodus, taking Israel back to Egypt (8:13; 9:3; 11:5). The idea created no growing tradition, even in the prophetic books, however, for it was too unthinkable. Once exile had happened, prophets found a way to speak of it as an act of God for the redemption (or re-creation) of God's people, but the materials preserved in Amos are too early to reflect those insights.

The prophet must announce the threat of exile and explain it, even though its ultimate purpose remains hidden. Explaining it does at least mean God continues the effort to remain in conversation with the people: "The Lord GOD has spoken;/ who can but prophesy?" (3:8 NRSV). Regularly the oracles begin with "Hear this word!" but Israel's failure to hear, to understand, and to obey dominates chapters 3–4, and their refusal to behave as the people of Yahweh is documented in chapters 5–6 and 8. Their election had meant Yahweh expected more of them than of the other nations (3:1-2). Yahweh admits it is "my" people upon whom the end will come (8:2), but their failure means something new will have to be done.

The Nations. Amos differs from the other prophetic books in taking up first Yahweh's dealings with all the nations surrounding Israel (except Egypt). The book makes no effort to explain why the nations are responsible to the God of Israel for their actions. Several proposals for the theology underlying Amos 1–2 will be noted in the commentary on those chapters. At this point, let us call these chapters (and 9:7) an expression of the "practical monotheism" of the book. Nothing is said about God's oneness or superiority to other deities, but the book begins with oracles against the nations as a way of asserting that Yahweh has the power to judge all who violate basic principles of justice.

Amos's interest in the relationship of the Gentile nations with Yahweh the God of Israel was taken up by the other prophets (cf. especially Isaiah 14; Ezekiel 28–32), who have left us with the claim that the downfall of nations throughout history must be traced directly to their failure to maintain justice within and among them. We cannot prove those prophets were wrong, for no nation has yet lived up to the standards of the Old Testament God. The litany of disasters in 4:6-12 may be reflected in all of history, which could be understood in the light of Amos's words as God's futile effort to get our attention.

Nature. The meaning of the hymn fragments that appear in 4:13; 5:8-9; and 9:5-6 has been widely discussed,[5] but their relationship to other hymns in the psalter that praise God's creative powers is clear. Elsewhere in the book of Amos, God threatens to turn nature against the people, making it an agent of divine judgment (e.g., 4:7-9; 7:1, 4; 8:8-9; 9:3*b*), and the hymns may have been included as reminders (since they are traditional language) that nature belongs to God, who thus has the power to use it according to the divine will. That general statement also includes the possibility that God may choose to make nature one of the primary agents of blessing, as in 9:13-14. That blessing cannot be expected until after the judgment has fallen, however.

The Future. The debated aspects of Amos's view of the future are two: Does the book offer any possibility of averting the doom it announces? Is there any way of integrating the promises of 9:11-15 with the negative message that dominates the rest of the book?

Only twice does the book contain an exhortation accompanied by a promise: "Seek the LORD and live" (5:6 NIV) and "Seek good and not evil,/ that you may live," followed by "it may be that the LORD, the God of hosts,/ will be gracious to the remnant of Joseph" (5:14, 15 NRSV). Some scholars have claimed this proves that Amos did not announce irrevocable judgment, but Hunter's thorough exegetical work supports those who say that at best the book does no more than hope that a few who are truly faithful may survive the coming disaster.[6] There is no future for the nation of Israel.

The second question involves consistency. The biographical approach will ask whether the same person could have announced both 9:8-10 and 9:11-15. Many scholars find that impossible to imagine; others ascribe the different messages to different parts of the prophet's career. Eschewing the biographical approach, we should reformulate the question so as to ask whether the book makes sense with this ending; in fact, these verses do not contradict the message of judgment in the rest of the book. They presuppose the fall of the "booth of David," the ruin of cities, and exile. The reference to David suggests a concern not for Amos's time, but for the end of the Davidic monarchy in the sixth century BCE. Even if these verses were produced in the eighth century, however, the promises they contain were not for the people of that time, for those people were on their way to death.

The new message of the book of Amos is that exile from the promised land is imminent. That means that a radically new stage in God's saving work is about to begin. It looks like the end of it, for Amos's word is "death," but eventually Ezekiel will add "resurrection" (Ezek 37:1-14). There is no hint of that in Amos, but it is important to deal with the Amos tradition as having always been a part of the larger prophetic tradition. These words introduce a new act in the history of salvation, leading us to ask why death must be the route God will take next. But it is not the last act, and Amos must always be read as part of the whole story of exile and restoration.

FOR FURTHER READING

Commentaries:

Andersen, Francis I., and David Noel Freedman. *Amos.* AB 24A. Garden City, N.Y.: Doubleday, 1989.

Harper, William Rainey. *A Critical and Exegetical Commentary on Amos and Hosea.* ICC. Edinburgh: T & T Clark, 1905.

Martin-Achard, Robert. *The End of the People of God: A Commentary on the Book of Amos.* ITC. Grand Rapids: Eerdmans, 1984.

Mays, James L. *Amos: A Commentary.* OTL. Philadelphia: Westminster, 1969.

Paul, Shalom. *Amos.* Hermeneia. Philadelphia: Fortress, 1991.

Wolff, Hans Walter. *Joel and Amos.* Hermeneia. Philadelphia: Fortress, 1977.

Other Studies:

Auld, A. G. *Amos.* Old Testament Guides. Sheffield: JSOT, 1986.

Carroll R., M. Daniel. *Amos—The Prophet and his Oracles: Research on the Book of Amos.* Louisville, Ky.: Westminster/John Knox Press, 2002.

Hasel, Gerhard F. *Understanding the Book of Amos: Basic Issues in Current Interpretations.* Grand Rapids: Baker, 1991.

Möller, Karl. *A Prophet in Debate: The Rhetoric of Persuasion in the Book of Amos.* JSOTSup 372. Sheffield: Sheffield Academic Press, 2003.

Park, Aaron W. *The Book of Amos as Composed and Read in Antiquity.* Studies in Biblical Literature 37. New York: Peter Lang, 2001.

Van der Wal, A. *Amos: A Classified Bibliography.* 3rd ed. Amsterdam: Free University Press, 1986.

ENDNOTES

1. Redaction criticism assumes books such as Amos have come into existence through a gradual process, with the original words of the prophet having been revised by later writers, then supplemented by successive layers of new oracles, in order to make their messages relevant to later times.

2. Claus Westermann, *Basic Forms of Prophetic Speech* (Philadelphia: Westminster, 1967) 181-88.

3. The simplest chiastic form is the pattern ABB′A′. More elaborate patterns may have a clear midpoint; e.g., ABCDED′C′B′A′.

4. Amos's concern is usually for the northern kingdom, but the book occasionally speaks of the traditions of Israel as a whole (2:9-11; 3:1-2; 9:7) or specifically of Judah (2:4-5; 6:1).

5. J. L. Crenshaw, *Hymnic Affirmations of Divine Justice: The Doxologies of Amos and Related Texts in the Old Testament,* SBLDS 24 (Missoula, Mont.: Scholars Press, 1975); Thomas Edward McComisky, "The Hymnic Elements of the Prophecy of Amos: A Study of Form-Critical Methodology," *JETS* 30 (1987) 139-57; J. D. W. Watts, "An Old Hymn Preserved in the Book of Amos," *JNES* 15 (1956) 33-39.

6. A. Vanlier Hunter, *Seek the Lord! A Study of the Meaning and Function of the Exhortations in Amos, Hosea, Isaiah, Micah, and Zephaniah* (Baltimore: St. Mary's Seminary and University Press, 1982) 56-105.

THE BOOK OF
OBADIAH

SAMUEL PAGÁN

THE BOOK

The book of the prophet Obadiah—the shortest in the Old Testament—presents a clear message of judgment against the people of Edom. It begins with the word "vision" (v. 1), which reveals the prophetic intent, the tone of the message, and the nature of the literature, and it ends with an affirmation of the kingdom and sovereignty of God, a word of hope (v. 21). The prophet elaborates on earlier traditions—e.g., the day of the Lord—and applies them to his immediate historical situation (the Israelite community of Jerusalem), and then to the exile of the people into Babylonia.

Obadiah is one of the least read prophetic writings in the Bible. It is a short book and does not provide much information about the author and the historical setting in which it was written. Moreover, at the literary level, a section of the message of Obadiah (vv. 1 b-6) is similar to Jeremiah 49.

The book of Obadiah belongs to a type of literature that heralds God's judgment to come upon the nations near Israel. These prophecies may have been preserved by the cultic circles in Jerusalem. The oracles of judgment against the nations constitute an important element in the biblical prophetic literature. Prophecies against Edom are also found in Isaiah (21:11-12), Jeremiah (49:7-22), Ezekiel (25:12-14), Amos (1:11-12), and Malachi (1:2-5; see also Isa 11:14; Jer 25:21; Lam 4:21; Joel 4:19).

In the Hebrew canon, the book of Obadiah is fourth in order among the minor prophets, between Amos and Jonah. Perhaps this order stems from the fact that Obadiah and Amos have similar themes: both prophets emphasize the day of the Lord. It is important to point out, moreover, that thematic connections are also found with the book of Joel; the proclamation of the day of the Lord presented in Joel 3:2, 14 is included in Amos 9:11-12

and emerges again in Obadiah 15 a-21. Some scholars think that Obadiah 1-14 is a commentary on Joel 3:19, and Obadiah 15-21 on Amos 9:12.

In most Septuagint manuscripts, the longer books (Hosea, Amos, Micah) are followed by shorter ones (Joel, Obadiah, Jonah). Such an ordering may reflect a criterion for order based on a book's length. Nonetheless, the length of Obadiah does not seem to be the main reason for placing it between Joel and Jonah in the Septuagint. Instead, the thematic relationship between Joel 3 and Obadiah and the interest in chronology manifested by the translators of the Septuagint were probably more important factors in establishing that order.[1]

It is difficult to determine precisely the date the book was written, since the historical information it provides is scant. Some scholars have proposed the ninth century BCE, referring to the Edomite rebellion against Joram (2 Kgs 8:20-22). Others, however, have placed the composition of the book at a much later date, at the middle of the fifth century BCE, after the exile of the people of Israel to Babylonia, during the Edomite occupation of the Negev.[2]

Nevertheless, historical, literary, and theological analysis of the book suggests the exilic period, particularly the years immediately following the crisis in Jerusalem (687/686 BCE), as the most probable date of the composition of Obadiah. Edom's attitude to the destruction of Jerusalem and the exile of Judahites helps to illumine Obadiah's historical context. Moreover, during that same period—at the beginning of the sixth century BCE—a literature with similar theological and literary tendencies developed (cf. Ps 137:7; Lam 4:18-22; Ezek 25:12-14; 31:1-15). These writings manifest resentment against the Edomites similar to that presented in the book of Obadiah. That anti-Edomite perspective also occurs in subsequent works. For example in 1 Ezra 4:45, the Edomites are identified as the ones who set fire to the Jerusalem Temple, when the Jews were devastated by the Chaldeans.

THE PROPHET

There is not much information about the prophet Obadiah. A tradition included in the Babylonian Talmud[3] identifies him as the servant of Ahab (1 Kgs 18:3-16), allied with Elijah and the protector of the prophets of the Lord (Jerome knew this tradition). Nevertheless, it is difficult to imagine an official of the king in the ninth century BCE who prophesied exclusively concerning relations between Judah and Edom three centuries later. Furthermore, there is no historical basis for equating the two characters. This tradition probably stemmed from the interest, attested in the Talmud, of identifying the author of each book of the Bible, along with the fact that very little information on this small prophetic book was available.

The Masoretic Text vocalized the name of the prophet Obadiah as עבדיה (ʿōbadyâ, "worshiper of Yahweh"); the Septuagint used Αβδιου (Abdiou); and the Vulgate rendered the name as Abdias, "servant of Yahweh." These variants in pronunciation produce alternate ways of understanding the same name. Some scholars have thought that the name "Abdias," beyond identifying a person, is symbolic. However, in ancient Israel, the name was fairly common. At least twelve people with that name are mentioned in the Old Testament; moreover, Obed, one of the variants of "Obadiah," is applied to six additional persons, including the grandfather of King David (Ruth 4:21-22; Matt 1:5).

Obadiah was a prophet of Yahweh. The prophet probably lived during the sixth century BCE, delivered his message in Jerusalem, and had at least some religious or cultic training. He was familiar with the prophetic traditions of judgment against the nations and was particularly versed in the anti-Edomite language, as seen in the similarities and parallels with Jeremiah 40; Ezek 25:12-14; Joel 1:15; 2:5, 32; 3:3, 17; and Amos 9:12. The style of Obadiah's oracles demonstrates his great communicative ability and literary skill. Perhaps, like Amos (Amos 7:10-15), he was not a professional prophet, but was called by God for a specific task.

The theme of the lordship of Yahweh (v. 21) perhaps echoes the enthronement psalms (Psalms 47; 93; 96–99), which made a prominent contribution to the worship liturgy in the Temple. The historical focus of the book (vv. 11-16) implies that it reflects the political relationship between Judah and Edom, after the catastrophe of 587/586 BCE and Israel's exile into Babylonia. Obadiah may have witnessed the destruction of Jerusalem and the capture of the people of Judah.

JUDAH AND EDOM

The territory of Edom is located to the south of the Dead Sea and is surrounded by deserts to the east and the south. To the west is a mountainous region that extends south to the Gulf of Aqaba. To the north, the Zered stream separated Edom and Moab. This small territory measured approximately seventy miles north to south and fifteen miles east to west. A characteristic of the region is the reddish color of its rocks and mountains; that geological trait may explain its name: אדום (ʾĕdôm) signifies this red region.

The Edomites arrived and settled that region around the year 1300 BCE, sometime before the Israelites arrived in Canaan. The history of the relations between these peoples is characterized by animosity and hostility. Edom is regularly included in the catalogue of judgment oracles against the nations that surround Israel.[4]

Some passages of the OT allude to the fraternal relationship between Israel and Edom; they are identified as "brother" peoples (Genesis 25; 27; 36; Num 20:14-21; Deut 2:4-8; 23:7; Jer 49:7-11; Amos 1:11-12; Mal 1:2-4). Two fundamental conclusions can be drawn from these texts: First, the term "brothers" does not always connote a bond of friendship or camaraderie between peoples. Second, the fraternal relationship between Israel and Edom stems from complex events in the histories of these nations.[5] The struggle between the twins in Rebekah's womb (Genesis 25) symbolizes such enmity and hostility between Israel and Edom.

The people of Israel and Edom have displayed great mutual hostility throughout the ages. According to the narrative in Num 20:14-21, the Israelites, on their journey from Egypt to the promised land, requested permission from the king of Edom to pass through that territory, but he refused them permission. That disdainful attitude marked the beginning of intense enmity between the two nations. The resentment reached its peak when Jerusalem was captured by the Babylonians in 587/586 BCE. The Edomites may have joined in the destruction and helped the plunderers of Jerusalem (Ps 137:7). Moreover, the Edomites helped to capture fugitives who had fled from Judah (Obad 14). Because of the lack of solidarity with the neighboring people of Israel, God is determined to punish Edom.

The difficulties and conflicts between the two peoples were evident from at least the time of King David (2 Sam 8:13-14), and possibly even from the time of King Saul, when Edom was listed among Israel's enemies (1 Sam 14:47). This history of enmity continued throughout the monarchic period to the fall of Judah and the destruction of Jerusalem by the Babylonians (2 Kings 25; Obad 11-14).[6]

During the exile and, subsequently, during the Persian period, neither of these peoples was in a political or military position to manifest resentment or conflict. Judah was a minor district in the Persian provincial system, whereas Edom, distant from the main events of the political powers of that day, experienced pressures from Arab groups that were attempting to take possession of its lands.

After the Babylonian exile, a group of Edomites moved to the south of Palestine to protect itself from the Nabataean Arab groups in the area that was later known as Idumaea, a word that derives from "Edom." Herod the Great was known as an Idumean, a term that reflects the hostility of the Jews toward the Edomites and their resentment toward Herod.

LITERARY STRUCTURE

One theory concerning the structure of the book divides the work into two major sections: (1) vv. 1-4, 15b and (2) vv. 15a, 16-21. This theory reflects the thematic and stylistic differences between these two sections. The first part refers to specific historical problems: the destruction of Jerusalem in the year 587/586 BCE and the attitude of the Edomites concerning that crisis. The rest of the work emphasizes eschatological issues related to God's judgment: the coming of the day of the Lord.

According to the scholars who propose this structure, the book portrays a transition from history to eschatology. Moreover, v. 16 presents an abrupt change in the target audience; the first part of the message is addressed to Edom, the second to Judah. Moreover, the second part of the book has been divided into several sections that reveal stylistic differences: v. 15a, vv. 16-18, and vv. 19-21.

A second theory for explaining the literary and stylistic complexities of the book of Obadiah also divides the work into two sections, but recognizes only vv. 1-18 as original to the prophet. Verses 19-21 were added later to emphasize eschatological hope. Some scholars have identified, in the first section of the book, oracles of the prophet that were subsequently compiled and edited to form the book.

Another theory attempts to explain the book as essentially one literary unit. The author developed his message from ideas and themes of numerous oracles spoken earlier against the nations and preserved in Jerusalem and incorporated into Obadiah's prophecy. Obadiah formulated his message in the light of Jerusalem's destruction, the exile, and the reaction of the Edomites during the 587/586 catastrophe.

The book can be divided into three major sections: (1) the proclamation of judgment against Edom (vv. 2-9); (2) the indictment and reasons for judgment (vv. 10-14, 15b); and (3) the announcement of the day of the Lord (vv. 15a, 16-21).

By studying the book of Obadiah as a literary unit, one can discover several important elements that are intimately related. There is a gradual progression in the development of the ideas: from the proclamation of judgment on Edom to the description of its sins during Judah's crisis and finally to the general theme of the day of the Lord with respect to the nations and the survival of a remnant of God's people. Nevertheless, the primary theme is God's judgment against Edom. God, according to the message of the prophet, is the Lord of the earth and will see to it that the territory of Judah is returned to God's people.

From a structural and thematic standpoint, the book may also be studied as a set of six short poems in chiastic form. This analysis underscores the theological importance of the work.[7] The chiastic structure, which presents the themes of the poem in parallel form, takes the shape ABCA′B′C′, with the following themes:

A vv. 1-4 God will humble Edom
B vv. 5-7 Edom will be attacked and abandoned by its allies
  C vv. 8-11 Edom is judged for remaining passive during the slaughter of its brothers and sisters
  C´ vv. 12-14 Edom should not have rejoiced at the defeat of Judah and should not have plundered and delivered up the survivors of the Jerusalem catastrophe
B´ vv. 15-18 God's people will return to rule on Mount Zion
A´ vv. 19-21 God will save God's people

The main emphasis occurs at the center of the book (sections C and C´): Edom will be judged for its attitude against God's people in their time of crisis and need.

OBADIAH'S RELATIONSHIP TO OTHER PROPHETS

The literary unity of the book does not overshadow its diverse components and influences from oral and written sources. Perhaps the material used by Obadiah is of ritual or liturgical origin; however, the range of the prophet's thematic and literary resources is difficult to determine.

The relationship between Obadiah and other prophets, particularly Jeremiah, has been the focus of much study and research.[8] Specifically, we can identify similarities between Obad 1-6 and Jeremiah 49. According to some scholars, Obadiah used the oracles of Jeremiah to formulate his own prophetic proclamation. Others believe that the book of Jeremiah includes the material that had been prepared by Obadiah. Both points of view claim that one of the two authors relied on the material of the other.

A better explanation may be that both works rely on prophetic material that already existed in cultic and prophetic circles in Jerusalem. Stylistic and thematic analysis of both works reveals literary, textual, and thematic continuity, which may be explained on the basis of that hypothesis.[9]

1—Parallels:		2—Similarities:	
Obadiah	Jeremiah	Obadiah	Jeremiah
1a	49:7	8	49:7
1b-4	49:14-16	9	49:22
5-6	49:9-10a	16	49:12

Study of Obadiah, moreover, reveals thematic and literary contact with other prophetic books, particularly with Joel, Amos, and Ezekiel. The parallels and similarities again underscore the importance of prophetic material against other nations, which circulated among the prophetic and cultic groups in Jerusalem. The brief oracle against Edom included in Ezek 25:12-14 and the theme of the day of the Lord of Amos 9:12 are clear examples. Obadiah also bears strong similarities to the book of Joel:

Obadiah	Joel
11	3:3
15	1:15
16	3:17
18	2:5
21	2:32

Such comparisons between Obadiah and Jeremiah and Joel indicate that these prophets used oral or written sources of prophetic oracles against Edom for developing their own message.

THEOLOGY

The theology of the book of Obadiah is intimately related to the historical reality that characterized the prophet's ministry. After the triumph of the Babylonian armies over Judah and Jerusalem, the citizens were left demoralized and humiliated as they had seen their country devastated, national institutions dismantled, and many of their leaders deported (2 Kgs 2:5). The prophet's theology had to take into consideration the political, social, and spiritual condition of the people, while appropriately responding to the theological expectations of the community. After the exile, the community of Judah and Jerusalem struggled to survive, to reorganize national life, and to comprehend the theological implications of the events that had befallen them.

The message of Obadiah is judgment for Edom and hope for the Yahwistic community. Although the work is not a systematic theological treatise and instead the prophetic word in the face of a national crisis,[10] one may identify four important themes.

Divine Justice. After the devastation of Jerusalem in 587/586 BCE, a divine manifestation of judgment against Edom was needed because of its part in Judah's catastrophe.

To balance the theological crisis created by the destruction of Jerusalem, the religious and political center of the Yahwistic community, Obadiah used and developed a theology of divine justice. God would intervene and punish those who had been involved in the plunder of Jerusalem: Edom. In vv. 2-9, Edom's destruction is announced. In vv. 10-14, the nature of Edom's crimes is developed. Verse 15*b* emphasizes the punishment warranted by Edom's betrayal of Judah and offense against God.

The Day of the Lord. Tied to the theme of God's justice is the theme of the day of the Lord. But this theme is also linked to the idea of holy war—the belief that God is able and willing to intervene to defeat decisively the enemies of God's people. The day of the Lord also implies the judgment and destruction of those enemies as well as victory and salvation for God's people.

The book of Lamentations identifies two important phases in the manifestation of the day of the Lord (Lam 1:21; 2:21-22) during the crisis of 587/586 BCE. The first phase takes place during the fall of Jerusalem, the destruction of the Temple, and the devastation of the Judahite state. The second phase involves the reaction of Judah's enemies to the slaughter and affliction of the people. Obadiah may have taken that double motif from the book of Lamentations and incorporated it into his message against Edom. The destruction of Edom will result from a new manifestation of the day of the Lord: first, because the Edomites had been accomplices to the Babylonians' intervention against Judah and, second, because they had taken advantage of the crisis to plunder and destroy the city. The destruction of Edom is the logical result of the just actions of a God who responds to the needs of people and does not allow injustice to reign. The people of Judah had received the divine penalty for their sins and actions in violation of the covenant. The book of Obadiah presents the theology of the day of the Lord and the manifestation of divine judgment, now applied to the people of Edom.

The Lord of History. The prophet's theology underscores the ability of the God of Israel to intervene in history and to vent the divine furor against the people of Edom. In ancient days, when nations would go to war, they believed their gods would be present in battle. According to that theology, the people of Judah might have been dismayed and frustrated at a God who was not able to defeat the gods of the Babylonians and the Edomites.

Obadiah's theology affirms that the God of Israel was not defeated and will manifest power in history so as to judge the people who have taken advantage of Judah's defeat in order to plunder it and take over its territory. The affirmation that the Lord is God over history runs counter to the Edomites' view of themselves. The destruction of Edom will not be a chance event but the result of the righteous action of the God of history.

The Kingdom of the Lord. The message of Obadiah ends with a statement concerning the people's future. After the national catastrophe, the future of the Jewish community will be radically transformed. The vindication of the people will be a reality, thanks to divine intervention that will restore the national borders and establish a theocracy in the world (vv. 19-20). Mount Zion will be reestablished as the capital of a renewed and liberated people. The book culminates with an ardent affirmation of faith and hope: "the kingdom shall be the LORD's" (v. 21).

THE TEXT OF THE BOOK

The Hebrew text of the book of Obadiah has been quite well preserved. Scholars frequently use the parallel passage of Jeremiah 49 to revise and amend difficult parts of Obad 1-5. That process of revision and textual amendment, however, must be made without violating the literary integrity of either document (see vv. 19-20). The Septuagint can also be of great assistance in studying the text of Obadiah; nonetheless, the Greek vocalization of poetic portions of the Masoretic Text should be used with careful critical judgment.[11]

Textual corrections that should be made to the book include changing the word נֶחְפְּשׂוּ (*nehĕpśu*; "ransacked," NIV; "pillaged," NRSV) from the plural to the singular (v. 6); revocalizing the Hebrew text, in accordance with the ancient versions, to clarify the sense of the text in vv. 7, 13, 17, 21; and, in v. 20, interpreting a strange expression that has been added to the original text. Some scholars maintain that in several places the text has suffered transpositions during the process of textual transmission (e.g., v. 15). Generally, it is believed that the topographical and geographical references in vv. 19-20 were added at an early stage of the text's history.[12] In this evaluation and analysis of the structure and style of the work, the text's integrity is respected so as to avoid inappropriate amendments and transpositions.

FOR FURTHER READING

Allen, Leslie C. *The Books of Joel, Obadiah, Jonah, and Micah*. NICOT. Grand Rapids: Eerdmans, 1976.

Ben Zvi, Ehud. *A Historical-Critical Study of the Book of Obadiah*. BZAW 242. Berlin: de Gruyter, 1996.

Clark, David, and Norm Mundhenk. *A Translator's Handbook on the Books of Obadiah and Micah*. New York: United Bible Societies, 1982.

Coggins, R. J., and S. P. Re'emi. *Israel Among the Nations: Nahum, Obadiah, Esther*. ITC. Grand Rapids: Eerdmans, 1985.

Dicou, Bert. *Edom, Israel's Brother and Antagonist: The Role of Edom in Biblical Prophecy and Story*. JSOTSup 169. Sheffield: Sheffield Academic Press, 1994.

Limburg, James. *Hosea–Micah*. Interpretation. Atlanta: John Knox, 1988.

Mason, R. *Micah, Nahum, Obadiah*. Sheffield: JSOT, 1991.

Myers, J. "Edom and Judah in the Sixth-Fifth Centuries B.C." In *Near Eastern Studies in Honor of William Foxwell Albright*. Edited by H. Goedicke. Baltimore: John Hopkins University Press, 1971.

Raabe, Paul R. *Obadiah: A New Translation and Commentary*. AB 24D. New York: Doubleday, 1996.

Snyman, S. D. "Cohesion in the Book of Obadiah," *ZAW* 101 (1989) 59-71.

Watts, J. D. W. *Obadiah: A Critical Exegetical Commentary*. Grand Rapids: Eerdmans, 1969.

Wolff, Hans Walter. *Obadiah and Jonah: A Commentary*. Minneapolis: Augsburg, 1986.

ENDNOTES

1. See Hans Walter Wolff, *Obadiah and Jonah: A Commentary* (Minneapolis: Augsburg, 1986) 17-18.

2. See Hans Walter Wolff, *Obadiah and Jonah: A Commentary*, 18-19.

3. *Sanhedrin* 39b.

4. See B. C. Cresson, "Israel and Edom: A Study of the Anti-Edom Bias in the Old Testament Religion" (Ph.D. diss., Duke University, 1963).

5. See W. Brueggemann, *Genesis*, Interpretation (Atlanta: John Knox, 1982); G. von Rad, *Genesis*, OTL (Philadelphia: Westminster, 1972).

6. See J. R. Barlett, "The Land of Seir and the Brotherhood of Edom," *JTS* 20 (1969) 1-20.

7. See L. F. Bliese, "Chiastic and Homogeneous Metrical Structure Enhanced by Word Patterns in Obadiah." Unpublished United Bible Societies paper, 1991.

8. See, e.g., Leslie C. Allen, *The Books of Joel, Obadiah, Jonah, and Micah*, NICOT (Grand Rapids: Eerdmans, 1976) 133-36, 140-43.

9. D. Stuart, *Hosea–Jonah*, WBC (Waco: Word, 1987) 415-16.

10. See R. J. Coggins, *Israel Among the Nations: Nahum, Obadiah, Esther*, ITC (Grand Rapids: Eerdmans, 1985) 74-76.

11. See *Preliminary and Interim Report on the Hebrew Old Testament Text Project*, vol. 5. (New York: UBS, 1980) 297-301.

12. Leslie C. Allen, *The Books of Joel, Obadiah, Jonah and Micah*, 137.

THE BOOK OF
JONAH

PHYLLIS TRIBLE

The book of Jonah bombards the reader with verbal activity from the heavens through the sea and the dry land into the netherworld. This noisy story of just forty-eight verses is nevertheless silent about compelling questions: Who wrote it? Under what circumstances? How? When? Where? Why? The silence has invigorated scholars. Of the many topics they debate, six inform this introduction: composition, date, genre, literary features, theology, and purpose.

COMPOSITION

Heterogeneous Elements. Although Jonah is a coherent narrative, heterogeneous elements compose it. The fictitious character Jonah most likely derives from a reference in 2 Kgs 14:25 to the historical "servant" of Yahweh, "Jonah son of Amittai, the prophet, who was from Gath-hepher" (NRSV). Chapter 1 of the book incorporates a virtually self-contained story of sailors delivered from a storm at sea. Chapter 2, the report of Jonah's being swallowed and vomited by a fish, suggests an independent tradition belonging to the genre of miraculous tales. The psalm Jonah prays while in the fish indicates a poetic provenance distinct from the narrative. Chapter 3 incorporates another virtually self-contained story of the Ninevites' being saved from a threat of destruction. Chapter 4, the extended dialogue between Jonah and Yahweh, with few references to the rest of the narrative, suggests yet another tradition, belonging perhaps to tales of holy men brought to accountability (cf., e.g., Num 22:15-35; 1 Kgs 19:1-18).

Linguistic diversity also contributes to the heterogeneous character of the book. It includes the appearance of different divine appellatives: "Yahweh," "Elohim," "ha-Elohim," and "Yahweh Elohim." Although the differences are in some instances explainable, in others they appear arbitrary. For example, the report about the Ninevites appropriately uses the generic "Elohim" for God rather than the distinctive Israelite name "Yahweh" (3:5-10). By contrast, the ending of the story inexplicably introduces the combination "Yahweh Elohim" (4:6), only to drop it subsequently (4:7-11) for the indiscriminate use of "Elohim" three times and "Yahweh" one time.[1]

The Psalm. The presence of the psalm (Jonah 2:2-9) within the prose narrative poses a major compositional problem. For two centuries it has provoked a storm of controversy. Critics debate whether the author of the narrative or a different author composed it. They wonder whether the narrative originated with the psalm or the psalm was added to the narrative. If it was an addition, they seek to determine who included it: the author of the narrative or an editor. Until the last few decades, the dominant stance challenged the pre-critical assumption of literary unity to build the case that an editor inserted the psalm. That stance has now shifted to argue that the psalm belongs to the original story, whether the author composed it or not.[2] But the matter is far from settled.

Scholars who struggle with the status of the psalm have collected an arsenal of criteria by which to render judgment. It includes linguistics, genre, vocabulary, content, context, theology, structural design, plot development, and character portrayal. In the use of these criteria every point set forth elicits a counterpoint and every counterpoint a point. For instance, Vanoni argues against the original inclusion of the psalm because it speaks of deliverance while Jonah is in the belly of the fish; Limburg argues for the original inclusion of the psalm because it speaks of deliverance while Jonah is in the belly of the fish.[3] Different understandings of deliverance yield different understandings of the same setting. From another perspective, Landes and Trible agree that Jonah exhibits a symmetrical design.[4] Landes then contends that the psalm supports the design and so belongs to the original story. Trible contends that the psalm disturbs the design and does not belong to the original story. In contrast to these scholars, Sasson observes that both authors and editors have stakes in establishing symmetry; therefore, this criterion is itself unreliable for determining the status of the psalm in the book.[5] Critics on all sides of the issue use the same criteria to support opposite conclusions.

The traditional debate about the psalm appears to be at a draw. The sociology of knowledge, constantly overturning itself, makes first one way of perceiving and then another more attractive. Current thinking poses the question differently. It does not ask if the psalm is an insertion; instead, it asks how the psalm functions in the story. Function neither requires nor disavows harmony, though many critics assume the former. They interpret the psalm as the genuine piety of Jonah, and they seek continuity between it and the narrative.[6]

Conclusion. Heterogeneous elements in Jonah attest to a rich heritage of traditions that feed the story. Although their provenance belongs to a lost history, their presence shows that the book did not emerge *de novo*. Some traditions may have circulated originally in oral form, as the abundance of repetition in words, phrases, and larger units indicates. But some may have come from written material that itself employed repetition along with other literary devices. In the end, an unknown author appropriated all these diverse traditions to craft a coherent narrative of superb artistry. A composite history produced a unified story. Apart from the unsettled issue of the psalm, the integrity of the whole garners scholarly respect.

DATE

Introduction. Unlike most prophetic literature, Jonah fails to locate itself in a particular historical setting. It has no superscription that places the book in the reigns of the kings of Israel and Judah (e.g., Hos 1:1; Amos 1:1) or in the exile (e.g., Ezek 1:1-3) or in the post-exilic era (e.g., Hag 1:1; Zech 1:1); nor does the story contain references to known historical events.

Proposals. Various efforts to date the book have not succeeded.[7] (1) An older argument that the text contains "Aramaisms" and thus belongs to the post-exilic era falters in the light of philological studies. They show that most of these words are characteristic of northern Israelite-Phoenician usage and further that Aramaic and Phoenician linguistic phenomena were present in Hebrew before, as well as after, the exile. (2) The view that the Hebrew perfect tense in the translation "Nineveh was" (נינוה היתה *nînĕwēh hāyĕtâ*, 3:3) indicates a time long after the city had fallen in 612 BCE falters on a point of grammar. This tense form occurs elsewhere as a feature of Hebrew narrative style rather than as a device for dating (cf., e.g., Gen 29:17; Exod 9:11). (3) The idea that the alleged nonhistorical phrase "king of Nineveh" (rather than king of Assyria) indicates a time after the demise of the Assyrian Empire falters on an invalid assumption. Similar phrases identifying historical kings with their royal residences occur in the Bible (e.g., 1 Kgs 21:1; 2 Kgs 1:3). (4) The proposal that Jonah is late literature because it "quotes" other biblical books falters on its own reasoning. Literary affinities do not in themselves establish dependency, and dependency does not in itself establish late dating. (5) Equally unreliable are attempts to date Jonah by its theology, whatever an individual critic declares it to be. Nothing anchors the book theologically to a particular period in Israelite history.

With no secure evidence to date Jonah, scholars have wandered throughout seven centuries to find it a home. Two dates set the boundaries. The reference in 2 Kgs 14:23-25 to Jonah son of Amittai in the reign of Jeroboam II posits the eighth century BCE as the *terminus a quo*. The reference in the Wisdom of ben Sira 49:10 to the "book of the twelve" prophets posits the second century BCE as the *terminus ad quem*. Within these boundaries every century has been proposed.[8] Although a majority of opinions clusters around the sixth, fifth, and fourth centuries, it but shows how indeterminate is the date. The book may belong to the pre-exilic, exilic, or post-exilic period. Dating it becomes even more elusive if a history of composition lies behind the present form.

Conclusion. Some critics still try to date Jonah, but others turn from the quest. Decades ago von Rad cautioned against letting conjectures about the matter cloud interpretation.[9] Citing the caution, Limburg minimizes the importance of the issue for understanding the book.[10] Similarly,

Sasson finds inconclusive all the arguments and deems the enterprise itself less useful than often assumed.[11] To have available so many centuries for dating undermines the goal of historical specificity and renders any conclusion suspect. Perhaps the best interpretive efforts allow Jonah to move among centuries.

GENRE

Introduction. The single issue on which scholars agree unanimously is the uniqueness of Jonah among the Book of the Twelve Prophets. Unlike all the others, it tells a story about a presumed prophet (though never so called) rather than relating oracles spoken by a prophet. Yet scholarly unanimity shatters as soon as the question of genre arises. Proposed classifications include allegory, didactic story, fable, fairy tale, folktale, historical account, legend, *Märchen*, *māšāl*, midrash, myth, novella, parable, parody, prophetic tale, saga, satire, sermon, short story, and tragedy. This broad spectrum indicates confusion about the meaning of genre, lack of standard nomenclature for genres, and different understandings of the same genre. The spectrum attests also to scholarly extravagances and to the peculiar character of Jonah within the canon.

The genres of folktale, parable, satire, and midrash receive attention here. Each of them illumines dominant literary features of Jonah while showing the inadequacy of any single designation to encompass the story.

Folktale. The genre of folktale designates traditional prose stories, oral or written, in which the realms of fantasy and reality mingle freely.[12] Such stories emerge in cultures all over the world, from ancient times to the present.

Folkloristic Motifs. Jonah abounds in folkloristic motifs.[13] Chapters 1 and 2 report the flight of a disobedient man, the threat of a storm at sea, the casting of lots to determine who is the guilty party, the expulsion of the guilty one, the resulting cessation of the storm, and the opportune presence of an animal to save the one thrown overboard.

Parallels to these motifs appear in folk literature of diverse cultures and times. From Buddhist literature comes the story of one Mittavindaka, who, disobeying his mother, puts out to sea.[14] After six days, the ship ceases to move. The sailors cast lots to determine the one responsible for the trouble, and three times the lots fall on Mittavindaka. As the sailors remove him from the ship onto a raft, they express the wish not to perish because of the misdeed of this young man (cf. Jonah 1:14). Thereafter the ship continues without difficulty. In Western literature the Italian tale *Pinocchio* contains several episodes reminiscent of Jonah, including a storm at sea that endangers the boat on which Gepetto, the father of Pinocchio, travels.[15] When the boat sinks, a shark swallows Gepetto. The same fate befalls Pinocchio as he seeks to rescue his father (cf. Jonah 1:17). Although the shark is not a friendly animal, it does save them from drowning. Later they emerge unharmed from the great fish. Stories with comparable motifs appear in the literature of ancient Egypt, Greece, and New Guinea.[16]

Chapters 3 and 4 of Jonah also contain folkloristic motifs. They include the appearance of royalty and nobility contrasted with common people, a royal proclamation that miraculously effects total repentance, the indiscriminate mingling of people and animals, the fantastic growth and demise of a wonder plant, and the timely appearances of worm, wind, and sun to cause distress.

Parallels abound.[17] In European tales like "Cinderella" and "Brother Frolick's Adventures," royalty interacts with peasantry, and royal decrees are frequently issued for all peoples in a kingdom (cf. Jonah 3:5-7). In such stories as "The Faithful Beasts" and "The Little Tales About Toads," the worlds of animals and humans freely mingle. Wonder plants are central in "The Royal Turnip," "The Enchanted Trees," and "Jack and the Beanstalk." In this last tale, the beanstalk grows up overnight (cf. Jonah 4:10). Folk stories with comparable motifs appear in Burmese, Hindu, and Japanese literature as well.[18]

Problems. Though Jonah contains innumerable folkloristic motifs, several problems attend its classification under this genre. First, altogether absent in folktales but everywhere present in Jonah is the transcendent and omnipotent deity who directs the action. Although the tales allow for the supernatural in the forms of fairies, witches, gremlins, spells, and enchantments, they have no place for the Creator "God of heaven, who made the sea and the dry land" (Jonah 1:9 NRSV). Second, folktales eschew historical and geographical references to use fictitious times, places, and characters. By contrast, the fictitious Jonah borrows his name from an identifiable eighth-century figure (2 Kgs 14:25), and the fictitious story specifies the historical locales of Joppa, Tarshish, and Nineveh (Jonah 2:2-3). Third, folktales privilege entertainment over instruction, but the book of Jonah reverses the emphasis. To call Jonah a folktale is to classify some, but not all, of its content.

Parable. The Concept of Comparison. The Hebrew term מָשָׁל (*māšāl*) and its Greek equivalent παραβολή (*parabolē*) cover literature as diverse in length and discourse as the proverb (cf. the book of Proverbs), the taunt song (Isa 14:4*b*-21), the dirge (Mic 2:1-5), the woe pronouncement (Hab 2:6-19), the oracle (Num 23:7-10), and the allegory (Ezek 17:3-10; 20:45-48; 24:3-5).[19] Even where the word *māšāl* does not itself occur, the concept extends to brief narratives like Jotham's fable about trees seeking a king (Judg 9:8-15), Nathan's tale about the ewe lamb (2 Sam 12:1-4), the woman of Tekoa's story about her two sons (2 Sam 14:4-43), and Isaiah's song of the vineyard (Isa 5:1-6). In all these instances the comprehensive genre *māšāl* focuses on the idea of comparison between something said and something intended.

Critics who call Jonah a *māšāl* (or parable) identify different comparisons for it. One view holds that Jonah represents recalcitrant Israel compared to Nineveh, which represents the receptive nations of the world. Another sees Jonah as the model of justice compared to Yahweh as the model of mercy. Still another deems Jonah the negative model of reproachable conduct compared to Nineveh, the positive model of repentance, and to Yahweh, the positive model of compassion.[20] These differences tend to undermine the concept of comparison as a stable criterion for deciding the genre of the book.

In measuring Jonah by known parables within the Hebrew Bible, Sasson finds other problems.[21] He notes as a minor point that Jonah exceeds the usual length of a parable and as a major point that Jonah lacks at its conclusion what a standard parable offers—namely, an explanation of the story told. For instance, Nathan interprets for David the meaning of the parable of the ewe lamb with the punch line, "You are the man!" (2 Sam 12:7 NRSV). The woman of Tekoa instructs David in the meaning of her parable of the two sons with the punch line, "In giving this decision the king convicts himself" (2 Sam 14:13 NRSV). Similarly,

the song of the vineyard discloses its meaning in the climactic last stanza, which identifies the vineyard as Israel and Judah (Isa 5:7). The conclusion of Jonah, however, does not move to an explanation. Neither the narrator nor Yahweh nor Jonah shifts to another plane of meaning. The plant remains the plant; the Ninevites remain the Ninevites (4:10-11).

Other Concepts. For some scholars the genre of parable pertains more to the internal literary feature of surprise and hyperbole than to comparison.[22] Surprises in Jonah include a prophet's going to a foreign land to deliver his message rather than speaking on his native soil against another nation, the mass conversion of the Ninevites, the violent storm, the miraculous fish, and the wonder plant. These incidents combine the extraordinary and the improbable to yield hyperbole and thus to mark Jonah as a parable. Yet surprise and hyperbole are surely not unique to parables. Folktales, for example, contain them.

For Christian readers prone to draw their understanding of parable from the Gospels, other obstacles prevail in so classifying Jonah. The stories told by Jesus are more economical in detail and length than is the book of Jonah. They are also embedded texts, narratives within larger narratives, but Jonah is an independent narrative. Although like Jonah they contain extravagances, unlike Jonah they report natural rather than miraculous events.[23] Their main characters are less well developed than is the character Jonah. Most tellingly, the stories of Jesus, unlike the story of Jonah, do not include God as a character. From the perspective of the Gospels, then, Jonah is far too theological to be a parable.[24]

In summary, different understandings of what constitutes a parable and different understandings of Jonah as a parable pose numerous difficulties for this classification. As a compromise term, "parable-like" attests the problem.[25]

Satire. The genre of satire uses irony, derision, wit, invective, and related phenomena to attack a specific target.[26] Though the attack has a serious purpose, humor mediates it.

In the process the grotesque, the absurd, and the fanciful may come into play. A preponderance of these features within a story confirms it as satire.

Most scholars who call the book of Jonah satire view Jonah himself as the target of attack. Overall, he is self-centered and self-willed, mouthing piety incongruous with his behavior. He is narrow minded and rebellious. Reacting with anger to the total success of his own preaching, he becomes a caricature of a prophet.

Satiric Details. Numerous details support a satiric reading of the story.[27] Though the name "Jonah son of Amittai" means "dove son of faithfulness," Jonah descends (1:3, 5) rather than soars; he disobeys rather than remains faithful. In boarding a ship to Tarshish in the west, he takes the opposite direction from Nineveh in the east. The narrator ridicules him by reporting that he snores in the bottom of the ship while the sailors work mightily to outlast the storm (1:5). The non-Israelite captain of the ship further ridicules him by urging him to pray to his own god and by using the same imperatives with which Yahweh has already addressed him, "Arise, call" (1:6; cf. 1:2). Jonah's subsequent answer to the sailors' questions traps him in a contradiction of his own making. He seeks to flee from the presence of Yahweh, whom he acknowledges to be "God of heaven, who made the sea and the dry land" (1:9 NRSV).

The satire continues when Jonah proposes that the sailors hurl him into the sea (1:12). Death by drowning would be a certain way to achieve flight from Yahweh. But the ploy does not work, because Yahweh appoints a fish to swallow Jonah (1:17). Even the negative connotation (cf., e.g., Exod 15:12; Num 16:28-34) of the verb "swallow" (בלע *bālaʿ*) ridicules him. He does not die but instead prays an incongruous psalm of thanksgiving while in the belly of the fish (2:2-9). The ridicule of Jonah and by Jonah climaxes with the concluding line of the psalm, "Deliverance belongs to the LORD!" (2:9 NRSV). Thereupon Yahweh orders the fish to "vomit" (קיא *qîʾ*) Jonah out. This infelicitous verb delivers its own satire.

Upon reaching Nineveh, Jonah delivers a five-word pronouncement upon the city. It parodies prophetic discourse (3:4). Making no explicit claim to speak "the word of Yahweh," Jonah uses the ambiguous verb "overturn" (הפך *hāpak*; NRSV, "overthrown"). It belies his intention, for Nineveh overturns through repentance, not destruction (3:5-10). Humor attends the city's earnest repentance. The animals, like the human beings, clothe themselves in sackcloth, mourn, and fast. In saving Nineveh, Yahweh undercuts

the messenger and his message. So the outcome humiliates Jonah, and he turns angry.

Irony, humor, parody, fantasy, and the absurd permeate the remainder of the story. Jonah uses a credo about God's mercy (4:2-3) to justify his own unmerciful attitude. His petulant behavior defies his pious words. That behavior extends to his sulking outside the city in a self-made booth and under a God-given plant (4:5). Puns, such as the association of the noun "shade" (צל *ṣēl*) with the verb "to save" (נצל *nāṣal*), help to support absurd features in the closing incidents: a plant growing up overnight, a single worm causing the plant's instant demise, and the sun beating upon the head of Jonah, who is sheltered presumably by his own booth (4:5-8). Jonah comes across as a ridiculous character, shifting his mood from delight to defiance. Fittingly, the sun attacking his head mocks his hardheadedness.

According to one interpretation, the question at the end of the book (4:10-11) ironically juxtaposes Jonah's self-pity to Yahweh's gratuitous pity for Nineveh.[28] Another proposal finds the irony in similarity. Jonah's self-pity regarding the plant parallels Yahweh's self-pity regarding Nineveh. The deity spares the city for selfish reasons. In that case, however, a satire attacking Jonah ironically becomes a vindication of him—or ironically becomes an attack on Yahweh.

Problems. Although satiric elements mark Jonah, whether they confirm it as satire opens up unsettled and unsettling problems, first between authorial intention and reader response and then among different readers. What authorial indicators secure satire as the genre of the book? Do generally agreed- upon satiric features become a license for inventing others? To what extent is satire in the eye of the beholder? For example, some readers find Jonah's prayer inside the fish an expression of genuine piety, but others deem it distortion and farce. Some readers chuckle to picture animals clothed in sackcloth and sitting upon ashes, but others see pathos and poignancy. How much satire does the book yield and how much do readers contribute? Jonah may have both less and more levity and gravitas than readers intend.[29]

A related problem concerns the target(s) being attacked. Are the sailors being ridiculed in their seeking to appease a storm god by hurling wares to the sea? Are they being ridiculed for lack of nautical acumen when they try to steer the ship to shore during a storm? Are the Ninevites being ridiculed when they command their animals to repent? Is nature being ridiculed when it is commanded to act unnaturally: A fish to swallow and vomit up a human being? A tree to pop up overnight? A single worm to fell a tree? Is Yahweh being ridiculed as a deity who can be duped by instant and mass conversions? Is Yahweh being ridiculed in arguing with angry Jonah? If a reader decides the book is a satire, then it may present more targets than one would like. At any rate, shifting targets decenter the claim that Jonah is the object of attack.[30]

Yet another problem centers on the character of Jonah. Does it remain constant throughout the book? Is he consistently disobedient, self-centered, and angry? The psalm (2:2-9) challenges this reading, as does the final question (4:10-11). If Jonah's character is not forever static or negative, then even the pronounced satire upon him does not cover the whole story.

Proposals that the book of Jonah is a satire have their limits. The difficulties extend also to the larger question of whether the Hebrews satirized or whether the genre of satire fits biblical literature.[31]

Midrash. Derived from the Hebrew verb דרשׁ (*dāraš*), meaning "to seek" or "to inquire," the noun *midrash* designates a type of literature, oral or written, that explicates a biblical passage. A midrash is a commentary that endeavors to make a particular text meaningful and relevant. Although midrash flourished in rabbinic literature, its origins are earlier. They include references to the midrash of the prophet Iddo in 2 Chr 13:22 and to the midrash on the book of Kings in 2 Chr 24:27.[32]

Proposals. Taking a cue from the latter reference, Karl Budde proposed long ago that the book of Jonah is a midrash on 2 Kgs 14:25.[33] Just as "Jonah son of Amittai, the prophet," spoke favorably about God's goodness to the sinful kingdom Israel, so the story of Jonah uses him to extend the divine mercy to sinful foreigners. Other scholars have seen the book as a midrash on prophetic literature.[34] For instance, the decree against Nineveh provides commentary on oracles against foreign nations in Jeremiah and Ezekiel. Though these oracles appear as absolute, they remain conditional (e.g., Jer 18:7-8; 25:5; Ezekiel 26–28). Accordingly, Jonah's pronouncement of certain doom results in repentance and deliverance (3:3, 10).

Another view holds that Jonah himself provides the text for the midrash.[35] It is the credo he recites about the character of Yahweh as "gracious . . . and merciful, slow to anger, and abounding in steadfast love, and ready to relent from punishing" (4:2b NRSV). Different versions of the credo appear throughout the Bible in different contexts with different meanings.[36] Choosing one version (cf. Joel 2:13), the author of Jonah built the narrative around it.

Two literary devices signal the centrality of the credo. First, its content binds the story together. In 1:3, the narrator reports that "Jonah arose to flee to Tarshish" but gives no reason for his flight. In 4:2, Jonah recites the attributes of Yahweh as the reason "why I hastened to flee to Tarshish." The device of delayed information joins the beginning and ending of the story to produce literary and theological coherence. Second, a conventional clause of disclosure introduces the credo: "for now I know that. . . . " It serves a deictic function, directing attention to a climactic utterance (cf. Gen 22:12b ; Exod 18:11; 1 Kgs 17:24). By using this device, Jonah points the reader and Yahweh to the heart of his problem: a quarrel with the compassionate nature of God.

The story explicates the credo. Chapters 1 and 2 portray Jonah trying to deny or ignore the gracious and merciful God. He attempts physical flight (1:3), psychological flight (1:5b), and existential flight (1:12, 15), but each time Yahweh saves him. Chapter 3 shows Jonah capitulating to the gracious and merciful God, who subsequently spares Nineveh. Chapter 4 depicts angry Jonah berating Yahweh for being merciful. Yahweh then takes over, not to berate Jonah but to extend mercy to him. Plant, worm, sun, and wind play their parts in the divine lesson. Through them the gracious God does not allow Jonah to perish. Divine compassion is itself the last word (4:11). From beginning (cf. 4:2b) to end, the book comments in narrative form on the ancient credo. The story is a midrash.

Problems. To classify Jonah as a midrash is not without problems, beginning with the word *midrash* itself. Its meaning can be slippery and imprecise.[37] Further, the appearances of the word *midrash* only in the late book of Chronicles (c. fourth century BCE) may imply that the genre was unavailable for earlier traditions. If Jonah was consciously conceived as a midrash, why does the term itself not appear in the story? How appropriate is the credo for encompassing the narrative? Conversely, how appropriate is the narrative for interpreting the credo?

The affirmation of God as "gracious . . . and merciful" links the opening of chapter 1 (1:1-3) to all that transpires in chapter 3. The ending of chapter 3 further links itself to the credo through identical vocabulary and theology: God "repenting of evil" (3:10; 4:2b). The credo then becomes the basis for the events of chapter 4. It supplies the rationale for Jonah's anger and his persistent wish to die. Moreover, it accounts for the continuing deeds and words of Yahweh on behalf of Jonah, and it leads to the question about divine pity at the end.

Omitted from this overview, however, is the sea narrative (1:4–2:11). Yahweh's hurling of a ferocious storm that threatens to destroy innocent lives hardly describes the activity of a merciful God who is slow to anger. The subsequent prayer of the sailors recognizes divine power (1:14), it does not acknowledge divine compassion. Even when the outcome is salvific, neither the sailors nor the narrator invokes the merciful and gracious God. In several respects, then, the sea narrative undermines the credo as the text for the entire story.

But another way of reading claims the credo. It holds that Jonah's behavior throughout the sea crisis is tacit recognition of the merciful God whom he so resents. In other words, he has knowledge that the sailors lack, and his knowledge shapes the narrative. His instructions to them, for instance, carry the hidden assurance of divine mercy (1:12). And the mercy comes with the cessation of the storm. Moreover, the opportune appearance of the fish signals the mercy that Jonah knows about and rejects. From this perspective the credo undergirds the sea narrative. Yet such a reading minimizes the reality of the storm for the sailors as well as the wrathful portrayal of Yahweh.

Conclusion. In its richness, complexity, and distinctiveness, the book of Jonah resists the categorizing endemic to genres. Although the designations folktale, parable, satire, and midrash illuminate the story to varying degrees, none of them embraces it fully. Perhaps the best interpretive efforts allow Jonah freedom to move among genres.

LITERARY FEATURES

Introduction. Jonah is a literary gem. Even a reading in English can detect exquisite properties in its structure, characters, plot, and style. Jonah 1:1 opens, "Now the word of the LORD came to Jonah son of Amittai, saying" (NRSV). Chapter 3:1 repeats these words, except for the appositive, and adds the telling phrase "a second time." The repetition, plus the addition, signals that the narrative falls into two major scenes.[38] At the beginning of each scene appear the primary characters, Yahweh and Jonah. The other characters, all unnamed, come in groups, each with a leader. They divide between the scenes: the sailors and their captain; the Ninevites and their king. Natural phenomena also play major roles: wind, storm, sea, dry land, and fish in scene one; animals, plant, worm, sun, and wind in scene two. The plot moves by divine activities, with human and natural responses marking the turning points. Throughout the narrative a host of literary features enhances the theology. The present discussion offers but an overview.[39]

External Design. Jonah is divided into two parts: scene one is chapters 1-2; scene two is chapters 3-4).[40]

(1) The preponderance of repetitions between the openings of scenes one (1:1-3) and two (3:1-4a) secures the division as it stresses the commanding power of Yahweh's word. This constant word compels Jonah to respond. His different responses, first disobedience and then obedience, set in motion the actions of both scenes.

(2) The responses of the sailors (1:5) and the Ninevites (3:4b) correspond in number, order, and kind, though not in vocabulary. First come contrasting inward responses: the sailors fear; the Ninevites believe. Second come corresponding articulated responses: the sailors cry; the Ninevites call. Third come contrasting outward responses: the sailors throw away; the Ninevites put on. The narrator draws favorable portraits of both groups as they appeal to the deity אלהים (ĕlōhîm). These portraits contrast strikingly with that of Jonah.

(3) From each group of foreigners emerges its unnamed leader (1:6; 3:6-9). The captain of the sailors makes a brief appearance; the king of Nineveh takes a major role. Their speeches differ, but the conclusions converge in syntax, vocabulary, and theology. Each opens with a rhetorical expression that anticipates but does not guarantee salvation.

"Perhaps," says the captain; "Who knows?" says the king. Each uses the designation "the god" (הָאֱלֹהִים *hāʾĕlōhîm*). Each concludes with the words "and we will not perish." The foreign leaders proclaim a theology of hope that understands the freedom of God. They make clear that whereas prayers and other cultic acts are appropriate—indeed, required—responses to impending disaster, the outcome nonetheless belongs solely to the deity.

(4) The verb "perish" (אבד *ʾābad*), used by the captain and the king, appears in two other places. The sailors use it in scene one (1:14) and Yahweh in scene two (4:10). These four occurrences provide balance and emphasis.

(5) At the endings (2:1-11; 4:2-11) the verb "appoint" (מנה *mānâ*; "provided," NIV), appears once in scene one (1:17) and three times in scene two (4:6, 7, 8). Each time Yahweh is the subject, and nature is the object. Each time Yahweh uses nature to deal with Jonah.

(6) Within the external design, symmetry and asymmetry contend. For example, the reports of impending disaster differ in length, type of discourse, and characters (1:4; 3:4b). The extended focus on the sailors vies with a short look at the Ninevites (1:7-15; 3:10). The ending of scene two (4:2-11) exceeds in length the ending of scene one (2:1-11). If the overall symmetry produces rhythm, contrast, emphasis, and continuity, the asymmetry disrupts the rhythm to give contrast and emphasis through discontinuity.

Structural and Stylistic Features. (1) Throughout Jonah, sentences with three main clauses, sometimes doubled, produce a rhythm that facilitates the grasping of content (e.g., 1:3-5, 15-16; 3:5, 7c-8a ; 4:7). An alternate structure provides variation through the use of four independent clauses (e.g., 2:1-2a, 11; 3:3-4a ; 3:6b ; 4:5). Occasionally some clauses depart from conventional Hebrew syntax to place subject before verb, a reversal that effects contrast and emphasis. In direct discourse, three kinds of sentences prevail: imperative, interrogative, and cohortative or jussive. Yahweh (1:2; 3:2), the captain (1:6), the sailors (1:7-8), and Jonah (4:3) use the imperative. The captain (1:6), the sailors (1:7-8, 10-11), the king (3:9), Jonah (4:2a), and Yahweh (4:4, 9-11) all use the interrogative, sometimes directly and other times rhetorically. The sailors (1:7) and most especially the king (3:7-8) use the cohortative or the jussive.

(2) The phenomenon of repetition permeates the story. It emphasizes themes to build unity and cohesion. A number of verbs occur three or more times each: "arise" (קום *qûm*), "call" (קרא *qārāʾ*), "know" (ידע *yādaʿ*), "hurl" (טול *ṭûl*), "fear" (ירא *yārēʾ*), "turn" (שוב *šûb*), "make" (עשה *ʿāśâ*), "repent" (נחם *nāḥam*), "appoint" (מנה *mānâ*), "go" (בוא *bôʾ*), "walk" (הלך *hālak*), and "perish" (אבד *ʾābad*). Certain nouns and adjectives appear often: "great" (גדול *gādôl*), fourteen times; "evil" (רעה *rāʿâ*), nine times; "sea" (ים *yām*), eleven times; and "life" or "self" (נפש *nepeš*), three times. Several phrases and clauses appear two or more times: "to flee to Tarshish," "the presence of Yahweh," "that the sea may be quiet," "call to Yahweh or God," "prayed to Yahweh," "is anger good." Six sets of cognate accusatives increase the use of repetition: "fear a fear," "vow a vow," "sacrifice a sacrifice," "call a call," "evil an evil," "delight a delight."

Unusual Vocabulary. Although the many repetitions suggest that the vocabulary is not large, nonetheless it contains a number of unusual words and words used in unusual ways. Five terms are unique to Jonah: ספינה (*sĕpînâ*; the second occurrence of the two words translated "ship" in 1:5), יתעשת (*yitʿaššēt*, "will think," 1:6), קריאה (*qĕrîʾâ*, "calling," 3:2), קיקיון (*qîqāyôn*, "plant," 4:6, 7, 9, 10), and חרישית (*ḥăr îšît*, "strong" or "fierce," 4:8). In addition, four verbs take on unique meanings: חשב (*ḥāšab*, "think"), applied to the inanimate object "ship" (1:4); שתק (*šātaq*, "be quiet"), applied to the sea (1:11-12); חתר (*ḥātar*, "dig" or "hollow out"), applied to the activity of rowing (1:13); and זעף (*zāʿap*, "be enraged"), applied to the sea (1:15). Rare also is the noun מלחים (*mallāḥîm*) for sailors (1:5; cf. only Ezek 27:9, 27, 29). (Elsewhere in Jonah the word translated "sailors" is simply אנשים [*ʾănāšîm*], "men.") The phrase החבל רב (*rab haḥḥōbēl*, 1:6), often translated by the single word "captain," literally means "the chief of the ropes." The noun חבל (*ḥōbēl*) occurs only here and in Ezek 27:8, 27-29.

The clustering of unusual vocabulary within chapter 1 bespeaks the distinctiveness of this seafaring incident within the Hebrew Bible. Some of the words also mark the peculiar style of the narrator in conveying information and ideas. To ascribe thought to the ship (1:4) intensifies its plight. To portray the captain as a handler of ropes (1:6) provides a choice detail about the operation of the ship. To describe rowing as "digging" (1:13) shows the desperation of the sailors (or a lack of nautical knowledge by the author?).

Overall, the vocabulary of Jonah is common and simple, unique and varied. It demonstrates a creative use of words and indicates a cosmopolitan outlook.

Rhetorical Devices. The creative use of words includes rhetorical devices. Some are available in translation, but many only in Hebrew. A sampling indicates their diversity and value.

(1) Alliteration, assonance, and related devices provide aesthetic and thematic emphasis. The alternation of the Hebrew particles מה (mâ) and מ (m) in the four questions that the sailors ask Jonah produces a staccato effect that achieves force and urgency: "What," "where," "what," and "where" (1:8). Jonah's answer, עברי אנכי (ʿibrî ʾānōkî), pleases the ear as he articulates his national identity, "A Hebrew am I" (1:9). The internal vowels in the phrase חנון ורחום (ḥannûn wĕraḥûm) resound in the description of God as "gracious" and "merciful" (4:2d). Repetition and rhyme enclose the opening line of the psalm (2:2). Its first and last words begin with the consonant "q" (ק qôp) and end with the vowel "i" (קראתי qārāʾtî, "I call"; and קולי qôlî, "my voice"). Several devices interplay in the clause "the ship thought itself to break up" (1:4). The two verb forms חשבה להשבר (ḥiššĕbâ lĕhiššābēr, "thought itself to break up") yield assonance with the vowels i, e, a, and i, a, e. These words also exhibit onomatopoeia; they sound like their meaning—namely, boards cracking from the force of water. The entire clause exemplifies prosopopoeia, the representation of an inanimate object by a human attribute.

(2) Chiasm, a syntactic structure that inverts the order of sentences or words, is a favorite rhetorical device. For instance, the narrated discourse in the fish episode begins and ends with sentences that have Yahweh as subject (2:1, 11). Between them come sentences with Jonah as subject (2:11). Thus the pattern is ABBʹAʹ. The report of Jonah's entering Nineveh (3:3-4a) inverts the order of the nouns: Jonah (A), Nineveh (B), Nineveh (Bʹ), Jonah (Aʹ). Beyond single words, chiasms in Jonah extend to entire verses.

(3) Merism, the division of the whole into parts, identifies the description of the cosmos as the heavens, the sea, and the dry land (1:9b). The device also occurs in the references to the total population of Nineveh as "from the greatest to the smallest" (3:5) and "the human and the animal" (3:7b).

(4) Synecdoche, in contrast to merism, substitutes parts for the whole. This device identifies the phrase "the herd and the flock," representing the animal population (3:7b).

(5) Puns enliven Jonah.[41] The opposite verbs עלה (ʿālâ, "go up") and ירד (yārad, "go down") play off each other. The evil of Nineveh goes up (ʿlh) to Yahweh (1:2); Jonah goes down (yrd) to Joppa, to the ship, and to the hold of the ship (1:3, 5). Jonah goes down (yrd) to the land, but Yahweh brings up (ʿlh) Jonah's life from the pit (2:6). A wordplay between the phrase "from his throne" (מכסאו mikkisʾô) and the verb "be covered" (כסה kāsâ) assists in depicting the transformation in the king of Nineveh (3:6b). The word טעם (ṭaʿam), rendered "proclamation" in 3:7, carries the concrete meaning of taste and the figurative meaning of judgment. Its use prepares for a pun on the first instruction, "let them not taste" (אל־יטעמו ʾal-yiṭʿāmû). The hope that God may "turn from his fierce anger" literally reads "from the burning of his nostrils" (3:9). After God fulfills the hope, Jonah "becomes angry," a description that literally reads, "it burned to him." What God has turned from inflames Jonah. Wordplay gives the incendiary contrast.

(6) A different kind of rhetorical device is the strategy of delayed information. In 1:1-3, Jonah makes no verbal reply to the command of Yahweh. Only much later (4:2) does the reader learn that Jonah did speak at that time, whether within himself or aloud to Yahweh. When Jonah talks to the sailors (1:9), he does not tell them that he is fleeing from Yahweh. Later the narrator supplies the information (1:10). When the plant withers, the narrator does not report Jonah's reaction (4:7). At the end, Yahweh gives it (4:10). The strategy of delayed information contributes to the surprise and suspense of the story.

Imagery. Overview. The storyteller uses a wide range of imagery. Cosmically it extends from the heavens above (1:9) to the dry land and the sea (1:9) to the depths of the netherworld (2:2). Geographically it extends east to west, from Tarshish (1:3) to Nineveh (3:3), with Joppa (1:3) and possibly Jerusalem (2:4, 7) in between. Vivid language presents the horrors of a storm at sea: the ship tossing to and fro, about to be dashed to pieces, and the frantic efforts of the sailors in hurling wares overboard and in rowing (1:4-5, 11, 13). Equally vivid language reports dangers on dry land: the destructive power of wind and sun beating upon the head of Jonah (4:8). Ritual activities enlarge the imagery: lot casting (1:7), mourning (3:5-8*a*), praying (1:14; 2:2-9), sacrificing (1:15; 2:9), vowing (1:15; 2:9), and worshiping in the Temple (2:4, 7). Varieties of life similarly expand the narrative world: people, animals, and a plant. All these images attest to the cosmopolitan purview of the storyteller.

Gender Imagery. Gender imagery in Jonah clusters around the theme of life and death. This subject requires careful explication, beginning with the distinction between grammar and identity. Comparative studies show that grammatical gender is primarily an issue of syntax rather than of sexual identity.[42] Masculine and feminine nouns, whether animate or inanimate, are not in themselves the equivalent of male and female. These linguistic data constrain the interpretation of certain feminine grammatical nouns and verbs in Jonah 1–2 that metaphorically suggest female activity and anatomy.

(1) The feminine noun אניה (*'ŏniyyâ*), one of two words used for the ship, first claims attention because it appears before its verb, thereby reversing the usual order of Hebrew syntax (1:4*a*). As already observed, the verb itself, חשבה להשבר (*ḥiššĕbâ lĕhiššābēr*, "thought to break up"), increases attention because it represents an inanimate object with a human attribute. Figuratively, the total combination yields a female persona for the ship: She thinks that she is cracking up.

(2) In the next verse (1:5) occurs the second word for "ship," ספינה (*sĕpînâ*). It appears in the phrase reporting that Jonah went down to "the innards of the ship" (ירכתי הספינה *yarkĕtê has-sĕpînâ*, 1:5*b*). Both of these nouns, "innards" and "ship," are gramatically feminine forms. Building upon the female persona of the thinking ship, the phrase suggests (though it does not specify) a uterine image: the inner recesses where Jonah lies in slumber. But the nautical body cannot shield Jonah. His presence in the "womb" of the ship threatens *her* life as well as his own. Destruction invades the place of conception.

(3) The two phrases about Jonah's being in "the belly of the fish" (1:17; 2:1) pose different images tied to different grammatical genders. The masculine plural noun translated "belly" (מעה *mē'eh*) signifies internal parts. Three places in the Bible it parallels the grammatical feminine noun בטן (*beten*) to acquire the meaning "womb" (Gen 25:23; Isa 49:1; Ps 71:6; cf. Ruth 1:11). That meaning is excluded in Jonah 1:17, where the word for "fish" (דג *dāg*) is masculine gender; but it acquires validity in Jonah 2:1, where the word for "fish" (דגה *dāgâ*) is feminine gender.

The switch from the masculine to the feminine gender for "fish" has intrigued readers through the centuries.[43] No one knows why it happened, what it means, or if it is important. Nonetheless, like the imagery of "the innards of the ship" (1:5*b*), the phrase "from the belly of the fish" in 2:1 evokes the womb. Once again, though this time not by his own choice, Jonah resides in a place of conception that harbors destruction. His presence in the ichthyic "womb" threatens his life.

(4) In the psalm that Jonah prays from within the mother fish, he cries to Yahweh "from the womb of Sheol" (מבטן שאול *mibbeten šĕ'ôl*, 2:3*a*; neither the NIV nor the NRSV chooses this translation). Here the grammatical feminine noun *beten* describes the depths of the underworld. The word climaxes the uterine descent (regression) of Jonah, first into the "innards" of the ship, then into the "belly" of the female fish, and at last beneath earth and sea to the "womb" of Sheol, the most deadly of residences. Tied to the verb *yrd* ("went down") in chapters 1 and 2, this imagery embodies the issue of life and death, of womb and tomb.[44]

Summary. Though the book of Jonah is silent on many critical questions, it speaks eloquently as a literary document. Design, structure, style, vocabulary, imagery, character portrayals, plot development, and rhetorical devices fashion an exquisite narrative abounding in interpretive offerings. Consummate artistry bears theological profundities.

THEOLOGY

Complexities mark the theology of Jonah. This overview begins with themes and moves to a narrative scanning of the book.

Themes. Prophetic Call. Jonah's resistance to the call from Yahweh is not unique. Moses shrank from speaking to Pharaoh (Exod 3:10–4:17); Elijah fled from denouncing the regime of Ahab (1 Kgs 19:1-18); Jeremiah recoiled from prophesying to the nations (Jer 1:4-10). Yet Jonah exceeds them all in his defiance. The phrase "from the presence of Yahweh" (1:3) signals not just resistance but outright disobedience. Contrary to the view that Jonah flees because he believes that Yahweh is confined to the land of Israel, the phrase indicates that Jonah recognizes Yahweh's presence and power in Nineveh. To flee from the divine presence is not to escape God but to reject the divine call.

Motives vary for resisting a call. Moses and Jeremiah thought themselves inadequate for the task (Exod 3:11, 4:10; Jer 1:6). Elijah feared for his own life (1 Kgs 19:3, 10). Amos and Isaiah found the message too dreadful to announce (e.g., Amos 7:2, 5; Isa 6:9-13). At first Jonah gives no reason for his resistance. Near the end, he offers an explanation that contrasts with those of his predecessors (4:2-3). He is not concerned about his qualifications; he does not fear for his life; and he does not resist because Yahweh commands him to preach doom. Instead, his objection is the certain knowledge that doom for Nineveh can be averted because God repents of evil. Whereas some prophets shrank from preaching because they saw no hope, Jonah refuses because he knows there is hope. Whereas some prophets complained about the wrath of Yahweh (e.g., Jer 20:7-9), Jonah protests the love of God.

The futility of resisting the call also permeates prophetic literature. Yahweh repeatedly overruled the objections of Moses and sent him to Pharaoh. Yahweh evicted Elijah from Mount Horeb and sent him back to Syria and Israel with a political and prophetic mandate. Yahweh held Isaiah and Amos to their respective assignments, and Yahweh bluntly informed Jeremiah that he had no choice. Similarly, Yahweh pursues Jonah on sea and dry land. By the end of scene one, Jonah has exhausted his efforts to disobey. At the beginning of scene two, without a word he goes to Nineveh as Yahweh commands. But his response is at best "giving in," resignation to the inevitable. At worst it is another way of resisting: to oppose through external obedience; to say yes but mean no.

Jonah's behavior after he fulfills his mission recalls Elijah's after the mighty contest on Mount Carmel (1 Kgs 18:20-46). Elijah leaves first his homeland and then the city of Beersheba, sits under a broomtree, and later makes his way to the cave at Mount Horeb. Jonah leaves Nineveh, builds a booth, and in time finds himself sitting under a miraculous plant. Like Elijah, he pleads that Yahweh take away his life (1 Kgs 19:4; Jonah 4:3). But the circumstances differ. Suffering from exhaustion, Elijah is zealous that Yahweh's will prevail. Suffering from anger, Jonah is defiant that Yahweh's will has prevailed. Along the way, both narratives involve extensive use of nature. Ravens feed Elijah (1 Kgs 17:4-6); a fish swallows Jonah (Jonah 2:1). Wind, earthquake, and fire signify the absence of God for Elijah (1 Kgs 19:11-12); plant, worm, wind, and sun signify the presence of God for Jonah (Jonah 4:7-8).

Elijah and Jonah are alone among the prophets in being sent to foreign lands. Each addresses God out of a sense of dejection and self-pity, and Yahweh responds with questions that the deity later repeats (1 Kgs 19:9, 13; Jonah 4:4, 9). The questions confront the prophets with the folly of self-concern.

Comparisons of Jonah with other prophets highlight the commonalities and particularities in his call. More than the others, he rails against the inevitability of obedience. In capitulation he continues to resist. He even turns the success of his mission into an accusation that itself tests the character of Yahweh to be merciful to a defiant messenger.[45]

Nineveh. As the object of Jonah's mission, Nineveh poses interpretive challenges. According to the table of nations, Nimrod the mighty hunter founded the city (Gen 10:8-12). Zephaniah condemned it for arrogance and forecast its destruction shortly before that event in 612 BCE (Zeph 2:13-15). Nahum assailed it as the "city of bloodshed" (Nah 3:1), described its evil in great detail, and rejoiced in its destruction. From this prophetic perspective, the historical Nineveh was evil incarnate; it justly deserved its fate.

In decisive ways the book of Jonah counters this portrait. (1) Yahweh, the very God in whose name Zephaniah and Nahum prophesied, repeatedly describes Nineveh as "the great city" (1:2; 3:2; 4:11), and the narrator even declares it a city "great to God" (3:3). Although Yahweh once ascribes "evil" to it (1:2), never is it called "the evil city." Indeed, God recognizes that it turns from evil (3:10). (2) The books of Zephaniah and Nahum denounce Nineveh and see its destruction as the will of Yahweh. But the book of Jonah shows no hatred toward the city. Jonah's own quarrel is not with the city but with God. Unlike those prophetic oracles of judgment, the story shows compassion for Nineveh and sees its salvation as the will of Yahweh. (3) Zephaniah and Nahum concentrate exclusively upon the violence of Nineveh. Although the book of Jonah refers to the evil and the violence of the city (1:2; 3:8, 10), it neither details nor dwells on these horrors. Instead, it emphasizes the religious sensitivities of the city. The people of Nineveh believe in God, engage in acts of penance, and repent (3:5-10). The repenting of God (3:10) then confirms these deeds as genuine. (4) Zephaniah and Nahum describe the historical Nineveh; Jonah depicts the legendary Nineveh. Beyond the identity of name and size, the two cities meet, briefly but profoundly, at the place of evil. Then they depart, radically and profoundly, at the place of repentance. As a result, prophetic imagination does not offer two attitudes toward one Nineveh; rather, it dares to offer two Ninevehs and thus to relativize historical certitude.[46]

Ecology. With a focus on human beings and their environment, ecology constitutes a prominent theological theme throughout Jonah. Yahweh first acts as the subject of a verb whose object is nature. The deity hurls a great wind that produces a great storm upon the sea, which in turn threatens the animated ship and its sailors (1:4). Countering the disobedience of one creature, Yahweh sets nature over against many. A single human response precipitates a hostile environment.

The sailors seek to appease the sea by offering it inanimate wares (1:5). Then they seek to escape the storm by returning to dry land (1:13). At last they succeed in calming the sea by sacrificing the culprit Jonah (1:15). They give to nature one of their own. Concerted human deeds restore harmony to a hostile environment. But the sailors take no credit for restoring the ecological balance. Instead, they worship Yahweh (1:16).

The next episode begins with Yahweh again the subject of a verb whose object is nature. The deity appoints a great fish to swallow Jonah (1:17). This animal of the sea mediates between the deity and the human being. Whether it performs a benign or malignant function remains a moot question. The verbs used for its actions carry negative meanings: "swallow" (בלע bāla') and "vomit" (קיא qî'). The former suggests that the fish is a hostile environment for Jonah; the latter suggests that Jonah is a hostile substance for the fish. The natural creature rejects the human creature. But the rejection is not an independent move by the fish. As with the swallowing, it happens because Yahweh decrees it.

A contrasting view observes that the psalm (2:1-9) depicts the fish as a friendly environment. It saves Jonah from the hostile sea; it becomes God's answer to Jonah's cry of distress; it is the place where deliverance happens. Yet the Jonah of the prose narrative does not want to be saved. Having sought flight from Yahweh in several unsuccessful ways, he proposes that the sailors throw him into the sea (1:12). From that perspective, drowning would be his salvation; the raging sea would ironically be his rescuer. But the fish thwarts his wish. The natural creature defies the human creature. Yet again, the defiance is not an independent move. Yahweh controls the fish.

The ecological theme continues in Nineveh, but with marked differences. The animals take their orders from the king rather than from God. Moreover, these natural creatures are not instruments for human or divine purposes; instead, they participate with human beings in acts of repentance. The salutation of the royal decree addresses the population as "the human and the animal" (3:7). Then it emphasizes the latter by the accompanying phrase "the herd and the flock." The instruction that follows commands them not to graze and not to drink water. It requires them to dress in sackcloth, to call to God with strength, and to turn from evil. Throughout, the decree treats animals on a par with human beings. The intent is not ridicule but respect, not parody but pathos. Nineveh cares for its animal population. Positing a link between the social and the animal order, the city symbolizes the cultivated earth.[47] An urban environment seeks the well-being of natural creatures.

At the close of the story, under the aegis of divine appointments, nature benevolent and malevolent instructs Jonah. A miraculous plant shades him; he delights in the plant (4:6). A worm kills the plant (4:7); he pities the plant (4:10). A fierce wind blows upon him, and the sun attacks his head; he faints and asks to die (4:8). Yahweh uses these experiences to argue divine pity for Nineveh. God describes the great city as a socionatural environment with humans by the thousands and animals galore. The deity acknowledges what the king knows: In issues of life and death, the animals of Nineveh matter alongside the people. On this strong ecological note, the book ends.

Justice Versus Mercy. Recent efforts to elucidate the theology of Jonah focus on the theme of justice versus mercy.[48] According to this view, Jonah the creature speaks for justice, which he finds violated in Yahweh's sparing of Nineveh (4:2). The city deserves punishment; no sudden repentance can compensate for its violence and evil. Yahweh the Creator speaks for mercy, which the deity freely gives to Nineveh. Despite Jonah's pronouncement (3:4), Yahweh has the sovereign right to do as the deity wills—in this case, to be gracious to whom God will be gracious (4:3; cf. Exod 33:19).

This theological formulation holds problems, beginning with the lack of any vocabulary for divine justice on the lips of Jonah—indeed, with the absence of the word "justice" (מִשְׁפָּט *mišpāṭ*) from the entire book. Jonah never frames his quarrel with God that way; he never accuses Yahweh of not being just. That view scholars deduce from his accusation that God is merciful (4:2). But objection to mercy does not necessarily mean approval of justice; it may signify, for instance, a desire for vengeance. Moreover, though the attributes of justice and mercy "are not necessarily synonymous,"[49] neither are they necessarily antonymous (cf. Mic 6:8).

If Jonah had wished to promote justice over against mercy, he might have quoted a different version of the credo. In proclaiming Yahweh "merciful and gracious," Exod 34:6-7 juxtaposes God's "forgiving iniquity . . . " with God who will "by no means [clear] the guilty,/ but [visit] the iniquity of the parents/ upon the children . . . to the third and fourth generation" (NRSV; cf. Num 14:18; Nah 1:2-3). In that version, mercy does not exclude judgment. Jonah might have charged, then, that Yahweh acted unjustly in sparing Nineveh, for the deity cleared the guilty rather than visit iniquity upon them. But Jonah does not quote that version, and he does not argue that way. The credo he recites says nothing about iniquity and punishment. It belongs instead to a countertradition (cf. Joel 2:13) that proclaims God "repenting of evil."[50] (The NIV renders the Hebrew "relents from sending calamity" and the NRSV "ready to relent from punishing.") In Ps 103:8-11, the tradition says outright that the "merciful and gracious" Yahweh "does not deal with us according to our sins nor repay us according to our iniquities." Jonah's appropriation of this tradition does not support the contention that he speaks for justice over against mercy.[51]

Another problem afflicts the juxtaposition of justice and mercy. These categories produce one-dimensional readings of both Jonah and God. Jonah becomes thereby the negative model and God the positive.[52] To be sure, abundant evidence discredits Jonah, but he is not altogether a static character. His behavior shifts from taciturn to loquacious and his mood from thanksgiving to delight to anger. Beyond his self-referential focus, Yahweh's attribution of pity to him (4:10) hints at a different facet of his character. The developing portrait of Jonah is not then totally negative. As for Yahweh, the portrait is not altogether positive. Though God repents of evil toward Nineveh, Yahweh endangers innocent sailors. The deity's hurling the great wind (1:4) displays neither justice nor mercy but menacing power. Like Jonah, Yahweh is not a one-dimensional character. Overall, the contrast between justice and mercy does not do justice to the theologies of the book.

A Narrative Scanning. Theologies at Sea. Yahweh first appears as a commanding presence bent on using Jonah to do the divine bidding. God is power, yet power defied. When Jonah disobeys, the deity replaces imperative speech with violent action. Yahweh summons nature to exact vengeance. The deity hurls a wind; it stirs a storm. So excessive is this fury for retaliation that it lashes out indiscriminately, endangering a thoughtful ship and innocent sailors. Although ignorant of the cause of the storm, the captain seeks a theological solution: "Perhaps" the god of Jonah will show favor "so that we do not perish" (1:6 NRSV). In recognizing the sovereign freedom of God, these words turn on irony. The deity from whom the captain seeks salvation is the very deity who threatens disaster. The irony builds when Jonah describes Yahweh as "God of heaven, who made the sea and the dry land" (1:9 NRSV). The traditional formula proclaims the creative power of God while the narrative itself presents the destructive power.

Jonah's orthodox theology evokes from the sailors great fear. The object of their fear is unspecified (1:10), but their experience is terrifying. The sea rages with increasing ferocity. So the sailors pray to the aggrieved and angry deity of Jonah. Asking that they not perish, they affirm the freedom of Yahweh to do as the deity pleases (1:14). The answer to their prayer follows their expelling Jonah to the sea. It ceases to rage. As the sailors respond with proper cultic acts, their fear transfers from the experience of the storm (1:5, 10) to the worship of Yahweh (1:16). After all, violent actions by this God have compelled them to make a human sacrifice in order to be spared a destruction they do not deserve. Divine wrath has manipulated human characters to achieve its end. Throughout the event Yahweh never even speaks to the sailors.

Appointing a fish to swallow Jonah, Yahweh continues to use nature against Jonah. Though the psalm he recites accents deliverance, a destructive portrait of the deity persists. Yahweh has cast Jonah into the sea, away from the divine presence (2:3-4). This coercive God next returns Jonah to dry land, there to confront him again with the commanding presence.

Chapters 1–2 assault characters and readers with conflicting portrayals of God. The creator vies with the destroyer, the punisher with the rescuer. Divine sovereignty and freedom spell vengeance, vindictiveness, and violence. That Yahweh should take cosmic action, hurling upon the sea a terrible wind all because puny Jonah had disobeyed, bespeaks crushing power. (Among other biblical characters, Job would surely understand what Jonah has stirred up.) The benign outcome for the sailors neither lessens nor justifies the use of nature to inflict indiscriminate suffering upon the innocent. This God is made of stern stuff, and it is not the stuff of justice or of mercy. Issues of theodicy flood these chapters.

Theologies in Nineveh. The second time around Yahweh wins over Jonah. Divine power overwhelms human disobedience. Jonah goes to Nineveh. The deity then withdraws to await the response of the Ninevites to Jonah's ambiguous pronouncement. Like the sailors, the Ninevites are god oriented; unlike the sailors, they are not innocent. The king himself acknowledges their evil and violence (3:8). Nonetheless, like the captain, he sounds a cautious note of hope based on a theological premise. If the captain appeals to the possible favor of God, the king appeals to the possible repentance: "Who knows? God may relent . . . so that we do not perish" (3:9 NRSV).

This premise introduces a theology of repentance, new to the story. It sets up a correlation, neither inevitable nor necessary, but yet possible, between human and divine turning. The repentance of the Ninevites may effect the repentance of God. And so it comes to pass. The Ninevites turn from evil; God turns from evil (3:10). In contrast to the dissonant theologies of chaps. 1–2, chap. 3 yields harmony. It works on a *quid pro quo* basis, an equal exchange between God and the people of Nineveh. Mutuality and reciprocity eliminate evil without resorting to punishment. Repentance substitutes for retribution. But the theology of repentance carries disturbing irony. Whereas the sailors experience the fury of Yahweh, the Ninevites experience the saving power.

Divine repentance angers Jonah. It provides the single verbal link to the credo he recites about God's being "gracious and merciful . . . repenting of evil" (4:2). Jonah does not question the authenticity of Nineveh's action; what bothers him is God's matching response. Yet in reciting the credo, Jonah expands the meaning of repentance beyond reciprocity. Rather than being just a correlary to Nineveh's repentance, God's repentance parallels God's mercy. Though different, the theologies of repentance and mercy work well together, binding parts of chapters 3 and 4. Each of them stands in bold contrast to the theologies of retribution and violence that characterize chapters 1 and 2. Strikingly, Jonah himself never complains about the latter, only about the former.

Theologies Beyond Nineveh. As the story moves to its ending, the theological mix becomes more dissonant. A series of natural appointments—plant, worm, and wind—achieves divine purposes. Once again destructive elements emerge within God. Yahweh does not show regard for the plant in its own right; a worm can destroy it with impunity. Just as Yahweh once hurled a great wind upon the sea because of Jonah's disobedience (1:4), so now the deity appoints a scorching wind to disturb Jonah and allows the sun to beat upon his head (4:8). The power of God to manipulate nature for weal or woe continues.

To each of the natural appointments Jonah responds. The first and third responses show him as self-centered. Shaded by the plant, he delights in it. Buffeted by the wind and beaten by the sun, he asks to die. In between, when the plant dies, his response is not reported. It emerges later to become the basis of yet another theology (cf. 4:7 with 4:10), and that theology upsets Jonah's orthodox understanding of mercy.

New vocabulary signals the new theology. In the last two verses of the book, Yahweh introduces the verb חוס (ḥûs) with Jonah and then the deity as subject. Most often translated "pity" or "show compassion" (though both the NIV and the NRSV use the weak word "concern"), the verb supplies Jonah's missing response in 4:7 to the death of the plant. He pitied the plant. Unlike the responses that surround it, this one is not self-centered.[53] The response of ḥûs signifies disinterested compassion. It shows that there is more to Jonah than Jonah has shown.

By analogy with Jonah, the verb ḥûs reports something new about Yahweh. The deity develops the argument through natural rather than revealed theology. It moves from the human to the divine, from the understandable to the mysterious, from Jonah's pity for the plant to Yahweh's pity for Nineveh. Alongside similarities, the argument through analogy carries dissimilarities. Jonah has no power over the plant. He can neither stop its destruction nor restore it to life. But he does pity the plant after its demise. By contrast, Yahweh's pity for Nineveh prevents the city's demise. The deity has total power over the city and its outcome. In exercising that sovereignty, Yahweh acts in a way new to the story. Yet the deity accounts for ḥûs not through divine revelation but through human sensibility for the natural world. Jonah's ḥûs argues for Yahweh's ḥûs. If the analogy is flawed, nonetheless the argument moves the story to another level of theological insight.

In the movement Yahweh acknowledges for the first time a non-utilitarian view of nature. Jonah pities the plant as a plant. His disinterested compassion forms the premise for Yahweh's disinterested compassion in Nineveh. So Yahweh characterizes the city not according to its evil, to its deeds, and to its repentance (see 3:10), but according to its size, to its ignorance, and to its animals. And Yahweh pities these animals as animals. Unlike the fish and the worm, they are not instruments of divine power. "Pity" (ḥûs), then, signals a new theology of ecology. If earlier the Ninevites understood the integrity of the animal creation (3:7-8), now Yahweh embraces that understanding.

The theology of 4:10-11 differs from repentance, mercy, and their interplay (though it is compatible with them).[54] As vocabulary new to the story, ḥûs distinguishes this understanding of Yahweh from the attributes cited in the credo. Yahweh shows compassion on the city not because it repents but because Yahweh chooses to show compassion on it. The story yields then two theologies of grace. If the first is understandable, the second is inexplicable; it does not fit the orthodox credo. Indeed, it is even more incredulous (qal wāḥōmer)[55] than Jonah's compassion for the plant. In this move from understandable to inexplicable mercy, Yahweh the creator affirms a sovereignty and freedom that borders on caprice. And if on this occasion caprice is compassion, what guarantee does Yahweh give that, on another occasion, it will not be destruction?[56] (Again, Job would understand well Jonah's plight.)[57]

Summary. Despite scholarly propensities to derive one consistent message from Jonah, the book reverberates with a cacophony of theologies.[58] Sovereignty, freedom, creation, retribution, vindictiveness, violence, repentance, mercy, pity, and caprice sound major dissonances. Though at places the harshness fades into harmony (primarily chap. 3), as a whole the disjunctions prevail. Yet they belong to a unified composition exquisitely wrought. Rather than taming the dissonances to produce a single theology, those interpretations that allow them to flourish witness best to the story—and to its God.

PURPOSE

The purpose of the Jonah narrative is not known. Far from deterring speculations, however, that ignorance has encouraged them. Two flaws characterize most efforts: tying the purpose to a presumed date and concentrating on parts of the story as if they equal the whole. A survey of major proposals shows the possibilities and limitations of the subject.

Israel and the Nations. The older view that Jonah espouses universalism to combat the nationalism and exclusionism fostered by the reforms of Ezra and Nehemiah has withered for lack of evidence.[59] The book contains no allusions to the reform measures of the fifth century BCE, nor does it portray Jonah as a nationalist. Its universalism is not an attack on Israel; its tone is not polemical; its contents do not report enmity between Israel and the Gentiles.[60] Correspondingly, the book is not a missionary tract to convert non-Israelites. Jonah does not disparage the gods of the sailors or try to make them Yahweh worshipers. Even when, after the storm, they worship Yahweh, they do not repudiate their own gods. Furthermore, the report on the repentance of the Ninevites says nothing about their conversion to Yahwism. The theological vocabulary of chapter 3 restricts itself to the generic term אלהים (ĕlōhîm, "god"). Unlike Second Isaiah, for instance, Jonah does not denounce foreign deities or proclaim Yahweh as the only God (cf. Isa 44:9-20; 45:14-25). Neither the theme of polemic against nationalistic Israel nor that of conversion for the nations accounts for the purpose of the book.

Although disavowing these particular formulations, some recent attempts sound related ideas. Ackerman thinks Jonah is designed to help Jews in Jerusalem recover from the Babylonian exile, to help them reckon with the apparent injustice of God toward their nation in relation to other nations that have not been punished for even greater sins.[61] Fretheim envisions a despairing and even cynical post-exilic community in Jerusalem, dismayed that the God who has let it down nonetheless requires it to give hope to the enemy.[62] Gitay proposes that the story aims to prepare the way theologically for cooperation with foreign rulers during the Babylonian and Persian periods.[63] Allen writes of a "self-centered" post-exilic community whom the book challenges "to face up to the unwelcome truth of God's sovereign compassion for foreigners and beasts."[64] Wolff thinks that Jonah seeks to overcome through irony the "gloomy concern" with themselves of the Jews in the Hellenistic period and so to effect "the assent of the religious egoist to Yhwh's pity for all human beings."[65] Despite scant evidence for all such dates and statements of purpose, their tenacity perdures.

Unfulfilled Prophecy. Another approach holds that Jonah proposes to address the issue of unfulfilled prophecy. Bickerman contrasts Jeremiah's view that human repentance effects divine repentance with Jonah's view that God's word of doom, once spoken, must not be changed.[66] The book of Jonah then surmounts this antithesis. Although Jeremiah and other prophets predicted that God would destroy Jerusalem, a prediction that came to pass, the author of Jonah teaches "the restored and still sinful city" that if God can spare Nineveh, there is yet hope for the salvation of Jerusalem. Rofé adopts a similar reading.[67] Surveying views about the fulfillment of prophecy found in Deuteronomy, Kings, Jeremiah, and Ezekiel, he concludes that the book of Jonah fits this milieu. Yahweh's salvation of Nineveh confirms Jonah in his previous knowledge that, even though he would like Yahweh to keep the divine word, Yahweh repents of evil. Thus Nineveh has a right to exist, apart from the fulfillment of prophecy.[68]

Repentance. Still another approach subordinates unfulfilled prophecy to the theme of repentance. The possibility of repentance mitigates any absolute declaration of destruction. In developing this idea, Clements finds parallels between Jonah and Jeremiah, Ezekiel, and the deuteronomic history.[69] He argues that, in the aftermath of the exile, many leaders asserted the necessity of repentance as the key to Israel's future. Belonging to the same theological scene, the book of Jonah teaches, through the use of Nineveh, this possibility for Israel. The purpose is to show that human repentance elicits divine repentance.

Efforts to locate purpose in the issues of unfulfilled prophecy and repentance underscore important themes that nevertheless fail to encompass the book. They substitute parts for the whole. From the beginning of the sea story in chapter 1 through the expulsion of Jonah from the fish at the end of chapter 2, neither prophecy nor repentance surfaces as a concern. The vocabulary of repentance appears only in chapter 3 and in 4:2. Chapter 4 does not consider the pronouncement of Jonah (3:4), the repentance of Nineveh, or the issue of unfulfilled prophecy. Indeed, at no place does the book even use the word "prophecy." Parts of Jonah may contribute to these topics, but the topics do not themselves define its purpose.

Rejection of Purpose. Certain literary approaches to Jonah question the value or validity of specifying its purpose. Clines proposes that if readers view the book of Jonah as a story, they can relax about seeking its intent. The book may "have nothing in particular to 'teach' but be an imaginative story . . . in which various serious concerns of the author are lightly and teasingly sketched."[70] (But then to sketch these concerns becomes itself a purpose.) Craig acknowledges that the book is "highly charged ideological literature," but he, too, takes pains to deny it a didactic purpose. Instead, it is polyphonic literature in which "several independent and legitimate points of view . . . work and often struggle together to assert themselves." Craig's rejection of the word "didactic" rests on assigning it the meanings of "militaristic" and "doctrinal." Yet he writes that near the end of the story Yahweh offers Jonah "a practical lesson" (itself a didactic word) whose outcome eschews rational coherence to present "the mystery of divine compassion."[71]

Conclusion. The book of Jonah does not disclose its purpose, and speculation has not secured it. This uncertainty matches the meager knowledge about its origin, date, composition, genre, and setting. Nonetheless, the book offers an abundance of literary treasures, theological complexities, and hermeneutical possibilities. It lends itself to multiple uses and readings in a variety of settings and for a variety of purposes.[72] Interpretations that remain faithful to the diversities and the mysteries best convey the challenges that this cacophonous story provides contemporary communities of faith.

FOR FURTHER READING

Commentaries:

Allen, Leslie C. *The Books of Joel, Obadiah, Jonah and Micah.* Grand Rapids: Eerdmans, 1976.

Limburg, James. *Jonah.* OTL. Louisville: Westminster/John Knox, 1993.

Sasson, Jack M. *Jonah.* AB 24B. New York: Doubleday, 1990.

Simon, Uriel. *Jonah.* Translated by Lenn J. Schramm. JPS Torah Commentary. Philadelphia: Jewish Publication Society, 1999.

Wolff, Hans Walter. *Obadiah and Jonah.* Translated by Margaret Kohl. Minneapolis: Augsburg, 1977.

Other Studies:

Ben Zvi, Ehud. *Signs of Jonah: Reading and Rereading in Ancient Yehud.* JSOTSup 367. Sheffield: Sheffield Academic Press, 2003.

Craig, Kenneth M., Jr. *A Poetics of Jonah: Art in the Service of Ideology.* Columbia: University of South Carolina Press, 1993.

Fretheim, Terence E. *The Message of Jonah: A Theological Commentary.* Minneapolis: Augsburg, 1977.

Gaines, Janet Howe. *Forgiveness in a Wounded World: Jonah's Dilemma.* Studies in Biblical Literature 5. Atlanta: Society of Biblical Literature, 2003.

Magonet, Jonathan. *Form and Meaning: Studies in Literary Techniques in the Book of Jonah.* BLS 8. Sheffield: Almond, 1983.

Sherwood, Yvonne. *A Biblical Text and Its Afterlives: The Survival of Jonah in Western Culture.* Cambridge: Cambridge University Press, 2000.

Trible, Phyllis. *Rhetorical Criticism: Context, Method, and the Book of Jonah.* GBS.OTS. Minneapolis: Fortress, 1994.

ENDNOTES

1. Efforts to solve the problem have not fully succeeded. For bibliography and critique, see Phyllis Lou Trible, "Studies in the Book of Jonah" (Ph.D. diss., Columbia University, 1963; University Microfilm International, order no. 65-7479) 82-87; Jack M. Sasson, *Jonah,* AB 24B (New York: Doubleday, 1990) 17-18.

2. For a summary of the controversy through the 1950s, see Phyllis Lou Trible, "Studies in the Book of Jonah," 75-82. For more recent discussions, see, e.g., George M. Landes, "The Kerygma of the Book of Jonah," *Int.* 21 (1967) 3-31; G. H. Cohn, *Das buch Jona im Lichte der biblischen Erzählkunst,* SSN 12 (Assen: Van Gorcum, 1969) 25-26, 92-94; James S. Ackerman, "Satire and Symbolism in the Song of Jonah," in *Traditions in Transformation,* ed. Baruch Halpern and Jon D. Levenson (Winona Lake, Ind.: Eisenbrauns, 1981) 213-46; Jonathan Magonet, *Form and Meaning: Studies in Literary Techniques in the Book of Jonah,* BLS 8 (Sheffield: Almond, 1983) 39-54; Hans Walter Wolff, *Obadiah and Jonah,* trans. Margaret Kohl (Minneapolis: Augsburg, 1986) 128-32, 140-42.

3. Gottfried Vanoni, *Das Buch Jona: Literar-und formkritische Untersuchung* (St. Ottilien: Eos Verlag, 1978) 29-35; James Limburg, *Jonah: A Commentary,* OTL (Louisville: Westminster/John Knox, 1993) 31-33.

4. George M. Landes, "The Kerygma of the Book of Jonah," 16-18, 25-30; Phyllis Lou Trible, "Studies in the Book of Jonah," 184-92.

5. Jack M. Sasson, *Jonah,* 203-4.

6. E.g., George M. Landes, "The Kerygma of the Book of Jonah," and James Limburg, *Jonah: A Commentary,* 31-33.

7. See George M. Landes, "Jonah, Book of," in *The Interpreter's Dictionary of the Bible, Supplementary Volume* (IDBSup) (Nashville: Abingdon, 1976) 490.

8. A sampling of proposals covers the gamut. For the eighth century, see G. F. Hasel, *Jonah, Messenger of the Eleventh Hour* (Mountain View, Calif.: Pacific Publishing Assn., 1976) 95-98; Yehezkel Kaufmann, *The Religion of Israel*, trans. Moshe Greenberg (New York: Schocken, 1972) 282-86. For the seventh century, see E. F. C. Rosenmüller, *Prophetae Minores* (1827) 344-47. For the sixth century, see George M. Landes, "Linguistic Criteria and the Date of the Book of Jonah," *Eretz Israel* 16 (1982) 147-70. For the fifth century, see Elias Bickerman, *Four Strange Books of the Bible* (New York: Schocken, 1967) 29; Terence E. Fretheim, *The Message of Jonah* (Minneapolis: Augsburg, 1977) 34-37. For the fifth or fourth century, see Leslie C. Allen, *The Books of Joel, Obadiah, Jonah, and Micah*, NICOT (Grand Rapids: Eerdmans, 1976) 185-88. For the fourth or third century, see Hans Walter Wolff, *Obadiah and Jonah: A Commentary*, 76-78. For the third century, see Frederick Carl Eiselen, *The Prophetic Books of the Old Testament*, vol. 2 (New York: The Methodist Book Concern, 1923) 462-67; Andre Lacocque and Pierre-Emmanuel Lacocque, *Jonah: A Psycho-Religious Approach to the Prophet* (Columbia: University of South Carolina Press, 1990) 26-48.

9. Gerhard von Rad, *Old Testament Theology*, 2 vols., trans. D. M. G. Stalker (New York: Harper & Row, 1962, 1965) 2:291-92.

10. James Limburg, *Jonah: A Commentary*, 31.

11. Jack M. Sasson, *Jonah*, 27-28. George M. Landes now concurs that Jonah cannot be dated with precision; see his review of Sasson's book in *JBL* 111 (1992) 130.

12. See Hermann Gunkel, *The Folktale in the Old Testament*, trans. Michael D. Rutter with intro. by John W. Rogerson (Sheffield: Almond, 1987); Stith Thompson, *The Folktale* (Berkeley: University of California Press, 1977); V. Propp, *Morphology of the Folktale*, trans. Laurence Scott, 2nd rev. ed., ed. Louis A. Wagner with intro. by Alan Dundes (Austin: University of Texas Press, 1973); Patricia G. Kirkpatrick, *The Old Testament and Folklore Study*, JSOTSup 62 (Sheffield: JSOT, 1988).

13. For a fuller exposition, see Phyllis Lou Trible, "Studies in the Book of Jonah," 144-52.

14. See E. Hardy, "Jona c. 1 und Jit. 439," *ZDMG* 50 (1896) 153.

15. Carlo Collodi, *The Pinocchio of E. Collodi*, trans. and annotated James T. Teahan (New York: Schocken, 1985).

16. See Phyllis Lou Trible, "Studies in the Book of Jonah," 147-49; for other parallels, cf. Elias Bickerman, *Four Strange Books of the Bible* 9-49.

17. See esp. *The Complete Fairy Tales of the Brothers Grimm*, trans. with intro. by Jack Zipes (New York: Bantam, 1992).

18. See Phyllis Lou Trible, "Studies in the Book of Jonah," 150-51; for other parallels, see Elias Bickerman, *Four Strange Books of the Bible*, 9-49.

19. See George M. Landes, "Jonah: A Māšāl?" in *Israelite Wisdom: Theological and Literary Essays in Honor of Samuel Terrien*, ed. John G. Gammie et al., (Missoula, Mont.: Scholars Press, 1978) 137-46.

20. See George M. Landes, "Jonah: A Māšāl?", ed. John G. Gammie et al., (Missoula, Mont.: Scholars Press, 1978), 146-49.

21. Jack M. Sasson, *Jonah*, 335-37.

22. See Leslie C. Allen, *The Books of Joel, Obadiah, Jonah and Micah*, 175-81, who draws upon the redefinition of parable given by Dan Otto Via, Jr., *The Parables* (Philadelphia: Fortress, 1967) 2-25.

23. On natural extravagances, see Mary Ann Tolbert, *Perspectives on the Parables* (Philadelphia: Fortress, 1979) 89-91.

24. For the older understanding of parable as a simple story with a central point and its inapplicability to Jonah, see Phyllis Lou Trible, "Studies in the Book of Jonah" 158-61.

25. See Brevard S. Childs, *Introduction to the Old Testament as Scripture* (Philadelphia: Fortress, 1979) 419, 421-22.

26. See Northrop Frye, *Anatomy of Criticism: Four Essays* (Princeton, N.J.: Princeton University Press, 1957, 1971) 223-39; Gilbert Highet, *The Anatomy of Satire* (Princeton, N.J.: Princeton University Press, 1962); Leonard Feinberg, *Introduction to Satire* (Ames: Iowa State University Press, 1967).

27. For the sketch provided here, see David Marcus, *From Balaam to Jonah: Anti-prophetic Satire in the Hebrew Bible* (Atlanta: Scholars Press, 1995) 1-27, 93-159; Millar Burrows, "The Literary Category

of the Book of Jonah," in *Translating and Understanding the Old Testament*, ed. Harry Thomas Frank and William L. Reed (Nashville: Abingdon, 1970) 80-107; James S. Ackerman, "Satire and Symbolism in the Song of Jonah," in *Traditions in Transformation*, ed. Baruch Halpern and Jon D. Levenson (Winona Lake, Ind.: Eisenbrauns, 1981) 227-29; cf. Andre Lacocque and Pierre-Emmanuel Lacocque, *Jonah: A Psycho-Religious Approach to the Prophet* 26-48.

28. See, e.g., Burrows, "The Literary Category of the Book of Jonah," 99; David Marcus, *From Balaam to Jonah: Anti-prophetic Satire in the Hebrew Bible*, 117-19.

29. For contrasting points of view, cf. Jack M. Sasson, *Jonah*, 329-40, esp. 331, with R. P. Carroll, "Is Humor Also Among the Prophets?" in *On Humour and the Comic in the Hebrew Bible*, ed. Yehuda T. Radday and Athalya Brenner, JSOTSup 92 (Sheffield: Almond, 1990) 169-89, esp. 171, 180-81, and with Judson Mather, "The Comic Art of the Book of Jonah," *Soundings* 65 (1982) 280-91.

30. Note the tension in the claim by Marcus that the book is "a satire on the prophet himself" and the acknowledgment that "the Ninevites are also ridiculed." Is the target, then, so "clearly defined?" (David Marcus, *From Balaam to Jonah*, 95, 121-22, 158, etc.).

31. See Jack M. Sasson, *Jonah*, 331-34, and George M. Landes, review of Lacocque and Lacocque, *Jonah: A Psycho-Religious Approach to the Prophet*, *JBL* 111 (1992) 131. On the related, yet distinct, genre of parody, see John A. Miles, Jr., "Laughing at the Bible: Jonah as Parody," *JQR* (New Series) 65 (1975) 168-81; cf. Adele Berlin, "A Rejoinder to John A. Miles, Jr., with Some Observations on the Nature of Prophecy," *JQR* (New Series) 66 (1976) 227-35. See also Arnold J. Band, "Swallowing Jonah: The Eclipse of Parody," *Prooftexts* (1990) 177-95.

32. On midrash, see Renée Bloch, "Midrash," *Dictionnaire de la Bible*, Supplement 5 (Paris: Librairie Letouzey et Ane, 1957) cols. 1263-1281; Addison G. Wright, *The Literary Genre Midrash* (Staten Island, N.Y.: Alba House, 1967); H. L. Strack and G. Stemberger, *Introduction to the Talmud and Midrash* (Minneapolis: Fortress, 1992) 254-68.

33. Karl Budde, "Vermutungen zum 'Midrasch des Büches der Könige,'" *ZAW* 12 (1892) 37-51.

34. E.g., A. Feuillet, "Les Sources du Livre de Jonas," *RB* 54 (1947) 161-86; A. Robert and A. Tri-cot, *Guide to the Bible I*, trans. Edward P. Arbez and Martin R. P. McGuire (New York: Desclee, 1960) 506.

35. See Phyllis Lou Trible, "Studies in the Book of Jonah," 167-68; 273-79.

36. Exodus 34:6-7 is the earliest formulation. Others include Num 14:18; Deut 7:8-10; 2 Chr 30:9; Neh 9:17, 31; Pss 86:5, 15; 103:8; 111:4; 112:4; 145:8; Joel 2:13; Nah 1:3; Neh 9:17, 31. For comparisons, see Gottfried Vanoni, *Das Buch Jona: Literar-und formkritische Untersuchung* (St. Ottilien: Eos Verlag, 1978) 138-41; Jack M. Sasson, *Jonah*, 280-83; Michael Fishbane, *Biblical Interpretation in Ancient Israel* (Oxford: Clarendon, 1985) 335-50; Thomas B. Dozeman, "Inner-Biblical Interpretation of Yahweh's Gracious and Compassionate Character," *JBL* 108 (1989) 207-23; James L. Crenshaw, *Joel*, AB 24C (New York: Doubleday, 1995) 135-38.

37. See Shaye J. D. Cohen, *From the Maccabees to the Mishnah* (Philadelphia: Westminster, 1987) 204-9.

38. On the phrase "a second time" (שֵׁנִית *šēnît*) as the introduction to parallel units, cf. Gen 22:11 and 22:15.

39. For a full discussion, see Phyllis Lou Trible, "Studies in the Book of Jonah" 184-202; Phyllis Trible, *Rhetorical Criticism: Context, Method, and the Book of Jonah* (Minneapolis: Fortress, 1994) 107-22. Cf. Kenneth M. Craig, Jr., *A Poetics of Jonah: Art in the Service of Ideology* (Columbia: University of South Carolina Press, 1993); Herbert Chanan Brichto, "'And Much Cattle': YHWH's Last Words to a Reluctant Prophet," in *Toward a Grammar of Biblical Poetics* (New York: Oxford University Press, 1992) 67-87.

40. See chart in Trible, *Rhetorical Criticism*, 110-11.

41. See Baruch Halpern and Richard Elliott Friedman, "Composition and Paronomasia in the Book of Jonah," *HAR* 4 (1980) 79-92.

42. See Bruce K. Waltke and M. O'Connor, *An Introduction to Biblical Hebrew Syntax* (Winona Lake, Ind.: Eisenbrauns, 1990) 96-110.

43. For proposals, see Jack M. Sasson, *Jonah*, 155-57.

44. In a quasi-Jungian reading, Ackerman uses the recesses of the ship, the belly of the fish, and the womb of Sheol, along with Nineveh (3:4-10) and the booth (4:5), to argue that Jonah repeatedly seeks

shelters that give him a "womb/death-like security" (James S. Ackerman, "Satire and Symbolism in the Song of Jonah," 239-43). In its concern with archetypal rather than metaphorical concepts, that reading diverges from the one proposed here. Neither Nineveh nor the booth offers a womblike metaphor. Nineveh is not described as an enclosed or walled city. Although the booth ostensibly provides Jonah shade as he sits under it, it need not be an enclosed space. Furthermore, Jonah himself builds the booth, unlike the ship, the fish, and Sheol. Again unlike them, the booth occupies the surface of the land; it does not yield imagery of the depths.

45. For Jonah as a reflection on prophets and prophecy, see Amos Funkenstein, *Perceptions of Jewish History* (Berkeley: University of California Press, 1993) 64-70. Cf. Band's view that the book is a parody on a prophet's career that over time got reinterpreted to become the reverse—namely, "a prophetic book with a prophetic message" (Arnold J. Band, "Swallowing Jonah: The Eclipse of Parody," esp. 191-94).

46. Cf. the proposal that Nineveh in the book of Jonah be viewed through the lens of the Hellenistic rather than the ancient Near Eastern world. See Thomas M. Bolin, "'Should I Not Also Pity Nineveh?' Divine Freedom in the Book of Jonah," *JSOT* 67 (1995) 109-20. This proposal is tied to the unstable assumption of a late date for Jonah.

47. See Funkenstein, *Perceptions of Jewish History*, 66.

48. See, e.g., James S. Ackerman, "Jonah," in *The Literary Guide to the Bible*, ed. Robert Alter and Frank Kermode (Cambridge: Belknap, 1987) 240-42; Athalya Brenner, "Jonah's Poem Out of and Within Its Context," in *Among the Prophets: Language, Image and Structure in the Prophetic Writings*, ed. Philip R. Davies and David J. A. Clines, JSOTSup 144 (Sheffield: JSOT, 1993) 190-92. A variation of this view contrasts justice and sovereignty; see Terence E. Fretheim, "Jonah and Theodicy," *ZAW* 90 (1978) 227-37; Jonathan Magonet, *Form and Meaning: Studies in Literary Techniques in the Book of Jonah*, 107-12.

49. See Jack M. Sasson, *Jonah*, 316.

50. See Thomas B. Dozeman, "Inner-Biblical Interpretation of Yahweh's Gracious and Compassionate Character," 207-23.

51. See David Marcus, *From Balaam to Jonah: Anti-prophetic Satire in the Hebrew Bible*, 156; cf.

Yehezkel Kaufmann, *The Religion of Israel*, 282-86, who understands that Jonah's formulation contrasts with that of Exod 34:6-7 but still describes the theological issue of the book as "justice versus mercy."

52. See e.g., Althalya Brenner, "Jonah's Poem Out of and Within Its Context," 191-92; cf. George M. Landes, "Jonah: A Māšāl?" in *Israelite Wisdom*, ed. John G. Gammie et al. (Missoula, Mont.: Scholars Press, 1978) 149.

53. Contra Herbert Chanan Brichto, " 'And Much Cattle': YHWH's Last Words to a Reluctant Prophet," 78-79.

54. See Hans Walter Wolff, *Obadiah and Jonah*, 87; Elias Bickerman, *Four Strange Books of the Bible*, 44; David Noel Freedman, "Did God Play a Dirty Trick on Jonah at the End?" *BR* 6 (1990) 26-31; Kenneth M. Craig, Jr., *A Poetics of Jonah: Art in the Service of Ideology* (Columbia: University of South Carolina Press, 1993) 158-59.

55. The rabbinic phrase *qal wāhōmer* signifies an argument "all the more" (*a fortiori*) than the one from which it precedes. The argument moves from the small to the great (*ad minori ad maius*). See L. Jacobs, "The *Qal Va-homer* Argument in the Old Testament," *BSO(A)S* 35 (1972) 221-27.

56. Cooper moves the argument for divine caprice in 4:10-11 toward God's destructive wrath. See Alan Cooper, "In Praise of Divine Caprice: The Significance of the Book of Jonah," in *Among the Prophets: Language, Image and Structure in the Prophetic Writings*, ed. Philip R. Davies and David J. A. Clines (Sheffield: JSOT, 1993) 144-63. See also Thomas M. Bolin, " 'Should I Not Also Pity Nineveh?' Divine Freedom in the Book of Jonah," *JSOT* 67 (1995) esp. 117-20.

57. The relationship of Jonah to wisdom theologies, especially to Job, remains an undeveloped topic. See Hans Walter Wolff, *Jonah*, 87; Leslie C. Allen, *The Books of Joel, Obadiah, Jonah, and Micah*, 191.

58. Cf. Hans Walter Wolff, *Jonah*: "The writer is not a systematic theologian" (87-88).

59. See R. E. Clements, "The Purpose of the Book of Jonah," VTSup 28 (Leiden: E. J. Brill, 1975) 16-20; cf. Yehezkel Kaufmann, *The Religion of Israel*, 282-83.

60. See Elias Bickerman, *Four Strange Books of the Bible*, 14-28.

61. See James S. Ackerman, "Jonah," 234, 242.

62. See Terence E. Fretheim, *The Message of Jonah* (Minneapolis: Augsburg, 1977) 190-91.

63. See Yehoshua Gitay, "Jonah: The Prophecy of Anti-rhetoric," in *Fortunate the Eyes That See*, ed. Astrid B. Beck et al. (Grand Rapids: Eerdmanns, 1995) 203-6.

64. See Leslie C. Allen, *The Books of Joel, Obadiah, Jonah and Micah*, 190-91.

65. See Hans Walter Wolff, *Obadiah and Jonah: A Commentary*, 86.

66. See Elias Bickerman, *Four Strange Books of the Bible* (New York: Schocken, 1967) 38-45.

67. See Alexander Rofé, "Classes in the Prophetical Stories: Didactic Legend and Parable," VTSup 26 (1974) 155-57.

68. Cf. Childs, who posits two editions for the book. The first ties the purpose of accounting for unfulfilled prophecy to the right of the Creator to let mercy override prophecy for the sake of the entire creation; the second amplifies creation theology in terms of the nations, with Nineveh as the case study. Brevard S. Childs, *Introduction to the Old Testament as Scripture*, 421-26.

69. See R. E. Clements, "The Purpose of the Book of Jonah," 20-21.

70. See David J. A. Clines, "Story and Poem: The Old Testament as Literature and as Scripture," *Int.* 34 (1980) 119. Cf. Marcus, who says that "no message is advocated; rather Jonah himself is satirized" (*From Balaam to Jonah: Anti-prophetic Satire in the Hebrew Bible*, 156-58).

71. See Kenneth M. Craig, Jr., *A Poetics of Jonah: Art in the Service of Ideology*, 159-65.

72. Cf. Jack M. Sasson, *Jonah*, 326.

THE BOOK OF
MICAH

DANIEL J. SIMUNDSON

The book of Micah, attributed to an eighth-century Judean prophet, numbers sixth among the twelve minor prophets. Like some other brief biblical books, it is sometimes overlooked. Many Christians are familiar with certain verses from Micah, yet they may not be aware of their source. The promise of a time of peace when nations will "beat their swords into plowshares" (Mic 4:3), the prophecy about a new ruler to come from the town of Bethlehem (5:2), and the response to the question of what the Lord requires of them, signal Micah's importance. But the book also contains other riches worthy of serious study by those wishing to grow in knowledge of Micah's world and of the God whose words the prophet claims to proclaim.

THE PROPHET
AND HIS HISTORICAL SETTING

We know very little about the prophet Micah (whose name means "Who is like [Yahweh]?"). A superscription (1:1) associates him with the reigns of three Judean kings: Jotham (742–735 BCE), Ahaz (735–715), and Hezekiah (715–687). Perhaps he was a younger contemporary of the prophet Isaiah. Unlike Jerusalem Isaiah, however, Micah was from Moresheth, a small village lying southwest of Judah's capital city.

Despite its paucity of explicit biographical information, the collection bearing Micah's name discloses something of the prophet's theology and religious fervor: his identification with the poor and oppressed (e.g., 2:9); the certainty that he had been called to prophesy by Yahweh (3:8); and his anger at the Judean leaders responsible for Jerusalem's impending doom (Micah 3). A century later, when the prophet Jeremiah predicted the destruction of Jerusalem and its temple, certain elders of the land quoted Micah's oracle (Mic 3:12) about Jerusalem's demise (Jer 26:18-19). They reminded their audience that King Hezekiah heeded Micah's prophecy and turned to the Lord, averting the disaster that he had predicted. Perhaps the people should likewise take seriously what Jeremiah was saying.

Scholars have attempted to identify the period of Micah's prophetic ministry more specifically. The consensus is that his earliest prophecies preceded the destruction of the city of Samaria and the fall of the northern kingdom of Israel in 722 (1:6-7)[1]. Some have suggested that he began to prophesy in the 730's, though not earlier.[2] Most scholars have associated his threats to the city of Jerusalem with Sennacherib's invasion in 701 BCE, although a minority would confine his career to a shorter span, ending perhaps within a decade after it had begun.[3]

The latter half of the eighth century BCE was a time of great transition. In the first half of that century, both Judah and Israel prospered because the great powers of the ancient Near East, preoccupied with other matters, did not torment them. That situation changed very rapidly after 746, however, when Tiglath-pileser III came to power in Assyria. A succession of short and unsuccessful kingships, foolhardy efforts at rebellion, and the resurgence of Assyrian power in the region led to the fall of the northern kingdom of Israel and its capital city, Samaria, in 722 BCE. Judah avoided a similar fate but paid a high price for its subservience to Assyria—huge tributes, loss of complete independence, and corruption of its traditions by the incorporation of religious practices of the dominant foreign power. Into this time of great change, when the fortunes of God's people had already declined and promised to get even worse, Micah stepped forward to provide a theological interpretation of crucial events facing the nation and its people.

The situation of ordinary citizens was of great concern to Micah. He felt compassion for the poor and dispossessed, and held the leaders responsible for their suffering. We can learn something about the people's social and economic situation from Micah's condemnation of their rulers, merchants, and prophets. Similar words from Micah's contemporary, Isaiah, add to our picture of a society where the rich and powerful used their influence to exploit the vulnerable and to create even greater inequalities of wealth and influence (e.g., Isa 5:8-10; 10:1-2). The economic situation of the poor was further aggravated by programs of armament and fortification in efforts to hold off the threat from foreign empires (see 2 Chronicles 32). The tribute demanded by Assyria from its vassal states also added to the problem. The wealth needed to buy off Assyria had to come from someone, and the poor surely paid more than their share. Further, Jerusalem grew in population at about this time, probably as a result of a large influx of refugees after the fall of Samaria. Archaeological evidence provides limited verification of this picture, which is drawn mostly from biblical material.[4] Chapters 16–19 of 2 Kings provide further details about this time of historical upheaval from the perspective of the deuteronomic historian.

LITERARY CONCERNS

Like other OT books, Micah has been carefully examined by biblical scholars using the methods of analysis common to the trade. Specialists have been, and many still are, preoccupied with matters of authorship and history of composition (redaction).[5] Conservative scholars have tended to attribute to Micah as much of the book as is rationally possible. A majority of scholars, however, have ascribed most of chaps. 1–3, but very little of chaps. 4–7, to Micah (perhaps some verses in chap. 6, and 7:1-7, but virtually nothing in 4–5). The challenge, as they see it, is to locate post-Micah materials in specific times and places and to trace the gradual growth of the book. More recently certain literary approaches, including rhetorical criticism, have encouraged scholars to bracket questions of original authorship and redaction history and to concentrate on interpreting the book as a whole in its final, canonical form.

With the exception of its superscription (1:1), the book of Micah consists of poetry, not prose. Characteristic features of Hebrew poetry—e.g.,

synonymous parallelism (the repetition of a thought, albeit with important variations in vocabulary, grammatical forms, and syntax; see, for example 3:6), traditional word pairs, metaphors, and similes—appear throughout the book.

Scholars interested in form criticism find examples of many literary genres in the book of Micah: judgment and salvation oracles, lament, lawsuit, disputation speech, prayer, and hymn. The prophet used these various forms drawn from different aspects of life to shape, enliven, and intensify the important messages that he felt called to speak. Many scholars question whether Micah ever spoke the promises of salvation contained in the collection. If his primary calling was to warn of impending doom (as suggested by Jer 26:18), would he have diluted the urgency of that message by concomitantly proclaiming words of hope? Would doing so soften his message, allowing listeners who should repent to fall back on a false security that God would never abandon them after all? We will ponder these questions as we move through the book of Micah.

Efforts to find some unifying principle for the present organization of the book of Micah have led to a number of suggestions. Although shorter units are generally isolated without much difficulty, the task of identifying major structural divisions has proven elusive. The book seems more a collection of materials than a carefully planned, coherent work. Abrupt transitions, sudden shifts between condemnation and promise, and alternations in personal pronouns and gender abound. Yet even scholars who do not discern much overall coherence in Micah must decide how to divide the book into major parts for their analysis of its content. In general, four basic ways to divide the book have emerged.

(1) At first glance, Micah seems to divide into three parts: Chapters 1–3 consist of brief words of judgment against Samaria and oracles against Jerusalem (except for words of promise in 2:12-13); chaps. 4–5 contain words of salvation (except for more hard words of judgment in 4:9-10; 5:10-15); and chaps. 6–7 are a mixture of judgment oracles, leading finally to hope. For this introduction, we will divide Micah into these three major units, although this division leaves some problems with the intrusion of salvation promises in the first section and more judgment

oracles in the second section. Many scholars who have divided Micah in this way have assumed that the prophet spoke only judgment oracles and that, therefore, most of what is authentic to Micah appears in the first three chapters.

(2) Several scholars argue in favor of dividing Micah into the following three major units: chaps. 1–2; 3–5; and 6–7. Each section begins with the imperative "hear," indicating the beginning of a major structural unit. Further, each of these three units moves from judgment to hope, a rather common flow seen often in biblical materials. The imperative "hear" also appears in 3:9 and 6:9, but these occurrences are considered by proponents of this view to be of secondary structural importance, echoing 3:1 and 6:1.[6] This way of making sense out of the overall structure of Micah has a certain appeal, though it seems not to deal adequately with the apparent major break between chapters 3 and 4.

(3) Another alternative is to divide the book into two major parts: chaps. 1–5 and 6–7. Again, both of these sections begin with "hear." Further, both begin with a lawsuit in which the prosecutor makes a case against the accused. Mays suggests that the first section is addressed to all nations, offering them a choice between submission and punishment. The second section is addressed to Israel.[7]

(4) A further way to divide Micah entails separating 7:8-20 as a closing liturgy spoken by the people. The other divisions remain the same as in the first hypothesis: Chapters 1–3 expose guilt and pronounce judgment with a brief interpolation in 2:12-13; chaps. 4–5 promise future salvation for Jerusalem and Israel; 6:1–7:7 is the work of a post-exilic social critic making a contemporary application of Micah's message; and 7:8-20 is a liturgical passage.[8]

THE TEXT

Although some scholars complain about the poor state of preservation of the Hebrew text of Micah the overall meaning is usually apparent. There are, however, some passages that are very difficult to translate (such as 1:10-16; 2:7-10; 6:9-12; and 7:11-12), as will become obvious when one compares the differing solutions proposed by the NIV and the NRSV translators. Occasionally, translators must acknowledge in a footnote that the Hebrew text is uncertain.

THEOLOGICAL ISSUES

Micah is a rich resource for the theological tasks of the preacher, the teacher, and the pastoral caregiver. Sometimes troubling and sometimes comforting, Micah provides insights into the nature of God and to the way humans relate to God and to each other. Some passages from Micah may strike us as "answers" to our deepest questions of meaning. Other texts disturb us and raise hard questions about what we are doing with our lives. In some cases, Micah may drive us to other biblical texts for words of assurance and a renewed sense of acceptance by God. Theological issues that the reader will encounter in the book of Micah include the following:

1. Despite its brevity, the book of Micah presents a complex variety of ways in which Yahweh relates to humanity. God seemingly acts differently in some situations than in others. God is angry and destructive, but the same God overflows with compassion and pity and comforting promises that abandonment will never be permanent. God is judge and savior, acts in the world and remains hidden, has a special covenant with the people of Israel and cares for the whole world. How can God be all of this and more? What is the true nature of God, the God who remains when all the present terrible events are history?

2. The anger of God is an issue too often avoided. Prophetic books like Micah do not permit us to sidestep it. Many people believe they have experienced God's anger, especially if they have suffered great trials in their own lives. Too often the church has not provided an opportunity for them to think about this issue. The book of Micah gives one an occasion to reflect upon God's wrath.

3. What does God expect from us? Micah answers that question in 6:6-8. Are we saved by our piety, our sacrifices, the way we perform and participate in liturgy? Are we saved by our ethical practices? Can we ever be good enough? What about God's grace and forgiveness? Can we save ourselves through proper understanding, the correct theological formulation, a right reading of the Holy Scriptures? Micah helps us think about these questions, even as we continue to struggle with how to be right before God.

4. The interpretation of disaster and suffering as judgment for sin needs constantly to be examined. Micah clearly states that the calamities the people will endure are the consequence of human behavior. All will suffer, though their leaders are most culpable. When bad things happen, is there always some sin lurking in the background that explains human suffering and sustains our belief in a just God? The doctrine of retribution retains its hold in the lives of many faithful people. The book of Micah gives an occasion to think about it, to see what is valid and what needs critique, what should be applied personally and communally, and what should be rejected as not fitting one's own circumstances.

5. From whom do the prophets (or other proclaimers of a word from God) receive their authority? What makes a prophet true or false? Often, prophets are judged to be true or false on the basis of the accuracy of their predictions (Deut 18:22; Jer 28:9). Why does the message of Micah end up in a canonical book, whereas many of ancient Israel's prophets were either forgotten or remembered only as those with whom true prophets had to contend?

6. The task of the prophet can be very painful. Often the prophets tried to say no when God placed a heavy task upon them. Their message often includes a painful criticism, and the listeners' first impulse is to reject the message and condemn and isolate the messenger. Unless the prophet actually hates those addressed, the message of doom will bring personal pain. Although we know very little about Micah, we can detect in his laments the inner pain that all proclaimers of God's Word must sometimes feel.

7. How does one articulate a message of hope that is honest, realistic, and able to revive the spirit of one who has been crushed? There are wonderful words of hope in Micah. Promises contained there continue to sustain and comfort troubled persons in our own day. The promises of hope in Micah remain a rich pastoral resource.

8. For Christians, the passage about a new ruler to come from Bethlehem (5:2-5) bears special significance. We are uplifted by it every Advent and Christmas season. What does Micah really say about the coming Messiah and the new age? Did Jesus fulfill these prophecies? In what way? Is there still more to come, if Micah's hopes for the future are to be fully realized?

9. When is the appropriate time to speak of hope? This is a very important question for scholars of the book of Micah. Many debates about the authenticity of certain oracles in the book are based

on the assumption that Micah would not have issued a word of hope when his main motive was to announce judgment. Could Micah utter doom and hope at the same time? Does hope come only after disaster, when it is no longer appropriate to speak of destruction? When people have lost everything they become desperate to hear words of encouragement. In public preaching and private counseling, when is it time to proclaim the law, the consequences of continuing misdeeds, the need for repentance? Should we wait until someone has finally "hit the bottom" before we begin to speak of hope? The struggle to discern the right word for the right time remains very much with us.

FOR FURTHER READING

Allen, Leslie C. *The Books of Joel, Obadiah, Jonah, and Micah.* NICOT. Grand Rapids: Eerdmans, 1976.

Anderson, Francis L. and David Noel Freedman. *Micah: A New Translation with Introduction and Commentary.* AB 24E. New York: Doubleday, 2000.

Ben Zvi, Ehud. *Micah.* FOTL 21B. Grand Rapids, Mich.: Eerdmans, 2000.

Hillers, Delbert R. *Micah: A Commentary on the Book of the Prophet Micah.* Hermeneia. Philadelphia: Fortress, 1984.

Jacobs, Mignon R. *The Conceptual Coherence of the Book of Micah.* Sheffield: Sheffield University Press, 2001.

Kaiser, Walter C., Jr. *Micah–Malachi.* Communicator's Bible. Dallas: Word, 1992.

Limburg, James. *Hosea–Micah.* Interpretation. Atlanta: John Knox, 1988.

Mays, James L. *Micah: A Commentary.* OTL. Philadelphia: Westminster, 1976.

Wagenaar, Jan A. *Judgment and Salvation: The Composition and Redaction of Micah 2-5.* VTSup 85. Leiden: Brill, 2001.

Wolff, Hans W. *Micah: A Commentary.* Minneapolis: Augsburg, 1990.

ENDNOTES

1. See, e.g., James Limburg, *Hosea–Micah,* Interpretation (Atlanta: John Knox, 1988) 3.

2. Hans W. Wolff, *Micah: A Commentary* (Minneapolis: Augsburg, 1990) 2-3.

3. Mays dates Micah's activity to a short time in 701 BCE before Sennacherib's invasion. See James L. Mays, *Micah*, OTL (Philadelphia: Westminster, 1976) 16. Wolff dates Micah's public activity to a short time between 733–722 BCE. See Hans W. Wolff, *Micah: A Commentary*, 8.

4. Delbert R. Hillers, *Micah: A Commentary on the Book of the Prophet Micah*, Hermeneia (Philadelphia: Fortress, 1984) 5.

5. See especially Mays and Wolff; Hillers, by contrast, expresses little confidence in the results of redaction criticism.

6. Leslie C. Allen, *The Books of Joel, Obadiah, Jonah, and Micah*, 258. Limburg supports this three-part division, *Hosea–Micah*, 159.

7. James L. Mays, *Micah*, 3.

8. Hans W. Wolff, *Micah*, 17-18.

THE BOOK OF
NAHUM

FRANCISCO O. GARCÍA-TRETO

NINEVEH AND ASSYRIA

The book of Nahum presents a difficult question to readers of the Bible. Why does Nahum, a Judean prophet, focus his attention on the fortunes of Nineveh, a distant Mesopotamian city? Simply to say that Nineveh was one of the major cities of Assyria and the main residence of the last Assyrian kings does not explain its importance for the author of this Hebrew poem. The fall of Nineveh in 612 BCE must have been one of the most momentous events during the time when the book of Nahum was written. Still, it is a challenge to understand the strong antipathy the poet manifests against the city and his joy at its doom.

Situated on the banks of the Tigris River, in today's northern Iraq, ancient Nineveh's remains lie beneath two mounds, Kuyunjik and Nebi Yunus, in what is now the city of Mosul. The Nineveh of Nahum's time was the premier city of the Late Assyrian Empire, from which Ashurbanipal (668–627), the last powerful king of Assyria, reigned. The Late Assyrian Empire comprised the reigns of six major kings and lasted from the second half of the eighth century BCE to the fall of Nineveh in 612 BCE.[1] It was precisely these six kings who cast the strongest shadows upon the political and cultural existence of Israel and Judah. Relatively unimportant in themselves, these two kingdoms found themselves, along with a number of their Syro-palestinian neighbors, caught up in an expansionist Assyrian policy, which aimed at Assyrian control of Egyptian trade.

The first of the six kings was Tiglath-pileser III, who invaded Palestine and captured Gaza in 734. As 2 Kings 15–16, for example, shows "Pul" (a diminutive of the name "Tiglath-pileser") exacted tribute from both Israel and Judah. From then on, Assyria remained a major and generally unwelcome player in the politics of the Palestinian states. His successor, Shalmaneser V, reigned for only four years, but was the one who conquered the Northern Kingdom in 722. In the same year, Sargon II put an end to Shalmaneser's life and reign.

The Late Assyrian Kings	
Tiglath-pileser III ("Pul")	744–727 BCE
Shalmaneser V	726–722
Sargon II	721–705
Sennacherib	704–681
Esarhaddon	680–669
Ashurbanipal	668–627 (631?)
The Collapse	626–609
Ashur-etil-ilani	630?–627?
Sinsharrishkun	626–612
Ashur-uballit II	611–609

Sargon II was the founder of Assyria's last dynasty. His son Sennacherib was the Assyrian king who devastated Judah in 701, sacked Lachish and other cities, and exacted heavy tribute from Hezekiah after besieging him in Jerusalem "like a bird in a cage," as Sennacherib's annals boast. He also chose to make Nineveh his capital, where he erected a magnificent royal palace as his residence and seat of government. The darkest years of Assyrian vassalage for Judah were those of the long reign of Hezekiah's son Manasseh (687–642), who ruled in Jerusalem under three Assyrian overlords: Sennacherib, Esarhaddon, and Ashurbanipal. While the deuteronomistic history's judgment on Manasseh as the worst of the kings of Judah (2 Kings 21) does not mention Assyria, it stands to reason that Judean nationalists, as well as Yahwistic monotheists, would have considered Assyria to be the wellspring of Manesseh's treason and apostasy. Sennacherib successfully crushed a long-standing Babylonian rebellion, and his forces destroyed the city of Babylon in 689. Esarhaddon, coming to the throne in 680, misguidedly turned his attention to the conquest of Egypt, which the Assyrian army invaded in 671. Assyria's armed might was fearsome, and Assyrian propaganda sought to inspire fear as a means of augmenting that might. Esarhaddon's westward move nevertheless constituted a serious mistake that led to irreducible Egyptian resistance and, more dangerously, pulled forces away from the eastern frontiers where the real threat to Assyria's survival lay.

Ashurbanipal managed temporarily to undo some of the worst results of his predecessor's policies, successfully quelling Babylonian rebellion and waging war against Elam, but with the mixed result of freeing the hand of the Medes to become a greater threat to Assyria. Ashurbanipal also inherited Esarhaddon's Egyptian entanglement, as a result of which the sack of No-Amon (the Egyptian capital city of Thebes) by the Assyrians, referred to in Nah 3:8-10, took place in 663.

Babylonia was to be Assyria's nemesis, destined to bring about the destruction of Nineveh. The Babylonians had long harbored rebellion against domination by their northern neighbors. Nabopolassar, who became king in Babylon in 626, formed an alliance with the Medes and brought the rule of Assyria to an end in a war highlighted by the fall of the cities of Asshur in 614 and of Nineveh in 612.

It is easy to see how a Judean consciousness, formed by well over one hundred years of Assyrian hegemony and buttressed by brutal militarism and propaganda, could react with elation at the news of Assyria's collapse. The Judahites perceived that Yahweh had accomplished Nineveh's downfall. What could be more natural than to cast the defeat of a long-hated oppressor as the long-sought after deliverance finally granted by "a jealous and avenging God"?

THE STRUCTURE OF THE BOOK

Sketching an outline of Nahum's forty-seven verses has not been a simple task, as a comparison of three of the standard English commentaries makes clear. Perhaps the least helpful attempt is that of Charles L. Taylor, who simply distinguished "the Acrostic Poem (1:1-9)" from "the Long Poem (1:11–3:19)" and bridged the gap between these two parts with "a Series of Marginal Notes (1:10, 12, 13, 15, 2:2)."[2] More detailed, and certainly more helpful, are the more recent proposals of Elizabeth Achtemeier and J. J. M. Roberts, both of whom apply form-critical categories in their analyses of the composition.[3] On the one hand, Achte-

meier recognizes 1:1 as a title, and then distinguishes six sections: (1) an opening hymn (1:2-11); (2) an oracle against Balial/Nineveh (1:12-15); (3) a judgment oracle in the form of a prophetic vision (2:1-13); (4) a woe oracle (3:1-7); (5) a taunt song (3:8-13); and (6) a final oracle (3:14-19) in two parts: a taunt song (3:14-17) and a funeral dirge (3:18-19). On the other hand, after the superscription (1:1), Roberts identifies four related oracles: (1) one "of reassurance to Judah (1:2–2:1)"; followed by (2) an "oracle threatening the Assyrian king (2:2-14)"; then (3) "a hoy-[woe] oracle against Nineveh (3:1-17)"; and, finally, (4) another "against the king of Assyria (3:18-19)."

Nonetheless, a powerful poetic composition such as Nahum, with its strong thematic integrity, demands a sustained reading from beginning to end. The theme is the fall of Assyria, which Nahum interprets as Yahweh's act of deliverance for his people Judah and defeat of his/their enemy Assyria. One's reading of Nahum must be informed, to be sure, by the perspectives and conclusions of critical analysis, but it must also allow literary sensibility full play. The poetic power of Nahum depends in great part on the cumulative impact of image upon image, metaphor upon metaphor. This accumulation of images rises to a pitch close to incoherence as the poet describes the destruction of the Assyrian capital and the fate of its inhabitants. Although analysis of the individual elements in the composition helps the reader to understand the poet's craft, only a sustained reading of the book as a whole will let the interpreter feel its literary power.

In agreement with Roberts, I recognize a main break at the end of 1:15 (2:1 in the Masoretic Text), which divides the poem into two major sections. The theme of the first part (1:2-15) is the appearance of Yahweh as the divine avenger, a warrior who defends the people and destroys their assailants, challenges the Assyrian enemy, who has dared to oppress Judah, and proclaims victory and salvation to Judah. The second section of Nahum (2:1–3:19) envisions the downfall of Nineveh, portraying it so vividly that the poetry takes on an almost incantatory character, as if it were an attempt to bring the events to pass magically by visualizing them. Certain formal elements used by the poet characterize parts of both sections—the incomplete alphabetic acrostic

(1:2-8) in the first or the woe-oracle (3:1-17) in the second—but the presence of these elements is not to be taken as grounds for marking major discontinuities within the sections. Nahum in this sense works as a collage, assembling literary material in the service of a larger poem.

THEME

The theme that Nahum's poetry so powerfully expresses—the avenging wrath of Yahweh redressing Assyrian oppression and abuse of power by Nineveh—will raise serious questions for theologically and ethically sensitive readers, particularly in the light of the horrors of war motivated by nationalism and tribalism. It is clear that the church has not been able easily to integrate Nahum's message into its liturgical usage; Nahum shares with Obadiah the dubious distinction of being the only prophetic books that do not appear in the Revised Common Lectionary, and probably for similar reasons. Elizabeth Achtemeier makes a strong attempt to face the problem in the introduction to her commentary by insisting that we let Nahum "be a book about God," and that Nahum's message then must be that God, the sole arbiter of human history, will not let the wicked go unpunished. In her analysis, the use of "evil" (רעה *r'â*) in 1:11 and 3:19 forms an inclusio that not only frames but also provides the theological key to the book: "evil introduced and evil done away form the inclusio of the thought of the book."[4]

Such a reading raises questions and leaves unanswered issues about the theology of Nahum. Can God's punishment of violence and oppression partake of that same violence and oppression? What difference is there between the Assyrians and their foes the Medes and Babylonians? Or, as Isaiah 10 recognizes, if Assyria's depredations have been committed as "the rod of [God's] anger," no matter how guilty Assyria is, is not its crime at least in part an initiative of divine justice? Such a notion implicates God in human acts of violence and death-dealing destruction, which are always impossible to qualify as absolutely good.

Another aspect of the ethical problem that Nahum poses is the lack of distinction the book makes between the guilty and the innocent, even (especially) among the Ninevites. There is no lack of examples of a much more precise sense of justice in the Hebrew Bible. Where, for example, is the overriding concern for the life of guiltless human beings (even in Sodom!) that Abraham expresses and that God agrees to in Genesis 18? Or the intellectual struggle to devise a scheme of personal condemnation or vindication according to personal guilt or innocence (even among the exiles) of Ezekiel 18? Finally, where is the lesson of God's love for all life (even in Nineveh), which the hapless prophet is taught in the last verse of the book of Jonah: "And should I not be concerned about Nineveh, that great city, in which there are more than a hundred and twenty thousand persons who do not know their right hand from their left, and also many animals?" (Jonah 4:11 NRSV)? Perhaps the book of Nahum might serve to spur the church toward ethical and theological discussion of these issues, on which no one can claim that this book speaks the last, or the most unexceptionable, word.

DATE AND PROVENANCE

The book cannot have been written before the fall of Thebes in 663 BCE, to which it alludes in 3:8. Moreover, the book seems to anticipate the fall of Nineveh, rather than report it, so that it must have been written before 612. Most scholars narrow this fifty-year window by assuming that the expectation of the fall of Nineveh probably developed after Nabopolassar and the Medes had actually begun to demolish Assyrian military power, so that shortly before 612 is the most likely judgment. A Judean provenance is likely, and given the genre of the work, we may assume that it was produced by a prophet-poet. But as the section on the superscription will suggest, nothing can be said for certain about the author.

FOR FURTHER READING

Achtemeier, Elizabeth. *Nahum–Malachi.* Interpretation. Atlanta: John Knox, 1986.

Cathcart, Kevin J. "Nahum, Book of." In David Noel Freedman, ed., *The Anchor Bible Dictionary.* New York: Doubleday, 1992. 4:998-1000.

O'Brien, Julia M. *Nahum.* Readings: A New Bible Commentary. Sheffield: Sheffield Academic Press, 2002.

Roberts, J. J. M. *Nahum, Habakkuk, and Zephaniah: A Commentary*. OTL. Louisville: Westminster/John Knox, 1991.

ENDNOTES

1. The fifteen years or so between the death of Ashurbanipal and the fall of Nineveh remain obscure to historians. Two kings seem to have ruled the rapidly collapsing empire, Ashur-etel-ilani and Sinsharrishkun, but little is known of their reigns. For three years after the fall of Nineveh, another, Ashur-uballit II, was nominally the last king of Assyria, until the last elements of the Assyrian army were defeated and dispersed in 609 BCE.

2. Charles L. Taylor, Jr., "Nahum," in *The Interpreter's Bible* (Nashville: Abingdon, 1956) 6:957-969.

3. Elizabeth Achtemeier, *Nahum–Malachi* (Atlanta: John Knox, 1986); and J. J. M. Roberts, *Nahum, Habakkuk, and Zephaniah*, OTL (Louisville: Westminster/John Knox, 1991).

4. Elizabeth Achtemeier, *Nahum–Malachi*, 5-7.

THE BOOK OF
HABAKKUK

THEODORE HIEBERT

The message of Habakkuk has become known to the church primarily through a single phrase, "the just shall live by faith" (2:4), the phrase quoted by the apostle Paul in his letter to the Romans (1:17 KJV). In fact, the brief section of Habakkuk in which this phrase occurs, Hab 2:1-4, along with Hab 1:1-4, are the only texts from Habakkuk selected for public reading in Christian worship in the Revised Common Lectionary. This key phrase, though brief and quoted by Paul without reference to the larger context of which it is a part, lies at the heart of the prophet's message and provides a useful starting point for interpreting the book of Habakkuk. This phrase can only be understood fully, however, through an examination of its place in the book of Habakkuk as a whole and of its relationship to the concrete experiences of the prophet.

THEOLOGICAL ISSUES

Habakkuk's central concern for justice places him solidly in the tradition of Israel's prophets. Like his predecessor Isaiah and his contemporary Jeremiah, Habakkuk calls attention to and criticizes the miscarriage of justice in the political, judicial, and economic institutions of Judah and of its capital, Jerusalem. Also in the tradition of Israel's prophets, he predicts the demise of this unjust society as the result of coming events in which God will punish its unjust leaders and reestablish equity and proper order.

Unlike other prophets in the biblical canon, however, Habakkuk gives prominent attention to a persistent and troubling problem that challenges this prophetic confidence in God's justice: the perseverance of injustice in the world. Even in the very events and agents understood by Habakkuk as instruments by which divine justice will be done, injustice seems to be present. Real-world politics appear to be continually at odds with the prophetic passion for justice

and faith in God's just rule. This problem, maintaining a belief in God's just rule in spite of an unjust world, is the central issue around which the book of Habakkuk as a whole has taken shape.

The challenge of believing in the ultimate power of justice in a world that appears to be overwhelmingly unjust is one of the most difficult existential struggles the religious person must face. Among biblical writers, Habakkuk was not alone in wrestling with it. Job, to whom Habakkuk is often compared, faces this issue more directly perhaps than does any other biblical figure, though within the context of his own family rather than in the wide realm of international politics, with which Habakkuk is concerned. The book of Job explores the religious crisis of a good and honest man who experiences a series of unprovoked catastrophes that force him to challenge the views in Israel's wisdom traditions of God's just rule. Such challenges are also raised in the context of Israelite worship. In the psalms of lament, the most common psalm type in the psalter, psalmists cry to God based on experiences of suffering and misfortune and plead for God to rectify wrongs and restore order. On occasion, a prophetic figure, such as Habakkuk's contemporary, Jeremiah, will question God's reliability and administration of justice in the world. But these occasions are rare in prophetic literature. No prophet confronts the issue of a just God and an unjust world in the direct and forceful way that Habakkuk does.

LITERARY STRUCTURE

The literary structure within which this topic is explored in the book of Habakkuk is built on a debate between the prophet and God, composed of two arguments. In the first argument, the prophet opens the debate with a complaint deploring the lack of justice in Judean society and God's failure to act against it (1:2-4). God responds by describing an astonishing, imminent event: a Chaldean invasion, designed to bring down Judah's corrupt government and put an end to its unjust policies and practices (1:5-11). In the second argument, the debate moves to a new level. The prophet again initiates the exchange with a complaint, this time questioning the justice of the divine plan itself: the Chaldean invasion. In his second complaint, Habakkuk describes the corruption of the Chaldeans, the very instrument by which God planned to render judgment and restore justice (1:12–2:1). Again, God responds, thereby completing the second exchange of speeches.

But just here, in the second divine response, the high point toward which the debate between the prophet and God has been building—the point at which the final resolution of Habakkuk's problem is expected—we encounter the book's key literary and exegetical challenges. The first of these challenges is the deciphering and translation of the difficult Hebrew in God's brief response to Habakkuk (2:2-4). Does it contain a new divine argument or merely promise a response in the future, one that is to be found perhaps in the subsequent sections of the book? The second major challenge is the relationship to the preceding debate of the literary units that follow this response. The first of these units is neither a prophetic complaint nor a divine response, but a collection of sayings spoken by conquered nations and peoples to ridicule the Chaldean oppressor (2:5-20). The second of these units, introduced by a superscription, often a sign of later editorial activity (3:1) and accompanied by musical notations characteristic of the book of Psalms (3:1, 3, 9, 13, 19), is an elaborate victory hymn describing God's appearance as a conquering warrior (3:2-19). The way in which one understands the relationship of these concluding literary sections to one another and to the previous dialogue determines to a great extent the way in which one interprets the ultimate message of the book.

The basic picture of the shape of the book of Habakkuk and its message that emerges from this exegesis discloses three stages of literary and theological development in the book's compilation. The first is represented by the judgment speech delivered to Judah (Hab 1:5-11), expressing the traditional prophetic theology of divine justice according to which Judah's sins will be justifiably punished by a foreign invader. The second stage is the incorporation of this oracle into the elaborate debate (Hab 1:12–2:4), in which this traditional theology of divine justice is questioned and then reconstructed in the second divine response (2:1-4) and in the wisdom of conquered peoples (2:5-20). The third stage involves the addition by later disciples of Habakkuk of an archaic victory hymn interpreted as the future intervention of God to restore absolute justice on earth (3:1-19). Within the framework of such a literary and theological development lie the most reliable clues for understanding the full sense of Habakkuk's claim: "The just shall live by his faith" (2:4 KJV).

HISTORICAL SETTING

Habakkuk has provided little concrete data to identify the historical events and political situation that led to his religious crisis and ensuing debate with God. The superscription of the book (1:1) contains no information, as do many superscriptions of prophetic books (Isa 1:1; Jer 1:1-3), about the particular kings within whose reigns the prophet spoke. Further, the language in which Habakkuk conducts the debate at the heart of the book is general and archetypal in nature. The key players in the political drama that raised such serious questions for Habakkuk—unrestrained oppressors and helpless victims—are regularly designated by the nonspecific terms "the wicked" and "the righteous" (1:4, 13; 2:4; cf. 3:13).

The starting point for understanding the book within a particular historical period is its one concrete political reference: the mention of the Chaldeans in 1:6. "Chaldean" is the name used by biblical historians (2 Kgs 25:1-13; 2 Chr 36:17) and prophets (Jer 21:4; Ezek 23:23) for the Neo-Babylonians under the rule of the powerful king Nebuchadnezzar II (605–562 BCE), who sacked Jerusalem in 597 and destroyed it completely in 586 BCE. These Neo-Babylonians first became a major force in the ancient Near East under the rule of Nebuchadnezzar's father, Nabopolassar, who declared himself king of Babylon in 626 BCE.

Habakkuk's prediction of an invasion of Babylonian armies (1:5-11) certainly predated their first siege of Jerusalem in 597 and probably also their first appearance in the coastal plain adjacent to Judah in

604 BCE. Otherwise, the prediction would hardly have been astonishing or unbelievable (1:5). On the other hand, a Neo-Babylonian invasion of Judah would not have been even conceivable until 605 BCE, when the Babylonians defeated the Assyrians and the Egyptians at Carchemish, four hundred miles north of Jerusalem, to establish their supremacy in the west. It is likely, therefore, that Habakkuk's announcement of the Chaldean invasion was delivered between these events, in 605–604 BCE, the fifth year of the reign of Jehoiakim, king of Judah, whose corrupt regime is described in 1:2-4.[1]

The central question that drives the book of Habakkuk—the persistence of injustice, even in the divine judgment on Judah at the hands of the Chaldeans—logically arises, however, from Habakkuk's firsthand experience of the Chaldeans themselves. Thus the description of abuses by the Neo-Babylonian invader in Habakkuk's second complaint (1:12–2:1) and the composition and compilation of the debate with God over divine rule in chaps. 1 and 2 derive from the period between Nebuchadnezzar's first invasion in 597 and his destruction of Jerusalem in 586 BCE, the era of the reign of Zedekiah, a Judean placed in power by the Neo-Babylonian regime. Habakkuk's career and his fervent struggle with divine justice are to be viewed, therefore, against the backdrop of the final, turbulent days of Jerusalem and its great Davidic dynasty.

The historical period within which the victory hymn in chap. 3 was composed and became part of the book of Habakkuk has been the subject of much discussion and debate. An earlier generation of scholars, represented in the bibliography by G. A. Smith, believed the poem to have been composed and added to Habakkuk in the post-exilic period, long after Habakkuk's career, the fall of Jerusalem, the Babylonian exile, and the initial efforts by the returned exiles to rebuild Jerusalem and Judah. Most contemporary scholars, including Achtemeier, Gowen, Haak, and Roberts as cited in the bibliography, have by contrast come to regard this hymn as an authentic work of Habakkuk himself, composed during the final, troubled days of Jerusalem, which gave rise to his debate with God in chaps. 1–2. A sizable body of evidence suggests, however, that the hymn in Habakkuk 3 is an archaic composition, added to the corpus of Habakkuk in the post-exilic period in order to emphasize God's final victory over evil. This evidence will be described in the commentary.

SOCIAL LOCATION

No direct information is provided in the book's superscription, or in Habakkuk's speeches themselves, that allows us to determine the social location of this prophet or his family within Judean society. Because his speeches share certain features of the psalms, and because chap. 3 contains musical annotations characteristic of the psalter, some have suggested that Habakkuk was a cult prophet—that is, a prophet employed by the Temple to deliver divine oracles within the liturgies and rituals of this institution.[2] The evidence is not decisive, with scholars differing on Habakkuk's relationship to the Temple and its priestly officials. Habakkuk's own struggle with the question certainly arose out of his prophetic office (1:1), as it did for Jeremiah; but the influence of the Temple upon his thought is more difficult to assess. As the biblical evidence from the psalter, from Job, and from Jeremiah, mentioned above, indicates, the question of God's justice and reliable rule in the world was raised in a variety of social contexts in ancient Israel. In the end, the problem of believing in the ultimate power of justice in an unjust world is such a basic one that it transcends particular social locations and political crises.

FOR FURTHER READING

Achtemeier, Elizabeth. *Nahum–Malachi.* Interpretation. Atlanta: John Knox, 1986.

Anderson, Francis I. *Habakkuk: A New Translation and Commentary.* AB 25. New York: Doubleday, 2001.

Gowen, Donald E. *The Triumph of Faith in Habakkuk.* Atlanta: John Knox, 1976.

Haak, Robert D. *Habakkuk.* VTSup 44. Leiden: Brill, 1991.

Hiebert, Theodore. *God of My Victory: The Ancient Hymn in Habakkuk 3.* HSM 38. Atlanta: Scholars Press, 1986.

Roberts, J. J. M. *Nahum, Habakkuk, and Zephaniah.* OTL. Louisville: Westminster/John Knox, 1991.

Smith, George Adam. *The Book of the Twelve Prophets.* Volume 2 of *The Expositor's Bible.* London: Hodder and Stoughton, 1898.

ENDNOTES

1. J. J. M. Roberts, *Nahum, Habakkuk, and Zephaniah*, OTL (Louisville: Westminster/John Knox, 1991) 82-84, 95.

2. Sigmund Mowinckel, *The Psalms in Israel's Worship*, trans. D. R. Ap-Thomas (New York: Abingdon, 1967) 2:93, 147, 150; J. H. Eaton, "The Origin and Meaning of Habakkuk 3," *ZAW* 76 (1964) 144-71.

THE BOOK OF
ZEPHANIAH

ROBERT A. BENNETT

THE PROPHET AND THE
SETTING OF HIS MINISTRY

The book of Zephaniah stands in the ninth position of the collection of Hebrew prophetic literature called the Book of the Twelve. Zephaniah's three chapters represent the collected oracles or divinely inspired sermons of the late seventh century BCE prophet Zephaniah ben Cushi. All that we know about Zephaniah ben Cushi comes from the title or introduction to this work and from inferences drawn from the oracles.

In the style typical of such collections, the title or opening verse identifies the author by name and background, the date and location of his activity, plus a basis for speaking in God's name. Zephaniah 1:1 tersely gives the call or right to speak simply as "The word of the LORD that came to Zephaniah," followed by a genealogical lineage going back some four generations to an ancestor named Hezekiah, and then concludes by locating this ministry during the reign of King Josiah (640–609 BCE).

The unusually long genealogy—the norm is one or two generations—suggests that the last name is of special significance. It may point to King Hezekiah (715–687 BCE) himself, the last reforming king before Josiah. Moreover, the prophet's full name, Zephaniah ben Cushi, is noteworthy because in usual Hebrew parlance "Cushi" means "African" and prefixed with the word בֶּן (ben, "son"/"child of") suggests an African heritage. The name "Zephaniah" represents a combination of the divine name prefaced with a form of the Hebrew word whose meaning is "hide" or "protect" (צְפַנְיָה ṣĕpan-yāh), thus "Yahweh protects."[1] The rest of what we know about Zephaniah ben Cushi must be gleaned from the content of his preaching. Given his knowledge of the city (1:10-13), its temple rites (1:7-8), and it hierarchy (1:8-6; 3:3-4), plus his concern (1:12-13) and compassion (3:7, 14, 17)

for its citizenry, Zephaniah must have been a Jerusalemite with connections to its Temple and the royal family. The dominant motif and single-minded message of his preaching, the coming day of the Lord, both as judgment (1:7–2:4) and as salvation (3:9-20), derives from cultic rites of the Jerusalem Temple. The sins of the community singled out for attack in his oracles as the root causes of the impending destruction—idolatry, syncretism, and the adoption of foreign dress and customs—are among those prohibited during the reforms of Josiah (2 Kgs 23:4-14). These in turn correspond to sins attacked in the deuteronomic law code (Deuteronomy 12–26), which was rediscovered and then promulgated under Josiah.

The content as well as the imagery found in Zephaniah's oracles reflects the union of ancient northern, pre-monarchic Yahwistic traditions of holy war and the divine warrior, plus equally ancient southern Jerusalem/Zion traditions of Yahweh as creator and as king. This merger was fostered after the fall of the northern kingdom (722 BCE) under the reform movements of Hezekiah and, subsequently, Josiah. The literary history of Deuteronomy reflects this joining together of traditions. The prophetic voices of Isaiah and Micah, followed some seventy years later by Zephaniah ben Cushi and then Jeremiah, each in his own way preached a message marked by wrathful vindication wrought by a divine warrior and divine promise associated with Jerusalem/Zion. More specifically, Zephaniah's oracles on the coming day of the Lord exhort one to do what is right and to reject what is wrong or face dire consequences (cf. the ancient Sinai covenant tradition in Deut 30:19), while also concluding with confident assurances for the faithful and with hymns celebrating God as king (3:12-18).

The historical and political setting of Zephaniah's ministry can be reconstructed from evidence present in the central unit of the book, the oracles against the (foreign) nations (2:5-15; 3:8). These accounts of God's dealings with Judah's near and distant neighbors not only give some inkling of the geopolitics of the ancient Near East during the seventh century BCE, but also mark the transition within the book of Zephaniah between the message of doom and the message of hope. Indeed, this unit itself opens on the note of judgment and ends just prior to Zephaniah's promises to Judah and Jerusalem, which are prefaced with a word of hope for the nations (3:9).

The oracle against the nations is a standard part of the prophetic repertoire, occurring in Amos 1–2, Isaiah 13–23, Jeremiah 46–51, and Ezekiel 25–32. The earliest example of an oracle used against a foreign nation is found in the story of the Moabite seer Balaam, who, though called upon to curse the invading Israelites, instead blesses them on their way into the promised land (Numbers 22–24). This account from the pre-monarchic period is set within the context of holy war, where it is God who fights on behalf of the Israelites. This same setting continues in the monarchic period when Isaiah opens his oracles against the nations by calling for holy war against Babylon (Isa 13:1-16).

Zephaniah ben Cushi's oracles against Judah's near neighbors (2:5-11), inhabitants of the Palestinian land bridge linking Asia in the north with Africa to the south, reflect the changed political situation within the region when young Josiah was placed on the throne of Judah in 640 BCE (2 Kgs 21:19-26; 22:1-2). Assyria, which had destroyed the northern kingdom of Israel and forced surviving Judah in the south to pay tribute, to cede territory, and to adopt Assyrian cult figures and other practices, was now in decline and no longer the dominant power within Syria-Palestine. This opening segment of the oracles against the nations assumes that Judah's servile status has passed and can now be interpreted as an opening salvo in the nation's efforts to regain territory lost to its neighbors during the Assyrian hegemony (2:7-9).[2]

The oracles against Judah's more distant neighbors, Cush/Nubia—rulers of Egypt during Hezekiah's reign who had helped to thwart Assyria's capture of Jerusalem (2:12) and hated Assyria to the north (2:13-15)—likewise give hints of their geopolitical setting. Assyria had captured Thebes in 633 BCE, spelling the end of the Cushite 25th Dynasty of Egypt. Still, Assyria's own capital, Nineveh, d uld fall not many years later in 612 BCE. Oracles linking these events occur in Zephaniah's later contemporary, Nahum (Nah 3:8-13). Likewise, the setting of Zephaniah's oracles is clearly one in which the prowess of Cushite Egypt has passed, though still remembered, and the fate of Assyria has already been sealed. However, Zephaniah does not consider the next major international power, even though his later contemporaries within the prophetic movement, Habakkuk and then Jeremiah, will point to the rise of the Neo-Babylonians.

Zephaniah's was the first prophetic voice to be raised in Judah against its people's disobedience to God since the time of Isaiah, some seventy years earlier during Hezekiah's reign. Isaiah's oracles against the nations (Isaiah 13–23) included a warning to Hezekiah against an alliance with the Cushite rulers of Egypt (Isaiah 18), since elsewhere Isaiah proclaimed Assyria as God's chastening rod, later itself to be judged (Isa 10:5). Zephaniah 2:12-15 shows that both powers were in decline toward the end of the seventh century BCE, thereby giving Josiah and the deuteronomic reformers the hope of bringing Judah back to religious and political independence and renewed obedience to God.

Zephaniah's ministry, therefore, is best located in the city of Jerusalem at the very beginning of Josiah's deuteronomic reform movement, approximately between 630 and 620 BCE, close in time to the prophet Nahum's oracles celebrating the fall of Nineveh in 612 BCE (Zeph 2:13-15). Given the vivid descriptions of the sins being condemned and the single-minded earnestness of Zephaniah's proclamation of the devastating day of the Lord, it appeared likely that this preaching preceded the full implementation of the reforms and, indeed, may have helped to inspire and guide the direction of the sought-for changes in Jerusalem and Judah. Josiah's father, Amon (642–640) was killed in a palace coup. Josiah himself was placed on the throne by the "people of the land" (2 Kgs 21:24 NRSV) when he was only eight years old (2 Kgs 22:1). With the discovery of the "book of the law" in the eighteenth year of his reign (2 Kgs 22:3-20), its authentication, and its promulgation (2 Kings 23), the reform began in 621 BCE. The core of the book of Deuteronomy (Deuteronomy 12–26) became the basis of purifying Judah of the idolatry, paganism, and loss of faith in

God's will to act (2 Kings 22–23) resulting from Assyrian hegemony, which had been aided by Manasseh's and Amon's ready compliance. The reform effort was dealt a serious setback, however, with the untimely death of Josiah (609 BCE), who was killed in battle when attempting to stop Egyptian forces from aiding Assyria.

THE BOOK OF ZEPHANIAH: ITS COMPOSITION, FORM, AND STYLE

The book of Zephaniah is composed of the collected oracles of the prophet arranged according to subject matter, thereby yielding three major literary units: (a) oracles of divine judgment against Judah and Jerusalem (1:2–2:4); (b) oracles of divine judgment against the nations (2:5–3:8); and (c) oracles of divine promise to the nations and to Judah and Jerusalem (3:9-20). The literary form called "oracle" is the biblical prophets' stock-in-trade. It is the vehicle through which the prophet proclaims the divinely inspired Word of God to God's covenanted people.

Zephaniah's later contemporary, Jeremiah, sets the oracle within its proper context as one of several means of inspired leadership through which God directs the covenant community:

Instruction [תורה *tôrâ*] shall not perish from the priest, nor counsel [עצה *'ēṣâ*] from the wise, nor the word [דבר *dābār*] from the prophet. (Jer 18:18 NRSV)

Priestly *torah*, or law, is like catechism or instruction in God's commandments. Its equivalent in Greek would be διδαχή (*didachē*, "teaching"). Wisdom teachers provide counsel, advice, or guidance in human affairs based upon their vast store of empirically gained knowledge. The prophet is given a word or profound insight into the contemporary state of the divine-human relationship, which he or she feels compelled to express in as effective a way as possible. Again, it is Jeremiah who summarizes both the prophetic compulsion to speak and the dire consequences for the speaker and the audience as expressed in the imagery of the divine word as a consuming fire (Jer 5:14; 20:8-9).

The oracles of judgment and of promise presuppose the covenant relationship between God and the Hebrew people that was established under the leadership of Moses at Mount Sinai. God and people are yoked together as long as the people obey the commandments or covenant stipulations, which demand exclusive loyalty to Yahweh alone and just dealings with one's neighbor. Whereas obedience leads to life in the land of promise, disobedience leads to expulsion from the land, bondage, and death. The sanctions for maintaining covenantal loyalty are understood by all to be blessings of life or curses of death (e.g., Deuteronomy 28). Therefore, when Zephaniah ben Cushi preached a stern message of doom and disaster to a disobedient society, his audience knew the covenantal context out of which he spoke. Likewise, the faithful, humble remnant whom he singled out within that decadent society also knew that he spoke not only of judgment, but also of the promise that lay beyond the chastening and purifying destruction about to befall Judah and Jerusalem.

The oracles against the nations, though addressed to those outside the Sinai covenant bond, are also to be understood within a wider covenant context acknowledged by the Israelite community. The Israelites realized that their God was indeed Lord of the nations and that the divine word applied to all peoples, as in the Noah covenant (Genesis 9) and again as in the table of nations (Genesis 10), which shows how all nations are related. On the one hand, while it is the case that judgment against the nations is due them for attacking God's people and taking the promised land God had given them as part of their covenant bond (i.e., Zeph 2:8-9 against Moab and Ammon), it is also true that these oracles are motivated out of the belief that a universal or natural law of justice is at work, which no nation can violate without punishment. The oracles against the nations with which Amos opens his attack on the injustices of Judah and Israel (Amos 1–2) are replete with examples of threats against the nations for what we would call crimes against humanity and common human decency.[3]

This fundamental belief in God's lordship in the life of the covenant community, extending even to the nations of the earth, means that for prophet and for people the power of the divine word enunciated through the oracle was such that it not only foretold what was to be, but also helped to initiate the process of the oracle's fulfillment. The oracle was in essence a sentence of judgment handed down in the heavenly court, where God was judge and the prophet an officer of the court, announcing its decrees of guilt or innocence, of sentencing to death or imprisonment or release. Each prophet gave his or her statement about the particular crimes or covenant infractions of which the community was guilty, which was then followed by the judgment or punishment. Although the idiom of the law court was the chief social setting or institutional context of the prophetic oracle of judgment or that of promise, language of priestly ritual and of wisdom advice was also borrowed to drive home the statement of charges and impending punishment.

The form of Zephaniah ben Cushi's oracles follows the pattern that reflects the court of law, with terms and images also taken from temple ritual and school. His sermons are set in Jerusalem on the occasion of a major pilgrimage festival, most likely Ingathering (Tabernacles/Booths). With the dramatic image of God sweeping the earth clean, Zephaniah opens his diatribe about Judah's and Jerusalem's idolatry and religious syncretism. After getting the people's attention, the prophet introduces his central message about the coming day of the Lord by using an even more startling image, which has been borrowed from the temple ritual: sinners are the sacrifice and the fierce executors of God's will are invited guests (1:7-9). Zephaniah ben Cushi's close association with the ruling elite of Jerusalem enabled him to describe in vivid detail their sins against God as well as to capture the repetitive cadence of priestly ritual in his portrayal of the day of judgment as one full of terror and dread (1:14-16). The temple ritual celebrating God's advent as the divine warrior who destroys the enemies of the covenant community had been a festive occasion of great joy. However, Amos, preaching before the fall of the northern kingdom, had already warned that the sins of the people made them God's enemies and thus the objects of God's wrath (5:18-24).

Punishment for people who break the covenant with God takes many forms, usually occurring as military defeat. However, the prophet reaches back into ancient covenantal tradition to extend the repertoire of sentences for the many crimes of which his people are found guilty. These are expressed in various ways using the imagery of the reversal of creation (1:2-3; 2:4), denial of the fruits of one's labor (1:13), and barrenness of the land

(2:8-11, against Moab; 2:13-15, against Assyria).

For all the stern single-mindedness of the prophet, he apparently pleads with those whom he addresses within this courtroom-like setting. Twice at the conclusion of the oracles against the nations when Jerusalem is addressed, Zephaniah laments that the city has not learned from experience—that is, has not accepted "correction"/"instruction" (מוסר *mûsār*), an expression borrowed from the didactic rhetoric of the wisdom teachers (3:2, 7).[4] Among the resources such wisdom counsel provides is the ability to learn from life's experiences, here, perhaps, the fate of the northern kingdom and of other cities destroyed by God.

The central motif of the book of Zephaniah is the coming of the day of the Lord as a time of terrifying judgment against Judah and all the earth (1:14-18). The day of the Lord (יום־יהוה *yôm-Yahweh*) is the central referent around which the final canonical shape of the collected oracles is formed. In the oracles of judgment (1:2–2:4) the warnings of impending doom (1:7-13) repeatedly include the phrase "on that day" (1:7a, 8a, 9a, 10a; "at that time," 1:12a), and then in the description of that terrible moment itself (1:14-18), "day of the Lord" or simply "day" recurs cascade-like or as a thundering avalanche in practically every verse. The exhortatory pleading that follows (2:1-4), almost like a brief respite from the terrifying preceding scene, concludes this first unit of the book with a grace note, "perhaps you may be hidden/ on the day of the LORD's wrath" (2:3b NRSV).

The oracles against the nations (2:5–3:8), threatening universal destruction, similarly refer to "the day when I arise as a witness" (3:8 NRSV), but lead immediately into the oracles of promise with which the book ends (3:9-20). They open with the expressions "at that time" (3:9a) and "on that day" (3:11a). The tone changes dramatically in the promises, since now it is an occasion for rejoicing over God's just vindication that converts the nations (3:9) and allows the humble remnant to live in peace (3:11-13).

This central and unifying motif—the day of the Lord—is clearly expressed within the milieu of the Jerusalem Temple with which Zephaniah ben Cushi is closely related. The prophet has chosen a festival occasion such as Ingathering, when many pilgrims come to Jerusalem and the temple complex, at which to make his proclamation that the time of God's judgment against the sinful community was drawing near. The punning language in the Hebrew text—i.e., the opening image of God sweeping the earth of its inhabitants, essentially reversing the process of creation (1:2-3)—is closely related to the terminology for the festival of Tabernacles or Ingathering. The sins outlined and condemned (1:4-5) are closely related to the temple personnel and the observance of religious practices that profane the proper worship of God.

Another bold and imaginative device is the announcement of a special sacrifice in the Temple, where sinful Judah is the sacrificial offering and the invited guests are the appointed forces of its destruction (1:7-9). Zephaniah ben Cushi even adopts the priestly call to worship, "Be silent [הס has] before the Lord GOD!" (1:7a, as in the well-known invocation of Hab 2:20). Similar features occur in the festive calls to choral song (3:14) and in the priestly oracles that report God has heard the penitent's call for divine succor, "Do not fear . . . " (3:16b; cf. the salvation oracles in Isa 40:9; 41:10, 13; 43:1, 5). Furthermore, the language of the psalms, the hymnody of the Temple, seems to be reflected in oracles against the nations' judgment of foreign gods (2:11; cf. Ps 82:6-7) and in the affirmation that God is king in the oracles of promise (3:15b; cf. the enthronement psalms' proclamation of God as universal king, Psalms 93; 96–99).

Understanding this cultic setting helps one to understand the essential unity in these collected oracles, even as they move from announcement of doom to promise of peace, from a message for Judah/Jerusalem to words addressed to all nations. Within the general announcement of doom, the reader may also find authentic, though muted, signs of hope. These are the words to the humble remnant (2:3, 7, 9) and the reassurance of God's continued stabilizing influence within a corrupt society (3:5a), as well as the potential that the people may learn from the disasters, that they can take "correction"/"instruction" (mûsār, 3:7). Even the reversal of the Noah covenant (Gen 9:11) in Zeph 3:8b prepares the audience for the possibility of something good in the future: the lifting of the curse of many languages (Gen 11:9) in the promise of changed speech among the nations (Zeph 3:9). This motif marks the sudden and dramatic transition from words of judgment to words

of promise, using an image of God reversing creation. Since the collected oracles began using this device (Zeph 1:2-3), one may understand it as a rhetorical tool with which the prophet's audience was familiar and thus could easily grasp.

Moving from the universal to the particular, as in the opening oracles, the prophet then announces that "on that day" (3:11) the sentence of judgment against Jerusalem will be reversed for the humble remnant (3:11-13). The concluding victory song of joy (3:14-20) echoes these notes of changed circumstances. A temple choir is invoked to sing that Yahweh is king (3:14), as in the enthronement psalm (see Psalms 96; 98–99). Moreover, one hears a priestly oracle of blessing, "Do not fear" (3:16a NRSV), doubtless reminiscent of the solemn assembly that Amos condemned as premature (Amos 5:18-24). However, on the other side of judgment, this ceremony was appropriate, since it conformed to God's agenda of release. Zephaniah ben Cushi, who plumbed the depths of terror awaiting the wicked, could also envision another future for the humble remnant that survived.

The book of Zephaniah is marked by a distinctive literary style and poetic technique. Except for the superscription (1:1), the entire collection of oracles is written in poetic form. Assonance and repetition are key poetic devices in this work. The introductory oracle on universal destruction (1:2-6), for example, repeats the word "sweep" (Hebrew root אסף 'sp) four times, twice in the opening verse for added emphasis (אסף אסף 'āsōp 'āsēp), "I will utterly sweep away." The use of "from the face of the earth" and "humans"/ "humanity" (1:3) is an example of paronomasia, or repetition of similar sounding words, since the Hebrew for "earth" and "human" (אדמה 'ădāmâ and אדם 'ādām) sound very much alike. Similarly, the repetition of the expression "day of the LORD" (yôm-Yahweh) in the following oracle (1:7–2:4) is used for poetic effect. Assonance and a punning wordplay stand at the end of this oracle as a conclusion and as a transition to the oracles against the nations (2:5-15) that follow. Thus "Gaza shall be deserted [עזה עזובה 'azzâ 'ăzzûbâ] . . . and Ekron shall be uprooted [ועקרון תעקר wĕ'eqrôn tē'āqēr]" (2:4 NRSV), using similar sounds respectively for the place name and its attending verb.

Powerful metaphors, dramatic imagery, and clever turns of phrase occur throughout the book of Zephaniah. The literary devices that attend the prophet's great sermon on the day of the Lord (1:7–2:4) have had a lasting affect upon subsequent understanding of the universal day of judgment. Among the images used are the call to the sacrifice, where sinners are the offering and the invaders are invited guests (1:7), and the portrayal of God searching Jerusalem with lanterns to expose those who drink their lives away in the belief that God does not care and will not intervene (1:12). The depiction of God's appearance as warrior in that central oracle on the great day of judgment is one of the great poems to be found in the Bible. Indeed, it has influenced liturgies for the burial of the dead in Western Christianity through the medieval Latin hymn "Dies Irae" ("Day of Wrath"). Zephaniah ben Cushi's proclamation of the divine intervention as a day of great distress emerges out of a veritable cascade of nouns modifying the bass note-like repetition of the word "day" (יוֹם *yôm*):

That day will be a day of wrath,
  a day of distress and anguish,
a day of ruin and devastation,
  a day of darkness and gloom,
a day of clouds and thick darkness,
  a day of trumpet blast and battle cry.
                    (1:15-16a NRSV)

The prophet also has a penchant for drawing striking examples from the natural order to illustrate realities within the social order. Thus, for example, corrupt officials and judges are called "roaring lions" and "evening wolves" (3:3), while God's sure and righteous presence is likened to the dependability of the sunrise.

"Every morning he renders his judgment, / each dawn without fail" (3:5b NRSV). For all of his single-minded, dispassionate announcement of doom that would befall the wicked community, the prophet also envisions the righteous who pursue life under God's reign in pastoral serenity (3:13). Likewise, in the concluding victory song of release, there is a depiction of God as king and victorious warrior who rejoices and exults in the midst of the redeemed (3:17). Perhaps Zephaniah ben Cushi's audience was thus reminded of the account of King David dancing before the ark as it was brought to Jerusalem (2 Sam 6:12-15) or, perhaps, of the enthronement psalm in which nature rejoices over God's reign as righteous judge (Ps 98:7-9).

TEXT

The Hebrew manuscript tradition, called the Masoretic Text, upon which our English translations of the book of Zephaniah are based, is in very good condition. This is doubtlessly the result of the early collection and transmission into written form of Zephaniah's oracles by those who were drawn to the prophet's message and were intent upon seeing that it was preserved, especially until the time of its fulfillment. Such a motivation for preserving the words of a prophet is clearly noted in Zephaniah ben Cushi's later contemporary Habakkuk (Hab 2:2-3), and also in Jeremiah (Jer 36:27-32).

The earliest translation of the Hebrew manuscript, the Greek translation known as the Septuagint, which emerged from the Alexandrian diaspora community in third-century BCE Egypt, generally reflects and, therefore, supports the authenticity of the Masoretic Text. The Dead Sea Scrolls or Qumran Palestinian Hebrew MSS from the last two centuries BCE also reflect the consonantal text of the MT.

The few difficulties that do occur for the translator and interpreter of the Hebrew text are, for the most part, due to a lost or obscure meaning of a Hebrew word or a corruption of the text because of scribal or transmission errors. A literal translation of the MT behind Zeph 3:18, for example, does not make much sense. The NIV attempts to stay close to the MT in its translation of 3:18, with an alternative reading placed in its note on this verse. The NRSV follows the LXX and the Syriac Version of the Old Testament (Syr), opening this verse with the final line of 3:17c, as indicated in its notes. Other examples of these two approaches in the NIV and the NRSV to obscure texts in Zephaniah are to be found in the treatment of Zeph 1:4b and 3:17b. The latter involves the much-debated question of what to do with the MT's "he will be silent in his love," when the context—the lines immediately before and after—suggests, as in the LXX and the Syr, that it be read as "he will renew you in his love" (3:17b NRSV). The NIV, however, translates "he will quiet you with his love."

FOR FURTHER READING

Achtemeier, Elizabeth. *Nahum–Malachi.* Interpretation. Atlanta: John Knox, 1986.

Africa in Antiquity: The Arts of Ancient Nubia and the Sudan. 2 vols. New York: Brooklyn Museum, 1978.

Ball, Ivan J. *Zephaniah: A Rhetorical Study.* Berkeley, Calif.: Bibal, 1988.

Bennett, Robert. "Africa." In *Oxford Companion to the Bible.* Edited by Bruce Metzger and Michael Coogan. New York: Oxford, 1993.

———. "Africa and the Biblical Period," *HTR* 64 (1971) 483-500.

Ben Zvi, Ehud. *A Historical-Critical Study of the Book of Zephaniah.* BZAW 198. Berlin: DeGruyter, 1991.

Berlin, Adele. *Zephaniah.* AB 25A. New York: Doubleday, 1994.

House, Paul. *Zephaniah: A Prophetic Drama.* JSOTSup 69. Sheffield: Almond Press, 1988.

Kapelrud, Arvid. *The Message of the Prophet Zephaniah: Morphology and Ideas.* Oslo: Universitetsforlaget, 1975.

Kitchen, Kenneth. *The Third Intermediate Period in Egypt.* Warminster: Aris & Phillips, 1973.

Mokhtar, G., ed. *Ancient Civilizations of Africa.* Berkeley: University of California Press, 1990.

Rice, Gene. "The African Roots of the Prophet Zephaniah." *JRT* 36 (1979).

Roberts, J. J. M. *Nahum, Habakkuk, and Zephaniah.* OTL. Louisville: Westminster/John Knox, 1991.

Sweeney, Marvin A. *Zephaniah.* Minneapolis, Minn.: Fortress, 2003.

Taylor, Charles, "Zephaniah." In *The Interpreter's Bible.* Vol. 6. Nashville: Abingdon, 1956.

Thurman, Howard. *Deep River and The Negro Spiritual Speaks of Life and Death.* Richmond, Ind.: Friends United Press, 1975.

———. *A Track to the Water's Edge: The Olive Schreiner Reader.* New York: Harper & Row, 1973.

Tutu, Desmond. *The Words of Desmond Tutu: Selected by Naomi Tutu.* New York: Newmarket, 1989.

Washington, James M., ed. *Conversations with God: Two Centuries of Prayers by African Americans.* New York: HarperCollins, 1994.

ENDNOTES

1. On the name "Zephaniah," see Adele Berlin, *Zephaniah*, AB 25A (New York: Doubleday, 1994) 64-65, and J. J. M. Roberts, *Nahum, Habakkuk, and Zephaniah*, OTL (Louisville: Westminster/John Knox, 1991) 165-66.

2. See Duane L. Christensen, "Zephaniah 2:4-15: A Theological Basis for Josiah's Program of Political Expansion," *CBQ* 46 (1984) 669-82; cf. the critique by Adele Berlin, *Zephaniah*, 119-20.

3. Amos 1:3, 6, 9, 11, 13 list the crimes against humanity of Israel's neighbors.

4. Examples of wisdom tradition's use of "correction"/"instruction" (*mûsār*): Prov 1:2, 3, 7-8; 10:17; 15:32-33; 23:12, 23.

THE BOOK OF
HAGGAI

W. EUGENE MARCH

Little is known about the man for whom the book of Haggai is named. No family name or other information is provided here or in the only other place where Haggai is mentioned, Ezra 5:1; 6:14. His name seems etymologically related to the Hebrew stem חגג (ḥgg), which means "make a pilgrimage" or "observe a pilgrimage feast." H. W. Wolff suggests that the name, found often in extrabiblical, post-exilic sources, was popular because it was "an allusion to the birth on a feast day of the person so named."[1] Three other persons with names related to this stem are mentioned in the Bible: Haggith, 2 Sam 3:4; 1 Kgs 1:6, 11; 2:13; 1 Chr 3:2; Haggiah, 1 Chr 6:30; and Haggi, Gen 46:16; Num 26:15.

The absence of a family name suggested to Carol Meyers and Eric Meyers that Haggai had family connections that would have been problematic for the prophet if they were publicly announced.[2] David Petersen, on the other hand, considered the absence of genealogical detail concerning Haggai a deliberate means of focusing attention on the divine authority by which the prophet spoke.[3] Nonetheless, for whatever reason, Haggai, like Amos, Habakkuk, and Obadiah before him, is not provided with a lineage.

Efforts have been made to develop some kind of biographical profile for Haggai based on other details in the book. Early Jewish and Christian sources assumed that Haggai was a man at least seventy years old on the basis of Hag 2:3, but, according to Janet Tollington, this verse actually makes no claim concerning the prophet's age.[4] On the one hand, on the basis of his use of agricultural images, Haggai has been identified as a Judahite farmer who never left Palestine. On the other hand, he has been portrayed as one of those persons who returned from the exile determined to lead restoration efforts and overcome the lethargy of those who had escaped exile and remained in Judah. In truth, however, all such efforts to identify Haggai remain speculative. There is just not sufficient evidence within the book to draw a biographical sketch.

Probably the only thing that can be said for certain of Haggai is that he was remembered as a prophet with authority. Five times Haggai is called "the prophet" (Hag 1:1, 3, 12; 2:1, 10). The messenger formula, "thus says the LORD," employed so often in the prophetic literature, is prominent in Haggai as well (fully in Hag 1:2, 5, 7; 2:6, 11; abbreviated in Hag 1:8; 2:7, 9). The divine oracle formula, "says the LORD" or "saying of the LORD," is likewise frequent in this book (Hag 1:9, 13; 2:4, 9, 14, 17, 23). Haggai addressed both the governor and the high priest as one with authority (Hag 1:1, 12, 14; 2:2, 4). He dealt with matters of priestly teaching as one who stood outside the priestly circle but who, nonetheless, deserved a hearing (Hag 2:10-14). Unlike the professional cultic prophets prevalent before the Babylonian exile, whose false optimism had been so harmful to the nation, Haggai presented a message of hope grounded in the hard reality of a destroyed land. Although some have tried to associate Haggai with the prophets (sometimes called cultic prophets) who lived at or near Israel's shrines and who participated regularly in the worship there, it seems best to understand him as being outside of those circles. Rather, Haggai is best associated with the long tradition of classical prophets raised up by God to proclaim the Lord's word to Israel.[5]

One further aspect of Haggai's role as prophet should be noted. As already mentioned, he was closely linked to Zechariah in Ezra 5–6. The two prophets were pictured working in Jerusalem at the same time and toward the same goal. Yet there is no reference to the other prophet in either Haggai or Zechariah. This enigmatic silence only underscores the vagueness of detail concerning

Haggai the prophet. Petersen is indeed correct that, with so little biographical data, attention must be centered upon the message rather than the messenger.[6]

HISTORICAL CONTEXT

The work of Haggai, according to the book itself, was concentrated between August 29, 520 BCE, and December 18 of the same year, the second year of the reign of Persian King Darius (Hag 1:1, 15; 2:1, 10). Scholars basically accept these dates as authentic and believe the book was compiled in its present form only a short time after the prophet spoke, certainly before 515 BCE, when the work on the Temple initiated at Haggai's urging was completed.

That the Temple could be rebuilt and that life in Jerusalem could resume with a degree of safety and modest prosperity was the result of Persia's defeat of the Babylonians. When his army conquered the city of Babylon in 538 BCE, Cyrus the Persian ended the harsh Babylonian rule that had prevailed in most of Mesopotamia and Syria-Palestine for over seventy years (612–538 BCE). Very quickly Cyrus set about reorganizing the administration of not only Babylon but also the vast empire Babylon had established. Further, early in his reign, Cyrus issued a decree, now preserved in what is known as the Cyrus Cylinder. The decree ordered the return of sacred images and temple furniture taken by the Babylonians as spoils from the numerous cities they had conquered. This decree effected the return of some Judahite exiles with a mandate and financial support to reconstruct the Temple (Ezra 1:2-4; 6:2-5). This decree may also explain why the writer of Second Isaiah, rejoicing at the prospect of the return from exile, conferred upon Cyrus the title of "Messiah," the Lord's "anointed" (Isa 45:1).

Cyrus was succeeded by Cambyses, his son, who ruled eight years (530–522 BCE). Cambyses extended Persian control into Egypt. While on his way home from his western military campaign, he received word of a revolt and suddenly died. The circumstances of Cambyses' death are unclear, but one of his officers, Darius, a blood relative although not a son, took over.[7] Darius returned home and put down the revolt. For the next two years, Darius dealt with rebellion in a number of cities. Then, with his rule finally established, Darius I the Great guided the Persian Empire until his death in 486 BCE.

Under Cyrus's administrative plan, Judah was governed as a large satrapy (province) called "Babylon and Beyond the River." "Beyond the River" had Samaria as its administrative center. Due to Cambyses' ambitions in Egypt, Syria-Palestine began to evolve into a separate district. By the time Darius I took over, a "governor" (פחה *peḥâ*) named Ushtani was in charge of the whole satrapy of "Babylon and Beyond the River," while a subordinate named Tattenai (also called *peḥâ* in Ezra 6:6, 13) administered that part of the satrapy called "Beyond the River." It is likely that the pressure to remove Judah from Samaria's direct administrative control began when Zerubbabel was appointed and dispatched to Judah around 523–522 BCE, though full regional autonomy was not to be realized until later in the fifth century.[8]

The socioeconomic situation of Judah at the time of Haggai can only be described broadly. Recent studies, well summarized by Petersen, highlight three aspects of the situation.[9] First, the economy was not particularly productive. Jerusalem, the major market and trading center of the region, was still recovering from the devastation of 587 BCE. Limited labor resources and relatively poor land combined to produce minimal economic return. Agricultural specialization in wine and olives became necessary in order to survive, but the end result of the specialization was the entrenchment of the more wealthy over against the poor.

A second phenomenon that dominated Judah's society was the concentration of community life around the Temple. As primarily the royal chapel of the monarchy before the exile, the Temple had played an important, though much more limited, role. The people as a whole did not go to the Temple. It was the sanctuary of the king and his household. After the people's return from the exile, however, the Temple became the center of social and economic activity in a way never seen during the days of the kings. Such temple-centered civil societies became typical all across Syria-Palestine during the Persian period. Judah's relatively sparse population and small territory (smaller than the state of Rhode Island), centered economically, socially, politically, and religiously around Jerusalem, made the Temple the religious and civic symbol it had never been before.

Finally, land distribution and administration took on a new look in the post-exilic community. When families had been exiled in 587 BCE, their land had been taken by people who had remained. When the deportees began to return under the auspices of the Persian authorities, conflicts inevitably arose. Elsewhere in the Persian Empire a new institution was developing that was adapted to the circumstances of Judah. Known as the אבות בית (bêt 'ābôt), the "fathers' house," it functioned as a collective, holding and administering land. In theory, members of a particular "house" were related genealogically from tribal times, but this was more myth than reality. Membership lists for some of these "houses" (e.g., Neh 7:61-62) indicate that people who had been in exile were integrated with those who had stayed behind. Thus land, taken possession of by those to whom it had not originally belonged, was shared with the returnees whose families had once been landowners. These collectives became the institution by which land was redistributed, and some measure of stability and productivity was brought back into the land.

During Haggai's time there was no longer a society defined by national borders with its own king and national religion. Rather, a community organized in landholding collectives with the Temple of the Lord as its administrative, economic, and religious center began to emerge. The shape of the society was not nearly as clear in Haggai's era as it would become one hundred years later. The prophet's task was to assist in these early stages of the process by pressing the need for rebuilding the Temple, and this he did vigorously.

THE BOOK OF HAGGAI

The most immediate impression that the book of Haggai makes on the reader is its chronologically ordered set of five units, presenting speeches made by the prophet and the circumstances of those speeches. Unlike most of the other prophetic books, which appear primarily as collections of unconnected, undated oracles, Haggai exists more in the form of a narrative or a drama. The narrative has five episodes: Hag 1:1-11; 1:12-15a; 1:15b-2:9; 2:10-19; 2:20-23, with a date assigned to each

unit. In the two brief chapters that comprise this book, a narrative spanning approximately three and one-half months is presented and arranged according to the appropriate dates:

Hag 1:1	First day, sixth month, second year of King Darius	Aug 29, 520 BCE
Hag 1:15a	twenty-fourth day, sixth month, second year of King Darius	Sept 21, 520 BCE
Hag 1:15b–2:1	twenty-first day, seventh month, second year of King Darius	Oct 17, 520 BCE
Hag 2:10	twenty-fourth day, ninth month, second year of King Darius	Dec 18, 520 BCE
Hag 2:20	twenty-fourth day, ninth month, second year of King Darius	Dec 18, 520 BCE

It seems clear that the book is intended to preserve and interpret words spoken by a prophet at critical points in the history of the community.

The type of narrative found here may be characterized as "brief apologetic historical narrative."[10] During the sixth century BCE, the distinctive style of prose represented here developed and may also be seen in other historical works influenced by the deuteronomists. Other examples of such a genre are found in 2 Kings 22–23; and Jeremiah 26; 36; 37–41. The book of Haggai aims to remember the positive community achievement represented by the rebuilding of the Temple and to emphasize Haggai's role in that event. Thus it might well be entitled, according to Petersen, "The story of Haggai's involvement in the restoration of Judah."[11]

There is wide agreement that the composition of the book had at least two phases: the preservation of the words of the prophet, probably by a disciple, and then the development of the narrative structure in which the present material is presented. The completion of the narrative was accomplished not long after the events remembered, and certainly before the temple project was completed (515 BCE). The narrative was fashioned by supplying a connective framework that provided context and, to a degree, interpretation (cf. Hag 1:1, 13, 12-13a, 14-15; 2:1-2, 10, 20-21a).[12] R. Mason has rightly demonstrated the many connections of the Haggai narrative with the deuteronomists (as opposed to relationships with the chronicler, which has been suggested by others).[13] Apart from debate concerning the original placement of Hag 2:15-19 and its possible connection to Hag 1:15a, there is general agreement on the date of the basic composition of Haggai.[14]

The message of Haggai is straightforward: Rebuild the Temple and therein witness and give testimony to the reign of God, both in the present and in the future. This twofold character of the message needs to be remembered. If only the present context is emphasized, the book might be read as too mundane, too concerned with the obvious need to rebuild the community. With the future (some would say eschatological) dimensions in mind, however, Haggai's words remind his hearers that the work of God's people always points beyond the present moment to the continuation of God's work and fulfillment of all the divine purpose.

FOR FURTHER READING

Commentaries:

Meyers, Carol L., and Eric M. Meyers. *Haggai and Zechariah 1–8: A New Translation, Introduction, and Commentary.* AB 25B. Garden City, N.Y.: Doubleday, 1987.

Petersen, David L. *Haggai and Zechariah 1–8.* OTL. Philadelphia: Westminster, 1984.

Stuhlmueller, Carroll. *Rebuilding with Hope: A Commentary on the Books of Haggai and Zechariah.* ITC. Grand Rapids: Eerdmans, 1988.

Wolff, Hans Walter. *Haggai.* Translated by Margaret Kohl. Minneapolis: Augsburg, 1988; German edition in *BK* series 1986.

Other Studies:

Boda, Mark J. *Haggai & Zechariah Research: A Bibliography.* Tools for Biblical Studies 5. Leiden: Deo, 2003.

Kessler, John. *The Book of Haggai: Prophecy and Society in Early Persian Yehud.* VTSup 91. Leiden: Brill, 2002.

Mason, R. "The Purpose of the 'Editorial Framework' of the Book of Haggai," *VT* 27 (1977) 413-21.

Tollington, Janet E. *Tradition and Innovation in Haggai and Zechariah 1–8.* JSOTSup 150. Sheffield: JSOT, 1993.

ENDNOTES

1. Hans Walter Wolff, *Haggai*, trans. Margaret Kohl (Minneapolis: Augsburg, 1988; German edition in *BK* series 1986) 37.

2. Carol L. Meyers and Eric M. Meyers, *Haggai and Zechariah 1–8*, AB 25B (Garden City, NY: Doubleday, 1987) 8.

3. David L. Petersen, *Haggai and Zechariah 1–8*, OTL (Philadelphia: Westminster, 1984) 18-19.

4. Janet E. Tollington, *Tradition and Innovation in Haggai and Zechariah 1–8*, JSOTSup 150 (Sheffield: JSOT, 1993) 52-53.

5. See Janet E. Tollington, *Tradition and Innovation in Haggai and Zechariah 1–8*, 61, 76; Wolff, *Haggai*, 16-17.

6. David L. Petersen, *Haggai and Zechariah 1–8*, 18-19.

7. David L. Petersen, *Haggai and Zechariah 1–8*, 22.

8. David L. Petersen, *Haggai and Zechariah 1–8*, 24-27.

9. David L. Petersen, *Haggai and Zechariah 1–8*, 28-31.

10. David L. Petersen, *Haggai and Zechariah 1–8*, 35, citing W. Rudolph, *Haggai–Sacharja 1–8/9–14 Maleachi*, KAT (1976).

11. David L. Petersen, *Haggai and Zechariah 1–8*, 34, citing W. Rudolph, *Haggai–Sacharja 1–8/9–14 Maleachi*, KAT (1976).

12. Janet E. Tollington, *Tradition and Innovation in Haggai and Zechariah 1–8*, 23; but for different suggestions, see Carroll Stuhlmueller, *Rebuilding with Hope: A Commentary on the Books of Haggai and Zechariah*, ITC (Grand Rapids: Eerdmans, 1988) 14; and Hans Walter Wolff, *Haggai*, 18.

13. R. Mason, "The Purpose of the 'Editorial Framework' of the Book of Haggai," *VT* 27 (1977) 415-18.

14. Hans Walter Wolff, *Haggai*, 59-62.

THE BOOK OF
ZECHARIAH

BEN C. OLLENBURGER

The book of Zechariah comes next to last in the "Book of the Twelve," or what are sometimes called the minor prophets. The literature now gathered under the name of Zechariah exists in at least two quite distinct parts. Since the seventeenth century, scholars have argued that some or all of chaps. 9–14 was written by someone other than the author of chaps. 1–8 and that the two sections were written at different times. Joseph Mede noted that Matt 27:9 attributes the statement about the thirty shekels of silver in Zech 11:13 to Jeremiah. In defense of the New Testament's accuracy, Mede argued that Zechariah 9–11 was indeed written by Jeremiah, a century earlier than Zechariah.[1] Since Medes' time, the substantial differences between chaps. 1–8 and all of 9–14 have led all but the most conservative scholars to see these two parts of the book as coming from different hands. Thus the major structural division in the book occurs between chaps. 1–8 and 9–14, which reflect sections now known as First and Second Zechariah.

FIRST ZECHARIAH

Structure, Form, and Composition. Within chaps. 1–8 a series of eight visions (1:7–6:15) is framed by a pair of sermons. The first of these sermons (1:1-6) is brief and retrospective. It reports a call to repentance, modeled on the preaching of the "former prophets" to the forebears, and the community's positive response. In style and vocabulary, vv. 1-6 strongly resemble the second, much longer sermon that comprises chaps. 7–8. There, too, the preaching of the former prophets is of key importance, as is the refusal of the forebears to respond to their words. This lack of a response led to Yahweh's judgment, devastation, and the difficult circumstances from which Yahweh now promises to deliver the community (7:8-14; 8:1-8). However, nowhere in the longer sermon, or in the visions, is there a call to repentance like that of

1:3: "Return to me, says the LORD of hosts, and I will return to you" (NRSV). On the contrary, in both the sermons and the visions the reversal of communal fortunes is Yahweh's own initiative (8:11). The precise language of 1:3 occurs elsewhere only in Mal 3:7, although it shares the perspective of the prophetic speeches in Chronicles (e.g., 2 Chr 30:6; cf. Joel 2:12-14). It seems that Zechariah's editors have composed a brief sermon on the basis of chaps. 7–8, but from a different theological perspective, which now serves as a preface to the visions: Yahweh's gracious announcements in the remainder of First Zechariah—especially Yahweh's promises to "return" (1:16; 8:3)—are now prefaced by, and predicated on, the community's repentance or return to Yahweh. In this way, Zechariah's editors have interpreted Zechariah in the direction of Haggai.

These editors have done so as well by providing a chronological framework for both the sermons and the visions in the superscriptions to each part (1:1, 7; 7:1), which link Zechariah's activity with Haggai's. The first chapter of the book of Haggai attributes the community's ills to its ignoring the Temple, which "lies in ruins" (Hag 1:9 NRSV), and exhorts them to rebuild it (1:8). Conversely, Haggai's second chapter attributes the community's dramatically improved fortunes to the people's beginning to work on temple reconstruction (Hag 2:15-19). Haggai's exhortation in chap. 1 is dated in the sixth month, and his reflections in chap. 2 are dated in the ninth month (2:10, 18). The redactors of Zechariah placed Zech 1:2-6 squarely between these two dates, sometime in the eighth month (1:1). In this way, they urge us to interpret the community's "return" in Zech 1:6 along lines provided by Haggai 1, as the theological premise of what Zechariah sees in his visions.

At the heart of First Zechariah are the visions, dated late in the eleventh month (1:7). They are arranged in chiastic fashion, with the first and the

---

last visions framing the others. The arrangement of the visions corresponds to their varying foci; in the first (1:8-17) and last (6:1-8) visions, the focus extends to the whole world. The focus first narrows to Judah and then to Jerusalem and finally to the lampstand—symbol of Yahweh's presence—in chap. 4; it then expands outward again to encompass the whole world. At one stage in the book's composition, this arrangement probably included seven visions, with chap. 4 as their center and pivot.[2] These visions, excluding chap. 3, are variations on a common pattern, in which Zechariah converses with an interpreting angel:

1. Zechariah reports a vision: "I saw. . . . "
2. He describes a sign: "and there before me was/were. . . ."
3. He asks: "What is this/are these?"
4. The angel identifies the sign: "This is/these are. . . . "
5. The angel interprets the sign.[3]

Chapter 3 departs significantly from this pattern to focus on Joshua the high priest. This chapter was probably added secondarily, increasing the number of visions to eight and giving them this arrangement:

(1) 1:8-17 Horses and riders patrolling the earth
  (2) 1:18-21 Four horns and four smiths
  (3) 2:1-5 Jerusalem without limits
    (4) 3:1-10 Joshua the high priest
    (5) 4:1-6a, 10b-14 The lampstand
  (6) 5:1-4 A flying scroll
  (7) 5:5-11 A flying ephah
(8) 6:1-8 Horses and chariots patrolling the earth

The addition of chap. 3 is not the only way in which editorial activity has affected the character of the visions. Intruding into what is now the fifth vision is an oracle addressed to Zerubbabel (4:6b-10a), described in Haggai as the "governor of Judah" (Hag 1:1). The oracle in Zechariah 4 identifies Zerubbabel as the temple builder, a role assigned in Zech 6:9-15 to an anonymous but expected "branch"—a royal figure from David's line, also expected in 3:8. Editorial activity here reflects uncertainty and perhaps disagreement about the role of Zerubbabel, to whom Haggai attaches extraordinary expectations (Hag 2:20-23). Further, there is some evidence that the first three visions, in chaps. 1 and 2, were once an independent collection. With their accompanying oracles

(1:14-17; 2:6-13[10-17]), these visions respond to the distress expressed in 1:12, envisioning Yahweh's return to Jerusalem, the elimination of oppression by the nations, Yahweh's action against Babylon and the nations, and the gathering of Jerusalem's people—and people from the nations—as God's people, culminating with Yahweh's dwelling in Zion. As a response to these things, all flesh is to be silent (2:13). With what was, at one stage in the formation of the book, the next vision (chap. 4), Zechariah has to be roused as if from sleep, suggesting that the visions in chaps. 4–6 were added to form a collection of seven, with chap. 3 added subsequently as a supplement to chap. 4.

The visionary material in First Zechariah includes oracles as well. These are identified by formulae introducing them or within them, including "thus says Yahweh" (messenger formula, 1:14), "says Yahweh" (oracle formula, 2:5), and "the word of Yahweh came to . . . " (revelation formula, 4:8). The oracles in chaps. 1–2 are integrally related to the content of the visions they follow, by interpreting or expanding on them. The oracular conclusion to chap. 3, in vv. 6-10, issues in an address to Joshua, as is also the case with Zerubbabel in 4:6-10a. In contrast, the oracular conclusion (6:9-15) to the vision sequence bears a less evident relation to the vision preceding it.

The oracles that follow Zechariah's visions constitute an extended sermon. In chaps. 7–8, Zechariah is not a seer of visions but a prophet and an interpreter of the tradition. The superscription in 7:1 dates the sermon approximately two years after the visions. In its content, and especially in what it promises for the future, the sermon is closely related to the material in chaps. 1–2.

The Date and Setting of First Zechariah.

Each of the superscriptions in First Zechariah, like those in Haggai, dates the material in the reign of Darius, king of Persia, either to his second year (1:1, 7) or to his fourth (7:1). These correspond to 520 and early 519, and to 518 BCE. Darius was third in the succession of Persian emperors, the first of whom, Cyrus, led Persia in displacing Babylon as the imperial power controlling the Mediterranean region. Cyrus made it Persian policy, after 539 BCE, to repatriate populations that had been exiled to Babylon, a policy celebrated in Ezra 1:1-4. The policy continued under Cambyses and then Darius, who assumed the throne in 522 BCE. He secured his reign against militant opposition in 520, the year assigned to Zechariah's first sermon and his visions. The Persian policy toward exiles, especially under Darius, was motivated by more than benevolence. It was designed to foster loyalty in the provinces and to provide efficient means of imperial control, including the collection of revenues. To this end, Darius supported or mandated the reconstruction of provincial institutions—religious, social, and economic—under authorized local leadership. Central among these institutions, in Judah's case as elsewhere, was the Temple; by Persian design, it was the administrative, cultic, and financial center of an essentially agrarian economy.

Under Persian organization, Judah (or in its Aramaic form, "Yehud") was part of the satrapy "Beyond the River," administered from Babylon. Whether it had provincial status, with its own governor, is a matter of dispute, but it does seem probable. According to Ezra, Zerubbabel and Joshua led a group of the golah—Jewish exiles—from Babylon to Judah and two years later initiated the rebuilding of the Temple (Ezra 2:1-2; 3:8-9). Haggai assumes that Zerubbabel and Joshua were Judah's leaders, as governor and high priest (Hag 1:1). In that case, and also by Persian design, it was members of the golah, repatriated from Babylon, who assumed civic and cultic authority in Judah, most of whose population had not been exiled. But in the Persian period, following the Babylonian conquest earlier in the sixth century BCE, Judah was only a fraction of its former self. In area, it comprised approximately 900 square miles, about the size of the greater Chicago metropolitan area, with a population only a third as large as it was earlier. Jerusalem's population, perhaps six or seven thousand before its destruction in 586 BCE, numbered only a few hundred in 520.[4] Zechariah's expectation that Judah's towns would overflow with goods (1:17), and that Jerusalem's population would exceed the capacity of any walls (2:4[8]; cf. 8:5), takes on new light in view of these data; he expects that Yahweh will reverse present conditions and past ones.

Basic Themes in First Zechariah. (1) Reversal is itself a persistent theme of chaps. 1–8. It is expressed within the visions, where Yahweh will reverse the relative situations of Judah/Jerusalem and the nations (1:14-17), and in the long sermon, where the reversal of Judah's fortunes is joined with a reversal of Yahweh's stance toward the community (8:10-13).

(2) But reversal, whether in the abstract or in relation to specific circumstances, is subordinate to Zechariah's implicit and explicit claim that Yahweh is "lord of the whole earth" (4:14). This claim does not easily comport with that of an empire like that of the Persians. Zechariah affirms the sovereignty of Israel's God.

(3) In the logic of the Zion tradition, in which Zechariah stands, Yahweh's lordship—Yahweh's dominion—is exercised from the divine dwelling place, Zion. In this regard, everything, and every kind of reversal, depends on God's return to Zion, which Zechariah's visions and sermons announce. God is specially related to a certain place.

(4) Within the community, leadership will be shared between the high priest and a royal figure (3:8-10; 4:10b-14; 6:9-15). However, one does not have the sense that this is a real-life political program. Rather, the "civic" authority is the subject of future expectation, of a messianic sort associated with David. In both 3:8-10 and 6:9-15, the priests are principally to bear witness to the promise of this coming "branch" of David.

(5) The Temple will be the locus of Yahweh's presence and dominion, symbolized by the lampstand in chap. 4. However, unlike Haggai, Zechariah nowhere urges the community to initiate or to continue building the Temple. Its reconstruction, under charge of the royal "branch," will correspond to the newly ordered world that Zechariah envisions and announces.

(6) This newly ordered world has a social and moral character that contrasts with the past and the present. The land will be purged of its guilt (3:9) and of its wickedness (5:1-11). In the future, truthfulness, justice, and peace will characterize the people of Judah (8:10-19). Moral transformation is not the condition of God's return, but results from it.

(7) Throughout, First Zechariah expects that other nations will be included in the glorious future promised to Judah and Jerusalem. Robbed of their destructive powers (1:18-21[2:1-4]) and witnessing to God's presence, they will be included among Yahweh's people (2:15[11]; 8:20-23). As with several other themes, this one deserves to be called eschatological.

Zechariah the Prophet. The literature associated with him provides few details about Zechariah. The superscriptions (1:1, 7) identify Zechariah as the son of Berechiah and the grandson of Iddo. The book of Ezra describes Zechariah as the close colleague of Haggai (Ezra 5:1-2; 6:14). Indeed, Ezra never mentions one without the other. This view is reflected in the editing of Zechariah 1–7, which coordinates, through the chronological references, Zechariah's activity with Haggai's. In one detail, Ezra disagrees with the superscriptions in Zech 1:1, 7. While these name Berechiah as Zechariah's father and Iddo as his grandfather, Ezra 5:1 and 6:14 say that Zechariah was the "son of Iddo." They make no mention of Berechiah. Perhaps Iddo was a family name. The names "Iddo" and "Berechiah" are used frequently in the OT, and there is no way to determine from which family Zechariah the prophet descended.

SECOND ZECHARIAH

Second Zechariah (chaps. 9–14) presents a complex and often discordant vision of the future, and in a literary style vastly different from those of First Zechariah. Apart from chap. 11, the prophetic persona so prominent in First Zechariah is completely absent from these chapters, as are any concrete references to their occasion. They refer to no identifiable person, no Zerubbabel or Joshua, and no Zechariah; they provide sparse and uncertain clues to their date; and the religious, social, and political concerns they address can be inferred only with great difficulty, and only tentatively. If our Bibles did not bind these latter chapters together with the first eight, we may find few reasons to connect them with Zechariah.[5] Indeed, some have suggested that Zechariah 9–11; 12–14; and Malachi are a three-part prophetic collection, two parts of which are now joined artificially to Zechariah 1–8.[6] Among the reasons for this suggestion is the presence in Zech 9:1; 12:1; Mal 1:1 of a phrase that occurs in each of these verses and nowhere else; it can be translated: "oracle of the word of Yahweh,"[7] though neither the NIV nor the NRSV translates it this way.

Structure, Form, and Composition. The material in these chapters is visionary, in the broadest sense of the term—it envisions the future. Of course, this is true of much prophetic literature and particularly of First Zechariah. However, two interrelated features of Second Zechariah mark its unusual visionary character. First, to articulate the vision, it refers extensively to other OT texts. Envisioning the future is here a literary and even an exegetical activity.[8] To some extent, this is true of First Zechariah as well; its visions and oracles draw especially on Isaiah and Jeremiah. But in contrast to the symmetrical arrangement of visions and oracles of Zechariah 1–6, Second Zechariah exhibits a profusion of genres: "invectives, threats, heraldic odes, promises, extended metaphors, symbolic actions," and others, in a form more "anthology-like" than symmetrical.[9]

Second, as a way of envisioning the future, Zechariah 9–14 *re*-envisions the past. For example, the poems in chaps. 9 and 10 not only draw from earlier texts, but also portray the future as a recapitulation and thus as a restoration, without a single specific reference to present circumstances. The description of Yahweh's march in 9:1-8 could be set in almost any period of Judah's history,[10] and 10:11 speaks as if Assyria and Egypt were still the world's great imperial powers. The past, and precisely God's action on behalf of Israel, is paradigmatic, and these poems draw from earlier texts to construct the paradigm. The narrative in 11:4-14 complicates this paradigm, suggesting conflict and disintegration rather than restoration. Although it is an autobiographical narrative, this text can be read as a symbol of Israel's history—and its future. Even the ominous announcements in 12:2-3 and 14:1-2 that the world will gather for war against Jerusalem recapitulate the past. Once before, "all the kingdoms of the earth" fought against Jerusalem (Jer 34:1; Zech 12:3), with exile the result (Zech 14:2). On the other hand, the future envisioned in Zechariah 12, and much more so in chap. 14, is not simply a restoration; it is utopia.[11] While restoration leaves intact conditions that can lead again to disintegration and exile, the utopian future of chaps. 12 and 14 eliminates those conditions. Here the future becomes radically discontinuous with the past, and such radical discontinuity involves violent conflict. These chapters depict a world at war, with its focus on Jerusalem. In Second Zechariah, the ordered world of First Zechariah is fractured, awaiting a new ordering.[12]

These observations make plausible the suggestion that Second Zechariah comprises two collections, chaps. 9–11 and 12–14, each designated as "an oracle" (מַשָּׂא *maśśā'*). The differences between them involve style and rhetoric, as well as content. For example, the first collection makes extensive use of subordinate causal or explanatory clauses introduced by כִּי (*kî*, "because" or "for"), characteristic of prophetic speech. This conjunction occurs twenty times in chaps. 9–11, but only four times in 12–14, three of them in 13:3-5. By contrast, the phrase "on that day" punctuates chaps. 12–14, where it occurs seventeen times (in reference to the future, it occurs only at 9:16 within chaps. 9–11).

Still, the material within each of these collections (9–11; 12–14) is not all of a piece. The narrative of 11:4-14 departs abruptly from the eschatological visions in chaps. 9–10, and the continuity between and within those two chapters is editorial. Forming a part of this continuity is the motif of sheep (or the flock) and shepherds, which first appears in 9:16. It is picked up again in 10:2 and then in 11:1-3, and is explored at length in 11:4-14. Finally, in 11:15-17, the shepherd suffers a violent punishment. Similarly, chaps. 12 and 14 present different scenarios of the future, and they are separated by 13:2-6, which predicts the elimination of prophets. But chap. 13 has links to both chap. 12 and chap. 14. The elimination of prophets is joined to the cleansing offered the house of David (12:10; 13:1-2), and the stabbing of prophets (13:3) echoes the stabbing or piercing of an anonymous victim in 12:10. The conclusion of chap. 13, in vv. 7-9, envisions another kind of cleansing, by fire, which will kill one-third of the population. This motif introduces the war and exile of 14:1-2. For these reasons Zechariah 13 is pivotal within the second collection (chaps. 12–14), which is distinct from 9–11.

While it is evident that chaps. 9–11 and 12–14 are two collections, their independence is only relative. In its concluding verses, chap. 13 returns to the sheep/shepherd motif of chaps. 9–11. In 13:7 the shepherd is struck with a sword and the sheep scattered. This is the only occurrence of the motif in chaps. 12–14, and it echoes 11:17; there, too, the shepherd encounters a sword. The act of violence against the shepherd has a different meaning in the two passages, but it does forge a connection between the two larger collections, or "oracles." Just as chap. 13 is pivotal within chaps. 12–14, so also chap. 11 is pivotal between chaps. 9–10 and 12–14.

Date and Setting. It is clear in Zech 11:17 and 13:7 that the shepherd is a figure of leadership of or within the community. This is not obvious in 10:2, and it is not the case in 11:1-3. Neither is it made explicit in either 11:4-17 or 13:7-9 exactly what leader(s) or what form of leadership—civil, cultic, prophetic—is in view. However, Zechariah 11 and the larger context of chap. 13 strongly suggest conflict within the community—i.e., within the community that can be described as Yahweh's sheep (9:16). Since the work of Otto Plöger,[13] and more recently of Paul Hanson, it has become common to interpret Second Zechariah against the background of intra-communal conflict. Such interpretation is rendered problematic by the very obscurity of the texts, by the absence of concrete references to people or events, and thus by permanent uncertainty about the times and circumstances in which these texts were written, collected, edited, and published. However, it seems clear enough that there is a conflict between the future as restoration, envisioned in chaps. 9–10, and the utopia envisioned in chaps. 12 and 14. And it may be that the nature of that conflict is reflected in chaps. 11 and 13.

Second Zechariah cannot be dated with any certainty; in addition, its several chapters, or parts of them, may come from different times. Proposals range from the seventh to the second century BCE. Chapters 12–14 are related to changes in Persian policy toward Judah and Jerusalem at the time of Nehemiah, just after the middle of the fifth century BCE. At this time, Persia sought to strengthen its control over, and military defenses within, the eastern Mediterranean area and to more effectively centralize the administration of Judah in Jerusalem.[14] Such social changes as these efforts brought about do not explain Second Zechariah, but they provide a plausible occasion for the violence and salvation that Jerusalem is expected to suffer, according to chaps. 12 and 14.

Theological Issues. Second Zechariah attests quite diverse expectations of the future. But in all cases the future depends on the action of God. Second Zechariah is a radically theocentric text; the only action it expressly enjoins on the community is to rejoice, and this injunction is addressed to Zion/Jerusalem at the entrance of its king (9:9). As in First Zechariah, the Zion tradition is prominent here, especially in chaps. 9 and 14. As do Zechariah's visions, Second Zechariah expects a future royal figure in the line of David. But this expectation, clearly expressed in 9:9-10 and implicit in 10:4-5, becomes complicated in chaps. 11–13 and is entirely absent from chap. 14. And again, like First Zechariah, the second part of the book envisions a world newly ordered, re-created, by God's initiative. But it comes to see the way to the future as fraught with conflict, suffering, and death. Perhaps for that reason Second Zechariah figures prominently in the NT's passion narratives.

FOR FURTHER READING

Achtemeier, Elizabeth. *Nahum–Malachi.* Interpretation. Atlanta: John Knox, 1986.

Baldwin, Joyce. *Haggai, Zechariah, Malachi.* Tyndale Old Testament Commentaries. Downers Grove, Ill.: Inter-Varsity, 1972.

Boda, Mark J. and Michael H. Floyd, eds. *Bringing Out the Treasure: Inner Biblical Allusion in Zechariah 9-14.* JSOTSupp 370. London: Sheffield Academic Press, 2003.

Calvin, John. *Commentaries on the Twelve Minor Prophets,* vol. 5. Grand Rapids: Eerdmans, 1950.

Conrad, Edgar W. *Zechariah.* Readings: A New Biblical Commentary. Sheffield: Sheffield Academic Press, 1999.

Hanson, Paul D. *The Dawn of Apocalyptic.* Philadelphia: Fortress, 1975.

Larkin, Katrina J. A. *The Eschatology of Second Zechariah.* Kampen: Pharos, 1994.

Love, Mark Cameron. *The Evasive Text: Zechariah 1-8 and the Frustrated Reader.* JSOTSup 296. Sheffield: Sheffield Academic Press, 1999.

Luther, Martin. *Lectures on the Minor Prophets.* Vol. 3: *Zechariah; Luther's Works,* vol. 20. St. Louis: Concordia, 1973.

Mason, Rex. *The Books of Haggai, Zechariah, and Malachi.* CBC. Cambridge: Cambridge University Press, 1977.

———. *Preaching the Tradition: Homily and Hermeneutics After the Exile.* Cambridge: Cambridge University Press, 1991.

Merrill, Eugene H. *Haggai, Zechariah, Malachi: An Exegetical Commentary.* Chicago: Moody, 1994.

Meyers, Carol L., and Eric M. Meyers. *Haggai and Zechariah 1-8,* and *Zechariah 9–14* AB 25B, 25C. New York: Doubleday, 1987, 1993.

Mitchell, Hinckley G. *A Critical and Exegetical Commentary on Haggai and Zechariah.* ICC. Edinburgh: T & T Clark, 1912.

Petersen, David L. *Haggai and Zechariah 1–8.* OTL. Philadelphia: Westminster, 1984

———. *Zechariah 9–14 and Malachi.* OTL. Louisville: Westminster John Knox, 1995.

Redditt, Paul L. *Haggai, Zechariah, Malachi.* NCB. Grand Rapids: Eerdmans, 1995.

Smith, Ralph L. *Micah–Malachi.* WBC. Waco: Word, 1984.

ENDNOTES

1. See J. Baldwin, *Haggai, Zechariah, Malachi* (Atlanta: John Knox, 1986) 63.

2. Carol L. Meyers and Eric M. Meyers, *Haggai and Zechariah 1-8,* AB 25B (Garden City, NY: Doubleday, 1987) 8.

3. Michael Fishbane, *Biblical Interpretation in Ancient Israel* (Oxford: Clarendon, 1985) 448.

4. Meyers and Meyers, *Haggai and Zechariah 1-8,* 24-25; and the same authors, "Demography and Diatribes: Yehud's Population and the Prophecy of Second Zechariah," in *Scripture and Other Artifacts,* ed. M. Coogan, J. Exum, L. Stager (Louisville: Westminister/John Knox, 1994) 268-85.

5. But see Rex A. Mason, "The Relation of Zech. 9–14 to Proto-Zechariah," *ZAW* 88 (1976) 227-39.

6. D. Peterson, *Zechariah 9–14 and Malachi,* OTL (Louisville: Westminster/John Knox, 1995) 2-3.

7. Eugene H. Merrill, *Haggai, Zechariah, Malachi: An Exegetical Commentary* (Chicago: Moody, 1994) 240.

8. Katrina J. A. Larkin, *The Eschatology of Second Zechariah* (Kampen: Pharos, 1994) 27-39.

9. Meyers and Meyers, *Haggai and Zechariah 1–8,* 46-47.

10. P. Hanson, *The Dawn of Apocalyptic* (Philadelphia: Fortress, 1975) 316.

11. Shemaryahu Talmon, "The Concept of Masiah and Messianism in Early Judaism," in *The Messiah: Developments in Earlier Judaism and*

Christianity, ed. James H. Charlesworth (Minneapolis: Fortress, 1992) 79-115.

12. Brevard Childs, *Introduction to the Old Testament as Scripture* (Philadelphia: Fortress, 1979) 483.

13. Otto Plöger, *Theocracy and Eschatology* (Oxford: Blackwell, 1968) 78-96.

14. Carol Meyers and Eric Meyers, Zechariah 9–14, AB 25C (New York: Doubleday, 1993) 20-23.

THE BOOK OF
MALACHI

EILEEN M. SCHULLER, O.S.U.

Malachi is the final book in the collection of the Twelve Prophets. Although the order of these books may have varied when the Bible was copied in manuscript form, in present-day Christian Bibles, Malachi concludes the entire prophetic section and is the final book of the whole of the Old Testament. As such, many readers have seen it as a transition to the New Testament, as "the skirt and boundary of Christianity" to use Tertullian's phrase. In most Hebrew manuscripts and in modern Jewish Bibles, Malachi functions differently: It is "the seal of the Prophets." It concludes both the Book of the Twelve (Hosea–Malachi) and the larger unit of Prophets (Joshua–Malachi), and it is followed by the section called Writings.

The book of Malachi is a relatively short collection of fifty-five verses. As expected in a book that belongs to the corpus of Prophets, in it we find words from God delivered through a human agent, words of both judgment and salvation, directed to "Israel" (1:1), either to the people as a whole or to the priests specifically (1:6; 2:1). But we also hear the voices of the people and the priests in response. Indeed, one of the distinctive features of the book is the way that priests and people articulate their questions and state their complaints in a way that sets up the dynamic of an ongoing dialogue. Finally, in addition to the words of God and the words of the people, the book also includes a brief editorial introduction (1:1), one verse of narration (3:16), and an epilogue (4:4-6).

Many readers have the sense that with the book of Malachi the prophetic corpus per se and the OT as a whole end not with a bang, but with a whimper. The book does not belong to the time when Israel and Judah were political powers on the stage of the world empires, but comes from the postexilic period, when Judah (or Yehud, as it was sometimes called) had been reduced to a minor administrative unit in the vast Persian Empire.[1]

The book is written in what is, at best, elevated and crafted prose, though not devoid of imagery and structure. This is not the rich lyrical poetry of a prophet like Isaiah. Throughout much of the book the prophet is concerned with details of animal sacrifice, the payment of tithes, bored priests, unfaithful husbands, and complaining laity. What deliverance is promised will come in the distant future when the Lord "will come to his temple" (3:1 NIV), but the description of that final eschatological scenario is frustratingly brief and sparse in imaginative detail. Some sections (esp. 2:10-16) are very difficult to interpret, and individual verses (e.g., 2:15) are hopelessly corrupt in the Hebrew so that only a combination of emendation and guesswork yields any intelligible meaning. The prophet is quoted directly only twice in the NT (Mal 1:2-3 in Rom 9:13 and Mal 3:1 in Mark 1:2/Matt 11:10/Luke 7:27), and only small selections from Malachi are included in most Christian lectionaries (usually Mal 3:1-4; 4:1-2).

And yet the book is not without strength or appeal. Many years ago G. von Rad warned about the modern tendency to judge the later prophets against some artificial norm of a "great age of prophecy" and find them wanting, precisely because they are not Isaiah, Jeremiah, or Ezekiel. Von Rad concluded that "the only proper question is whether these prophets, in giving the message they did, were true ministers to their day."[2] Some years before Malachi, the prophet Zechariah had aptly described this period after the exile, when Israel had lost its king and political independence and was struggling to learn new ways to survive, as "the day of small things" (Zech 4:10 NRSV). It was in "this day of small things" that Malachi continued the established prophetic tradition and introduced new perspectives for his time and for the generations to come.

Within these four short chapters, for example, we find a particularly rich and creative reworking and integration of the major covenant themes that inspired the earlier prophets.[3] The passion for justice, the concern for the widow and orphan and laborer of the eighth-century prophets is combined with a focus on Temple, cult, and priesthood that both reflects and addresses the centrality of these institutions for the post-exilic community. In line with similar developments in Joel, Zechariah 9–14, and Isaiah 56–66, Malachi 3–4 attests to a lively eschatological expectation and introduces certain new concepts (such as the "book of remembrance" [3:16]) connected with the firm hope that "the day is coming" (4:1 NRSV). Throughout subsequent centuries in Second Temple Judaism, Malachi's description of the "covenant with Levi" (2:4 NRSV) played a formative role in the development of a rich body of literature around the figure of Levi (e.g., *Jubilees* 30–32, the *Testament of Levi*, and the Aramaic Levi Document). Similarly, the promise that Elijah will come "before the great and terrible day of the LORD" (4:5 NRSV) generated a wealth of legends and traditions in Judaism and was of crucial importance for the early Christian community as it sought to understand both John the Baptist and Jesus and the relationship between them (see Matt 11:10-14; Mark 9:13; Luke 7:24).

AUTHOR, DATE,
AND HISTORICAL CONTEXT

Scholars have long debated whether "Malachi" is to be taken as the personal name of a specific prophet or as a title, "my messenger" (מלאכי *mal'ākî*), derived from the expression in 3:1: "See, I am sending my messenger" (NRSV). I will follow established convention and use Malachi as a name, but as the commentary at 1:1 discusses in greater detail, this does not imply that we can know anything about the specific individual who was the intermediary in the transmission of these words from God. These oracles are basically anonymous and function independently of the person of the prophet.

Similarly, the book of Malachi is curiously ahistorical. There are no references to specific persons or events that would enable us to situate these words on the larger stage of world history, and many of the abuses the prophet condemns are generic to almost any period of biblical—or human—history. There is general consensus that

the book comes from the time after the Babylonian exile; the references to a governor (not a king) in 1:8 and to the destruction of the kingdom of Edom (1:2-5) as well as certain linguistic features all point to the period of the Persian Empire (539–332 BCE). The date is certainly somewhat later than the prophets Haggai and Zechariah—that is, after the reestablishment of the Temple in 515 BCE.

Often these oracles are fixed more precisely in the decades immediately before Ezra and Nehemiah, c. 480–450 BCE. It is certainly true that many of the abuses condemned in Malachi are related to major concerns of the books of Ezra and Nehemiah: provision for sacrifices (Neh 10:32-39; 13:31; Mal 1:6-14); payment of tithe (Neh 10:37-39; 13:10-14; Mal 3:8-12); definition of community boundaries through regulation of acceptable marriage partners (Ezra 9–10; Neh 11:23-27; Mal 2:10-12); exploitation of the disadvantaged (Neh 5:1-13; Mal 3:5). Moreover, it is generally assumed that Malachi came first and was relatively ineffectual with his prophetic message, so that real reform was effected only with the concrete measures enacted by Ezra and Nehemiah. Although such a scenario is not impossible, it is much more speculative than often admitted and depends on a multitude of assumptions.[4] Many of the issues in Malachi are not as similar in detail to conditions at the time of Ezra–Nehemiah as appears on first glance, and such generic abuses could have been found at almost any time during the Persian period.

In addition to reading Malachi through the lens of Ezra–Nehemiah, scholars have looked for other clues that might establish a more precise date for the prophet: linguistic analysis of the Hebrew language in the book; the relative placement of Malachi 3–4 on an evolutionary line of development of eschatological scenarios; comparison of the language with the technical terminology of the Deuteronomic and Priestly codes. But attempts to use such criteria for dating Malachi have proved problematic and fundamentally inconclusive. Recently some commentators have turned to the work of archaeologists, historians, and social scientists for help in understanding Jewish life under Persian domination.[5] Studies of settlement patterns and the size and material culture of sites in the early part of Persian rule do support the sense gleaned from the book of Malachi of a small and relatively poor community, without solid economic resources or great hopes, a community that could well ask, "Where is the God of justice?" (2:17 NRSV) and expect vindication only in a future day of direct divine intervention. Yet a certain caution must be exercised when attempting to draw precise sociological and historical conclusions from these oracles. Malachi is a prophet and, as such, condemns specific abuses in society from the perspective of God's law and the fundamental covenant reality of Israel's existence. It is simplistic, however, to conclude that his depiction of laxity, corruption, unfaithfulness, and indifference reflects the total reality of life under the rule of the Persian Empire.

Furthermore, it is surely significant that these oracles were not handed down with reference to specific historical events. In pointed contrast to the editorial process that produced the books of Haggai and Zechariah—one that judged the oracles of Haggai and Zechariah could be understood only by knowing the exact year, month, and day of their deliverance (Hag 1:1; 2:1, 10, 20; Zech 1:1, 7; 7:1)—the process of collecting and editing that led to the book of Malachi never considered such knowledge essential to reading these words of the Lord. If we take that editorial process seriously, we are in fact discouraged from seeking such historical precision, or at least assuming that such knowledge would somehow be the key to understanding this material.

TEXT, FORM, AND STRUCTURE

The Hebrew text of Malachi presents few major problems that seriously affect the meaning. Fragments from Mal 2:10–4:6 have been preserved as part of one of the Minor Prophets scrolls found at Qumran from about 150–125 BCE[6] Perhaps a few words in another manuscript are from Mal 3:6-7.[7] These are our earliest Hebrew copies of the book, and they preserve some interesting divergent readings and perhaps a different order for the whole collection,[8] but they will not dramatically change our understanding of the book.

Scholars have sometimes tried to separate the original core of prophetic material from the secondary additions by a redactor.[9] Yet apart from the superscription in 1:1 and the final verses in 4:4-6, there is little consensus on what might be secondary additions (1:12-14; 2:11-12; 3:1b-4; 3:13–4:3 are most frequently proposed as secondary). In any case, this short book gives little evidence of having

undergone as lengthy and complex a process of development as is often postulated for other prophetic books.

The formation of the book cannot be separated from the question of how the Book of the Twelve (the "Minor Prophets") was put together. Indeed, some scholars suggest that the very existence of Malachi as a separate book (rather than as an anonymous collection of oracles or as a continuation of the material in Zech 9:1 and 12:1) came about precisely at the stage when the prophetic material was organized so that there would be exactly twelve books.[10] However, so little is known about the whole process of the formation of the Book of the Twelve that elaborate reconstructions about how this larger context shaped the book of Malachi are highly speculative and abstract.

Certain features of the book's structure are puzzling in the light of how the rest of the prophetic corpus is arranged. For instance, the traditional prophetic formula "thus says the LORD of hosts" occurs some twenty-two times, but it does not delineate short individual oracular units in the same way as in an earlier book like Amos. Although at times the phrase seems to be scattered at random, the repetition of this classic formula makes the book sound "prophetic," even though the individual units are quite different in form and structure from anything found in other prophetic literature.

The book falls clearly into six distinctive units of varying length: 1:2-5; 1:6–2:9; 2:10-16; 2:17–3:5; 3:6-12; 3:13–4:3. There is a basic common structure to each unit: an opening affirmation, whether in the form of a statement or a question; a response that calls into question in some way what was said; and an explication and amplification that reaffirms the initial word. But within this general pattern, there is considerable diversity and fluidity in the way each unit is developed.

Perhaps the most distinctive feature of the book is the repeated use of questions—twenty-two in only fifty-five verses. The questions are not all of one type. Some are rhetorical with a self-evident reply: "Is not Esau Jacob's brother?" (1:3 NRSV); "Did not one God create us?" (2:10 NIV); "Will anyone rob God?" (3:8 NRSV). Others are accusatory: "If then I am a father, where is the honor due me?" (1:6 NRSV); "When you offer blind animals in sacrifice, is that not wrong?" (1:8 NRSV). The most profound question, "Where is the God of justice?" (2:17 NIV), is not put to God directly, but quoted indirectly: "Yet you say . . . 'Where is the God of justice?' " (2:17 NRSV). The questions put directly to God are most often "how" questions: "How have you loved us?" (1:2 NRSV); "How have we despised your name?" (1:6 NRSV); "How have we polluted it [you]?" (1:7 NRSV); "How have we wearied him?" (2:17 NIV); "How shall we return?" (3:7 NRSV); "How do we rob you?" (3:8 NIV); "How have we spoken against you?" (3:13 NRSV).

Although the genre has been described variously as "prophetic disputation," "discussion," "catechetical," or "lawsuit," none of these terms really fits the book as a whole. Other prophets certainly made use of questions (e.g., Isa 40:27-28; Jer 2:14, 23, 29, 32; Amos 5:20; Mic 2:7; Hag 1:4; 2:3; some twenty-five questions in Zechariah 1–8), but in these prophets the questions are not as central to the entire book as they are in Malachi. It is difficult to decide precisely how much this format reflects the prophet's actual style of speaking and how much it is a literary and rhetorical device, perhaps stemming from the stage when the material was put into written form. What is certain is that a new style of prophetic discourse is in the process of development, a style both more dialogical and more argumentative than in the earlier prophets.

FOR FURTHER READING

Commentaries:

Achtemeier, Elizabeth. *Nahum–Malachi.* Interpretation. Atlanta: John Knox, 1986.

Glazier-McDonald, Beth. *Malachi: The Divine Messenger.* SBLDS 98. Atlanta: Scholars Press, 1987.

Kaiser, Walter C., Jr. *Malachi: God's Unchanging Love.* Grand Rapids: Baker Book House, 1984.

Petersen, David L. *Zechariah 9–14 and Malachi.* OTL. Louisville: Westminster/John Knox, 1995.

Redditt, Paul L. *Haggai, Zechariah, Malachi.* NCB. Grand Rapids: Eerdmans, 1995.

Smith, Ralph L. *Micah–Malachi.* WBC 32. Waco, Tex.: Word, 1984.

Verhoef, Pieter A. *The Books of Haggai and Malachi.* NICOT. Grand Rapids: Eerdmans, 1987.

Other Studies:

Hugenberger, Gordon Paul. *Marriage as Covenant: A Study of Biblical Law and Ethics Governing Marriage, Developed from the Perspective of Malachi.* VTSup 52. Leiden: E. J. Brill, 1994.

Mason, Rex. *Preaching the Tradition: Homily and Hermeneutics After the Exile.* Cambridge: Cambridge University Press, 1990.

O'Brien, Julia M. *Priest and Levite in Malachi.* SBLDS 121. Atlanta: Scholars Press, 1990.

Weyde, Karl William. *Prophecy and Teaching: Prophetic Authority, Form Problems, and the Use of Traditions in the Book of Malachi.* BZAW 288. Berlin: de Gruyter, 2000.

ENDNOTES

1. The precise status of the territory of the former kingdom of Judah and the city of Jerusalem within the Persian Empire remains a matter of scholarly debate. For a good summary of the issues and alternatives, see D. Petersen, *Zechariah 9–14 and Malachi*, OTL (Louisville: Westminster John Knox, 1995).

2. G. von Rad, *Old Testament Theology*, vol. 2 (London: SCM, 1975) 278-79.

3. See S. L. McKenzie and H. N. Wallace, "Covenant Themes in Malachi," *CBQ* 45 (1983) 549-63.

4. For an attempt to relate Malachi very specifically to Ezra and Nehemiah, see W. J. Dumbrell, "Malachi and the Ezra-Nehemiah Reforms," *Reformed Theological Review* 35 (1976) 42-52. Another proposed dating for Malachi is to place him precisely in the years between the first and second visits of Nehemiah to Jerusalem—that is, immediately after 433 BCE (as argued most recently by P. A. Verhoef, *The Books of Haggai and Malachi*, NICOT [Grand Rapids: Eerdmans, 1987] 156-60).

5. For an exploratory effort to raise many of these questions, see the two volumes of collected essays edited by P. Davies, *Second Temple Studies 1: Persian Period*, JSOTSup 117 (Sheffield: Sheffield Academic, 1991), and T. C. Eskenazi and K. H. Richards, *Second Temple Studies 2: Temple Community in the Persian Period*, JSOTSup 175 (Sheffield: Sheffield Academic, 1994). For a recent survey of the literature, see T. C. Eskenazi, "Current Perspectives on Ezra-Nehemiah and the Persian Period," *Currents in Research 1* (1993) 59-86.

6. 4QXII^a. For a preliminary discussion of the most significant fragments, see R. E. Fuller, "Text-Critical Problems in Malachi 2:10-16," *JBL* 110 (1991) 47-57.

7. 4QXII^c. The Qumran manuscripts of the Twelve Prophets will be published by R. E. Fuller in *Discoveries in the Judaean Desert* (Oxford: Clarendon, forthcoming).

8. In 4QXII^a, the last verses of Malachi are followed by another column of text that seems to come from Jonah. This order is not attested in any other manuscripts.

9. For example, see P. L. Redditt, "The Book of Malachi in Its Social Setting," *CBQ* 56 (1994) 240-55. Redditt delineates core oracles and secondary additions and draws conclusions about the sociological setting of both.

10. J. Nogalski, *Redaction Processes in the Book of the Twelve*, BZAW 218 (New York: Walter de Gruyter, 1993) 182-212. Nogalski sees a very close link between the material in Malachi and Zechariah 1–8 and seeks to explain how it became separated in the formation of the Book of the Twelve.

PART TWO:
APOCRYPHA

THE BOOK OF
TOBIT

IRENE NOWELL, O.S.B.

The book of Tobit tells the story of a good man named Tobit who seems to suffer without cause. In performing an act of charity, burying a dead man, he is struck with blindness and made dependent on his wife. He is so aggrieved by a quarrel with her that he prays to die. Meanwhile, in another city, a young woman named Sarah also prays to die because she has been married seven times, and each husband has died on the wedding night. God hears their prayers and sends the angel Raphael to heal them each of their distress.

Tobit remembers some money he has deposited in another city and sends his son Tobiah to get it. Tobiah and Tobit hire a guide, the angel Raphael in disguise, who not only leads Tobiah to the house of Raguel, Sarah's father, but also helps Tobiah catch a fish whose parts will be useful in healing both his father and Sarah. Raphael instructs Tobiah to ask for Sarah's hand in marriage. Tobiah burns the parts of the fish to drive away the demon who is killing Sarah's husbands; then he and Sarah pray and sleep happily through the night. Meanwhile Raguel, fearing the death of another son-in-law, has dug a grave. When he and his wife, Edna, discover that Tobiah and Sarah are well, they hold a fourteen-day wedding feast. Raphael, who has gone after Tobit's money, returns to the feast with Gabael, who has held the money in deposit.

Tobiah's parents are worried sick, however, because their son is late in returning. So Tobiah and his wife set out with Raphael on the return journey. As soon as Tobiah sees his father, he uses the remaining parts of the fish to heal his blindness. When the two men attempt to pay the guide, Raphael reveals his identity and instructs them to praise God. Tobit's song of praise is the last and longest prayer in this book, which contains prayers or blessings by every character except Anna, Tobit's wife, and Raphael. After a long and happy life, Tobit calls for Tobiah and Sarah, along with their children, to give them a final instruction. After their deaths, Tobiah gives both his parents and his parents-in-law honorable burials. Finally Tobiah himself dies at the age of 117.

TEXT AND LANGUAGE

The origins of the book of Tobit are somewhat murky. The book is available to us in three Greek recensions, several fragments of four Aramaic and one Hebrew manuscript, the Old Latin version, and the Latin Vulgate. The presence of Aramaic and Hebrew manuscripts at Qumran led to the conclusion that the original language was Semitic, although whether Hebrew or Aramaic is debatable. Most scholars lean toward Aramaic.[1]

The Qumran manuscripts are fragmentary, however. Thus for a primary text one of the Greek recensions is necessary. There are three Greek recensions: G^I, represented by two manuscripts, Vaticanus (B) and Alexandrinus (A); G^{II}, represented by the Sinaiticus MS, and G^{III}, preserved in MSS 44, 106, and 107. G^{II} has a strong Semitic flavor, many narrative details, and is substantially longer than the others. It has two major gaps, however—4:7-19 and 13:6-10. G^I is written in a more idiomatic Greek and is shorter and more concise than G^{II}. G^{III} is fragmentary, preserved only from 6:9 to 13:8.[2]

The Old Latin version (VL) represents G^{II} and is useful in correcting and reconstructing S. The Vulgate, Jerome says, was translated rapidly (in one day!) from an Aramaic version. Much of it is dependent on VL. Therefore, it is of less value textually than VL. However, it does provide some interesting interpretations of the story. The Qumran manuscripts support the priority of G^{II}.

DATE

Speculation concerning the date of the book of Tobit has ranged from the seventh century BCE to the third century CE, with a definite preference for the third to second centuries BCE. There are several reasons to support this date with regard to *terminus a quo*. The confusion concerning historical and geographical data in seventh-century Assyria excludes an early date for the book. The title "law of Moses" or "book of Moses" (Tob 6:13; 7:11-13) became current after the writing of the books of Chronicles (4th cent. BCE; cf. 2 Chr 23:18; 25:4; 30:16). The author of Tobit presumes the authority of the prophets as proclaimers of God's Word (14:4). The prophets were canonized around 200 BCE. The fact that the Jews did not accept the book of Tobit in their canon also indicates a late date for the work.

The Maccabean revolt provides the *terminus ad quem*. There is no evidence in Tobit of the turmoil caused by the persecution begun by Antiochus IV Epiphanes (175–164). The emphasis on endogamy, a practice that died out in the first century BCE, the absence of comment on resurrection of the dead, whether belief or non-belief, and the discovery of copies of the book at Qumran support a *terminus ad quem* in the second century. Fitzmyer suggests that the Aramaic in the Qumran fragments represents the period between the end of the second century BCE and the beginning of the second century CE.[3] The most probable date for the writing of the book of Tobit, then, is between 200 and 180 BCE.

PLACE

The most difficult question concerning the origin of the book of Tobit concerns place. Palestine, Egypt, and Mesopotamia have been suggested as possibilities. Assyria and Persia are usually rejected because of the inaccurate geographical references. The eastern diaspora is a stronger possibility.

The other major area of the diaspora, Egypt, is also possible. Some connections exist between Tobit and the Elephantine papyri (5th cent. BCE). One source of Tobit is the story of Ahiqar (see the section "The Story of Ahiqar," below), an Aramaic copy of which was found at Elephantine. The marriage contract discovered among the same papyri is very similar to the words of Raguel at the wedding of Sarah and Tobiah.[4] Yet there are also several arguments against Egypt. It seems unlikely that a story written in Aramaic would originate in second-century Egypt. Upper Egypt appears to be a faraway place when the demon is banished there (Tob 8:3).

The third possibility is Palestine. The chief objection to this locale is the setting of the story in the diaspora. Nonetheless, the interest in Jerusalem and its cult may indicate Palestinian provenance. The evidence does not allow a definite conclusion concerning the place of origin of our book.

CANONICAL STATUS

The book of Tobit is not included in the Hebrew Scriptures and thus is not a part of the Old Testament in the Protestant tradition. It is, however, contained in the Septuagint, the ancient Greek translation of Jewish holy books, and was translated by Jerome and included in the Latin Vulgate. Thus it remains part of the Old Testament canon for Roman Catholics and for the Orthodox churches.

GENRE

The book of Tobit is a work of narrative prose with several prayers in poetic form. The question of its historicity has been widely debated. There are several arguments against its literal historicity. First, inaccuracies appear in the report of Assyrian history. Sargon II (721–705) is missing from the recital of kings in chapter 1, perhaps echoing 2 Kgs 17:1-6 and 18:9-13, in which Sargon is not mentioned. The Assyrian king responsible for the deportation of Naphtali from Galilee, the deportation that presumably included Tobit, was Tiglath-Pileser III (745–727), not Shalmaneser V as Tob 1:2 states. Second, the first-person narrative in the opening chapters may signal questionable historicity. Authors of antiquity sometimes used first-person narrative to make the teller of the tale, and not the author, responsible for its truth.[5] However, Miller argues that the redactors of texts such as Tobit, the Genesis Apocryphon, and Nehemiah preserved the first-person narrative whenever it was available precisely because it was valued as "original autobiography."[6] Third, the religious principles of the book are more consistent with the period of the author (2nd cent. BCE) than the period in which the story is set

(8th–7th cents. BCE). Thus, while there may be a historical nucleus to the book, its primary function is not the telling of history. Rather, it has a didactic purpose: to teach and illustrate basic principles of religious faith.

The book of Tobit bears many characteristics of a "romance" that is cast as a successful quest.[7] The genre, however, is affected by the biblical context. The book also has many features of the Hebrew short story, as defined by Campbell.[8] Its characters are ordinary people whose everyday lives become signs of the working of God's providence. The religious purpose of the author is shown by the subject matter and by the use of biblical models and imagery. It is, however, a late example of the genre. A folktale element predominates, and the distinction between legend and Hebrew short story is blurred.

Hence, the book of Tobit belongs to a mixed genre, created to respond to the needs of the post-exilic community to which its author belonged, a genre shared with Esther, Judith, and Susanna.[9] Overall, the book of Tobit is best described as a Hebrew romance.

Other literary forms appear in the book, specifically poetic prayers (3:2-6, 11-15; 8:5-8, 15-17; 11:14-15; 13:1-18)[10] and wisdom speeches (4:3-21; 12:6-10; 14:3-11). The wisdom speeches, which contain several proverbs, may also be classified as farewell discourses.[11]

SOURCES FOR THE PLOT

The Grateful Dead. The plot of the center section of Tobit, the travelogue (chaps. 5–12), is derived from the folktale "The Grateful Dead."[12] The basic story of the Grateful Dead, as found in a widespread collection of folktales, concerns a man who impoverishes himself to ransom and bury a corpse that is being mistreated by the dead man's creditors. Shortly thereafter, when the poor man is on a journey, he is joined by a stranger who offers to be his servant in return for half of whatever the hero might acquire.

At this point the folktales diverge. The version best known in the Near East and in Eastern Europe is the form that is related to the book of Tobit. In this form the tale is combined with the tale of "The Monster in the Bridal Chamber." The hero in this combination of tales is advised by the stranger to marry a wealthy princess whose former bridegrooms have all perished in the bridal chamber. The stranger then keeps watch on the wedding night and slays the serpent that emerges from the mouth of the princess to kill the hero. Subsequently, the stranger demands half the bride as his payment, but as he threatens to divide the bride with his sword (or actually does), another serpent(s) comes out of the bride, and she is freed from enchantment. The stranger then reveals himself as the grateful dead man whom the hero had buried.[13]

Several similarities exist between this story and the plot of Tobit. Tobit is impoverished because of his practice of burying the dead. His son Tobiah (the hero has been divided into two characters of similar name) is accompanied on a journey by a mysterious stranger who advises him to marry a bride whose husbands have all died on the wedding night. Through the advice and service of the stranger, Tobiah survives the wedding night, and the bride is freed from enchantment. The stranger is offered payment of half the goods acquired on the journey (not, however, half the bride). He then reveals his identity and disappears.

The Story of Ahiqar. A second major source for the plot is the story of Ahiqar (NAB; NRSV, "Ahikar"), who appears in the book of Tobit in four passages (1:21-22; 2:10; 11:18; 14:10). The story seems to have been written originally in Aramaic sometime in the sixth century BCE.[14] Fragments of the story in Aramaic were found at Elephantine and have been dated to the fifth century BCE. The story of Ahiqar appears in several languages: Syriac, Arabic, Armenian, and Slavonic, and fragments in Ethiopic and Greek. These versions are much later than the Aramaic fragments.

The story of Ahiqar consists of a narrative portion and a set of proverbs. The narrative tells the story of the life of Ahiqar, a royal official at the courts of Sennacherib and Esarhaddon. Because he is childless, Ahiqar adopts Nadin,[15] his nephew, and trains him to succeed to his royal position. But Nadin, treacherous and ungrateful, accuses Ahiqar of disloyalty to the king. Ahiqar is condemned to death, but is secretly rescued by the executioner whose life Ahiqar had saved earlier. He remains hidden in a cave under his own house until the king, challenged to a contest of wisdom by the pharaoh of Egypt, expresses the wish that Ahiqar still lived. Thereupon Ahiqar emerges from hiding, answers the pharaoh's challenge, and is restored to his former honor. Meanwhile, Nadin is imprisoned and dies.[16] The proverbs of Ahiqar are probably older than the narrative and were presumably added to the story to strengthen the impression of Ahiqar's wisdom.

Similarities between the story of Ahiqar and the book of Tobit can be seen both in content and in literary form. The life of Ahiqar resembles in broad strokes the life of Tobit. Both are faithful men who are unjustly plunged into darkness, but who, because of righteousness, are saved from death and restored to life. The story of Ahiqar is told in first-person narrative, similar to the beginning of the book of Tobit. The wisdom speech of Tobit to his son Tobiah (4:3-21) echoes proverbs in the story of Ahiqar.

General knowledge of the story of Ahiqar is presumed by the author of the book of Tobit. Ahiqar is made a relative of Tobit (1:21), ostensibly to enhance Tobit by connecting him with such a renowned sage. Ahiqar uses his position to help Tobit in his distress (1:21-22; 2:10). He and Nadin come to rejoice in Tobit's joy (11:18). In the final reference to Ahiqar, Tobit recounts a synopsis of Ahiqar's life (14:10-11).

Just as the journey of Tobiah (the central section) rests on the outline of the folktale combination of the "Grateful Dead"/"Monster in the Bridal Chamber," so also the life of Tobit (chaps. 1–4; 13–14; the frame) rests on the outline of the story of Ahiqar. The influence of these two sources clarifies the interweaving of first-person narrative, wisdom sections and prayers, and the theme of innocent suffering and vindication with the folktale quest for a bride.

These two sources, however, are insufficient to explain the motivations and the progress of the plot in the book of Tobit. The book is permeated with biblical themes and principles. Folktale elements from the "Grateful Dead"/"Monster in the Bridal Chamber" have been changed in conformity with the tenets of biblical faith. The grateful dead man has been replaced by an angel. The hero is now represented by two figures: the father-hero and the son-hero. The father-hero buries the dead out of respect for biblical injunctions (e.g., Deut 21:23) and is both tested and rewarded for his fidelity. The son-hero wins the bride, not because he buried the dead, but because he has a right to her by Mosaic law (Tob 6:12-13; 7:10; cf. Num 36:8-9). The marriage is planned in heaven (Tob 6:18; 7:11). The bride is delivered from the demon by God, who sends an angel to instruct the hero in exorcism and prayer (6:17-18; 8:2-9). The angel demands no payment but is offered half of the recovered money (12:15).

Modifications have also been made in the borrowing from Ahiqar. Ahiqar himself has been made a Jew. The figure of the son differs in the two stories. In Ahiqar, Nadin is an adopted son; in Tobit, Tobiah is a natural son. Nadin is a classic example of the ungrateful son; Tobiah is an example of the devoted, faithful son. The just man in the two stories is vindicated for different reasons. Tobit is vindicated simply because he is righteous; Ahiqar is vindicated because of a specific form of righteousness, almsgiving.

The Joseph Story. L. Ruppert proposes the Joseph story (Genesis 37; 39–50) as the link between extra-biblical sources and the biblical tradition that is fundamental to the book of Tobit.[17] The Joseph story, the basic biblical analogue to Tobit, is the third and most significant element that must be considered in outlining its plot. In the Joseph story, as in the book of Tobit, an elderly father sends a beloved son (Benjamin), whom he entrusts to a companion (Reuben or Judah; Gen 42:37; 43:8-9), on a dangerous journey to a distant land to obtain relief from a current need. The travelers recognize that the father's life is so bound up in that of the son that if the son should die, the father would go down to the nether world in grief (Gen 44:30-31; cf. Tob 6:15).

Upon his arrival the son meets a near relative (Joseph/Raguel) who inquires about his father's health (Gen 45:3; Tob 7:4-5). After the close kinship is revealed, the travelers are welcomed with tearful embraces (Gen 45:14-15; cf. Tob 7:6-8; Gen 43:27-30).[18] Meanwhile, although the father (or mother; note that in Tobit it is Edna who inquires concerning Tobit's health) fears the son's death (Gen 37:33-35; 43:14; cf. Tob 10:4, 7), the son escapes danger (Gen 39:1-6; 44:1–45:3; cf. Tob 6:3-4; 8:2-9) and is reunited with the father (Gen 46:30; cf. Tob 11:9-10).[19] With tearful embraces the father (or mother) proclaims readiness to die (Gen 46:30; Tob 11:9; cf. Tob 11:14). As the story draws to a close, the father summons his son(s) and grandchildren to his deathbed, asks for an honorable burial, and makes a statement about the future and about return to the homeland (Gen 47:27–48:2, 15-22; cf. Gen 50:24; Tob 14:3-

8; 13:5). There is a final poetic speech by the father concerning the future (Genesis 49:1; Tobit 13).[20]

Biblical Type Scenes. In addition to the outline from part of the Joseph story, the central scene of the book of Tobit has another biblical analogue. Tobiah's betrothal (7:1-17), including the preceding departure from the father (5:17-22) and subsequent departure from the bride's home (10:7-13), is modeled on the biblical type scene of betrothal.[21] The two betrothal scenes closest in pattern to Tob 7:1-17 are Isaac's (Gen 34:1-67) and Jacob's (Gen 29:1-30). Genesis 29:4-6 appears almost verbatim in Tob 7:3-5. In addition, each passage is linked to Tobit by a particular key word. The link to Isaac's betrothal scene is εὐοδόω (euodoō, "prosper," "make successful"). The link to Jacob's betrothal scene is ὑγιαίνω (hygiainō, "to be well"). The scenes are also similar in structure.

Two points of correspondence link Tobiah's betrothal scene with that of Moses (Exod 2:15-21): the number seven (a folktale element) and the name of the father-in-law. Seven daughters meet Moses at the well. The father of Moses' future bride is named Raguel (or Reuel). Moses' departure from his father-in-law (Exod 4:18a) also resembles the corresponding scenes in Tobit (10:11) and in Genesis (24:54-61).

The Book of Job. A final pattern influencing the book of Tobit appears in the book of Job. The structure of the two books is similar. Each book contains a "framing" section that sets the stage in the beginning and summarizes the situation at the end (Job 1:1–2:13; 42:7-17; Tob 1:1–3:17; 12:1–14:15). The central action is set into this frame (Job 3:1–42:6; Tob 4:1–11:18). The progress of Tobit's life is modeled on that of Job. Each man suffers bodily affliction, even though he is righteous (Job 2:7; 27:6; Tob 1:3; 2:10); each is grieved by the sharp words of a wife (Job 2:9-10; Tob 2:14–3:1) and prays for death (Job 7:15; Tob 3:2-6). After his testing, each man is vindicated and rewarded (Job 42:7-17; Tob 14:1-3). Imagery of light and darkness is prevalent in both books. More than a quarter of the occurrences of the words אוֹר ('ôr, "light") and חֹשֶׁךְ (hōšek, "darkness") in the Hebrew Bible are in the book of Job. The story of Tobit moves from light to darkness and back to light.

Conclusion. The outline of the plot of the book of Tobit is shaped by several sources. Extra-biblical literature has contributed the patterns of two folktales—the "Grateful Dead"/"Monster in the Bridal Chamber," and the story of Ahiqar—which form respectively a basis for the central travelogue and for the framing story of the just, guiltless man who suffers but is finally vindicated. Biblical literature has contributed four elements: The story of Joseph functions as a pattern for incorporating the story of Tobit into the flow of salvation history; the betrothal scene from the ancestor stories serves as a model for the central scene in Tobit; the book of Job provides a model for the structure of the book of Tobit, the life of its principal character, and its basic imagery; and finally, the story is set in, and permeated by, a context of faith. As Zimmermann says, "The woof comes from the folklore of mankind, and the warp and the pattern, the vitality and the color, come from the religious experience of the Jewish people."[22]

It is not similarities to a pattern, however, but the variations that are significant[23] The differences between the book of Tobit and the folktales derive largely from the biblical context. The differences between the book of Tobit and its biblical models can be attributed to the influences of a different time and a different historical situation. The location differs from the ancestor stories. The need for burial of the dead, though a prominent theme in Genesis,[24] arises from a different cause. The essence of a just life—fear of God and charity toward others—remains constant, but the ways in which justice is enacted differ for the characters in Tobit, who lived in exile, from the ancestors, who lived in Egypt and among the Canaanites. The outline of the plot of Tobit derives from several sources; however, the unique expression of this particular plot reflects the needs and preoccupations of the second-century diaspora.[25]

LITERARY ARTISTRY

The Narrator. There are two narrators in the book of Tobit: the first-person narrator of 1:3–3:1 and the third-person narrator of 3:17 through the end of the book. A bridge consisting of two prayers and the introduction of two new characters connects them, but it is unclear whether Tobit remains the narrator in the bridge.[26] The third-person narrator is unobtrusive, reliable, omniscient, and brief. The first-person narrator, by contrast, is more limited in perspective, less knowledgeable and less neutral.[27]

Dialogue and Reticence. The bulk of the story in the book of Tobit is carried by dialogue. Alter suggests the analysis of (1) the characters' own speech, particularly the first reported speech; (2) contrasting dialogue between characters; and (3) the discontinuity between speech and reticence.[28] The first reported speech of each character, with the exception of Raphael and Sarah, occurs in the first scene in which that character appears. The first speech is significant as a revelation of character. Comparing the speech of various characters is also instructive regarding character. For example, Tobit speaks with greater breadth than does Anna, who speaks in short questions. Also, Tobiah asks many questions and speaks with the haste of youth, whereas Raphael makes long speeches and is generally a vehicle of information (a fitting task for an angel).

The economy of the biblical author is most evident in the reticence of the characters. The most striking example is Sarah, whose only words are spoken in prayer (3:11-15; 8:8). Several times characters simply disappear from a scene (e.g., Tobiah in 2:3-8; 5:10–6:6; 7:11*b*–8:3; 8:20-21; Raphael in 7:9-17; 10:7-13; 11:9-15).

A frequent feature of dialogue shared in common by all speakers is inclusion—that is, beginning and ending a speech with the same word or phrase (e.g., "take courage" [θάρσει *tharsei*] in 5:10; "welcome" [ὑγιαίνων ἔλθοις *hygiainōn elthois*] in 5:14; "child" [παιδίον *paidion*] in 5:17; "will leave in good health/return in good health" [ὑγιαίνων πορεύσεται/ὑποστρέψει ὑγιαίνων *hygiainōn poreusetai/hypostrepsei hygiainōn*] in 5:21-22; "eat and drink" [φάγε καὶ πίε *phage kai pie*] in 7:10-11; "take courage, daughter" [θάρσει θύγατερ *tharsei thygater*] in 7:17; "take courage, child" [θάρσει παιδίον *tharsei paidion*] in 8:21; "my child has perished" [ἀπώλετο τὸ παιδίον μου *apōleto to paidion mou*] in 10:4, 7; "how much shall I pay him?" [πόσον αὐτῷ δώσω τόν μισθόν/πόσον αὐτῷ ἔτι δῶ μισθόν *poson autō dōsō ton misthon/poson autō eti dō misthon*] in 12:2-3).

Irony. There are two major and several minor types of irony in the book of Tobit. The basic conflict of the book—the problem that the apparent consequence of doing good is not prosperity but suffering—is an example of the "general irony of events."[29] The veiled identity of Raphael constitutes an example of the second major type of irony, "dramatic irony," in which the readers know what the characters do not.[30] Raguel's digging of the unnecessary grave (8:9-18) is also an example of dramatic irony. The "irony of self-betrayal" is evident in the contradiction between Anna's words and her actions, for she continues to watch the road even though she declares that Tobiah is dead. Irony carries the main theme of the book of Tobit: God blesses the righteous and punishes the wicked; yet God remains free. This final type of irony may be called "divine irony."

Imagery and Key Words. The book is built on a basic opposition between death and life. Only chap. 9 has no mention of death or burial. In addition to words referring specifically to death and life, the concept is imaged through the opposition between night and day, darkness and light, blindness and vision. Tobit's blindness is the physical symbol of the opposition between light and darkness, life and death. It ranks him with sinners as well as with the dead.

A group of abstract terms supports the basic opposition of death and life. Key words on the positive side of the opposition center around healing: health and wellness, safety and salvation, mercy and prosperity are frequently mentioned. With these gifts comes joy. The prayers are particularly filled with expressions of joy. The negative side of the opposition is represented by two clusters of words. The main characters experience and fear distress and reproach. Their distress has two consequences: grief and prayer for deliverance.

One of the major tenets of the book is that these contrasting realities of life and death, suffering and health, joy and sorrow, are in God's hands. The life-and-death opposition manifested in the characters' lives is reflected in the portrait of Jerusalem in the final chapters. For a time, Jerusalem will be desolate, but at the proper time it will be rebuilt.

Another set of key words serves to describe the characters in the book. Four adjectives are used consistently to describe Tobit: "noble/beautiful" (καλός *kalos*); "good" (ἀγαθός *agathos*); "righteous" (δίκαιος *dikaios*); and "charitable/merciful" (ἐλεήμων *eleēmōn*). The cognate nouns of two of these words, "charity" and "righteousness," along with "truth/fidelity" (ἀλήθεια *alētheia*), form an inclusio that frames the book

(1:3; 14:9). Tobit exhorts Tobiah and his children, and also the whole people, to these virtues. These words appear also in descriptions of Raphael (5:14, 22) and in his exhortation to Tobit and Tobiah (12:6-8, 11). They describe not only the character of Tobit, but also the nature of God (3:2; 13:6). Thus the four key words characterize God, God's messenger, and the human characters in the book. God is noble and good, just and merciful. The messengers sent by God to assist human beings manifest the same qualities. Human beings, in response, are called to be noble and good, just and merciful.

Two further images in the book serve as symbols. The fish that attempts to swallow Tobiah's foot (6:3) is a symbol of death. The number seven is a symbol of completion. Sarah loses seven bridegrooms.[31] Tobiah is the eighth husband; he ends the sorrow brought by the previous seven. He is adjured to bring joy to her heart, beginning with the fourteen-day (twice seven) wedding feast (8:20). Then the two return home to celebrate another seven happy days (11:18). Their children number seven sons (14:3). The messenger of God's providence, sent to bring God's healing and joy to this family, is Raphael, one of the seven angels who stand before God (12:15).

THEOLOGY

The Providence of God. A basic premise of the book is that God cares for human beings. God's plan shapes human history, affecting both individual lives and national destinies. Individual lives are woven together in a common journey. The circle of interwoven lives widens from the individual (Tobit) to the larger family, to the whole people, and finally to all nations who will come to Jerusalem.

The agents of God's providence are an angel, human beings, and natural objects and events. The developed figure of the angel (messenger) is one of the major contributions of the book of Tobit to Old Testament theology. The angel Raphael functions as guide and protector, conveyor of information, mediator of prayer, and one who tests. His words and identity, however, are veiled and ambiguous. God's work through him is not immediately obvious to the other characters in the story.

The primary agents of God's providence in this book are human persons. The clearest example is found in the actions of Tobiah. Through his obedi-

ence, God heals both Tobit and Sarah. God's providence is also shown through natural materials, such as the medicinal properties of the fish organs.

The Justice of God. The book of Tobit also asserts that God is just. The understanding of God's justice is expressed in the theory of retribution: God rewards the just and punishes the wicked. The apparent contradiction of this theory, found in the suffering of the just man Tobit, generates the conflict of the plot. How can God be just if the apparent consequence of doing good is not prosperity but suffering? Only at the end is it clear that Tobit's unflinching faith is justified: The wicked are indeed punished (the destruction of Nineveh), and the just are rewarded (the prosperity of Tobit and his family).

The Freedom of God. Although Tobit ultimately receives reward, the story of his life demonstrates that the doctrine of retribution is not a simple equation. The concept of God in this book is not that of a deterministic fate, but of a personal God who is merciful and just, caring and provident, and who blesses the righteous out of the depths of divine freedom.

The Virtuous Life. The book of Tobit provides a guide and an example for human living. The virtuous life is demonstrated first of all in three sets of relationships in family life: the relationship between parents and children; the marriage relationship; and respect for women. The relationship between parents and children is characterized by instruction, obedience, respect, and love.

There are several examples of the faithful and supportive marriage relationship. The relationships between husband and wife for each of the three married couples differ, but love is expressed in each. The interaction between Tobit and Anna is the liveliest of the three and portrays both positive and negative sides of the relationship. The relationship between Raguel and Edna is less obvious, but there is evidence of mutual interdependence and support. The relationship between Tobiah and Sarah is set firmly upon trust in God's plan and obedience to God's law. It begins with prayer, in which marriage is seen as a gift from God. Raguel, Edna, and Tobit all express the hope that marriage will bring joy, and they regard children as a blessing. They recognize marriage not only as a bond between two people, but also as a bond between families.

The respect for women shown throughout the book is also an element of virtuous family life. The three female characters are carefully drawn and are given significant roles and distinct personalities. Sarah, although the most silent and passive character in the story, reveals in her prayer that she is strong in self-knowledge, capable of deliberation, and has been instructed in the law and in prayer. She is "sensible and beautiful" (6:12). Edna, who never appears without Raguel, has a more limited role and autonomy than Anna. Nonetheless both women are respected by their husbands and are contributing members of their families. Tobit's grandmother Deborah is honored for her instruction of the young Tobit. Women are regarded as competent persons, capable of relating to God through prayer and obedience to the law, capable of providing help and support to their husbands, capable of instructing and guiding their children. They do not, however, have public responsibilities in either the economic or the religious sphere. They are seen primarily in relationship to their families.[32]

Two virtues are expressed not only within the family, but also within the wider kinship group. The first is ἐλεημοσύνη (eleēmosyne), which is translated as "almsgiving," "charity," or "mercy." This virtue, mentioned in the inclusio that frames the book (1:3; 14:9), is linked to the major statement of the book that God rewards the just and punishes the wicked. What God rewards is almsgiving.[33] The second virtue exercised within the kinship group is hospitality. Raguel, whose character is modeled on that of Abraham, is the primary example of the hospitable person. The hospitality of Tobit can be seen in the alacrity with which he greets Raphael (5:10), his joyous welcome of his daughter-in-law Sarah (11:17), and the feasts he hosts (2:2; 11:17-18). Tobiah follows his father's example in inviting Gabael to join the wedding feast in Ecbatana (9:2, 5-6).

Both eleēmosyne and hospitality are limited in the book of Tobit to one's own kindred and people (1:3, 8, 16-18; 2:2-3; 4:17). The diaspora setting of the story helps to explain the limitation to the covenant community. Survival as a people depended on mutual support. Fear of being led astray or contaminated by non-believers encouraged exclusivity. Yet the separation from non-Jews, though evident in matters of food (1:10-11) and marriage (1:9; 4:12-13), does not extend to contempt for other peoples, such as appears in Ezra–Nehemiah or the books of Maccabees.

The relationship of the righteous person to God is characterized by observance of the law and the practice of prayer. Tobit himself is the primary example of faithful observance (1:6-11). He exhorts his son to the same careful observance (chap. 4). Observance of the law is expected not only with regard to detailed external practices, but also through an inner spirit of piety toward God and charity toward neighbor. The relationship with God is to be characterized by fear (4:21; 14:6), love (14:7), and sincerity (4:6; 13:6; 14:7). The habit of prayer is the most pervasive expression of inner devotion to God.[34] The book has been called "a school of prayer";[35] the frequency of prayer and its incorporation at major turning points of the plot indicate its importance. The story is a graphic illustration that prayer is answered. The continual turning to God in prayer indicates that God is the real hero and principal actor of the book. The virtuous life, learned through prayer and the law, is modeled on God, who is righteous, merciful, and truthful.[36]

FOR FURTHER READING

Craghan, John. Esther, Judith, Tobit, Jonah, Ruth. OTM 16. Edited by C. Stuhlmueller and M. McNamara. Wilmington, Del.: Michael Glazier, 1982.

Dancy, John C., W. J. Fuerst, and R. J. Hammer. The Shorter Books of the Apocrypha. Edited by P. R. Ackroyd et al. Cambridge: Cambridge University Press, 1972.

Fitzmyer, J. A. Tobit: Qumran Cave 4, xiv. DJD 19. Edited by M. Broshi et al. Oxford: Clarendon, 1995.

Fitzmeyer, Joseph A. Tobit. Commentaries on Early Jewish Literature. New York: de Gruyter, 2003.

Hanhart, R. Tobit. Septuaginta, Vetus Testamentum Graecum 8/5. Göttingen: Vandenhoeck & Ruprecht, 1983.

MacDonald, Dennis R., ed. Mimesis and Intertextuality in Antiquity and Christianity. Studies in Antiquity and Christianity 1. Harrisburg, PA.: Trinity, 2001.

Moore, Carey A. Tobit. AB 40A. Garden City, N.Y.: Doubleday, 1996.

Nickelsburg, G. W. E. "Tobit." In Harper's Bible Commentary. Edited by J. L. Mays. New York: Harper & Row, 1988.

ENDNOTES

1. See, e.g., J. A. Fitzmyer, "The Aramaic and Hebrew Fragments of Tobit from Qumran Cave 4," *CBQ* 57 (1995) 671. See also C. A. Moore, *Tobit,* AB 40A (Garden City, N.Y.: Doubleday, 1996) 33-39, for further discussion.

2. See R. Hanhart, *Tobit,* Septuaginta; Vetus Testamentum Graecum 8/5 (Göttingen: Vandenhoeck & Ruprecht, 1983) 29-36.

3. Fitzmyer, "The Aramaic and Hebrew Fragments of Tobit from Qumran Cave 4," 667.

4. See "Contract of Mibtahiah's Third Marriage," *ANET* 222; see also R. Vattioni, "Studi e note sul libro di Tobia," *Aug 10 (1940) 277.*

5. B. E. Perry, *The Ancient Romances: A Literary-Historical Account of Their Origins* (Berkeley: University of California Press, 1967) Appendix 3, 325-26.

6. J. E. Miller, "The Redaction of Tobit and the Genesis Apocryphon," *JSP* 8 (1991) esp. 56-57.

7. See N. Frye, *Anatomy of Criticism* (Princeton, N.J.: Princeton University Press, 1957) 187-93; R. Scholes and R. Kellogg, *The Nature of Narrative* (New York: Oxford University Press, 1966) 228.

8. E. F. Campbell, Jr., "The Hebrew Short Story: A Study of Ruth," in *A Light unto My Path, Festschrift for J. M. Myers,* ed. H. N. Bream, R. D. Heim, and C. A. Moore (Philadelphia: Temple University Press, 1974) 91.

9. See O. Loretz, "Roman und Kurzgeschichte in Israel," *Wort und Botschaft des Alten Testaments,* ed. J. Schreiner (Würzburg: Echter, 1969) 325.

10. For an excellent analysis of the prayers found in the book, see P. J. Griffin, "The Theology and Function of Prayer in the Book of Tobit" (Ph.D. diss., The Catholic University of America, 1984).

11. A. A. Di Lella, "The Deuteronomic Background of the Farewell Discourse in Tob 14:3-11," *CBQ* 41 (1979) 380n. 1.

12. See K. Simrock, *Der Gute Gerhard und die dankbaren Todten* (Bonn: Marcus, 1856) 131-32; G. H. Gerould, *The Grateful Dead,* publications of the Folklore Society 60 (London: D. Nutt, 1980; reprinted, Folcroft, Pa.: Folcroft Library Editions, 1973) 7.

13. See S. Thompson, *The Folktale* (New York: Dryden, 1946) 50-53, for the basic synopsis. See G. H. Gerould, *The Grateful Dead,* 47-75, for a description of folktales from several places that demonstrate the combination he calls the Grateful Dead and the Poison Maiden.

14. J. M. Lindenberger, *The Aramaic Proverbs of Ahiqar* (Baltimore: Johns Hopkins University Press, 1983) 16-20.

15. This spelling of the name is found in the Qumran fragments 4QTob[d], 11:18.

16. See the synopsis of this story in J. M. Lindenberger, *The Aramaic Proverbs of Ahiqar,* 3-4. See also J. R. Harris in F. C. Conybeare, J. R. Harris, and A. S. Lewis, *The Story of Ahikar* (London: C. J. Clay & Sons, 1898) viii-x.

17. L. Ruppert, "Zur Function der Achikar-Notizen im Buch Tobias," *BZ* 20 (1976) 232-37. For the links between Ahiqar and the Joseph story, see also S. Niditch and R. Doran, "The Success Story of the Wise Courtier: A Formal Approach," *JBL* 96 (1977) 179-93.

18. G. Priero, *Tobia,* ed. S. Garofalo, 2nd ed., La Sacra Bibbia (Turin: Marietti, 1963) 37, comments on the frequency of tears in Tobit (e.g., 2:7; 3:1, 10; 5:18; 7:6-8, 16; 9:6; 10:4, 7; 11:9, 14). They are, perhaps, an echo of the frequent tears in the Joseph story (Gen 37:35; 42:30; 45:14-15; 47:29; 50:1, 17).

19. Note that in the Joseph story two beloved sons are separated from the father and are feared dead, Joseph and Benjamin. In the book of Tobit there is only one, Tobiah.

20. Ruppert, "Zur Function der Achikar-Notizen im Buch Tobias," 114-15.

21. R. Alter, *The Art of Biblical Narrative* (New York: Basic Books, 1981) 51.

22. F. Zimmermann, *The Book of Tobit: An English Translation with Introduction and Commentary,* Dropsie College Edition, JAL (New York: Harper and Bros., 1958) 12.

23. R. Alter, *The Art of Biblical Narrative,* 52.

24. I. Abrahams, "Tobit and Genesis," *JQR* 5 (1893) 348-50, was the first to point out the connection between Tobit and Genesis in the concentration on burial.

25. See O. Loretz, "Roman und Kurzgeschichte in Israel," *Wort und Botschaft des Alten Testaments,* ed. J. Schreiner (Würzburg: Echter, 1969) 324-25.

26. J. E. Miller, "The Redaction of Tobit and the Genesis Apocryphon," *JSP* 8 (1991) 54-55.

27. See D. McCracken, "Narration and Comedy in the Book of Tobit," *JBL* 114 (1995) 403-9. I am grateful to McCracken for correcting my over-

simplification regarding the differences between the two narrative voices.

28. R. Alter, *The Art of Biblical Narrative,* 182-83.

29. D. C. Muecke, *Irony* (London: Methuen & Co., 1970) 67.

30. D. C. Muecke, *Irony,* 64-66.

31. J. Craghan lists seven calamities for Tobit also. See Craghan, *Esther, Judith, Tobit, Jonah, Ruth,* OTM 16, ed. C. Stuhlmueller and M. McNamara (Wilmington, Del.: Michael Glazier, 1982) 138.

32. See B. Bow and G. W. E. Nickelsburg, "Patriarchy with a Twist: Men and Women in Tobit," in *Women Like This: New Perspectives on Jewish Women in the Greco-Roman World,* ed. Amy-Jill Levine (Atlanta: Scholars Press, 1991) 127-43.

33. See P. J. Griffin, "A Study of *Eleēmosynē* in the Bible with Emphasis upon Its Meaning and Usage in the Theology of Tobit and Ben Sira" (MA thesis, The Catholic University of America, 1982), for a thorough treatment of the structural and narrative significance of *eleēmosynē* in the book of Tobit. He notes that the word *eleēmosynē* appears more often in the book of Tobit than in any other OT book (22 times, compared to 13 times in Sirach; 7 times in Proverbs; 4 times in Isaiah; 3 times in Psalms; twice each in Deuteronomy, the Song of Songs, Baruch, and Daniel; and once in Genesis), and that its semantic development is one of the major contributions of the book of Tobit to OT theology. P. Deselaers defines *eleēmosynē* as "community building activity" (*solidarische handeln*). See Paul Deselaers, *Das Buch Tobit: Studien zu seiner Entstehung, Komposition, und Theologie,* OBO 43 (Freiburg [Schwiez]/Göttingen: Universtätsverlag/Vandenhoeck und Ruprecht, 1982) 348-58.

34. See P. J. Griffin, "The Theology and Function of Prayer in the Book of Tobit".

35. J. Goettmann, "Le livre des conseils ou le miroir du Juste engagé dans le monde," *BVC* 21 (1958) 36.

36. See A. A. Di Lella, "The Deuteronomic Background of the Farewell Discourse in Tob 14:3-11," 386-87.

THE BOOK OF
JUDITH

LAWRENCE M. WILLS

The book of Judith is a Jewish novel, likely written in about 100 BCE, that celebrates the victory over a foreign power by the hand of a woman. Although never part of Jewish Scriptures, it did become part of the Christian Bible, now consigned to the apocrypha. The anonymous author probably wrote in Hebrew, although there is no copy of a Hebrew original still in existence, and no fragments or quotations of it were discovered among the Dead Sea Scrolls.

It falls naturally into two parts. In the first part (chaps. 1–7), Nebuchadnezzar, king of the Assyrians, is engaged in a major campaign against Arphaxad, king of the Medes. Many of the nations to the west refuse to ally with Nebuchadnezzar, but he proceeds against Arphaxad nevertheless and defeats him easily. He then turns against the nations who spurned him, which include Judea and Samaria, and commissions his general Holofernes to mobilize vast numbers of troops to invade these nations, moving inexorably toward Judea. His forces pause below the mountain village of Bethulia, which must be taken in order for him to move through its pass and proceed on to take Jerusalem; and he commences a siege that cuts off the water to the village. The first part thus ends with a pause in the action, as the Israelites contemplate the disaster that is about to befall them.

In the second part (chaps. 8–16), Judith is introduced as a beautiful, wealthy, and pious Jewish widow who has lived a life of prayer and fasting in a special tent or booth on the roof of her estate. She emerges from this relative seclusion to put into motion a plan to thwart the enemy advance. She leaves Bethulia with her favorite maid and goes to the enemy camp. There she captivates Holofernes and his soldiers and lies to manipulate Holofernes to her ends. Hoping to seduce Judith, Holofernes drinks wine until he is quite drunk and passes out, whereupon Judith takes this opportunity to slice off his head with his own sword. Carrying the head with them, she and her maid return to their village, display the head on the wall, and instruct the villagers to attack the Assyrians the next day. When the Assyrians see that their general has been beheaded, they flee and are decisively beaten by the Israelites.

Popular among both Jews and Christians over the centuries, the story of Judith has nevertheless suffered from strongly ambivalent reactions in the modern period. The interest in biblical history and "higher criticism" that developed in the nineteenth century left Judith out of the picture. By genre, it seemed like a romance or fiction; as history, it was—and is—suspect; in its theology, it was unremarkable; in its depiction of moral character, it presented a heroine who was often considered either morally tainted or decidedly dangerous. As a result, the book of Judith has been viewed as offensive, ludicrous, or—worst of all—irrelevant for biblical theology. Only with the rise of feminist studies of the Bible and an interest in the female characters has a new appreciation for the book developed. This interest has remained strong and has produced a wealth of new studies and a much more positive appreciation for Judith.

HISTORICAL SITUATION AND DATE

Judith begins with a dating formula (using the year of the reign of a major king) that is like the accounts in the biblical history books (1 Kgs 15:1; 16:15, 29; 2 Kgs 12:1; 13:1); yet, the first personage encountered, Nebuchadnezzar, king of the Assyrians, is clearly implausible. Nebuchadnezzar was king of the Babylonian Empire, not the Assyrian, and since both Nebuchadnezzar and the Assyrian Empire were well known to Jews, an accidental error is inconceivable. This one historical impossibility is followed by a number of other difficulties. In the first two chapters alone, we meet the presumably important King Arphaxad of the Medes, who is unknown to history, and geographical problems of all sorts arise with the place-names: Some are unknown; some are in the wrong place. Perhaps most serious of all, however, is what we find at 5:18-19. Achior has faithfully recounted Israelite and Jewish history, but then proceeds to describe events that occurred *after* both Nebuchadnezzar and the Assyrians had long since disappeared. The audience would clearly have been aware of the historical and geographical inaccuracies and would likely have understood the book accordingly as a work of fiction. Some scholars have sought to solve this problem by arguing that the two parts of the book (the military campaigns of chaps. 1–7 and the response of Judith in chaps. 8–16) are of unequal value historically and that there is still a historical kernel to the book, or that to avoid persecution the book makes use of fictitious personages to refer to contemporary leaders, much as the members of the Qumran sect referred to Romans as Kittim. This is not likely, however, because the entire work bespeaks a period of triumph and freedom from external oppression, not a secret text of hope in a time of adversity.

The earliest known references to the story of Judith come in the first century CE. The book probably influenced the description of Deborah in the *Biblical Antiquities* of the author known as Pseudo-Philo,[1] and the first reference by name to the story of Judith is by Clement of Rome, a Christian author who wrote near the end of the first century. He incorporates the story positively, with no hint of a concern about the historical problem, and when Judith is quoted by the later Christian fathers, there is likewise no question as to the historicity of the text. Judith is not quoted as scripture by Jews, but is the subject of legendary treatment, and no one among Jewish authors objects or comments on the reliability of the text. Through the medieval period Judith is treated as a revered figure, but rarely does anyone raise any historical questions. When we come to Martin Luther, however, we encounter a very modern-sounding criticism. In his preface to the book of Judith, he writes, "It hardly squares with the historical accounts of the Holy Scriptures, especially Jeremiah and Ezra."[2] His solution to this problem is also very modern and has in fact become the accepted scholarly consensus: "Some people think this is not an account of historical events but rather a beautiful religious fiction. . . . Such an interpretation strikes my fancy, and I think that the poet deliberately and painstakingly inserted the errors of time and name in order to remind the reader that the book should be taken and understood as that kind of a sacred, religious composition."

Although the stated historical setting in the era of the Assyrian Empire still pushed some scholars to argue for an early dating—that is, before the exile in 587 BCE—most now focus on evidence that it was written at a much later period. There are terms and personages that correspond to the period of the Persian rule of Judea (539–332 BCE) and other terms and ideas that correspond to the period of Greek rule (332–165 BCE) or to the period of the independent Judea under the Maccabees (or Hasmoneans; 165–63 BCE), when Greek customs were still influential in Jewish life. Moore has conveniently listed the terms and names in each category, the most important of which are given here.[3] For dating in the Persian period, we note especially that in 350 and 343 BCE there were invasions of the west by Artaxerxes III Ochus of Persia that were similar in scope to the fictitious invasion by Nebuchadnezzar and Holofernes. He came as far as Egypt (see Jdt 1:10). More important, he had a general named Holofernes and a counselor, probably a eunuch, named Bagoas (cf. Jdt 12:11). Thus the connections to Judith are very strong and suggest at least that the memory of this invasion fired the imagination of the author of Judith. In addition, there are a number of terms that are associated with the Persian era, even though they might also have lingered in the popular consciousness long afterward.

There are no precisely datable Greek terms or ideas, but several motifs—the wearing of garlands and olive wreaths, the worship of a king as a god, and people reclining instead of sitting at table—could have entered in any time after 332 BCE. Some of the most convincing datable motifs arise in connection with the Hasmoneans (the dynastic name of the Maccabees), who achieved independence from the Greeks (Seleucids) in 165 BCE. The high priest as a political and military leader, the ascendancy of the Jerusalem council, and the close similarity between the exhibiting of Holofernes' head and the exhibiting of the head of Nicanor after he had been defeated by Judah the Maccabee (1 Macc 7:43-50; 2 Macc 15:30-32) all speak for a date after the Maccabean revolt.

Even more important for consideration, the *ideals* expressed in Judith correspond closely to the ideals of the later Hasmonean rulers, especially John Hyrcanus I (135–104 BCE) and Alexander Janneus (103–78 BCE). Hyrcanus in 107 BCE annexed Samaria, the provincial designation of the northern half of the old kingdom of Israel. He thus realized a Hasmonean dream of reestablishing the approximate borders of David's and Solomon's united Israel.[4] A dating of the book in this period would even provide a possible origin of "Nebuchadnezzar, king of the Assyrians." Assyria in biblical prophecies was often read as Syria in the literature of this period; thus "Nebuchadnezzar king of the Assyrians" could have been read as a satirical reference to "Antiochus, king of the Syrians," from whom the Maccabees had gained their independence.[5] In the process of annexing Samaria, John Hyrcanus also destroyed the Samaritan temple on Mt. Gerizim, and so rid the land of cult practices not strictly based on the hegemony of Jerusalem. This illuminates Judith's otherwise very odd statement in 8:18-20 that the Jews had successfully rooted out the worship of "gods made with hands." Further, the conversion of Achior, though it would find some precedents in ancient Jewish tradition, would be more comprehensible in the light of John Hyrcanus's move to convert the Idumaeans to Judaism by force. One could argue that the forced annexation of Samaria and the forced conversion of Idumaeans would not lead to such warm relations as are depicted in Judith, but to the Hasmoneans the annexation and conversion would be seen as liberation, and this is precisely why Judith is at such pains to *idealize* them. The boldness of Judith's affirmations make most sense in a situation where unity is imposed. The book of Judith thus idealizes Samaria and Judea together as "Israel" and does not have, as some scholars have suggested, a hidden Samaritan identity. To be sure, other scholars argue that the author of Judith is secretly opposed to the rule of the Hasmoneans, but the agreements with the Hasmonean rulers far outweigh the possible challenges within the text.[6] Even if Judith were a subversive text within the Hasmonean kingdom, that would still at least date the text in the period that is here proposed.

It has also been suggested that the author was a Samaritan because of the importance of the regions of Samaria, a Sadducee because of the coordination of Judith's practices with the temple administration, or a Pharisee because of the practices of fasting and prayer.[7] Arguing against the first two possibilities are the idealized union of Judea and Samaria into "Israel" (noted above) and the Hasmonean idealization of the high priesthood as a governing office. Whether the author was a Pharisee is impossible to determine, but it should be noted that the practices of the protagonist provide a parallel to the development of fasting, penitence, and prayer of the Pharisees and others in the Judaism of this period. It is likely, then, that the anonymous author lived in Palestine and wrote in Hebrew near the end of the second century BCE. A narrative tradition that may have arisen in the Persian period was possibly utilized, which would explain the Persian parallels;[8] but the concerns of the author clearly point to a composition in the later historical context.

GENRE

Although Judith was included as part of the canon of the Christian Bible as a historical text and was so understood by many, in the modern world a number of scholars have considered it a novel or a romance (the terms are essentially interchangeable) on the analogy of Greek novels. The classicist Ulrich von Wilamowitz judged it a novel, as did Ruth Stiehl, Franz Altheim, and Moses Hadas.[9] Although the Jewish texts are shorter than their Greco-Roman counterparts, they are earlier and should perhaps be considered important parts of a broad international literary development that includes, in addition to the main Greek and Roman novels, smaller novels that arise from various indigenous ethnic groups of the Hellenistic world.[10]

Some scholars have emphasized the similarity of Judith to oral folk narratives and have pressed this category as a genre designation.[11] While this similarity is very important (see below), the present shape of Judith is like the other written novels of the period. To be sure, Jewish novels sometimes developed out of pre-existing narratives, which may in turn have been derived from oral legends. The development from oral legend to novel can be seen in the combination of originally independent stories in Daniel 1:1–6 with the visions of Daniel

7:1–12 to form a larger whole, and then later in the addition of the Prayer of Azariah and the Song of the Three Jews and Susanna to form the apocryphal version of Daniel. The development toward the novel can also be discerned in certain other contemporary Jewish works, such as *Testament of Joseph* from the *Testaments of the Twelve Patriarchs, Testament of Job, and Testament of Abraham,* which begin to take on a novelistic coloring as a keener interest in description and character development gives rise to an expansion of the narrative. Other contemporary texts seem to be like histories in that they do not appear to be intended as fictions, and yet they also tend toward an exciting narration of the protagonists' personal situations: *2 Maccabees, 3 Maccabees, Artapanus,* and the *Tobiad Romance,* and *Royal Family of Adiabene from Josephus's Antiquities of the Jews* 12.154-236, 20.17-96.[12] The novelistic developments should be seen as experiments that push toward the creation of a new art form. In addition to the more obvious elements of the novel, such as rousing action, international sweep, wealth, danger, sex, violence, and use of dialogue, more subtle themes are woven into the text that include the use of everyday characters, domestic settings, and the exploration of the interior life of psychology and emotion. In addition, in both the Greek and the Jewish novels, there is a strong focus on the female protagonist. But while the Greek novels of antiquity portray a young couple in love, separated by challenging circumstances, in the Jewish novels a vulnerable woman is often more alone at the center. She is often directly involved with her extended family, but she faces the trials of life and death alone.

The character of Judith has similarities to two types of characters in Greek novels. In some ways, such as in respect to her beauty, wealth, and piety, she is like the young heroines; in terms of being a self-directed and commanding figure and a widow, she is also like some of the Greek widows.[13] The widows, however, are not generally depicted positively, but are sexually driven, powerful, and sinister, controlling the protagonists' lives. Jerome makes a comparison between Gentile widows and Christian widows that is illuminating: "Gentile widows are wont to paint their faces with rouge and white lead, to flaunt in silk dresses, to deck themselves in gleaming jewels, to wear gold necklaces, to hang from their pierced ears the costliest Red Sea pearls, and to reek of musk."[14] Jerome's stereotype is thus similar to that of the Greek novels; it is all the more striking, then, that Judith does all these things as well, albeit in the service of God, and is seen positively throughout. Another similarity to the Greek novels is the fact that the female protagonist is so much more engaging and active than the male protagonists. This aspect is also found as a genre trait in the Greek novels,[15] but is emphasized even more in Judith. Still, there is one important way in which Judith differs from the Greek and the Jewish novels: the invulnerability of the heroine. The Greek and Jewish novels all feature a vulnerable heroine, and usually a vulnerable hero as well, but Judith is not buffeted by events. She is more like the male hero of epic.

The classical historian Moses Hadas was so convinced that Judith is related to the Greek novels that he objected to just those aspects of the text that are dissimilar to the other novels. A story of a Greek widow in Plutarch, *Amatorius* 2, for example, is very similar to Judith. She remains chaste and curries the favor of a powerful man who she secretly knows killed her husband. Finally she poisons both the suitor and herself and dies triumphantly. In the Greek novel *An Ephesian Tale* by Xenophon of Ephesus, the beautiful young Anthia must also kill a suitor who is trying to rape her. The tragic ending in Plutarch seems appropriate in Greek narrative, and the innocent and threatened heroine in Xenophon seems appropriate as well, but the author of Judith is judged by Hadas to have missed the point of the genre. "What makes the Judith story awkward is the mixed atmosphere of piety and license; the erotic has come in [as in the Greek novels], and shows its leering face despite the author's efforts to smother it in piety. If the constraints of the religious motivation (in itself admirable) are removed, the story would spring back into the pattern of Greek romance."[16] We will turn again below to the heroic Judith, and can perhaps explain the source of the problem as Hadas sees it.

A remaining issue concerning the Jewish novels is whether they were considered historically true or were treated in the ancient world as fictitious, as scholars now often consider them to be. Although many of the known novelistic works were eventually canonized as part of the Christian Bible, it is not clear that these writings were all considered historical at the time of their writing. Several of them contain an obvious historical error that would likely have been easily recognized as such by the audience: Esther becomes a Jewish queen of Persia; in Dan 5:31 Babylon falls to "Darius the Mede" (Darius was a famous Persian king); Tob 14:15 refers to Xerxes king of Media (Xerxes was also a famous Persian king); and in *Joseph and Aseneth*, Joseph rises to become pharaoh until a young prince reaches maturity. Judith's Nebuchadnezzar, king of the Assyrians, is simply another example of this phenomenon, even though it may be the most outrageous historical mistake of all. The audience would have understood why these two evil empires were combined in Judith, and would have applauded it, but they would never have been fooled into thinking this was a retelling of actual historical events. It is this aspect of these novels that helps to define their genre and distinguish them from other prose narratives, like the Gospels.

LITERARY ASPECTS OF JUDITH

The literary qualities of Judith are significant, but it is often a challenge to describe the attractions of a work of "popular," as opposed to "classical," literature.[17] Popular novels have a function to entertain, perhaps to instruct, but are often perceived as falling short of the higher criteria of excellence that have been arrived at in the study of "classical" literature. Still, it is unfair, and ultimately inaccurate, to apply the standards of classical literature rigidly to popular literature. The latter will come up short, and the essential nature of such literature, and its positive qualities and social function may be missed. Just as the moral ideals in Judith were questioned by commentators in the modern period, so also the literary qualities of the book have often been dismissed by those who misperceived its literary genre and function. These criticisms fall into two categories: the disproportionate length of the first part concerning the rise of the military threat to Bethulia and the rhetorical excesses of the whole.

Cowley, who appreciated other literary qualities about the book, took the author to task for creating a first half that takes too long to come to the introduction of the heroine.[18] Dancy was less kind: "Dramatically [the first half] is spoiled by tedious descriptions and confusions, stylistically by exaggerations and empty rhetoric."[19] Even Alonso-Schökel, who set the tone for the literary-critical approaches, denigrated the first part in favor of the second.[20] It seems that most critics were unappreciative of the first part and failed to recognize its contribution to the narrative as a whole. The first part, which is not quite half of the book (even if the Song of Judith at the end is omitted), does *seem* to be longer; actually, the greater share of attention is devoted to the events in the second part. The reader's impression is that the first part is taken up with military movements and engagements, but it is really mostly talk. The talk is, first of all, a way of revealing the characters of Nebuchadnezzar and Holofernes and how they will try to attain world domination, but it is also a means to introduce Achior into the story, his view of the role of Israel in history, the reactions of the Israelites to the crisis, and what is religiously at stake. But these are far from plodding; they develop all the issues of the context of Judith's decisive act. And since Judith was probably read as entertainment, it simply would not do to have the climactic scene arrive too soon.

On the question of the rhetorical excesses, in general, these were perhaps noted most emphatically by Pfeiffer: "The turgid style, the patent exaggerations, the stately pomp and ceremony throughout, unrelieved by a sense of humor, give to the book a baroque rather than a classic appearance."[21] It is quite revealing of his lack of sympathy for the genre that he says that the book of Judith does not have a sense of humor. Quite the opposite is the case.

In response to these criticisms, it is important to see popular literature in its proper context. It is precisely the goal of the author of Judith to impress the reader with an unrestrained exuberance and to have an immediate impact. The author of Judith makes an art of excess: the descriptions of the troops, the artificial geographical sweep, the pillage and destruction, the gory central scene—all of these serve to keep the reader riveted. This is the same approach that is found in other novelistic works, both Jewish and Greek. It should also be noted that the author of Judith did not work with established models of what the novel genre should look like; the novel was a bold experiment, only in the first stages of development. Nonetheless, the author had introduced innovative improvements over the other novels. Whereas some of the more primitive novels of this period were characterized by duplicated scenes (the Additions to Esther) or separate small narratives strung together (the Additions to Daniel), Judith attains a length that is larger than the other novels of the apocrypha, and yet maintains a smooth, taut narrative. To be sure, there are two different movements to the story, but there is a logical relationship between them, and the author exercises many literary gifts. In many ways, Judith is the best constructed of the Jewish novels.

Toni Craven made a major breakthrough in the literary appreciation of the whole of the book when she identified certain aspects of the function of the first part.[22] There are many parallels and contrasts between the first part of the book and the second and, in addition, parallels and contrasts within each part. This results in a complex and intentional structuring of the two parts that greatly enriches the reading experience, *once one is prepared for such a reading.* Some of the most important correspondences can be represented thus:

First half
  A Campaign against disobedient nations; the
    people surrender (1:1–3:10)
    B Israel is "greatly terrified"; Joakim pre-
      pares for war (4:1-15)
      C Holofernes talks with Achior; Achior is
        expelled (5:1–6:13)
      C′ Achior is received in Bethulia; Achior
        talks with the people (6:14-21)
    B′ Holofernes prepares for war; Israel is
      "greatly terrified" (7:1-5)
  A′ Campaign against Bethulia; the people want
    to surrender (7:6-32)

Second half
  A Introduction of Judith (8:1-8)
    B Judith plans to save Israel (8:9–10:9a)
      C Judith and her maid leave Bethulia
        (10:9b-10)
        D Judith overcomes Holofernes
          (10:11–13:10a)
      C′ Judith and her maid return to Bethulia
        (13:10b-11)
    B′ Judith plans to destroy Israel's enemy
      (13:12–16:20)
  A′ Conclusion about Judith (16:21-25)

Craven's discernment of the pattern of parallels and contrasts allows a much more sympathetic— and ultimately enjoyable—reading of the first half of the book. Each half is in the form of a chiasm— that is, a structure that resembles the Greek letter *chi,* or X, and in which motifs in the first half are repeated in the second, except reversed.[23] This allows each part to have an effective center, yet move to a culmination. The first part ends with a calm that is not a resolution; it is the dread of Holofernes' attack. The question hanging over the Jews is, "Who is lord, Nebuchadnezzar or God?" The second part removes the Israelites' fear of Holofernes and answers that question resoundingly, "God is Lord and works even through the hand of a woman." The structuring of the narrative is simple and complex at the same time. There are numerous structural relationships, yet they point to a single overall arc: rising action, denouement, falling action.

In addition to the pattern of balanced parallels and oppositions of motifs that Craven analyzed, we can detect several other important narrative operations as well. First, there is a typical hero pattern in the novel. This common cross-cultural narrative structure usually portrays a male hero, sometimes withdrawn from society, who comes forward when the community is threatened by a larger-than-life monster and slays it. At this point, there are essentially two resolutions of the story: either a comic one or a tragic one. In the comic resolution (usually associated with myths and fairy tales), the hero returns to a celebration with the community, and peace and fertility are restored to the land. In the tragic ending (usually associated with epic poetry and tragedy), the hero either dies in the process or returns to a community in which he cannot really participate. Judith can easily be seen as an adaptation of the hero pattern: In the beginning, she is outside of society in the tent on her roof. She comes out of seclusion to "arm" herself in beautiful garments, moves forward to engage the monster, slays the monster, and returns to a celebration of the community. The ending is closer to the comic resolution, although this question will be taken up again in regard to the ending of the work. The similarity of Judith to heroic narratives has been noted by various scholars. Coote has suggested the cross-cultural tale pattern more typical of the heroine called "wife disguised as a man frees her husband," which depicts a faithful wife (here, Judith is a "wife" of Israel) who disguises herself as a man to rescue her husband.[24] However, it seems more likely that what we see in Judith is not a female pattern such as this, but a more radical adaptation of a male warrior-hero pattern. The role reversal in Judith and the flouting of normal sexual taboos is much stronger than in most heroine tales of disguise.[25]

The hero pattern is a broad and varied phenomenon, occurring in all parts of the world, and it has attracted the attention of scholars who see the possibility of isolating a "monomyth," a single narrative structure that is the model of all hero tales worldwide. While this goal may never be attained in detail, it is clear that there are common patterns of the hero narrative and that comparing Judith with some of the reconstructions of cross-cultural patterns could be instructive. The best-known attempt to isolate a single pattern with variations is that of Joseph Campbell.[26] His summary of the typical hero story pattern—and the vast majority of the narratives he cites concern male heroes—is as follows (slightly simplified): The mythological hero, setting forth from his hut or castle, proceeds to the threshold of adventure. There he encounters a shadow presence that guards the passage. The hero may defeat or conciliate this power and go alive into the kingdom of the dark. Beyond the threshold the hero journeys through a world of unfamiliar, yet strangely intimate, forces, some of which severely threaten him. When he arrives at the nadir of the mythological world, he undergoes a supreme ordeal and gains his reward. The triumph may be represented as the hero's theft of the boon he came to gain. The final work is that of return; the hero reemerges from the kingdom of dread. The boon that he brings restores the world.

The elements of the narrative are very similar to the book of Judith: the departure of the hero, the crossing of the threshold into a dark region of danger (see below on the gates of Bethulia as a threshold), the trials of the hero and the slaying of a monster (in this case, Holofernes), the stealing of a great boon to humanity (the head of Holofernes), the return of the hero, the reentry into society by crossing the threshold again, and the restoration of peace. What we have in the case of Judith is a

hero narrative cast in a more realistic setting that brings down to earth many of the elements of the story pattern. Further, Campbell's analysis helps us to understand why some of the characters of Judith are so one-dimensional. The literary or theological value of the book of Judith is not contained in the development of Judith's character or in an analysis of evil as embodied in Holofernes. The complexity that usually makes characters interesting is not present. Judith does not grow as a character and is not mixed of good and evil qualities. It is emphasized that she is wise, virtuous, and capable; but she does not discover anything about herself (cf. in this regard Esther 4). She is like the figures of myth, who are likewise often one-dimensional. The hero of myth is born fully formed in his heroic traits. The remarkable virtues of this person, according to Campbell, are more predestined than achieved in the course of life. Thus both the hero and the monster reach their end by destiny. There is very little need to create multidimensional characters.

The hero pattern is thus the overarching structure for the book of Judith, but contained within it are interesting smaller structures as well that serve to illuminate important segments of the departure and return of the hero. One of these is the preparation of Judith, or her transition out of her life of quietism in chap. 8. It is best described as what anthropologists would call a "rite of passage," a ritually marked transition that involves separation from society, a liminal period in which normal markers of social order, such as age, class, gender, or status, are obliterated and sacred information is imparted, and incorporation or aggregation back into the social order with a new status.[27] At 8:11-27, Judith has scolded the rulers of Bethulia for being weak willed and has told them that she has a plan to deliver them. She then must prepare herself, and enters into a state of ritual cleansing and self-abnegation in which she uncovers her mourning garments, prays, bathes, and then reclothes herself in rich apparel and cosmetics. The scene is remarkably similar to the central prayer scenes of the female protagonists in the Additions to Esther and *Joseph and Aseneth*.[28] At a turning point near the middle of the narrative, the female protagonist turns to prayer and begins a process of penitence and self-abasement. She condemns her beauty, puts on sackcloth as a garment of mourning, prays, and afterward reclothes herself in beautiful garments and emerges to perform her mission (see also the much less stylized scenes in Tob 3:10-15 and Sus 22:1-23).

This scene is related to Jewish penitential theology that developed in the post-exilic period, already found, for instance, in Nehemiah 9, Daniel 9, some of the psalms, and Baruch and the Prayer of Manasseh in the apocrypha, and emerging later in Jas 4:8-10. The themes emphasized in these texts differ, as do the content of their prayers. Still, in all the Jewish novels except Judith, the introspective female protagonist is buffeted and psychologically tested.[29] The amount of space devoted to this issue and the depth of the psychological interest vary from Susanna (the least attention) to *Joseph and Aseneth* (the most), but it is interesting that Judith is not psychologically buffeted despite her situation. Moore compares the prayer in Judith with that of Add. Esth 14:1-19,[30] but misses this crucial difference. Neither does Judith show any penitence. Esther, and even more so Aseneth, purifies herself by a penitence that involves an abject self-abasement. The rituals of mourning are incorporated, which would be typical in the Bible in a moment of crisis, but Esther goes beyond this; it has become a quasi-ascetic repudiation of those aspects of her body associated with her beauty: "Instead of costly perfumes she covered her head with ashes and dung, and she utterly humbled her body; every part that she loved to adorn she covered with her tangled hair" (Add. Esth 14:2). The heroines' awareness of sin, associated with their bodies, is overwhelming in Esther and *Joseph and Aseneth*. Yet Judith knows nothing of this. Even her fasts do not appear to have an explicit penitential aspect. Judith undergoes an experience of transformation without being transformed. The author takes up the paradigm and the literary pattern of the buffeted Jewish heroine who is penitent and prayerful, but gives her no recognition of sin. She is simply perfect as she is.

In addition, another important segment of the hero's quest, crossing the threshold into the sphere of darkness and danger and returning again,[31] is marked very clearly in the narrative as an important passage as well. Craven notes in her structural arrangement of Judith a correspondence between the departure of Judith and her maid through the gates of Bethulia at 10:9*b*-10 and their return at 13:10*b*-11. These corresponding scenes contain a number of important, ritualized elements. When Judith, with the help of her maid, has prepared for her quest by means of the dressing scene, she commands the town elder Uzziah, "Order the gate of the town to be opened." Accompanying her departure is a series of gestures of Uzziah and the townspeople that are typical of the departure scenes in heroic poetry . When the two return again she also says, "Open, open the gate!" which marks clearly the return of the hero and her incorporation back into the safety of the known village. Although there is still a battle to be fought when she returns, the immediate danger to her—and especially to her honor as a pious Jewish woman—is while she is in the liminal period between her going and coming. This is also the period in which she flaunts her sexuality, engages in deceit and manipulation, and murders Holofernes. It is also the dramatic center of the book.

Aside from these structural elements of the novel, there are also certain aspects of the literary style that deserve attention. Judith utilizes a number of techniques that enliven the narrative: anticipation of future events; retardation and acceleration of plot; vivid visual description; and irony and humor. Concerning the anticipation of events that appear later in the text, we must assume that the story of Judith was well known, whether from oral tradition or from written narratives, such as the present text. This would be quite likely if, as discussed above, an older narrative tradition from the Persian period was at the core of the present Hasmonean-era text. Anticipation is a way of building suspense about future events, but it also introduces a kind of irony—that is, a perception on the part of the audience about what they think will happen that is different from the perspective of the characters. The anticipation in Judith is sometimes suspenseful, sometimes ironic and humorous. It is suspenseful when Achior's exile to the village of Bethulia anticipates his witness there to the events that are about to unfold. It is ironic and humorous when statements that are made take on a different meaning in the light of anticipated events, such as Holofernes' blustery statement to Achior: "You shall not see my face again until I take revenge on this race!" (6:5). Anticipation can often be seen in the irony of many of the statements in Judith's and Holofernes' dialogue (e.g., 11:6; 12:4).

The retardation and acceleration of the plot are among the most effective techniques of the author, creating excellent pacing of the narrative. This is often accomplished by the alternation of narrative and dialogue, action and rest, and alternation of location, but most often by the use of vivid description.[32] The audience fully anticipates the beheading of Holofernes—they know that is what the story is about—to such an extent that the amount of text that goes before it has surprised many critics. Just as the Gospel of Mark has been characterized as a passion story with a long introduction,[33] so also Judith is a beheading with a long introduction. With this in mind, one can see chaps. 1–7 as a series of episodes that use retardation and acceleration, in addition to alternation of types of discourse, to set the stage for the climactic decapitation. Chapter 1 launches immediately into a military drama between two great world powers, followed by a rest (1:16). The narrative moves again into a brisk description of military events and another rest (3:10). Israel's response to war follows, which is described almost like military preparations (4:1-15). There are several extended dialogues following (5:1–6:9), after which there are intrigues that involve a combination of vivid description with some retardation of the plot and dialogue, as Achior is expelled from Holofernes' camp and welcomed into Bethulia (6:10–7:18). In 10:11-23 we find a similar combination of vivid description, plot retardation, and dialogue as Judith reverses the direction of Achior's movement and goes from Bethulia to Holofernes' camp.[34] From 11:1 to 12:18 there is dialogue, and then at the climactic scene in Holofernes' tent, we find slight retardation of the plot as Judith approaches Holofernes (12:19–13:7), and then acceleration of the plot as Judith beheads Holofernes, collects the head and the tent canopy, moves through the camp, climbs up the mountain and back to Bethulia, all in three verses (13:8-10)! The military campaign at the end of Judith (15:1-7) is also told in the same quick, bold strokes as the military campaigns at the beginning of Judith.

If there is one literary device that most characterizes the book of Judith, however, it would be irony. In this respect Judith is in good company; irony is at the center of the Gospel of John, the book of Jonah, and Plato's portrait of Socrates.[35] The irony is ubiquitous in Judith and plays on several levels.[36] On the broadest level, it is found in the unexpected development that the great Assyrian general Holofernes is felled by the hand of a woman. This is the central irony that underlies the structure of the book as a whole, and it is referred to often, both in Judith's prayer in chap. 9, and in the Song of Judith in chap. 16. The irony spills over into the dialogue, creating an extended train of ironic utterances, as characters time and again speak words that have one meaning for them and another for the audience. Judith, who is very clever, seems to be uttering double entendres intentionally, playing with Holofernes as a cat plays with a mouse. But Holofernes is also prone to making pronouncements that will come back to haunt him; he is too obtuse to realize what is going on around him. The two strands of ironic statements—Judith's and Holofernes'—thus proceed simultaneously through much of the novel. Related to this is the discrepancy between Holofernes' self-understanding and the pitiable end for which he is destined. His bloated self-image clouds his judgment, so that he not only sees in himself what he wants to see, but also he sees in Judith only what he chooses. If Holofernes had been clever enough to catch Judith's irony, he would have been clever enough to avoid her trap, even get the best of her. But he was not. Surrounding these larger ironies are smaller examples that are still significant. Nebuchadnezzar claims to be "lord of the whole world" (2:5); yet the narrative confirms that God is lord, and this will be proved, not on the great battlefields or in the famous cities of the ancient Near East, but outside the tiny mountain village of Bethulia. Also Achior, though an Ammonite, is more stalwart in his defense of Israel than is Uzziah, one of the rulers of Bethulia. We may note one last example of irony that also relates to the moral evaluation of Judith: She is fastidious about the observance of kosher laws, and yet she violates Jewish views of the permissible actions of a pious widow. This irony lies at the center of Judith's liminal actions.

BIBLICAL PARALLELS

The reader familiar with the Bible will immediately recognize in Judith parallels to many biblical stories. The text is indeed a rich tapestry of biblical allusions. The most important of these are listed and analyzed by Dubarle,[37] and here the most important ones will be mentioned. In addition to the explicit references to Abraham, Isaac, and Jacob (Jdt 8:25-27) and to Simeon (Jdt 9:2-4), there are evident influences of narrative motifs from many biblical texts.

The fact that the main character is a woman naturally attracts our attention to biblical stories that focus on female characters. The general theme of the ruse of a woman recurs in biblical literature, from Rebekah's manipulation to secure the birthright for her son Jacob in Genesis 27, to Tamar's ruse to have sex with her father-in-law in order to raise up a child in the name of her dead husband in Genesis 38.[38] Rahab the prostitute's aid to the two spies sent into Jericho (Joshua 2:1; 6:22-25) bears more than a passing resemblance to parts of Judith. It is not simply that Judith also "plays the harlot" with Holofernes; Rahab, like Achior, is also a non-Israelite who joins Israel, and her speech (Josh 2:9-14) is very similar to Achior's speech in Judith 5. At several points in the HB there is an execution of a warrior by a woman, which was considered a shameful form of death. In Judg 9:50-55, Abimelech is killed by a woman who drops a millstone upon him. Emphasized here is that Abimelech does not want to die at the hand of a woman, a mark of shame that is found also in Jdt 16:5 (see also 2 Sam 4:5-12; 20:14-22).

The most important of the parallels to women in active roles, however, is the story of Deborah the prophet in Judges 4:1–5, and especially the role of Jael in murdering the general Sisera. In Judges 4, the prose version of the story, King Jabin of Canaan has sent his general Sisera to attack the Israelites. Deborah the prophet instructs Barak to lead the Israelites out to fight Sisera. She promises Barak that the Lord will defeat Sisera and adds, "The LORD will sell Sisera into the hand of a woman." Barak routs the forces of Sisera, but Sisera himself takes refuge in the tent of Jael. He lies down, and while he is sleeping, Jael takes a tent peg and drives it through his head. Judges 5 is then a victory song of Deborah in celebration. The most obvious similarities to Judith are the heroism of a woman who gives courage to her people in a time of oppression by a foreign power, her call to arms to the men to defend themselves, and also the murder scene in which a woman—now not Deborah

but Jael—kills the general of the foreign king. More specifically we may note that both women are very strong, patriotic people and that the execution scenes both take place in a tent while the general is incapacitated and lying down.[39] The victory song of Judith is partly modeled on the Song of Deborah and also on Moses' Song of the Sea in Exodus 15. In a fascinating development, we also see that a first-century CE retelling of Bible history, Pseudo-Philo's *Biblical Antiquities* 30-31, modifies the story of Deborah by adding elements evidently drawn from Judith.[40] The influence of the stories has now moved in the opposite direction!

There are similarities as well to male warriors and leaders in the Bible. Judith is not only like Deborah, but she is also like the other judges and prophets who arise when God hears the prayers of the people (Jdt 4:13; cf. Judg 2:11-23), to give the land rest from oppression for a number of years afterward (Jdt 16:25; cf. Judg 3:11, 30; 5:31).[41] We note, for example, Ehud's killing of Eglon, king of Moab (Judg 3:12-30). Once Ehud has assassinated the king in his inner chamber, Ehud leaves the doors closed so that the servants are pacing without, wondering what is taking the king so long. This is played to comic effect, just as is the analogous scene in Jdt 14:14-18.

Other texts have left their mark on Judith, not just in the similarity of the motifs, but in the use of words as well: Abram's (Abraham's) pursuit of the captors of Lot in Genesis 14 (cf. Judith 15), the motif of the complaining of the people in Exodus 17 (cf. Judith 7), the story of David and Goliath in 1 Samuel 17 (cf. Judith 13), the bluster of Nebuchadnezzar in Daniel 2-4 and the insistence that the king be worshiped as a god in Daniel 6 (cf. Judith 2), and the repentance in sackcloth, even for the cattle, in Jonah 3:5-8 (cf. Jdt 4:10). Some of these parallels may result from the oral circulation of good story motifs, but others are either much too close to be independent or use similar words. Thus the essence of Judith is not a literary rendition of an originally oral story, as may be the case for Tobit, Esther, or Daniel 1:1–6. Judith uses broad folklore themes, to be sure, but the parallels reveal an author at work who is borrowing heavily from a number of biblical texts and weaving them together into a unified story. Dubarle likens this process to the "anthological style" of other post-exilic Jewish works and of such Christian texts as Luke 1:1–2.[42] It would be wrong, however, to say that Judith is an imaginative interpretation that simply mines and develops a number of biblical passages. For one thing, non-Jewish traditions can also be postulated that are in many cases just as close as the biblical: the Ugaritic epic of Aqhat, for example, tells the story of the woman Paghat, who, enraged over the death of her brother Aqhat, avenges him by inebriating his murderer and slaying him while he is on his bed.[43] The use of written texts in the composition of another written text does not preclude the use also of motifs and themes from oral tradition,[44] but what is important here is that Judith is not just the sum total of the myriad motifs that it appears to borrow, now strung together. It uses these many building blocks, and yet still reflects the single vision of a talented author who communicates the exuberance of Judith's freedom in a new genre, the novel.

FOR FURTHER READING

Commentaries:

Cowley, Arthur E. "The Book of Judith." In *APOT* 1:242-67.

Dancy, J. C. *The Shorter Books of the Apocrypha.* CBC. Cambridge: Cambridge University Press, 1972.

Enslin, Morton S., and Solomon Zeitlin. *The Book of Judith.* JAL VIII. Leiden: Brill, 1972.

Moore, Carey A. *Judith.* AB 40. Garden City, N.Y.: Doubleday, 1985.

Other Studies:

Alonso-Schökel, Luis. *Narrative Structures in the Book of Judith.* Berkeley, Calif.: Center for Hermeneutical Studies in Hellenistic and Modern Culture, 1974.

Bal, Mieke. "Head Hunting: 'Judith' on the Cutting Edge of Knowledge." *JSOT* 63 (1994) 3-34.

Brenner, Athalya, ed. *A Feminist Companion to Esther, Judith and Susanna.* Sheffield: Sheffield Academic, 1995.

Craven, Toni. *Artistry and Faith in the Book of Judith.* Chico, Calif.: Scholars Press, 1983.

Elder, Linda Bennett. "Judith." In Elisabeth Schüssler Fiorenza, ed. *Searching the Scriptures.* Vol. 2. New York: Crossroad, 1993–94.

Garrard, Mary. "Judith." In *Artemisia Gentileschi: The Image of the Female Hero in Italian Baroque Art.* Princeton: Princeton University Press, 1989.

Jacobus, Mary. "Judith, Holofernes, and the Phallic Woman." In *Reading Women: Essays in Feminist Criticism.* New York: Columbia University Press, 1986.

Lacocque, André. *The Feminine Unconventional: Four Subversive Figures in Israel's Tradition.* Minneapolis: Fortress, 1990.

Levine, Amy-Jill. "Sacrifice and Salvation: Otherness and Domestication in the Book of Judith." In *"No One Spoke Ill of Her": Essays on Judith.* Edited by James C. VanderKam. Atlanta: Scholars Press, 1992.

McNeil, Brian. "Reflections on the Book of Judith." *The Downside Review* 96 (1978) 199-207.

Milne, Pamela. "What Shall We Do with Judith? A Feminist Assessment of a Biblical 'Heroine.' " *Semeia* 62 (1993) 37-58.

Pervo, Richard I. "Aseneth and Her Sisters: Women in Jewish Narrative and in the Greek Novels." In *"Women Like This": New Perspectives on Jewish Women in the Greco-Roman World.* Edited by Amy-Jill Levine. Atlanta: Scholars Press, 1991.

Skehan, Patrick. "The Hand of Judith." *CBQ* 25 (1963) 94-110.

Stocker, Margarita. *Judith, Sexual Warrior: Women and Power in Western Culture.* New Haven: Yale University Press, 1998.

VanderKam, James C., ed. *"No One Spoke Ill of Her": Essays on Judith.* Atlanta: Scholars Press, 1992.

Wills, Lawrence M. *The Jewish Novel in the Ancient World.* Ithaca: Cornell University Press, 1995.

ENDNOTES

1. Richard I. Pervo, "Aseneth and Her Sisters: Women in Jewish Narrative and in the Greek Novels," in *"Women Like This": New Perspectives on Jewish Women in the Greco-Roman World*, ed. Amy-Jill Levine (Atlanta: Scholars Press, 1991) 159 n. 71.

2. Martin Luther, *Luther's Works*, 55 vols. (Philadelphia: Muhlenberg, 1960) 35:337-38.

3. Carey A. Moore, *Judith*, AB 40 (Garden City, N.Y.: Doubleday, 1985) 50-55, 67-70.

4. Lee I. A. Levine, "The Age of Hellenism: Alexander the Great and the Rise and Fall of the Hasmonean Kingdom," in *Ancient Israel: A Short History from Abraham to the Roman Destruction of the Temple*, ed. Hershel Shanks (Englewood Cliffs, N.J.: Prentice Hall, 1988) 186-89.

5. George W. E. Nickelsburg, *Jewish Literature Between the Bible and the Mishnah* (Philadelphia: Fortress, 1981) 109.

6. Arguing for the subversive position of Judith over against the Hasmonean rulers are André, Lacocque, *The Feminine Unconventional: Four Subversive Figures in Israel's Tradition* (Minneapolis: Fortress, 1990) 41, and Jan Willem van Henten, "Judith as Alternative Leader: A Rereading of Judith 7:1–13," in *A Feminist Companion to Esther, Judith and Susanna*, ed. Athalya Brenner (Sheffield: Sheffield Academic, 1995) 243-44. Carey A. Moore, *Judith*, 67-70, is in agreement with the position adopted here.

7. See Carey A. Moore, *Judith*, 70-71; Toni Craven, *Artistry and Faith in the Book of Judith* (Chico, Calif.: Scholars Press, 1983) 118-20.

8. George W. E. Nickelsburg, *Jewish Literature Between the Bible and the Mishnah*, 108-9.

9. Ulrich von Wilamowitz et al., *Die griechische und lateinische Literatur und Sprache*, 3rd ed. (Leipzig: Teubner, 1912) 189; Ruth Stiehl and Franz Altheim, *Die aramäische Sprache unter den Achaimeniden* (Frankfurt am Main: Vittorio Klostermann, 1963) 200; Moses Hadas, *Hellenistic Culture: Fusion and Diffusion* (New York: Norton, 1959) 165-66.

10. J. R. Morgan and Richard Stoneman, *Greek Fiction: The Greek Novel in Context* (London: Routledge, 1994); Lawrence M. Wills, *The Jewish Novel in the Ancient World* (Ithaca: Cornell University Press, 1995). Greek novels can be found in B. P. Reardon, *Collected Ancient Greek Novels* (Berkeley: University of California Press, 1989), and William F. Hansen, *Anthology of Ancient Greek Popular Literature* (Bloomington: Indiana University Press, 1998).

11. Mary P. Coote, "Response," in Luis Alonso-Schökel, *Narrative Structures in the Book of Judith* (Berkeley, Calif.: Center for Hermeneutical Studies in Hellenistic and Modern Culture, 1974) 21-26; Pamela Milne, "What Shall We Do with Judith? A Feminist Reassessment of a Biblical Heroine," *Semeia* 62 (1993) 37-58.

12. Lawerence M. Wills, *The Jewish Novel in the Ancient World*, 16-30, 185-211. A good English translation of some of the non-canonical Jewish texts listed here, with scholarly introductions, can be found in James H. Charlesworth, *The Old Testament Pseudepigrapha*, 2 vols. (Garden City, N.Y.: Doubleday, 1985).

13. Achilles Tatius, *Leucippe and Clitophon* 5-8; Heliodorus, *An Ephesian Story*, 7-8.

14. Jerome, *Epistle* 127.3, quoted in Pervo, "Aseneth and Her Sisters," 156-57.

15. David Konstan, *Sexual Symmetry: Love in the Ancient Novel and Related Genres* (Princeton: Princeton University Press, 1994).

16. Moseo Hadas, *Hellenist Culture*, 169.

17. Lawrence M. Wills, *The Jewish Novel in the Ancient World* 1-39, 212-45; William F. Hansen, *Anthology of Ancient Greek Popular Literature*, 3-13.

18. Arthur E. Cowley, "The Book of Judith," in *APOT* 1:242-43.

19. J. C. Dancy, *The Shorter Books of the Apocrypha*, CBC (Cambridge: Cambridge University Press, 1972) 68.

20. Alonso-Schökel, *Narrative Structures in the Book of Judith*, 5.

21. Robert H. Pfeiffer, *History of New Testament Times* (New York: Harper and Bros., 1949) 299.

22. Toni Craven, *Artistry and Faith in the Book of Judith*, 60-62.

23. On chiasm see also Adele Berlin, "Introduction to Hebrew Poetry," *The New Interpreter's Bible*, 12 vols. (Nashville: Abingdon, 1994) 4:310, and using the language of "concentric construction," Michael Kolarcik, S.J., "The Book of Wisdom," *NIB, 5:443-46*.

24. Mary P. Coote, "Response," in Luis Alonso-Schökel, *Narrative Structures in the Book of Judith* (Berkeley, Calif.: Center for Hermeneutical Studies in Hellenistic and Modern Culture, 1974) 21-26.

25. Pamela Milne, "What Shall We Do with Judith?" A Feminist Reassessment of a Biblical Heroine," 37-58, also looks to the male hero narrative pattern isolated by Heda Jason, "Ilja of Murom and Tzar Kalin: A Proposal for a Model for the Narrative Structure of an Epic Struggle," *Slavica Hierosylimitana*, 5-6 (1981) 47-55. An interest-

ing study of the "female hero" in modern literature also explores the adaptation of the male hero pattern in modern novels about women. See Carol Pearson and Katherine Pope, *The Female Hero in American and British Literature* (New York: Bowker, 1981).

26. Joseph Campbell, *The Hero with a Thousand Faces* (New York: Pantheon, 1949) esp. 245-46. On Judith as a heroic quest, see Mary Garrard, "Judith," in *Artemisia Gentileschi: The Image of the Female Hero in Italian Baroque Art* (Princeton, N.J.: Princeton University Press, 1989) 281.

27. Arnold van Gennep, *The Rites of Passage* (Chicago: University of Chicago Press, 1960); Victor Turner, "Betwixt and Between: The Liminal Period in Rites de Passage," in *The Forest of Symbols: Aspects of Ndembu Ritual* (Ithaca: Cornell University Press) 93-111.

28. Lawrence M. Wills, *The Jewish Novel in the Ancient World*, 224-32; Alice Bach, *Women, Seduction and Betrayal in Biblical Narrative* (New York: Cambridge University Press, 1997) 202-3.

29. Lawerence M. Wills, *The Jewish Novel in the Ancient World*, 147-48.

30. Carey A. Moore, *Judith*, 195-97.

31. Joseph Campbell, *Hero with a Thousand Faces*, 90-91.

32. On alternation of location, see Toni Craven, *Artistry and Faith in the Book of Judith*, 61; on description, see Luis Alonso-Schökel, *Narrative Structures in the Book of Judith*, 7.

33. Martin Kähler, *The So-Called Historical Jesus and the Historic, Biblical Christ* (Philadelphia: Fortress, 1964) 80.

34. On the "exchange" of Achior and Judith, see Adolfo Roitman, "Achior in the Book of Judith: His Role and Significance," in *"No One Spoke Ill of Her": Essays on Judith*, ed. James C. VanderKam (Atlanta: Scholars Press, 1992) 31-45.

35. Carey A. Moore, *Judith*, 78-85.

36. See Gail R. O'Day, "The Gospel of John," *NIB*, 9:566, 813-15.

37. A. M. Dubarle, *Judith: Formes et sens des diverses traditions*, 2 vols. (Rome: Pontifical Biblical Institute, 1966) 1:137-64.

38. Esther Fuchs, "Who Is Hiding the Truth? Deceptive Women and Biblical Androcentrism," in *Feminist Perspectives on Biblical Scholarship*, ed. Adela Yarbro Collins (Chico, Calif.: Scholars Press, 1985) 137-44.

39. Sidnie Ann White, "In the Steps of Jael and Deborah: Judith as Heroine," in *"No One Spoke Ill of Her": Essays on Judith*, ed. James C. VanderKam (Atlanta: Scholars Press, 1992) 5-16.

40. Richard I. Pervo, "Aseneth and Her Sisters: Women in Jewish Narrative and in the Greek Novels," 159n. 71.

41. Sidnie Ann White, "In the Steps of Jael and Deborah," 12; Jan Willem van Henten, "Judith as Alternative Leader: A Rereading of Judith 7:1–13," in *A Feminist Companion to Esther, Judith and Susanna*, ed. Athalya Brenner (Sheffield: Sheffield Academic, 1995) 243-44.

42. A. M. Dubarle, *Judith*, 1:137-64.

43. *ANET*, 155.

44. Susan Niditch, *Oral World and Written Word: Ancient Israelite Literature* (Louisville: Westminster/John Knox, 1996) 8-24.

THE ADDITIONS TO ESTHER

SIDNIE WHITE CRAWFORD

The so-called Additions to Esther, found in the Greek versions of Esther (LXX and AT), make the book of Esther a very different literary work from that in the Hebrew Bible (MT). The additions add drama, plumb the emotional depths of the characters, add information to fill in the gaps of the MT, and, most important, supply an overt religious element that is lacking in the MT. To fully appreciate the LXX version of Esther, it is helpful to read it in its entirety, as it is found in the apocrypha of the NRSV. The Additions are not all from the same author, nor were they all composed in the same language. Josephus, who was certainly familiar with LXX, does not use all the Additions (e.g., he does not include Add. A), perhaps indicating that he did not know them all or did not consider them original.[1]

The most striking change in the LXX version of Esther is the addition of religious elements. The additions continually mention God, and the LXX redactor introduces the name of God within the (translated) text of the MT:

"to fear God and obey his commandments"
   (2:20)
"call upon the Lord" (4:8)
"and the Lord drove sleep from the king that
   night" (6:1)
"for God is with him" (6:13).

Also, the Additions contain a dream sent by God (Addition A), prayers by Mordecai and Esther, fasting explicitly directed toward God, a manifest concern for keeping the purity laws, especially those concerning food and marriage, a mention of the Temple (all in Addition C), and a Gentile acknowledgment of the power of the God of Israel (Addition E).[2] The effect of all these changes is that God becomes the hero of the Greek story, and the importance of human action is greatly lessened; the LXX redactor makes clear to the reader that God acts to save the Jews and that, because of God's protective concern for the Jews, the outcome of the crisis is never in doubt.

This change in emphasis also leads to changes in the main human characters, Mordecai and Esther. Mordecai, as the recipient of the dream sent by God, becomes a typical biblical hero, like Joseph or Daniel, and is the chief human character in the drama. Esther, on the other hand, loses status from her portrayal in the MT: She becomes a romantic and emotional heroine, as in the Hellenistic romance novel, and, as such, is less attractive to modern readers.[3]

FOR FURTHER READING

See "The Book of Esther."

ENDNOTES

1. Josephus, *Antiquities of the Jews*, Book XI.

2. Carey A. Moore, *Daniel, Esther and Jeremiah: The Additions*, AB 44 (Garden City, N.Y.: Doubleday, 1977) 158-59.

3. For LXX Esther as a Hellenistic romance novel, see Lawrence M. Wills, *The Jew in the Court of the Foreign King*, HDR 26 (Minneapolis: Fortress, 1990) 197.

THE BOOK OF WISDOM

BY MICHAEL KOLARCIK, S.J.

This book has been referred to over the centuries and still today as the book of Wisdom (from the Vulgate) or the Wisdom of Solomon (from the Septuagint). The latter title derives from the middle section of the book where the unnamed speaker is immediately recognized as Solomon—the king who preferred the wisdom of God to fame and riches. In Jewish tradition, Solomon became a model for the "true sage" in whom the best of human wisdom and the most ardent faithfulness to the ways of God were joined. Standing under the authority of this figure of Solomon, the unknown author of this work presents us with a dramatic exhortation to seek justice. It is the gift of wisdom that makes it possible to live justly and to receive friendship with God. The extraordinary deliverance of the Israelites from Egypt and the subsequent guidance through the desert testify to the strength of justice and to the wisdom of God. These three concerns—the exhortation to justice, the gift of wisdom, and the deliverance from Egypt—make up the rich tapestry of the three main sections of the Wisdom of Solomon.

The style of writing is clearly poetic with a strong emphasis on paradoxical and forceful images rather than on logical arguments. Yet the images are arranged and orchestrated in such a way as to sustain an argument for justice and faithfulness. In the first part of the book, the Hebrew poetic device of parallelism between lines is used to great effect—so much so that earlier scholars presumed the text had been written first in Hebrew and subsequently translated into Greek, as in the case of Sirach. But the use of such Greek words as those representing "immortality" (ἀθανασία athanasia) and "incorruptibility" (ἀφθαρσία aphtharsia) makes it difficult to imagine a Hebrew original. In any event, we have no references to a Hebrew text of Wisdom, and the most ancient manuscripts that relate the book of Wisdom are in Greek. Furthermore, the latter part of the book makes use of a freer prosaic style of writing that reveals the author's familiarity and ease with Greek prose.

AUTHOR, DATE, AND PLACE OF COMPOSITION

The first unambiguous reference to the book of Wisdom stems from the second century CE in the writings of Irenaeus (c. 140–202 CE). Two references are made to Wis 2:24 and 12:10: "Everyone follows the desires of his depraved heart, nurturing a wicked jealousy through which death entered the world";[1] "from generation to generation the Lord gives an opportunity to repent to all those who desire to return."[2] References become multiple in the writings of Clement of Alexandria (c. 175–230 CE), who continuously refers to the book of Wisdom and treats it as a canonical book. The book of Wisdom is cited among the list of books held to be canonical by the church in the Muratorian Canon (c. 180–190 CE). Interestingly, in the Muratorian Canon, the book of Wisdom is located among the canonical books of the New Testament.

Although Origen (c. 185–255 CE) cites the book of Wisdom among his writings and commentaries on Scripture, he shares the uncertainty of its canonical status with others. Jerome follows Origen's hesitancy and accepts as canonical the twenty-two books of the Hebrew canon (according to a certain combination of books), the number of which corresponds to the twenty-two letters of the Hebrew alphabet. The greatest impetus for the formal inclusion of the book of Wisdom in the canon of Scripture came from Augustine (354–430 CE). For Augustine, the long and venerable reading of the book of Wisdom in the liturgy by all Christians revealed its veritable canonical status.[3]

However, it was very clear to early Christian writers like Origen and Augustine that the Solomonic authorship of the book was practically impossible. Although many candidates had been proposed (from the nephew of Ben Sira to Philo of Alexandria), there was no consensus regarding the authorship of this fascinating work.

The great affinity between many phrases in the book of Wisdom and in the writings of Philo (c. 20 BCE–50 CE) has brought attention to their relationship. Although they share a common set of concerns and many phraseological affinities, there are no clear citations between them. It would be tempting to see in the book of Wisdom the result of Philo's personal attempt to write a more religious and poetic work over and above the philosophical and allegorical works for which he is famous. The greatest stumbling block to identifying Philo as the author of the book of Wisdom is his penchant for allegorical interpretation and its absence in Wisdom. Similarly, although Wisdom's personification of wisdom bears similarities to the Logos theology of Philo, the former does not employ platonic philosophical categories as Philo does. Still, the affinities between the two testify to the distinct likelihood that they shared a common cultural background and could not have been far apart in time.

The relationship of the book of Wisdom to Philo suggests the Roman period of Alexandria to be the likely time frame for the book's composition (30 BCE–40 CE). There are many factors to support this time frame and the location of Alexandria in Egypt for the book's composition. The particular nuances of numerous Greek words and phrases, for example, in the book of Wisdom belong to the first century CE.[4]

The tension between the Jewish community and the Greeks in Alexandria under Roman rule explains the many concerns for justice that abound in the book of Wisdom. Moreover, the author's familiarity with Greek poetry and philosophy as well as the author's presupposition that the reader is conversant with Hellenism would suggest a cultural center with strong Jewish participation. Alexandria provides precisely such a cultural context. Under Ptolemy I (323–285), Alexandria became the capital of Egypt. With its museum and library, Alexandria soon became the leading center of Hellenistic philosophy and art. It is not surprising, then, that Alexandria became the focus for the translation of the Hebrew Bible into Greek.[5]

According to Philo, the Jewish population in Egypt reached one million,[6] and much of it lived in Alexandria. Although that number may be an exaggeration, there is no doubt that the Jewish community was a major force in the economic and cultural fabric of the city. The Jews formed their own *politeuma*, an organization with economic and educational rights. Such Jewish literary figures as Aristobulos (180–145 BCE) and Philo show how far the Jewish community had integrated many aspects of Hellenism into its own tradition. Whether they gained access to the gymnasium or established their own educational centers parallel to those of the Greeks is difficult to establish. What is certain is that their leading figures were thoroughly conversant with Hellenism.

The tension that the author of the book of Wisdom highlights between justice and injustice, between the Egyptians and the righteous, also mirrors the tension between the Jewish community and other inhabitants of Alexandria. Although Alexandrian Jews had been granted certain rights by Emperor Augustus in continuity with the policies of the Ptolemies, the poll tax that was introduced in 24 BCE threw the status of the Jewish community into question. The criteria for applying the tax made a distinction among Greek citizens who were exempt, Hellenes who paid a lower tax, and the Egyptian natives who paid the tax in full. The Jews of Alexandria sought to establish Greek citizenship, and the Greeks vehemently barred them from doing so.

The tension reached tragic proportions in 38 CE when the Jews were attacked in a pogrom-like manner. Synagogues were destroyed or desecrated with portraits of Caligula bearing divine titles. The following year, Philo himself led the Jewish delegation to Emperor Caligula to argue for the rights that had originally been granted them by Augustus. But no positive results were forthcoming. With the assassination of Caligula in 41 CE, the Jews revolted in Alexandria. This led the new Emperor Claudius to settle the dispute once and for all with his forceful letter to the Alexandrians in 41 CE. The letter of Claudius essentially maintained the status quo. Greeks were reprimanded for their hostility toward the Jewish community, but the Jews were told to be satisfied with their position and not to strive for Greek citizenship. In effect, even though the letter brought a certain peace to Alexandria, it was a bitter blow to the Jewish community. Without access to the gymnasium, the Jews had no access to Alexandrian citizenship. This restriction paved the way for future strife and rebellion, which would eventually see the annihilation of the Jewish community in Alexandria during Trajan's suppression of the Jewish revolt in 115–117 CE.[7]

This combination of a thorough familiarity with and respect for the best in Hellenism that the Jewish community manifested, as well as the tension between the Greeks and the Jewish community, makes Alexandria the likely site for the composition of the book of Wisdom. The argument that Wisdom could not have been written in Alexandria if Philo does not mention it or quote it is quite weak if, in fact, Philo and the writer of Wisdom were contemporaries.

The question as to whether the New Testament writers were familiar with the book of Wisdom is difficult to resolve. There are, however, special affinities between Paul and John and the book of Wisdom. But the common phraseology and ideas are general enough to suggest that they arise from common concerns and values rather than from literary dependency.

INFLUENCES

The two major influences on the author's thought and arguments in the book of Wisdom are Hellenism and the Hebrew Bible itself. Throughout the argumentation and imaginative language employed in the work, the author essentially retains a Hebrew mentality while conversing in language familiar to various strains within Hellenism. The author has not gone as far as Philo did in applying philosophical categories from Middle Platonism to the interpretation of the biblical stories. Yet, as in the case of Philo, Middle Platonism provided distinctions and concepts that the Wisdom author employed.

Hellenism is, of course, a wide cultural umbrella that covers diverse philosophical systems and cultural values. With Platonism we can see points of contact all through the author's argumentation: the respect for beauty, the advantage of virtue, the superiority of the soul, the relationship between body and soul, the ethical perspective on justice and injustice. A certain contact may exist between Epicureanism and the author's presentation of the wicked person's project in life (Wisdom 2). In this case, the author was making reference to a popular ethical stance of pleasure that the disciples of Epicurus postulated. The author seems to have borrowed a number of terms and phrases from Stoic philosophers without using them in the precise manner of the Stoics. The Stoic concern to convey a coherent presentation of reality that is permanent and in flux is reflected in the interpretation of the plagues. The Neo-Pythagoreans especially flourished in Alexandria in the Roman period and, with their insistence on heavenly immortality, offered a counterbalance to the Stoics. Other motifs that are close to the Pythagoreans find an echo in the imagery of the book of Wisdom: the order of numbers (Wis 11:20b), the metaphor of music for order and harmony in the universe (Wis 19:18), the seriousness of perjury (Wis 14:28-31).

However, the prime source for the author of Wisdom is Scripture itself. Throughout every section of the book of Wisdom, the author makes reference to authoritative images, concepts, and stories from the Torah, the Prophets, and the Writings.

In the first section, Wis 1:1–6:21, the images from the creation and fall episodes form a veritable backdrop for the author's arguments on justice, death, and immortality (Genesis 1–3). Moreover, there is a particular concentration on successive images from Isaiah 52–58 that highlights the author's arguments against injustice and in favor of justice (the suffering servant, the sterile woman, the eunuch, the just, divine judgment).

In the second section, Wis 6:22–11:1, the author builds on the personification of wisdom exemplified in Proverbs 8 and Sirach 24. The prayer for wisdom that the figure of Solomon articulates in Wisdom 9 is formulated through the author's adaptation of Solomon's night vision in 1 Kings 3 and 2 Chronicles 1. Finally, Wisdom 10 is a eulogy of salvation history that recounts wisdom's role in saving and guiding humanity from the time of creation right up to the events of the exodus from Egypt.

The third and largest section, Wis 11:2–19:22, has been termed a "midrash" on the events of the exodus from Egypt and the journeying in the desert. The books of Exodus and Numbers provide the backdrop for the author's extended treatment of the liberation of the Israelites from Egypt. There are two large digressions on God's power and mercy and on the critique of false worship. In the course of these digressions, the author makes continuous reference to the prophets. Although the image of the covenant itself does not command a central focus in the book, such related features to the covenant as election, God's faithfulness, and the responsibility of humans to decide and act constantly emerge throughout all sections of the book.

UNITY

One feature that may be striking, at first, from a surface reading of the book of Wisdom is the great divergence of imagery and style among its three large sections. The first section displays a dramatic struggle between injustice and virtue, against which the images of life and death constantly emerge. It is a forceful exhortation to justice as if the issue of justice is a matter of life and death for the author and the reader alike. The second section moves almost indiscernibly to a contemplative tranquility. Here the author offers eloquent praise to the wisdom that comes from God and that guides humans effortlessly in their journeys. In the third section, the positive role of wisdom appears to recede into the background, and it is God who intervenes directly in the affairs of the wicked and the righteous during the exodus events. The conflict between the wicked and the just, which we found already in the first part of the book, is exemplified again in the exodus narrative.

All of these differences between the major sections of the book of Wisdom have led scholars to postulate divergent authors for the respective sections. However, studies on the unity of the language have essentially dispelled the theories of diverse authorship, even though different styles of writing were employed. At most, the author may have written these sections over a longer period of time. The surface dissimilarities among the three sections are matched by their deep unity of imagery and purpose.

One particular image that is used throughout all three sections of the book is the positive role of the cosmos. In the first section, the positive function of the forces of creation is set in relief against the back-

drop of the struggle between justice and injustice. It is the cosmos itself that God arms to wage a battle against injustice. In the second section, wisdom's role to save humanity is assured through wisdom's presence at the creation of the world and humanity. Wisdom and the cosmos are intertwined in order to bring life and prosperity to the just and the wise. In the third section, the author emphasizes the role of the forces of creation in bringing justice to the wicked and sustenance to the righteous.

In terms of the unity of purpose, each section focuses on a particular concern within the author's overarching argument. The author is attempting to bolster the faith of the Jewish community under attack by powerful forces (such as those present in the Alexandrian community during Roman rule). The first section is an exhortation to justice that attempts to strip away the facade of the power of injustice and unfaithfulness. It would have been attractive to many Jews to give up their tradition in favor of Greek citizenship. The author counters such deprecation of the Jewish tradition by unmasking the powerlessness of injustice in the face of virtuous justice. Essentially, it is a dissuasion from injustice and death. The second section is more of a persuasion to the faith through the beauty and power of wisdom and virtue. Finally, the last part of the second section (chap. 10) and the midrashic treatment of the exodus events (chaps. 11–19) give historical support to the author's message. The wisdom of God has continuously accompanied humanity to bring the righteous to prosperity and well-being even through trials and tribulation (chap. 10). God has intervened with the forces of the cosmos itself to bring the wicked to justice and to sustain the righteous (chaps. 11–19).

GENRE

The book of Wisdom in its entirety does not fit into any particular genre. The work is the result of a creative and imaginative writer who has produced a rather unique piece of literature. Two forms of discourse that stem from Aristotelian rhetoric have been proposed: *Protreptic* discourse, which is governed by exhortation and persuasion, and the *Epideictic* discourse of the *Encomium*, which praises a figure and entertains throughout a sustained argument.[8] Both genres, however, include exhortation and praise. The question is,

Which is at the service of the other? Since we are lacking extant sources and examples of these forms of literature from the time of the book of Wisdom, it is not an issue that can be easily decided. David Winston has summarized well the situation regarding the genre: "It is thus extremely difficult to determine whether Wisdom is an epideictic composition with an admixture of protreptic, or essentially a protreptic with a considerable element of epideictic."[9]

The author makes use of several forms of writing throughout the work. There is the *diatribe*, especially noticeable in the first part, where the author sets up speakers in order to critique their arguments. There are *literary diptychs*, which make use of the comparing and contrasting features of *synkrisis*. These are especially noticeable in the first part of the book, where the lives of the just are contrasted with the lives of the wicked, and in the later part of the book, where the Egyptians are contrasted with the Israelites. The second part of the work makes use of the *eulogy* in order to sustain the contemplation of the beauty and attractiveness of wisdom. Finally, though it is difficult to call the style of writing known as a *midrash* a genre because of its loose structure, it is clear that the author makes use of this general style of interpretation when treating biblical texts. In the first part of the book, the author employs a series of images from Isaiah in a manner that has been called midrashic or homiletic.[10] In commenting on the events of the exodus in the last part of the book, the author is clearly following the events as recounted in Exodus and Numbers and attempting to give them a specific interpretation from a unique point of view. This is typical of midrashic writing. All of these styles of writing have been combined by a skilled writer who was able to make use of devices and forms according to the movement of the argument.

STRUCTURE

The book of Wisdom is a highly structured literary work. It is helpful for the interpretation of specific passages to keep in mind the overall structure of the book and the structure of individual sections. The structures that give shape to the author's argument and arrangement of images are often dense. They help to bring images in relation to each other, both for comparison and for contrast.

There are two literary structures that the author particularly favors: the concentric structure and the parallel structure of literary diptychs. A concentric structure derives its name from the geometric image of circles sharing a common center (ABCDD'C'B'A'). By paralleling phrases, images, or types of speech at the beginning of a unit to the end, the author skillfully draws the reader's attention to comparisons, to contrasts, and to development. Often the center of such a unit contains a focus of concentration. Parallel structures draw together images or ideas in parallel fashion (ABCDA'B'C'D'). The term *literary diptych* is derived from iconography, where two images are set side by side for the purpose of complementarity or contrast. The parallel structure of literary diptychs is particularly suited for developing and emphasizing contrasts.

The opening section of the book is formulated in a rather elegant concentric structure:

A		1:1-15	exhortation to justice warning against death
	B	1:16–2:24	speech of the wicked their defense of injustice through power and might
		C 3:1–4:20	three diptychs contrast the just with the wicked the defense of injustice by the wicked is dismantled
	B´	5:1-23	speech of the wicked their confession of error
A´		6:1-21	exhortation to wisdom against warning injustice

Even within this concentric structure, the parallel diptych system is used in the central unit, where the situation of the just is contrasted with that of the wicked:

3:1-13*a*	— the just are in the hand of God
	— the wicked will be punished
3:13*b*–4:6	— the just who appear fruitless will bear much fruit
	— the wicked who appear fruitful will not benefit from their wickedness
4:7-20	— the virtuous youth who dies is with God
	— the aged wicked will be condemned by the youth

The second section of the book of Wisdom contains two concentric structures—7:1–8:21, Solomon's desire for wisdom, and 9:1-18, Solomon's prayer for wisdom—and a parallel structure of diptychs—10:1-21, where God's wisdom is shown to have intervened in the life of humanity in order to save the just.

A	7:1-6	Solomon is mortal and limited
B	7:7-12	Wisdom is superior to all goods
C	7:13-22a	God is the guide of wisdom God gives knowledge and wealth
D	7:22b–8:1	eulogy of wisdom twenty-one attributes of wisdom
C′	8:2-9	Solomon desires to have wisdom as a bride Wisdom knows all things and is a source of wealth
B′	8:10-16	Wisdom grants success and fame
A′	8:17-21	as a child, Solomon was gifted but still needs God's wisdom

The concentric structure of chapter 9:

A	9:1-3	God has formed humanity through wisdom
B	9:4	Solomon asks for the wisdom that sits beside God's throne
C	9:5-6	Solomon is weak and limited
D	9:7-8	yet called to be king and judge over God's people
E	9:9	Wisdom knows what is pleasing to God
F	9:10ab	prayer for God to send wisdom
E′	9:10c-11	so that Solomon may learn what is pleasing to God
D′	9:12	Solomon will judge God's people justly
C′	9:13-17a	for human beings are weak and burdened
B′	9:17b	unless God's wisdom and Spirit come from on high
A′	9:18	and through wisdom humanity is saved

Chapter 10 consists of seven brief diptychs that show how wisdom accompanied various persons from the Torah and helped them against adversaries: (1) 10:1-3, Adam/Cain; (2) 10:4, Noah/those who perished in the flood; (3) 10:5, Abraham/the nations of Babel; (4) 10:6-8, Lot/those who perished in the cities of the plain and his wife; (5) 10:6-12, Jacob/Esau and his personal enemies; (6) 10:13-14, Joseph/his brothers and Potiphar's wife; (7) 10:15-21, the Israelites and Moses/their oppressors.

The final section of the book is a rather developed series of five diptychs that relate the punishment of the plagues to a particular sin of the Egyptians. The contrast in each diptych focuses on the means of punishment against the oppressors and the means of salvation in favor of the righteous. In addition, two major digressions occur within the second diptych. The digression on false worship (chaps. 13–15) is formulated in three parts that progress from the least blameworthy to the most blameworthy: (1) 13:1-9, philosophers incur slight blame; (2) 13:10–15:13, idol worship is condemned; (3) 15:14-19, the idol and animal worship of Egypt is severely condemned.

The central section of the critique that treats idol worship specifically is organized concentrically:

A	13:10-19	gold, silver, stone, wooden idols—carpenter
B	14:1-10	reflection on God's providential care
C	14:11-31	invention and result of idolatry punishment of idolatry
B′	15:1-6	reflection on God's mercy and power
A′	15:7-13	clay idols—potter

MAJOR CONTRIBUTIONS

Death, Immortality, Justice. The author advances significantly the formal treatment of the status of an individual human being after death. Although the problem of God's faithfulness to the just who suffer arose in such works as Job and Ecclesiastes, the unambiguous declaration of the survival of the individual is a late phenomenon (Dan 12:2-3; 2 Macc 7:9). The background for the author's unambiguous declaration of human immortality is the covenantal faithfulness of God to the just. God is faithful to the just, and no torment will destroy them; God's grace and mercy remain with the elect (3:1-9).

The Five Diptychs and the Seven Antitheses in the Book of Wisdom

Causal relationship 11:16		Antithetical relationship 11:5, 13
Sins	**Plagues**	**Blessings**
1. 11:6-14 killing of infants	1. 11:6-14 undrinkable water	water in the desert
2. 11:15–16:14 animals adored	2. 16:1-4 animals suppress the appetite	delicious animals (quails)

1st digression 11:17–12:27 — God's power and mercy to save and to punish
2nd digression 13–15 — the origins of false worship
minor digression 16:5-14 — the brazen serpent; God has power over life and death

	3. 16:5-14 animals that kill	the saving brazen serpent
3. 16:15-29 refusal to recognize the true God	4. 16:15-29 rain, hail; creation destroys by fire; lack of food	creation saves; the manna resists burning by fire
4. 17:1–18:4 enslaving the Hebrews	5. 17:1–18:4 captivity by darkness	pillar of fire in the darkness Aaron stops the destroyer
5. 18:5–19:21 killing of infants in river	6. 18:5-25 death of the firstborn	Israel passes through the Red Sea
	7. 19:1-9 drowning in the sea	

minor digression 18:20-25—
minor digression 19:6-12— Creation

Although the language the author employs to convey the belief in an afterlife is Greek, a uniquely Hebraic ethical understanding is given to that language. The author sustains the idea of the survival of the just after death with such words as "immortal" (Wis 1:15; 3:4; 4:1; 8:17; 15:3) and "incorruptible" (2:23; 6:18-19). But an ethical perspective is brought in to condition this notion of immortality. The author is not positing an inherent immortality that all humans possess. Rather, immortality depends on the inner life of virtue. Immortality is the divine life toward which all human beings have been destined from the dawn of creation (Wis 2:23). But the decisions and actions of human beings that affect others determine the quality of final life.

A life of justice and virtue leads to immortality (Wis 3:4; 6:17-20). A life of injustice and wickedness leads to death (Wis 1:16; 2:24; 5:17-23). Death here is understood not simply as the experience of mortality, which the just experience as well, but as divine judgment. Similarly, the immortal life of the just is not presented as an inherent quality, but as the result of a positive divine judgment over one's decisions and actions (Wis 5:15-16). Although the author's presentation of the immortality of the just could be reconciled with the notion of a bodily resurrection, nowhere is a bodily resurrection formally posited in the book of Wisdom.

Even the notion of justice, which figures so dominantly throughout the book, retains its Hebraic nuances rather than the Greek qualities of balance and equality that are associated with justice. The two perspectives are not incompatible, but for the author of the book of Wisdom justice involves the support and respect for the weak. Solomon asks for wisdom to be able to judge God's people justly (Wis 9:12). Injustice is identified as oppressing and exploiting the weak and defenseless. The wicked employ their power to oppress the widow, the aged, the poor, and the just (Wis 2:12-20).

Personification of Wisdom. In focusing on the wisdom of God through personification, the author picks up the sapiential traditions from Proverbs 8 and Sirach 24. However, what is unique to the author of the book of Wisdom is the emphasis on the specific role of wisdom both in creation and in human affairs. The wisdom that comes from God is able to help humans because it was present at creation. As a result of this, wisdom is a bridge between humans and God. Wisdom knows God's works, knows what is pleasing to God, and brings friendship with God.

The author integrates the current Greek views of wisdom with the Hebrew sapiential tradition of the personification of wisdom. For the Greeks, wisdom is essentially a means of gaining knowledge, both cosmic and divine. For the Wisdom author, wisdom lives with God and is revealed and given to humans by God. The wisdom that comes from God is a gift that brings to completion the wisdom through which humans were formed at creation. According to the author's anthropology, human beings have been shaped and formed by the wisdom of God in such a way that they yearn to be completed by the wisdom of God, which comes only as a gift. Solomon provided the ideal figure through which the author presents this anthropology. He is presented as naturally gifted, yet as realizing the limitations of his being and yearning for the wisdom that comes from God.

It is not surprising, then, to see how the author attaches the wisdom of God to the just. Injustice is inimical both to the structures of the cosmos and to the human heart. Wisdom flees from the unjust and the wicked, but waits for the just and actively seeks them out.

The author has gone as far as possible in the personification of God's wisdom without creating a separate entity as an intermediate being between human beings and God. Wisdom is the manner in which God has created the world and fashioned the human heart. Wisdom is the manner in which God continuously intervenes in history both to save the just and to thwart the designs of injustice.

CANONICAL STATUS

The canonical status of the book of Wisdom differs among the Christian communities. Discussion regarding the book's status hinged essentially on the acceptance or rejection of the wider canon of the LXX, the Greek version of the Old Testament. The doubt regarding its acceptance can be traced to the strong voice of Jerome (345–419 CE), who preferred the smaller canon of the Hebrew Scriptures. The authoritative voice of Augustine provided the greatest impetus for acceptance. In the ambit of the Latin Church, the Council of Carthage (397 CE) and the letter of Innocent I to the Bishop of Toulouse (405 CE) follow the list of canonical books presented by Augustine.[11]

The acceptance of the wider canon was settled definitively in the Roman Church at the Council of Trent (1546 CE). The Orthodox Church accepted the Roman canons of Scripture at the Council of Jerusalem in 1672. But since the eighteenth century a renewed discussion has emerged among the Orthodox communities regarding the inspiration of the deuterocanonical books. The Protestant and Reformed traditions follow the lead of Martin Luther, who was inspired by Jerome's preference for the smaller canon. However, even Martin Luther accepted the deuterocanonical/apocryphal books as inspirational reading while withholding their canonical status. So it is not surprising to note that one of Wisdom's best modern commentaries stems from the pen of a Protestant scholar.[12] Since there is little doubt as to the Jewish origin of the work, Jewish scholars also study Wisdom as a source for understanding the currents of Jewish thought during the Hellenistic period.[13]

FOR FURTHER READING

Cheon, Samuel. *The Exodus Story in the Wisdom of Solomon: A Study in Biblical Interpretation.* JSOPSup 23. Sheffield: Sheffield Academic Press, 1997.

Kolarcik, Michael. *The Ambiguity of Death in the Book of Wisdom (1–6).* AnBib 127. Rome: Pontifical Biblical Institute, 1991.

Larcher, C. *Le Livre de la Sagesse ou La Sagesse de Salomon.* Vols. 1-3. Études Biblique, nouvelle série. 1, 3, 5. Paris: Gabalda, 1983–85.

———. *Études sur le Livre de la Sagesse.* Études Bibliques. Paris: Gabalda, 1969.

Nickelsburg, George W. E. *Resurrection, Immortality and Eternal Life in Intertestamental Judaism.* HTS 26. Cambridge, Mass.: Harvard University Press, 1972.

Reese, James M. *Hellenistic Influence on the Book of Wisdom and Its Consequences.* AnBib 41. Rome: Pontifical Biblical Institute, 1970.

Taylor, Richard J. "The Eschatological Meaning of Life and Death in the Book of Wisdom I-V," *ETL* 42 (1966) 72-137.

Vílchez, José. *Sabiduría.* Sapienciales V. Nueva Biblia Española. Estella: Editorial Verbo Divino, 1990.

Winston, David. *The Wisdom of Solomon.* AB 43. New York: Doubleday, 1979.

Wright, Addison G. "Wisdom." *NJBC.* Englewood Cliffs, N.J.: Prentice Hall, 1990.

ENDNOTES

1. Irenaeus *Against Heresies* 3:4.

2. Irenaeus *Against Heresies*, 7:5.

3. Augustine *Patrologia latina* 44.979-980.

4. For a discussion on the time frame for many words and phrases employed in the Wisdom of Solomon see David Winston, *The Wisdom of Solomon*, AB 43 (New York: Doubleday, 1979) 20-25. Winston places the date for the composition of Wisdom around the reign of Caligula (37–41 CE), though it could very well have been written over a longer period of time.

5. See *The Letter of Aristeas* c. 150–100 BCE.

6. Philo *Flaccus* 43.

7. For a thorough treatment of the ambiguous status of the Jews in Alexandria during the Roman period, see Martin Hengel, *Judaism and Hellenism*, trans. J. Bowden (Philadelphia: Fortress, 1974).

8. Aristotle *The Art of Rhetoric* III.xiv. 10-xv.9.

9. D. Winston, book review, *CBQ* 48 (1986) 527.

10. J. Suggs, "Book of Wisdom II, 10-V: A Homily Based on the Fourth Servant Song," *JBL* 76 (1957) 26-33.

11. Augustine, *De Doctrina Christiana* 2,8; *PL* 34, 40.

12. C. L. W. Grimm, *Das Buch der Weisheit* (Leipzig: Hirzel, 1837).

13. Y. Amir, "The Figure of Death in 'The Book of Wisdom,' " *JJS* 30 (1979) 154-78.

THE BOOK OF
SIRACH

BY JAMES L. CRENSHAW

In English Bibles the titles for the book under consideration lack consistency. The NRSV calls it "Ecclesiasticus, or the Wisdom of Jesus Son of Sirach." The TNK, or new Jewish translation, opts for "Ecclesiasticus," a title derived from many Latin Vulgate manuscripts. The GNB uses "Sirach: the Wisdom of Jesus, Son of Sirach (Ecclesiasticus)," and the REB has "Ecclesiasticus or the Wisdom of Jesus son of Sirach." I will refer to the book as Sirach and designate its author as Ben Sira.

WISDOM LITERATURE
IN THE BIBLE

The books of Proverbs, Job, and Ecclesiastes differ markedly from the rest of the Old Testament, in both style and content. Their closest parallels occur outside the Bible, particularly in ancient Egyptian and Mesopotamian literature associated with educational contexts, either in the training of courtiers or the instruction of temple personnel. On the basis of sustained interest in wisdom within these biblical texts, scholars have labeled them "wisdom literature."[1] Specialists in Egyptian and Mesopotamian literature have adopted this nomenclature,[2] although it brings together texts with quite different settings and purposes.

Egyptian literature in this genre arose in the third millennium BCE in connection with the instruction of rulers, at first given by pharaohs and later by counselors who taught potential rulers. Several texts have survived the ravages of time, including *The Instruction of Ptah-hotep, The Instruction of Amenemope, The Instruction of Ani, The Instruction of Ankhsheshanky,* and Papyrus Insinger. In addition, several scribal texts illuminate the educational enterprise, attesting to lazy students and vigorous disciplinary measures by teachers. A text called *A Satire of the Trades* or *The Teaching for Duauf* makes fun of several occupations and praises the profession of the scribe above all others.[3]

Scribal texts from Sumerian times in ancient Mesopotamia describe conditions at the school house (*edubba*) and indicate that similar conditions existed there as in Egypt. A Sumerian instruction attributed to *Šuruppak* advises his son about the duties of kingship. An early prototype of the book of Job and a collection of Sumerian proverbs round out this early literature from Sumer.[4] Babylonian texts of this kind include *Counsels to a Prince*, various collections of proverbs, and parallels to the books of Job (*I Will Praise the Lord of Wisdom, The Babylonian Theodicy*) and Ecclesiastes (*The Dialogue of a Master and His Slave*).[5] *The Sayings of Ahiqar*, an Aramaic document, purports to have come from an adviser to an Assyrian king, Sennacherib (704–681 BCE). This text of early "Jewish" wisdom was enormously popular, being translated into several languages.[6] Although very little evidence of Canaanite wisdom has been preserved, many interpreters think that these peoples must also have had such texts.[7]

Resemblances between biblical wisdom and these extra-biblical texts from Egypt and Mesopotamia sometimes are so striking that a relationship of some kind appears likely. Most noteworthy is the case of *The Instruction of Amenemope* and a collection within the book of Proverbs, specifically Prov 22:17–23:33, where eleven sayings overlap.[8] The similarities between the book of Job and earlier prototypes from Mesopotamia are only slightly less remarkable, as is the affinity of Ecclesiastes with the ideas put forward in *The Dialogue of a Master and His Slave* and the *Epic of Gilgamesh*, a story about a hero who goes in search of eternal life and retrieves a branch from the tree of life, thanks to advice from the survivor of the flood, Utnapishtim, only to lose it to a serpent.[9]

These close similarities in teachings from three distinct environments in the ancient Near East illustrate a characteristic of wisdom literature: its tendency to present ideas in a universalistic context, one grounded in creation.[10] To the sages, truth was not bound by national ties. Nothing specifically Israelite appears in the books of Proverbs, Job, and Ecclesiastes. Scholars have often noted an absence in these texts of anything about the patriarchs Abraham, Isaac, and Jacob; nothing about early leaders like Moses, Joshua, Samuel; no mention of the judges; no celebration of Israelite kings—except to attribute wisdom literature to Solomon—and no mention of the prophets or a covenant between the Lord and Israel, a special people. In short, the entire history of salvation is missing from these texts. For this reason, wisdom literature has been largely ignored until recently in efforts to describe the theology of the Bible.[11]

Besides being applicable to all people, wisdom literature addresses the fundamental question, "What promotes well-being?" It offers advice on coping with difficult circumstances, in a sense giving parental counsel to growing children, but also offering popular advice to people of all ages. One type of wisdom literature explores existential questions, chiefly the matter of innocent suffering and what this implies about divine justice. Naturally, this questioning attitude does not stop short of asking about death and its consequences.[12]

Another characteristic of this literature is its preoccupation with the search for wisdom, which appears as a feminine personification associated with God in the creative process. She also actively woos young men to deeper intellectual and moral pursuits; in this endeavor she has a rival, folly, also personified as a woman. Often called a foreign woman, or strange, she seduces young men with the aid of powerful rhetoric (cf. Prov 9:17).[13]

The extent of biblical wisdom has elicited considerable debate, some interpreters wishing to broaden the category to include much of the Bible (e.g., Genesis 1–11; Deuteronomy; the story of David's rise to power and the succession, 2 Samuel 9–20; 1 Kings 1–2; Esther; Jonah).[14] These attempts merely demonstrate the fact that sages did not own a distinct vocabulary but used the ordinary language of their time. Their influence does seem to manifest itself in the book of Psalms, especially in 37; 49; and 73.

Sirach definitely belongs to biblical wisdom, although its teachings represent a transition from a nonspecific national audience to Jewish hearers whose intellectual heritage faces obliteration by Hellenism. Its author, Ben Sira, unites the unique legacy of Israel's saving history to the wisdom tradition. Although the language echoes that within the book of Proverbs, the content weaves together an account of the merciful guidance of Israel's Lord with advice on coping with life's eventualities. Like the book of Proverbs, Sirach also praises personified wisdom, further elaborating a myth of her activity at creation and identifying her with the accessible Mosaic law. Ben Sira describes the various professions, like *The Satire of the Trades*, and evidences a strong personal piety resembling that in *The Instruction of Ani*.[15]

A new dimension in Sirach, the praise of Israel's "saints" (men of piety), relates Israelite spiritual leadership to the guidance of wisdom. The other wisdom text, also from the Apocrypha, that develops this approach to Israel's history is the book of Wisdom. Its author praises personified wisdom, now a hypostasis (or manifestation) of God's essential character, and describes the period of the exodus from Egypt as one during which wisdom guided God's people into freedom. Prayer and praise unite in this thoroughly Hellenistic text, one composed in Greek and making extensive use of Greek rhetoric.[16]

THE ORIGINAL TITLE
OF THE BOOK AND ITS CONTENTS

The title of this book in most Greek manuscripts identifies its genre and author: Σοφία Ἰησοῦ υἱοῦ Σιραχ (*Sophia Iēsou huiou S(e)irach*, "the Wisdom of Jesus the son of Sirach"). A shorter form occurs in the Syriac text: the Wisdom of Bar Sira (the Wisdom of the Son of Sira). And an altogether different title appears in the Latin tradition, where one finds such descriptive categories as the church book (Ecclesiasticus) in the Vulgate and *Parabolae* ("Wise Sayings") in a Hebrew copy, according to Jerome. On two occasions later Jewish writers preface a citation from Sirach with the words המשל אמר (*hammōšēl 'āmar*, "the one who spoke in Proverbs"). The tenth-century Jewish scholar Saadia refers to Sirach as ספר מוסר (*sēper mûsār*, "the book of Discipline/Instruc-

tion"), and Rabbi Joseph calls it משלי בן סרא
(*mišlê ben sirā'*, "The Proverbs of the Son of Sira").

Although the opening chapter of Sirach has not survived in the Hebrew manuscripts, a remark in Sir 50:27 attributes the book to Simeon ben Eleazar ben Sira, and Sir 51:30 adds: "Thus far the words of Simeon, the son of Jeshua, who is called Ben Sira. The Wisdom of Simeon, the son of Jeshua, the son of Eleazar, the son of Sira." The name "Simeon" (Σίμων *Simōn*) seems to have come from Sir 50:1, 24a; the probable name of the author is Jeshua ben Eleazar ben Sira. Most Greek and Latin manuscripts partially confirm the identity of the author, reading "the Wisdom of Jesus son of Sira" and "the book of Jesus son of Sirach" respectively. The *ch* ending on Sirach in Greek manuscripts represents either a Greek χ (*chi*), indicating an indeclinable word, or the Hebrew א (*'aleph*).

The prologue to the book, written by Ben Sira's grandson, confirms the tradition that identifies the author's name with Jeshua (Jesus). Ben Sira's patronymic includes the name of his father (Eleazar) and his grandfather (Sira). Within the book several self-references occur, identifying Ben Sira as a professional wise man, describing his disciplined life-style, and inviting young boys to study in his academy.[17]

The first of several authorial self-references, 24:30-34 (cf. 34:12-13; 39:12-15, 32-35; 41:16; 43:32; 50:25-29; 51:1-30) implies that Ben Sira understood his teachings as inspired utterances that began small but grew unexpectedly, like a canal expanding into a huge stream. His own learning, directed initially toward personal enjoyment ("I will water my garden/ and drench my flower-beds" [24:31 NRSV]), soon lost its selfish character and became available to everyone ("Observe that I have not labored for myself alone,/ but for all who seek wisdom" [24:34 NRSV]). In 33:16-18, Ben Sira repeats the latter remark; in doing so he compares himself to gleaners following grape pickers. This image suggests an awareness that the period of divine inspiration is rapidly coming to an end ("Now I was the last to keep vigil," 33:16). Later rabbinic teaching limited the era of divine inspiration to that begun by Moses and ended by Ezra. In the context of discussing the wide experience of educated persons, he mentions extensive travel and the danger associated with journeys in the ancient world (34:9-13).

Within an elaborate treatment of various professions in his day, Ben Sira demonstrates the advantages of being a scholar (38:24–39:11). The similarities to a popular Egyptian text, *The Instruction for Duauf,* often called *A Satire of the Trades,* has long been known and commented on, although the texts differ in tone and subject matter. (Ben Sira does not satirize, and his list of vocations is much shorter.) Having given his strong endorsement of the scribe's profession, yet without disparaging the works of one's hands, Ben Sira states that he has more to say, being full like the full moon, and invites students to blossom comparably, joining knowledge and worship (39:12-15). He proceeds to sing praise to the Creator:

> So from the beginning I have
> been convinced of all this
> and have thought it out and
> left it in writing:
> All the works of the Lord are good,
> and he will supply every need in its time.
> (39:32-33 NRSV)

Expressing a teacher's desire for respect, Ben Sira urges students to observe his instruction (41:16). In the Greek text of 43:32 (but not in the Hebrew) which has the plural "we," Ben Sira acknowledges the inevitable mystery that humans encounter when reflecting on transcendence: "Many things greater than these lie hidden,/ for I have seen but few of his works" (NRSV). An epilogue, 50:25-29, expresses Ben Sira's extreme animosity toward Samaritans, Idumeans, and Philistines (Hellenists), along with some comments reflecting an entirely novel idea in Hebraic thought: pride of authorship.

> Instruction in understanding and knowledge
> I have written in this book,
> Jesus son of Eleazar son of
> Sirach of Jerusalem,
> whose mind poured forth wisdom.
> Happy are those who concern
> themselves with these things,
> and those who lay them to
> heart will become wise.
> For if they put them into practice,
> they will be equal to anything,
> for the fear of the Lord is their path.
> (50:27-29 NRSV)

The final chapter, consisting of a prayer, an autobiographical poem on wisdom, and an appeal to readers (51:1-30), is rich with personal references, although employing literary conventions. This practice of using traditional language of self-reference already appears in the book of Proverbs (cf. Prov 4:1-9) and Ecclesiastes (Eccl 1:12–2:2 and throughout the book).[18] For this reason, some of the self-references in Sirach may reveal nothing about the author's personal experiences (e.g., adventures during traveling).

The information that Ben Sira enjoyed the leisurely status of a professional teacher suggests that one can find in Sirach the sort of teachings he conveyed to his students. The book stands in the tradition of Proverbs and Ecclesiastes, especially the former. It consists, therefore, of brief aphorisms, maxims, and clever statements in poetic form having to do with practical daily existence.[19] Like the initial collection in Proverbs (Proverbs 1–9), the sayings in Sirach frequently make up brief paragraphs on a particular topic. The subjects range widely, extending from inner feelings, like a sense of shame,[20] to external behavior, such as slander, from deeply religious acts of charity to self-serving conduct at banquets, from proper attitudes toward money to the disgrace of being reduced to begging, from various kinds of friends to the trouble occasioned by bad daughters, and much more.

The teachings also take up existential issues, such as sickness and death,[21] wrestling with the ethical question of whether one should consult a physician, who in popular imagination was seen to interfere with divine punishment for sin. Ben Sira takes no refuge in belief in a future life, and that refusal to do so allows the matter of divine justice—or more correctly its absence—to press heavily on him, as it did on the author of the book of Job.[22] This vexing problem surfaces frequently in argumentative contexts, suggesting that Ben Sira encountered a vocal group who denied God's just governance of the world. Ben Sira subscribed to traditional religious teachings and expressed his own faith quite tangibly, either in prayer or in hymnic praise. Moreover, he identified the divine revelation in the Torah with the figure of wisdom, who descended from heaven to dwell in Jerusalem. True knowledge, as he saw it, consisted of worship, its origin and destination.

Ben Sira's teachings have no discernible order, except for the lengthy section praising faithful men

(אנשי חסד 'anšê ḥesed; 44:1–50:24), and even there some confusion occurs as to actual sequence.[23] Occasional vocatives ("my son") give the book an appearance of actual classroom use, although this form of address is standard in wisdom literature, occurring in ancient Sumerian and Egyptian instructions and in Proverbs. The expressions "father" and "son" eventually came to be used for "teacher" and "student." The advice in the book of Sirach certainly accords with the supposition that a professional teacher is busily at work in Jerusalem preparing his Jewish students to cope with reality in a Hellenistic environment (50:27).

Viewing the book as a text for the academy, Wolfgang Roth understands the book in terms of "seven teaching units set off from each other through brief passages that reassure and encourage the struggling student."[24] In his view, the book moves from simple matters to more complex ones on the assumption that students learn by stages. Moreover, Ben Sira uses himself as an example, describing his own progress from early discipline to later success. Marking the stages of a student's progress, an exhortation to prepare for testing (2:1-18) leads to instruction about filial devotion and duty to associates (2:7–4:10). A call to cling to wisdom (4:11-19) then introduces section two, an instruction on sincerity and justice, on humility, consistency, and friendship (4:20–6:17). An exhortation to accept wisdom's fetters follows introducing section three, teaching about social issues (7:1–14:19). The fourth section (15:11–23:27) praises students for staying in Wisdom's shelter, debates the matter of free will, and closes with a discourse by Wisdom (24:1-27). The fifth section (25:1–33:15) deals with social relationships in general, giving a "mini-sociology of early Judaism." The sixth section (33:19–39:11), introduced by a report on Ben Sira's progress (33:16-18), deals with such intimate issues as dreams and the inner springs of piety (providence, prayer, temperance, and illness), "a sort of mini-psychology." The seventh section (39:16–50:24) begins with a reflection on divine presence in human thinking and experience (39:16–42:14) and treats God's presence in the universe (42:15–43:35), reaching its climax in the praise of faithful Israelites (44:1–50:24), "a theological survey."[25]

THE HISTORICAL SETTING

A prologue introduces the Greek translation of Sirach. Ben Sira's grandson, who rendered the Hebrew text into Greek for the Jewish community in Egypt, gives the precise date of his arrival in Egypt as the thirty-eighth year of Euergetes. That epithet was applied to only two Lagid rulers, Ptolemy III Euergetes I (246–221 BCE) and Ptolemy VII Physkon Euergetes II (170–164, and 146–117 BCE). Only the latter king held office long enough to meet the translator's specified thirty-eight years; the date 132 BCE, therefore, marks his entry into Egypt. The translation was completed after the death of Euergetes II in 117 BCE (note the participle συγχρονίσας [sygchronisas], which ordinarily implies simultaneity, hence, "I was there as long as Euergetes reigned").[26]

Ben Sira lavishly praises a high priest named Simeon, son of Jochanan (called Onias in some Greek MSS). From 219 to 196 BCE, Simeon II was high priest in Jerusalem, which accords well with the information provided by Ben Sira's grandson. The grandfather lived during Simeon's rule over the religious life of the Jews, and Ben Sira vividly describes an occasion in which the high priest presided over the ritual at the Temple on a special holy day, perhaps the Day of Atonement, or possibly the daily whole offering.[27] The tone of Ben Sira's remarks about Simeon suggests that he had already died.

Assuming that Ben Sira lived during Simeon's tenure as high priest, when did he die? One thing is certain: He does not mention the social chaos that erupted during the Maccabean revolt against Syrian oppression in 167 BCE, although that seethed for some time prior to open resistance. In 175 BCE the Seleucid ruler Antiochus IV Epiphanes came to power, intensifying the policy of Hellenization already in force. Jason, the son of the high priest Simeon, joined in this effort, having replaced his own brother, Onias III, in that office, a prize secured through a bribe of 360 silver talents, plus the promise to hasten Hellenization through the construction of a gymnasium in Jerusalem. According to 2 Macc 4:23-26, the prize of the office of high priest later went to Menelaus, who offered an even higher sum to Antiochus.

In 167 BCE, this Seleucid king went so far as to proscribe Judaism, forbidding the celebration of festivals and sacrifices, the practice of circumcision and observance of dietary laws, and setting up a statue of Zeus over the altar in the Temple at Jerusalem. The horrified author of Dan 8:13; 9:27; 11:31; and 12:11 designates this statue "the abomination of desolation." Ben Sira has nothing to say about these disturbing events, and one can plausibly assume that he died before they took place. On the basis of a somewhat nostalgic depiction of Simeon, seemingly directed at his successor, Onias, and urging him to imitate his father's good deeds, scholars generally date Sirach in the period between 195 and 180 BCE. A date c. 185 BCE seems likely.[28]

Seleucid kings had not always looked on Jews as enemies. Antiochus III the Great (223–187 BCE) waged aggressive campaigns from Asia Minor to India, then turned his attention to Egypt. He was defeated at Raphia in 217 by Ptolemy IV Philopator, but succeeded in crushing the Egyptian army at Panium in 198 during the reign of Ptolemy V Epiphanes (203–181 BCE). The Jewish historian Josephus claims that the Jews assisted Antiochus in these early years, providing supplies and elephants and fighting to remove the garrison of Egyptian soldiers in the citadel at Jerusalem.

In gratitude, Antiochus made a number of concessions: (1) to help defray the cost of daily sacrifices; (2) to exempt from taxation the materials for building the Temple; (3) to obligate the people to live according to the Torah; (4) to exempt from taxation the senate, priests, scribes, and sacred singers; (5) to exempt Jerusalem citizens from taxation for three years; and (6) to let the remaining citizens reduce their taxes by a third and to emancipate slaves.[29] When the Syrians were routed by Romans at Magnesia in 190 BCE, the situation changed noticeably, and, pressed for revenues, Antiochus rescinded the exemptions from taxes and reduced the privileges previously granted to Jews. In 187, Antiochus was assassinated at Elymais while attacking one of Bel's sacred places to make payment to Rome. His son, Seleucus IV Philopator (187–175 BCE), succeeded him. Seleucus's treatment of the Jews was somewhat ambiguous, at first restoring the privileges earlier granted them by his father, but later sending Heliodorus to confiscate the treasures in the Temple at Jerusalem (2 Macc 3:4-40). In 175, Seleucus IV Philopator was assassinated, and Antiochus IV Epiphanes

(175–164 BCE) assumed the reins. Among Jews he earned the nickname "Epimanes" ("Madman"), from his cruel treatment of them.[30]

The internal situation reflected the political climate abroad. Opportunists chose sides, hoping to find themselves on the side of the eventual winners in the struggle for power. Competing families—Tobiads and Oniads—strove for popular support, and old rivalries—Jews versus Samaritans— extended the dissension beyond the streets of Jerusalem. Avarice and greed ran free, touching the highest office, turning the religious priesthood into a coveted prize up for grabs to the highest bidder. Jason's and Menelaus's willingness to compromise ancestral practices in favor of Greek ways demonstrates the degradation of the priesthood and explains Ben Sira's glowing praise of Simeon, who stood as a sharp contrast to the weak son, Onias III. Antiochus IV Epiphanes's removal of Onias showed how far a foreign ruler was willing to go in carrying out his policy of Hellenization.

A few allusions in Sirach may suggest the volatile situation. In 50:25-26, Ben Sira voices contempt for Idumeans, Philistines (Hellenizers), and Samaritans, and in 7:4-7; 40:25-26; and 50:1, 23-24 (Hebrew text) he may criticize contenders for the office of high priest. Finally, the prayer for renewed deeds of deliverance and signs of divine leadership (36:1-22) suggests that Ben Sira thought that belief in the ancient experience of divine watchcare could soon disappear from the collective memory.[31] Nevertheless, such remarks fall readily within the historical situation envisioned by an activity for Ben Sira between 200 and 180 BCE.

FORMS OF EXPRESSION

Ben Sira stands in a venerable tradition of wisdom teachers.[32] His speech forms resemble those in Proverbs, Job, and Ecclesiastes, which he studied thoroughly (along with the Torah and prophetic literature).[33] Truth statement and instruction, the base forms of the מָשָׁל (māšāl), loosely translated "proverb" but etymologically implying a likeness and an authoritative word, occur with great frequency.

Truth Statements. Often called sentences, truth statements capture fleeting insights and express them in poetic form so as to seize the imagination and linger in memory. They capture the experience of many and couch it in words that individualize the discovery, giving it a timeless quality. Such aphorisms and maxims have the force of legal injunction in some societies;[34] ancient Israelites employed them as incontrovertible evidence. They need only be spoken to command assent: "A new friend is like new wine;/ when it has aged, you can drink it with pleasure" (9:10b NRSV). Who can deny that "all living beings become old like a garment,/ for the decree from of old is, 'You must die!' " (14:17 NRSV)? These sentences pronounce judgment on human nature: "A rich person does wrong, and even adds insults;/ a poor person suffers wrong, and must add apologies" (13:3 NRSV); "Like music in time of mourning is ill-timed conversation,/ but a thrashing and discipline are at all times wisdom" (22:6 NRSV).[35] Long experience with poor learners rests behind this one: "Whoever teaches a fool is like one who glues potsherds together,/ or who rouses a sleeper from deep slumber" (22:9 NRSV). Fools in biblical wisdom were morally bankrupt, not devoid of intellect.

These ancient truth statements came in various forms: "Better are the God-fearing who lack understanding/ than the highly intelligent who transgress the law" (19:24 NRSV). Echoing a sentiment within Proverbs, this truth statement expresses the pathos of being dependent on others: "Better is the life of the poor under their own crude roof/ than sumptuous food in the house of others" (29:22 NRSV). Failing to speak at the right time evokes the following comment: "Better are those who hide their folly/ than those who hide their wisdom" (41:15 NRSV).

Numerical sayings enable teachers to combine similar things to achieve maximum effect when the last item finally appears:

I take pleasure in three things,
  and they are beautiful in the sight of God
  and of mortals:
agreement among brothers and sisters,
  friendship among neighbors,
and a wife and a husband who
  live in harmony.   (25:1 NRSV)

Sometimes these sayings become somewhat wordy:

Two kinds of individuals multiply sins,
  and a third incurs wrath.
Hot passion that blazes like a fire
  will not be quenched until it
    burns itself out;
one who commits fornication with
  his near of kin
will never cease until the fire
  burns him up.   (23:16 NRSV)

At two things my heart is grieved,
  and because of a third anger comes over me:
a warrior in want through poverty,
  intelligent men who are treated contemptu-
  ously, and a man who turns back from
  righteousness to sin—
  the Lord will prepare him for the sword!
                          (26:28 NRSV)

Some truth statements are introduced by a particle of existence; e.g., שׁ (*yēš*, "there is").[36]

Some [*yēš*] people keep silent and are
    thought to be wise,
  while others are detested for being talkative.
Some people keep silent because
    they have nothing to say,
  while others keep silent because
    they know when to speak.   (20:5-6 NRSV)

There are those who work and
    struggle and hurry,
  but are so much the more in want.
There are others who are slow and need help,
  who lack strength and abound in poverty;
but the eyes of the Lord look
    kindly upon them;
  he lifts them out of their lowly condition
and raises up their heads
  to the amazement of the many.
                        (11:11-13 NRSV)

There is the gift that profits you nothing,
  and the gift to be paid back double.
                          (20:10 NRSV)

Some truth statements take the form of benedic-
tion or malediction, blessing and curse: "Happy are
those who do not blunder with their lips,/ and need
not suffer remorse for sin./ Happy are those whose
hearts do not condemn them,/ and who have not

given up their hope" (14:1-2 NRSV). Ben Sira characterizes pursuit of wisdom in this manner:

Happy is the person who meditates on wisdom
    and reasons intelligently,
  who reflects in his heart on her ways
    and ponders her secrets,[37]
pursuing her like a hunter,
    and lying in wait on her paths;
  who peers through her windows
    and listens at her doors;
  who camps near her house
    and fastens his tent peg to her walls;
  who pitches his tent near her,
    and so occupies an excellent lodging place;
  who places his children under her shelter,
    and lodges under her boughs;
  who is sheltered by her from the heat,
    and dwells in the midst of her glory.
                          (14:20-27 NRSV)

The benedictions contrast mightily with these
maledictions: "Woe to timid hearts and to slack
hands,/ and to the sinner who walks a double
path!/ Woe to the fainthearted who have no trust!/
Therefore they have no shelter./ Woe to you who
have lost your nerve!/ What will you do when the
Lord's reckoning comes?" (2:12-14 NRSV). These
two forms reflect the sapiential tendency to think in
polarities, making clear distinctions between the
wise and fools, good and evil.

The simple sentence, or *māšāl*, also occurs as a
rhetorical question: "Whose offspring are worthy of
honor?/ Human offspring./ Whose offspring are worthy of honor?/ Those who fear the Lord./ Whose offspring are unworthy of honor?/ Human offspring./
Whose offspring are unworthy of honor?/ Those who
break the commandments" (10:19 NRSV). Apostrophe, direct rhetorical address, livens the speech about
death in 41:1-2: "O death, how bitter is the thought
of you/ to the one at peace among possessions,/ who
has nothing to worry about and is prosperous in
everything,/ and still is vigorous enough to enjoy
food!/ O death, how welcome is your sentence/ to
one who is needy and failing in strength,/ worn
down by age and anxious about everything;/ to one
who is contrary, and has lost all patience!" (NRSV).[38]

Instruction. The other base form, instruction,
sets the tone for Ben Sira's teaching, for he speaks as
an authoritative figure addressing students. The direct

address varies from the usual בְּנִי (*bĕnî*), "my son," to "holy sons" (39:13), "children" (3:1), "my children" (23:7; 41:14), and "you who need instruction" (51:23). His prescriptive advice, often resembling brief paragraphs on specific topics, is reinforced with warnings and admonitions, the proverbial dangling carrot employed to motivate people. Frequently, refrains set this material apart from what precedes or follows.

Throughout the book positively expressed instructions alternate with negative ones: "Honor your father by word and deed,/ that his blessing may come upon you" (3:8 NRSV); "Do not glorify yourself by dishonoring your father,/ for your father's dishonor is no glory to you" (3:10 NRSV). Frequently these instructions lack motivation, e.g., "Do not be ashamed to confess your sins,/ and do not try to stop the current of a river" (4:26 NRSV). Sometimes a series of instructions is followed by a single motivating clause: "My child, do not cheat the poor of their living,/ and do not keep needy eyes waiting./ Do not grieve the hungry/ or anger one in need./ Do not add to the troubles of the desperate,/ or delay giving to the needy . . . for if in bitterness of soul some should curse you,/ their Creator will hear their prayer" (4:1-6 NRSV). The appeal to reward for good conduct balances threats aimed at misbehavior: "Give to the Most High as he has given to you,/ and as generously as you can afford./ For the Lord is the one who repays,/ and he will repay you sevenfold" (35:12-13 NRSV).

Ben Sira demonstrates a fondness for refrains and repetitive phrases, as if stopping the readers in midthought and suspending them there: "You who fear the Lord, wait for his mercy;/ do not stray, or else you may fall./ You who fear the Lord, trust in him,/ and your reward will not be lost./ You who fear the Lord, hope for good things,/ for lasting joy and mercy" (2:7-9 NRSV; cf. 2:15-17). Similarly:

> Question a friend; perhaps he did not do it;
> or if he did, so that he may not do it again.
> Question a neighbor; perhaps he did not say it;
> or if he said it, so that he may not repeat it.
> Question a friend, for often it is slander;
> so do not believe everything you hear.
>
> .   .   .   .   .   .
>
> Question your neighbor before you threaten
> him;
> and let the law of the Most High take its
> course.   (19:13-15, 17 NRSV)

Other Literary Forms. Besides the two base forms, truth statement and instruction, several other forms of literary expression liven Ben Sira's teaching. He includes two prayers, a rare feature in earlier wisdom (cf. Prov 30:7-9 for a profound invocation of help, presumably from above).[39] In 22:27–23:6, Ben Sira asks for effective control over his speech and thoughts, as well as mastery of pride and illicit sensual desire. This moving expression of piety addresses God as "O Lord, Father and Master of my life" and as "O Lord, Father and God of my life" (23:1, 4 NRSV). Ben Sira welcomes divine chastisement as early warning against repeating one's sins, lest one also become subject to human mockers. The other prayer, 36:1-22, invokes the "God of All," Yahweh, the sacred name of the deity in Jewish literature, and the "God of the ages." Here Ben Sira gives vent to frustration over God's apparent inactivity, praying for renewed signs and defeat of enemies, hastening the day of reckoning.[40] He longs for the return of all exiled Jews, and he asks for pity on Zion. Remembering ancient recitations of Yahweh's mighty deeds on Israel's behalf, together with prophetic promises yet unfulfilled, Ben Sira begs the Lord to confirm the truth of both in his own time.

Several hymns also appear in Sirach, most notably 42:15–43:33 and 51:1-12 (the Hebrew text of MS B after 51:12 has another hymn of sixteen verses modeled on Psalm 136).[41] In these hymns, Ben Sira extols the wonders of the created world in the same way the author of Job did. The awesome power of the Creator and a humble awareness of mystery, still unseen, establish the mood for these hymns. Ben Sira knows that human eyes merely touch the surface, but his exquisite use of poetic imagery suggests that even this limited knowledge is something marvelous. He mentions the way pools put on ice like a breastplate, and he describes frost as pointed thorns. The rapid descent of snow reminds him of birds in the sky. Such poetic flourish does not detract from the impression of order and precision, the existence of complementary pairs, and the purposive attention to design and function where the heavenly bodies are concerned.[42]

Two didactic compositions resemble the hymns, but their mood places more distance between the singer and the Creator (16:24–17:14; 39:12-35).

One has the feeling that these learned meditations grew out of rational reflection and studious instruction. Exploring the place of human beings in the universe, they affirm a legitimate role for everything, even those things that seem out of place in a harmonious universe. These didactic compositions function as a defense of divine justice, like the debate form,[43] which Ben Sira uses freely.

Also known from Egyptian wisdom literature, this device to stave off dissent first appears within the Bible in Ecclesiastes: "Do not say, 'Who can have power over me?'/ for the Lord will surely punish you./ Do not say, 'I sinned, yet what has happened to me?'/ for the Lord is slow to anger. . . . Do not say, 'His mercy is great,/ he will forgive the multitude of my sins,'/ for both mercy and wrath are with him,/ and his anger will rest on sinners" (Eccl 5:3-4, 6 NRSV). This debate form warns against presuming too much about God's patience, mercy, and sovereignty. It challenges those who think they can sin with impunity: "Do not say, 'I am hidden from the Lord,/ and who from on high has me in mind?/ Among so many people I am unknown,/ for what am I in a boundless creation?' " (16:17 NRSV).

In two places Ben Sira sings wisdom's praise (1:1-10; 24:1-23), moving beyond Job 28, where wisdom remains altogether inaccessible to human beings, and Prov 8:1-36, where she is present alongside Yahweh as the first act of creation. Ben Sira affirms this earlier tradition, attesting to her innate inaccessibility and declaring her the initial creative act. At the same time, he insists that the Lord dispensed wisdom on all God's works and on those who love God (1:1-10). According to Sirach 24, wisdom searched the whole world for a suitable resting place until the Creator chose Israel as her place of residence. In Zion she blossomed and produced fruit, inviting those who desired her to eat their fill. Ben Sira identifies wisdom with the Mosaic law, making it accessible to everyone in Israel. The universal motif of wisdom's covering the earth like mist gives way to a particularistic tradition. The erotic relationship between wisdom and students, present in Proverbs 8–9, achieves new expression in an acrostic poem that concludes Sirach (51:13-20, 30), an earlier form of which was discovered in cave 11 at Qumran.[44]

Ben Sira also heaps praise on a select group of ancestral heroes (Sir 44:1–50:24).[45] He walks through the gallery of biblical characters, and in doing so prepares the way for a eulogy on the high priest of his day, Simeon. These descriptions resemble Greek encomia in some respects,[46] but suitable antecedents from biblical literature exist.[47] The choice of heroes, highly selective, betrays a decided preference for priestly figures[48] and for others who contributed to Israel's cult in some material way. One looks in vain for a woman in the list, despite the presence of remarkable females in the sacred traditions (e.g., Deborah, Huldah, Hannah, Samson's mother, Ruth). Pride of position goes to Aaron and Phinehas, with Moses, David, Solomon, Hezekiah, Josiah, Zerubbabel, and Joshua being invoked for their part in reforming and strengthening the cult of the temple. Prophets who make the list do so on the basis of miraculous acts rather than oracular proclamations. The sequence of heroes follows the canonical divisions, first those characters whose lives are recorded in the Pentateuch; then prophets, including Job; and finally Nehemiah, from the writings. An afterthought leads Ben Sira to return to the beginning, Enoch, and work backward to Adam.

BEN SIRA'S USE OF BIBLICAL TRADITIONS

Although Ben Sira patterns his teaching after Israel's wisdom literature, the extensive praise of ancestral heroes moves outside that body of texts to embrace the whole Hebrew canon.[49] This appeal to special revelation and its confessional attestations marks a radical departure from the books of Proverbs, Job, and Ecclesiastes. Sacred history thus becomes subject matter for consideration, and that shift compromises the fundamental character of wisdom as accessible to all people, regardless of nationality or geographical location.

To be sure, the author of Proverbs 1–9 introduces the notion of divine legislation (תורה *tôrâ*) and discipline (מוסר *mûsār*), together with the concept of reprehensible conduct (תועבה *tôʿēbâ*), all of which come perilously close to providing a link with Deuteronomy. Their non-specific use with reference to the will of God and its punitive action against despicable behavior complicates matters and prevents firm resolution of the question of whether the author had Deuteronomy in mind when using these ideas. With Ben Sira, the issue is no longer ambiguous.

The integration of sacred history and wisdom instruction pervades the entire book of Sirach, not just 44:1–50:24. Allusions to Israel's history as recorded in the canon of his day function as examples of praiseworthy conduct and as warnings against deeds that provoke divine anger. No longer content to study nature and human nature in search of instructive analogies, Ben Sira draws freely on the special relationship between an elect people and its deity. He actually quotes King David's response to divine anger occasioned by obedience to a command to number the people, a perplexing story of a vacillating deity that prompted the chronicler to introduce Satan as the instigator of David's action. According to 2 Sam 24:14, David opted to take his chances with an angry Yahweh in preference to three years of famine or three months of fleeing from enemies. Ben Sira observes: "Let us fall into the hands of the Lord,/ but not into the hands of mortals;/ for equal to his majesty is his mercy,/ and equal to his name are his works" (2:18 NRSV).

From the book of Genesis, Ben Sira alludes to Adam (Sir 33:10; 40:1), to Eve (Sir 25:24),[50] to Lot (Sir 16:8), to Sodom and Gomorrah (Sir 39:23), to the fallen angels (Sir 16:7), to the flood (Sir 40:10), to the covenant with Noah (Sir 17:12), to the image of God (Sir 17:3), to the creation account (Sir 39:16, 21), and to Jacob's descendants (Sir 23:12). Given the dearth of biblical references to Adam and Eve outside Genesis, Ben Sira's clear mention of Adam in 40:1—only the Greek text has the proper name in 33:10—and his placing on Eve the sole responsibility for the origin of sin show that he was influenced by a growing trend to speculate about such biblical persons as Adam, Eve, and Enoch.

Allusions to incidents associated with the signal event of Israelite history, the exodus, also occur. Ben Sira mentions the six hundred thousand Israelites who perished in the wilderness because of their idolatrous conduct (Sir 16:9-10), as well as the tree that turned bitter water sweet (Sir 38:5). He refers to Yahweh as the "Holy One" (Sir 4:14) and mentions the Sinaitic legislation transmitted through Moses to the people (Sir 24:23).

Sometimes Ben Sira alludes to a cluster of ideas from specific biblical themes. In 24:1-12, he refers to the Yahwistic notion of creation by means of a heavenly mist; to the pillar of cloud that symbol-ized Yahweh's guiding presence with the Israelites under Moses' leadership; to the tabernacle, also a sign of Yahweh's coming to meet the chosen spokesman for the wandering people; to sacred names—Israel/Jacob, Jerusalem—and to an elect people. Similarly, 36:1-17 mentions divine signs and wonders, echoing those associated with the exodus from Egypt and its immediate aftermath; the regular cultic recitation of Yahweh's "mighty deeds" (צדקות ṣĕdāqôt); the tribes of Jacob and their inheritance, the land promised to Abraham; the people on whom the divine name Yahweh had been pronounced; Israel, the firstborn of God; Zion, the city of God's sanctuary; unfulfilled prophecies uttered in Yahweh's name; and Aaron's priestly blessing.

Such allusions to the major sacral traditions, creation and exodus, also appear within didactic psalms, becoming at times somewhat tedious. Ben Sira stops short of giving a detailed account of these historical events connected with the wilderness, thus avoiding the tedium of learned psalmography (cf. Psalms 78; 105; 106; 136). The surprising aspect of his selection from Israel's sacred story is what he does not choose. Given the illustrative force of Joseph's refusal to succumb to seduction, the powerful negative potential of Saul, the perennial temptation to idolatry afforded by the story about Balaam, and so forth, one marvels at Ben Sira's reticence. When warning against the dangers of uncontrolled passion, he does not appeal to the examples of David and Bathsheba or Amnon and Tamar (cf. 6:2-4). To combat the strong lure of Hellenism, especially for young men, Ben Sira does not use the episode about Balaam or even the incident involving Elijah and the prophets of Baal.[51]

Ben Sira may very well have alluded to far more biblical texts than suggested thus far, inasmuch as his language frequently echoes ideas from them. For example, the designation of the Lord as compassionate and merciful (2:11)[52] undoubtedly reflects an abbreviated version of Exod 34:6-7, the ancient proclamation to Moses of the divine attributes. This oft-cited creed—only the positive attributes—left an indelible print on subsequent characterizations of Yahweh. Ben Sira often offers advice that has its point of reference in ancient teachings, such as the command to honor one's parents (Sir 3:3), although he provides a different rationale for such filial allegiance than one finds in the Decalogue.

Comparison with a wisdom text later than Ben Sira is instructive, for the author of the book of Wisdom also weaves sacred story into his instructions, always without specific names of the persons being recalled (Wis 10:1–19:22). He traces the long account of Israel in Egypt and the escape into the wilderness without ever naming anyone. The clear implication is that the audience knew the story intimately and filled in the missing names. This author adheres to the story line from beginning to end. The resulting treatment approaches the type of interpretation known as midrash, a running commentary on a biblical text. Furthermore, this midrash-like interpretation heightens the psychological features of a divine drama between Israel's God and the Egyptians. Their offense, idolatry, provides focus for the entire analysis.

The characters behind the story in Wis 10:1–19:22 include Adam, Cain, Abel, Noah, Abraham, Isaac, Lot, Lot's wife, Jacob, Esau, Joseph, and Moses. The full narrative explores the familiar events in considerable detail, leaving little to the imagination. Nevertheless, the incidents lead up to and set the stage for a sharp attack on idolatry, including three explanations for its appeal to the popular imagination (the aesthetic, a parent's grief over a son, a desire to honor a distant emperor).

With a single exception, Ben Sira withholds the names of persons to whom he refers in 1:1–43:33. That one specific reference is Lot (Sir 16:8). Ben Sira does mention Jacob, but the reference seems always to be national, hence synonymous with Israel. In the section praising ancestral heroes (Sir 44:1–50:24), Ben Sira specifically names the individuals under discussion. The difference probably relates to the literary form being employed; one mentions the name of the deceased in a "eulogy."

The practice of rehearsing ancient history by means of allusions raises the question, "Who was the intended audience?" In the light of the expense of owning scrolls of the entire Bible, one may reasonably conclude that both Ben Sira and the author of the book of Wisdom directed their teachings to a small group of prospective scribes. These young men would have studied the Scriptures just as Ben Sira is said to have done. Still, one cannot rule out the possibility that communal worship, especially singing the didactic psalms, and parental teaching may have familiarized the people with certain biblical traditions, particularly the story of the beginnings.

In some ways, Sirach resembles the book of Tobit, Baruch, the *Testament of the Twelve Patriarchs*, and *Pirqe 'Abot*, devotional literature from the wider Jewish environment. The author of Tobit emphasizes acts of piety as an expression of loyalty to the Mosaic law and regularly lifts up a voice in prayer. In Tob 12:6-10 the angel Raphael assumes the venerable role of wisdom teacher, insisting that "a little with righteousness is better than wealth with wrongdoing" (Tob 12:8 NRSV) and promising reward for virtuous living. Tobit both prays for and experiences divine activity; like Job, his misfortune was eventually reversed. The poem on wisdom in Bar 3:9–4:4 does not integrate mythic themes concerning wisdom's function at creation with the notion that wisdom finds concrete expression in the law of Moses. Instead, it proceeds in the manner of Job 28, stressing the inaccessibility of wisdom to all but God, who passed it on to Israel in the Torah.[53] The *Testament of the Twelve Patriarchs* transcends the ritual features of worship in favor of ethical dimensions to an unprecedented degree; Ben Sira endeavors to combine the two.[54] Like *Pirqe 'Abot*, Ben Sira offers ethical advice to students steeped in torah piety.

BEN SIRA AND HELLENISM

Occasional similarities between Sirach and Greek authors raise the issue of Ben Sira's dependence on popular Hellenistic philosophers.[55] The comparison of death to falling leaves in 14:18 (and in the *Iliad* vi.146-149) belongs to folk wisdom. The image would naturally occur to anyone who gave much thought to the process of growth and decay in nature and among humans. Ben Sira proclaims at one point: "He is the All." This expression was common in Stoic philosophy, but Ben Sira could easily have arrived at such an understanding of God on the basis of his reading of Isa 45:5-7 and Deut 32:39. Unlike Stoic thinkers, Ben Sira did not equate God with the created universe. The Stoic ideal of world citizenship did not drive out Ben Sira's conviction that God had chosen Israel as a special heritage.[56]

Ben Sira's affirmation of physicians shows that he did not reject Greek ideas without careful consideration (Sir 38:1-15). He combines traditional Jewish belief about sin and disease with Hellenistic teachings, although the two seem mutually contradictory. In the end, piety prevailed, and because both Greeks and Jews prayed for healing, he could argue for combining the physician's treatment with fervent prayer. Greek customs and ideas filled the air Ben Sira breathed, expressing themselves in many ways: a eulogy of ancestors, the notion of a rational universe with perfectly balanced pairs, human freedom and divine providence, dining customs, pride of authorship, and much more.

The last two deserve further comment. Ben Sira refers to the Hellenistic practice of selecting a person to preside over a banquet, and he gives advice on fulfilling that honor in an acceptable manner (Sir 32:1-13). He even mentions the reward for good service, the customary wreath awarded for leadership. His advice on table etiquette in 31:12-24 presupposes dinners like Greek banquets followed by symposia. Such dinners included contests at drinking wine, musical entertainment, speeches demonstrating wit and wisdom, seating of guests according to rank, and a blessing to the gods at the end of the dinner.

Greek pride of authorship influenced Ben Sira so strongly that he departed from the usual anonymity or pseudonymity of those who composed the books of Proverbs, Job, and Ecclesiastes. He saw no particular virtue in attributing his teachings to King Solomon; given the nature of the book, he could not have done so, for the praise of ancestral heroes required an author from a much later time than the Solomonic era. The author of the book of Wisdom avoided a historical resume that would place him in the second or first centuries.

Egyptian influence can probably be detected in the comparison of professions in 38:24–39:11, although this text differs fundamentally from the *Satire of the Trades*. Ben Sira offers no hint of satire in describing the work of the farmer, the artisan, the smith, and the potter. Instead, he merely points out that their work consumes both time and energy, leaving no opportunity for study. In no way does he disparage their contribution to society, which he thinks depends on what they do for survival. The Egyptian *Instruction for Duauf*, or the *Satire of the Trades*, ridicules considerably more occupations than the four Ben Sira mentions. Both Ben Sira and the Egyptian author

contrast the scribe's profession with all other kinds of work; their intent was to attract students to intellectual pursuits.

The ethic of caution based on shame and regard for one's reputation as expressed in Sirach closely resembles that in Papyrus Insinger; similarities also exist between this late Egyptian instruction and Ecclesiastes.[57] If Ben Sira relies on this work, he varies it in significant ways (cf. Sir 6:13; 13:1–42:2; 32:23; 41:11-13). His allusion to the bee to illustrate the importance of tiny things hardly confirms dependence on Papyrus Insinger, for such an analogy seems like a natural conclusion to an observant reader.

Links with Aramaean wisdom through the *Sayings of Ahiqar*, although possible, may derive from folk tradition: the futility of opposing a turbulent stream (*Ahiqar* 3.83 and Sir 4:26) and the revelation of character through the clothes one wears (*Ahiqar* 2.39 and Sir 19:29-30).[58] Anyone could easily draw these conclusions without having heard or read either work.

This meager evidence of Greek influence on Ben Sira[59] indicates that he drew far more extensively from biblical literature than from extra-biblical, even when trying to persuade Jews that their legacy was just as universal as Greek philosophy. That was the point of identifying the Mosaic law with cosmic wisdom. Ben Sira's teachings demonstrate an awareness of the seductive power of Hellenism, especially to young people, and he wages battle for the next generation of Jews. This struggle introduces new types of discourse: psychological and philosophical arguments in the service of theodicy, discussion of free will and determinism, reflection about two ways (Sir 2:12). In essence, he sought to provide rational backing for his ancestral heritage.[60] The assertion that wisdom comes from the Lord constitutes a declaration of war against Hellenism, where it was a product of human inquiry. Ben Sira dismisses all astrological speculation—and apocalyptic—as sheer arrogance or pride. "Be content with the knowledge God has bestowed on you" sums up his attitude toward striving to unlock hidden mysteries.[61]

Did Ben Sira venture forth into the Hellenistic world as an ambassador like John, the father of Eupolemus, who was sent to Rome to negotiate a treaty (cf. 2 Macc 4:11), or Philo, who represented the Jews of Alexandria before Caligula? Did Ben Sira occupy a position as judge or counselor in the *gerousia?* Did he work as a scribe in the Temple? Perhaps one could say more about his relationship with Hellenism if these questions could be answered.

RELIGIOUS TEACHINGS IN SIRACH

The two primary themes in the book, fear of the Lord[62] and wisdom,[63] are interwoven from first to last, making it difficult to determine the dominant one. The author of Proverbs 1–9 subjugated piety to knowledge, viewing the fear of the Lord as the main ingredient and first principle of learning. Wisdom thus consisted of something above and beyond obedience to God, although religion comprised its very core. For Ben Sira, fear of the Lord has no rival, not even the acquisition of wisdom: "How great is the one who finds wisdom!/ But none is superior to the one who fears the Lord./ Fear of the Lord surpasses everything;/ to whom can we compare the one who has it?" (25:10-11 NRSV). Like the word translated "wisdom" (חכם *ḥākām*), the expression "fear of the Lord" (יראי יהוה *yirê yhwh*) appears often in Sirach (over fifty times).

Such elevation of religion prompts Ben Sira to conclude that wisdom's garland and root exist in the fear of the Lord, making religious achievement the sole justification for pride (Sir 10:22). Human wisdom expresses itself in deeds of kindness, true obedience to the law of Moses. Divine wisdom manifests itself in the Torah. Whereas the later wisdom has assumed the form of legal statute and passionate exhortation, men and women have no excuse for choosing folly. It has been said that wisdom manifests itself subjectively as fear of the Lord and objectively as the law of Moses.[64]

Ben Sira urges submission to the yoke of divine discipline (מוסר *mûsār*), noting that it withholds itself like its name. Acknowledging the difficulty encountered by most students when they first endeavor to become wise, he describes wisdom as a hard taskmaster until people have demonstrated their worth. In time, however, she shows herself as the ardent lover, making them consider her earlier afflictions as nothing. This erotic language for intellectual curiosity and obedience to the Lord links up with the passionate discourse about love for God in the book of Deuteronomy.

Another theme pervading Sirach concerns God's justice and mercy. Ben Sira subscribes to the traditional belief in God's justice, but he knows that skepticism has imprinted itself indelibly on the minds of his audience. He uses the standard arguments—that God waits patiently, giving sinners an opportunity to repent; that things can change in a moment; that the hour of death will settle the score; that suffering serves as a test of character or as discipline; that human knowledge is partial; that praise is the proper response—and seeks to improve on them from Greek arguments about the design of the universe and punishment by mental and psychological anxiety.[65] He refuses to endorse an answer that seems to have been emerging slowly in the Jewish community: the conviction that righteous individuals will receive eternal life (17:27-28).[66] The Greek and Syriac texts introduce this belief at crucial junctures (Sir 7:17*b*; 48:11*b*; Greek II, Sir 2:9*c*; 16:22*c*; 19:19; Syriac, Sir 1:12*b*, 20; 3:1*b*). In this respect, Ben Sira resembles later Sadducees rather than Pharisees, who believed in life after death. That conservative tendency on the part of Ben Sira explains why he places so much emphasis on preserving honor or reputation, the one thing that survives after a person dies (Sir 41:11-13).

The origin of sin in a perfect universe placed a special burden on defenders of divine justice, particularly when it was attributed to the Creator. The serpent's presence in the garden indirectly indicted the Lord. Later biblical texts compromise divine justice further, insisting that God overrides human freedom, forcing pharaohs and others to persist in obstinacy. Ben Sira stoutly resisted such ideas, for he believed that everyone acts with absolute freedom (Sir 15:11-20). Nevertheless, he realized that irresistible forces put extraordinary pressure on free will (Sir 33:11-13). That ambiguity characterizes much biblical thinking about sin, but Ben Sira brings the issue of free will into the arena of public discussion.

Ben Sira's frequent attribution of mercy to the deity stands out when one observes the rarity of this idea in earlier wisdom literature. If an individual can rely on reward for virtuous conduct, the presupposition of much earlier wisdom, then divine mercy really does not fit into the picture. That understanding probably explains why sages did not characterize God as merciful. The shift takes place in Sirach, perhaps because earlier optimism had faded under the barrage of questions in the books of Job and Ecclesiastes.[67] Historical circumstances no longer favored such optimistic reading of the human situation, if they ever did, and a greater consciousness of human frailty produces existential anxiety. The extent to which such alarm over sinful dominance and the sorry future of the human race, both in this life and in the next, can be grasped by studying 2 Esdras. In the light of the weighty burden hanging over humanity, Ben Sira takes some comfort in divine compassion. The source of his confidence in God's mercy lies outside the wisdom literature, most likely in the ancient creedal confession in Exod 34:6-7.

The God whom Ben Sira worshiped was the Creator, a concept at the very heart of wisdom thinking.[68] This majestic fashioner of an orderly universe saw whatever transpired and therefore ruled with exact justice. This sovereign demanded social justice (Sir 4:8-10), the demonstration of one's true worship through ritual *and* charitable deeds, as well as pure thoughts. Ben Sira honors God as father, shepherd, and judge (Sir 18:13, 40; 23:1, 4; 51:10; 16:12-14).

It was noted earlier that Ben Sira did not believe in life beyond the grave, and in this regard he could be labeled a proto-Sadducee. Rejecting a meaningful existence after death alone hardly suffices to place him in the camp with later Sadducees, for he shared this skepticism with virtually all OT authors (Psalm 73; Isa 26:19; and Dan 12:2 being the only exceptions). Like the Sadducees of the first century CE, Ben Sira had strong interests, if not actual membership, in the priesthood. Moreover, he belonged to the elite ranks of upper-class citizens, and with this status came ultraconservatism aimed at maintaining the status quo. In addition, the temple cult represented the center of religious life for him, despite a commendable concern for doing acts of kindness when the occasion presented itself. In a sense, he understood the fundamentals of hasidic piety, but he never let the emotions seize control.

Later Pharisaism lacked this elitism and the strong attachment to the temple cult; it also appealed to the masses much more readily than did Sadduceeism. The destruction of the Temple in 70 CE brought the sacrificial cult to an end, as well as placing the priesthood in jeopardy. The Pharisees were able to continue their worship in synagogues, which offered a natural setting for prayer and religious training of the young. Ben Sira's influence may well have suffered along with the priests whose life centered in the Temple. The sectarians at Qumran also cared deeply about the temple cult, but Ben Sira did not share their strong attention to divine mystery. Nor did he subscribe to their apocalyptic fervor, midrashic exegesis, celibacy, and so much more.

BEN SIRA'S ATTITUDE TOWARD WOMEN

Much has been said about biblical patriarchalism,[69] a subjecting of women to their husbands' whims and placing them in the category of property to be disposed of at will. Daughters depended on their fathers to arrange marriages, husbands could negate solemn oaths taken by their wives, and women usually did not inherit property. Husbands could marry more than one wife, but women had no such freedom. Two standards operated in the area of sexual misconduct, and husbands punished wives for infidelity. In a sense, primary responsibility for sin's origin fell to a woman, and a prophet could even personify evil as a woman (Zech 5:5-11). In traditional lore, if not also in fact, a father could sacrifice his daughter if he so wished (Jephthah), but sons were equally vulnerable (Isaac).

We should not lose sight of the fact that the male authors of the biblical texts often portrayed women in a highly favorable light (cf. the depiction of Samson's mother over against that of Manoah,[70] Ruth, Deborah, and Susanna). They may have acknowledged the threat presented by the notorious foreign woman of Proverbs,[71] but they balanced this figure with wisdom, personified as a woman, and with the portrait of an ideal wife. To be sure, they also personified folly as a female and praised the wife in Prov 31:10-31, largely from the point of view of the husband whom she benefits. Numerous instances of mutual love between husband and wife in the Bible suggest that not all women considered themselves oppressed. Sages considered good wives gifts of God, and the unknown author of 1 Esdr 3:1–4:41 praises woman as the strongest thing on earth, exceeded only by truth and its Author.[72] The erotic passion expressed in Song of Songs testifies to a society that values the power stronger than death that draws men and women to each other.

Nevertheless, rare expressions of misogynism reveal the darker side of Israelite society, the result of centuries of double standards and jokes that have long since lost their humor. The author of Ecclesiastes expresses disdain over his, or someone else's, inability to discover a single trustworthy woman, although he does proceed to indict men almost equally, giving them only one one-thousandth of an advantage over women (Eccl 7:23-29). The heroine Judith stands above all the men in the little town of Bethulia as courageous, virtuous, and pious (Jdt 8:1-34; 15:8-10). In the book of Tobit, both Anna and Sarah appear above reproach (Tob 2:11-14; 3:7-15), suggesting that misogynistic views may have been less dispersed than has often been claimed. Examination of the Greco-Roman environment and of rabbinic Judaism reveals rampant misogynism, making the attitude of the Bible toward women look tame by comparison.[73]

Ben Sira inherits the mixed biblical tradition with respect to women, but he may be subject to Hellenistic views as well. In any event, he adds a new dimension, the discussion of daughters as a separate category.[74] Moreover, he places the adjective "wicked" (רעה *rāʿâ*) before the noun "daughters" (בנות *bānôt*). His obscene characterization of them as opening their quiver for every arrow (Sir 26:12) represents the ultimate in disrespect, and his rancorous opinion that the birth of a daughter is a loss (Sir 22:3) can hardly be justified by anxiety over what that entails—finding a husband for her, securing her virginity until marriage and her faithfulness afterward, worrying about her ability to bear children. Worse still, he places the entire blame for sin and death on the first woman (Sir 25:24) and apparently makes the ridiculous statement that a man's wickedness is better than a woman's goodness.[75]

The positive evaluation of woman also finds expression in Sirach, demonstrating Ben Sira's awareness that life without women would be drab, indeed. He recognizes the value of a faithful wife, and he sees the pathos of impossible "love" (using the image of a eunuch who beholds a desirable young woman and groans). Ben Sira scolds foolish old men who stray from their nests like birds, and he mentions restless sighing brought on by loneliness. His erotic appreciation for a woman's physical beauty seems boundless, issuing in effusive language based on the holy artifacts in the Temple ("Like the shining lamp on the holy lampstand,/ so is a beautiful face on a stately figure./ Like golden pillars on silver bases;/ so are shapely legs and steadfast feet" [Sir 26:17-18 NRSV]).

THE PRAISE OF ANCESTRAL HEROES

Such lavish praise of women did not induce Ben Sira to include a woman in his praise of loyal people, which comprises the last major section of the book, 44:1–50:24. If his primary criterion for selection relates to their contribution to and active participation in the temple cult, then silence with regard to women is mandated. That particular perspective certainly applies to Moses, Aaron, Phinehas, David, Solomon, Hezekiah, Josiah, Zerubbabel, Jeshua, Nehemiah, and Simeon. A secondary criterion, the desire to achieve canonical coverage, may explain the inclusion of Joshua and Caleb, along with the unnamed Judges, and the prophetic figures Nathan, Elijah, Elisha, Isaiah, Ezekiel, Job(!), and the unnamed twelve. That leaves two royal reprobates, Rehoboam and Jeroboam, and three priestly villains (Korah, Dathan, and Abiram) who merely stand out because of their infamy. Perhaps the addition of pre-Israelite worthies—Enoch, Noah, Abraham, Isaac, Jacob at first, then Enoch, Joseph, Shem, Seth, Enosh, and Adam later—represents a feeble effort to universalize the list.

This unusual journey through the portrait gallery of notables has recently been described as a complete reading of epic history that served as a mythic etiology for Judaism in the period of the Second Temple.[76] The hypothesis runs like this: The hymn consists of a tripartite architectonic structure with transitional units: (1) the establishment of covenants with the conquest of the land as transition; (2) the history of the prophets and kings, with the story of the restoration as transition; and (3) the climax in Simeon the high priest. Themes unite the figures within each major unit, for example, the promise of a blessing joins together the individuals from Abraham to Jacob. The poem resembles an encomium with four parts: (1) a prooemium in 44:1-15, (2) a genealogy in 44:17–49:16, (3) the narration of the subject's achievements in 50:1-21, and (4) an epilogue in 50:22-24.

According to this theory, Sir 49:14-16 serves as a bridge linking past and present, juxtaposing Adam and Simeon in a manner that renders praise of the latter both appropriate and effective. This praise commemorates rather than entertains, although many rhetorical encomiastic devices occur, such as amplification by syncrisis (the juxtaposition of opposites for rhetorical effect), hyperbole, rhetorical questions, appeal to experience acquired through traveling, a reference to a person's character and reputation for good deeds, the claim that words cannot adequately describe an individual, and an assertion that a person's contribution to society lacks precedent. Thus far, the theory.

The hypothesis would be more persuasive if Ben Sira had used the four essential characteristics of encomia (prooemium, ancestry, deeds, epilogue) in proper proportion and in a manner so that they could easily be recognized.[77] Stated differently, if Ben Sira borrowed the form of an encomium, he changed it radically. Moreover, the chronicler provides a number of parallels to Ben Sira's use of biblical material, remaining silent about embarrassing aspects of David's character and dropping people from the record. Everything in the list could easily have occurred to a Jewish sage with no knowledge of Greek encomia. Most of the rhetorical features above occur in the Samson narrative, as well as in numerous other stories in the Hebrew Bible.

Why does Ben Sira overlook Ezra?[78] Was the omission intentional? At least five competing explanations for this anomaly deserve consideration. First, the socioeconomic circumstances had changed radically between the late fourth and early second centuries BCE in Jerusalem, making mixed marriage a matter of indifference.[79] This view assumes that Ezra's strict legislation concerning marriage with foreigners failed because it did not take into account long-standing practice among the Jews. Ben Sira, on this view, remained quiet about Ezra out of embarrassment over his strict policy and the ensuing suffering it generated.

A second explanation focuses on the venerable profession of scribes, to which Ben Sira belonged. In Ezra's day scribes had become narrowly and exclusively oriented toward the Mosaic law, but Ben Sira understands the scribal profession much more broadly. For him, an interest in the law went hand in hand with research in the tradition of the wise. To some degree, Ben Sira transforms the office of priest-scribe into that of teacher, whose authority rests ultimately on scholarship, insights, and communicative ability.[80]

A third response to the silence about Ezra focuses on the state of the priestly office during the immediate period after Simeon's death. Although Simeon's son and successor, Onias III, was a pious leader, he lacked the qualities of bold leadership. Like Ezra, he was a political quietist. For this reason, Ben Sira did not want to laud Ezra as someone whom Onias could emulate. Instead, Ben Sira skips over Ezra and commends Onias's father, hoping to stimulate a desire on the son's part to pattern his actions after his father and predecessor in the office of high priest.[81]

A fourth explanation for Ben Sira's omission of Ezra in the list of ancestral heroes takes its cue from a feature common to several individuals—active participation in constructing or repairing the Temple.[82] In this view, Ezra was omitted in favor of Nehemiah, whose vital role in repairing the wall of the city was essential to the successful operation of the cult.

A fifth attempt to explain Ben Sira's failure to mention Ezra focuses on the chronicler's championing of Levites, which did not accord with the elevation of the Aaronide priestly lineage in Ben Sira. For this reason, he did not wish to mention a scribe who championed the cause of a rival priestly group.[83]

Two other prominent omissions call for comment, Joseph and Saul. In the body of the poem, one expects a reference to Joseph after the mention of Jacob, but it does not occur. The name "Joseph" appears in a brief "afterthought," along with the pre-deluvians Shem, Seth, and Adam (Sir 49:14-16; Enoch occurs here for a second time but is missing in the Masada text and the Syriac). Perhaps Joseph's connection with the northern tribes of Ephraim and Manasseh and his blessing of these sons gave the appearance of approving the despised Samaritans, who now occupied the area originally granted to Ephraim and Manasseh. The active campaign waged by the Tobiads in Transjordan and the leaders of Samaria against the policies of Simeon II and the Tobiads in Jerusalem may have generated sufficient antipathy to cause Ben Sira to remain silent about Joseph. Alternatively, Ben Sira may have removed the name of Joseph to blot out any record of his role as adviser to the pharaoh. Again, in the light of Onias III's switch of allegiance from the Seleucids to the Ptolemaic ruler, Ben Sira may have avoided giving the impression that he approved this shift.

Naturally, these attempts to explain Ben Sira's silence about Joseph presuppose the secondary character of the name in Sir 49:15. Viewing his presence in the latter text as comparison rather than praise lacks persuasiveness; excising the entire unit 49:14-16 as secondary solely to restore a sequence of two persons, Nehemiah and Simeon II, who were responsible for engineering improvements in Jerusalem, seems problematic at best.[84]

One further notable omission is the first king, Saul. The biblical story ascribes enough negative features to his character to explain the lack of any reference to him. In addition, his rivalry with David and his connection with northern tribal groups made Saul an unlikely candidate for Ben Sira's list of worthy men.

SIRACH AND THE CANON

The preface to Sirach, written by Ben Sira's grandson, refers to the law, the prophets, and the other writings, suggesting that the first two divisions of the Hebrew Bible existed as distinct entities and that the third group may or may not have been relatively fixed in his day. Ben Sira's praise of ancestral heroes supports this evidence, pushing the date back to the early second century BCE for at least two closed units, the law and the prophets.[85] He knows the chief characters in Genesis through Deuteronomy, and he mentions Isaiah, Jeremiah, Ezekiel, and the Twelve, as well as prominent persons from the Former Prophets (Joshua, Judges, Samuel, and Kings). Unfortunately, he does not provide enough information to enable scholars to identify the exact books making up the third category. Among them he mentions Job and Nehemiah, but he probably knew Psalms and other books as well.[86]

Although Sirach was excluded from the Hebrew Bible, it was frequently cited in rabbinic circles until the tenth century CE, occasionally introduced by the formula "it is written," which indicates Scripture.[87] Akiba, the noted rabbi of the second century (d. c. 132 CE), thought it belonged among the חסונים (ḥisōnîm, "outside") or extra-

canonical books, those that did not, in the language of the day, "defile the hands." A severe penalty accompanied their reading, forfeiture of any participation in the next life.[88] The same assessment of Sirach appears in *Tosephta*,[89] which states that the book does not defile the hands. Nevertheless, Sirach is quoted eighty-two times in the Talmud and other rabbinical writings.

Recent evidence from Masada and Qumran confirms that the Jewish communities in the area of the Dead Sea viewed the book as sacred, for the copy from Masada and the two tiny fragments from Cave 2 at Qumran are written stichometrically, with parallel columns, the first half of each colon beginning on the right side and the second half appearing on the left side. Moreover, the inclusion of Sirach in the Septuagint and the Palestinian revisions of this Greek text and the Hebrew indicate its acceptance as sacred. The formulation of specific criteria for canonicity, resulting from the debates associated with the so-called council of Jamnia and related discussions, automatically excluded Sirach, if one limits inspiration to the period from Moses to Ezra. In addition, several aspects of the book are closer to Sadducaic teaching than to Pharisaic, and this may have influenced its checkered history.

The situation is equally ambiguous in Christian tradition. The presence of the book of Sirach in the Septuagint implied at least quasi-sacred character, but the translator of the Vulgate, Jerome, denied a place in the canon to the additional books, labeling them deuterocanonical.[90] These books include 1–2 Esdras, Tobit, Judith, the Additions to Esther, the book of Wisdom, Sirach, Baruch, the Letter of Jeremiah, the Song of the Three Jews, Susanna, Bel and the Dragon, the Prayer of Manasseh, and 1–2 Maccabees. Augustine disagreed with Jerome's estimate, considering all the books in the Septuagint equally authoritative.

Following Jerome, Martin Luther rejected the sacred character of the additional books in the Septuagint, which he called apocrypha and placed in a separate group between the two Testaments in his German translation of 1534. John Calvin rejected these books altogether. Nevertheless, the Apocrypha appeared in the King James translation in English until the third decade of the nineteenth century, when they were removed for a combination of reasons, partly theological and partly economic. The Roman Catholic Church still considers these books sacred, but deuterocanonical, except for 1–2 Esdras and the Prayer of Manasseh.

The author of the Epistle of James was particularly fond of Sirach.[91] Other works of the early church used Sirach as a source of inspiration, including the *Didache,* the *Shepherd of Hermas,* and the *Epistle of Barnabas.* So did the church father Clement of Alexandria. The early Latin fathers included Sirach as one of the five books written by Solomon, and Cyprian accepted its sacred character. This position eventually prevailed at the Council of Trent.

THE TEXT

Slightly more than two-thirds of Sirach has survived in Hebrew manuscripts (approx. 68 percent).[92] Between 1896 and 1900, the Cairo Geniza, a place for discarded sacred texts in the old synagogue in Cairo, yielded four distinct manuscripts of Sirach (A, B, C, D), dating from the tenth to the twelfth centuries. Another leaf (E) was discovered in 1931, and additional fragments of B and C came to light in 1958 and 1960. Three years later a fragmentary and mutilated scroll, resembling B, was discovered at Masada. In 1982 a new leaf of Sirach from the Cairo Geniza was identified (F). These manuscripts contain the following texts from Sirach:[93]

A	3:6*b*–16:26 (six leaves)
B	30:11–33:3; 35:11; 38:27*b*, 39:15*c*–51:30 (nineteen leaves, written stichometrically)
C	4:23, 30-31; 5:4-7, 9-13; 6:18*b*-19, 28, 35; 7:1-2, 4, 6, 17, 20-21, 23-25; 18:31*b*–19:3*b*, 20:5-7; 37:19, 22, 24, 26; 20:13; 25:8, 13, 17-24; 26:1-2*a* (a florilegium)
D	36:29–38:1*a* (one leaf)
E	32:16–34:1 (one leaf, written stichometrically)
F	31:24–32:7; 32:12–33:8 (one leaf, written stichometrically)

A fragment from Cave 2 at Qumran has Sir 6:20-31 in stichometric arrangement (only the ends of the lines have survived).

The Greek text exists in two forms: (1) codices such as the four major uncials: Sinaiticus, Vaticanus, Alexandrinas, and Ephraemi; and (2) a longer form in the Lucianic rescension and Origen's recension of the Septuagint. The Old Latin and Vulgate used the Greek text of Sirach, which has also influenced the *Peshitta* to some degree.

Both the Greek and the Hebrew texts contain titles for individual sections (Greek, 20:27; 23:7; 24:1; 30:1, 16; 44:1; 51:1; Hebrew, 31:12 = Greek 34:12; 41:14; 44:1) and transitions (42:25 to 43:1; 43:33 to 44:1; 49:16 to 50:1). In the Hebrew text an extra psalm resembling Psalm 136 follows Sir 51:12 (cf. 11QPs[a]). The sequence from Sirach 31 to 36 differs in the Hebrew, the Vulgate, and the Syriac from the Greek, which offers a less likely order at this point.

FOR FURTHER READING

Commentaries, Concordances, Monographs:

Barthelemy, D., and O. Rickenbacher. *Konkordanz zum hebräischen Sirach.* Göttingen: Vandenhoeck & Ruprecht, 1973.

Coggins, Richard J. *Sirach.* Guides to the Apocrypha and Pseudepigrapha. Sheffield: Sheffield Academic Press, 1998.

Hengel, Martin. *Judaism and Hellenism.* 2 vols. Philadelphia: Fortress, 1974.

Lee, T. R. *Studies in the Form of Sirach 44–50.* SBLDS 75. Atlanta: Scholars Press, 1986.

Mack, Burton L. *Wisdom and the Hebrew Epic: Ben Sira's Hymn in Praise of the Fathers.* Chicago Studies in the History of Judaism. Chicago: University of Chicago Press, 1985.

Marböck, J. *Weisheit im Wandel: Untersuchungen zur Weisheitstheologie Bei Ben Sira.* BBB 37. Bonn: Peter Hanstein, 1971.

Mulder, Otto. *Simon the High Priest in Sirach 50: An Exegetical Study of the Significance of Simon the High Priest as Climax to the Praise of the Fathers in Ben Sira's Concept of the History of Israel.* Supplements to the Journal for the Study of Judaism 78. Leiden: Brill, 2003.

Oesterley, W. O. E. *The Wisdom of Jesus the Son of Sirach or Ecclesiasticus.* Cambridge: Cambridge University Press, 1912.

Sanders, J. T. *Ben Sira and Demotic Wisdom.* SBLMS 28. Chico, Calif.: Scholars Press, 1983.

Schrader, Lutz. *Leiden und Gerechtigkeit. Studien zu Theologie und Textgeschichte des Sirach-*

buches. BBET 27. Frankfurt am Main: Peter Lang, 1994.

Skehan, Patrick, and Alexander A. Di Lella. *The Wisdom of Ben Sira*. AB 39. New York: Doubleday, 1987.

Snaith, John G. *Ecclesiasticus or The Wisdom of Jesus, Son of Sirach*. CBC, NEB. Cambridge: Cambridge University Press, 1974.

Stadelmann, Helga. *Ben Sira als Schriftgelehrter: Eine Untersuchung zum Berufsbild des vor-Maccabäischen Sofer unter Berucksichtigung seines Verhältnisses zu Priester-, Propheten und Weisheitslehretum*. WUNT 2/6. Tübingen: Mohr, 1981.

Trenchard, W. C. *Ben Sira's View of Women: A Literary Analysis*. Brown Judaic Studies 38. Chico, Calif.: Scholars Press, 1982.

Wischmeyer, Oda. *Die Kultur des Buches Jesus Sirach*. BZNW 77. Berlin: Walter de Gruyter, 1994.

Yadin, Yigael. *The Ben Sira Scroll from Masada*. Jerusalem: Israel Exploration Society, 1965.

Ziegler, J. *Sapientia Iesu Filii Sirach*. Septuaginta 12/2. Göttingen: Vandenhoeck & Ruprecht, 1965.

Other Studies:

Crenshaw, James L. *Old Testament Wisdom*. Atlanta: John Knox, 1981.

————. "Sirach." *Harper Bible Commentary*. San Francisco: Harper & Row, 1988.

————. *Urgent Advice and Probing Questions: Collected Writings on Old Testament Wisdom*. Macon, Ga.: Mercer University Press, 1995.

Day, John, Robert P. Gordon, and H. G. M. Williams, eds. *Wisdom in Ancient Israel*. Cambridge: Cambridge University Press, 1995.

Duesberg, H. *Les Scribes Inspirés: Introduction aux livres sapientiaux de la Bible*. 2 vols. Paris: Maredsous, 1966.

Gammie, John G., and Leo G. Perdue, eds. *The Sage in Israel and the Ancient Near East*. Winona Lake: Eisenbrauns, 1990.

Levine, Amy-Jill, ed. *"Women Like This": New Perspectives on Jewish Women in the Greco-Roman World*. Atlanta: Scholars Press, 1991.

Murphy, Roland E. *The Tree of Life: An Exploration of Biblical Wisdom Literature*. ABRL. New York: Doubleday, 1990.

Nickelsburg, G. W. E. *Jewish Literature Between the Bible and the Mishnah: A Historical and Literary Introduction*. Philadelphia: Fortress, 1981.

Perdue, Leo G., Bernard Brandon Scott, and William Johnston Wiseman, eds. *In Search of Wisdom: Essays in Memory of John Gammie*. Louisville: Westminster/John Knox, 1993.

Rad, Gerhard von. *Wisdom in Israel*. Nashville: Abingdon, 1972.

Schnabel, E. J. *Law and Wisdom from Ben Sira to Paul: A Traditional Historical Inquiry into the Relation of Law, Wisdom, and Ethics*. WUNT 2/16. Tübingen: Mohr, 1985.

ENDNOTES

1. One can obtain entry into this realm of discourse from several introductions, most notably James L. Crenshaw, *Old Testament Wisdom* (Atlanta: John Knox, 1981); Gerhard von Rad, *Wisdom in Israel* (Nashville: Abingdon, 1972); and Roland E. Murphy, *The Tree of Life* (New York: Doubleday, 1990), Several volumes of collected essays cover the entire spectrum of ancient wisdom, particularly *The Sage in Israel and the Ancient Near East*, eds. John G. Gammie and Leo G. Perdue (Winona Lake: Eisenbrauns, 1990); *In Search of Wisdom*, eds. Leo G. Perdue, Bernard Brandon Scott, and William Johnson Wiseman (Louisville: Westminster/John Knox, 1993); James L. Crenshaw, *Urgent Advice and Probing Questions* (Macon, Ga.: Mercer University Press, 1995); and *Wisdom in Ancient Israel*, eds. John Day, Robert P. Gordon, and H. G. M. Williamson (Cambridge: Cambridge University Press, 1995).

2. W. G. Lambert, *Babylonian Wisdom Literature* (Oxford: Clarendon, 1960); and Miriam Lichtheim, *Late Egyptian Wisdom Literature in the International Context: A Study of Demotic Instructions*, OBO 52 (Fribourg: Fribourg University Press, 1983).

3. Miriam Lichtheim, *Ancient Egyptian Literature*, 3 vols. (Berkeley: University of California Press, 1973, 1976, 1980), includes wisdom literature among other genres, offering fresh translations of all the texts referred to above.

4. In addition to Lambert's translation of these texts, see Bendt Alster, *The Instructions of Šuruppak: A Sumerian Proverb Collection*, Meso-

potamia 2 (Copenhagen: Akademisk Forlag, 1974); *Studies in Sumerian Proverbs*, Mesopotamia 3 (Copenhagen: Akademisk Forlag, 1975); and *Proverbs of Ancient Sumer: The World's Earliest Proverb Collection* (Bethesda, Md.: CDL, 1996).

5. Translations can be found in *Ancient Near Eastern Texts Relating to the Old Testament*, ed. James B. Pritchard, 3rd ed. (Princeton, N.J.: Princeton University Press, 1969).

6. James M. Lindenberger, *The Aramaic Proverbs of Ahiqar* (Baltimore: Johns Hopkins University Press, 1983).

7. No satisfactory study exists, as one can readily see from Loren R. Mack-Fisher's two entries in Gammie and Perdue, *The Sage in Israel and the Ancient Near East*. The first, "A Survey and Reading Guide to the Didactic Literature of Ugarit: Prolegomenon to a Study on the Sage" (67-80) suffers badly from an ill-defined grasp of wisdom literature, and the second, "The Scribe (and Sage) in the Royal Court at Ugarit" (109-15) fares no better.

8. See Harold C. Washington, *Wealth and Poverty in the Instruction of Amenemope and the Hebrew Proverbs*, SBLDS 142 (Atlanta: Scholars Press, 1994); Glendon E. Bryce, *A Legacy of Wisdom: The Egyptian Contribution to the Wisdom of Israel* (Lewisburg: Bucknell University Press, 1979). Both assess the relationship between these two texts from different countries. Nili Shupak, *Where Can Wisdom Be Found? The Sage's Language in the Bible and in Ancient Egyptian Literature*, OBO 130 (Fribourg & Göttingen: University Press & Vandenhoeck & Ruprecht, 1993), offers a valuable analysis of linguistic affinities between Israelite and Egyptian sages.

9. Alexander Heidel, *The Gilgamesh Epic and Old Testament Parallels* (Chicago: University of Chicago Press, 1946); Jeffrey Tigay, *The Evolution of the Gilgamesh Epic* (Philadelphia: Fortress, 1982); Jeffrey Tigay, *Empirical Models for Biblical Criticism* (Philadelphia: Fortress, 1985); Jack M. Sasson, "Gilgamesh Epic," *ABD* 2:1024-1027; William L. Moran, "The Gilgamesh Epic: A Masterpiece from Ancient Mesopotamia," in *Civilizations of the Ancient Near East*, ed. Jack M. Sasson (New York: Scribner's, 1995) 4:2327-2336.

10. Leo G. Perdue, *Wisdom and Creation: The Theology of Wisdom Literature* (Nashville: Abingdon, 1994).

11. In addition to the last-cited work, see Ronald E. Clements, *Wisdom in Theology* (Grand Rapids: Eerdmans, 1992). William P. Brown, *Character in Crisis: A Fresh Approach to the Wisdom Literature of the Old Testament* (Grand Rapids: Eerdmans, 1996), emphasizes the development of moral character in the sapiential literature; Joseph Blenkinsopp, *Wisdom and Law in the Old Testament* (Oxford: Oxford University Press, 1995), draws attention to the ordering of society in ancient Israel, one dubiously located in the school by E. W. Heaton, *The School Tradition of the Old Testament* (Oxford: Clarendon, 1994). Lennart Boström, *The God of the Sages: The Portrayal of God in the Book of Proverbs*, CBOTS 29 (Lund: Almqvist & Wiksell, 1990); James L. Crenshaw, "The Concept of God in Old Testament Wisdom," in Perdue et al., *In Search of Wisdom*, 1-18 (reprinted in Crenshaw, *Urgent Advice and Probing Questions*, 191-205), and James L. Crenshaw, "The Contemplative Life," in Sasson, *Civilizations of the Ancient Near East*, 4:2445-2457.

12. James L. Crenshaw, "The Shadow of Death in Qoheleth," in *Israelite Wisdom* (Philadelphia: Fortress, 1979) 205-16; reprinted in Crenshaw, *Urgent Advice and Probing Questions*, 573-85.

13. J. N. Aletti, "Seduction et parole en Proverbs 1–9," *VT* 27 (1977) 129-44.

14. Donn F. Morgan, *Wisdom in the Old Testament Traditions* (Atlanta: John Knox, 1981). James L. Crenshaw, "Method in Determining Wisdom Influence upon 'Historical' Literature," *JBL* 88 (1969) 129-42 (=Crenshaw, *Urgent Advice and Probing Questions*, 312-25) evaluates such attempts to find wisdom in various parts of the OT.

15. A shift from confident self-reliance, characteristic of early Egyptian wisdom, seems to occur in the new kingdom with Ani and Amenemope and to grow stronger with the passing of time, as evidenced by demotic instructions (Papyrus Insinger and the *Instruction of Ankhsheshanky*).

16. See James L. Crenshaw, "The Restraint of Reason, the Humility of Prayer," in Crenshaw, *Urgent Advice and Probing Questions*, 206-21.

17. Wolfgang Roth, "Sirach: The First Graded Curriculum," *The Bible Today* 29 (1991) 298-302, thinks the book was used as a textbook. The curious silence about circumcision and the sabbath, noted by J. Marböck, *Weisheit im Wandel: Untersuchungen zur Weisheitstheologie bei Ben Sira*,

BBB 37 (Bonn: Peter Hanstein, 1971) 93, shows that, whatever its use, a certain haphazardness exists. The same principle was operative in law codes in the Bible, where significant gaps occur, and in ethical texts, such as Proverbs, that omit many important areas of life.

18. For different views about the frequency of first-person language in Ecclesiastes and its function, see James L. Crenshaw, *Ecclesiastes*, OTL (Philadelphia: Westminster, 1987); and Michael V. Fox, *Qoheleth and His Contradictions*, JSOTSup 71 (Sheffield: Almond, 1989).

19. Research in the area of OT wisdom has made significant progress, yet without actually clarifying the precise sociological context within which ancient sages worked. For an understanding of the complex issues, see Gerhard von Rad, *Wisdom in Israel* (London: SCM, 1972); James L. Crenshaw, *Old Testament Wisdom* (Atlanta: John Knox, 1981); Roland E. Murphy, *The Tree of Life* (New York: Doubleday, 1990); R. N. Whybray, *The Intellectual Tradition in the Old Testament* (Berlin: Walter de Gruyter, 1974); Claus Westermann, *The Roots of Wisdom* (Louisville: Westminster/John Knox, 1995); Claus Westermann, *Forschungsgeschichte zur Weisheitsliteratur 1950–1990*, AzT 71 (Stuttgart: Calwer, 1991); Stuart Weeks, *Israelite Wisdom*, OTM (Oxford: Clarendon, 1994).

20. Jack T. Sanders, "Ben Sira's Ethics of Caution," *HUCA* 50 (1979) 73-106.

21. Friedrich Vinzenz Reiterer, "Deutung und Wertung des Todes durch Ben Sira," *Die Alttestamentliche Botschaft als Wegweisung: Festschrift für Heinz Reinelt*, ed. Josef Zmijemski (Stuttgart: Katholisches Bibelwerk, 1990) 203-36; the focus of attention in this article falls on Sir 41:1-4. L. J. Prockter, " 'His Yesterday and Yours Today' (Sir 38:22): Reflections on Ben Sira's View of Death," *J Sem* 2 (1990) 44-56, claims that Ben Sira combines Jewish piety with the best of popular Hellenistic philosophy, accepting life and death as part of God's providential order, like a good Stoic.

22. On theodicy as perceived by biblical authors, see James L. Crenshaw, ed., *Theodicy in the Old Testament* (Philadelphia: Fortress, 1983), particularly the opening essay, "Introduction: The Shift from Theodicy to Anthropodicy," 1-16. See also Crenshaw, *Urgent Advice and Probing Questions*, 141-54.

23. Interpreters usually emphasize the random character of the teachings in Sirach, viewing the book as a compendium of the accumulated lectures of a lifetime of work, with no fundamental structure. Rejecting a theory of accidental juxtaposition of wholly unrelated teachings, Wolfgang Roth, "On the Gnomic-Discursive Wisdom of Jesus Ben Sirach," *Semeia*, 17 (1980) 59-79, thinks Ben Sira wrote an original book consisting of 1:1–23:27 and 51:1-30, later supplementing this first edition with three additional units (24:1–32:13; 32:14–38:23; 38:24–50:24, 29). A prologue introduces each new section (24:1-29; 32:14–33:15; 38:24–39:11), and an autobiographical note intervenes between the prologue and the body of the unit (in contrast to the original edition, where prologues occur [1:1–2:18; 4:11-19; 6:18-37; 14:20–15:10], but no autobiographical note). Roth sees 39:2-3 as programmatic for Ben Sira's "hermeneutic-pedagogic theory: from understanding to explanation, from assimilation to exposition, from learning to teaching, from apprenticeship to mastery" (ibid., 63). In Ben Sira's oral instructions (e.g., 6:35; 17:10; 25:9; 42:15–43:33; 44–50), he sees a forerunner to *haggadah* (homiletic discourse); in other teachings (18:30–19:30; 20:27-31; 31:12–32:13) he recognizes early *halakah* (legal instruction). Roth thinks Ben Sira's warning against exceeding the scope of assignments (3:21-22) means exactly that: Stick to the day's lesson (ibid., 64). Roth also believes that Ben Sira organized the original four sections alphabetically: אב (*'āb*, "father") in 3:1-16; בשת (*bōšet*, "shame") in 4:20-28; גאוה (*gā'ôt* "arrogance") in 7:17 and 10:5-18; דעת (*da'at*, "knowledge") in 16:25*b*–23:27, following the order of the first four letters in the Hebrew alphabet (ibid., 74). The first two sections comprise, in Roth's view, elementary instruction; the third section "is more hortative-ethical and society oriented in character," while the fourth is more explorative-theological and individualistic (ibid., 74-75).

24. Wolfgang Roth, "On the Gnomic-Discursive Wisdom of Jesus Ben Sirach," *Semeia*, 17 (1980) 302.

25. Wolfgang Roth, "On the Gnomic-Discursive Wisdom of Jesus Ben Sirach," *Semeia*, 17 (1980) 298-302.

26. Rudolf Smend, *Die Weisheit des Jesus Sirach erklärt* (Berlin: Reimer, 1906) 3-4.

27. F. O'Fearghail, "Sir 50, 5-21: Yom Kippur or The Daily Whole Offering," *Bib* 59 (1978) 301-16, argues that Ben Sira describes the daily whole offering rather than the Day of Atonement. Alexander Di Lella accepts this view; see Patrick W. Skehan and Alexander A. Di Lella, *The Wisdom of Ben Sira*, AB 39 (New York: Doubleday, 1987) 550-51.

28. James D. Martin, "Ben Sira—A Child of His Time," in *A Word in Season: Essays in Honour of William McKane*, eds. James D. Martin and Philip R. Davies, JSOTSup 42 (Sheffield: JSOT, 1986) 141-61, examines Ben Sira's teachings in the light of emerging apocalypticism in the Jewish world. The changing circumstances associated with the Babylonian defeat of Jerusalem and dislocation of a large segment of the Judean populace contributed to an attitude quite different from earlier optimism. Portions of the books of Ezekiel (chaps. 38–39), Isaiah (chaps. 26–29), and Zechariah (chaps. 9–14) reflect an early apocalypticism (sometimes called proto-apocalypticism). Full-blown developments occur in the books of Daniel and Revelation. Apocalyptic thought includes, among other things, a belief in a transcendent God (momentarily inactive in Israel's history), the temporary victory of evil, and imminent judgment on all peoples. This message assumes the form of revelation attributed to ancient worthies but kept hidden for years, strange imagery involving animals and beasts, coded language, heavenly journeys, visions, and martial conflicts. Sometimes a work asks difficult questions and ponders the existence of wickedness in a world supposedly ruled by a benevolent deity (cf. 2 Esdras, a masterpiece that asks why God's people are subjected to such harsh treatment from persons less devout than they). The idea of a final battle between the forces of good and the forces of evil finds expression in *The Wars of the Sons of Light Against the Sons of Darkness*, a text from Qumran; earlier expressions of this conflict occur in Ezekiel 38–39 and Joel 3–4 (Eng. 2:28-32; 3:1-21). The closest kinship with Ben Sira's panegyric of the fathers exists, in Martin's view, in Wisdom and 1 Maccabees (ibid., 145); such cult-centered historiography may thus be the origin of apocalyptic's historical expression (ibid., 147), although Ben Sira opposes idle speculation and apocalyptic excesses (ibid., 154). For Ben Sira in the Hellenistic context, see Martin Hengel, *Judaism and Hellenism*, I-II (Philadelphia: Fortress, 1974) 131-53.

29. Josephus *Antiquities of the Jews* 12.138-144.

30. Skehan and Di Lella, *The Wisdom of Ben Sira*, 8-16, sketches this history and locates Ben Sira within the general period 250–175 BCE, with Sirach being written when Ben Sira was an old man, probably about 180 BCE. This interpretation of the data has obtained the status of consensus, rare among biblical critics.

31. J. Marböck, "Das Gebet um die Rettung Zions Sir 36, 1-22 (Gr: 33.9-13a; 36, 16b-22) im zusammenhang der Geschichtsschau ben Siras," in *Memoria Jerusalem*, ed. J. B. Bauer (Jerusalem and Graz: Akademische Druck-und Verlagsanstalt, 1977) 93-116. In examining this remarkable prayer, Marböck points out that Ben Sira's appeal for renewed action on behalf of an elect people accords with Sir 17:17, which refers to Israel as Yahweh's special portion.

32. Walter Baumgartner, "Die literarischen Gattungen in der Weisheit des Jesus Sirach," *ZAW* 34 (1914) 161-98; James L. Crenshaw, "Sirach," *Harper Bible Commentary* (San Francisco: Harper & Row, 1988) 836-54; James L. Crenshaw, "Wisdom," in *Old Testament Form Criticism*, ed. John H. Hayes, TUMS 2 (San Antonio: Trinity University Press, 1974) 225-64. See also James L. Crenshaw, *Urgent Advice and Probing Questions* (Macon, Ga.: Mercer University Press, 1995).

33. J. L. Koole, "Die Bibel des Ben-Sira," *OTS* 14 (1965) 374-96; Douglas E. Fox, "Ben Sira on OT Canon Again: The Date of Daniel," *WTJ* 49 (1987) 335-50; T. Middendorp, *Die Stellung Jesu Ben Siras zwischen Judentum und Hellenismus* (Leiden: Brill, 1973); Eckhard J. Schnabel, *Law and Wisdom from Ben Sira to Paul: A Tradition-Historical Enquiry into the Relation of Law, Wisdom, and Ethics* (Tübingen: J. C. B. Mohr, 1985). The last two authors calculate the extent of Ben Sira's allusions to scripture (70 allusions to the Torah, 46 to historical books, 51 to prophetic books, and over 160 to the writings, according to Middendorp's reckoning). A more exacting criterion for establishing an allusion would reduce the number appreciably.

34. The advisory nature of sentences, as opposed to mandatory instructions, can no longer be maintained. See James L. Crenshaw, *Prophetic Conflict*, BZAW 124 (Berlin and New York; Walter de Gruyter, 1971), excursus B, "'eṣa and *dabar:*

The Problem of Authority/Certitude in Wisdom and Prophetic Literature," 116-23; James L. Crenshaw, "Wisdom and Authority: Sapiential Rhetoric and Its Warrants," *Congress Volume Vienna 1980,* SVTP 32 (Leiden: Brill, 1981) 10-29 (see also Crenshaw, *Urgent Advice and Probing Questions,* 326-43); Claus Westermann, "Weisheit im Sprichwort," *Schalom. Festschrift A. Jepsen* (Stuttgart: Calwer Verlag, 1971) 73-85; Claus Westermann, *The Roots of Wisdom* (Louisville: Westminster/ John Knox, 1995); Friedemann W. Golka, *The Leopard's Spots* (Edinburgh: T & T Clark, 1993).

35. John J. Pilch, " 'Beat His Ribs While He Is Young' (Sir 30:12): A Window on the Mediterranean World," *BTB* 23 (1993) 101-13, examines the ancient understanding of parenting, concluding that respect for parents was more important than actual deeds and that strict (harsh) discipline fit nicely into such a worldview. His use of modern Mediterranean concepts raises the question of how appropriate is the analogy. Modern educators question the universality of the statement about the value of corporal punishment.

36. On this type of proverbial saying, see Pancratius C. Beentjes, " 'Full Wisdom Is Fear of the Lord.' Ben Sira 19, 20-20, 31: Context, Composition and Concept," *EstBib* 47 (1989) 27-45, esp. 37-40. In the existing Hebrew manuscripts, שׁ (*yēš*) occurs 64 times, involving 46 different verse lines; in 20:5-6, 22-23 they appear in "absolute condensation" (ibid., 37).

37. Martin, "Ben Sira—A Child of His Time," 154, thinks of the warning against seeking hidden things as being aimed at apocalyptic speculation. Others think it refers to Hellenistic philosophy.

38. The rhetorical device apostrophe occurs in the final acrostic (alphabetic poem) to capture students' interest and to give the impression of intimacy.

39. On prayer in wisdom literature, especially in Sirach, see James L. Crenshaw, "The Restraint of Reason, the Humility of Prayer," in Crenshaw, *Urgent Advice and Probing Questions,* 206-21. See also James L. Crenshaw, *Origins: Early Judaism and Christianity in Historical and Ecumenical Perspective,* Brown Judaic Studies, forthcoming.

40. Several scholars have addressed the issue of eschatology and messianism in Sirach, usually reaching a minimalist position that only hints of each appear. See James D. Martin, "Ben Sira's Hymn to the Fathers: A Messianic Perspective," in *Crises and Perspectives: Studies in Ancient Near Eastern Polytheism, Biblical Theology, Palestinian Archaeology and Intertestamental Literature: Papers Read at the Joint British-Dutch Old Testament Conference Held at Cambridge, U.K., 1985,* Oudtestamentische Studien, deel 24, ed. A. S. Van der Woude (Leiden: E. J. Brill, 1986) 107-23; Stanley Frost, "Who Were the Heroes? An Exercise in Bitestamentary Exegesis, with Christological Implications," in *The Glory of Christ in the New Testament,* eds. L. D. Hurst and N. T. Wright (Oxford: Clarendon, 1987) 65-172; Burton L. Mack, "Wisdom Makes a Difference: Alternatives to 'Messianic' Configuration," in *Judaisms and Their Messiahs at the Turn of the Christian Era,* eds. Jacob Neusner, William Scott Green, and Ernest S. Frerichs (Cambridge: Cambridge University Press, 1987) 15-48; Robert Hayward, "The New Jerusalem in the Wisdom of Jesus Ben Sira," *ScanJT* 6 (1992) 123-38. A. Caquot, "Ben Sira et le Messianisme, *Sem* 16 (1966) 43-68, finds no evidence for messianism in Sirach. Hayward contrasts the lackluster Greek translation of Sirach 36 with the vibrant Hebrew, arguing that the grandson thought too much emphasis had been put on Zion in the past, an era that was "dead and gone" (Hayward, "The New Jerusalem in the Wisdom of Jesus Ben Sira," 137).

41. C. Deutsch, "The Sirach 51 Acrostic: Confession and Exhortation," *ZAW* 94 (1982) 400-409, studies "the passage as the statement of the sage, the focus of the acrostic." Deutsch emphasizes the affective language and lessons from Ben Sira's own life. Pamela F. Foulkes, " 'To Expound Discipline': The Portrait of the Scribe in Ben Sira," *Pacifica* 7 (1994) 75-84, thinks of Ben Sira as a reflective scholar fit for judicial or ambassadorial posts.

42. Marböck calls it "very abstract, indeed almost philosophical." See J. Marböck, *Weisheit im Wandel: Untersuchungen zur Weisheitstheologie bei Ben Sira,* BBB 37 (Bonn: Peter Hanstein, 1971) 137.

43. On the debate form, see James L. Crenshaw, "The Problem of Theodicy in Sirach: On Human Bondage," *JBL* 94 (1975) 47-64. See also Crenshaw, *Urgent Advice and Probing Questions,* 155-74.

44. James A. Sanders, *The Dead Sea Psalms Scroll* (Ithaca, N.Y.: Cornell University Press, 1967); James A. Sanders, *The Psalms Scroll of Qumran Cave 11 (11 Q Psaᵃ)*, DJD 4 (Oxford: Clarendon, 1965). Sanders interprets the psalm as highly erotic, but see T. Muraoka, "Sir 51:13-30. An Erotic Hymn to Wisdom?" *JSJ* 10 (1979) 166-78.

45. The panegyric on ancestral worthies has generated considerable discussion, the most thorough recent studies being those of Burton L. Mack, *Wisdom and the Hebrew Epic: Ben Sira's Hymn in Praise of the Fathers*, Chicago Studies in the History of Judaism (Chicago: University of Chicago Press, 1985); Thomas R. Lee, *Studies in the Form of Sirach 44–50*, SBLDS 75 (Atlanta: Scholars Press, 1986). Other important essays include Maurice Gilbert, "L'eloge de la Sagesse [Siracide 24]," *Revue Théologique* 5 (1974) 326-48; Edmond Jacob, "L'Histoire d'Israel vue par Ben Sira," in *Mélanges bibliques rédigés en l'honneur de André Robert* (Paris: Bloud and Gay, 1958) 288-94.

46. Lee understands the section lauding Israel's heroes as an encomium (a Greek device praising a notable figure; it consisted of a prooemium, a genealogy, a narration of the person's accomplishments, and an epilogue with its concluding exhortation). The object of praise, in this view, is Simeon, not Israel's ancestors. See Lee, *Studies in the Form of Sirach 44–50*, 81. The record of Simeon's predecessors is proof from example. Mack thinks in terms of a hymn with decidedly encomiastic features (*Wisdom and the Hebrew Epic*). Chris A. Rollston, "The Non-Encomiastic Features of Ben Sira 44–50" (M.A. thesis, Emmanuel School of Religion, Johnson City, Tennessee, 1992), challenges their interpretation.

47. The unknown authors of the book of Wisdom and 1 Maccabees imitate Ben Sira's recitation of ancient history with emphasis on human accomplishments. Biblical antecedents of Ben Sira glorify God even when referring to similar history (cf. Psalms 68; 77–78).

48. J. G. Snaith, "Ben Sira's Supposed Love of Liturgy," *VT* 25 (1975) 167-74, plays down the author's priestly interests in favor of prophetic social justice, but John F. A. Sawyer, "Was Jeshua Ben Sira a Priest?" *Proceedings of the Eighth World Congress of Jewish Studies*, Div. A. (Jerusalem: World Union of Jewish Studies, 1982) 65-71, and Saul M. Olyan, "Ben Sira's Relationship to the Priesthood," *HTR* 80 (1987) 261-86, argue persuasively for identifying Ben Sira as a priest/sage. H. Stadelmann, *Ben Sira als Schriftgelehrter*, WUNT 6 (Tübingen: Mohr-Siebeck, 1980), develops the thesis that Ben Sira was a priestly, learned scribe.

49. J. G. Snaith, "Quotations in Ecclesiasticus," *TThS* 18 (1967) 1-12, finds very little citation of Scripture in Sirach. Other interpreters think Ben Sira made use of an anthological style, using brief phrases with telling effect. On the larger problem of citations, see *It Is Written: Scripture Citing Scripture. Essays in Honour of Barnabas Lindars, SSF*, eds. D. A. Carson and H. G. M. Williamson (Cambridge: Cambridge University Press, 1986).

50. Jack Levison, "Is Eve to Blame? A Contextual Analysis of Sirach 25:24," *CBQ* 47 (1985) 617-23, makes an interesting case for understanding the reference in this verse (Sir 25:24) as being directed to wicked wives, no thanks to whom husbands die. Levison rightly observes that elsewhere Ben Sira implies that death belongs to the natural order of things. An allusion to Eve in the context of discussing evil wives seems entirely natural, however, and Levison must assume remarkable gaps in Ben Sira's expression, which are supplied by brackets in Levison's translation: "From the [evil] wife is the beginning of sin, / and because of her we [husbands] all die." Moreover, the evidence from the use of γυνή (gynē (ἀπὸ; γυναικός *apo gynaikos*) is inconclusive, for the word refers to "wife" and to "woman" generally. Levison's claim that women are depraved is then cancelled by a recognition that good wives benefit husbands. Finally, the text from Cave 4 at Qumran entitled "The Wiles of the Wicked Woman," to which Levison alludes, deals with a mythic reality, personified evil, just as Sir 25:24, on the traditional reading, refers to the primal myth. See R. Moore, "Personification of the Seduction of Evil: 'The Wiles of the Wicked Woman,'" *RevQ* 10 (1979–81) 505-19. Levison's attempt to reorient scholarly thinking about Sir 25:24 resembles Norbert Lohfink's reading of Eccl 7:23-29: "War Kohelet ein Frauenfeind?" in *La Sagesse de l'Ancien Testament*, ed. Maurice Gilbert (Leuven: University Press, 1979) 259-87.

51. Mary Douglas, *In the Wilderness: The Doctrine of Defilement in the Book of Numbers* (Sheffield: Academic Press Limited, 1995), inter-

prets the Balaam story as satire directed at the harsh policies of Ezra and Nehemiah. A text from Deir 'Alla attests the popularity of the prophetic legend in relatively late times.

52. See James L. Crenshaw, "Who Knows What YHWH Will Do? The Character of God in the Book of Joel," in *Fortunate the Eyes That See: Essays in Honor of David Noel Freedman in Celebration of His Seventieth Birthday,* eds. Astrid B. Beck et al. (Grand Rapids: Eerdmans, 1995) 185-96.

53. Lewis J. Prockter, "Torah as a Fence Against Apocalyptic Speculation: Ben Sira 3:17-24," *Proceedings of the Tenth World Congress of Jewish Studies,* Div. A (Jerusalem: World Union of Jewish Studies, 1990) 245-52. Prockter writes: "To seek in heaven what is already on earth, namely Torah given once and for all to Moses, is not only foolish but perilous. To seek what is 'beyond you' is to display pride, and by so doing to wilfully cut yourself off from God, who reveals his will to the humble here below, not to those trying to ascend to the heavenly *hekhalot* (3:17-20)" (ibid., 251). On the limitations to knowledge generally, see James L. Crenshaw, "Wisdom and the Sage: On Knowing and Not Knowing," *Proceedings of the Eleventh World Congress of Jewish Studies,* Div. A (Jerusalem: World Union of Jewish Studies, 1994) 137-44.

54. J. G. Snaith, "Ben Sira's Supposed Love of Liturgy," *VT* 25 (1975), emphasizes the teachings about social justice in Sirach. Ben Sira maintains a healthy balance between observing the niceties of cultic ritual and deeds of kindness, and he provides theological underpinnings for both in divine commands and the nature of Yahweh as merciful. Otto Kaiser, "Die Begrundung der Sittlichkeit im Buche Jesus Sirach," *ZTK* 55 (1958) 51-63, examines the basis for ethical actions in Sirach.

55. T. Middendorp, *Die Stellung Jesus ben Siras zwischen Judentum und Hellenismus* (Leiden: Brill, 1973), overstresses Ben Sira's dependence on Hellenistic thinkers. The fault lies in his method, for similarities in phrases and ideas between Sirach and various Greek philosophers indicate literary dependence only when (1) the language and concepts are otherwise unique to Hellenism and (2) similarities in biblical literature are lacking. Moreover, two other factors enter the picture: Only a limited sample of Jewish literature from the ancient world has survived, and intelligent people can arrive at similar ideas independ-

ently. Even the expression "He is the all" does not necessarily derive from Stoic thinkers, for biblical precedent exists (Deut 32:39; Isa 45:5-7). These caveats notwithstanding, Ben Sira does show Hellenistic influence in the way he understands the universe as an orderly arrangement of complementary pairs. His almost mathematical tone in describing the universe, his endorsement of physicians, his description of banquets and symposia, and his pride of authorship place him squarely within the Hellenistic world. On the broader issue, see Jonathan Goldstein, "Jewish Acceptance and Rejection of Hellenism," in *Jewish and Christian Self-Definition,* eds. E. P. Sanders et al. (Philadelphia: Fortress, 1981) 2:64-87.

56. Stoic influence on Ben Sira has also been exaggerated; for a sober assessment, see David Winston, "Theodicy in Ben Sira and Stoic Philosophy," in *Of Scholars, Savants, and Their Texts,* ed. Ruth Link-Salinger (New York: Peter Lang, 1989) 239-49. An earlier study, Raymond Paultrel, "Ben Sira et le Stoicisme," *RSR* 51 (1963) 535-49, challenges Smend's claim that Ben Sira declares war against Hellenism. Paultrel also remarks on the omissions within such a long work as Sirach, noting Ben Sira's silence about angels, the Messiah, and the prohibition against images (ibid., 547).

57. J. T. Sanders, "Ben Sira's Ethics of Caution," *HUCA* 50 (1979); *Ben Sira and Demotic Wisdom,* SBLMS 28 (Chico, Calif.: Scholars Press, 1983). On the influence of "Papyrus Insinger" on Qoheleth, see James L. Crenshaw, *Ecclesiastes,* OTL (Philadelphia: Westminster, 1987), and for a modern translation of the Egyptian text, see Miriam Lichtheim, *Ancient Egyptian Literature,* 3 vols. (Berkeley: University of California Press, 1973–80) 3:184-217.

58. These references come from Edmond Jacob, "Wisdom and Religion in Sirach," in *Israelite Wisdom: Theological and Literary Essays in Honor of Samuel Terrien,* eds. John G. Gammie et al. (Missoula: Scholars Press, 1978) 250. They do not appear in James M. Lindenberger, *The Aramaic Proverbs of Ahiqar* (Baltimore: Johns Hopkins University Press, 1983), but the popular sayings attributed to Ahiqar have survived in various translations, chiefly Syriac, Armenian, Arabic, and Slavonic. See Lindenberger, *The Aramaic Proverbs of Ahiqar,* 354. The saying about stopping a river occurs frequently in ancient literature.

59. Martin Hengel, *Judaism and Hellenism*, 2 vols. (Philadelphia: Fortress, 1974) 1:115-254, examines the extent of Hellenistic influence on Jewish literature of the last three centuries before the emergence of the church.

60. Ryan thinks of Ben Sira's "holistic response to the divisions within Israel" as a "comprehensive act of identification." See Michael D. Ryan, "The Act of Religious Identification in Ben Sirach and Paul," *The Drew Gateway* 54 (1983) 4-16.

61. Ben Sira acknowledges that the intellect can only touch the surface of divine mystery; at the same time, he wishes to assert that God has revealed to Israel all that is necessary for living in obedience to Yahweh. Maintaining a balance so as to discourage idle speculation, whatever its nature, was no easy matter. This struggle to appreciate the revelation of Torah without discrediting a sense of the unknown and unknowable has persisted in Judaism. Michael Fishbane, *The Garments of Torah: Essays in Biblical Hermeneutics* (Bloomington: Indiana University Press, 1989), treats this problem with his usual freshness and passion.

62. Joseph Haspecker, *Gottesfurcht bei Jesus Sirach: Ihre religiöse Struktur und ihre literarische und doctainäre Bedeutung*, AnBib 30 (Rome: Pontifical Biblical Institute, 1967), argues forcefully that the fear of God, not wisdom, occupies the prominent position in Sirach.

63. Gerhard von Rad, *Wisdom in Israel* (Nashville: Abingdon, 1972) 242, insists that wisdom subordinates everything else to it. The summary statement in 50:27 that Ben Sira poured forth wisdom from his heart does not settle the issue, for 50:29 balances knowledge with action. For Ben Sira, wisdom expressed itself in religious devotion ("fear of the Lord").

64. "Subjectively, wisdom is the fear of God; objectively, the Mosaic lawbook (chapter 24)." ("Subjektiv ist die Weisheit daher die Gottesfurcht, objektiv ist sie das Gesetzbuch Moses, c 24.") This succinct statement appears in Rudolf Smend, *Die Weisheit des Jesus Sirach erklärt* (Berlin: Reimer, 1906) xxiii.

65. See these works by James L. Crenshaw: *Theodicy in the Old Testament* (Philadelphia: Fortress, 1983); "Theodicy," in *Anchor Bible Dictionary*, 6 vols. (New York: Doubleday, 1992) 6:444-47; and "The Problem of Theodicy in Sirach: On Human Bondage," *JBL* 94 (1975).

66. Vincenz Hamp, "Zukunft und Jenseits im Buche Sirach," *Alttestamentliche Studien, Festschrift Nötscher*, BBB 1 (Bonn: Hanstein, 1950) 86-97. Hamp finds no evidence that Ben Sira thought of retribution in the next life.

67. James L. Crenshaw, "The Concept of God in Old Testament Wisdom," in *In Search of Wisdom: Essays in Memory of John Gammie*, eds. Leo G. Perdue, Bernard B. Scott, and William J. Wiseman (Louisville: Westminster John Knox, 1993) 1-18, explores the function of the idea of mercy in Sirach. Earlier optimism has given way to a sense of utter dependence on God's compassion; obedience has become more difficult and temptations harder to resist, perhaps because of declining influence from the family. Moreover, confidence in divine sovereignty, as well as faith that God works wonders on Israel's behalf, has begun to fade.

68. See the recent analysis of creation theology in Leo G. Perdue, *Wisdom and Creation: The Theology of Wisdom Literature* (Nashville: Abingdon, 1994).

69. Phyllis Trible, *God and the Rhetoric of Sexuality* (Philadelphia: Fortress, 1978); Phyllis Trible, "Depatriarchalizing in Biblical Interpretation," *JAAR* 41 (1973) 30-48.

70. James L. Crenshaw, *Samson* (Atlanta: John Knox, 1978) 65-98.

71. Carol A. Newsom, "Woman and the Discourse of Patriarchal Wisdom: A Study of Proverbs 1–9," in *Gender and Difference in Ancient Israel*, ed. Peggy L. Day (Minneapolis: Fortress, 1989) 142-60; Joseph Blenkinsopp, "The Social Context of the 'Outsider Woman' in Proverbs 1–9," *Bib* 72 (1991) 457-73.

72. James L. Crenshaw, "The Contest of Darius' Guards in 1 Esdras 3:1-5:3," in *Images of Man and God: The Old Testament Short Story in Literary Focus*, ed. Burke O. Long (Sheffield: Almond, 1981) 74-88, 119-20. See also Crenshaw, *Urgent Advice and Probing Questions*, 222-34.

73. Charles E. Carlston, "Proverbs, Maxims, and the Historical Jesus," *JBL* 99 (1980) 87-105, esp. 95-97, gives some examples of maxims in the Greco-Roman world that denigrate women. Patrick W. Skehan and Alexander A. Di Lella, *The Wisdom of Ben Sira*, 91, also give some repugnant maxims about women culled from M. R. Lefkowitz and M. B. Fant, *Women's Life in Greece and Rome* (Baltimore: Johns Hopkins University

Press, 1982). Di Lella wishes to judge Ben Sira in the light of attitudes prevalent in his own time, a valid procedure.

74. Karla G. Bohmbach, "With Her Hands on the Threshold: Daughters and Space in the Hebrew Bible" (Ph.D. diss., Duke University, 1996).

75. W. C. Trenchard, *Ben Sira's View of Women: A Literary Analysis*, BJS 38 (Chico, Calif.: Scholars Press, 1982), goes too far in condemning Ben Sira for hostility to women. The positive treatment of some women, like the negative attitude toward some others, requires proper nuancing. On this problem, see Maurice Gilbert, "Ben Sira et le femme," *RTL* 7(1967) 426-42. Modern corrective to such thinking receives impetus from Brenner, ed. *A Feminist Companion to Wisdom Literature* (Sheffield: Sheffield Academic Press, 1995).

76. Burton L. Mack, *Wisdom and the Hebrew Epic: Ben Sira's Hymn in Praise of the Fathers*, Chicago Studies in the History of Judaism (Chicago: University of Chicago Press, 1985). R. A. F. MacKenzie, "Ben Sira as Historian," in *Trinification of the World: A Festschrift in Honor of F. E. Crowe*, eds. T. A. Dunne and J. M. Laport (Toronto: Regis College Press, 1978) 313-27. MacKenzie observes that Ben Sira does not mention the Babylonian exile in his account of Israel's heroes. Was there any compelling reason to do so? After all, he concentrates on the high points, illustrating them with the names of persons involved in those momentous events.

77. Rollston illustrates the difficulty of proving literary dependence when an author adapts material or exercises exceptional selectivity. The resulting product differs appreciably from the presumed source, casting doubt on the presumption itself. See Chris A. Rollston, "The Non-Encomiastic Features of Ben Sira 44–50."

78. Peter Höffken, "Warum schwieg Jesus Sirach über Esra," *ZAW* 87 (1975) 184-201, argues that Ben Sira omitted Ezra from the list of ancestral worthies because of his championing of Levites. Ben Sira rejects the chronicler's plea for the levitical priesthood and returns to the earlier priestly emphasis on the Aaronide line. Höffken understands the choice of the priestly tradition as theological. Christopher Begg, "Ben Sirach's Non-Mention of Ezra," *BN* 42 (1988) 14-18, finds the key to Ben Sira's silence about Ezra in his absence from participation in building projects related to the Temple. Begg detects no anti-Levitical polemic in Sirach.

79. Changing socioeconomic circumstances may explain many emphases in Sirach, on which see Martin Hengel, *Judaism and Hellenism*, 2 vols. (Philadelphia: Fortress, 1974).

80. Ben Sira does not stand in the direct line of Ezra, whose responsibility for instructing the people in the law of their God was tantamount, and yet both men were teachers. Ben Sira links up much more closely with the unknown authors of Proverbs, but with decisive differences. He embraces the entire sacral tradition and integrates it into wisdom instruction.

81. With the assassination of the weak Onias III, Simeon's line came to an end. According to P. C. Beentjes, " 'The Countries Marveled at You.' King Solomon in Ben Sira 47:12-22," *BTfuT* 45 (1984) 13, Ben Sira's goal in writing the history of Israel was "the perpetuation of and the succession of the priestly dynasty of Simeon and his descendants," their rule signifying divine activity.

82. P. C. Beentjes, "Hezekiah and Isaiah: A Study on Ben Sira xlviii 15-25," *OTS* 25 (1989) 77-88, esp. 81-82, calls attention to differences between the biblical account of Hezekiah's fortifications and that by Ben Sira.

83. Peter Höffken, "Warum schwieg Jesus Sirach über Esra."

84. Christopher Begg, "Ben Sirach's Non-Mention of Ezra," *BN* 42 (1988).

85. Harry M. Orlinsky, "Some Terms in the Prologue to Ben Sira and the Hebrew Canon," *JBL* 110 (1991) 483-90, insists that the first two divisions of the HB were already fixed in the time of Ben Sira's grandson, hence should be capitalized—Law and Prophets.

86. The inclusion of Job among the prophets accords with an ancient Jewish tradition, although the book usually appears, in varying sequence, among the Writings.

7. Israel Levi, "Sirach, the Wisdom of Jesus the Son of," *The Jewish Encyclopedia* 11 (New York and London: Funk and Wagnalls, 1905) 390-92, discusses the book's popularity among Jews and Christians.

88. *Sanhedrin* 28a.

89. *Yadayim* 2.13.

90. According to Gilbert, "The Book of Ben Sira: Implications for Jewish and Christian Traditions," in *Jewish Civilization in the Hellenistic-Roman Period*,

ed. Shamaryahu Talmon (Sheffield: JSOT, 1991) 87, Jerome quotes Ben Sira eighty times in his works.

91. Luke Timothy Johnson, *The Letter of James*, AB 37A (New York: Doubleday, 1995) 33-34, calls attention to similarities and differences between wisdom literature generally and the Epistle of James. Hubert Frankemolle, "Zum Thema des Jakobusbriefe im Kontext der Rezeption von Sir 2:1-18 und 15:11-20," *BN* 48 (1989) 21-49, stresses the affinities, at least in one respect.

92. Patrick W. Skehan and Alexander A. Di Lella, *The Wisdom of Ben Sira*, AB 39 (New York: Doubleday, 1987) 53.

93. Patrick W. Skehan and Alexander A. Di Lella, *The Wisdom of Ben Sira*, 52.

THE BOOK OF
BARUCH

BY ANTHONY J. SALDARINI

The book of Baruch is a five-chapter pseudepigraphic work attributed to Baruch, the highly placed Jerusalem scribe who appears in the book of Jeremiah (chaps. 32; 36; 43; 45). It is often called 1 Baruch to distinguish it from *2* and *3 Baruch*, apocalyptic narratives from the late first and second centuries CE and from *4 Baruch*, or *Paraleipomena of Jeremiah*, a narrative about the destruction of the Temple in 586 BCE. Baruch is part of a cluster of writings associated with the prophet Jeremiah and the destruction of the Temple in 586 BCE. It is extant in Greek, though parts or all of it were translated from a Hebrew original. In the Septuagint it immediately follows the book of Jeremiah and precedes Lamentations; in the Vulgate it follows Lamentations and includes the Letter of Jeremiah as a sixth chapter. Baruch is recognized as canonical by Roman Catholics and the Orthodox communities. It is not recognized as canonical by the Jewish and Protestant communities, but is classified with the apocrypha.

Many commentators have described Baruch as a very derivative, composite work, lacking in originality and unity, and "substandard" in comparison with the Hebrew Bible. Carey Moore, for example, explains that the Christian church bypassed Baruch because "the book's literary style, which at best is uneven in quality, was not sufficiently strong or memorable to compensate for the book's theological and religious weaknesses, especially in the book's lack of originality and consistency."[1] Such comments imply that Baruch and other Second Temple Jewish literature reflect a time of decline. They fail to appreciate the vitality and creativity of Second Temple Jewish literature, of which Baruch is an example. Like all prayers and poems of that era, Baruch uses biblical words, phrases, themes, and ideas. But Baruch and Second Temple literature are notable for their innovative uses of biblical traditions to meet new circumstances and to express intense community distress and aspirations.

STRUCTURE, UNITY, AND GENRES

Baruch may be divided into four uneven parts, the first two of which are prose and the second two, poetry: (1) narrative introduction (1:1-14); (2) prayer of confession and repentance (1:15–3:8); (3) wisdom poem of admonition and exhortation (3:9–4:4); (4) poem of consolation and encouragement (4:5–5:9). Their distinctive styles, themes, and language have led commentators to postulate multiple authors or to deny to the book any coherence or substantial unity. Although the parts of Baruch are based on biblical and Second Temple models and may have been written independently before being incorporated into the final work, the final author has linked the parts with words, themes, and traditions so that they work together to form a rhetorical and literary unity. Such composite works, which underwent extensive editing, are common in Second Temple literature (see, e.g., *1 Enoch; Testaments of the Twelve Patriarchs*) as well as in the Bible (see, e.g., Daniel and especially the versions of the book of Jeremiah to which Baruch is related). In Baruch the final author has melded the parts into a dramatic whole. After he sets the scene in the introduction, he moves from suffering and repentance for sin (1:15–3:8) to devotion, to wisdom and obedience, and to God's commands (3:9–4:4); he concludes with encouragement to persevere in suffering and with the promise of divine intervention (4:5–5:9).

LANGUAGES

Baruch is extant in a Greek version that was probably translated from a Hebrew original. Translations of Baruch into Latin, Syriac, Coptic,

Ethiopic, Armenian, and Arabic have also survived. The Syriac version is especially helpful in interpreting the Greek. The majority of scholars agree that the Greek of the prayer of confession and repentance, along with the introduction (1:1–3:8), was translated from Hebrew. The Greek contains Hebraisms (e.g., 2:26, literally in Greek, "where your name has been called over it") and translation errors (e.g., 1:9, where the Greek translator chose the wrong meaning for the Hebrew מסגר [masgēr], which can refer either to "prisoners" or to "smiths." In general, a comparison of the Greek version of Jeremiah with Baruch 1:15–3:8 indicates that the same person translated both Jeremiah and Baruch from Hebrew.[2] Whether the wisdom poem and the poem of consolation and encouragement derive from Hebrew originals is still debated, though a successful retroversion of these poems into Hebrew with extensive commentary by David Burke has tipped the balance toward a Hebrew original.[3]

DATES AND PROVENANCE

Since Baruch contains four distinct sections, many scholars assign separate dates to them and another to the final form of the book. Modern commentators generally place the final form somewhere in the Greco-Roman period, from 300 BCE to 135 CE, not in the Babylonian period assigned it by the narrative frame. Beyond that there is little consensus. All acknowledge that the book contains only the vaguest allusions to events contemporary with the author(s) and that since the book is couched in traditional language, it has a "timeless" quality. Arguments for the dates of the book and its parts depend upon the Greek translation of the book, literary relationships with other works, and the tone and atmosphere of the whole book.

1. The Greek Translation of Baruch 1:1–3:8. As noted in the section on language, the prayer of confession and repentance was translated from Hebrew into Greek by the same person who translated Jeremiah. Since the grandson of Ben Sira, who translated the Wisdom of Ben Sira (Ecclesiasticus) into Greek in Egypt by 116 BCE, refers to the Law and the Prophets as a well-known and accepted collection in the Greek-speaking community of Alexandria, the Greek version of Baruch 1:1–3:8 must have been completed before 116 BCE.

2. Literary Relationships. The prayer of confession and repentance (Baruch 1:15–2:18) has a detailed literary relationship with the Hebrew prayer of repentance in Dan 9:4-19. Many have interpreted Baruch 1:15–2:8 as dependent on Daniel 9 and thus later than 165 BCE.[4] However the type of dependency and the dates of both works are uncertain. Even though the prayer in Baruch is much more expansive that that in Daniel, both may have independently adapted an earlier prayer that is now lost. Even if Baruch depends on Daniel 9, the prayer in Daniel 9 is probably an earlier work incorporated into the apocalyptic visions of Daniel 7–12.[5]

The poem of consolation and encouragement (Baruch 4:5–5:9) contains a passage (Baruch 5:5-9) that has a close literary relationship with *Psalms of Solomon* 11. Commentators have frequently used this relationship to date either the poem of consolation and encouragement or the whole of the book of Baruch, but uncertainties about the literary relationship and the date of *Psalms of Solomon* 11 undermine the arguments for the date of Baruch. Many commentators have argued that the author of Baruch used *Psalms of Solomon* 11 because they see Baruch as more tightly organized and literarily unified.[6] But other commentators have argued that *Psalms of Solomon* is dependent on Baruch.[7] On the other hand, the poem is so traditional in language and thought that both *Psalms of Solomon* 11 and Baruch 5 could be independent variations on a common source.

Thus arguments that the whole of Baruch or at least the last section is based on the date of the *Psalms of Solomon* (after the Roman conquest in 63 BCE, since these psalms allude to Pompey, the Roman general) rest on shaky ground. In addition, some commentators think that *Psalms of Solomon* 11 may have been an earlier poem incorporated into the collection.[8] If so, then the author of Baruch would have had access to this psalm before 63 BCE.

In summary, a hypothesis of a common source for the *Psalms of Solomon* 11 and Bar 5:5-9 is more consonant with the shared themes, forms, and expressions found in Second Temple Jewish prayers. The author of Baruch draws upon widespread and deeply felt hopes for the vindication and reconstitution of Israel as a nation under God's protection. Baruch's literary relationships with Daniel 9 and *Psalms of Solomon* 11 locate Baruch solidly within the Second Temple period but do not support a more precise date. Similarly, the thought and wording throughout Baruch depend on the biblical Law and Prophets, especially Deuteronomy, Jeremiah, and Isaiah 40–66. Thus Baruch is probably from the Hellenistic period (late 4th cent. BCE on), when the OT canon began to take shape and became communally recognized.

3. Internal Evidence. The internal atmosphere of the book and allusions to its time of composition are vague and sometimes contradictory. The introduction (1:1-14), which assumes goodwill toward the reigning monarchs for whom it requests prayers, contrasts to the final prayer of consolation and encouragement, which manifests intense anger against the oppressive nations (see 4:31-35). The chronology of the introduction understands the deportation as a recent event (1:11-12), but the wisdom poem alludes to an exile of long duration (2:4-5; 3:10-11; 4:2-3). In the introduction either the Temple is standing (1:10) or sacrifices are being offered at the Temple site in Jerusalem, but in the prayer of repentance the Temple has been destroyed (2:26). As noted previously the content of the prayers resembles that of Second Temple literature in general and does not help with dating.

4. Conclusion. The Greek period (332–63 BCE) is the most probable setting for most of the materials in Baruch, and within that period the second century has found most favor with commentators.[9] The lack of a detailed polemic and crisis atmosphere leads Moore to place Baruch early in the second century BCE, before the Maccabean war with Antiochus IV (167–164 BCE) and the conflicts with his successors.[10] Others, such as Goldstein (followed by Steck), put it after the Maccabean war.[11] Other scholars differ and put Baruch in the Roman-Herodian period (63 BCE–70 CE) with its simultaneous accommodation to Roman rule and fierce resentment of oppression. Others associate the hope of restoration in Baruch with the aftermath of the destruction of the Temple by the Romans in 70 CE.[12] In the end, no firm and widely persuasive conclusion has been reached because the urgent prayers of Israel, the lamentation over the sufferings of exile, and the hopes for the restoration of Israel and Jerusalem are common themes in Jewish literature from the sixth century BCE to the second century CE and have a protean quality that allows them to be applied to various situations.

PLACE, AUTHORSHIP, AUDIENCE, AND PURPOSE

Baruch as a whole is oriented toward Jerusalem. The author addresses a personified Jerusalem and her inhabitants; and Jerusalem addresses the exiles, her former inhabitants. The prayers and exhortations seek the restoration of Jerusalem and her inhabitants. Exile is a temporary state, to be ended by God's intervention. Thus Baruch probably originated in Jerusalem. The author knew thoroughly the biblical and Second Temple traditions and supported worship at the Temple, the holiness of Jerusalem, the restoration of Israel, and obedience to the Torah. Baruch, the pseudonymous author chosen for the book, was a highly placed Jerusalem scribe in the time of Jeremiah. The author may also have been a teacher or an official in Jerusalem, part of a learned circle devoted to the study and promotion of the traditions of Israel. In the swirl of Hellenistic conflicts and threats to safety, the author sought to influence the outlooks, commitments, and policies of the Jerusalem leadership and people. Political, social, cultural, and religious groups were numerous and varied during this period. The book of Baruch encouraged all to adhere to the traditional deuteronomic theology, the wisdom of Israel articulated in the Torah, the commandments as a guide for life, and the post-exilic prophetic hopes for restoration of Jerusalem and Israel. It sought to clarify and establish the political, social, and religious traditions of Israel in Jewish society and to guide Jews in their responses to oppressive imperial rule and attractive foreign culture.

THOUGHT AND THEOLOGY

Baruch draws upon the traditions of Israel as they developed from the Babylonian exile (586 BCE) through the Second Temple period. Each of the parts of Baruch has been influenced by different biblical books and traditions—for example, but not exclusively, 1:15–3:8 by Daniel 9, Jeremiah, and Deuteronomy; 3:9–4:4 by Job 28 and the wisdom tradition, and 4:5–5:9 by Isaiah 40–66. The theological emphases of each section correspond to their literary genres and purposes. The confession and prayer of repentance addresses God with the liturgically proper title "Lord" and petitions for forgiveness. The wisdom poem addresses God with the most general and universal Greek word for "God", θεός (*theos*), in the manner of international wisdom. Despite that, the author identifies true wisdom with the biblical law (Torah) and wise behavior with obedience to God's commandments, as do other second-century writings, such as Sirach (Ecclesiasticus) 24. The poem of consolation and encouragement promises the eventual restoration of Israel and Jerusalem and the overcoming of the nations who dominate and oppress them. Here God is frequently designated as eternal or everlasting, as befits God's comprehensive, long-term restorative role.

The particularities of Baruch can best be seen against the background of the outlooks, political stances, and religious programs of other Jewish literature and groups in the Second Temple period. Contrary to many sectarian polemical texts, such as those found at Qumran, Baruch does not distinguish between those Jews who are faithful to a certain way of keeping the law and those who are unfaithful. The author of Baruch invites all Jews to acknowledge the nation's sinfulness, to repent, to obey the commandments, and to hope for divine assistance. He desires the reunification of all exiles with the Judeans in the land, and his norms for correct attitudes and behavior are drawn from the mainstream biblical traditions without emphasis on special practices or beliefs. The arguments over laws and calendar found in the book of *Jubilees*, the *Damascus Document*, and other works are entirely absent.

Baruch does not promote any of the new beliefs and world views that appeared in apocalyptic literature. Like the Hebrew Bible (except for Daniel 12), Baruch does not look forward to life after death but expects divine intervention and restoration of Israel in this world. The nations, which have persecuted Israel, will be punished and subjugated; but no messiah will come to defeat them or lead Israel, nor is any universal judgment or wholesale destruction envisioned. Rather, the desired result of the restoration is for Israel to dwell in its land in peace. Special revelations and cosmic battles between good and evil, such as those found in Daniel, do not appear here.

The author of Baruch has produced a middle-of-the-road, traditional theology to which Israel can adhere under all circumstances. Baruch's very generality and lack of originality, for which it has often been criticized, made it attractive and available to Jews of every inclination. The book seems to have been especially useful to Jews in the Greek-speaking diaspora, since it survived in Greek.

Baruch has not been greatly or directly influential on Christian literature. It shares with Christianity a stress on confession and repentance for sin, but both derived it from the Hebrew Bible. The sin of sacrificing to demons rather than to God appears in 1 Cor 10:20 and Baruch 4:5, but both may be dependent on Deut 32:17. Both Baruch and Paul attack Greco-Roman wisdom as false (Baruch 3:16-28; 1 Cor 1:18-25), but no direct literary relationship can be established.

The wisdom poem in Baruch may have had a literary influence on Paul's Letter to the Romans and the Gospel of John. Paul's argument that one does not need to ascend to heaven or descend into the abyss to find righteousness (Rom 10:6-8) is based on Deut 30:12-14, a text that has also influenced Baruch 3:29-30. Baruch stresses both the impossibility of humans' finding wisdom on their own and the presence of wisdom among humans as a divine gift (Baruch 3:36–4:1). This interpretation and elaboration of Deuteronomy accords closely with Paul's analysis of the divine gift of righteousness brought by Jesus.

Baruch 3:29–4:4 also speaks of wisdom in a way parallel to the Gospel of John's discourse about Jesus the son of God in John 3:13-21 and 31-36. In both Baruch and John humans cannot ascend to heaven to get wisdom, but rather wisdom in Baruch and the son of the Father in John descend from heaven to humans as a divine gift. In Baruch, wisdom is associated with life, light, and salvation, as is Jesus in John. Wisdom understood as the law dwells with Israel in Baruch just as Jesus dwells with humans as the truth, the word, and the way in John. In Deuteronomy 30, Baruch, and John, God's presence on earth (commandments, wisdom, Jesus) is available to all who will accept it.[13]

FOR FURTHER READING

Commentaries:

Fitzgerald, Aloysius. "Baruch." *New Jerome Biblical Commentary.* Edited by Raymond Brown et al. Englewood Cliffs, N.J.: Prentice-Hall, 1990.

Harrington, Daniel J. "Baruch." In *Harper's Bible Commentary.* Edited by James L. Mays. San Francisco: Harper & Row, 1988.

Moore, Carey A. *Daniel, Esther, and Jeremiah: The Additions.* AB 44. Garden City, N.Y.: Doubleday, 1977.

Steck, Odil Hannes. *Dask apokryphe Baruchbuch: Studien zu Rezeption und Konzentration "kanonischer" Überlieferung.* Göttingen: Vandenhoeck & Ruprecht, 1993.

Whitehouse, O. C. "1 Baruch." In *The Apocrypha and Pseudepigrapha of the Old Testament.* Volume 1. Edited by R. H. Charles. Oxford: Clarendon, 1913.

Other Studies:

Nickelsburg, George W. E. "The Bible Rewritten and Expanded." In *Jewish Writings of the Second Temple Period.* Edited by Michael E. Stone. Philadelphia: Fortress, 1984.

———. *Jewish Literature Between the Bible and the Mishnah.* Philadelphia: Fortress, 1981.

Schürer, Emil, Geza Vermes, Fergus Millar, and Martin Goodman. *The History of the Jewish People in the Age of Jesus Christ (175 B.C.–A.D. 135).* Volume 3.2. Edinburgh: T & T Clark, 1987.

ENDNOTES

1. Carey A. Moore, *Daniel, Esther and Jeremiah: The Additions,* AB 44 (Garden City, N.Y.: Doubleday, 1977) 261.

2. Emanuel Tov, *The Septuagint Translation of Jeremiah and Baruch: A Discussion of an Early Revision of the LXX of Jeremiah 29–52 and Baruch 1:1–3:15,* HSM 8 (Missoula, Mont.: Scholars Press, 1976) 111-33.

3. David G. Burke, *The Poetry of Baruch: A Reconstruction and Analysis of the Original Hebrew Text of Baruch 3:9–5:9,* SBLSCS 10 (Chico, Calif.: Scholars Press, 1982). A hundred years previously J. J. Kneucker, *Das Buch Baruch. Geschichte und Kritik, Übersetzung, und Erklärung* (Leipzig: Brockhaus, 1879), also provided a retroversion with extensive comments. For arguments pro and con see R. H. Pfeiffer, *History of New Testament Times with an Introduction to the Apocrypha* (New York: Harper, 1949) 417-21, and George W. E. Nickelsburg, "The Bible Rewritten and Expanded" in *Jewish Writings of the Second Temple Period,* ed. Michael E. Stone (Philadelphia: Fortress, 1984) 144-45.

4. E.g., Odil Hannes Steck, *Das apokryphe Baruchbuch: Studien zu Rezeption und Konzentration "kanonischer" Überlieferung* (Göttingen: Vandenhoeck & Ruprecht, 1993) 88-92, 286,

argues that Baruch used Daniel 9 as it appears in the context of Daniel 7–12 and like that text it stems from the Maccabean crisis in the 160s BCE.

5. John J. Collins, *Daniel,* Hermeneia (Minneapolis: Fortress, 1993) 359, notes correctly that "the prayer in Daniel 9 is a traditional piece that could have been composed at any time after the Exile."

6. Carey A. Moore, *Daniel, Esther, and Jeremiah: The Additions,* 314-16, argues that the close parallels are confined to Baruch 5:5-9 and that the past tenses inserted into 5:8-9 indicate that Baruch is secondary to the Psalms of Solomon. But he also argues that Baruch 5:5-9 was added to the end of Baruch at a later date, so that the parallels with Psalms of Solomon cannot be used to date Baruch. Rather, Baruch 4:5–5:4 could be from the early second century or even the previous two centuries BCE. Jonathan A. Goldstein, "The Apocryphal Book of Baruch," *PAAJR* 46-47 (1979-80) 191-92n. 41, argues against Moore's case for the secondary nature of Baruch 5:5-9.

7. Wilhelm Pesch, "Die Abhängigkeit des 11. Salomonischen Psalms vom letzten Kapitel des Buches Baruch," *ZAW* 67 (1955) 251-63; David G. Burke, *The Poetry of Baruch,* 30, following Pesch; Hannes Steck, *Das apokryphe Baruchbuch,* 240-42, further argues that Baruch 4:5–5:9 is so integrally related to the whole of Baruch that it is an original composition and never existed as an independent poem.

8. George W. E. Nickelsburg, "The Bible Rewritten and Expanded," 145n. 327.

9. See the detailed survey of numerous scholars of the past two centuries in David G. Burke, *The Poetry of Baruch,* 26-29.

10. Carey A. Moore, *Daniel, Esther, and Jeremiah: The Additions,* 260.

11. Jonathan A. Goldstein, "The Apocryphal Book of Baruch"; Hannes Steck, *Das apokryphe Baruchbuch,* 294-303; George W. E. Nickelsburg, *Jewish Literature Between the Bible and the Mishnah* (Philadelphia: Fortress, 1981) 113-14, opts for either the early second century BCE or the Maccabean period. According to Goldstein, the author of Baruch was promoting peaceful coexistence with the Seleucids through cooperation with Antiochus V after the death of his father, the notorious Antiochus IV, and after the rededication of the Temple. In this scenario, the hostility toward the

nations would be a response to the oppression suffered during and after the reign of Antiochus IV Epiphanes, and the goodwill toward the ruling powers in the introduction (1:11-12) would reflect the gradually emerging detente with the Seleucids.

12. Doron Mendels, "Baruch, Book of," *ABD* 1:620, prefers either post-70 or early second century BCE. Emil Schürer, Geza Vermes, Fergus Millar, and Martin Goodman, *The History of the Jewish People in the Age of Jesus Christ (175 B.C.–A.D. 135)*, vol. 3.2 (Edinburgh: T & T Clark, 1987) 737-38, suggest that the introduction, the compilation of Baruch, and perhaps the last section (4:5–5:9) are post-70 CE.

13. For an analysis of the detailed relationships between John and Baruch, see Norman R. Petersen, *The Gospel of John and the Sociology of Light: Language and Characterization in the Fourth Gospel* (Valley Forge, Pa.: Trinity, 1993) 114-19.

THE LETTER OF
JEREMIAH

ANTHONY J. SALDARINI

The Epistle of Jeremiah survives in Greek as well as in many versions, such as Syriac, Arabic, Coptic, Ethiopic, and Latin. In some Greek mss (e.g., Alexandrinus, Vaticanus) and in the Syriac Hexapla and the Arabic, the epistle is separated from Baruch by Lamentations. In later LXX and other Syriac mss and in the old Latin, the epistle comes right after Baruch. In the Vulgate, the KJV, and Catholic Bibles, the epistle is included as chapter 6 of Baruch, which itself follows Jeremiah.

GENRE AND LITERARY STRUCTURE

The superscription of the epistle (v. 1) identifies it as a copy of a letter sent by the prophet Jeremiah to Judean prisoners who were about to be shipped to Babylon. The next six verses (vv. 2-7) directly address the exiles in a form consistent with a letter and also provide a narrative framework for the document. However, the rest of the epistle consists of satirical parodies and polemics against idols[1] and prophetic admonitions and warnings,[2] all of which have literary links with the Hebrew Bible, especially the book of Jeremiah.[3] Whether the epistle is thought of as an ancient letter depends on how flexibly the letter genre is understood.[4] The first seven verses of the epistle parallel the letter Jeremiah sent to the Babylonian exiles (Jeremiah 29),[5] and the epistle is clearly meant to supplement the materials found in the book of Jeremiah. Although the epistle's language is very much like a tract, it also addresses the exiles in its exhortatory refrains as one would address the recipients of a letter.

After the introduction (vv. 1-7), the polemics, instructions, and exhortations may be divided into ten sections: vv. 8-16, vv. 17-23, vv. 24-29, vv. 30-40*a*, vv. 40*b*-44, vv. 45-52, vv. 53-56, vv. 57-65, vv. 66-69, and vv. 70-73. Each division concludes with a refrain, which argues that the statues of the gods are not really gods and, therefore, should not be feared: "From this it is evident that they are not gods; so do not fear them" (v. 16; similarly vv. 23, 29, 65, 69); "Why then must anyone think that they are gods, or call them gods?" (v. 40; similarly vv. 44, 51, 56, 72). Similar rhetorical questions and statements also appear within sections four (v. 30), six (vv. 47, 49, 51), and eight (vv. 59, 64). These refrains keep before the reader the main themes of the epistle, "beware of becoming at all like the foreigners or of letting fear for these gods possess you" (v. 5), and "It is you, O Lord, whom we must worship" (v. 6). The fear motif comes from Jeremiah 10, which has influenced the whole epistle: "Their idols are like scarecrows in a cucumber field,/ and they cannot speak;/ they have to be carried,/ for they cannot walk./ *Do not be afraid of them,*/ for they cannot do evil,/ nor is it in them to do good" (Jer 10:5, italics added; cf. Ep Jer 5, 70). Thus the Epistle of Jeremiah, despite its repletion, transmits a unified message within the Jeremiah tradition. The Targum on Jer 10:11 says that the Aramaic slogan in that verse was quoted from this epistle, but the Targum is a late and unreliable source for this kind of information. However, the theme of Jer 10:11, "The gods who did not make the heavens and the earth shall perish from the earth and from under the heavens" (NRSV), fits well the content and focus of the epistle.

Within this narrative and thematic framework, the epistle's polemical observations and arguments are repeated frequently, often without discernible order. This repetition has led commentators to outdo one another in criticizing it. Ball wonders how a work "so formless, so confused, so utterly destitute of the graces of style" could have been preserved in the Alexandrian canon. "We are presented with a voluble but ill-connected succession of propositions, bearing little visible relation to each other beyond general animus against idolatry."[6] Torrey agreed more briefly: "It is a formless composition, rambling and repetitious."[7] Carey Moore describes the epistle more precisely: "Apart from a not infrequent uncertainty as to the antecedents of its pronouns, the text is intelligible enough; but its images, analogies, and comparison are rarely new and never memorable. After the first three or four stanzas there is no further development or progression of thought; rather, the same old observations and arguments are rehashed."[8]

Others have seen more structure to the argument. The Greek conjunction γάρ (*gar*, "for") links arguments and observations in vv. 7, 8, 17, 24, 30, 50, 53, 60, 66, and 70. (These connectives are not always translated in the NRSV.) Similarly, the connective particle δέ (*de*) appears in v. 43 and the conjunction οὖν (*oun*, "therefore") in vv. 49, 51, 56, and 64. Although the lines of argument and coherence are often unclear, a recent study has divided the argument into two parts (vv. 8-29 and 30-73), with each subdivided into three sections (vv. 8-16, 17-23, 24-29 and vv. 30-65 [with subdivisions], 66-69, 70-73.)[9] Suffice it to say that the epistle marshals abundant, related evidence against the reality of the gods, but it lacks a tightly structured argument.

In form and content the Epistle of Jeremiah is closely related to the Hebrew Bible and other Second Temple literature. The rejection of statues and images of God as well as of other gods is found in the Ten Commandments (Exod 20:3-5; Deut 5:7-9) and other biblical laws (Exod 34:17; Lev 19:4; 26:1; Deut 4:16, 23; 27:15). But the Epistle of Jeremiah addresses the danger of idolatry in exile (cf. Deut 4:27-28) more specifically by drawing upon the prophetic and cultic polemics against idols (Pss 115:3-8; 135:15-18; Isa 40:18-20; 41:6-7; 44:9-20; 46:1-8; Hab 2:18-19). These materials have been drawn into the Jeremiah tradition and organized under the influence of the polemic against idols in Jer 10:1-16 and the letter to the exiles in Jeremiah 29.[10] Presumably the author of the Epistle of Jeremiah sought to address new dangers by gathering and reinterpreting the anti-idol materials in the prophets, especially Jeremiah. The epistle was one of a number of Second Temple compositions that addressed the problem of idolatry through polemic and parody (see Wis 13:10-19; 15:7-13; Bel and the Dragon; *Jub.* 12:2-5; 20:8-9). The author, who probably wrote in Hebrew, used the Hebrew version of Jeremiah, not

the Greek. The image of the scarecrow in the cucumber patch (v. 70) comes from the Hebrew of Jer 10:5, but is missing in the Greek.

In a recent study, R. G. Kratz argues that the Epistle of Jeremiah is an orderly interpretation and rewriting of Jer 10:1-16 for a new situation rather than a random borrowing of themes and motifs. Thus Jer 10:2-3*a* and Ep Jer 4–6 each introduces its respective polemics. Jeremiah 10:3*b*-5*a* (along with Jer 10:9, 14) provided the themes of the first part of the epistle (vv. 8-29), and Jer 10:5*b*-16 the themes for the second, longer and more complex part (vv. 30-73).[11] Kratz places the epistle within the chronological framework of the Jeremiah tradition, which was itself undergoing extensive editing during the Persian and Greek periods. The writer of the epistle was adapting the Jeremiah tradition to his own situation in the third century BCE, which required long-term resistance to idolatry.[12] Thus the Epistle of Jeremiah is not a pale imitation of Jeremiah; rather, it is part of a vital and developing complex of prophetic traditions that were giving guidance to Jewish communities in the Hellenistic age.

LANGUAGE, DATE AND PLACE

The Epistle of Jeremiah has survived only in Greek as part of the LXX. The earliest ms evidence for the epistle is a very fragmentary copy of vv. 43-44 in Greek.[13] However, a number of peculiarities in the Greek suggest that it was translated from a Hebrew original.[14] The clearest translation error, corrected by most English versions, is found in v. 72. The Greek reads, literally: "From the purple and marble that rot upon them [the statues of the gods] you will know that they are not gods." Since marble does not rot, the statement is incoherent. However, the Hebrew word for "marble" or "alabaster" (שֵׁשׁ *šēš*) also means "linen," which here would refer to the statues' clothing, which does rot. Similarly, in v. 12 the Greek says literally that the statues "cannot save themselves from rust and food" (the NRSV's "rust and corrosion" comes from a Greek variant reading). The translator probably read the Hebrew letters מאכל (*m'kl*) as מַאֲכָל (*maʾăkāl*), "food," rather than as מֵאֹכֵל (*mēʾōkēl*), "the devourer," that is, a moth. Thus the Hebrew original referred to rust corroding the metal overlay of the statues and moths eating away at the clothing. Elsewhere, in the middle of an argument that the statues of the gods are powerless, they are said to be "like crows between heaven and earth" (v. 55), an unusually obscure simile. However, the Hebrew consonants for the word "crows" (ערבים 'rbym) could easily have been confused with "clouds" (עבים 'bym) by the translator. Other suggested mistranslations are less certain but improve the text. In "for just as someone's dish is useless when it is broken" (v. 17), "someone's dish" (אדם כלי kly 'dm; lit., "dish of a man") in Hebrew may have resulted from a misreading of כלי אדמה (kly 'dmh), "ceramic/earthen disk" (lit., "dish of earth"). In general, the Greek of the epistle has many Semitic characteristics and can be easily retroverted into Hebrew, so the likelihood of a Hebrew original is generally accepted.

The epistle can be assigned no secure date. It has been most frequently placed in the Hellenistic period (332–63 BCE). The Qumran Greek ms fragment of vv. 43-44 mentioned above was copied in about 100 BCE. The epistle may be referred to in 2 Macc 2:2, which recounts that Jeremiah "instructed those who were being deported [to Babylon] not . . . to be led astray in their thoughts on seeing the gold and silver statues and their adornment" (NRSV). The cover letter of 2 Maccabees (2 Macc 1:1-9) is dated in 124 BCE, and the letter it introduces (2 Macc 1:10–2:18) is generally thought to be earlier, perhaps soon after the rededication of the Temple in 164 BCE. These two pieces of external evidence suggest that the Epistle of Jeremiah was composed in the second century or earlier. Some commentators have taken the reference to seven generations (v. 3) literally and calculated a period of 280 years from 597 or 586 to the late fourth century (317 and 306 BCE).[15] But chronological notices of this kind are conventional and symbolic. Jeremiah speaks of seventy years (Jer 25:12; 29:10) and three generations (Jer 27:7). Daniel reinterpreted this period into seventy weeks of years (Dan 9:2, 24-27), and it may be that the author is here engaged in a similar enterprise. If so, then such chronological notices are not accurate indicators for the document's date of composition. The content and purpose of the epistle, to delegitimate other gods so that Israel will not worship them, are so general that they may pertain to any time in the Persian and Greek periods.[16]

The narrative framework of the introduction refers to the Babylonian period and to Babylonian gods. More substantively, the types of statues, processions, dressing, feeding, and care of the gods that are alluded to and mocked in the polemics of the epistle (vv. 15-22, 29-39, 40-44, 57-58) match closely what we know of Babylonian worship.[17] But Babylonian worship continued throughout the Persian and Greek periods, and Greeks, Egyptians, Syrians, and Mesopotamians worshiped and used statues of gods in analogous and similar ways. In addition, polemics and parodies against the gods were common in Hellenistic literature.[18] Thus the author of the Hebrew original of the epistle may have been in the Babylonian[19] or Judean Jewish community. There is no sign of specifically Egyptian influence except for the mention of cats (v. 22), which were first domesticated in Egypt.

THEMES

The extensive attack on the Near Eastern gods supports the main theme and goal of the Epistle of Jeremiah: that Israel should worship only the God of the Bible (v. 6) and not fear foreign gods (v. 5). The list of polemical charges brought against the statues of the gods is long, detailed, and repetitious. In general, the author lists exhaustively the gods' lack of all the attributes and aptitudes generally expected of gods in the ancient Near East. In making this attack, the epistle contrasts the ancient intuition of divine power and presence in the statues with the perceptible inactivity of those images of the gods.[20] The author repeats constantly that the gods are made of wood overlaid with gold and silver (vv. 30, 39, 55, 57-58, 70-71) and that they, far from being creators, were made by human craftsmen (vv. 4, 8-9, 39, 45-47, 50, 57) who themselves will die (v. 46). The gods cannot care for themselves or help themselves in time of crisis (vv. 12-15, 18-21, 24, 27, 55). They cannot move, but must be carried (vv. 4, 26-27, 55, 68) and must be clothed by humans (vv. 9-11). They cannot speak, see, or touch (vv. 8, 19, 41); in short, they have no breath or life within them (vv. 25, 27).

These gods cannot do good or evil for their worshipers or for themselves (vv. 34-38, 48-49, 53, 64, 67). They do not rule the heavens (vv. 60-63), make or break kings (vv. 34, 53, 66), fight wars, enforce judgments, help their clients, or protect themselves from theft (vv. 14-15, 18, 53-55, 57-59). Their wooden cores, metal plating, and clothing deteriorate (vv. 12, 20, 72). They are served by dishonest priests who steal from them (vv. 10, 28, 33). Their cults are improper and impure (judged by biblical standards), because priests have torn clothing and shaved heads (vv. 31-32) and because impure women and prostitutes serve them (vv. 11, 29-30, 42-43). As a result, these gods bring dishonor and shame upon their worshipers (vv. 26, 39-40, 47, 72-73).

FOR FURTHER READING

Commentaries:

Ball, Charles J. "Epistle of Jeremy." in *Apocrypha and Pseudepigrapha of the Old Testament.* Edited by R. H. Charles. Oxford: Clarendon, 1913.

Fitzgerald, Alysius. "Baruch." *New Jerome Biblical Commentary.* Edited by Raymond Brown et al. Englewood Cliffs, N.J.: Prentice-Hall, 1990.

Harrington, Daniel J. "Letter of Jeremiah." In *Harper's Bible Commentary.* Edited by James L. Mays. San Francisco: Harper & Row, 1988.

Moore, Cary A. *Daniel, Esther, and Jeremiah: The Additions.* AB 44. Garden City, N.Y.: Doubleday, 1977.

Other Studies:

Nickelsburg, George W. E. "The Bible Rewritten and Expanded." In *Jewish Writings of the Second Temple Period.* Edited by Michael E. Stone. Philadelphia: Fortress, 1984.

———. *Jewish Literature Between the Bible and the Mishnah.* Philadelphia: Fortress, 1981.

Schürer, Emil, Geza Vermes, Fergus Millar, and Martin Goodman. *The History of the Jewish People in the Age of Jesus Christ (175 B.C.–A.D. 135).* Vol. 3.2. Edinburgh: T & T Clark, 1987.

ENDNOTES

1. Wolfgang M. W. Roth, "For Life, He Appeals to Death (Wis 13:18): A Study of Old Testament Idol Parodies," *CBQ* 37 (1975) 21-47, esp. 40-42.

2. Irene Taatz, *Frühjüdische Briefe: Die paulinischen Briefe im Rahmen der offiziellen religiösen Briefe des Frühjudentums* (Göttingen: Vandenhoeck & Ruprecht, 1991) 57-58.

3. For the invocation of the letter form for its authoritative status, even when the genre was not sustained, see Philip S. Alexander, "Epistolary Literature," in *Jewish Writings of the Second Temple Period,* ed. Michael E. Stone (Assen/Philadelphia: Van Gorcum/Fortress, 1984) 584-85 and n. 26.

4. For the broad use of the term *epistle* or *letter* to name ancient documents, see Philip S. Alexander, "Epistolary Literature," 581 and n. 13.

5. Reinhard G. Kratz, "Die Rezeption von Jeremia 10 und 29 im Pseudepigraphen Brief des Jeremia," *JSJ* 26 (1995) 19.

6. Charles J. Ball, "Epistle of Jeremy," *APOT,* 597.

7. C. C. Torrey, *The Apocryphal Literature* (New Haven: Yale University Press, 1945) 65.

8. Carey A. Moore, "Jeremiah, Additions to," *ABD* 3:704.

9. Reinhard G. Kratz, "Die Rezeption von Jeremia 10 und 29 im Pseudepigraphen Brief des Jeremia," 2-31, with a chart on 6-7.

10. W. Roth, "For Life, He Appeals to Death (Wis 13:18)," 41, notes that all the motifs in Jer 10:1-16 appear in the Epistle of Jeremiah.

11. Reinhard G. Kratz, "Die Rezeption von Jeremia 10 und 29 im Pseudepigraphen Brief des Jeremia," 14-15.

12. Reinhard G. Kratz, "Die Rezeption von Jeremia 10 und 29 im Pseudepigraphen Brief des Jeremia," 20-21, 26-29.

13. M. Baillet et al., *Les "Petites Grottes" de Qumrân: Textes,* DJD 3 (Oxford: Clarendon, 1962) 7Q2, 143.

14. The most influential case in English was made by Charles J. Ball, "Epistle of Jeremy," 597-98.

15. See Charles J. Ball, "Epistle of Jeremy," 596; Carey A. Moore, *Daniel, Esther, and Jeremiah: The Additions,* AB 44 (Garden City, N.Y.: Doubleday, 1977) 328, 334-35.

16. Reinhard G. Kratz, "Die Rezeption von Jeremia 10 und 29 im Pseudepigraphen Brief des Jeremia," 30, suggests that the Epistle of Jeremiah is a response to Hellenistic worship that uses the book of Jeremiah in a new way.

17. For a convenient summary of the archaeological evidence for Babylonian worship, see Philip J. King, "Jeremiah and Idolatry," in *Eretz-Israel: Archaeological, Historical and Geographical Studies,* Joseph Aviram Volume 25 (Jerusalem: Israel Exploration Soci-

ety, 1996) 31*-36*. See also Wolfgang M. W. Roth, "For Life, He Appeals to Death (Wis 13:18)," 51, on the Babylonian evidence in the Epistle of Jeremiah. The most extensive case for the Babylonian gods as objects of polemic was made by Weigand Naumann, "Untersuchungen über den apokrynphen Jeremiahsbrief," *BZAW* 25 (1913) 3-31.

18. See the parallels cited in George W. E. Nickelsburg, "The Bible Rewritten and Expanded," 148n. 341.

19. Reinhard G. Kratz, "Die Rezeption von Jeremia 10 und 29 im Pseudepigraphen Brief des Jeremia," 2, suggests a Hebrew or Aramaic original addressed to the Babylonian community and a third-century BCE Greek translation of the Epistle of Jeremiah.

20. For the Mesopotamian gods, see A. L. Oppenheim, *Ancient Mesopotamia: Portrait of a Dead Civilization* (Chicago: University of Chicago Press, 1964) 171-227; T. Jacobsen, "The Graven Image," in *Ancient Israelite Religion: Dedicated to Frank M. Cross*, ed. P. Miller et al. (Philadelphia: Fortress, 1987) 15-32; Philip J. King, "Jeremiah and Idolatry," 33*.

THE ADDITIONS TO
DANIEL

BY DANIEL L. SMITH-CHRISTOPHER

THE GREEK TRANSLATION
OF THE OLD TESTAMENT

The importance of the Greek translations of the Old Testament for biblical and textual research is hard to exaggerate. Indeed, Ernst Würthwein states that the Septuagint is so significant that "apart from it both Christendom and Western Culture would be inconceivable."[1] But how these Greek versions were produced is a controversial subject in scholarly debate.

According to the *Letter of Aristeas*, which scholars date from about the second century BCE into the first century CE, Ptolemy II Philadelphus commissioned the translation of the Jewish Scriptures to be a part of his great library at Alexandria. The text was miraculously translated by seventy-two elders in precisely seventy-two days, thus it was named "Septuagint." The translation was read and proved to be without error by the Jewish community itself. The story gives us the impression that there was one book that was considered "the" Greek version of the Old Testament. But scholarly views of the origin of the Septuagint suggest that the production was considerably more complex than a single event or version, and furthermore had much more to do with the need of Jews in the diaspora for a version of the Bible in their newly adopted language, Greek. The need for a Greek version of the Hebrew Bible sometime after Alexander's conquests of the ancient Near East, therefore, is a measure of cultural change and social transformation in the Jewish community. Scholarly study of the Greek versions of Daniel focuses on two older Greek versions of the book of Daniel: the Old Greek or LXX version and the "Theodotion" version. Moore points out that in the story of Susanna, the differences between the LXX and the Theodotion versions are the greatest, while in the Song of the Three the differ-ences are not very significant.[2] Bel and the Dragon occupies a middle position.

Although the entire Theodotion Old Testament is usually dated to the second century CE, the book of Daniel itself presents special problems. Since the Theodotion version of Daniel is cited in the New Testament, the book of Daniel that became a part of the later Theodotion version must itself be older. This Theodotion version of Daniel, however, became the accepted version for the Christian church, over the Old Greek version. In this commentary, I will use the Theodotion text and occasionally draw attention to differing readings in the LXX.

When these Greek translations were produced, many of the books of the Hebrew Bible were expanded with material that may or may not go back to a Hebrew or Aramaic original. Although, in the case of the additions to Daniel, many scholars argue that these stories do go back to Semitic originals, no evidence of a Semitic language version of these stories has been found as yet.

Writing as a Protestant scholar, I regard it a pity that Protestants generally have little exposure to the Greek additions to Daniel because of Luther's insistence on the Hebrew text as the acceptable canon of the Old Testament, as opposed to the traditional Christian use of the Greek canon of the Old Testament, which included these Deutero-canonical works. Apart from any theological issues of what constituted the canon (which is a doctrinal issue that quite properly has little bearing on scholarly and historical study of texts), these additions are fascinating indicators of concerns and issues in the Jewish community in the late Hellenistic period. A study of the additional Greek material about figures like Jeremiah, Daniel, Esther, and Joseph reveals further concerns with themes of intercultural contact, political occupation and exile, and the traditions of facing foreign power with faith in God's redeeming power. Such issues were on the minds of Jews in Hellenistic and Roman occupied Near Eastern territories from the second century BCE into the common era. We will see in these additions to Daniel that many of the themes of the canonical book of Daniel—sovereignty, resistance, and idolatry, for example—are developed and expanded upon. This also means that a key to understanding these additions, as much as the canonical stories of Daniel, is the experience of disenfranchisement and loss of self-determination that exile, as well as political occupation in one's own homeland, involves.

FOR FURTHER READING

See The Book of Daniel

ENDNOTES

1. Ernst Würthwein, *The Text of the Old Testament*, trans. E. F. Rhoades (Grand Rapids: Eerdmans, 1979) 57.

2. C. A. Moore, *Daniel, Esther, and Jeremiah: The Additions*, AB 44 (Garden City, N.Y.: Doubleday, 1977) 16.

THE FIRST BOOK OF
MACCABEES

ROBERT DORAN

The first and second books of the Maccabees describe the revolt of the Jews in Judea against the Seleucid Empire in the second century BCE. They are two separate works, as 2 Maccabees is not the sequel to 1 Maccabees but an independent telling of the same events. Both works, in different ways, deal with the problem of how Jews were to maintain their own cultural and religious identity within the larger empire of the Seleucids. Both works show how friction grew between the inhabitants of Judea and the Seleucid monarch Antiochus IV Epiphanes, until he decided to outlaw the practice of Judaism within Judea, leading to the profanation of the Temple in Jerusalem. In response to this attack on their culture and religion, various groups of Jews rose up in revolt, spearheaded by the Maccabean family. First Maccabees begins with the actions of Antiochus IV against the Jews and the profanation of the Temple, and it focuses on the first generation of the Maccabees, sometimes called the Hasmoneans, from the father Mattathias through his sons Judas, Jonathan, and Simon. During this time, the Temple was retaken and purified, and the independence of Judea was proclaimed in 142/41 BCE. The narrative ends with the death of Simon in 135/34 BCE. The narrative of 2 Maccabees is preceded by two letters addressed by the Jews in Judea to the Jews in Egypt, requesting that the Egyptian Jews celebrate the Feast of the Purification of the Temple—i.e., the Feast of Hanukkah. The first letter is dated to 124 BCE, while the second purports to be written in the time of Judas Maccabeus. The narrative portion of 2 Maccabees begins in the reign of Antiochus IV's predecessor, Seleucus IV. It provides more details about events leading up to the oppression of Judea in Jerusalem, highlights the martyrdom of Jewish resisters, and concentrates on the figure of Judas Maccabeus. The account ends while Judas is still alive after the defeat of the Seleucid commander Nicanor in 161 or 160 BCE.

HISTORICAL BACKGROUND

The Ancient Near Eastern Setting. Once the dust had settled from the battles over who would inherit Alexander the Great's conquests, three major powers had emerged in the eastern Mediterranean: the Macedonian Empire, the Ptolemaic Empire based in Egypt, and the Seleucid Empire. The Seleucid Empire was the true heir to the Achaemenid, or Persian, Empire. It stretched from the western coast of Asia Minor to present-day Afghanistan and was the largest of the Hellenistic kingdoms. The Seleucid Empire also lay claim to Coelesyria, which the Ptolemaic Empire had controlled since 301 BCE. Size brought its own problems, and the Seleucid kings would see their territory whittled away during the third century BCE. In the west, partly as a result of the Celtic invasions in Asia Minor in 278–277 BCE, various states in Asia Minor arose—Bithynia, Pontus, Cappadocia, and the Attalids at Pergamum. In the east, Bactria and Parthia seceded. Although the Seleucid kings kept an interest in their Iranian possessions, no doubt for reasons of military defense, they did not maintain as strong an influence as in Syria and Mesopotamia. Antiochus III reasserted Seleucid authority in Iran during his expedition there (212–205/4 BCE), for which he assumed the title "Great King," but Parthia and Bactria remained unconquered, and Seleucid control of eastern Iran remained rather superficial. Antiochus III also sought to restore Seleucid control over western Asia Minor and marched into Coelesyria in 202 BCE. He seized control of Coelesyria, Phoenicia, and Palestine with a decisive victory over the Ptolemaic forces at Panium in 200 BCE.

Antiochus's attempt to restore the Seleucid kingdom to its former glory failed, however, for a new player had entered the power game in the eastern Mediterranean. Rome, however hesitatingly and clumsily, was emerging as the dominant

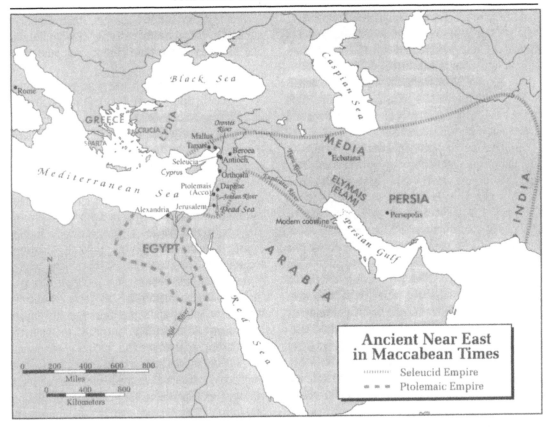

Ancient Near East in Maccabean Times

········· Seleucid Empire

■ ■ ■ Ptolemaic Empire

force. By its victories over Philip V of Macedonia at Cynoscephalae in 197 BCE, over Philip's son Perseus at Pydna in 168 BCE, and finally over the Achaean League in 146 BCE, Rome gained complete control of Macedonia and Greece. Antiochus III also fell before the Romans at Magnesia in 190 BCE, and the subsequent Treaty of Apamea in 188 BCE took away most of his possessions in Asia Minor and saddled him with a heavy indemnity. When Antiochus IV attempted to extend Seleucid influence into Egypt, the Roman envoy C. Popillius Laenas delivered to him the senate's order that he leave Egypt, and he did so in humiliation. Rome was the dominant power in the East from the second century on. The weaker party in any dispute would appeal to Rome, and Rome's representatives were frequently in the East investigating conflicts and advising the senate on solutions.

The Ptolemaic and Seleucid empires would continue, however, although wracked by dynastic struggles between rival claimants to the throne. The Seleucid Empire ended when Pompey the Great annexed Syria in 64 BCE; the Ptolemaic Empire formally lasted longer, ending when Cleopatra VII committed suicide in 30 BCE. While weak, these empires could still muster impressive forces. Antiochus VII Sidetes invaded Judea in 135/34 BCE, besieging Jerusalem and reinstating Seleucid rule, if only for a brief time. Later, about 112 BCE, John Hyrcanus could not resist the incursions of Antiochus IX Cyzicenus. When Alexander Jannaeus, king of Judea 103–76 BCE, tried to extend his territory west to the port of Ptolemais (Akko) early in his reign, he was decisively defeated by Ptolemy IX Soter II (Lathyrus); later, about 88 BCE, he was defeated by the Seleucid monarch Demetrius III Eucaerus.

Judea. When Antiochus III defeated the Ptolemaic forces at Panium in 200 BCE, he forthwith gained control of the small city-state of Judea. Judea had been ruled by the Ptolemies for over a century, but the details of its administration remain very hazy, since the sources at our disposal are not concerned with these sociopolitical questions.[1] Following is a discussion of the main narrative sources used to search out life in pre-Maccabean Jerusalem.

(1) First Maccabees provides almost no details of Judean life before the revolt. It does mention

that there were some anonymous "renegades" who wanted Jews to conform to the way of life of the nations round about and so had a gymnasium built in Jerusalem (1 Macc 1:11-15).

(2) Second Maccabees provides more details about the high priests in Jerusalem and their role in the building of a gymnasium. It gives names and events not otherwise recorded.

(3) The Jewish historian Josephus, writing at the end of the first century CE, provides information about Jerusalem in the pre-Maccabean period in his works *The Jewish War* and *Antiquities of the Jews*. The latter work in particular includes citations of official letters by Seleucid rulers about the Jews. It also contains a narrative about one Jewish family, the Tobiads, which is usually called the Tobiad romance.[2] This story tells of the rise to prominence of Joseph the Tobiad, who took over the role of tax collector for the Egyptian Ptolemies from his uncle, the miserly high priest Onias. Josephus tells the story in a most confusing way, but some scholars believe that they can glean some historical data from this fanciful account and date the events to the rule of Ptolemy III Euergetes (246–221 BCE). According to this story, the seven oldest sons of Joseph fought against their younger half brother, Hyrcanus, and this rivalry was in part responsible for the Seleucids' intervening in Judah to offset the Ptolemaic connections of Hyrcanus.

(4) The last part of the canonical book of Daniel also recounts the events preceding and during the reign of Antiochus IV in the visions of Daniel 7–12. The events are cast in the form of a symbolic vision, with the kings of the south, the Ptolemies, waging war against the kings of the north, the Seleucids. The exact significance of some of the references is unclear.

(5) The first book of *Enoch*, a pseudepigraphic work (portions of which have been found among the Dead Sea Scrolls), also recounts in symbolic form the history of Israel up to the time of the Maccabees (*1 Enoch* 83–90). Here the symbols are of animals fighting against one another.

(6) The work of Jesus ben Sira, a teacher in Jerusalem around 190–170 BCE, evidences a deep concern for the role of wisdom in creation. True wisdom comes from God, and Ben Sira identifies divine wisdom with the Torah, or Law of Moses (Sir 24:8-29). He places great emphasis on proper worship in the Temple.

From these various sources, then, scholars attempt to piece together a sense of what life was like in Judea in the third century BCE, and what happened there.

From a decree found in Josephus, we know that Antiochus III affirmed the right of the Jews to live according to their ancestral religion.[3] He also mentioned that the Jews had a "council" (γερουσία *gerousia*), but we do not know precisely who its members were (probably wealthy aristocracy) or how they were chosen. Although Antiochus does not mention the high priest in his letter, the Greek historian Hecataeus of Abdera, who wrote around 300 BCE, stated that the high priest was a leading figure in civil as well as religious matters. Hecataeus's work is reported by a later Greek writer of the first century BCE, Diodorus Siculus.[4] In his idealized picture of the Jews, Hecataeus wrote that Moses appointed priests to be "judges in all major disputes, and entrusted to them the guardianship of the laws and customs. For this reason the Jews never have a king, and authority over the people is regularly vested in whichever priest is regarded as superior to his colleagues in wisdom and virtue. They call this man the high priest, and believe he acts as a messenger to them of God's commandments."[5]

Ben Sira (50:1-21) also lavishes praise on the high priest of his own day, Simon son of Onias, and notes how Simon built the walls of the temple enclosure and fortified the city against siege. The Tobiad romance has the high priest in charge of paying tribute to the Ptolemies, although the point of the story is the transfer of this power to a non-priest, Joseph the Tobiad. Scholars have deduced from this that the high priest was the only authority in Judea, but we do not know whether the Ptolemies or the Seleucids installed another imperial functionary alongside the high priest.

Nothing much changed through the transfer of power from the Ptolemies to the Seleucids. However, the defeat of Antiochus III by the Romans in 190 BCE put the Seleucid Empire under a heavy indemnity. The description of the attempt by Seleucus IV, Antiochus's successor, to obtain money from the Jerusalem Temple as told in 2 Maccabees 3 should be seen in the light of the Seleucid emperor's need for money to keep up payment of that indemnity. More important, the author of 2 Maccabees recounts how Jason, the brother of the high priest Onias III, outbid his brother to take from him the office of high priest (2 Macc 4:7-10). We do not know if previously every high priest had to pay for reinstatement at the advent of a new ruler, but the accession of Antiochus IV saw the bestowal of the high priesthood on the highest bidder. The narrative of 2 Maccabees in particular forces us to consider the competition and rivalries among various groups in pre-Hasmonean Jerusalem. Following is a highlight of important areas for the reader to keep in mind while working through 1 and 2 Maccabees.

Factions in Jerusalem. In any discussion of the causes of the rebellion in Judea, one has to remember that the small state of Judea (traveling about twenty miles in any direction from Jerusalem would take one outside its territory) was ruled by wealthy priestly and lay families. At times, this situation is described as an ideal one: "the holy city was inhabited in unbroken peace and the laws were strictly observed" (2 Macc 3:1 NRSV). The high priest is described by Sirach as being surrounded by the whole congregation, lifting up their hands and voices in unison and harmony as they worshiped God (Sir 50:1-21). Such an idyllic picture is, however, rudely countered by the descriptions of factional fighting and murder committed by one group against another (see, e.g., 2 Macc 4:3).

Several influential families can be identified from the sources: the Oniad family of Zadokite high priests, Onias III and Jason (2 Macc 3:1; 4:7); the Bilgah family, Simon, Menelaus, and Lysimachus (2 Macc 3:4; 4:23-29); the Hakkoz family, John and Eupolemus (1 Macc 8:17; 2 Macc 4:11); the Jehoiaribs, i.e., the Hasmonean family; the family of Jakim, Alcimus (1 Macc 7:5); and the Tobiads.[6] Although the Tobiads, who were lay leaders and not priests, do not appear at all in 1 and 2 Maccabees, Josephus in one account describes how the sons of Tobias urged Antiochus IV to invade Jerusalem.[7] It is also important to keep in mind that other wealthy lay families vied for power and prestige in Judea. As for the priestly families, it seems significant that the chronicler, in the lists of ancestral houses of the priests apart from the high priest Zadok, mentions the other four families (1 Chr 24:7, 10, 12, 14). Hakkoz's descendants were barred from the priesthood after the return from exile because their family name could not be found in the genealogical entries (Ezra 2:61-63), but their presence in the list in Chronicles as well as their diplomatic activity in the second century BCE (2 Macc 4:11; 1 Macc 8:17) attests to their continued prominence. From the narrative in 2 Maccabees, one can see how the Bilgah family seized the opportunity offered by the split in the Zadokite family between Onias and his brother Jason and how the Hakkoz family sided with the Hasmoneans, while Alcimus of the family of Jakim pursued his own quest for power. Thus the causes of the Maccabean revolt must be seen as having arisen from the competition between ambitious families in the small city-state of Judea.

There are other signs that all was not well in Judea. The discoveries at Qumran have shown that discontent was present in the third century BCE. In *1 Enoch* 1-16, part of a pseudepigraphic work dated to the third century BCE, a story similar to that of Gen 6:1-8 is told of how angels from heaven brought sin and pollution upon the earth. The story is paradigmatic for the way the author of *1 Enoch* and his community viewed their world as one of disorder and confusion. Later, in the second century BCE, the author of the book of Daniel depicted the history of the world from the Babylonians to the Greeks as chaotic and bestial (Daniel 7). Within Judaism itself there was dissension over the cultic calendar as seen in the book of *Jubilees*, which favors a solar instead of a lunar-solar calendar. There was debate over other legal questions as well, if 4QMMT found at Qumran is to be dated early. Even the traditionalist Ben Sira includes in his work a prayer for the deliverance of Jerusalem and the Jewish nation from foreign oppression (Sir 36:1-22). Within both 1 and 2 Maccabees we also meet a group called the Hasideans (1 Macc 2:42; 7:13; 2 Macc 14:6). We do not know who they were, but their choice of name—"pious," "loyal ones"—suggests that they thought others were not so pious and loyal as they. The *Damascus Document* also hints that members of its exclusivist group were found throughout Judea.[8] Clearly, not everyone thought that all was well in Judea.

Persecution by Antiochus IV. The accounts of the persecution enforced by Antiochus IV Epiphanes differ in 1 and 2 Maccabees. Here is a schematic outline of the events:

A Synoptic Chart of Antiochus's Persecution

1 Maccabees	2 Maccabees
1. "Renegades" ask to be like other nations; they build a gymnasium.	The high priest Jason asks to build a gymnasium as a way to adopt the Greek way of life. The high priest Menelaus commits acts of sacrilege, which lead to an uprising of the people.
2. An arrogant Antiochus IV invades Egypt, plunders it, and then plunders Jerusalem and the Temple.	After Antiochus IV's second invasion of Egypt, a civil war breaks out between Jason and Menelaus. In response to this, a bestial Antiochus plunders the Temple.
3. Two years later, a military garrison is set up in Jerusalem.	Antiochus installs governors in Judea and in Samaria. He then commands another attack on Jerusalem.
4. Sometime later, Antiochus IV imposes a cult on Judea, profanes the Temple, and prohibits the Mosaic Law.	Finally, Antiochus IV outlaws Judaism in Judea, profanes the Temple, and installs another cult.
5. When news reaches Antiochus that the Temple has been recaptured and purified by the Jews, he dies.	Antiochus IV dies before the Temple is purified.

The two accounts are basically the same, but with important differences that will be discussed in the commentary. Both accounts agree that some Jews built a gymnasium and that Antiochus IV imposed a cult on Jerusalem. The characterization of Antiochus IV differs in both. In 1 Maccabees, Antiochus IV is arrogant from the start and seeks to impose a unified worship and behavior throughout his empire. In 2 Maccabees, he is at first portrayed neutrally, then as sympathetic, but finally as enraged against the Jews. Second Maccabees shows that the cult was imposed after a series of disturbances and uprisings in Jerusalem, and it places much of the blame on the unruly passions of the emperor. On the other hand, 1 Maccabees states that the cult was imposed because the emperor wished all nations to be the same and to give up their particular customs (1 Macc 1:41-42). Antiochus is thus portrayed in 1 Maccabees as zealous in the spread of Hellenization, of striving to conform everyone to Greek customs, while in 2 Maccabees he is shown initially as encouraging the adoption of Greek customs by some Jews.

It must be said that Antiochus IV was not a Hellenizing zealot. He certainly wanted to keep the Seleucid Empire together, but all evidence suggests that he encouraged the maintenance of local customs and traditions and did not seek to suppress them. We should see as rhetorical polemic, therefore, the statement in 1 Macc 1:41 concerning a decree to force all peoples to abandon their customs. However, we should also be sensitive to the pressure there must have been to learn the ways of the Seleucids. The Seleucid monarch was extremely powerful, and it would have been in the best interests of rulers within his empire to be on good terms with him. What we find is that during the reigns of Antiochus III and Antiochus IV a number of older cities were recognized as *poleis* (πόλεις), i.e., Greek cities, and were renamed. Obviously this was thought to be a beneficial step for the cities concerned—indeed, a goal to strive for.

The high priest Jason must have thought so, because he had Jerusalem renamed as Antioch-at-Jerusalem (2 Macc 4:9, 19) and built a gymnasium, an exercise and educational establishment that every "decent" Greek city was supposed to have. One must also recognize, however, that we know almost nothing about what this process of renaming entailed. Did the renaming of an ancient city like Jerusalem as Antioch-at-Jerusalem necessarily signify the adoption of a new constitution? Was the *gerousia* under Antiochus III different from that under Antiochus IV and his successors? Earlier scholars argued that, theoretically, if not in practice, a new constitution was adopted, but the minimal evidence seems to support the continuance of older customs. In addition, nothing indicates that citizenship in Antioch-at-Jerusalem was limited to wealthy friends of Jason. As for the gymnasium, we simply do not know what its curriculum was; evidence from what took place in Athens should be applied cautiously to Jerusalem, since each city controlled its own educational process. What we do know is that the people in the gymnasium would have been taught to speak Greek, as well as to carry out the exercises and sports that any well-reared Greek citizen would have learned. The emperor would certainly have had interpreters available, but the ability to become a member of the club by partaking in gymnastic exercises and by conversing in Greek would no doubt have made for a more amicable relationship with the powerful monarch. Moreover, the renaming of Jerusalem around 175 BCE and the building of a gymnasium brought about no local upheaval, even though the author of 2 Maccabees sees it as the start of the Hellenization and the religious factionalism it produced (2 Macc 4:11-17).

The trouble developed following a series of events. Factional war broke out between the high priest Menelaus and the former high priest Jason while Antiochus IV was campaigning in Egypt. Antiochus's reaction to this revolt was to enter Jerusalem by force, massacre the population, and pillage the Temple (2 Macc 5:1-21). Antiochus appointed overseers in Jerusalem and over the Samaritans (2 Macc 5:22-23). Later, there were two more missions against Jerusalem, one by Apollonius, captain of the Mysians (1 Macc 1:29-35; 2 Macc 5:24-26), and one by Geron the Athenian, to compel the Jews to abandon their laws (1 Macc 1:44-51; 2 Macc 6:1-2). Since these missions were probably not mere whims, it seems safe to conclude that the populace of Jerusalem and Judea was considered by the Seleucid authorities to be

restless and that the decision to stamp out forcibly the practice of Judaism was the final step in a series of unsuccessful attempts to settle affairs in Jerusalem. Indeed, the persecution was limited to Judea, Samaria (2 Macc 6:2), and neighboring Greek cities (2 Macc 6:8-9). Jews in other major cities of the Seleucid Empire, such as Antioch, were not, so far as we know, affected.

The persecution aimed at every aspect of Jewish observance. Torah scrolls were burned, circumcision was forbidden, and the sabbath was not to be observed. Jews were forced to participate at pagan festivals and compelled to eat pork. Observance of Torah was outlawed under threat of death. The Temple was profaned and turned into a temple for pagan festivals.

A great deal of energy has been spent trying to pinpoint exactly which cult was imposed upon Jerusalem by Antiochus IV. The sources tell us that the temple was dedicated to Zeus Olympios (2 Macc 6:2), that a desolating sacrilege and an altar were placed on top of the altar of burnt offering in the temple courtyard (1 Macc 1:54, 59; 4:43-44), and that both the king's birthday and the feast day of the god Dionysos were celebrated monthly (2 Macc 6:7). There may also have been temple prostitutes (2 Macc 6:4). The term "desolating sacrilege" (βδέλυγμα ἐρημώσεως *bdelygma erēmōseōs*, 1 Macc 1:54) is the same as that found in Dan 9:27; 11:31, where the Hebrew (משמם שקוצים *šiqqûṣîm mĕšōmēm*) is a play on the name "Ba ʾal Shamen," or "Lord of Heaven," the Syrian counterpart of Zeus Olympios. Based on this, some scholars have argued that the cult was Syro-Canaanite, assuming that one cult substituted for another. However, 1 Macc 1:47 speaks of many altars, sacred precincts, and shrines for idols, and 2 Macc 10:2 details that altars had been built in the public square of Jerusalem and also that there were sacred precincts. Rather than the imposition of the worship of one god in place of Yahweh, it seems that the worship of many gods, including Dionysus and Zeus Olympios, took place. Thus regular paganism, characterized by the worship of many gods and goddesses, was introduced.

Antiochus IV would later change his mind and revoke the persecution (2 Macc 11:27-33), but the enigma still remains as to why he started a policy so at variance with the usual workings of the Hellenistic world, wherein states normally respected the existing gods and cultic practices of the various cities. Antiochus III and Seleucus IV had supported the cult in Jerusalem. Scholars have attempted to find a specific answer to the problem. Suggestions that Antiochus was either crazy or a zealous Hellenizer do not explain why only this small area of his kingdom was affected. Goldstein has suggested that Antiochus IV, a former hostage in Rome, was attempting to set up an empirewide Antiochian citizenship similar to Roman civic and religious programs, but his ingenious theory lacks supporting data.[9] Other scholars have sought an explanation from within the factions in Jerusalem. E. Bickermann argued brilliantly that the initiative for the persecution came from the "Hellenizers" in Jerusalem, who wanted to reform Judaism and remove the barriers that separated Jews from Gentiles;[10] the persecution of opponents would have followed Jewish models of persecution such as that carried out by Jehu (2 Kings 9–10). V. Tcherikover did not follow the notion of a Reform Judaism, but stressed that the Hellenizers were an upper-class elite, whereas the common people were staunchly anti-Hellenistic.[11] He speculated that the people, led by the legal and spiritual leaders, the scribes, attempted to throw out both Jason and Menelaus; it was their pious revolt that led to Antiochus's persecution and the installation of a Syrian military colony, which set up its own worship in the Jerusalem Temple. Goldstein agreed with both Bickermann, in holding that the religion imposed was a kind of polytheistic Judaism, and Tcherikover, in that the religion was brought in by Antiochus's military colony in Jerusalem, a colony made up of Jewish soldiers who followed that kind of practice.[12] K. Bringmann stressed that, while Menelaus created the new religion in line with the Syrian military colony, Antiochus issued the orders primarily to consolidate his own power and to provide a stable source of revenue.[13]

I have emphasized that Antiochus IV, when he gained the Seleucid throne in 175 BCE, quickly knew that the Ptolemies were eager to renew hostilities to regain Coelesyria. The Ptolemies would have invaded in 180 BCE if Ptolemy V Epiphanes had not been assassinated. Once his widow had died in 176 BCE, the new government did little to conceal its hostile intentions and, in fact, finally attacked in late 170 or early 169 BCE. In this atmosphere of hostility on his southern border, Antiochus IV would have wished to have a region favorable to him and so acceded to Jason's request to rename Jerusalem. The gymnasium with its attached *ephebium* would have trained young men in military exercises for possible use as auxiliary forces. When Antiochus IV was rebuffed from Egypt by the Romans in 168 BCE, he may have felt even more strongly the need for a secure southern border and hence the imposition of paganism in Judea. However, I would not wish to hold that Antiochus was guided only by political concerns, as one cannot easily separate religion and politics in the ancient world. Rather, Antiochus IV may have heard stories that the Jews had a misanthropic attitude toward other nations, as stated even in the positive account of Hecataeus of Abdera, who wrote that "as a result of their expulsion from Egypt, [Moses] introduced an unsocial and intolerant mode of life."[14] Antiochus may have decided that this aspect of religious polity had to be suppressed. Why this institution of paganism required the burning of the books of the Law, the prohibition of circumcision, and the end of the daily offering in the Temple remains an enigma. Given the meager quality of our sources and their highly polemical stance, scholars will continue to debate and put forward explanations.

The Sequel to the Revolt. The last event recorded in 1 and 2 Maccabees is the death of Simon Maccabeus in 135/34 BCE. It is hinted that he was succeeded by his son John Hyrcanus, who would rule from 135/34 to 104 BCE. After repulsing the attempted coup of his brother-in-law Ptolemy, John was forced to submit to Seleucid forces under Antiochus VII Sidetes and to pay tribute. After Antiochus died in 129 BCE while campaigning against Parthia, the Seleucid throne remained weak, and John Hyrcanus seized the opportunities offered by this Syrian weakness. During the course of his thirty-year reign, the territory of Judea expanded enormously to the east, north, and south. Early in his career, John captured two fortified towns in Transjordan: Medeba and Samoga. Then he turned north and captured Shechem and Mount Gerizim; he also subdued the Samaritans and destroyed their temple. Then he marched south to Idumea and captured its two main cities, Adora and Marisa. Late in his reign, he conquered the Macedonian colony at Samaria and also captured Scythopolis. The details of how John accomplished this expansion are debated, in part because the dating of a document preserved by Josephus is disputed.[15] Does it belong early in John's reign at the time of Antiochus VII or later, during the reign of Antiochus IX? If later, then John Hyrcanus's forces are seen to be weak and unable to resist Seleucid attacks. We know that John Hyrcanus hired mercenaries, but how many and how effective a fighting force are unknown.[16] Could he have successfully controlled the area he is said to have conquered without some support from the native populations? Hyrcanus was certainly the strong man of the area, but how were the forcibly circumcised Idumeans so compliantly integrated into the Jewish way of life?[17] Although facing some internal opposition in his thirty-year reign,[18] Hyrcanus succeeded in forging a Jewish state such as had not existed from pre-exilic times. Josephus lavishly praises him and states that he was the only person to unite in himself the roles of ruler, priest, and prophet.

Hyrcanus's son, Aristobulus I, ruled for one year (104–103 BCE). He continued the policy of expansion and appropriated Galilee.[19] Aristobulus is said by Josephus to have transformed the government into a kingdom and to have put the diadem on his own head.[20] His successor, his brother Alexander Jannaeus (103–76 BCE), was continually embroiled in foreign and domestic wars. Josephus gives a list of the territory conquered by Alexander: northern Transjordan; most of the coastal cities as far north as Caesarea, Idumea, Samaria, and Galilee—a kingdom almost as large as Solomon's.[21] Such a major territorial expansion raises questions about the identity of those persons introduced into the new realm. Aristobulus is said to have forced inhabitants of Galilee who wished to remain in the country to be circumcised and to live according to the laws of the Jews.[22] During the expansion under Alexander Jannaeus, the city of Pella is said to have been razed because its inhabitants would not promise to accept and practice the ancestral customs of the Jews.[23] These statements raise the question of what being a "Jew" meant. Did it mean merely that the conquered cities were to be under the control of the king of Judea? Or did it mean, as the requirement of circumcision suggests, that the conquered population was to be treated as resident aliens in the land, following the commands of Exod 12:48; 22:20; and throughout Deuteronomy? What was their status vis-à-vis the citizens of Judea? Who would determine that all the male inhabitants of every village were circumcised? The incorporation of so many towns with different cultural traditions would have sparked a debate over what it meant to be a Jew—a native-born citizen of Judea, or one who was circumcised and followed the requirements of the resident alien, or someone who was circumcised and followed all the Torah?

THE ETHICS OF VIOLENCE

War dominates these books. They include stories of incredible courage under torture, as in the stories of Eleazar and the mother who encouraged her seven sons to die rather than transgress the Mosaic Law (2 Macc 6:18–7:42). There are stories of great daring, as in the story of another Eleazar who attempted to attack and kill the king and so end the battle. Eleazar fought through the ranks of the opposing army and killed an elephant on which he thought the king was riding, even though he knew that it would mean his own death, sacrificing his own life for those of his comrades and his nation (1 Macc 6:43-46). The story of Razis (2 Macc 14:37-46) shows a man ready to die rather than be captured, a mentality that was much admired in the ancient world. As Euripides the Greek playwright said, "Not death is evil, but a shameful death."[24] There are stories of night raids and tactical maneuvers, the stuff of which thrilling movies are made.

But woven into these accounts is a much more disquieting thread, for we find stories in which whole towns are razed. Throughout the accounts of the battles against neighboring cities in Gilead runs the refrain "and killed every male by the edge of the sword" (1 Macc 5:28 NRSV; see also 1 Macc 5:35, 51). Cities are burned to the ground. In one grisly scene, the army of Judas as well as the men, women, and children they are bringing back to Judea walk over the bodies of their slain enemies (1 Macc 5:51). In another scene, a lake near a town seems to be running over with the blood of those slain by the Maccabean forces (2 Macc 12:13-16). The delight in the destruction of human life seems almost palpable.

These stories imitate those found in the book of Judges. In trying to understand the ethics of violence in the books of the Maccabees, the analysis that Susan Niditch has made of the war accounts in the Hebrew Scriptures is very informative.[25] Niditch categorizes some of the narratives of the destruction of whole cities, in particular the killing of human beings, as narratives that portray the Israelites as instruments of God's justice, requiting the sins and misdeeds of their opponents. We see just such an attitude in the books of the Maccabees, as the Gentiles are consistently depicted as attempting to destroy the Maccabean forces without provocation (1 Macc 5:1; 2 Macc 12:2). Such an attitude also lies behind the ethnic cleansing that Simon pursues as he forces the inhabitants of Gazara and Beth-zur to leave; in the case of Gazara, he purifies the city (1 Macc 13:43-47; 11:65-66). The campaigns are also seen as purifying God's land of idol worship.

There are other instances in the books of Maccabees that fit Niditch's category of the ideology of expediency, an ideology in which force is used to instill terror. When the citizens of Antioch rebel against King Demetrius, Jonathan brutally suppresses the uprising as his troops fan out through the city and kill about one hundred thousand persons (1 Macc 11:41-51). Here Jonathan is portrayed as using brutal tactics to stop the revolt quickly. His tactics succeed, and he wins great renown.

For those who have been reared in the just-war tradition, which justifies waging war only as a last resort and prohibits attacking innocent civilians and annihilating defeated enemies, these stories do not provide an example that we would wish to follow. The books of the Maccabees are replete with judgments on their opponents as barbarous, godless, and sinful. There is no attempt to see the opponents as fellow human beings. War and the defeat of the enemy are glorified. In reading these stories, then, we have to realize that they tell us a great deal, not about how we ought to behave, but about what kind of group produced them. As Niditch states, "the more stable a group or person is, the surer they are of their identity, the less likely they are to be warlike, and the less rigid and totalistic their war ideologies are likely to be."[26] We can begin to understand that the communities out of which these books came felt themselves to be under attack and knew that their existence depended on building up their own self-esteem by denigrating their opponents. When we read these books, then, we can empathize with the protagonists in their struggles and seek to understand their point of view, but without sympathizing with their war practices and their demonization of their enemies. What reading these books should do is strengthen our commitment to explore ways to implement policies that embody the perspective of just-war theory. We should not be anesthetized by these stories of slaughter, but resolve that war and violence should be the last resort to settle conflicts, and that conflict will never make us forget that our enemies are human. If wars and conflicts result from insecurity and a sense of injustice, we must work to bring social justice and fair treatment to all nations and peoples. We must strive to bolster the self-image of all.

The books of 1 and 2 Maccabees also force readers to confront the problem of self-defense versus pacifism, particularly in the narrative of Jews who, despite attempting to live their lives in solitude, are hunted down and killed (1 Macc 2:29-41). Within this narrative, the right to defend oneself and one's country is strikingly affirmed. What we have to remember in reading these books is that there were no constraints on the emperor's will. If he wanted to, he could order the execution of all who opposed his will. The non-violent techniques used by Gandhi in India and by Martin Luther King, Jr., in the United States worked to a certain extent because both India under British rule and the United States are societies in which the rule of law constrains what leaders and police can do. Such techniques would have been of no avail in the Seleucid regime. To preserve one's own heritage and culture when threatened, one had to defend oneself. There was no escape. These books on war, therefore, while they affirm the right of a society to defend itself by recourse to war, do not address the question of the right of an individual in today's society to object conscientiously to serving in the military. That is another issue.

Finally, these books about war and events of the public arena reflect a male perspective. Women appear even less than in works like the *Iliad*. We learn that Jonathan and Simon had sons, but no mention is made of their wives. When women do appear in the stories, it is in the role of mother, as in the martyrdom stories (1 Macc 1:60; 2 Macc

6:10; 7), or as an image to describe social upheaval with the women leaving their houses and being seen in the streets (2 Macc 3:19-21). These are very male-dominated works.

THE DATING OF EVENTS

How to harmonize the dates given in the books of Maccabees has long puzzled commentators. Chronology in the study of Judaism is always complicated by the fact that the lunar-solar calendar was never perfect, being off by about ten days. Moreover, when trying to chart the events recounted in 1 and 2 Maccabees, scholars have been faced with inconsistencies between the two books (e.g., while 1 Macc 6:20 dates Lysias's second expedition to 150 of the Seleucid era, 2 Macc 13:1 dates it to 149 of the Seleucid era). Further confusion sets in when we realize that there were two systems for calculating the dates of the Seleucid era, which was held to begin from the conquest of Babylonia by Seleucus I. One system started the year following the Macedonian calendar, which began in the autumn, and so year 1 of the Seleucid Macedonian system would correspond to the time of autumn 312 to autumn 311 BCE. The second system, following the Babylonian calendar, started the year in spring, and so year 1 of the Seleucid Babylonian system would be from spring 311 to spring 310 BCE. The author of 1 Maccabees uses the Jewish names of the months (1:54; 4:52; 7:43, 49; 14:27; 16:14) and places the Festival of Booths in the seventh month (10:21), presuming a system beginning in spring. However, he dates the death of Antiochus IV to the year 149 of the Seleucid era (6:16), whereas the Babylonian cuneiform tablets, which also use a calendar that begins in spring, date Antiochus's death in 148 of the Seleucid era. Scholars have outlined three solutions to keep all the dates in balance and maintain the basic reliability of the sources:

(1) There is one system of dating in 1 Maccabees that begins in autumn 312.[27] According to this chronology, the suppression of Jewish worship would have begun in 168 BCE, and the Temple would have been purified in December 165 BCE. One problem for this solution is found at 10:21, where the Feast of Booths is said to occur in Tishri, the seventh month, presupposing a calendar beginning in spring.

(2) There are two systems of dating in 1 Maccabees, one for internal Jewish events, like festivals, that begins, like the Seleucid Babylonian system, in spring 311 BCE, and one for external events, such as the dates for Seleucid expeditions, that is based on the Seleucid Macedonian system, which began in autumn 312 BCE.[28] According to this chronology, Antiochus's persecution would have begun in 167 BCE, and the Temple would have been purified in December 164 BCE.

(3) There are two systems of dating in 1 Maccabees, as in theory 2, except that the calendar for dating internal Jewish events would have begun in spring 312 BCE.[29] According to this system, the suppression of Jewish worship would be dated to 168 BCE and the purification of the Temple to 165 BCE.

Deciding upon one from among these theories is exceedingly complex. Bickermann's theory, theory 2, is the one most widely accepted. Most scholars hold that the author of the epitome in 2 Maccabees followed the Seleucid Macedonian system.

STYLE, WORLDVIEW, AND DATE

First Maccabees opens with a prologue that speaks of Alexander the Great and his exploits (1 Macc 1:1-10), but the narrative covers events from sometime after the accession of Antiochus IV Epiphanes in 175 BCE until the death of Simon Maccabeus in 135/34 BCE. Furthermore, the book is structured around the Hasmonean family. After a description of the apostasy of some from Judaism and the subsequent persecution when Antiochus tries to force all peoples to abandon their native customs (1:41), the narrative focuses on the patriarch Mattathias and his three sons—Judas, Jonathan, and Simon—as they lead the fight against those who wish to do away with their ancestral religion.

Style. Although 1 Maccabees gives the appearance of a straightforward narrative, it is not so straightforward as it seems. The author intersperses various documents into the narrative to provide the proper aura of documentation required to foster belief in the historical correctness of the account. (The authenticity of some of these documents has been disputed.) Yet this is a narrative interspersed with traditional poetic passages and whose syntax imitates that of narrative sections of the Hebrew Scriptures. It is, then, a narrative that consciously aims at incorporating its story into the tradition of the Hebrew Scriptures. It is not a retelling of Hebrew Scriptures as, for example, the pseudepigraphic book of *Jubilees*, which recounts the primeval history of humanity and the history of God's chosen people up to the time of Moses, or as the *Temple Scroll* from Qumran,[30] which restates much of the legislation from Exodus, Leviticus, and Deuteronomy. Rather, 1 Maccabees perceives the events it tells as another reenactment of the events of the Hebrew Scriptures. This is seen in the way the author views the execution of the Hasideans in 7:16 as being in accordance with the words of Ps 79:2-3—that is, the author sees the words of the psalm actualized in the events of his own day. This view of present-day events reflecting the Scriptures can be compared to the way the Qumran covenanters and the authors of the Gospels interpret the psalms and the prophets as talking about events in their own history. The author has not written a simple presentation of facts, but has woven a highly textured narrative.

That the syntax of 1 Maccabees reflects the narrative sections of the Hebrew Scriptures can be seen in the opening sentence, which begins as so many Hebrew narratives (e.g., Joshua, Judges, Ruth, 2 Samuel) begin and is then followed by a string of clauses all connected by "and." In addition, the Greek of 1 Maccabees is filled with Semitisms much like those in the LXX. There are also places in the text where one can understand what is going on if one presupposes that an original Hebrew text has been misunderstood or mistranslated (e.g., 9:2; possibly 3:37; and the enigmatic transliteration at 14:27). All this has led scholars to posit that 1 Maccabees was originally written in Hebrew and that our present text is a translation, while the original Hebrew text is missing. The Greek translator follows closely the translation style of other portions of the Hebrew Scriptures, so that one can often reconstruct what the original Hebrew text would have looked like. As the discoveries at Qumran have shown, writings in Hebrew were plentiful at this time, and so a writing in Hebrew should not surprise us.

The author also at times shows the inner connections of incidents by inserting literary linkages. For example, at 1 Macc 3:37, the author states that Antiochus IV was going through the upper provinces and then repeats the phrase at 6:1, thus binding Antiochus into the whole first series of actions and successes of the Hasmoneans. The same technique of intercalation is used to set the alliance of Jonathan with Rome between two attacks by commanders of Demetrius (11:63; 12:24). The author also carefully places in the narrative the documents that show the growing prestige and power of the Hasmoneans.

Even though the original text of 1 Maccabees was probably written in Hebrew, one should be aware of what a careful job the Greek translator has done. He shows considerable awareness of the Greek translation of the Hebrew Scriptures, but also is able to show connections in his choice of Greek phrasing and sections. For example, the use of the same root for the verb and the noun at 2:42 and 7:12 ("there united [συνήχθησαν *synēchthēsan*] . . . a company [συναγωγή *synagōgē*]"; "there appeared [ἐπισυνήχθησαν *episynēchthēsan*] . . . a group [*synagōgē*]") and the repetition of the same phrases throughout 7:1-25 bind the section together (see also 9:58-73). It is, for the most part, a thoughtful translation.

Worldview. That the author of the books of Maccabees wrote in Hebrew in imitation of the style of the Hebrew Scriptures was no accident. The author consciously set out to show how the Maccabean revolt closely followed ancestral traditions. Particularly noteworthy is the way the author has spliced the narrative with poetic compositions that echo traditional psalms of lament and rejoicing. Just as the author of the Gospel of Luke used hymns in the opening chapters of his work to give his Gospel a traditional flavoring, so too did this earlier author. The author also models his heroes on biblical antecedents. Mattathias's opening act of rebellion explicitly echoes that of Phinehas in Num 25:6-13. Mattathias, as he lies dying, gives his testament, as Jacob had done (Genesis 49), and commissions his sons just as Moses had commissioned Joshua (Deut 31:7-23; Josh 1:6-9) and David had commissioned Solomon (1 Chr 22:13; 28:20). The Maccabeans are also related to the former judges of Israel. The most explicit reference to these judges is at 9:73, where Jonathan is said to "judge" Israel; Jonathan's election to succeed Judas also shows the influence of Jephthah's election (Judg 10:18; 11:6-11). The structural principle of the book of Judges is that when the Israelites do what is wrong in the eyes of the Lord, they are punished, but when they cry out, the Lord raises up someone to deliver

Chronology of 1 and 2 Maccabees

Dates:		Events:	References:		
BCE	Seleucid[1] Calendar		1 Maccabees	2 Maccabees	Daniel
333–323		Conquests of Alexander the Great	1:1-9		7:7; 11:3-4
202		Antiochus III invades Coelesyria, begins Fifth Syrian War			
200		Antiochus III defeats Ptolemy V at Paneas			11:5
198		Antiochus III controls Coelesyria, including Judea; Jews allowed to live by their own law			
196		Onias III becomes high priest			
190		Roman army defeats Antiochus III at Magnesia			11:18
		Treaty of Apamea; Antiochus V taken as hostage to Rome			
187		Death of Antiochus III, succeeded by Seleucus IV			11:19
180		Ben Sira finishes his writings			
		Heliodorus's attempt to loot the Temple		3:1-40	11:20
		Simon schemes against Onias		4:1-6	
175	137	Death of Seleucus IV, accession of Antiochus IV	1:10-15	4:7	7:8, 23-25; 11:21
		Jason appointed high priest (Onias deposed)		4:7	9:26a; 11:22?
		Hellenization of Jerusalem begins		4:7-17	
172		Menelaus appointed high priest (Jason deposed)		4:23-50	
171/170		Sixth Syran War between antiochus IV and Ptolemy VI			
170/169		Antiochus IV invades Egypt	1:16-19		
169	143	Syrian attack on Jerusalem	1:20-28[2]	5:11-14	11:28
169		Antiochus IV's second invasion of Egypt;	5:1		11:29
		Roman ultimatum to withdraw obeyed;			11:30a
		Jason's coup attempt		5:5-10	
167	145	Second Syrian attack on Jerusalem:			9:26b; 11:30b
		Massacre by Apollonius	1:29-32	5:21-26	9:12-14?
		Construction of the citadel (Akra)	1:33-40		
		Enforced Hellenization by Antiochus IV	1:41-50		
		Judaism outlawed, Temple defiled	1:51-64	6:1-10	9:27; 11:31-35; 12:11
		Maccabean revolt in Modein	2:1-28		
		Slaughter of innocents on sabbath	2:29-38	6:11	
		Guerilla attacks led by Mattathians	2:39-48		
166	146	Death of Mattathias	2:49-70		
		Martyrdoms of Eleazar; seven brothers, and mother		6:12–7:42	
		Judas becomes leader of the revolt	3:1-9	8:1-8	
		Judas's early victories:	3:10-26	8:5	
		Apollonius defeated at Lebonah	3:10-12		
		Seron defeated at Beth-horon	3:13-26		
165	147	Antiochus IV's campaign to Persia	3:27-37		
		Victory over Seleucid armies led by Ptolemy, Nicanor, and Gorgias	3:38–4:25	8:8-29; 11:1-15	
164	148	Amnesty offer gained by Menelaus			
		First expedition of Lysias	4:28-35	11:1-15	
	148	Peace negotiations of Lysias and the role of the Romans		11:16-21, 34-38	
	149	Death of Antiochus IV, accession of			
		Antiochus V Eupator (Lysias regent)[3]	6:1-17	9:1-29; 10:10-11	11:40-45
		Cleansing and rededication of the Temple	4:36-61	10:1-9	
		Restoration of ancestral customs by Antiochhus V		11:22-26	
		Jewish defensive campaigns:			
		Idumea	5:3-5, 65a	10:14-23	
		Ammon	5:6-8		
		Gilead	5:9-13, 24-51	8:30-33; 10:24-38; 12:17-31	
		Galilee	5:14-23		
		Philistia	5:65b-68		
		Siege of the citadel by Judas	6:18-27		

Chronology of 1 and 2 Maccabees (continued)

Dates: BCE	Seleucid[1] Calendar	Events:	References: 1 Maccabees	2 Maccabees	Daniel
162	150	Seleucid invasion led by Lysias:	6:28-63	13:1-26[4]	
		Execution of Menelaus		13:3-8	
		Battle near Modein		13:9-17	
		Siege of Beth-zur	6:28-31, 49-50	13:18-22	
		Battle at Beth-zechariah	6:32-47		
		Siege of Jerusalem	6:48-54		
		Peace made with Lysias	6:55-63	13:23-26	
161	151	Demetrius I ascends:	7:1-7	14:1-2	
		Lysias and Antiochus IV executed			
		First Seleucid campaign led by Bacchides:	7:8-25		
		Alcimus appointed high priest	7:9-18	14:3-10	
		Seleucid invasion led by Nicanor:	7:26-50	14:11—15:37	
		Defeated by Judas at Caphar-salama		End of 2 Maccabees	
		Defeated by Judas at Adasa			
		Judas's Treaty with Rome	8:1-32		
160	152	Second Seleucid campaign by Bacchides:	9:1-53		
		Death of Judas Maccabeus at Elasa	9:18		
		Jonathan appointed "ruler and leader"	9:28-31		
159	153	Death of Alcimus; no high priest appointed	9:54-57		
157		Third Seleucid campaign by Bacchides:	9:58-73		
		Siege of Bethbasi	9:62-69		
		Peace made with Jonathan	9:70-73		
152	160	Revolt of Alexander Balas (Epiphanes)	10:1-14		
		Jonathan appointed high priest	10:15-21		
		Demetrius makes overtures to Jonathan	10:22-47		
151		Alexander defeats Demetrius (who is slain)	10:48-50		
150	162	Alexander weds Cleopatra	10:51-66		
147	165	Demetrius II invades Seleucia	10:67-68		
		Jonathan defeats Apollonius at Jamnia	10:69-89		
145	167	Ptolemy VI of Egypt defeats Alexander Balas;			
		Demetrius II made king	11:1-19		
		Jonathan's alliance with Demetrius II	11:20-38, 41-53		
		Trypho sets up Antiochus VI as king	11:39-40, 54-56		
		Jonathan's alliance with Antiochus VI	11:57—12:38		
		Trypho usurps the throne	12:39		
143		Jonathan slain by Trypho	12:40-53; 13:23-30		
		Simon becomes leader	13:1-22		
142	170	Simon's alliance withh Demetrius II;			
		Judean independence	13:31-42		
		Simon conquers Gazara	13:43-48		
141	171	Citadel in Jerusalem captured	13:49-53		
140	172	Demetrius II captured and imprisoned	14:1-3		
		Diplomacy with Rome and Sparta	14:16-24		
		Simon appointed high priest	14:25-49		
138	174	Antiochus VII grants rights to Simon	15:1-9		
		Antiochus VII defeats Trypho	15:10-14		
		Renewed ties with Rome	15:15-24		
		Campaign led by Cendebeus against Jews	15:37—16:10		
135/34	177	Simon and sons murdered by Ptolemy	16:11-17		
		John Hyrcanus becomes high priest	16:18-24		

1. Dates given in 1 or 2 Maccabees.
2. 1 Maccabees records this attack following Antiochus's first invasion of Egypt, 2 Maccabees following his second invasion.
3. 1 Maccabees places the death of Antiochus IV after the cleansing of the Temple.
4. Dated 149 (163 BCE) in 2 Maccabees.

them, and the land is at peace while that judge lives (Judg 2:16-18; 3:7-11). That same principle is operative in 1 Maccabees. Judas turns away God's anger (3:8) as he becomes the savior of Israel (9:21), under whom the land is at peace—if only for a while (7:50). When the land is in great distress after Judas's death, Jonathan is chosen to lead the people, and he succeeds so well that the sword no longer hangs over Israel (9:73). When destruction again threatens after Jonathan's capture, Simon takes command, and soon the country is at peace again (14:4). The ideology of the Judges also appears in the way towns are put under the ban and whole towns and their inhabitants are destroyed (5:28, 35, 44). Judas acts toward Ephron in accordance with the regulations of Deut 20:10-15 (1 Macc 5:45-51), and Simon's ethnic cleansing of Gazara/Gezer (1 Macc 13:47-48) attempts to follow the command not to have any covenant with the inhabitants of the land and to tear down their altars (Deut 7:1-6; Judg 2:1-2). The author of 1 Maccabees also frequently uses the term "foreigners" (ἀλλόφυλοι *allophyloi*) to describe the Gentiles (3:41; 4:12, 22, 26, 30; 5:15, 66, 68; 11:68, 74), a term often found in Judges and 1 Samuel.

It is also important to note how the Jewish enemies of the Hasmoneans are characterized: They are the lawless (1 Macc 2:44; 3:5-6; 7:5; 9:23, 58, 69), the workers of lawlessness (1 Macc 3:6; 9:23), sinners (1 Macc 2:44, 48, 62), and impious persons (1 Macc 3:8; 6:21; 7:5-9; 9:73). More significantly, they are "renegades" (παράνομοι *paranomoi*; see 1 Macc 1:11; 10:61; 11:21), a term used to describe those who would lead Israel astray (Deut 13:12-15), to characterize those who attacked and raped the Levite's concubine and so started a civil war (Judg 19:22), and to describe the followers of Jeroboam, who brought on the split of David's kingdom (2 Chr 13:7). The author of 1 Maccabees uses only these labels to describe the Jewish opponents of the Hasmoneans—with one exception, Alcimus. Except for the high priest Alcimus, the enemies' names would be forever forgotten if not for 2 Maccabees. The author thus uses labels effectively to emphasize that the Hasmonean party is right and its enemies wrong, to set up a strong us/them dichotomy.

The author of 1 Maccabees thus frames his narrative in biblical imagery. His heroes have been raised up by God to defend the people, just like the judges before them. The Hasmoneans are skillfully portrayed as upholding the traditional ancestral faith while their enemies are destroyers of the social fabric, those who bring in foreign ways. The opposition to foreigners extends to the Seleucids and to the Ptolemies, but not to the Romans. The Romans are portrayed as trustworthy and loyal, whereas the Ptolemies and the Seleucids are consistently untrustworthy. This may evidence a proper lack of knowledge of the Roman way of handling affairs, but it also shows how the author is willing to view in a favorable light anyone who does not attempt to wrest away Israel's independence, for this is the aim of the author—to celebrate the gaining of independence—and this is what he means by proclaiming the Hasmoneans the family through whom deliverance was given to Israel (5:62; cf. 13:41-42).

Date. It is not known who wrote 1 Maccabees, when or where it was written, or when it was translated into Greek. Since Josephus seems to base his account on the Greek version, it must have been translated sometime before the end of the first century CE. The fact that it was written in Hebrew, as well as the accuracy of some of its geographical data, suggests that it was composed in Israel. Its style of writing suggests someone well-versed in the traditional Scriptures of Israel. The erudite echoing of the Hebrew Scriptures suggests someone from the scribal class, or someone educated by a teacher like Sirach.

Scholars have consistently used two factors in determining a date for 1 Maccabees: its pro-Hasmonean stance and its concluding sentence, which refers to the annals of the high priesthood of John Hyrcanus (who ruled until 104 BCE). Bar-Kochva has suggested that the author, by the vividness and accuracy of his descriptions of the battles of Judas, must have been an eyewitness to the events and was, therefore, writing early in the reign of John Hyrcanus.[31] However, a vivacious writing style and accurate geography can be achieved by others besides eyewitnesses. Most scholars have combined the above two factors to suggest a date late in Hyrcanus's reign or just after his death. S. Schwartz has argued, however, that the pro-Hasmonean stance of the author and his keeping of foreigners at arm's length are in conflict with what we know happened during the lengthy reign of Hyrcanus and his successors, when whole groups were incorporated into the area controlled by Hyrcanus. (For details on the reign of John Hyrcanus, see the section "Historical Background," above.) Schwartz therefore proposed a date early in Hyrcanus's reign, before such assimilation began. Schwartz's point is well taken, but the conclusion to the book still sounds as it if were written after the death of John Hyrcanus; thus Schwartz proposes that it was added later.[32] I would suggest that one should look more carefully at the assumption that the work is pro-Hasmonean. It clearly approves the gaining of independence, describes the Hasmonean founders as biblical heroes, and claims that they were the family through whom deliverance came to Israel. It is striking, however, that the author portrays Simon as having died while drunk at a banquet, which need not have been mentioned. There is also contrast between the utopian picture of Roman government in chapter 8 and the one-man rule imposed by Simon (14:41-45). Therefore, 1 Maccabees may be seen as a critique of the developments that had taken place under Hyrcanus and his successors, opposing the assimilation of non-Jews (which Schwartz points to), and the increasingly regal life-style of the Hasmoneans. Thus it is plausible to date 1 Maccabees to shortly after the death of John Hyrcanus.

FIRST AND SECOND MACCABEES IN JEWISH AND CHRISTIAN TRADITION

The events recounted in 1 and 2 Maccabees were, and are, celebrated in the Jewish community with the Feast of Hanukkah. In that festival, God's miraculous deliverance of the covenant people from their oppressors is remembered. The message of Hanukkah has been meaningful to a community that has sought to preserve its traditional beliefs and customs in an often hostile environment. Such a community could always look back and recall how the Seleucid kings had tried to stamp out Judaism, but were prevented from doing so by God's working through the Maccabees. In this way, the community could be reassured that it would never be deserted by God. Particularly symbolic of that deliverance is a story found not in 1 and 2 Maccabees, but in the later rabbinic tradition. This story recounts how the Jews, when they retook the city of Jerusalem and were preparing to reinstate proper worship in the Temple, found only one jar of oil for the temple lamps, which would have lasted but a single day. Miraculously, that one jar kept the lamps lighted for eight days. Enemies had tried to snuff out Judaism, but it had survived. This tradition also extolled the martyrdom accounts, particularly that of the mother and her seven sons (2 Maccabees 7), which was expanded by naming the mother Hannah and by the addition of more grisly torments for the martyrs. Much later, the heroism of the Maccabees in resisting oppression and defending their own culture and religion was especially meaningful in the nineteenth-century Zionist movement.

Early Christian communities also found the message of 1 and 2 Maccabees congenial. Not only could this record of events be used to validate the book of Daniel as prophetic and true, but also the story of a community faithful to God's commandments in the face of an idolatrous oppressor resonated with the life situation of many Christians in the Roman Empire. The books were particularly recommended for their martyrdom accounts. The feast of the Maccabean martyrs was celebrated at Antioch in Syria; at Carthage in North Africa, center of a Christian community determined not to be polluted by the contagion of the outside world, the martyrs were extolled. The great Christian thinker of the third century CE, Origen of Alexandria, wrote to exhort Christians to undergo martyrdom: "What dead person could be more deserving of praise than he who of his own choice elected to die for his religion? This is what Eleazar did, who welcoming death with honor rather than life with ignominy, went up to the rack to die of his free choice" (see 2 Macc 6:19).[33] The characters in 1 and 2 Maccabees still provide examples of endurance to what one believes in, even if that endurance means death.

FOR FURTHER READING

Bar-Kochva, Bezalel. *Judas Maccabeus.* Cambridge: Cambridge University Press, 1988.

Bartlett, John R. *First Maccabees.* Guides to the Apocrypha and Pseudepigrapha. Sheffield: Sheffield Academic Press, 1998.

Bickerman, Elias. *The God of the Maccabees: Studies on the Meaning and Origin of the Maccabean Revolt.* SJLA 32. Leiden: Brill, 1979.

Bringmann, Klaus. *Hellenistische Reform und Religionsverfolgung in Judäa: Eine Untersuchung zur jüdisch-hellenistische Geschichte*

(175–163 v. Chr). Göttingen: Vandenhoeck and Ruprecht, 1983.

Doran, Robert. *Temple Propaganda: The Purpose and Character of 2 Maccabees*. Washington, D.C.: Catholic Biblical Association, 1981.

Geller, M. J. "New Information on Antiochus IV from Babylonian Astronomical Diaries," *BSO(A)S* 54 (1991) 1-4.

Goldstein, Jonathan A. *1 Maccabees*. AB 41. Garden City, N.Y.: Doubleday, 1976.

———. *2 Maccabees*. AB 41A. Garden City, N.Y.: Doubleday, 1983.

Grabbe, Lester L. *Judaism from Cyrus to Hadrian*. 2 vols. Minneapolis: Fortress, 1992.

Harrington, Daniel J. *The Maccabean Revolt: Anatomy of a Biblical Revolution*. Wilmington, Del.: Michael Glazier, 1988.

Momigliani, Arnaldo. "The Second Book of Maccabees," *CP* 70 (1975) 81-88.

Mørkholm, Otto. *Antiochus IV of Syria*. Copenhagen: Gyldendalske Boghandel, 1966.

Schürer, Emil. *The History of the Jewish People in the Age of Jesus Christ (175 BC–AD 135)*. 3 vols. Revised by G. Vermes, F. Millar, M. Goodman. Edinburgh: Clark, 1973–87.

Sievers, Joseph. *The Hasmoneans and Their Supporters: From Mattathias to the Death of John Hyrcanus*. Atlanta: Scholars Press, 1991.

———. *Synopsis of the Greek Sources for the Hasmonean Period: 1-2 Maccabees and Josephus, War 1 and Antiquities 12-14*. SubBi 20. Rome: Pontifical Biblical Institute, 2001.

Tcherikover, Victor. *Hellenistic Civilization and the Jews*. Philadelphia: Jewish Publication Society, 1961.

ENDNOTES

1. A full listing of these sources can be found in the work by Lester L. Grabbe, *Judaism from Cyrus to Hadrian*, 2 vols. (Minneapolis: Fortress, 1992), and in the revised edition of Emil Schüerer, *The History of the Jewish People in the Age of Jesus Christ*, rev. ed., 4 vols. (Edinburgh: T & T Clark, 1973–87). The interested reader may consult the full discussion in those works.

2. Josephus *Antiquities of the Jews* 12.157-236.

3. Josephus *Antiquities of the Jews* 12.138-146.

4. Diodorus Siculus 40.3.1-8.

5. Diodorus Siculus 40.3.5.

6. Josephus *Antiquities of the Jews* 12.158-236.

7. Josephus *The Jewish War* 1.31-32.

8. CD 12:19.

9. Jonathan A. Goldstein, *I Maccabees*, AB 41 (Garden City, N.Y.: Doubleday, 1976) 104-21.

10. Elias Bickermann, *The God of the Maccabees: Studies on the Meaning and Origin of the Maccabean Revolt*, SJLA 32 (Leiden: Brill, 1979).

11. V. Tcherikover, *Hellenistic Civilization and the Jews* (Philadelphia: Jewish Publication Society, 1961).

12. Jonathan A. Goldstein, *2 Maccabees*, AB 41A (Garden City, N.Y.: Doubleday, 1983) 98-112.

13. K. Bringmann, *Hellenistische Reform und Religionsverfolgung in Judäa: Eine Untersuchung zur jüdisch-hellenistische Geschichte (175–163 v. Chr)* (Göttingen: Vandenhoeck and Ruprecht, 1983).

14. Diodorus Siculus 40.3.4.

15. Josephus *Antiquities of the Jews* 14.249-250.

16. See Josephus *Antiquities of the Jews* 13.249.

17. See Josephus *Antiquities of the Jews* 13.257-258; 15.253-256.

18. Josephus *The Jewish War* 1.67-68.

19. See Josephus *Antiquities of the Jews* 13.318-319.

20. See Josephus *Antiquities of the Jews* 13.301.

21. See Josephus *Antiquities of the Jews* 13.395-397.

22. See Josephus *Antiquities of the Jews* 13.318-319.

23. See Josephus *Antiquities of the Jews* 13.397.

24. Euripides *Fragments*, as quoted by Epictetus *Discourses* 2.1.

25. S. Niditch, *War in the Hebrew Bible: A Study of the Ethics of Violence* (New York: Oxford, 1993).

26. S. Niditch, *War in the Hebrew Bible: A Study of the Ethics of Violence*, 21.

27. K. Bringmann, *Hellenistische Reform und Religionsverfolgung in Judäa: Eine Untersuchung zur jüdisch-hellenistische Geshichte (175–163 v. Chr)*, 15-40; J. VanderKam, "Hanukkah: Its Timing and Significance According to 1 and 2 Maccabees," *JSP* (1987) 23-40.

28. E. Bickermann, *The God of the Maccabees: Studies on the Meaning and Origin of the Maccabean Revolt*, 155-58.

29. L. Grabbe, "Maccabean Chronology:

167–164 or 168–165 BCE?" *JBL* 110 (1991) 59-74.

30. 11QTemple.

31. Bezalel Bar-Kochva, *Judas Maccabeus* (Cambridge: Cambridge University Press, 1988).

32. S. Schwartz, "Israel and the Nations Round-about: 1 Maccabees and the Hasmonean Expansion," *Journal of Jewish Studies* 42 (1991) 16-30.

33. Origen *To the Martyrs* 22.

THE SECOND BOOK OF MACCABEES

ROBERT DORAN

THE EPITOME,
2 MACCABEES 2:19–15:39

The Second Book of Maccabees is not a continuation of the First Book of Maccabees, but a completely independent work. It covers some of the same material as 1 Maccabees, but in a very different fashion. The story starts during the reign of Seleucus IV Philopator (187–175 BCE) and ends with the defeat of Nicanor in 161 BCE, providing much more detail than 1 Maccabees does about the parties and factions in Jerusalem prior to the persecution by Antiochus VI Epiphanes. The letters preserved in 2 Maccabees 11 are particularly important in reconstructing the events of this period. The book has a formal prologue and epilogue and is structured around three attacks on the Jerusalem Temple: (1) by Heliodorus under Seleucus IV (3:1-39); (2) under Antiochus IV Epiphanes (3:40–10:8); and (3) the final assault by Nicanor under Demetrius I (10:9–15:37).

Style. In contrast to 1 Maccabees, which was originally written in Hebrew and then translated into Greek, the bulk of 2 Maccabees (2:19–15:39, often referred to as the epitome) was written in the typical Greek style of the day. The prologue evidences knowledge of Hellenistic historiographical conventions, as do the reflections that the author (commonly called the epitomist) inserts into the narrative at 4:16-17; 5:17-20; 6:12-17. The narrative reveals an author who loves to indulge in metaphors and word play. The author also strives to heighten the emotional effect of the narrative on his readers or listeners, as in the scene of distress at Heliodorus's approach to the Temple (3:15-22), the attention given to the mother and her seven sons (chap. 7), the emotional turnaround of Antiochus IV (chap. 9), and the distress of the priests at the insults of Nicanor (14:13-36). This emotional heightening is helped by the author's focusing on individual confrontations—Heliodorus and the high priest, and Nicanor and Judas in the first battle (chap. 8).

The narrative also abounds in tales of the miraculous, as in the graphic descriptions of the epiphanies of God's deliverance of the people at 3:24-28; 5:2-4; 10:29-30; 11:8-11. The presentation of these angelic helpers parallels the stories about divine helpers that one finds in Greco-Roman literature and is further evidence of the author's acquaintance with Greek literature. One could argue, in fact, that the narrative of the epitome falls within the Greek literary genre of epiphanic collections, which tell of the way a god defends his or her temple.

Worldview. While the narrative shows the influence of Greco-Roman literary conventions, the author has used these conventions to portray a confrontation between Judaism (2:21; 8:1; 14:38) and Hellenism (4:13). As far as we know, this is the first appearance of the term "Judaism." For this author, the Jews are the civilized norm, whereas the Greeks are barbarians (2:21; 10:4). The Jewish scribe Eleazar, and not his opponents, is the one who acts nobly (6:18-31). This attitude of separation of Jews from non-Jews is particularly evident in the author's discussion of the gymnasium in Jerusalem. For him, this change in educational system symbolizes the destruction of the Jewish ancestral religion, and he is particularly violent toward Jews participating in the gymnasium.

Although the author stresses that it is always non-Jews who instigate troubles against the Jews, who only defend themselves and their ancestral religion (10:12-14; 12:1-2), he goes out of his way to show that Jews and Gentiles can get along harmoniously. Non-Jews protest the execution of Onias (4:35) and the members of the Jewish council (4:49); the people of Scythopolis treat the Jews kindly during bad times (12:30-31). Even Antiochus IV claims that the

Jews are good citizens and asks them to maintain their goodwill toward him and his son and heir (9:19-20, 26). Alcimus accuses the Jews under Judas of not being loyal citizens (14:6-10), but events prove him wrong as Judas makes an agreement with Nicanor and settles down to married life (14:20-25). What is striking about this narrative, in fact, is that the Jews are not portrayed as seeking to set up an independent realm. Rather, the story ends with the Jews able to celebrate their religion in peace, not with political independence. Judas seems quite happy to live a settled life under the Seleucids. This is in sharp contrast to the outlook of the author of 1 Maccabees, who views all Seleucids with suspicion.

The theology of the author has a distinctly deuteronomistic flavor about it. As long as the Jews obey the laws, God keeps them in peace, and they flourish. When they disobey, punishment comes (3:1; 4:16-17; 6:12-17). The author, therefore, shows Judas and his followers as strict observers of the sabbath (8:27) and other festivals (12:31) and links the Festival of Hanukkah to the older Feast of Tabernacles (10:6). The author is a strong believer in punishment fitting the crime, as seen in the fates of Jason and Menelaus, in the execution of Andronicus on the same spot where he had killed Onias (4:38), in the dismemberment of Nicanor (15:32-33), and in the providential care of God, who restores temple worship on the anniversary of the day that it had been profaned (10:5-6).

Date. The epitome of 2 Maccabees (2:19–15:39) is a shortened version of a no longer extant five-volume work by Jason of Cyrene. Scholars have speculated on how to reconstruct Jason's work and when he might have written it. At present, no sure answers to these questions can be given because all we have is the work of the epitomist. Scholars have also tried to reconstruct a "life of Judas" from the events common to both 1 and 2 Maccabees. One can certainly plot out from both books a sequence of battles in which Judas had engaged. But each book has its distinctive way of describing events. The fact that one account is a Greek translation of an original Hebrew text, whereas the other was written originally in Greek, is further reason to make one feel less than sanguine that any source document, in a meaningful sense of the term, can be recovered.

Who, then, was the epitomist of 2 Maccabees, and when and where did he write? We have even fewer clues to go on than with 1 Maccabees. Dates range from the second century BCE to the first century CE. Perhaps, since the text shows a friendly attitude toward the Romans, it might have been written before Pompey's entry into Jerusalem in 63 BCE. Momigliano has suggested that the epitome was written to accompany the first prefixed letter; therefore, the epitome would have been written in 124 BCE.[1] Yet, although one can make connections between the prefixed letters and the epitome, the author of the epitome makes no mention in his prologue that he was writing it to accompany a letter.

If there are no indications as to the date of the epitome, can one then suggest where it might have been written? Scholars have suggested, because it was written in Greek, that it must have come out of the diaspora, possibly from Alexandria, (given the great deal of literary activity by Jews there) or Antioch (since the Maccabean martyrs were celebrated there). The author's knowledge of events affecting Jews in Babylonia (8:20) and the author's polemic against Jews attending a gymnasium lend support to such a theory. Later inscriptional evidence from Cyrene shows that Jews did attend the gymnasium there. Therefore, one might conclude that the work was written by someone in the diaspora who was concerned that young Jewish men were beginning to attend the local gymnasium. The author wanted to write against that practice and yet still insist that Jews can be good and loyal residents wherever they live. But there is no reason why someone living in Jerusalem who was fluent in Greek could not have written it. The temptation to attend a gymnasium could be present anywhere in the Hellenistic world.

THE PREFIXED LETTERS, 1:1–2:18

The position of the two letters at the beginning of 2 Maccabees is quite perplexing. What is their connection to the epitome? Why were they added? From where do they come? Since the two letters are addressed to Alexandrian Jews, were they part of some letter archive in Alexandria? Each letter is quite different from the other. Most scholars would see the first letter as authentic but have serious questions regarding the authenticity of the second one. While the first letter follows the conventions of letters written in Aramaic/Hebrew, the second does not and yet abounds in Semitisms.

As mentioned above, Momigliano suggested that the epitome was written to accompany the first letter, but there is no explicit mention of this in either the letter or the prologue to the epitome. Also, the account of the death of Antiochus IV in the epitome cannot be reconciled with the account of his death in the second letter.

Yet connections can be seen between the letters and the epitome. While in 1 Maccabees Judas and his followers celebrate the purification of the Temple for eight days (1 Macc 5:56), only in the epitome and in the prefixed letters of 2 Maccabees is the festival explicitly connected with the Feast of Tabernacles (2 Macc 1:10, 18; 10:6). One might also note how both the first prefixed letter and the epitome use a Greek form—"to reconcile," "reconciliation" (καταλλάσσω *katallassō*; καταλλαγή *katallagē*)—which is very unusual in the LXX (2 Macc 1:5; 5:20; 7:33; 8:29). Finally, at the climactic battle against Nicanor, Judas's mission is divinely sanctioned and approved through the figure of the prophet Jeremiah (15:14-16), and Jeremiah figures prominently in the second letter (2:1-8). One should note, of course, that in the epitome the figure of Jeremiah is used to connect Judas with Israel's past, whereas in the letter Jeremiah's hiding of the temple vessels speaks of a discontinuity with the First Temple.

What binds the letters to the epitome most strongly is the connection between the Festival of Hanukkah and the Feast of Tabernacles in Kislev. The second letter dates itself to the lifetime of Judas (between 164 and 160 BCE), the first to 124 BCE. Perhaps the letters were added to the epitome sometime after 124 BCE, but exactly when is unknown. The most likely location of the writing, given the addressees of the letters, is Alexandria.

Finally, it is interesting to speculate whether the letters affect the message of the epitome. The addition of the first letter does not change the message much. The second letter, however, adds to the message of the epitome in several ways. Its emphasis on the continuity between the First and Second Temples and the connections it forges between Judas and Nehemiah underline God's concern with the covenant people and for their following covenant laws. In addition, the second letter concludes with a prayer for the ingathering of God's holy people (2 Macc 2:18). This prayer, which resonates with that of the priests at the miraculous rekindling of the temple fire (1:26-29), has eschatological overtones, especially given the concern that the Jews of the diaspora return to the holy land. The writer of the epitome, however, shows no concern for eschatology.

For more discussion of the historical background of 1 and 2 Maccabees, of the ethics of violence in both books, and of the place of 1 and 2 Maccabees in Jewish and Christian tradition, see the chapter on 1 Maccabees. See also the bibliography located there.

ENDNOTES

1. Momigliano, "The Second Book of Maccabees," *CP* 70 (1975) 83-84.

ABBREVIATIONS
AND
CHARTS, ILLUSTRATIONS,
AND MAPS

ABBREVIATIONS

GENERAL

BCE	Before the Common Era
CE	Common Era
c.	circa
cent.	century
cf.	compare
chap(s).	chapter(s)
d.	died
Dtr	Deuteronomistic historian
esp.	especially
fem.	feminine
f(f).	and following
HB	Hebrew Bible
lit.	literally
l(l).	line(s)
LXX	Septuagint
MS(S)	manuscript(s)
mg.	margin
masc.	masculine
MT	Masoretic Text
n(n).	note(s)
neut.	neuter
NT	New Testament
OG	Old Greek
OL	Old Latin
OT	Old Testament
par(s).	parallel(s)
pl(s).	plate(s)
sing.	singular
SP	Samaritan Pentateuch
v(v).	verse(s)
Vg	Vulgate
\\	between Scripture references indicates parallelism

BIBLE TRANSLATIONS

ASV	American Standard Version
CEV	Contemporary English Version
CSB	Catholic Study Bible
GNB	Good News Bible
JB	Jerusalem Bible
KJV	King James Version

NAB	New American Bible
NCB	New Century Bible
NEB	New English Bible
NIV	New International Version
NJB	New Jerusalem Bible
NKJV	New King James Version
NRSV	New Revised Standard Version
REB	Revised English Bible
RSV	Revised Standard Version
TLB	The Living Bible
TNK	Tanakh

BIBLICAL BOOKS (WITH THE APOCRYPHA)

Gen	Nah	1–4 Kgdms	John
Exod	Hab	Add Esth	Acts
Lev	Zeph	Bar	Rom
Num	Hag	Bel	1–2 Cor
Deut	Zech	1–2 Esdr	Gal
Josh	Mal	4 Ezra	Eph
Judg	Ps (Pss)	Jdt	Phil
1–2 Sam	Job	Ep Jer	Col
1–2 Kgs	Prov	1–4 Macc	1–2 Thess
Isa	Ruth	Pr Azar	1–2 Tim
Jer	Cant	Pr Man	Titus
Ezek	Eccl	Sir	Phlm
Hos	Lam	Sus	Heb
Joel	Esth	Tob	Jas
Amos	Dan	Wis	1–2 Pet
Obad	Ezra	Matt	1–3 John
Jonah	Neh	Mark	Jude
Mic	1–2 Chr	Luke	Rev

PSEUDEPIGRAPHICAL AND EARLY PATRISTIC BOOKS

Apoc. Ab.	*Apocalypse of Abraham*
Apoc. Adam	*Apocalypse of Adam*
2 Apoc. Bar.	Syriac *Apocalypse of Baruch*
3 Apoc. Bar.	Greek *Apocalypse of Baruch*
Apoc. Mos.	*Apocalypse of Moses*
As. Mos.	*Assumption of Moses*
Ascen. Isa.	*Ascension of Isaiah*
Barn.	*Barnabas*
1–2 Clem.	*1–2 Clement*
Did.	*Didache*
1 Enoch	Ethiopic Book of *Enoch*
2 Enoch	Slavonic Book of *Enoch*
3 Enoch	Hebrew Book of *Enoch*
Ep. Arist.	*Epistle of Aristeas*

Gos. Pet.	Gospel of Peter
Herm. Sim.	Shepherd of Hermas, Similitude
Ign. Eph.	Ignatius, To the Ephesians
Ign. Magn.	Ignatius, To the Magnesians
Ign. Phld.	Ignatius, To the Philadelphians
Ign. Pol.	Ignatius, To Polycarp
Ign. Rom.	Ignatius, To the Romans
Ign. Smyrn.	Ignatius, To the Smyrnaeans
Ign. Trall.	Ignatius, To the Trallians
Jub.	Jubilees
P. Oxy.	Oxyrynchus Papyri. Edited by B. P. Grenfell and A. S. Hunt.
Pss. Sol.	Psalms of Solomon
Sib. Or.	Sibylline Oracles
T. Benj.	Testament of Benjamin
T. Dan	Testament of Dan
T. Iss.	Testament of Issachar
T. Job	Testament of Job
T. Jud.	Testament of Judah
T. Levi	Testament of Levi
T. Naph.	Testament of Naphtali
T. Reu.	Testament of Reuben
T. Sim.	Testament of Simeon

DEAD SEA SCROLLS AND RELATED TEXTS

CD	Cairo Genizah text of the Damascus Document
DSS	Dead Sea Scrolls
8Hev XIIgr	Greek Scroll of the Minor Prophets from Nahal Hever
Q	Qumran
1Q, 2Q, 3Q, etc.	Numbered caves of Qumran yielding written material followed by abbreviation of biblical or apocryphal book (e.g., 1Q pHab) or numbered document (e.g., 1Q7)
1Q28b	Appendix b (Rule of the Blessings) to 1QS
1QH^a	Hodayot^a (Thanksgiving Hymns^a)
1QM	Milhamah (War Scroll)
1QpHab	Pesher Habakkuk
1QS	Serek Hayahad (Rule of the Community, Manual of Discipline)
1QS^a	Appendix a (Rule of the Congregation) to 1QS
1QS^b	Appendix b (Rule of the Blessings) to 1QS
4Q175	Testimonia (4QTest)
4Q246	Apocryphon of Daniel (Aramaic Apocalypse)
4Q298	Cryptic A: Words of the Sage to the Sons of Dawn
4Q385^b	4QApocryphon of Jeremiah^c
4Q389^a	4QApocryphon of Jeremiah^e
4Q390	4QPseudo-Moses^e
4Q394	Miqsat Ma'aśê ha- Torah^a (4QMMT^a)
4Q416	Sapiential Work Ab
4Q521	Messianic Apocalypse
4Q550Qproto-Esther $^{a-f}$	ProtoEsther, Aramaic, copies to
4QFlor (MidrEschat^a)	Florilegium (or Midrash on Eschatology^a)

4QMMT	*Halakhic Letter*
4QpaleoDeutr	Copy of Deuteronomy in paleo-Hebrew script
4QpaleoExod[m]	Copy of Exodus in paleo-Hebrew script
4QpNah	*Nahum Pesher*
4QpPss[a]	*Psalm Pesher A*
4QprNab ar	*Prayer of Nabonidus*
4QPs37	*Psalms Scroll*
4QpsDan	Pseudo-Daniel
4Qsam[a]	First copy of Samuel
4QTob	Copy of Tobit
11QMelch	*Melchizedek*
11QpHab	A fragment of the Habakkuk scroll
11QPs[a]	*Psalms Scroll[a]*
11QTemple	*Temple Scroll*
11QtgJob	*Targum of Job*

ORDERS AND TRACTATES IN MISHNAIC AND RELATED LITERATURE

To distinguish between the same-named tractates in the Mishna, Tosepta, Babylonian Talmud, and Jerusalem Talmud, *m.*, *t.*, *b.*, or *y.* precedes the title of the tractate.

ʾAbot	*ʾAbot*
ʾArak.	*ʾArakin*
B. Bat.	*Baba Batra*
B. Men	*Baba Meniʿa*
B. Qam.	*Baba Qamma*
Ber.	*Berakot*
Dem.	*Demai*
Git.	*Gittin*
Hag.	*Hagigah*
Hor.	*Horayot*
Hul.	*Hullin*
Ketub.	*Ketubbot*
Maʿaś.	*Maʿaśerot*
Meg.	*Megillah*
Menah.	*Menahot*
Mid.	*Middot*
Moʾed Qat.	*Moʾed Qatan*
Ned.	*Nedarim*
Pesah.	*Pesahim*
Qidd.	*Qiddušin*
Šabb.	*Šabbat*
Sanh.	*Sanhedrin*
Shekal	*Pesahim Shekalim*
Soïa	*Soïa*
Sukk.	*Sukka*
Taʿan.	*Taʿanit*
Tg. Neof.	*Targum Neofiti*
Yad.	*Yadayim*
Yoma	*Yoma (= Kippurim)*

Targumic Material

Tg. Esth. I, II	*First or Second Targum of Esther*
Tg. Neb.	*Targum of the Prophets*

Other Rabbinic Works

'Abot R. Nat.	*'Abot de Rabbi Nathan*
Pesiq. Rab.	*Pesiqta Rabbati*
Rab.	*Rabbah* (following abbreviation of biblical book—e.g., Gen. Rab. = Genesis Rabbah)
Sipra	*Sipra*
Song Rab.	*Song of Songs Rabbah*

Periodicals, Reference Works, and Serials

AB	Anchor Bible
ABD	*Anchor Bible Dictionary.* Edited by D. N. Freedman. 6 vols. New York, 1992
ABR	*Australian Biblical Review*
ABRL	Anchor Bible Reference Library
ACNT	Augsburg Commentaries on the New Testament
AcOr	*Acta orientalia*
AfO	*Archiv für Orientforschung*
AfOB	Archiv für Orientforschung: Beiheft
AGJU	Arbeiten zur Geschichte des antiken Judentums und des Urchristentums
AJP	*American Journal of Philology*
AJSL	*American Journal of Semitic Languages and Literature*
AJT	*American Journal of Theology*
AnBib	Analecta biblica
ANEP	*The Ancient Near East in Pictures Relating to the Old Testament.* Edited by J. B. Pritchard. Princeton, 1954
ANET	*Ancient Near Eastern Texts Relating to the Old Testament.* Edited by J. B. Pritchard. 3rd ed. Princeton, 1969
ANF	*The Ante-Nicene Fathers*
ANRW	*Aufstieg und Niedergang der römischen Welt: Geschichte und Kultur Roms im Spiegel der neueren Forschung.* Edited by H. Temporini and W. Haase. Berlin, 1972–
ANTC	Abingdon New Testament Commentaries
ANTJ	Arbeiten zum Neuen Testament und Judentum
APOT	*Apocrypha and Pseudepigrapha of the Old Testament.* Edited by R. H. Charles. 2 vols. Oxford, 1913
ASNU	Acta seminarii neotestamentici upsaliensis
ATANT	Abhandlungen zur Theologie des Alten und Neuen Testaments
ATD	Das Alte Testament Deutsch
ATDan	Acta theological danica
Aug	*Augustinianum*
BA	*Biblical Archaeologist*
BAGD	Bauer, W., W. F. Arndt, F. W. Gingrich, and F. W. Danker. *Greek-English Lexicon of the New Testament and Other Early Christian Literature.* 2nd ed. Chicago, 1979

BAR	*Biblical Archaeology Review*
BASOR	*Bulletin of the American Schools of Oriental Research*
BBB	Bonner biblische Beiträge
BBET	Beiträge zur biblischen Exegese und Theologie
BBR	*Bulletin for Biblical Research*
BDAG	Bauer, W., F. W. Danker, W. F. Arndt, and F. W. Gingrich. *Greek-English Lexicon of the New Testament and Other Early Christian Literature.* 3rd ed. Chicago, 2000
BDB	Brown, F., S. R. Driver, and C. A. Briggs. *A Hebrew and English Lexicon of the Old Testament.* Oxford, 1907
BDF	Blass, F., A. Debrunner, and R. W. Funk. *A Greek Grammar of the New Testament and Other Early Christian Literature.* Chicago, 1961
BEATAJ	Beiträge zur Erforschung des Alten Testaments und des antiken Judentum
BETL	Bibliotheca ephemeridum theologicarum lovaniensium
BEvT	Beiträge zur evangelischen Theologie
BHS	*Biblia Hebraica Stuttgartensia.* Edited by K. Elliger and W. Randolph. Stuttgart, 1983
BHT	Beiträge zur historischen Theologie
Bib	*Biblica*
BibInt	*Biblical Interpretation*
BibOr	Biblica et orientalia
BJRL	*Bulletin of the John Rylands University Library of Manchester*
BJS	Brown Judaic Studies
BK	*Bibel und Kirche*
BKAT	Biblischer Kommentar, Altes Testament. Edited by M. Noth and H. W. Wolff
BLS	Bible and Literature Series
BN	*Biblische Notizen*
BNTC	Black's New Testament Commentaries
BR	*Biblical Research*
BSac	*Bibliotheca sacra*
BSOAS	*Bulletin of the School of Oriental and African Studies*
BT	*The Bible Translator*
BTB	*Biblical Theology Bulletin*
BVC	*Bible et vie chrétienne*
BWA(N)T	Beiträge zur Wissenschaft vom Alten (und Neuen) Testament
BZ	*Biblische Zeitschrift*
BZAW	Beihefte zur Zeitschrift für die alttestamentliche Wissenschaft
BZNW	Beihefte zur Zeitschrift für die neutestamentliche Wissenschaft
CAD	*The Assyrian Dictionary of the Oriental Institute of the University of Chicago.* Chicago, 1956–
CB	*Cultura bíblica*
CBC	Cambridge Bible Commentary
CBQ	*Catholic Biblical Quarterly*
CBQMS	Catholic Biblical Quarterly Monograph Series
ConBNT	Coniectanea neotestamentica or Coniectanea biblica: New Testament Series
ConBOT	Coniectanea biblica: Old Testament Series
CP	*Classical Philology*
CRAI	Comptes rendus del l'Académie des inscriptions et belles-lettres
CRINT	Compendia rerum iudaicarum ad Novum Testamentum
CTM	*Concordia Theological Monthly*

DJD	Discoveries in the Judaean Desert
EB	Echter Bibel
EI	*Encyclopaedia of Islam.* 9 of 13 projected vols. 2nd ed. Leiden, 1954–
EKKNT	Evangelisch-katholischer Kommentar zum Neuen Testament
Enc	*Encounter*
EncJud	*Encyclopaedia Judaica.* 16 vols. Jerusalem, 1972
EPRO	Etudes préliminairies aux religions orientales dans l'empire romain
ErIsr	*Eretz-Israel*
EstBib	*Estudios bíblicos*
ETL	*Ephemerides theologicae lovanienses*
ETS	Erfurter theologische Studien
EvQ	*Evangelical Quarterly*
EvT	*Evangelische Theologie*
ExAud	*Ex auditu*
ExpTim	*Expository Times*
FAT	Forschungen zum Alten Testament
FB	Forschung zur Bibel
FBBS	Facet Books, Biblical Series
FFNT	Foundations and Facets: New Testament
FOTL	Forms of the Old Testament Literature
FRLANT	Forschungen zur Religion und Literatur des Alten und Neuen Testaments
FTS	Frankfurter Theologische Studien
GBS.OTS	Guides to Biblical Scholarship. Old Testament Series
GCS	Die griechische christliche Schriftsteller der ersten [drei] Jahrhunderte
GKC	*Gesenius' Hebrew Grammar.* Edited by E. Kautzsch. Translated by A. E. Cowley. 2nd ed. Oxford, 1910
GNS	*Good News Studies*
GTA	Göttinger theologischer Arbeiten
HAL	Koehler, L., W. Baumgartner, and J. J. Stamm. *Hebräisches und aramäisches Lexikon zum Alten Testament.* Fascicles 1–5, 1967–1995 (KBL3). ET: *HALOT*
HAR	*Hebrew Annual Review*
HAT	Handbuch zum Alten Testament
HBC	*Harper's Bible Commentary.* Edited by J. L. Mays et al. San Francisco, 1988
HBT	*Horizons in Biblical Theology*
HDB	*Hastings Dictionary of the Bible*
HDR	Harvard Dissertations in Religion
HeyJ	*Heythrop Journal*
HNT	Handbuch zum Neuen Testament
HNTC	Harper's New Testament Commentaries
HR	*History of Religions*
HSM	Harvard Semitic Monographs
HSS	Harvard Semitic Studies
HTKNT	Herders theologischer Kommentar zum Neuen Testament
HTR	*Harvard Theological Review*
HTS	Harvard Theological Studies
HUCA	*Hebrew Union College Annual*
IB	*Interpreter's Bible.* Edited by G. A. Buttrick et al. 12 vols. New York, 1951–1957
IBC	Interpretation: A Bible Commentary for Teaching and Preaching

IBS	*Irish Biblical Studies*
ICC	International Critical Commentary
IDB	*The Interpreter's Dictionary of the Bible.* Edited by G.A. Buttrick. 4 vols. Nashville, 1962
IDBSup	*Interpreter's Dictionary of the Bible: Supplementary Volume.* Edited by K. Crim. Nashville, 1976
IEJ	*Israel Exploration Journal*
Int	*Interpretation*
IRT	Issues in Religion and Theology
ITC	International Theological Commentary
JAAR	*Journal of the American Academy of Religion*
JAL	Jewish Apocryphal Literature Series
JANESCU	*Journal of the Ancient Near Eastern Society of Columbia University*
JAOS	*Journal of the American Oriental Society*
JBL	*Journal of Biblical Literature*
JETS	*Journal of the Evangelical Theological Society*
JJS	*Journal of Jewish Studies*
JNES	*Journal of Near Eastern Studies*
JNSL	*Journal of Northwest Semitic Languages*
JPS	Jewish Publication Society
JPSV	Jewish Publication Society Version
JQR	*Jewish Quarterly Review*
JR	*Journal of Religion*
JRH	*Journal of Religious History*
JSJ	*Journal for the Study of Judaism in the Persian, Hellenistic, and Roman Periods*
JSNT	*Journal for the Study of the New Testament*
JSNTSup	Journal for the Study of the New Testament: Supplement Series
JSOT	*Journal for the Study of the Old Testament*
JSOTSup	Journal for the Study of the Old Testament: Supplement Series
JSP	*Journal for the Study of the Pseudepigrapha*
JSPTSS	Journal of the Study of Pentecostal Theology Supplement Series
JSS	*Journal of Semitic Studies*
JTC	*Journal for Theology and the Church*
JTS	*Journal of Theological Studies*
KAT	Kommentar zum Alten Testament
KEK	Kritisch-exegetischer Kommentar über das Neue Testament (Meyer-Kommentar)
KPG	Knox Preaching Guides
LCL	Loeb Classical Library
LTQ	*Lexington Theological Quarterly*
MNTC	Moffatt New Testament Commentary
NA^{27}	*Novum Testamentum Graece*, Nestle-Aland, 27th ed.
NCBC	New Century Bible Commentary
NHS	Nag Hammadi Studies
NIB	*The New Interpreter's Bible*
NICNT	New International Commentary on the New Testament
NICOT	New International Commentary on the Old Testament
NIGTC	New International Greek Testament Commentary
NJBC	*The New Jerome Biblical Commentary.* Edited by R. E. Brown et al. Englewood Cliffs, 1990

NovT	*Novum Testamentum*
NovTSup	Supplements to Novum Testamentum
NPNF	*Nicene and Post-Nicene Fathers*, Series 1 and 2
NTC	New Testament in Context
NTD	Das Neue Testament Deutsch
NTG	New Testament Guides
NTS	*New Testament Studies*
NTTS	New Testament Tools and Studies
OBC	Oxford Bible Commentary
OBO	Orbis biblicus et orientalis
OBT	Overtures to Biblical Theology
OIP	Oriental Institute Publications
Or	*Orientalia* (NS)
OTG	Old Testament Guides
OTL	Old Testament Library
OTM	Old Testament Message
OTP	*Old Testament Pseudepigrapha*. Edited by J. H. Charlesworth. 2 vols. New York, 1983
OtSt	*Oudtestamentische Studiën*
PAAJR	*Proceedings of the American Academy of Jewish Research*
PEQ	*Palestine Exploration Quarterly*
PGM	*Papyri graecae magicae: Die griechischen Zauberpapyri*. Edited by K. Preisendanz. Berlin, 1928
PTMS	Pittsburgh Theological Monograph Series
QD	Quaestiones disputatae
RANE	Records of the Ancient Near East
RB	*Revue biblique*
ResQ	*Restoration Quarterly*
RevExp	*Review and Expositor*
RevQ	*Revue de Qumran*
RevScRel	*Revue des sciences religieuses*
RSR	*Recherches de science religieuse*
RTL	*Revue théologique de Louvain*
SAA	State Archives of Assyria
SBB	Stuttgarter biblische Beiträge
SBL	Society of Biblical Literature
SBLDS	Society of Biblical Literature Dissertation Series
SBLMS	Society of Biblical Literature Monograph Series
SBLRBS	Society of Biblical Literature Resources for Biblical Study
SBLSCS	Society of Biblical Literature Septuagint and Cognate Studies
SBLSP	*Society of Biblical Literature Seminar Papers*
SBLSS	Society of Biblical Literature Semeia Studies
SBLSymS	Society of Biblical Literature Symposium Series
SBLWAW	Society of Biblical Literature Writings from the Ancient World
SBM	Stuttgarter biblische Monographien
SBS	Stuttgarter Bibelstudien
SBT	Studies in Biblical Theology
SEÅ	*Svensk exegetisk årsbok*
SJLA	Studies in Judaism in Late Antiquity
SJOT	*Scandinavian Journal of the Old Testament*

SJT	*Scottish Journal of Theology*
SKK	Stuttgarter kleiner Kommentar
SNTSMS	Society for New Testament Studies Monograph Series
SOTSMS	Society for Old Testament Study Monograph Series
SP	Sacra pagina
SR	*Studies in Religion*
SSN	Studia semitica neerlandica
Str-B	Strack, H. L., and P. Billerbeck. *Kommentar zum Neuen Testament aus Talmud und Midrasch.* 6 vols. Munich, 1922–6161
SUNT	Studien zur Umwelt des Neuen Testaments
SVTP	Studia in Veteris Testamenti pseudepigrapha
TB	Theologische Bücherei: Neudrucke und Berichte aus dem 20. Jahrhundert
TD	*Theology Digest*
TDNT	*Theological Dictionary of the New Testament.* Edited by G. Kittel and G. Friedrich. Translated by G. W. Bromiley. 10 vols. Grand Rapids, 1964–1976
TDOT	*Theological Dictionary of the Old Testament.* Edited by G. J. Botterweck and H. Ringgren. Translated by J. T. Willis, G. W. Bromiley, and D. E. Green. 8 vols. Grand Rapids, 1974–
THKNT	Theologischer Handkommentar zum Neuen Testament
ThTo	*Theology Today*
TLZ	*Theologische Literaturzeitung*
TOTC	Tyndale Old Testament Commentaries
TQ	*Theologische Quartalschrift*
TS	Texts and Studies
TS	*Theological Studies*
TSK	*Theologische Studien und Kritiken*
TSSI	*Textbook of Syrian Semitic Inscriptions.* J. C. L. Gibson. Oxford, 1971–1982
TynBul	*Tyndale Bulletin*
TZ	*Theologische Zeitschrift*
UBS	United Bible Societies
UBS[4]	*The Greek New Testament*, United Bible Societies, 4th ed.
UF	*Ugarit-Forschungen*
USQR	*Union Seminary Quarterly Review*
UUA	Uppsala Universitetsårsskrift
VC	*Vigiliae christianae*
VT	*Vetus Testamentum*
VTSup	Vetus Testamentum Supplements
WA	*Weimar Ausgabe.* (Weimer ed.). M. Luther
WBC	Word Biblical Commentary
WBT	*Word Biblical Themes*
WMANT	Wissenschaftliche Monographien zum Alten und Neuen Testament
WTJ	*Westminster Theological Journal*
WUNT	Wissenschaftliche Untersuchungen zum Neuen Testament
ZAH	*Zeitschrift für Althebräistik*
ZAW	*Zeitschrift für die alttestamentliche Wissenschaft*
ZNW	*Zeitschrift für die neutestamentliche Wissenschaft und die Kunde de älteren Kirche*
ZTK	*Zeitschrift für Theologie und Kirche*

INDEX OF CHARTS, ILLUSTRATIONS, AND MAPS

CHARTS

ILLUSTRATIONS

MAPS

NOTES

NOTES

NOTES

NOTES

NOTES

CPSIA information can be obtained at www.ICGtesting.com
Printed in the USA
LVOW03*0453290514

387671LV00004B/32/P